THE COMPLETE
ELFQUEST®

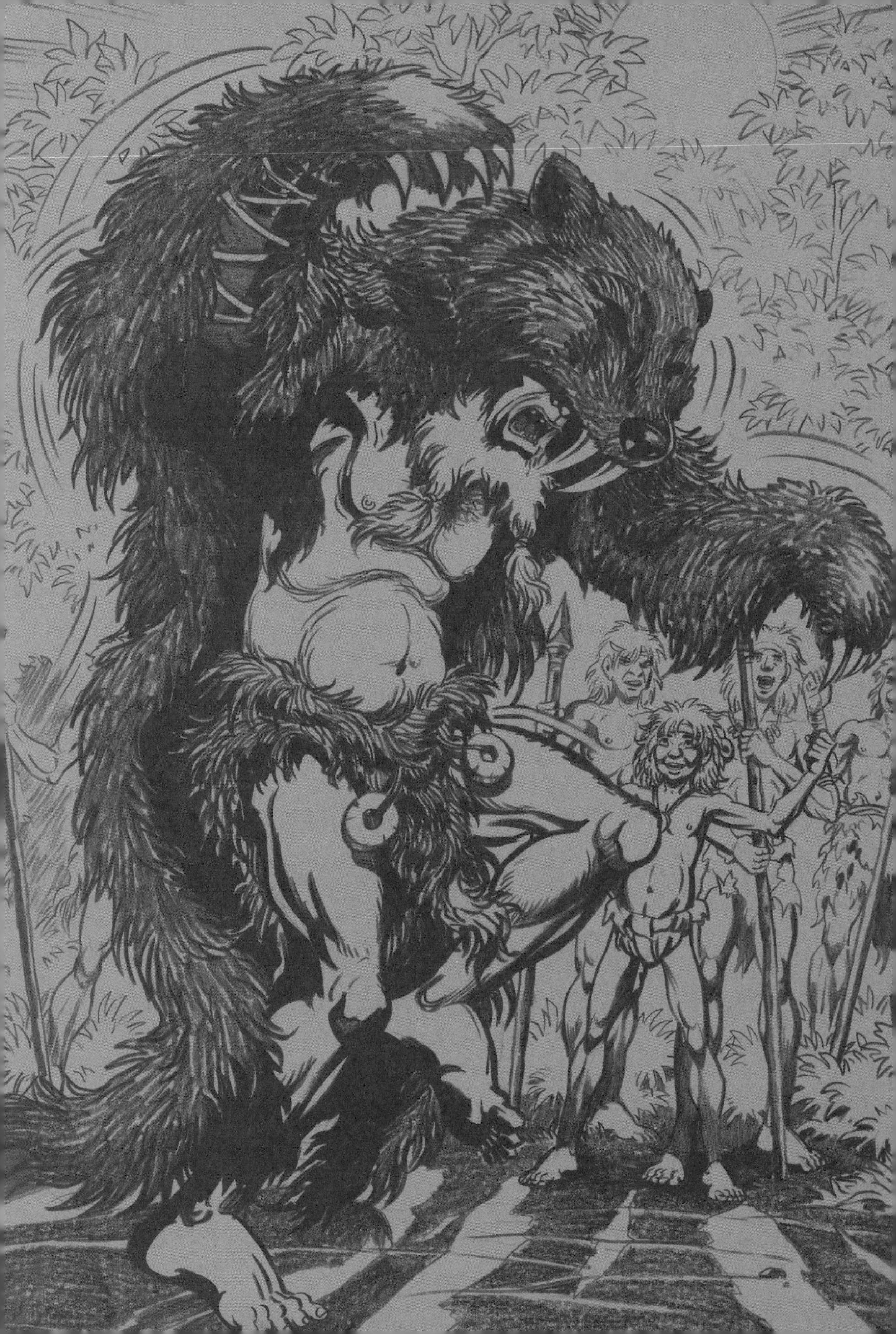

THE COMPLETE ElfQuest®

VOLUME SIX

BY WENDY AND RICHARD PINI

SONNY STRAIT
*(TROLL GAMES AND SOUL NAMES,
WOLFSHADOW, FULL CIRCLE)*

SCRIPTS BY
WENDY PINI
CHRISTY MARX
(WOLFRIDER!)

PENCILS BY
WENDY PINI
JEFF ZUGALE
(WOLFRIDER! PARTS 7-10)
CAROL LYON
(FULL CIRCLE)
SONNY STRAIT
*(TROLL GAMES AND SOUL NAMES,
WOLFSHADOW, FULL CIRCLE)*

INKS BY
WENDY PINI
SONNY STRAIT
(TROLL GAMES AND SOUL NAMES, WOLFSHADOW)
CAROL LYON
(FULL CIRCLE)

LETTERS BY
WENDY PINI
(HOMESPUN, TROLL GAMES AND SOUL NAMES)
RICHARD PINI
JOHN J HILL AND RYANE HILL

DARK HORSE BOOKS

President & Publisher MIKE RICHARDSON

Editor RACHEL ROBERTS

Assistant Editor JENNY BLENK

Designer SARAH TERRY

Digital Art Technician ALLYSON HALLER

NEIL HANKERSON Executive Vice President - TOM WEDDLE Chief Financial Officer
RANDY STRADLEY Vice President of Publishing - NICK McWHORTER Chief Business Development Officer
DALE LaFOUNTAIN Chief Information Officer - MATT PARKINSON Vice President of Marketing
CARA NIECE Vice President of Production and Scheduling - MARK BERNARDI Vice President of Book Trade and
Digital Sales - KEN LIZZI General Counsel - DAVE MARSHALL Editor in Chief - DAVEY ESTRADA Editorial Director
CHRIS WARNER Senior Books Editor - CARY GRAZZINI Director of Specialty Projects - LIA RIBACCHI Art
Director - VANESSA TODD Director of Print Purchasing - MATT DRYER Director of Digital Art and Prepress
MICHAEL GOMBOS Senior Director of Licensed Publications - KARI YADRO Director of Custom Programs
KARI TORSON Director of International Licensing - SEAN BRICE Director of Trade Sales

Published by Dark Horse Books
A division of Dark Horse Comics LLC
10956 SE Main Street
Milwaukie, OR 97222

First edition: November 2019
ISBN 978-1-50670-607-8
1 3 5 7 9 10 8 6 4 2
Printed in China

To find a comics shop in your area, visit comicshoplocator.com

THE COMPLETE ELFQUEST VOLUME 6

*This volume collects and reprints the comic books ElfQuest: Wolfrider! #1–#12, Homespun, Troll Names and Soul Games,
Heart's Way, The Jury, Wolfshadow, Full Circle, The Searcher and the Sword, and ElfQuest: Discovery #1–#4.*

TO THE KIDS WHO HAVE GROWN UP

AND PASS THE STORIES ON WITH LOVE,

EVEN TO THE THIRD AND FOURTH GENERATION.

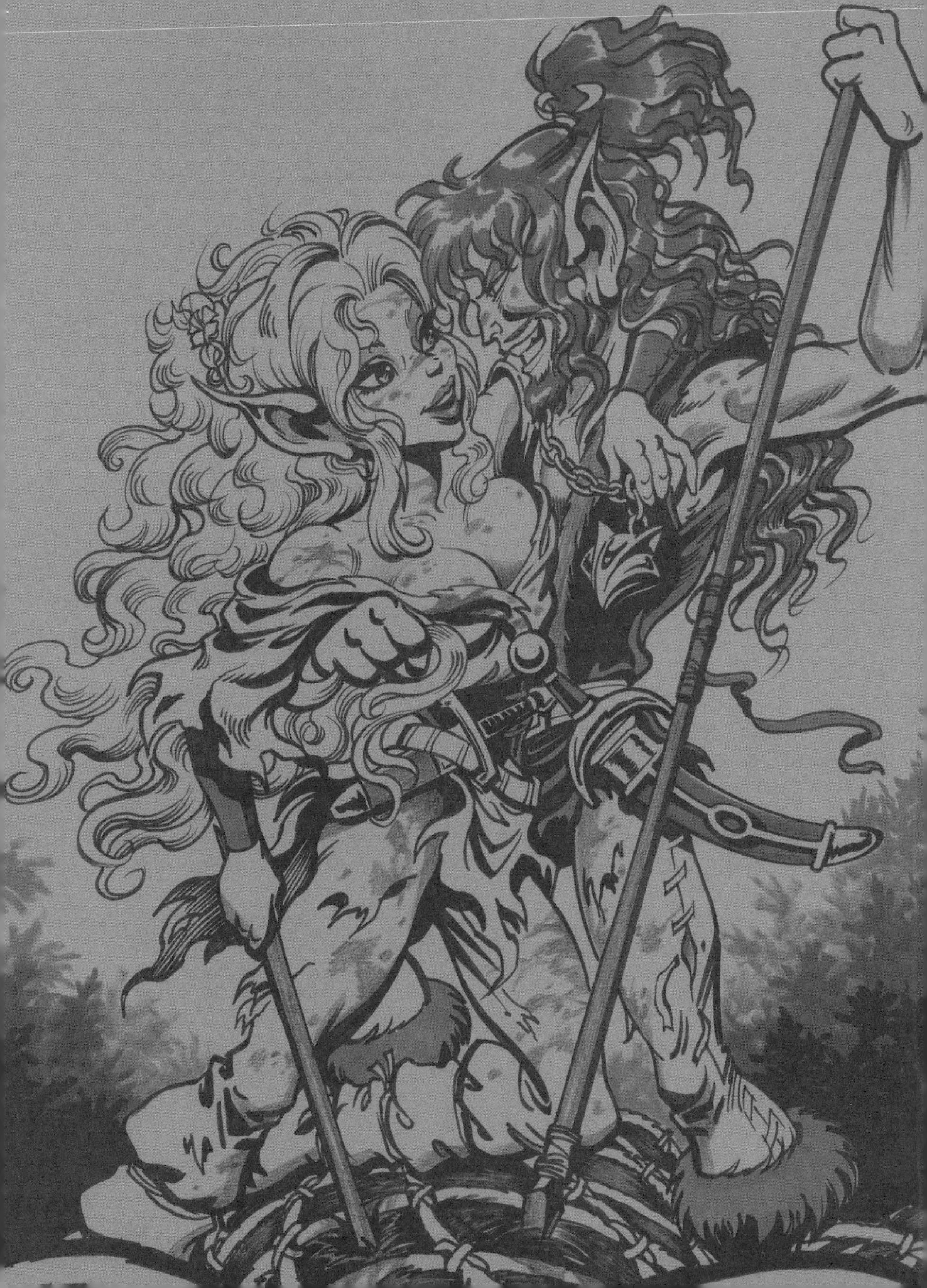

CONTENTS

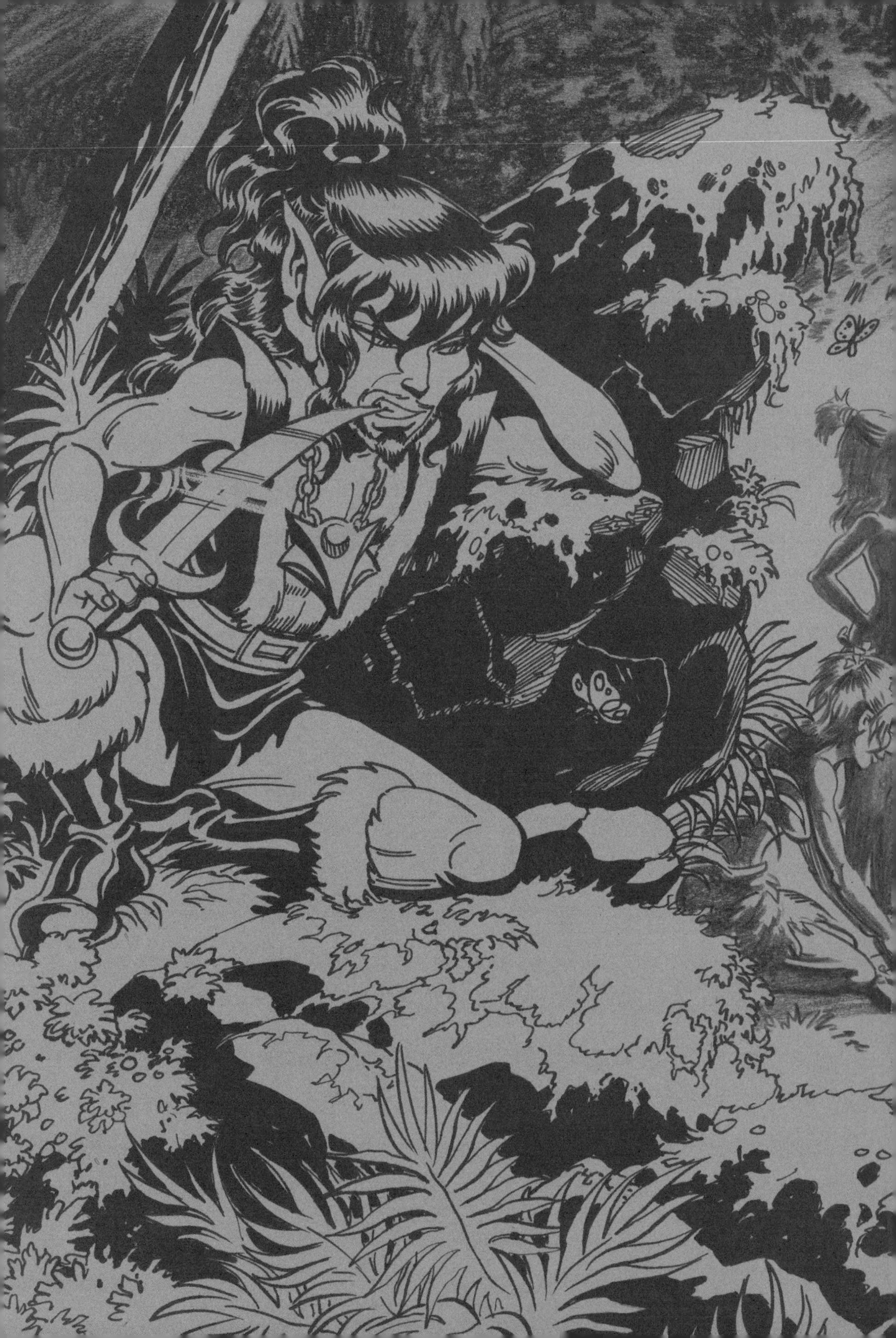

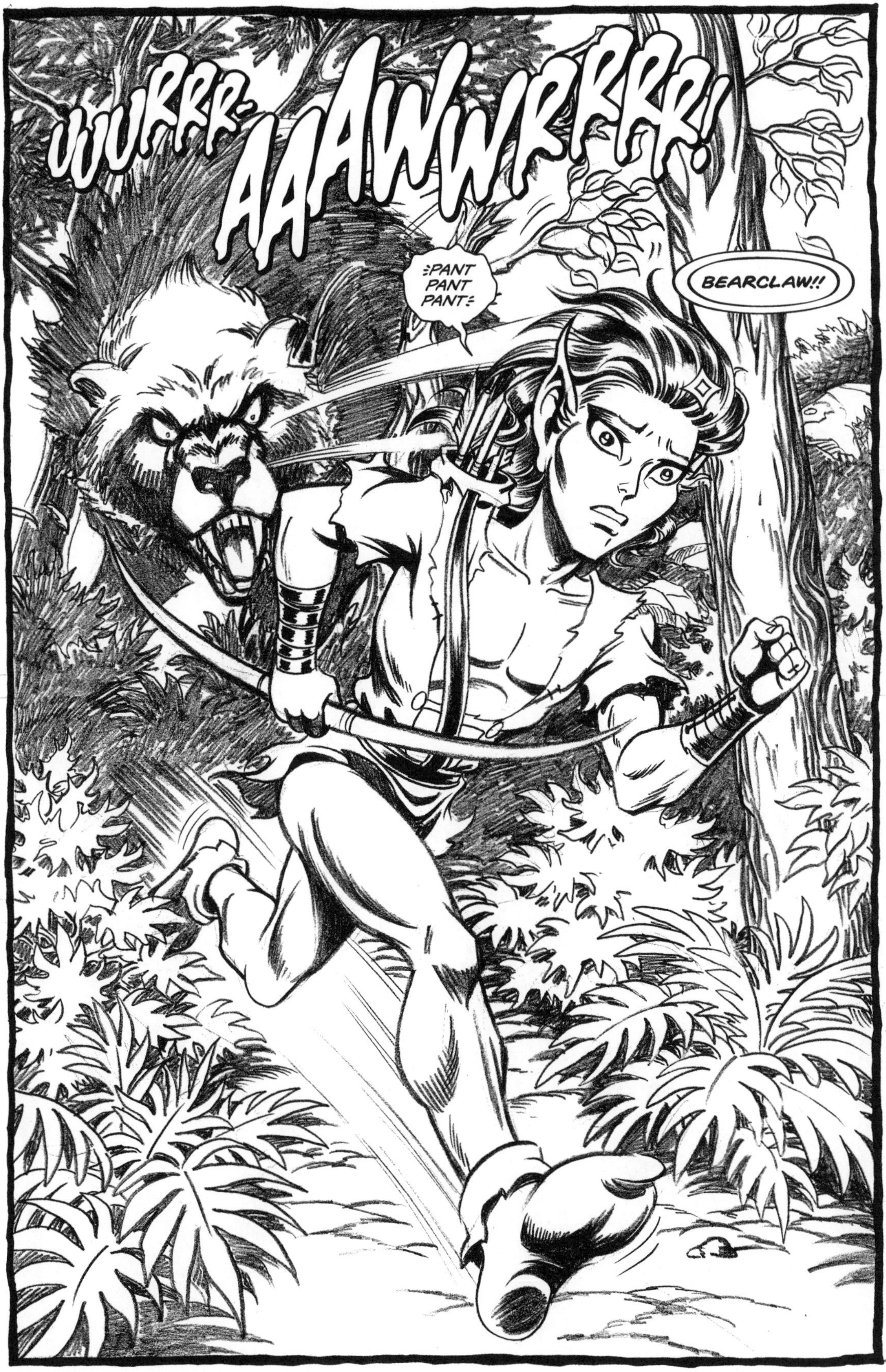
WURRR-AAAWWRRRR!
PANT PANT PANT
BEARCLAW!!

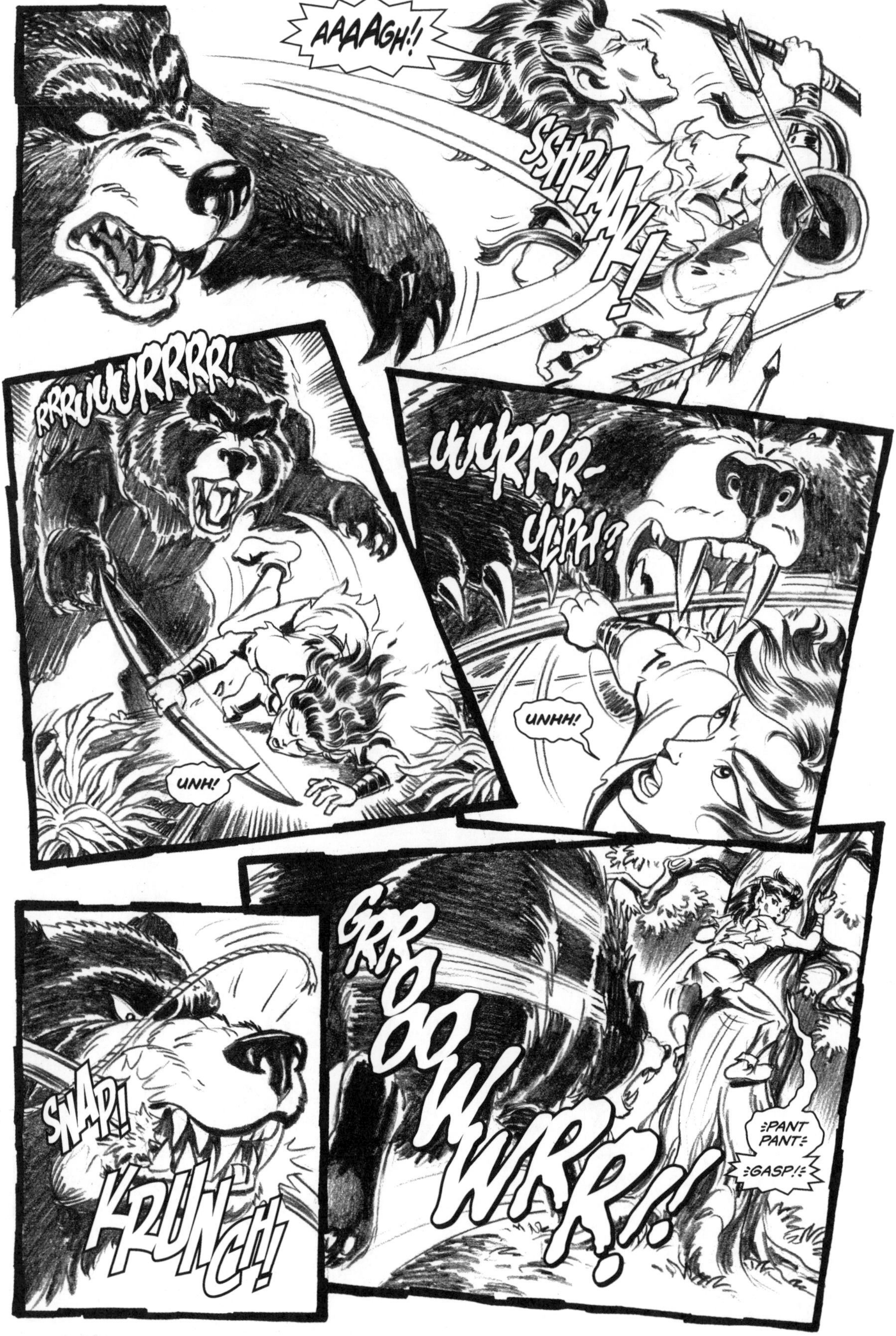
AAAAGH!!
SSHRAAAK!
RRRUUURRRR!
UNH!
UURRRR-ULPH?
UNHH!
SNAP!
KRUNCH!
GRROOOWWRR!!
PANT PANT
GASP!

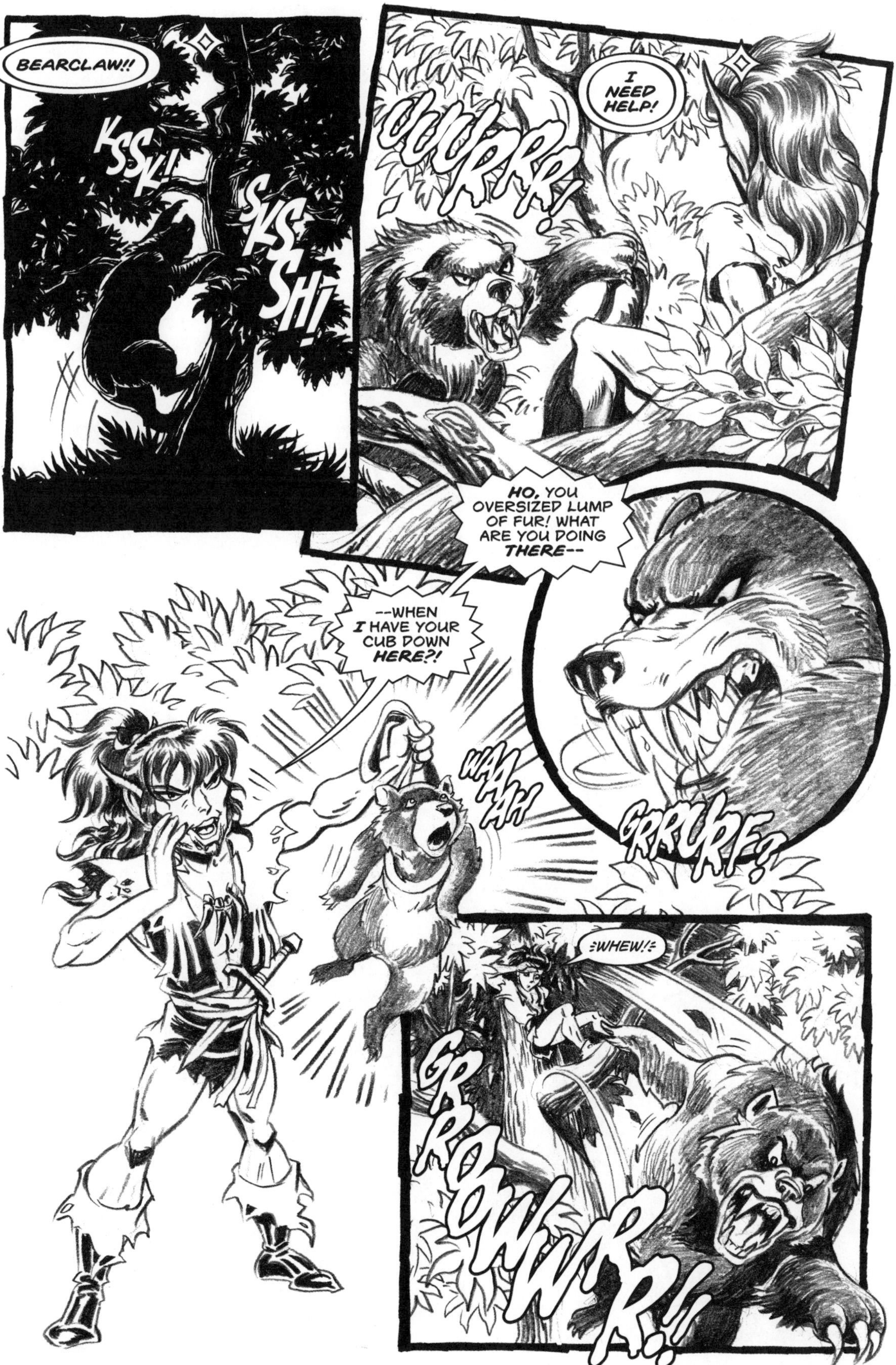
BEARCLAW!!
KSSK!
SKSSH!
I NEED HELP!
UUURRR!
HO, YOU OVERSIZED LUMP OF FUR! WHAT ARE YOU DOING THERE--
--WHEN I HAVE YOUR CUB DOWN HERE?!
WAAAH
GRRURF?!
WHEW!
GRROWWR!!

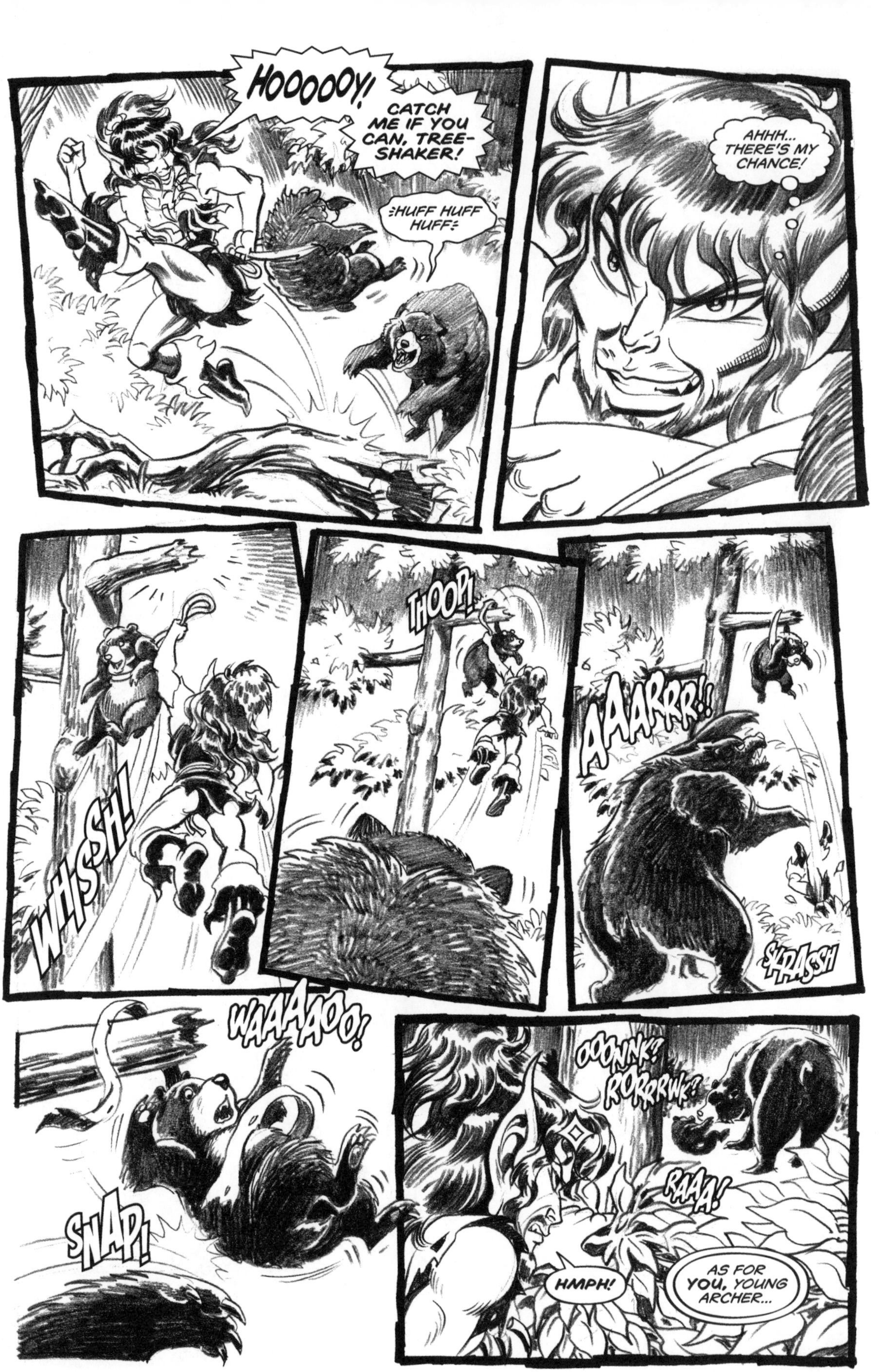
HOOOOOY!
CATCH ME IF YOU CAN, TREE-SHAKER!
HUFF HUFF HUFF
AHHH... THERE'S MY CHANCE!
WHISSSH!
THOOP!
AAARRR!!
SKRASSH
WAAAAOO!
SNAP!
OOONNK? RORRRWK?
RAAA!
HMPH!
AS FOR YOU, YOUNG ARCHER...

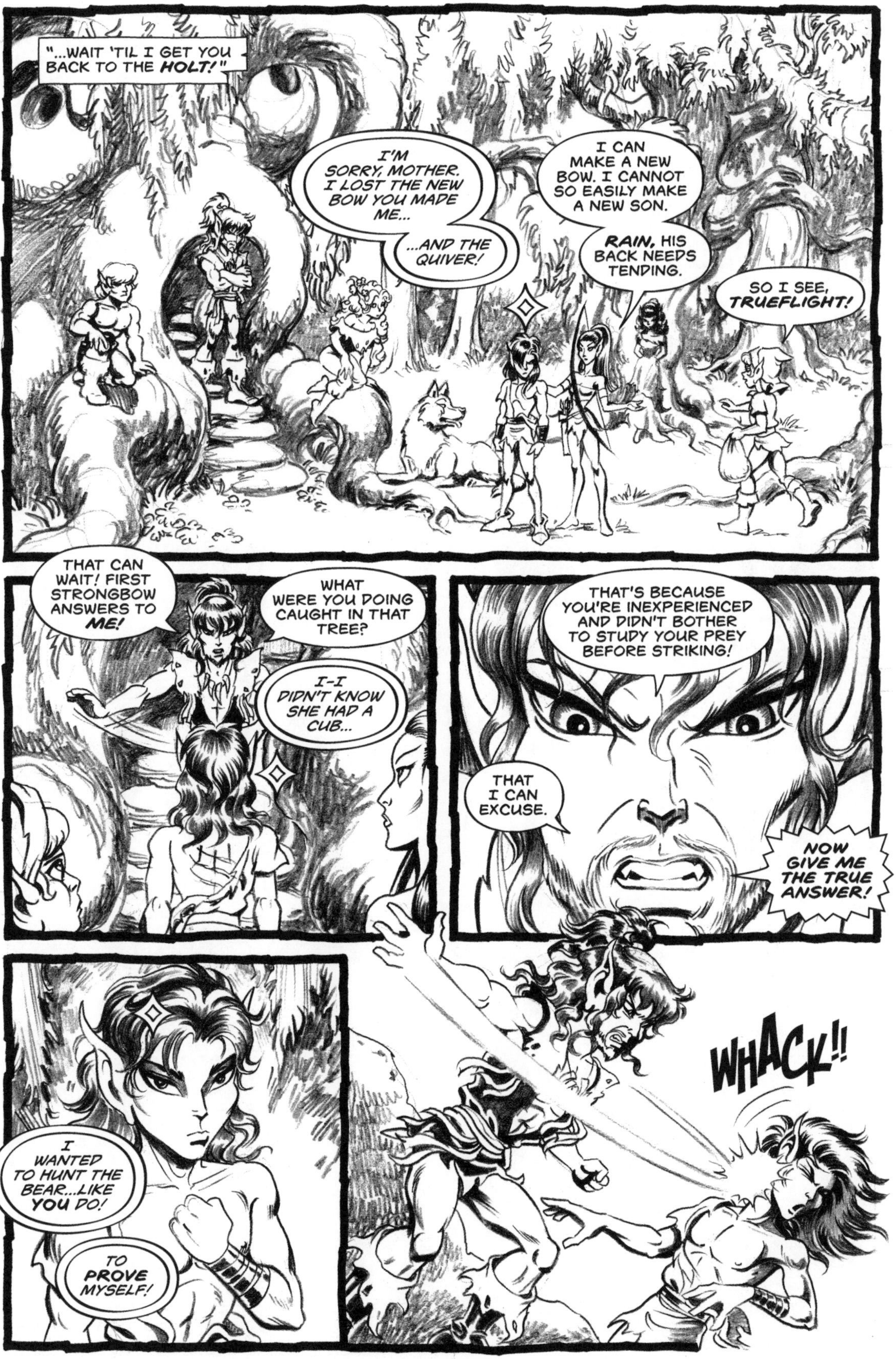
"...WAIT 'TIL I GET YOU BACK TO THE **HOLT!**"
I'M SORRY, MOTHER. I LOST THE NEW BOW YOU MADE ME...
...AND THE QUIVER!
I CAN MAKE A NEW BOW. I CANNOT SO EASILY MAKE A NEW SON.
RAIN, HIS BACK NEEDS TENDING.
SO I SEE, **TRUEFLIGHT!**
THAT CAN WAIT! FIRST STRONGBOW ANSWERS TO **ME!**
WHAT WERE YOU DOING CAUGHT IN THAT TREE?
I-I DIDN'T KNOW SHE HAD A CUB...
THAT'S BECAUSE YOU'RE INEXPERIENCED AND DIDN'T BOTHER TO STUDY YOUR PREY BEFORE STRIKING!
THAT I CAN EXCUSE.
NOW GIVE ME THE TRUE ANSWER!
I WANTED TO HUNT THE BEAR...LIKE **YOU** DO!
TO **PROVE** MYSELF!
WHACK!!

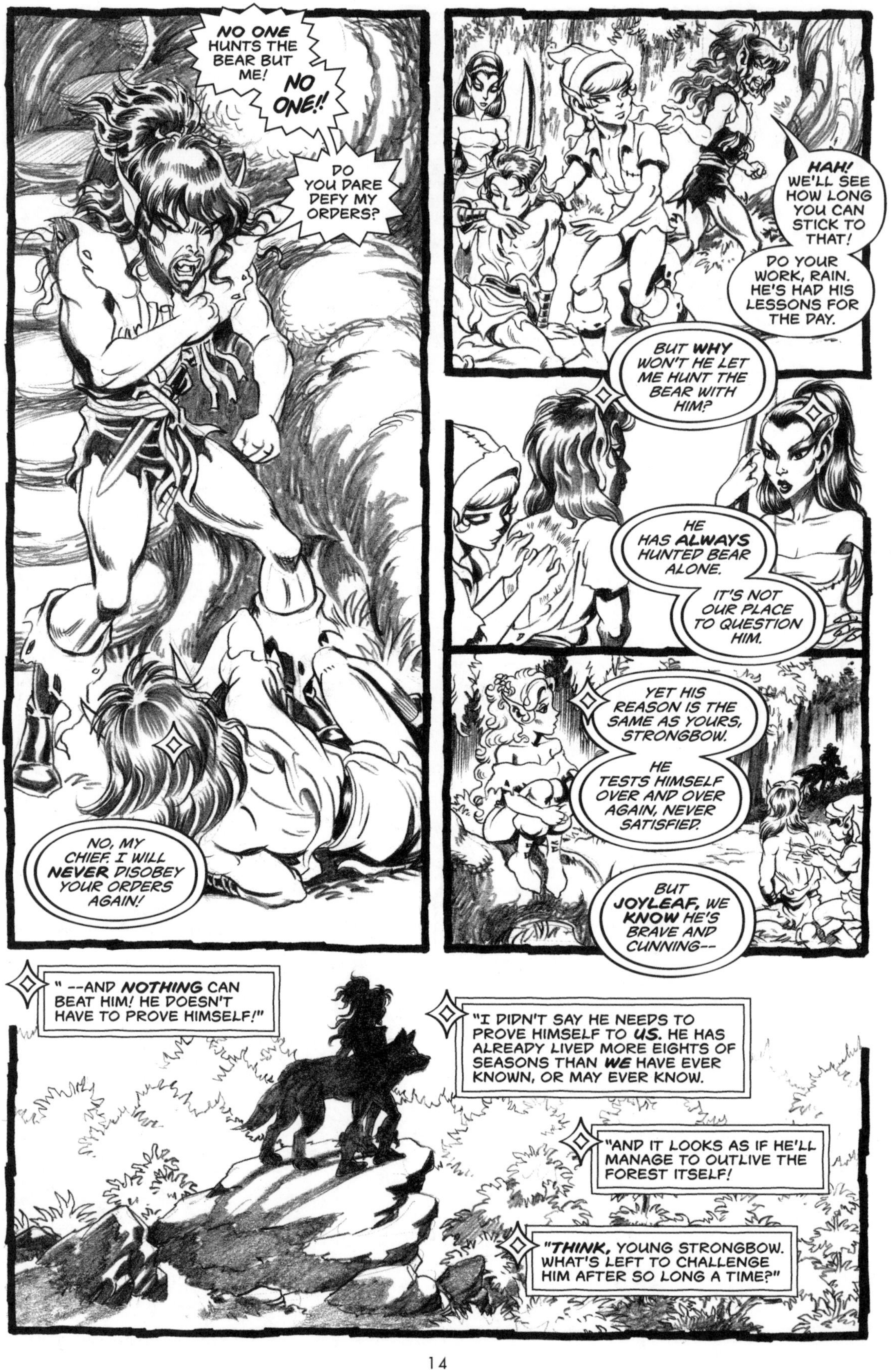
NO ONE HUNTS THE BEAR BUT ME!
NO ONE!!
DO YOU DARE DEFY MY ORDERS?
NO, MY CHIEF. I WILL NEVER DISOBEY YOUR ORDERS AGAIN!
HAH! WE'LL SEE HOW LONG YOU CAN STICK TO THAT!
DO YOUR WORK, RAIN. HE'S HAD HIS LESSONS FOR THE DAY.
BUT WHY WON'T HE LET ME HUNT THE BEAR WITH HIM?
HE HAS ALWAYS HUNTED BEAR ALONE.
IT'S NOT OUR PLACE TO QUESTION HIM.
YET HIS REASON IS THE SAME AS YOURS, STRONGBOW.
HE TESTS HIMSELF OVER AND OVER AGAIN, NEVER SATISFIED.
BUT JOYLEAF, WE KNOW HE'S BRAVE AND CUNNING--
" --AND NOTHING CAN BEAT HIM! HE DOESN'T HAVE TO PROVE HIMSELF!"
"I DIDN'T SAY HE NEEDS TO PROVE HIMSELF TO US. HE HAS ALREADY LIVED MORE EIGHTS OF SEASONS THAN WE HAVE EVER KNOWN, OR MAY EVER KNOW.
"AND IT LOOKS AS IF HE'LL MANAGE TO OUTLIVE THE FOREST ITSELF!
"THINK, YOUNG STRONGBOW. WHAT'S LEFT TO CHALLENGE HIM AFTER SO LONG A TIME?"

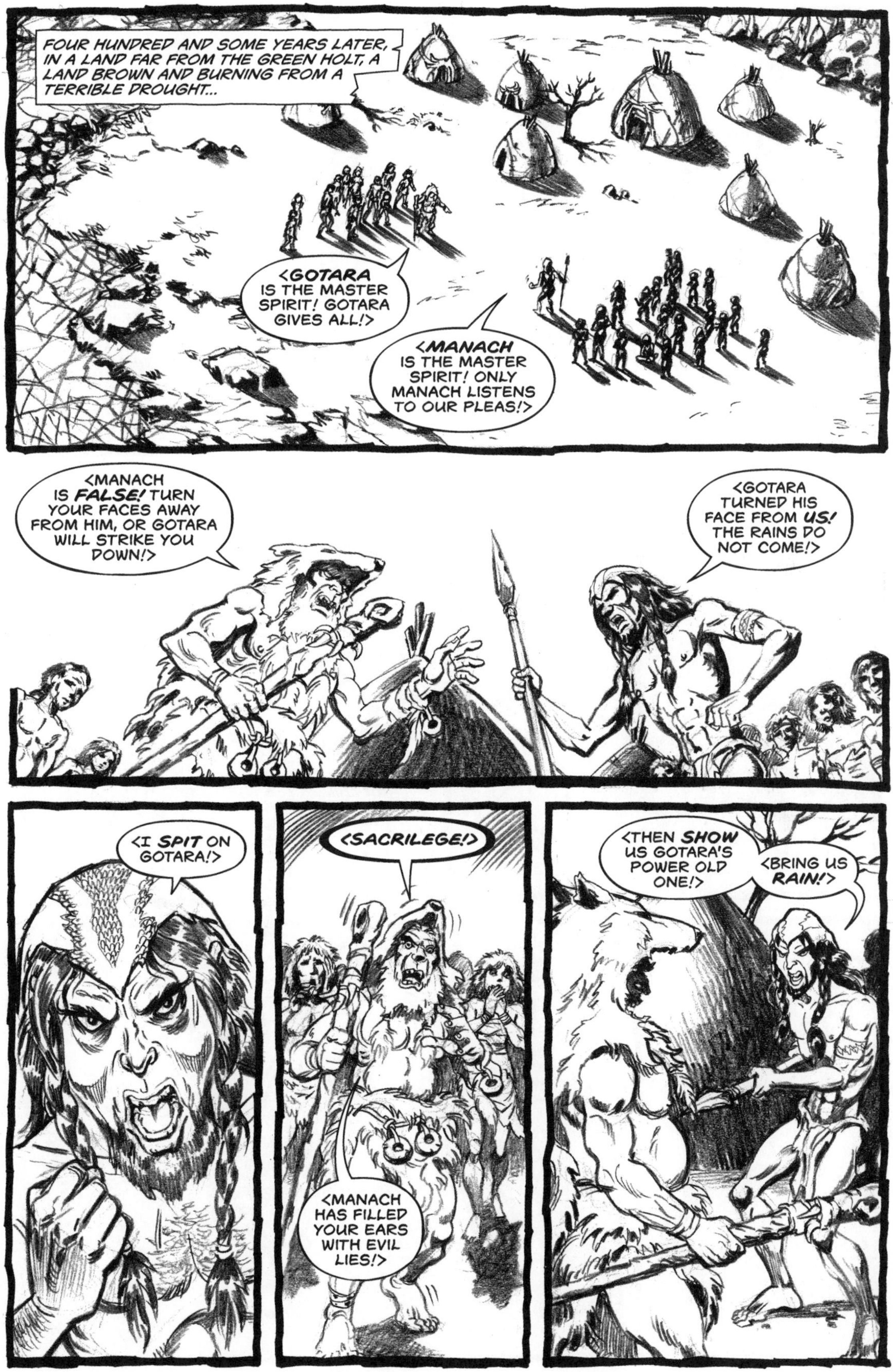

FOUR HUNDRED AND SOME YEARS LATER, IN A LAND FAR FROM THE GREEN HOLT, A LAND BROWN AND BURNING FROM A TERRIBLE DROUGHT...
<GOTARA IS THE MASTER SPIRIT! GOTARA GIVES ALL!>
<MANACH IS THE MASTER SPIRIT! ONLY MANACH LISTENS TO OUR PLEAS!>
<MANACH IS FALSE! TURN YOUR FACES AWAY FROM HIM, OR GOTARA WILL STRIKE YOU DOWN!>
<GOTARA TURNED HIS FACE FROM US! THE RAINS DO NOT COME!>
<I SPIT ON GOTARA!>
<SACRILEGE!>
<MANACH HAS FILLED YOUR EARS WITH EVIL LIES!>
<THEN SHOW US GOTARA'S POWER OLD ONE!>
<BRING US RAIN!>

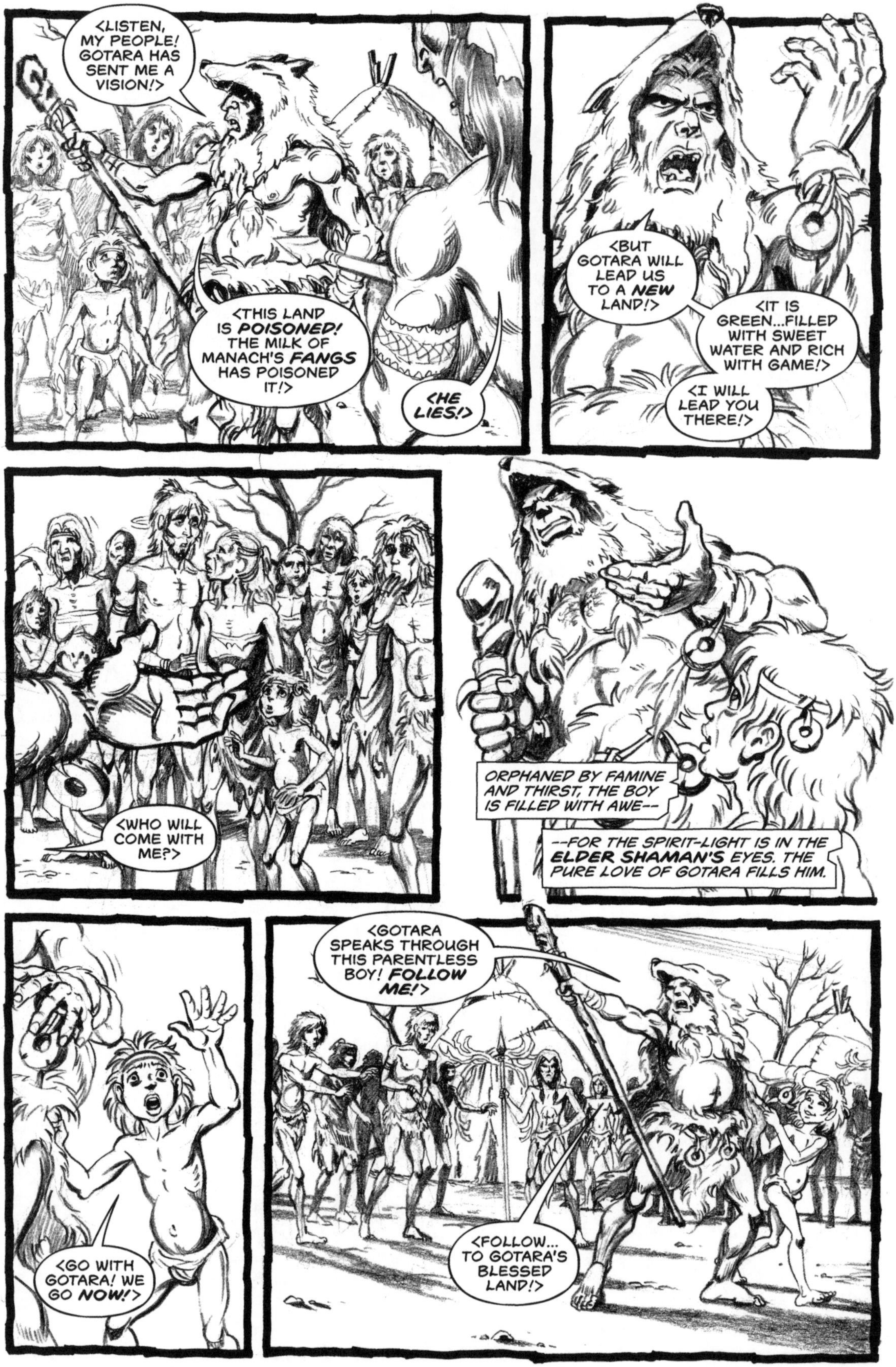
<LISTEN, MY PEOPLE! GOTARA HAS SENT ME A VISION!>
<THIS LAND IS **POISONED!** THE MILK OF MANACH'S **FANGS** HAS POISONED IT!>
<HE LIES!>
<BUT GOTARA WILL LEAD US TO A **NEW** LAND!>
<IT IS GREEN...FILLED WITH SWEET WATER AND RICH WITH GAME!>
<I WILL LEAD YOU THERE!>
<WHO WILL COME WITH ME?>
ORPHANED BY FAMINE AND THIRST, THE BOY IS FILLED WITH AWE--
--FOR THE SPIRIT-LIGHT IS IN THE **ELDER SHAMAN'S** EYES. THE PURE LOVE OF GOTARA FILLS HIM.
<GO WITH GOTARA! WE GO **NOW!**>
<GOTARA SPEAKS THROUGH THIS PARENTLESS BOY! **FOLLOW ME!**>
<FOLLOW... TO GOTARA'S BLESSED LAND!>

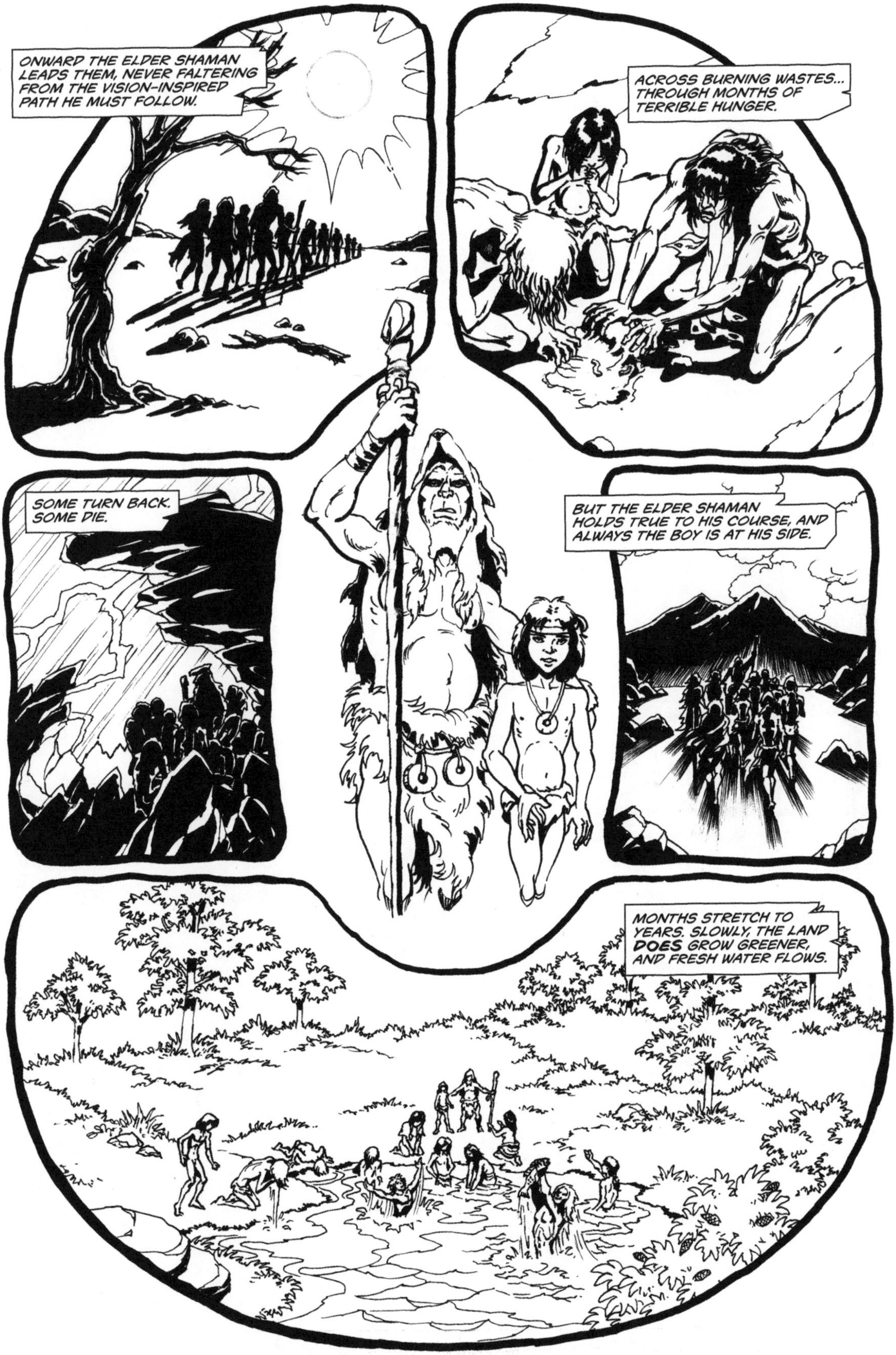
ONWARD THE ELDER SHAMAN LEADS THEM, NEVER FALTERING FROM THE VISION-INSPIRED PATH HE MUST FOLLOW.
ACROSS BURNING WASTES... THROUGH MONTHS OF TERRIBLE HUNGER.
SOME TURN BACK. SOME DIE.
BUT THE ELDER SHAMAN HOLDS TRUE TO HIS COURSE, AND ALWAYS THE BOY IS AT HIS SIDE.
MONTHS STRETCH TO YEARS. SLOWLY, THE LAND **DOES** GROW GREENER, AND FRESH WATER FLOWS.

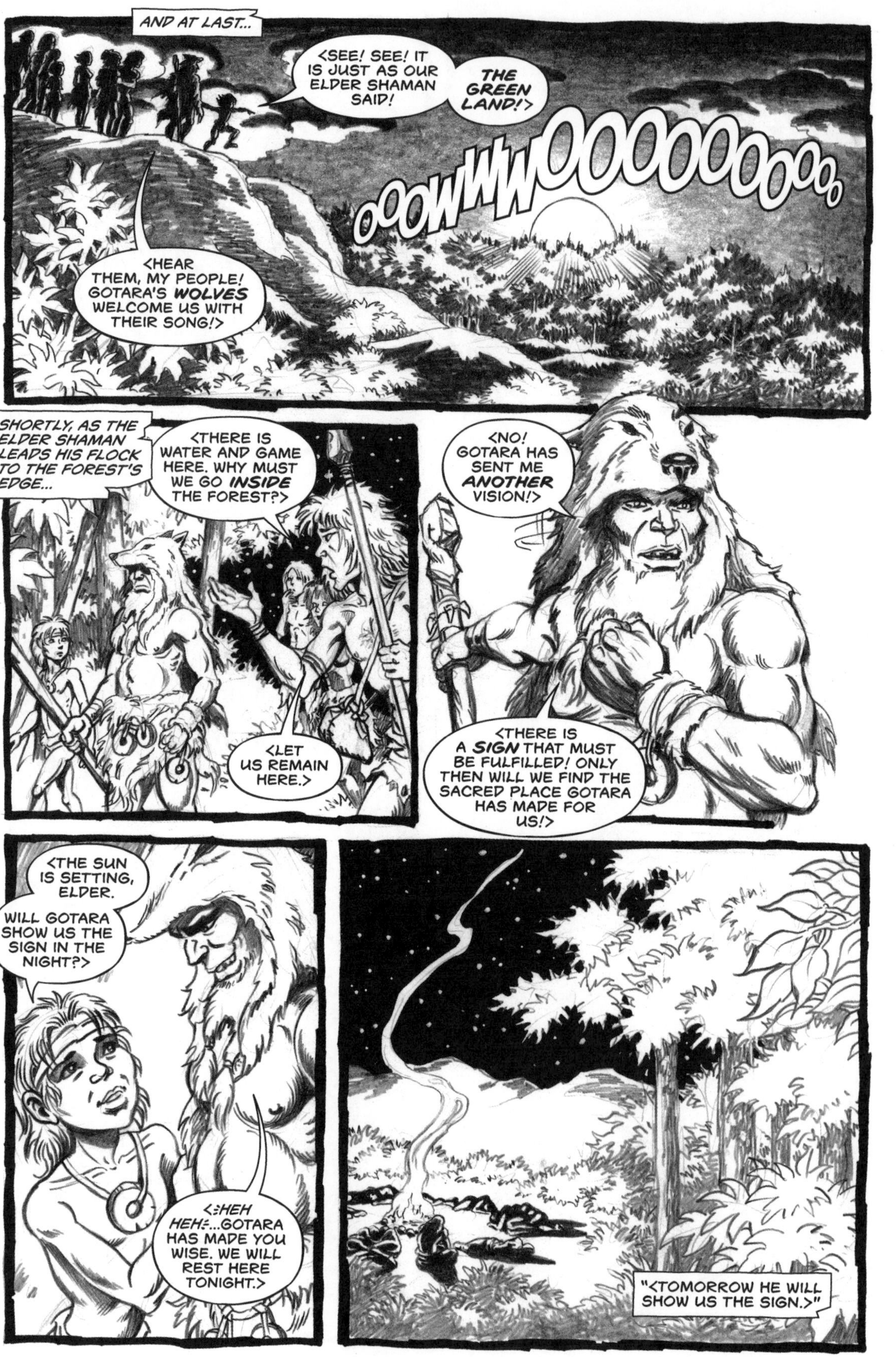
AND AT LAST...
<SEE! SEE! IT IS JUST AS OUR ELDER SHAMAN SAID!
THE GREEN LAND!>
OOOWWWOOOOOOOOOO
<HEAR THEM, MY PEOPLE! GOTARA'S WOLVES WELCOME US WITH THEIR SONG!>
SHORTLY, AS THE ELDER SHAMAN LEADS HIS FLOCK TO THE FOREST'S EDGE...
<THERE IS WATER AND GAME HERE. WHY MUST WE GO INSIDE THE FOREST?>
<LET US REMAIN HERE.>
<NO! GOTARA HAS SENT ME ANOTHER VISION!>
<THERE IS A SIGN THAT MUST BE FULFILLED! ONLY THEN WILL WE FIND THE SACRED PLACE GOTARA HAS MADE FOR US!>
<THE SUN IS SETTING, ELDER.
WILL GOTARA SHOW US THE SIGN IN THE NIGHT?>
<=HEH HEH=...GOTARA HAS MADE YOU WISE. WE WILL REST HERE TONIGHT.>
"<TOMORROW HE WILL SHOW US THE SIGN.>"

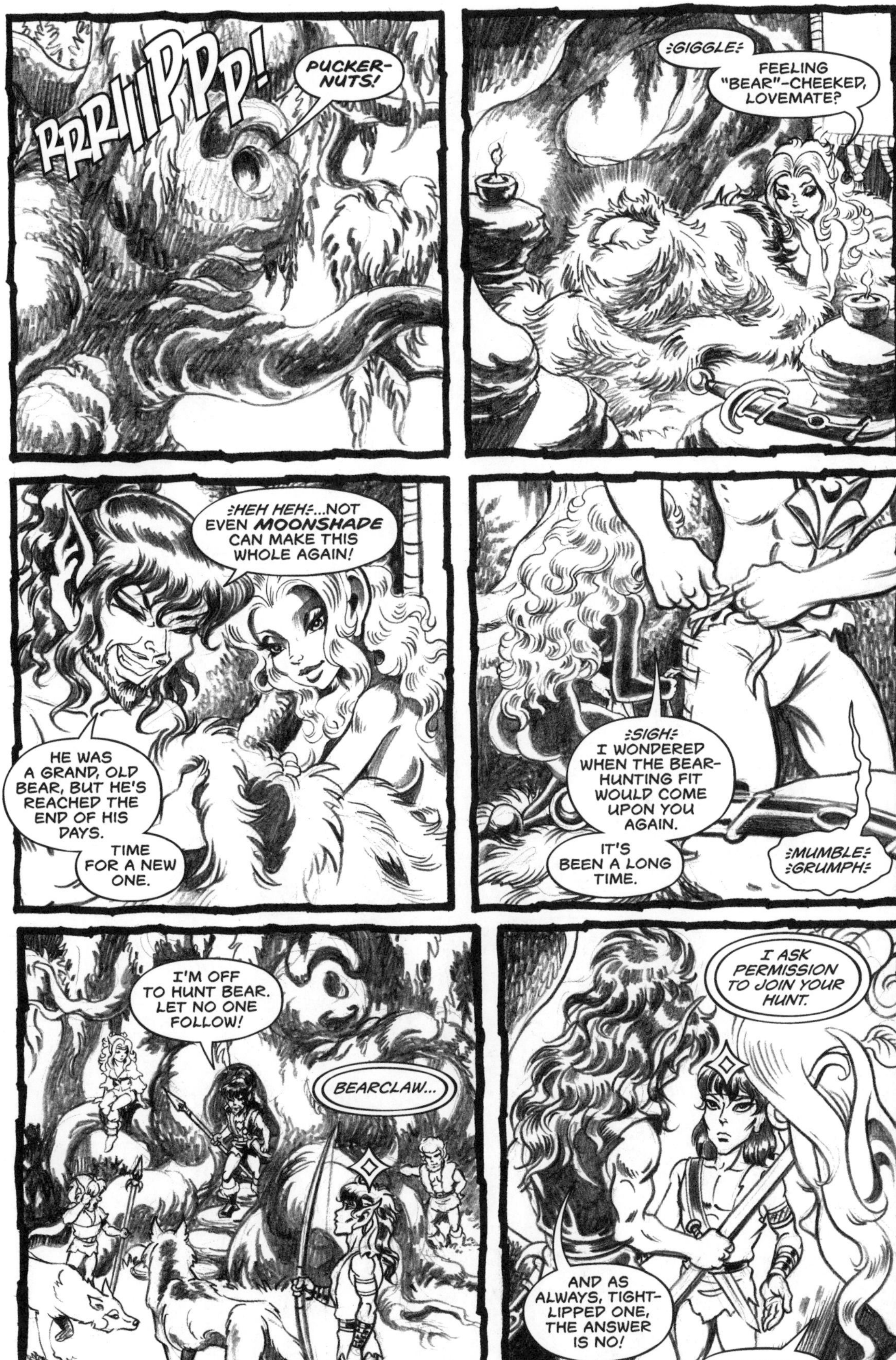
RRRIIIPPPp!
PUCKER-NUTS!
GIGGLE
FEELING "BEAR"-CHEEKED, LOVEMATE?
HEH HEH...NOT EVEN MOONSHADE CAN MAKE THIS WHOLE AGAIN!
HE WAS A GRAND, OLD BEAR, BUT HE'S REACHED THE END OF HIS DAYS.
TIME FOR A NEW ONE.
SIGH I WONDERED WHEN THE BEAR-HUNTING FIT WOULD COME UPON YOU AGAIN.
IT'S BEEN A LONG TIME.
MUMBLE GRUMPH
I'M OFF TO HUNT BEAR. LET NO ONE FOLLOW!
BEARCLAW...
I ASK PERMISSION TO JOIN YOUR HUNT.
AND AS ALWAYS, TIGHT-LIPPED ONE, THE ANSWER IS NO!
BEARCLAW...

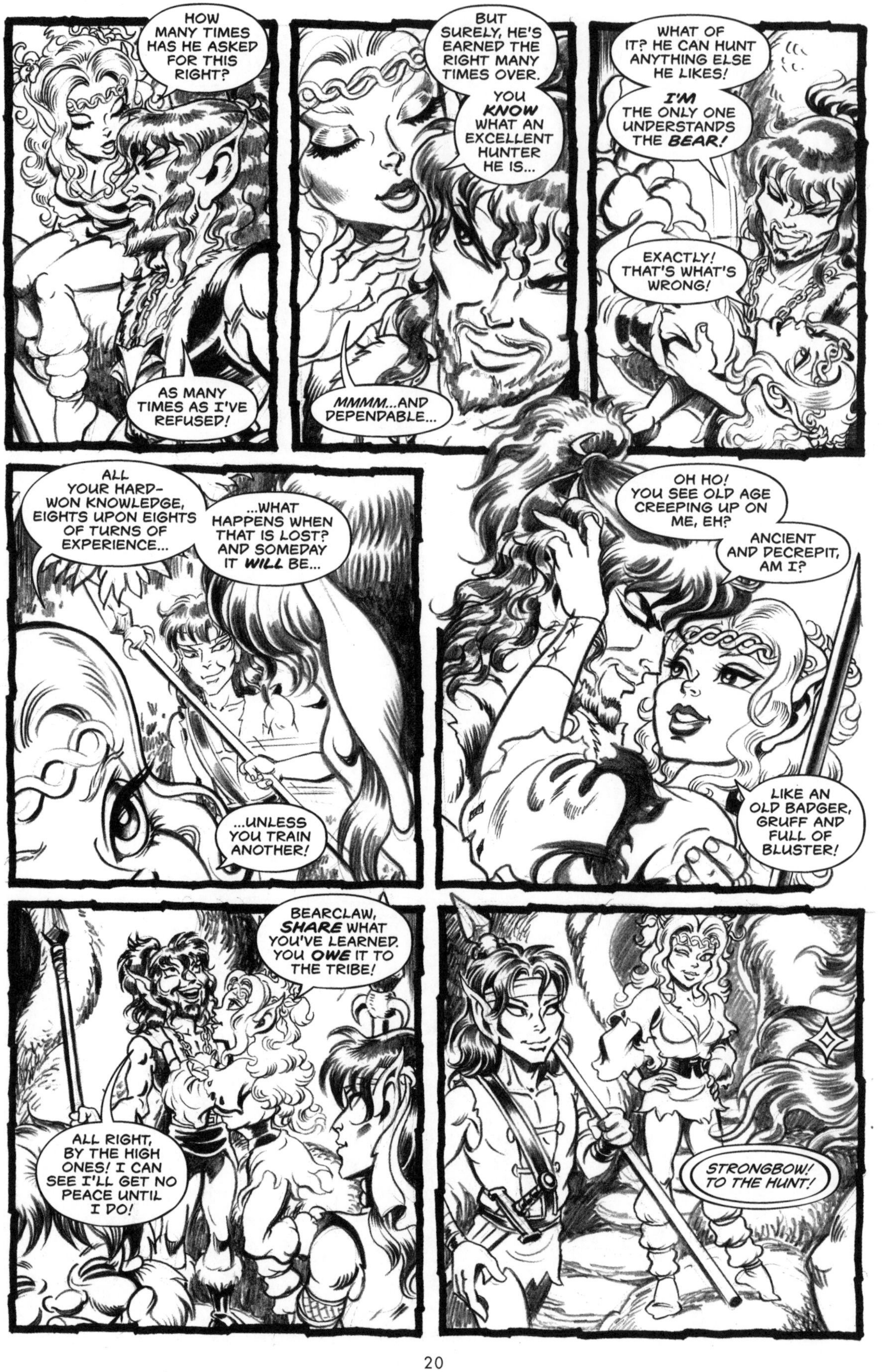
HOW MANY TIMES HAS HE ASKED FOR THIS RIGHT?
AS MANY TIMES AS I'VE REFUSED!
BUT SURELY, HE'S EARNED THE RIGHT MANY TIMES OVER.
YOU KNOW WHAT AN EXCELLENT HUNTER HE IS...
MMMM...AND DEPENDABLE...
WHAT OF IT? HE CAN HUNT ANYTHING ELSE HE LIKES!
I'M THE ONLY ONE UNDERSTANDS THE BEAR!
EXACTLY! THAT'S WHAT'S WRONG!
ALL YOUR HARD-WON KNOWLEDGE, EIGHTS UPON EIGHTS OF TURNS OF EXPERIENCE...
...WHAT HAPPENS WHEN THAT IS LOST? AND SOMEDAY IT WILL BE...
...UNLESS YOU TRAIN ANOTHER!
OH HO! YOU SEE OLD AGE CREEPING UP ON ME, EH?
ANCIENT AND DECREPIT, AM I?
LIKE AN OLD BADGER, GRUFF AND FULL OF BLUSTER!
BEARCLAW, SHARE WHAT YOU'VE LEARNED. YOU OWE IT TO THE TRIBE!
ALL RIGHT, BY THE HIGH ONES! I CAN SEE I'LL GET NO PEACE UNTIL I DO!
STRONGBOW! TO THE HUNT!

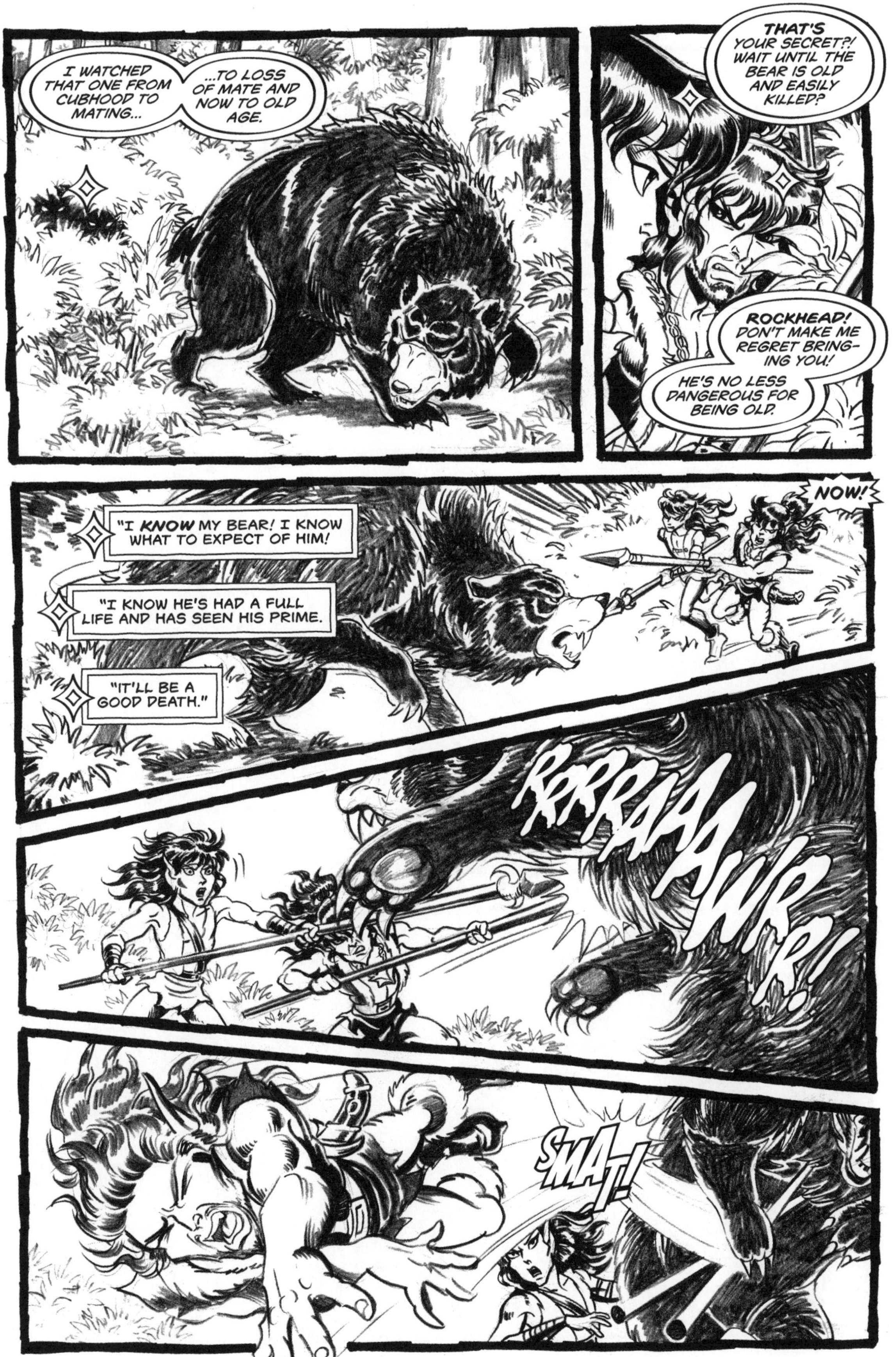

I WATCHED THAT ONE FROM CUBHOOD TO MATING...
...TO LOSS OF MATE AND NOW TO OLD AGE.
THAT'S YOUR SECRET?! WAIT UNTIL THE BEAR IS OLD AND EASILY KILLED?
ROCKHEAD! DON'T MAKE ME REGRET BRINGING YOU!
HE'S NO LESS DANGEROUS FOR BEING OLD.
NOW!
"I KNOW MY BEAR! I KNOW WHAT TO EXPECT OF HIM!
"I KNOW HE'S HAD A FULL LIFE AND HAS SEEN HIS PRIME.
"IT'LL BE A GOOD DEATH."
RRRRAAAAWRR!
SMAT!

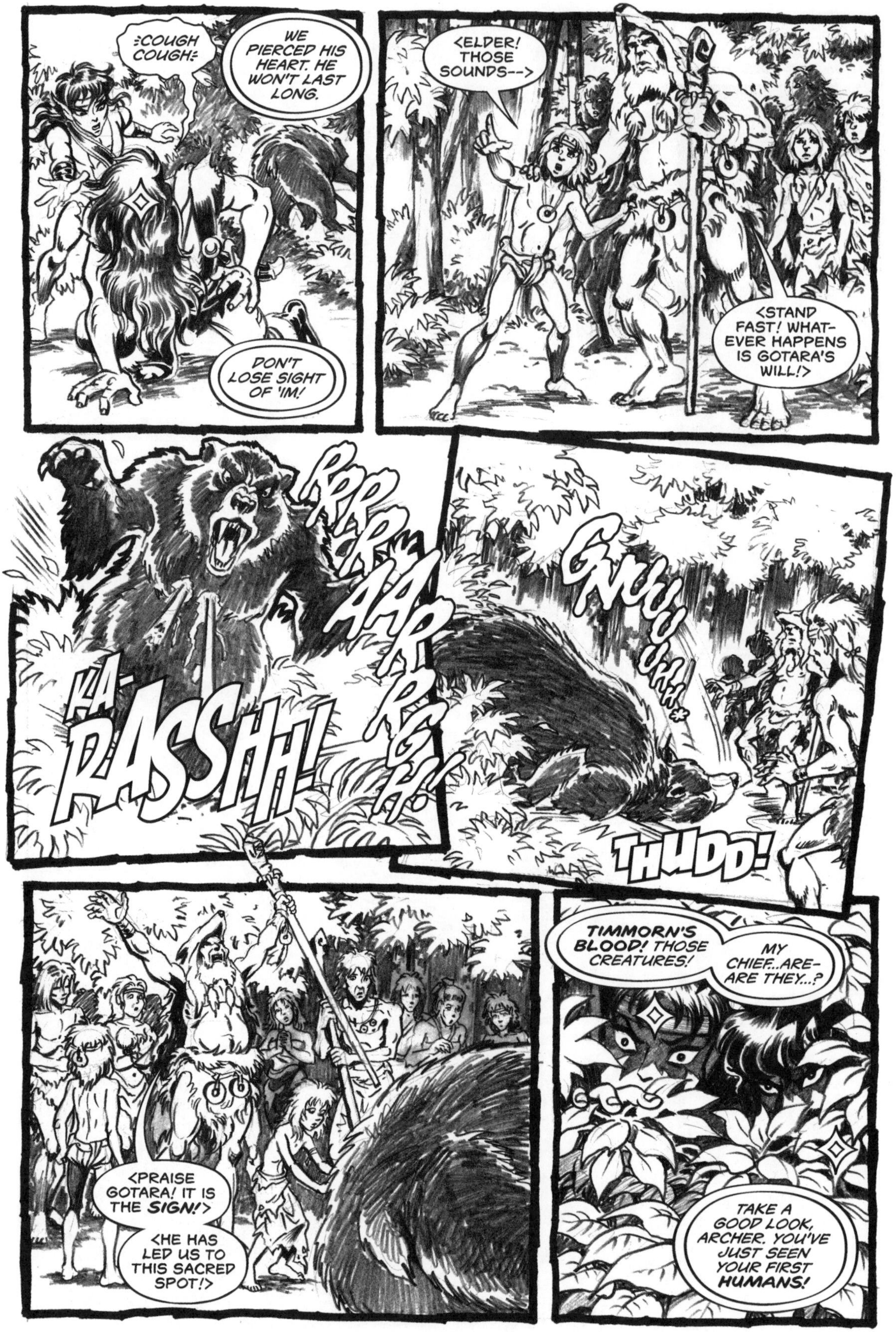
:COUGH COUGH:
WE PIERCED HIS HEART. HE WON'T LAST LONG.
DON'T LOSE SIGHT OF 'IM!
<ELDER! THOSE SOUNDS-->
<STAND FAST! WHATEVER HAPPENS IS GOTARA'S WILL!>
RRRRAARRGH!
KA-RASSHH!
GNUUUHH*
THUDD!
<PRAISE GOTARA! IT IS THE SIGN!>
<HE HAS LED US TO THIS SACRED SPOT!>
TIMMORN'S BLOOD! THOSE CREATURES!
MY CHIEF...ARE-ARE THEY...?
TAKE A GOOD LOOK, ARCHER. YOU'VE JUST SEEN YOUR FIRST HUMANS!

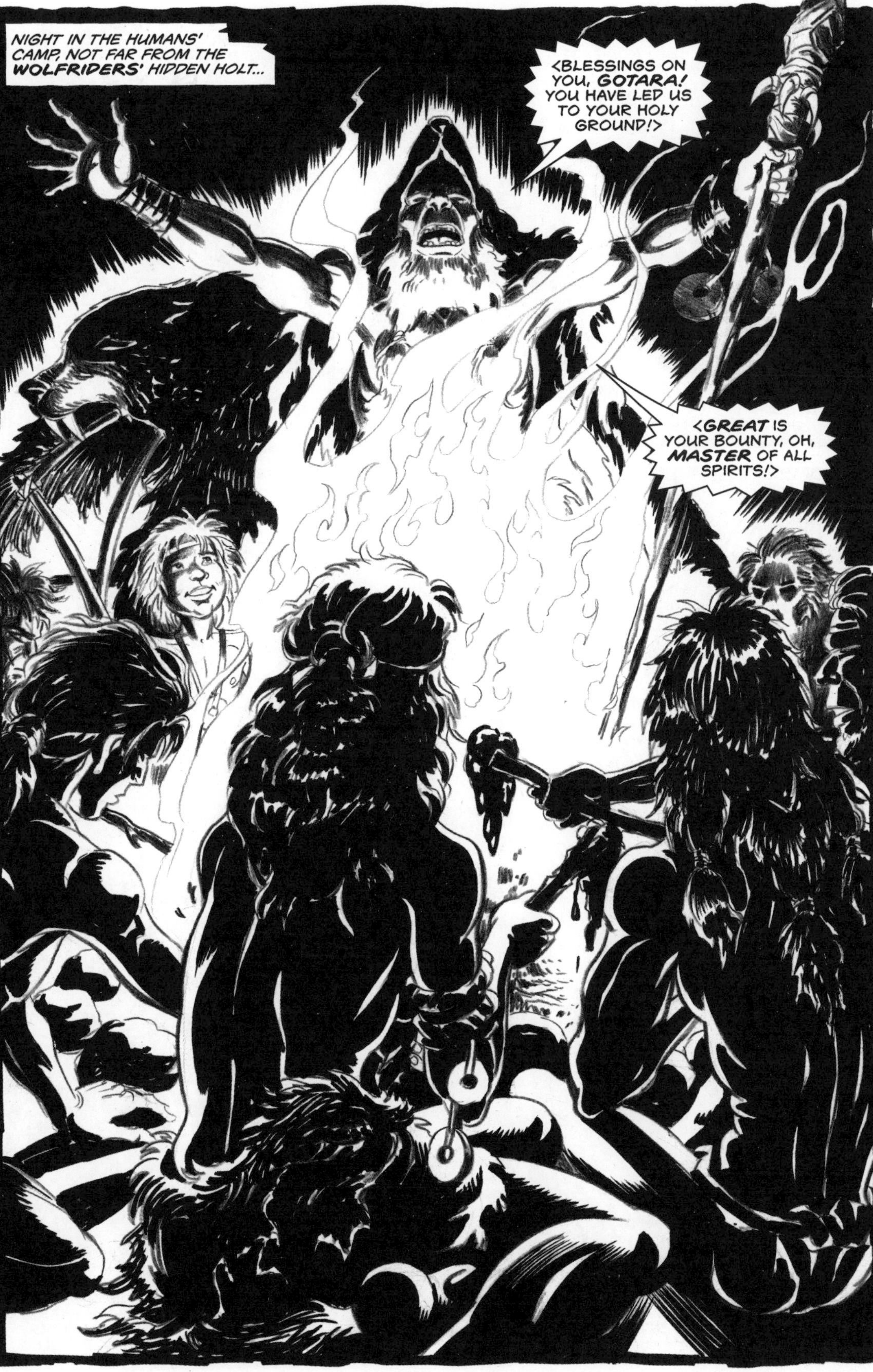
NIGHT IN THE HUMANS' CAMP, NOT FAR FROM THE WOLFRIDERS' HIDDEN HOLT...
<BLESSINGS ON YOU, GOTARA! YOU HAVE LED US TO YOUR HOLY GROUND!>
<GREAT IS YOUR BOUNTY, OH, MASTER OF ALL SPIRITS!>

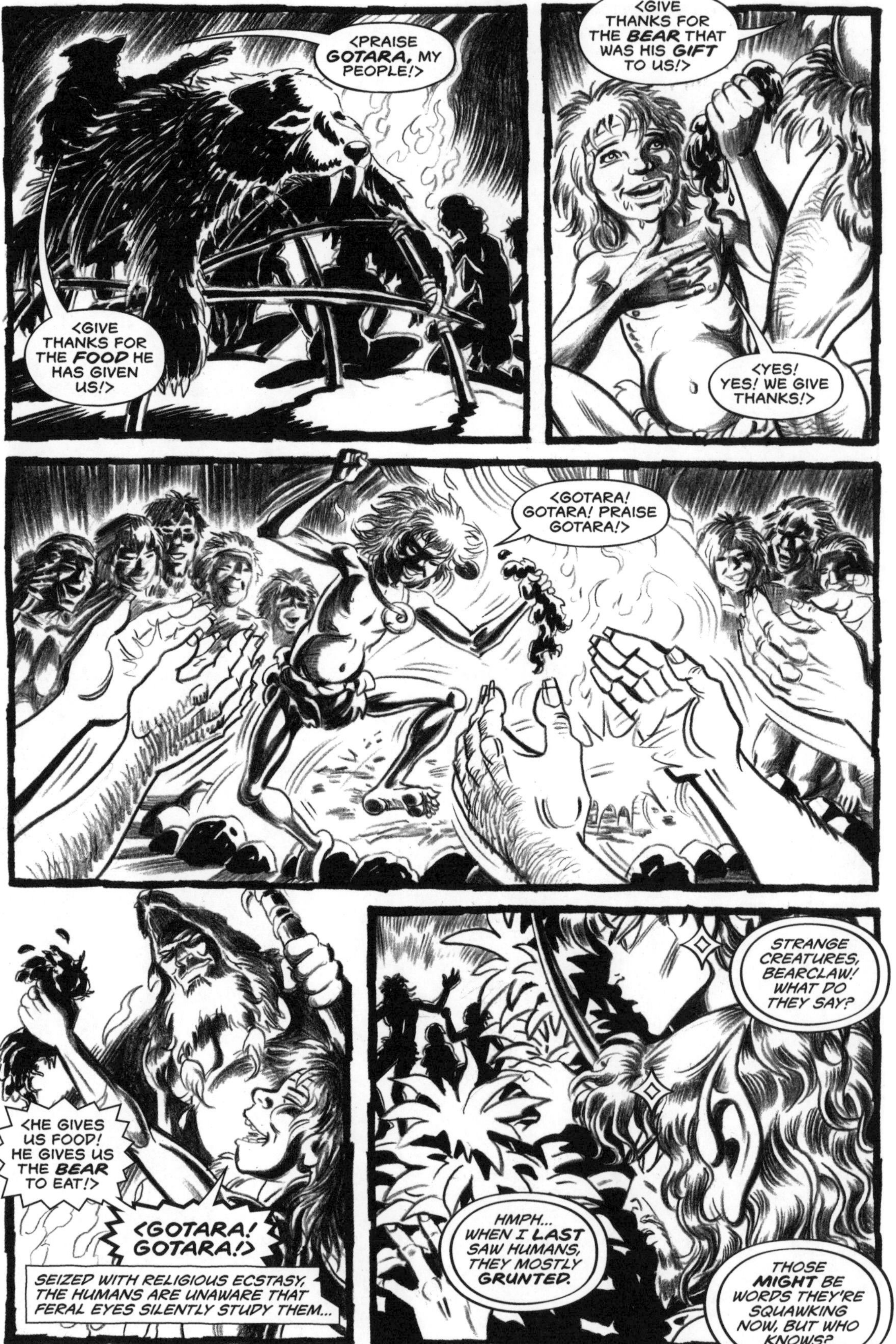

<PRAISE GOTARA, MY PEOPLE!>
<GIVE THANKS FOR THE FOOD HE HAS GIVEN US!>
<GIVE THANKS FOR THE BEAR THAT WAS HIS GIFT TO US!>
<YES! YES! WE GIVE THANKS!>
<GOTARA! GOTARA! PRAISE GOTARA!>
<HE GIVES US FOOD! HE GIVES US THE BEAR TO EAT!>
<GOTARA! GOTARA!>
SEIZED WITH RELIGIOUS ECSTASY, THE HUMANS ARE UNAWARE THAT FERAL EYES SILENTLY STUDY THEM...
STRANGE CREATURES, BEARCLAW! WHAT DO THEY SAY?
HMPH... WHEN I LAST SAW HUMANS, THEY MOSTLY GRUNTED.
THOSE MIGHT BE WORDS THEY'RE SQUAWKING NOW, BUT WHO KNOWS?

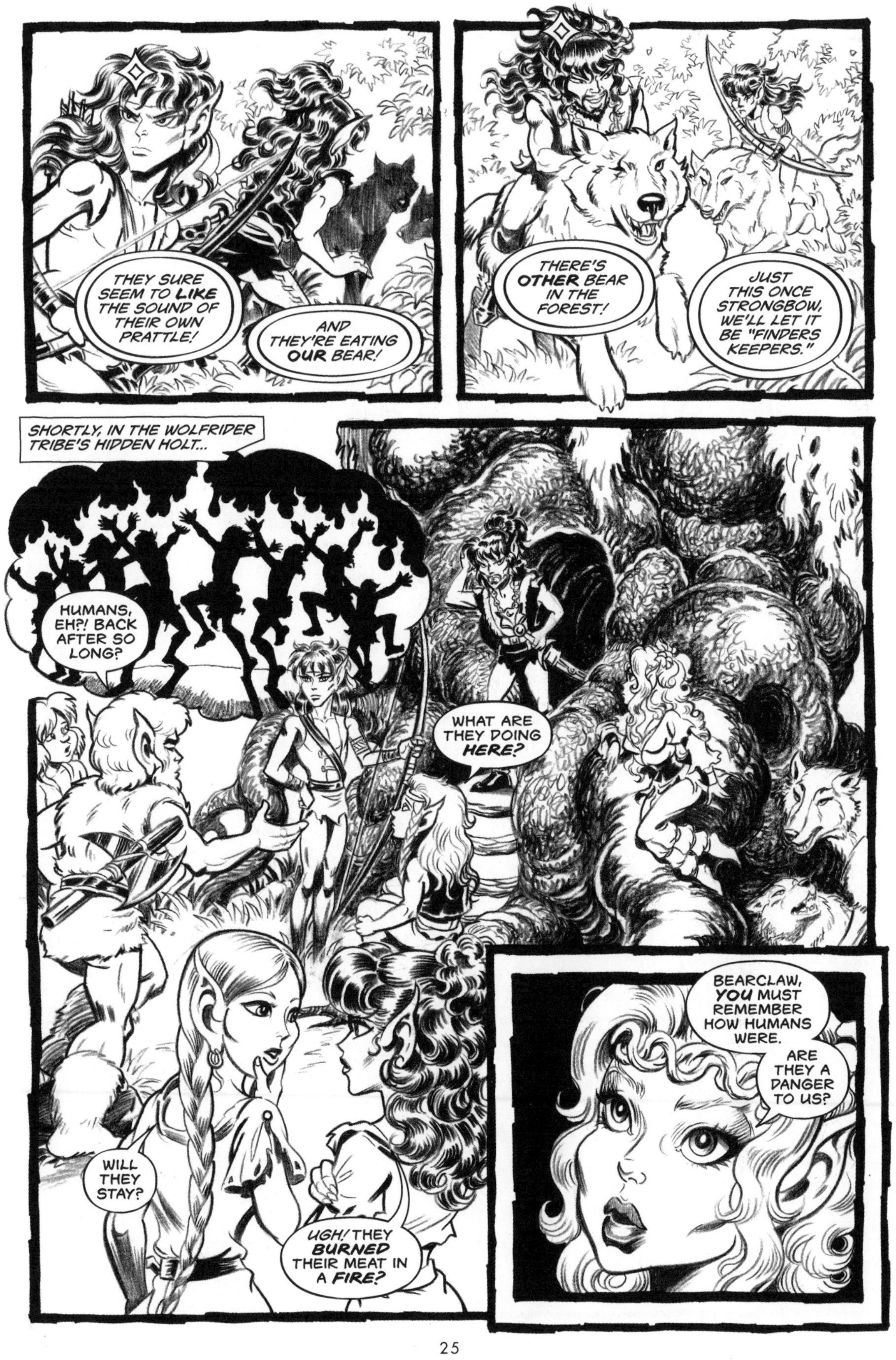
THEY SURE SEEM TO LIKE THE SOUND OF THEIR OWN PRATTLE!
AND THEY'RE EATING OUR BEAR!
THERE'S OTHER BEAR IN THE FOREST!
JUST THIS ONCE STRONGBOW, WE'LL LET IT BE "FINDERS KEEPERS."
SHORTLY, IN THE WOLFRIDER TRIBE'S HIDDEN HOLT...
HUMANS, EH?! BACK AFTER SO LONG?
WHAT ARE THEY DOING HERE?
WILL THEY STAY?
UGH! THEY BURNED THEIR MEAT IN A FIRE?
BEARCLAW, YOU MUST REMEMBER HOW HUMANS WERE.
ARE THEY A DANGER TO US?

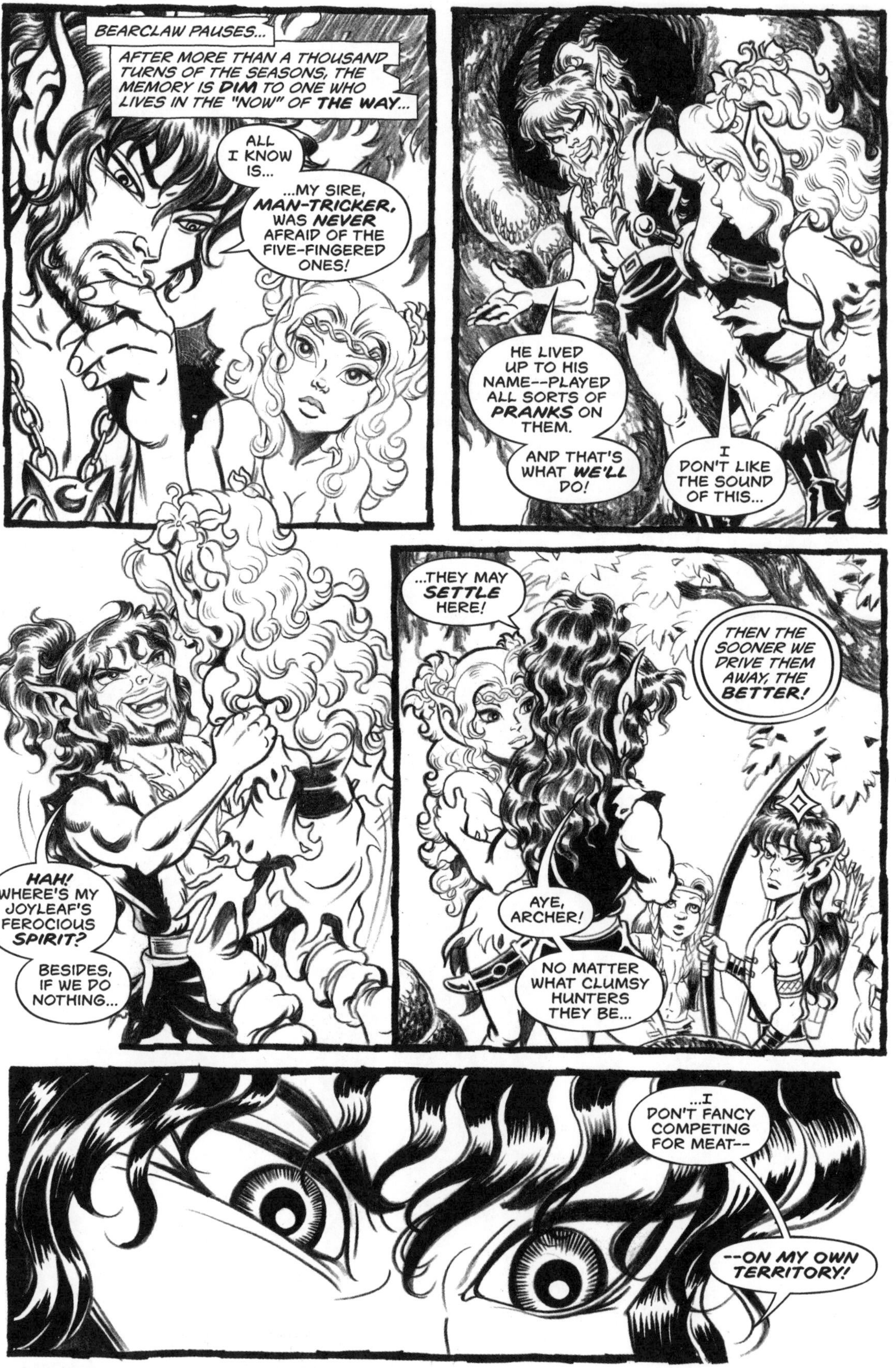
BEARCLAW PAUSES...
AFTER MORE THAN A THOUSAND TURNS OF THE SEASONS, THE MEMORY IS DIM TO ONE WHO LIVES IN THE "NOW" OF THE WAY...
ALL I KNOW IS...
...MY SIRE, MAN-TRICKER, WAS NEVER AFRAID OF THE FIVE-FINGERED ONES!
HE LIVED UP TO HIS NAME--PLAYED ALL SORTS OF PRANKS ON THEM.
AND THAT'S WHAT WE'LL DO!
I DON'T LIKE THE SOUND OF THIS...
HAH! WHERE'S MY JOYLEAF'S FEROCIOUS SPIRIT?
BESIDES, IF WE DO NOTHING...
...THEY MAY SETTLE HERE!
THEN THE SOONER WE DRIVE THEM AWAY, THE BETTER!
AYE, ARCHER!
NO MATTER WHAT CLUMSY HUNTERS THEY BE...
...I DON'T FANCY COMPETING FOR MEAT--
--ON MY OWN TERRITORY!

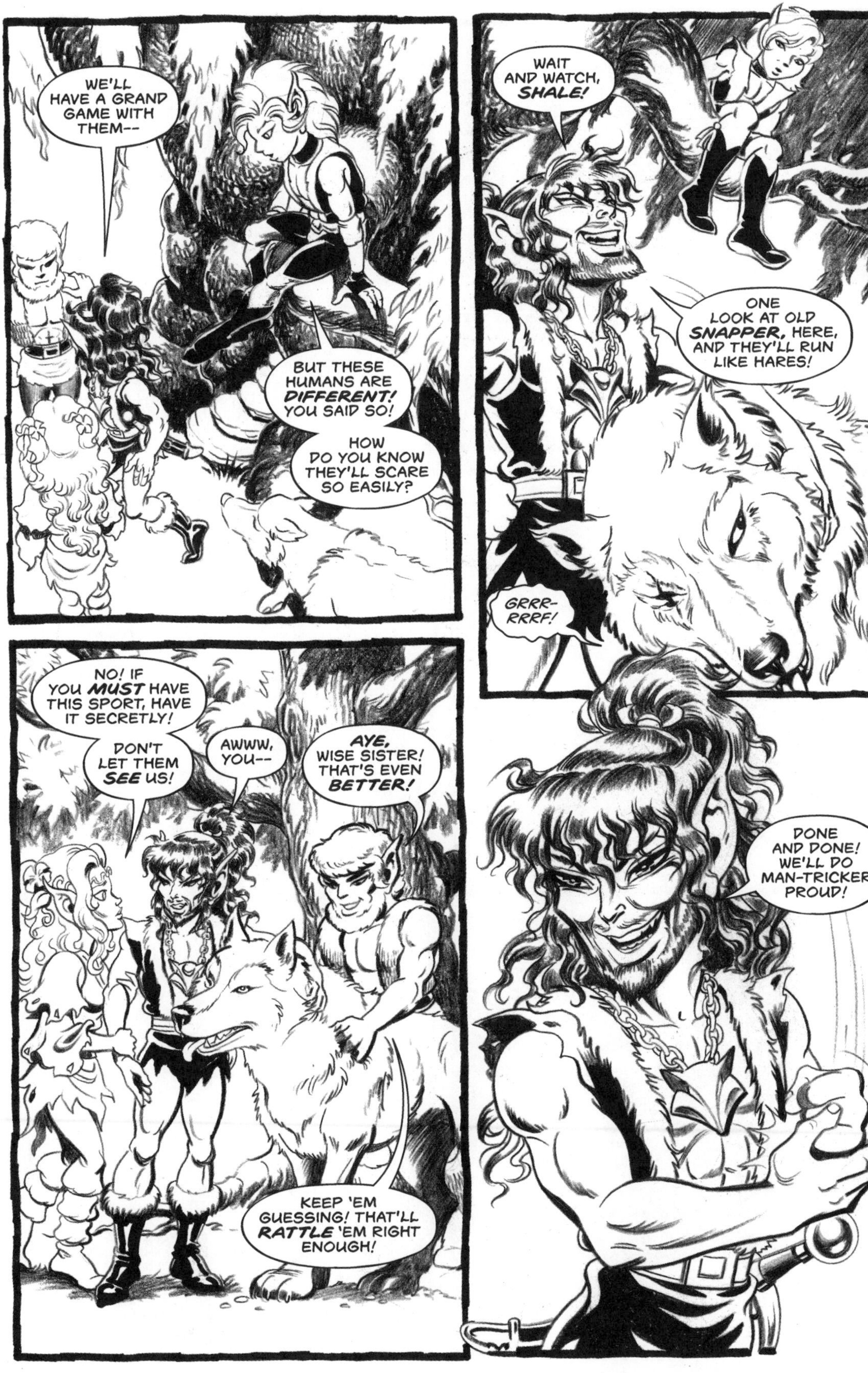
WE'LL HAVE A GRAND GAME WITH THEM--
BUT THESE HUMANS ARE DIFFERENT! YOU SAID SO!
HOW DO YOU KNOW THEY'LL SCARE SO EASILY?
WAIT AND WATCH, SHALE!
ONE LOOK AT OLD SNAPPER, HERE, AND THEY'LL RUN LIKE HARES!
GRRR-RRRF!
NO! IF YOU MUST HAVE THIS SPORT, HAVE IT SECRETLY!
DON'T LET THEM SEE US!
AWWW, YOU--
AYE, WISE SISTER! THAT'S EVEN BETTER!
KEEP 'EM GUESSING! THAT'LL RATTLE 'EM RIGHT ENOUGH!
DONE AND DONE! WE'LL DO MAN-TRICKER PROUD!

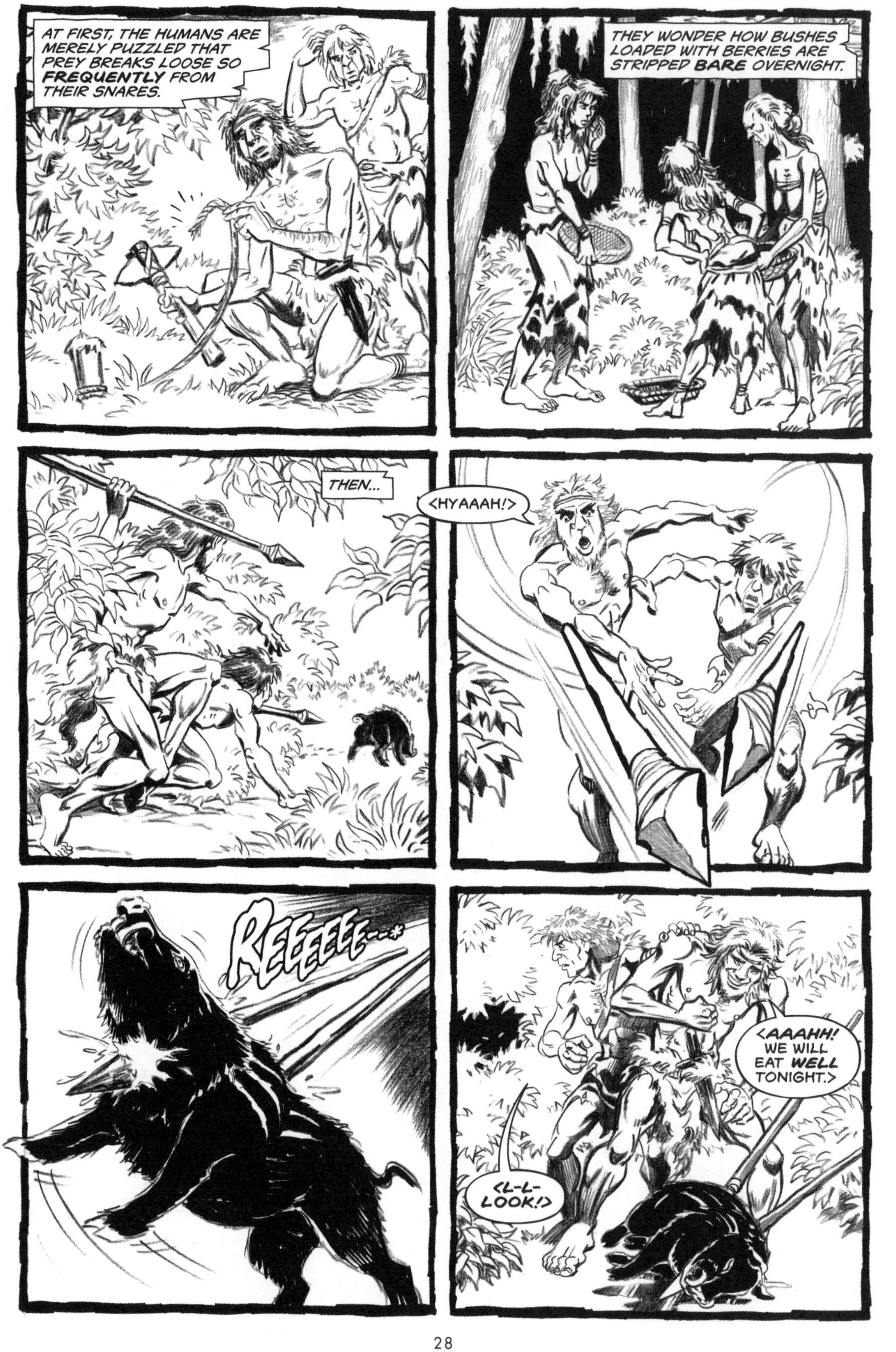
AT FIRST, THE HUMANS ARE MERELY PUZZLED THAT PREY BREAKS LOOSE SO **FREQUENTLY** FROM THEIR SNARES.
THEY WONDER HOW BUSHES LOADED WITH BERRIES ARE STRIPPED **BARE** OVERNIGHT.
THEN...
<HYAAAH!>
REEEEEE--*
<AAAHH! WE WILL EAT **WELL** TONIGHT.>
<L-L-LOOK!>

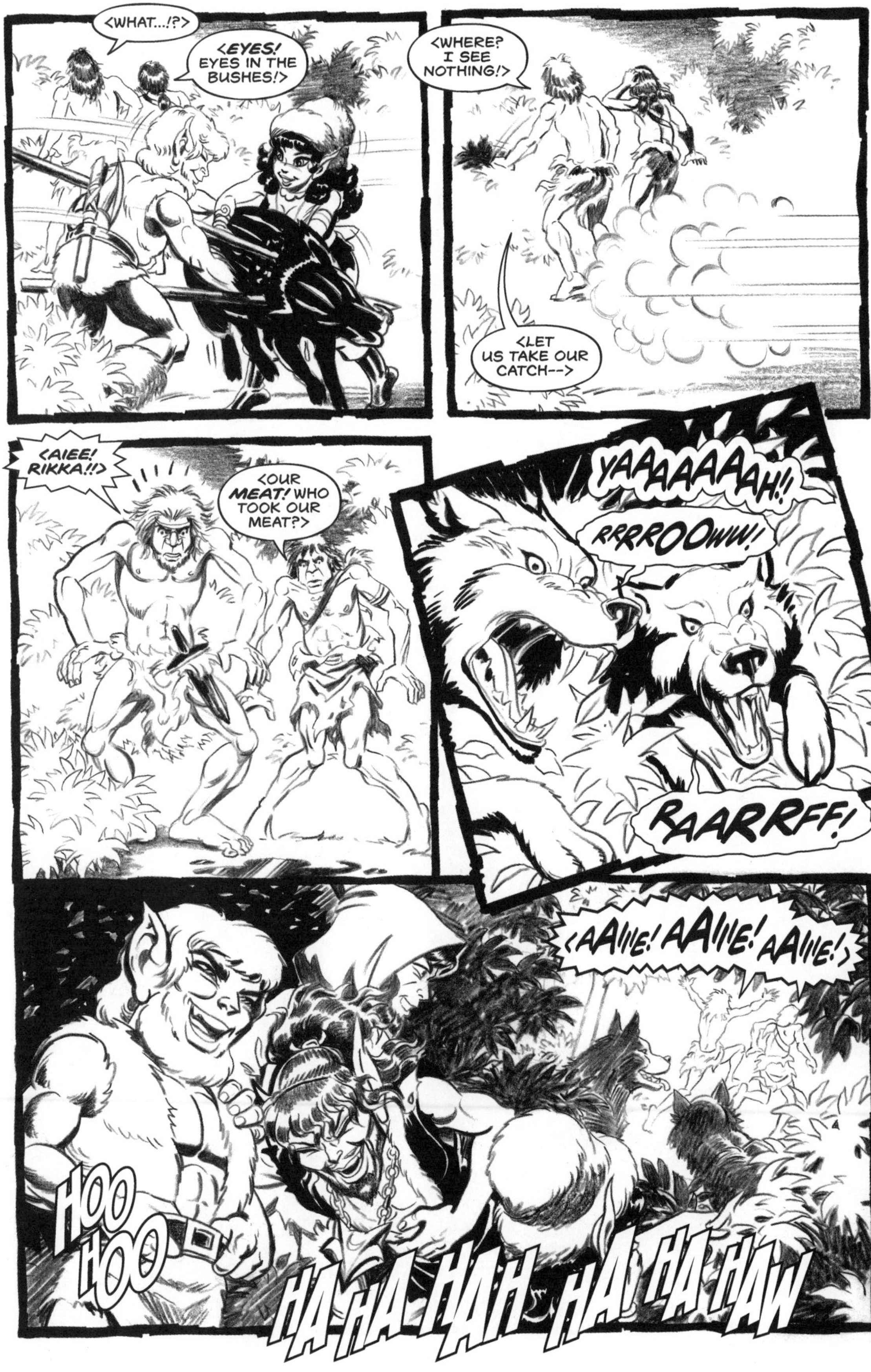
<WHAT...!?>
<EYES! EYES IN THE BUSHES!>
<WHERE? I SEE NOTHING!>
<LET US TAKE OUR CATCH-->
<AIEE! RIKKA!!>
<OUR MEAT! WHO TOOK OUR MEAT?>
YAAAAAAAAH!!
RRRROOWW!
RAARRFF!
<AAIIIE! AAIIIE! AAIIIE!>
HOO HOO
HA HA HAH HA! HA HAW

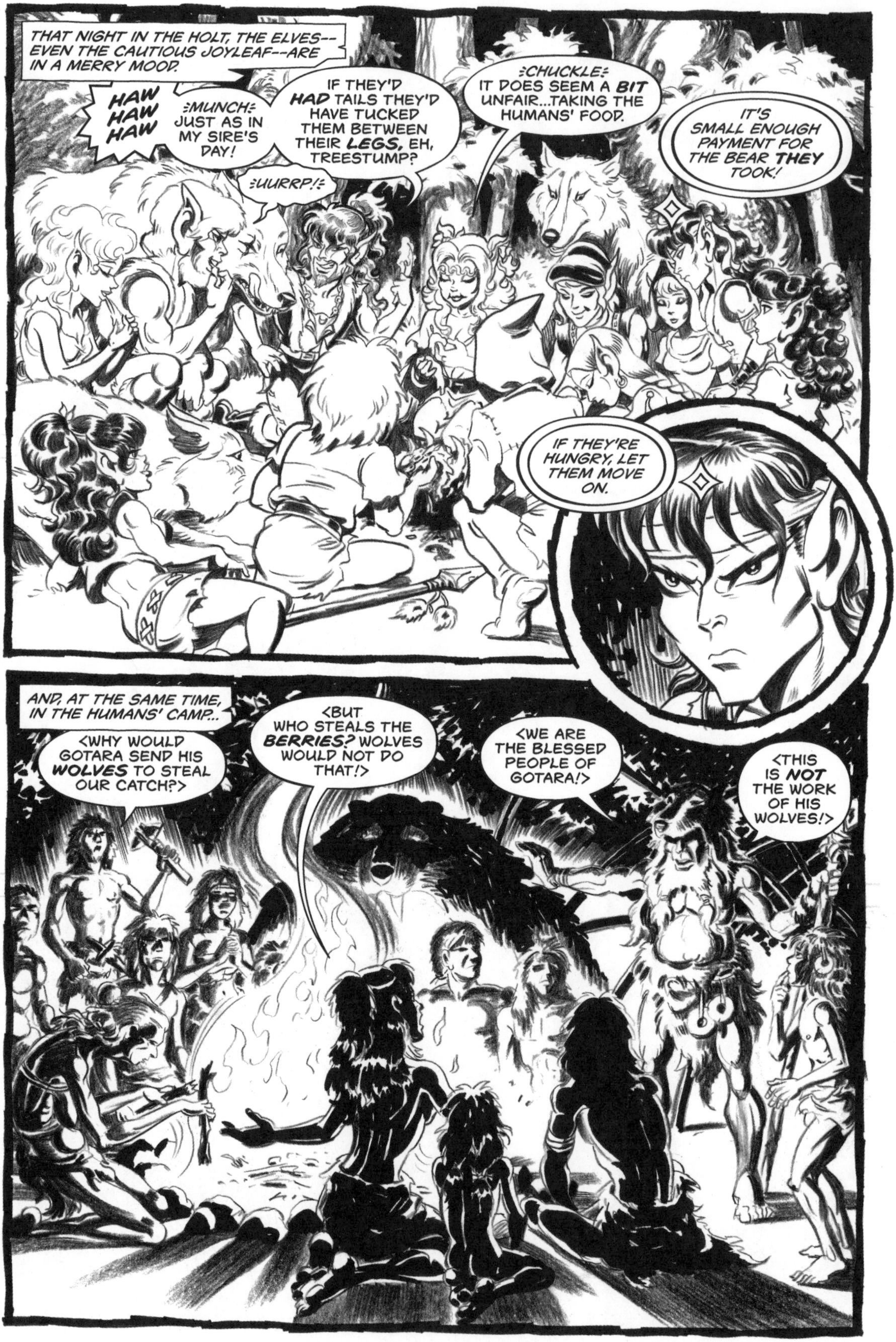
THAT NIGHT IN THE HOLT, THE ELVES-- EVEN THE CAUTIOUS JOYLEAF--ARE IN A MERRY MOOD.
HAW HAW HAW
:MUNCH: JUST AS IN MY SIRE'S DAY!
IF THEY'D HAD TAILS THEY'D HAVE TUCKED THEM BETWEEN THEIR LEGS, EH, TREESTUMP?
:UURRP!:
:CHUCKLE: IT DOES SEEM A BIT UNFAIR...TAKING THE HUMANS' FOOD.
IT'S SMALL ENOUGH PAYMENT FOR THE BEAR THEY TOOK!
IF THEY'RE HUNGRY, LET THEM MOVE ON.
AND, AT THE SAME TIME, IN THE HUMANS' CAMP...
<WHY WOULD GOTARA SEND HIS WOLVES TO STEAL OUR CATCH?>
<BUT WHO STEALS THE BERRIES? WOLVES WOULD NOT DO THAT!>
<WE ARE THE BLESSED PEOPLE OF GOTARA!>
<THIS IS NOT THE WORK OF HIS WOLVES!>

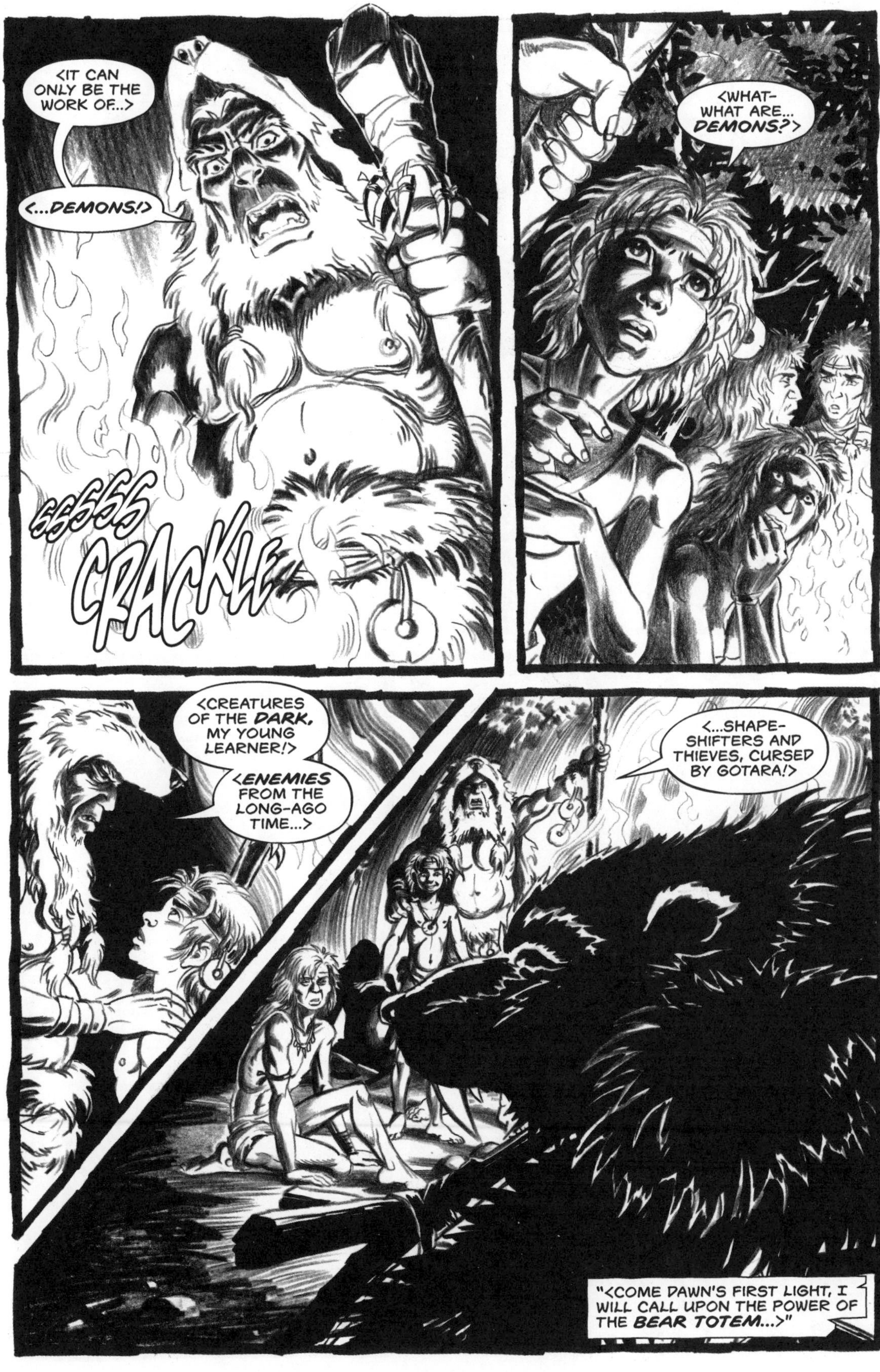
<IT CAN ONLY BE THE WORK OF...>
<...DEMONS!>
SSSSS
CRACKLE
<WHAT- WHAT ARE... DEMONS?>
<CREATURES OF THE DARK, MY YOUNG LEARNER!>
<ENEMIES FROM THE LONG-AGO TIME...>
<...SHAPE-SHIFTERS AND THIEVES, CURSED BY GOTARA!>
"<COME DAWN'S FIRST LIGHT, I WILL CALL UPON THE POWER OF THE BEAR TOTEM...>"

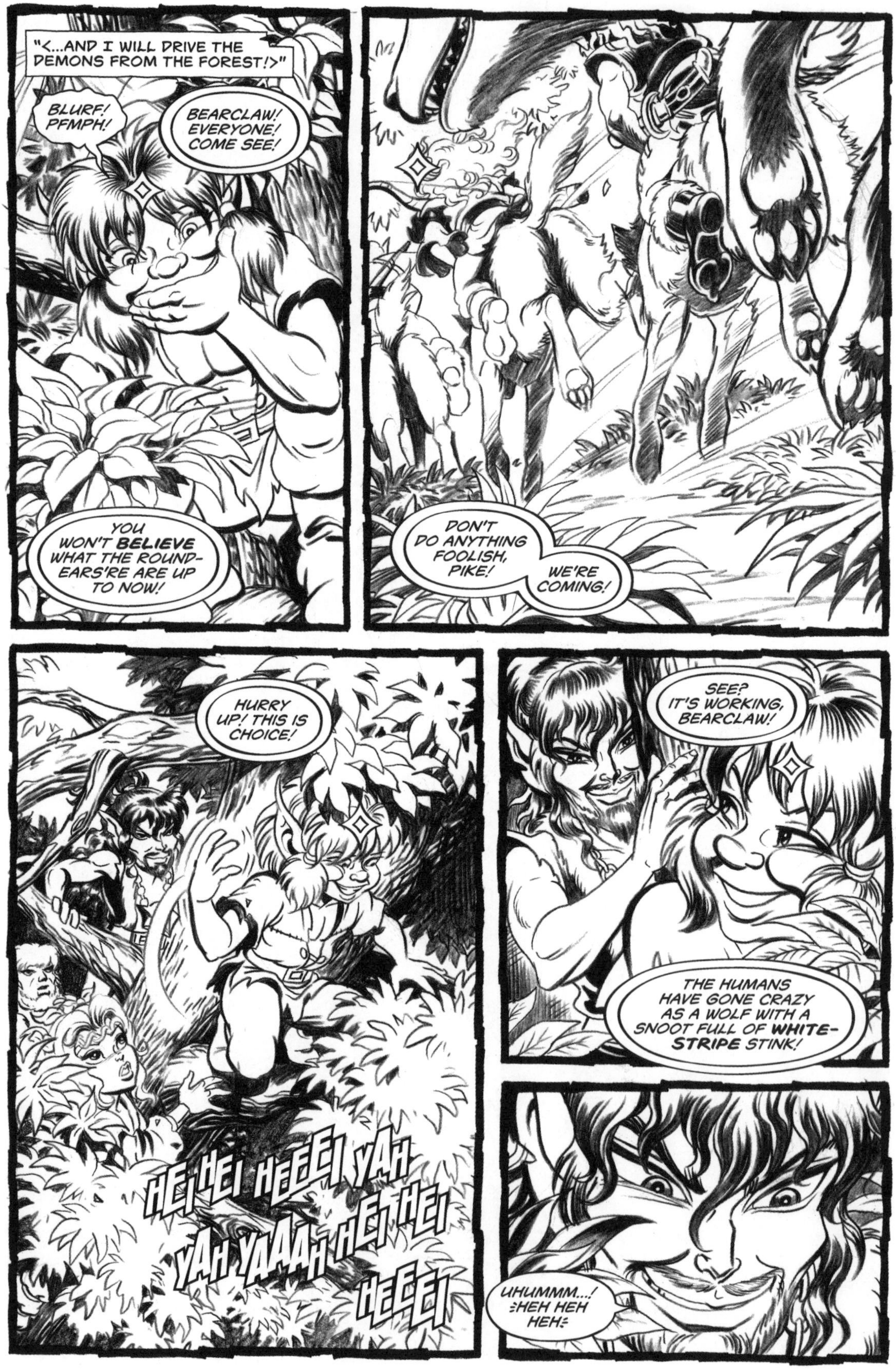
"<...AND I WILL DRIVE THE DEMONS FROM THE FOREST!>"
BLURF! PFMPH!
BEARCLAW! EVERYONE! COME SEE!
YOU WON'T BELIEVE WHAT THE ROUND-EARS'RE ARE UP TO NOW!
DON'T DO ANYTHING FOOLISH, PIKE!
WE'RE COMING!
HURRY UP! THIS IS CHOICE!
HEI HEI HEEEI YAH YAH YAAAH HEI HEI HEEEI
SEE? IT'S WORKING, BEARCLAW!
THE HUMANS HAVE GONE CRAZY AS A WOLF WITH A SNOOT FULL OF WHITE-STRIPE STINK!
UHUMMM...! HEH HEH HEH

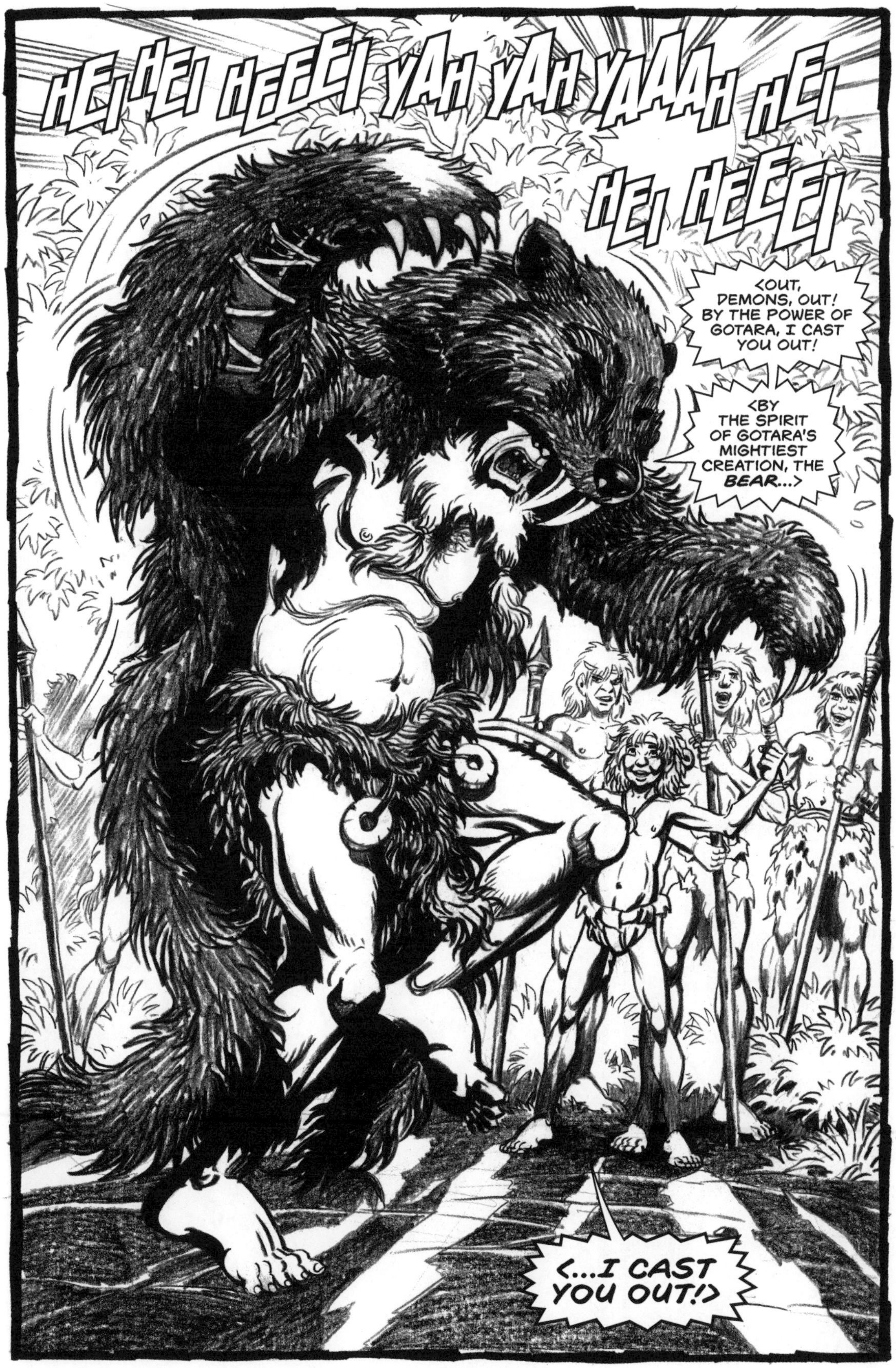
HEI HEI HEEEEI YAH YAH YAAAAH HEI HEI HEEEEI
<OUT, DEMONS, OUT! BY THE POWER OF GOTARA, I CAST YOU OUT!
<BY THE SPIRIT OF GOTARA'S MIGHTIEST CREATION, THE BEAR...>
<...I CAST YOU OUT!>

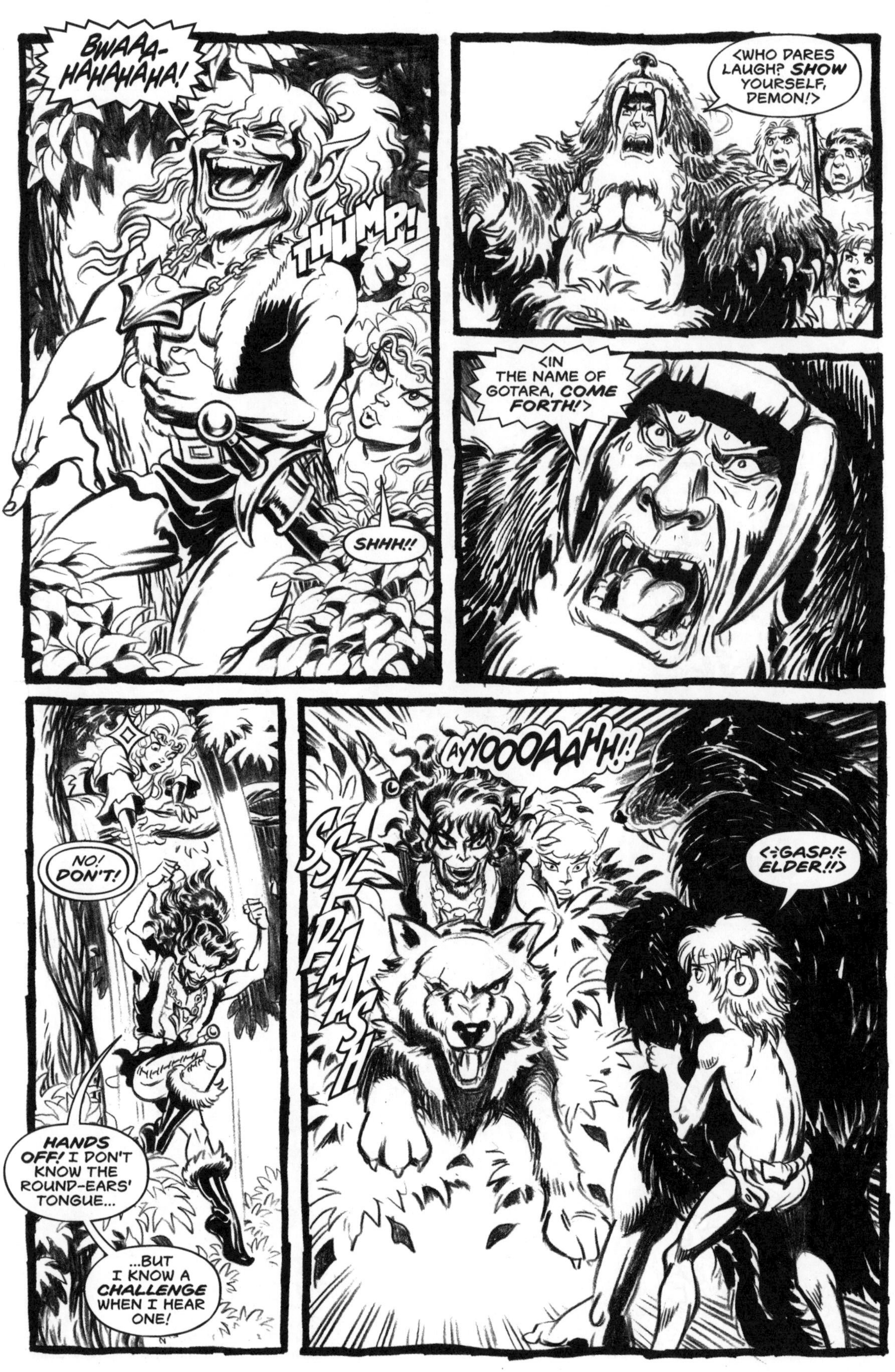
BWAAA-HAHAHAHA!
THUMP!
SHHH!!
<WHO DARES LAUGH? SHOW YOURSELF, DEMON!>
<IN THE NAME OF GOTARA, COME FORTH!>
NO! DON'T!
HANDS OFF! I DON'T KNOW THE ROUND-EARS' TONGUE...
...BUT I KNOW A CHALLENGE WHEN I HEAR ONE!
AYYOOOAAHH!!
SSKRAAASH
<-GASP!- ELDER!!>

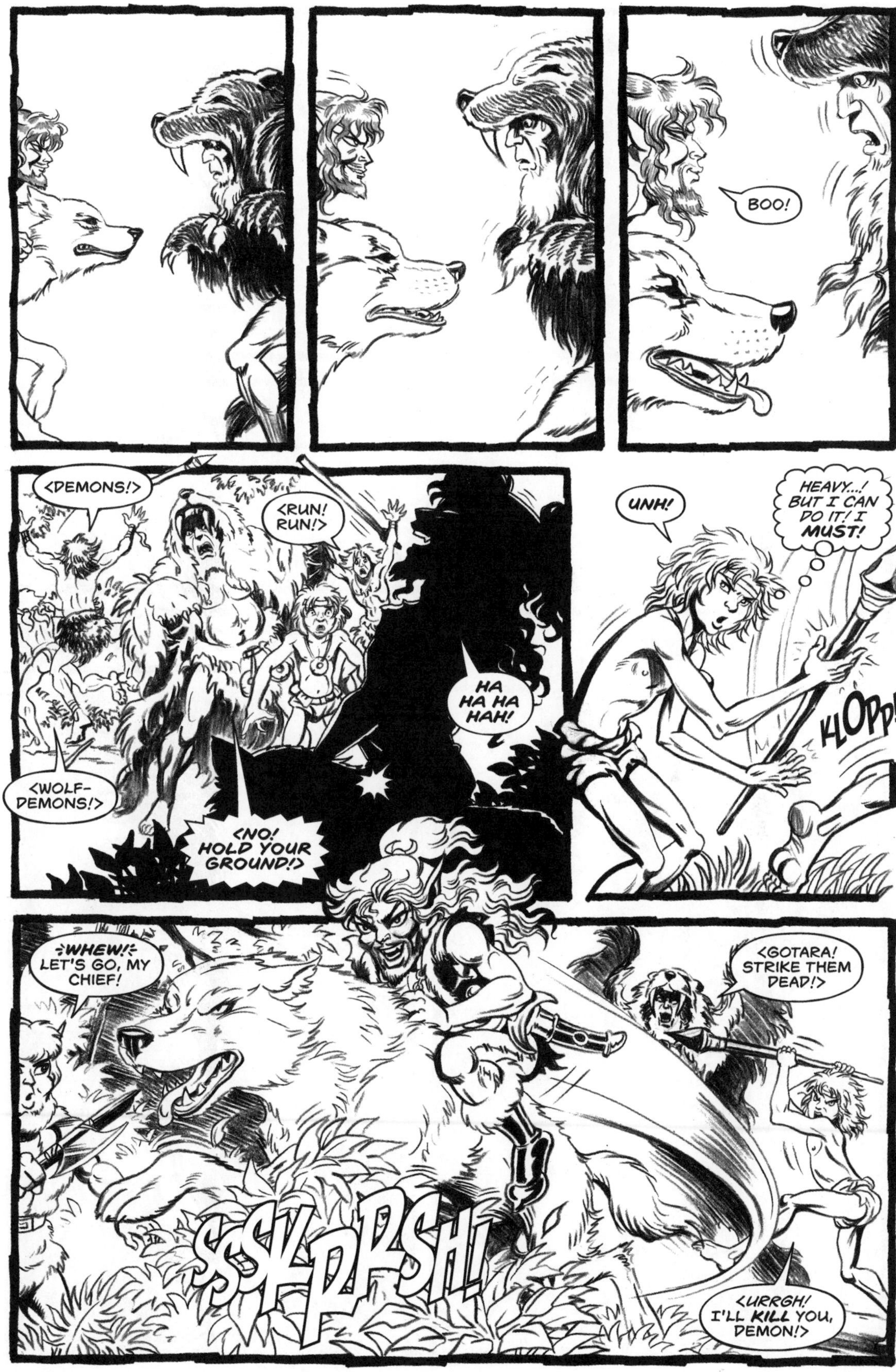
BOO!
<DEMONS!>
<RUN! RUN!>
HA HA HA HAH!
<WOLF-DEMONS!>
<NO! HOLD YOUR GROUND!>
UNH!
HEAVY...! BUT I CAN DO IT! I MUST!
KLOPP!
WHEW! LET'S GO, MY CHIEF!
<GOTARA! STRIKE THEM DEAD!>
SSSKRRSH!
<URRGH! I'LL KILL YOU, DEMON!>

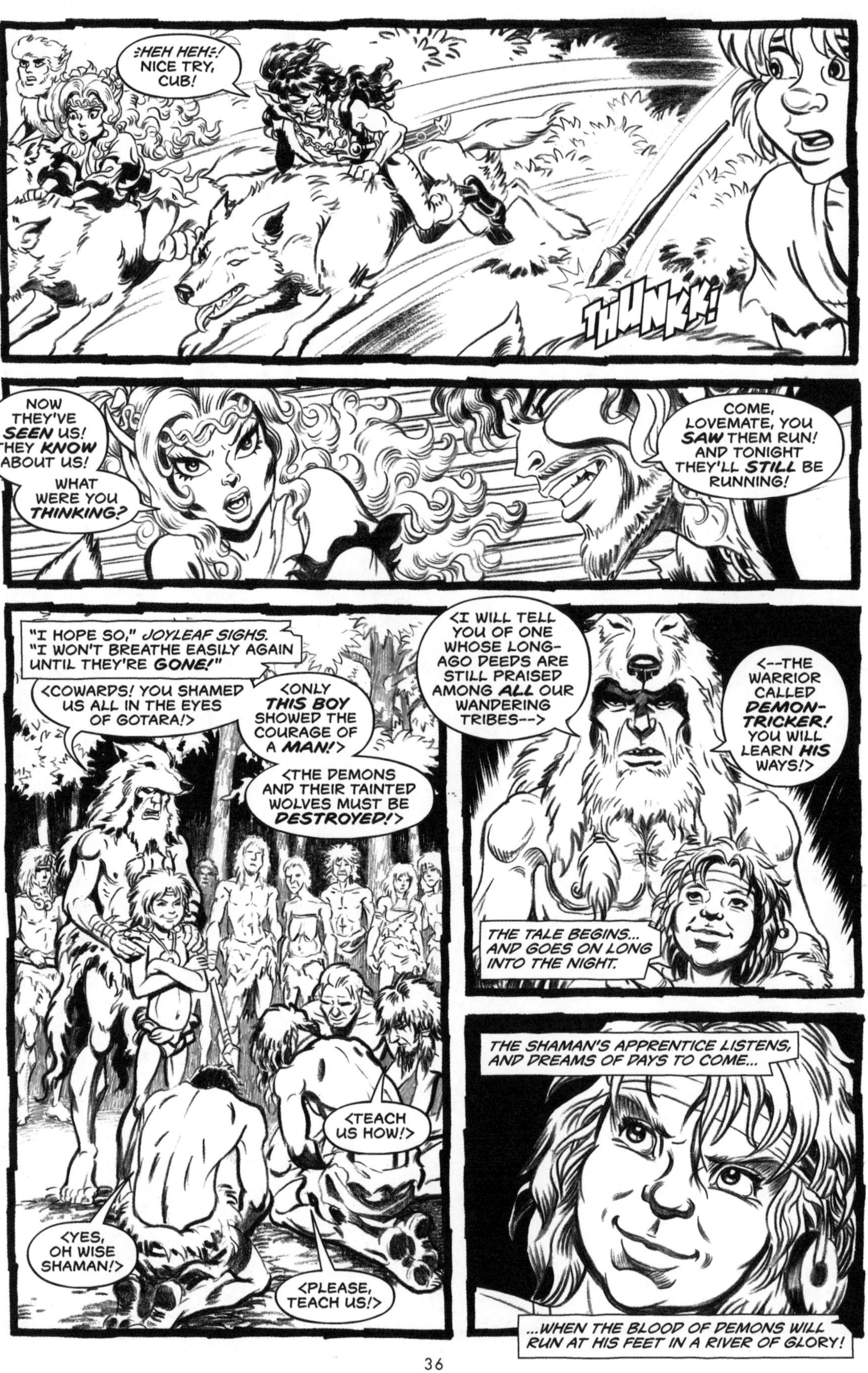
HEH HEH! NICE TRY, CUB!
THUNKK!
NOW THEY'VE SEEN US! THEY KNOW ABOUT US!
WHAT WERE YOU THINKING?
COME, LOVEMATE, YOU SAW THEM RUN! AND TONIGHT THEY'LL STILL BE RUNNING!
"I HOPE SO," JOYLEAF SIGHS. "I WON'T BREATHE EASILY AGAIN UNTIL THEY'RE GONE!"
<COWARDS! YOU SHAMED US ALL IN THE EYES OF GOTARA!>
<ONLY THIS BOY SHOWED THE COURAGE OF A MAN!>
<THE DEMONS AND THEIR TAINTED WOLVES MUST BE DESTROYED!>
<TEACH US HOW!>
<YES, OH WISE SHAMAN!>
<PLEASE, TEACH US!>
<I WILL TELL YOU OF ONE WHOSE LONG-AGO DEEDS ARE STILL PRAISED AMONG ALL OUR WANDERING TRIBES-->
<--THE WARRIOR CALLED DEMON-TRICKER! YOU WILL LEARN HIS WAYS!>
THE TALE BEGINS... AND GOES ON LONG INTO THE NIGHT.
THE SHAMAN'S APPRENTICE LISTENS, AND DREAMS OF DAYS TO COME...
...WHEN THE BLOOD OF DEMONS WILL RUN AT HIS FEET IN A RIVER OF GLORY!

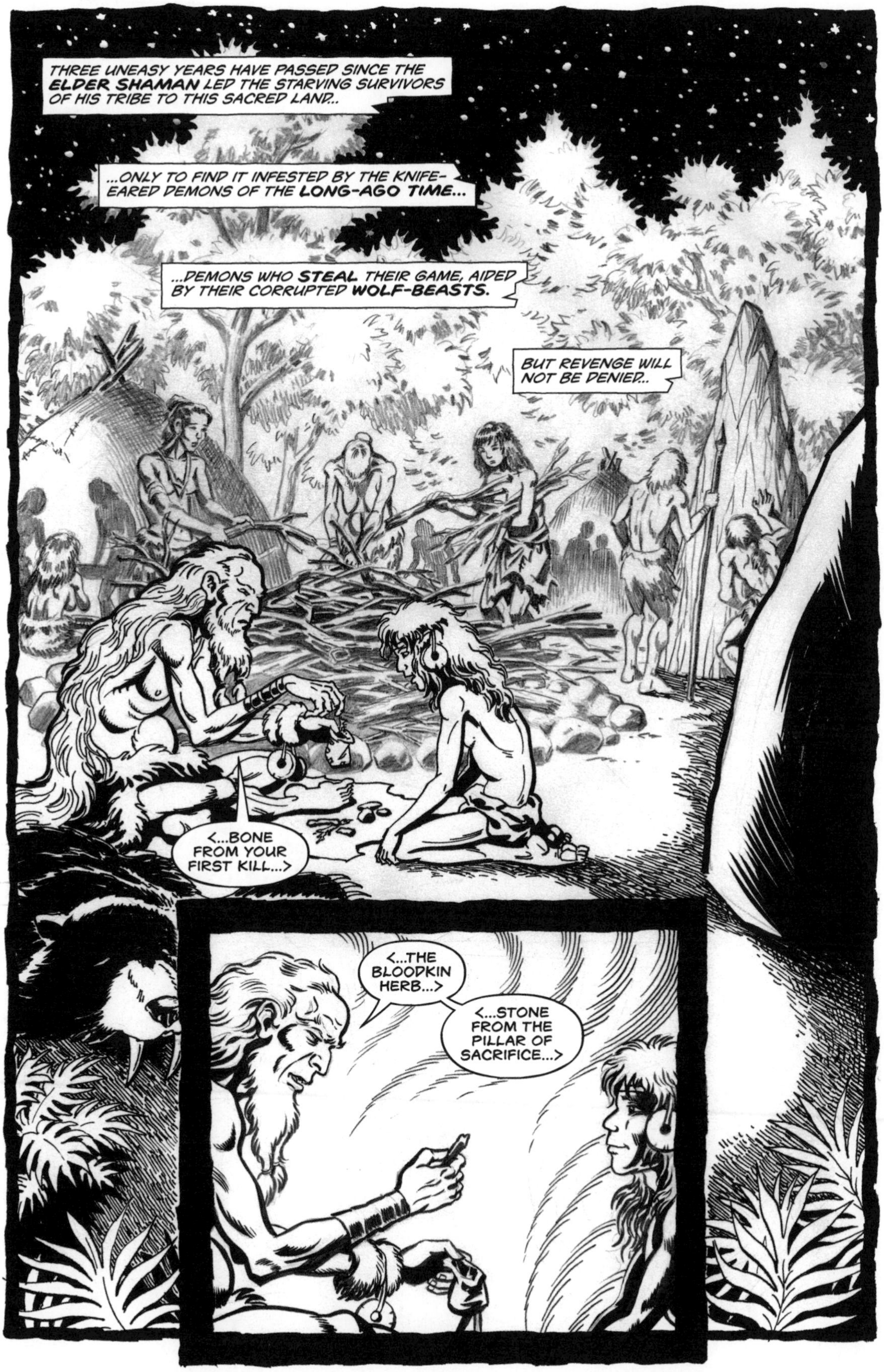
THREE UNEASY YEARS HAVE PASSED SINCE THE ELDER SHAMAN LED THE STARVING SURVIVORS OF HIS TRIBE TO THIS SACRED LAND...
...ONLY TO FIND IT INFESTED BY THE KNIFE-EARED DEMONS OF THE LONG-AGO TIME...
...DEMONS WHO STEAL THEIR GAME, AIDED BY THEIR CORRUPTED WOLF-BEASTS.
BUT REVENGE WILL NOT BE DENIED...
<...BONE FROM YOUR FIRST KILL...>
<...THE BLOODKIN HERB...>
<...STONE FROM THE PILLAR OF SACRIFICE...>

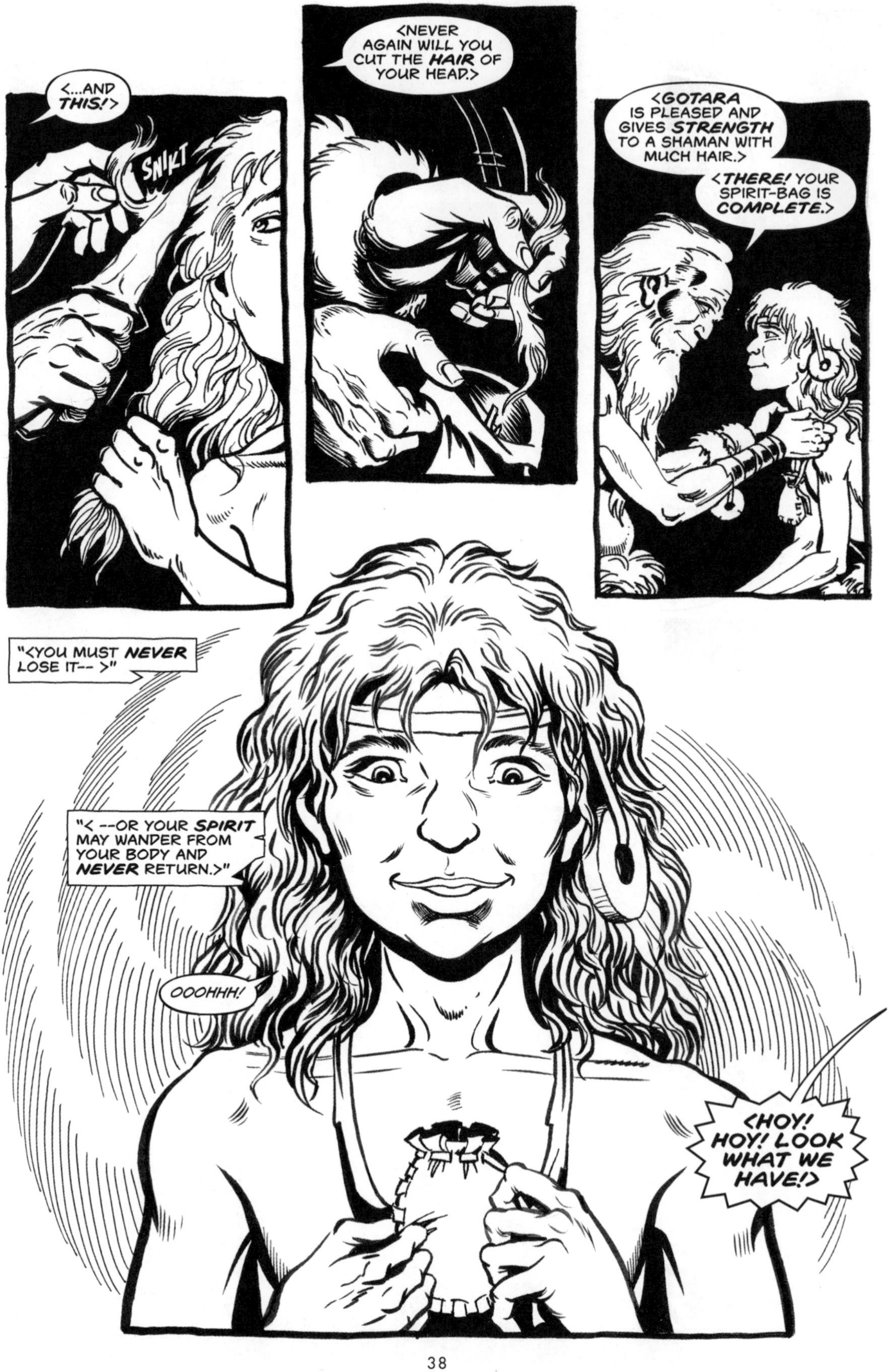

<...AND THIS!>
SNIKT
<NEVER AGAIN WILL YOU CUT THE HAIR OF YOUR HEAD.>
<GOTARA IS PLEASED AND GIVES STRENGTH TO A SHAMAN WITH MUCH HAIR.>
<THERE! YOUR SPIRIT-BAG IS COMPLETE.>
"<YOU MUST NEVER LOSE IT-- >"
"< --OR YOUR SPIRIT MAY WANDER FROM YOUR BODY AND NEVER RETURN.>"
OOOHHH!
<HOY! HOY! LOOK WHAT WE HAVE!>

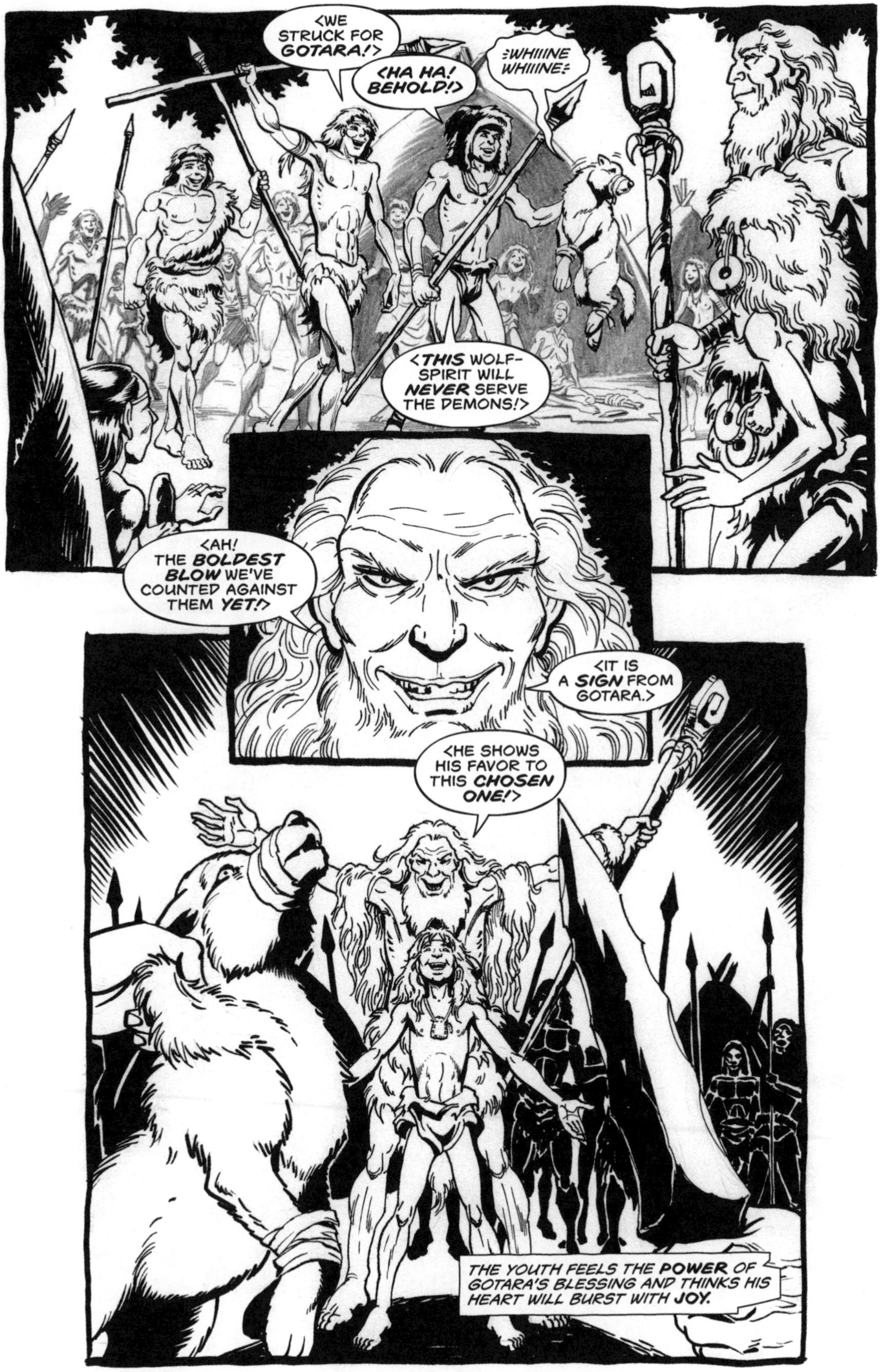

<WE STRUCK FOR GOTARA!>
<HA HA! BEHOLD!>
=WHIIINE WHIIINE=
<THIS WOLF-SPIRIT WILL NEVER SERVE THE DEMONS!>
<AH! THE BOLDEST BLOW WE'VE COUNTED AGAINST THEM YET!>
<IT IS A SIGN FROM GOTARA.>
<HE SHOWS HIS FAVOR TO THIS CHOSEN ONE!>
THE YOUTH FEELS THE POWER OF GOTARA'S BLESSING AND THINKS HIS HEART WILL BURST WITH JOY.

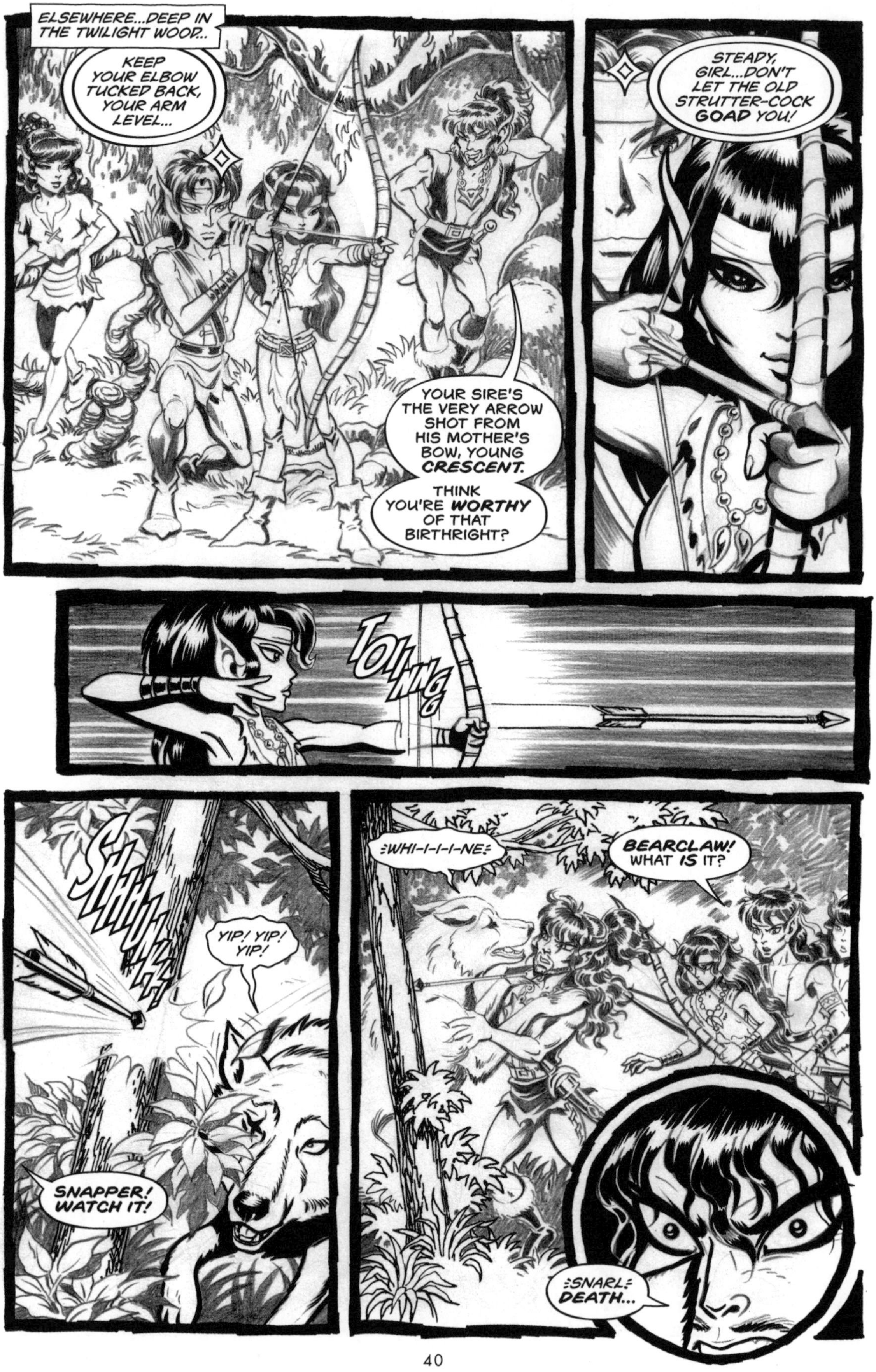
ELSEWHERE...DEEP IN THE TWILIGHT WOOD...
KEEP YOUR ELBOW TUCKED BACK, YOUR ARM LEVEL...
YOUR SIRE'S THE VERY ARROW SHOT FROM HIS MOTHER'S BOW, YOUNG CRESCENT.
THINK YOU'RE WORTHY OF THAT BIRTHRIGHT?
STEADY, GIRL...DON'T LET THE OLD STRUTTER-COCK GOAD YOU!
TOIUNNGG
SHHHUK
YIP! YIP! YIP!
SNAPPER! WATCH IT!
WHI-I-I-I-NE
BEARCLAW! WHAT IS IT?
SNARL
DEATH...

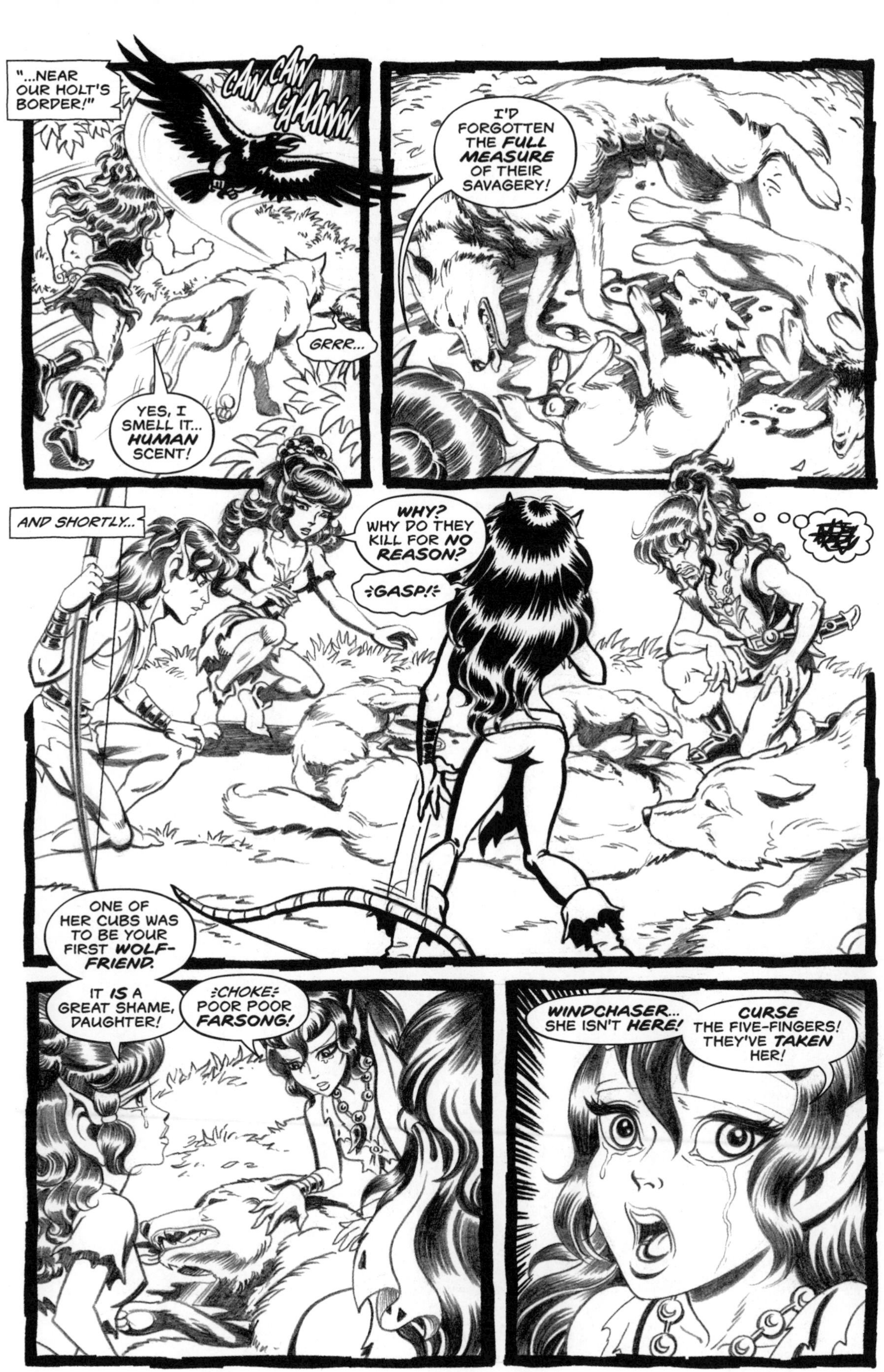
"...NEAR OUR HOLT'S BORDER!"
CAW CAW CAAAWW
YES, I SMELL IT... HUMAN SCENT!
GRRR...
I'D FORGOTTEN THE FULL MEASURE OF THEIR SAVAGERY!
AND SHORTLY...
WHY? WHY DO THEY KILL FOR NO REASON?
GASP!
ONE OF HER CUBS WAS TO BE YOUR FIRST WOLF-FRIEND.
IT IS A GREAT SHAME, DAUGHTER!
CHOKE POOR POOR FARSONG!
WINDCHASER... SHE ISN'T HERE!
CURSE THE FIVE-FINGERS! THEY'VE TAKEN HER!

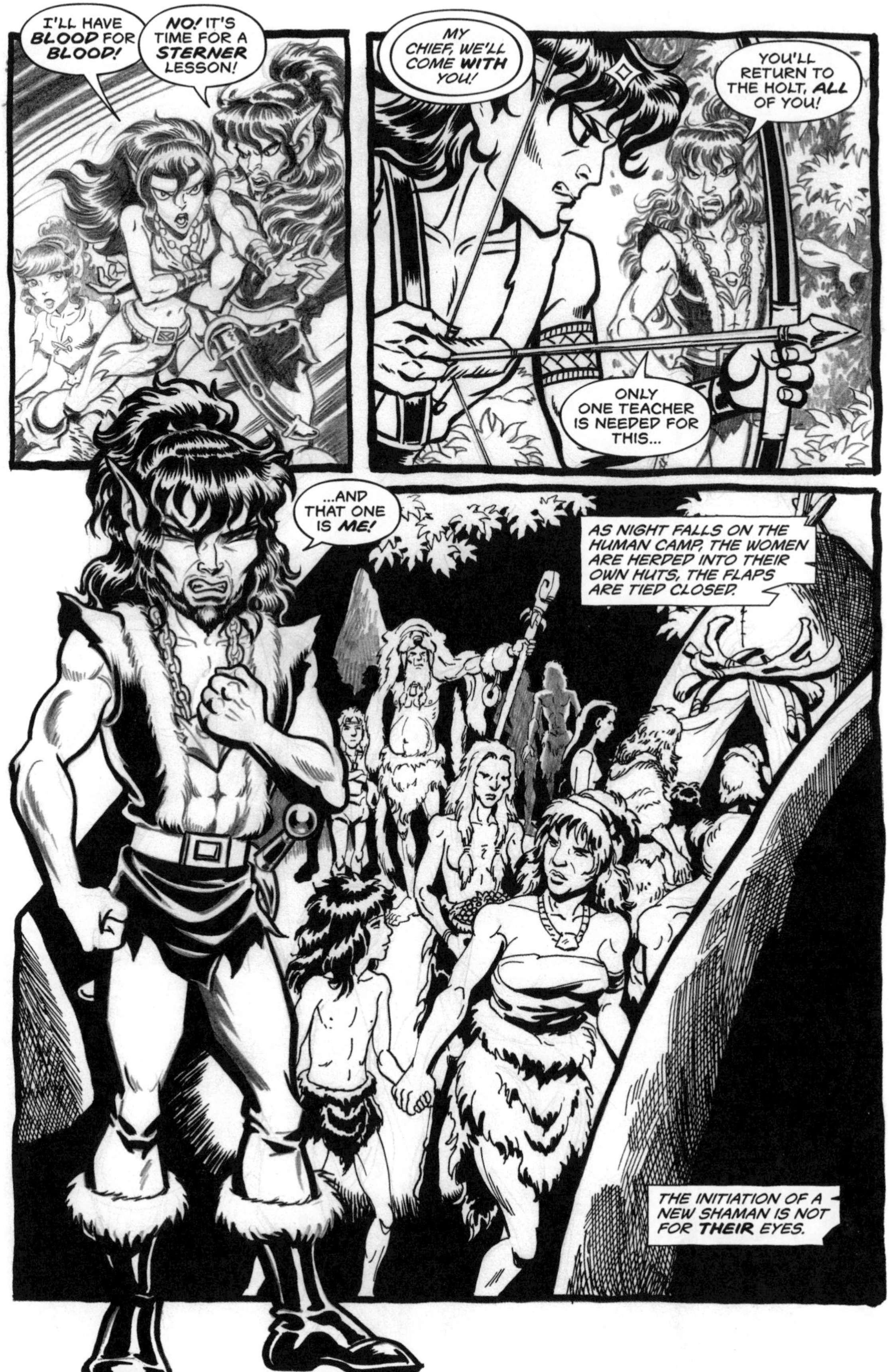

I'LL HAVE BLOOD FOR BLOOD!
NO! IT'S TIME FOR A STERNER LESSON!
MY CHIEF, WE'LL COME WITH YOU!
YOU'LL RETURN TO THE HOLT, ALL OF YOU!
ONLY ONE TEACHER IS NEEDED FOR THIS...
...AND THAT ONE IS ME!
AS NIGHT FALLS ON THE HUMAN CAMP, THE WOMEN ARE HERDED INTO THEIR OWN HUTS, THE FLAPS ARE TIED CLOSED.
THE INITIATION OF A NEW SHAMAN IS NOT FOR THEIR EYES.

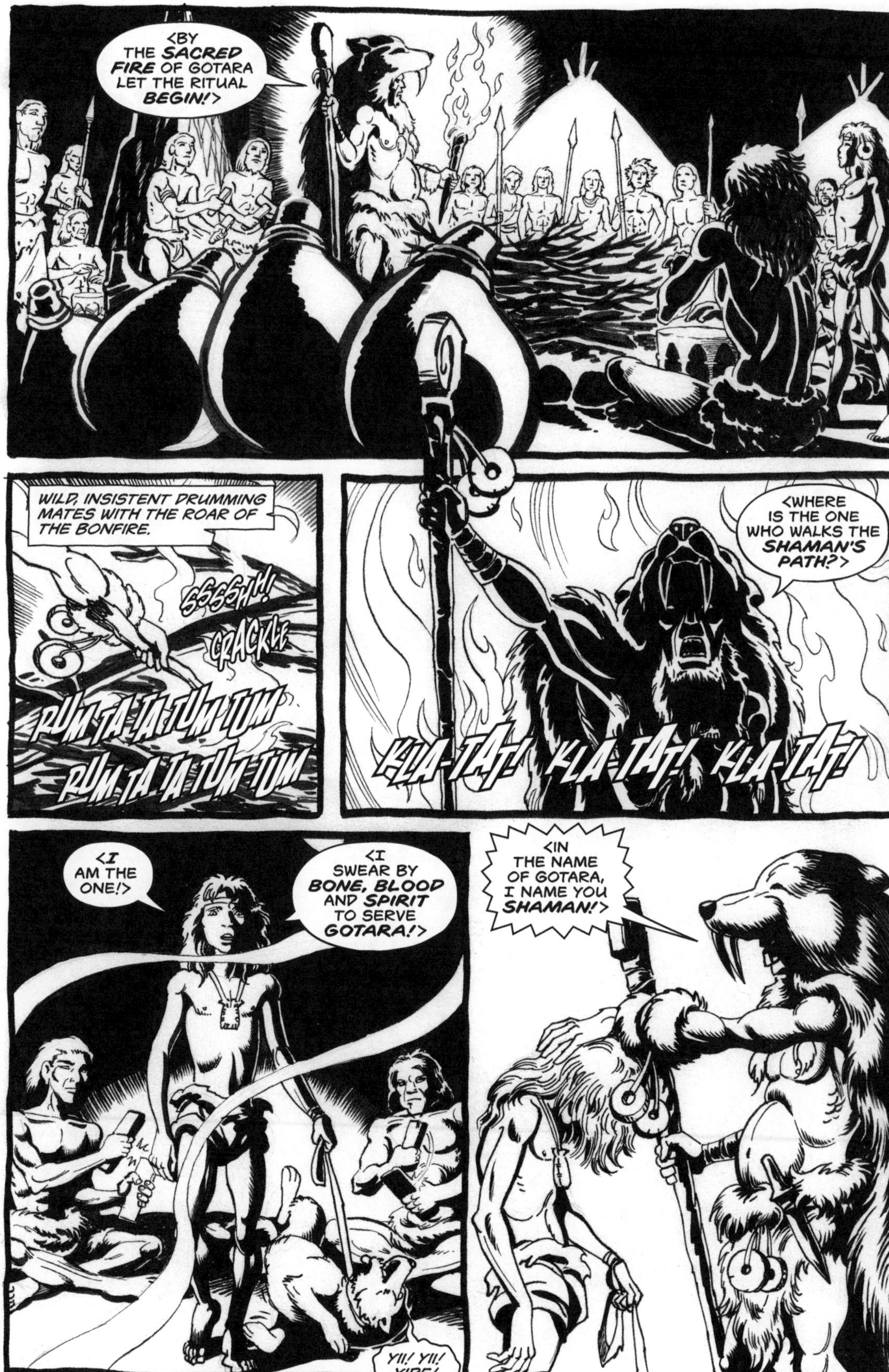

<BY THE SACRED FIRE OF GOTARA LET THE RITUAL BEGIN!>
WILD, INSISTENT DRUMMING MATES WITH THE ROAR OF THE BONFIRE.
SSSSHH!
CRACKLE
RUM TA TA TUM TUM
RUM TA TA TUM TUM
<WHERE IS THE ONE WHO WALKS THE SHAMAN'S PATH?>
KLA-TAT! KLA-TAT! KLA-TAT!
<I AM THE ONE!>
<I SWEAR BY BONE, BLOOD AND SPIRIT TO SERVE GOTARA!>
YII! YII! YIPE!
<IN THE NAME OF GOTARA, I NAME YOU SHAMAN!>

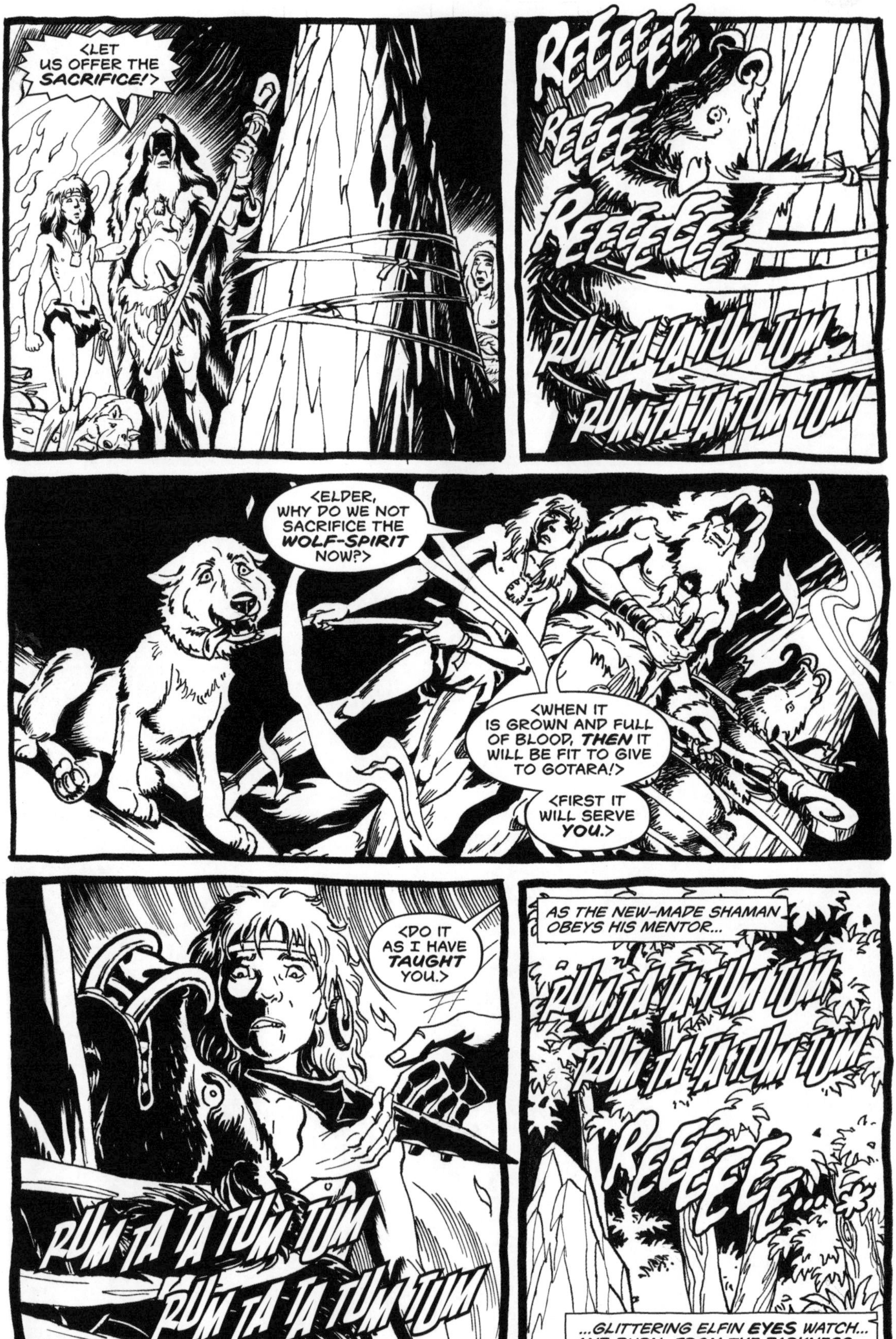

<LET US OFFER THE SACRIFICE!>
REEEEEE,
REEEE
REEEEEEE
RUM TA TA TUM TUM
RUM TA TA TUM TUM
<ELDER, WHY DO WE NOT SACRIFICE THE WOLF-SPIRIT NOW?>
<WHEN IT IS GROWN AND FULL OF BLOOD, THEN IT WILL BE FIT TO GIVE TO GOTARA!>
<FIRST IT WILL SERVE YOU.>
<DO IT AS I HAVE TAUGHT YOU.>
RUM TA TA TUM TUM
RUM TA TA TUM TUM
AS THE NEW-MADE SHAMAN OBEYS HIS MENTOR...
RUM TA TA TUM TUM
RUM TA TA TUM TUM
REEEEEE...
...GLITTERING ELFIN EYES WATCH... AND BURN...FROM THE DARKNESS.

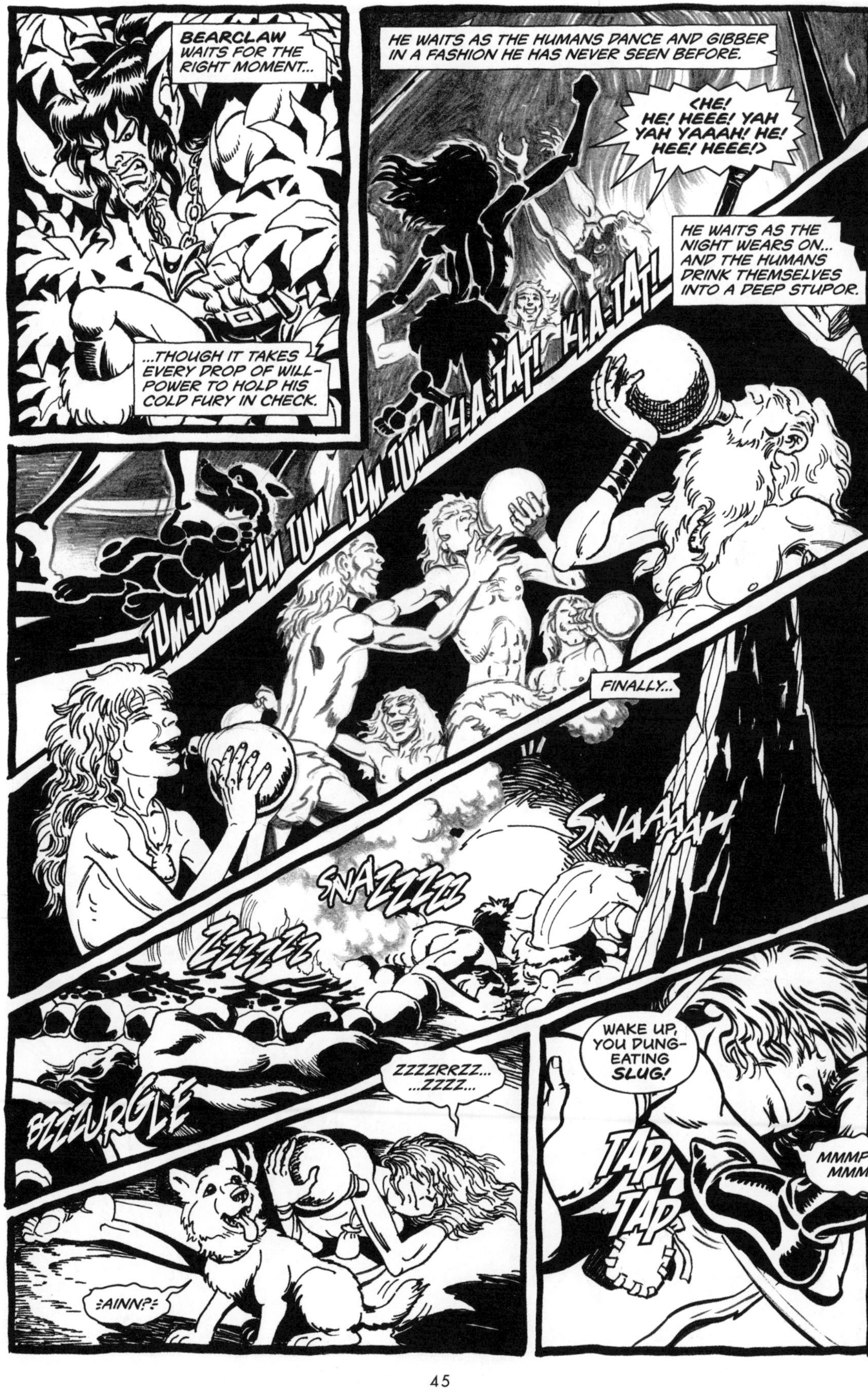
BEARCLAW WAITS FOR THE RIGHT MOMENT...
...THOUGH IT TAKES EVERY DROP OF WILL-POWER TO HOLD HIS COLD FURY IN CHECK.
HE WAITS AS THE HUMANS DANCE AND GIBBER IN A FASHION HE HAS NEVER SEEN BEFORE.
<HE! HE! HEEE! YAH YAH YAAAH! HE! HEE! HEEE!>
TUM TUM TUM TUM TUM TUM KLA-TAT! KLA-TAT!
HE WAITS AS THE NIGHT WEARS ON... AND THE HUMANS DRINK THEMSELVES INTO A DEEP STUPOR.
FINALLY...
SNAAAAH
SNAZZZZZ
ZZZZZZ
BZZZURGLE
ZZZZRRZZ... ...ZZZZ...
AINN?
WAKE UP, YOU DUNG-EATING SLUG!
TAP TAP
MMMPH-MMM?

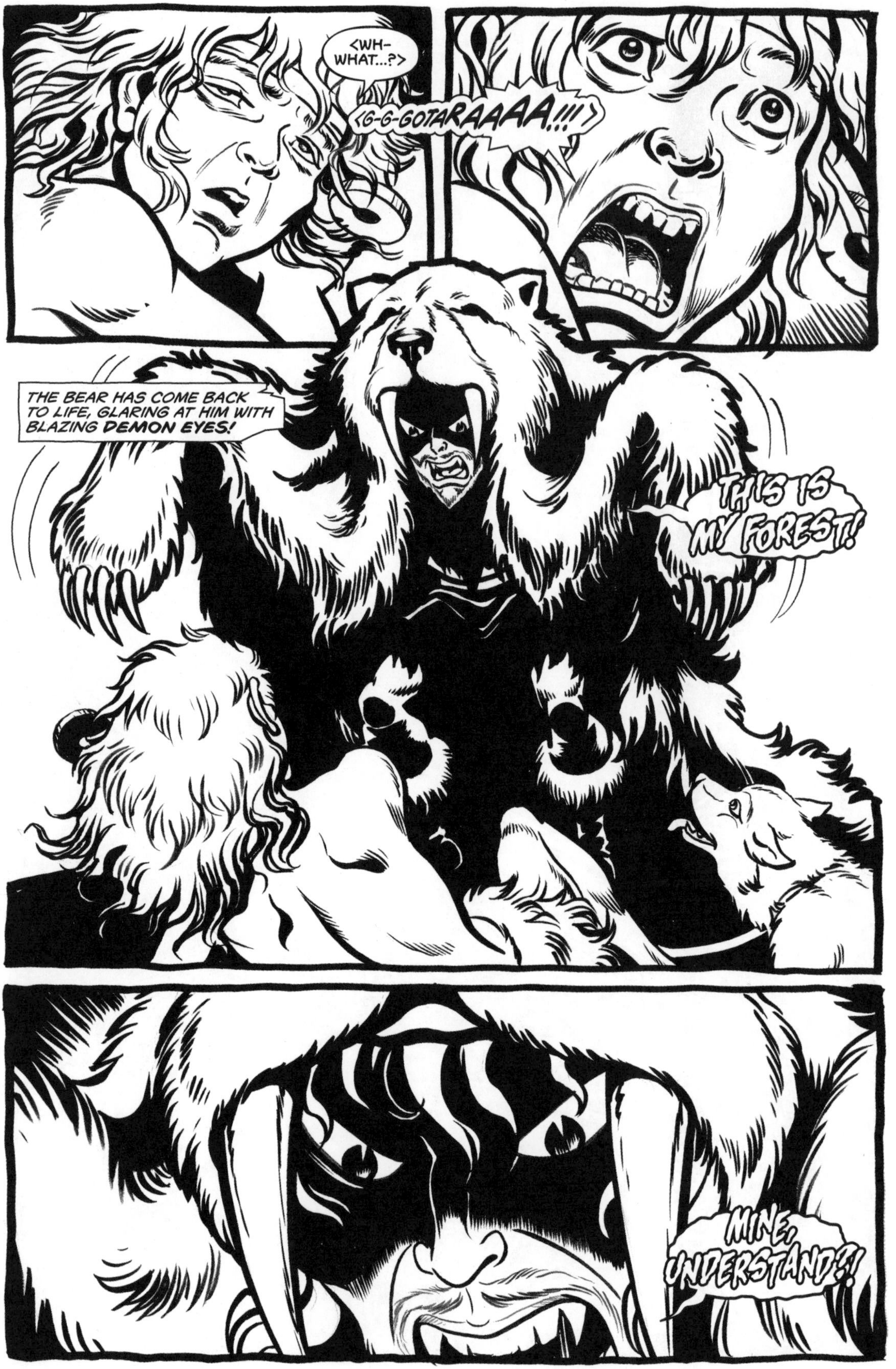
<WH- WHAT...?>
<G-G-GOTARAAAAA!!!>
THE BEAR HAS COME BACK TO LIFE, GLARING AT HIM WITH BLAZING DEMON EYES!
THIS IS MY FOREST!
MINE, UNDERSTAND?!

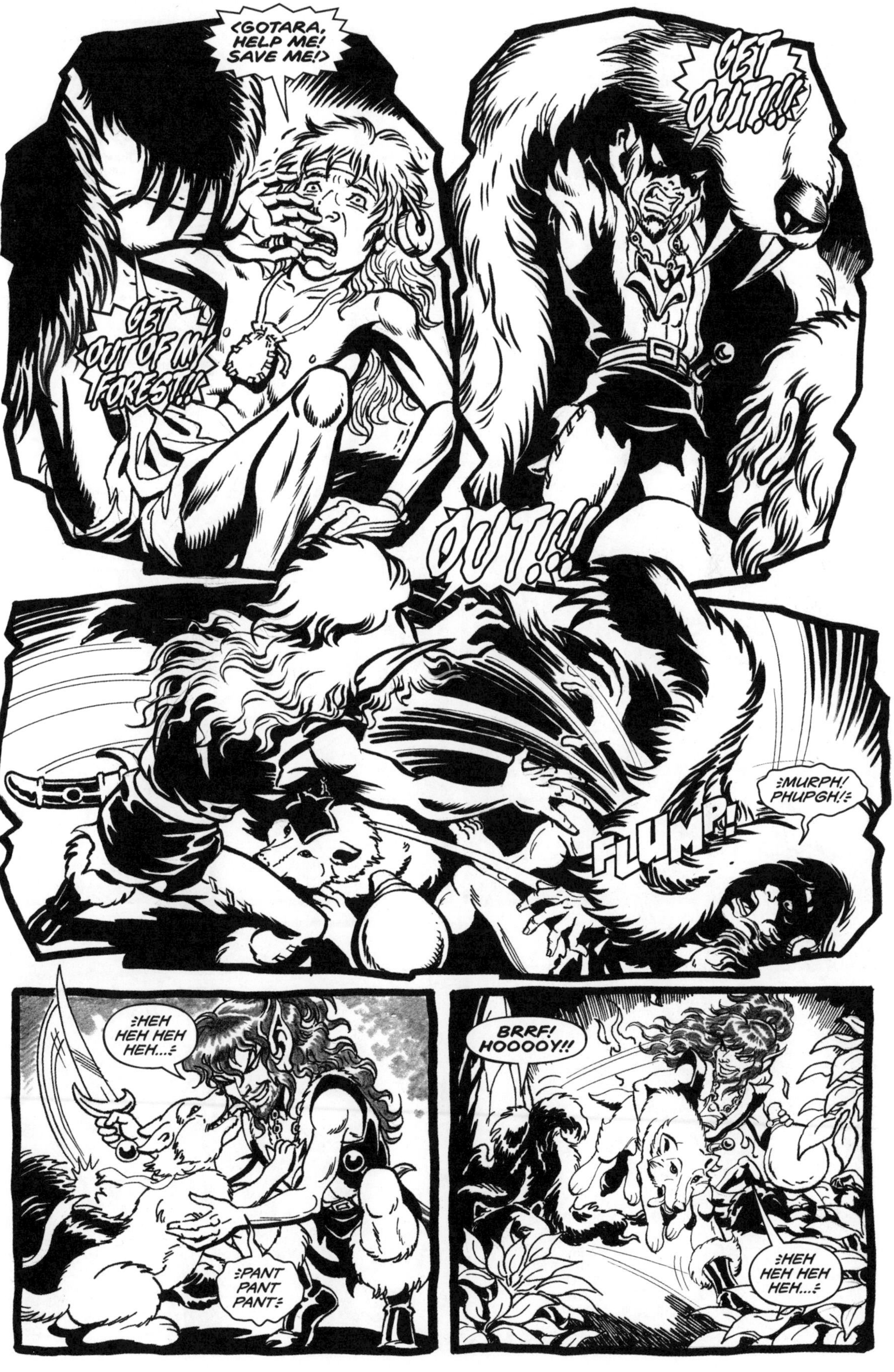

<GOTARA, HELP ME! SAVE ME!>
GET OUT OF MY FOREST!!!
GET OUT!!!
OUT!!!
MURPH! PHUPGH!
FLUMP!
HEH HEH HEH HEH...
PANT PANT PANT
BRRF! HOOOOY!!
HEH HEH HEH HEH...

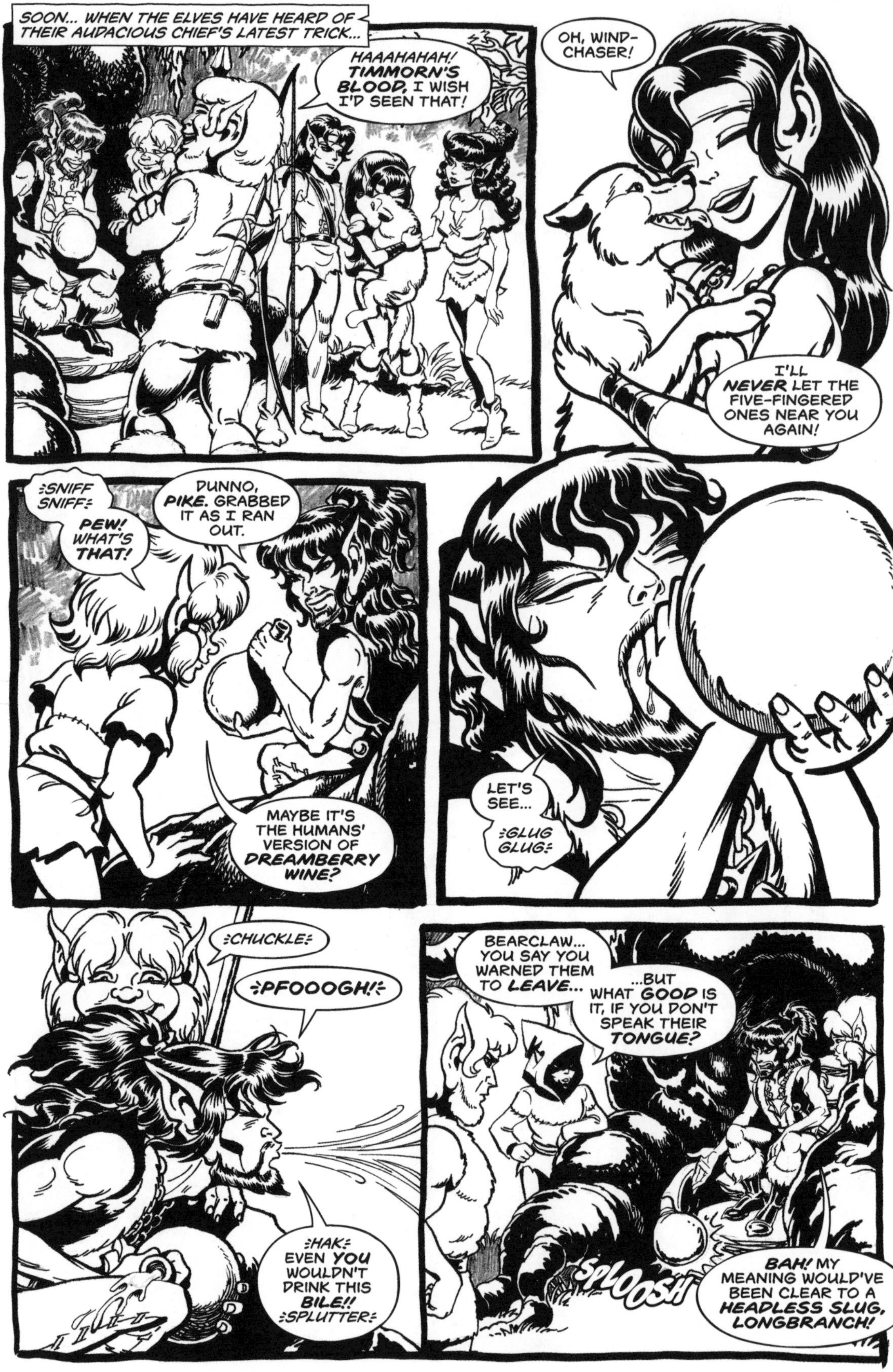
SOON... WHEN THE ELVES HAVE HEARD OF THEIR AUDACIOUS CHIEF'S LATEST TRICK...
HAAAAHAHAH! TIMMORN'S BLOOD, I WISH I'D SEEN THAT!
OH, WIND-CHASER!
I'LL NEVER LET THE FIVE-FINGERED ONES NEAR YOU AGAIN!
SNIFF SNIFF
PEW! WHAT'S THAT!
DUNNO, PIKE. GRABBED IT AS I RAN OUT.
MAYBE IT'S THE HUMANS' VERSION OF DREAMBERRY WINE?
LET'S SEE...
GLUG GLUG
CHUCKLE
PFOOOGH!
HAK
EVEN YOU WOULDN'T DRINK THIS BILE!!
SPLUTTER
BEARCLAW... YOU SAY YOU WARNED THEM TO LEAVE...
...BUT WHAT GOOD IS IT, IF YOU DON'T SPEAK THEIR TONGUE?
SPLOOSH
BAH! MY MEANING WOULD'VE BEEN CLEAR TO A HEADLESS SLUG, LONGBRANCH!

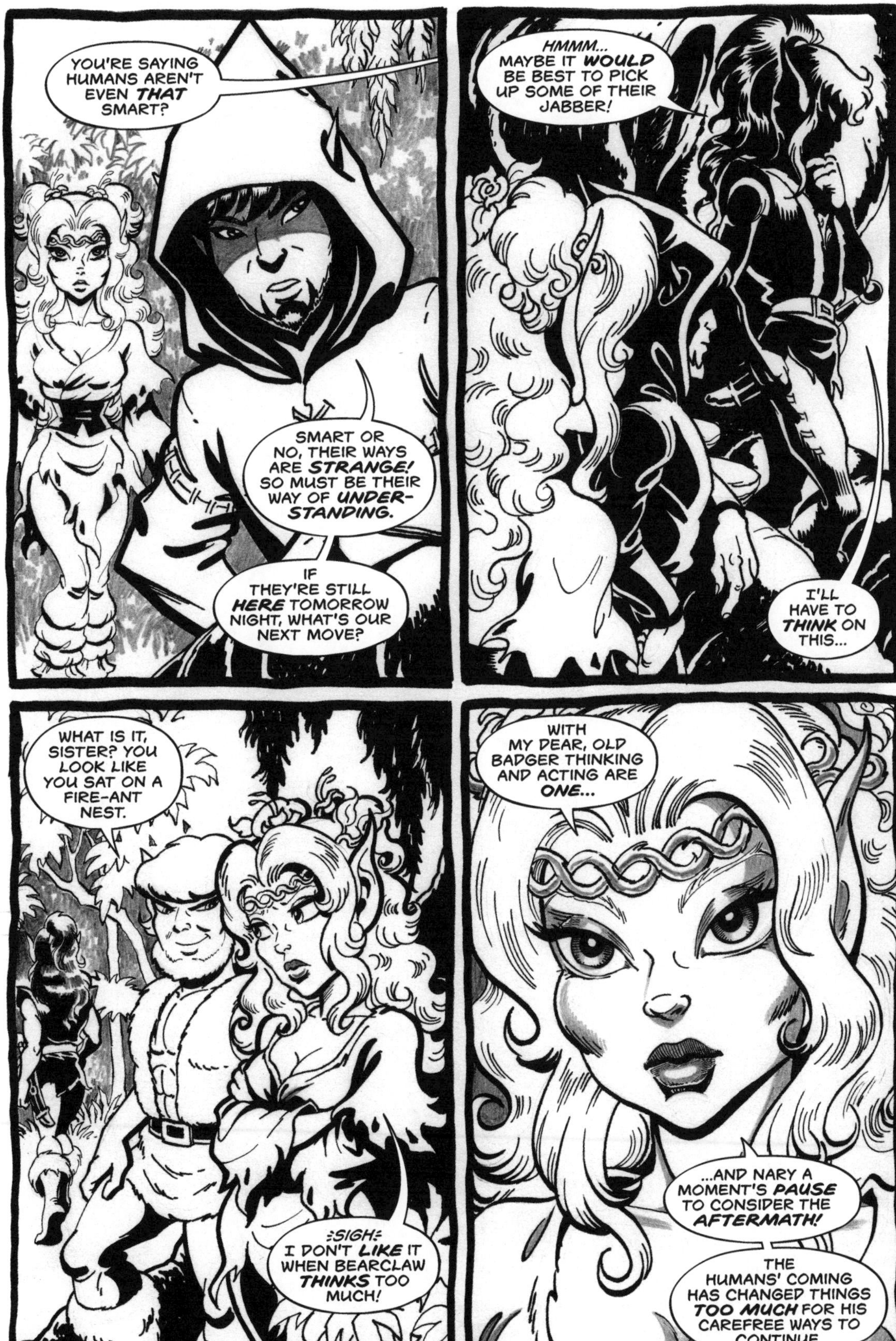
YOU'RE SAYING HUMANS AREN'T EVEN *THAT* SMART?
SMART OR NO, THEIR WAYS ARE *STRANGE!* SO MUST BE THEIR WAY OF *UNDER-STANDING.*
IF THEY'RE STILL *HERE* TOMORROW NIGHT, WHAT'S OUR NEXT MOVE?
HMMM... MAYBE IT *WOULD* BE BEST TO PICK UP SOME OF THEIR JABBER!
I'LL HAVE TO *THINK* ON THIS...
WHAT IS IT, SISTER? YOU LOOK LIKE YOU SAT ON A FIRE-ANT NEST.
:SIGH: I DON'T *LIKE* IT WHEN BEARCLAW *THINKS* TOO MUCH!
WITH MY DEAR, OLD BADGER THINKING AND ACTING ARE *ONE...*
...AND NARY A MOMENT'S *PAUSE* TO CONSIDER THE *AFTERMATH!*
THE HUMANS' COMING HAS CHANGED THINGS *TOO MUCH* FOR HIS CAREFREE WAYS TO CONTINUE.

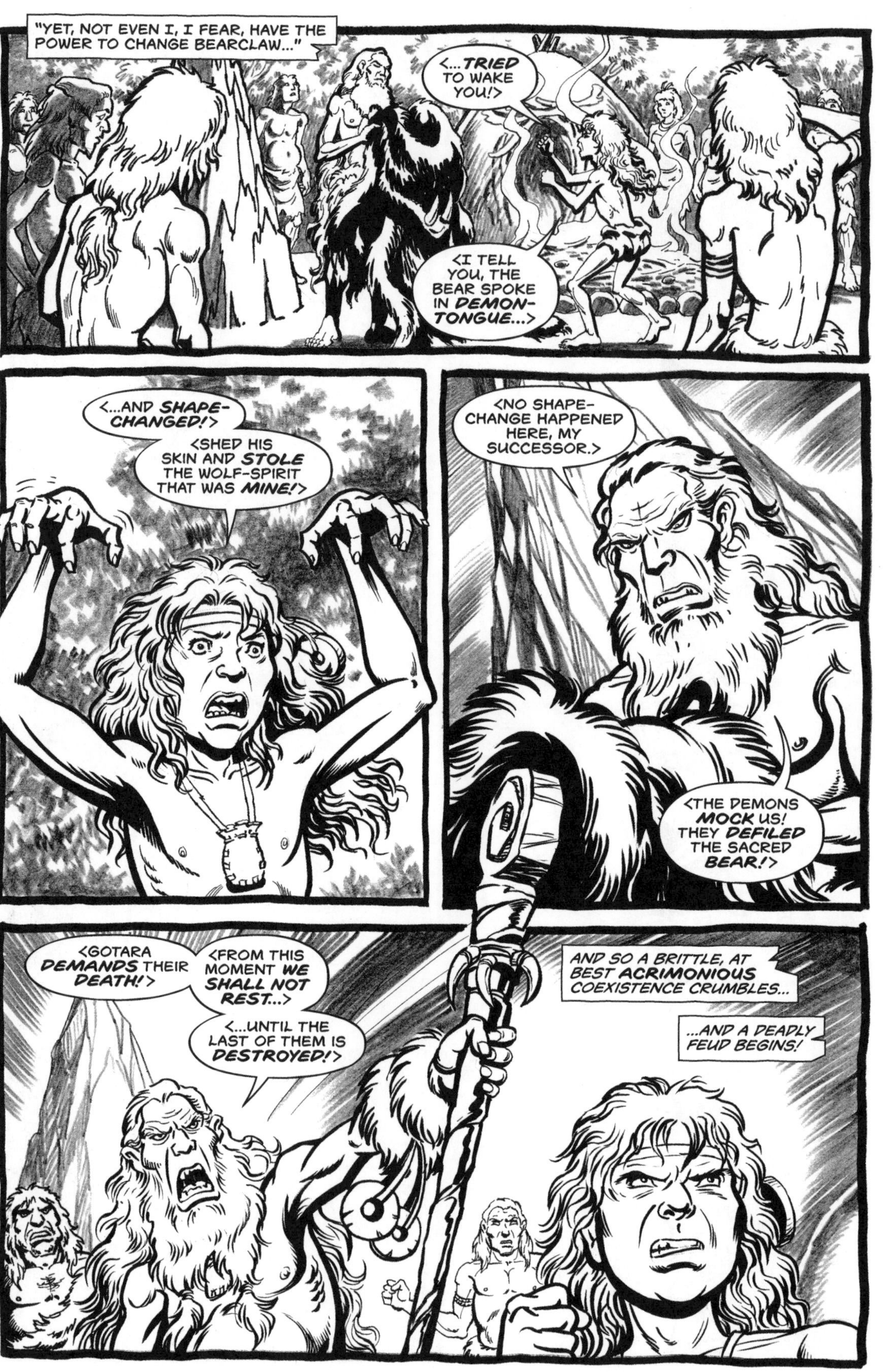
"YET, NOT EVEN I, I FEAR, HAVE THE POWER TO CHANGE BEARCLAW..."
<...TRIED TO WAKE YOU!>
<I TELL YOU, THE BEAR SPOKE IN DEMON-TONGUE...>
<...AND SHAPE-CHANGED!>
<SHED HIS SKIN AND STOLE THE WOLF-SPIRIT THAT WAS MINE!>
<NO SHAPE-CHANGE HAPPENED HERE, MY SUCCESSOR.>
<THE DEMONS MOCK US! THEY DEFILED THE SACRED BEAR!>
<GOTARA DEMANDS THEIR DEATH!>
<FROM THIS MOMENT WE SHALL NOT REST...>
<...UNTIL THE LAST OF THEM IS DESTROYED!>
AND SO A BRITTLE, AT BEST ACRIMONIOUS COEXISTENCE CRUMBLES...
...AND A DEADLY FEUD BEGINS!

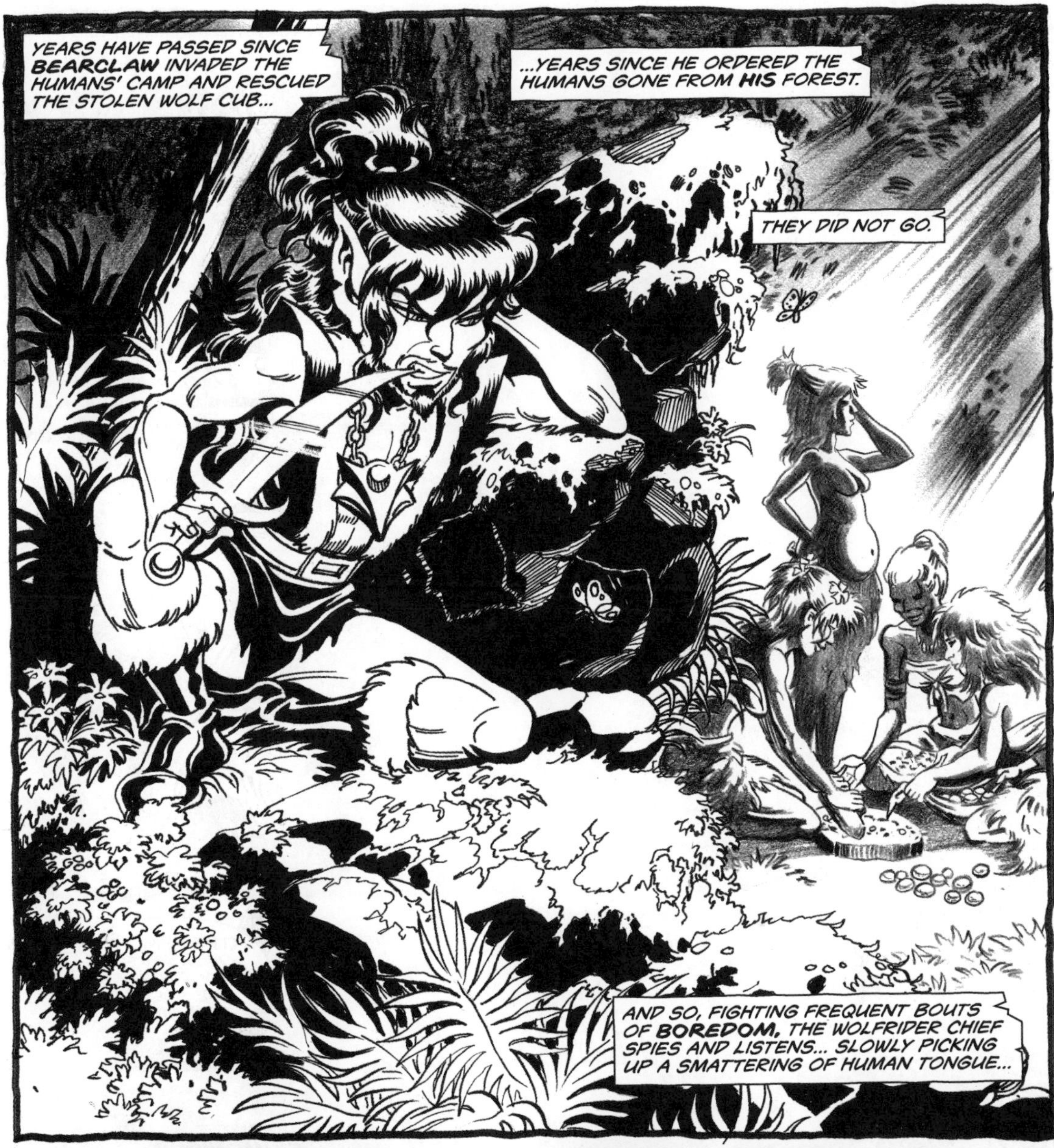
YEARS HAVE PASSED SINCE BEARCLAW INVADED THE HUMANS' CAMP AND RESCUED THE STOLEN WOLF CUB...
...YEARS SINCE HE ORDERED THE HUMANS GONE FROM HIS FOREST.
THEY DID NOT GO.
AND SO, FIGHTING FREQUENT BOUTS OF BOREDOM, THE WOLFRIDER CHIEF SPIES AND LISTENS... SLOWLY PICKING UP A SMATTERING OF HUMAN TONGUE...

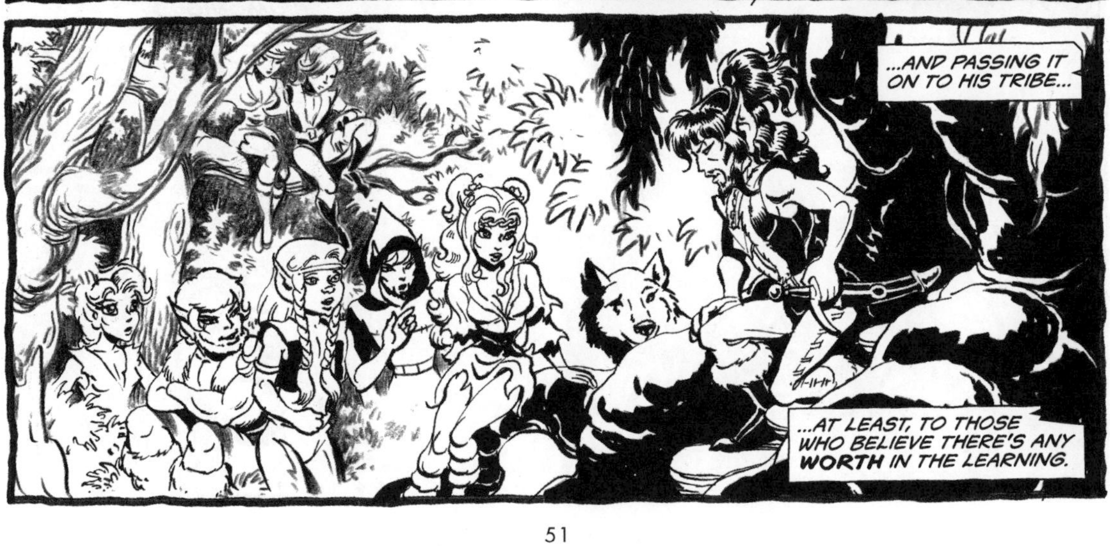
...AND PASSING IT ON TO HIS TRIBE...
...AT LEAST, TO THOSE WHO BELIEVE THERE'S ANY WORTH IN THE LEARNING.

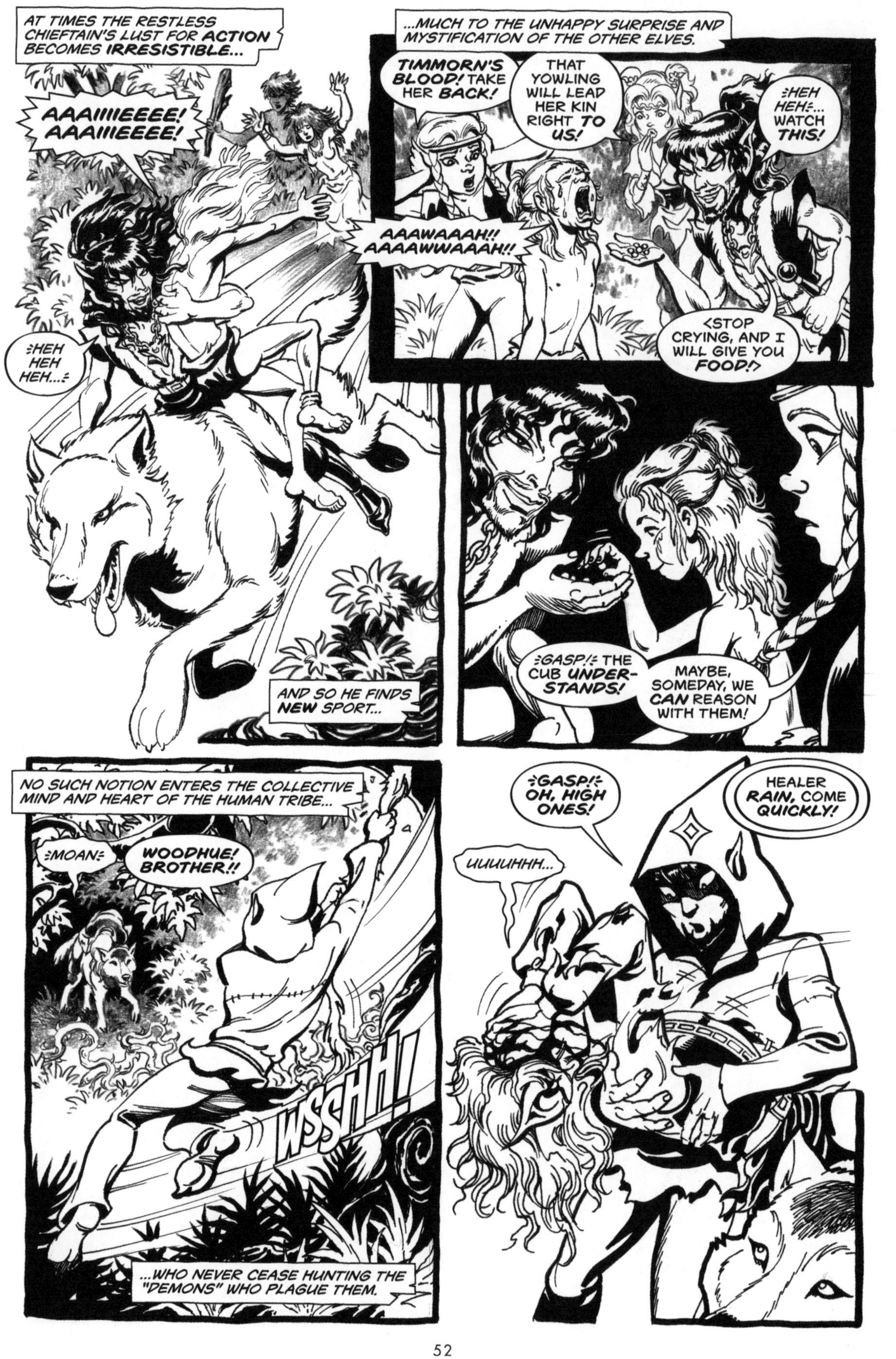
AT TIMES THE RESTLESS CHIEFTAIN'S LUST FOR ACTION BECOMES IRRESISTIBLE...
AAAIIIEEEE! AAAIIIEEEE!
:HEH HEH HEH...:
AND SO HE FINDS NEW SPORT...
...MUCH TO THE UNHAPPY SURPRISE AND MYSTIFICATION OF THE OTHER ELVES.
TIMMORN'S BLOOD! TAKE HER BACK!
THAT YOWLING WILL LEAD HER KIN RIGHT TO US!
:HEH HEH:... WATCH THIS!
AAAWAAAH!! AAAAWWAAAH!!
<STOP CRYING, AND I WILL GIVE YOU FOOD!>
:GASP!: THE CUB UNDER-STANDS!
MAYBE, SOMEDAY, WE CAN REASON WITH THEM!
NO SUCH NOTION ENTERS THE COLLECTIVE MIND AND HEART OF THE HUMAN TRIBE...
:MOAN:
WOODHUE! BROTHER!!
WSSHH!!
...WHO NEVER CEASE HUNTING THE "DEMONS" WHO PLAGUE THEM.
:GASP!: OH, HIGH ONES!
HEALER RAIN, COME QUICKLY!
UUUUHHH...

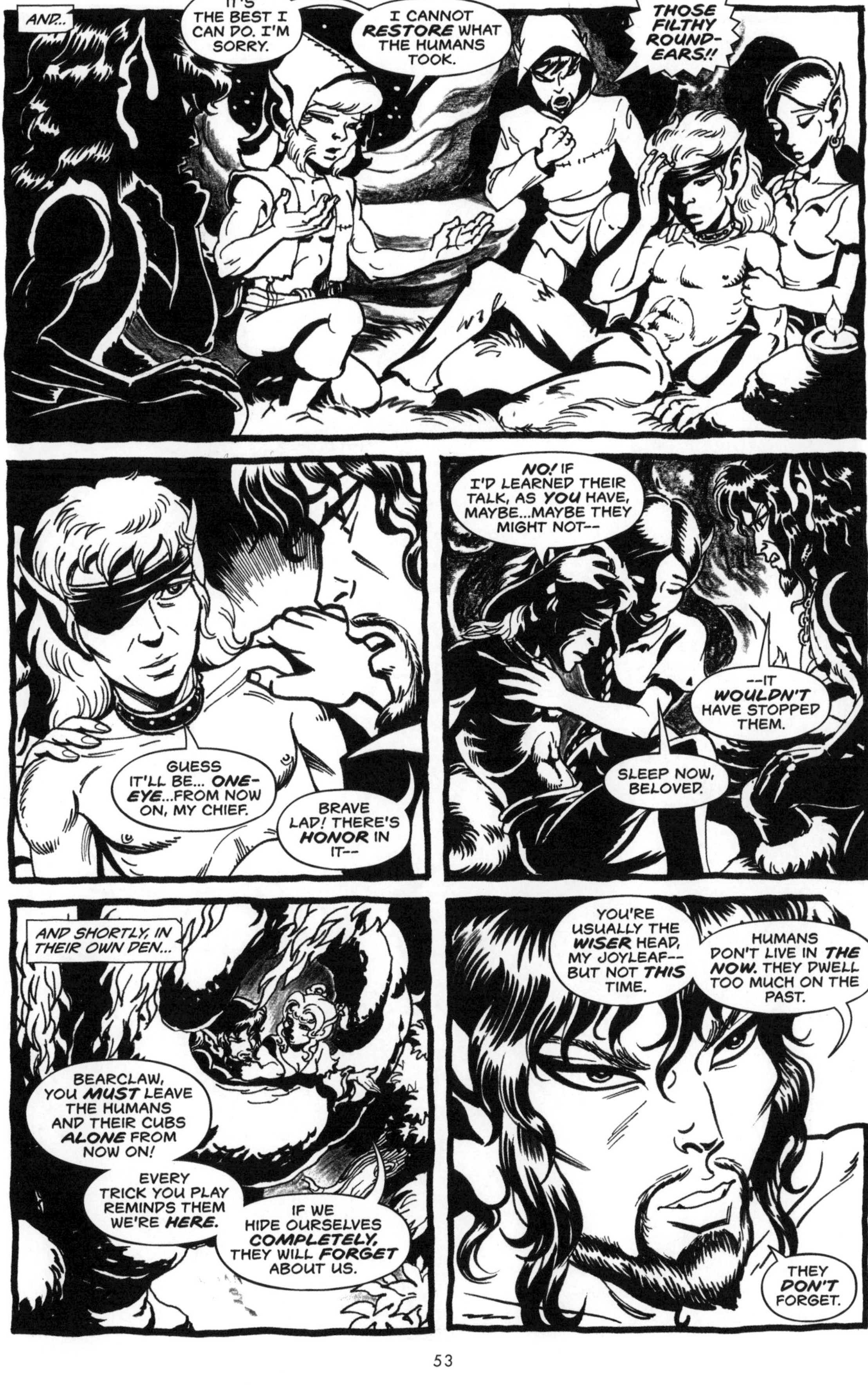
AND...
IT'S THE BEST I CAN DO. I'M SORRY.
I CANNOT RESTORE WHAT THE HUMANS TOOK.
THOSE FILTHY ROUND-EARS!!
GUESS IT'LL BE... ONE-EYE...FROM NOW ON, MY CHIEF.
BRAVE LAD! THERE'S HONOR IN IT--
NO! IF I'D LEARNED THEIR TALK, AS YOU HAVE, MAYBE...MAYBE THEY MIGHT NOT--
--IT WOULDN'T HAVE STOPPED THEM.
SLEEP NOW, BELOVED.
AND SHORTLY, IN THEIR OWN DEN...
BEARCLAW, YOU MUST LEAVE THE HUMANS AND THEIR CUBS ALONE FROM NOW ON!
EVERY TRICK YOU PLAY REMINDS THEM WE'RE HERE.
IF WE HIDE OURSELVES COMPLETELY, THEY WILL FORGET ABOUT US.
YOU'RE USUALLY THE WISER HEAD, MY JOYLEAF-- BUT NOT THIS TIME.
HUMANS DON'T LIVE IN THE NOW. THEY DWELL TOO MUCH ON THE PAST.
THEY DON'T FORGET.

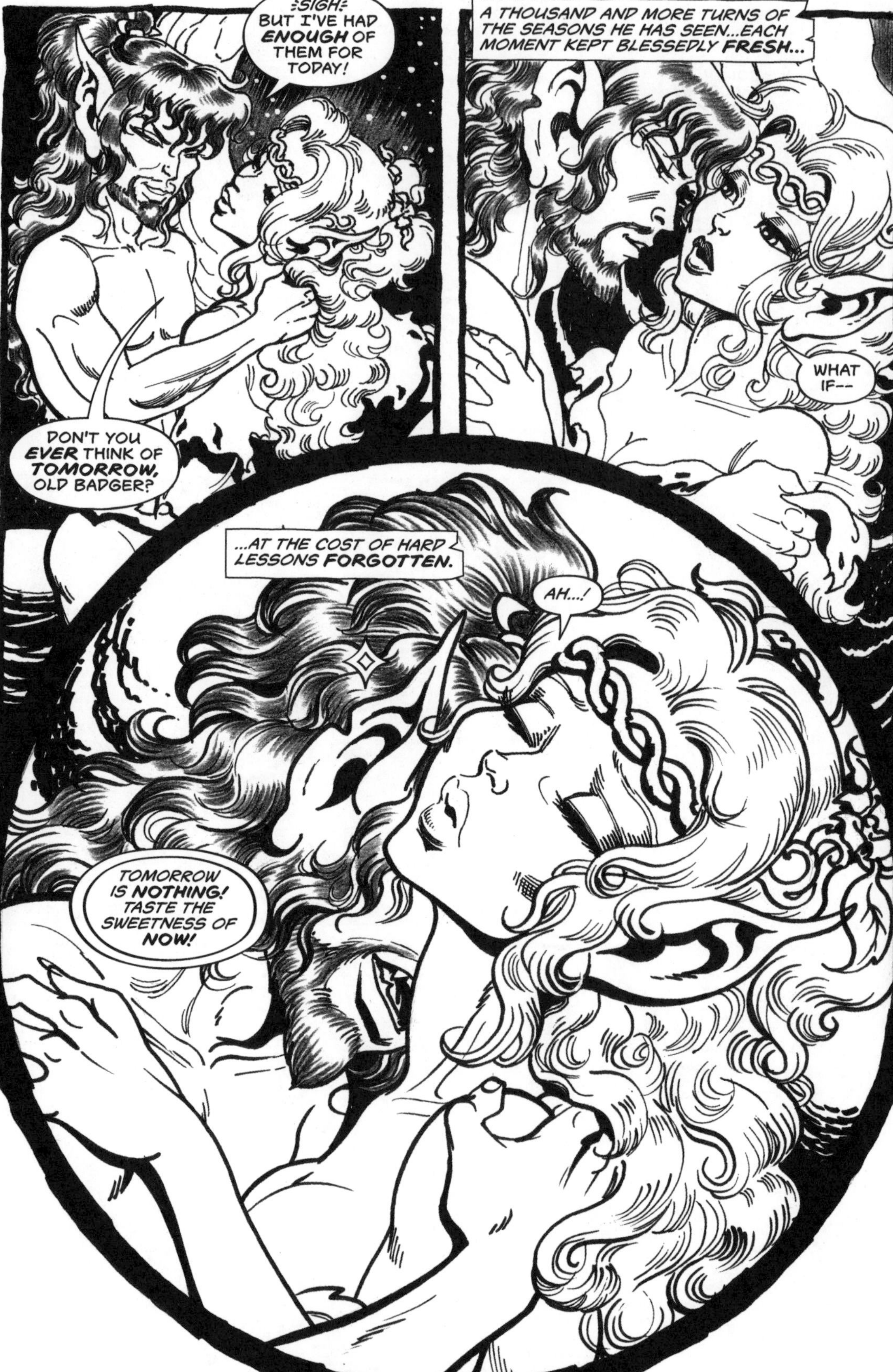

SIGH BUT I'VE HAD ENOUGH OF THEM FOR TODAY!
DON'T YOU EVER THINK OF TOMORROW, OLD BADGER?
A THOUSAND AND MORE TURNS OF THE SEASONS HE HAS SEEN...EACH MOMENT KEPT BLESSEDLY FRESH...
WHAT IF--
...AT THE COST OF HARD LESSONS FORGOTTEN.
AH...!
TOMORROW IS NOTHING! TASTE THE SWEETNESS OF NOW!

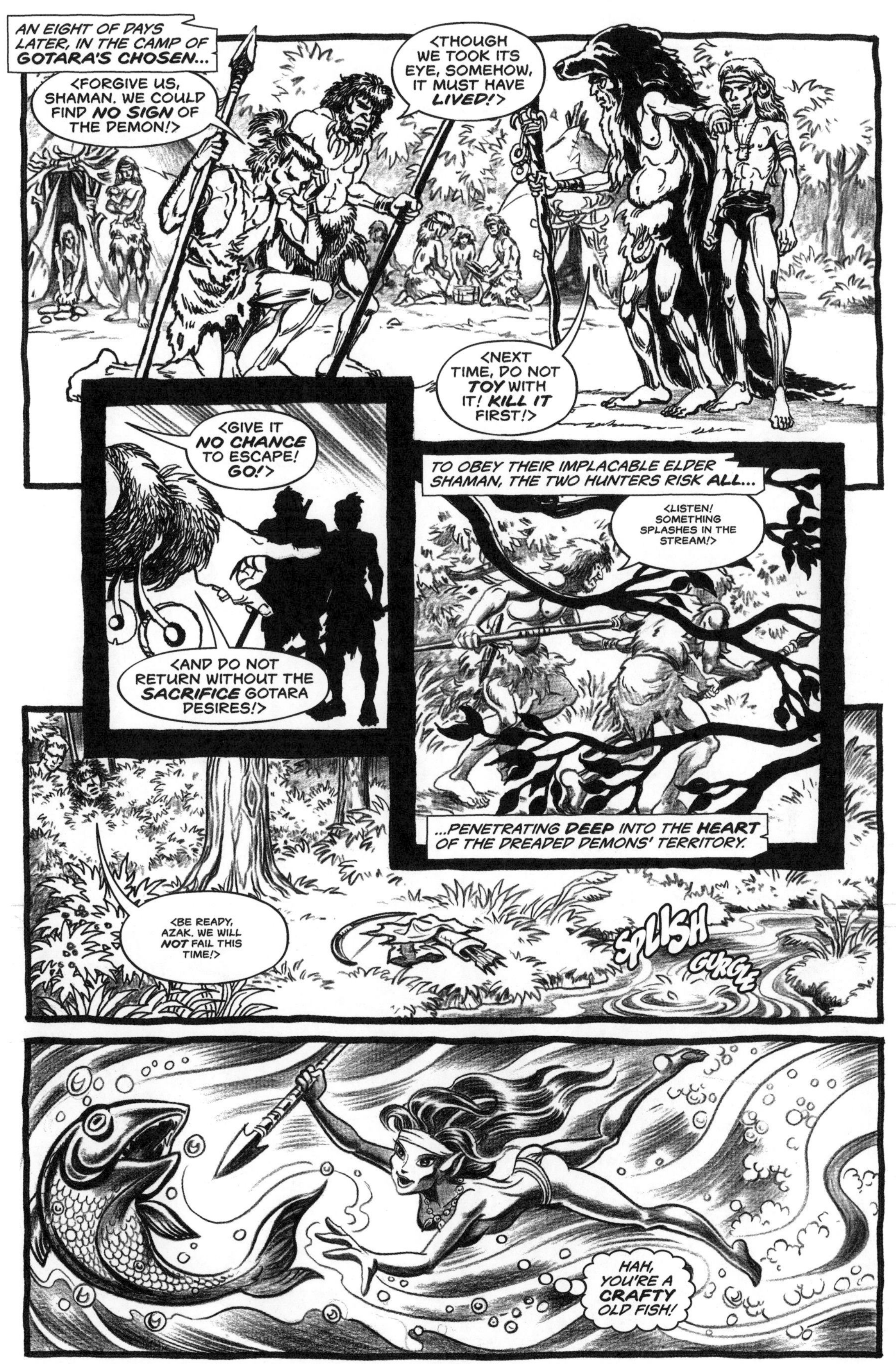

AN EIGHT OF DAYS LATER, IN THE CAMP OF GOTARA'S CHOSEN...
<FORGIVE US, SHAMAN. WE COULD FIND NO SIGN OF THE DEMON!>
<THOUGH WE TOOK ITS EYE, SOMEHOW, IT MUST HAVE LIVED!>
<NEXT TIME, DO NOT TOY WITH IT! KILL IT FIRST!>
<GIVE IT NO CHANCE TO ESCAPE! GO!>
<AND DO NOT RETURN WITHOUT THE SACRIFICE GOTARA DESIRES!>
TO OBEY THEIR IMPLACABLE ELDER SHAMAN, THE TWO HUNTERS RISK ALL...
<LISTEN! SOMETHING SPLASHES IN THE STREAM!>
...PENETRATING DEEP INTO THE HEART OF THE DREADED DEMONS' TERRITORY.
<BE READY, AZAK. WE WILL NOT FAIL THIS TIME!>
SPLISH
GURGLE
HAH, YOU'RE A CRAFTY OLD FISH!

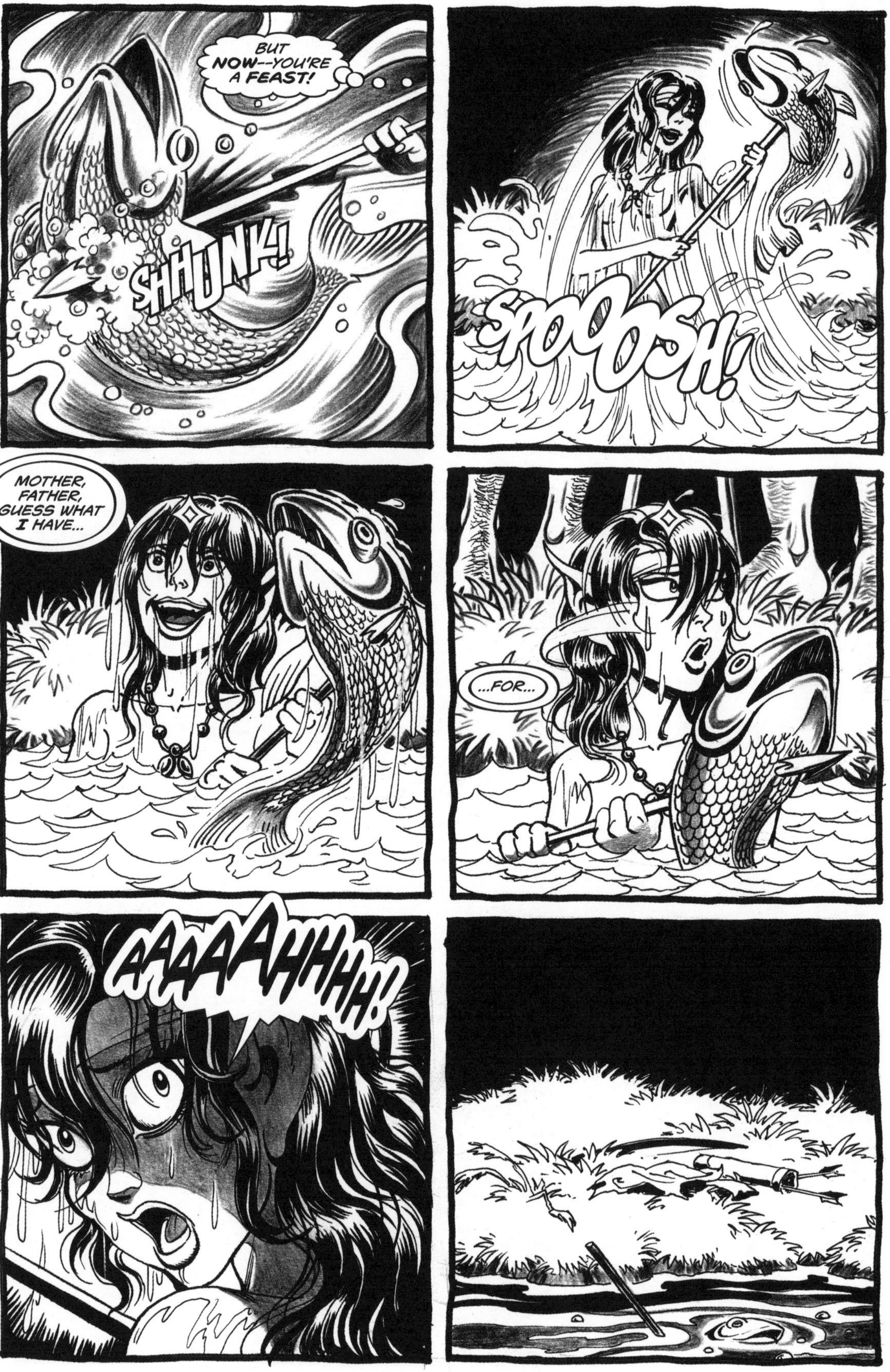
BUT NOW--YOU'RE A FEAST!
SHHUNK!
SPOOOSH!
MOTHER, FATHER, GUESS WHAT I HAVE...
...FOR...
AAAAAHHHH!

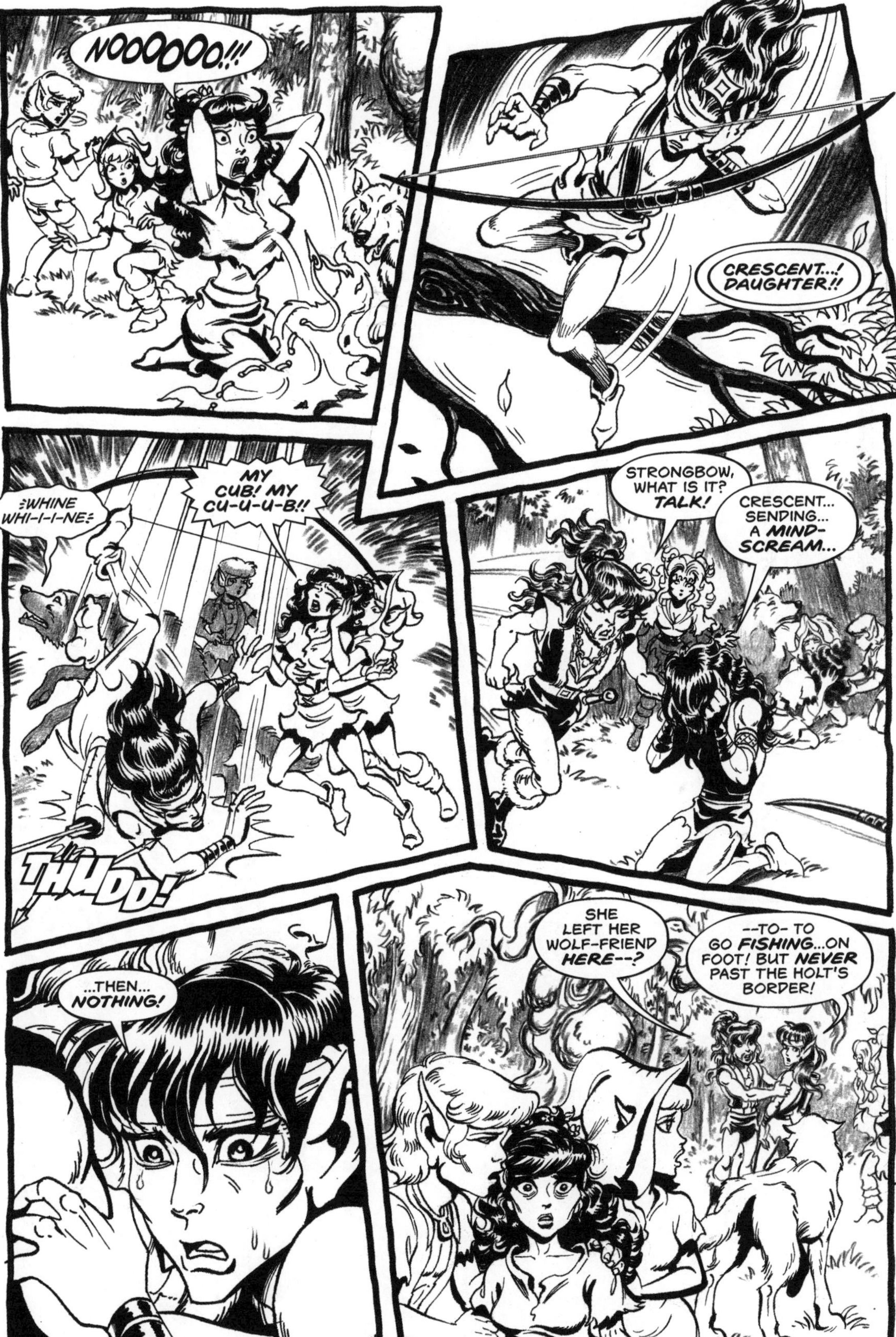
NOOOOOO!!!
CRESCENT...! DAUGHTER!!
WHINE WHI-I-I-NE
MY CUB! MY CU-U-U-B!!
THUDD!
STRONGBOW, WHAT IS IT? TALK!
CRESCENT... SENDING... A MIND-SCREAM...
...THEN... NOTHING!
SHE LEFT HER WOLF-FRIEND HERE--?
--TO- TO GO FISHING...ON FOOT! BUT NEVER PAST THE HOLT'S BORDER!

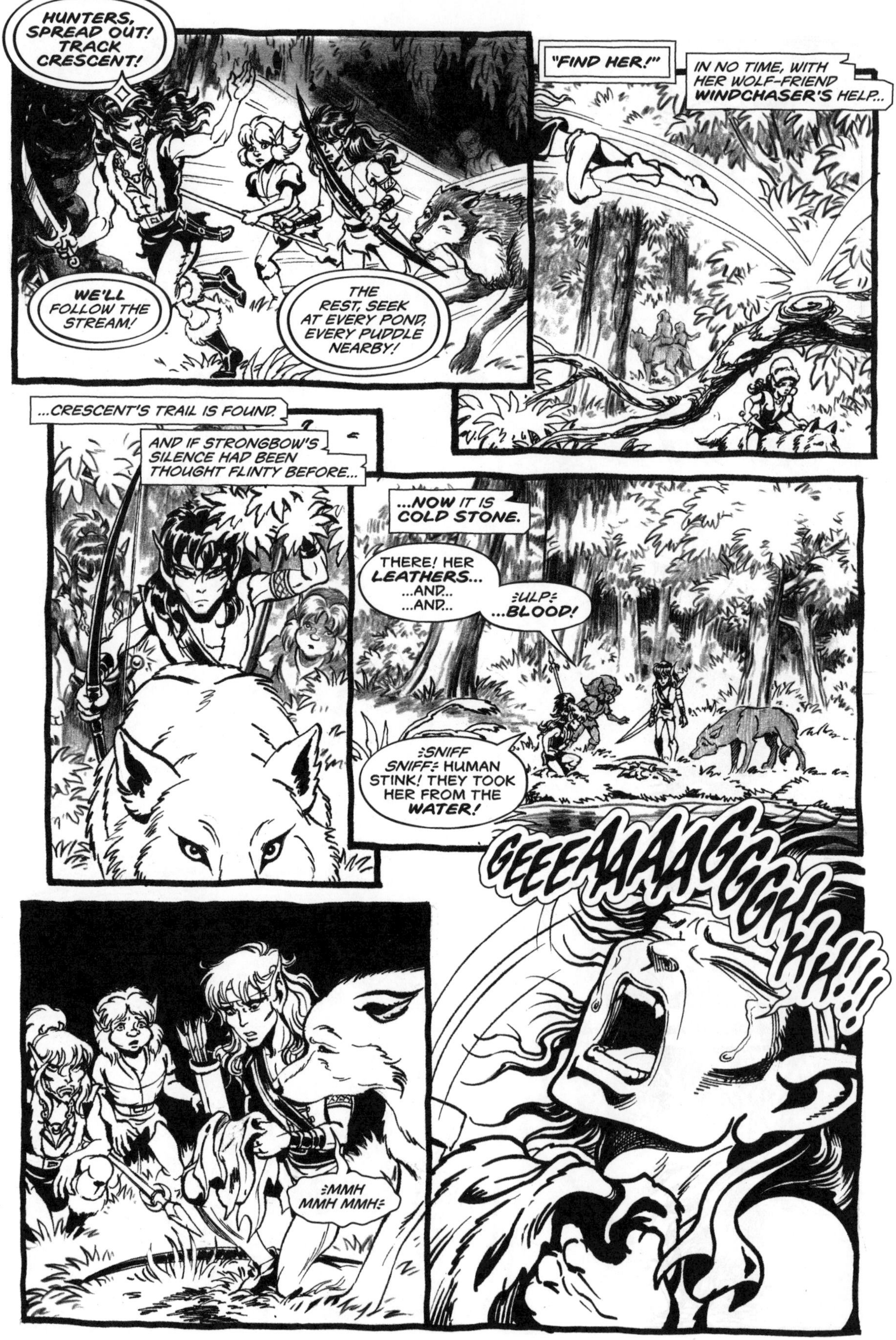

HUNTERS, SPREAD OUT! TRACK CRESCENT!
WE'LL FOLLOW THE STREAM!
THE REST, SEEK AT EVERY POND, EVERY PUDDLE NEARBY!
"FIND HER!"
IN NO TIME, WITH HER WOLF-FRIEND WINDCHASER'S HELP...
...CRESCENT'S TRAIL IS FOUND.
AND IF STRONGBOW'S SILENCE HAD BEEN THOUGHT FLINTY BEFORE...
...NOW IT IS COLD STONE.
THERE! HER LEATHERS... ...AND... ...AND...
ULP ...BLOOD!
SNIFF SNIFF HUMAN STINK! THEY TOOK HER FROM THE WATER!
MMH MMH MMH
GEEEAAAAGGGHHH!!!

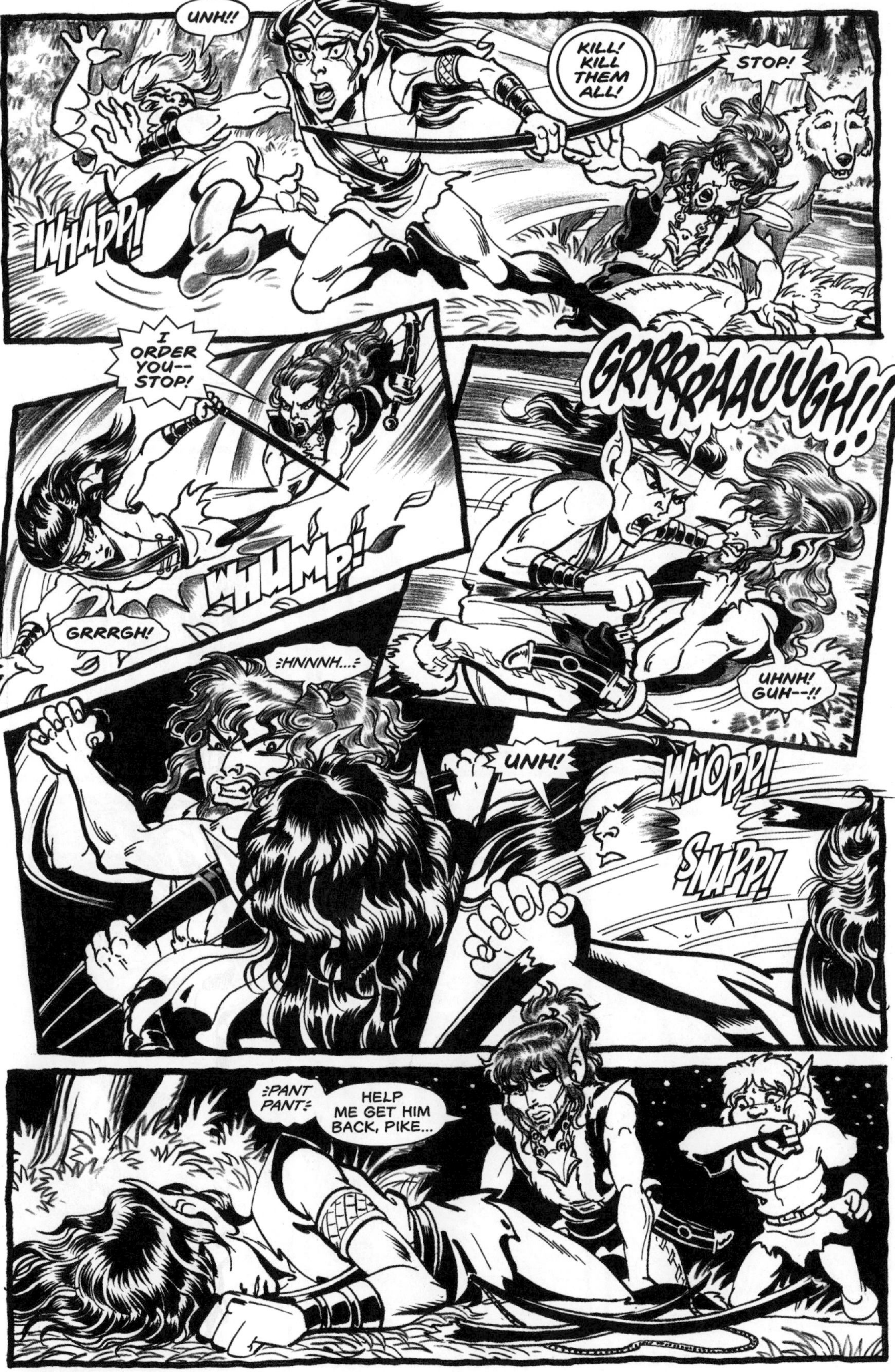
UNH!!
KILL! KILL THEM ALL!
STOP!
WHAPP!
I ORDER YOU-- STOP!
WHUMP!
GRRRGH!
GRRRRAAUUGH!!
HNNNH...
UHNH! GUH--!!
UNH!
WHOPP!
SNAPP!
PANT PANT
HELP ME GET HIM BACK, PIKE...

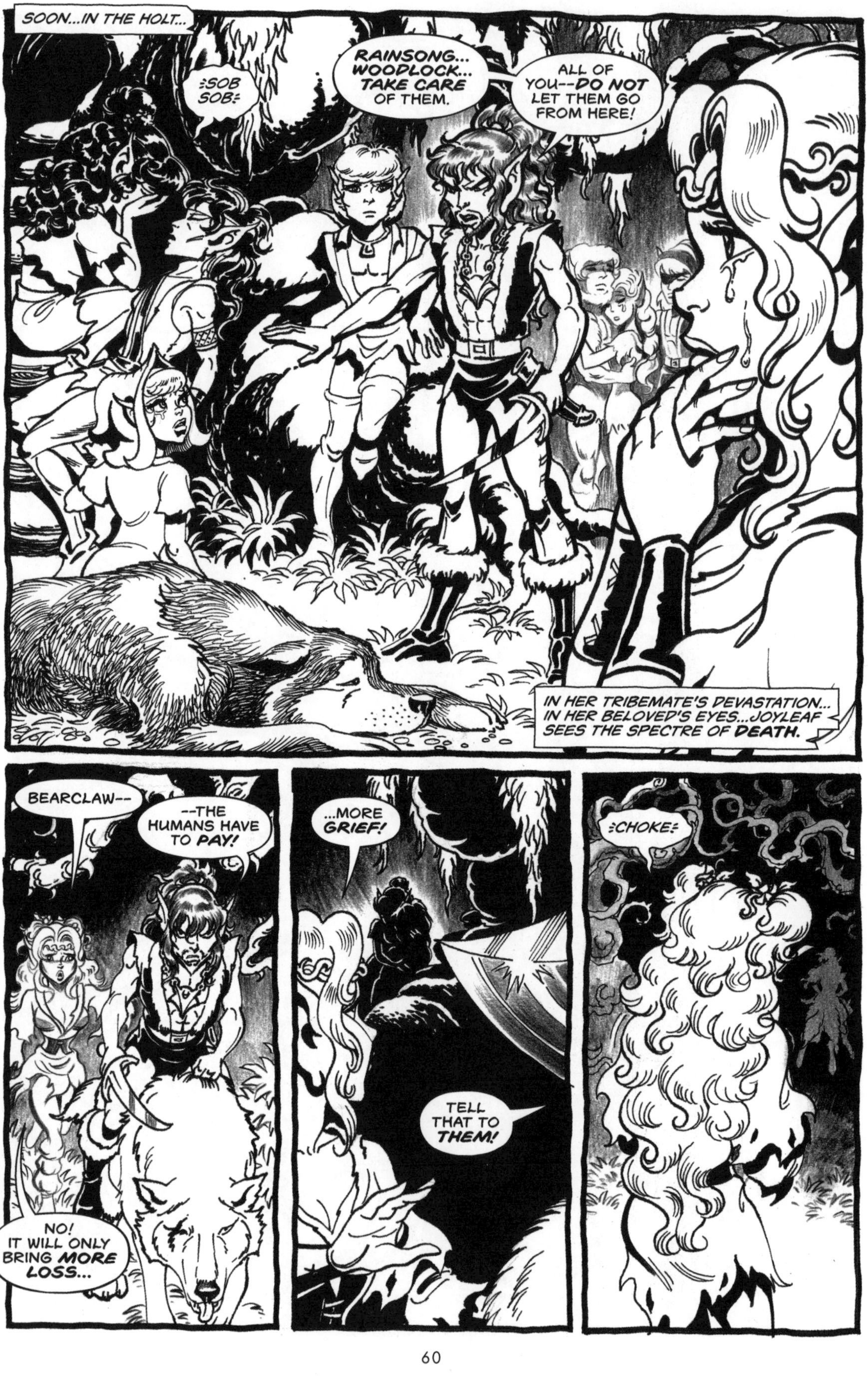

SOON...IN THE HOLT...
SOB SOB
RAINSONG... WOODLOCK... TAKE CARE OF THEM.
ALL OF YOU--DO NOT LET THEM GO FROM HERE!
IN HER TRIBEMATE'S DEVASTATION... IN HER BELOVED'S EYES...JOYLEAF SEES THE SPECTRE OF DEATH.
BEARCLAW--
--THE HUMANS HAVE TO PAY!
NO! IT WILL ONLY BRING MORE LOSS...
...MORE GRIEF!
TELL THAT TO THEM!
CHOKE

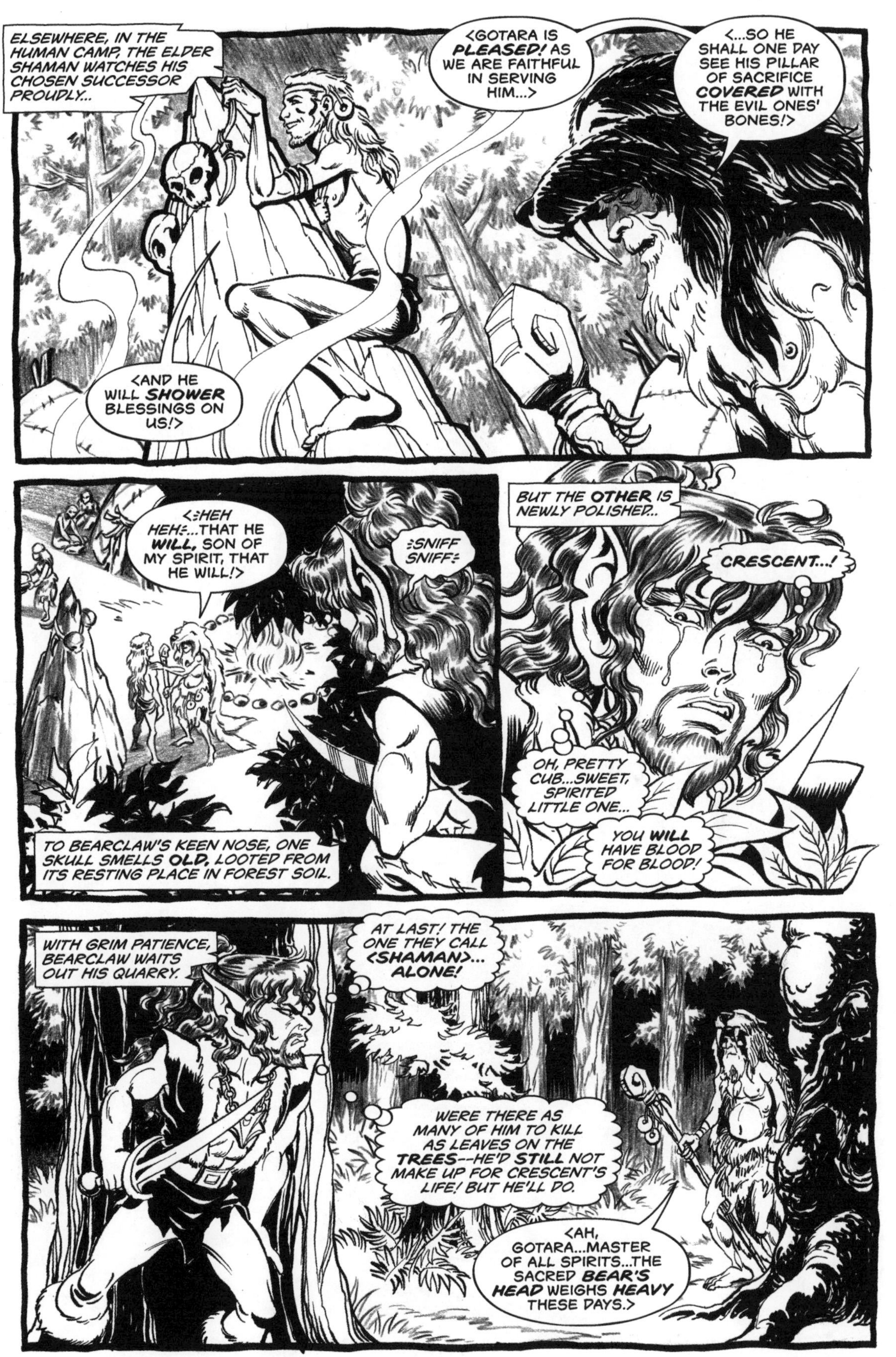
ELSEWHERE, IN THE HUMAN CAMP, THE ELDER SHAMAN WATCHES HIS CHOSEN SUCCESSOR PROUDLY...
<GOTARA IS PLEASED! AS WE ARE FAITHFUL IN SERVING HIM...>
<...SO HE SHALL ONE DAY SEE HIS PILLAR OF SACRIFICE COVERED WITH THE EVIL ONES' BONES!>
<AND HE WILL SHOWER BLESSINGS ON US!>
<-HEH HEH-...THAT HE WILL, SON OF MY SPIRIT, THAT HE WILL!>
-SNIFF SNIFF-
TO BEARCLAW'S KEEN NOSE, ONE SKULL SMELLS OLD, LOOTED FROM ITS RESTING PLACE IN FOREST SOIL.
BUT THE OTHER IS NEWLY POLISHED...
CRESCENT...!
OH, PRETTY CUB...SWEET, SPIRITED LITTLE ONE...
YOU WILL HAVE BLOOD FOR BLOOD!
WITH GRIM PATIENCE, BEARCLAW WAITS OUT HIS QUARRY.
AT LAST! THE ONE THEY CALL <SHAMAN>... ALONE!
WERE THERE AS MANY OF HIM TO KILL AS LEAVES ON THE TREES--HE'D STILL NOT MAKE UP FOR CRESCENT'S LIFE! BUT HE'LL DO.
<AH, GOTARA...MASTER OF ALL SPIRITS...THE SACRED BEAR'S HEAD WEIGHS HEAVY THESE DAYS.>

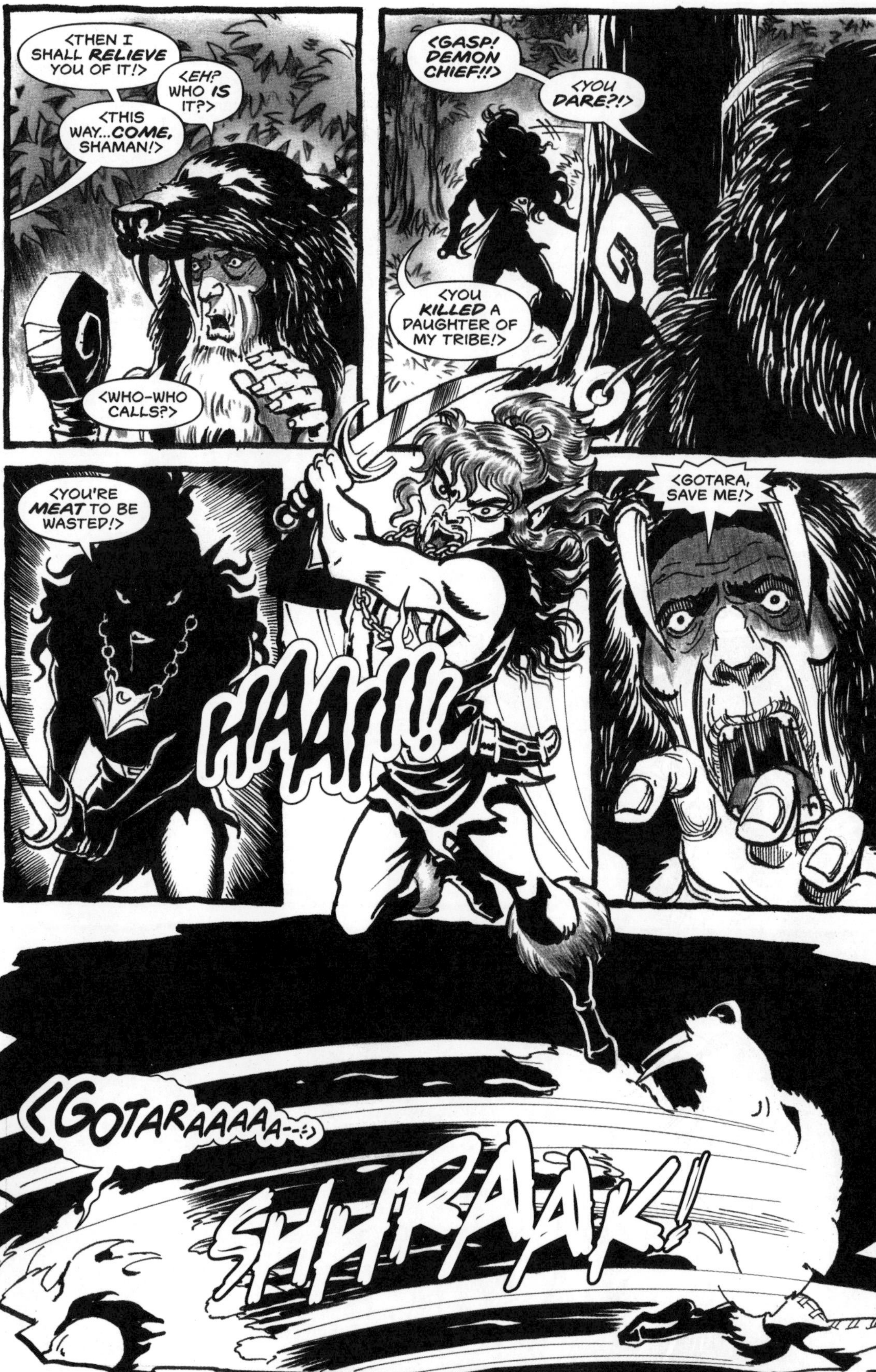
<THEN I SHALL RELIEVE YOU OF IT!>
<EH? WHO IS IT?>
<THIS WAY...COME, SHAMAN!>
<WHO-WHO CALLS?>
<GASP! DEMON CHIEF!!>
<YOU DARE?!>
<YOU KILLED A DAUGHTER OF MY TRIBE!>
<YOU'RE MEAT TO BE WASTED!>
HAAII!
<GOTARA, SAVE ME!>
<GOTARAAAAA--!>
SHHRAAK!

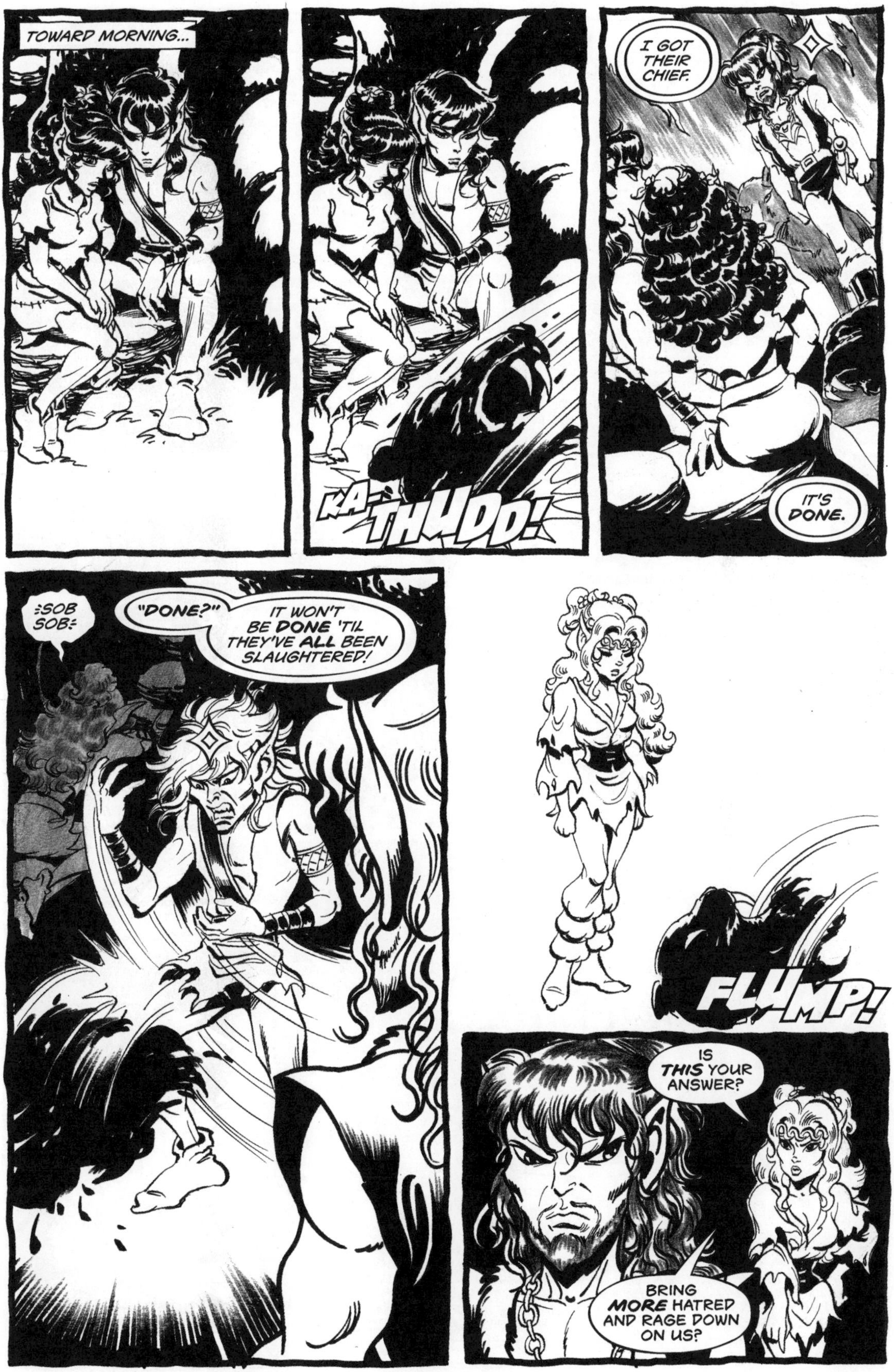
TOWARD MORNING...
KA-THUDD!
I GOT THEIR CHIEF.
IT'S DONE.
SOB SOB
"DONE?"
IT WON'T BE DONE 'TIL THEY'VE ALL BEEN SLAUGHTERED!
FLUMP!
IS THIS YOUR ANSWER?
BRING MORE HATRED AND RAGE DOWN ON US?

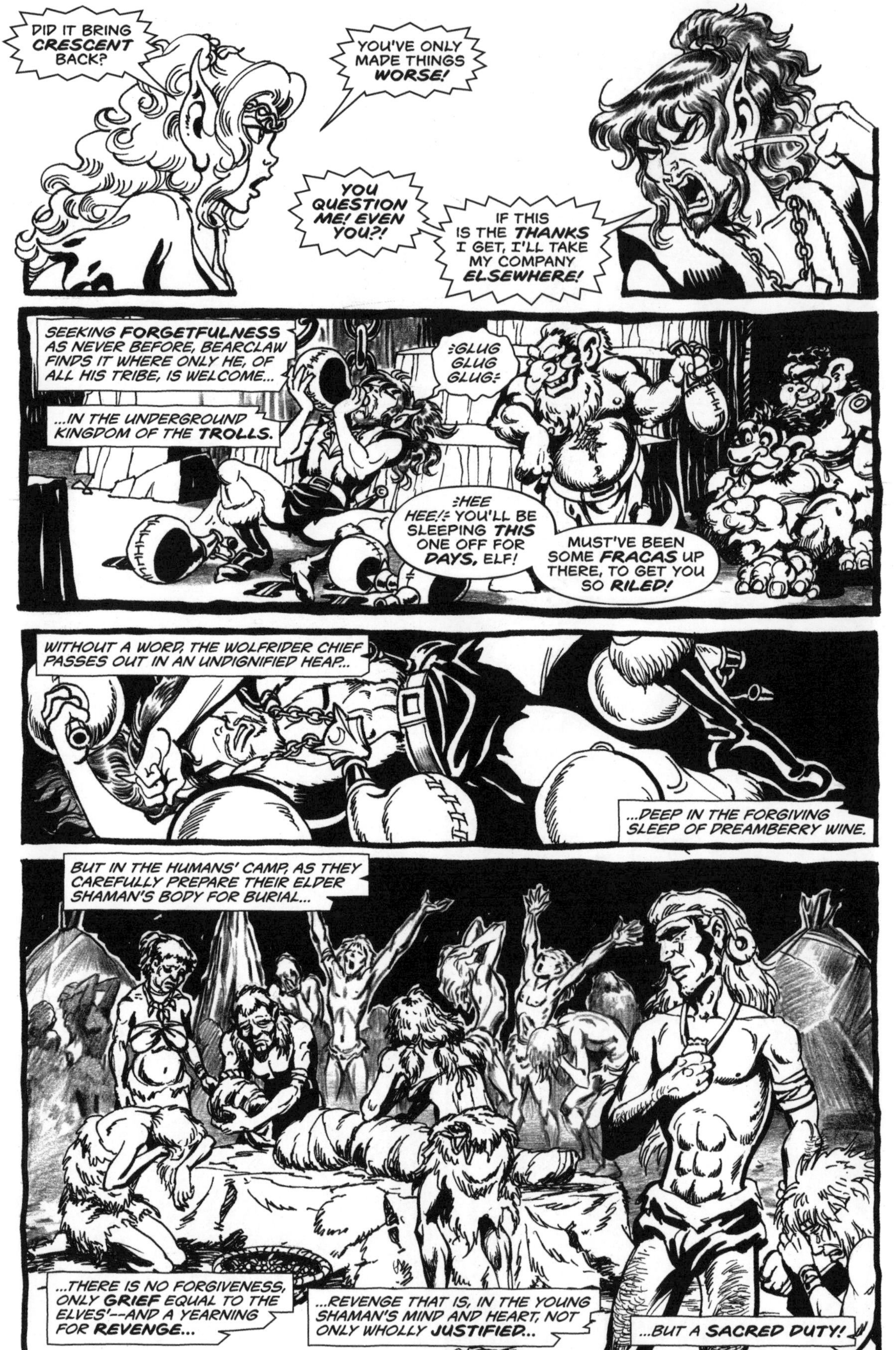
DID IT BRING CRESCENT BACK?
YOU'VE ONLY MADE THINGS WORSE!
YOU QUESTION ME! EVEN YOU?!
IF THIS IS THE THANKS I GET, I'LL TAKE MY COMPANY ELSEWHERE!
SEEKING FORGETFULNESS AS NEVER BEFORE, BEARCLAW FINDS IT WHERE ONLY HE, OF ALL HIS TRIBE, IS WELCOME...
...IN THE UNDERGROUND KINGDOM OF THE TROLLS.
GLUG GLUG GLUG
HEE HEE! YOU'LL BE SLEEPING THIS ONE OFF FOR DAYS, ELF!
MUST'VE BEEN SOME FRACAS UP THERE, TO GET YOU SO RILED!
WITHOUT A WORD, THE WOLFRIDER CHIEF PASSES OUT IN AN UNDIGNIFIED HEAP...
...DEEP IN THE FORGIVING SLEEP OF DREAMBERRY WINE.
BUT IN THE HUMANS' CAMP, AS THEY CAREFULLY PREPARE THEIR ELDER SHAMAN'S BODY FOR BURIAL...
...THERE IS NO FORGIVENESS, ONLY GRIEF EQUAL TO THE ELVES'--AND A YEARNING FOR REVENGE...
...REVENGE THAT IS, IN THE YOUNG SHAMAN'S MIND AND HEART, NOT ONLY WHOLLY JUSTIFIED...
...BUT A SACRED DUTY!

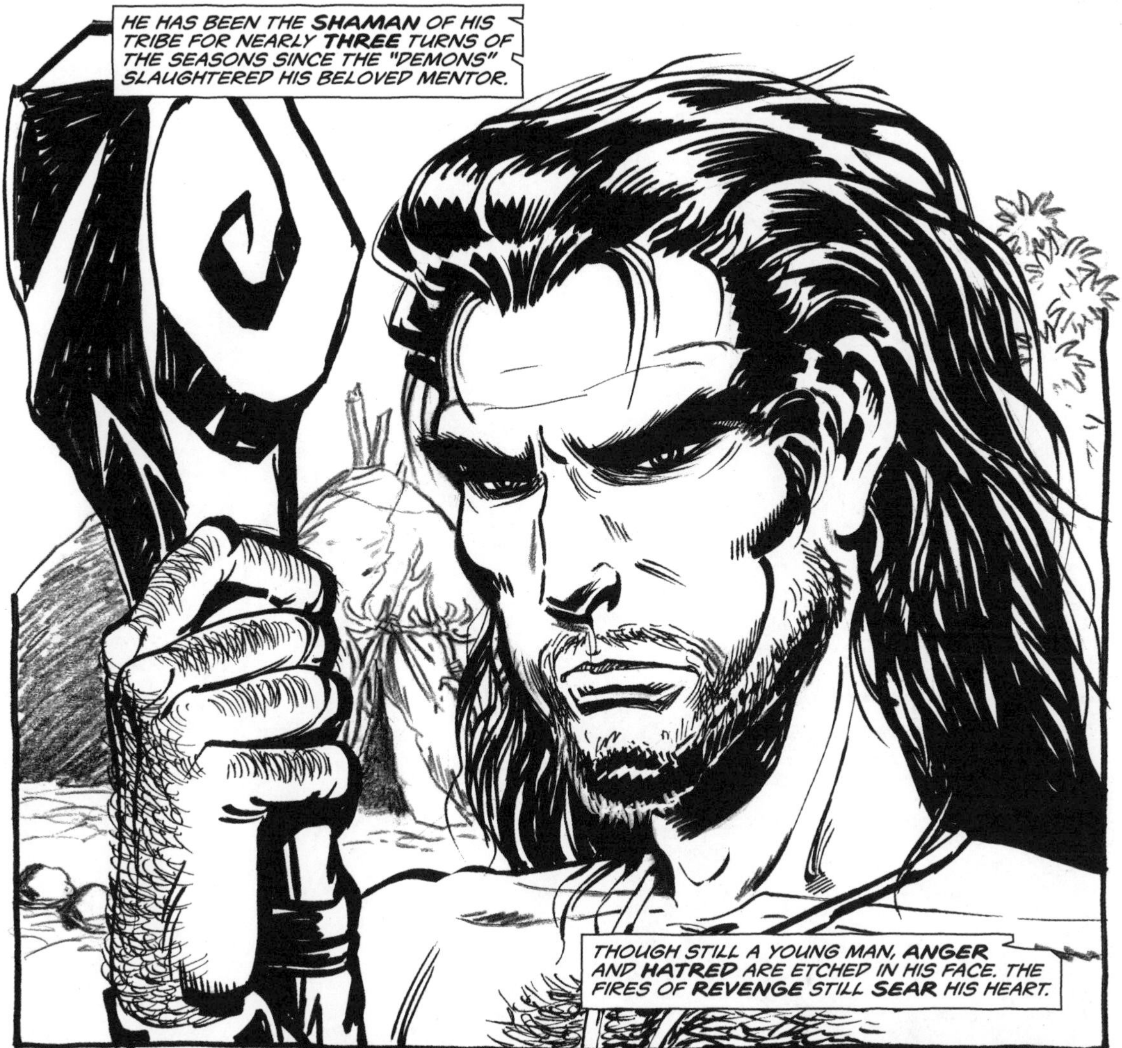
HE HAS BEEN THE SHAMAN OF HIS TRIBE FOR NEARLY THREE TURNS OF THE SEASONS SINCE THE "DEMONS" SLAUGHTERED HIS BELOVED MENTOR.
THOUGH STILL A YOUNG MAN, ANGER AND HATRED ARE ETCHED IN HIS FACE. THE FIRES OF REVENGE STILL SEAR HIS HEART.

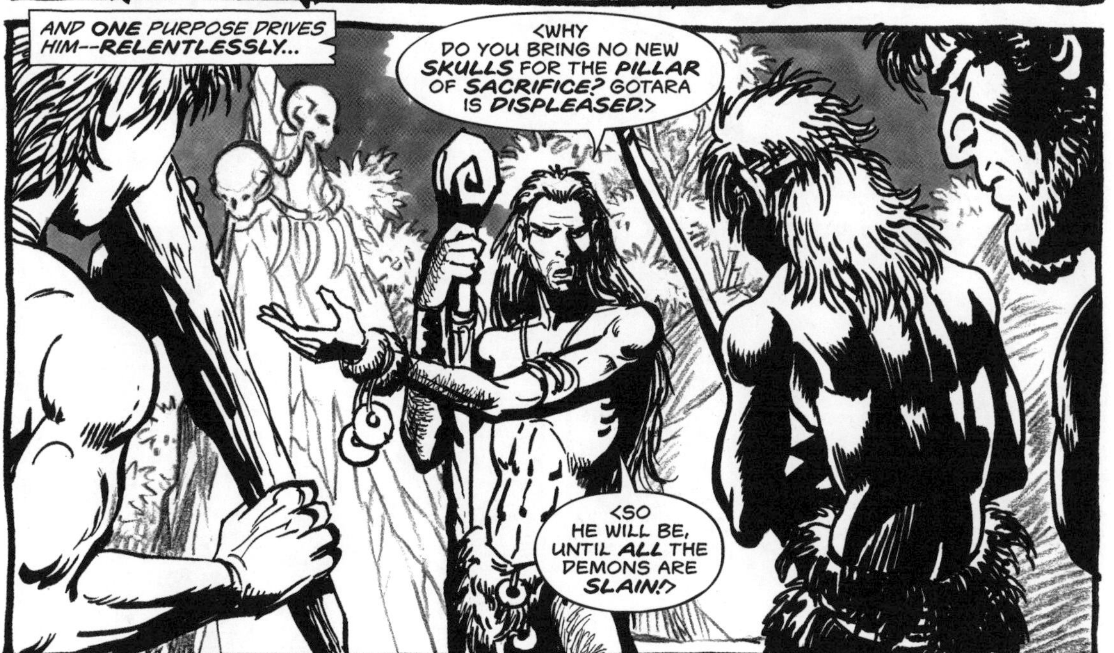
AND ONE PURPOSE DRIVES HIM--RELENTLESSLY...
<WHY DO YOU BRING NO NEW SKULLS FOR THE PILLAR OF SACRIFICE? GOTARA IS DISPLEASED.>
<SO HE WILL BE, UNTIL ALL THE DEMONS ARE SLAIN!>

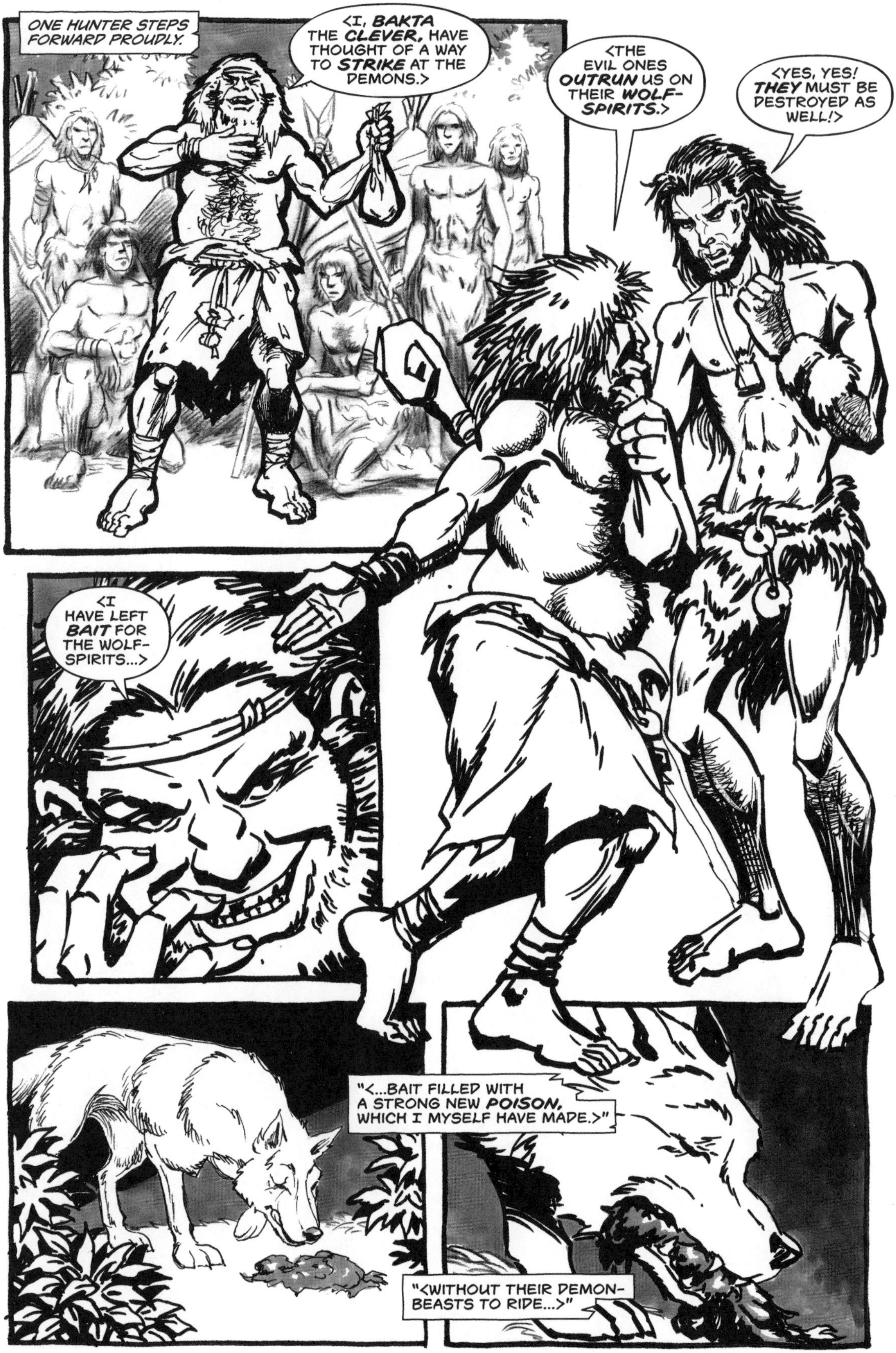
ONE HUNTER STEPS FORWARD PROUDLY.
<I, BAKTA THE CLEVER, HAVE THOUGHT OF A WAY TO STRIKE AT THE DEMONS.>
<THE EVIL ONES OUTRUN US ON THEIR WOLF-SPIRITS.>
<YES, YES! THEY MUST BE DESTROYED AS WELL!>
<I HAVE LEFT BAIT FOR THE WOLF-SPIRITS...>
"<...BAIT FILLED WITH A STRONG NEW POISON, WHICH I MYSELF HAVE MADE.>"
"<WITHOUT THEIR DEMON-BEASTS TO RIDE...>"

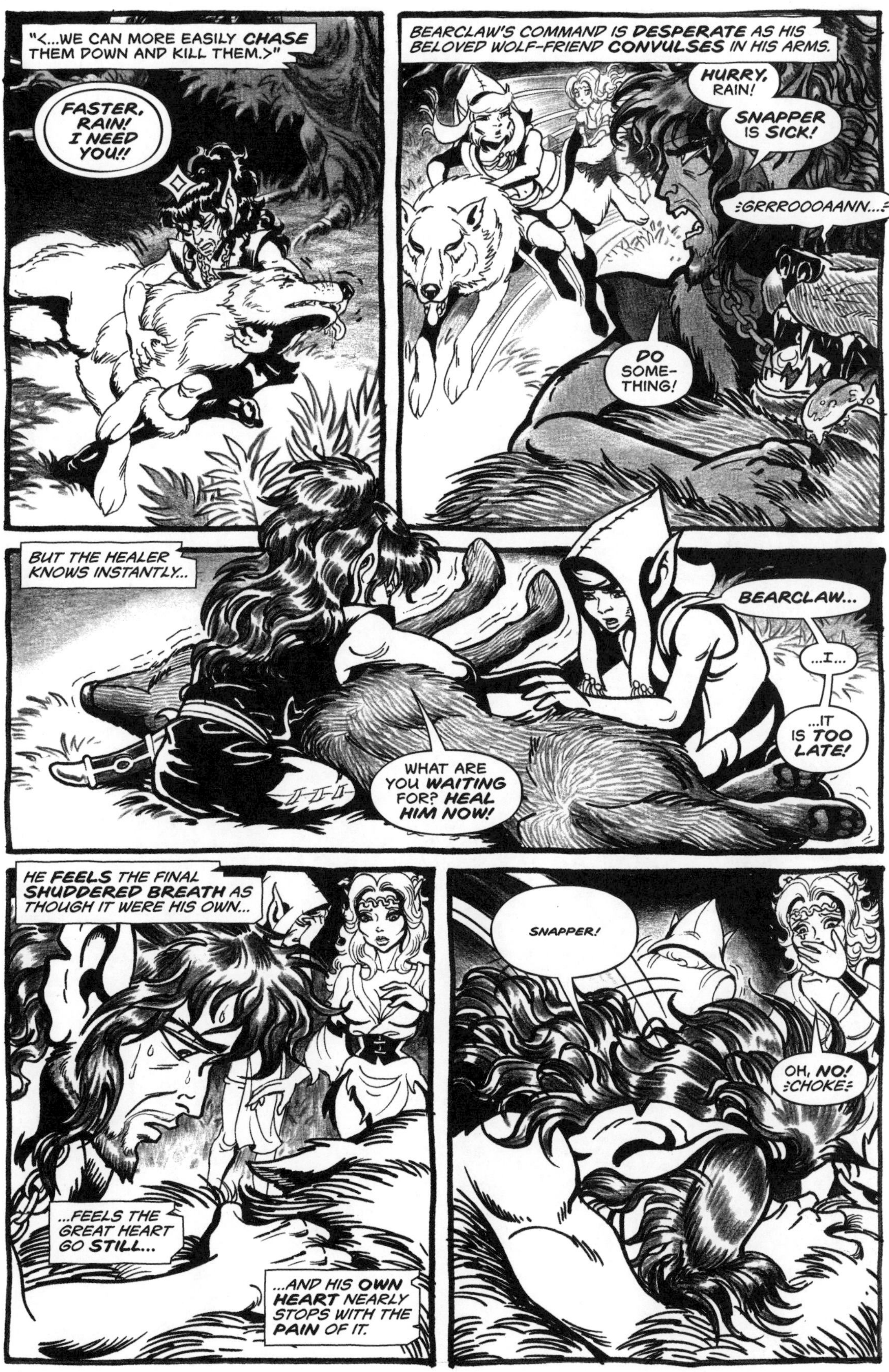
"<...WE CAN MORE EASILY CHASE THEM DOWN AND KILL THEM.>"
FASTER, RAIN! I NEED YOU!!
BEARCLAW'S COMMAND IS DESPERATE AS HIS BELOVED WOLF-FRIEND CONVULSES IN HIS ARMS.
HURRY, RAIN!
SNAPPER IS SICK!
GRRROOOAANN...
DO SOME-THING!
BUT THE HEALER KNOWS INSTANTLY...
BEARCLAW...
...I...
...IT IS TOO LATE!
WHAT ARE YOU WAITING FOR? HEAL HIM NOW!
HE FEELS THE FINAL SHUDDERED BREATH AS THOUGH IT WERE HIS OWN...
...FEELS THE GREAT HEART GO STILL...
...AND HIS OWN HEART NEARLY STOPS WITH THE PAIN OF IT.
SNAPPER!
OH, NO! CHOKE

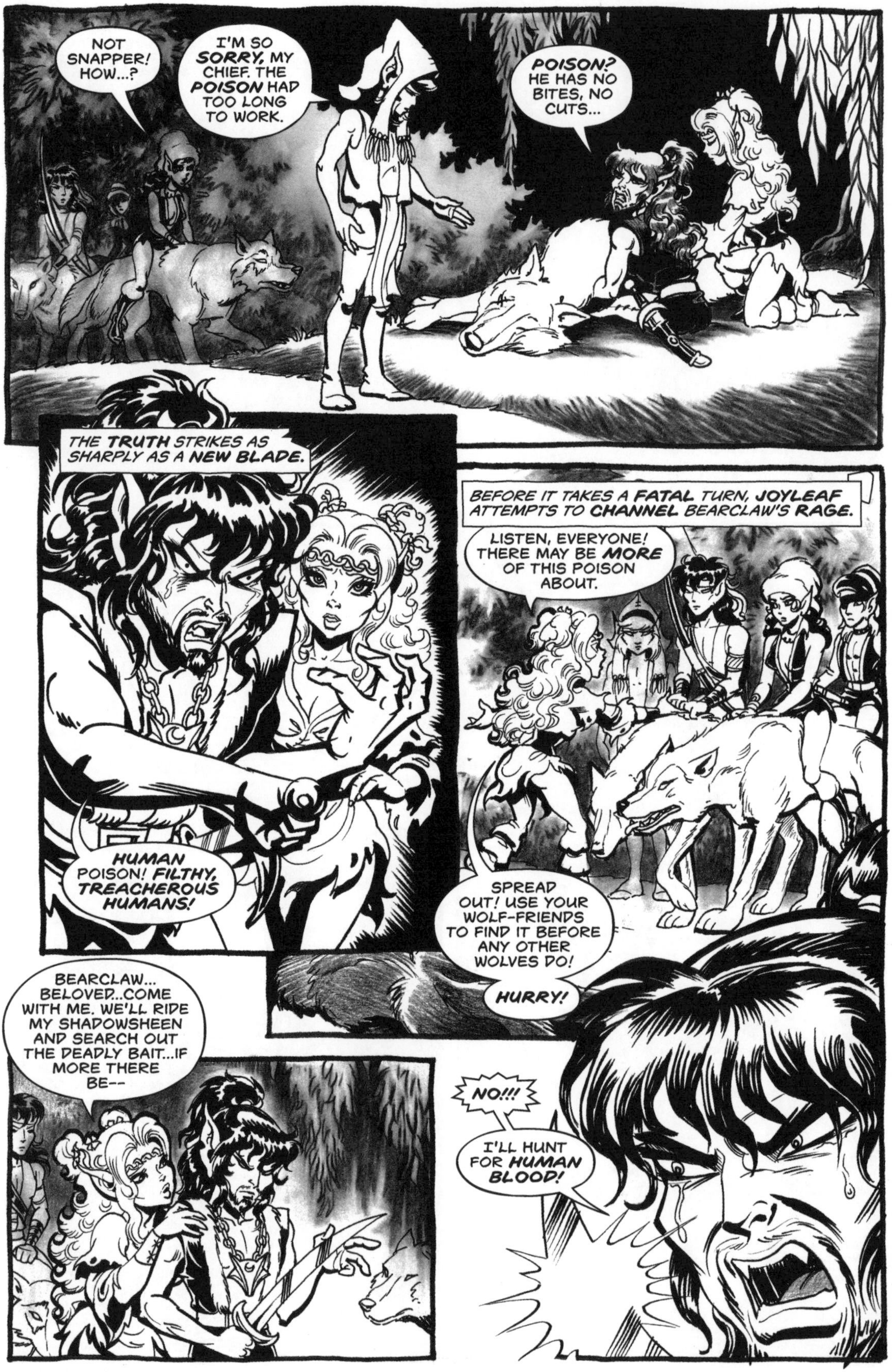

NOT SNAPPER! HOW...?
I'M SO SORRY, MY CHIEF. THE POISON HAD TOO LONG TO WORK.
POISON? HE HAS NO BITES, NO CUTS...
THE TRUTH STRIKES AS SHARPLY AS A NEW BLADE.
HUMAN POISON! FILTHY, TREACHEROUS HUMANS!
BEFORE IT TAKES A FATAL TURN, JOYLEAF ATTEMPTS TO CHANNEL BEARCLAW'S RAGE.
LISTEN, EVERYONE! THERE MAY BE MORE OF THIS POISON ABOUT.
SPREAD OUT! USE YOUR WOLF-FRIENDS TO FIND IT BEFORE ANY OTHER WOLVES DO!
HURRY!
BEARCLAW... BELOVED...COME WITH ME. WE'LL RIDE MY SHADOWSHEEN AND SEARCH OUT THE DEADLY BAIT...IF MORE THERE BE--
NO!!!
I'LL HUNT FOR HUMAN BLOOD!

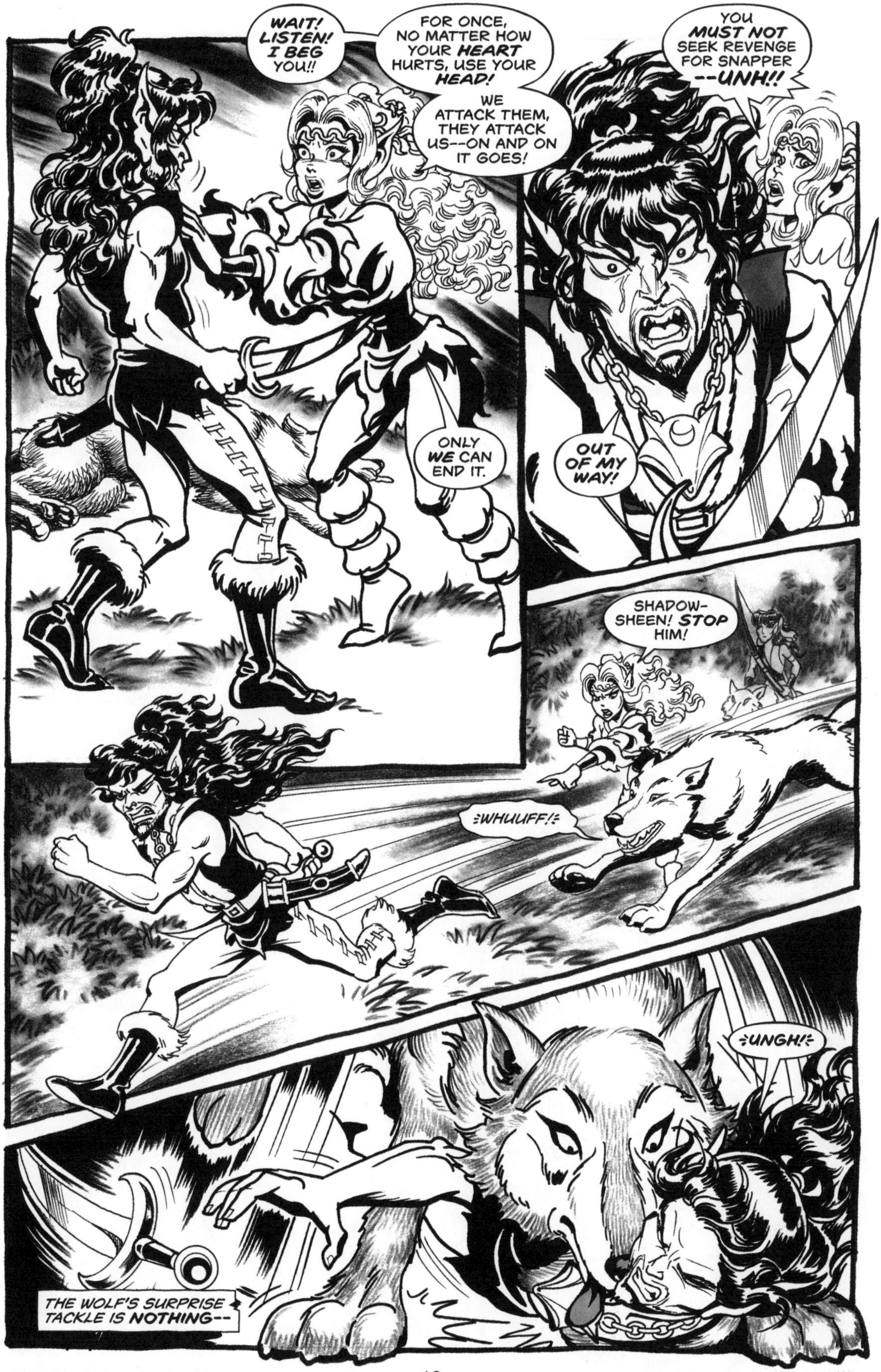
WAIT! LISTEN! I BEG YOU!!
FOR ONCE, NO MATTER HOW YOUR HEART HURTS, USE YOUR HEAD!
WE ATTACK THEM, THEY ATTACK US--ON AND ON IT GOES!
ONLY WE CAN END IT.
YOU MUST NOT SEEK REVENGE FOR SNAPPER --UNH!!
OUT OF MY WAY!
SHADOW-SHEEN! STOP HIM!
WHUUFF!
UNGH!
THE WOLF'S SURPRISE TACKLE IS NOTHING--

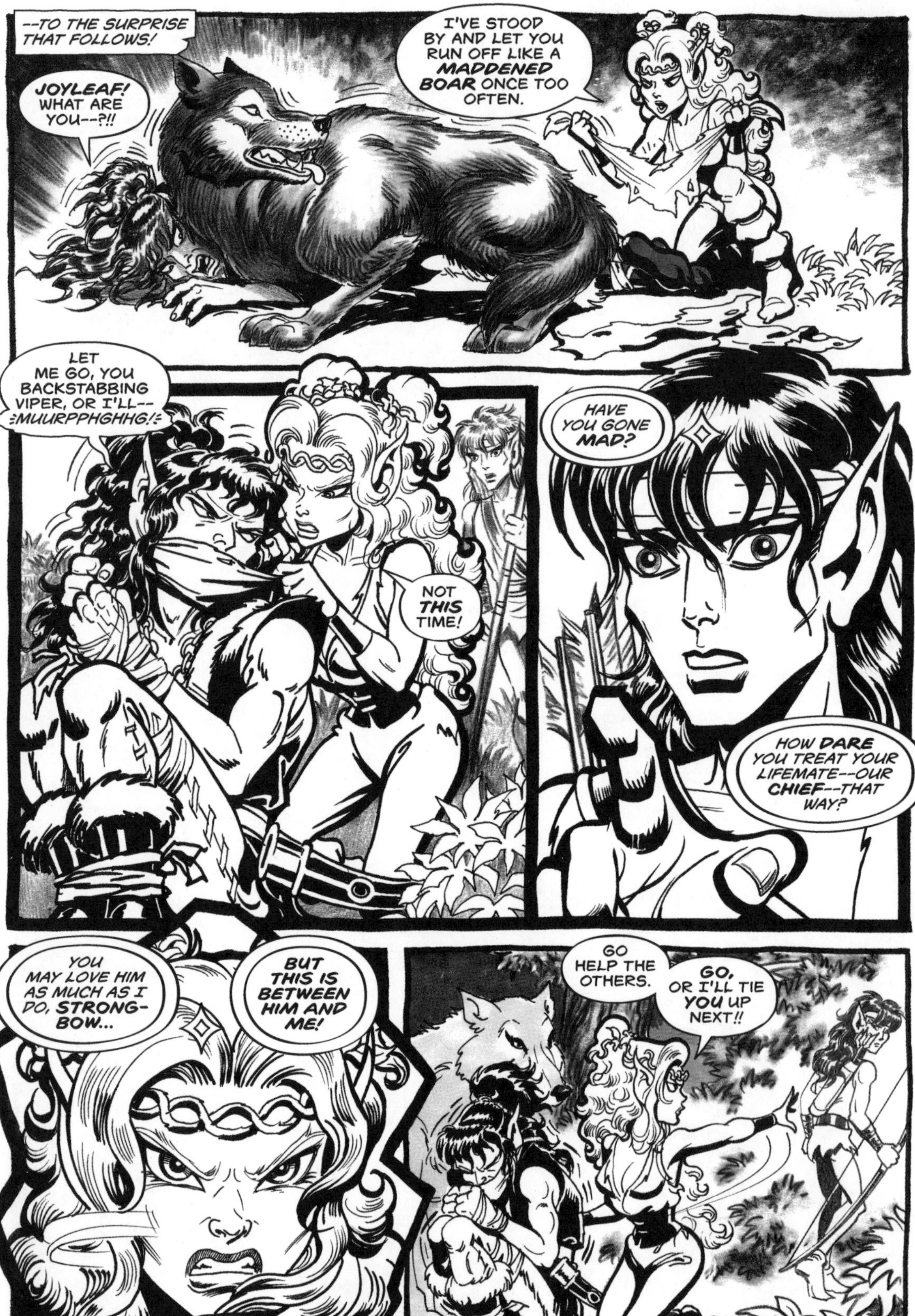
--TO THE SURPRISE THAT FOLLOWS!
JOYLEAF! WHAT ARE YOU--?!!
I'VE STOOD BY AND LET YOU RUN OFF LIKE A MADDENED BOAR ONCE TOO OFTEN.
LET ME GO, YOU BACKSTABBING VIPER, OR I'LL-- MUURPPHGHHG!
NOT THIS TIME!
HAVE YOU GONE MAD?
HOW DARE YOU TREAT YOUR LIFEMATE--OUR CHIEF--THAT WAY?
YOU MAY LOVE HIM AS MUCH AS I DO, STRONGBOW...
BUT THIS IS BETWEEN HIM AND ME!
GO HELP THE OTHERS.
GO, OR I'LL TIE YOU UP NEXT!!
WISELY, STRONGBOW CHOOSES NOT TO CONFRONT THIS SNARLING SHE-WOLF.

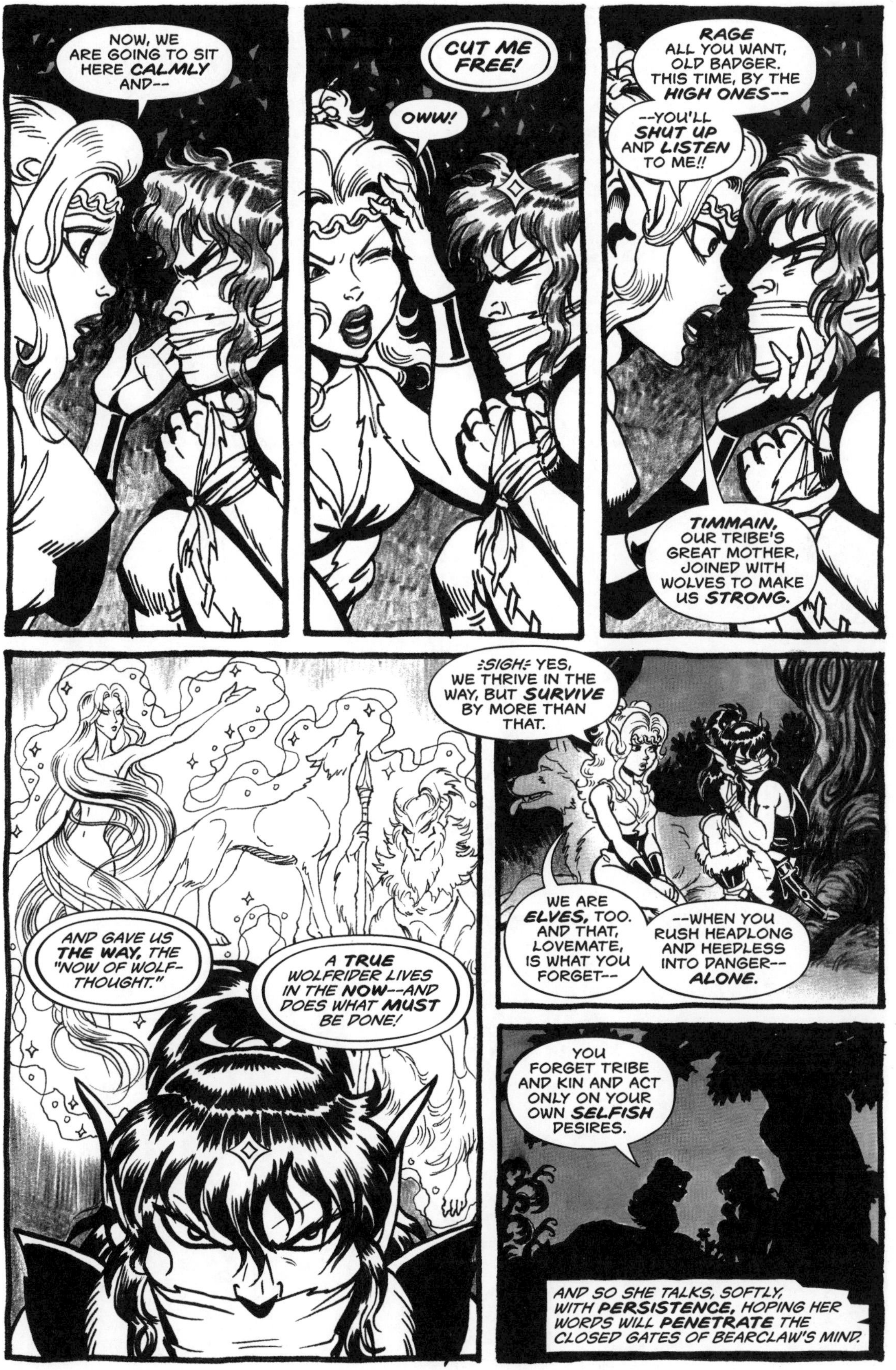
NOW, WE ARE GOING TO SIT HERE CALMLY AND--
CUT ME FREE!
OWW!
RAGE ALL YOU WANT, OLD BADGER. THIS TIME, BY THE HIGH ONES--
--YOU'LL SHUT UP AND LISTEN TO ME!!
TIMMAIN, OUR TRIBE'S GREAT MOTHER, JOINED WITH WOLVES TO MAKE US STRONG.
AND GAVE US THE WAY, THE "NOW OF WOLF-THOUGHT."
A TRUE WOLFRIDER LIVES IN THE NOW--AND DOES WHAT MUST BE DONE!
:SIGH: YES, WE THRIVE IN THE WAY, BUT SURVIVE BY MORE THAN THAT.
WE ARE ELVES, TOO. AND THAT, LOVEMATE, IS WHAT YOU FORGET--
--WHEN YOU RUSH HEADLONG AND HEEDLESS INTO DANGER--ALONE.
YOU FORGET TRIBE AND KIN AND ACT ONLY ON YOUR OWN SELFISH DESIRES.
AND SO SHE TALKS, SOFTLY, WITH PERSISTENCE, HOPING HER WORDS WILL PENETRATE THE CLOSED GATES OF BEARCLAW'S MIND.

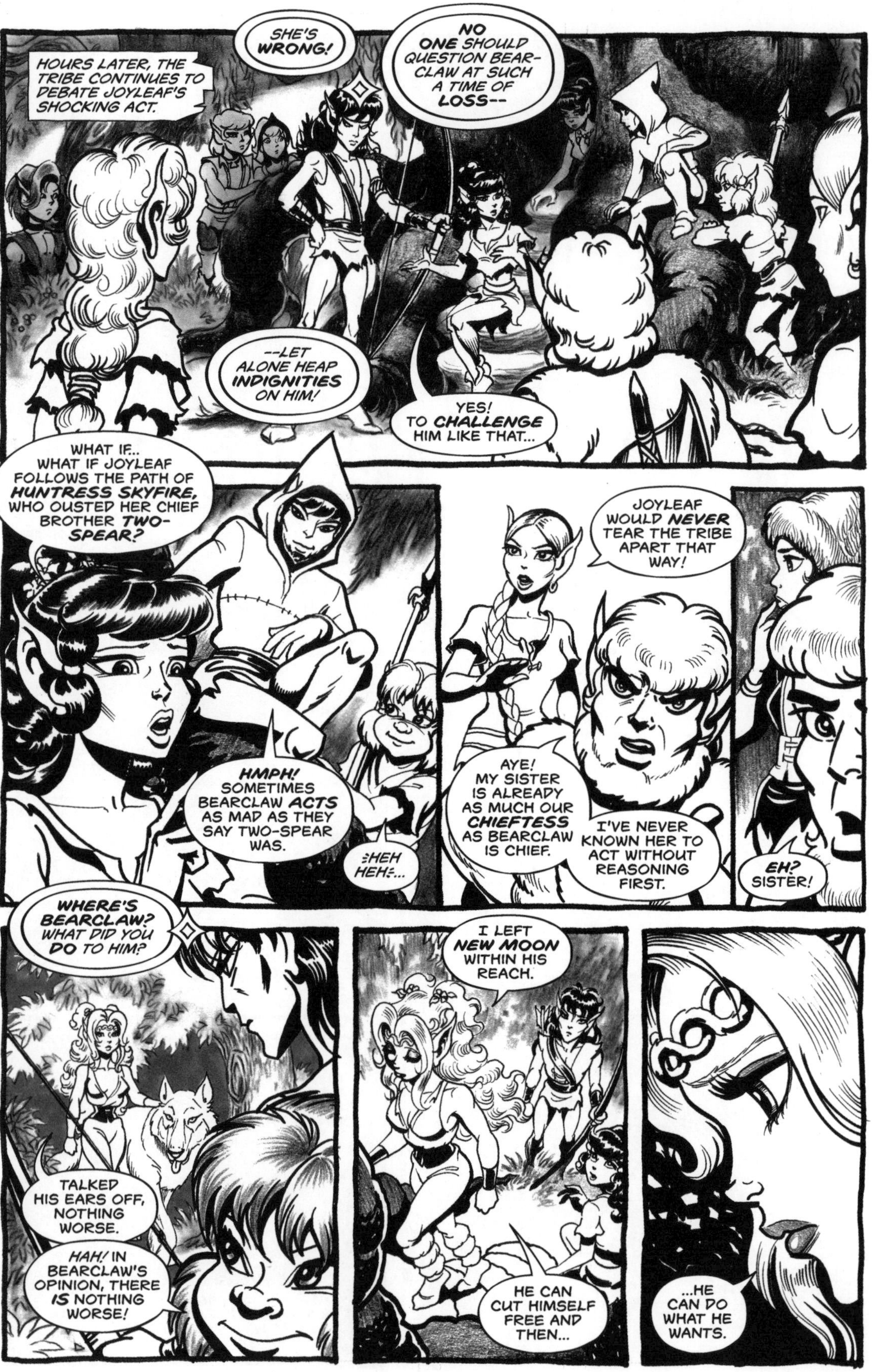
HOURS LATER, THE TRIBE CONTINUES TO DEBATE JOYLEAF'S SHOCKING ACT.
SHE'S WRONG!
NO ONE SHOULD QUESTION BEAR-CLAW AT SUCH A TIME OF LOSS--
--LET ALONE HEAP INDIGNITIES ON HIM!
YES! TO CHALLENGE HIM LIKE THAT...
WHAT IF.. WHAT IF JOYLEAF FOLLOWS THE PATH OF HUNTRESS SKYFIRE, WHO OUSTED HER CHIEF BROTHER TWO-SPEAR?
HMPH! SOMETIMES BEARCLAW ACTS AS MAD AS THEY SAY TWO-SPEAR WAS.
HEH HEH...
JOYLEAF WOULD NEVER TEAR THE TRIBE APART THAT WAY!
AYE! MY SISTER IS ALREADY AS MUCH OUR CHIEFTESS AS BEARCLAW IS CHIEF.
I'VE NEVER KNOWN HER TO ACT WITHOUT REASONING FIRST.
EH? SISTER!
WHERE'S BEARCLAW? WHAT DID YOU DO TO HIM?
TALKED HIS EARS OFF, NOTHING WORSE.
HAH! IN BEARCLAW'S OPINION, THERE IS NOTHING WORSE!
I LEFT NEW MOON WITHIN HIS REACH.
HE CAN CUT HIMSELF FREE AND THEN...
...HE CAN DO WHAT HE WANTS.

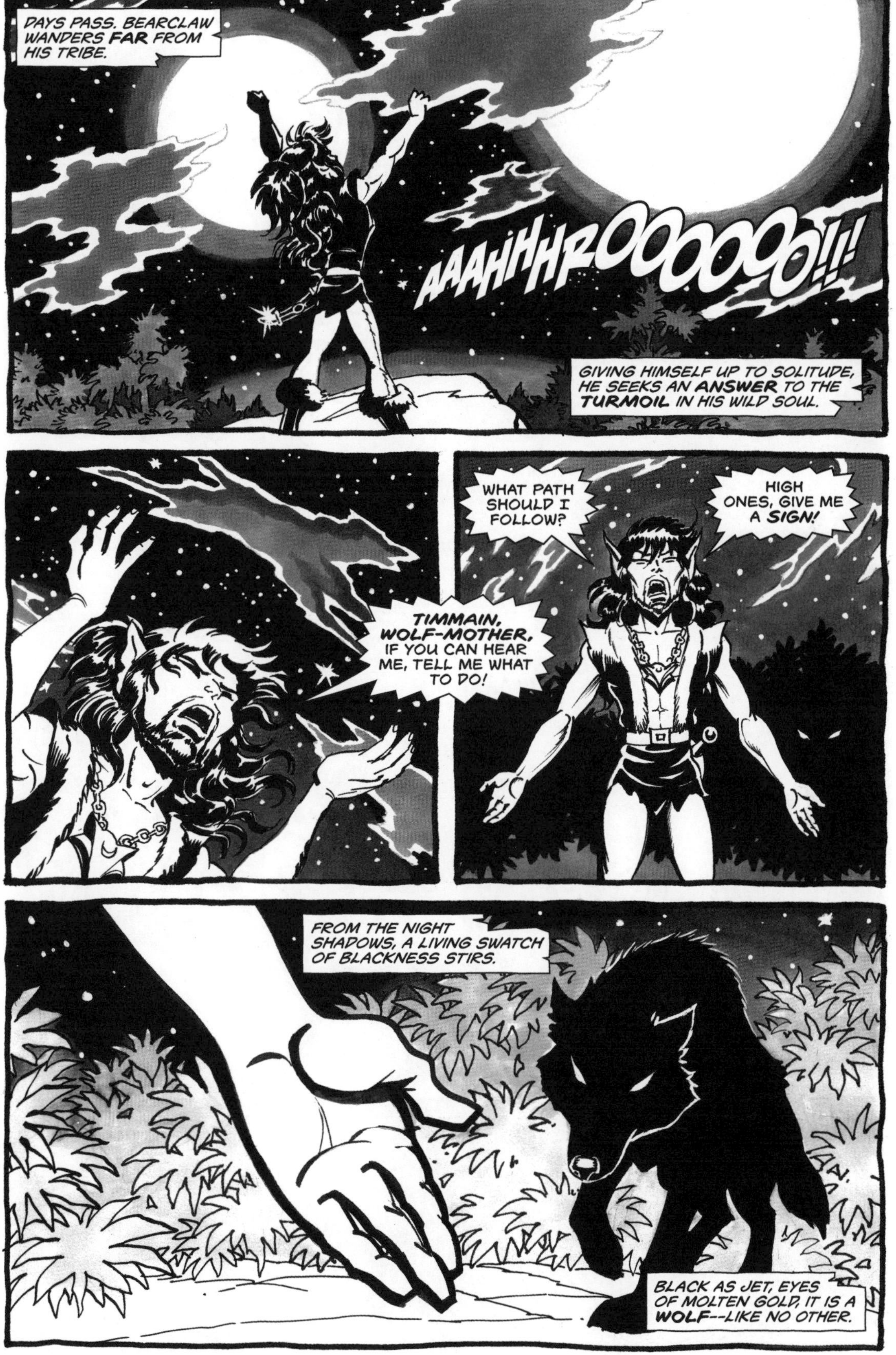
DAYS PASS. BEARCLAW WANDERS FAR FROM HIS TRIBE.
AAAHHHROOOOOOO!!!
GIVING HIMSELF UP TO SOLITUDE, HE SEEKS AN ANSWER TO THE TURMOIL IN HIS WILD SOUL.
TIMMAIN, WOLF-MOTHER, IF YOU CAN HEAR ME, TELL ME WHAT TO DO!
WHAT PATH SHOULD I FOLLOW?
HIGH ONES, GIVE ME A SIGN!
FROM THE NIGHT SHADOWS, A LIVING SWATCH OF BLACKNESS STIRS.
BLACK AS JET, EYES OF MOLTEN GOLD, IT IS A WOLF--LIKE NO OTHER.

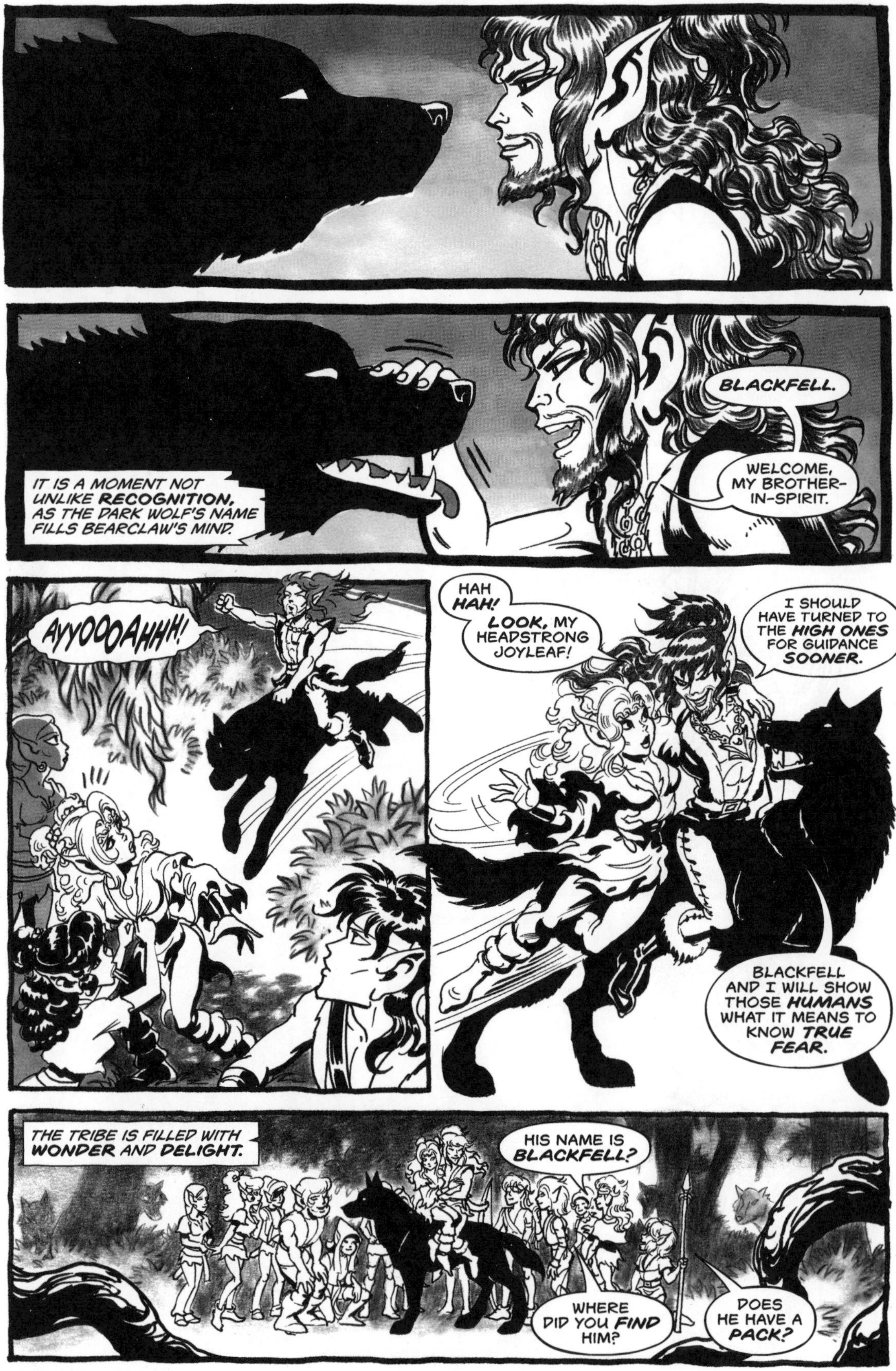
BLACKFELL.
WELCOME, MY BROTHER-IN-SPIRIT.
IT IS A MOMENT NOT UNLIKE RECOGNITION, AS THE DARK WOLF'S NAME FILLS BEARCLAW'S MIND.
AYYOOOAHHH!
HAH HAH! LOOK, MY HEADSTRONG JOYLEAF!
I SHOULD HAVE TURNED TO THE HIGH ONES FOR GUIDANCE SOONER.
BLACKFELL AND I WILL SHOW THOSE HUMANS WHAT IT MEANS TO KNOW TRUE FEAR.
THE TRIBE IS FILLED WITH WONDER AND DELIGHT.
HIS NAME IS BLACKFELL?
WHERE DID YOU FIND HIM?
DOES HE HAVE A PACK?

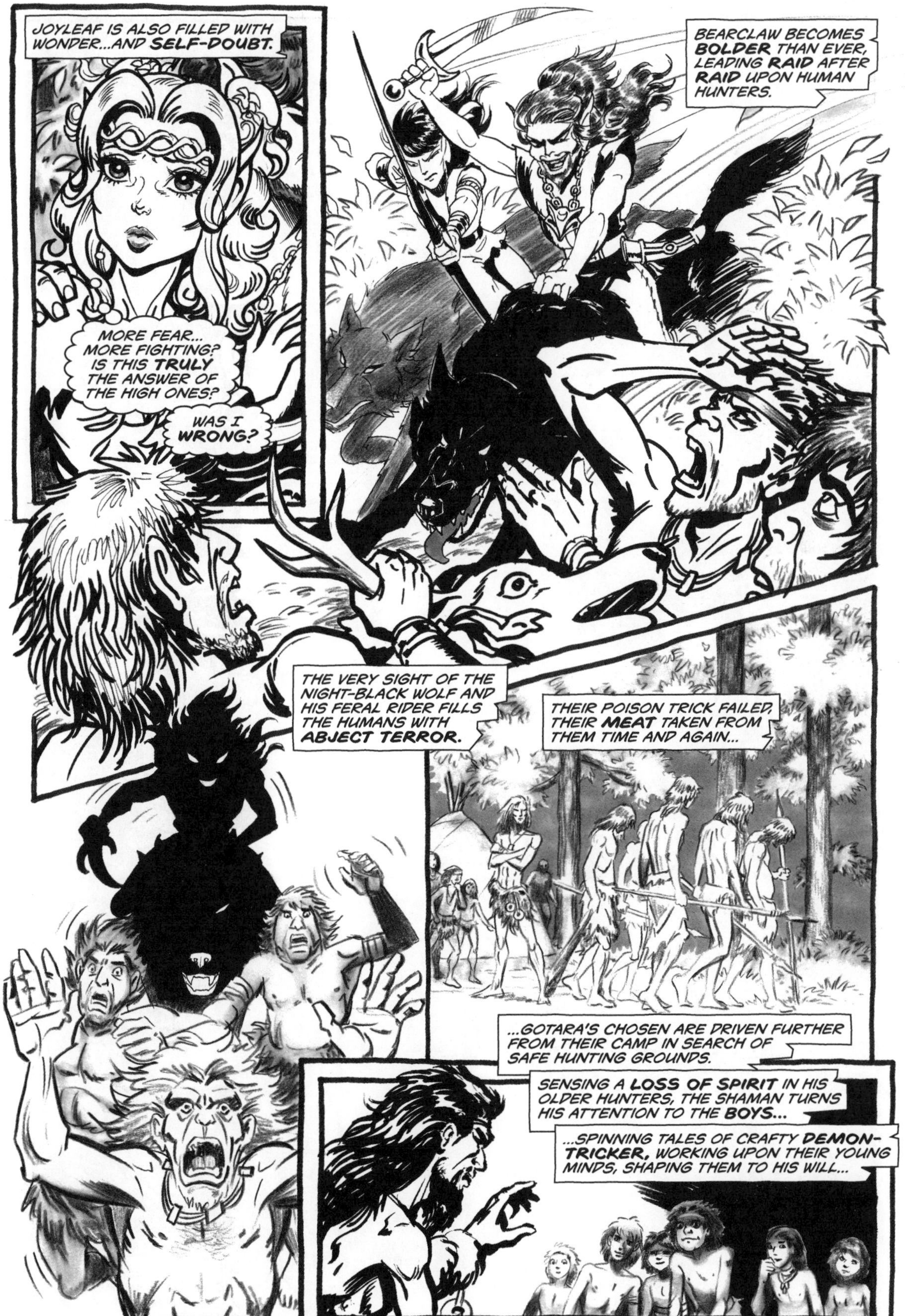

JOYLEAF IS ALSO FILLED WITH WONDER...AND SELF-DOUBT.
MORE FEAR... MORE FIGHTING? IS THIS TRULY THE ANSWER OF THE HIGH ONES?
WAS I WRONG?
BEARCLAW BECOMES BOLDER THAN EVER, LEADING RAID AFTER RAID UPON HUMAN HUNTERS.
THE VERY SIGHT OF THE NIGHT-BLACK WOLF AND HIS FERAL RIDER FILLS THE HUMANS WITH ABJECT TERROR.
THEIR POISON TRICK FAILED, THEIR MEAT TAKEN FROM THEM TIME AND AGAIN...
...GOTARA'S CHOSEN ARE DRIVEN FURTHER FROM THEIR CAMP IN SEARCH OF SAFE HUNTING GROUNDS.
SENSING A LOSS OF SPIRIT IN HIS OLDER HUNTERS, THE SHAMAN TURNS HIS ATTENTION TO THE BOYS...
...SPINNING TALES OF CRAFTY DEMON-TRICKER, WORKING UPON THEIR YOUNG MINDS, SHAPING THEM TO HIS WILL...

...WITH **TRAGIC** RESULTS FOR THE ELVES. **SHALE** AND **EYES-HIGH**...

...**SLAIN** BY TWO LADS TRYING TO EMULATE THEIR RENOWNED ANCESTOR, **DEMON-TRICKER.**

THIS IS **MY** FAULT! I CAN NO LONGER LET THE OTHERS LIVE **FREE.**

FROM NOW ON, **NO ONE** GOES FROM THE HOLT ALONE...

...**NO ONE!**

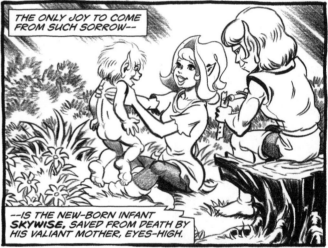

THE ONLY JOY TO COME FROM SUCH SORROW--

--IS THE NEW-BORN INFANT **SKYWISE,** SAVED FROM DEATH BY HIS VALIANT MOTHER, **EYES-HIGH.**

THE TRIBE BECOMES MOTHER AND FATHER TO HIM.

RAISED BY ALL, HE LEARNS WELL TO **LOATHE** AND **FEAR** THE HUMANS WHO **SLAUGHTERED** HIS PARENTS.

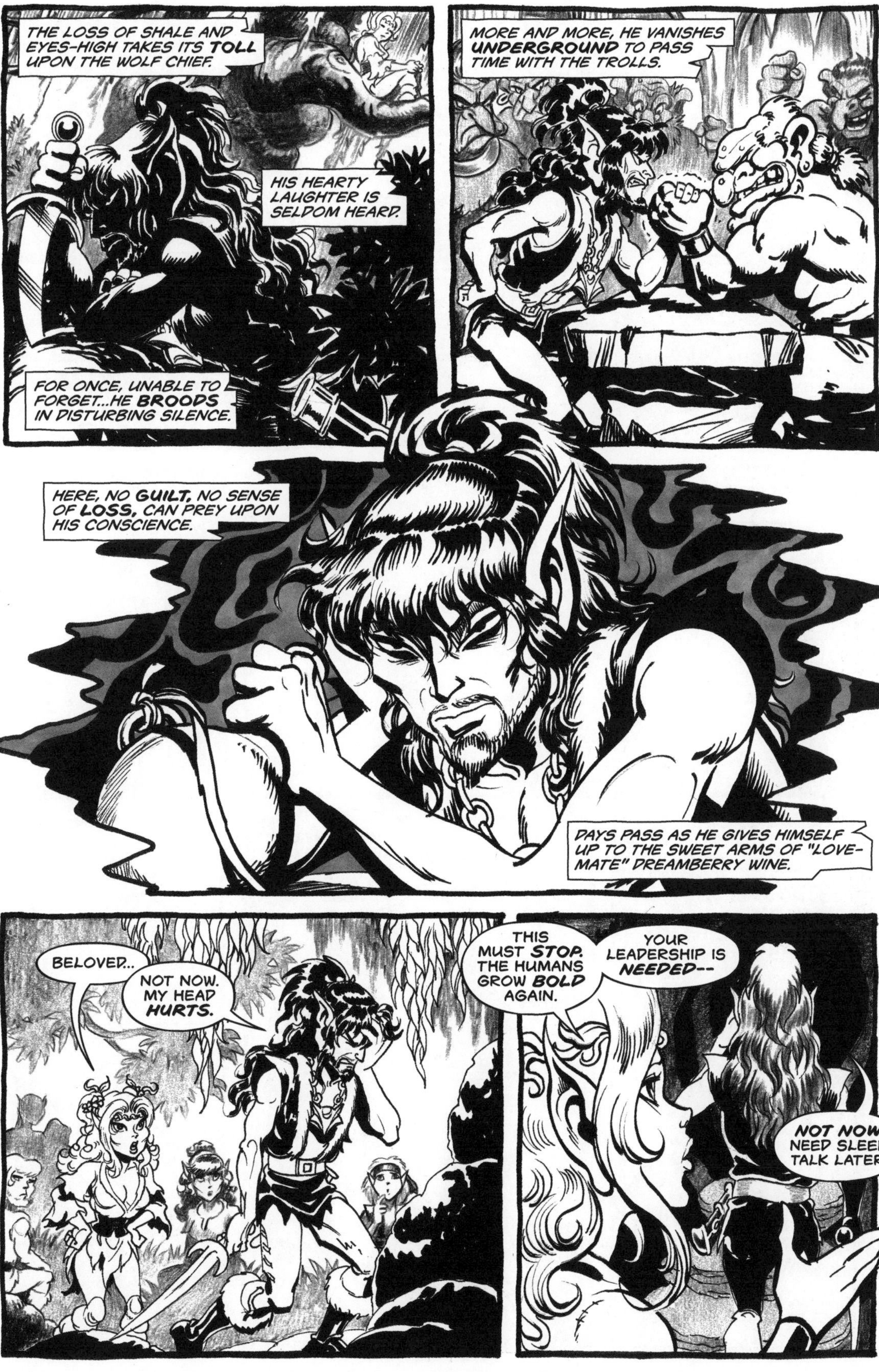
THE LOSS OF SHALE AND EYES-HIGH TAKES ITS TOLL UPON THE WOLF CHIEF.
HIS HEARTY LAUGHTER IS SELDOM HEARD.
FOR ONCE, UNABLE TO FORGET...HE BROODS IN DISTURBING SILENCE.
MORE AND MORE, HE VANISHES UNDERGROUND TO PASS TIME WITH THE TROLLS.
HERE, NO GUILT, NO SENSE OF LOSS, CAN PREY UPON HIS CONSCIENCE.
DAYS PASS AS HE GIVES HIMSELF UP TO THE SWEET ARMS OF "LOVE-MATE" DREAMBERRY WINE.
BELOVED...
NOT NOW. MY HEAD HURTS.
THIS MUST STOP. THE HUMANS GROW BOLD AGAIN.
YOUR LEADERSHIP IS NEEDED--
NOT NOW. NEED SLEEP. TALK LATER.

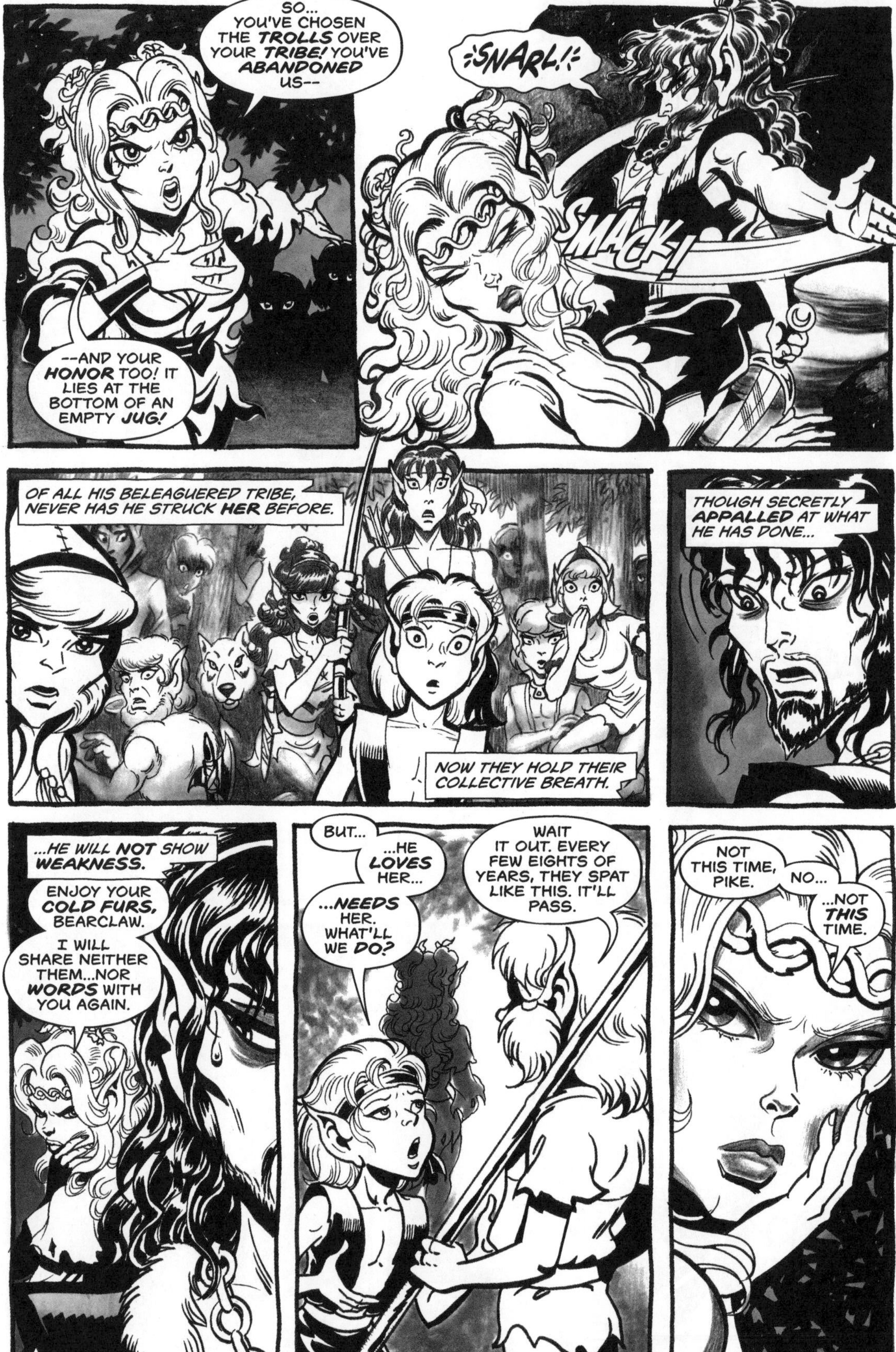
SO... YOU'VE CHOSEN THE TROLLS OVER YOUR TRIBE! YOU'VE ABANDONED US--
--AND YOUR HONOR TOO! IT LIES AT THE BOTTOM OF AN EMPTY JUG!
SNARL!
SMACK!
OF ALL HIS BELEAGUERED TRIBE, NEVER HAS HE STRUCK HER BEFORE.
NOW THEY HOLD THEIR COLLECTIVE BREATH.
THOUGH SECRETLY APPALLED AT WHAT HE HAS DONE...
...HE WILL NOT SHOW WEAKNESS.
ENJOY YOUR COLD FURS, BEARCLAW.
I WILL SHARE NEITHER THEM...NOR WORDS WITH YOU AGAIN.
BUT...
...HE LOVES HER...
...NEEDS HER. WHAT'LL WE DO?
WAIT IT OUT. EVERY FEW EIGHTS OF YEARS, THEY SPAT LIKE THIS. IT'LL PASS.
NOT THIS TIME, PIKE.
NO...
...NOT THIS TIME.

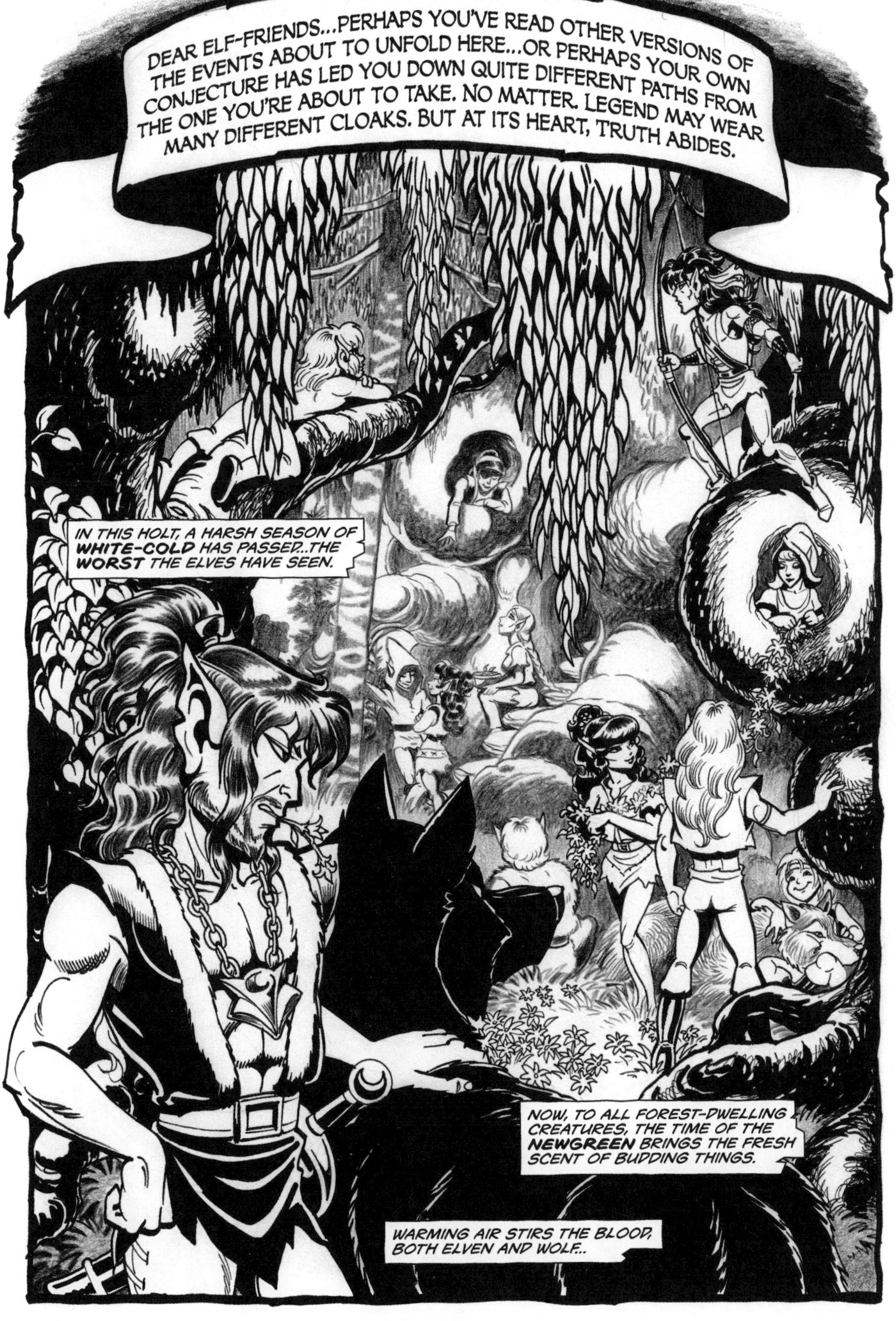
DEAR ELF-FRIENDS...PERHAPS YOU'VE READ OTHER VERSIONS OF THE EVENTS ABOUT TO UNFOLD HERE...OR PERHAPS YOUR OWN CONJECTURE HAS LED YOU DOWN QUITE DIFFERENT PATHS FROM THE ONE YOU'RE ABOUT TO TAKE. NO MATTER. LEGEND MAY WEAR MANY DIFFERENT CLOAKS. BUT AT ITS HEART, TRUTH ABIDES.
IN THIS HOLT, A HARSH SEASON OF WHITE-COLD HAS PASSED...THE WORST THE ELVES HAVE SEEN.
NOW, TO ALL FOREST-DWELLING CREATURES, THE TIME OF THE NEWGREEN BRINGS THE FRESH SCENT OF BUDDING THINGS.
WARMING AIR STIRS THE BLOOD, BOTH ELVEN AND WOLF...

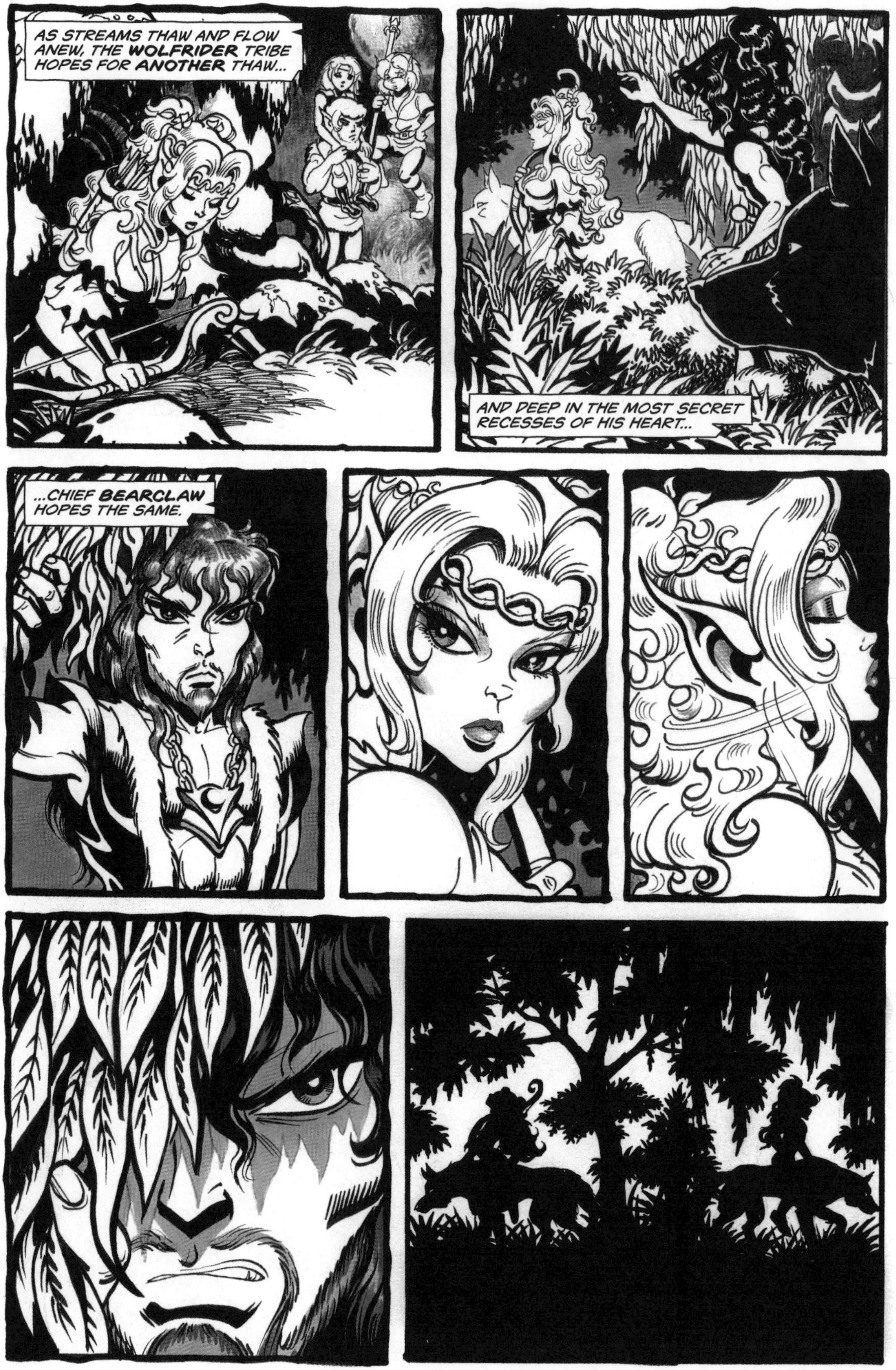
AS STREAMS THAW AND FLOW ANEW, THE WOLFRIDER TRIBE HOPES FOR ANOTHER THAW...
AND DEEP IN THE MOST SECRET RECESSES OF HIS HEART...
...CHIEF BEARCLAW HOPES THE SAME.

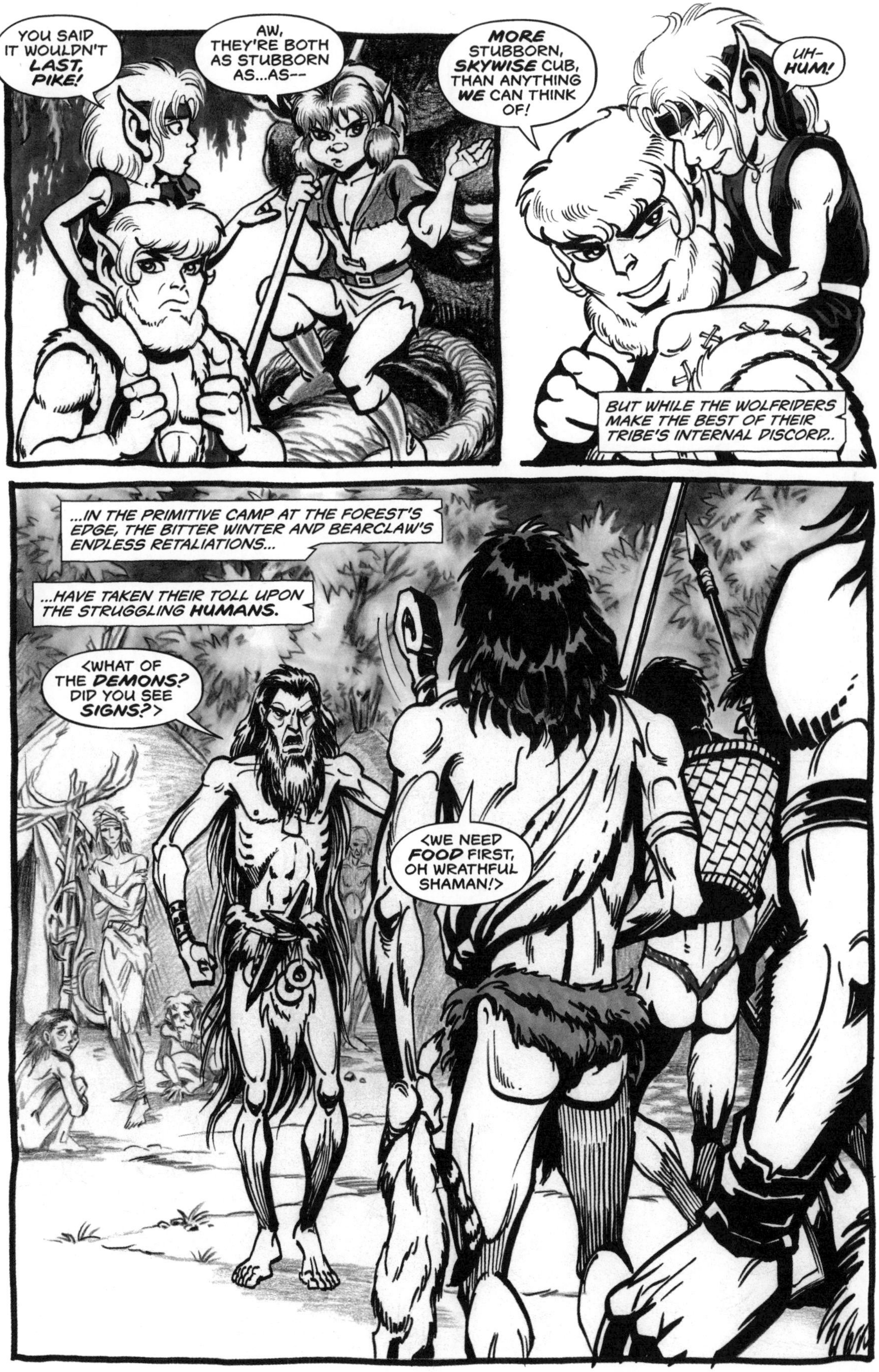
YOU SAID IT WOULDN'T LAST, PIKE!
AW, THEY'RE BOTH AS STUBBORN AS...AS--
MORE STUBBORN, SKYWISE CUB, THAN ANYTHING WE CAN THINK OF!
UH-HUM!
BUT WHILE THE WOLFRIDERS MAKE THE BEST OF THEIR TRIBE'S INTERNAL DISCORD...
...IN THE PRIMITIVE CAMP AT THE FOREST'S EDGE, THE BITTER WINTER AND BEARCLAW'S ENDLESS RETALIATIONS...
...HAVE TAKEN THEIR TOLL UPON THE STRUGGLING HUMANS.
<WHAT OF THE DEMONS? DID YOU SEE SIGNS?>
<WE NEED FOOD FIRST, OH WRATHFUL SHAMAN!>

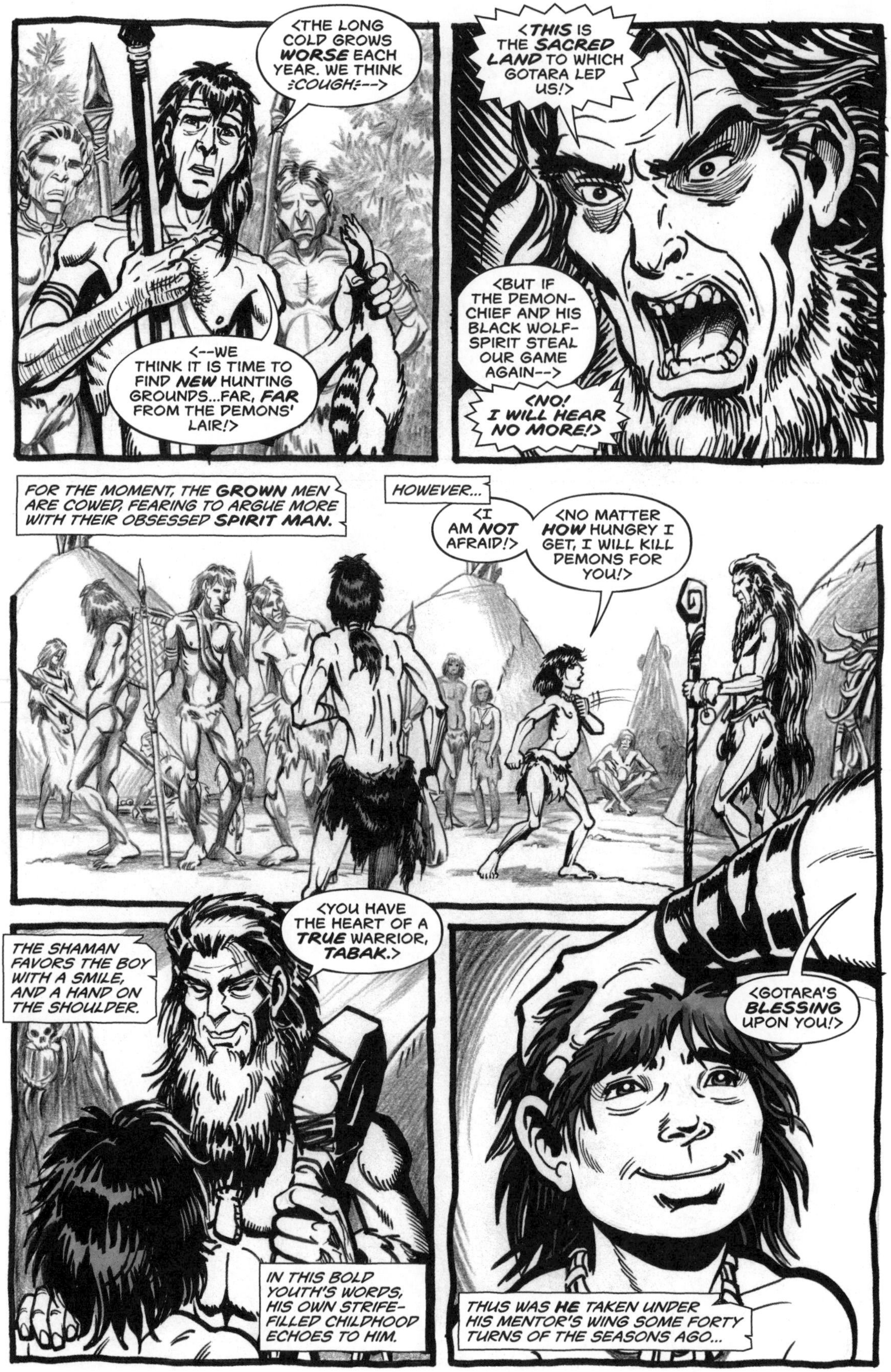
<THE LONG COLD GROWS WORSE EACH YEAR. WE THINK :COUGH:-->
<--WE THINK IT IS TIME TO FIND NEW HUNTING GROUNDS...FAR, FAR FROM THE DEMONS' LAIR!>
<THIS IS THE SACRED LAND TO WHICH GOTARA LED US!>
<BUT IF THE DEMON-CHIEF AND HIS BLACK WOLF-SPIRIT STEAL OUR GAME AGAIN-->
<NO! I WILL HEAR NO MORE!>
FOR THE MOMENT, THE GROWN MEN ARE COWED, FEARING TO ARGUE MORE WITH THEIR OBSESSED SPIRIT MAN.
HOWEVER...
<I AM NOT AFRAID!>
<NO MATTER HOW HUNGRY I GET, I WILL KILL DEMONS FOR YOU!>
THE SHAMAN FAVORS THE BOY WITH A SMILE, AND A HAND ON THE SHOULDER.
<YOU HAVE THE HEART OF A TRUE WARRIOR, TABAK.>
IN THIS BOLD YOUTH'S WORDS, HIS OWN STRIFE-FILLED CHILDHOOD ECHOES TO HIM.
<GOTARA'S BLESSING UPON YOU!>
THUS WAS HE TAKEN UNDER HIS MENTOR'S WING SOME FORTY TURNS OF THE SEASONS AGO...

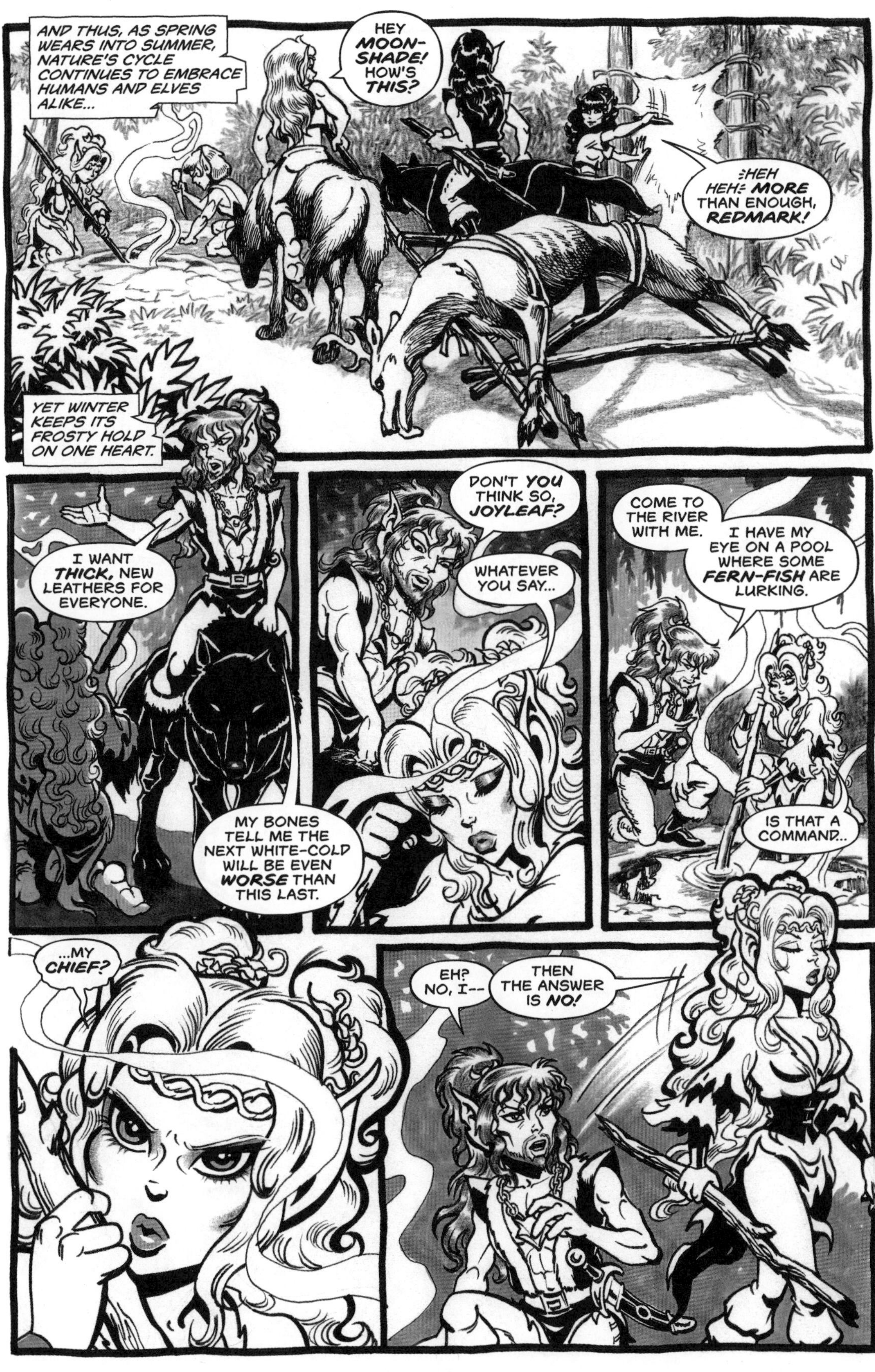
AND THUS, AS SPRING WEARS INTO SUMMER, NATURE'S CYCLE CONTINUES TO EMBRACE HUMANS AND ELVES ALIKE...
HEY MOON-SHADE! HOW'S THIS?
HEH HEH! MORE THAN ENOUGH, REDMARK!
YET WINTER KEEPS ITS FROSTY HOLD ON ONE HEART.
I WANT THICK, NEW LEATHERS FOR EVERYONE.
MY BONES TELL ME THE NEXT WHITE-COLD WILL BE EVEN WORSE THAN THIS LAST.
DON'T YOU THINK SO, JOYLEAF?
WHATEVER YOU SAY...
COME TO THE RIVER WITH ME.
I HAVE MY EYE ON A POOL WHERE SOME FERN-FISH ARE LURKING.
IS THAT A COMMAND...
...MY CHIEF?
EH? NO, I--
THEN THE ANSWER IS NO!

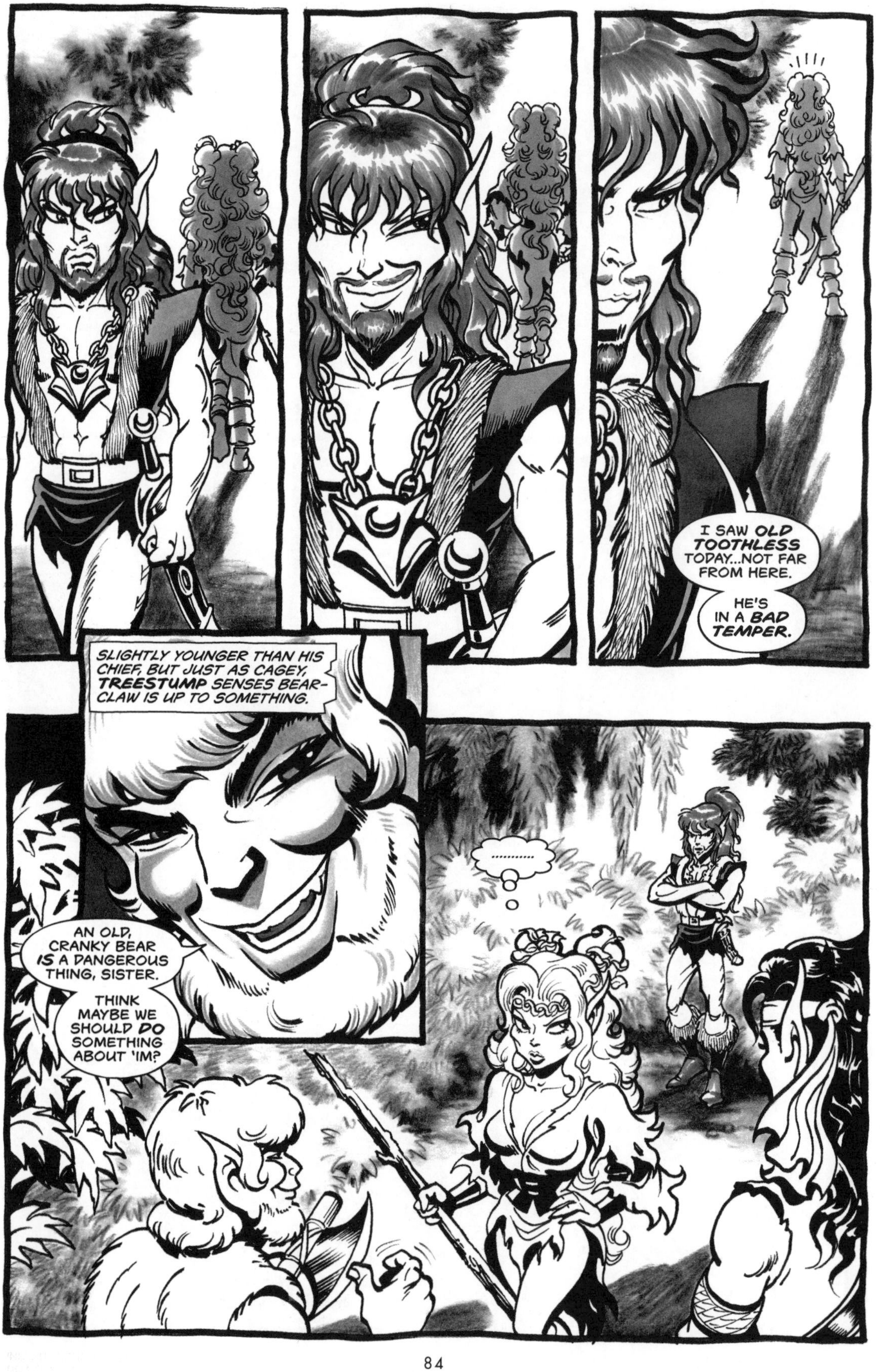
I SAW OLD TOOTHLESS TODAY...NOT FAR FROM HERE.
HE'S IN A BAD TEMPER.
SLIGHTLY YOUNGER THAN HIS CHIEF, BUT JUST AS CAGEY, TREESTUMP SENSES BEARCLAW IS UP TO SOMETHING.
....
AN OLD, CRANKY BEAR IS A DANGEROUS THING, SISTER.
THINK MAYBE WE SHOULD DO SOMETHING ABOUT 'IM?

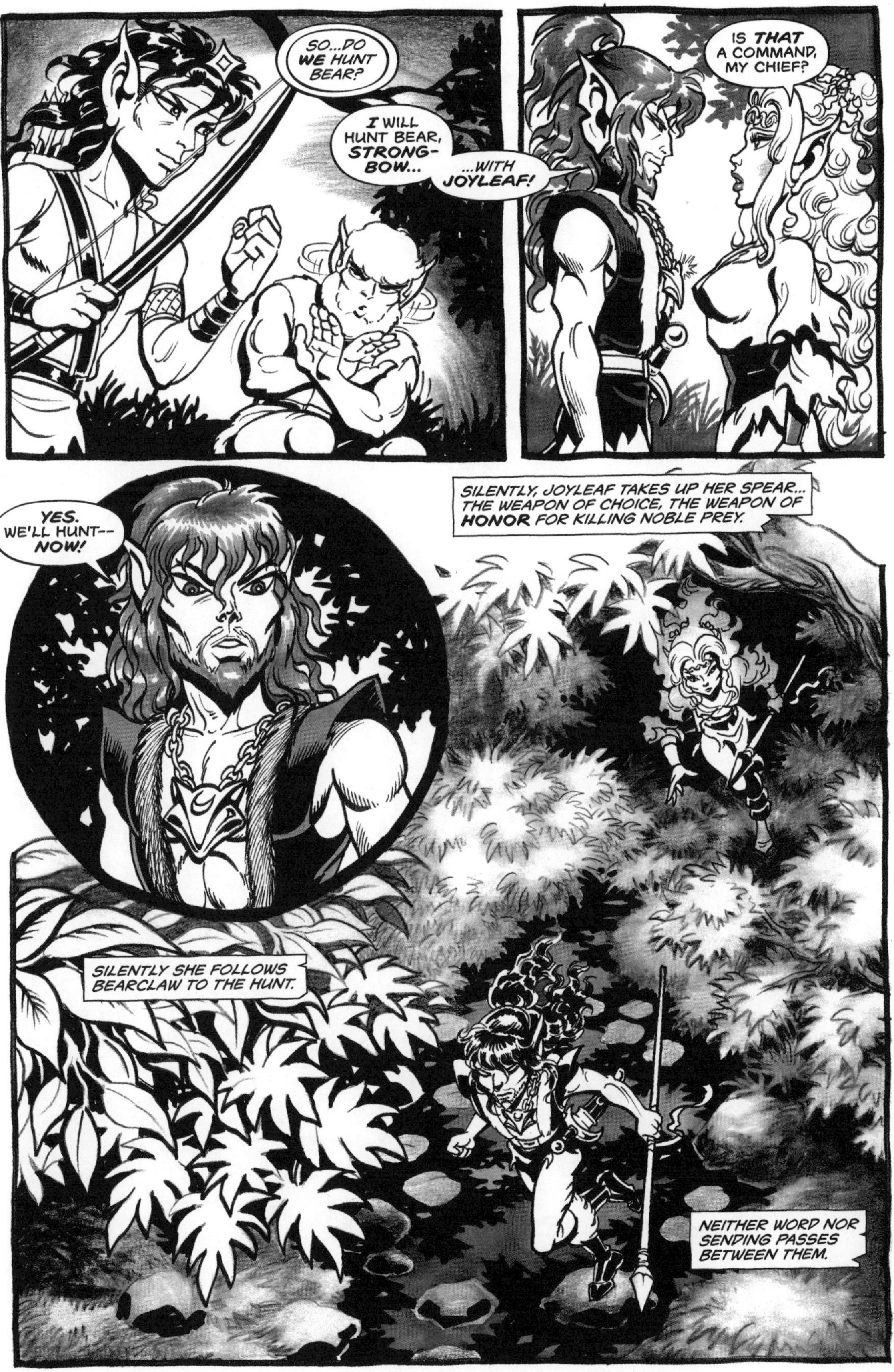

SO...DO WE HUNT BEAR?
I WILL HUNT BEAR, STRONGBOW...
...WITH JOYLEAF!
IS THAT A COMMAND, MY CHIEF?
YES. WE'LL HUNT-- NOW!
SILENTLY, JOYLEAF TAKES UP HER SPEAR... THE WEAPON OF CHOICE, THE WEAPON OF HONOR FOR KILLING NOBLE PREY.
SILENTLY SHE FOLLOWS BEARCLAW TO THE HUNT.
NEITHER WORD NOR SENDING PASSES BETWEEN THEM.

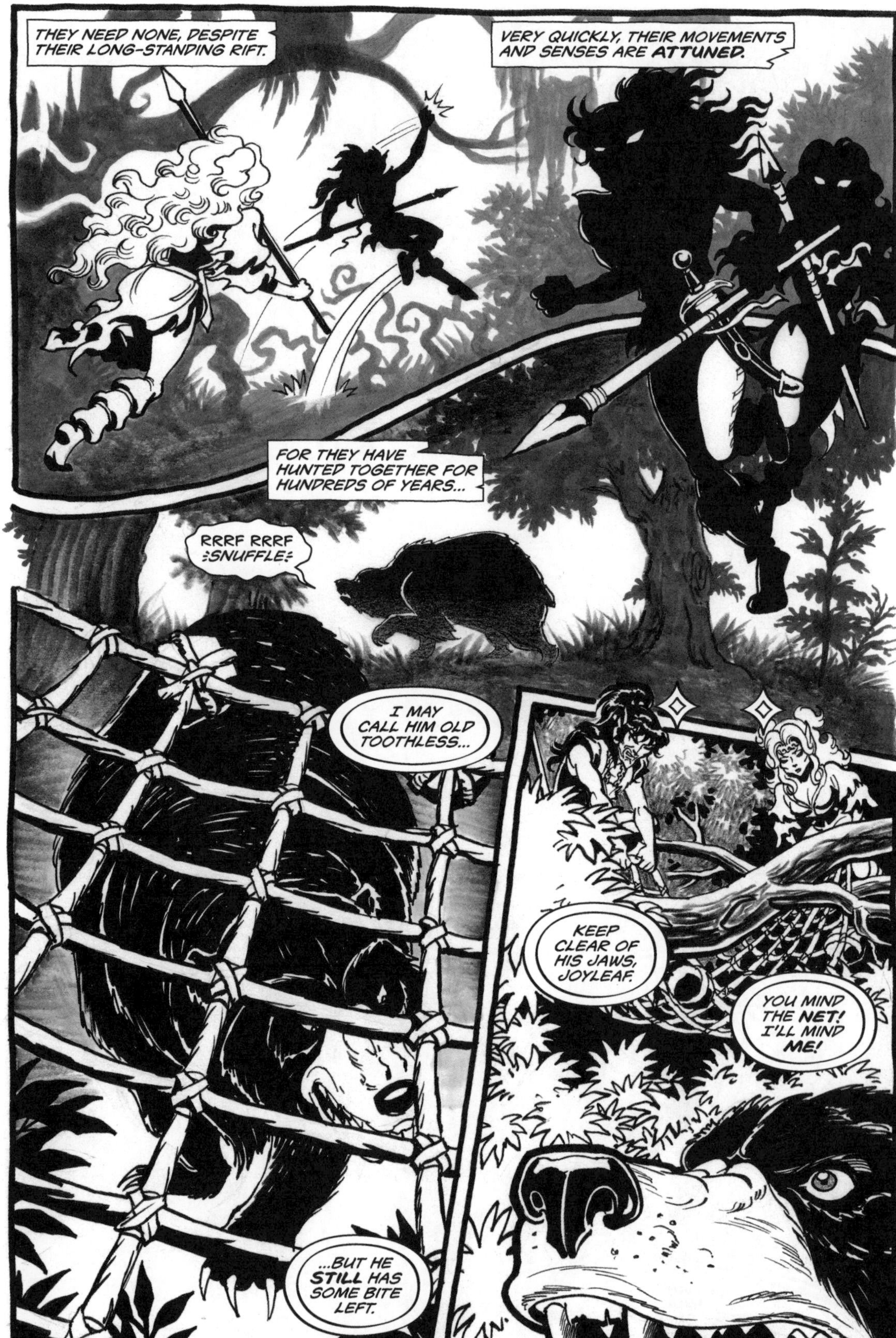
THEY NEED NONE, DESPITE THEIR LONG-STANDING RIFT.
VERY QUICKLY, THEIR MOVEMENTS AND SENSES ARE ATTUNED.
FOR THEY HAVE HUNTED TOGETHER FOR HUNDREDS OF YEARS...
RRRF RRRF :SNUFFLE:
I MAY CALL HIM OLD TOOTHLESS...
...BUT HE STILL HAS SOME BITE LEFT.
KEEP CLEAR OF HIS JAWS, JOYLEAF.
YOU MIND THE NET! I'LL MIND ME!

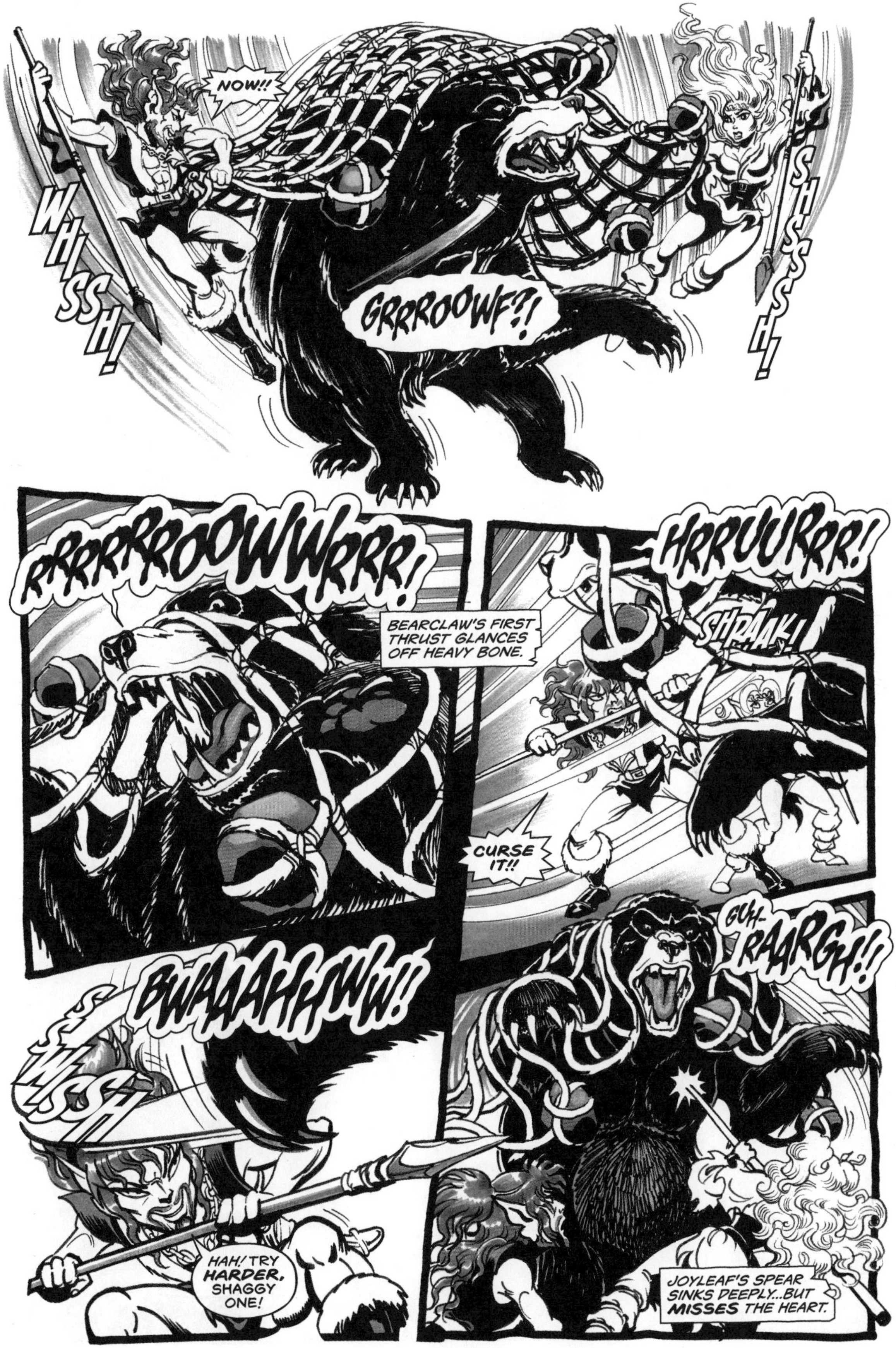
NOW!!
WHISSH!
SHSSSSH!
GRRROOWF?!
RRRRRROOWWRRR!
BEARCLAW'S FIRST THRUST GLANCES OFF HEAVY BONE.
HRRUURRR!
SHRAAK!
CURSE IT!!
BWAAAHHWW!
SWISH
HAH! TRY HARDER, SHAGGY ONE!
GUH-RAARGH!!
JOYLEAF'S SPEAR SINKS DEEPLY...BUT MISSES THE HEART.

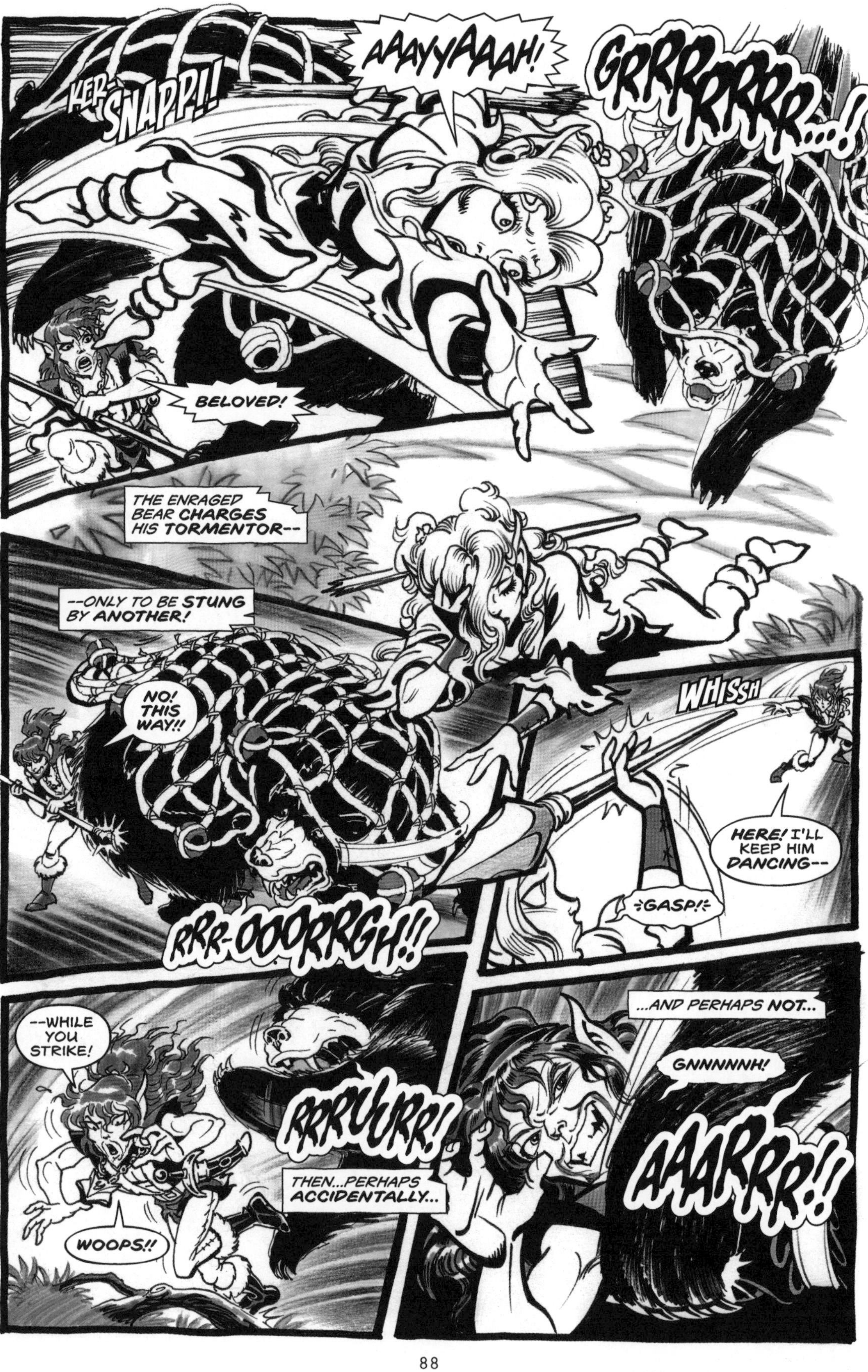
KER-SNAPP!!
AAAYYAAAH!
GRRRRRRR...!
BELOVED!
THE ENRAGED BEAR CHARGES HIS TORMENTOR--
--ONLY TO BE STUNG BY ANOTHER!
NO! THIS WAY!!
WHISSH
HERE! I'LL KEEP HIM DANCING--
GASP!
RRR-OOORRGH!!
--WHILE YOU STRIKE!
RRRUURR!
WOOPS!!
THEN...PERHAPS ACCIDENTALLY...
...AND PERHAPS NOT...
GNNNNNH!
AAARRR!!

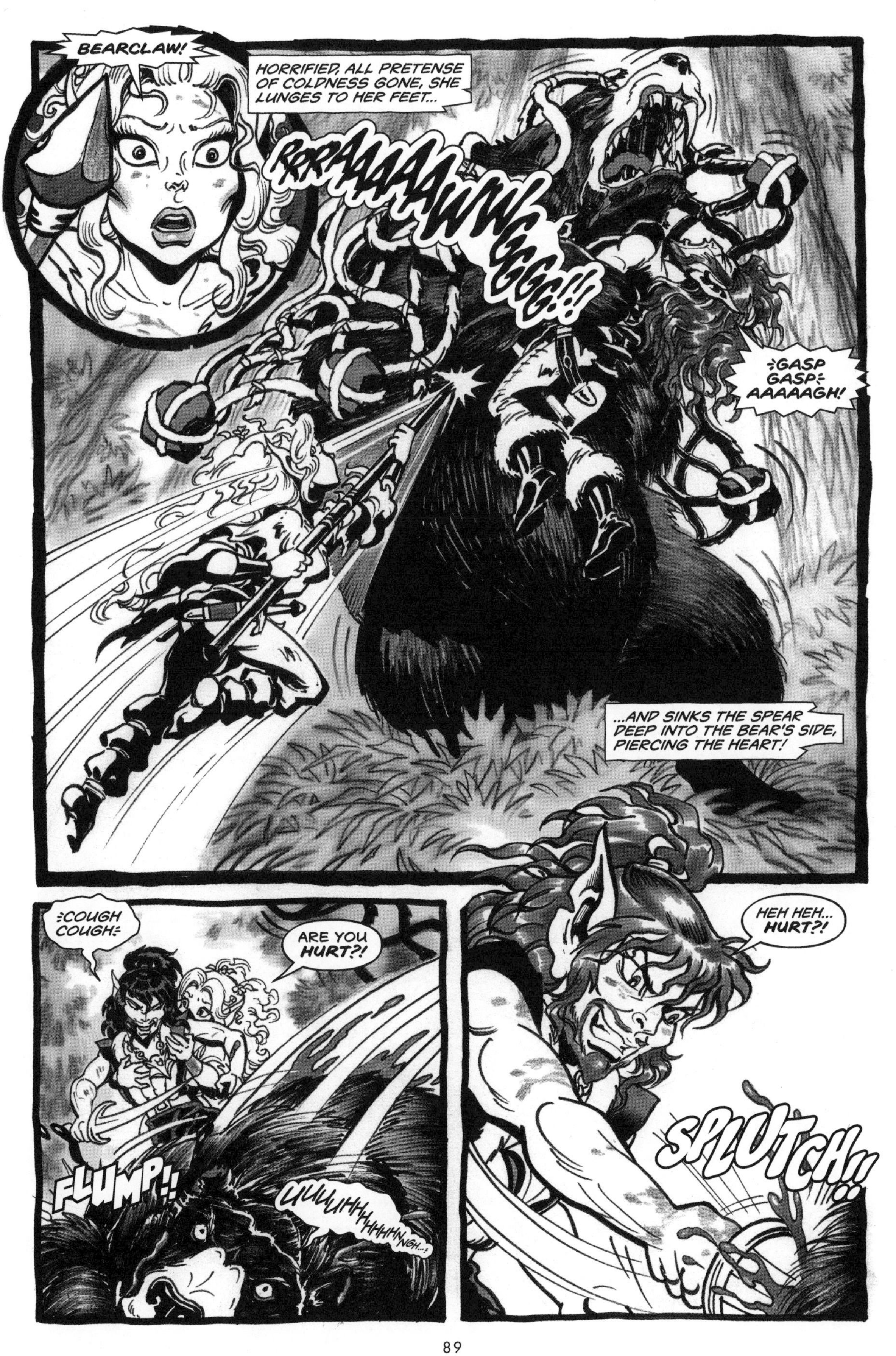
BEARCLAW!
HORRIFIED, ALL PRETENSE OF COLDNESS GONE, SHE LUNGES TO HER FEET...
RRRAAAAAAWWGGG!!
GASP GASP AAAAAGH!
...AND SINKS THE SPEAR DEEP INTO THE BEAR'S SIDE, PIERCING THE HEART!
COUGH COUGH
ARE YOU HURT?!
FLUMP!!
UUUUHHHHHHHNGH...
HEH HEH... HURT?!
SPLUTCH!!

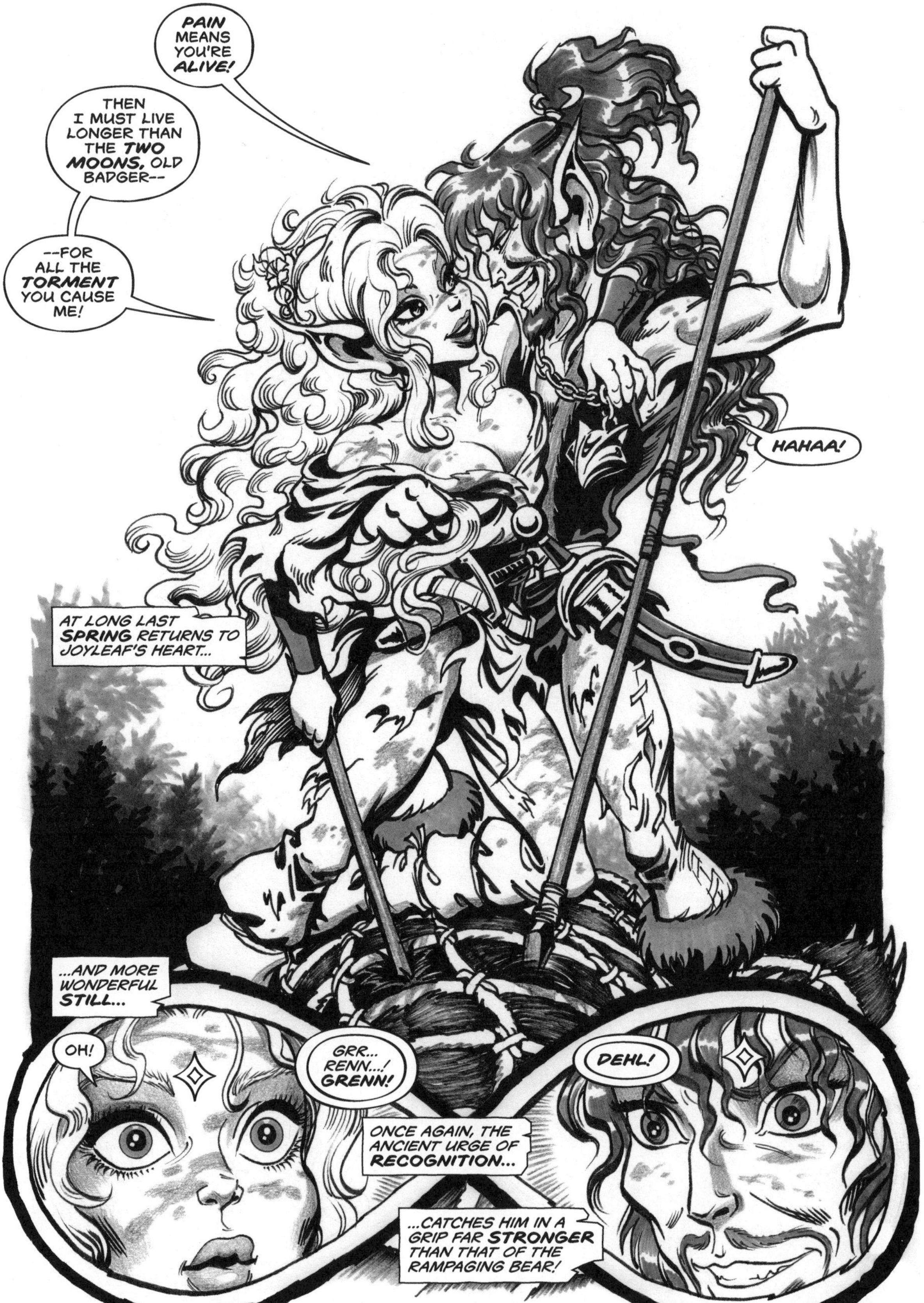
PAIN MEANS YOU'RE ALIVE!
THEN I MUST LIVE LONGER THAN THE TWO MOONS, OLD BADGER--
--FOR ALL THE TORMENT YOU CAUSE ME!
HAHAA!
AT LONG LAST SPRING RETURNS TO JOYLEAF'S HEART...
...AND MORE WONDERFUL STILL...
OH!
GRR... RENN...! GRENN!
DEHL!
ONCE AGAIN, THE ANCIENT URGE OF RECOGNITION...
...CATCHES HIM IN A GRIP FAR STRONGER THAN THAT OF THE RAMPAGING BEAR!

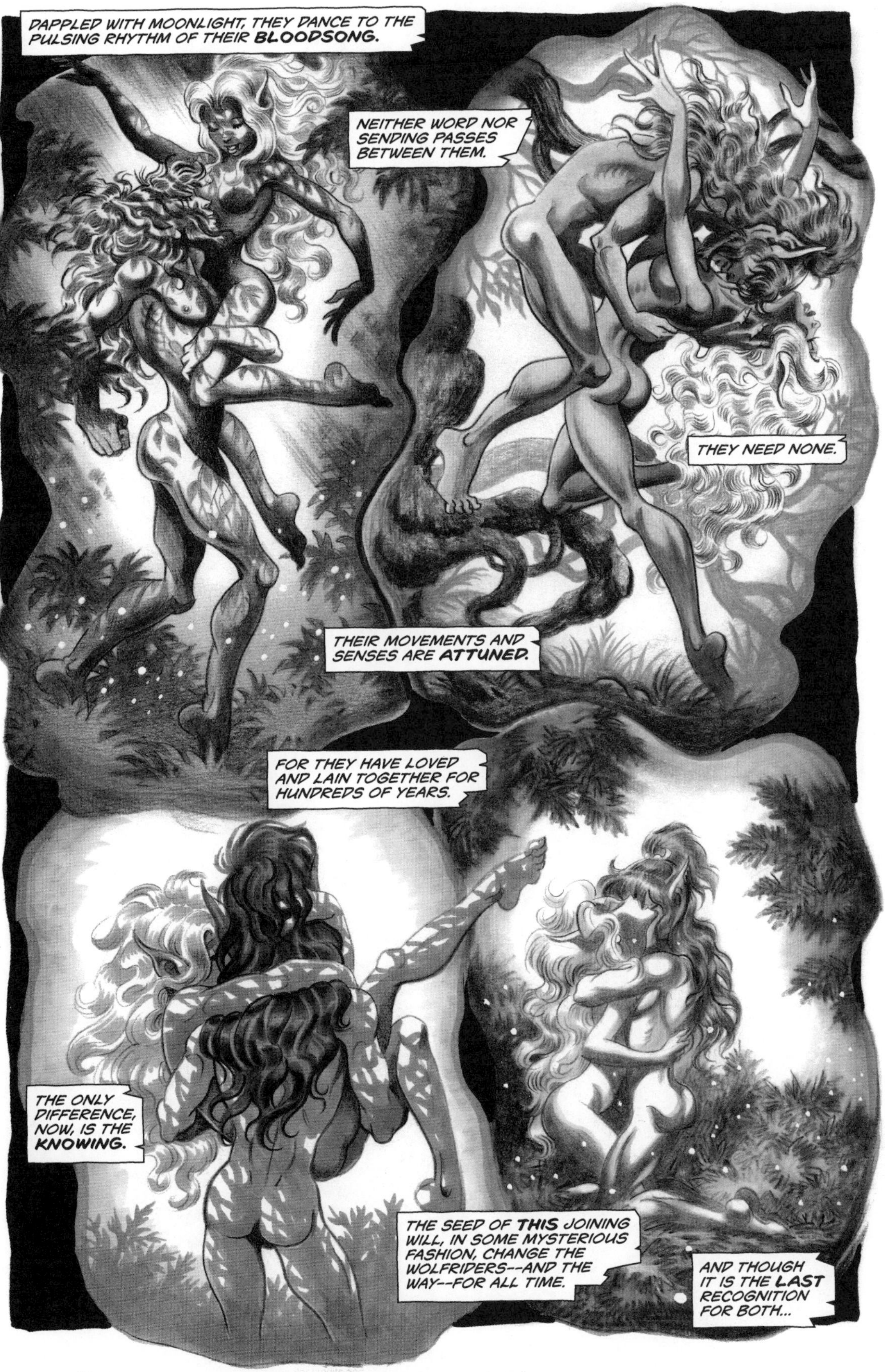
DAPPLED WITH MOONLIGHT, THEY DANCE TO THE PULSING RHYTHM OF THEIR **BLOODSONG.**
NEITHER WORD NOR SENDING PASSES BETWEEN THEM.
THEY NEED NONE.
THEIR MOVEMENTS AND SENSES ARE **ATTUNED.**
FOR THEY HAVE LOVED AND LAIN TOGETHER FOR HUNDREDS OF YEARS.
THE ONLY DIFFERENCE, NOW, IS THE **KNOWING.**
THE SEED OF **THIS** JOINING WILL, IN SOME MYSTERIOUS FASHION, CHANGE THE WOLFRIDERS--AND THE WAY--FOR ALL TIME.
AND THOUGH IT IS THE **LAST** RECOGNITION FOR BOTH...

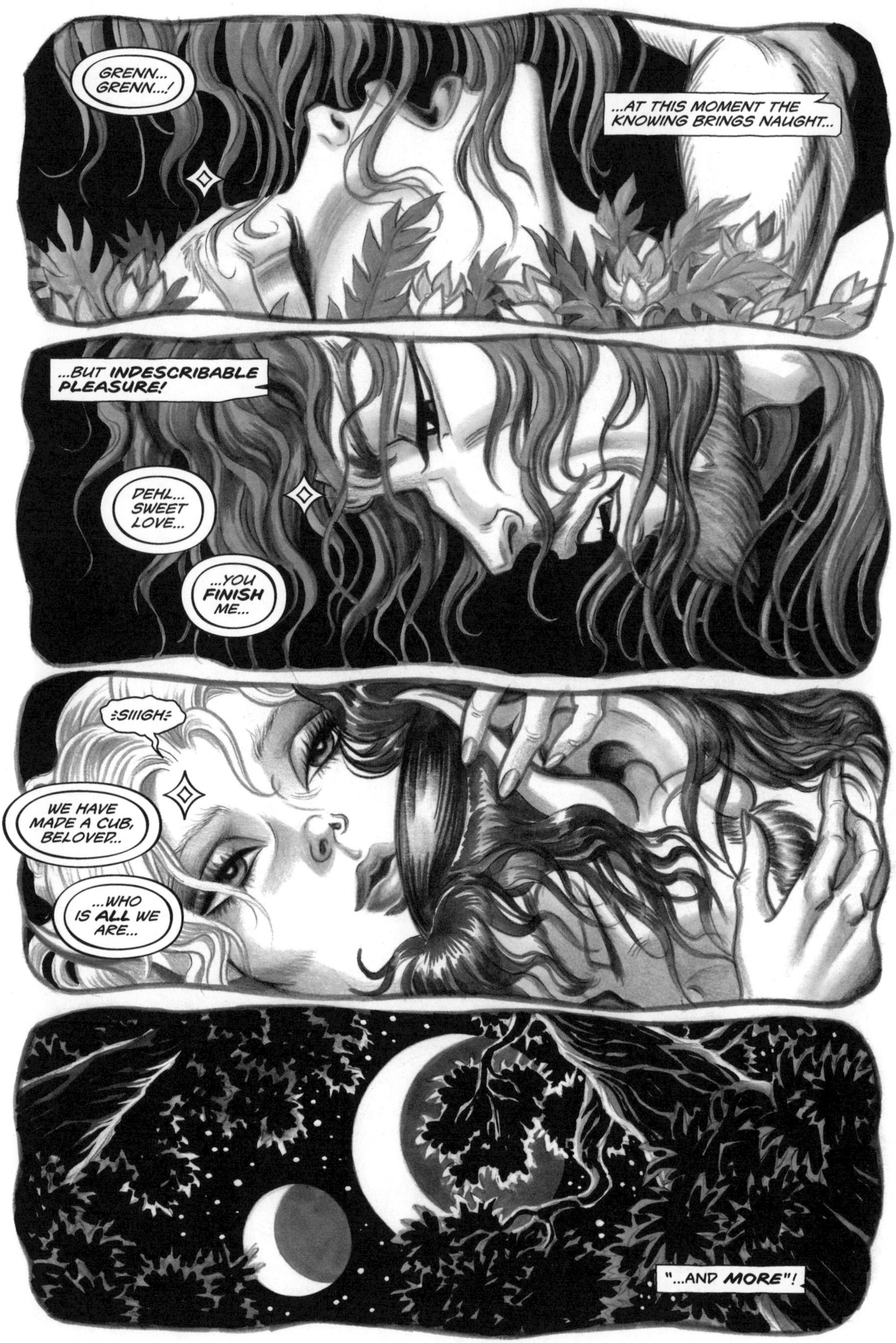
GRENN... GRENN...!
...AT THIS MOMENT THE KNOWING BRINGS NAUGHT...
...BUT INDESCRIBABLE PLEASURE!
DEHL... SWEET LOVE...
...YOU FINISH ME...
SIIIGH
WE HAVE MADE A CUB, BELOVED...
...WHO IS ALL WE ARE...
"...AND MORE"!

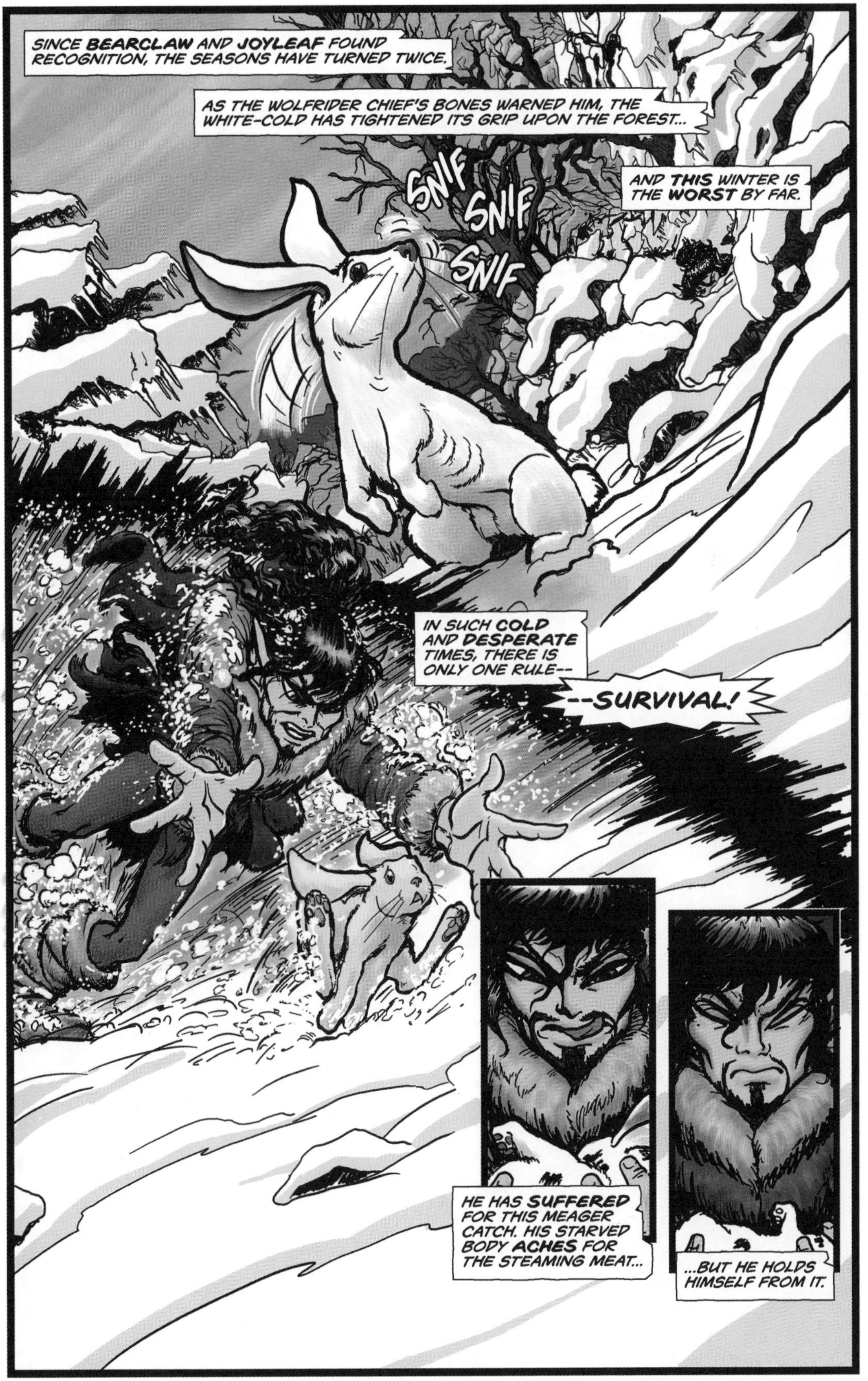
SINCE BEARCLAW AND JOYLEAF FOUND RECOGNITION, THE SEASONS HAVE TURNED TWICE.
AS THE WOLFRIDER CHIEF'S BONES WARNED HIM, THE WHITE-COLD HAS TIGHTENED ITS GRIP UPON THE FOREST...
AND THIS WINTER IS THE WORST BY FAR.
SNIF SNIF SNIF
IN SUCH COLD AND DESPERATE TIMES, THERE IS ONLY ONE RULE--
--SURVIVAL!
HE HAS SUFFERED FOR THIS MEAGER CATCH. HIS STARVED BODY ACHES FOR THE STEAMING MEAT...
...BUT HE HOLDS HIMSELF FROM IT.

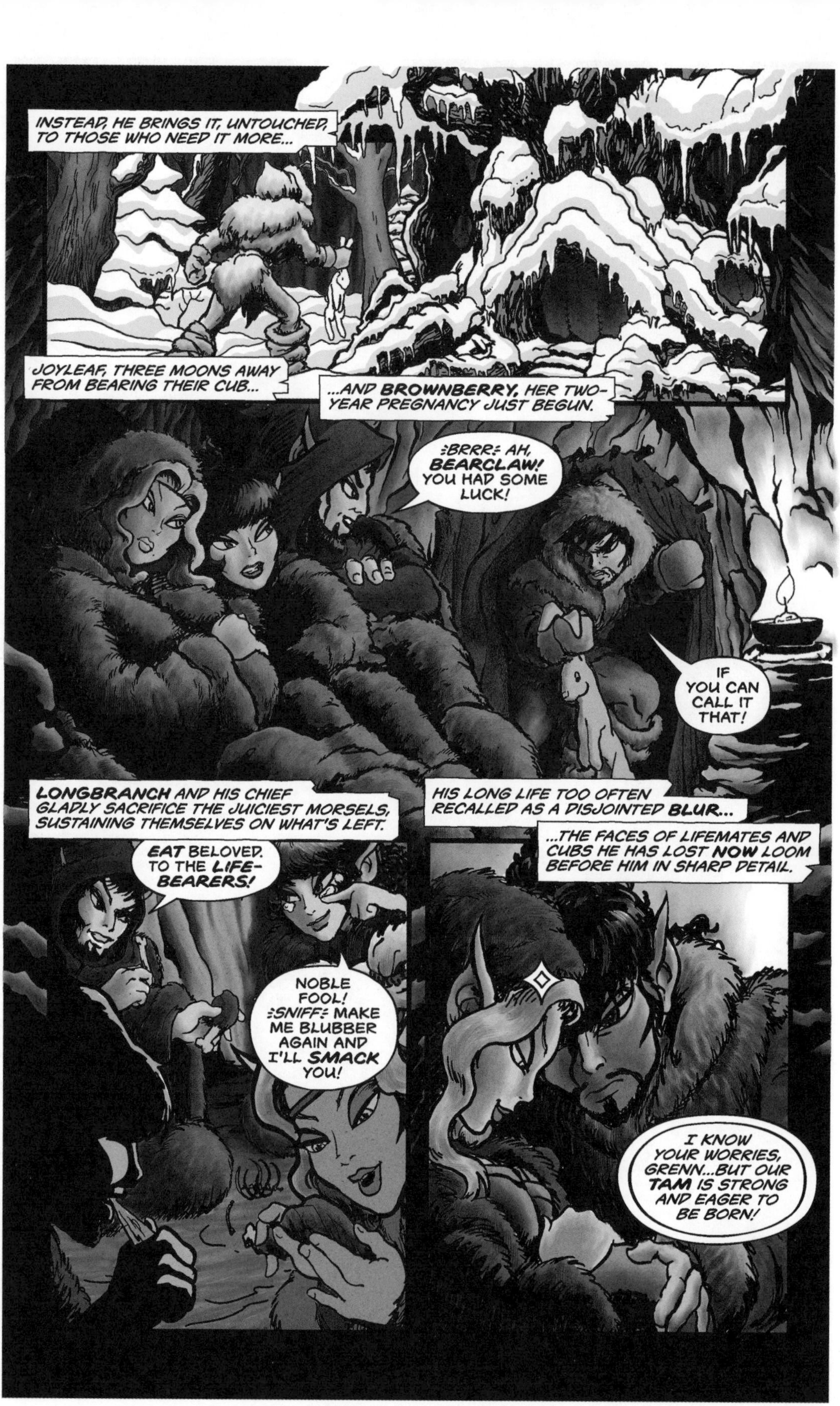
INSTEAD, HE BRINGS IT, UNTOUCHED, TO THOSE WHO NEED IT MORE...
JOYLEAF, THREE MOONS AWAY FROM BEARING THEIR CUB...
...AND BROWNBERRY, HER TWO-YEAR PREGNANCY JUST BEGUN.
BRRR AH, BEARCLAW! YOU HAD SOME LUCK!
IF YOU CAN CALL IT THAT!
LONGBRANCH AND HIS CHIEF GLADLY SACRIFICE THE JUICIEST MORSELS, SUSTAINING THEMSELVES ON WHAT'S LEFT.
EAT BELOVED. TO THE LIFE-BEARERS!
NOBLE FOOL! SNIFF MAKE ME BLUBBER AGAIN AND I'LL SMACK YOU!
HIS LONG LIFE TOO OFTEN RECALLED AS A DISJOINTED BLUR...
...THE FACES OF LIFEMATES AND CUBS HE HAS LOST NOW LOOM BEFORE HIM IN SHARP DETAIL.
I KNOW YOUR WORRIES, GRENN...BUT OUR TAM IS STRONG AND EAGER TO BE BORN!

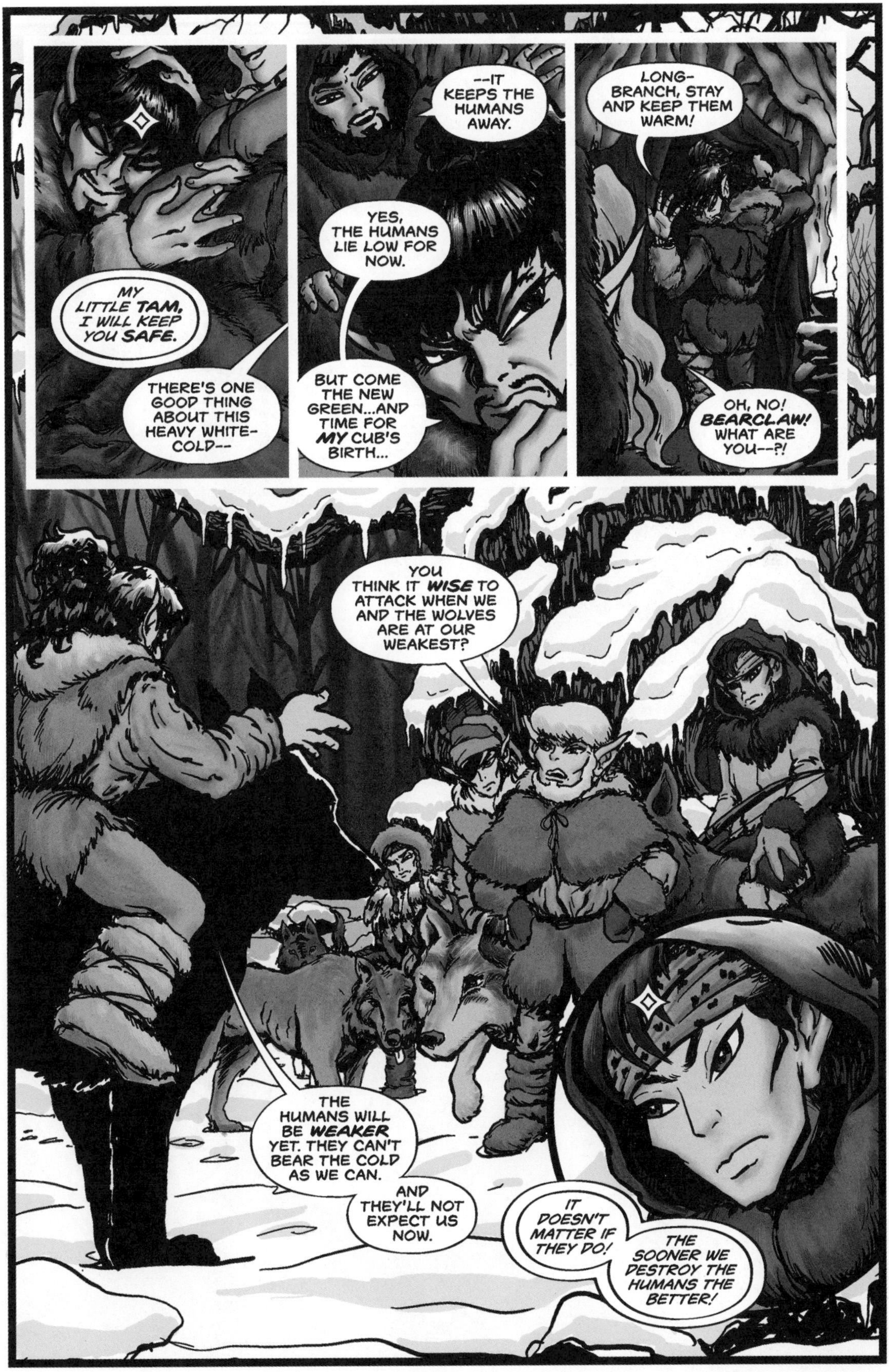
MY LITTLE TAM, I WILL KEEP YOU SAFE.
THERE'S ONE GOOD THING ABOUT THIS HEAVY WHITE-COLD--
--IT KEEPS THE HUMANS AWAY.
YES, THE HUMANS LIE LOW FOR NOW.
BUT COME THE NEW GREEN...AND TIME FOR MY CUB'S BIRTH...
LONG-BRANCH, STAY AND KEEP THEM WARM!
OH, NO! BEARCLAW! WHAT ARE YOU--?!
YOU THINK IT WISE TO ATTACK WHEN WE AND THE WOLVES ARE AT OUR WEAKEST?
THE HUMANS WILL BE WEAKER YET. THEY CAN'T BEAR THE COLD AS WE CAN.
AND THEY'LL NOT EXPECT US NOW.
IT DOESN'T MATTER IF THEY DO!
THE SOONER WE DESTROY THE HUMANS THE BETTER!

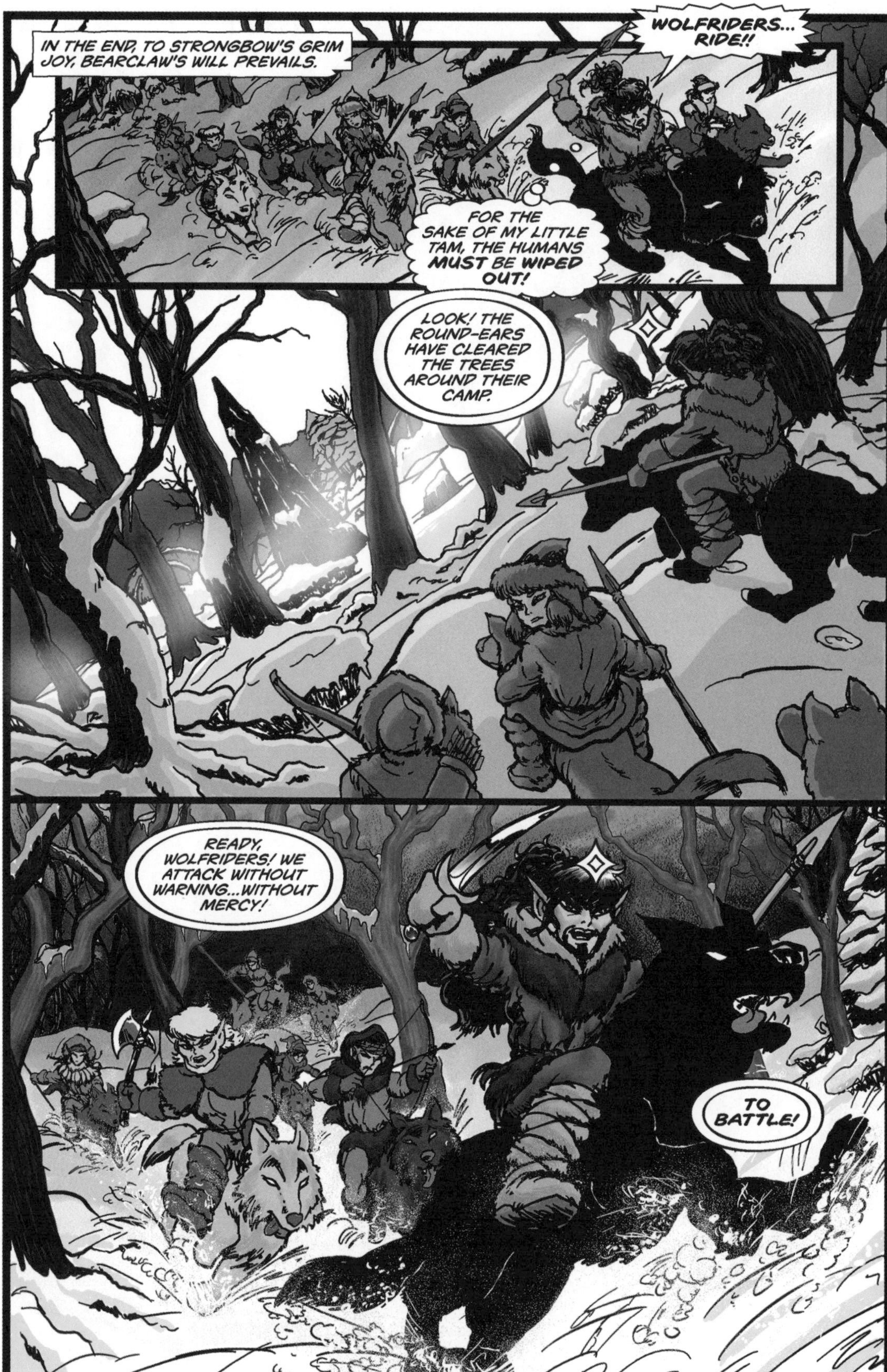

IN THE END, TO STRONGBOW'S GRIM JOY, BEARCLAW'S WILL PREVAILS.
WOLFRIDERS... RIDE!!
FOR THE SAKE OF MY LITTLE TAM, THE HUMANS MUST BE WIPED OUT!
LOOK! THE ROUND-EARS HAVE CLEARED THE TREES AROUND THEIR CAMP.
READY, WOLFRIDERS! WE ATTACK WITHOUT WARNING...WITHOUT MERCY!
TO BATTLE!

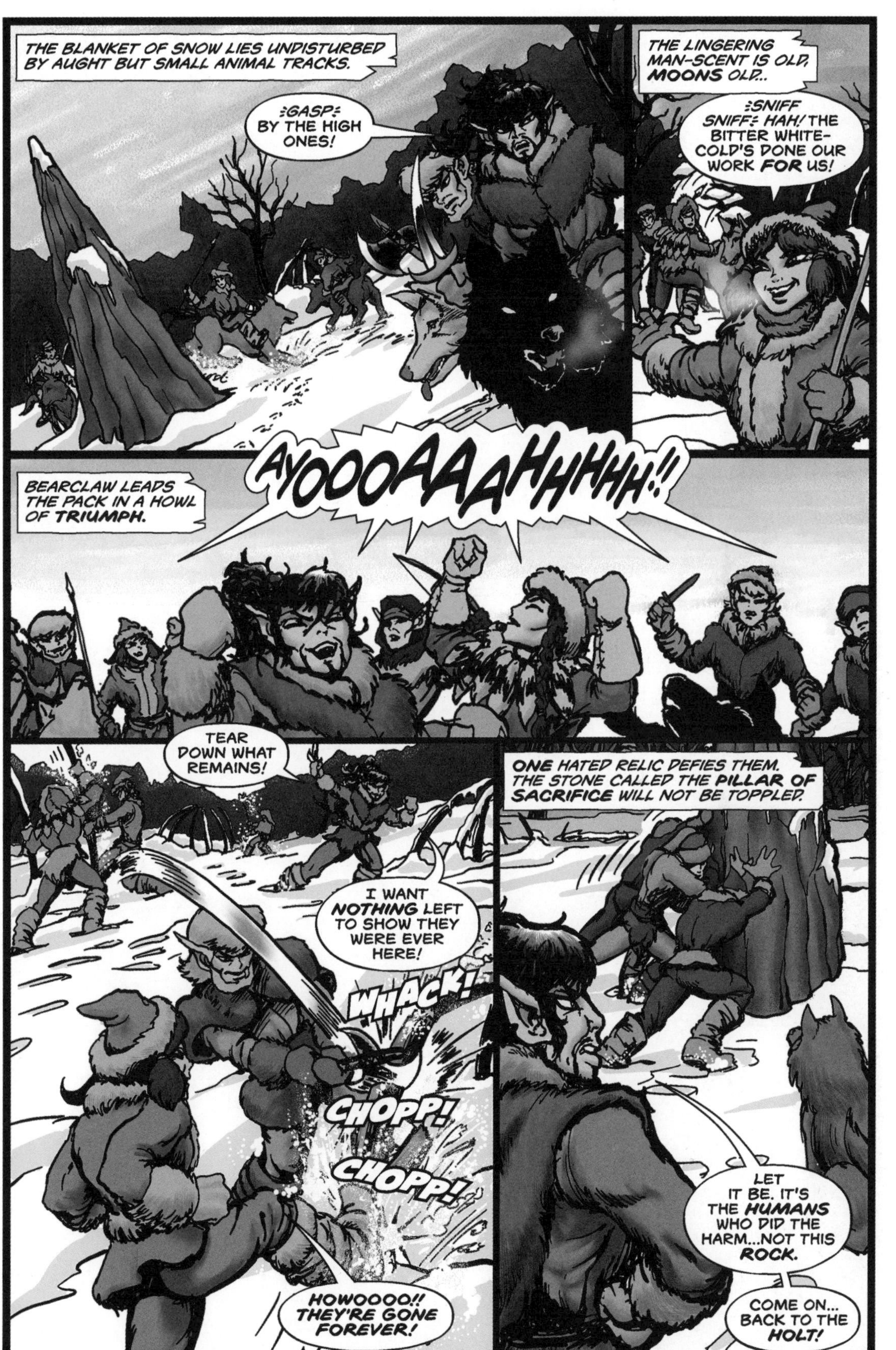

THE BLANKET OF SNOW LIES UNDISTURBED BY AUGHT BUT SMALL ANIMAL TRACKS.
GASP BY THE HIGH ONES!
THE LINGERING MAN-SCENT IS OLD, MOONS OLD..
SNIFF SNIFF HAH! THE BITTER WHITE-COLD'S DONE OUR WORK FOR US!
BEARCLAW LEADS THE PACK IN A HOWL OF TRIUMPH.
AYOOOAAAHHHHH!!
TEAR DOWN WHAT REMAINS!
I WANT NOTHING LEFT TO SHOW THEY WERE EVER HERE!
WHACK!
CHOPP!
CHOPP!
HOWOOOO!! THEY'RE GONE FOREVER!
ONE HATED RELIC DEFIES THEM. THE STONE CALLED THE PILLAR OF SACRIFICE WILL NOT BE TOPPLED.
LET IT BE. IT'S THE HUMANS WHO DID THE HARM...NOT THIS ROCK.
COME ON... BACK TO THE HOLT!

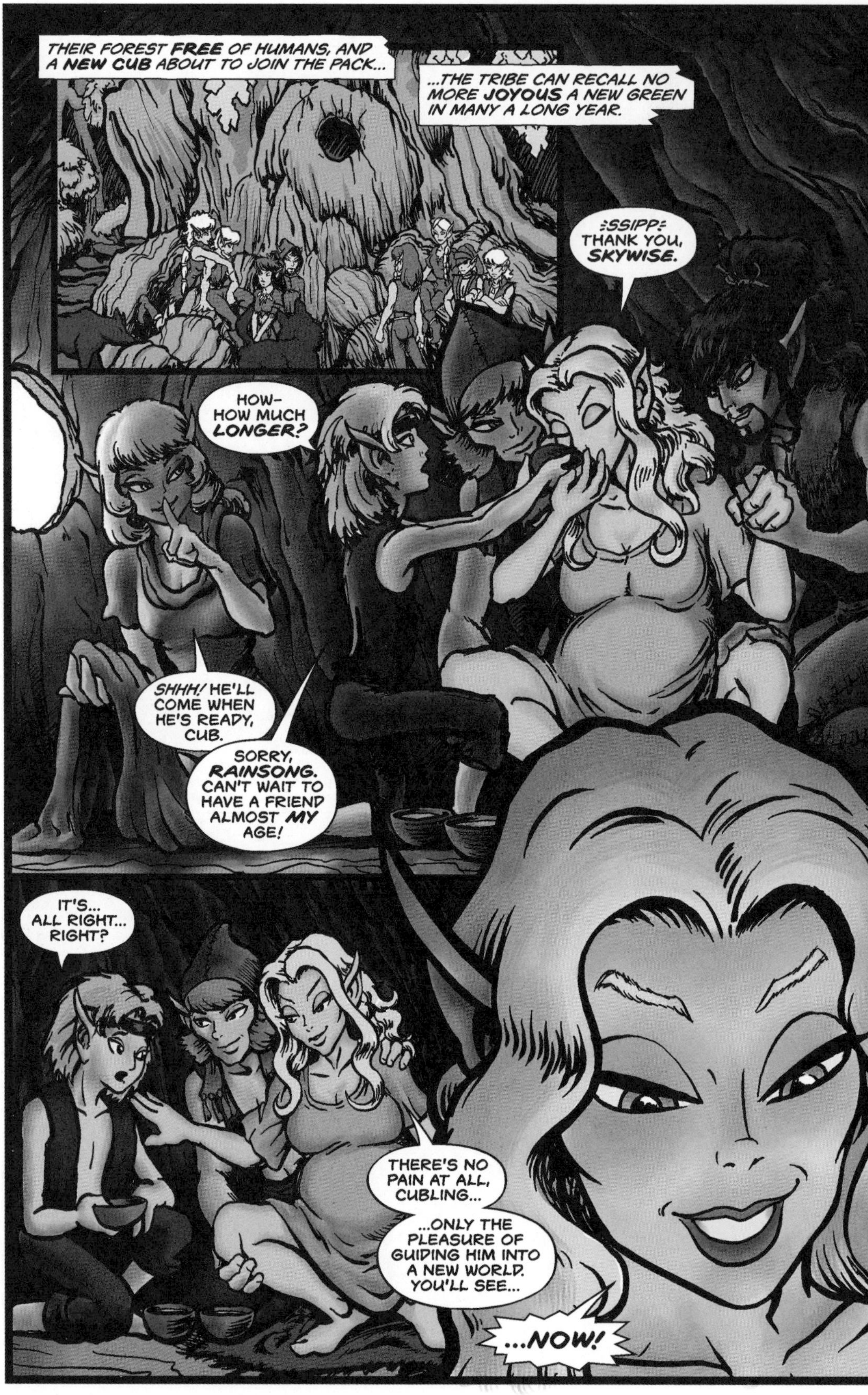
THEIR FOREST FREE OF HUMANS, AND A NEW CUB ABOUT TO JOIN THE PACK...
...THE TRIBE CAN RECALL NO MORE JOYOUS A NEW GREEN IN MANY A LONG YEAR.
:SSIPP: THANK YOU, SKYWISE.
HOW- HOW MUCH LONGER?
SHHH! HE'LL COME WHEN HE'S READY, CUB.
SORRY, RAINSONG. CAN'T WAIT TO HAVE A FRIEND ALMOST MY AGE!
IT'S... ALL RIGHT... RIGHT?
THERE'S NO PAIN AT ALL, CUBLING...
...ONLY THE PLEASURE OF GUIDING HIM INTO A NEW WORLD. YOU'LL SEE...
...NOW!

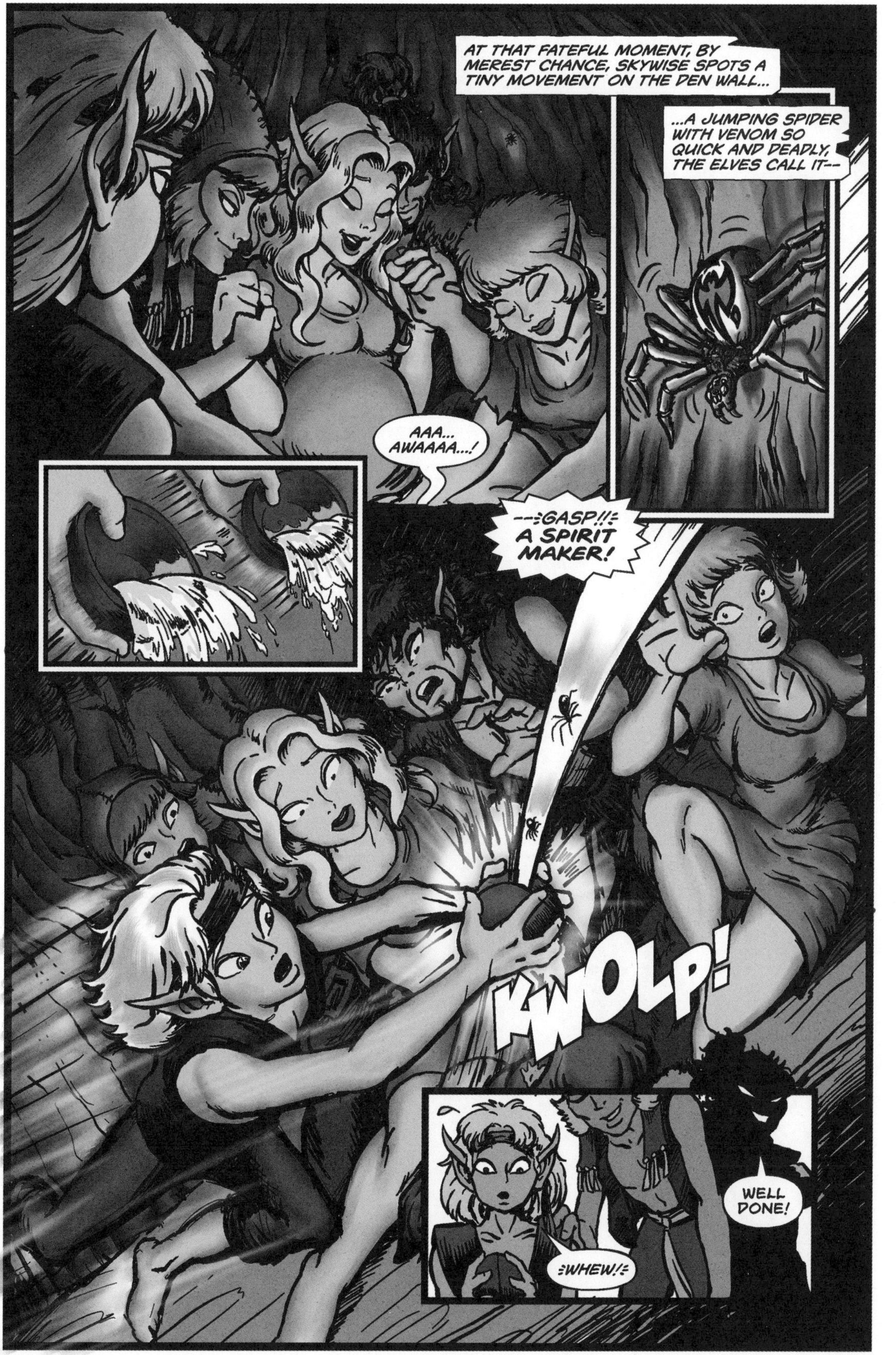

AT THAT FATEFUL MOMENT, BY MERREST CHANCE, SKYWISE SPOTS A TINY MOVEMENT ON THE DEN WALL...
...A JUMPING SPIDER WITH VENOM SO QUICK AND DEADLY, THE ELVES CALL IT--
AAA... AWAAAA...!
--:GASP!!: A SPIRIT MAKER!
KWOLP!
WELL DONE!
:WHEW!:

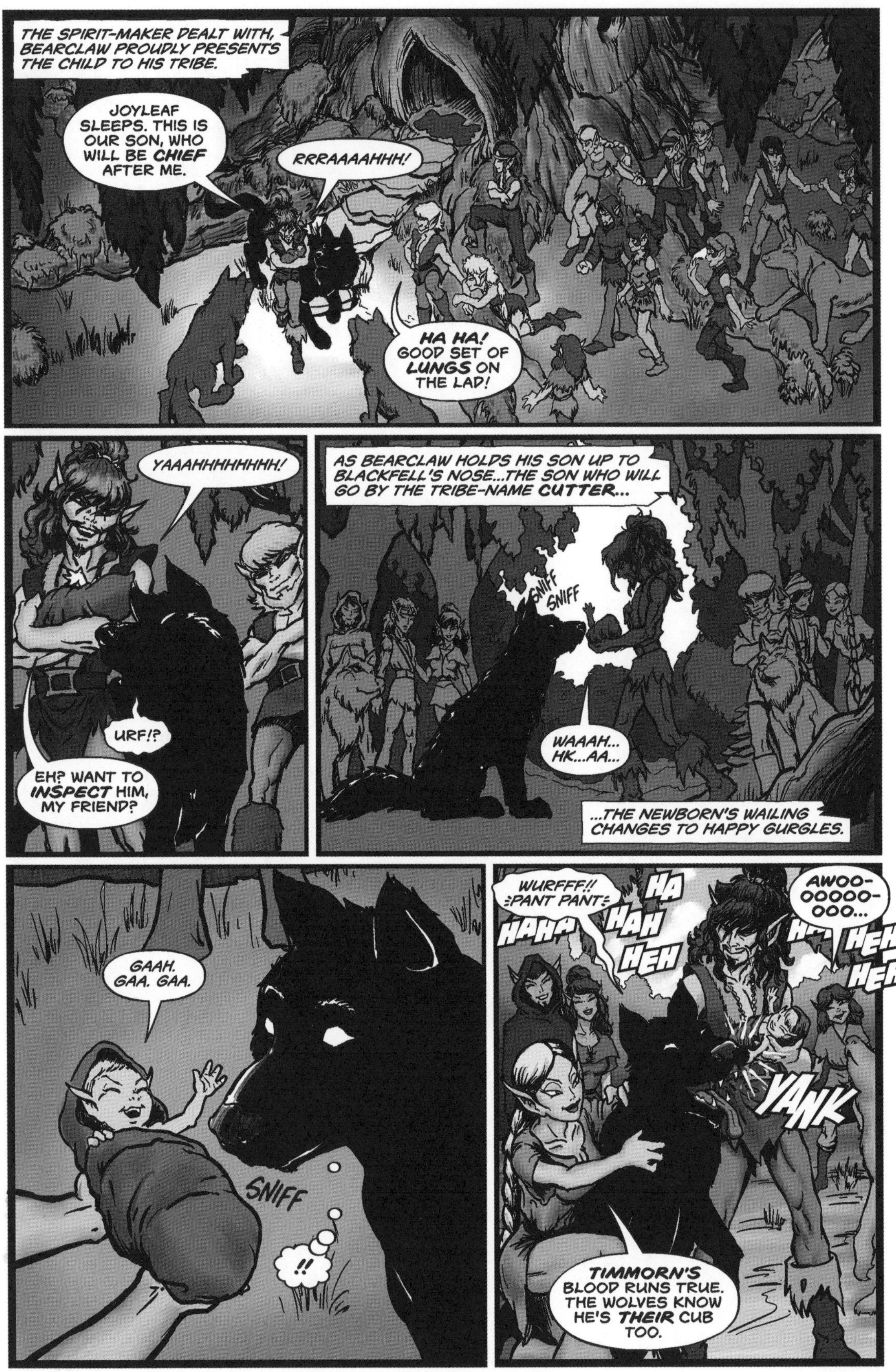

THE SPIRIT-MAKER DEALT WITH, BEARCLAW PROUDLY PRESENTS THE CHILD TO HIS TRIBE.
JOYLEAF SLEEPS. THIS IS OUR SON, WHO WILL BE CHIEF AFTER ME.
RRRAAAAHHH!
HA HA! GOOD SET OF LUNGS ON THE LAD!
YAAAHHHHHHHH!
URF!?
EH? WANT TO INSPECT HIM, MY FRIEND?
AS BEARCLAW HOLDS HIS SON UP TO BLACKFELL'S NOSE...THE SON WHO WILL GO BY THE TRIBE-NAME CUTTER...
SNIFF SNIFF
WAAAH... HK...AA...
...THE NEWBORN'S WAILING CHANGES TO HAPPY GURGLES.
GAAH. GAA. GAA.
SNIFF
!!
WURFFF!! PANT PANT
HAHA
HA HAH HEH
AWOO-OOOOO-OOO...
HEH HEH
YANK
TIMMORN'S BLOOD RUNS TRUE. THE WOLVES KNOW HE'S THEIR CUB TOO.

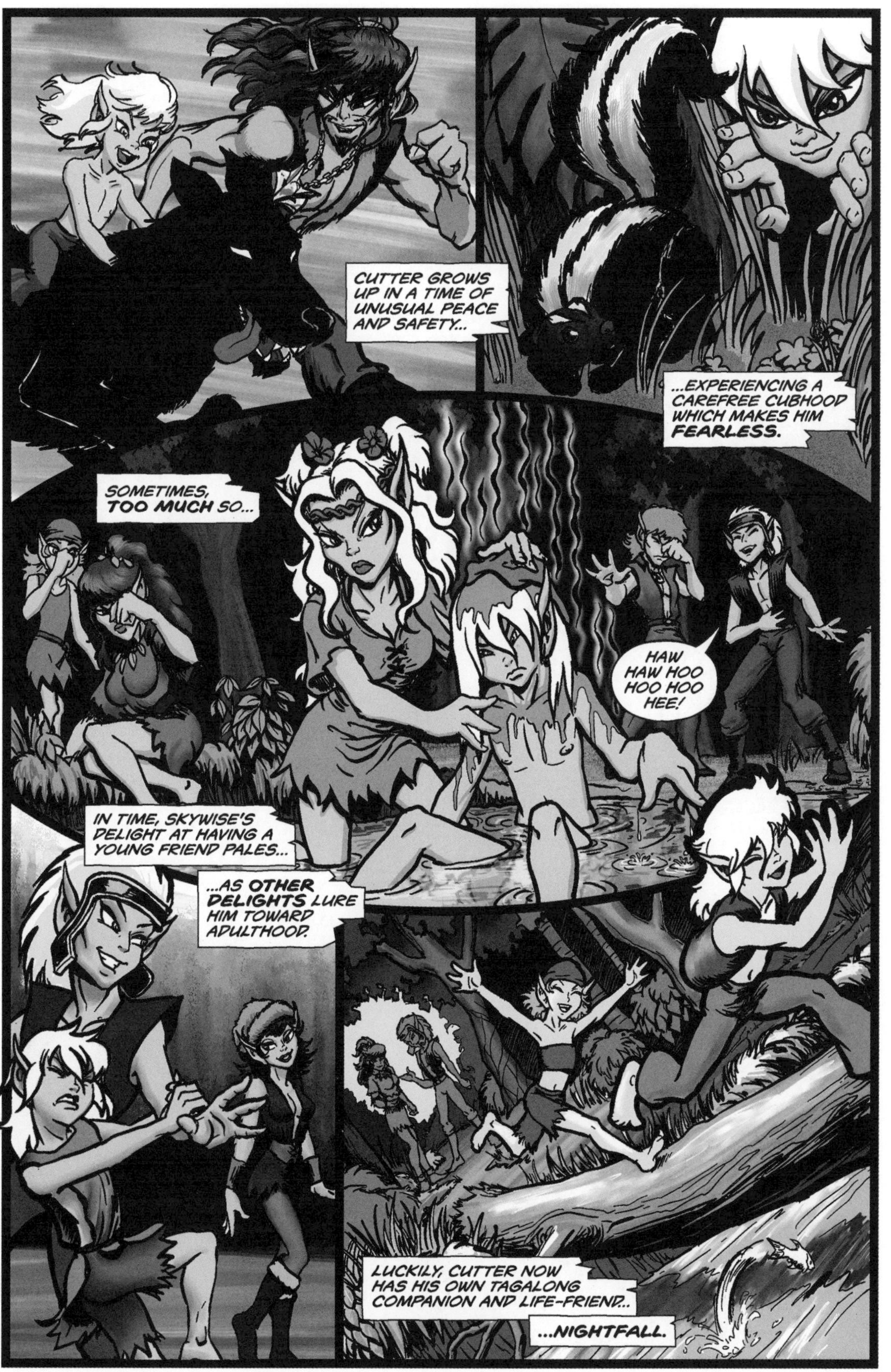
CUTTER GROWS UP IN A TIME OF UNUSUAL PEACE AND SAFETY...
...EXPERIENCING A CAREFREE CUBHOOD WHICH MAKES HIM FEARLESS.
SOMETIMES, TOO MUCH SO...
HAW HAW HOO HOO HOO HEE!
IN TIME, SKYWISE'S DELIGHT AT HAVING A YOUNG FRIEND PALES...
...AS OTHER DELIGHTS LURE HIM TOWARD ADULTHOOD.
LUCKILY, CUTTER NOW HAS HIS OWN TAGALONG COMPANION AND LIFE-FRIEND...
...NIGHTFALL.

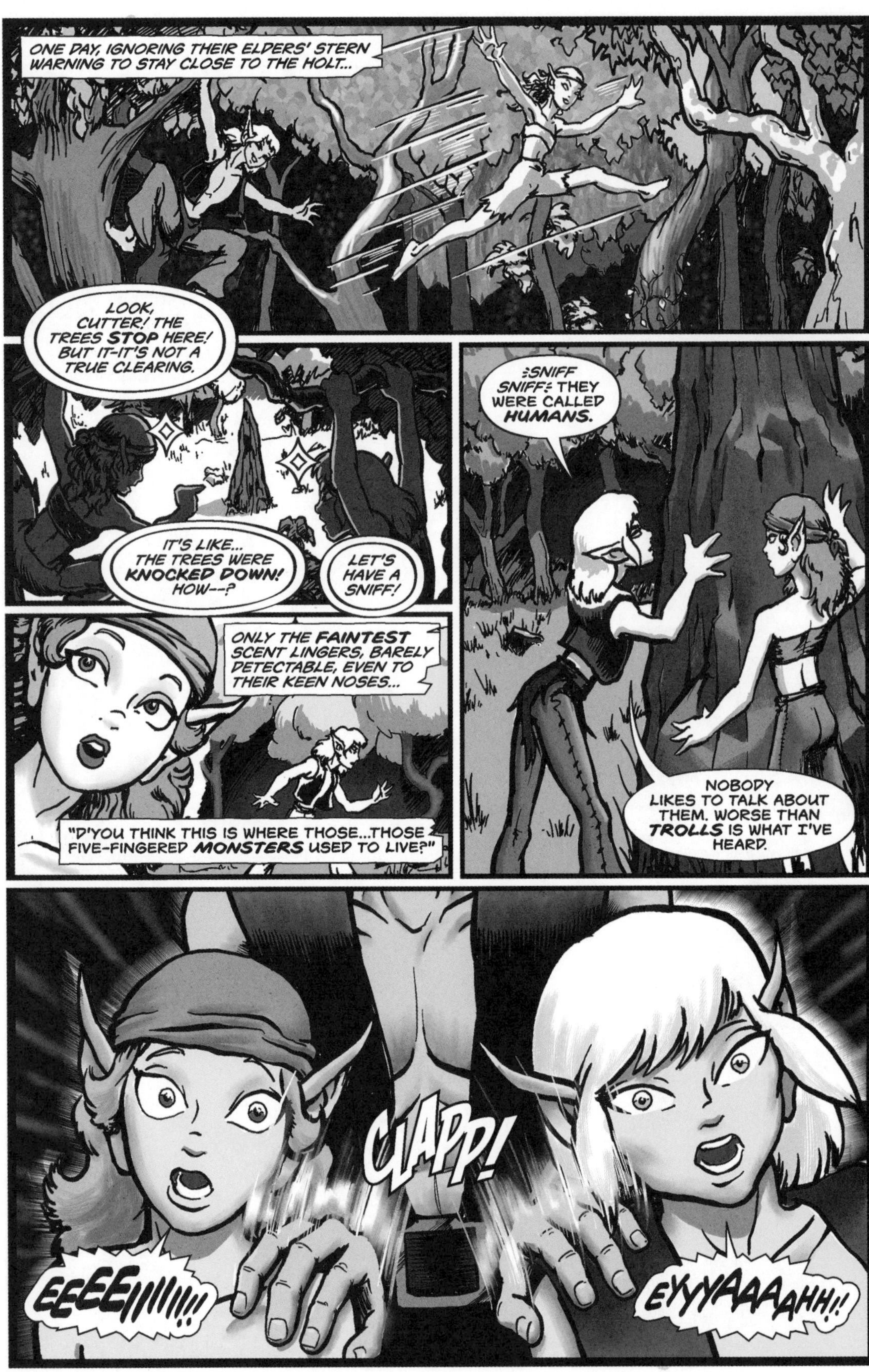
ONE DAY, IGNORING THEIR ELDERS' STERN WARNING TO STAY CLOSE TO THE HOLT...
LOOK, CUTTER! THE TREES STOP HERE! BUT IT-IT'S NOT A TRUE CLEARING.
IT'S LIKE... THE TREES WERE KNOCKED DOWN! HOW--?
LET'S HAVE A SNIFF!
SNIFF SNIFF THEY WERE CALLED HUMANS.
ONLY THE FAINTEST SCENT LINGERS, BARELY DETECTABLE, EVEN TO THEIR KEEN NOSES...
"D'YOU THINK THIS IS WHERE THOSE...THOSE FIVE-FINGERED MONSTERS USED TO LIVE?"
NOBODY LIKES TO TALK ABOUT THEM. WORSE THAN TROLLS IS WHAT I'VE HEARD.
CLAPP!
EEEEIIIIII!!!
EYYYAAAAAHH!!

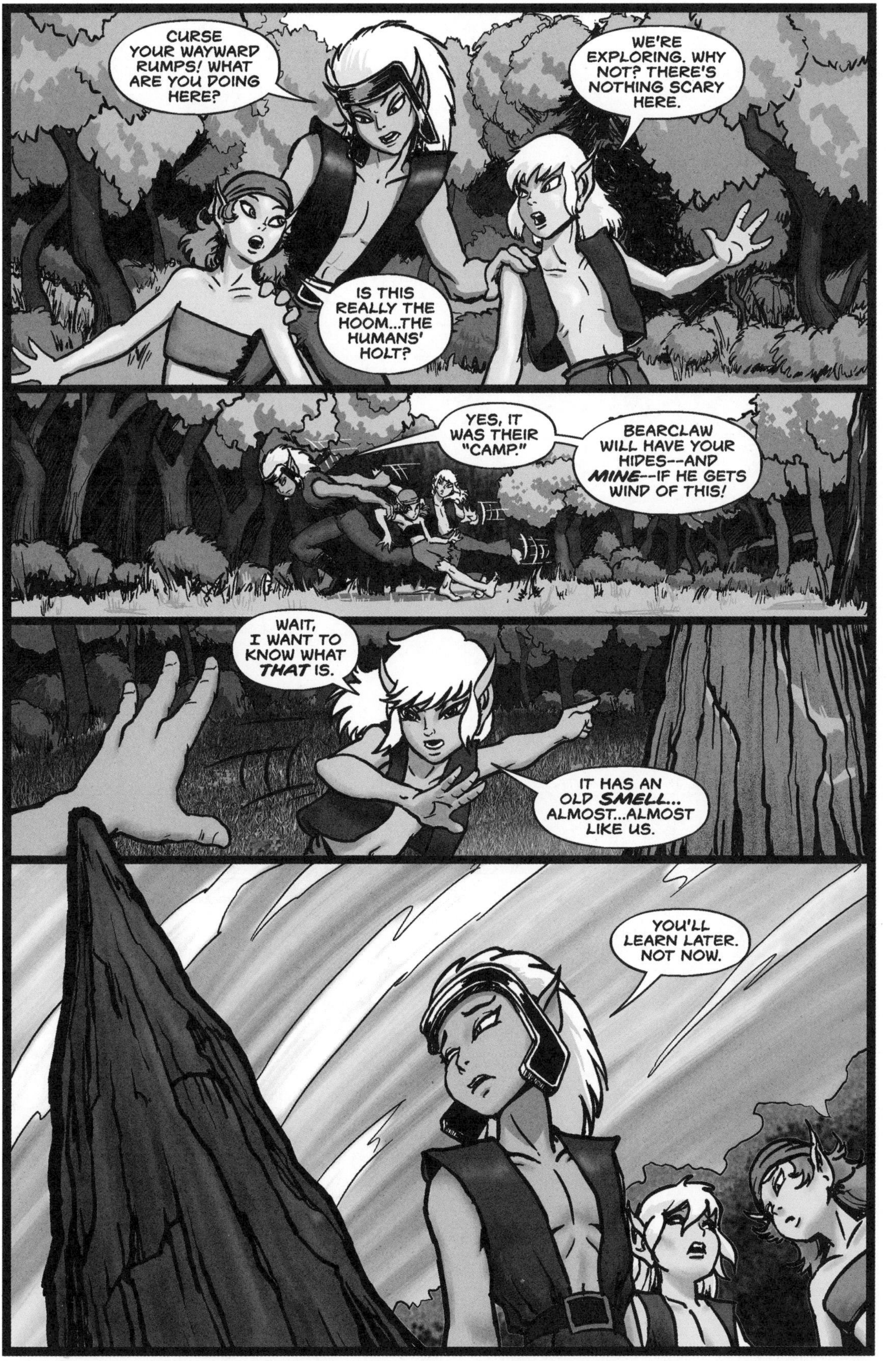
CURSE YOUR WAYWARD RUMPS! WHAT ARE YOU DOING HERE?
WE'RE EXPLORING. WHY NOT? THERE'S NOTHING SCARY HERE.
IS THIS REALLY THE HOOM...THE HUMANS' HOLT?
YES, IT WAS THEIR "CAMP."
BEARCLAW WILL HAVE YOUR HIDES--AND MINE--IF HE GETS WIND OF THIS!
WAIT, I WANT TO KNOW WHAT THAT IS.
IT HAS AN OLD SMELL... ALMOST...ALMOST LIKE US.
YOU'LL LEARN LATER. NOT NOW.

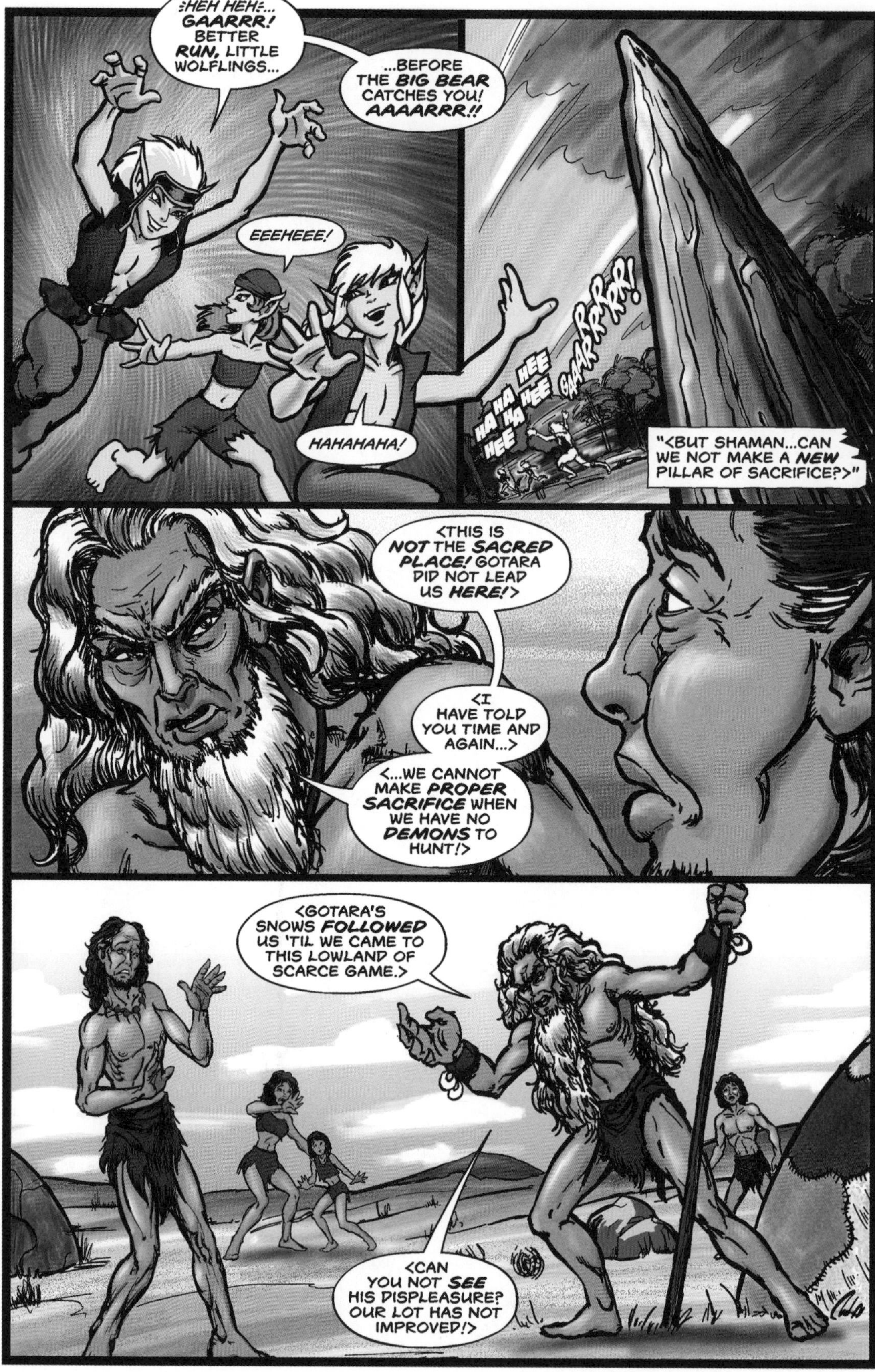
:HEH HEH:... GAARRR! BETTER RUN, LITTLE WOLFLINGS...
...BEFORE THE BIG BEAR CATCHES YOU! AAAARRR!!
EEEHEEE!
HAHAHAHA!
HA HA HEE
HA HA HEE HEE
GAAARRRRRR!
"<BUT SHAMAN...CAN WE NOT MAKE A NEW PILLAR OF SACRIFICE?>"
<THIS IS NOT THE SACRED PLACE! GOTARA DID NOT LEAD US HERE!>
<I HAVE TOLD YOU TIME AND AGAIN...>
<...WE CANNOT MAKE PROPER SACRIFICE WHEN WE HAVE NO DEMONS TO HUNT!>
<GOTARA'S SNOWS FOLLOWED US 'TIL WE CAME TO THIS LOWLAND OF SCARCE GAME.>
<CAN YOU NOT SEE HIS DISPLEASURE? OUR LOT HAS NOT IMPROVED!>

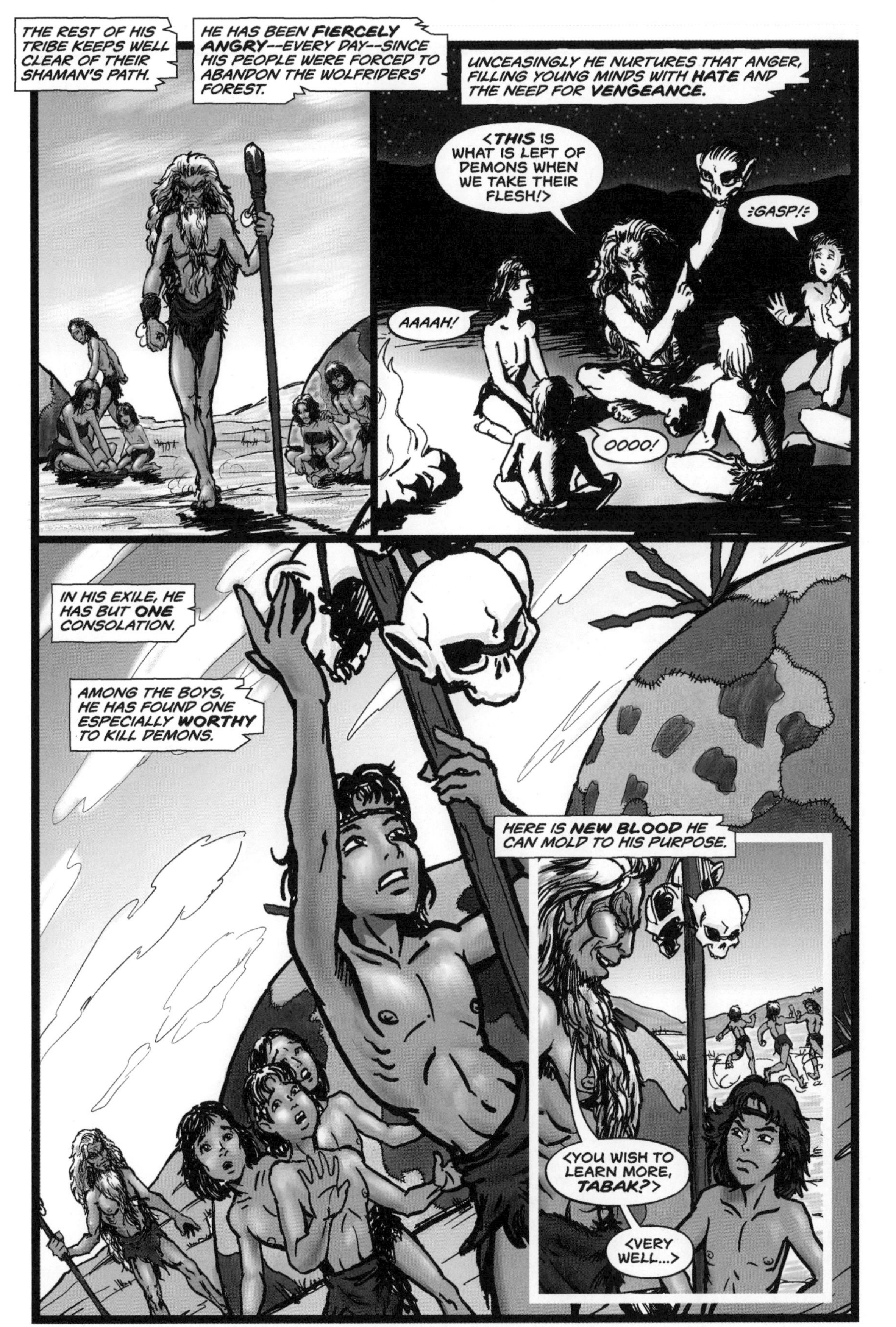
THE REST OF HIS TRIBE KEEPS WELL CLEAR OF THEIR SHAMAN'S PATH.
HE HAS BEEN FIERCELY ANGRY--EVERY DAY--SINCE HIS PEOPLE WERE FORCED TO ABANDON THE WOLFRIDERS' FOREST.
UNCEASINGLY HE NURTURES THAT ANGER, FILLING YOUNG MINDS WITH HATE AND THE NEED FOR VENGEANCE.
<THIS IS WHAT IS LEFT OF DEMONS WHEN WE TAKE THEIR FLESH!>
:GASP!:
AAAAH!
OOOO!
IN HIS EXILE, HE HAS BUT ONE CONSOLATION.
AMONG THE BOYS, HE HAS FOUND ONE ESPECIALLY WORTHY TO KILL DEMONS.
HERE IS NEW BLOOD HE CAN MOLD TO HIS PURPOSE.
<YOU WISH TO LEARN MORE, TABAK?>
<VERY WELL...>

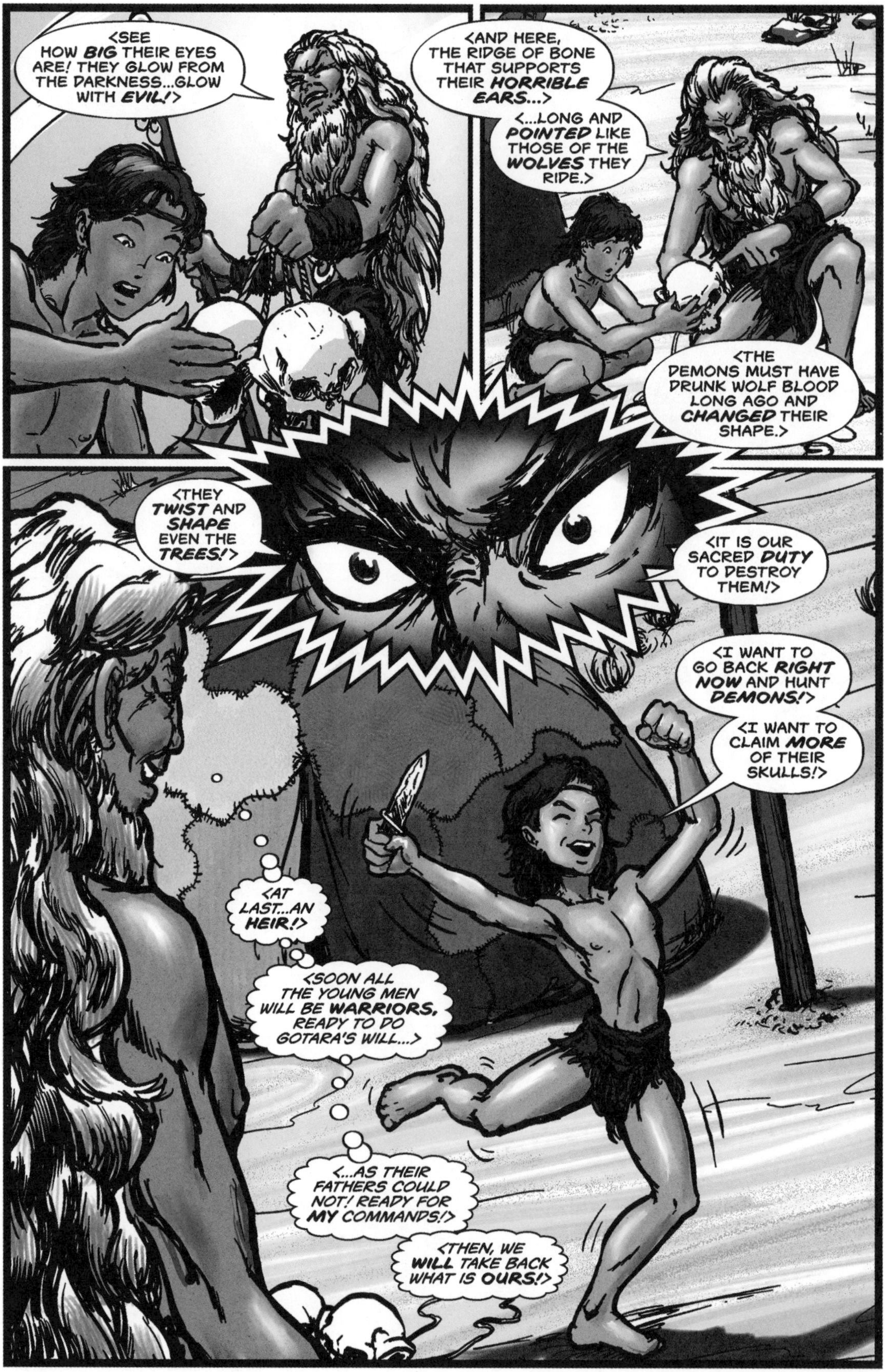

<SEE HOW BIG THEIR EYES ARE! THEY GLOW FROM THE DARKNESS...GLOW WITH EVIL!>
<AND HERE, THE RIDGE OF BONE THAT SUPPORTS THEIR HORRIBLE EARS...>
<...LONG AND POINTED LIKE THOSE OF THE WOLVES THEY RIDE.>
<THE DEMONS MUST HAVE DRUNK WOLF BLOOD LONG AGO AND CHANGED THEIR SHAPE.>
<THEY TWIST AND SHAPE EVEN THE TREES!>
<IT IS OUR SACRED DUTY TO DESTROY THEM!>
<I WANT TO GO BACK RIGHT NOW AND HUNT DEMONS!>
<I WANT TO CLAIM MORE OF THEIR SKULLS!>
<AT LAST...AN HEIR!>
<SOON ALL THE YOUNG MEN WILL BE WARRIORS, READY TO DO GOTARA'S WILL...>
<...AS THEIR FATHERS COULD NOT! READY FOR MY COMMANDS!>
<THEN, WE WILL TAKE BACK WHAT IS OURS!>

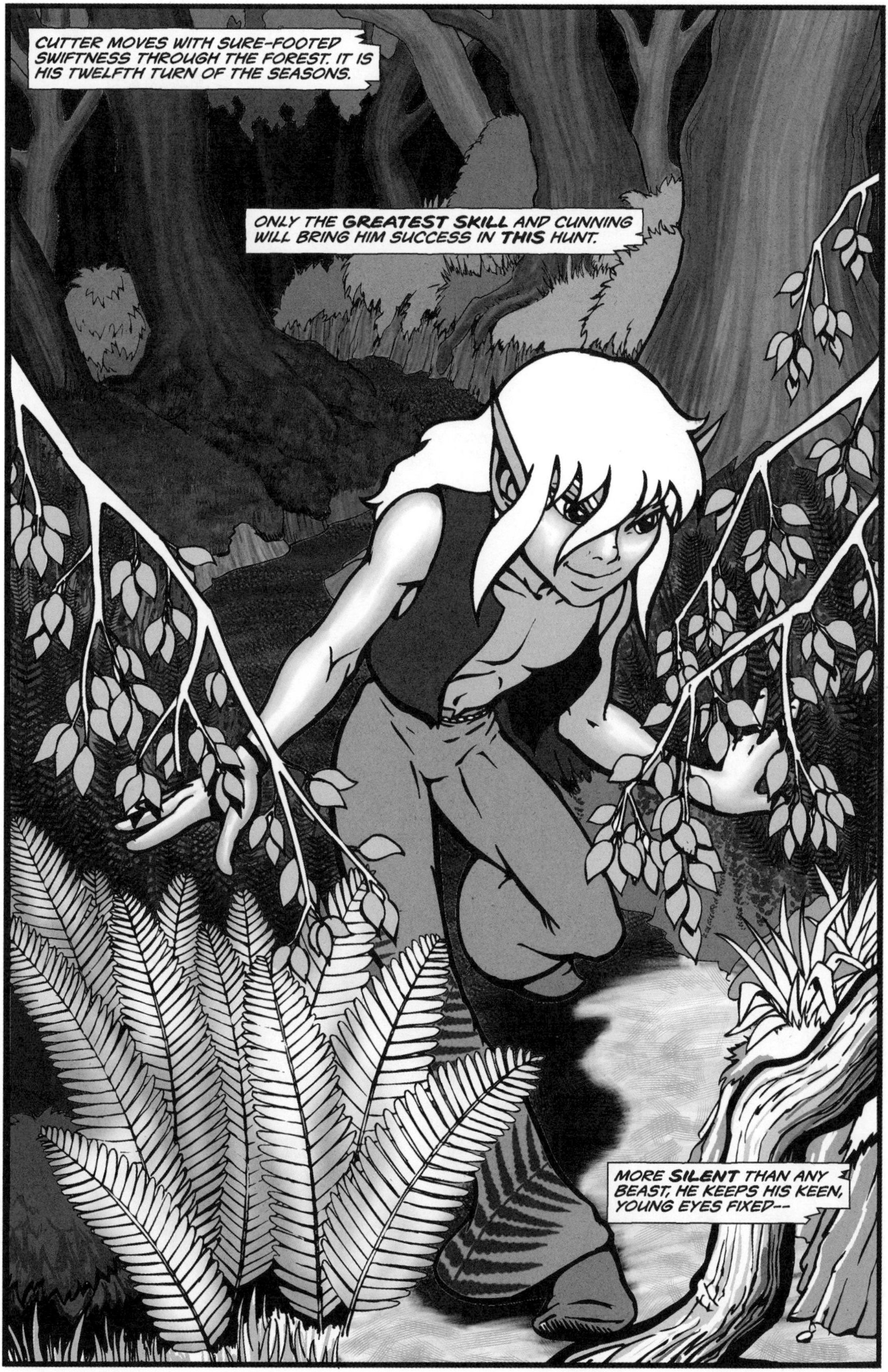
CUTTER MOVES WITH SURE-FOOTED SWIFTNESS THROUGH THE FOREST. IT IS HIS TWELFTH TURN OF THE SEASONS.
ONLY THE GREATEST SKILL AND CUNNING WILL BRING HIM SUCCESS IN THIS HUNT.
MORE SILENT THAN ANY BEAST, HE KEEPS HIS KEEN, YOUNG EYES FIXED--

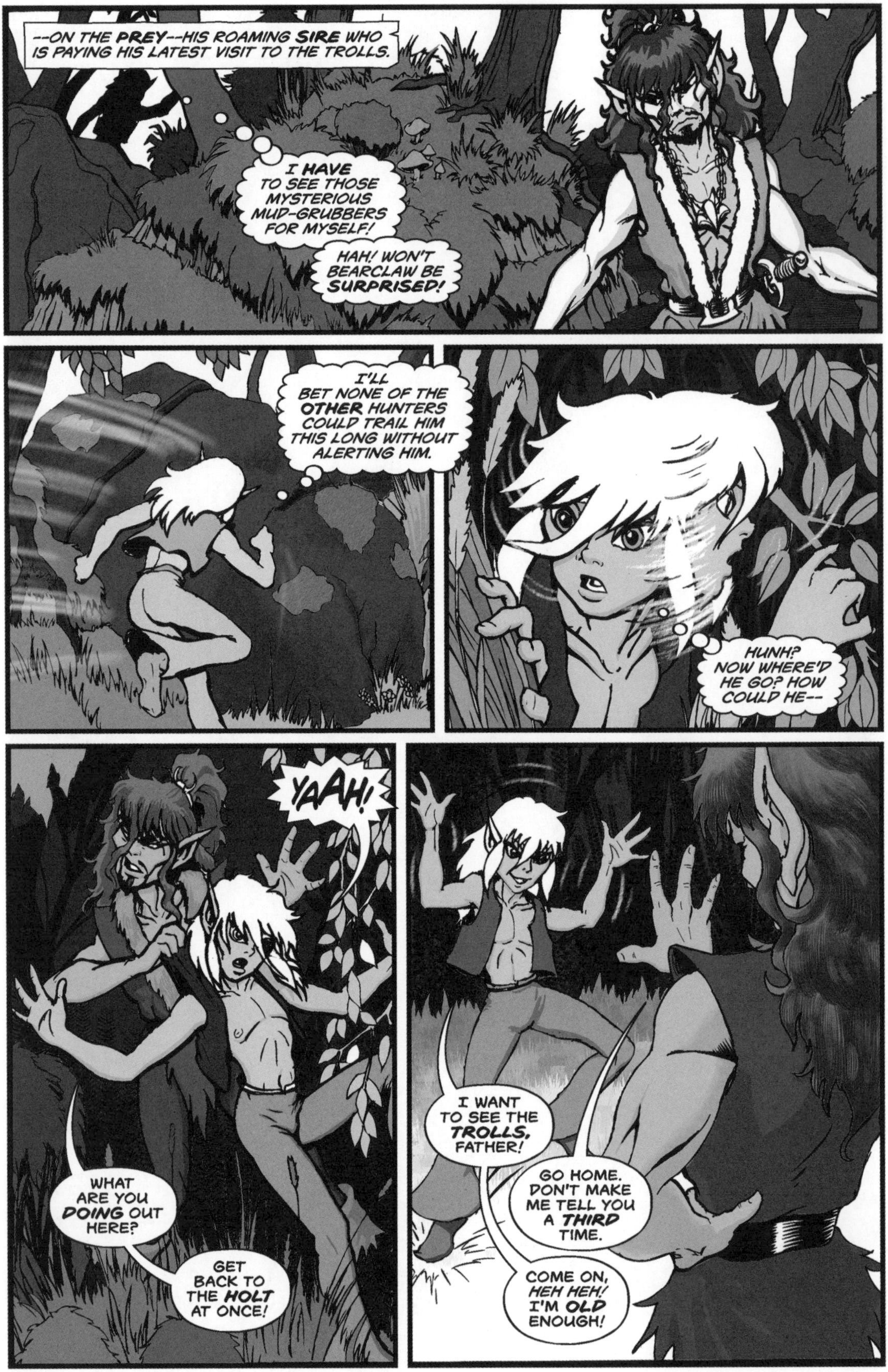
--ON THE PREY--HIS ROAMING SIRE WHO IS PAYING HIS LATEST VISIT TO THE TROLLS.
I HAVE TO SEE THOSE MYSTERIOUS MUD-GRUBBERS FOR MYSELF!
HAH! WON'T BEARCLAW BE SURPRISED!
I'LL BET NONE OF THE OTHER HUNTERS COULD TRAIL HIM THIS LONG WITHOUT ALERTING HIM.
HUNH? NOW WHERE'D HE GO? HOW COULD HE--
YAAH!
WHAT ARE YOU DOING OUT HERE?
GET BACK TO THE HOLT AT ONCE!
I WANT TO SEE THE TROLLS, FATHER!
GO HOME. DON'T MAKE ME TELL YOU A THIRD TIME.
COME ON, HEH HEH! I'M OLD ENOUGH!

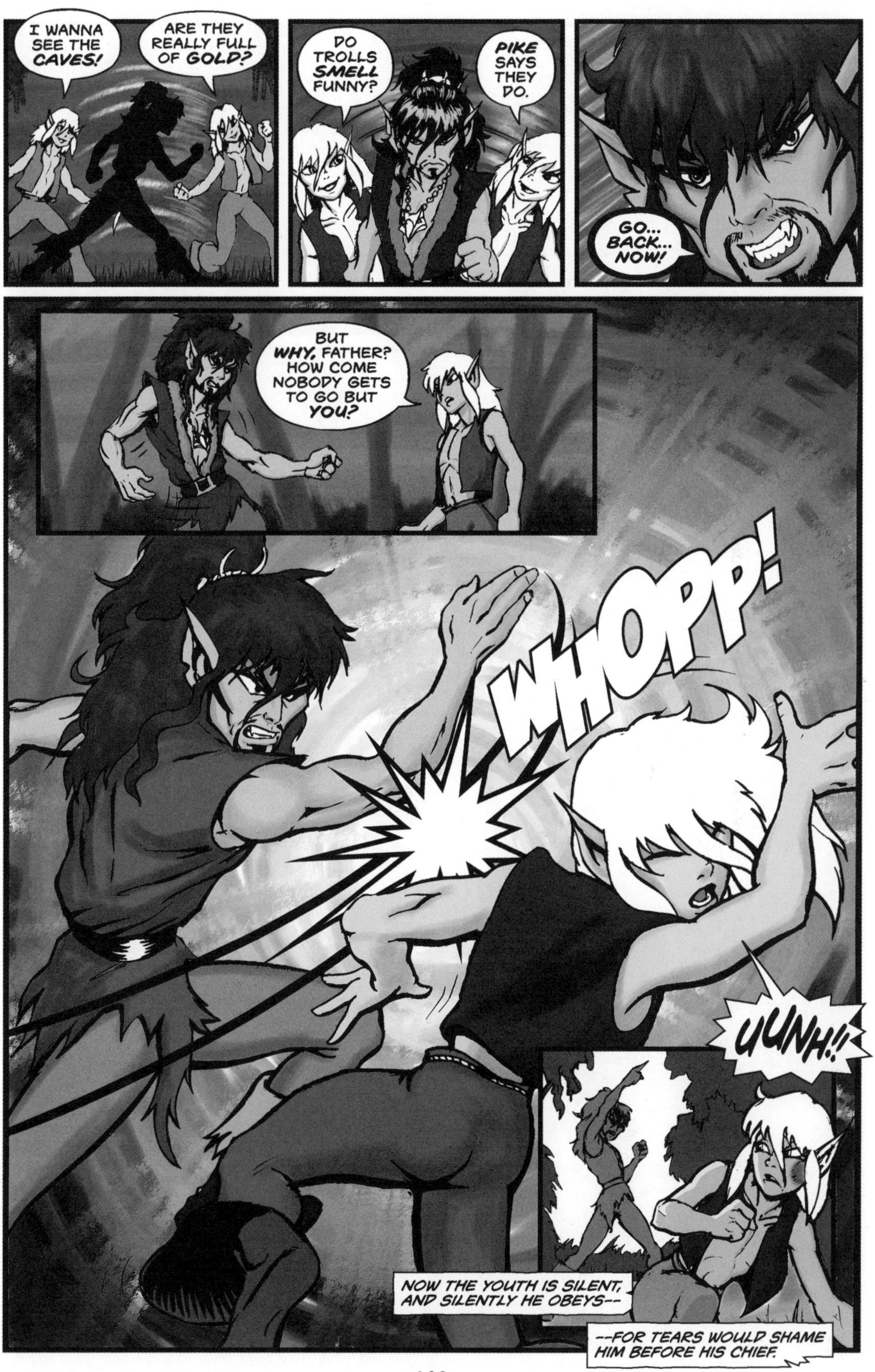
I WANNA SEE THE CAVES!
ARE THEY REALLY FULL OF GOLD?
DO TROLLS SMELL FUNNY?
PIKE SAYS THEY DO.
GO... BACK... NOW!
BUT WHY, FATHER? HOW COME NOBODY GETS TO GO BUT YOU?
WHOPP!
UUNH!!
NOW THE YOUTH IS SILENT, AND SILENTLY HE OBEYS--
--FOR TEARS WOULD SHAME HIM BEFORE HIS CHIEF.

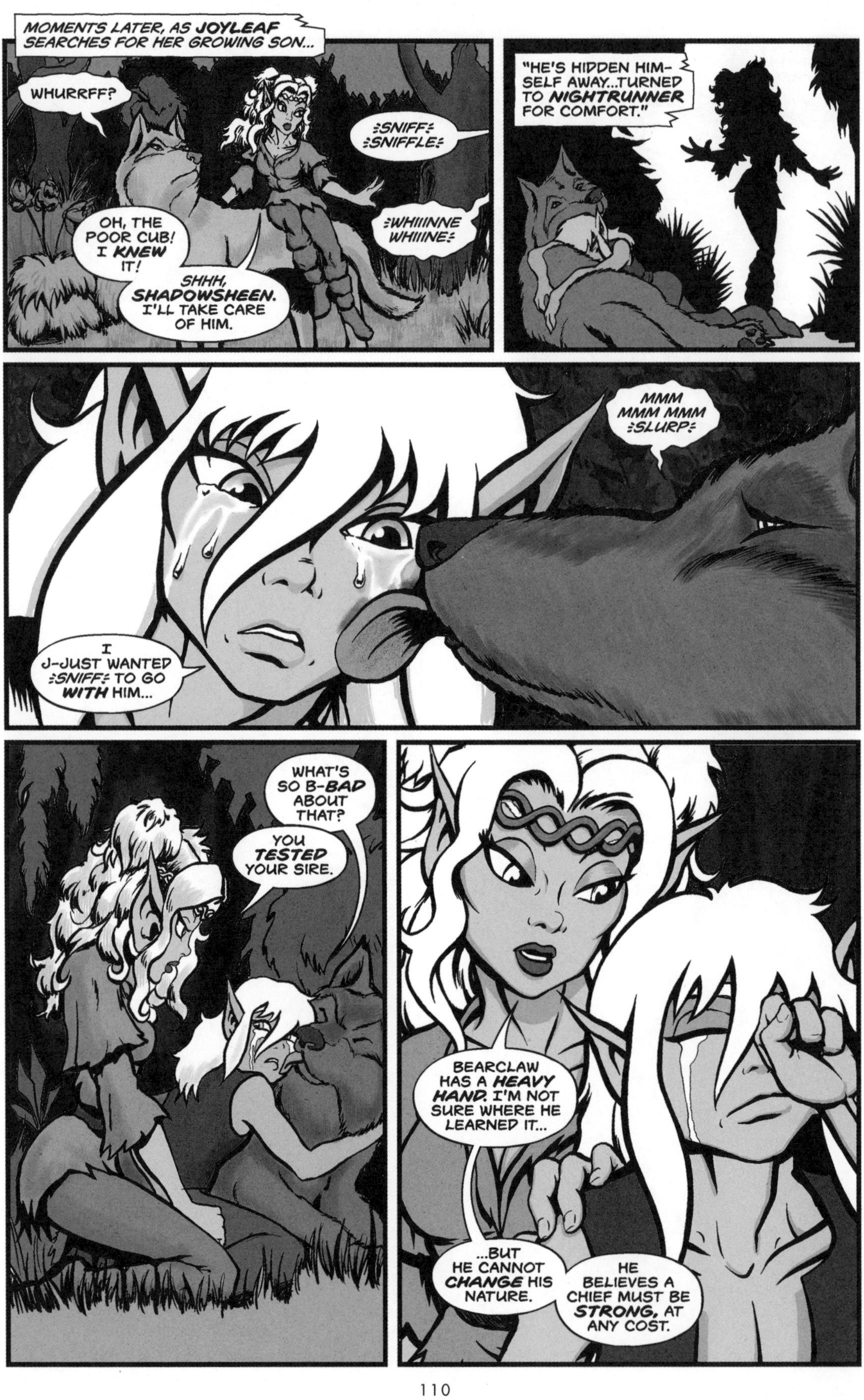
MOMENTS LATER, AS JOYLEAF SEARCHES FOR HER GROWING SON...
WHURRFF?
:SNIFF: :SNIFFLE:
OH, THE POOR CUB! I KNEW IT!
:WHIIINNE WHIIINE:
SHHH, SHADOWSHEEN. I'LL TAKE CARE OF HIM.
"HE'S HIDDEN HIMSELF AWAY...TURNED TO NIGHTRUNNER FOR COMFORT."
MMM MMM MMM :SLURP:
I J-JUST WANTED :SNIFF: TO GO WITH HIM...
WHAT'S SO B-BAD ABOUT THAT?
YOU TESTED YOUR SIRE.
BEARCLAW HAS A HEAVY HAND. I'M NOT SURE WHERE HE LEARNED IT...
...BUT HE CANNOT CHANGE HIS NATURE.
HE BELIEVES A CHIEF MUST BE STRONG, AT ANY COST.

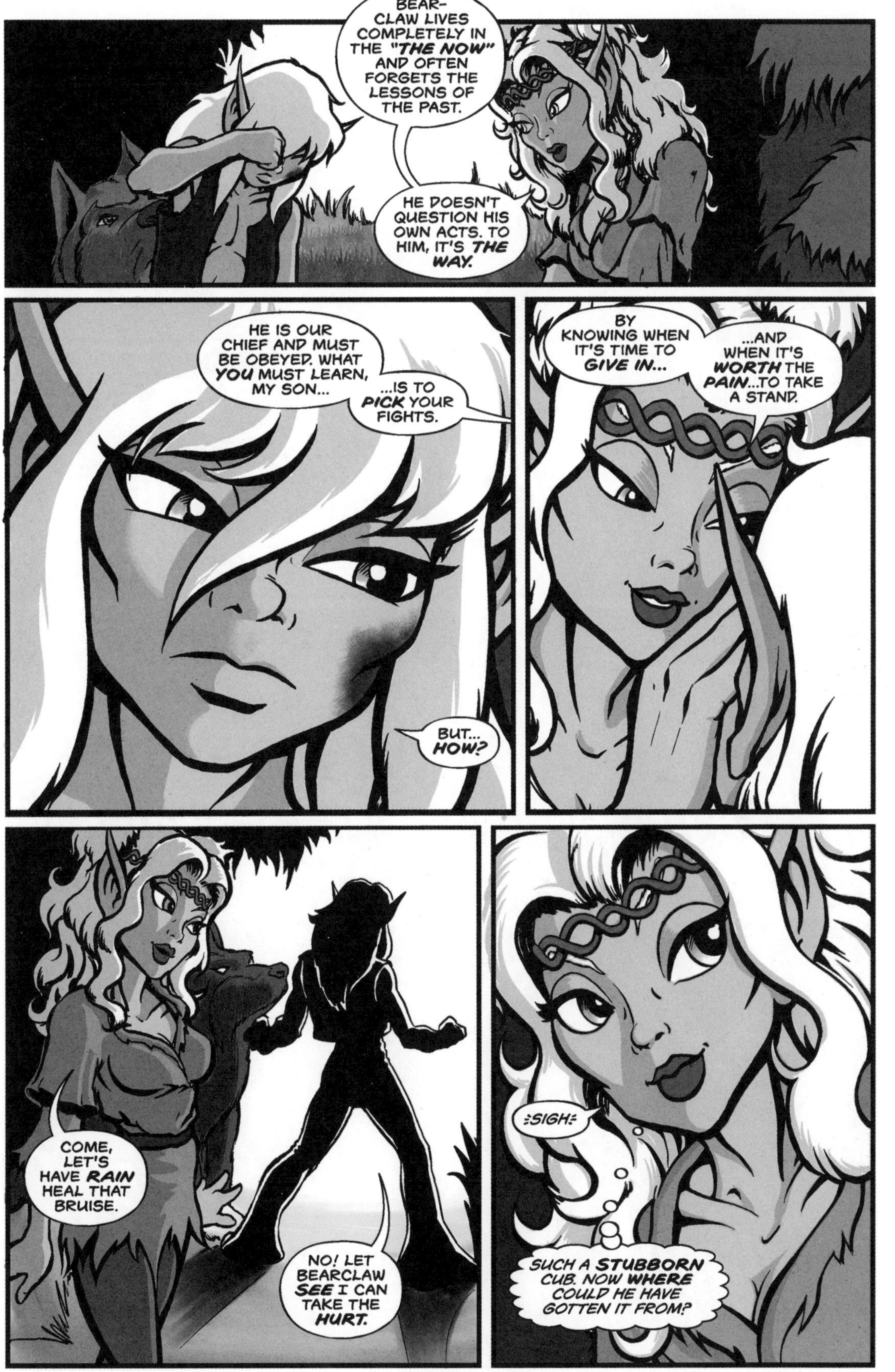
BEAR-CLAW LIVES COMPLETELY IN THE "THE NOW" AND OFTEN FORGETS THE LESSONS OF THE PAST.
HE DOESN'T QUESTION HIS OWN ACTS. TO HIM, IT'S THE WAY.
HE IS OUR CHIEF AND MUST BE OBEYED. WHAT YOU MUST LEARN, MY SON...
...IS TO PICK YOUR FIGHTS.
BUT... HOW?
BY KNOWING WHEN IT'S TIME TO GIVE IN...
...AND WHEN IT'S WORTH THE PAIN...TO TAKE A STAND.
COME, LET'S HAVE RAIN HEAL THAT BRUISE.
NO! LET BEARCLAW SEE I CAN TAKE THE HURT.
:SIGH:
SUCH A STUBBORN CUB. NOW WHERE COULD HE HAVE GOTTEN IT FROM?

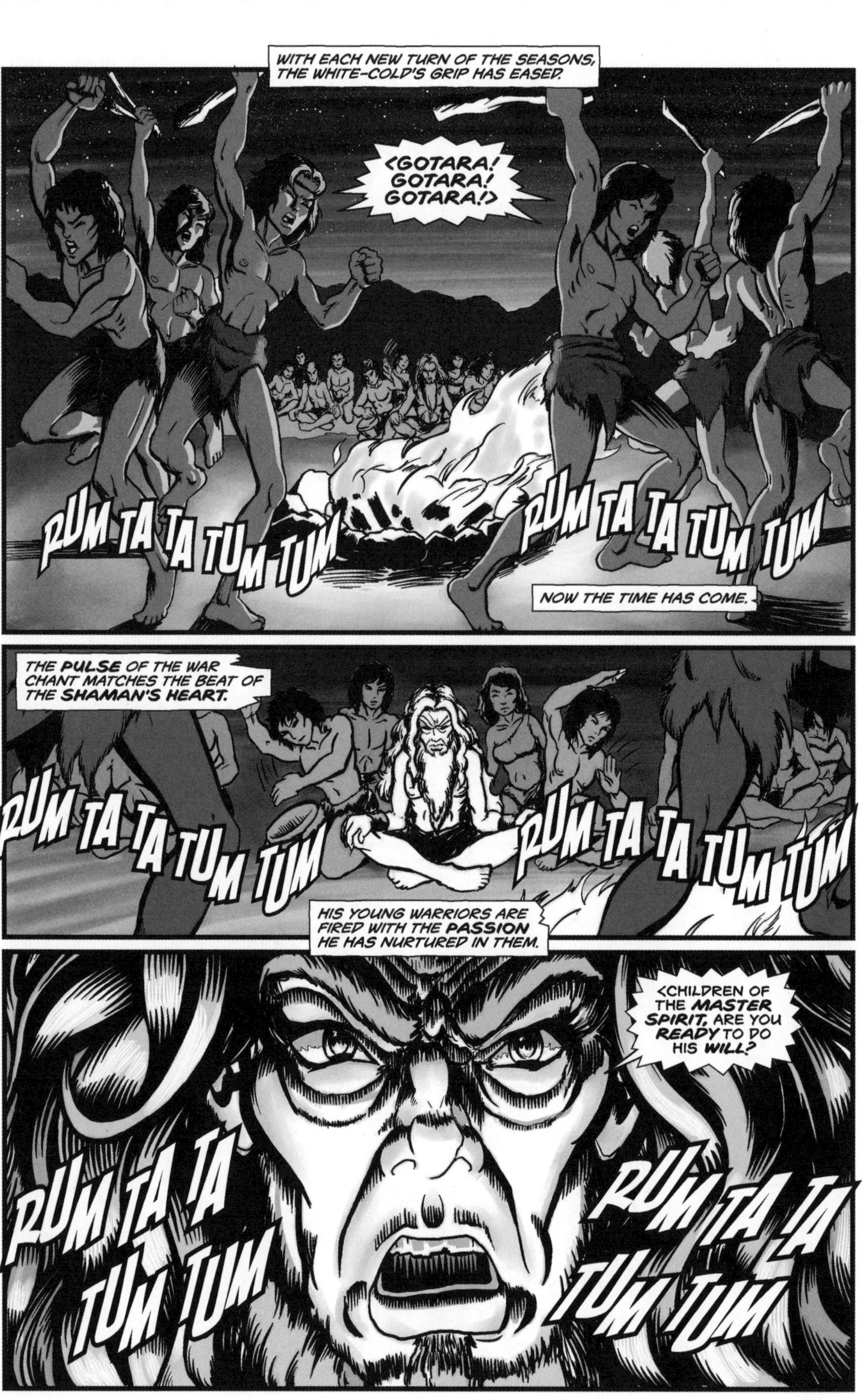
WITH EACH NEW TURN OF THE SEASONS, THE WHITE-COLD'S GRIP HAS EASED.
<GOTARA! GOTARA! GOTARA!>
RUM TA TA TUM TUM
RUM TA TA TUM TUM
NOW THE TIME HAS COME.
THE **PULSE** OF THE WAR CHANT MATCHES THE BEAT OF THE **SHAMAN'S HEART.**
RUM TA TA TUM TUM
RUM TA TA TUM TUM
HIS YOUNG WARRIORS ARE FIRED WITH THE **PASSION** HE HAS NURTURED IN THEM.
<CHILDREN OF THE **MASTER SPIRIT,** ARE YOU **READY** TO DO HIS **WILL?**
RUM TA TA TUM TUM
RUM TA TA TUM TUM

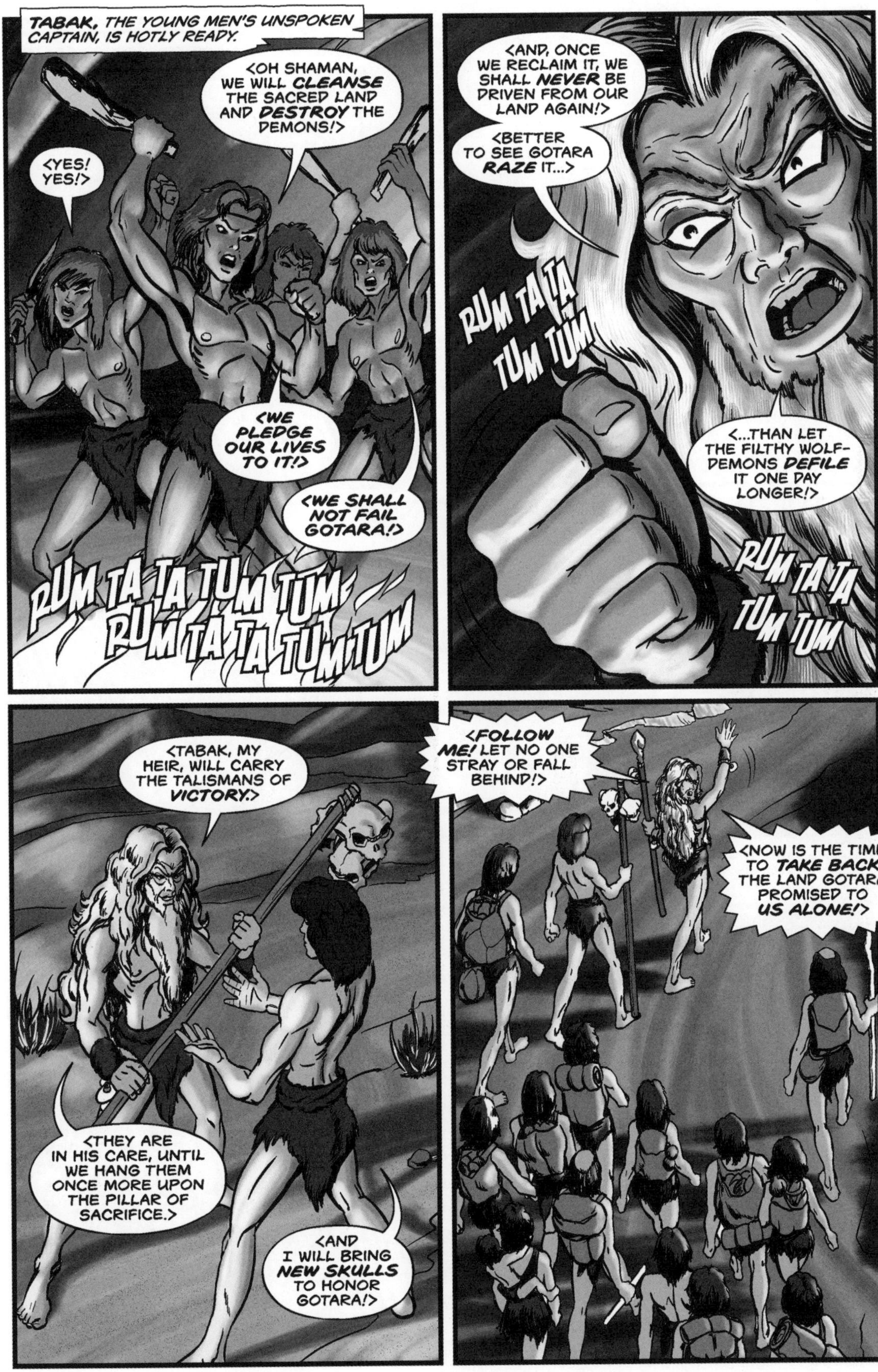
TABAK, THE YOUNG MEN'S UNSPOKEN CAPTAIN, IS HOTLY READY.
<OH SHAMAN, WE WILL CLEANSE THE SACRED LAND AND DESTROY THE DEMONS!>
<YES! YES!>
<WE PLEDGE OUR LIVES TO IT!>
<WE SHALL NOT FAIL GOTARA!>
RUM TA TA TUM TUM
RUM TA TA TUM TUM
<AND, ONCE WE RECLAIM IT, WE SHALL NEVER BE DRIVEN FROM OUR LAND AGAIN!>
<BETTER TO SEE GOTARA RAZE IT...>
RUM TA TA TUM TUM
<...THAN LET THE FILTHY WOLF-DEMONS DEFILE IT ONE DAY LONGER!>
RUM TA TA TUM TUM
<TABAK, MY HEIR, WILL CARRY THE TALISMANS OF VICTORY.>
<THEY ARE IN HIS CARE, UNTIL WE HANG THEM ONCE MORE UPON THE PILLAR OF SACRIFICE.>
<AND I WILL BRING NEW SKULLS TO HONOR GOTARA!>
<FOLLOW ME! LET NO ONE STRAY OR FALL BEHIND!>
<NOW IS THE TIME TO TAKE BACK THE LAND GOTARA PROMISED TO US ALONE!>

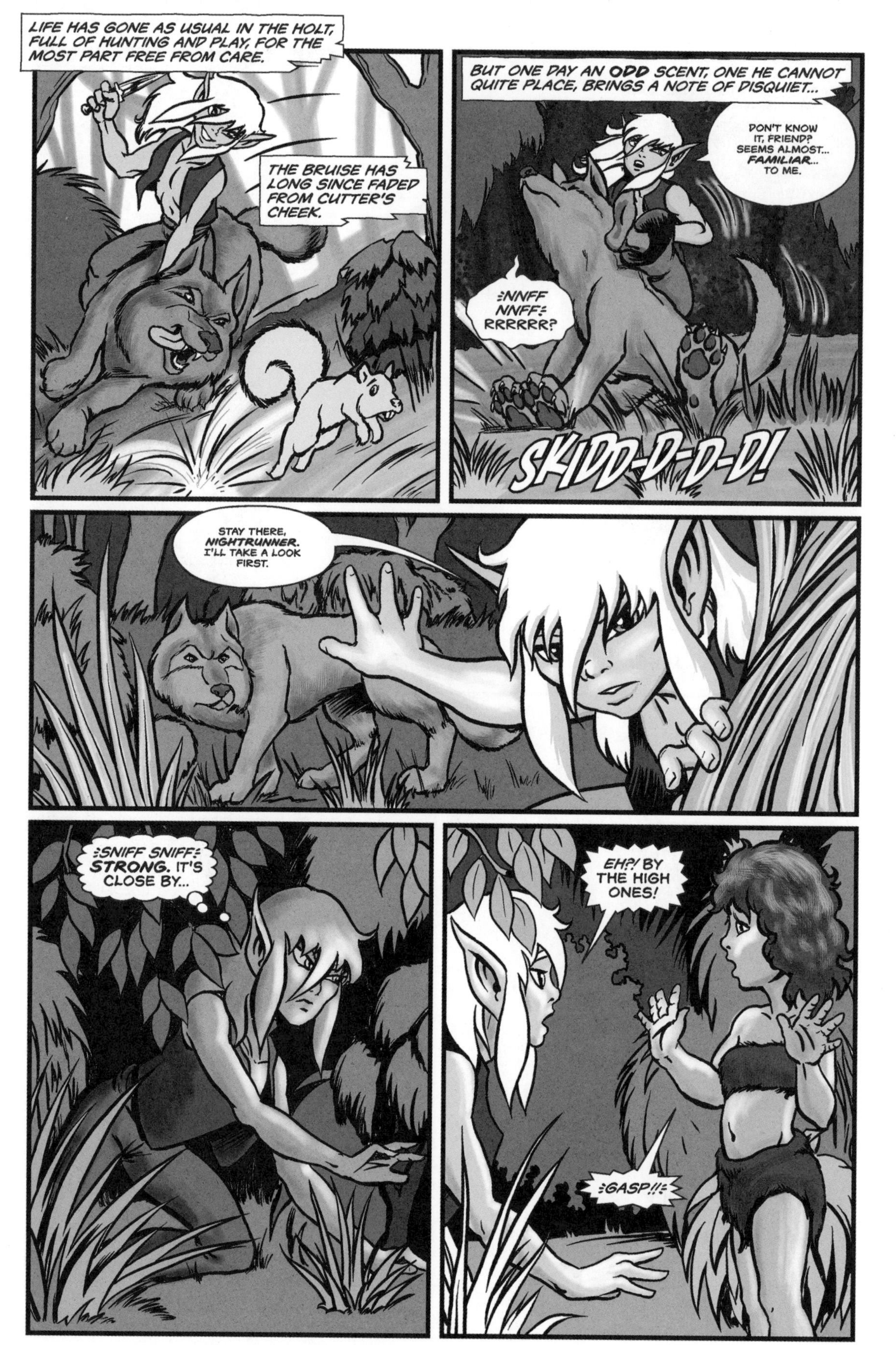

LIFE HAS GONE AS USUAL IN THE HOLT, FULL OF HUNTING AND PLAY, FOR THE MOST PART FREE FROM CARE.
THE BRUISE HAS LONG SINCE FADED FROM CUTTER'S CHEEK.
BUT ONE DAY AN ODD SCENT, ONE HE CANNOT QUITE PLACE, BRINGS A NOTE OF DISQUIET...
DON'T KNOW IT, FRIEND? SEEMS ALMOST... FAMILIAR... TO ME.
NNFF NNFF RRRRRR?
SKIDD-D-D-D!
STAY THERE, NIGHTRUNNER. I'LL TAKE A LOOK FIRST.
SNIFF SNIFF STRONG. IT'S CLOSE BY...
EH?! BY THE HIGH ONES!
GASP!!

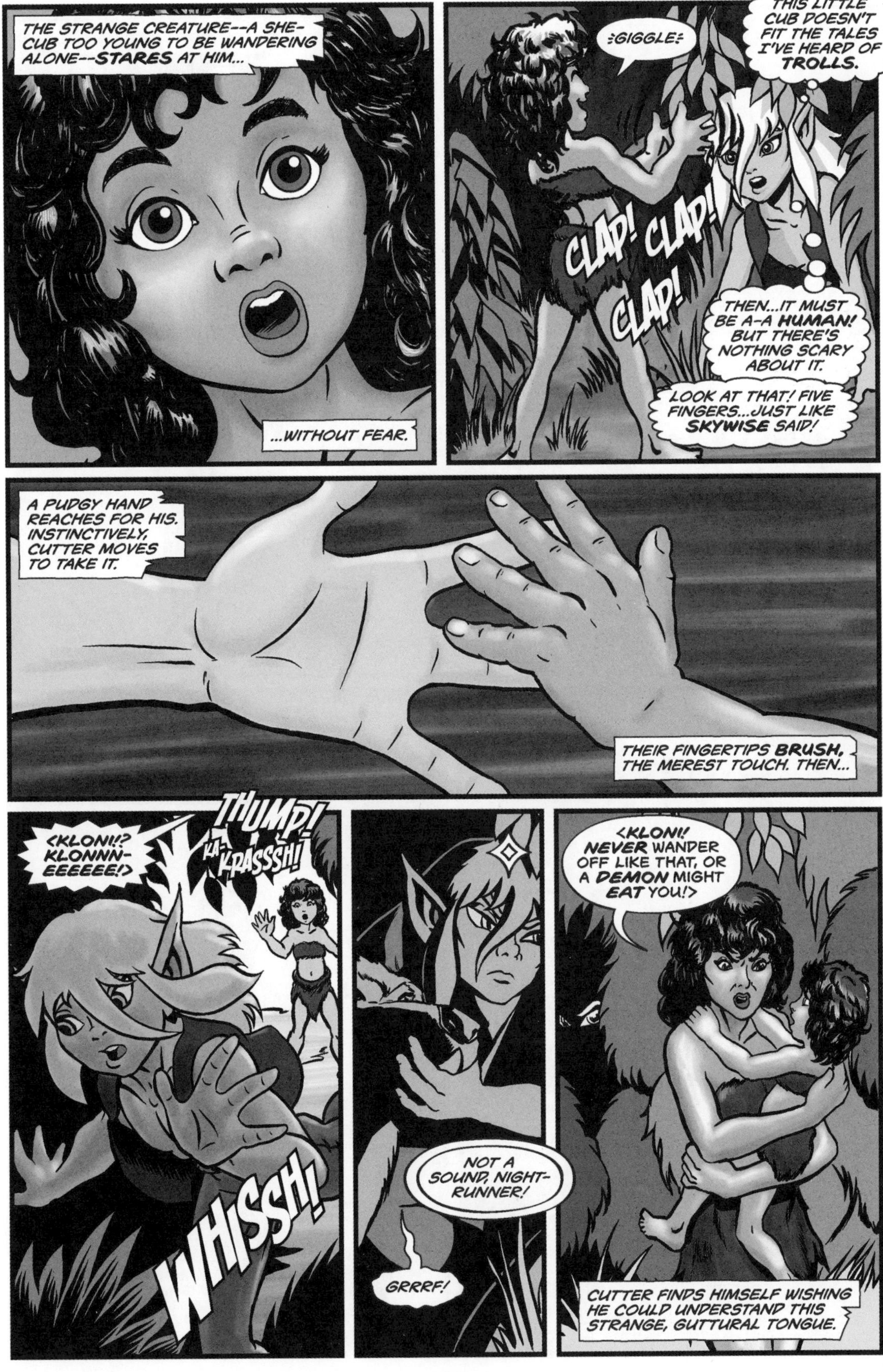
THE STRANGE CREATURE--A SHE-CUB TOO YOUNG TO BE WANDERING ALONE--STARES AT HIM...
...WITHOUT FEAR.
:GIGGLE:
THIS LITTLE CUB DOESN'T FIT THE TALES I'VE HEARD OF TROLLS.
CLAP! CLAP! CLAP!
THEN...IT MUST BE A-A HUMAN! BUT THERE'S NOTHING SCARY ABOUT IT.
LOOK AT THAT! FIVE FINGERS...JUST LIKE SKYWISE SAID!
A PUDGY HAND REACHES FOR HIS. INSTINCTIVELY, CUTTER MOVES TO TAKE IT.
THEIR FINGERTIPS BRUSH, THE MEREST TOUCH. THEN...
<KLONI!? KLONNN-EEEEEE!>
THUMP!
KA-KRASSSH!
WHISSH!
NOT A SOUND, NIGHT-RUNNER!
GRRRF!
<KLONI! NEVER WANDER OFF LIKE THAT, OR A DEMON MIGHT EAT YOU!>
CUTTER FINDS HIMSELF WISHING HE COULD UNDERSTAND THIS STRANGE, GUTTURAL TONGUE.

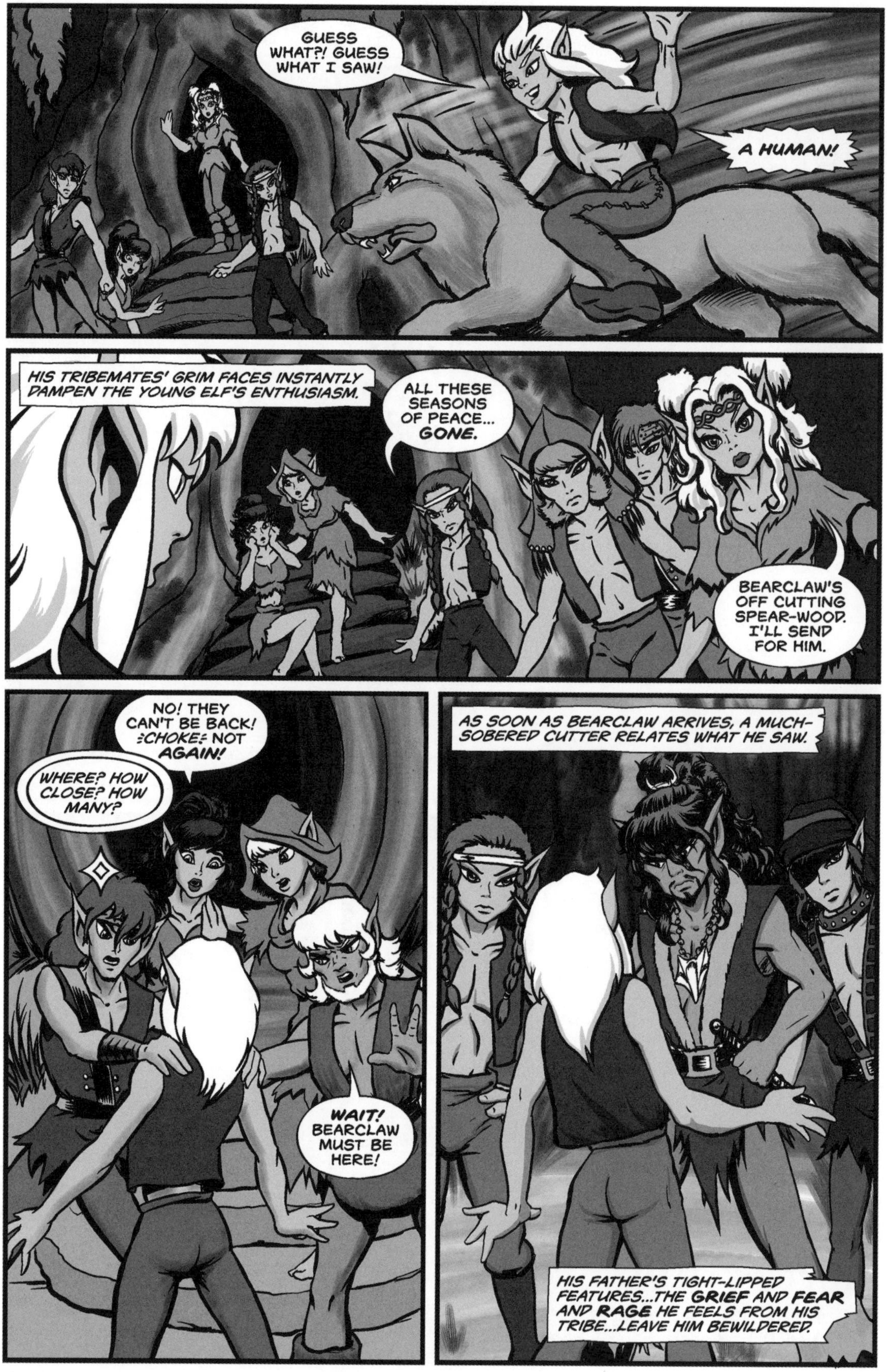
GUESS WHAT?! GUESS WHAT I SAW!
A HUMAN!
HIS TRIBEMATES' GRIM FACES INSTANTLY DAMPEN THE YOUNG ELF'S ENTHUSIASM.
ALL THESE SEASONS OF PEACE... GONE.
BEARCLAW'S OFF CUTTING SPEAR-WOOD. I'LL SEND FOR HIM.
NO! THEY CAN'T BE BACK! :CHOKE: NOT AGAIN!
WHERE? HOW CLOSE? HOW MANY?
WAIT! BEARCLAW MUST BE HERE!
AS SOON AS BEARCLAW ARRIVES, A MUCH-SOBERED CUTTER RELATES WHAT HE SAW.
HIS FATHER'S TIGHT-LIPPED FEATURES...THE GRIEF AND FEAR AND RAGE HE FEELS FROM HIS TRIBE...LEAVE HIM BEWILDERED.

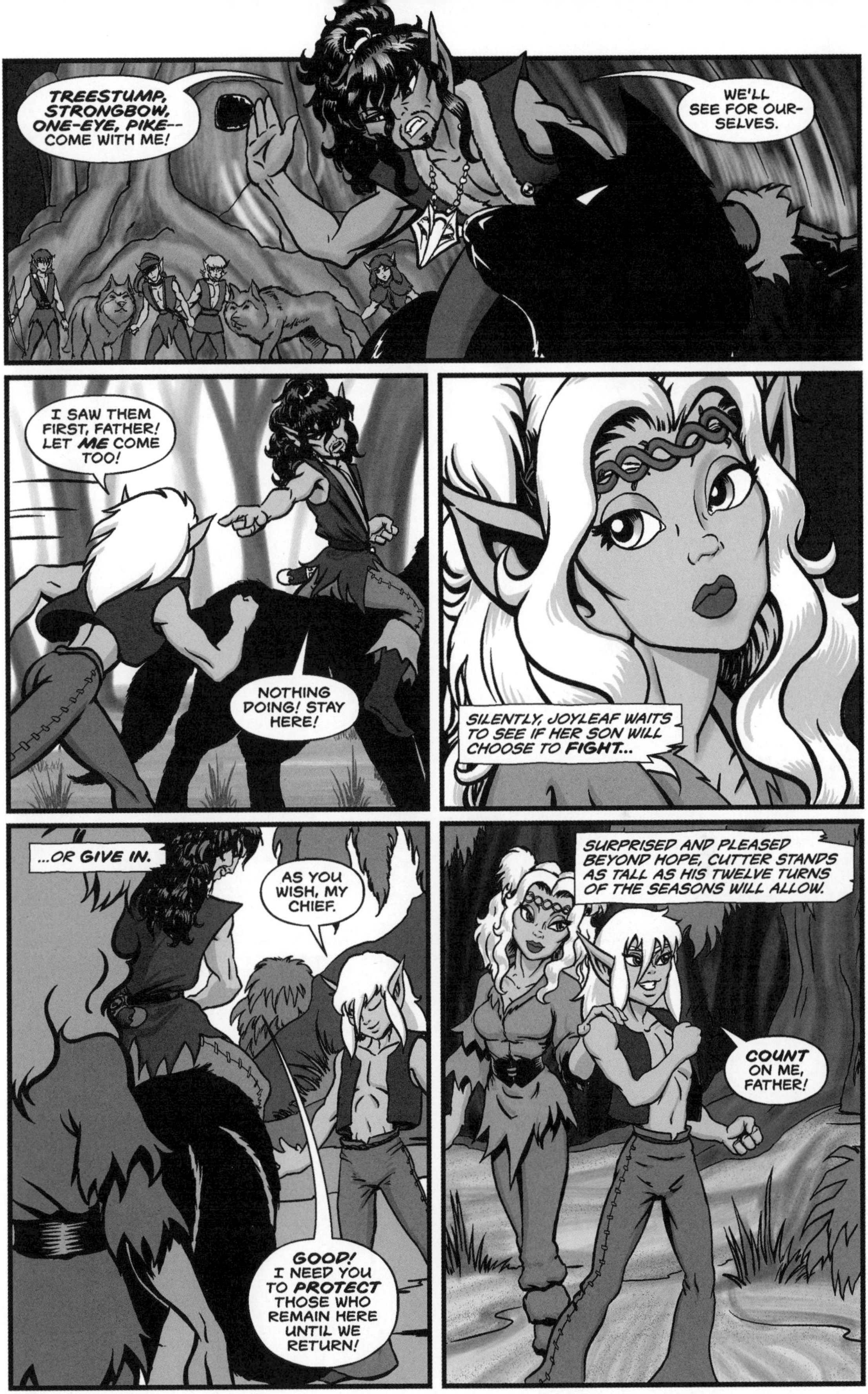
TREESTUMP, STRONGBOW, ONE-EYE, PIKE-- COME WITH ME!
WE'LL SEE FOR OUR-SELVES.
I SAW THEM FIRST, FATHER! LET ME COME TOO!
NOTHING DOING! STAY HERE!
SILENTLY, JOYLEAF WAITS TO SEE IF HER SON WILL CHOOSE TO FIGHT...
...OR GIVE IN.
AS YOU WISH, MY CHIEF.
GOOD! I NEED YOU TO PROTECT THOSE WHO REMAIN HERE UNTIL WE RETURN!
SURPRISED AND PLEASED BEYOND HOPE, CUTTER STANDS AS TALL AS HIS TWELVE TURNS OF THE SEASONS WILL ALLOW.
COUNT ON ME, FATHER!

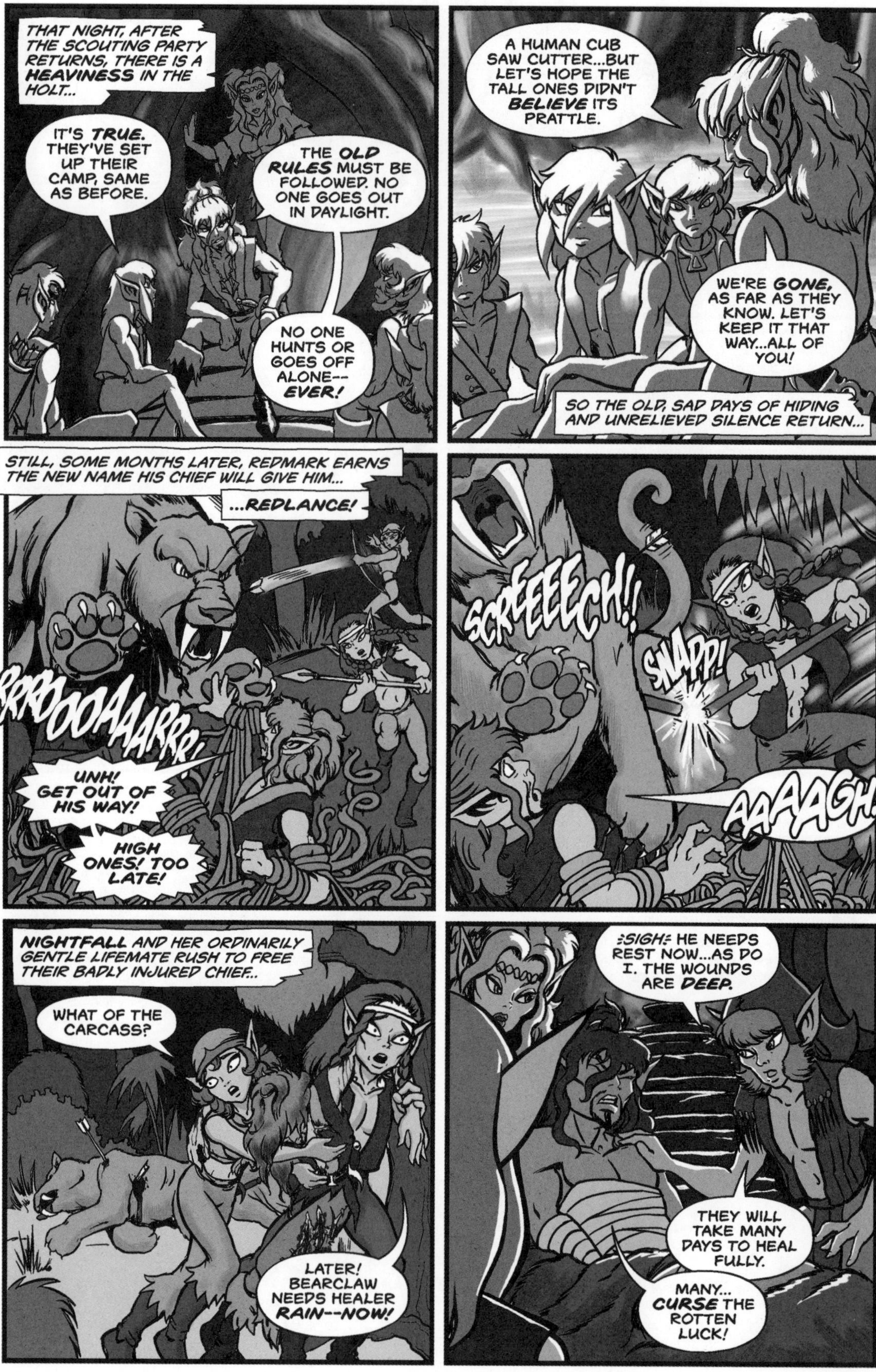
THAT NIGHT, AFTER THE SCOUTING PARTY RETURNS, THERE IS A HEAVINESS IN THE HOLT...
IT'S TRUE. THEY'VE SET UP THEIR CAMP, SAME AS BEFORE.
THE OLD RULES MUST BE FOLLOWED. NO ONE GOES OUT IN DAYLIGHT.
NO ONE HUNTS OR GOES OFF ALONE-- EVER!
A HUMAN CUB SAW CUTTER...BUT LET'S HOPE THE TALL ONES DIDN'T BELIEVE ITS PRATTLE.
WE'RE GONE, AS FAR AS THEY KNOW. LET'S KEEP IT THAT WAY...ALL OF YOU!
SO THE OLD, SAD DAYS OF HIDING AND UNRELIEVED SILENCE RETURN...
STILL, SOME MONTHS LATER, REDMARK EARNS THE NEW NAME HIS CHIEF WILL GIVE HIM...
...REDLANCE!
RRROOOAAARRR!
UNH! GET OUT OF HIS WAY!
HIGH ONES! TOO LATE!
SCREEEECH!!
SNAPP!
AAAAGH!!
NIGHTFALL AND HER ORDINARILY GENTLE LIFEMATE RUSH TO FREE THEIR BADLY INJURED CHIEF...
WHAT OF THE CARCASS?
LATER! BEARCLAW NEEDS HEALER RAIN--NOW!
:SIGH: HE NEEDS REST NOW...AS DO I. THE WOUNDS ARE DEEP.
THEY WILL TAKE MANY DAYS TO HEAL FULLY.
MANY... CURSE THE ROTTEN LUCK!

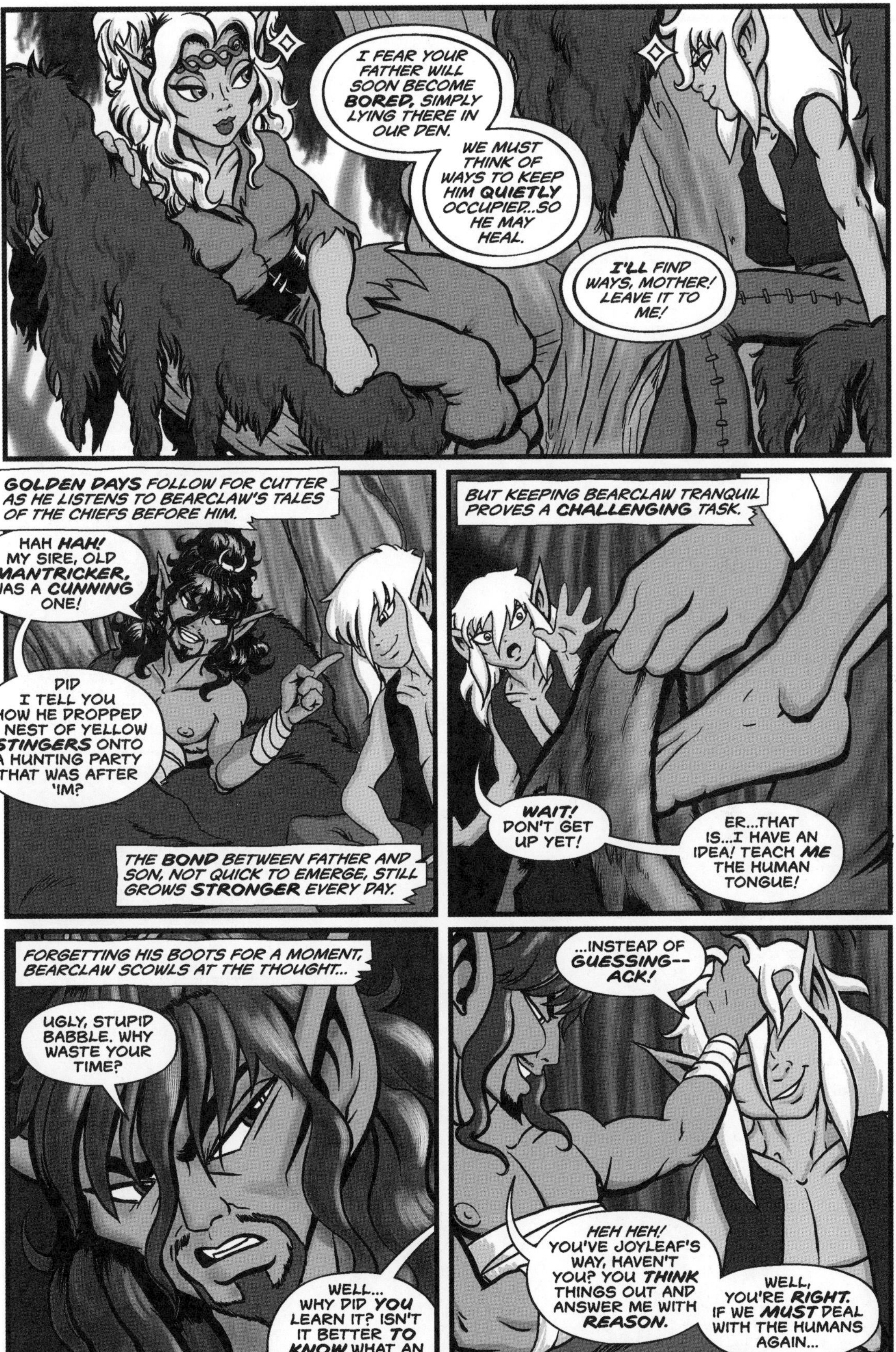
I FEAR YOUR FATHER WILL SOON BECOME BORED, SIMPLY LYING THERE IN OUR DEN.
WE MUST THINK OF WAYS TO KEEP HIM QUIETLY OCCUPIED...SO HE MAY HEAL.
I'LL FIND WAYS, MOTHER! LEAVE IT TO ME!
GOLDEN DAYS FOLLOW FOR CUTTER AS HE LISTENS TO BEARCLAW'S TALES OF THE CHIEFS BEFORE HIM.
HAH HAH! MY SIRE, OLD MANTRICKER, WAS A CUNNING ONE!
DID I TELL YOU HOW HE DROPPED A NEST OF YELLOW STINGERS ONTO A HUNTING PARTY THAT WAS AFTER 'IM?
THE BOND BETWEEN FATHER AND SON, NOT QUICK TO EMERGE, STILL GROWS STRONGER EVERY DAY.
BUT KEEPING BEARCLAW TRANQUIL PROVES A CHALLENGING TASK.
WAIT! DON'T GET UP YET!
ER...THAT IS...I HAVE AN IDEA! TEACH ME THE HUMAN TONGUE!
FORGETTING HIS BOOTS FOR A MOMENT, BEARCLAW SCOWLS AT THE THOUGHT...
UGLY, STUPID BABBLE. WHY WASTE YOUR TIME?
WELL... WHY DID YOU LEARN IT? ISN'T IT BETTER TO KNOW WHAT AN ENEMY'S SAYING?
...INSTEAD OF GUESSING-- ACK!
HEH HEH! YOU'VE JOYLEAF'S WAY, HAVEN'T YOU? YOU THINK THINGS OUT AND ANSWER ME WITH REASON.
WELL, YOU'RE RIGHT. IF WE MUST DEAL WITH THE HUMANS AGAIN...

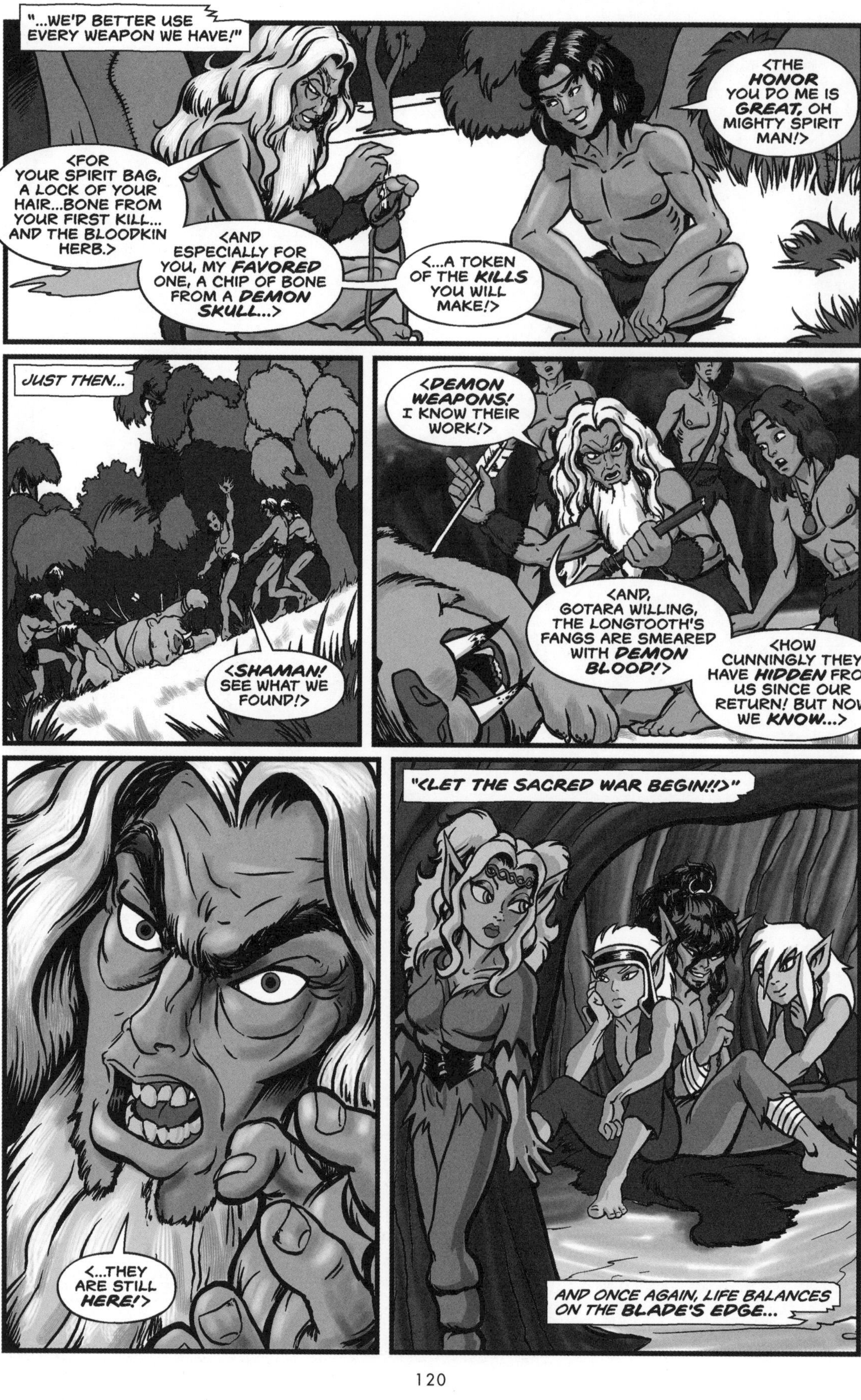
"...WE'D BETTER USE EVERY WEAPON WE HAVE!"
<FOR YOUR SPIRIT BAG, A LOCK OF YOUR HAIR...BONE FROM YOUR FIRST KILL... AND THE BLOODKIN HERB.>
<AND ESPECIALLY FOR YOU, MY FAVORED ONE, A CHIP OF BONE FROM A DEMON SKULL...>
<...A TOKEN OF THE KILLS YOU WILL MAKE!>
<THE HONOR YOU DO ME IS GREAT, OH MIGHTY SPIRIT MAN!>
JUST THEN...
<SHAMAN! SEE WHAT WE FOUND!>
<DEMON WEAPONS! I KNOW THEIR WORK!>
<AND, GOTARA WILLING, THE LONGTOOTH'S FANGS ARE SMEARED WITH DEMON BLOOD!>
<HOW CUNNINGLY THEY HAVE HIDDEN FROM US SINCE OUR RETURN! BUT NOW WE KNOW...>
<...THEY ARE STILL HERE!>
"<LET THE SACRED WAR BEGIN!!>"
AND ONCE AGAIN, LIFE BALANCES ON THE BLADE'S EDGE...

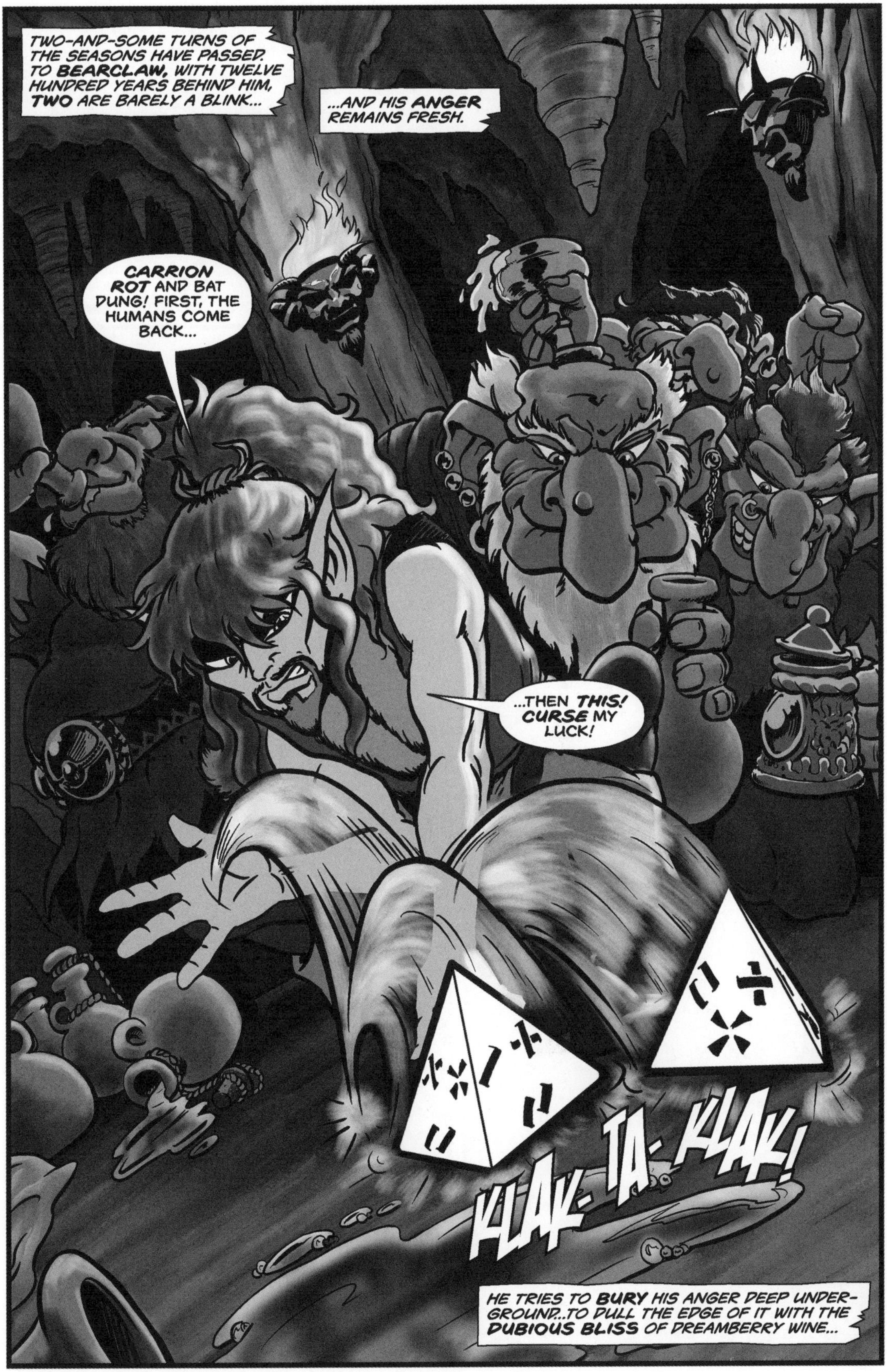
TWO-AND-SOME TURNS OF THE SEASONS HAVE PASSED. TO BEARCLAW, WITH TWELVE HUNDRED YEARS BEHIND HIM, TWO ARE BARELY A BLINK...
...AND HIS ANGER REMAINS FRESH.
CARRION ROT AND BAT DUNG! FIRST, THE HUMANS COME BACK...
...THEN THIS! CURSE MY LUCK!
KLAK-TA-KLAK!
HE TRIES TO BURY HIS ANGER DEEP UNDERGROUND...TO DULL THE EDGE OF IT WITH THE DUBIOUS BLISS OF DREAMBERRY WINE...

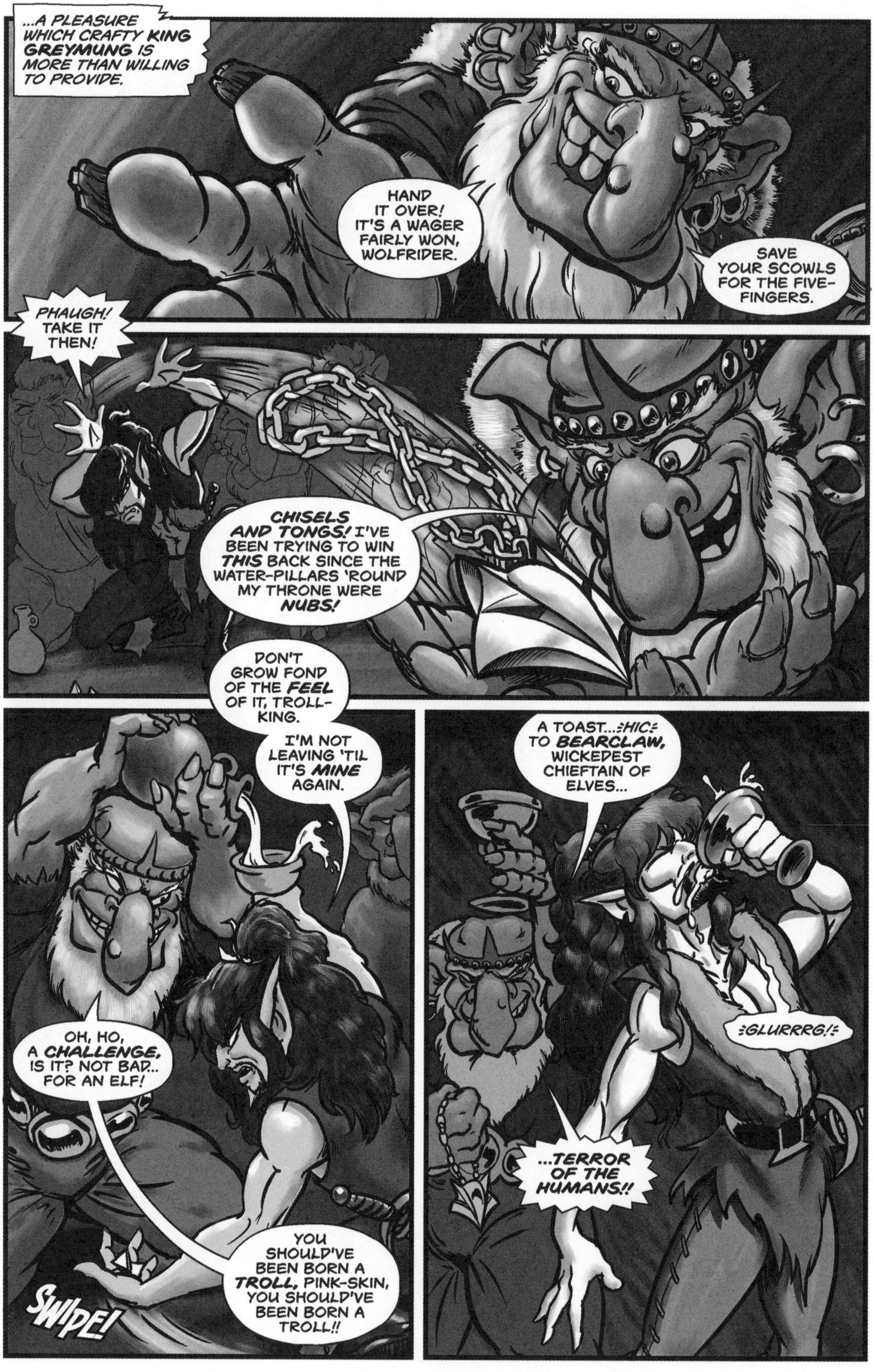
...A PLEASURE WHICH CRAFTY KING GREYMUNG IS MORE THAN WILLING TO PROVIDE.
HAND IT OVER! IT'S A WAGER FAIRLY WON, WOLFRIDER.
SAVE YOUR SCOWLS FOR THE FIVE-FINGERS.
PHAUGH! TAKE IT THEN!
CHISELS AND TONGS! I'VE BEEN TRYING TO WIN THIS BACK SINCE THE WATER-PILLARS 'ROUND MY THRONE WERE NUBS!
DON'T GROW FOND OF THE FEEL OF IT, TROLL-KING.
I'M NOT LEAVING 'TIL IT'S MINE AGAIN.
OH, HO, A CHALLENGE, IS IT? NOT BAD.. FOR AN ELF!
YOU SHOULD'VE BEEN BORN A TROLL, PINK-SKIN, YOU SHOULD'VE BEEN BORN A TROLL!!
SWIPE!
A TOAST... HIC TO BEARCLAW, WICKEDEST CHIEFTAIN OF ELVES...
GLURRRG!
...TERROR OF THE HUMANS!!

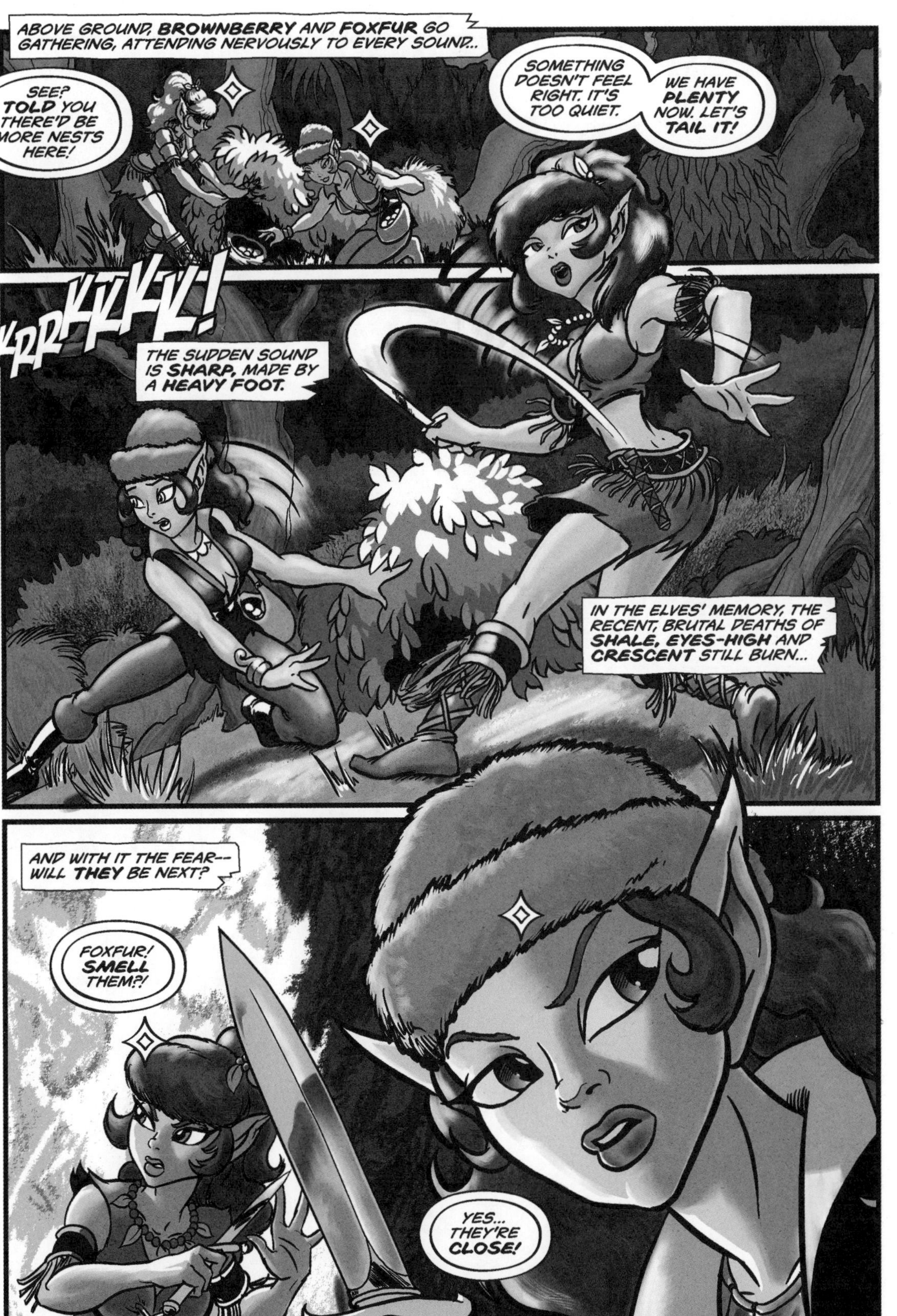
ABOVE GROUND, BROWNBERRY AND FOXFUR GO GATHERING, ATTENDING NERVOUSLY TO EVERY SOUND...
SEE? TOLD YOU THERE'D BE MORE NESTS HERE!
SOMETHING DOESN'T FEEL RIGHT. IT'S TOO QUIET.
WE HAVE PLENTY NOW. LET'S TAIL IT!
KRRKKKKK!
THE SUDDEN SOUND IS SHARP, MADE BY A HEAVY FOOT.
IN THE ELVES' MEMORY, THE RECENT, BRUTAL DEATHS OF SHALE, EYES-HIGH AND CRESCENT STILL BURN...
AND WITH IT THE FEAR-- WILL THEY BE NEXT?
FOXFUR! SMELL THEM?!
YES... THEY'RE CLOSE!

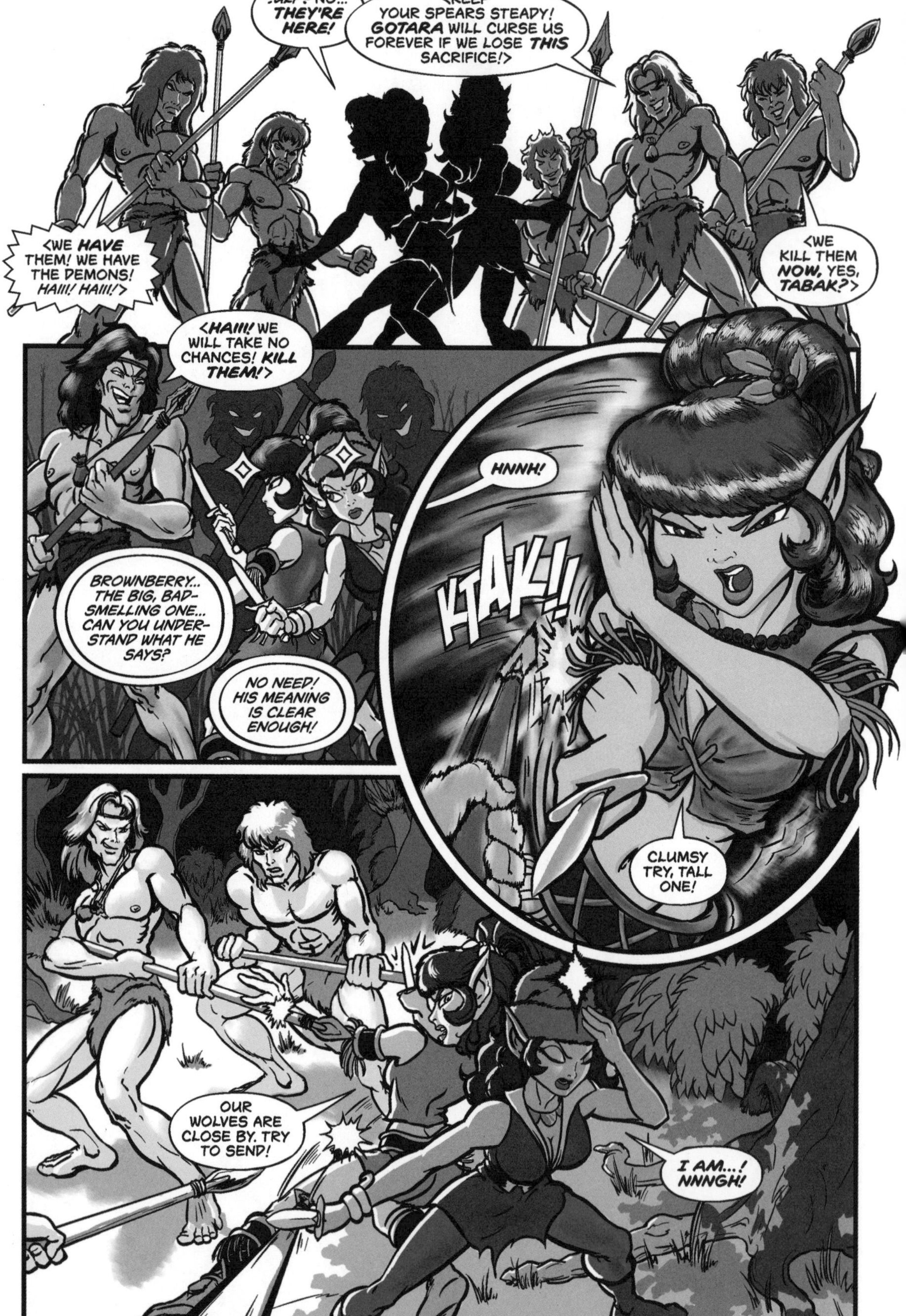
:ULP: NO... THEY'RE HERE!
<KEEP YOUR SPEARS STEADY! GOTARA WILL CURSE US FOREVER IF WE LOSE THIS SACRIFICE!>
<WE HAVE THEM! WE HAVE THE DEMONS! HAIII! HAIII!>
<WE KILL THEM NOW, YES, TABAK?>
<HAIII! WE WILL TAKE NO CHANCES! KILL THEM!>
BROWNBERRY... THE BIG, BAD-SMELLING ONE... CAN YOU UNDERSTAND WHAT HE SAYS?
NO NEED! HIS MEANING IS CLEAR ENOUGH!
HNNH!
KTAK!!!
CLUMSY TRY, TALL ONE!
OUR WOLVES ARE CLOSE BY. TRY TO SEND!
I AM...! NNNGH!

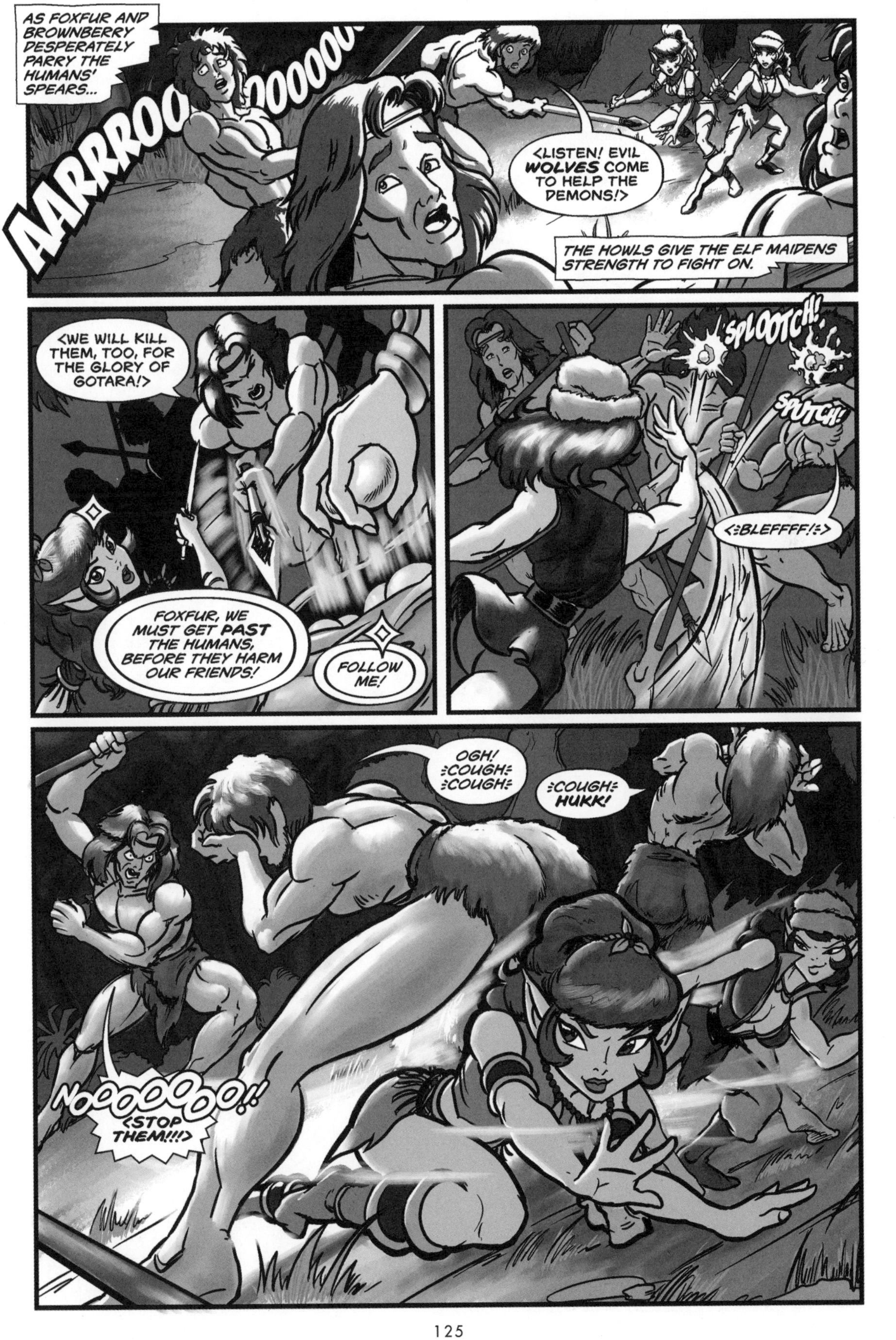

AS FOXFUR AND BROWNBERRY DESPERATELY PARRY THE HUMANS' SPEARS...
AARROOOOOOOOO
<LISTEN! EVIL WOLVES COME TO HELP THE DEMONS!>
THE HOWLS GIVE THE ELF MAIDENS STRENGTH TO FIGHT ON.
<WE WILL KILL THEM, TOO, FOR THE GLORY OF GOTARA!>
FOXFUR, WE MUST GET PAST THE HUMANS, BEFORE THEY HARM OUR FRIENDS!
FOLLOW ME!
SPLOOTCH!
SPUTCH!
<:BLEFFFF!:>
OGH! :COUGH: :COUGH:
:COUGH: HUKK!
NOOOOOOOO!! <STOP THEM!!!>

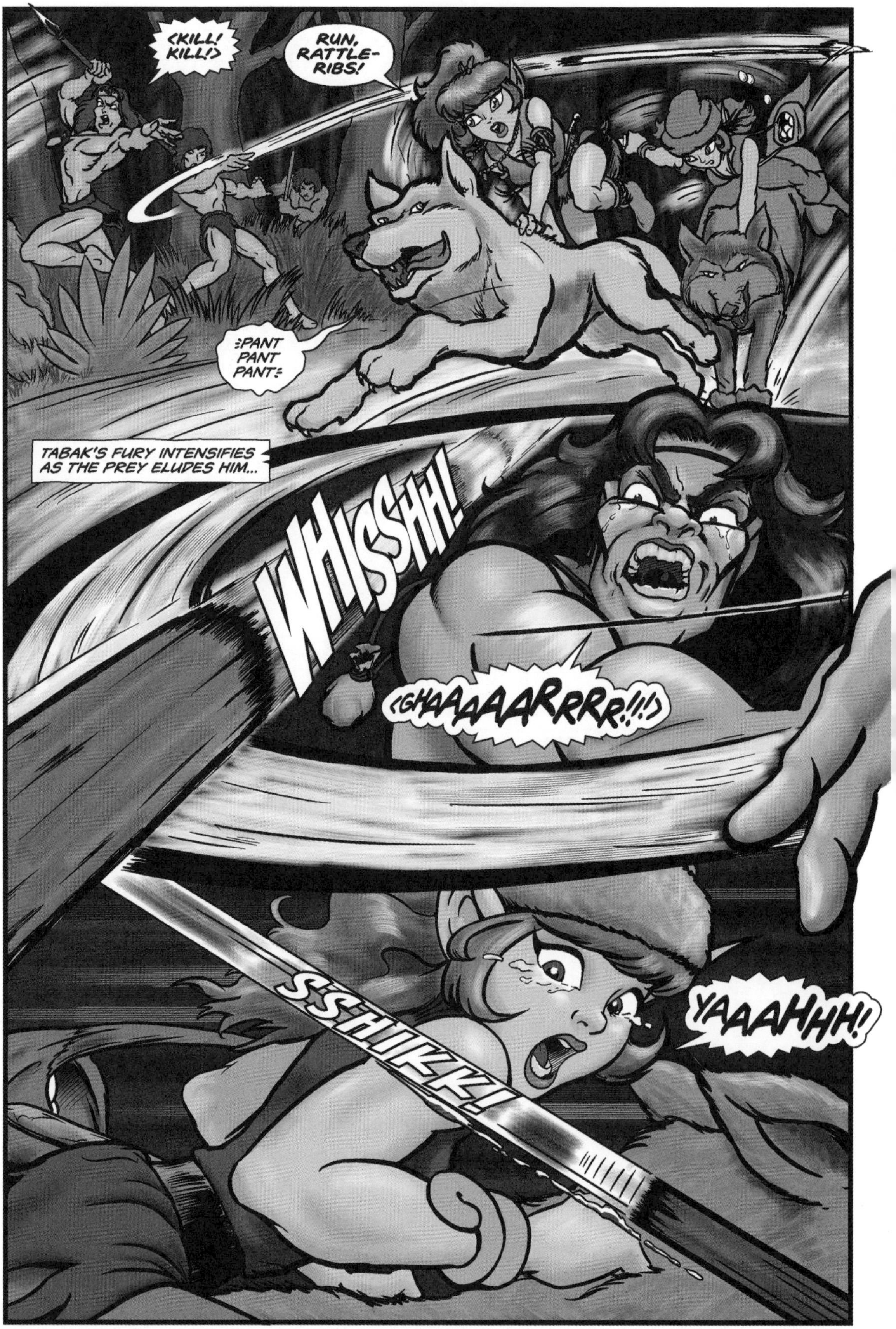

<KILL! KILL!>
RUN, RATTLE-RIBS!
:PANT PANT PANT:
TABAK'S FURY INTENSIFIES AS THE PREY ELUDES HIM...
WHISSHH!
<GHAAAAAARRRR!!!>
SSHIKK!
YAAAHHH!

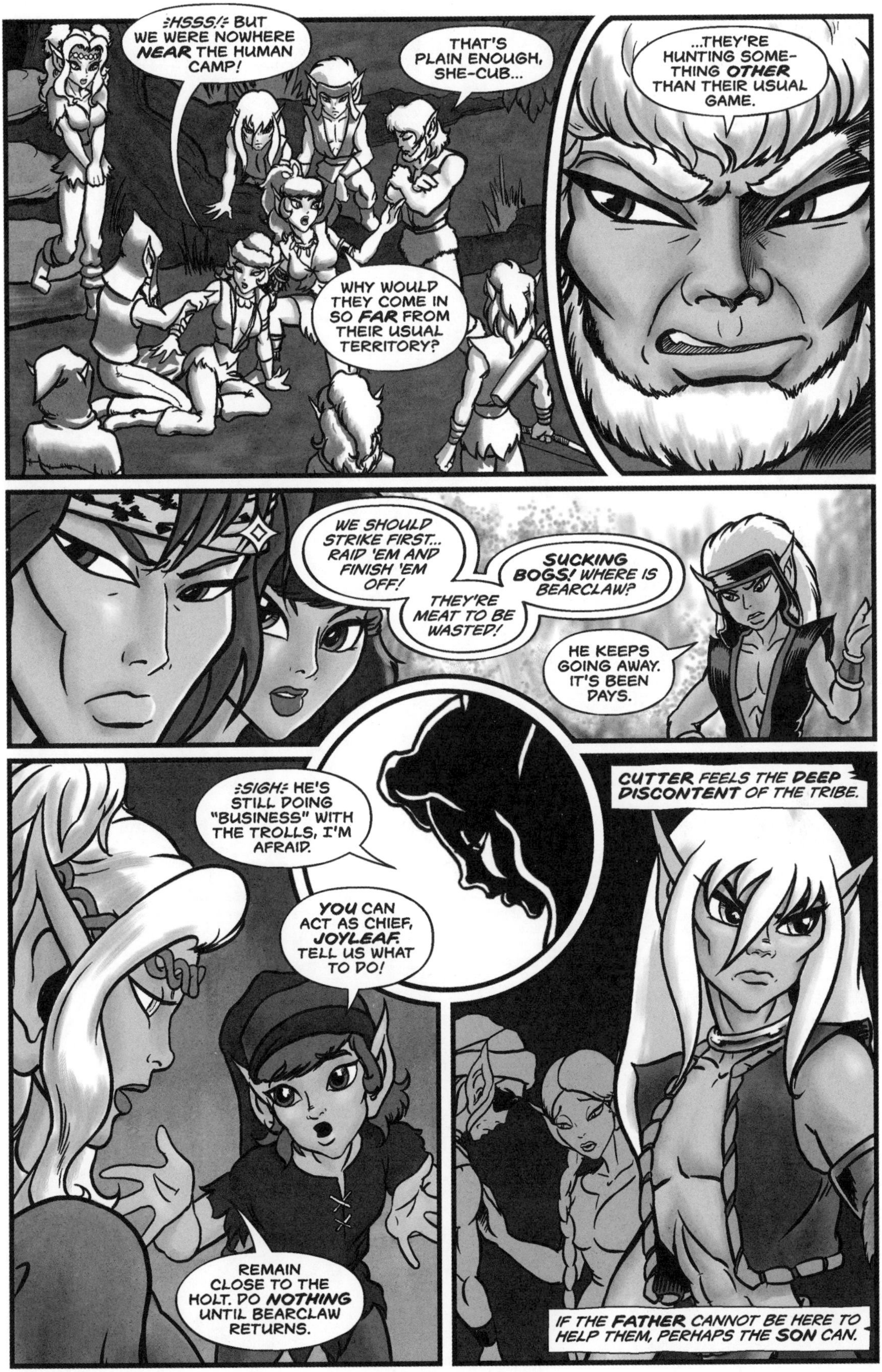
:HSSS!: BUT WE WERE NOWHERE NEAR THE HUMAN CAMP!
THAT'S PLAIN ENOUGH, SHE-CUB...
...THEY'RE HUNTING SOME-THING OTHER THAN THEIR USUAL GAME.
WHY WOULD THEY COME IN SO FAR FROM THEIR USUAL TERRITORY?
WE SHOULD STRIKE FIRST... RAID 'EM AND FINISH 'EM OFF!
THEY'RE MEAT TO BE WASTED!
SUCKING BOGS! WHERE IS BEARCLAW?
HE KEEPS GOING AWAY. IT'S BEEN DAYS.
:SIGH: HE'S STILL DOING "BUSINESS" WITH THE TROLLS, I'M AFRAID.
YOU CAN ACT AS CHIEF, JOYLEAF. TELL US WHAT TO DO!
REMAIN CLOSE TO THE HOLT. DO NOTHING UNTIL BEARCLAW RETURNS.
CUTTER FEELS THE DEEP DISCONTENT OF THE TRIBE.
IF THE FATHER CANNOT BE HERE TO HELP THEM, PERHAPS THE SON CAN.

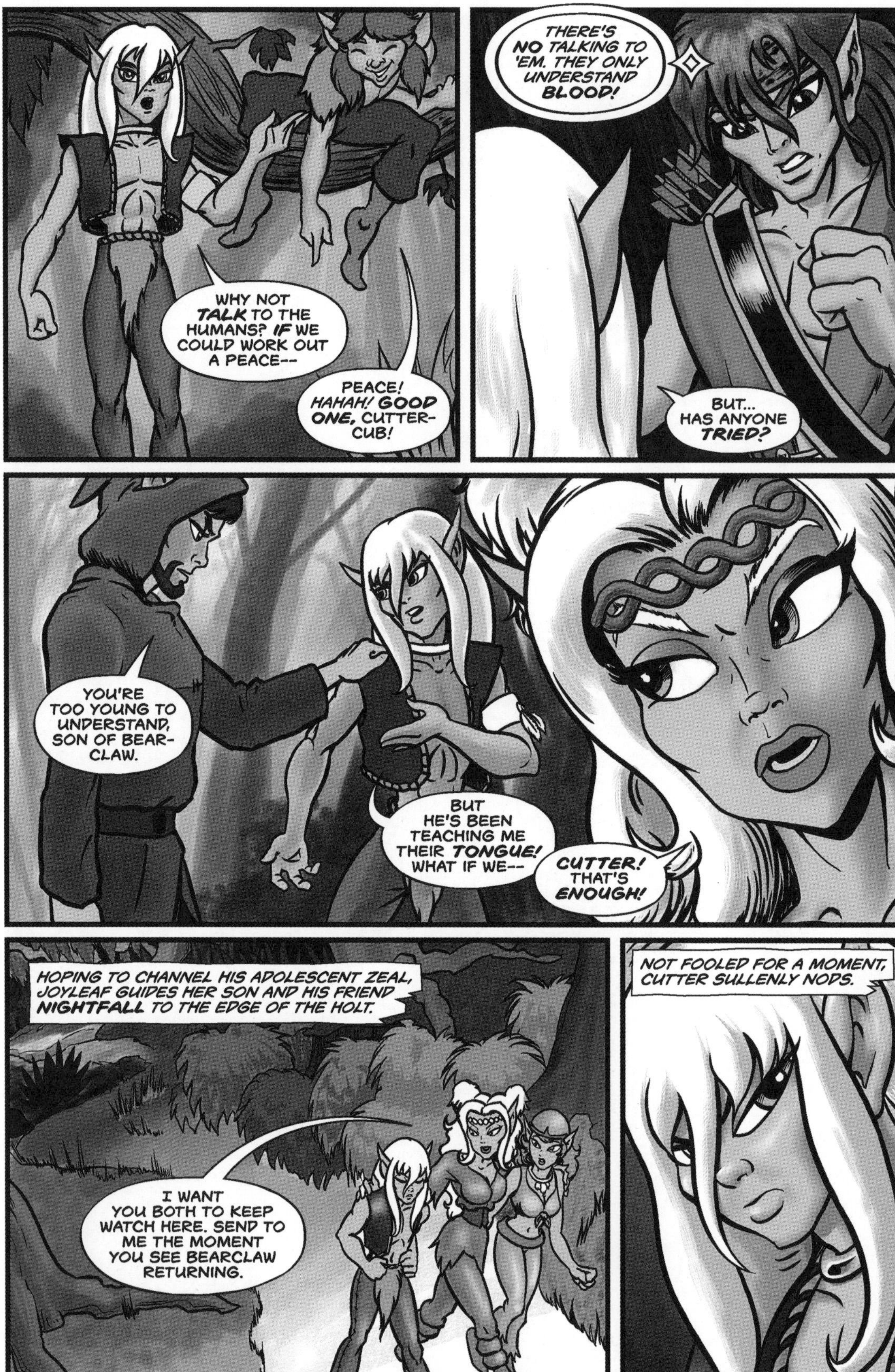
WHY NOT TALK TO THE HUMANS? IF WE COULD WORK OUT A PEACE--
PEACE! HAHAH! GOOD ONE, CUTTER-CUB!
THERE'S NO TALKING TO 'EM. THEY ONLY UNDERSTAND BLOOD!
BUT... HAS ANYONE TRIED?
YOU'RE TOO YOUNG TO UNDERSTAND, SON OF BEAR-CLAW.
BUT HE'S BEEN TEACHING ME THEIR TONGUE! WHAT IF WE--
CUTTER! THAT'S ENOUGH!
HOPING TO CHANNEL HIS ADOLESCENT ZEAL, JOYLEAF GUIDES HER SON AND HIS FRIEND NIGHTFALL TO THE EDGE OF THE HOLT.
I WANT YOU BOTH TO KEEP WATCH HERE. SEND TO ME THE MOMENT YOU SEE BEARCLAW RETURNING.
NOT FOOLED FOR A MOMENT, CUTTER SULLENLY NODS.

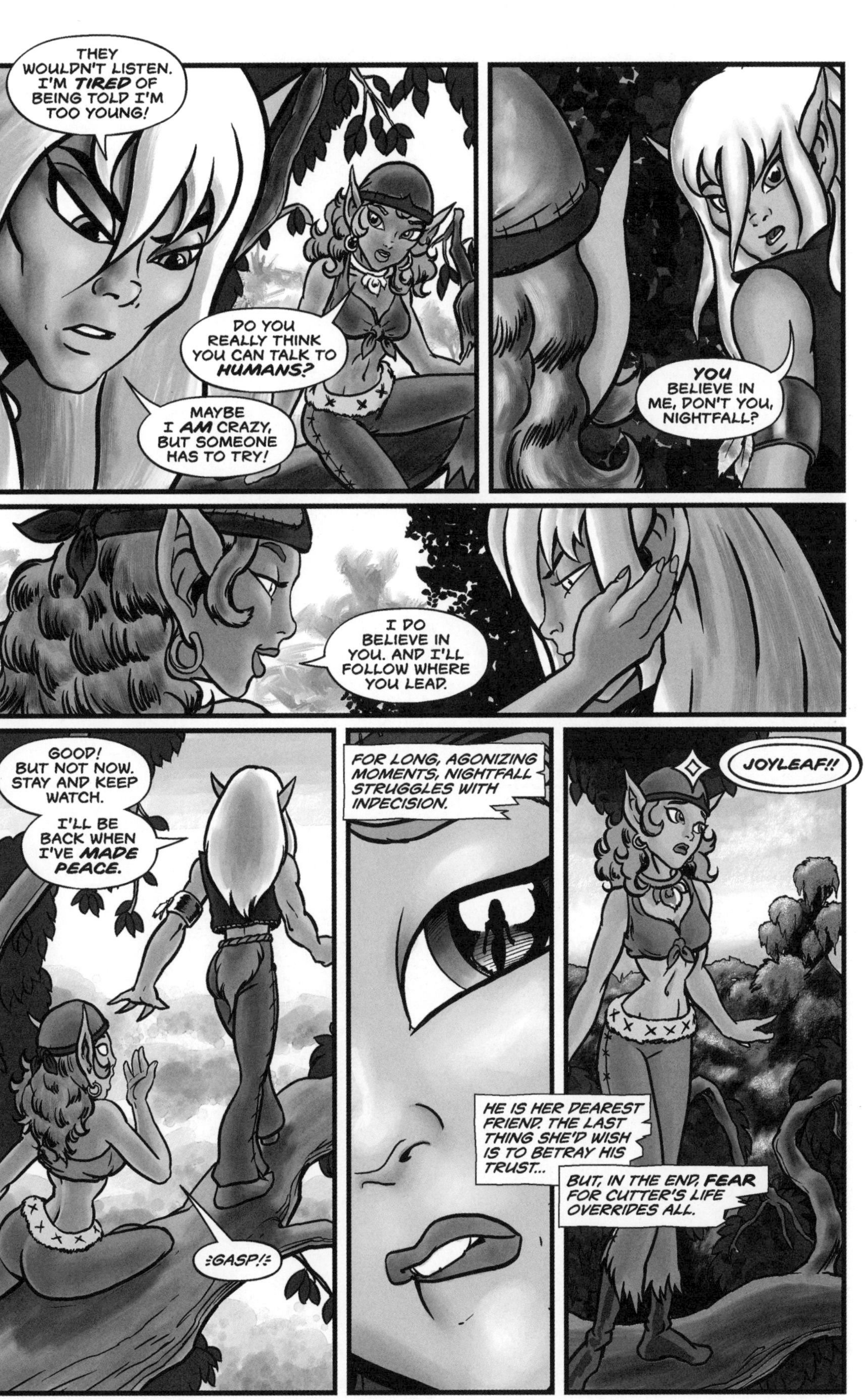
THEY WOULDN'T LISTEN. I'M TIRED OF BEING TOLD I'M TOO YOUNG!
DO YOU REALLY THINK YOU CAN TALK TO HUMANS?
MAYBE I AM CRAZY, BUT SOMEONE HAS TO TRY!
YOU BELIEVE IN ME, DON'T YOU, NIGHTFALL?
I DO BELIEVE IN YOU. AND I'LL FOLLOW WHERE YOU LEAD.
GOOD! BUT NOT NOW. STAY AND KEEP WATCH.
I'LL BE BACK WHEN I'VE MADE PEACE.
GASP!
FOR LONG, AGONIZING MOMENTS, NIGHTFALL STRUGGLES WITH INDECISION.
HE IS HER DEAREST FRIEND. THE LAST THING SHE'D WISH IS TO BETRAY HIS TRUST...
BUT, IN THE END, FEAR FOR CUTTER'S LIFE OVERRIDES ALL.
JOYLEAF!!

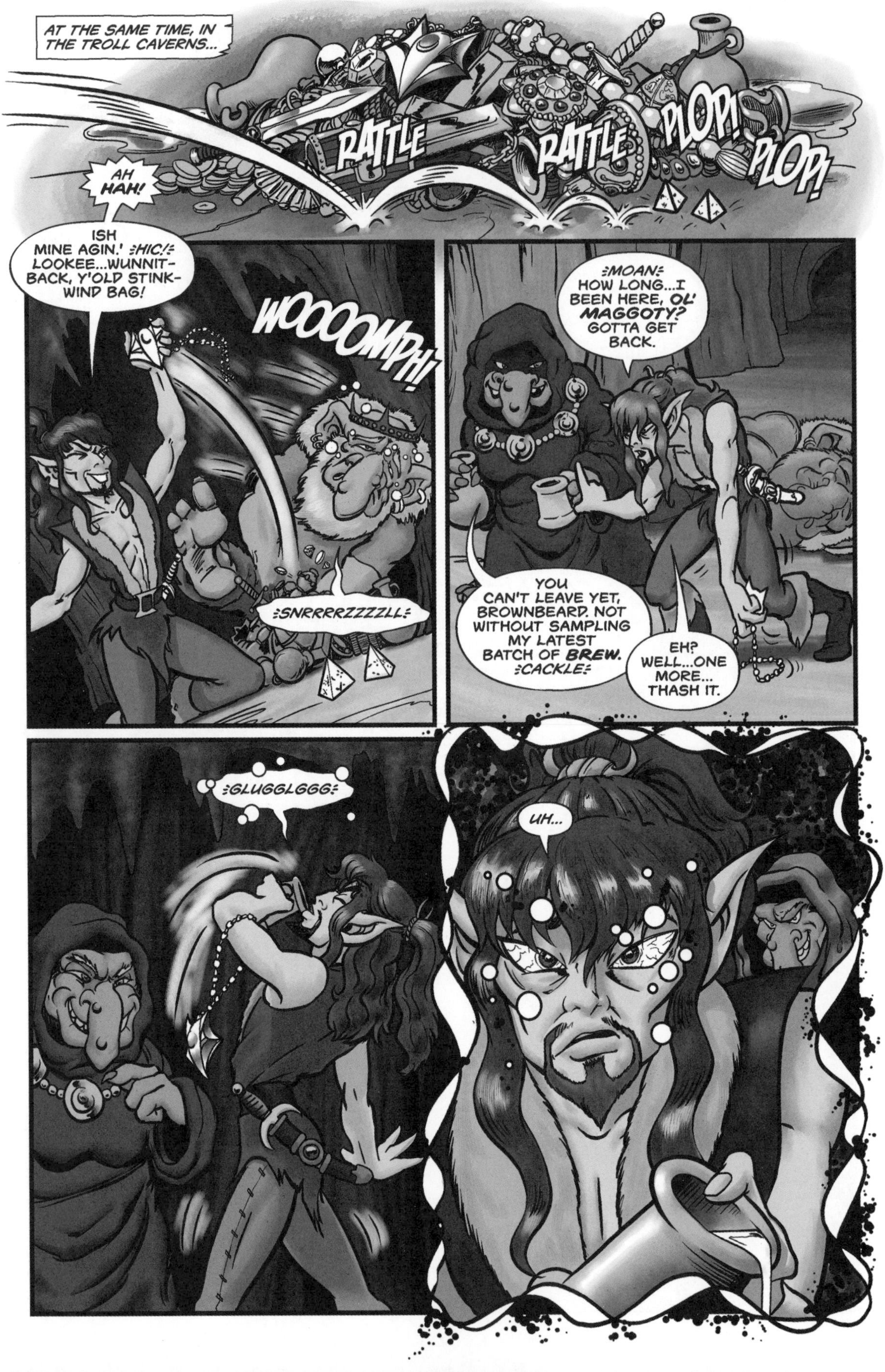
AT THE SAME TIME, IN THE TROLL CAVERNS...
RATTLE
RATTLE
PLOP!
PLOP!
AH HAH!
ISH MINE AGIN.' :HIC!: LOOKEE...WUNNIT-BACK, Y'OLD STINK-WIND BAG!
WOOOOMPH!
:SNRRRRZZZZLL:
:MOAN: HOW LONG...I BEEN HERE, OL' MAGGOTY? GOTTA GET BACK.
YOU CAN'T LEAVE YET, BROWNBEARD. NOT WITHOUT SAMPLING MY LATEST BATCH OF BREW. :CACKLE:
EH? WELL...ONE MORE... THASH IT.
:GLUGGLGGG:
UH...

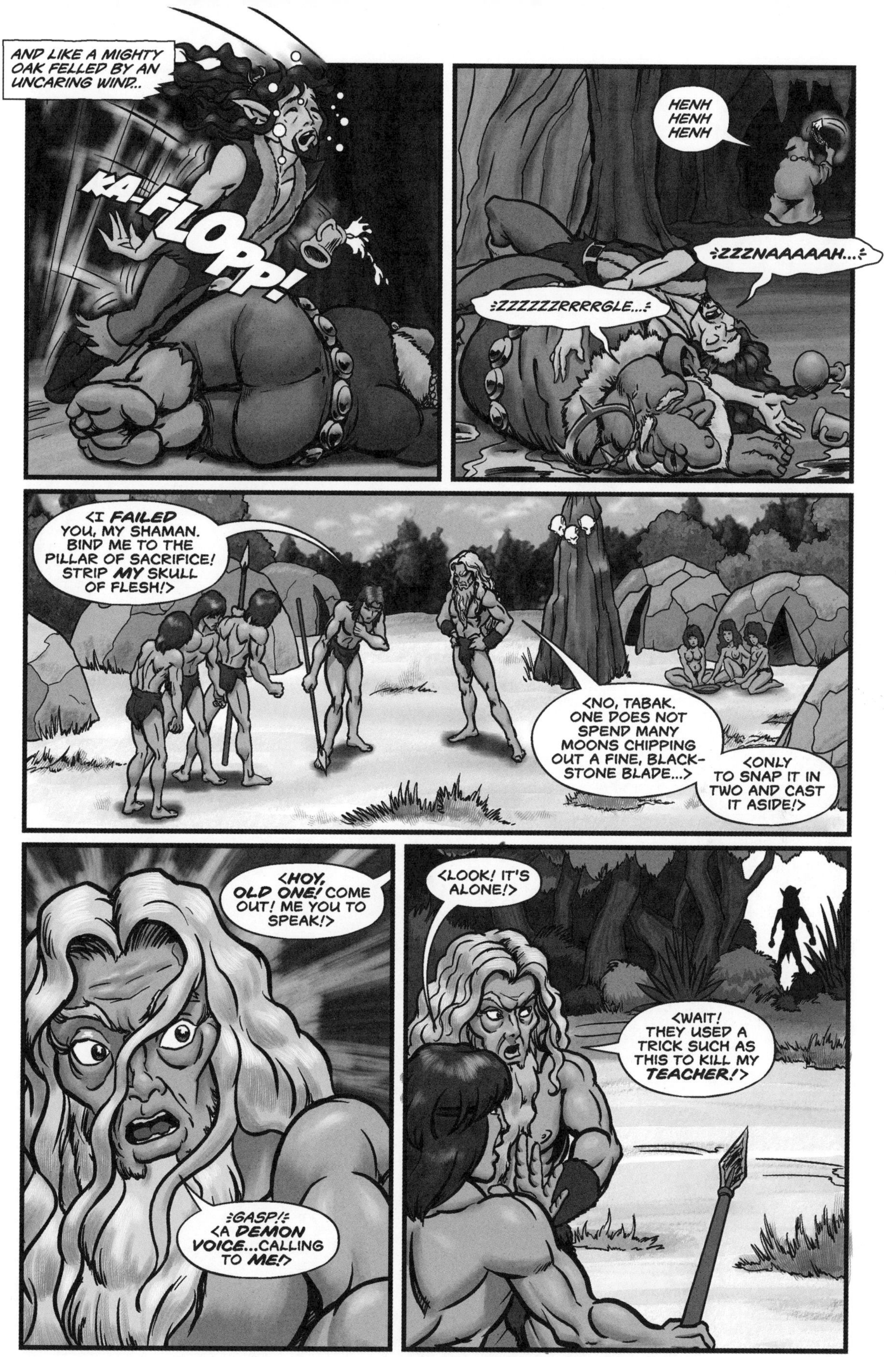
AND LIKE A MIGHTY OAK FELLED BY AN UNCARING WIND...
KA-FLOPP!
HENH HENH HENH
ZZZNAAAAAH...
ZZZZZZRRRRGLE...
<I FAILED YOU, MY SHAMAN. BIND ME TO THE PILLAR OF SACRIFICE! STRIP MY SKULL OF FLESH!>
<NO, TABAK. ONE DOES NOT SPEND MANY MOONS CHIPPING OUT A FINE, BLACK-STONE BLADE...>
<ONLY TO SNAP IT IN TWO AND CAST IT ASIDE!>
<HOY, OLD ONE! COME OUT! ME YOU TO SPEAK!>
GASP! <A DEMON VOICE...CALLING TO ME!>
<LOOK! IT'S ALONE!>
<WAIT! THEY USED A TRICK SUCH AS THIS TO KILL MY TEACHER!>

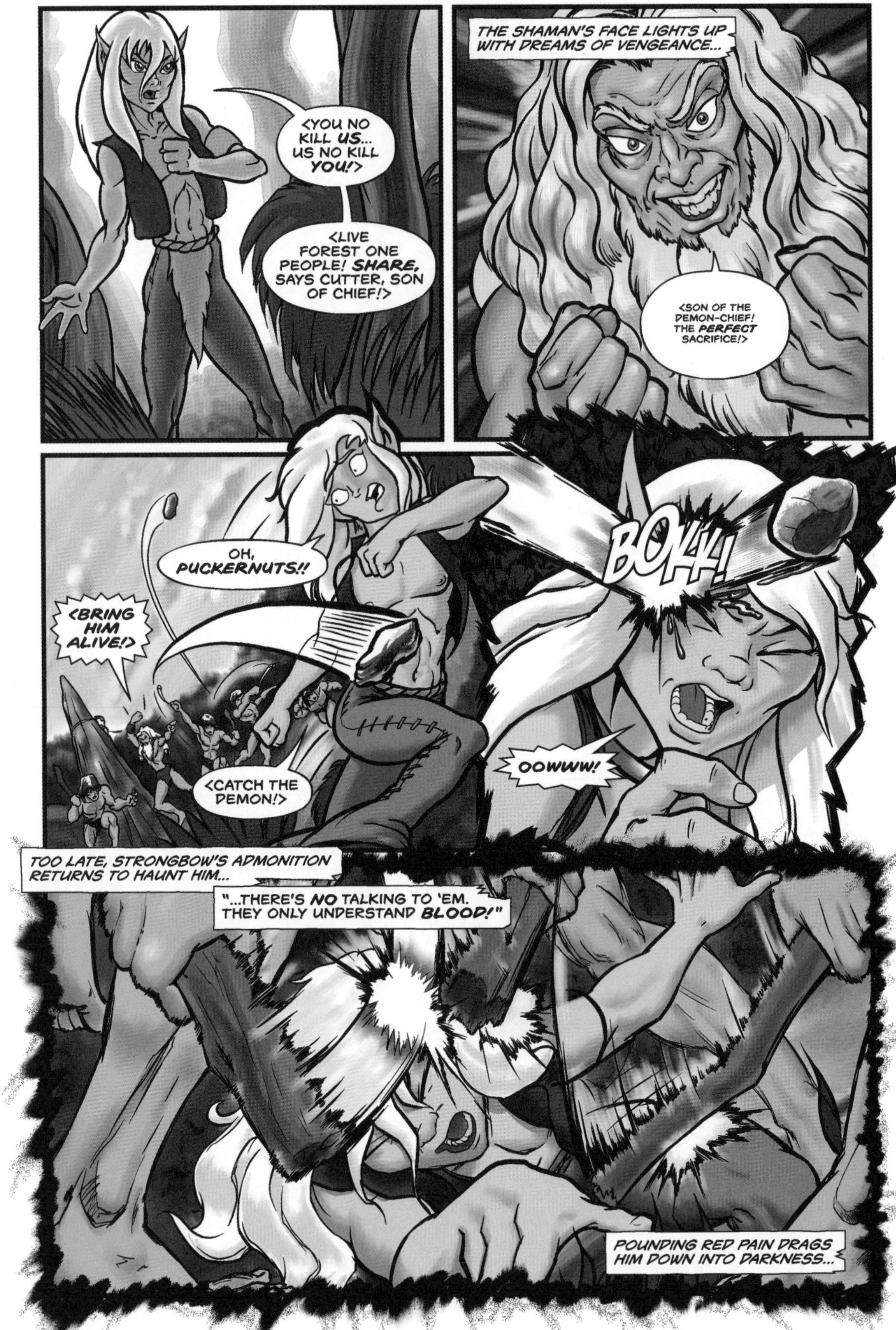
<YOU NO KILL US... US NO KILL YOU!>
<LIVE FOREST ONE PEOPLE! SHARE, SAYS CUTTER, SON OF CHIEF!>
THE SHAMAN'S FACE LIGHTS UP WITH DREAMS OF VENGEANCE...
<SON OF THE DEMON-CHIEF! THE PERFECT SACRIFICE!>
OH, PUCKERNUTS!!
<BRING HIM ALIVE!>
<CATCH THE DEMON!>
BOKK!
OOWWW!
TOO LATE, STRONGBOW'S ADMONITION RETURNS TO HAUNT HIM...
"...THERE'S NO TALKING TO 'EM. THEY ONLY UNDERSTAND BLOOD!"
POUNDING RED PAIN DRAGS HIM DOWN INTO DARKNESS...

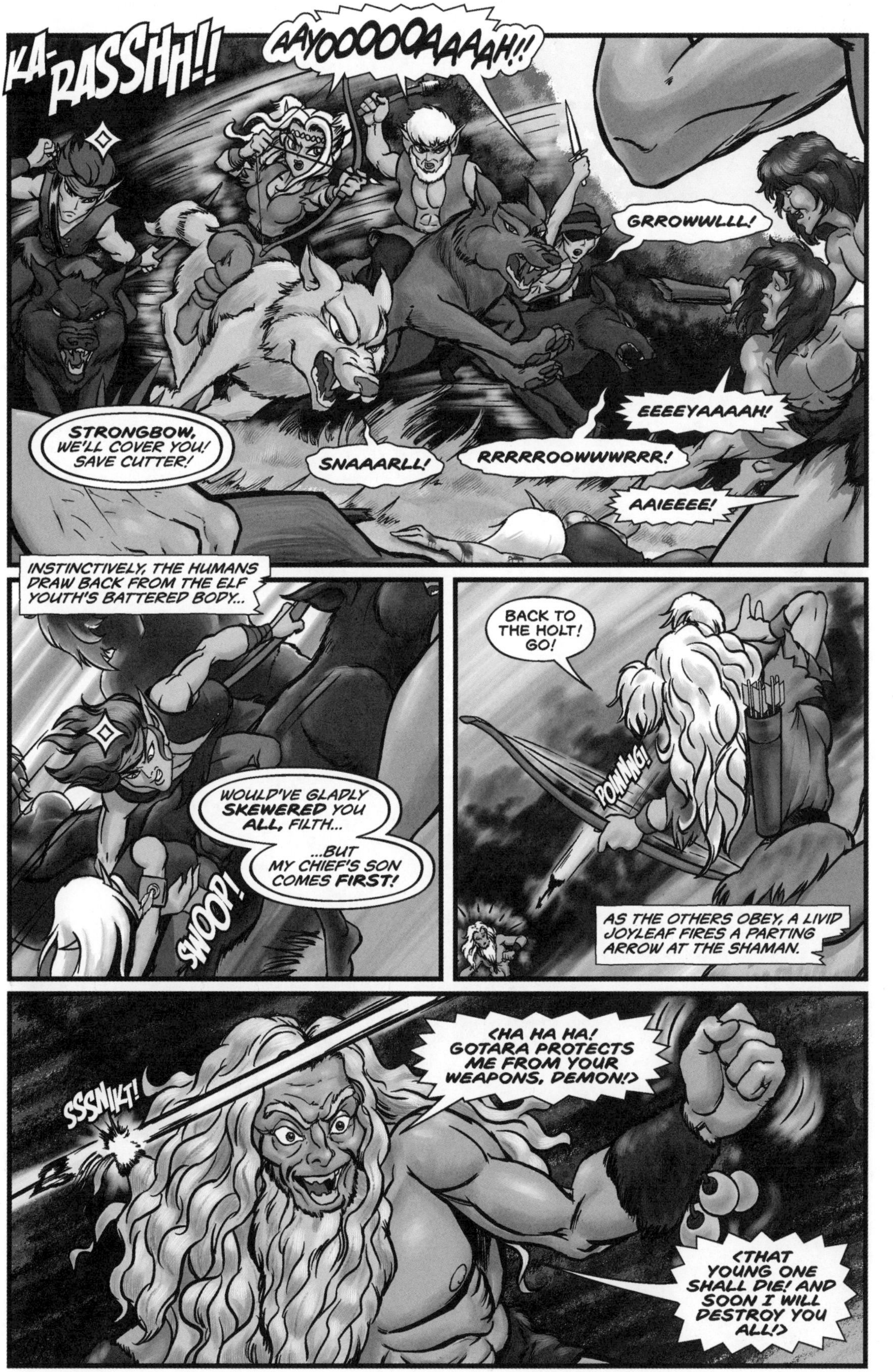
KA-RASSHH!!
AAYOOOOOAAAAAH!!
GRROWWLLL!
EEEEYAAAAH!
STRONGBOW, WE'LL COVER YOU! SAVE CUTTER!
SNAAARLL!
RRRRROOWWWRRR!
AAIEEEE!
INSTINCTIVELY, THE HUMANS DRAW BACK FROM THE ELF YOUTH'S BATTERED BODY...
WOULD'VE GLADLY SKEWERED YOU ALL, FILTH...
...BUT MY CHIEF'S SON COMES FIRST!
SWOOP!
BACK TO THE HOLT! GO!
POINNNG!
AS THE OTHERS OBEY, A LIVID JOYLEAF FIRES A PARTING ARROW AT THE SHAMAN.
SSSNIKT!
<HA HA HA! GOTARA PROTECTS ME FROM YOUR WEAPONS, DEMON!>
<THAT YOUNG ONE SHALL DIE! AND SOON I WILL DESTROY YOU ALL!>

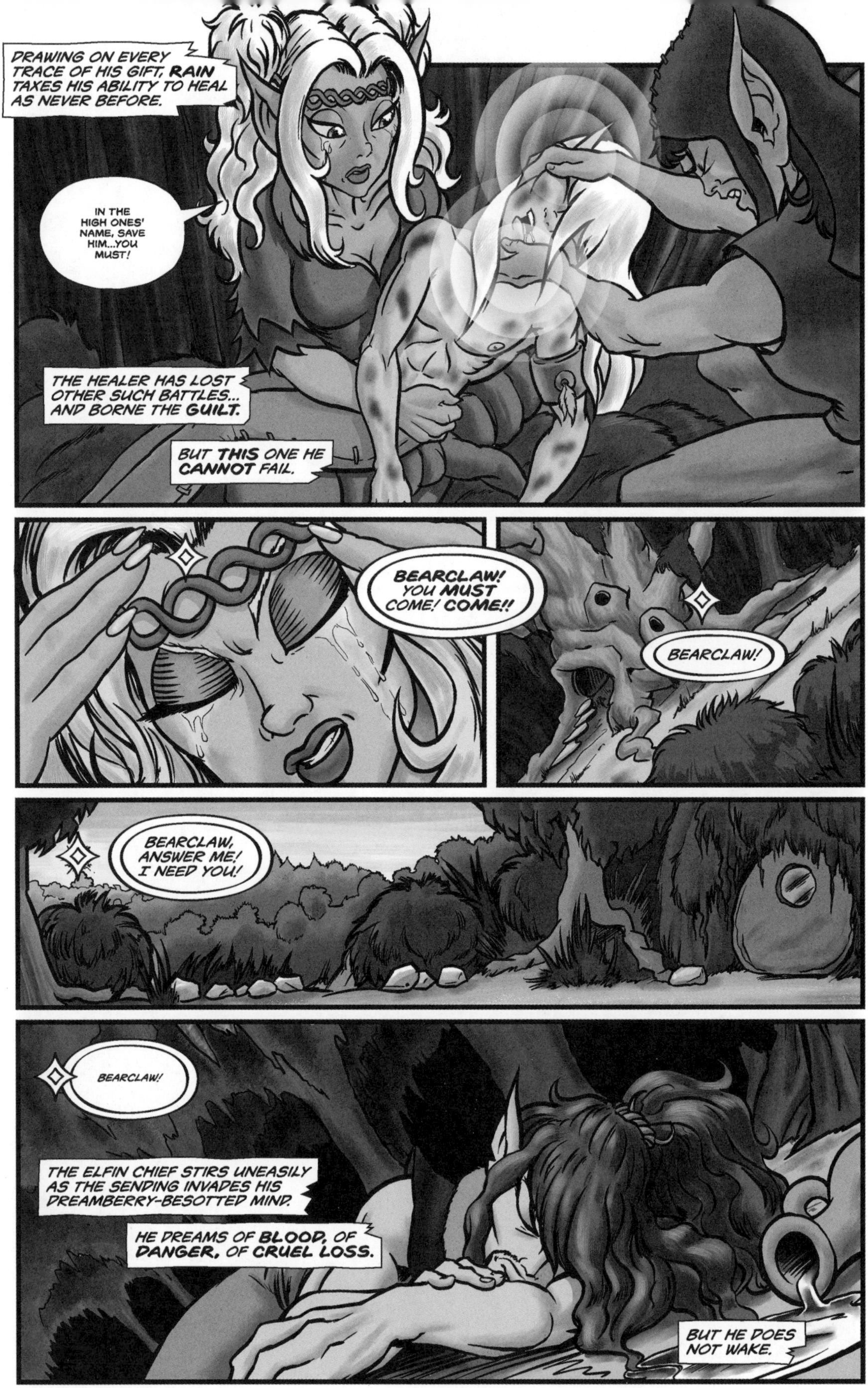
DRAWING ON EVERY TRACE OF HIS GIFT, RAIN TAXES HIS ABILITY TO HEAL AS NEVER BEFORE.
IN THE HIGH ONES' NAME, SAVE HIM...YOU MUST!
THE HEALER HAS LOST OTHER SUCH BATTLES... AND BORNE THE GUILT.
BUT THIS ONE HE CANNOT FAIL.
BEARCLAW! YOU MUST COME! COME!!
BEARCLAW!
BEARCLAW, ANSWER ME! I NEED YOU!
BEARCLAW!
THE ELFIN CHIEF STIRS UNEASILY AS THE SENDING INVADES HIS DREAMBERRY-BESOTTED MIND.
HE DREAMS OF BLOOD, OF DANGER, OF CRUEL LOSS.
BUT HE DOES NOT WAKE.

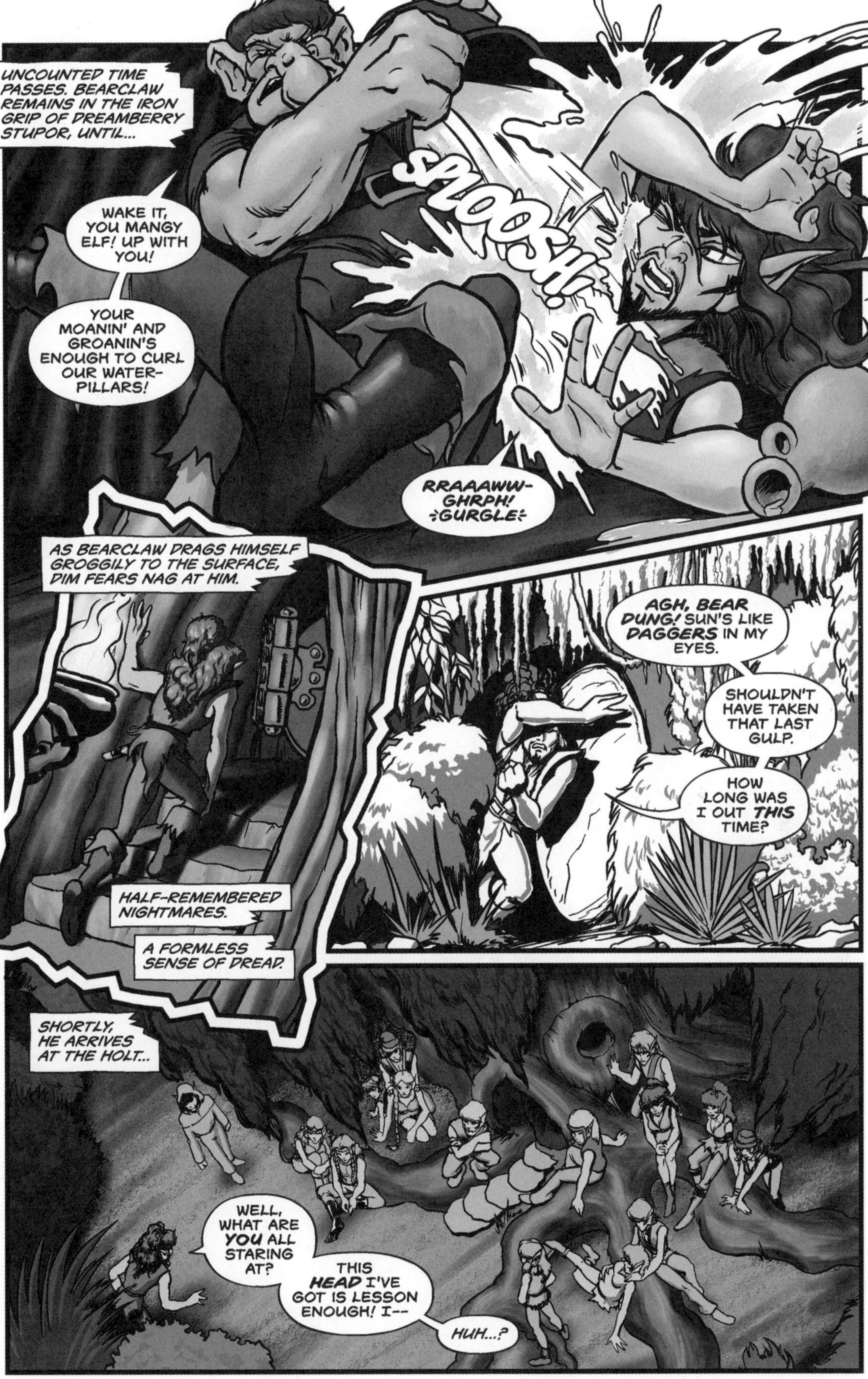
UNCOUNTED TIME PASSES. BEARCLAW REMAINS IN THE IRON GRIP OF DREAMBERRY STUPOR, UNTIL...
WAKE IT, YOU MANGY ELF! UP WITH YOU!
YOUR MOANIN' AND GROANIN'S ENOUGH TO CURL OUR WATER-PILLARS!
SPLOOSH!
RRAAAWW-GHRPH! GURGLE
AS BEARCLAW DRAGS HIMSELF GROGGILY TO THE SURFACE, DIM FEARS NAG AT HIM.
HALF-REMEMBERED NIGHTMARES.
A FORMLESS SENSE OF DREAD.
AGH, BEAR DUNG! SUN'S LIKE DAGGERS IN MY EYES.
SHOULDN'T HAVE TAKEN THAT LAST GULP.
HOW LONG WAS I OUT THIS TIME?
SHORTLY, HE ARRIVES AT THE HOLT...
WELL, WHAT ARE YOU ALL STARING AT?
THIS HEAD I'VE GOT IS LESSON ENOUGH! I--
HUH...?

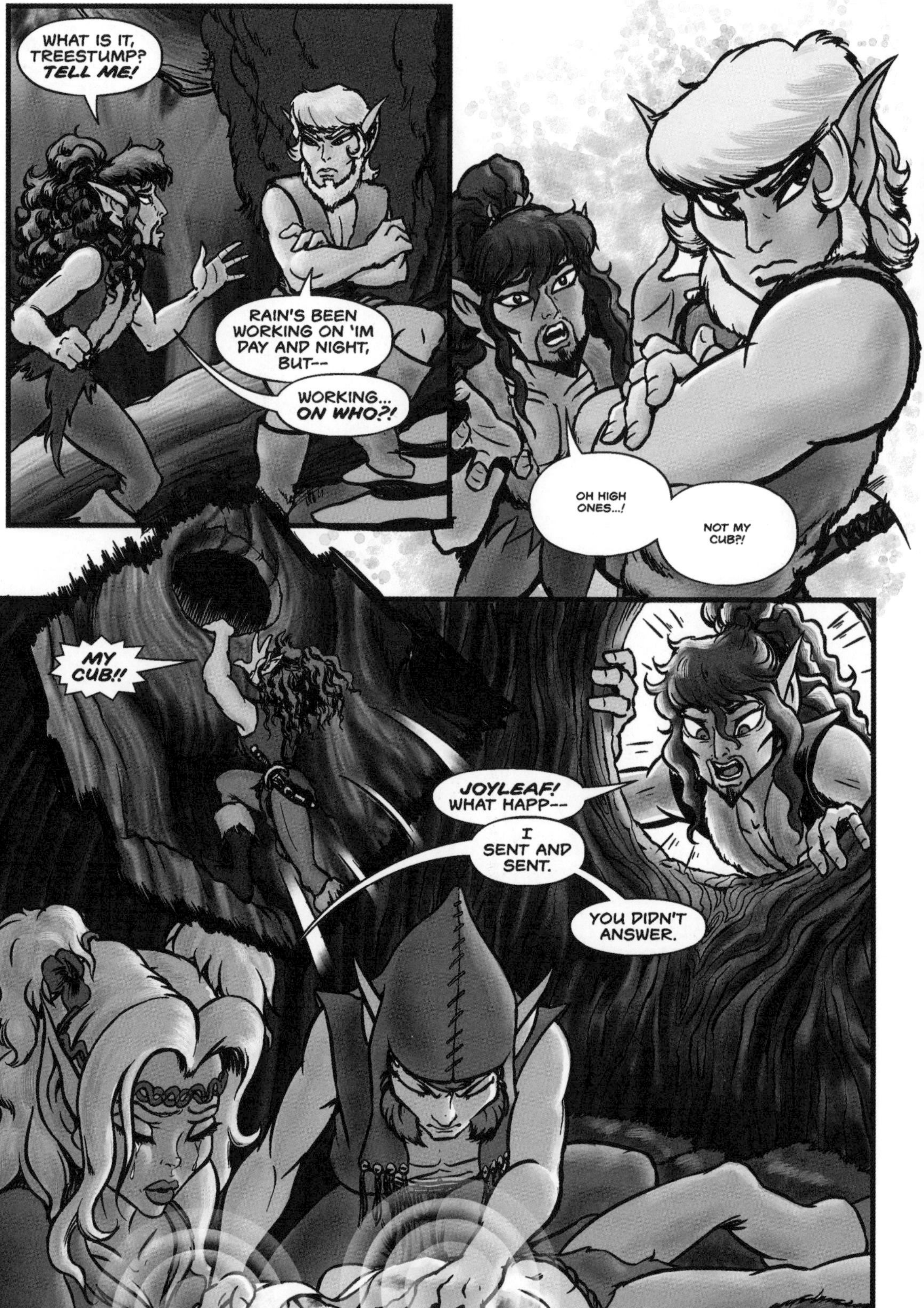
WHAT IS IT, TREESTUMP? TELL ME!
RAIN'S BEEN WORKING ON 'IM DAY AND NIGHT, BUT--
WORKING... ON WHO?!
OH HIGH ONES...!
NOT MY CUB?!
MY CUB!!
JOYLEAF! WHAT HAPP--
I SENT AND SENT.
YOU DIDN'T ANSWER.

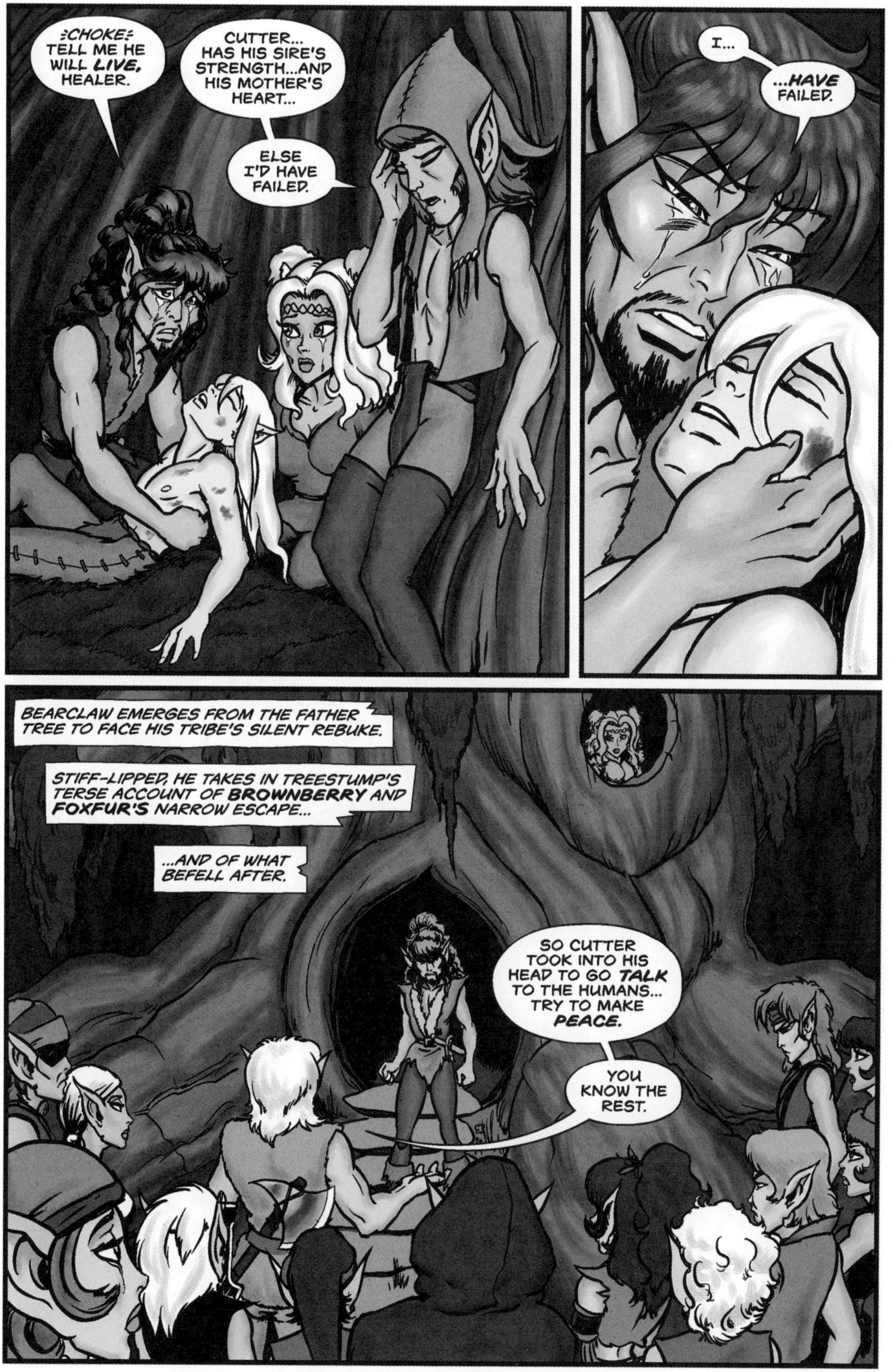

CHOKE
TELL ME HE WILL LIVE, HEALER.
CUTTER... HAS HIS SIRE'S STRENGTH...AND HIS MOTHER'S HEART...
ELSE I'D HAVE FAILED.
I...
...HAVE FAILED.
BEARCLAW EMERGES FROM THE FATHER TREE TO FACE HIS TRIBE'S SILENT REBUKE.
STIFF-LIPPED, HE TAKES IN TREESTUMP'S TERSE ACCOUNT OF BROWNBERRY AND FOXFUR'S NARROW ESCAPE...
...AND OF WHAT BEFELL AFTER.
SO CUTTER TOOK INTO HIS HEAD TO GO TALK TO THE HUMANS... TRY TO MAKE PEACE.
YOU KNOW THE REST.

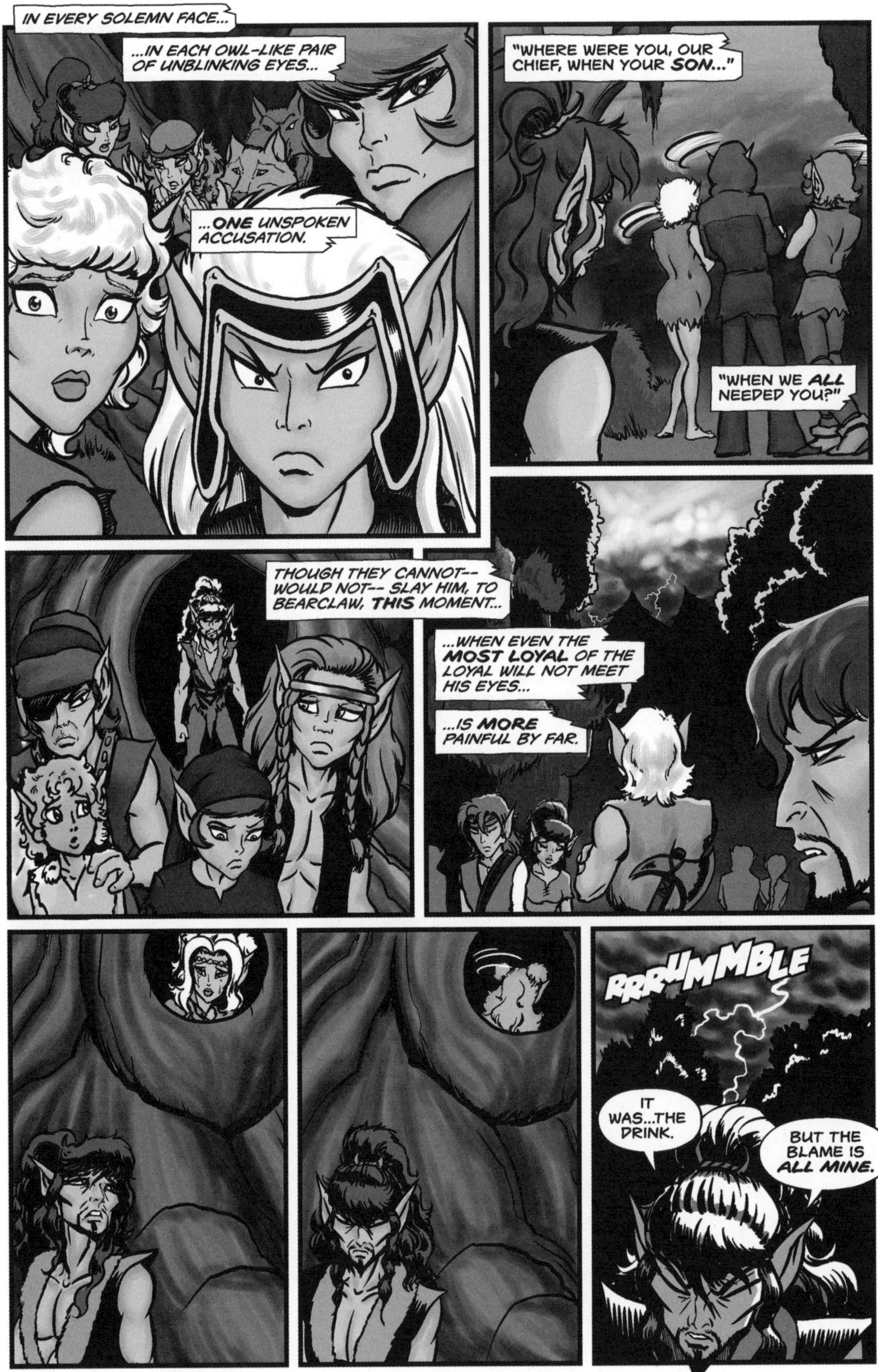
IN EVERY SOLEMN FACE...
...IN EACH OWL-LIKE PAIR OF UNBLINKING EYES...
...ONE UNSPOKEN ACCUSATION.
"WHERE WERE YOU, OUR CHIEF, WHEN YOUR SON..."
"WHEN WE ALL NEEDED YOU?"
THOUGH THEY CANNOT-- WOULD NOT-- SLAY HIM, TO BEARCLAW, THIS MOMENT...
...WHEN EVEN THE MOST LOYAL OF THE LOYAL WILL NOT MEET HIS EYES...
...IS MORE PAINFUL BY FAR.
RRRUMMBLE
IT WAS...THE DRINK.
BUT THE BLAME IS ALL MINE.

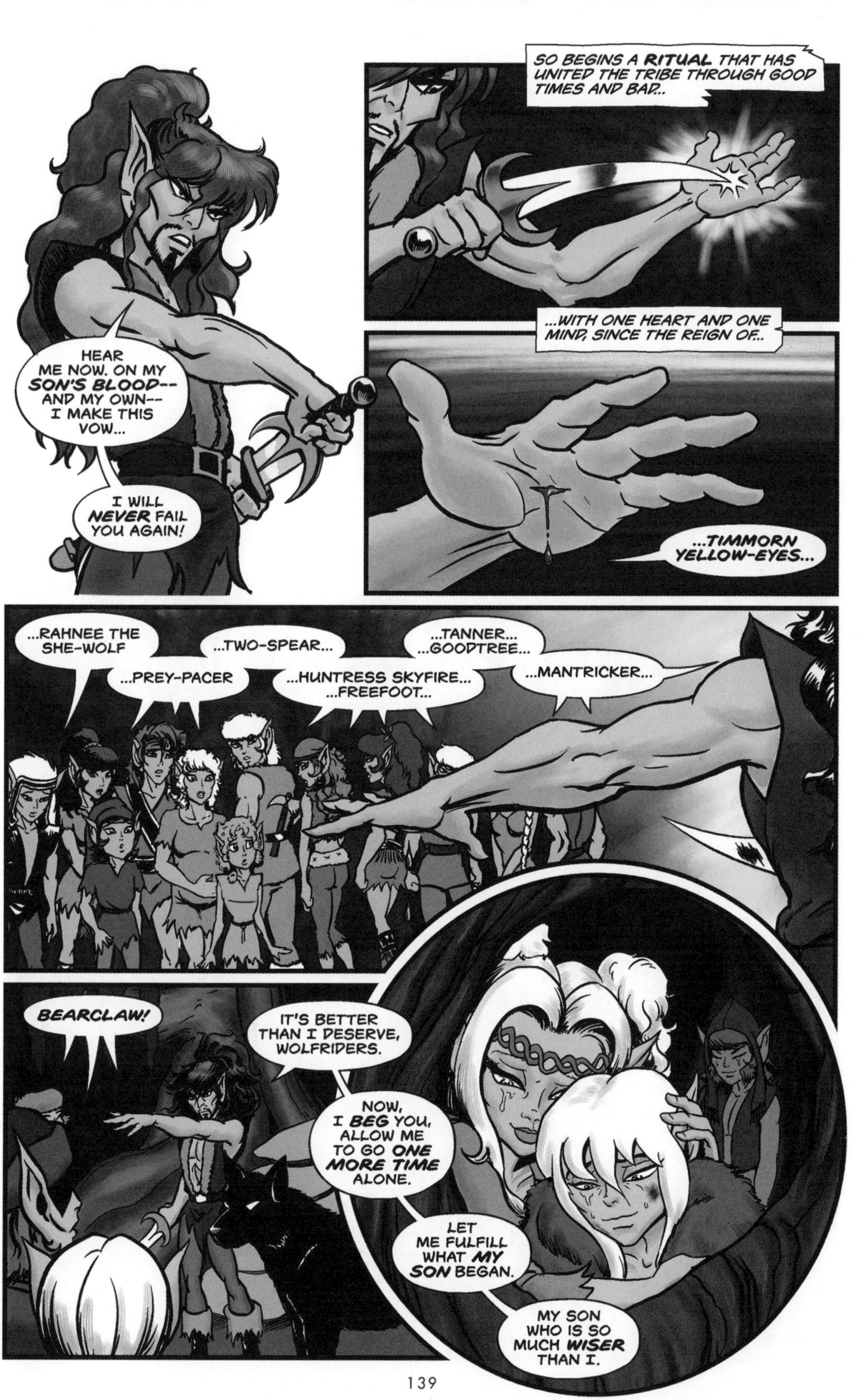
HEAR ME NOW. ON MY SON'S BLOOD-- AND MY OWN-- I MAKE THIS VOW...
I WILL NEVER FAIL YOU AGAIN!
SO BEGINS A RITUAL THAT HAS UNITED THE TRIBE THROUGH GOOD TIMES AND BAD...
...WITH ONE HEART AND ONE MIND, SINCE THE REIGN OF...
...TIMMORN YELLOW-EYES...
...RAHNEE THE SHE-WOLF
...PREY-PACER
...TWO-SPEAR...
...HUNTRESS SKYFIRE... ...FREEFOOT...
...TANNER... ...GOODTREE...
...MANTRICKER...
BEARCLAW!
IT'S BETTER THAN I DESERVE, WOLFRIDERS.
NOW, I BEG YOU, ALLOW ME TO GO ONE MORE TIME ALONE.
LET ME FULFILL WHAT MY SON BEGAN.
MY SON WHO IS SO MUCH WISER THAN I.

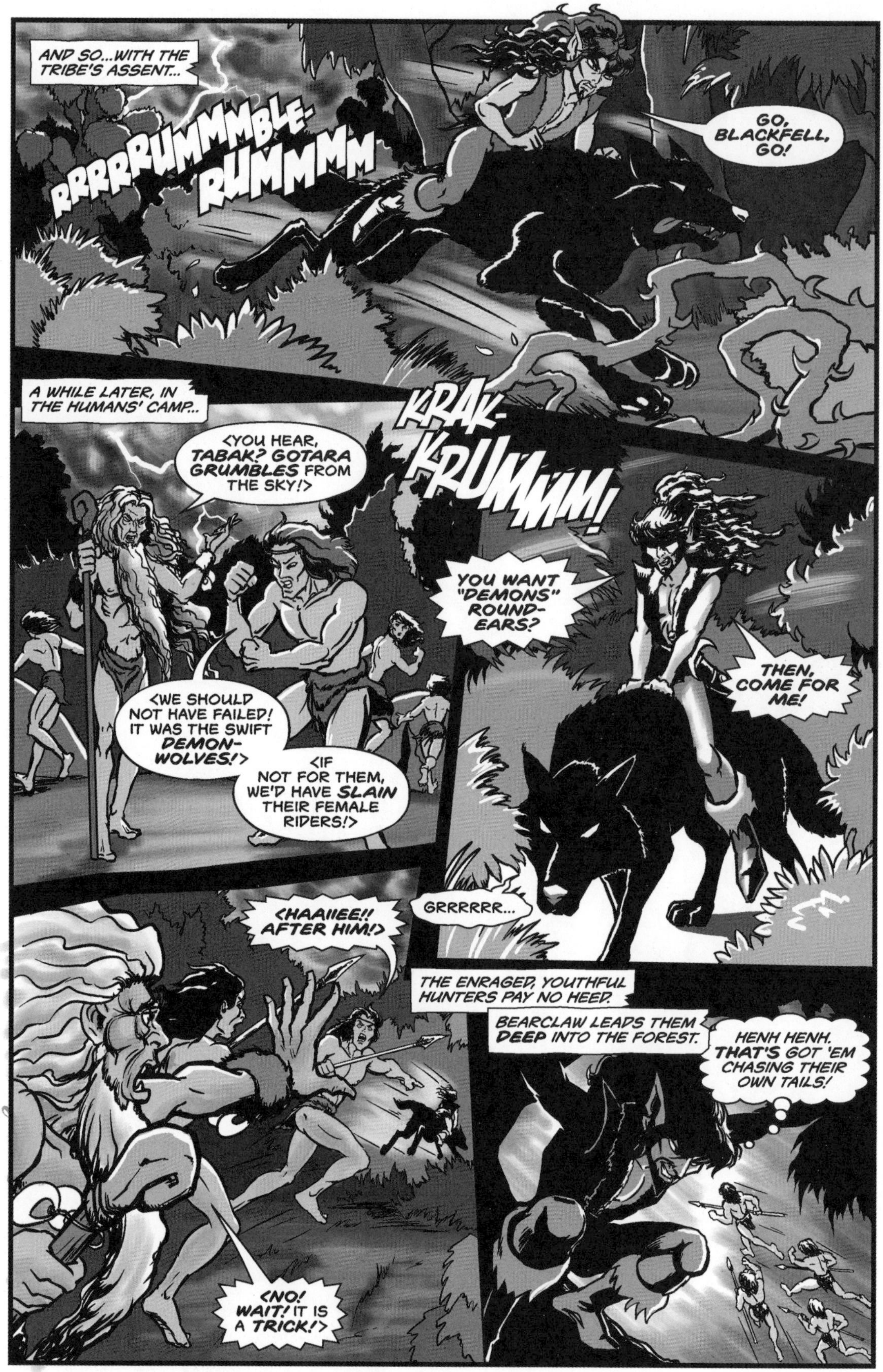
AND SO...WITH THE TRIBE'S ASSENT...
RRRRRUMMMBLE-RUMMMM
GO, BLACKFELL, GO!
A WHILE LATER, IN THE HUMANS' CAMP...
KRAK-KRUMMMM!
<YOU HEAR, TABAK? GOTARA GRUMBLES FROM THE SKY!>
<WE SHOULD NOT HAVE FAILED! IT WAS THE SWIFT DEMON-WOLVES!>
<IF NOT FOR THEM, WE'D HAVE SLAIN THEIR FEMALE RIDERS!>
YOU WANT "DEMONS" ROUND-EARS?
THEN, COME FOR ME!
GRRRRRR...
<HAAIIEE!! AFTER HIM!>
<NO! WAIT! IT IS A TRICK!>
THE ENRAGED, YOUTHFUL HUNTERS PAY NO HEED.
BEARCLAW LEADS THEM DEEP INTO THE FOREST.
HENH HENH. THAT'S GOT 'EM CHASING THEIR OWN TAILS!

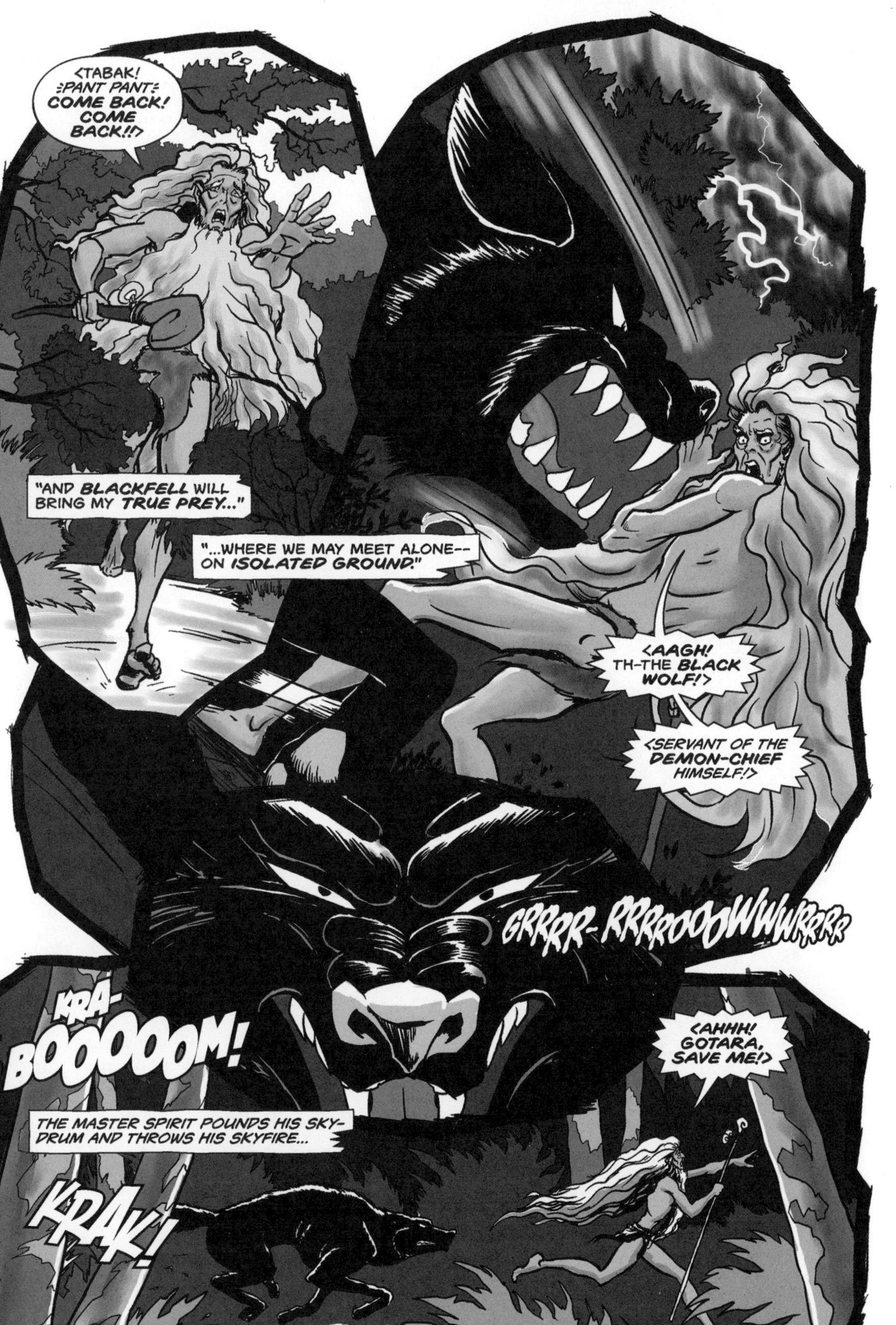
<TABAK! :PANT PANT: COME BACK! COME BACK!!>
"AND BLACKFELL WILL BRING MY TRUE PREY..."
"...WHERE WE MAY MEET ALONE-- ON ISOLATED GROUND."
<AAGH! TH-THE BLACK WOLF!>
<SERVANT OF THE DEMON-CHIEF HIMSELF!>
GRRRR- RRRROOOWWWRRRR
KRA-BOOOOOM!
<AHHH! GOTARA, SAVE ME!>
THE MASTER SPIRIT POUNDS HIS SKY-DRUM AND THROWS HIS SKYFIRE...
KRAK!
...YET THE SHADOW-BEAST DRIVES THE SHAMAN EVER DEEPER INTO AN UNKNOWN PART OF THE WOODS.

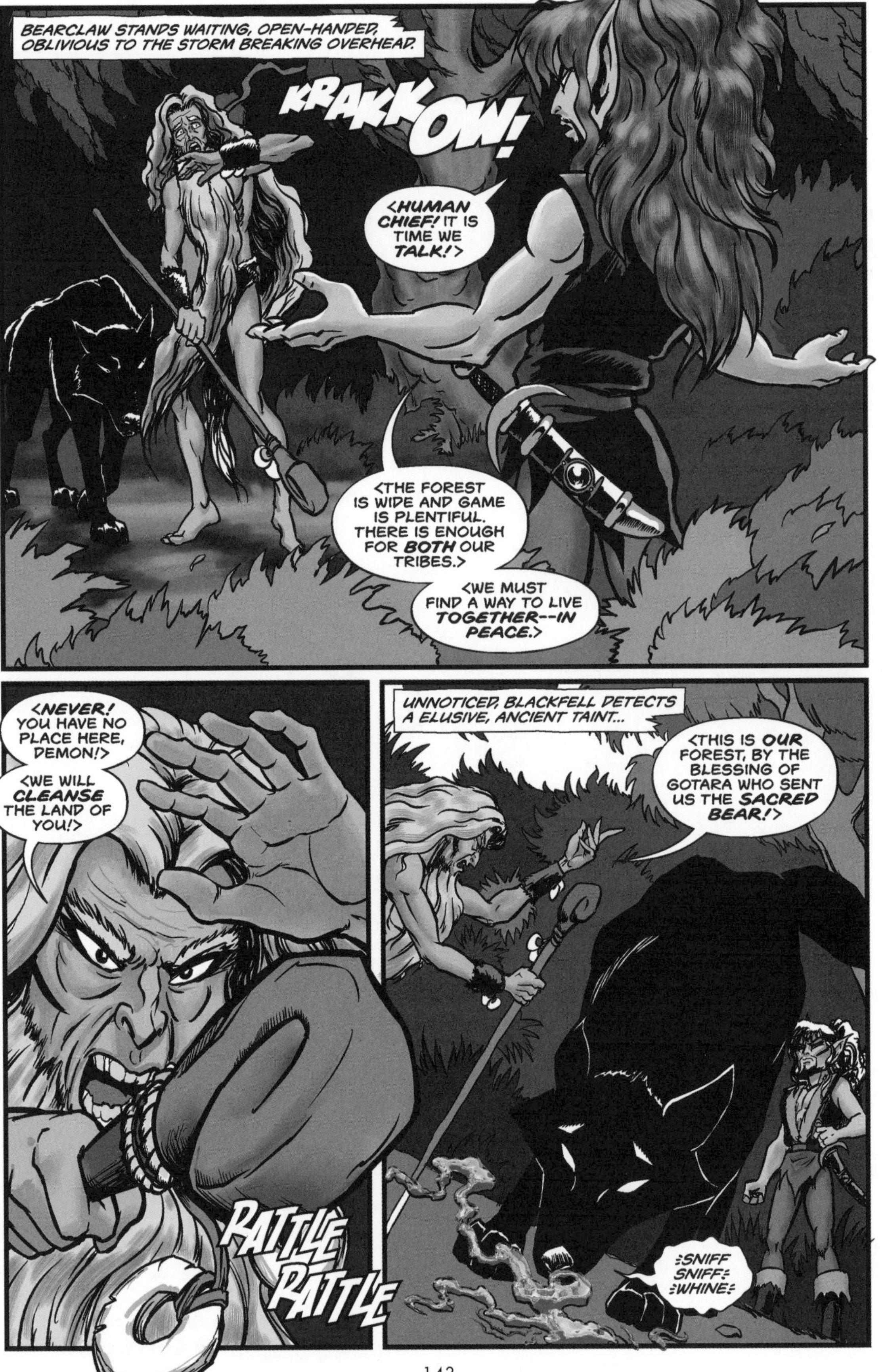
BEARCLAW STANDS WAITING, OPEN-HANDED, OBLIVIOUS TO THE STORM BREAKING OVERHEAD.
KRAKKOW!
<HUMAN CHIEF! IT IS TIME WE TALK!>
<THE FOREST IS WIDE AND GAME IS PLENTIFUL. THERE IS ENOUGH FOR BOTH OUR TRIBES.>
<WE MUST FIND A WAY TO LIVE TOGETHER--IN PEACE.>
<NEVER! YOU HAVE NO PLACE HERE, DEMON!>
<WE WILL CLEANSE THE LAND OF YOU!>
RATTLE RATTLE
UNNOTICED, BLACKFELL DETECTS A ELUSIVE, ANCIENT TAINT...
<THIS IS OUR FOREST, BY THE BLESSING OF GOTARA WHO SENT US THE SACRED BEAR!>
SNIFF SNIFF WHINE

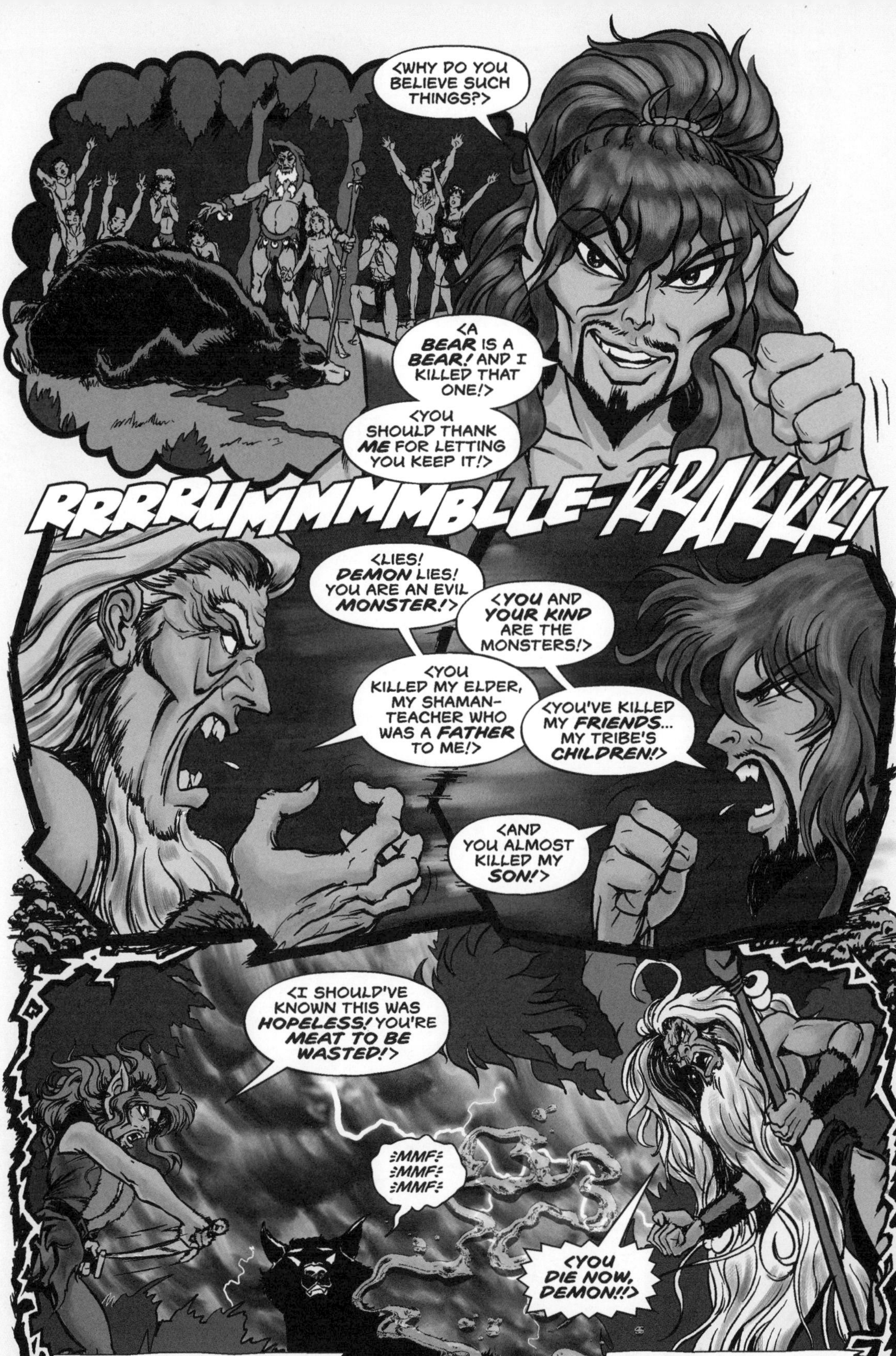

<WHY DO YOU BELIEVE SUCH THINGS?>
<A BEAR IS A BEAR! AND I KILLED THAT ONE!>
<YOU SHOULD THANK ME FOR LETTING YOU KEEP IT!>
RRRRUMMMMMBLLE-KRAKKK!
<LIES! DEMON LIES! YOU ARE AN EVIL MONSTER!>
<YOU AND YOUR KIND ARE THE MONSTERS!>
<YOU KILLED MY ELDER, MY SHAMAN-TEACHER WHO WAS A FATHER TO ME!>
<YOU'VE KILLED MY FRIENDS... MY TRIBE'S CHILDREN!>
<AND YOU ALMOST KILLED MY SON!>
<I SHOULD'VE KNOWN THIS WAS HOPELESS! YOU'RE MEAT TO BE WASTED!>
:MMF: :MMF: :MMF:
<YOU DIE NOW, DEMON!!>
BLINDED AND DEAFENED AGAIN BY HATE, NEITHER ELF NOR HUMAN HEAR THE WOLF'S AGITATED WHINES.
THEY CANNOT SEE, AS THE WOLF CAN, WHAT THEIR VIOLENT EMOTIONS HAVE AWAKENED...

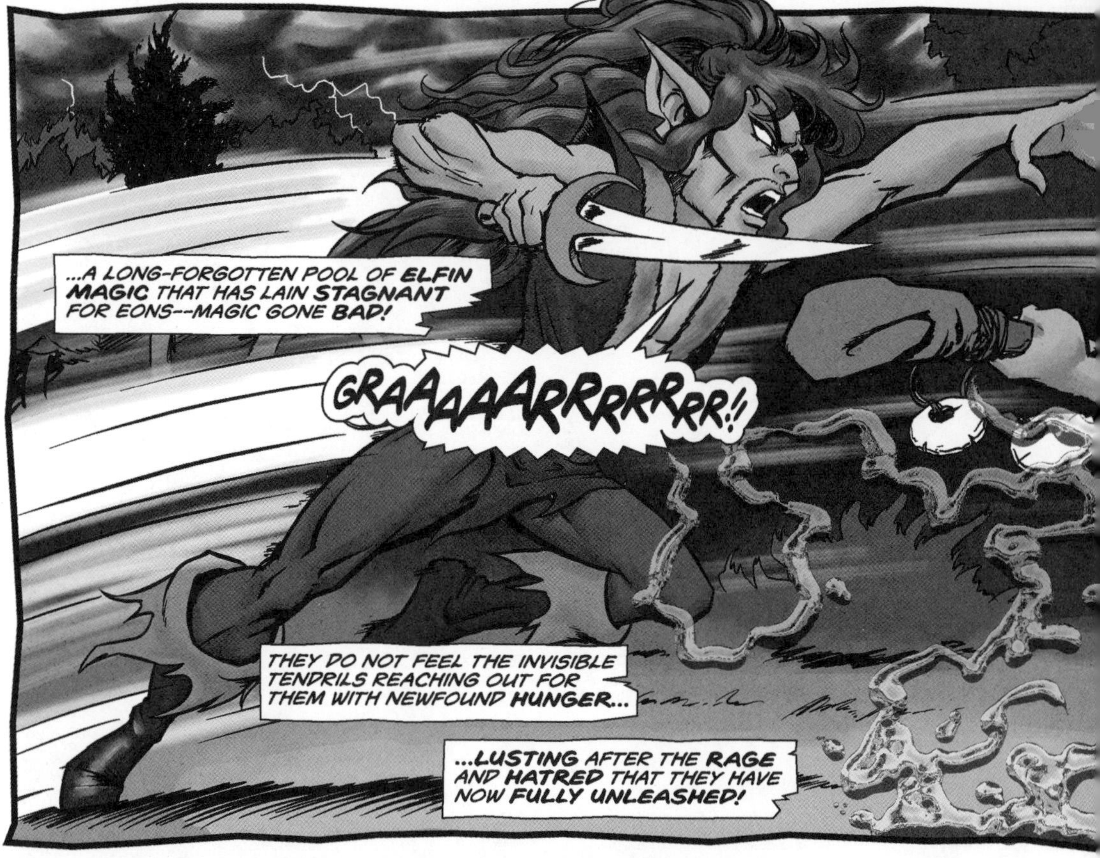
...A LONG-FORGOTTEN POOL OF ELFIN MAGIC THAT HAS LAIN STAGNANT FOR EONS--MAGIC GONE BAD!
GRAAAAARRRRRR!!
THEY DO NOT FEEL THE INVISIBLE TENDRILS REACHING OUT FOR THEM WITH NEWFOUND HUNGER...
...LUSTING AFTER THE RAGE AND HATRED THAT THEY HAVE NOW FULLY UNLEASHED!

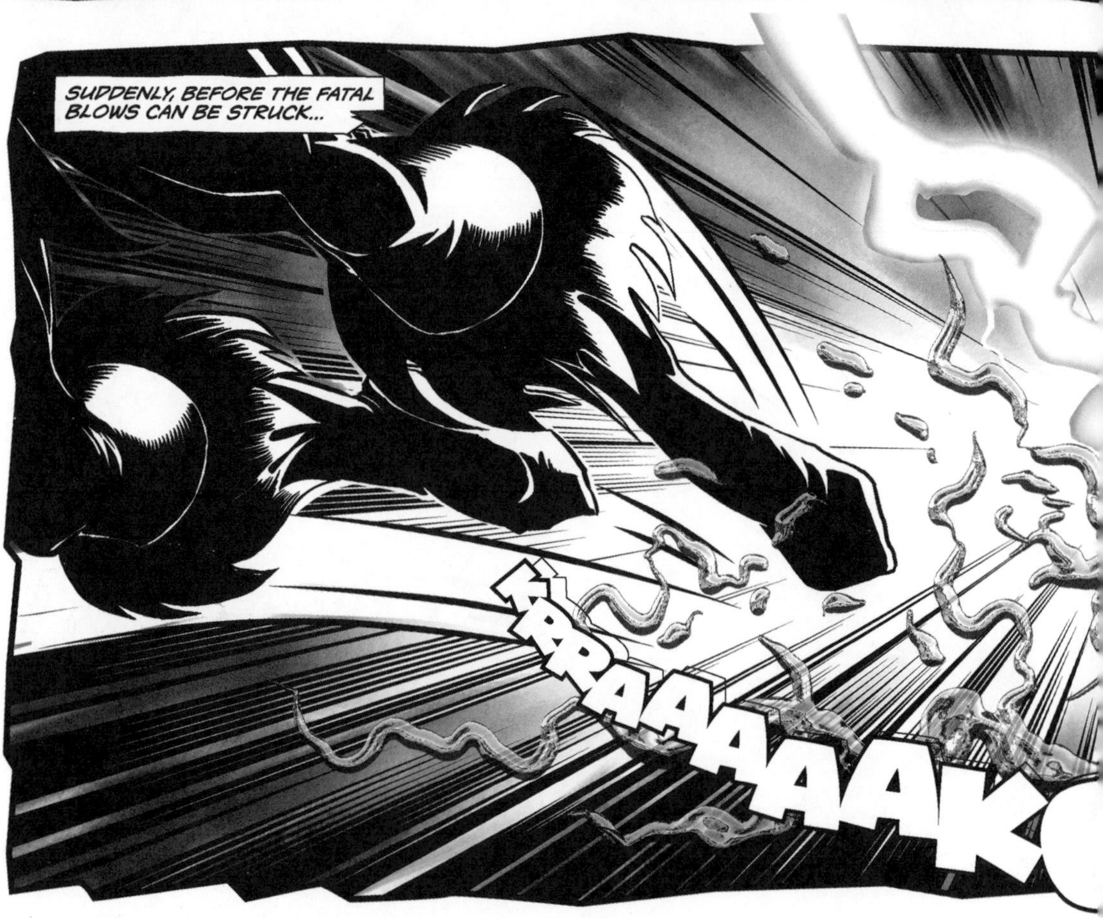
SUDDENLY, BEFORE THE FATAL BLOWS CAN BE STRUCK...
KRRAAAAAAK

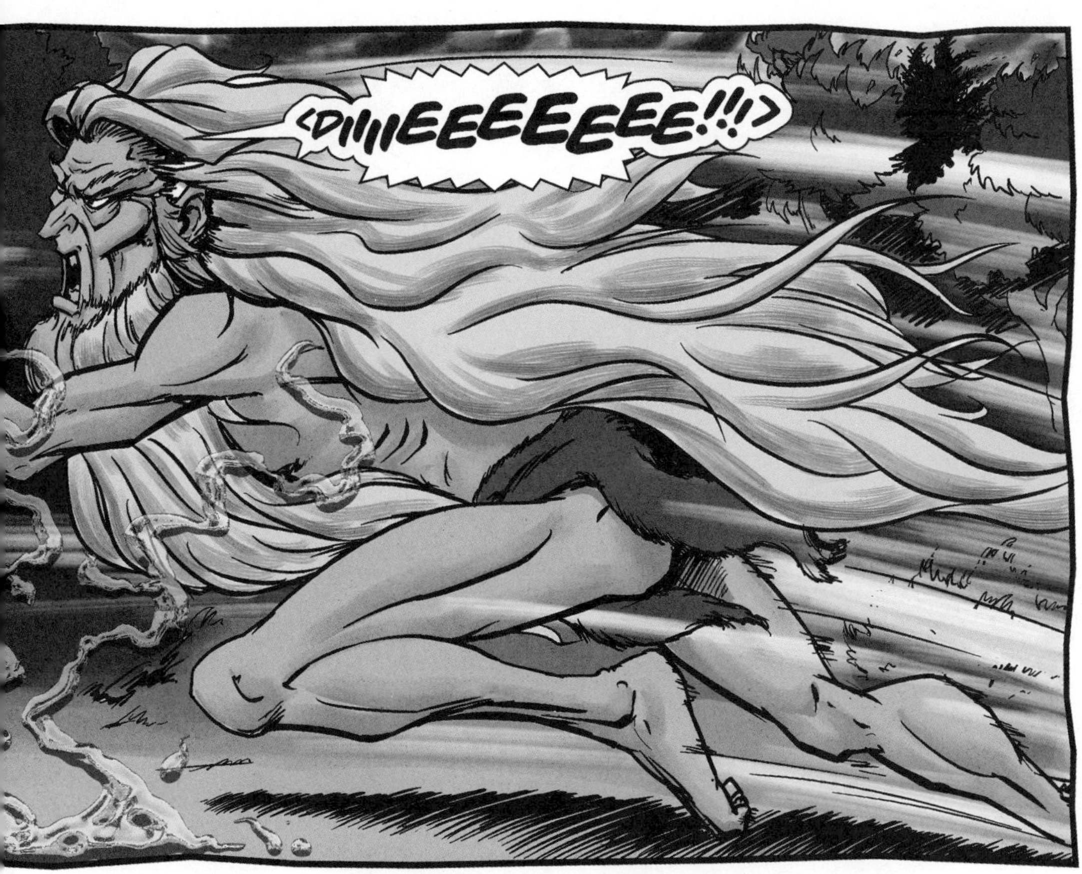
<DIIIIEEEEEEEEE!!!>

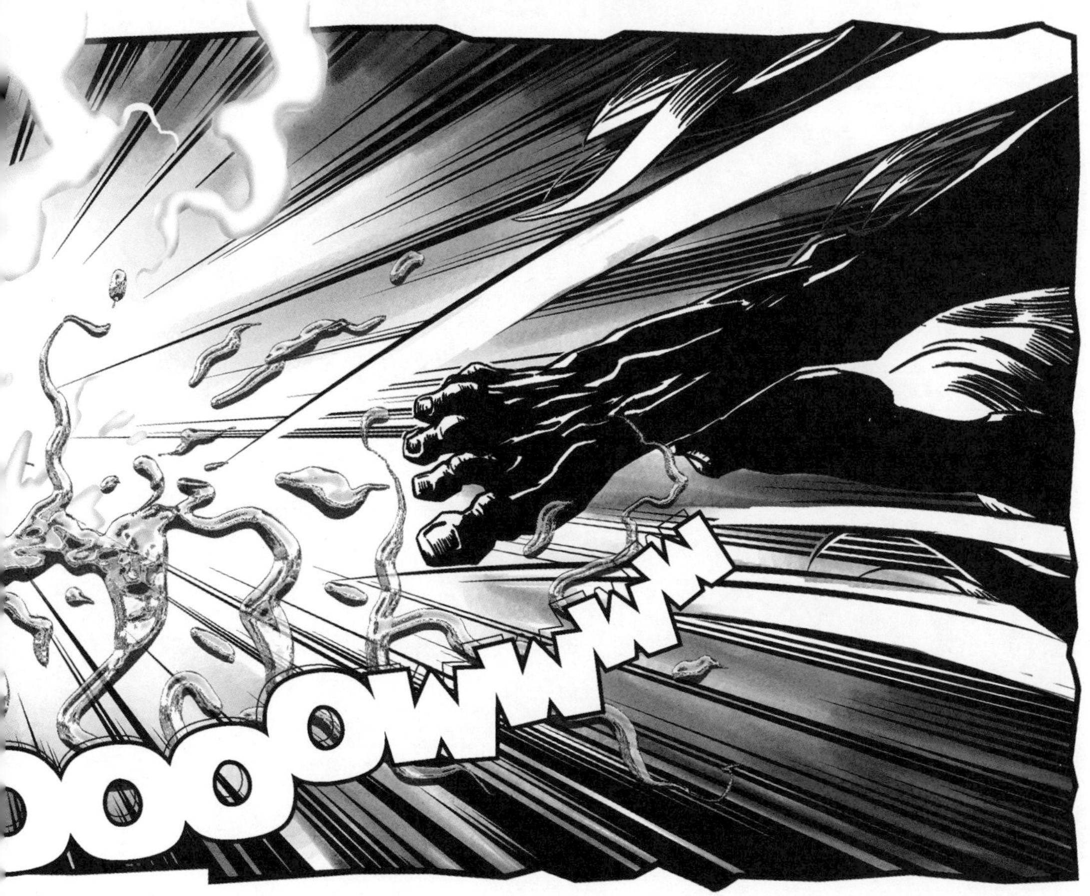
DOOOOWWWWN

UUUHHHH...

<OOHHHH....>

TSSSSSSSSSSSS...

FRANTICALLY, BLACKFELL DRAGS HIS ELF-FRIEND AWAY FROM THE QUESTING THREADS...

SO, TOO, THE HUMAN SOURCE OF SUSTENANCE ESCAPES THE SINISTER MAGIC'S THIRST.

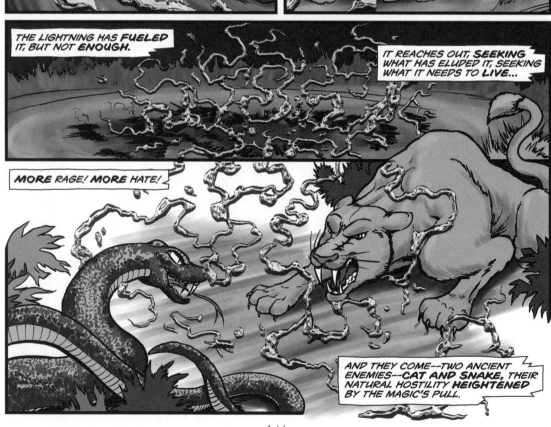

THE LIGHTNING HAS **FUELED** IT, BUT NOT **ENOUGH.**

IT REACHES OUT, **SEEKING** WHAT HAS ELUDED IT, SEEKING WHAT IT NEEDS TO **LIVE...**

MORE RAGE! **MORE** HATE!

AND THEY COME--TWO ANCIENT ENEMIES--**CAT AND SNAKE,** THEIR NATURAL HOSTILITY **HEIGHTENED** BY THE MAGIC'S PULL.

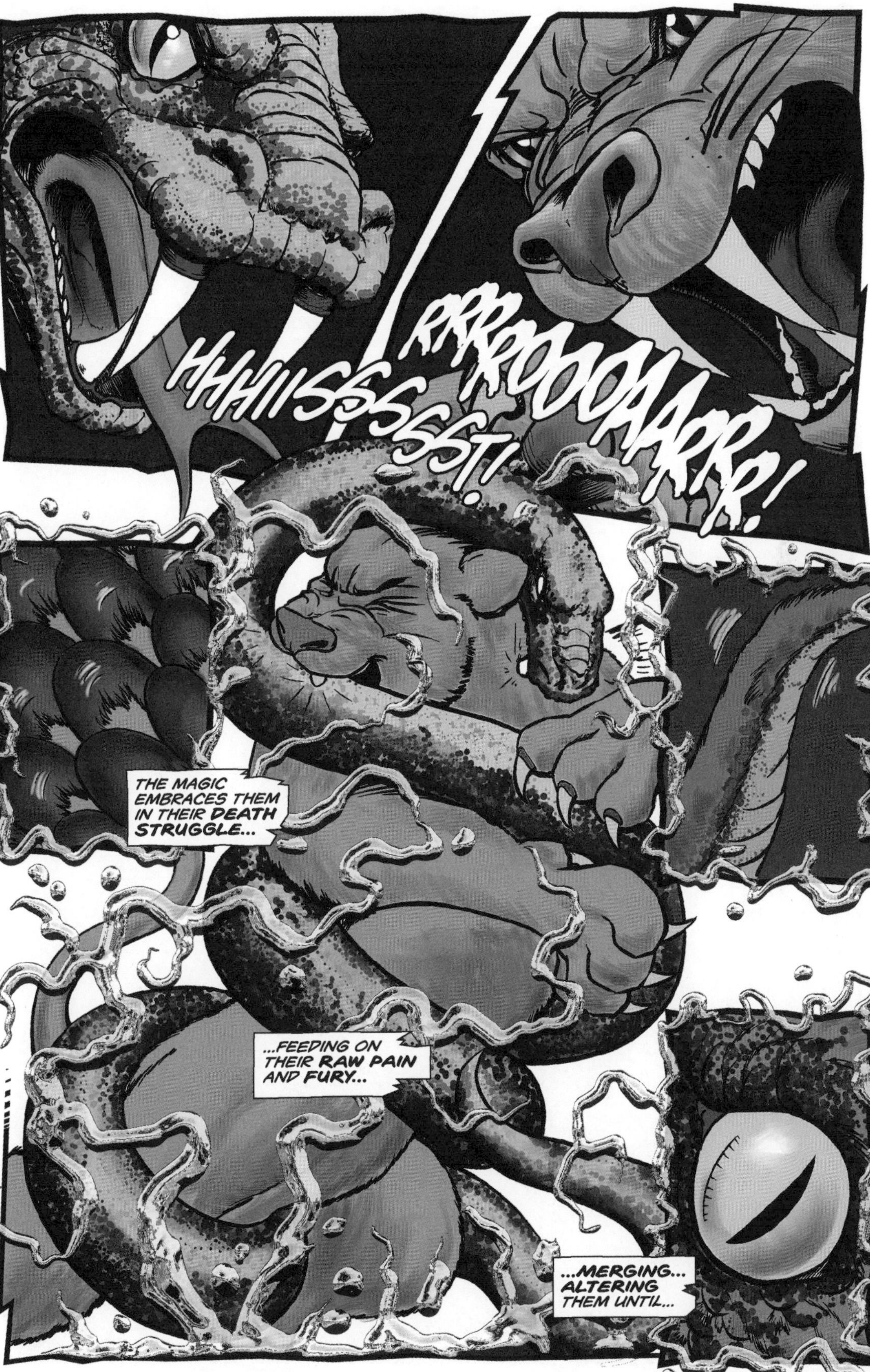
HHHIISSSSST!
RRRROOOOAARRR!
THE MAGIC EMBRACES THEM IN THEIR DEATH STRUGGLE...
...FEEDING ON THEIR RAW PAIN AND FURY...
...MERGING... ALTERING THEM UNTIL...

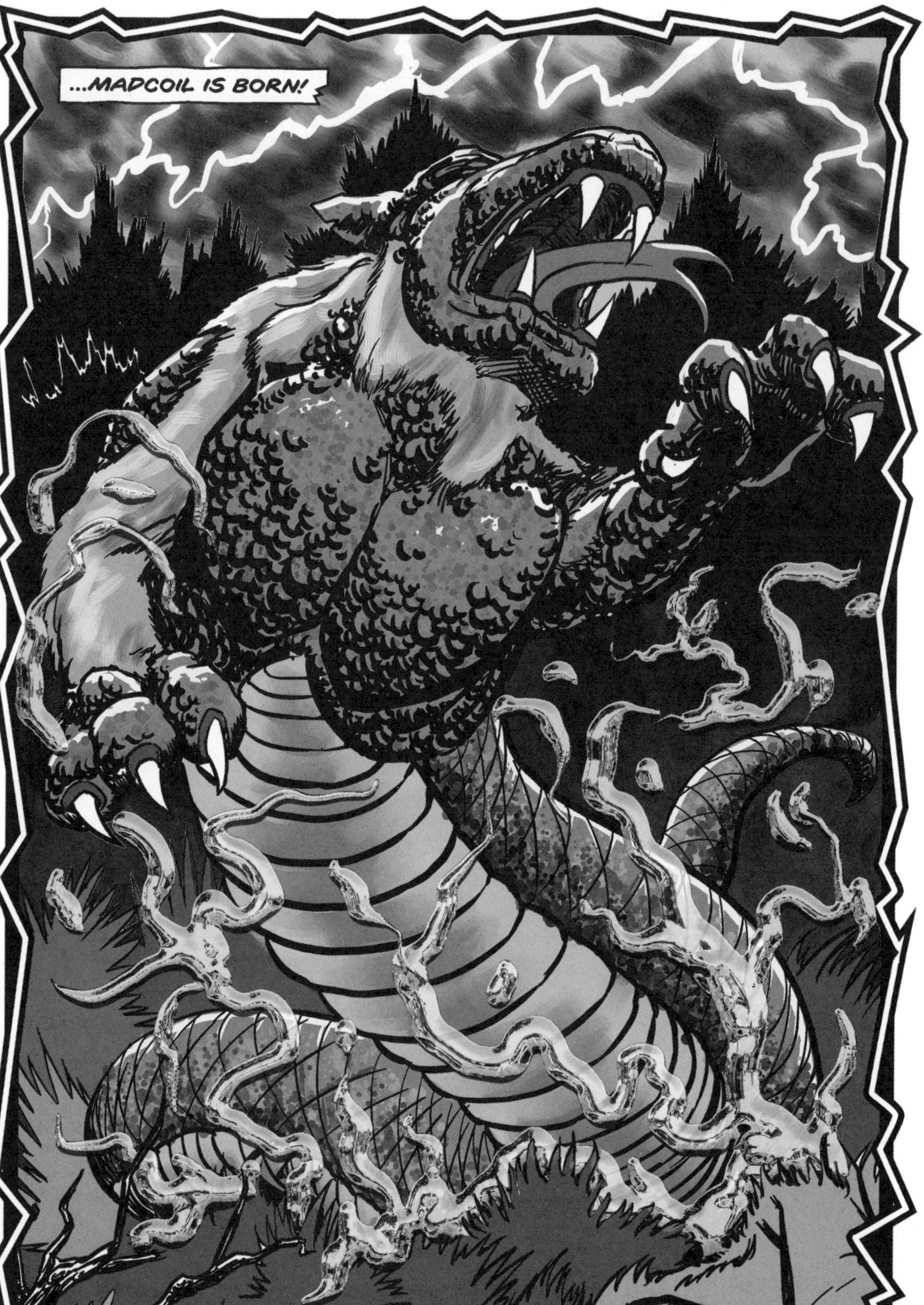
...MADCOIL IS BORN!

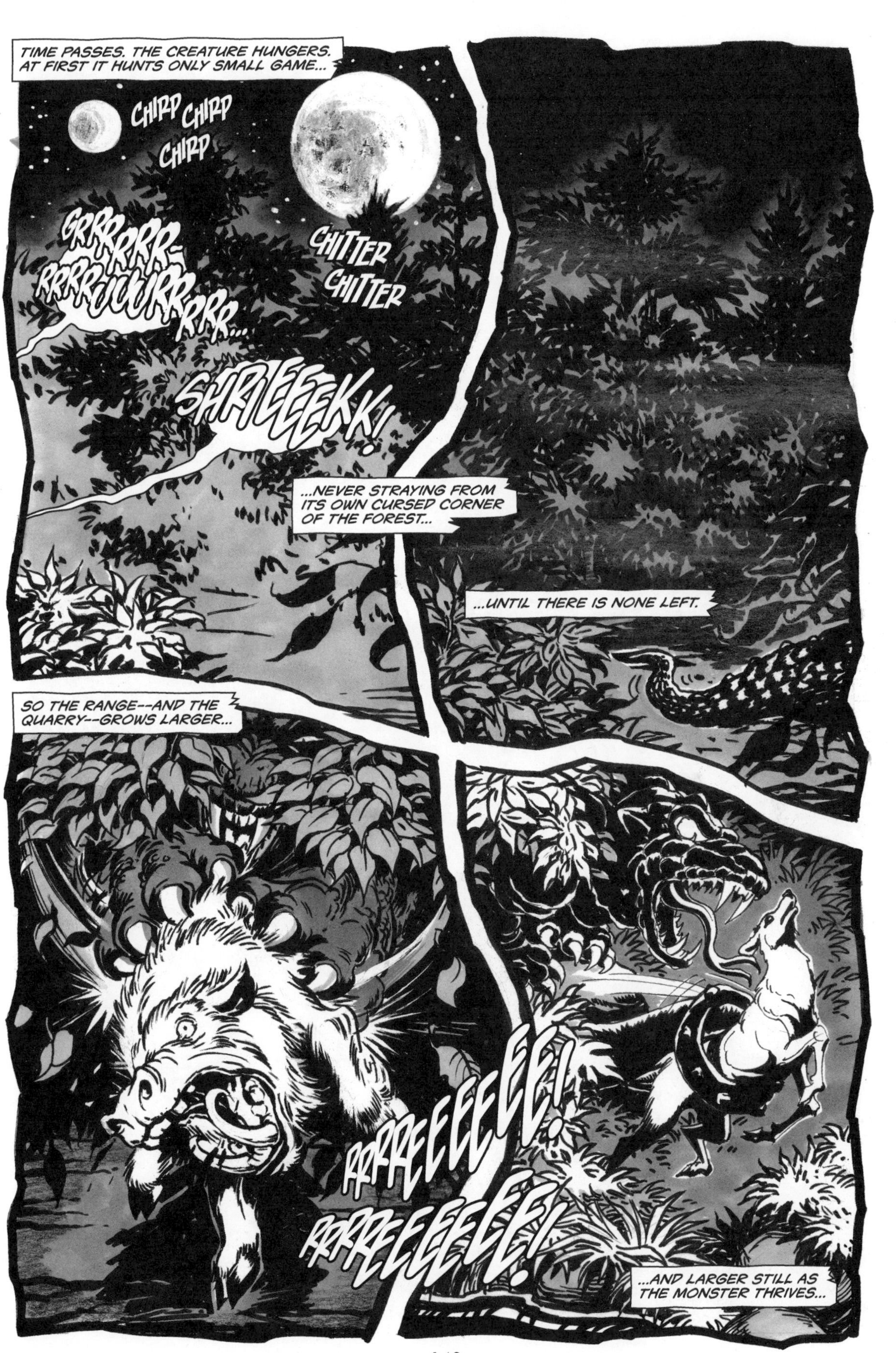

TIME PASSES. THE CREATURE HUNGERS. AT FIRST IT HUNTS ONLY SMALL GAME...
CHIRP CHIRP CHIRP
GRRRRRR-RRRRUUURRRRRR...
CHITTER CHITTER
SHRIEEEEKK!
...NEVER STRAYING FROM ITS OWN CURSED CORNER OF THE FOREST...
...UNTIL THERE IS NONE LEFT.
SO THE RANGE--AND THE QUARRY--GROWS LARGER...
RRRREEEEEEE!
RRRREEEEEEE!
...AND LARGER STILL AS THE MONSTER THRIVES...

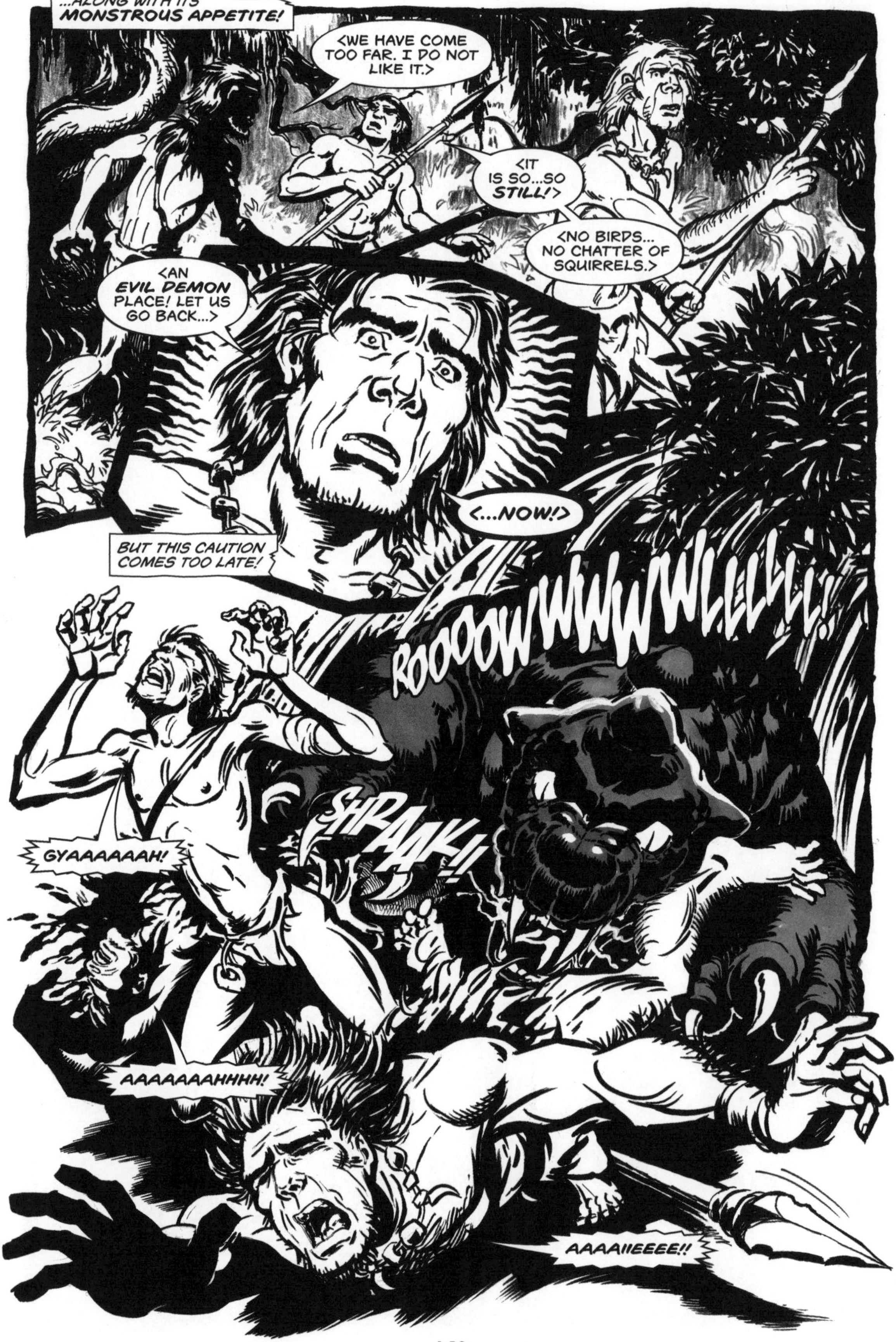

...ALONG WITH ITS MONSTROUS APPETITE!
<WE HAVE COME TOO FAR. I DO NOT LIKE IT.>
<IT IS SO...SO STILL!>
<NO BIRDS... NO CHATTER OF SQUIRRELS.>
<AN EVIL DEMON PLACE! LET US GO BACK...>
<...NOW!>
BUT THIS CAUTION COMES TOO LATE!
ROOOOWWWWWLLLLLL!
SHRAAK!!
GYAAAAAAAH!
AAAAAAAHHHH!
AAAAIIEEEE!!

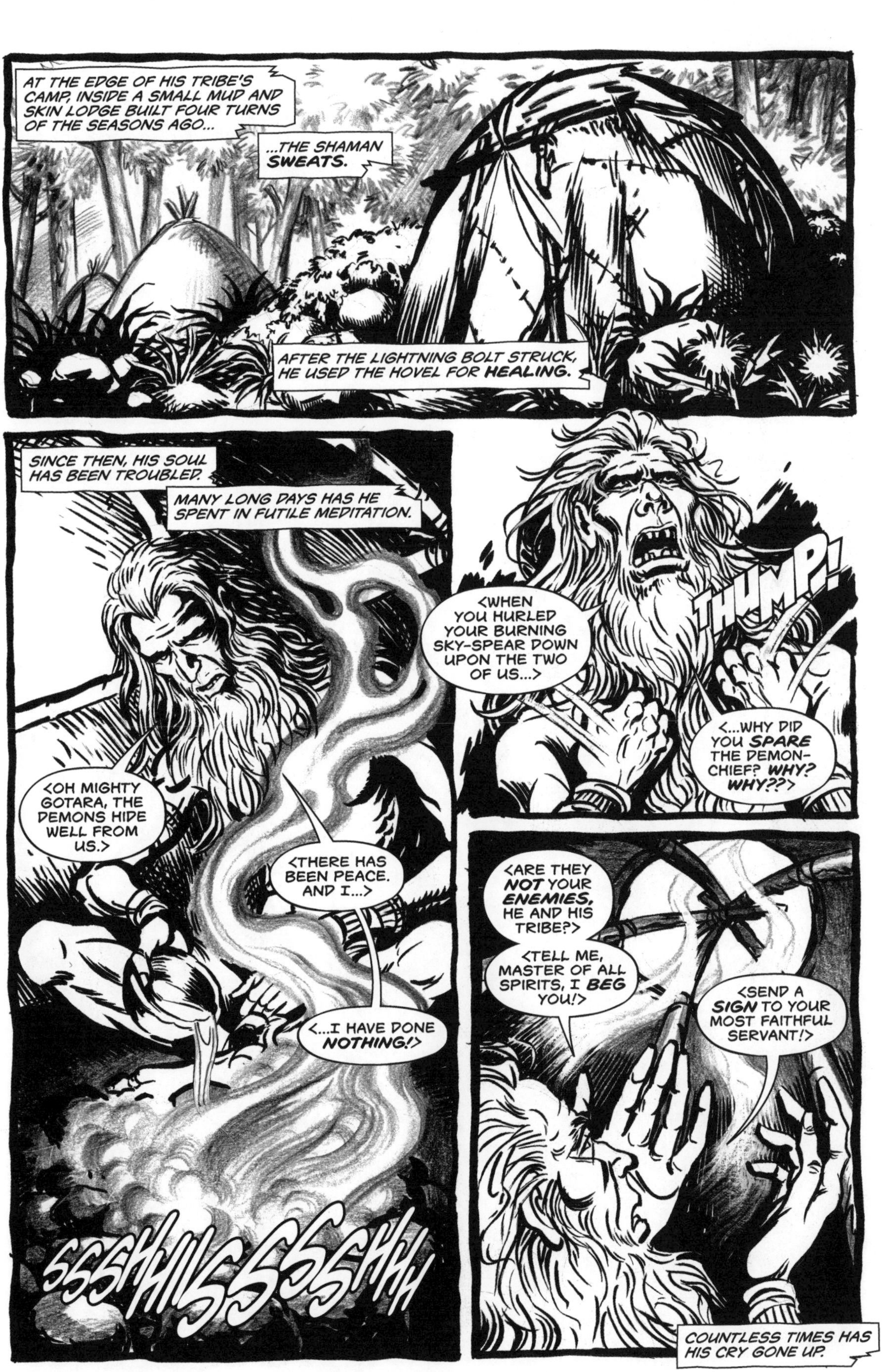
AT THE EDGE OF HIS TRIBE'S CAMP, INSIDE A SMALL MUD AND SKIN LODGE BUILT FOUR TURNS OF THE SEASONS AGO...
...THE SHAMAN SWEATS.
AFTER THE LIGHTNING BOLT STRUCK, HE USED THE HOVEL FOR HEALING.
SINCE THEN, HIS SOUL HAS BEEN TROUBLED.
MANY LONG DAYS HAS HE SPENT IN FUTILE MEDITATION.
<OH MIGHTY GOTARA, THE DEMONS HIDE WELL FROM US.>
<THERE HAS BEEN PEACE. AND I...>
<...I HAVE DONE NOTHING!>
SSSHHISSSSSHHH
<WHEN YOU HURLED YOUR BURNING SKY-SPEAR DOWN UPON THE TWO OF US...>
THUMP!
<...WHY DID YOU SPARE THE DEMON-CHIEF? WHY? WHY??>
<ARE THEY NOT YOUR ENEMIES, HE AND HIS TRIBE?>
<TELL ME, MASTER OF ALL SPIRITS, I BEG YOU!>
<SEND A SIGN TO YOUR MOST FAITHFUL SERVANT!>
COUNTLESS TIMES HAS HIS CRY GONE UP.

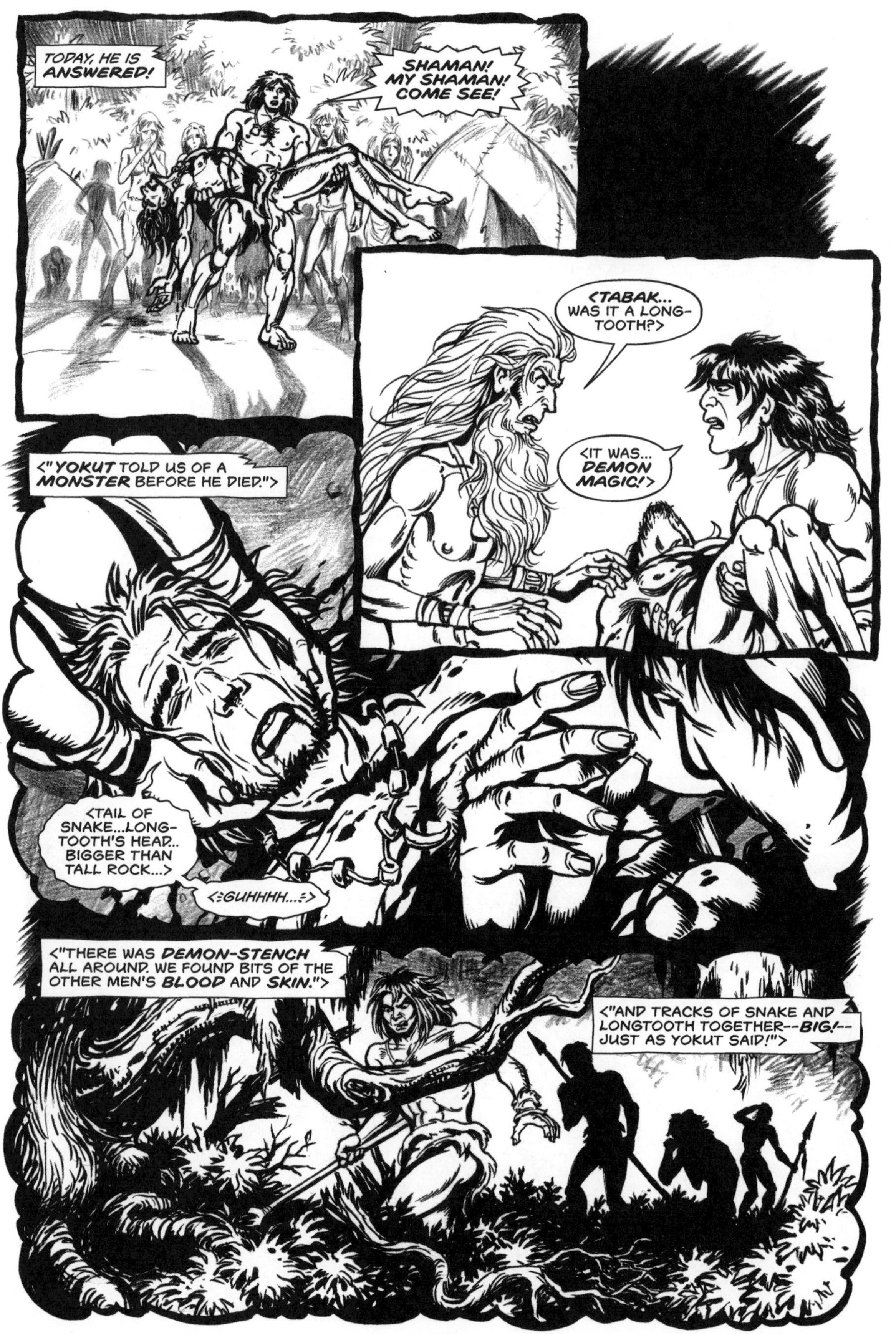
TODAY, HE IS ANSWERED!
SHAMAN! MY SHAMAN! COME SEE!
<TABAK... WAS IT A LONG-TOOTH?>
<IT WAS... DEMON MAGIC!>
<"YOKUT TOLD US OF A MONSTER BEFORE HE DIED.">
<TAIL OF SNAKE...LONG-TOOTH'S HEAD.. BIGGER THAN TALL ROCK...>
<:GUHHHH...:>
<"THERE WAS DEMON-STENCH ALL AROUND. WE FOUND BITS OF THE OTHER MEN'S BLOOD AND SKIN.">
<"AND TRACKS OF SNAKE AND LONGTOOTH TOGETHER--BIG!-- JUST AS YOKUT SAID!">

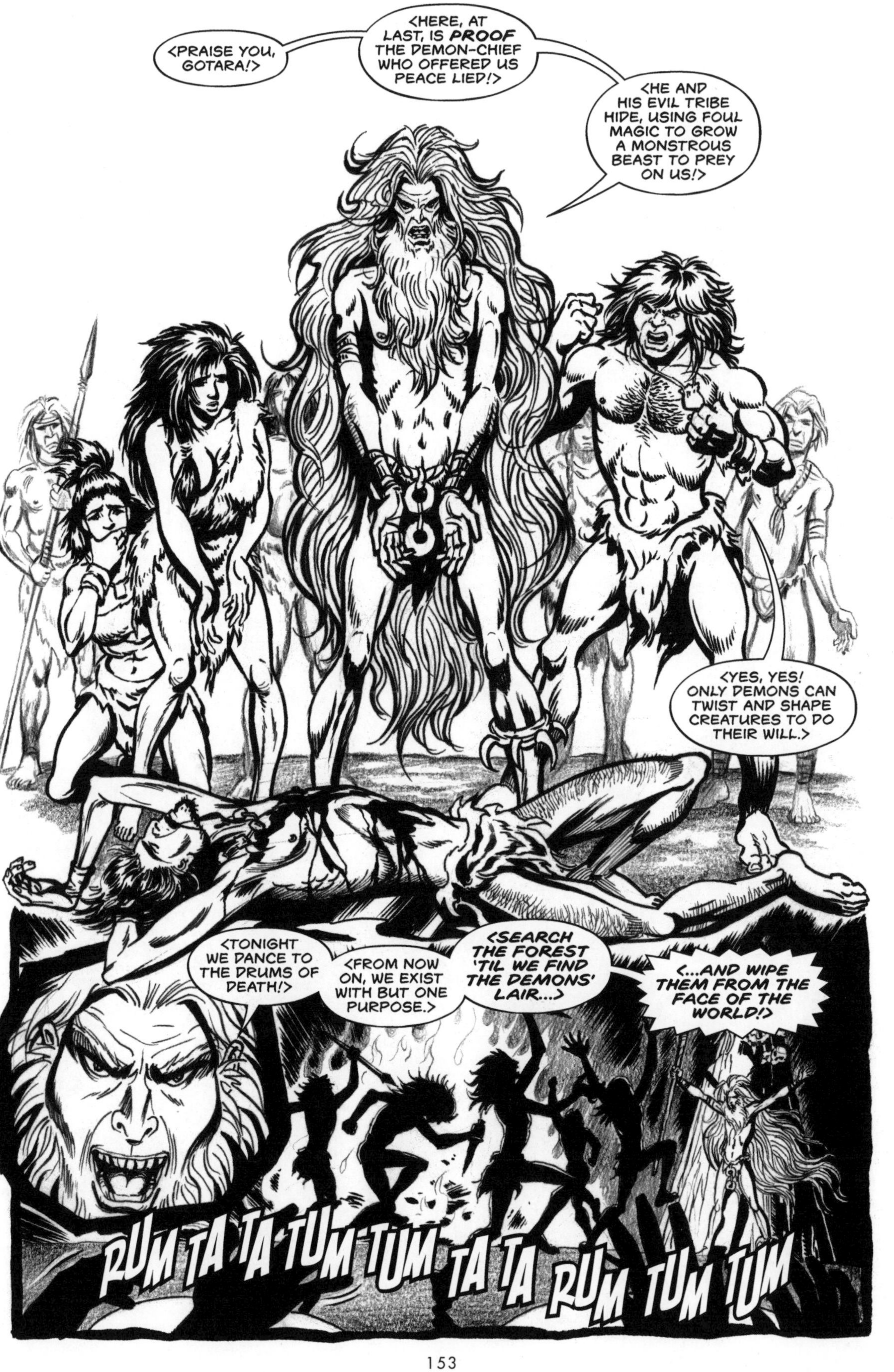
<PRAISE YOU, GOTARA!>
<HERE, AT LAST, IS PROOF THE DEMON-CHIEF WHO OFFERED US PEACE LIED!>
<HE AND HIS EVIL TRIBE HIDE, USING FOUL MAGIC TO GROW A MONSTROUS BEAST TO PREY ON US!>
<YES, YES! ONLY DEMONS CAN TWIST AND SHAPE CREATURES TO DO THEIR WILL.>
<TONIGHT WE DANCE TO THE DRUMS OF DEATH!>
<FROM NOW ON, WE EXIST WITH BUT ONE PURPOSE.>
<SEARCH THE FOREST 'TIL WE FIND THE DEMONS' LAIR...>
<...AND WIPE THEM FROM THE FACE OF THE WORLD!>
RUM TA TA TUM TUM TA TA RUM TUM TUM

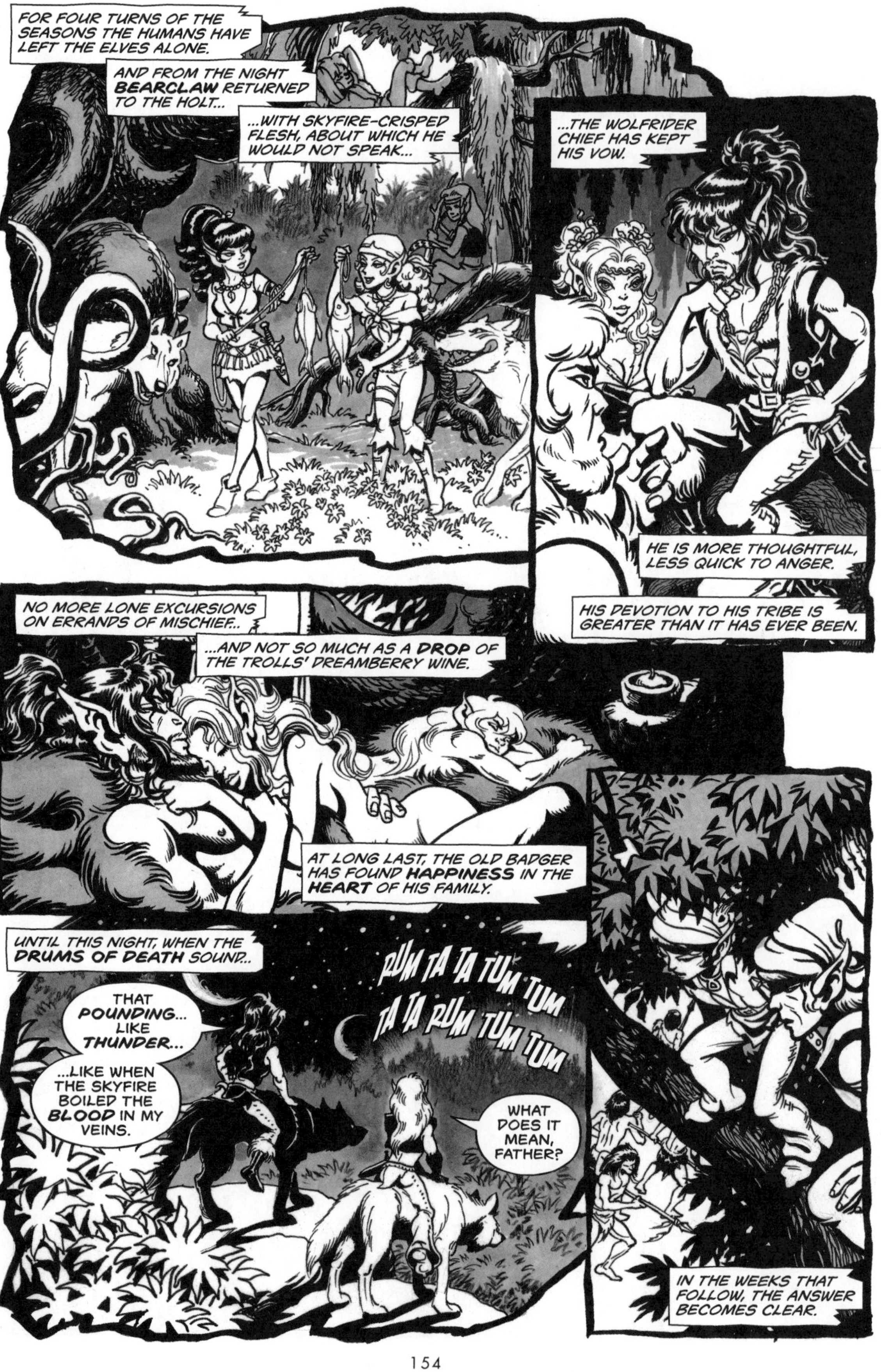
FOR FOUR TURNS OF THE SEASONS THE HUMANS HAVE LEFT THE ELVES ALONE.
AND FROM THE NIGHT BEARCLAW RETURNED TO THE HOLT...
...WITH SKYFIRE-CRISPED FLESH, ABOUT WHICH HE WOULD NOT SPEAK...
...THE WOLFRIDER CHIEF HAS KEPT HIS VOW.
HE IS MORE THOUGHTFUL, LESS QUICK TO ANGER.
HIS DEVOTION TO HIS TRIBE IS GREATER THAN IT HAS EVER BEEN.
NO MORE LONE EXCURSIONS ON ERRANDS OF MISCHIEF...
...AND NOT SO MUCH AS A DROP OF THE TROLLS' DREAMBERRY WINE.
AT LONG LAST, THE OLD BADGER HAS FOUND HAPPINESS IN THE HEART OF HIS FAMILY.
UNTIL THIS NIGHT, WHEN THE DRUMS OF DEATH SOUND...
RUM TA TA TUM TUM
TA TA RUM TUM TUM
THAT POUNDING... LIKE THUNDER...
...LIKE WHEN THE SKYFIRE BOILED THE BLOOD IN MY VEINS.
WHAT DOES IT MEAN, FATHER?
IN THE WEEKS THAT FOLLOW, THE ANSWER BECOMES CLEAR.

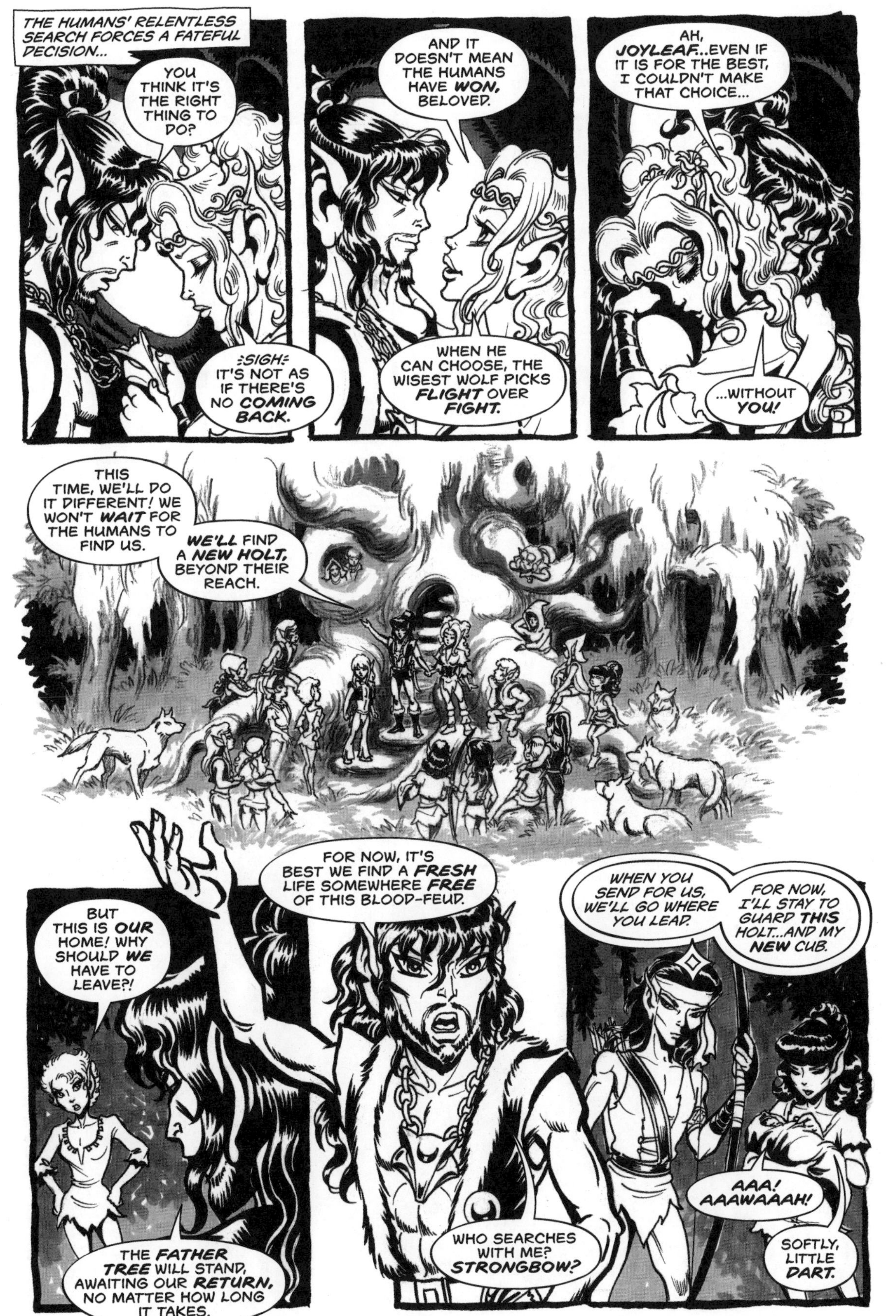
THE HUMANS' RELENTLESS SEARCH FORCES A FATEFUL DECISION...
YOU THINK IT'S THE RIGHT THING TO DO?
:SIGH: IT'S NOT AS IF THERE'S NO COMING BACK.
AND IT DOESN'T MEAN THE HUMANS HAVE WON, BELOVED.
WHEN HE CAN CHOOSE, THE WISEST WOLF PICKS FLIGHT OVER FIGHT.
AH, JOYLEAF...EVEN IF IT IS FOR THE BEST, I COULDN'T MAKE THAT CHOICE...
...WITHOUT YOU!
THIS TIME, WE'LL DO IT DIFFERENT! WE WON'T WAIT FOR THE HUMANS TO FIND US.
WE'LL FIND A NEW HOLT, BEYOND THEIR REACH.
BUT THIS IS OUR HOME! WHY SHOULD WE HAVE TO LEAVE?!
THE FATHER TREE WILL STAND, AWAITING OUR RETURN, NO MATTER HOW LONG IT TAKES.
FOR NOW, IT'S BEST WE FIND A FRESH LIFE SOMEWHERE FREE OF THIS BLOOD-FEUD.
WHO SEARCHES WITH ME? STRONGBOW?
WHEN YOU SEND FOR US, WE'LL GO WHERE YOU LEAD.
FOR NOW, I'LL STAY TO GUARD THIS HOLT...AND MY NEW CUB.
AAA! AAAWAAAH!
SOFTLY, LITTLE DART.

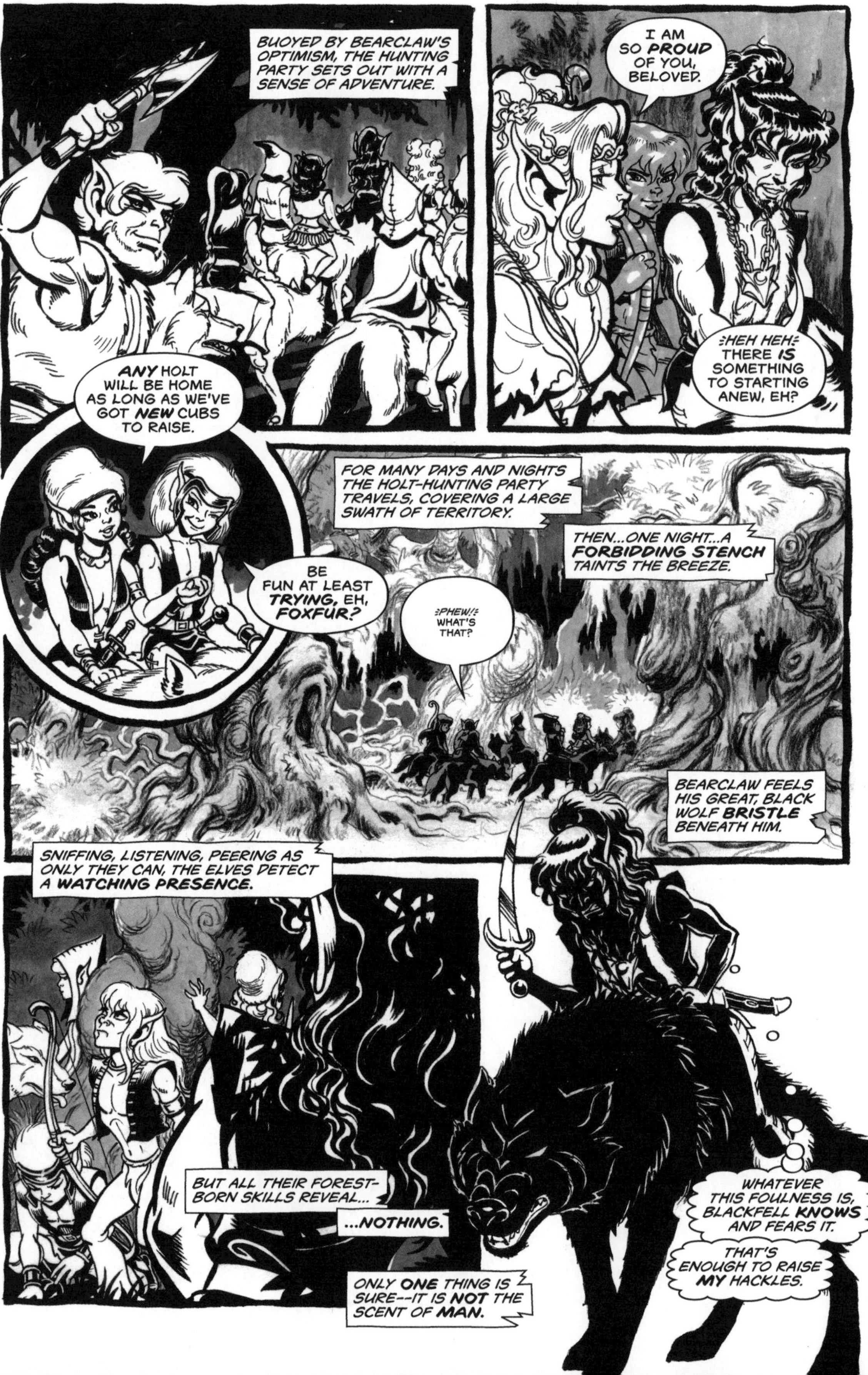
BUOYED BY BEARCLAW'S OPTIMISM, THE HUNTING PARTY SETS OUT WITH A SENSE OF ADVENTURE.
ANY HOLT WILL BE HOME AS LONG AS WE'VE GOT NEW CUBS TO RAISE.
I AM SO PROUD OF YOU, BELOVED.
HEH HEH THERE IS SOMETHING TO STARTING ANEW, EH?
BE FUN AT LEAST TRYING, EH, FOXFUR?
FOR MANY DAYS AND NIGHTS THE HOLT-HUNTING PARTY TRAVELS, COVERING A LARGE SWATH OF TERRITORY.
THEN...ONE NIGHT...A FORBIDDING STENCH TAINTS THE BREEZE.
PHEW! WHAT'S THAT?
BEARCLAW FEELS HIS GREAT, BLACK WOLF BRISTLE BENEATH HIM.
SNIFFING, LISTENING, PEERING AS ONLY THEY CAN, THE ELVES DETECT A WATCHING PRESENCE.
BUT ALL THEIR FOREST-BORN SKILLS REVEAL...
...NOTHING.
ONLY ONE THING IS SURE--IT IS NOT THE SCENT OF MAN.
WHATEVER THIS FOULNESS IS, BLACKFELL KNOWS AND FEARS IT.
THAT'S ENOUGH TO RAISE MY HACKLES.

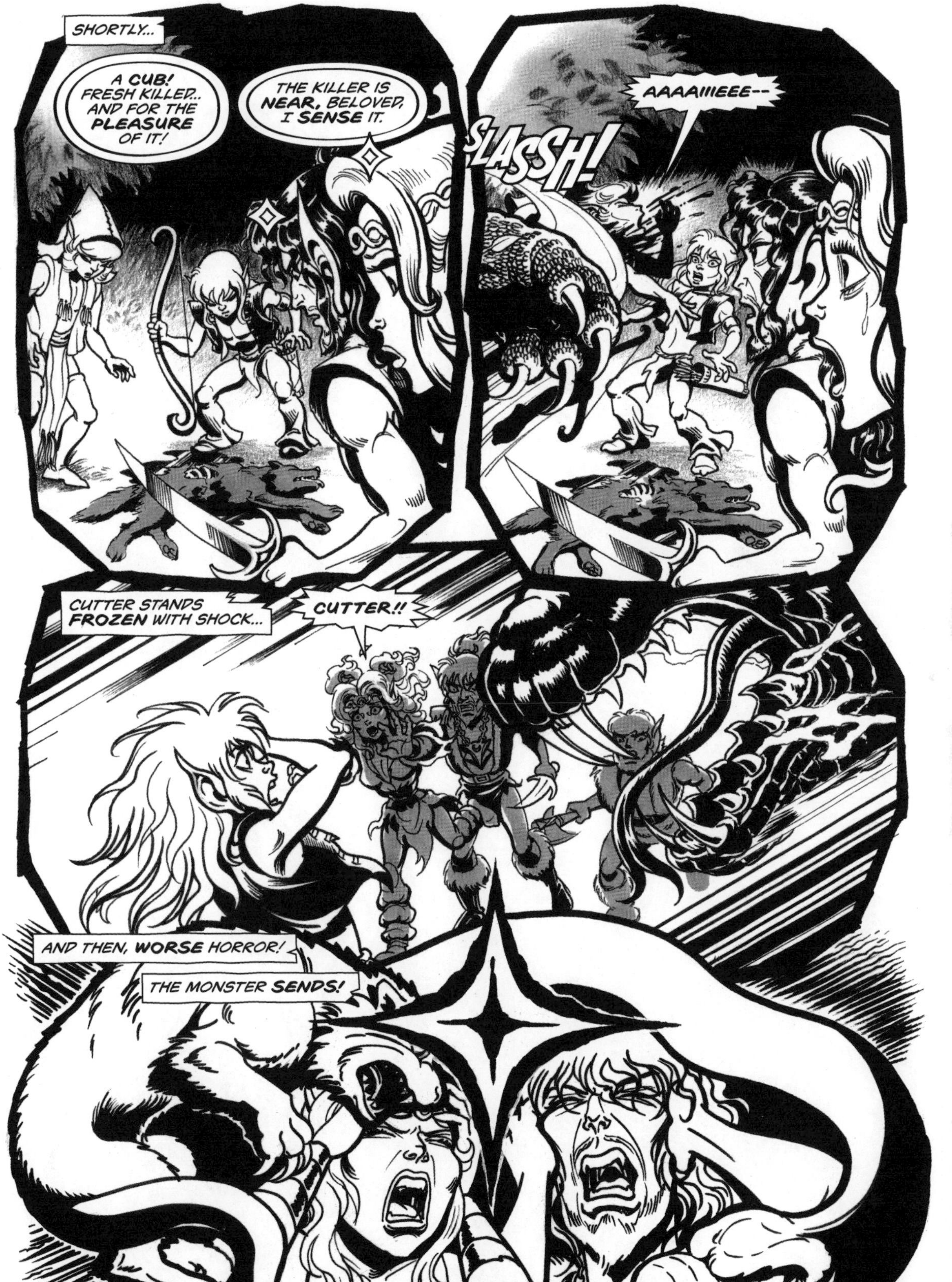
SHORTLY...
A CUB! FRESH KILLED... AND FOR THE PLEASURE OF IT!
THE KILLER IS NEAR, BELOVED, I SENSE IT.
AAAAIIIEEE--
SLASSH!
CUTTER STANDS FROZEN WITH SHOCK...
CUTTER!!
AND THEN, WORSE HORROR!
THE MONSTER SENDS!
BLOOD AND FIRE, CAT AND SNAKE JOINED BY TWISTED, ANCIENT MAGIC!

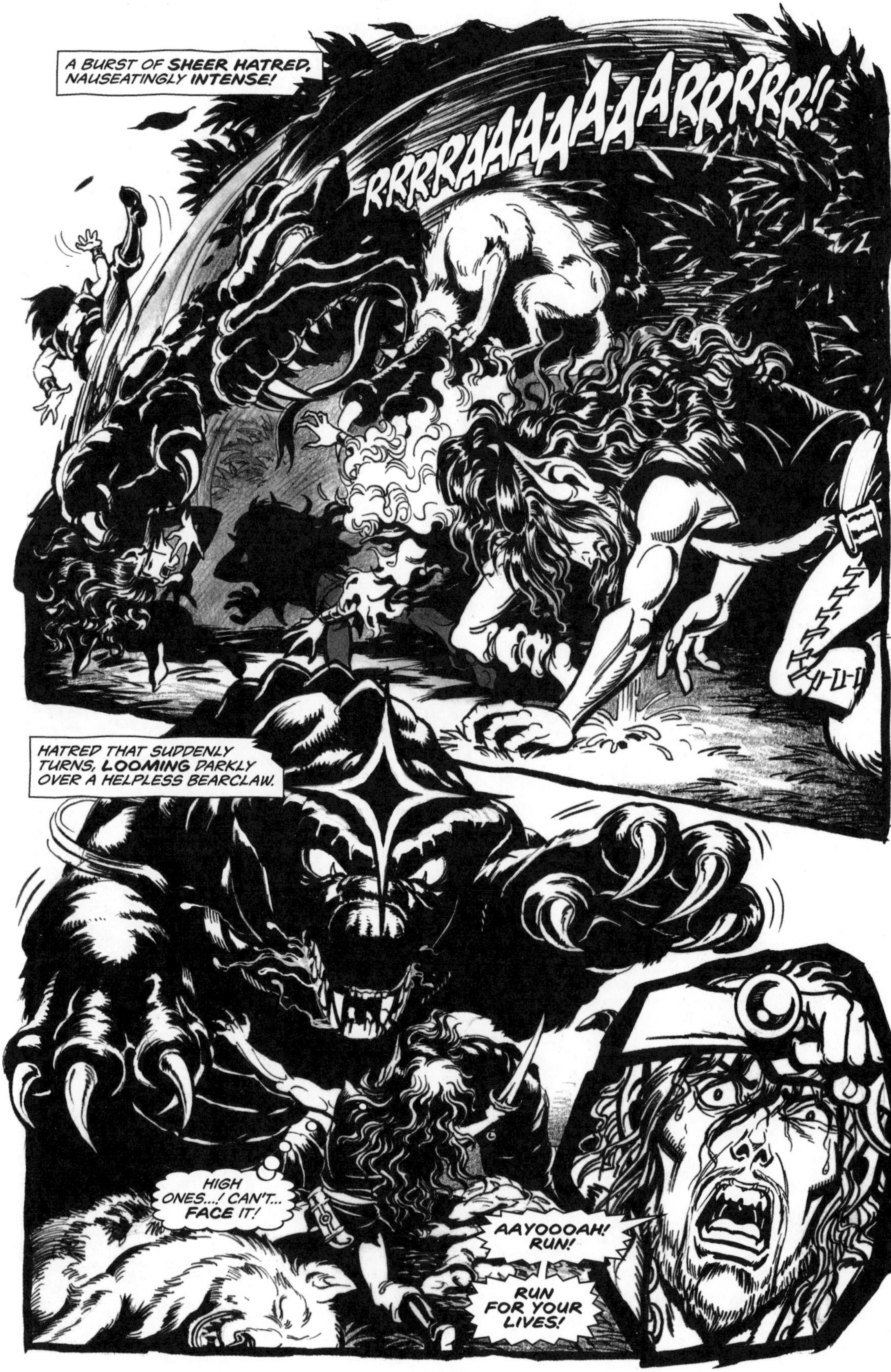
A BURST OF SHEER HATRED, NAUSEATINGLY INTENSE!
RRRRAAAAAAAAARRRRRR!!
HATRED THAT SUDDENLY TURNS, LOOMING DARKLY OVER A HELPLESS BEARCLAW.
HIGH ONES...! CAN'T... FACE IT!
AAYOOOAH! RUN!
RUN FOR YOUR LIVES!

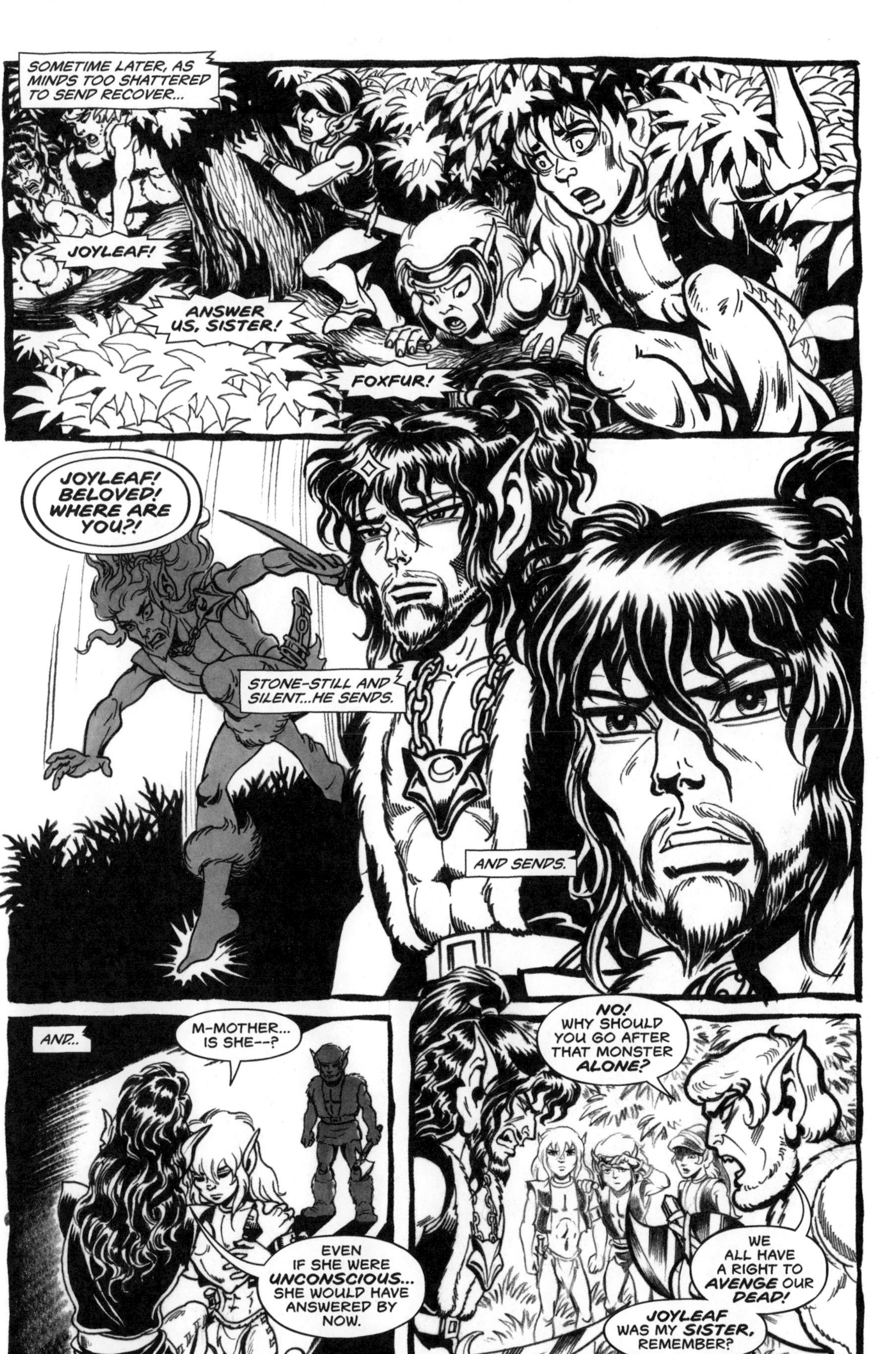
SOMETIME LATER, AS MINDS TOO SHATTERED TO SEND RECOVER...
JOYLEAF!
ANSWER US, SISTER!
FOXFUR!
JOYLEAF! BELOVED! WHERE ARE YOU?!
STONE-STILL AND SILENT...HE SENDS.
AND SENDS.
AND...
M-MOTHER... IS SHE--?
EVEN IF SHE WERE UNCONSCIOUS... SHE WOULD HAVE ANSWERED BY NOW.
NO! WHY SHOULD YOU GO AFTER THAT MONSTER ALONE?
WE ALL HAVE A RIGHT TO AVENGE OUR DEAD!
JOYLEAF WAS MY SISTER, REMEMBER?

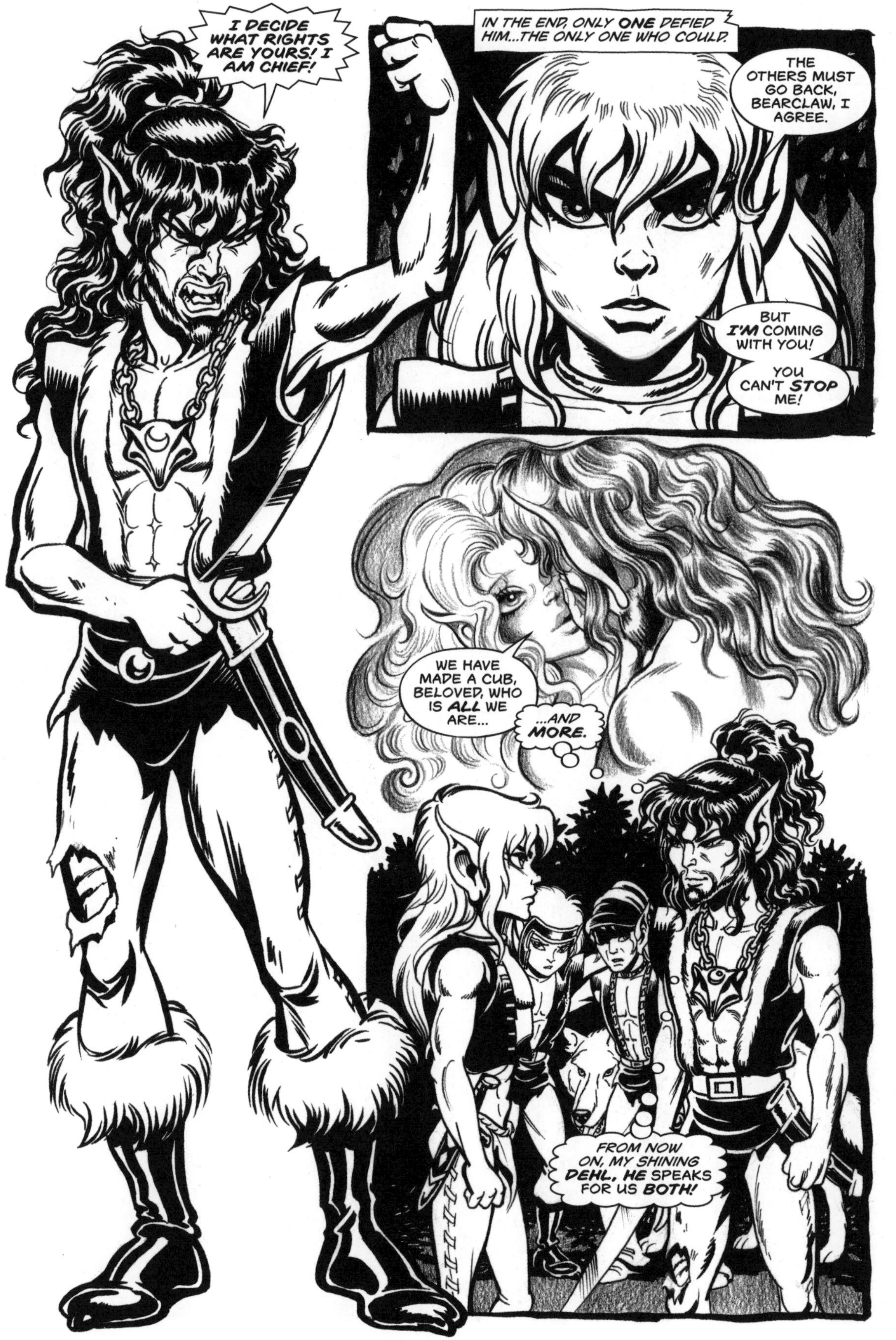
I DECIDE WHAT RIGHTS ARE YOURS! I AM CHIEF!
IN THE END, ONLY ONE DEFIED HIM...THE ONLY ONE WHO COULD.
THE OTHERS MUST GO BACK, BEARCLAW, I AGREE.
BUT I'M COMING WITH YOU!
YOU CAN'T STOP ME!
WE HAVE MADE A CUB, BELOVED, WHO IS ALL WE ARE...
...AND MORE.
FROM NOW ON, MY SHINING DEHL, HE SPEAKS FOR US BOTH!

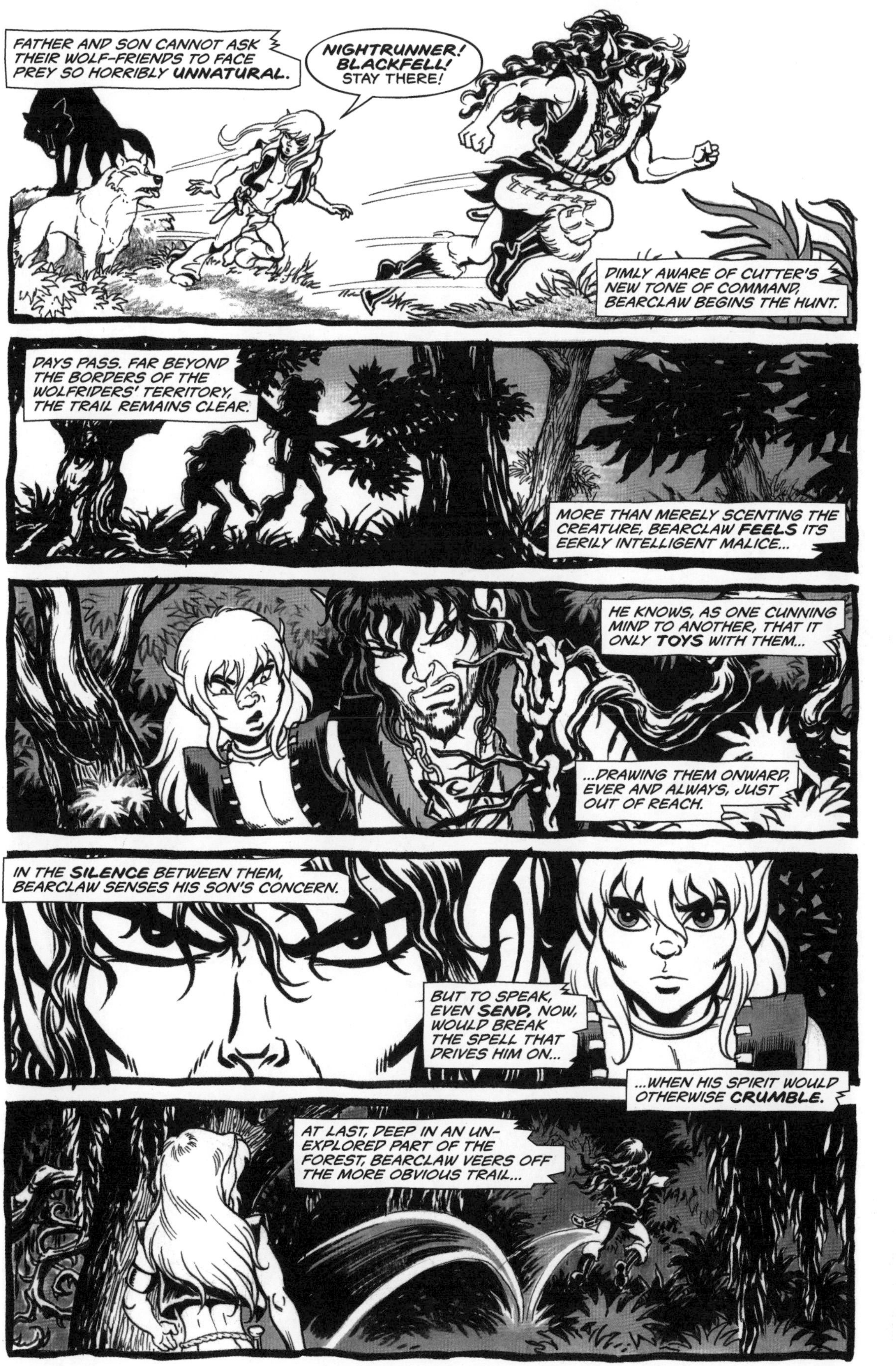

FATHER AND SON CANNOT ASK THEIR WOLF-FRIENDS TO FACE PREY SO HORRIBLY UNNATURAL.
NIGHTRUNNER! BLACKFELL! STAY THERE!
DIMLY AWARE OF CUTTER'S NEW TONE OF COMMAND, BEARCLAW BEGINS THE HUNT.
DAYS PASS. FAR BEYOND THE BORDERS OF THE WOLFRIDERS' TERRITORY, THE TRAIL REMAINS CLEAR.
MORE THAN MERELY SCENTING THE CREATURE, BEARCLAW FEELS ITS EERILY INTELLIGENT MALICE...
HE KNOWS, AS ONE CUNNING MIND TO ANOTHER, THAT IT ONLY TOYS WITH THEM...
...DRAWING THEM ONWARD, EVER AND ALWAYS, JUST OUT OF REACH.
IN THE SILENCE BETWEEN THEM, BEARCLAW SENSES HIS SON'S CONCERN.
BUT TO SPEAK, EVEN SEND, NOW, WOULD BREAK THE SPELL THAT DRIVES HIM ON...
...WHEN HIS SPIRIT WOULD OTHERWISE CRUMBLE.
AT LAST, DEEP IN AN UN-EXPLORED PART OF THE FOREST, BEARCLAW VEERS OFF THE MORE OBVIOUS TRAIL...

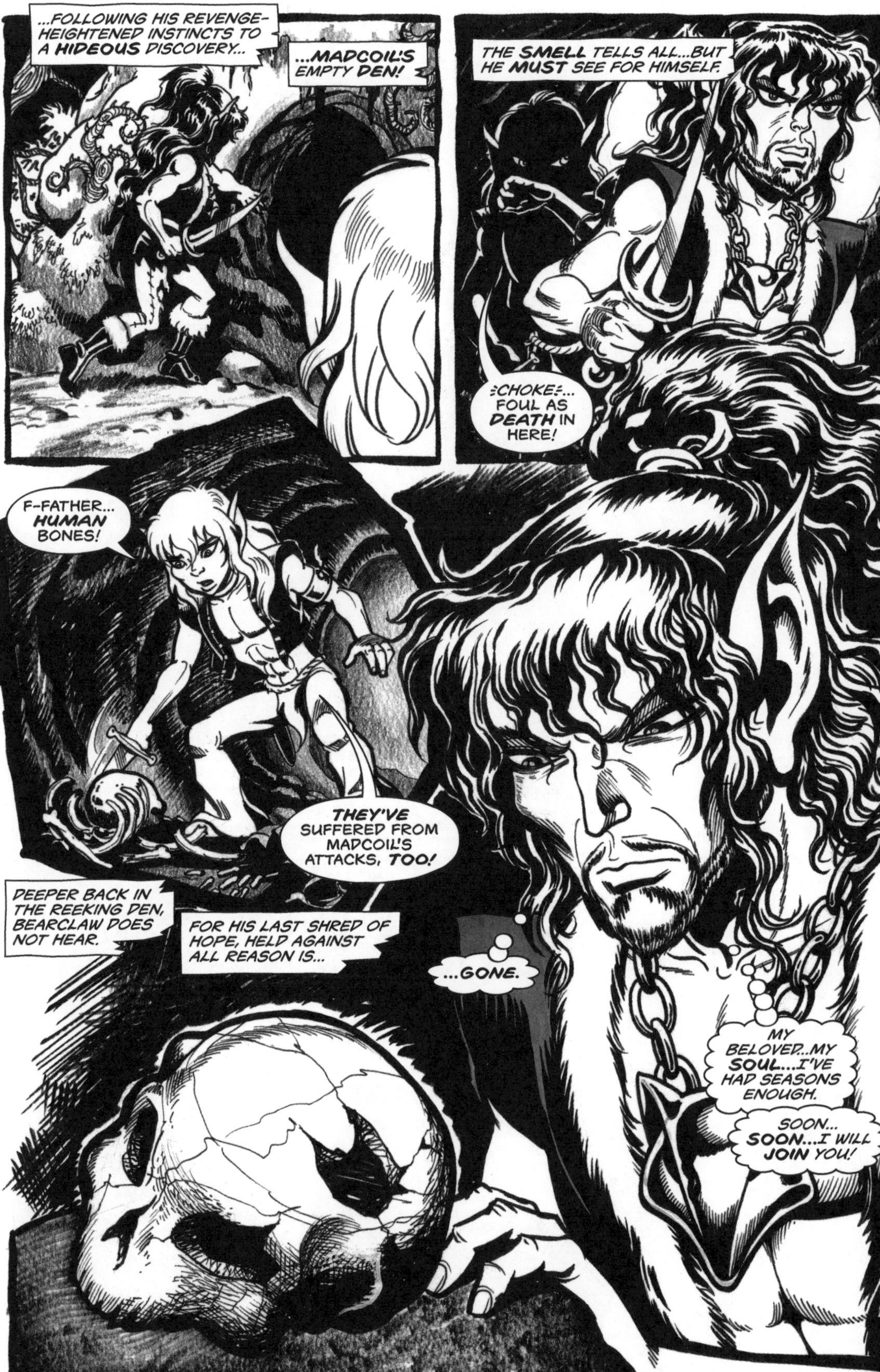
...FOLLOWING HIS REVENGE-HEIGHTENED INSTINCTS TO A HIDEOUS DISCOVERY...
...MADCOIL'S EMPTY DEN!
THE SMELL TELLS ALL...BUT HE MUST SEE FOR HIMSELF.
:CHOKE:... FOUL AS DEATH IN HERE!
F-FATHER... HUMAN BONES!
THEY'VE SUFFERED FROM MADCOIL'S ATTACKS, TOO!
DEEPER BACK IN THE REEKING DEN, BEARCLAW DOES NOT HEAR.
FOR HIS LAST SHRED OF HOPE, HELD AGAINST ALL REASON IS...
...GONE.
MY BELOVED...MY SOUL...I'VE HAD SEASONS ENOUGH.
SOON... SOON...I WILL JOIN YOU!

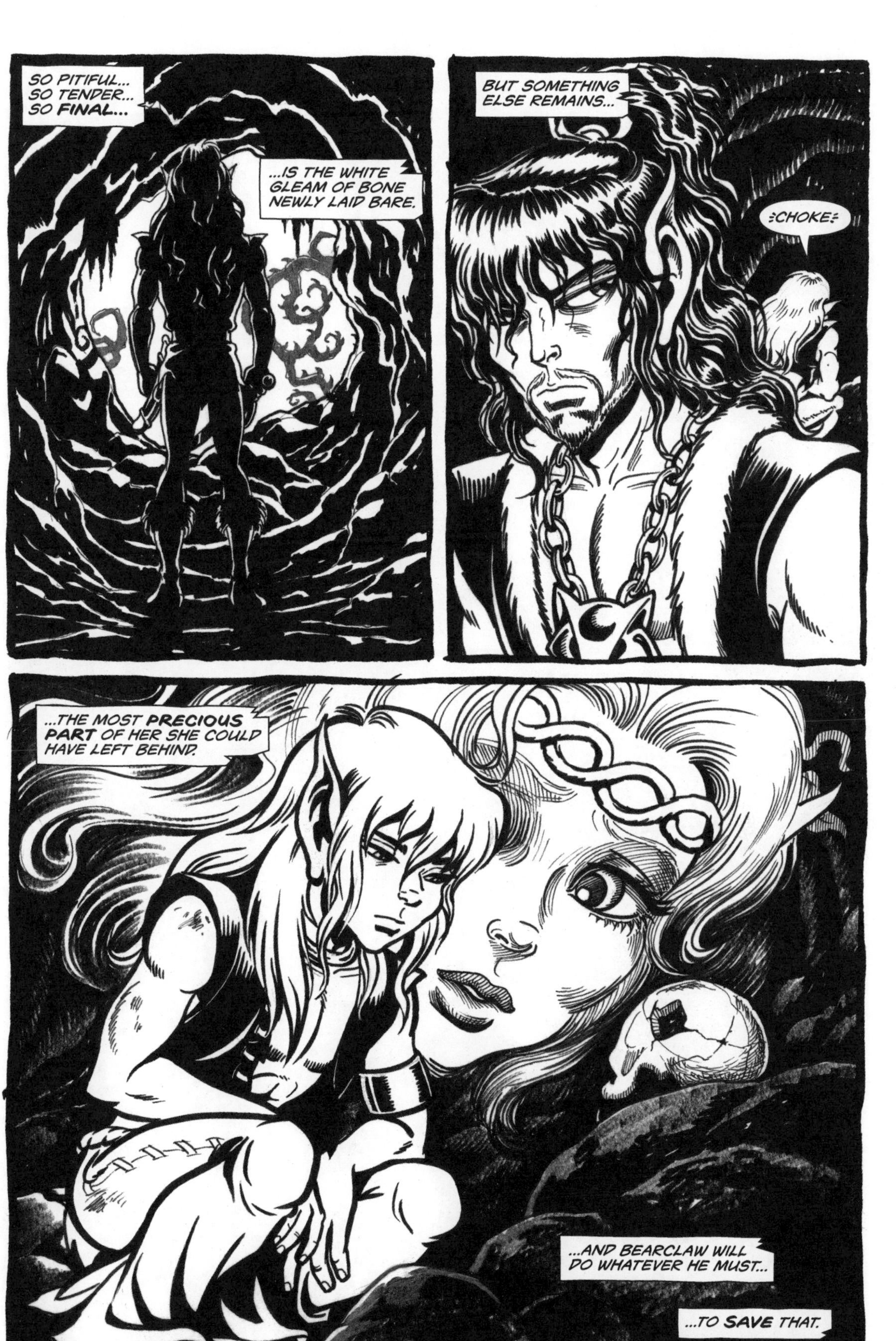
SO PITIFUL... SO TENDER... SO FINAL...
...IS THE WHITE GLEAM OF BONE NEWLY LAID BARE.
BUT SOMETHING ELSE REMAINS...
CHOKE
...THE MOST PRECIOUS PART OF HER SHE COULD HAVE LEFT BEHIND.
...AND BEARCLAW WILL DO WHATEVER HE MUST...
...TO SAVE THAT.

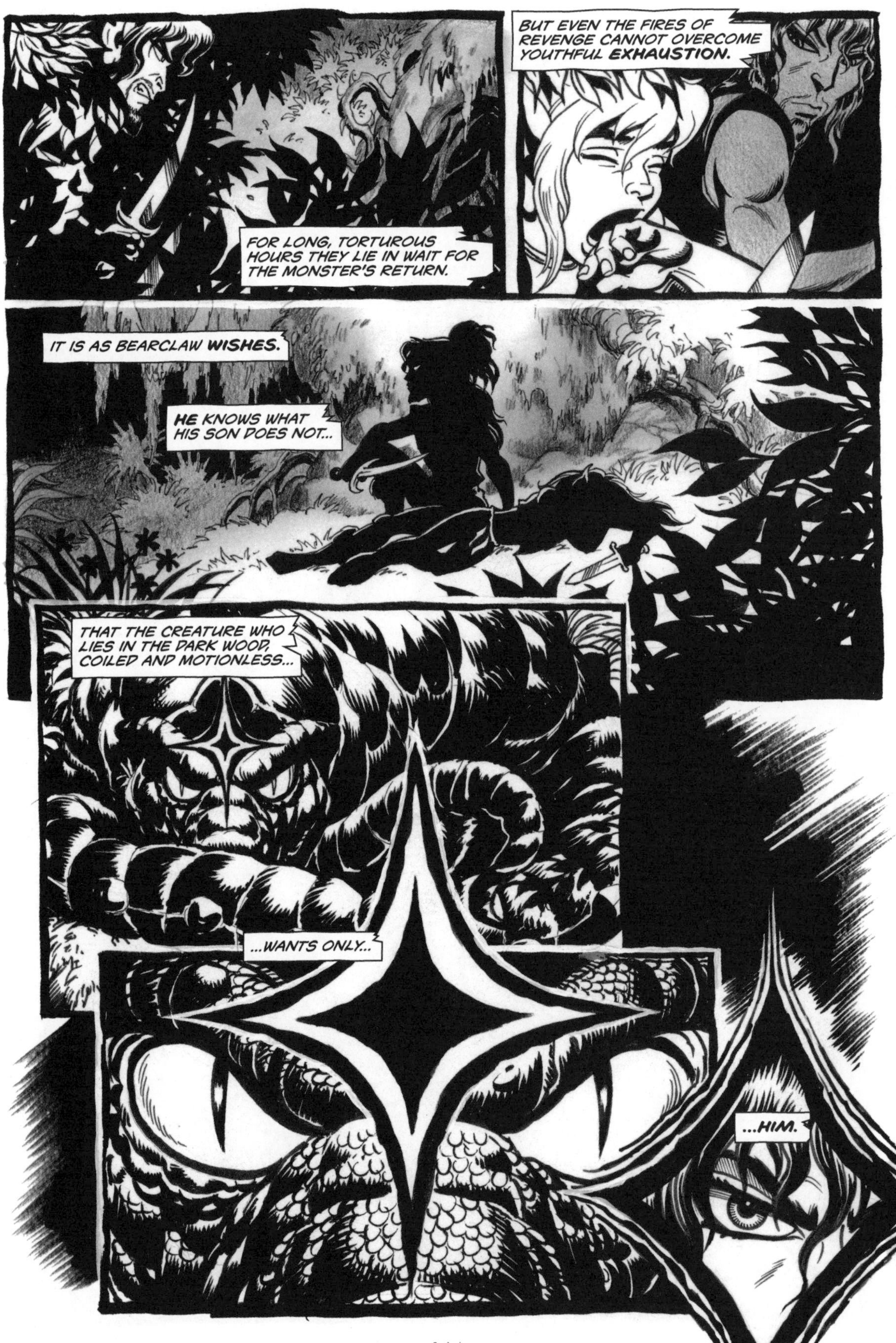
FOR LONG, TORTUROUS HOURS THEY LIE IN WAIT FOR THE MONSTER'S RETURN.
BUT EVEN THE FIRES OF REVENGE CANNOT OVERCOME YOUTHFUL EXHAUSTION.
IT IS AS BEARCLAW WISHES.
HE KNOWS WHAT HIS SON DOES NOT...
THAT THE CREATURE WHO LIES IN THE DARK WOOD, COILED AND MOTIONLESS...
...WANTS ONLY...
...HIM.

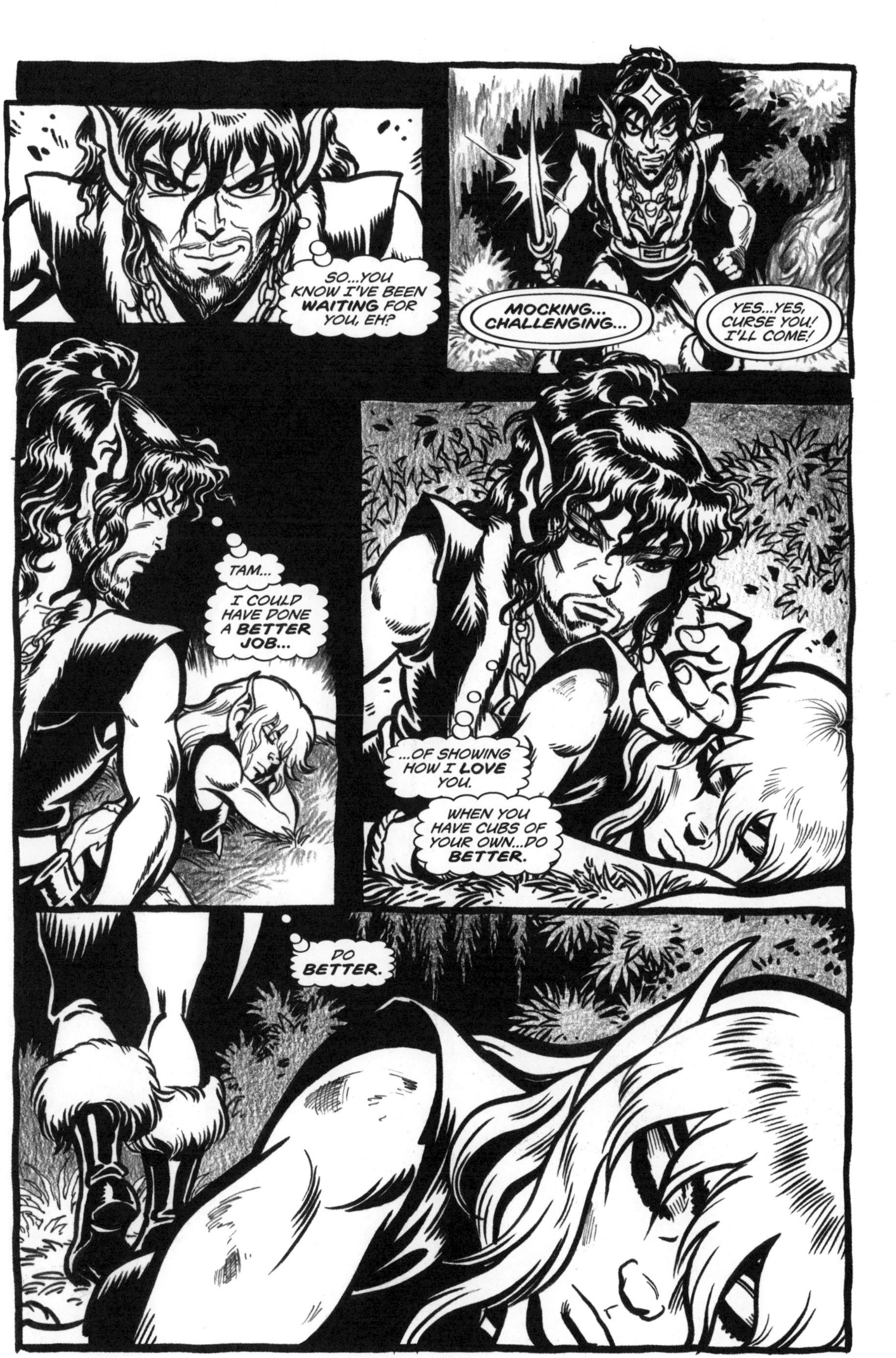
SO...YOU KNOW I'VE BEEN WAITING FOR YOU, EH?
MOCKING... CHALLENGING...
YES...YES, CURSE YOU! I'LL COME!
TAM...
I COULD HAVE DONE A BETTER JOB...
...OF SHOWING HOW I LOVE YOU.
WHEN YOU HAVE CUBS OF YOUR OWN...DO BETTER.
DO BETTER.

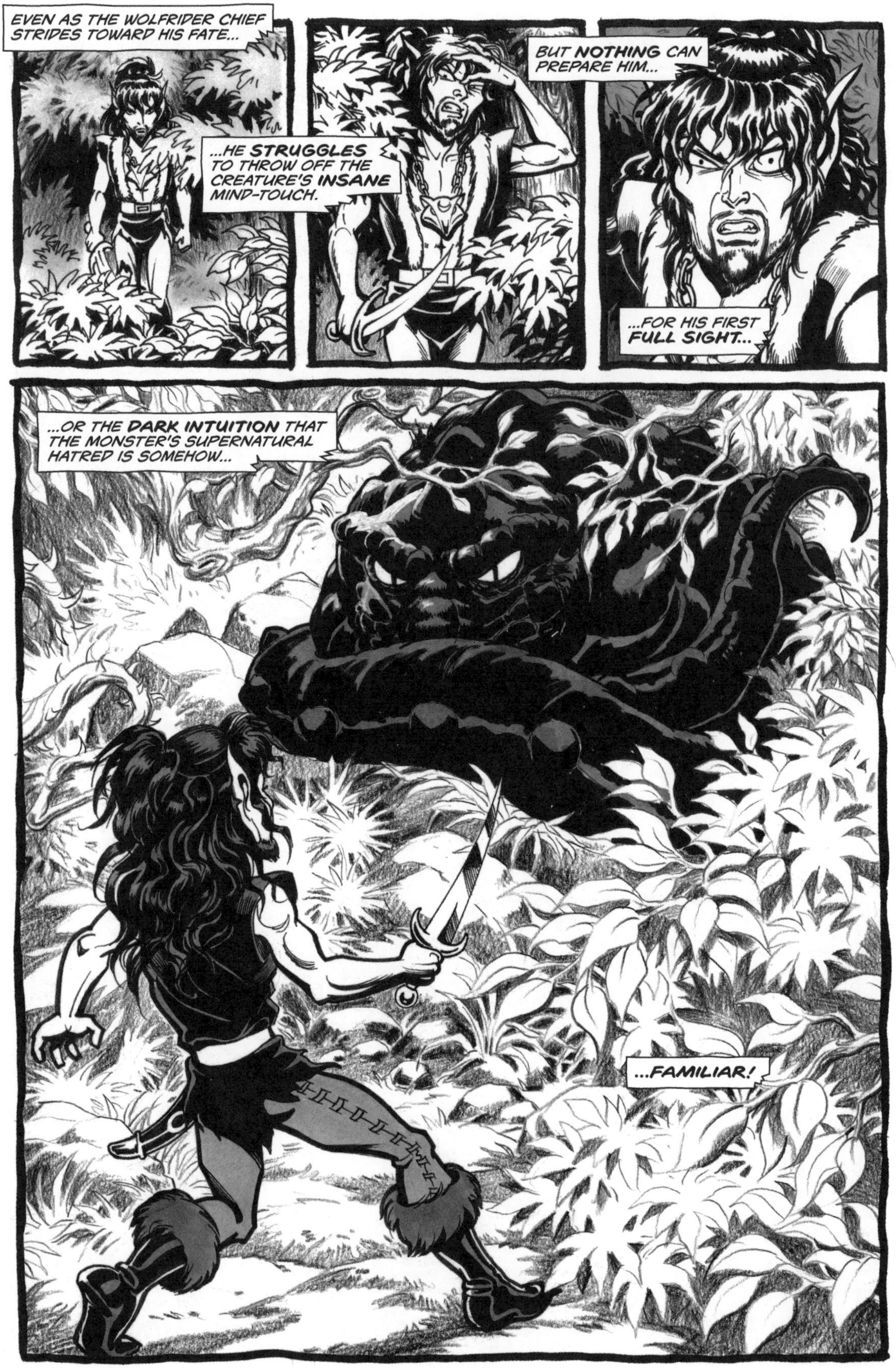
EVEN AS THE WOLFRIDER CHIEF STRIDES TOWARD HIS FATE...
...HE STRUGGLES TO THROW OFF THE CREATURE'S INSANE MIND-TOUCH.
BUT NOTHING CAN PREPARE HIM...
...FOR HIS FIRST FULL SIGHT...
...OR THE DARK INTUITION THAT THE MONSTER'S SUPERNATURAL HATRED IS SOMEHOW...
...FAMILIAR!

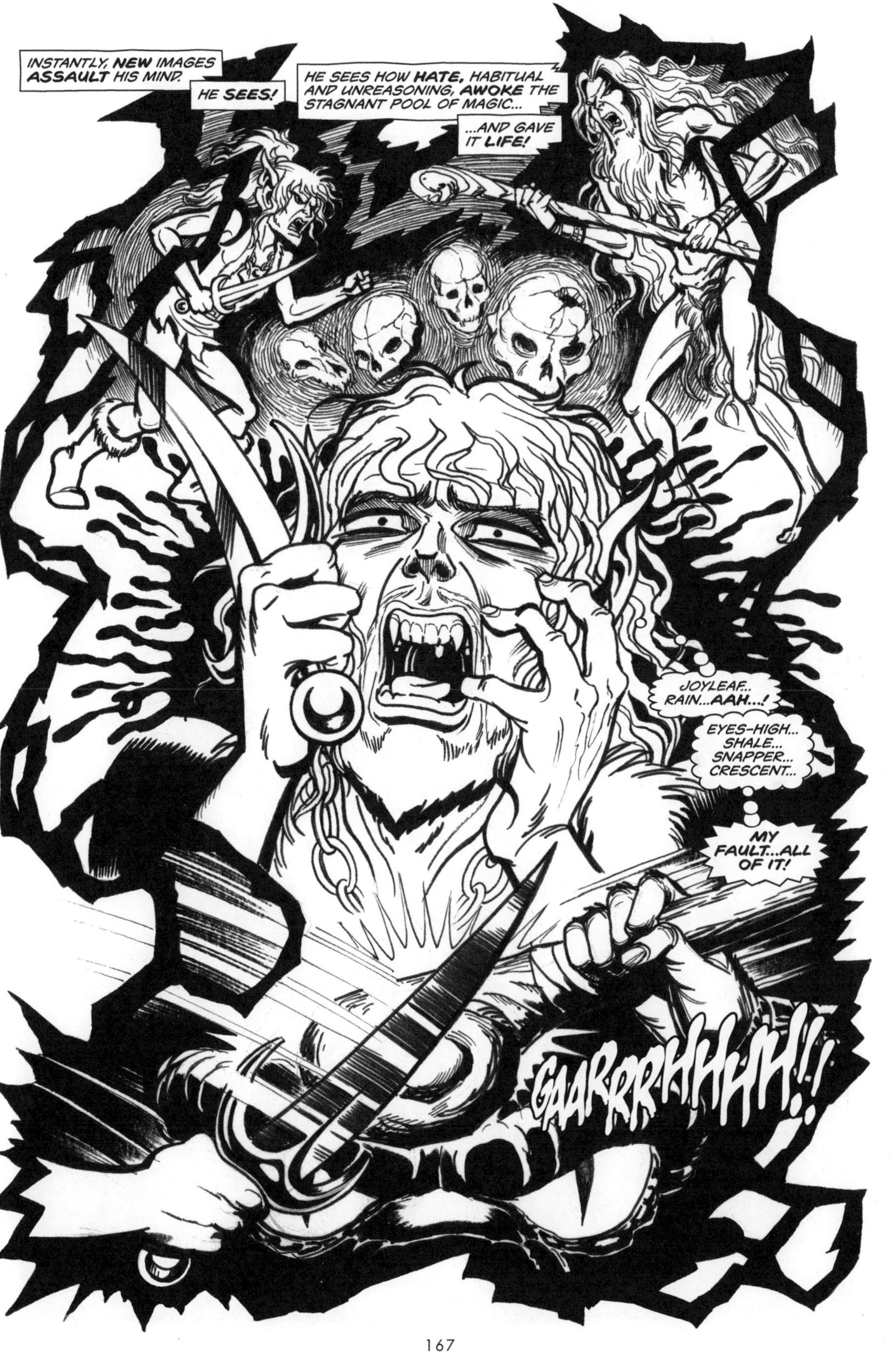
INSTANTLY, NEW IMAGES ASSAULT HIS MIND.
HE SEES!
HE SEES HOW HATE, HABITUAL AND UNREASONING, AWOKE THE STAGNANT POOL OF MAGIC...
...AND GAVE IT LIFE!
JOYLEAF... RAIN...AAH...!
EYES-HIGH... SHALE... SNAPPER... CRESCENT...
MY FAULT...ALL OF IT!
GAARRRHHHH!!!

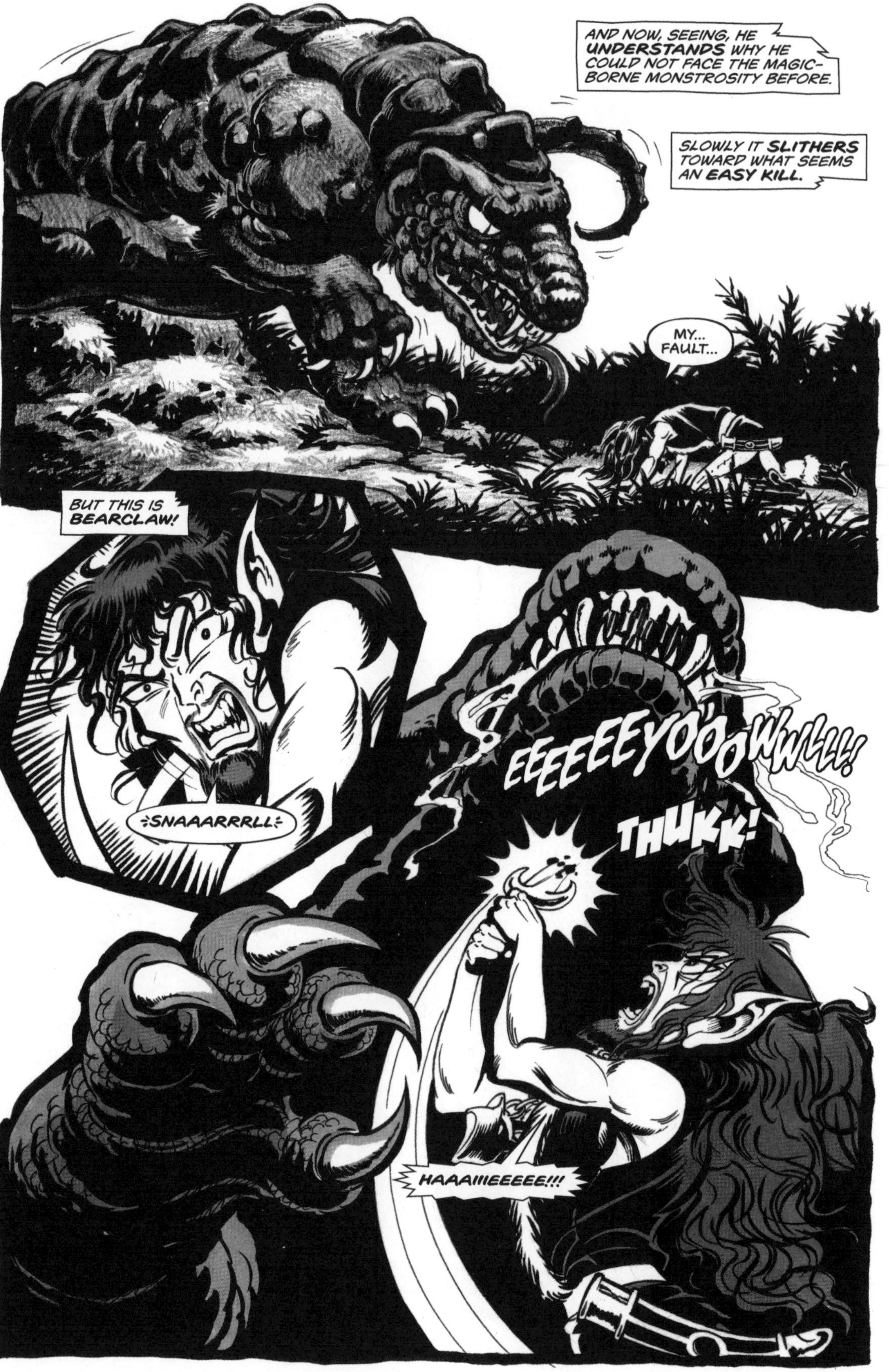
AND NOW, SEEING, HE UNDERSTANDS WHY HE COULD NOT FACE THE MAGIC-BORNE MONSTROSITY BEFORE.
SLOWLY IT SLITHERS TOWARD WHAT SEEMS AN EASY KILL.
MY... FAULT...
BUT THIS IS BEARCLAW!
SNAAARRRLL
EEEEEEYOOOOWWLLL!
THUKK!
HAAAIIIEEEEE!!!

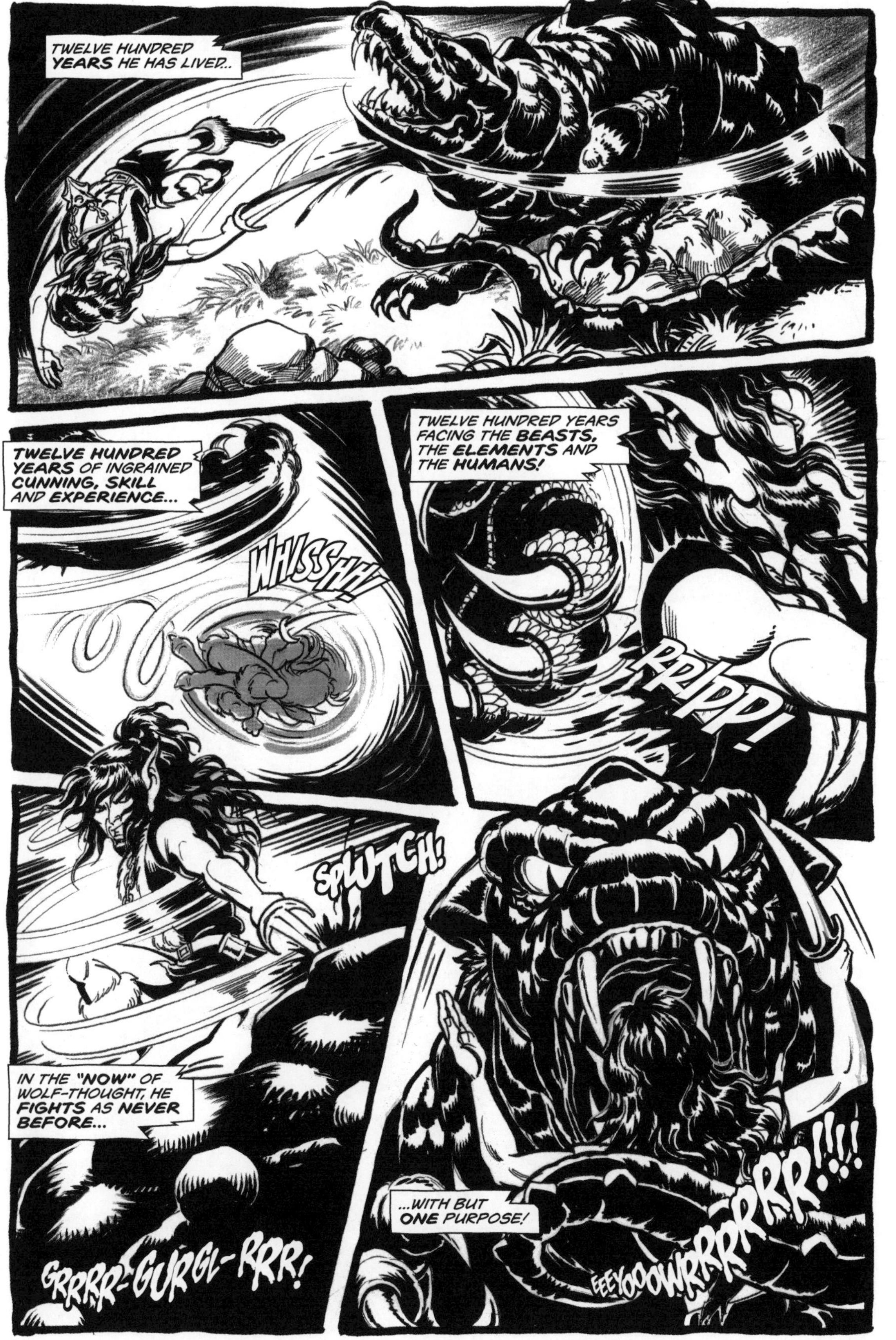

TWELVE HUNDRED YEARS HE HAS LIVED...
TWELVE HUNDRED YEARS OF INGRAINED CUNNING, SKILL AND EXPERIENCE...
WHISSHH!
TWELVE HUNDRED YEARS FACING THE BEASTS, THE ELEMENTS AND THE HUMANS!
RRIPP!
SPLUTCH!
IN THE "NOW" OF WOLF-THOUGHT, HE FIGHTS AS NEVER BEFORE...
GRRRR-GURGL-RRR!
...WITH BUT ONE PURPOSE!
EEEYOOOWRRRRRR!!!!!

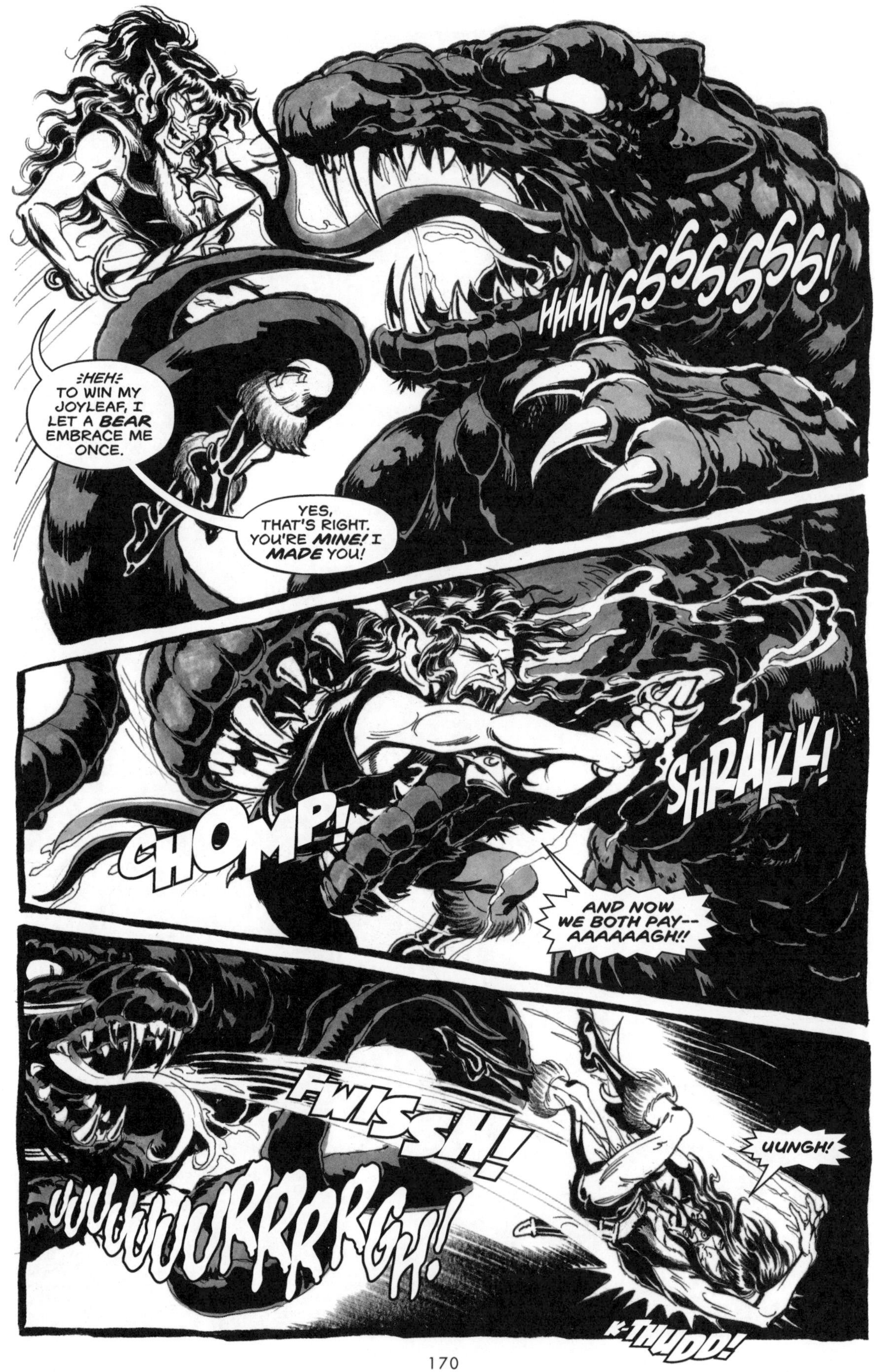
HHHHISSSSSSSS!
:HEH: TO WIN MY JOYLEAF, I LET A BEAR EMBRACE ME ONCE.
YES, THAT'S RIGHT. YOU'RE MINE! I MADE YOU!
SHRAKK!
CHOMP!!
AND NOW WE BOTH PAY-- AAAAAAAGH!!
FWISSH!
UUNGH!
UUUUUURRRRGH!
K-THUDD!

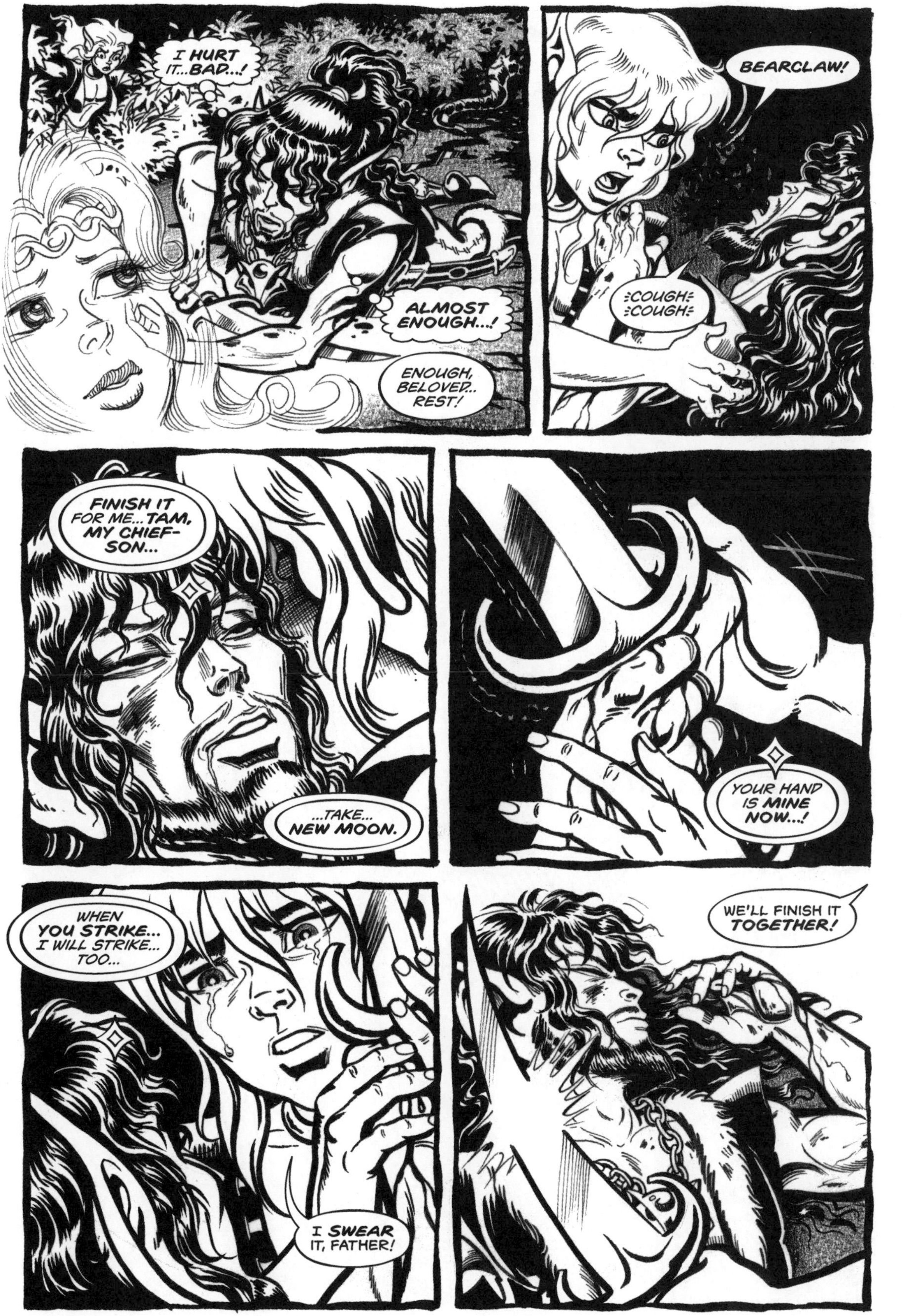
I HURT IT...BAD...!
ALMOST ENOUGH...!
ENOUGH, BELOVED... REST!
BEARCLAW!
COUGH COUGH
FINISH IT FOR ME...TAM, MY CHIEF-SON...
...TAKE... NEW MOON.
YOUR HAND IS MINE NOW...!
WHEN YOU STRIKE... I WILL STRIKE... TOO...
I SWEAR IT, FATHER!
WE'LL FINISH IT TOGETHER!

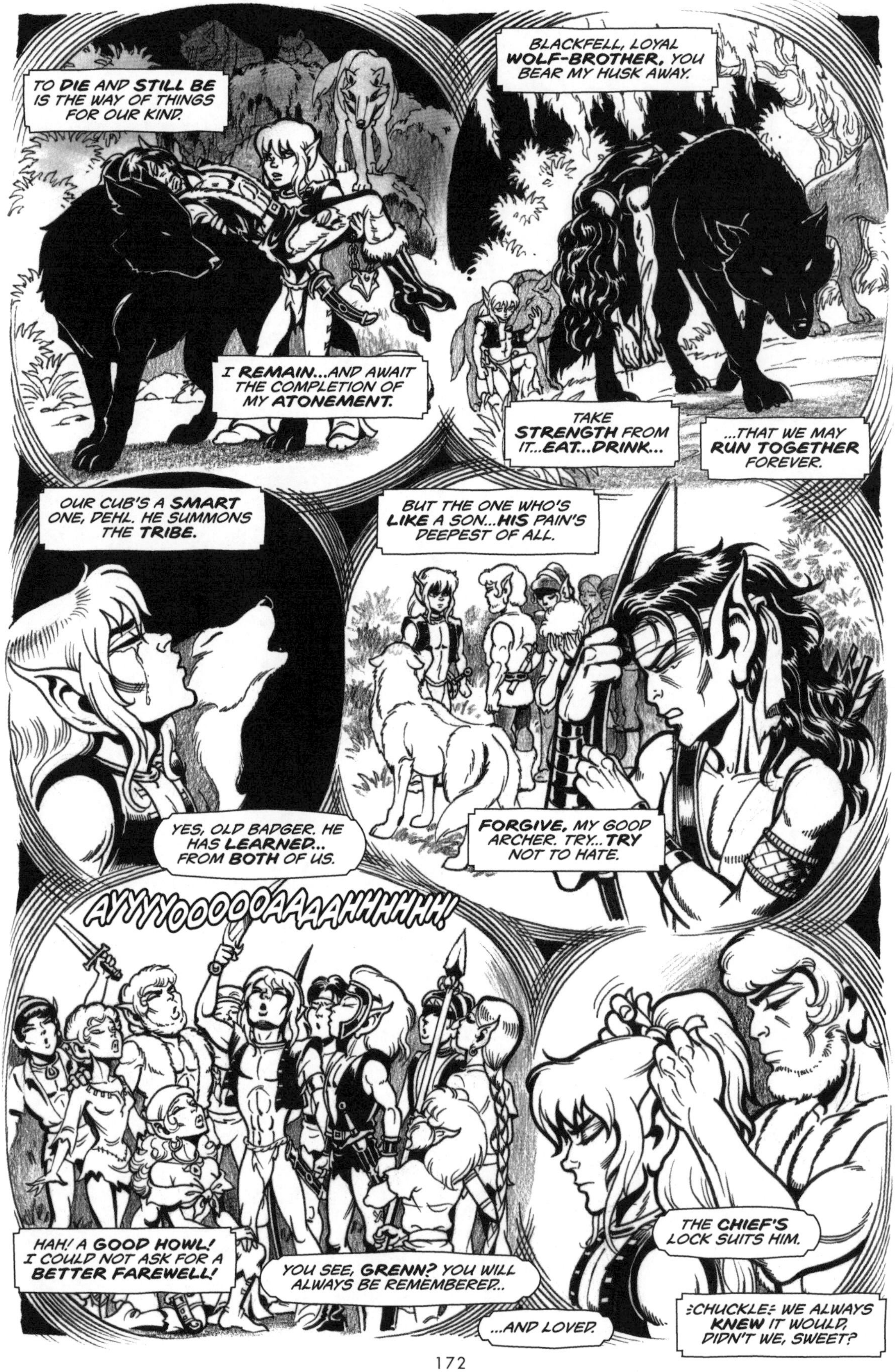
TO DIE AND STILL BE IS THE WAY OF THINGS FOR OUR KIND.
I REMAIN...AND AWAIT THE COMPLETION OF MY ATONEMENT.
BLACKFELL, LOYAL WOLF-BROTHER, YOU BEAR MY HUSK AWAY.
TAKE STRENGTH FROM IT...EAT...DRINK...
...THAT WE MAY RUN TOGETHER FOREVER.
OUR CUB'S A SMART ONE, DEHL. HE SUMMONS THE TRIBE.
YES, OLD BADGER. HE HAS LEARNED... FROM BOTH OF US.
BUT THE ONE WHO'S LIKE A SON...HIS PAIN'S DEEPEST OF ALL.
FORGIVE, MY GOOD ARCHER. TRY...TRY NOT TO HATE.
AYYYOOOOOAAAAHHHHHH!
HAH! A GOOD HOWL! I COULD NOT ASK FOR A BETTER FAREWELL!
YOU SEE, GRENN? YOU WILL ALWAYS BE REMEMBERED...
...AND LOVED.
THE CHIEF'S LOCK SUITS HIM.
:CHUCKLE: WE ALWAYS KNEW IT WOULD, DIDN'T WE, SWEET?

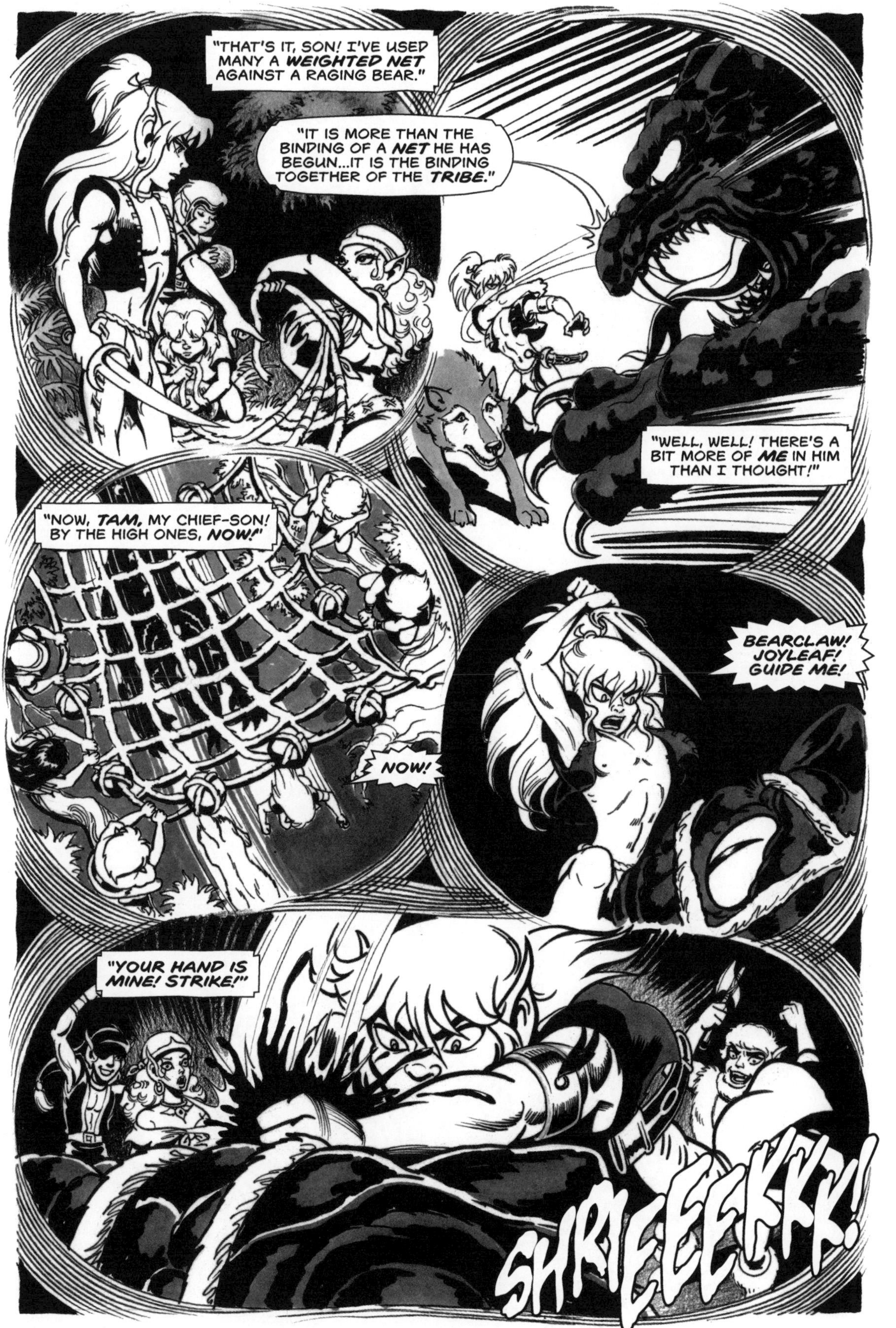
"THAT'S IT, SON! I'VE USED MANY A WEIGHTED NET AGAINST A RAGING BEAR."
"IT IS MORE THAN THE BINDING OF A NET HE HAS BEGUN...IT IS THE BINDING TOGETHER OF THE TRIBE."
"WELL, WELL! THERE'S A BIT MORE OF ME IN HIM THAN I THOUGHT!"
"NOW, TAM, MY CHIEF-SON! BY THE HIGH ONES, NOW!"
NOW!
BEARCLAW! JOYLEAF! GUIDE ME!
"YOUR HAND IS MINE! STRIKE!"
SHRIEEEKKK!

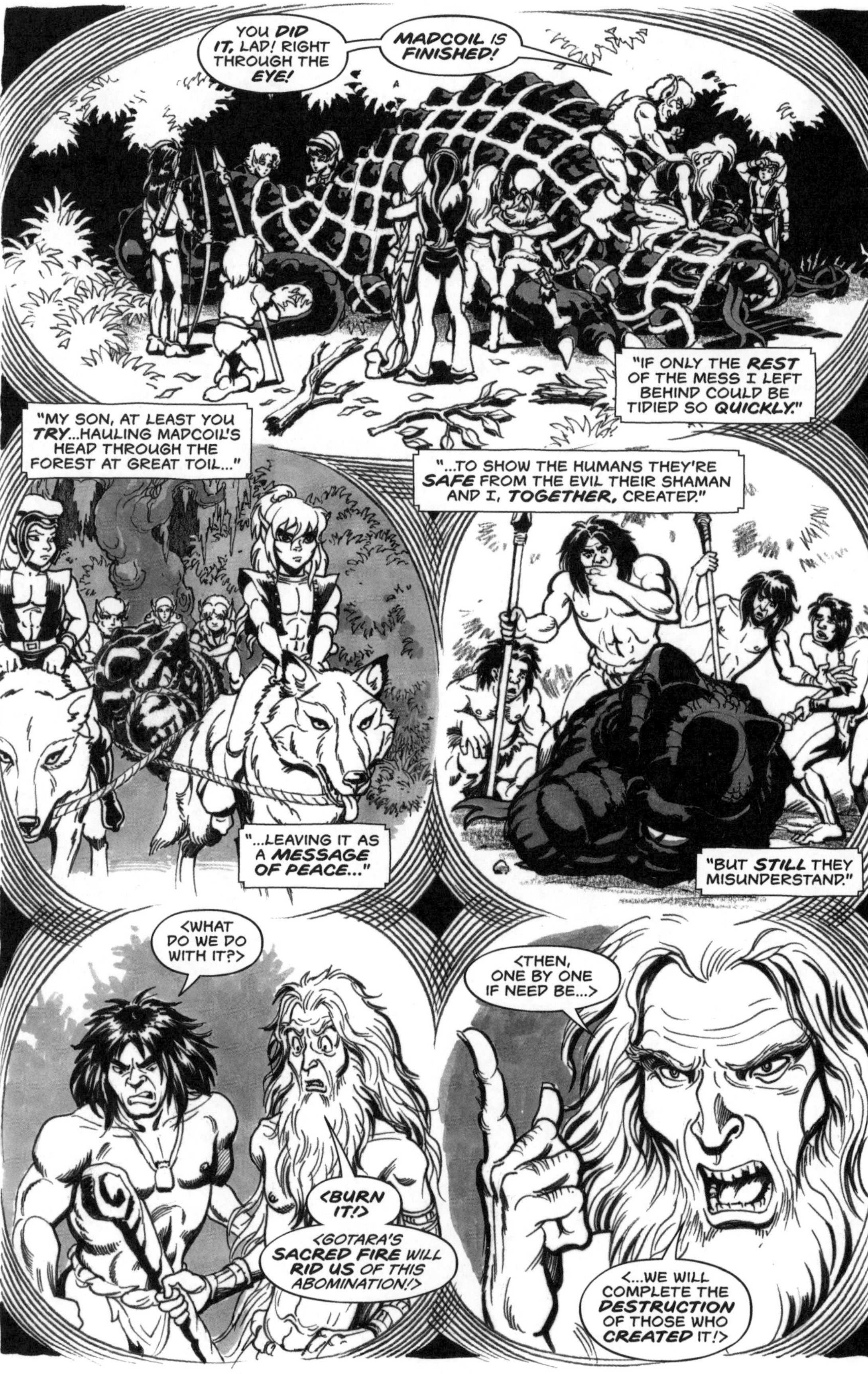

YOU DID IT, LAD! RIGHT THROUGH THE EYE!
MADCOIL IS FINISHED!
"IF ONLY THE REST OF THE MESS I LEFT BEHIND COULD BE TIDIED SO QUICKLY."
"MY SON, AT LEAST YOU TRY...HAULING MADCOIL'S HEAD THROUGH THE FOREST AT GREAT TOIL..."
"...LEAVING IT AS A MESSAGE OF PEACE..."
"...TO SHOW THE HUMANS THEY'RE SAFE FROM THE EVIL THEIR SHAMAN AND I, TOGETHER, CREATED."
"BUT STILL THEY MISUNDERSTAND."
<WHAT DO WE DO WITH IT?>
<BURN IT!>
<GOTARA'S SACRED FIRE WILL RID US OF THIS ABOMINATION!>
<THEN, ONE BY ONE IF NEED BE...>
<...WE WILL COMPLETE THE DESTRUCTION OF THOSE WHO CREATED IT!>

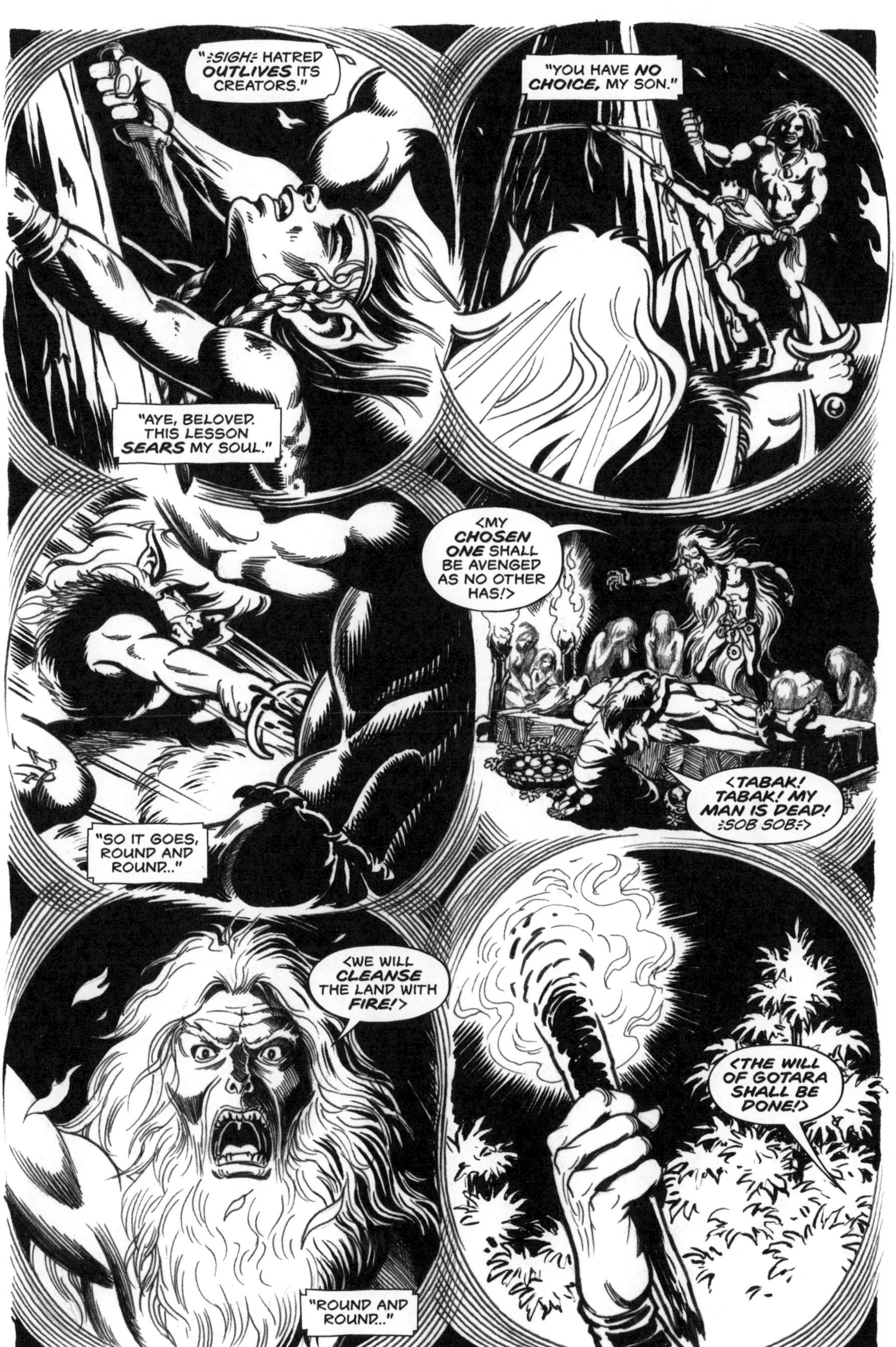
":SIGH: HATRED OUTLIVES ITS CREATORS."
"AYE, BELOVED. THIS LESSON SEARS MY SOUL."
"YOU HAVE NO CHOICE, MY SON."
"SO IT GOES, ROUND AND ROUND..."
<MY CHOSEN ONE SHALL BE AVENGED AS NO OTHER HAS!>
<TABAK! TABAK! MY MAN IS DEAD! :SOB SOB:>
<WE WILL CLEANSE THE LAND WITH FIRE!>
"ROUND AND ROUND..."
<THE WILL OF GOTARA SHALL BE DONE!>

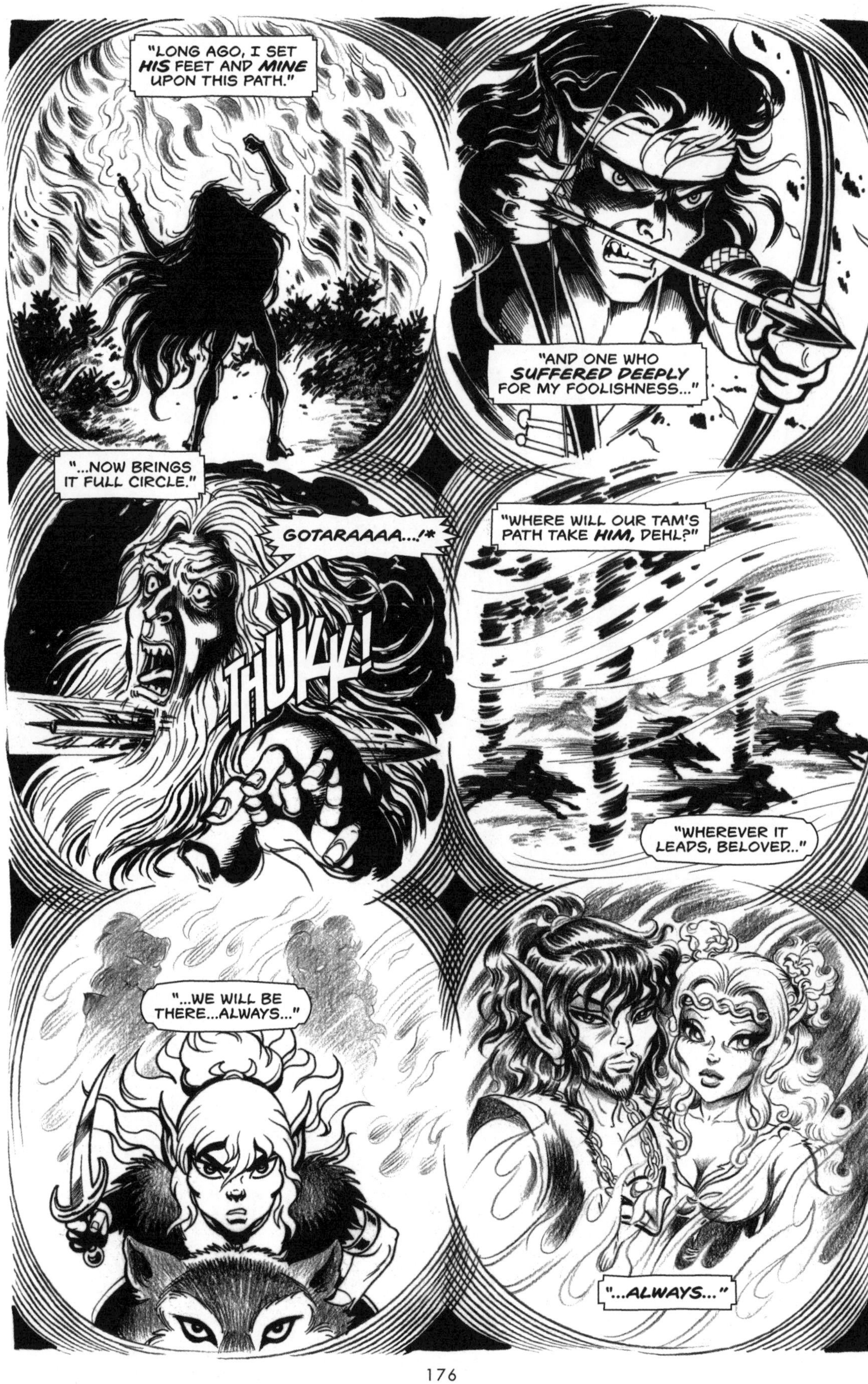
"LONG AGO, I SET HIS FEET AND MINE UPON THIS PATH."
"AND ONE WHO SUFFERED DEEPLY FOR MY FOOLISHNESS..."
"...NOW BRINGS IT FULL CIRCLE."
GOTARAAAA...!*
THUKK!
"WHERE WILL OUR TAM'S PATH TAKE HIM, DEHL?"
"WHEREVER IT LEADS, BELOVED..."
"...WE WILL BE THERE...ALWAYS..."
"...ALWAYS..."

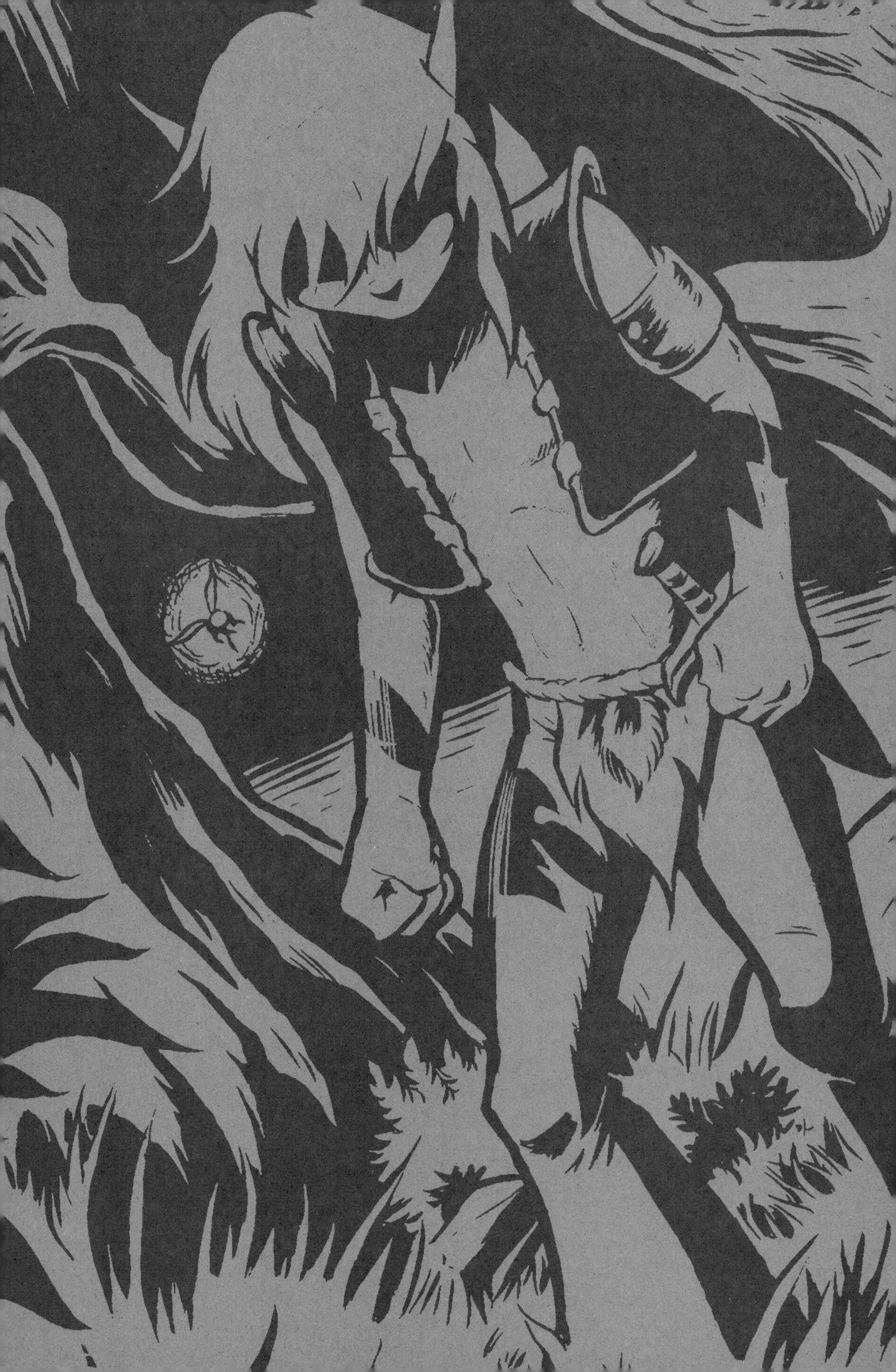

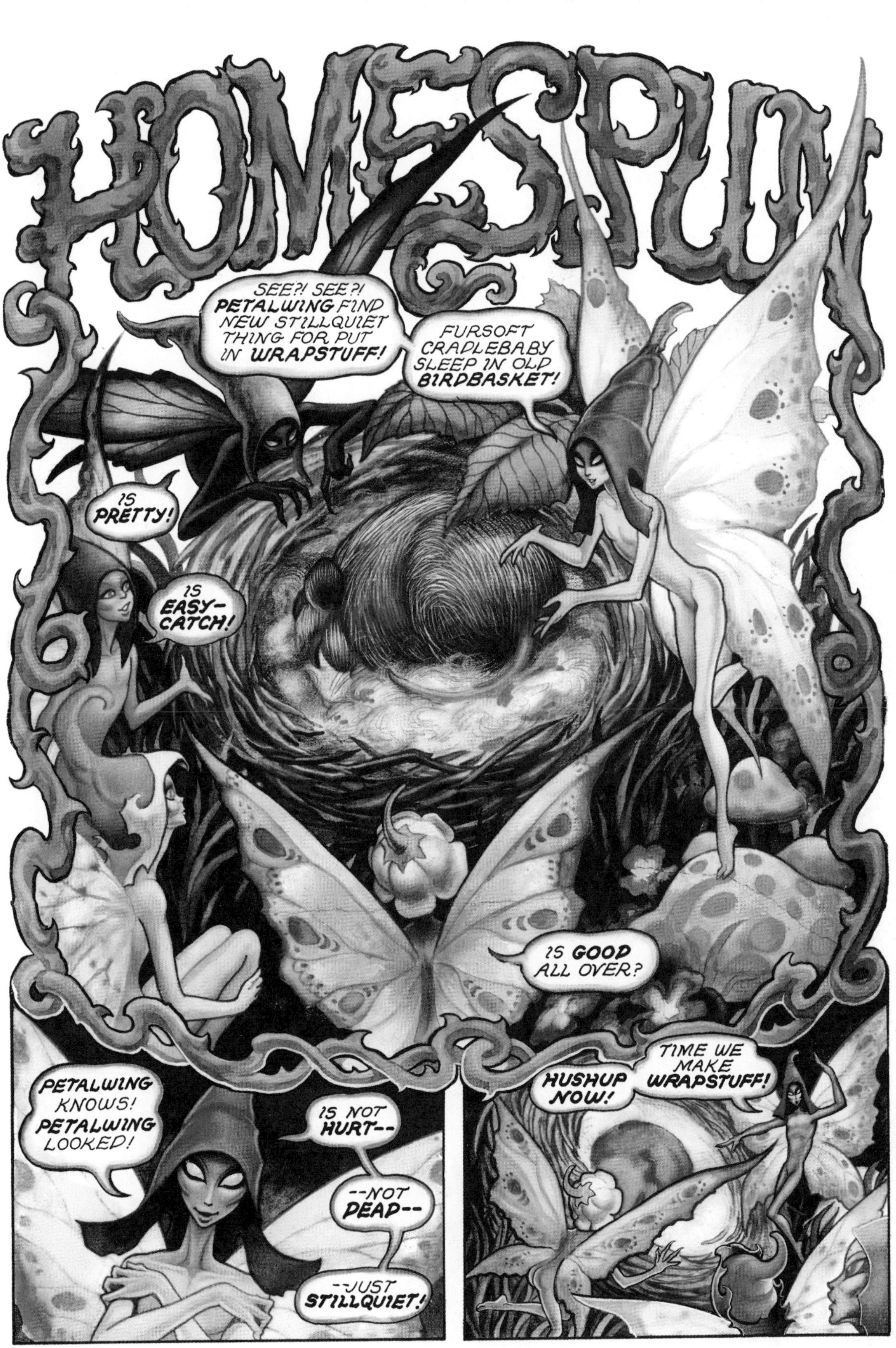
HOMESPUN
SEE?! SEE?! PETALWING FIND NEW STILLQUIET THING FOR PUT IN WRAPSTUFF!
FURSOFT CRADLEBABY SLEEP IN OLD BIRDBASKET!
IS PRETTY!
IS EASY-CATCH!
IS GOOD ALL OVER?
PETALWING KNOWS! PETALWING LOOKED!
IS NOT HURT--
--NOT DEAD--
--JUST STILLQUIET!
HUSHUP NOW!
TIME WE MAKE WRAPSTUFF!

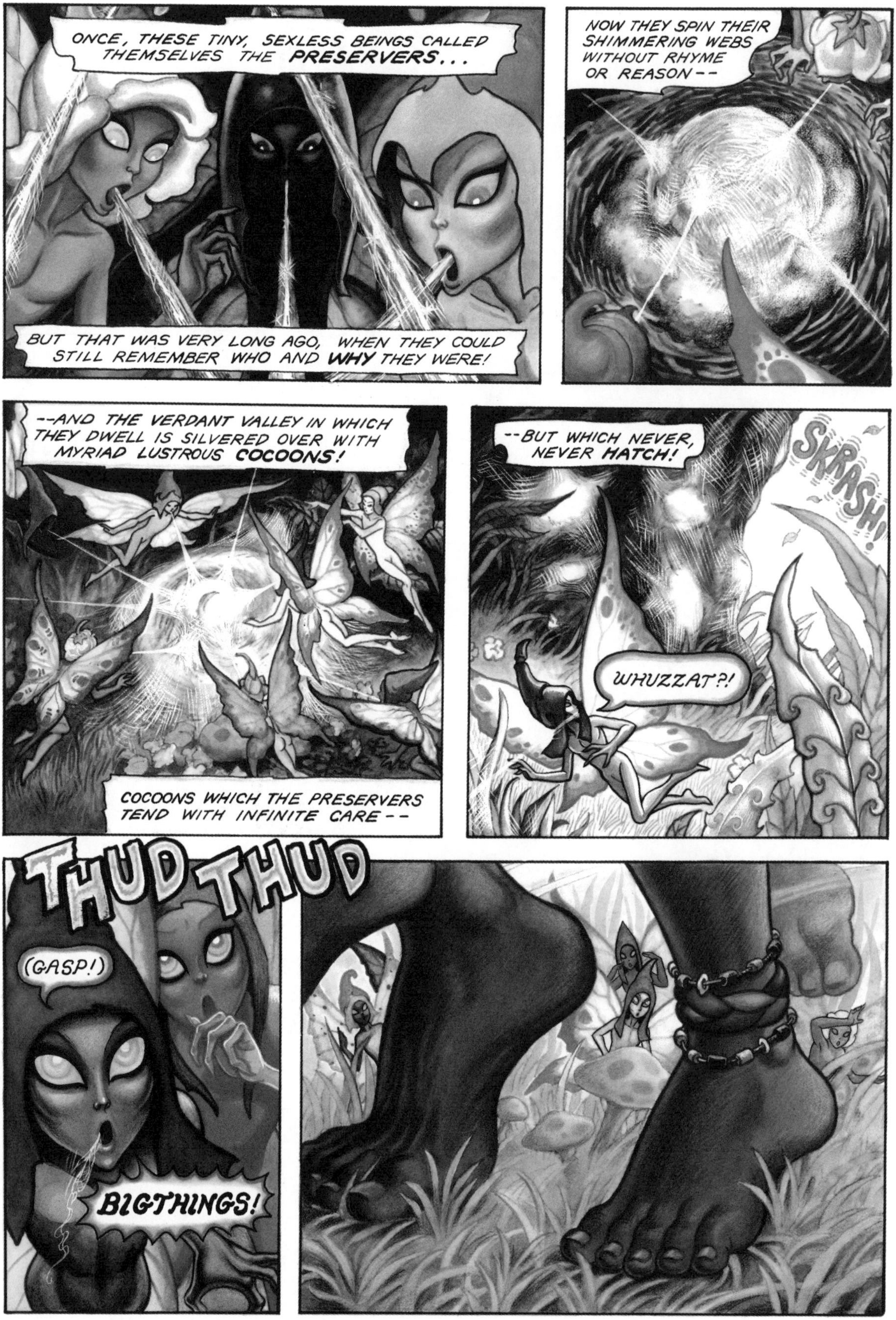

ONCE, THESE TINY, SEXLESS BEINGS CALLED THEMSELVES THE PRESERVERS...
BUT THAT WAS VERY LONG AGO, WHEN THEY COULD STILL REMEMBER WHO AND WHY THEY WERE!
NOW THEY SPIN THEIR SHIMMERING WEBS WITHOUT RHYME OR REASON--
--AND THE VERDANT VALLEY IN WHICH THEY DWELL IS SILVERED OVER WITH MYRIAD LUSTROUS COCOONS!
COCOONS WHICH THE PRESERVERS TEND WITH INFINITE CARE--
--BUT WHICH NEVER, NEVER HATCH!
SKRASH!
WHUZZAT?!
THUD THUD
(GASP!)
BIGTHINGS!

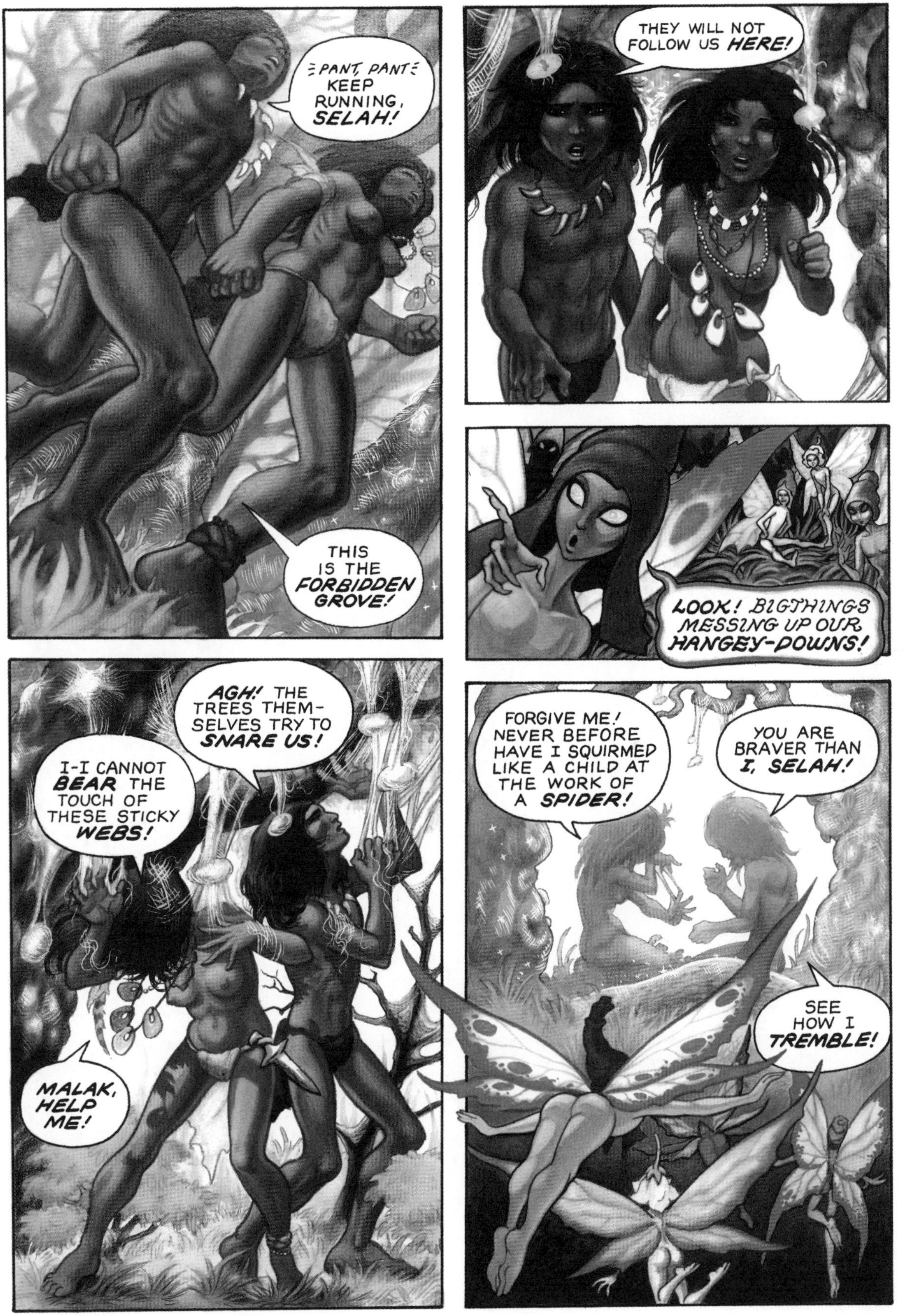
PANT, PANT KEEP RUNNING, SELAH!
THIS IS THE FORBIDDEN GROVE!
THEY WILL NOT FOLLOW US HERE!
LOOK! BIGTHINGS MESSING UP OUR HANGEY-DOWNS!
I-I CANNOT BEAR THE TOUCH OF THESE STICKY WEBS!
AGH! THE TREES THEM-SELVES TRY TO SNARE US!
MALAK, HELP ME!
FORGIVE ME! NEVER BEFORE HAVE I SQUIRMED LIKE A CHILD AT THE WORK OF A SPIDER!
YOU ARE BRAVER THAN I, SELAH!
SEE HOW I TREMBLE!

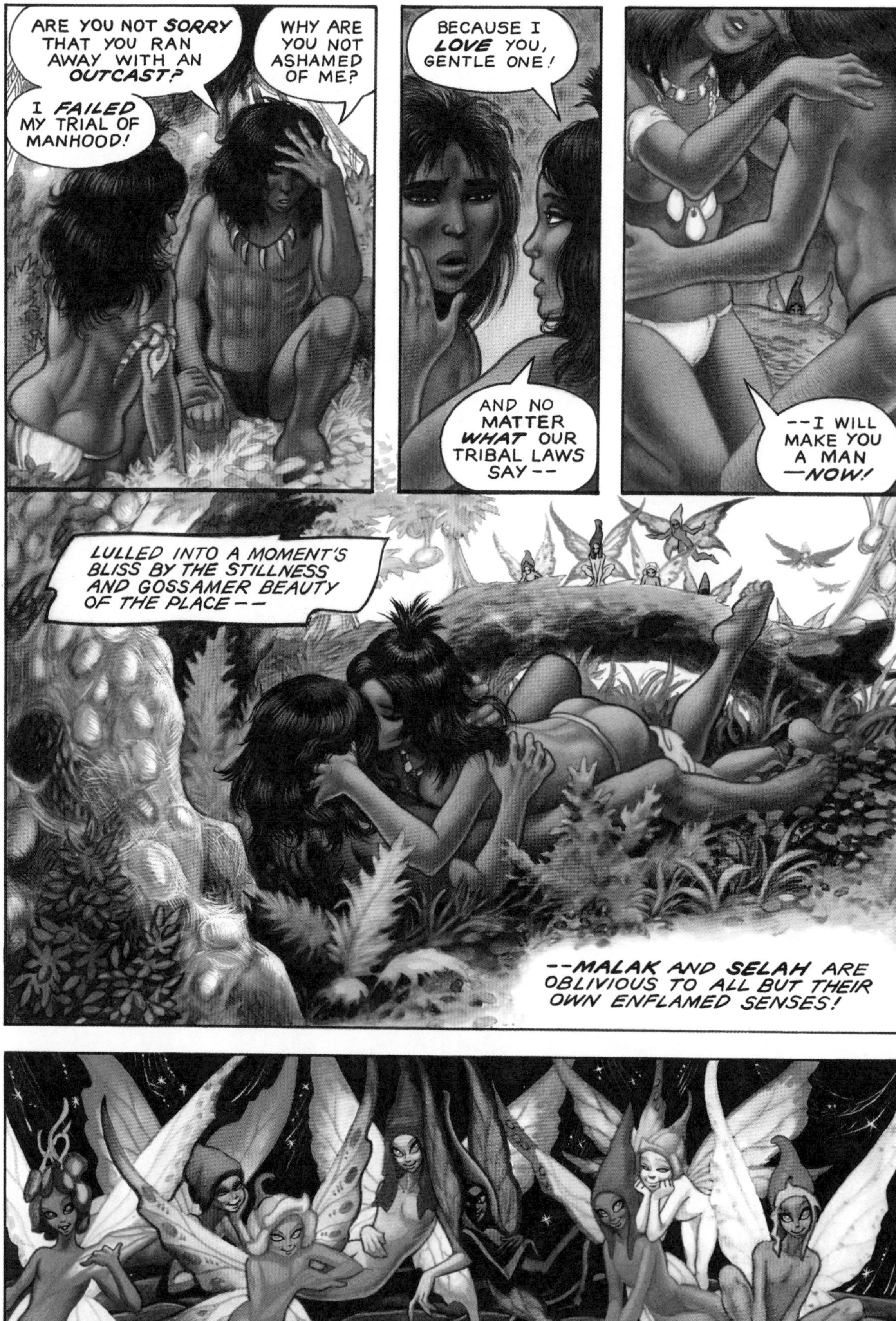
ARE YOU NOT SORRY THAT YOU RAN AWAY WITH AN OUTCAST?
I FAILED MY TRIAL OF MANHOOD!
WHY ARE YOU NOT ASHAMED OF ME?
BECAUSE I LOVE YOU, GENTLE ONE!
AND NO MATTER WHAT OUR TRIBAL LAWS SAY--
--I WILL MAKE YOU A MAN —NOW!
LULLED INTO A MOMENT'S BLISS BY THE STILLNESS AND GOSSAMER BEAUTY OF THE PLACE--
--MALAK AND SELAH ARE OBLIVIOUS TO ALL BUT THEIR OWN ENFLAMED SENSES!

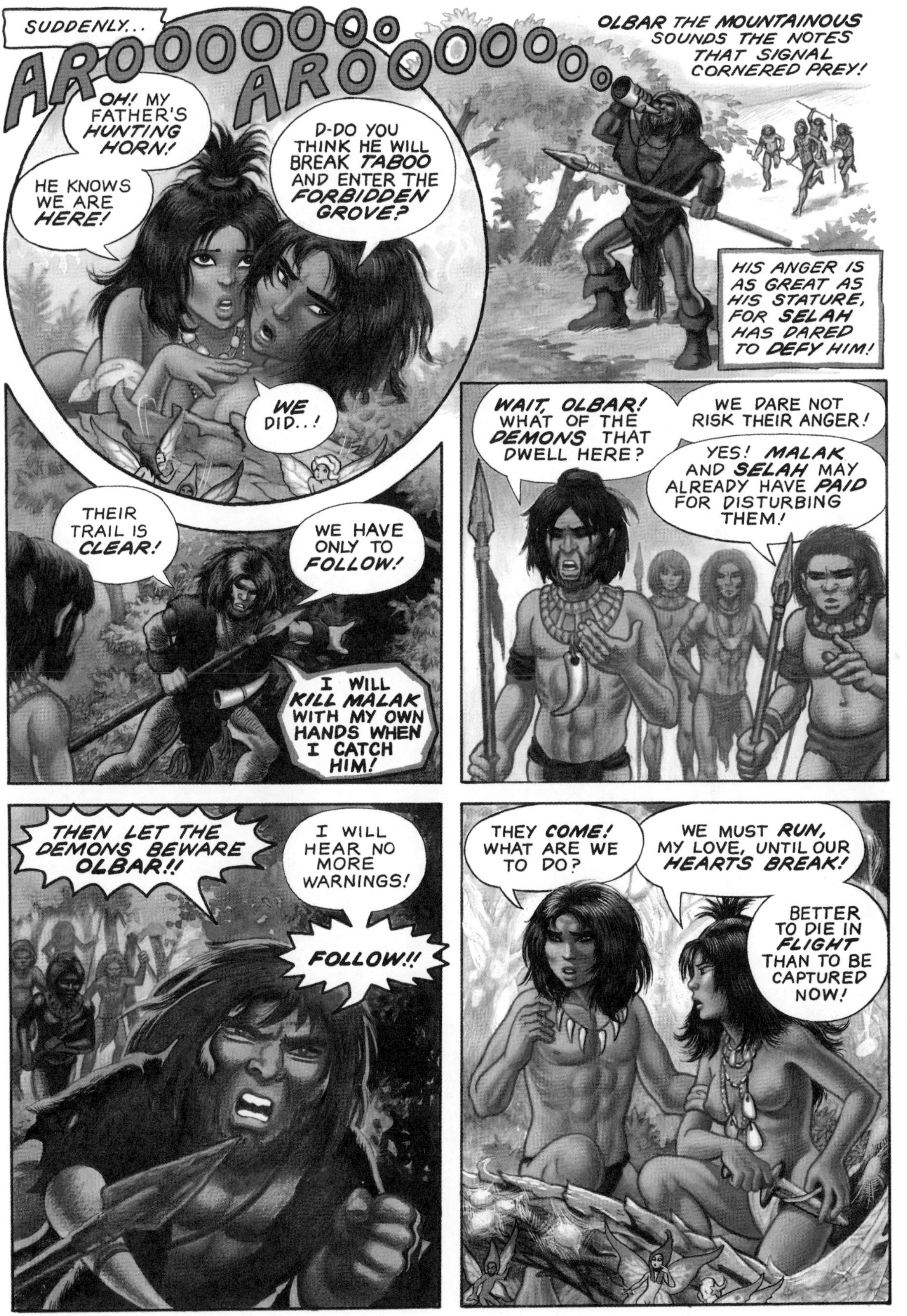
SUDDENLY...
AROOOOOOo
AROOOOOOo
OLBAR THE MOUNTAINOUS SOUNDS THE NOTES THAT SIGNAL CORNERED PREY!
OH! MY FATHER'S HUNTING HORN!
HE KNOWS WE ARE HERE!
D-DO YOU THINK HE WILL BREAK TABOO AND ENTER THE FORBIDDEN GROVE?
WE DID..!
HIS ANGER IS AS GREAT AS HIS STATURE, FOR SELAH HAS DARED TO DEFY HIM!
THEIR TRAIL IS CLEAR!
WE HAVE ONLY TO FOLLOW!
I WILL KILL MALAK WITH MY OWN HANDS WHEN I CATCH HIM!
WAIT, OLBAR! WHAT OF THE DEMONS THAT DWELL HERE?
WE DARE NOT RISK THEIR ANGER!
YES! MALAK AND SELAH MAY ALREADY HAVE PAID FOR DISTURBING THEM!
THEN LET THE DEMONS BEWARE OLBAR!!
I WILL HEAR NO MORE WARNINGS!
FOLLOW!!
THEY COME! WHAT ARE WE TO DO?
WE MUST RUN, MY LOVE, UNTIL OUR HEARTS BREAK!
BETTER TO DIE IN FLIGHT THAN TO BE CAPTURED NOW!

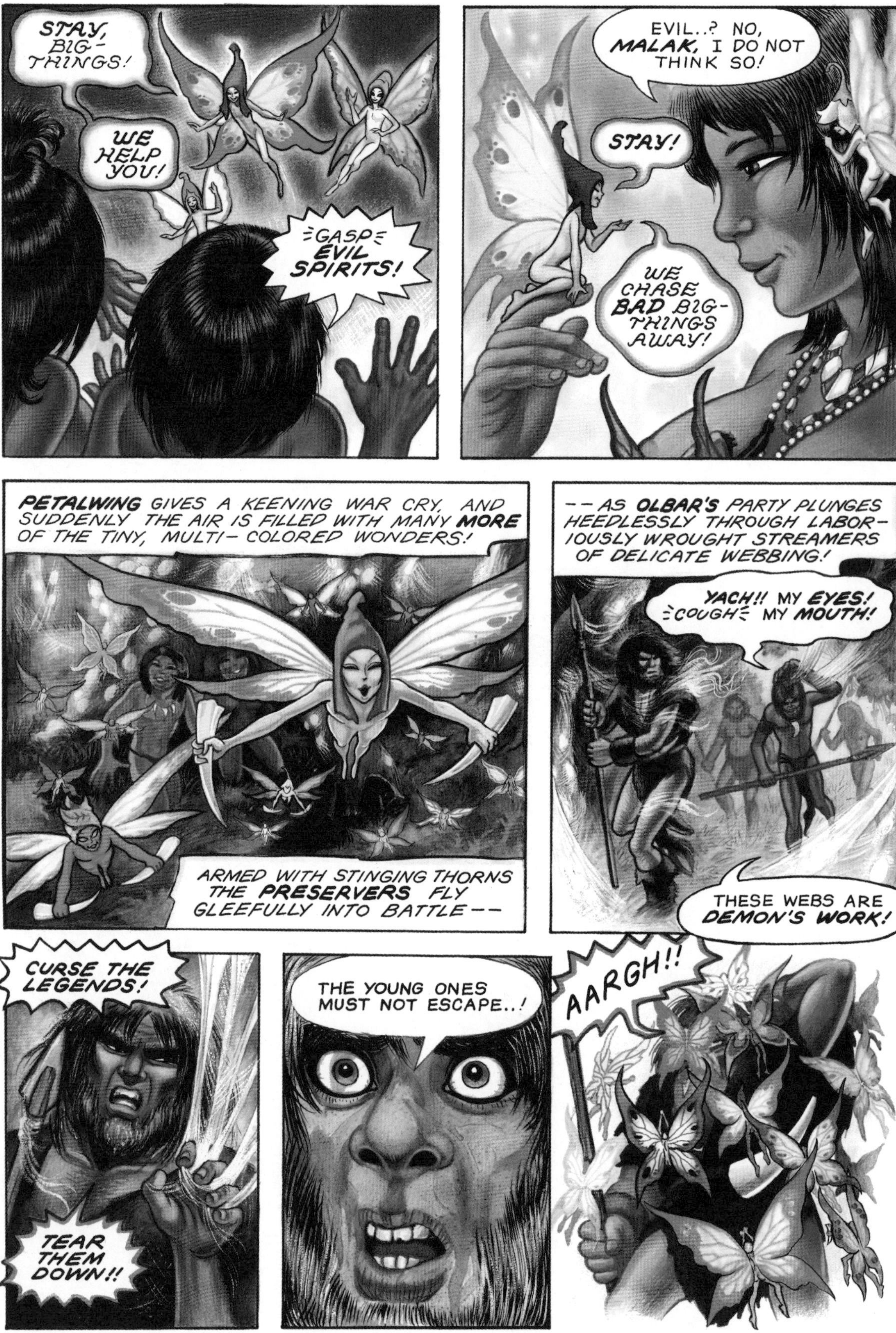
STAY, BIG-THINGS!
WE HELP YOU!
GASP EVIL SPIRITS!
EVIL..? NO, MALAK, I DO NOT THINK SO!
STAY!
WE CHASE BAD BIG-THINGS AWAY!
PETALWING GIVES A KEENING WAR CRY, AND SUDDENLY THE AIR IS FILLED WITH MANY MORE OF THE TINY, MULTI-COLORED WONDERS!
ARMED WITH STINGING THORNS THE PRESERVERS FLY GLEEFULLY INTO BATTLE--
--AS OLBAR'S PARTY PLUNGES HEEDLESSLY THROUGH LABORIOUSLY WROUGHT STREAMERS OF DELICATE WEBBING!
YACH!! MY EYES! COUGH MY MOUTH!
THESE WEBS ARE DEMON'S WORK!
CURSE THE LEGENDS!
TEAR THEM DOWN!!
THE YOUNG ONES MUST NOT ESCAPE..!
AARGH!!

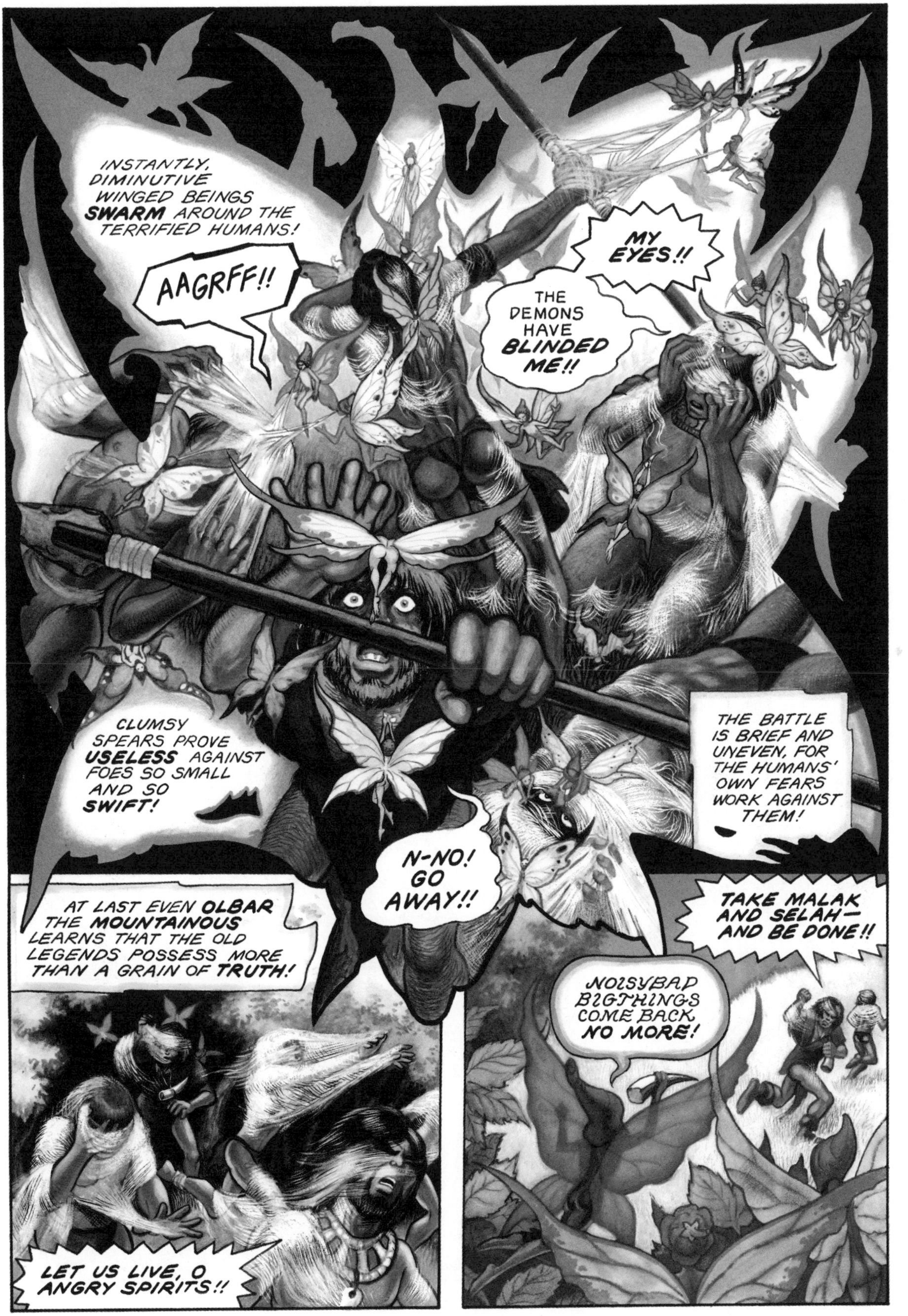
INSTANTLY, DIMINUTIVE WINGED BEINGS SWARM AROUND THE TERRIFIED HUMANS!
AAGRFF!!
MY EYES!!
THE DEMONS HAVE BLINDED ME!!
CLUMSY SPEARS PROVE USELESS AGAINST FOES SO SMALL AND SO SWIFT!
THE BATTLE IS BRIEF AND UNEVEN, FOR THE HUMANS' OWN FEARS WORK AGAINST THEM!
N-NO! GO AWAY!!
AT LAST EVEN OLBAR THE MOUNTAINOUS LEARNS THAT THE OLD LEGENDS POSSESS MORE THAN A GRAIN OF TRUTH!
LET US LIVE, O ANGRY SPIRITS!!
TAKE MALAK AND SELAH— AND BE DONE!!
NOISYBAD BIGTHINGS COME BACK NO MORE!

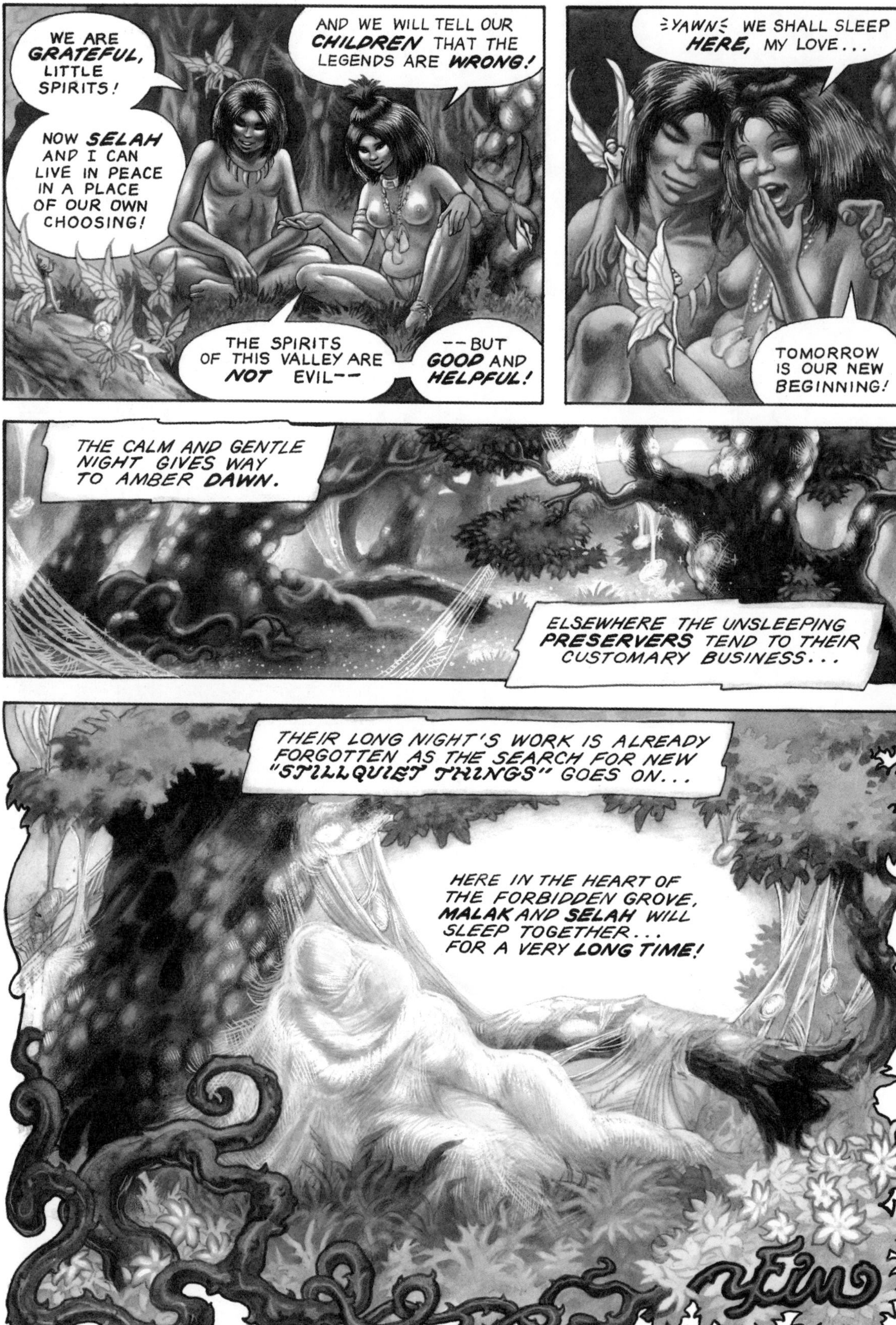
WE ARE GRATEFUL, LITTLE SPIRITS!
NOW SELAH AND I CAN LIVE IN PEACE IN A PLACE OF OUR OWN CHOOSING!
AND WE WILL TELL OUR CHILDREN THAT THE LEGENDS ARE WRONG!
THE SPIRITS OF THIS VALLEY ARE NOT EVIL--
--BUT GOOD AND HELPFUL!
YAWN WE SHALL SLEEP HERE, MY LOVE...
TOMORROW IS OUR NEW BEGINNING!
THE CALM AND GENTLE NIGHT GIVES WAY TO AMBER DAWN.
ELSEWHERE THE UNSLEEPING PRESERVERS TEND TO THEIR CUSTOMARY BUSINESS...
THEIR LONG NIGHT'S WORK IS ALREADY FORGOTTEN AS THE SEARCH FOR NEW "STILLQUIET THINGS" GOES ON...
HERE IN THE HEART OF THE FORBIDDEN GROVE, MALAK AND SELAH WILL SLEEP TOGETHER... FOR A VERY LONG TIME!
Fin

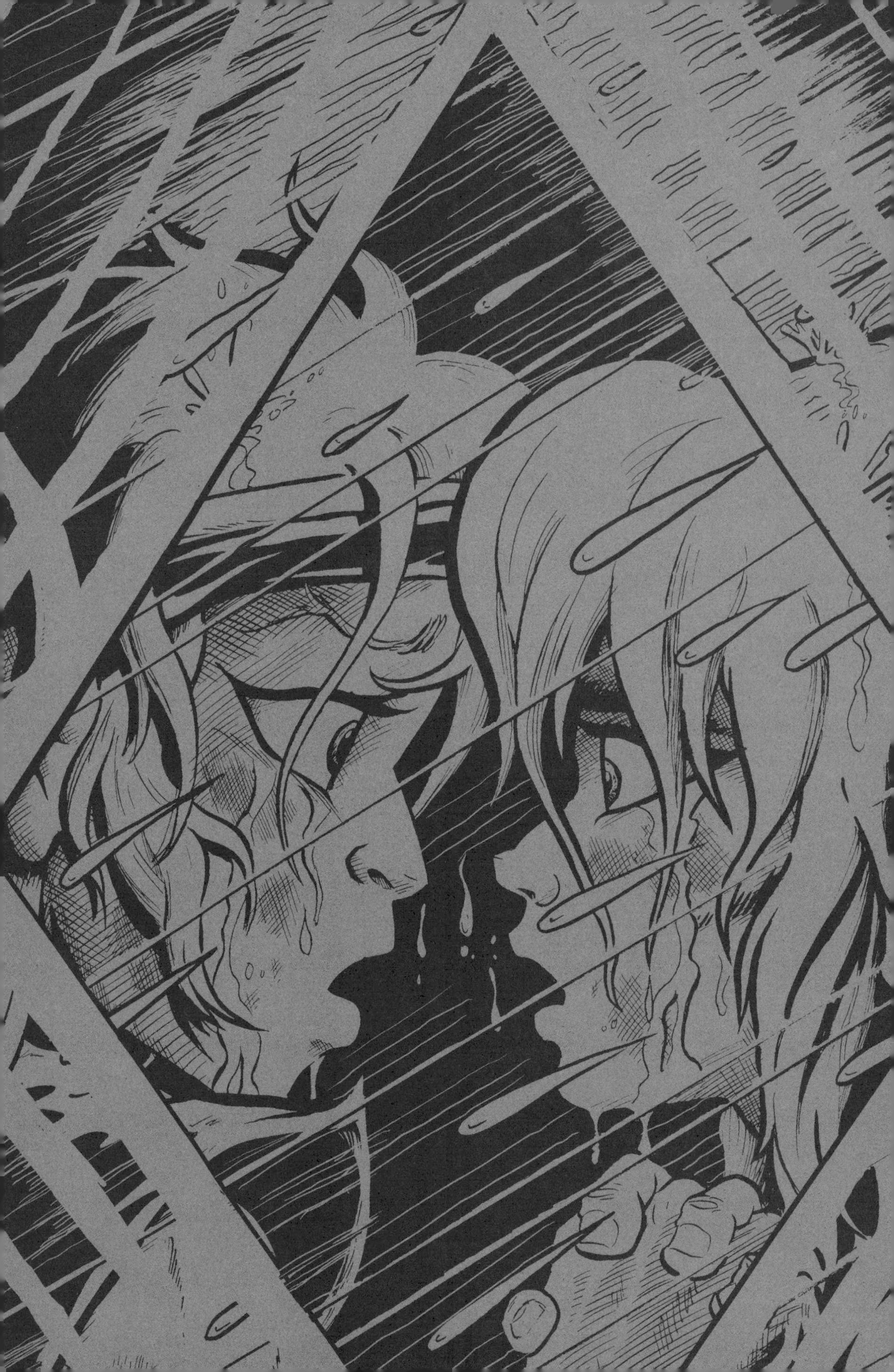

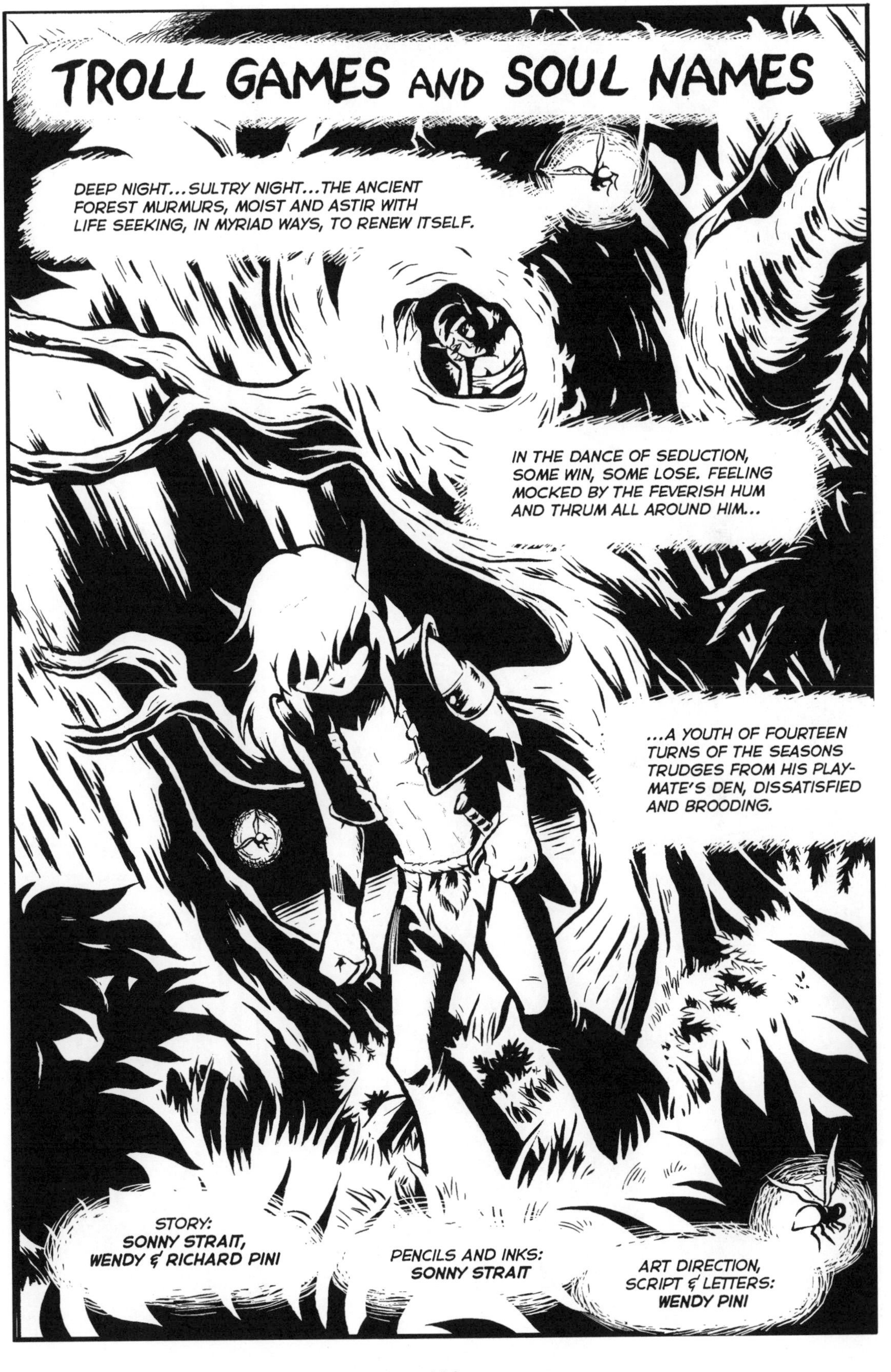
TROLL GAMES AND SOUL NAMES
DEEP NIGHT...SULTRY NIGHT...THE ANCIENT FOREST MURMURS, MOIST AND ASTIR WITH LIFE SEEKING, IN MYRIAD WAYS, TO RENEW ITSELF.
IN THE DANCE OF SEDUCTION, SOME WIN, SOME LOSE. FEELING MOCKED BY THE FEVERISH HUM AND THRUM ALL AROUND HIM...
...A YOUTH OF FOURTEEN TURNS OF THE SEASONS TRUDGES FROM HIS PLAY-MATE'S DEN, DISSATISFIED AND BROODING.
STORY: SONNY STRAIT, WENDY & RICHARD PINI
PENCILS AND INKS: SONNY STRAIT
ART DIRECTION, SCRIPT & LETTERS: WENDY PINI

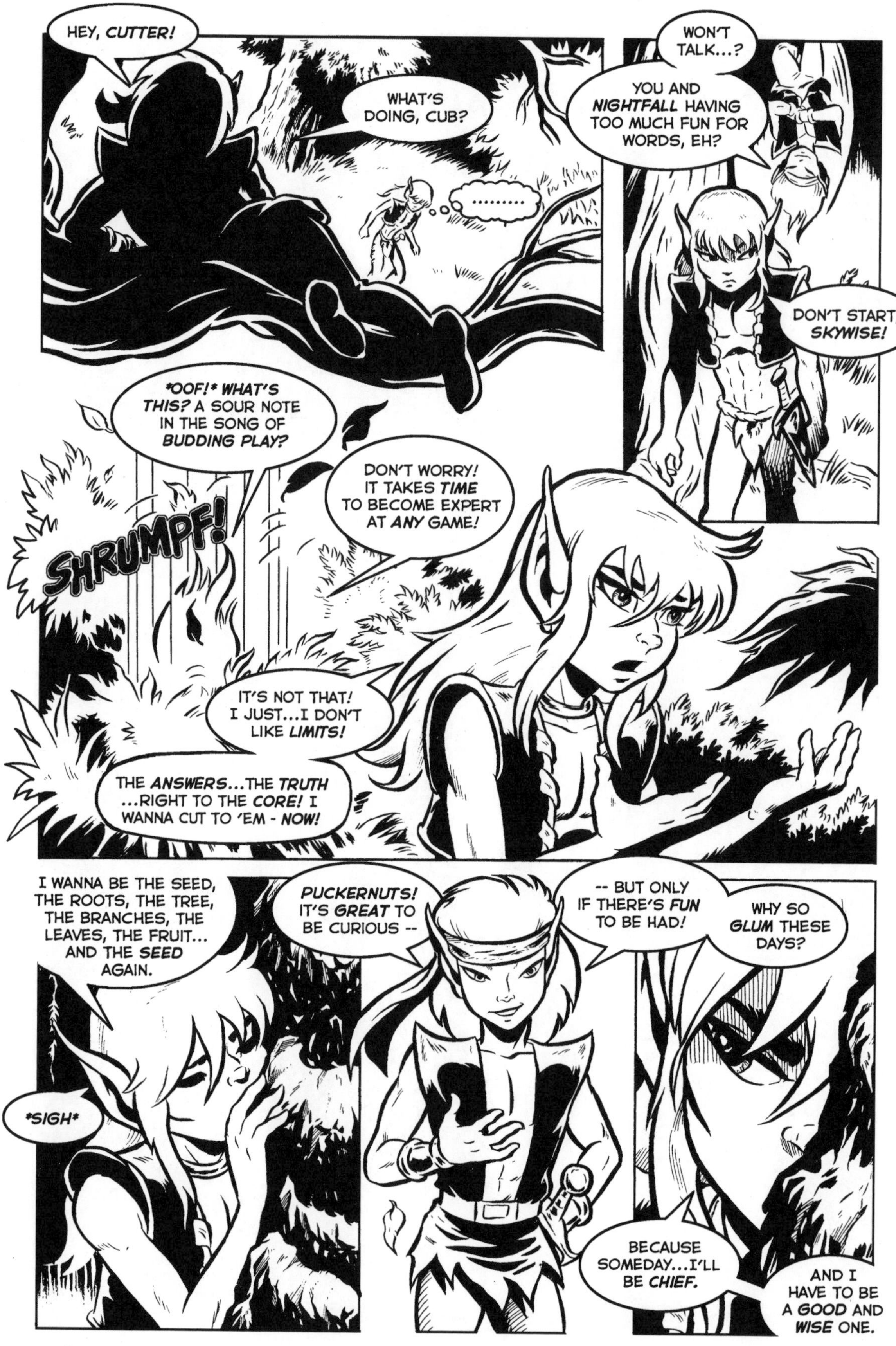

HEY, CUTTER!
WHAT'S DOING, CUB?
....
WON'T TALK...?
YOU AND NIGHTFALL HAVING TOO MUCH FUN FOR WORDS, EH?
DON'T START, SKYWISE!
OOF! WHAT'S THIS? A SOUR NOTE IN THE SONG OF BUDDING PLAY?
SHRUMPF!
DON'T WORRY! IT TAKES TIME TO BECOME EXPERT AT ANY GAME!
IT'S NOT THAT! I JUST...I DON'T LIKE LIMITS!
THE ANSWERS...THE TRUTH ...RIGHT TO THE CORE! I WANNA CUT TO 'EM - NOW!
I WANNA BE THE SEED, THE ROOTS, THE TREE, THE BRANCHES, THE LEAVES, THE FRUIT... AND THE SEED AGAIN.
SIGH
PUCKERNUTS! IT'S GREAT TO BE CURIOUS --
-- BUT ONLY IF THERE'S FUN TO BE HAD!
WHY SO GLUM THESE DAYS?
BECAUSE SOMEDAY...I'LL BE CHIEF.
AND I HAVE TO BE A GOOD AND WISE ONE.

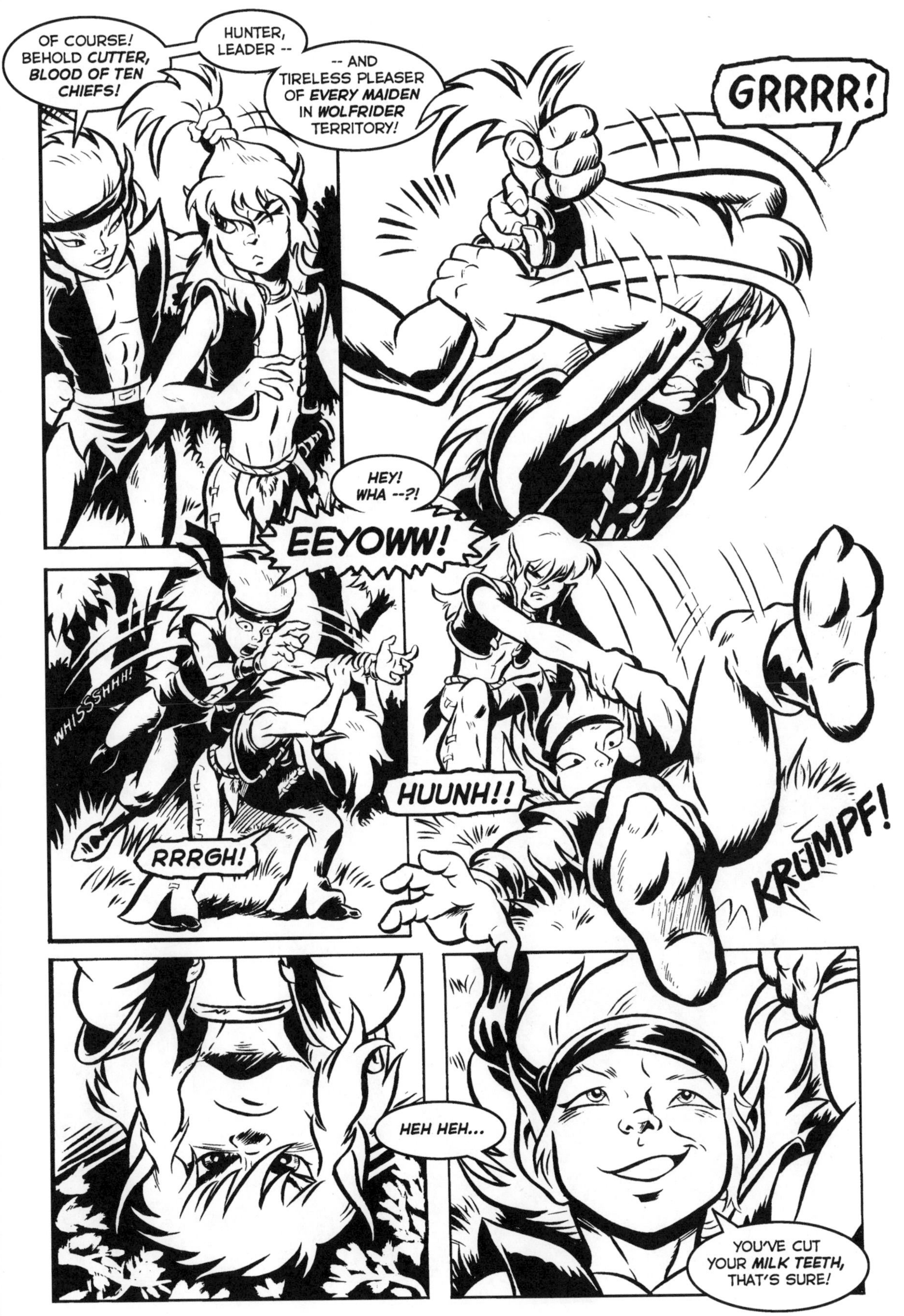
OF COURSE! BEHOLD CUTTER, BLOOD OF TEN CHIEFS!
HUNTER, LEADER --
-- AND TIRELESS PLEASER OF EVERY MAIDEN IN WOLFRIDER TERRITORY!
GRRRR!
HEY! WHA --?!
EEYOWW!
WHISSSHHH!
RRRGH!
HUUNH!!
KRUMPF!
HEH HEH...
YOU'VE CUT YOUR MILK TEETH, THAT'S SURE!

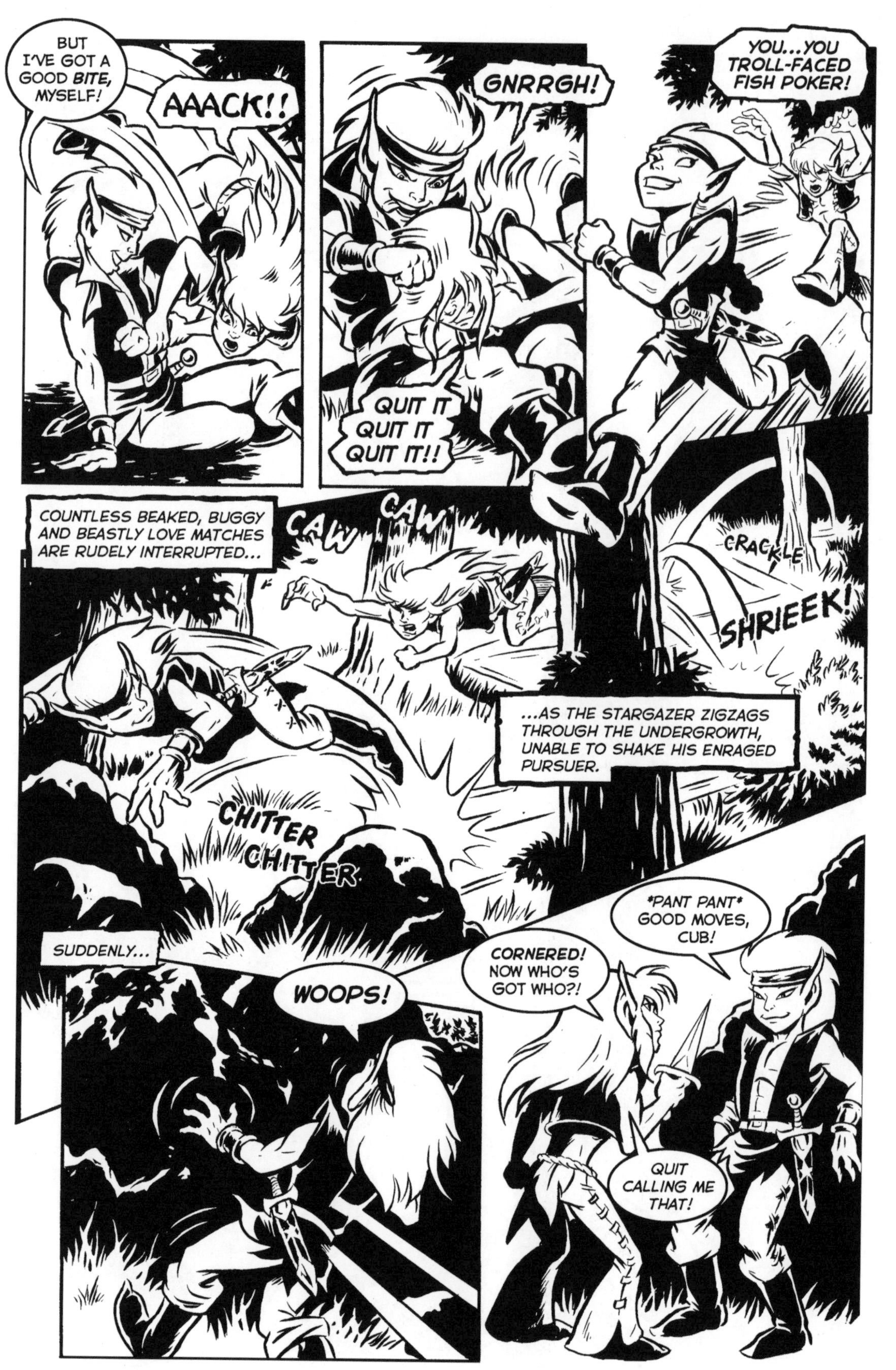
BUT I'VE GOT A GOOD BITE, MYSELF!
AAACK!!
GNRRGH!
QUIT IT QUIT IT QUIT IT!!
YOU...YOU TROLL-FACED FISH POKER!
COUNTLESS BEAKED, BUGGY AND BEASTLY LOVE MATCHES ARE RUDELY INTERRUPTED...
CAW CAW
CRACKLE
SHRIEEK!
...AS THE STARGAZER ZIGZAGS THROUGH THE UNDERGROWTH, UNABLE TO SHAKE HIS ENRAGED PURSUER.
CHITTER CHITTER CHITTER
SUDDENLY...
WOOPS!
CORNERED! NOW WHO'S GOT WHO?!
PANT PANT GOOD MOVES, CUB!
QUIT CALLING ME THAT!

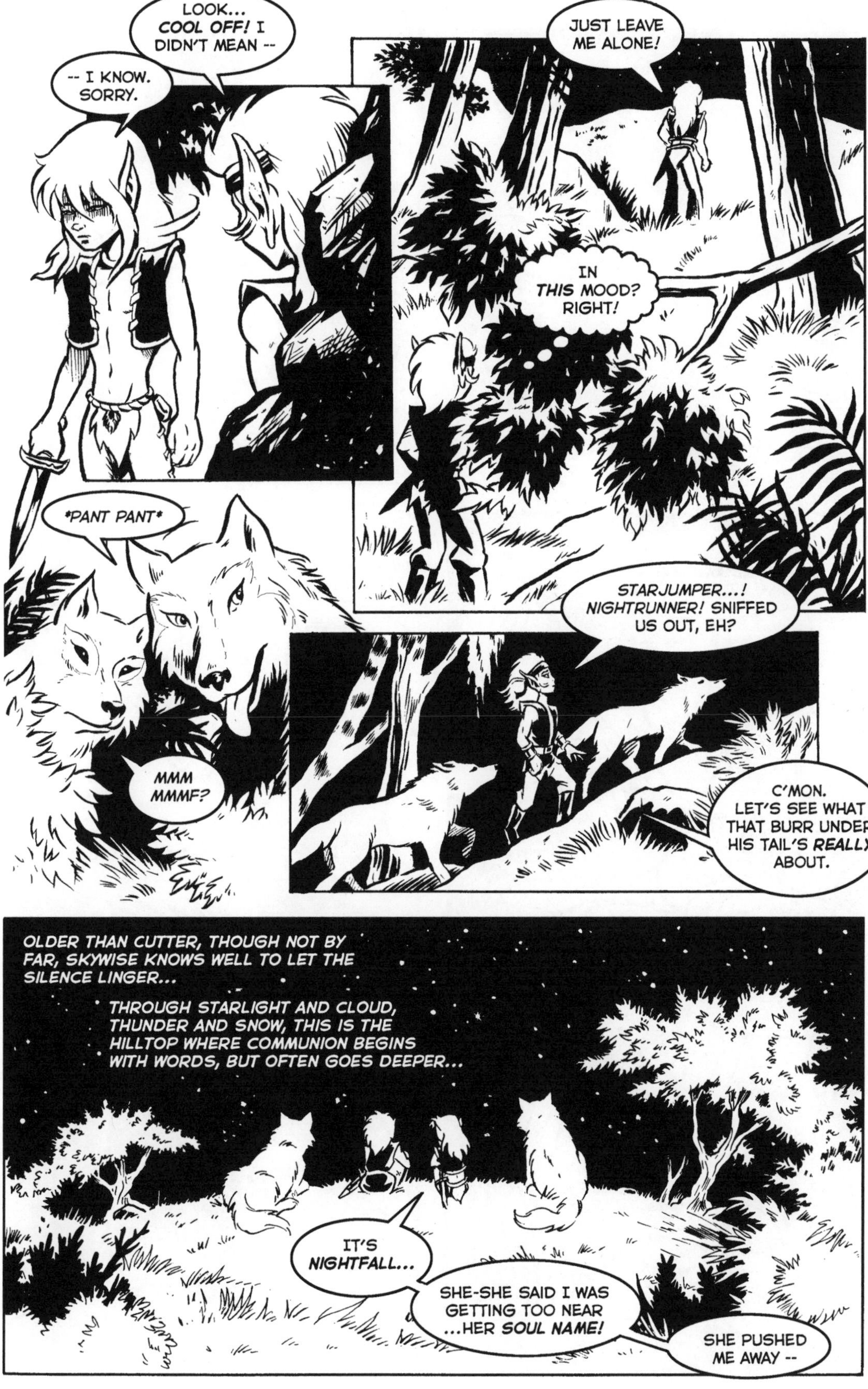
LOOK... COOL OFF! I DIDN'T MEAN --
-- I KNOW. SORRY.
JUST LEAVE ME ALONE!
IN THIS MOOD? RIGHT!
PANT PANT
MMM MMMF?
STARJUMPER...! NIGHTRUNNER! SNIFFED US OUT, EH?
C'MON. LET'S SEE WHAT THAT BURR UNDER HIS TAIL'S REALLY ABOUT.
OLDER THAN CUTTER, THOUGH NOT BY FAR, SKYWISE KNOWS WELL TO LET THE SILENCE LINGER...
THROUGH STARLIGHT AND CLOUD, THUNDER AND SNOW, THIS IS THE HILLTOP WHERE COMMUNION BEGINS WITH WORDS, BUT OFTEN GOES DEEPER...
IT'S NIGHTFALL...
SHE-SHE SAID I WAS GETTING TOO NEAR ...HER SOUL NAME!
SHE PUSHED ME AWAY --

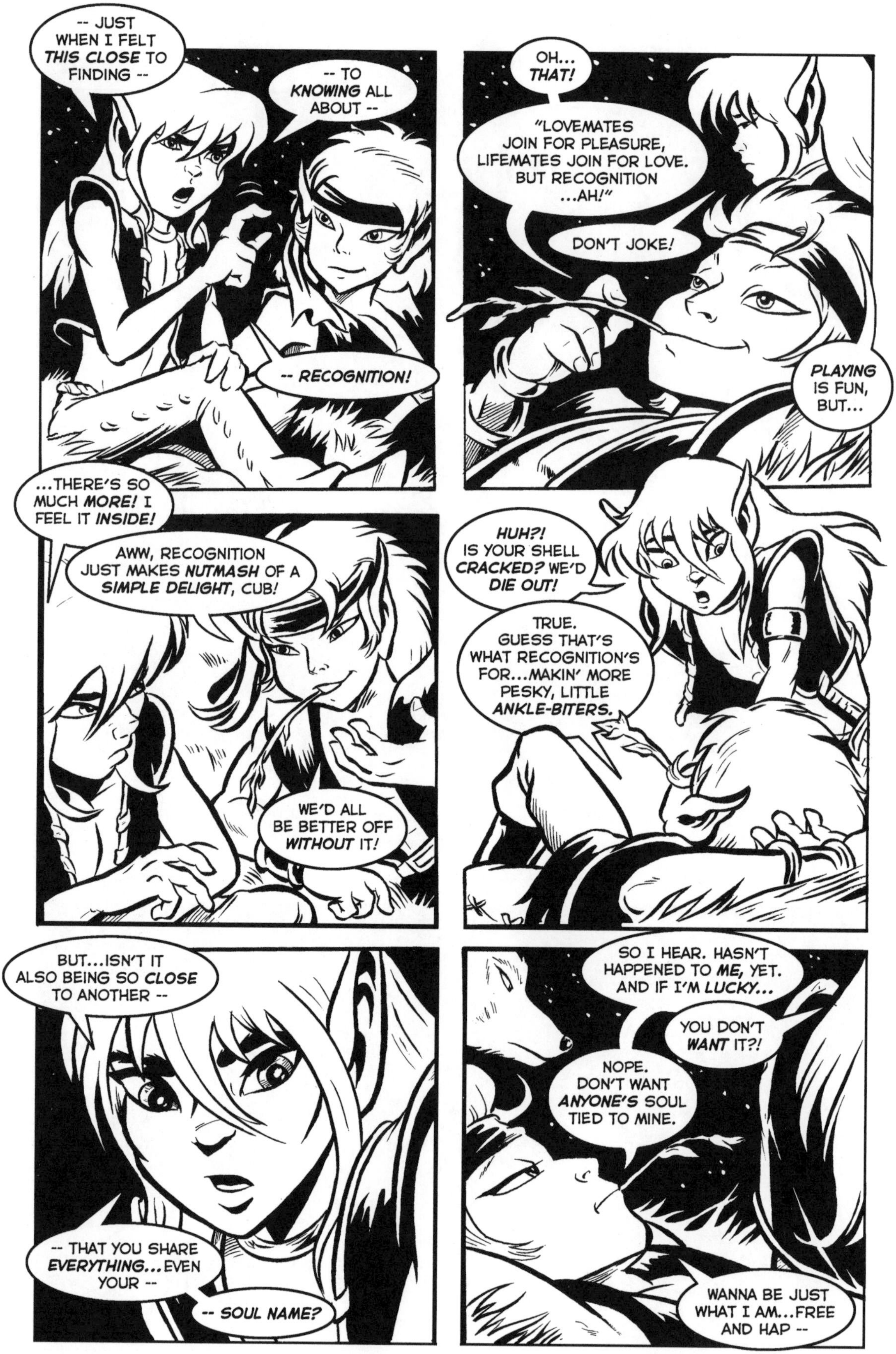
-- JUST WHEN I FELT *THIS CLOSE* TO FINDING --
-- TO *KNOWING* ALL ABOUT --
-- *RECOGNITION!*
OH... *THAT!*
"LOVEMATES JOIN FOR PLEASURE, LIFEMATES JOIN FOR LOVE. BUT RECOGNITION ...AH!"
DON'T JOKE!
PLAYING IS FUN, BUT...
...THERE'S SO MUCH *MORE!* I FEEL IT *INSIDE!*
AWW, RECOGNITION JUST MAKES *NUTMASH* OF A *SIMPLE DELIGHT*, CUB!
WE'D ALL BE BETTER OFF *WITHOUT* IT!
HUH?! IS YOUR SHELL *CRACKED?* WE'D *DIE OUT!*
TRUE. GUESS THAT'S WHAT RECOGNITION'S FOR...MAKIN' MORE PESKY, LITTLE *ANKLE-BITERS.*
BUT...ISN'T IT ALSO BEING SO *CLOSE* TO ANOTHER --
-- THAT YOU SHARE *EVERYTHING*...EVEN YOUR --
-- *SOUL NAME?*
SO I HEAR. HASN'T HAPPENED TO *ME,* YET. AND IF I'M *LUCKY...*
YOU DON'T *WANT* IT?!
NOPE. DON'T WANT *ANYONE'S* SOUL TIED TO MINE.
WANNA BE JUST WHAT I AM...FREE AND HAP --

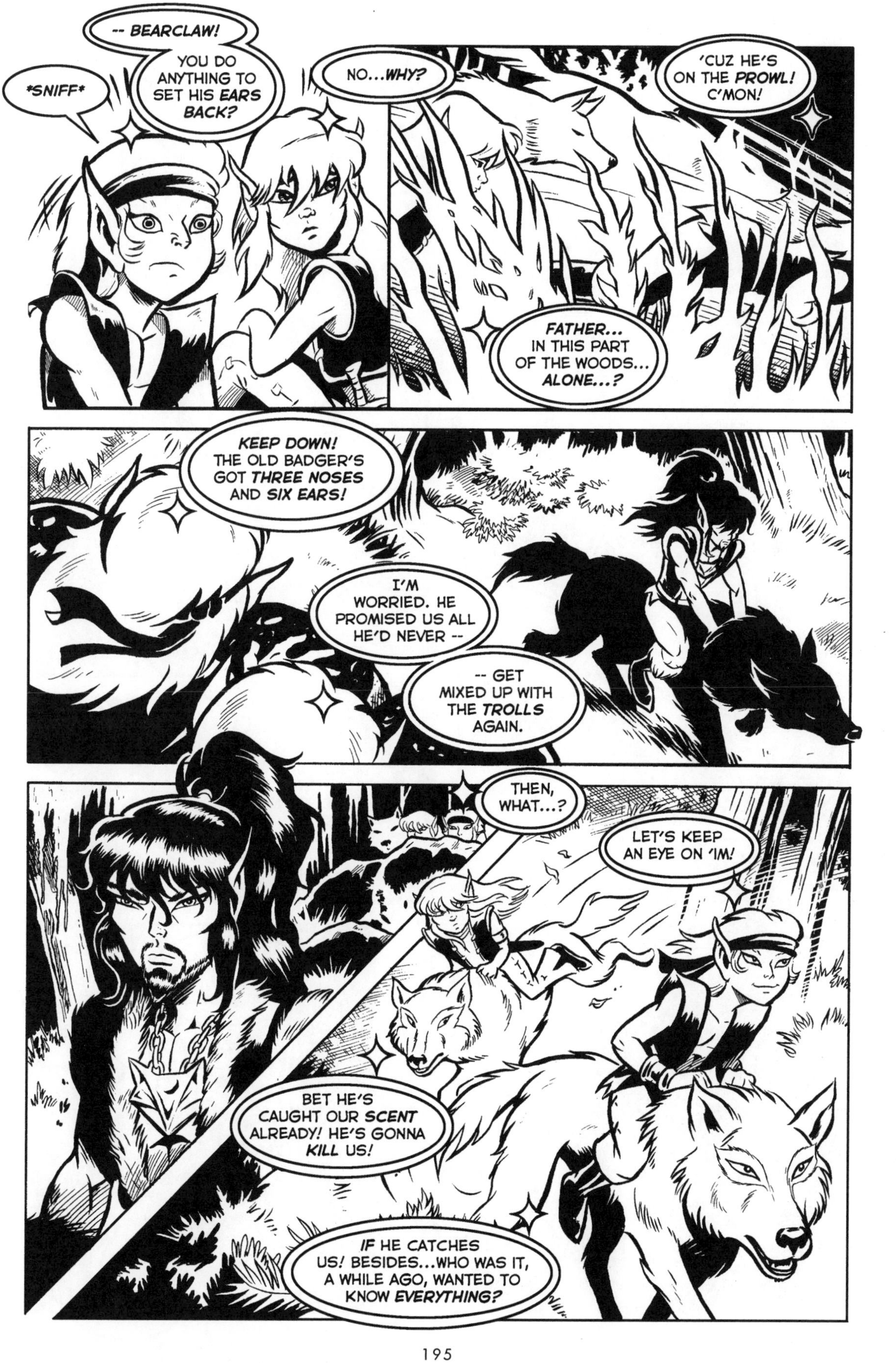
-- BEARCLAW!
YOU DO ANYTHING TO SET HIS EARS BACK?
SNIFF
NO...WHY?
'CUZ HE'S ON THE PROWL! C'MON!
FATHER... IN THIS PART OF THE WOODS... ALONE...?
KEEP DOWN! THE OLD BADGER'S GOT THREE NOSES AND SIX EARS!
I'M WORRIED. HE PROMISED US ALL HE'D NEVER --
-- GET MIXED UP WITH THE TROLLS AGAIN.
THEN, WHAT...?
LET'S KEEP AN EYE ON 'IM!
BET HE'S CAUGHT OUR SCENT ALREADY! HE'S GONNA KILL US!
IF HE CATCHES US! BESIDES...WHO WAS IT, A WHILE AGO, WANTED TO KNOW EVERYTHING?

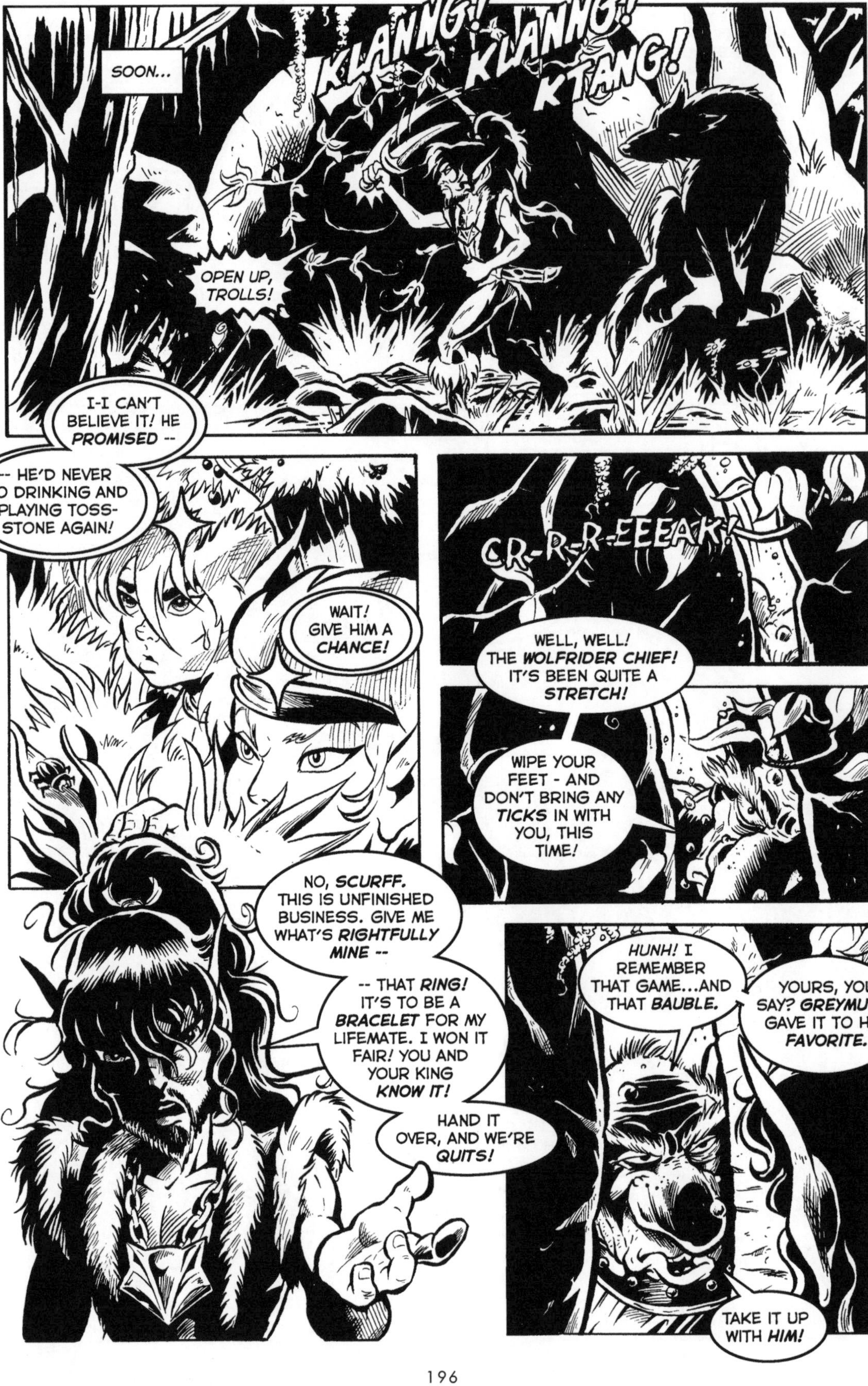
SOON...
KLANNG! KLANNG! KTANG!
OPEN UP, TROLLS!
I-I CAN'T BELIEVE IT! HE PROMISED --
-- HE'D NEVER GO DRINKING AND PLAYING TOSS-STONE AGAIN!
WAIT! GIVE HIM A CHANCE!
CR-R-R-EEEAK!
WELL, WELL! THE WOLFRIDER CHIEF! IT'S BEEN QUITE A STRETCH!
WIPE YOUR FEET - AND DON'T BRING ANY TICKS IN WITH YOU, THIS TIME!
NO, SCURFF. THIS IS UNFINISHED BUSINESS. GIVE ME WHAT'S RIGHTFULLY MINE --
-- THAT RING! IT'S TO BE A BRACELET FOR MY LIFEMATE. I WON IT FAIR! YOU AND YOUR KING KNOW IT!
HAND IT OVER, AND WE'RE QUITS!
HUNH! I REMEMBER THAT GAME...AND THAT BAUBLE.
YOURS, YOU SAY? GREYMUNG GAVE IT TO HIS FAVORITE.
TAKE IT UP WITH HIM!

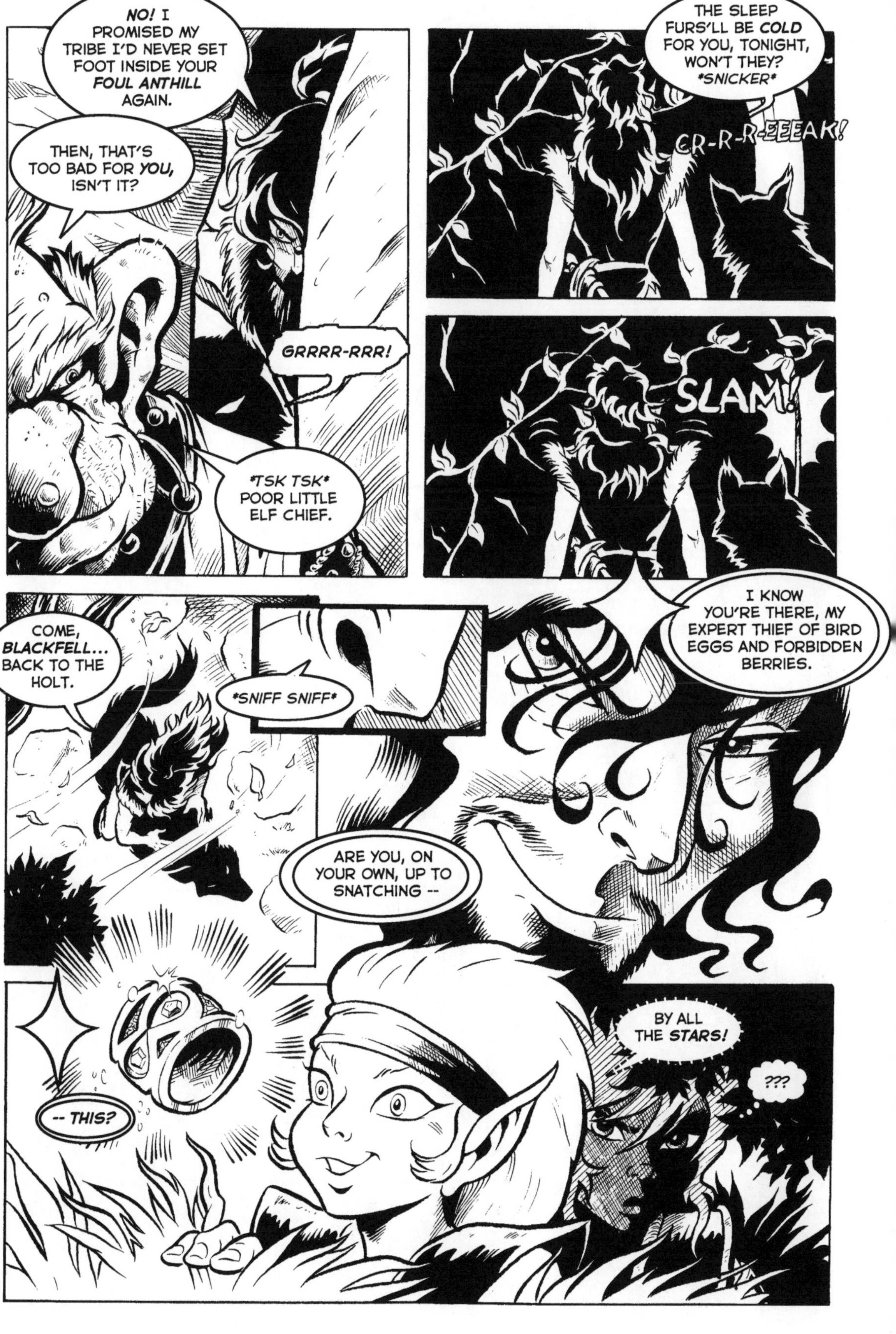
NO! I PROMISED MY TRIBE I'D NEVER SET FOOT INSIDE YOUR FOUL ANTHILL AGAIN.
THEN, THAT'S TOO BAD FOR YOU, ISN'T IT?
GRRRR-RRR!
TSK TSK POOR LITTLE ELF CHIEF.
THE SLEEP FURS'LL BE COLD FOR YOU, TONIGHT, WON'T THEY? *SNICKER*
CR-R-R-EEEAK!
SLAM!
COME, BLACKFELL... BACK TO THE HOLT.
SNIFF SNIFF
I KNOW YOU'RE THERE, MY EXPERT THIEF OF BIRD EGGS AND FORBIDDEN BERRIES.
ARE YOU, ON YOUR OWN, UP TO SNATCHING --
-- THIS?
BY ALL THE STARS!
???

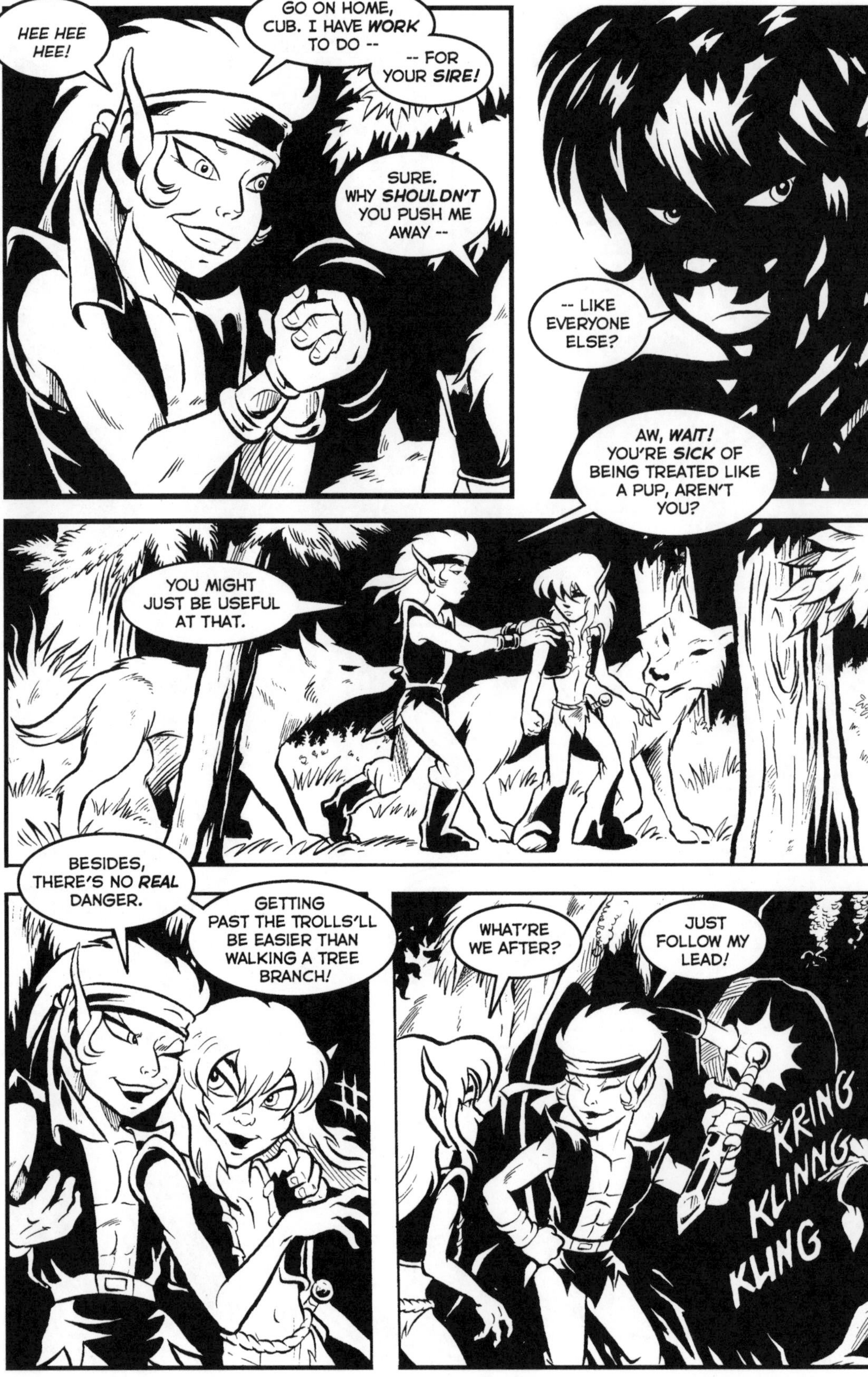
HEE HEE HEE!
GO ON HOME, CUB. I HAVE *WORK* TO DO --
-- FOR YOUR *SIRE!*
SURE. WHY *SHOULDN'T* YOU PUSH ME AWAY --
-- LIKE EVERYONE ELSE?
AW, *WAIT!* YOU'RE *SICK* OF BEING TREATED LIKE A PUP, AREN'T YOU?
YOU MIGHT JUST BE USEFUL AT THAT.
BESIDES, THERE'S NO *REAL* DANGER.
GETTING PAST THE TROLLS'LL BE EASIER THAN WALKING A TREE BRANCH!
WHAT'RE WE AFTER?
JUST FOLLOW MY LEAD!
KRING KLINNG KLING

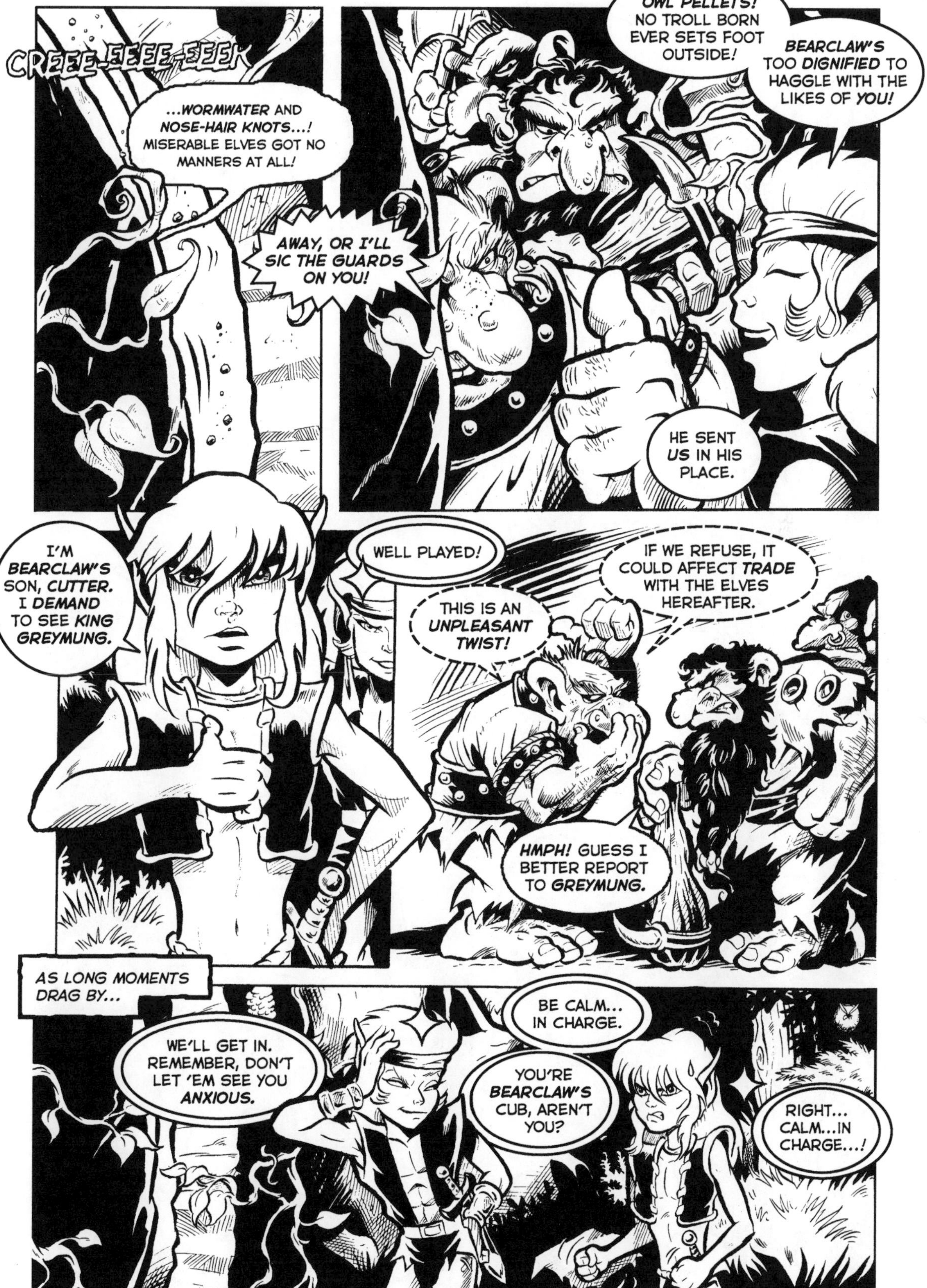
CREEE-EEEE-EEEK
...WORMWATER AND NOSE-HAIR KNOTS...! MISERABLE ELVES GOT NO MANNERS AT ALL!
AWAY, OR I'LL SIC THE GUARDS ON YOU!
OWL PELLETS! NO TROLL BORN EVER SETS FOOT OUTSIDE!
BEARCLAW'S TOO DIGNIFIED TO HAGGLE WITH THE LIKES OF YOU!
HE SENT US IN HIS PLACE.
I'M BEARCLAW'S SON, CUTTER. I DEMAND TO SEE KING GREYMUNG.
WELL PLAYED!
THIS IS AN UNPLEASANT TWIST!
IF WE REFUSE, IT COULD AFFECT TRADE WITH THE ELVES HEREAFTER.
HMPH! GUESS I BETTER REPORT TO GREYMUNG.
AS LONG MOMENTS DRAG BY...
WE'LL GET IN. REMEMBER, DON'T LET 'EM SEE YOU ANXIOUS.
BE CALM... IN CHARGE.
YOU'RE BEARCLAW'S CUB, AREN'T YOU?
RIGHT... CALM...IN CHARGE...!

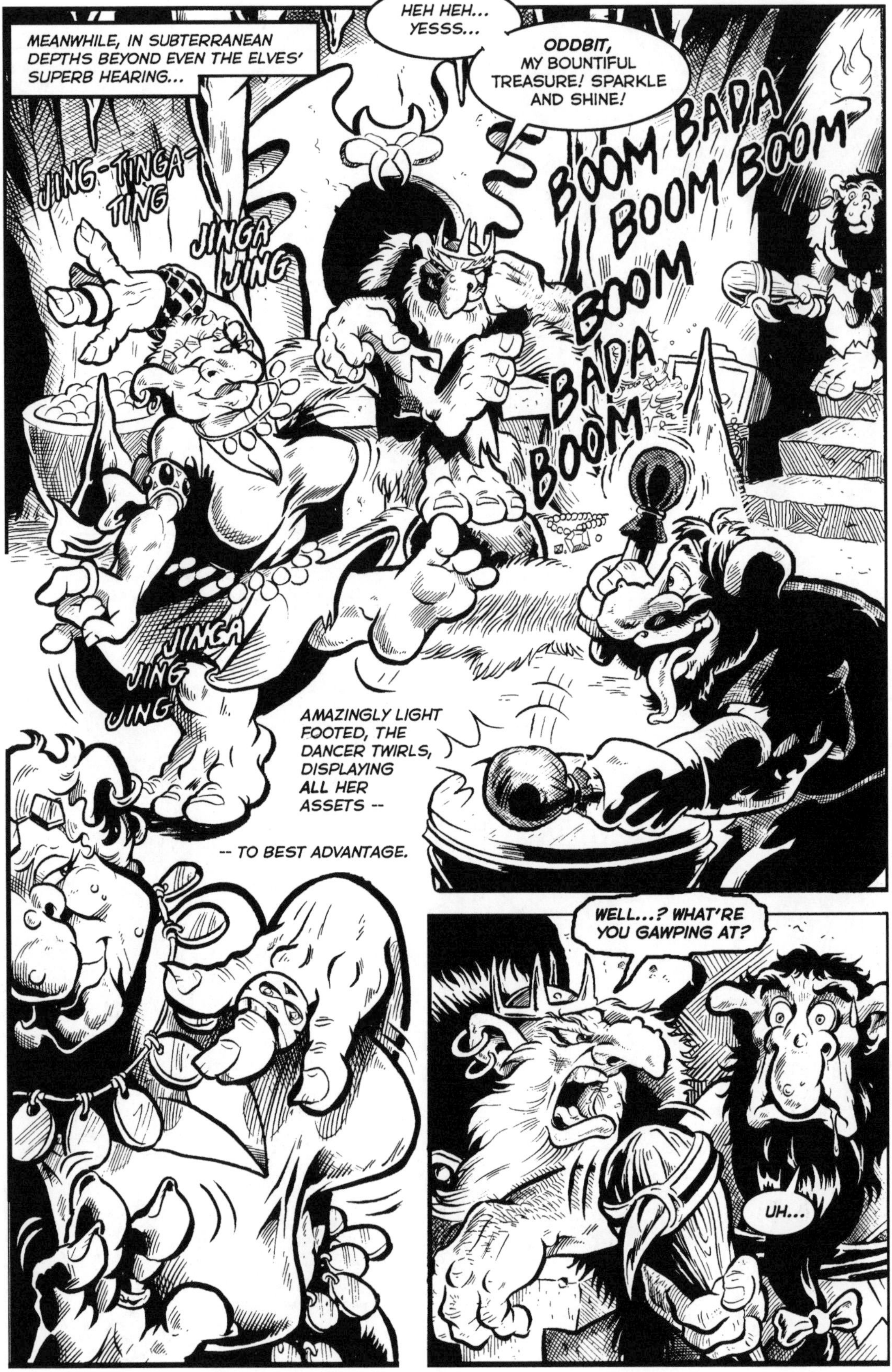
MEANWHILE, IN SUBTERRANEAN DEPTHS BEYOND EVEN THE ELVES' SUPERB HEARING...
HEH HEH... YESSS...
ODDBIT, MY BOUNTIFUL TREASURE! SPARKLE AND SHINE!
JING-TINGA-TING
JINGA JING
BOOM BADA BOOM BOOM
BOOM BADA BOOM
JINGA JING JING
AMAZINGLY LIGHT FOOTED, THE DANCER TWIRLS, DISPLAYING ALL HER ASSETS --
-- TO BEST ADVANTAGE.
WELL...? WHAT'RE YOU GAWPING AT?
UH...

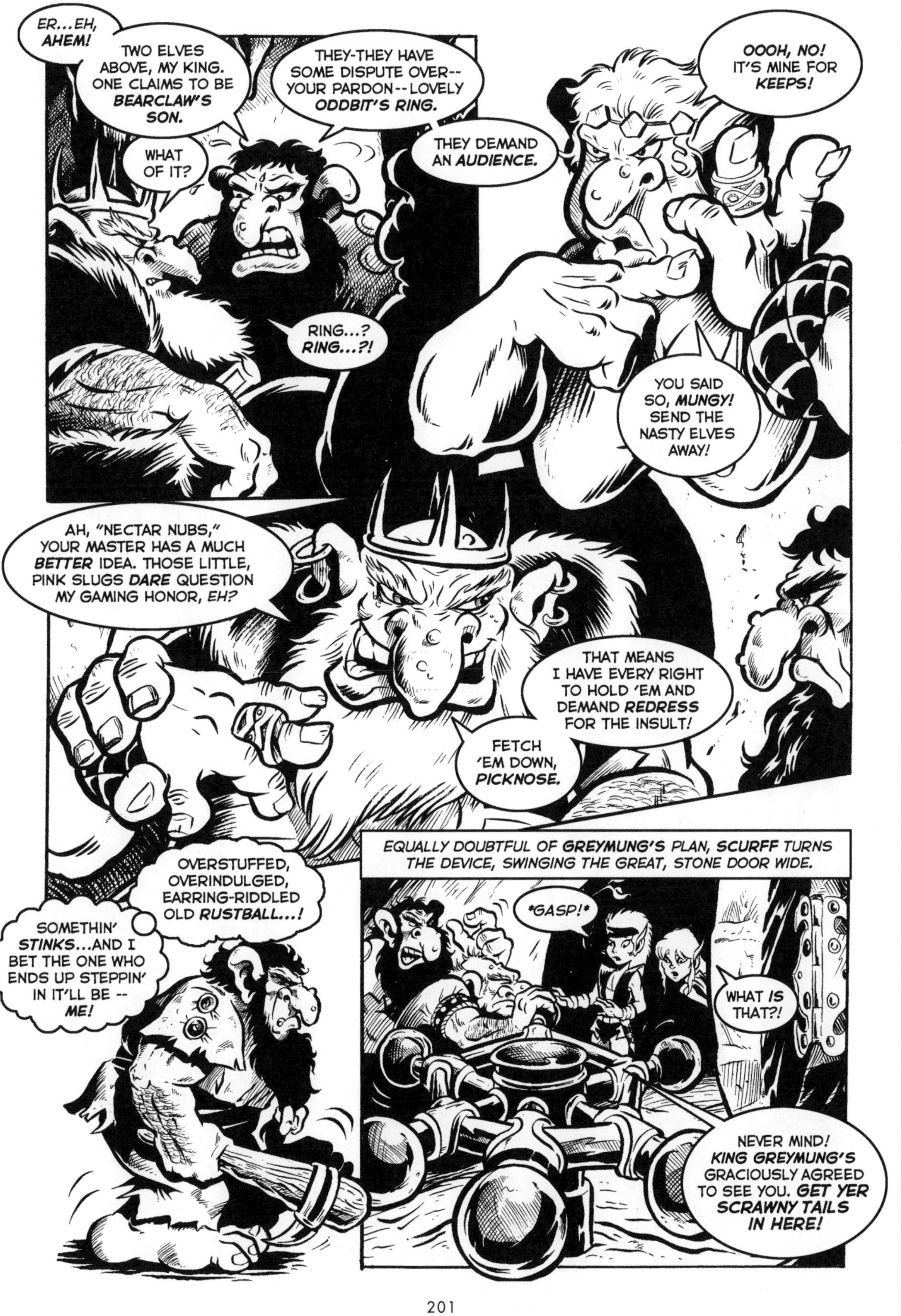
ER...EH, AHEM!
TWO ELVES ABOVE, MY KING. ONE CLAIMS TO BE BEARCLAW'S SON.
WHAT OF IT?
THEY-THEY HAVE SOME DISPUTE OVER-- YOUR PARDON--LOVELY ODDBIT'S RING.
THEY DEMAND AN AUDIENCE.
RING...? RING...?!
OOOH, NO! IT'S MINE FOR KEEPS!
YOU SAID SO, MUNGY! SEND THE NASTY ELVES AWAY!
AH, "NECTAR NUBS," YOUR MASTER HAS A MUCH BETTER IDEA. THOSE LITTLE, PINK SLUGS DARE QUESTION MY GAMING HONOR, EH?
THAT MEANS I HAVE EVERY RIGHT TO HOLD 'EM AND DEMAND REDRESS FOR THE INSULT!
FETCH 'EM DOWN, PICKNOSE.
OVERSTUFFED, OVERINDULGED, EARRING-RIDDLED OLD RUSTBALL...!
SOMETHIN' STINKS...AND I BET THE ONE WHO ENDS UP STEPPIN' IN IT'LL BE -- ME!
EQUALLY DOUBTFUL OF GREYMUNG'S PLAN, SCURFF TURNS THE DEVICE, SWINGING THE GREAT, STONE DOOR WIDE.
GASP!
WHAT IS THAT?!
NEVER MIND! KING GREYMUNG'S GRACIOUSLY AGREED TO SEE YOU. GET YER SCRAWNY TAILS IN HERE!

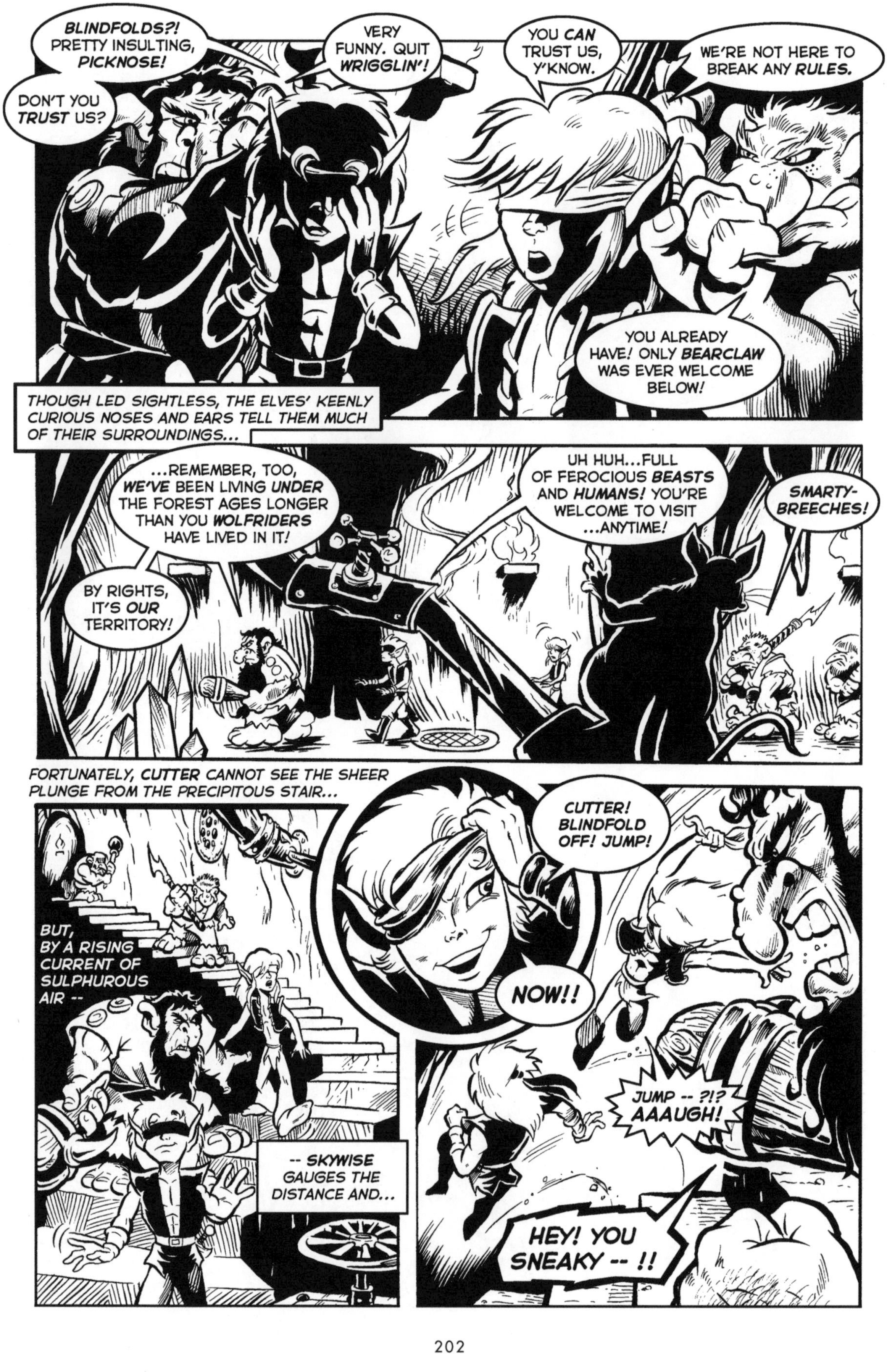

BLINDFOLDS?! PRETTY INSULTING, PICKNOSE!
DON'T YOU TRUST US?
VERY FUNNY. QUIT WRIGGLIN'!
YOU CAN TRUST US, Y'KNOW.
WE'RE NOT HERE TO BREAK ANY RULES.
YOU ALREADY HAVE! ONLY BEARCLAW WAS EVER WELCOME BELOW!
THOUGH LED SIGHTLESS, THE ELVES' KEENLY CURIOUS NOSES AND EARS TELL THEM MUCH OF THEIR SURROUNDINGS...
...REMEMBER, TOO, WE'VE BEEN LIVING UNDER THE FOREST AGES LONGER THAN YOU WOLFRIDERS HAVE LIVED IN IT!
BY RIGHTS, IT'S OUR TERRITORY!
UH HUH...FULL OF FEROCIOUS BEASTS AND HUMANS! YOU'RE WELCOME TO VISIT ...ANYTIME!
SMARTY-BREECHES!
FORTUNATELY, CUTTER CANNOT SEE THE SHEER PLUNGE FROM THE PRECIPITOUS STAIR...
BUT, BY A RISING CURRENT OF SULPHUROUS AIR --
-- SKYWISE GAUGES THE DISTANCE AND...
CUTTER! BLINDFOLD OFF! JUMP!
NOW!!
JUMP -- ?!? AAAUGH!
HEY! YOU SNEAKY -- !!

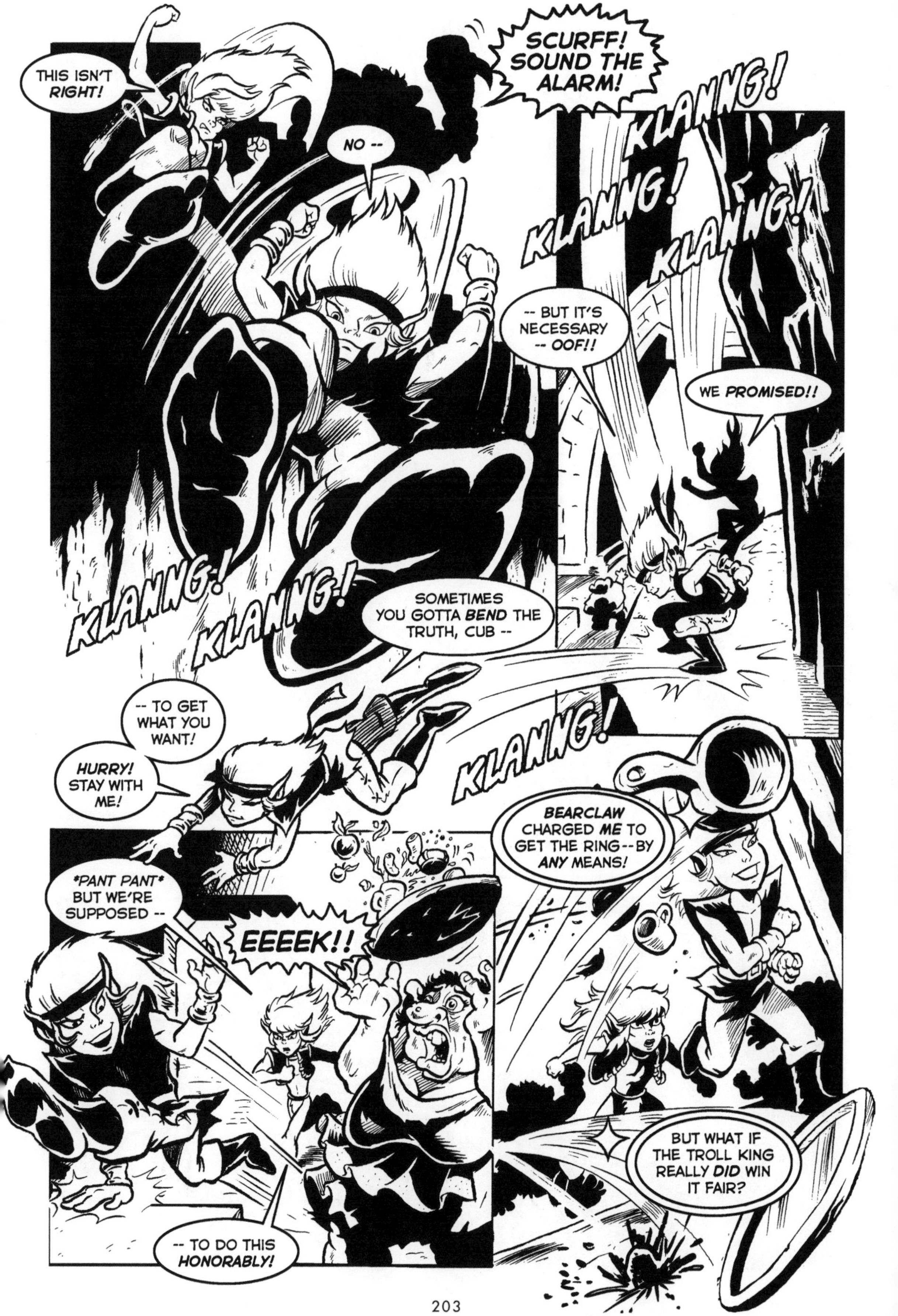

THIS ISN'T RIGHT!
SCURFF! SOUND THE ALARM!
NO --
KLANNG!
KLANNG!
KLANNG!
-- BUT IT'S NECESSARY -- OOF!!
WE PROMISED!!
KLANNG!
KLANNG!
SOMETIMES YOU GOTTA BEND THE TRUTH, CUB --
-- TO GET WHAT YOU WANT!
HURRY! STAY WITH ME!
KLANNG!
PANT PANT BUT WE'RE SUPPOSED --
EEEEK!!
-- TO DO THIS HONORABLY!
BEARCLAW CHARGED ME TO GET THE RING--BY ANY MEANS!
BUT WHAT IF THE TROLL KING REALLY DID WIN IT FAIR?

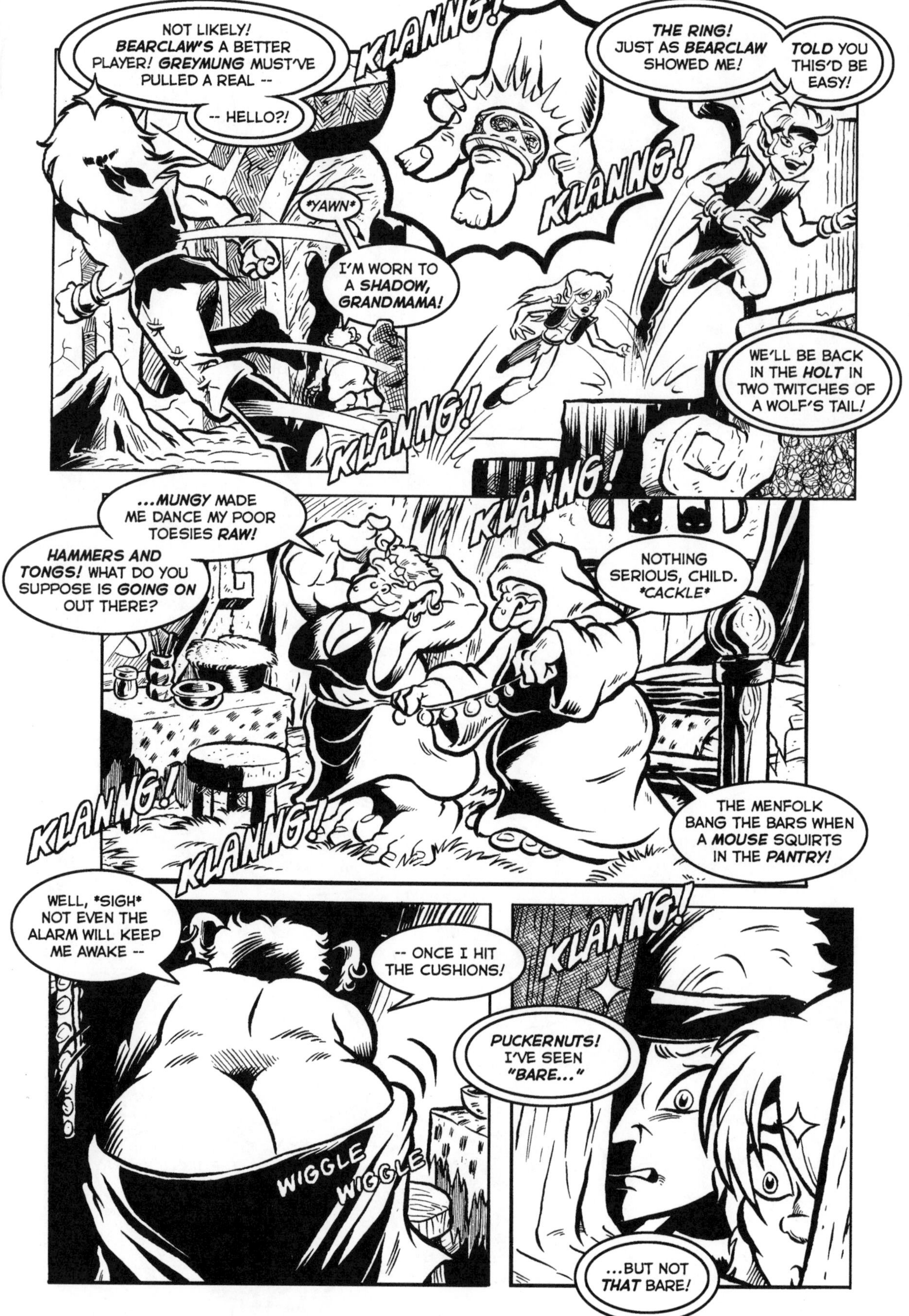
NOT LIKELY! BEARCLAW'S A BETTER PLAYER! GREYMUNG MUST'VE PULLED A REAL --
-- HELLO?!
KLANNG!
YAWN
I'M WORN TO A SHADOW, GRANDMAMA!
KLANNG!
THE RING! JUST AS BEARCLAW SHOWED ME!
TOLD YOU THIS'D BE EASY!
KLANNG!
WE'LL BE BACK IN THE HOLT IN TWO TWITCHES OF A WOLF'S TAIL!
KLANNG!
...MUNGY MADE ME DANCE MY POOR TOESIES RAW!
HAMMERS AND TONGS! WHAT DO YOU SUPPOSE IS GOING ON OUT THERE?
NOTHING SERIOUS, CHILD. *CACKLE*
KLANNG!
KLANNG!
THE MENFOLK BANG THE BARS WHEN A MOUSE SQUIRTS IN THE PANTRY!
WELL, *SIGH* NOT EVEN THE ALARM WILL KEEP ME AWAKE --
-- ONCE I HIT THE CUSHIONS!
WIGGLE WIGGLE
KLANNG!
PUCKERNUTS! I'VE SEEN "BARE..."
...BUT NOT THAT BARE!

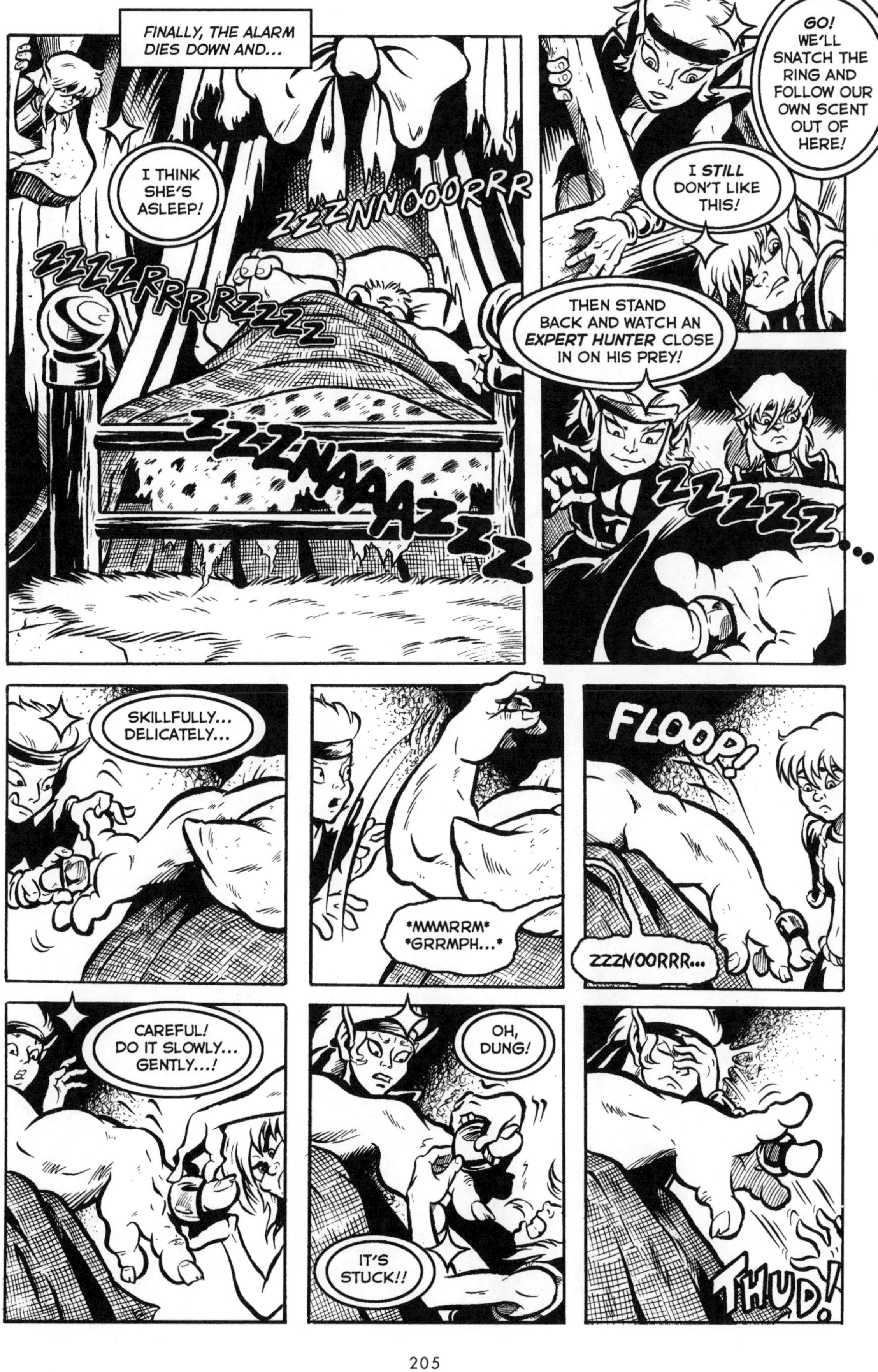
FINALLY, THE ALARM DIES DOWN AND...
I THINK SHE'S ASLEEP!
ZZZNNOOORRRR
ZZZZRRRRRZZZZZ
ZZZNAAAAZZZ
GO! WE'LL SNATCH THE RING AND FOLLOW OUR OWN SCENT OUT OF HERE!
I STILL DON'T LIKE THIS!
THEN STAND BACK AND WATCH AN EXPERT HUNTER CLOSE IN ON HIS PREY!
ZZZZZZ...
SKILLFULLY... DELICATELY...
MMMRRM *GRRMPH...*
FLOOP!
ZZZNOORRR...
CAREFUL! DO IT SLOWLY... GENTLY...!
OH, DUNG!
IT'S STUCK!!
THUD!

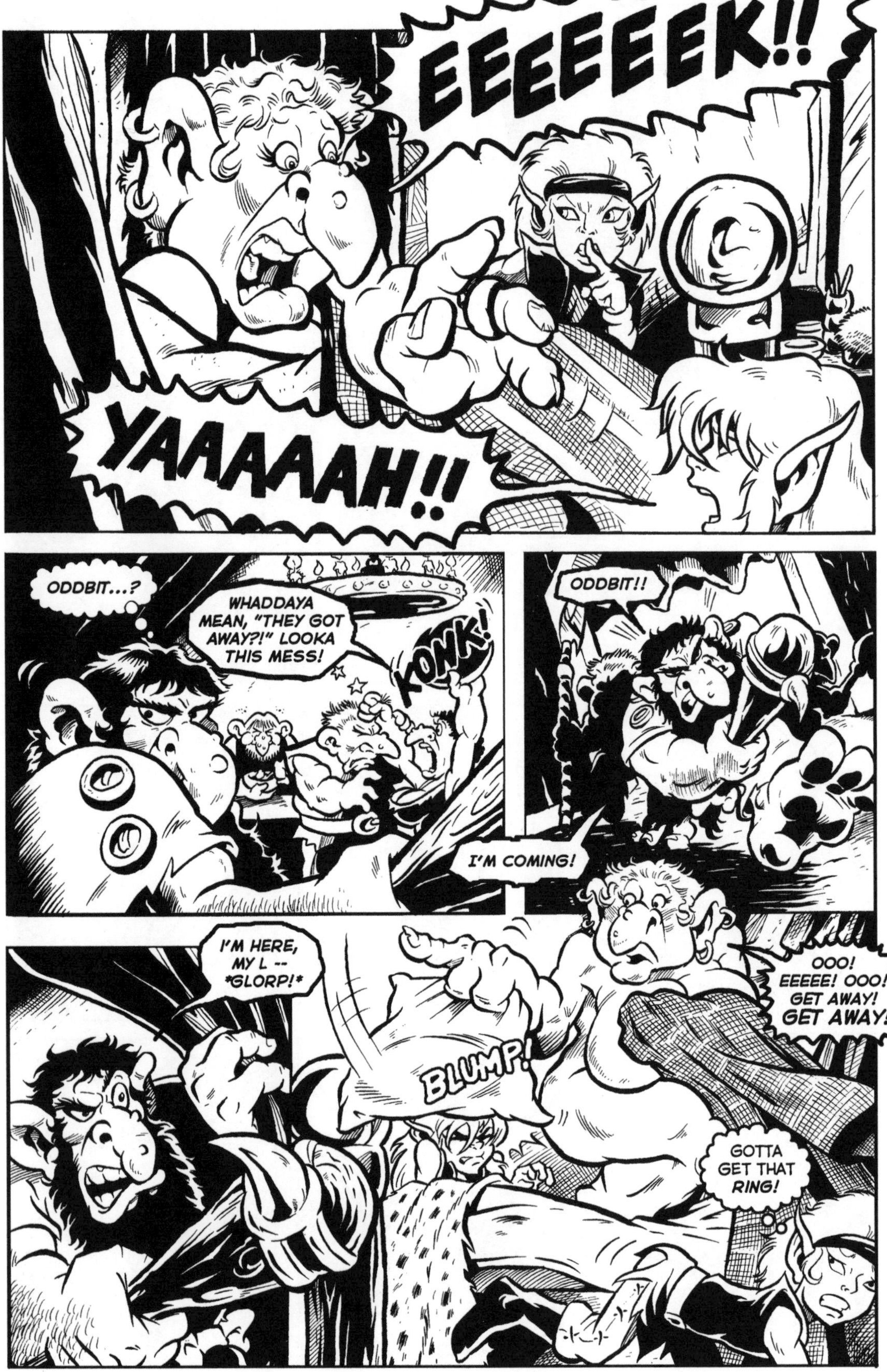
EEEEEEK!!
YAAAAAH!!
ODDBIT...?
WHADDAYA MEAN, "THEY GOT AWAY?!" LOOKA THIS MESS!
KONK!
ODDBIT!!
I'M COMING!
I'M HERE, MY L -- *GLORP!*
OOO! EEEEE! OOO! GET AWAY! GET AWAY!
BLUMP!
GOTTA GET THAT RING!

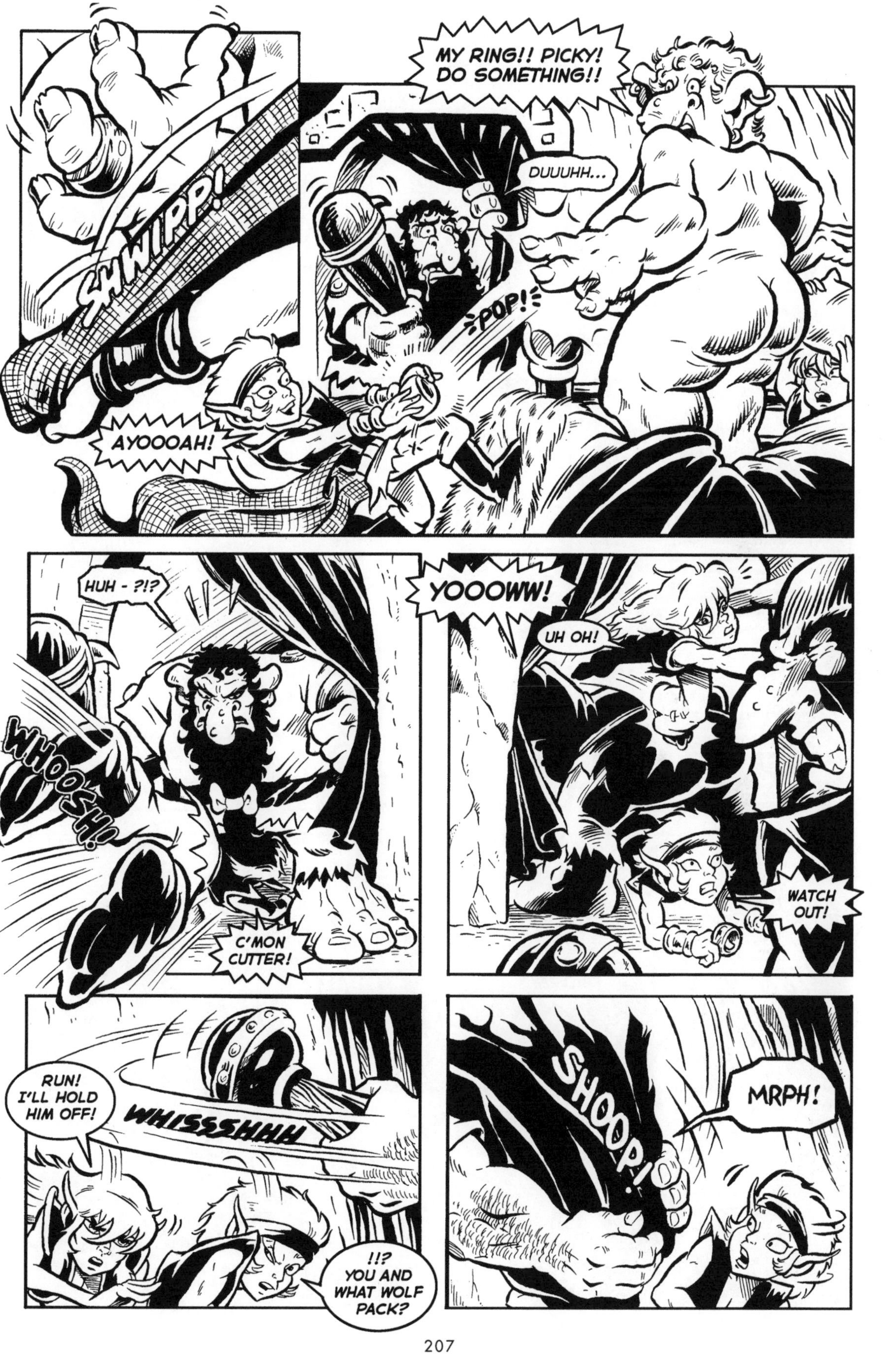
SHWIPP!
MY RING!! PICKY! DO SOMETHING!!
DUUUHH...
POP!
AYOOOAH!
HUH - ?!?
WHOOSH!
C'MON CUTTER!
YOOOWW!
UH OH!
WATCH OUT!
RUN! I'LL HOLD HIM OFF!
WHISSSHHH
!!? YOU AND WHAT WOLF PACK?
SHOOP!
MRPH!

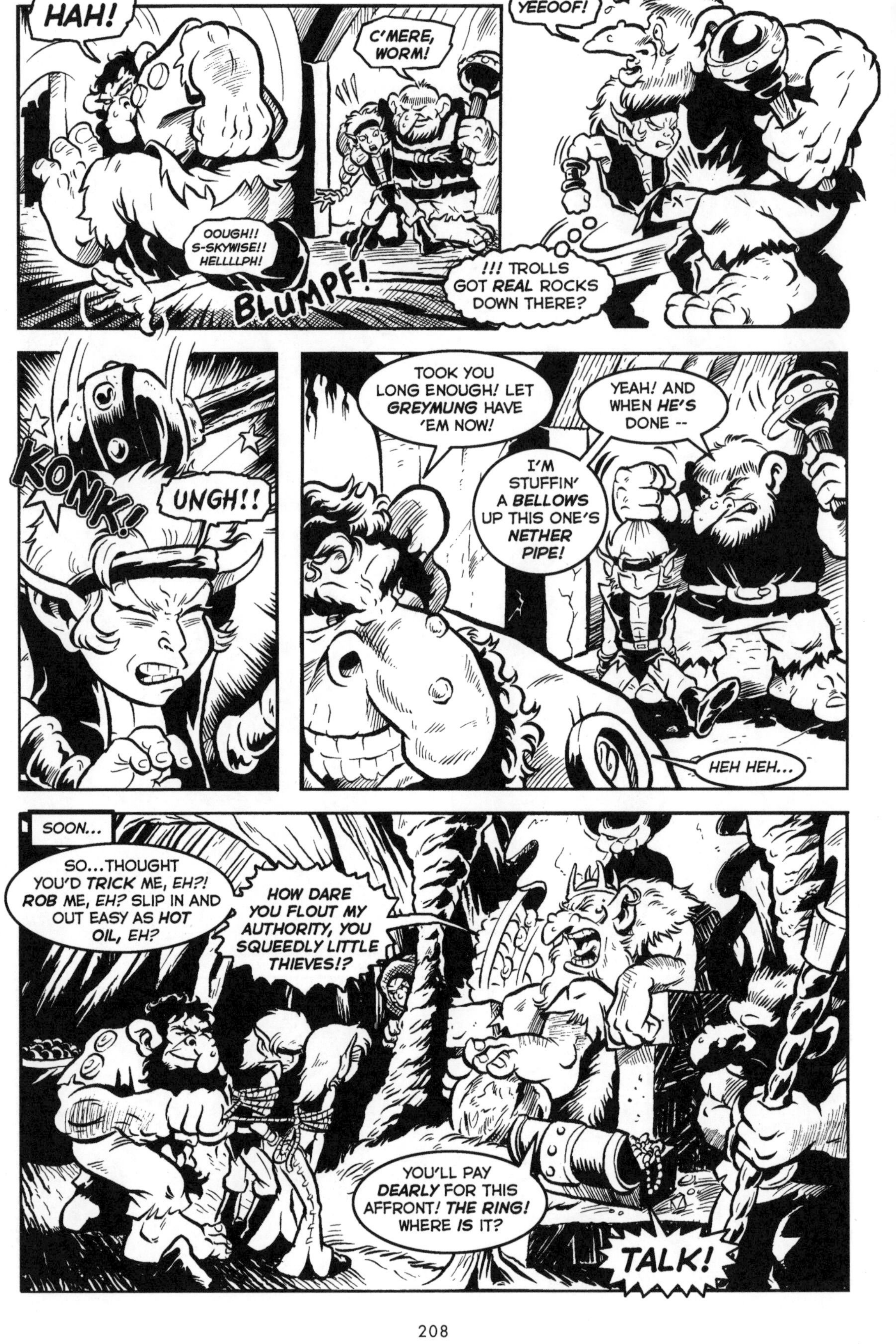
HAH!
OOUGH!! S-SKYWISE!! HELLLLPH!
BLUMPF!
C'MERE, WORM!
YEEOOF!
!!! TROLLS GOT REAL ROCKS DOWN THERE?
KONK!
UNGH!!
TOOK YOU LONG ENOUGH! LET GREYMUNG HAVE 'EM NOW!
YEAH! AND WHEN HE'S DONE --
I'M STUFFIN' A BELLOWS UP THIS ONE'S NETHER PIPE!
HEH HEH...
SOON...
SO...THOUGHT YOU'D TRICK ME, EH?! ROB ME, EH? SLIP IN AND OUT EASY AS HOT OIL, EH?
HOW DARE YOU FLOUT MY AUTHORITY, YOU SQUEEDLY LITTLE THIEVES!?
YOU'LL PAY DEARLY FOR THIS AFFRONT! THE RING! WHERE IS IT?
TALK!

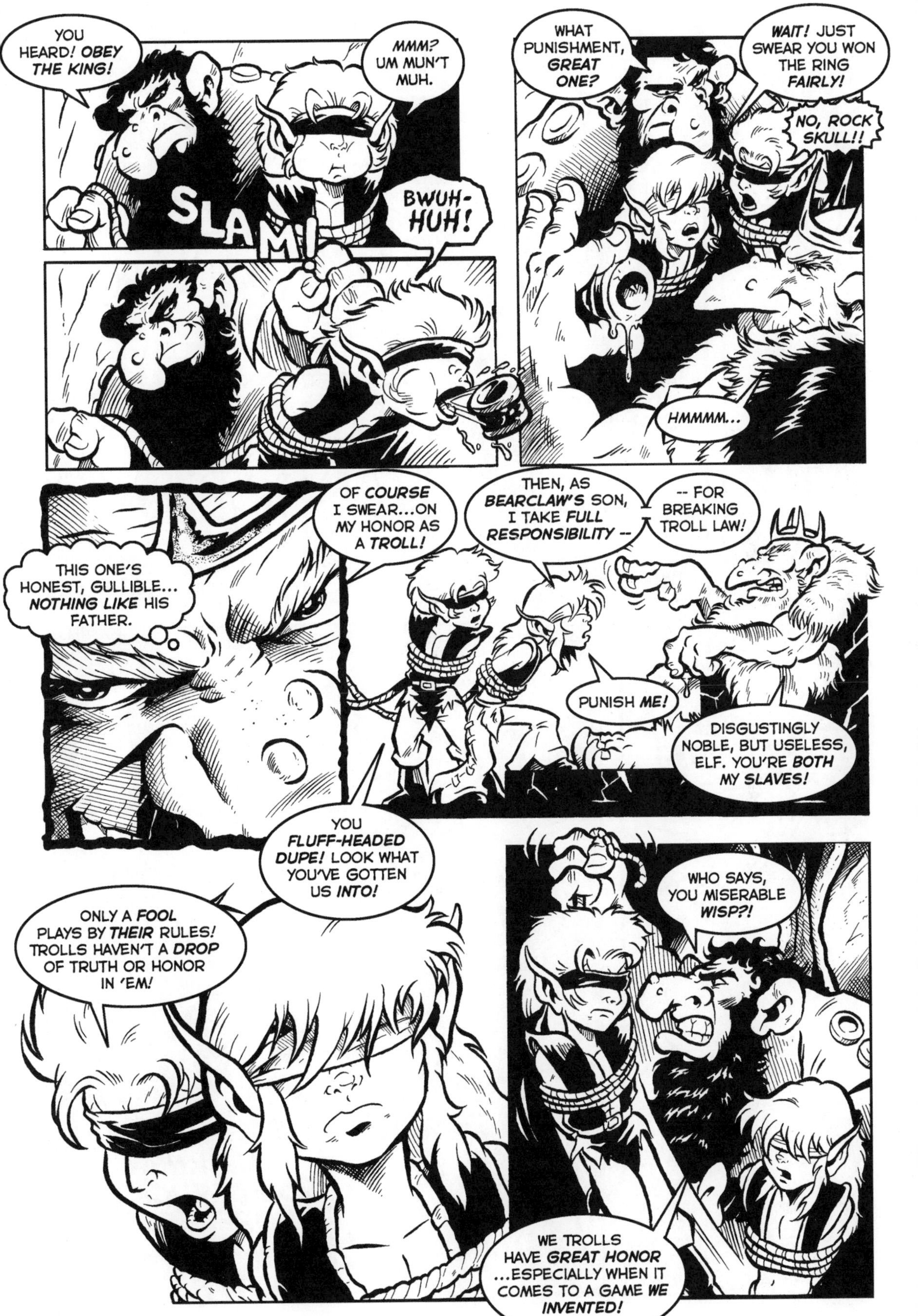

YOU HEARD! OBEY THE KING!
MMM? UM MUN'T MUH.
SLAM!
BWUH-HUH!
WHAT PUNISHMENT, GREAT ONE?
WAIT! JUST SWEAR YOU WON THE RING FAIRLY!
NO, ROCK SKULL!!
HMMMM...
THIS ONE'S HONEST, GULLIBLE... NOTHING LIKE HIS FATHER.
OF COURSE I SWEAR...ON MY HONOR AS A TROLL!
THEN, AS BEARCLAW'S SON, I TAKE FULL RESPONSIBILITY --
-- FOR BREAKING TROLL LAW!
PUNISH ME!
DISGUSTINGLY NOBLE, BUT USELESS, ELF. YOU'RE BOTH MY SLAVES!
YOU FLUFF-HEADED DUPE! LOOK WHAT YOU'VE GOTTEN US INTO!
ONLY A FOOL PLAYS BY THEIR RULES! TROLLS HAVEN'T A DROP OF TRUTH OR HONOR IN 'EM!
WHO SAYS, YOU MISERABLE WISP?!
WE TROLLS HAVE GREAT HONOR ...ESPECIALLY WHEN IT COMES TO A GAME WE INVENTED!

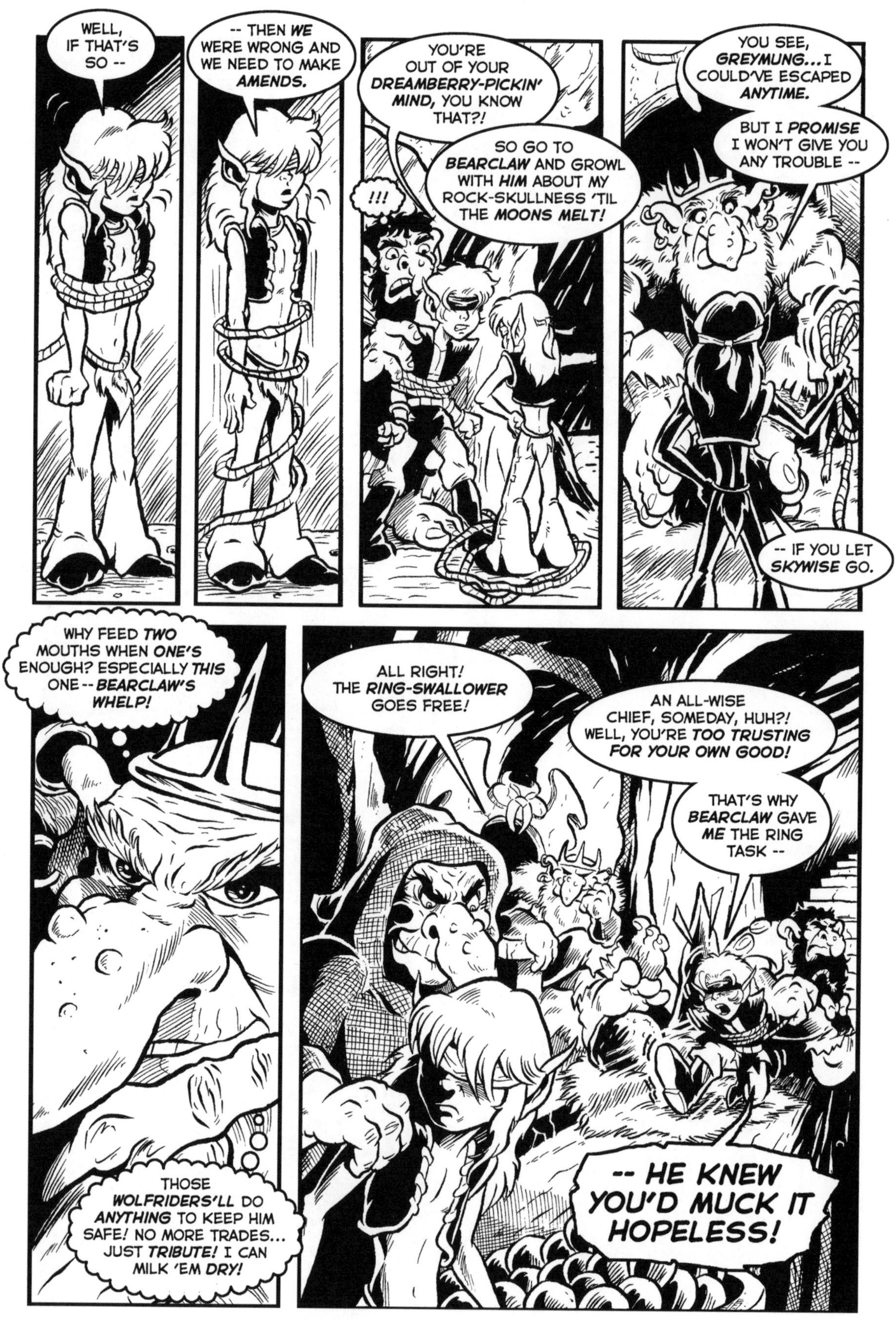

WELL, IF THAT'S SO --
-- THEN WE WERE WRONG AND WE NEED TO MAKE AMENDS.
YOU'RE OUT OF YOUR DREAMBERRY-PICKIN' MIND, YOU KNOW THAT?!
!!!
SO GO TO BEARCLAW AND GROWL WITH HIM ABOUT MY ROCK-SKULLNESS 'TIL THE MOONS MELT!
YOU SEE, GREYMUNG... I COULD'VE ESCAPED ANYTIME.
BUT I PROMISE I WON'T GIVE YOU ANY TROUBLE --
-- IF YOU LET SKYWISE GO.
WHY FEED TWO MOUTHS WHEN ONE'S ENOUGH? ESPECIALLY THIS ONE -- BEARCLAW'S WHELP!
THOSE WOLFRIDERS'LL DO ANYTHING TO KEEP HIM SAFE! NO MORE TRADES... JUST TRIBUTE! I CAN MILK 'EM DRY!
ALL RIGHT! THE RING-SWALLOWER GOES FREE!
AN ALL-WISE CHIEF, SOMEDAY, HUH?! WELL, YOU'RE TOO TRUSTING FOR YOUR OWN GOOD!
THAT'S WHY BEARCLAW GAVE ME THE RING TASK --
-- HE KNEW YOU'D MUCK IT HOPELESS!

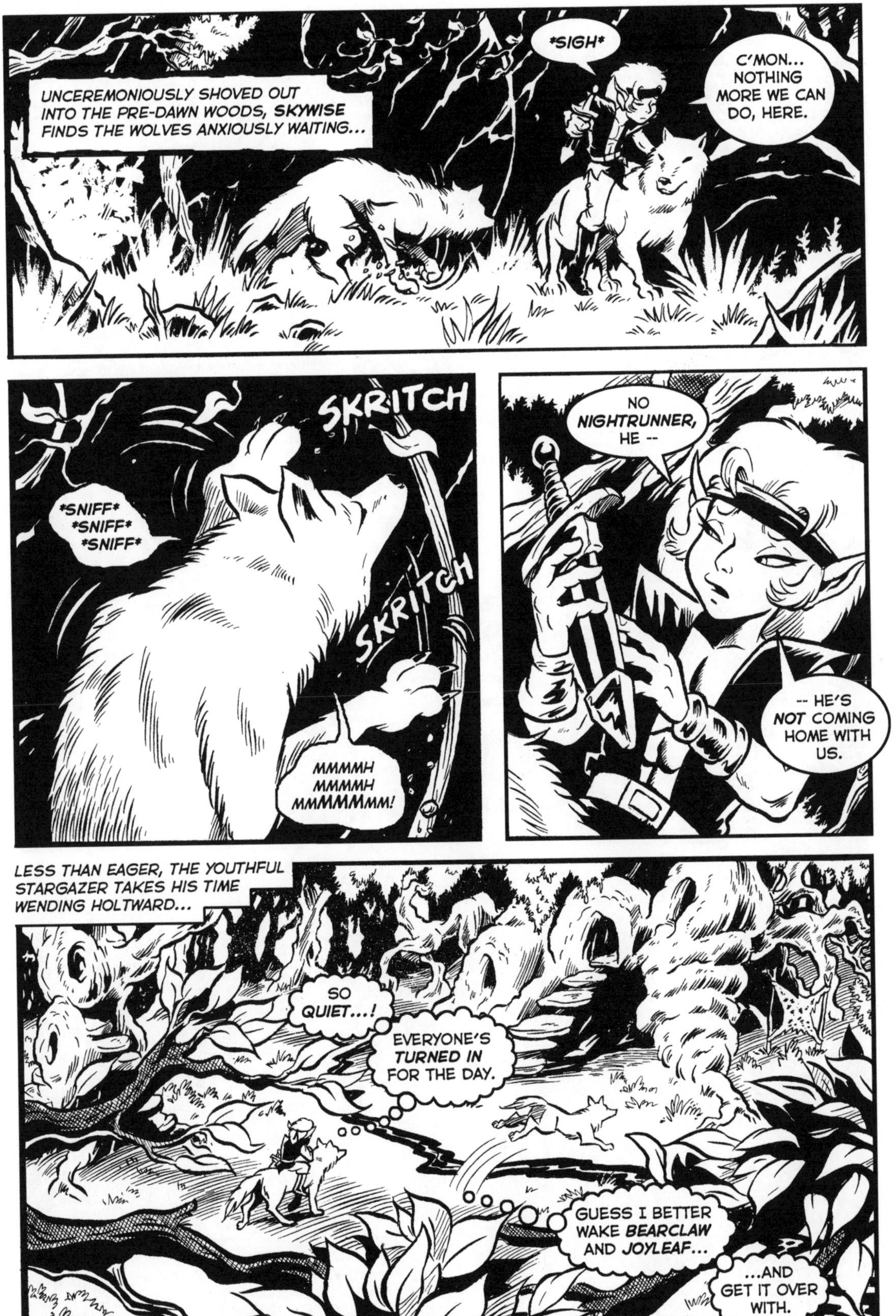
UNCEREMONIOUSLY SHOVED OUT INTO THE PRE-DAWN WOODS, SKYWISE FINDS THE WOLVES ANXIOUSLY WAITING...
SIGH
C'MON... NOTHING MORE WE CAN DO, HERE.
SKRITCH
SNIFF *SNIFF* *SNIFF*
SKRITCH
MMMMH MMMMH MMMMMmm!
NO NIGHTRUNNER, HE --
-- HE'S NOT COMING HOME WITH US.
LESS THAN EAGER, THE YOUTHFUL STARGAZER TAKES HIS TIME WENDING HOLTWARD...
SO QUIET...!
EVERYONE'S TURNED IN FOR THE DAY.
GUESS I BETTER WAKE BEARCLAW AND JOYLEAF...
...AND GET IT OVER WITH.

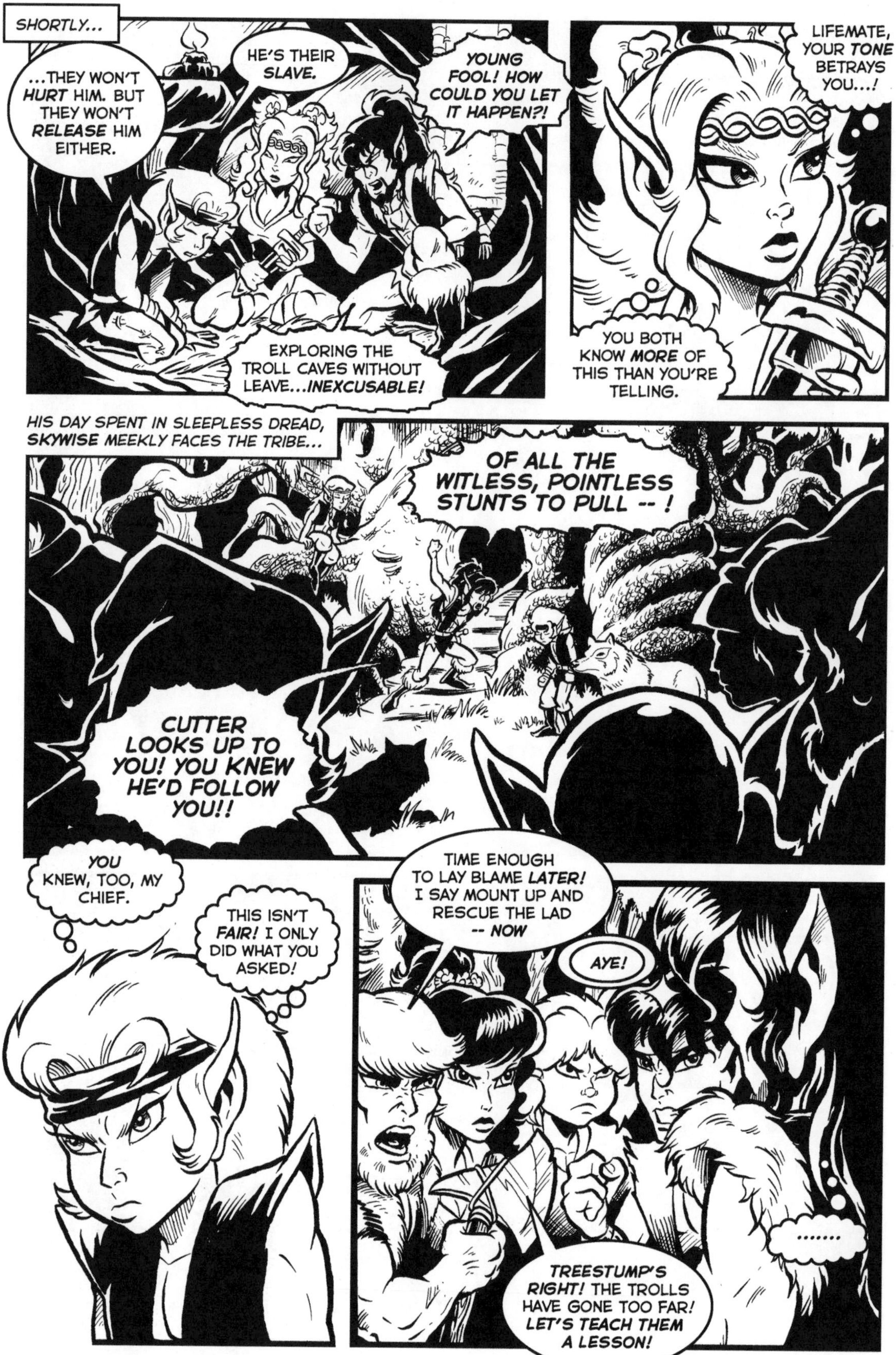
SHORTLY...
...THEY WON'T HURT HIM. BUT THEY WON'T RELEASE HIM EITHER.
HE'S THEIR SLAVE.
YOUNG FOOL! HOW COULD YOU LET IT HAPPEN?!
EXPLORING THE TROLL CAVES WITHOUT LEAVE...INEXCUSABLE!
LIFEMATE, YOUR TONE BETRAYS YOU...!
YOU BOTH KNOW MORE OF THIS THAN YOU'RE TELLING.
HIS DAY SPENT IN SLEEPLESS DREAD, SKYWISE MEEKLY FACES THE TRIBE...
OF ALL THE WITLESS, POINTLESS STUNTS TO PULL -- !
CUTTER LOOKS UP TO YOU! YOU KNEW HE'D FOLLOW YOU!!
YOU KNEW, TOO, MY CHIEF.
THIS ISN'T FAIR! I ONLY DID WHAT YOU ASKED!
TIME ENOUGH TO LAY BLAME LATER! I SAY MOUNT UP AND RESCUE THE LAD -- NOW
AYE!
....
TREESTUMP'S RIGHT! THE TROLLS HAVE GONE TOO FAR! LET'S TEACH THEM A LESSON!

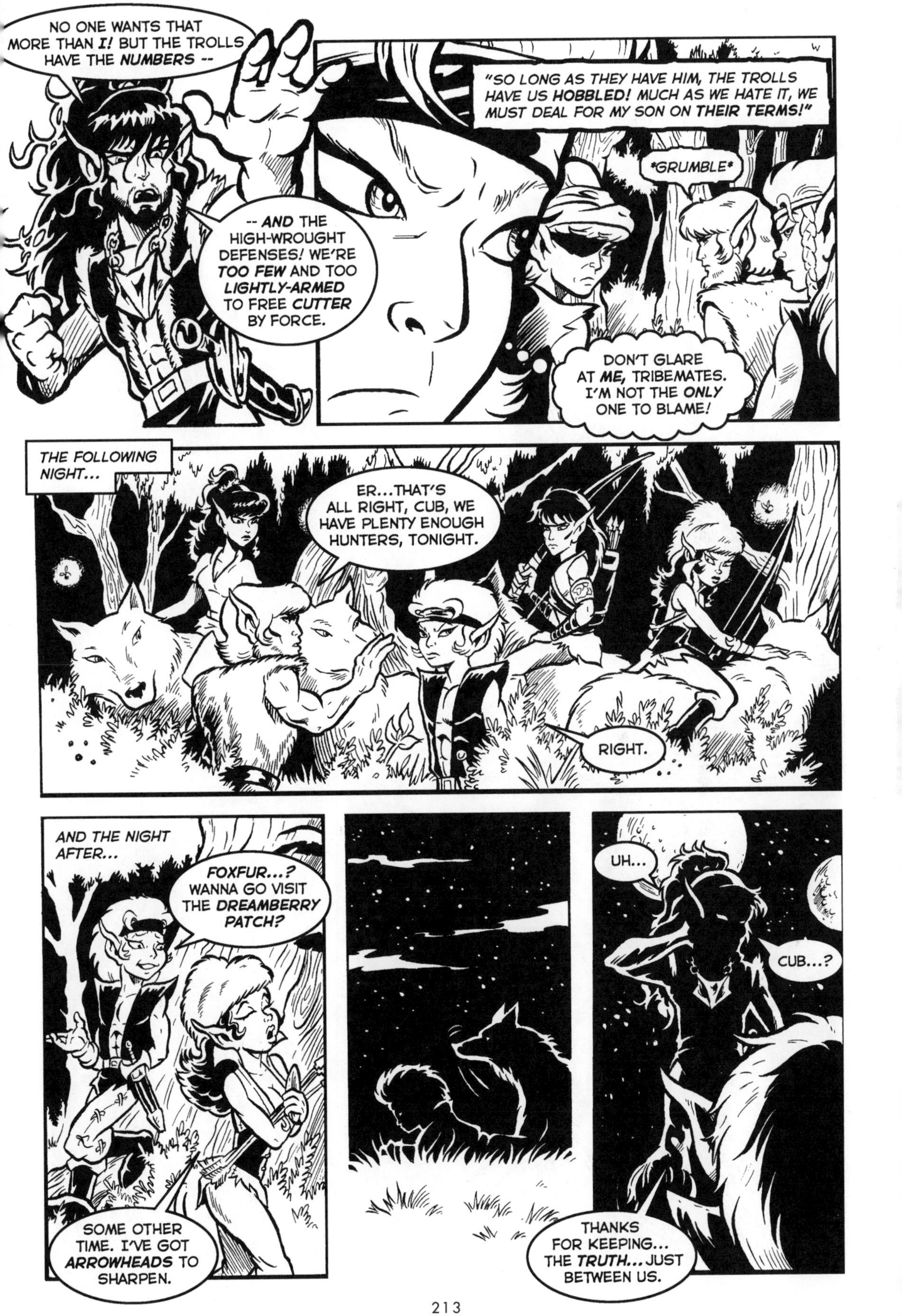
NO ONE WANTS THAT MORE THAN I! BUT THE TROLLS HAVE THE NUMBERS --
-- AND THE HIGH-WROUGHT DEFENSES! WE'RE TOO FEW AND TOO LIGHTLY-ARMED TO FREE CUTTER BY FORCE.
"SO LONG AS THEY HAVE HIM, THE TROLLS HAVE US HOBBLED! MUCH AS WE HATE IT, WE MUST DEAL FOR MY SON ON THEIR TERMS!"
GRUMBLE
DON'T GLARE AT ME, TRIBEMATES. I'M NOT THE ONLY ONE TO BLAME!
THE FOLLOWING NIGHT...
ER...THAT'S ALL RIGHT, CUB, WE HAVE PLENTY ENOUGH HUNTERS, TONIGHT.
RIGHT.
AND THE NIGHT AFTER...
FOXFUR...? WANNA GO VISIT THE DREAMBERRY PATCH?
SOME OTHER TIME. I'VE GOT ARROWHEADS TO SHARPEN.
UH...
CUB...?
THANKS FOR KEEPING... THE TRUTH... JUST BETWEEN US.

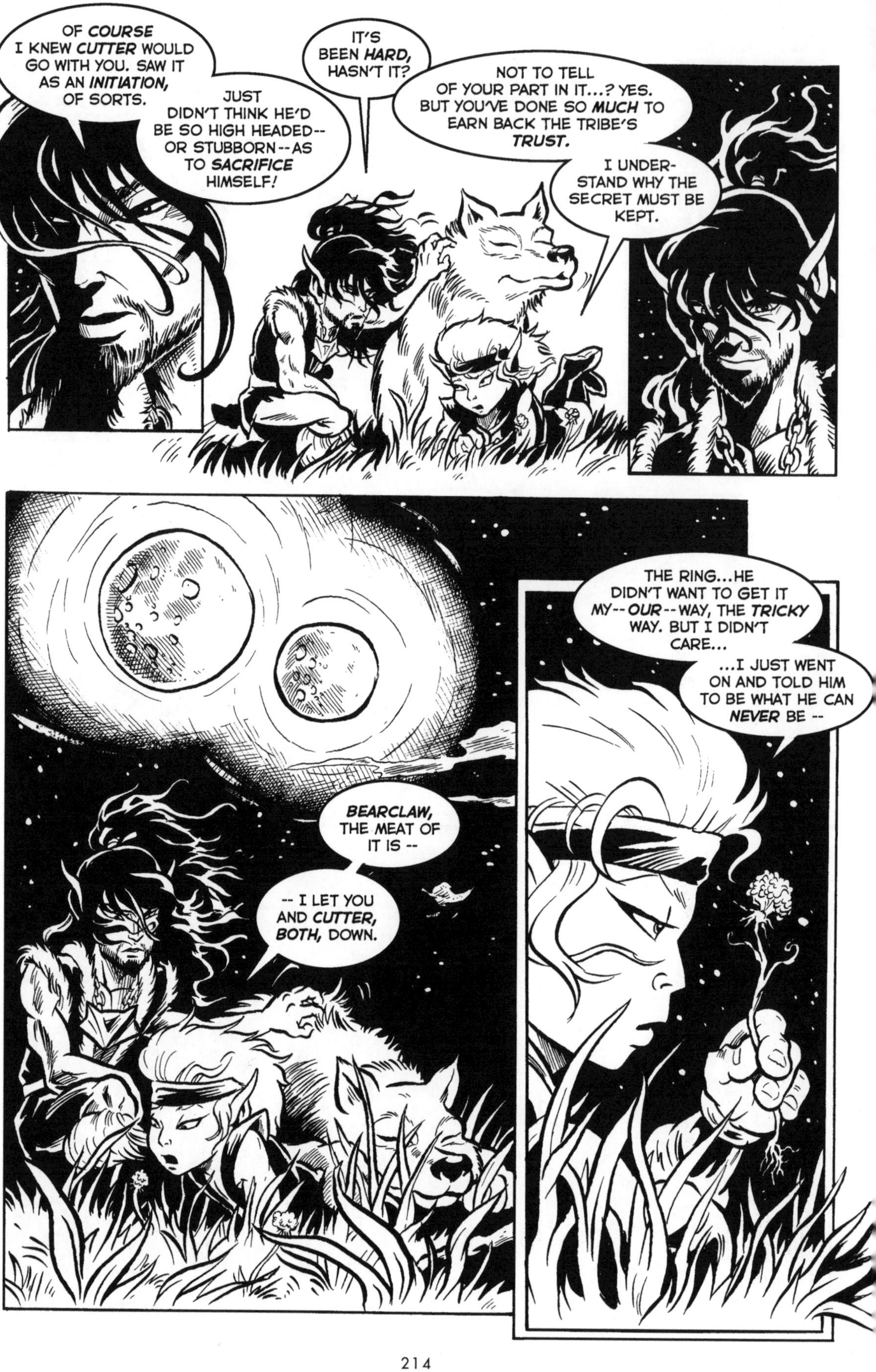
OF COURSE I KNEW CUTTER WOULD GO WITH YOU. SAW IT AS AN INITIATION, OF SORTS.
JUST DIDN'T THINK HE'D BE SO HIGH HEADED-- OR STUBBORN--AS TO SACRIFICE HIMSELF!
IT'S BEEN HARD, HASN'T IT?
NOT TO TELL OF YOUR PART IN IT...? YES. BUT YOU'VE DONE SO MUCH TO EARN BACK THE TRIBE'S TRUST.
I UNDER-STAND WHY THE SECRET MUST BE KEPT.
BEARCLAW, THE MEAT OF IT IS --
-- I LET YOU AND CUTTER, BOTH, DOWN.
THE RING...HE DIDN'T WANT TO GET IT MY--OUR--WAY, THE TRICKY WAY. BUT I DIDN'T CARE...
...I JUST WENT ON AND TOLD HIM TO BE WHAT HE CAN NEVER BE --

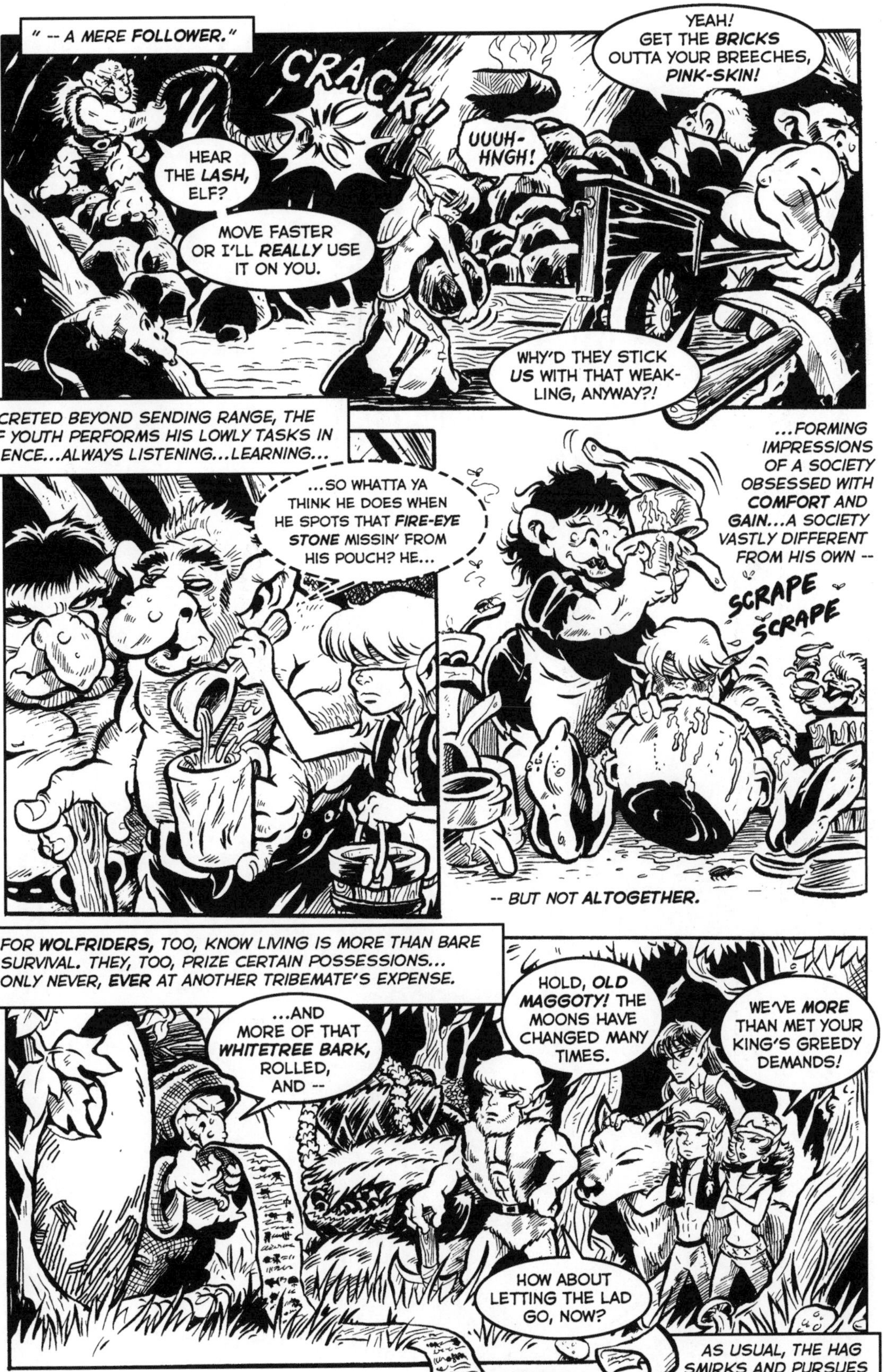
" -- A MERE FOLLOWER."
CRACK!
HEAR THE LASH, ELF?
MOVE FASTER OR I'LL REALLY USE IT ON YOU.
UUUH-HNGH!
YEAH! GET THE BRICKS OUTTA YOUR BREECHES, PINK-SKIN!
WHY'D THEY STICK US WITH THAT WEAK-LING, ANYWAY?!
SECRETED BEYOND SENDING RANGE, THE ELF YOUTH PERFORMS HIS LOWLY TASKS IN SILENCE...ALWAYS LISTENING...LEARNING...
...SO WHATTA YA THINK HE DOES WHEN HE SPOTS THAT FIRE-EYE STONE MISSIN' FROM HIS POUCH? HE...
...FORMING IMPRESSIONS OF A SOCIETY OBSESSED WITH COMFORT AND GAIN...A SOCIETY VASTLY DIFFERENT FROM HIS OWN --
SCRAPE
SCRAPE
-- BUT NOT ALTOGETHER.
FOR WOLFRIDERS, TOO, KNOW LIVING IS MORE THAN BARE SURVIVAL. THEY, TOO, PRIZE CERTAIN POSSESSIONS... ONLY NEVER, EVER AT ANOTHER TRIBEMATE'S EXPENSE.
...AND MORE OF THAT WHITETREE BARK, ROLLED, AND --
HOLD, OLD MAGGOTY! THE MOONS HAVE CHANGED MANY TIMES.
WE'VE MORE THAN MET YOUR KING'S GREEDY DEMANDS!
HOW ABOUT LETTING THE LAD GO, NOW?
AS USUAL, THE HAG SMIRKS AND PURSUES HER SYMBOL-DRAWN LIST.

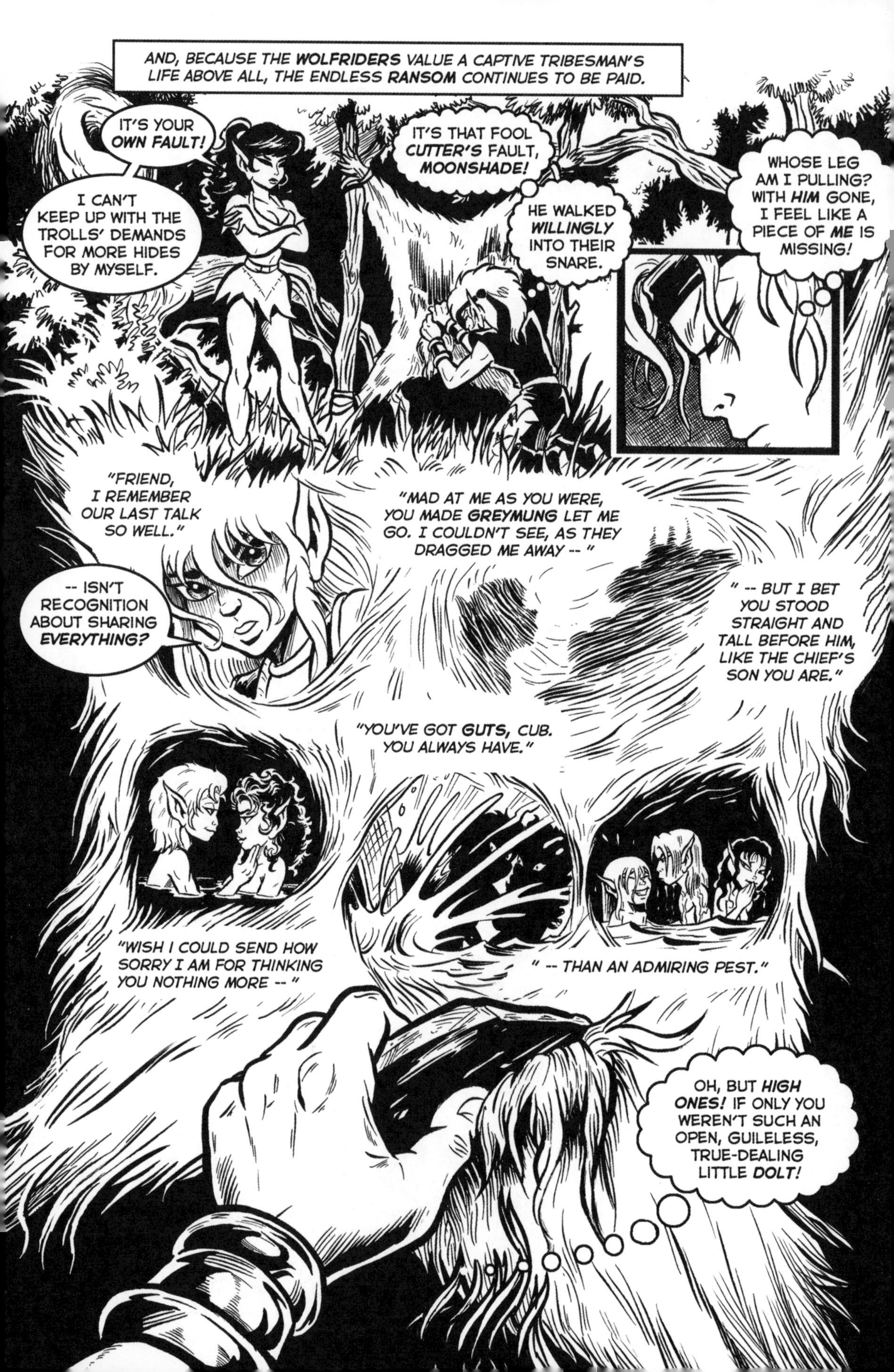
AND, BECAUSE THE WOLFRIDERS VALUE A CAPTIVE TRIBESMAN'S LIFE ABOVE ALL, THE ENDLESS RANSOM CONTINUES TO BE PAID.
IT'S YOUR OWN FAULT!
I CAN'T KEEP UP WITH THE TROLLS' DEMANDS FOR MORE HIDES BY MYSELF.
IT'S THAT FOOL CUTTER'S FAULT, MOONSHADE!
HE WALKED WILLINGLY INTO THEIR SNARE.
WHOSE LEG AM I PULLING? WITH HIM GONE, I FEEL LIKE A PIECE OF ME IS MISSING!
"FRIEND, I REMEMBER OUR LAST TALK SO WELL."
-- ISN'T RECOGNITION ABOUT SHARING EVERYTHING?
"MAD AT ME AS YOU WERE, YOU MADE GREYMUNG LET ME GO. I COULDN'T SEE, AS THEY DRAGGED ME AWAY -- "
" -- BUT I BET YOU STOOD STRAIGHT AND TALL BEFORE HIM, LIKE THE CHIEF'S SON YOU ARE."
"YOU'VE GOT GUTS, CUB. YOU ALWAYS HAVE."
"WISH I COULD SEND HOW SORRY I AM FOR THINKING YOU NOTHING MORE -- "
" -- THAN AN ADMIRING PEST."
OH, BUT HIGH ONES! IF ONLY YOU WEREN'T SUCH AN OPEN, GUILELESS, TRUE-DEALING LITTLE DOLT!

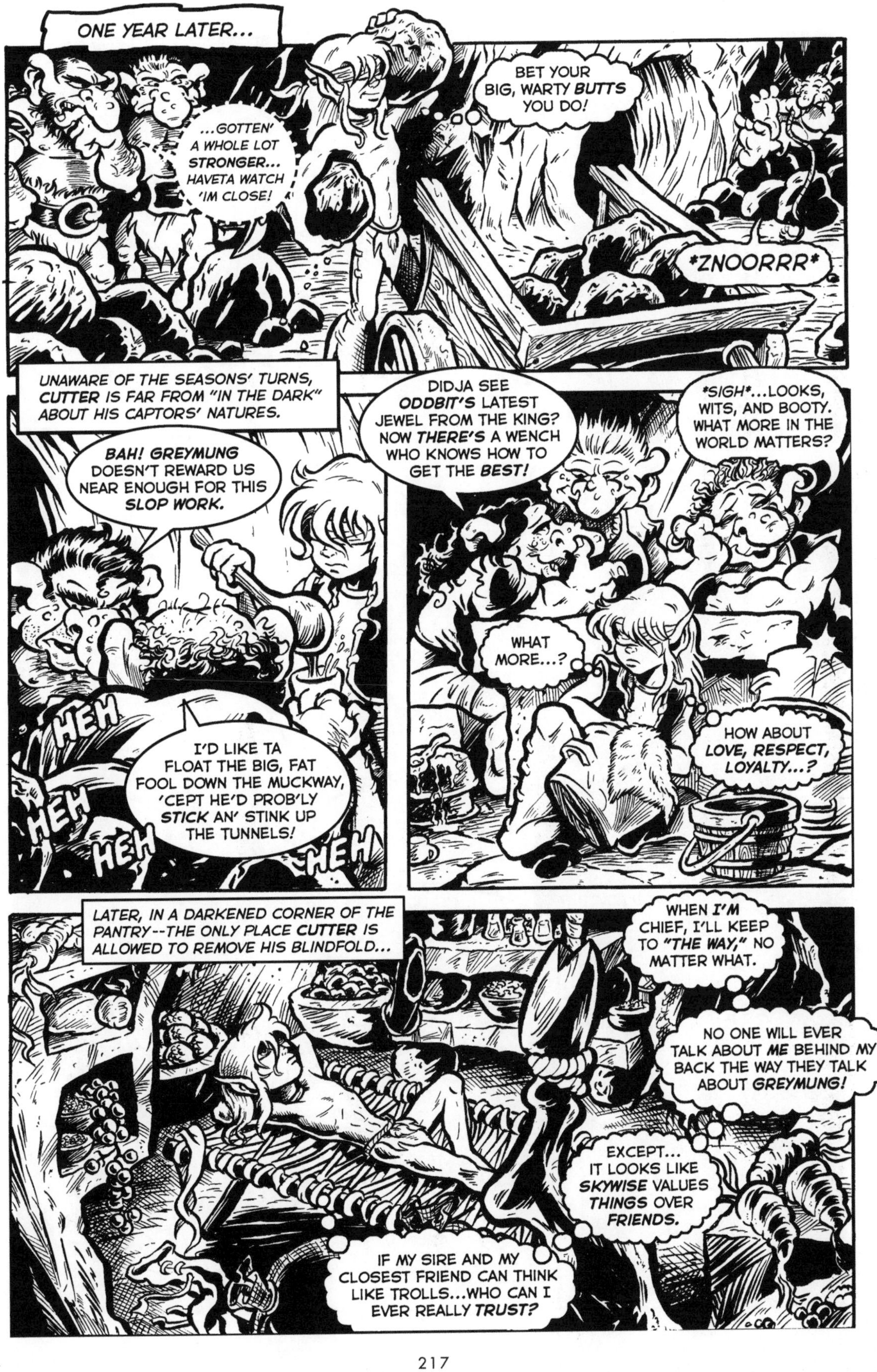
ONE YEAR LATER...
...GOTTEN' A WHOLE LOT STRONGER... HAVETA WATCH 'IM CLOSE!
BET YOUR BIG, WARTY BUTTS YOU DO!
ZNOORRR
UNAWARE OF THE SEASONS' TURNS, CUTTER IS FAR FROM "IN THE DARK" ABOUT HIS CAPTORS' NATURES.
BAH! GREYMUNG DOESN'T REWARD US NEAR ENOUGH FOR THIS SLOP WORK.
I'D LIKE TA FLOAT THE BIG, FAT FOOL DOWN THE MUCKWAY, 'CEPT HE'D PROB'LY STICK AN' STINK UP THE TUNNELS!
HEH HEH HEH HEH
DIDJA SEE ODDBIT'S LATEST JEWEL FROM THE KING? NOW THERE'S A WENCH WHO KNOWS HOW TO GET THE BEST!
SIGH...LOOKS, WITS, AND BOOTY. WHAT MORE IN THE WORLD MATTERS?
WHAT MORE...?
HOW ABOUT LOVE, RESPECT, LOYALTY...?
LATER, IN A DARKENED CORNER OF THE PANTRY--THE ONLY PLACE CUTTER IS ALLOWED TO REMOVE HIS BLINDFOLD...
WHEN I'M CHIEF, I'LL KEEP TO "THE WAY," NO MATTER WHAT.
NO ONE WILL EVER TALK ABOUT ME BEHIND MY BACK THE WAY THEY TALK ABOUT GREYMUNG!
EXCEPT... IT LOOKS LIKE SKYWISE VALUES THINGS OVER FRIENDS.
IF MY SIRE AND MY CLOSEST FRIEND CAN THINK LIKE TROLLS...WHO CAN I EVER REALLY TRUST?

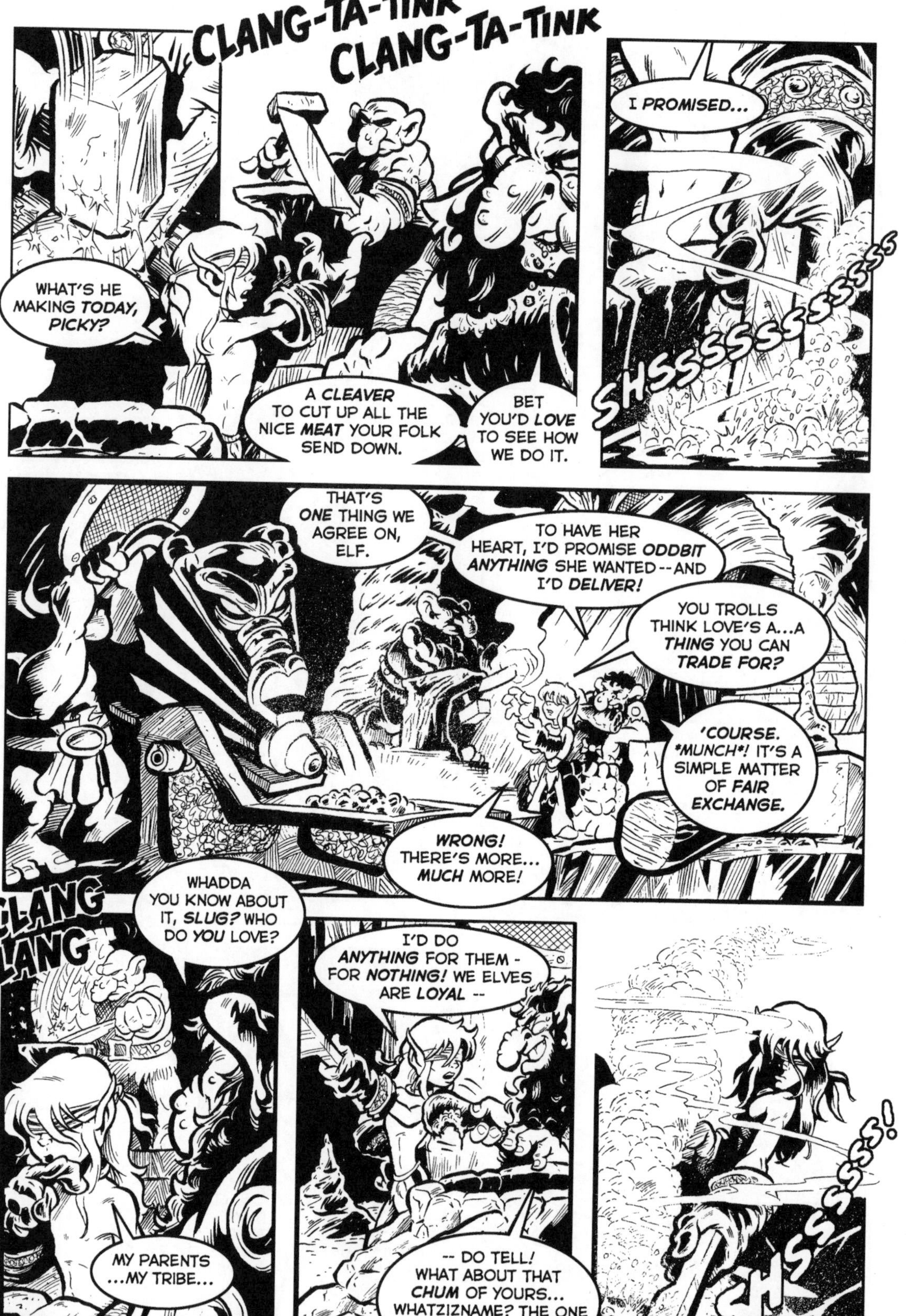
CLANG-TA-TINK
CLANG-TA-TINK
WHAT'S HE MAKING TODAY, PICKY?
A CLEAVER TO CUT UP ALL THE NICE MEAT YOUR FOLK SEND DOWN.
BET YOU'D LOVE TO SEE HOW WE DO IT.
I PROMISED...
SHSSSSSSSSSSSS
THAT'S ONE THING WE AGREE ON, ELF.
TO HAVE HER HEART, I'D PROMISE ODDBIT ANYTHING SHE WANTED--AND I'D DELIVER!
YOU TROLLS THINK LOVE'S A...A THING YOU CAN TRADE FOR?
'COURSE. *MUNCH*! IT'S A SIMPLE MATTER OF FAIR EXCHANGE.
WRONG! THERE'S MORE... MUCH MORE!
CLANG
CLANG
WHADDA YOU KNOW ABOUT IT, SLUG? WHO DO YOU LOVE?
MY PARENTS ...MY TRIBE...
I'D DO ANYTHING FOR THEM - FOR NOTHING! WE ELVES ARE LOYAL --
-- DO TELL! WHAT ABOUT THAT CHUM OF YOURS... WHATZIZNAME? THE ONE WHO GOT YOU INTO THIS?
SHSSSSSSS!

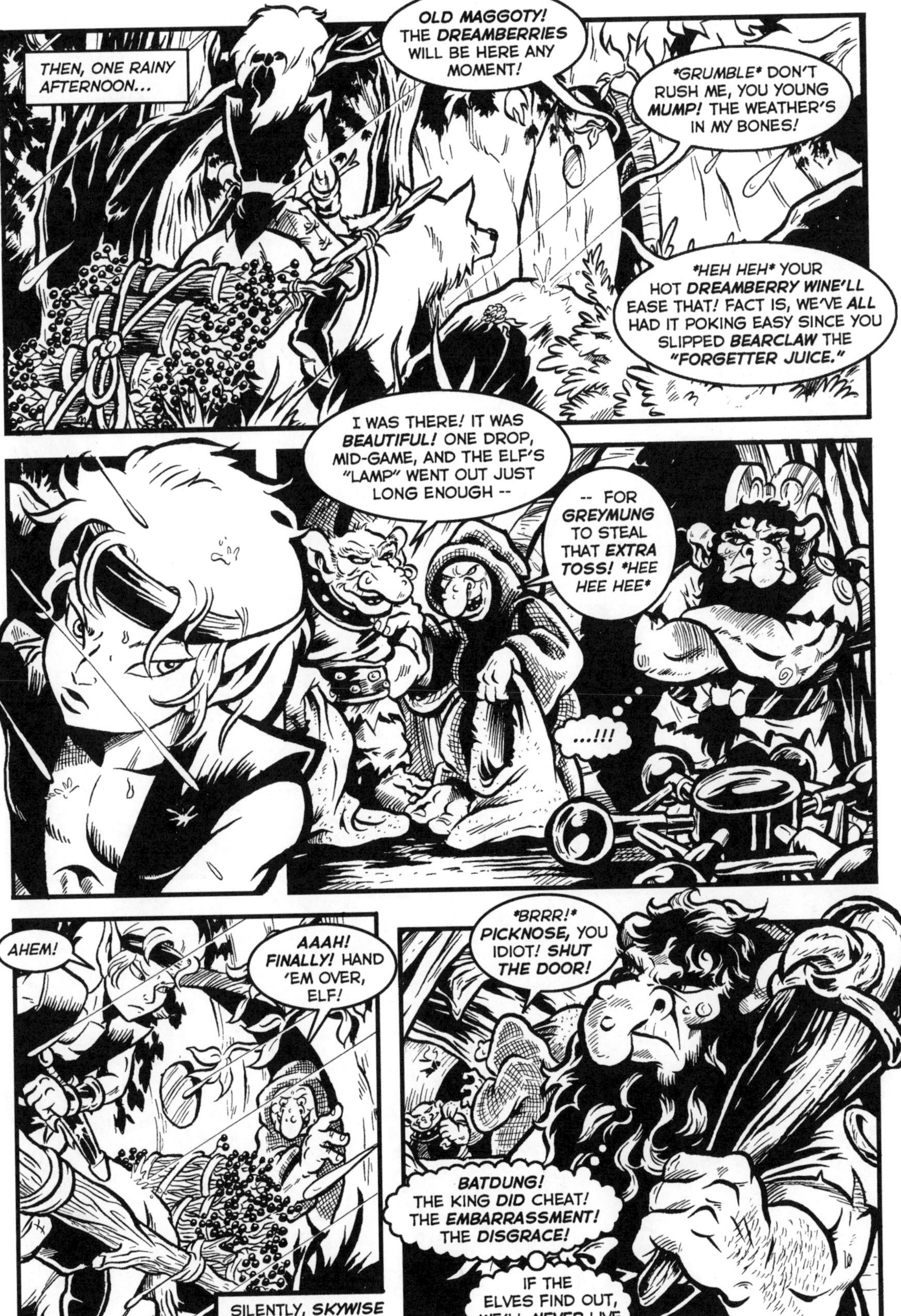
THEN, ONE RAINY AFTERNOON...
OLD MAGGOTY! THE DREAMBERRIES WILL BE HERE ANY MOMENT!
GRUMBLE DON'T RUSH ME, YOU YOUNG MUMP! THE WEATHER'S IN MY BONES!
HEH HEH YOUR HOT DREAMBERRY WINE'LL EASE THAT! FACT IS, WE'VE ALL HAD IT POKING EASY SINCE YOU SLIPPED BEARCLAW THE "FORGETTER JUICE."
I WAS THERE! IT WAS BEAUTIFUL! ONE DROP, MID-GAME, AND THE ELF'S "LAMP" WENT OUT JUST LONG ENOUGH --
-- FOR GREYMUNG TO STEAL THAT EXTRA TOSS! *HEE HEE HEE*
...!!!
AHEM!
AAAH! FINALLY! HAND 'EM OVER, ELF!
SILENTLY, SKYWISE OBEYS AND...
BRRR! PICKNOSE, YOU IDIOT! SHUT THE DOOR!
BATDUNG! THE KING DID CHEAT! THE EMBARRASSMENT! THE DISGRACE!
IF THE ELVES FIND OUT, WE'LL NEVER LIVE IT DOWN!

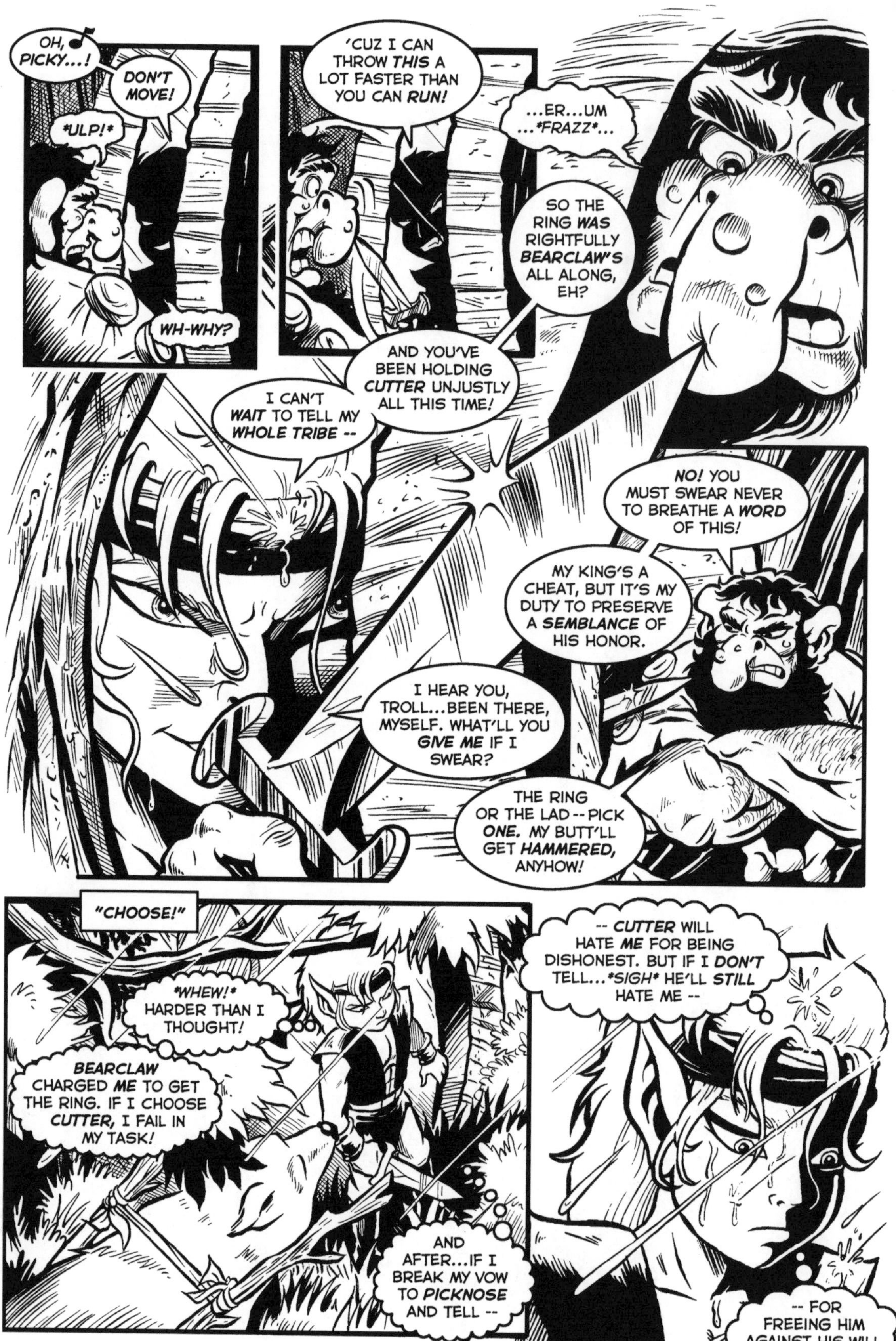

OH, PICKY...!
DON'T MOVE!
ULP!
WH-WHY?
'CUZ I CAN THROW THIS A LOT FASTER THAN YOU CAN RUN!
...ER...UM ...*FRAZZ*...
SO THE RING WAS RIGHTFULLY BEARCLAW'S ALL ALONG, EH?
AND YOU'VE BEEN HOLDING CUTTER UNJUSTLY ALL THIS TIME!
I CAN'T WAIT TO TELL MY WHOLE TRIBE --
NO! YOU MUST SWEAR NEVER TO BREATHE A WORD OF THIS!
MY KING'S A CHEAT, BUT IT'S MY DUTY TO PRESERVE A SEMBLANCE OF HIS HONOR.
I HEAR YOU, TROLL...BEEN THERE, MYSELF. WHAT'LL YOU GIVE ME IF I SWEAR?
THE RING OR THE LAD--PICK ONE. MY BUTT'LL GET HAMMERED, ANYHOW!
"CHOOSE!"
WHEW! HARDER THAN I THOUGHT!
BEARCLAW CHARGED ME TO GET THE RING. IF I CHOOSE CUTTER, I FAIL IN MY TASK!
AND AFTER...IF I BREAK MY VOW TO PICKNOSE AND TELL --
-- CUTTER WILL HATE ME FOR BEING DISHONEST. BUT IF I DON'T TELL...*SIGH* HE'LL STILL HATE ME --
-- FOR FREEING HIM AGAINST HIS WILL AND WORD.

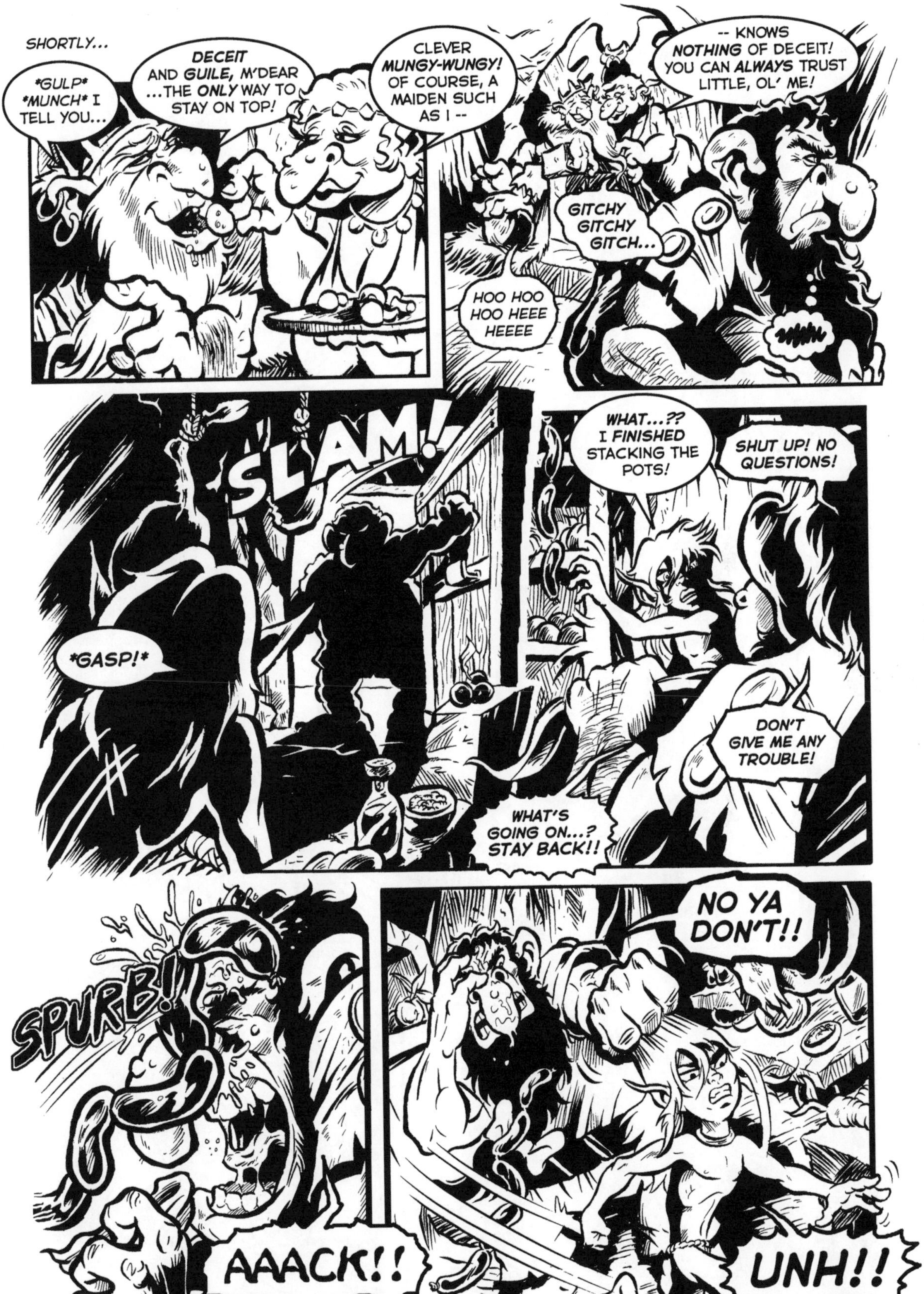
SHORTLY...
GULP *MUNCH* I TELL YOU...
DECEIT AND GUILE, M'DEAR ...THE ONLY WAY TO STAY ON TOP!
CLEVER MUNGY-WUNGY! OF COURSE, A MAIDEN SUCH AS I --
-- KNOWS NOTHING OF DECEIT! YOU CAN ALWAYS TRUST LITTLE, OL' ME!
GITCHY GITCHY GITCH...
HOO HOO HOO HEEE HEEEE
SLAM!
GASP!
WHAT...?? I FINISHED STACKING THE POTS!
SHUT UP! NO QUESTIONS!
DON'T GIVE ME ANY TROUBLE!
WHAT'S GOING ON...? STAY BACK!!
SPURB!
AAACK!!
NO YA DON'T!!
UNH!!

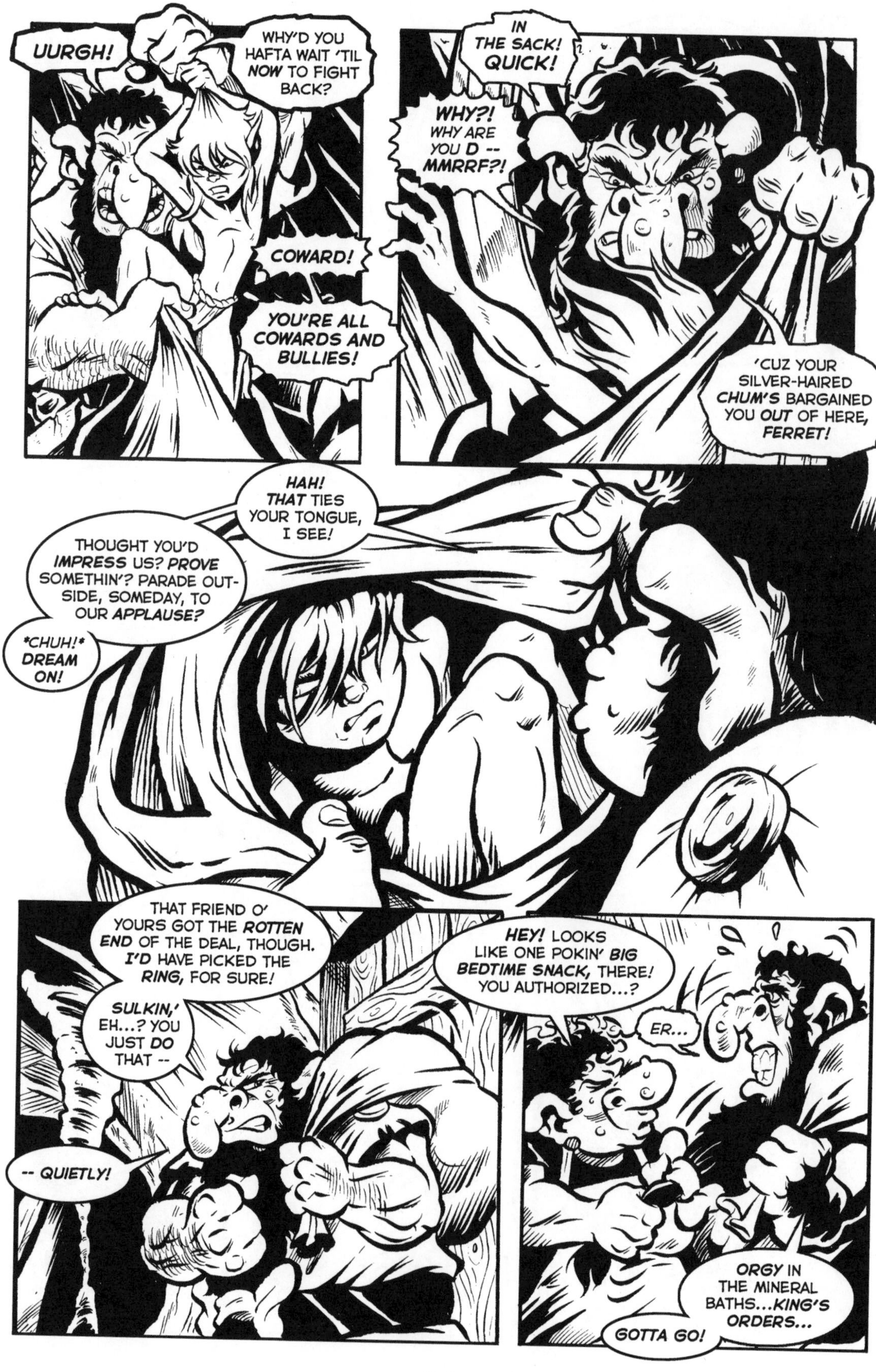
UURGH!
WHY'D YOU HAFTA WAIT 'TIL NOW TO FIGHT BACK?
COWARD!
YOU'RE ALL COWARDS AND BULLIES!
IN THE SACK! QUICK!
WHY?! WHY ARE YOU D -- MMRRF?!
'CUZ YOUR SILVER-HAIRED CHUM'S BARGAINED YOU OUT OF HERE, FERRET!
HAH! THAT TIES YOUR TONGUE, I SEE!
THOUGHT YOU'D IMPRESS US? PROVE SOMETHIN'? PARADE OUT-SIDE, SOMEDAY, TO OUR APPLAUSE?
CHUH! DREAM ON!
THAT FRIEND O' YOURS GOT THE ROTTEN END OF THE DEAL, THOUGH. I'D HAVE PICKED THE RING, FOR SURE!
SULKIN,' EH...? YOU JUST DO THAT --
-- QUIETLY!
HEY! LOOKS LIKE ONE POKIN' BIG BEDTIME SNACK, THERE! YOU AUTHORIZED...?
ER...
ORGY IN THE MINERAL BATHS...KING'S ORDERS...
GOTTA GO!

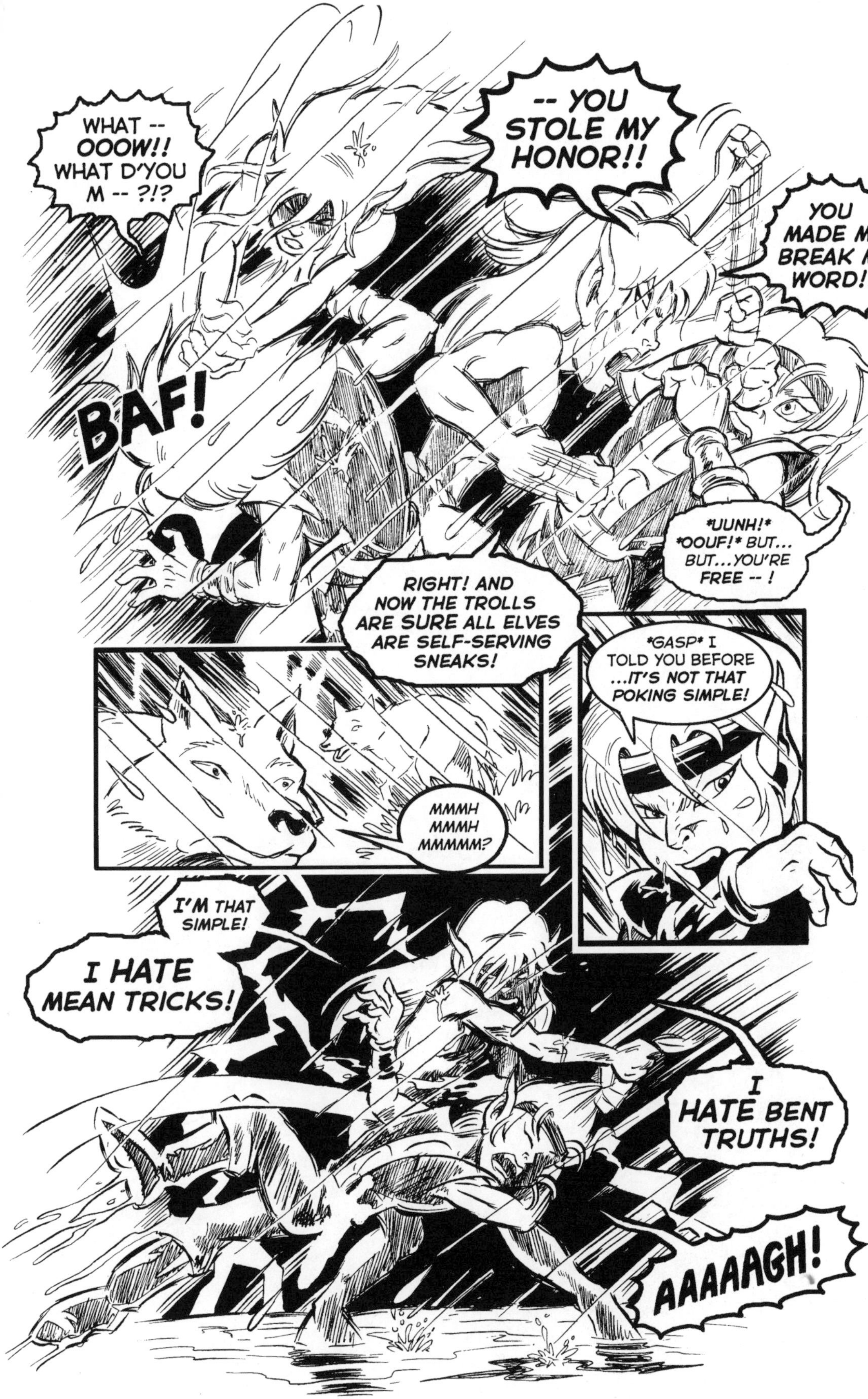
WHAT -- OOOW!! WHAT D'YOU M -- ?!?
-- YOU STOLE MY HONOR!!
YOU MADE ME BREAK MY WORD!!
BAF!
UUNH! *OOUF!* BUT... BUT...YOU'RE FREE -- !
RIGHT! AND NOW THE TROLLS ARE SURE ALL ELVES ARE SELF-SERVING SNEAKS!
MMMH MMMH MMMMM?
GASP I TOLD YOU BEFORE ...IT'S NOT THAT POKING SIMPLE!
I'M THAT SIMPLE!
I HATE MEAN TRICKS!
I HATE BENT TRUTHS!
AAAAAGH!

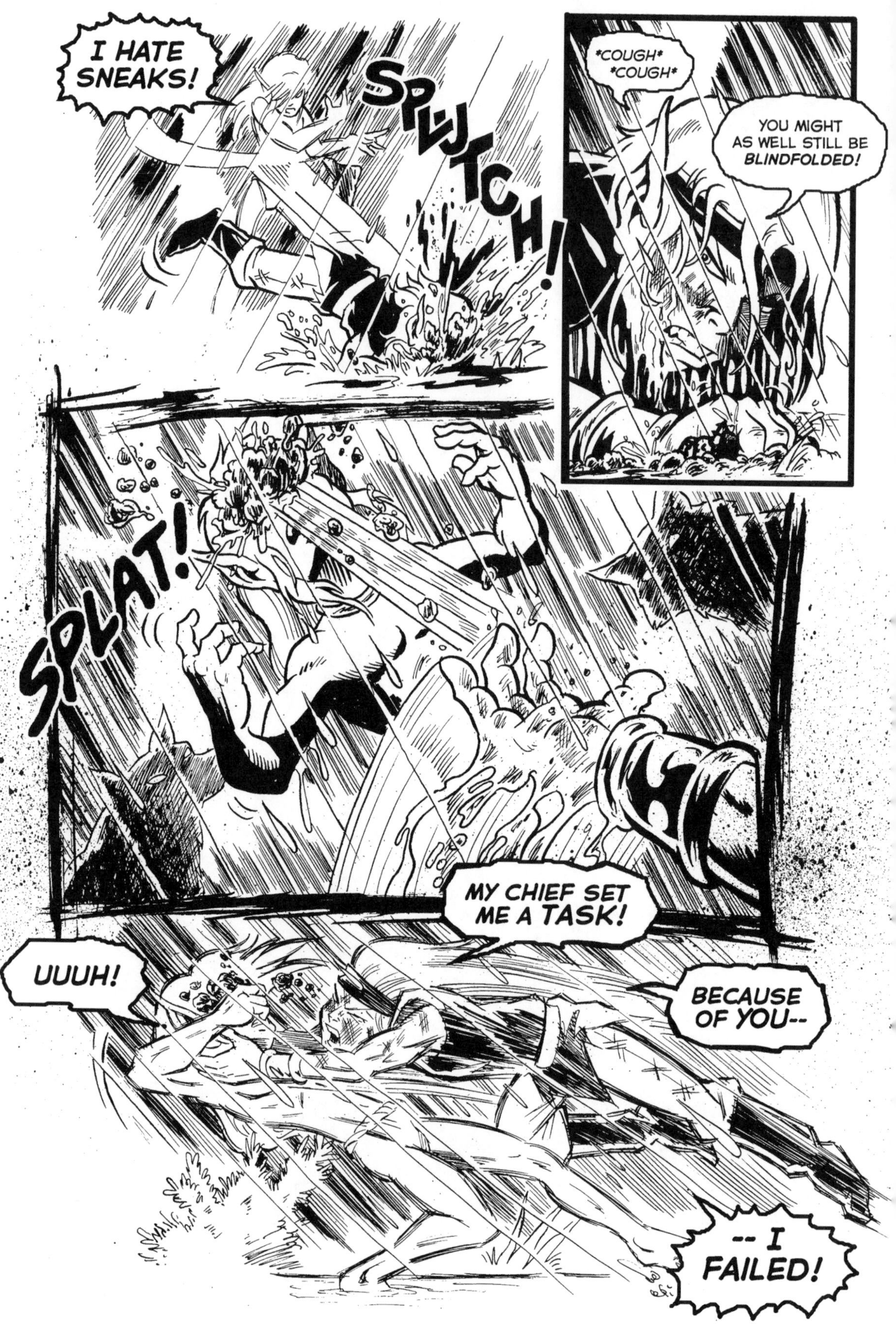
I HATE SNEAKS!
SPLUTCH!
COUGH *COUGH*
YOU MIGHT AS WELL STILL BE BLINDFOLDED!
SPLAT!
MY CHIEF SET ME A TASK!
UUUH!
BECAUSE OF YOU--
-- I FAILED!

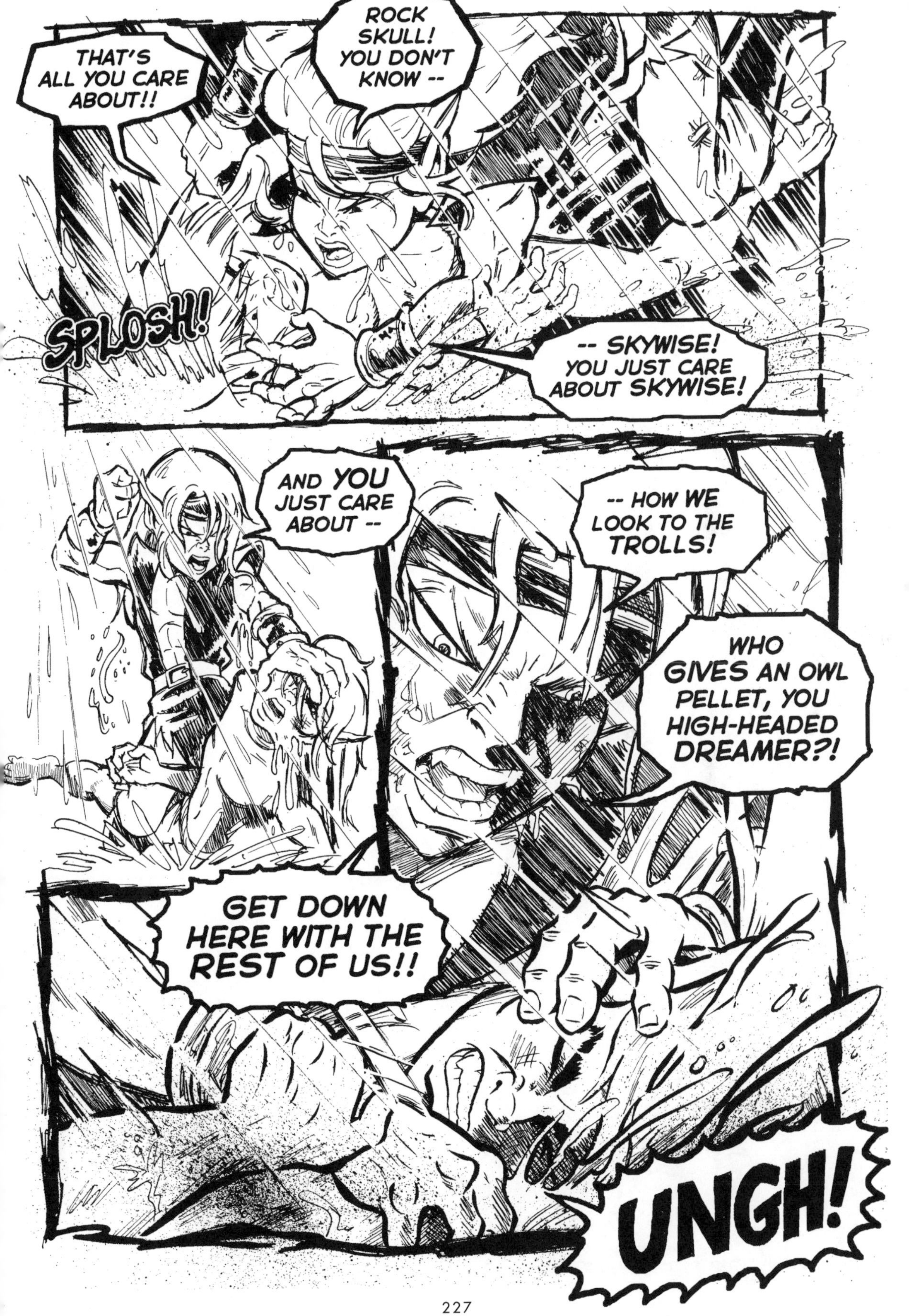
THAT'S ALL YOU CARE ABOUT!!
ROCK SKULL! YOU DON'T KNOW --
SPLOSH!
-- SKYWISE! YOU JUST CARE ABOUT SKYWISE!
AND YOU JUST CARE ABOUT --
-- HOW WE LOOK TO THE TROLLS!
WHO GIVES AN OWL PELLET, YOU HIGH-HEADED DREAMER?!
GET DOWN HERE WITH THE REST OF US!!
UNGH!

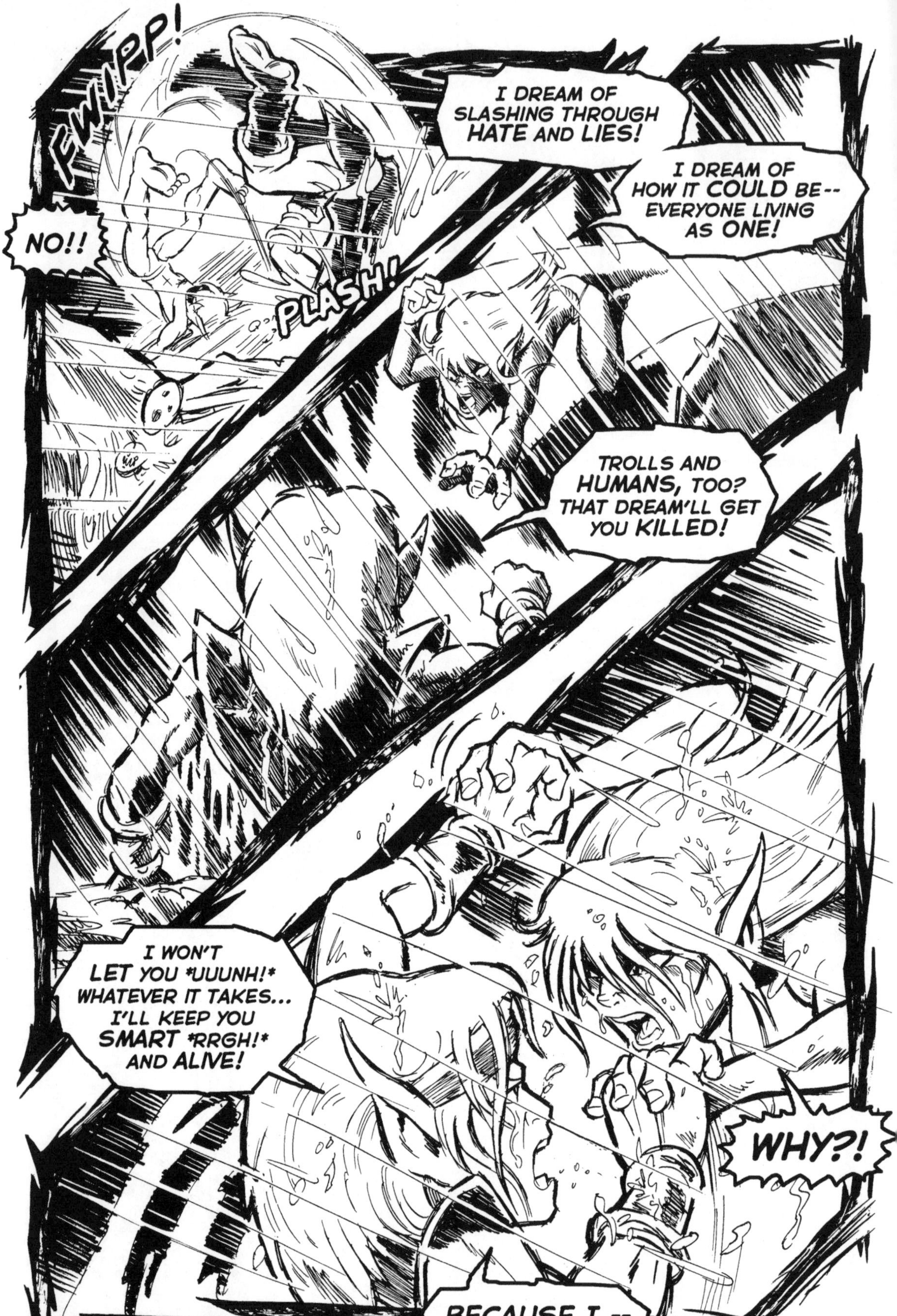

FWIPP!
I DREAM OF SLASHING THROUGH HATE AND LIES!
NO!!
PLASH!
I DREAM OF HOW IT COULD BE-- EVERYONE LIVING AS ONE!
TROLLS AND HUMANS, TOO? THAT DREAM'LL GET YOU KILLED!
I WON'T LET YOU *UUUNH!* WHATEVER IT TAKES... I'LL KEEP YOU SMART *RRGH!* AND ALIVE!
WHY?!
BECAUSE I --

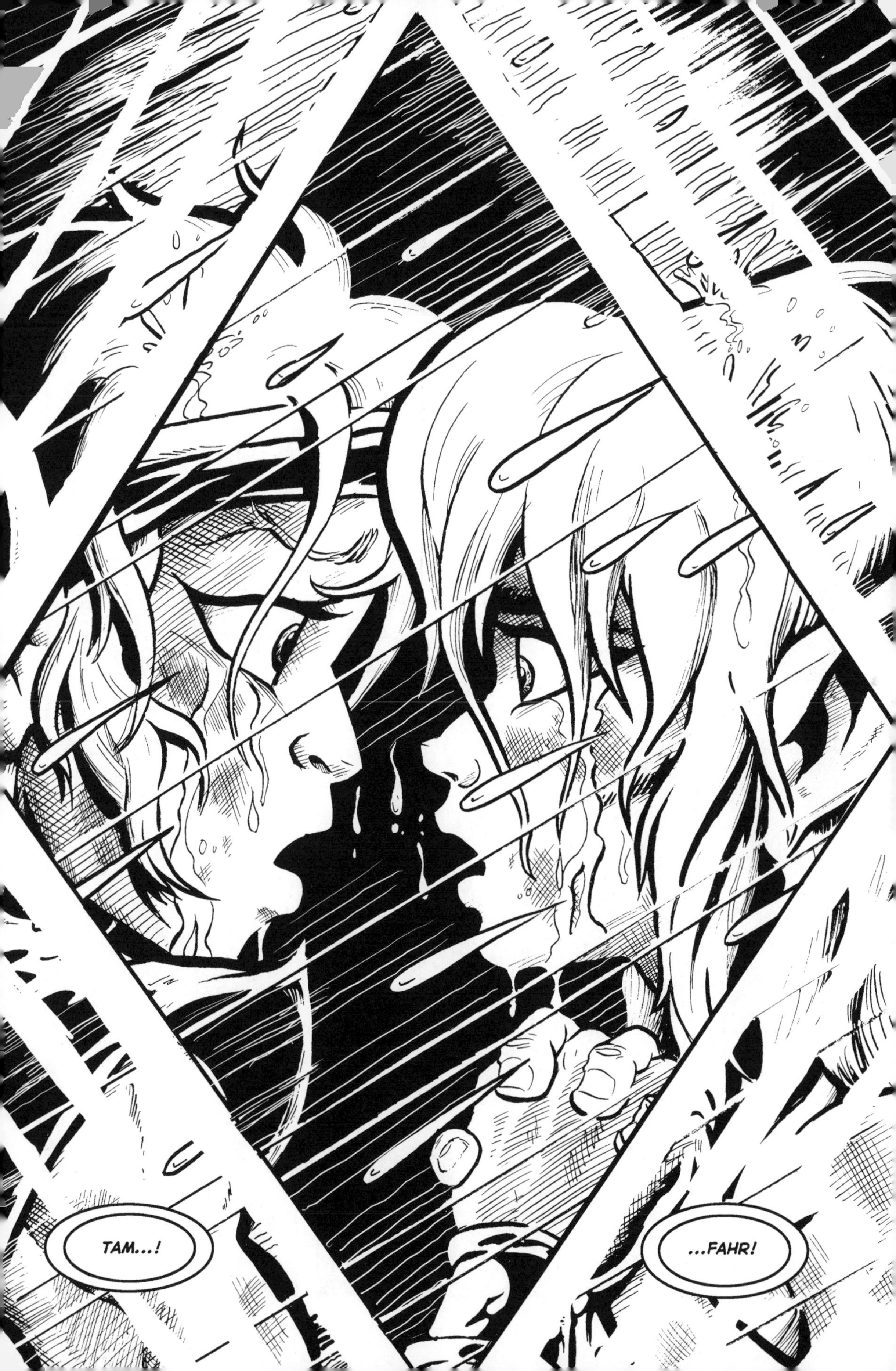
TAM...!
...FAHR!

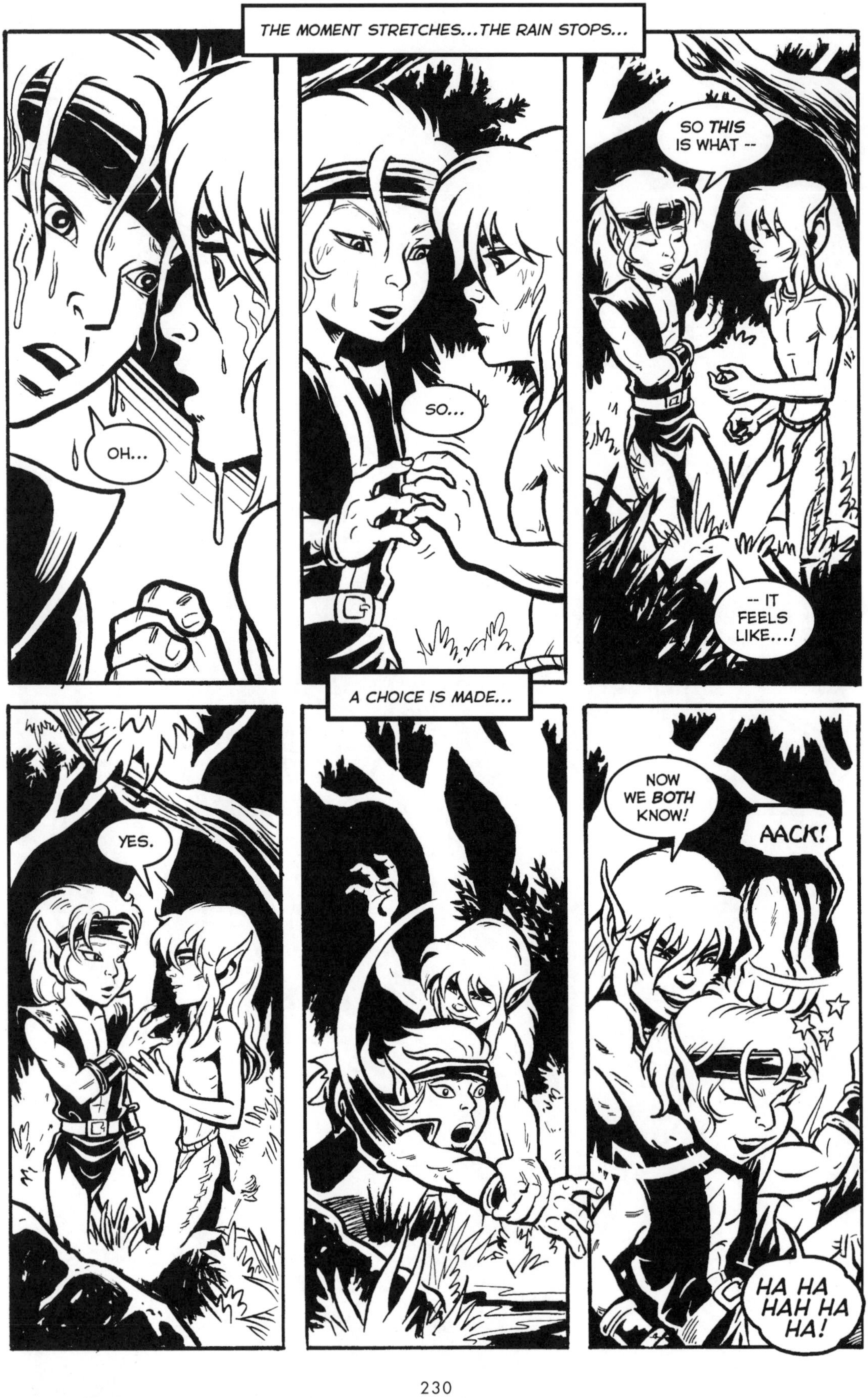
THE MOMENT STRETCHES...THE RAIN STOPS...
OH...
SO...
SO *THIS* IS WHAT --
-- IT FEELS LIKE...!
A CHOICE IS MADE...
YES.
NOW WE *BOTH* KNOW!
AACK!
HA HA HAH HA HA!

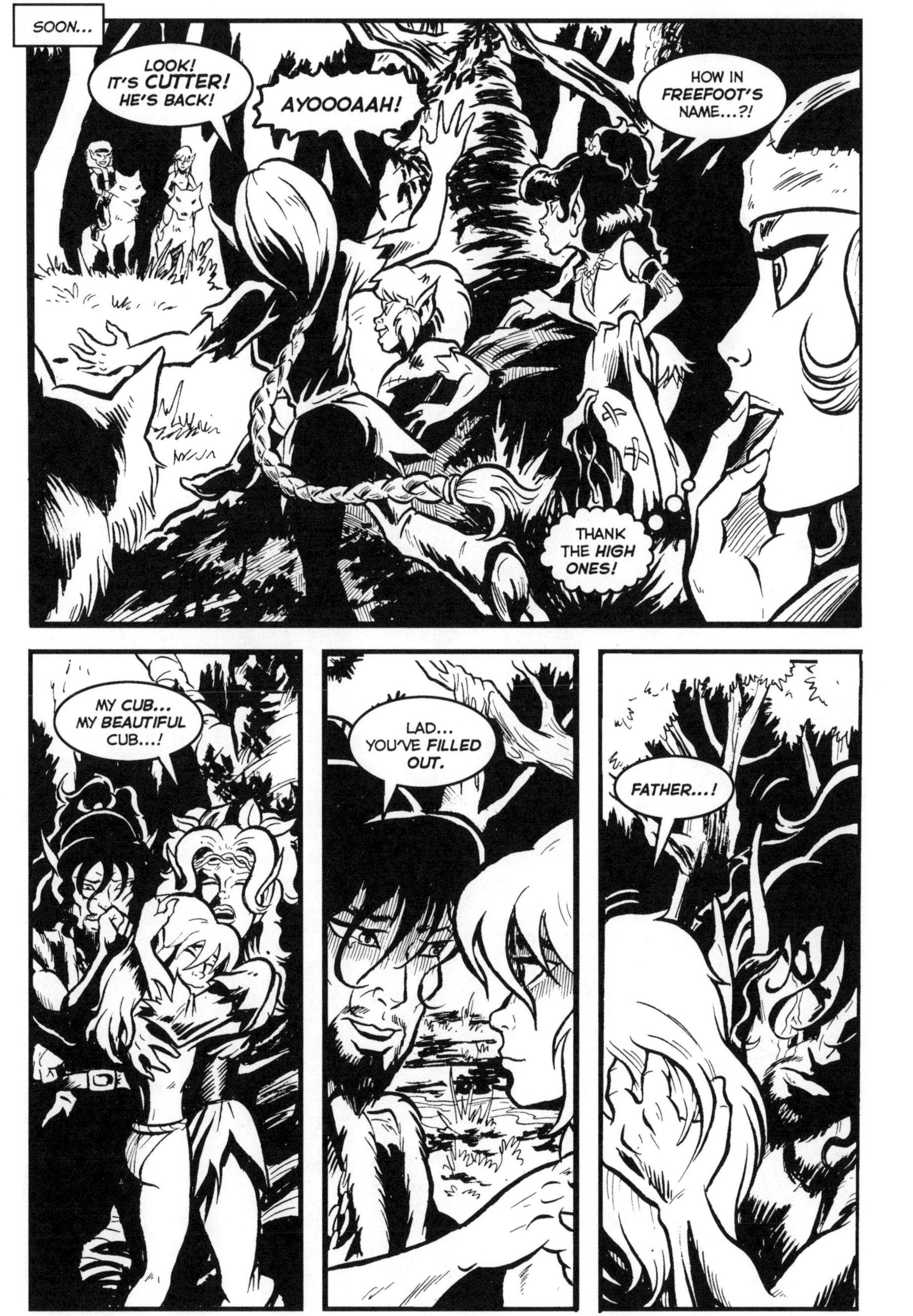
SOON...
LOOK! IT'S CUTTER! HE'S BACK!
AYOOOAAH!
HOW IN FREEFOOT'S NAME...?!
THANK THE HIGH ONES!
MY CUB... MY BEAUTIFUL CUB...!
LAD... YOU'VE FILLED OUT.
FATHER...!

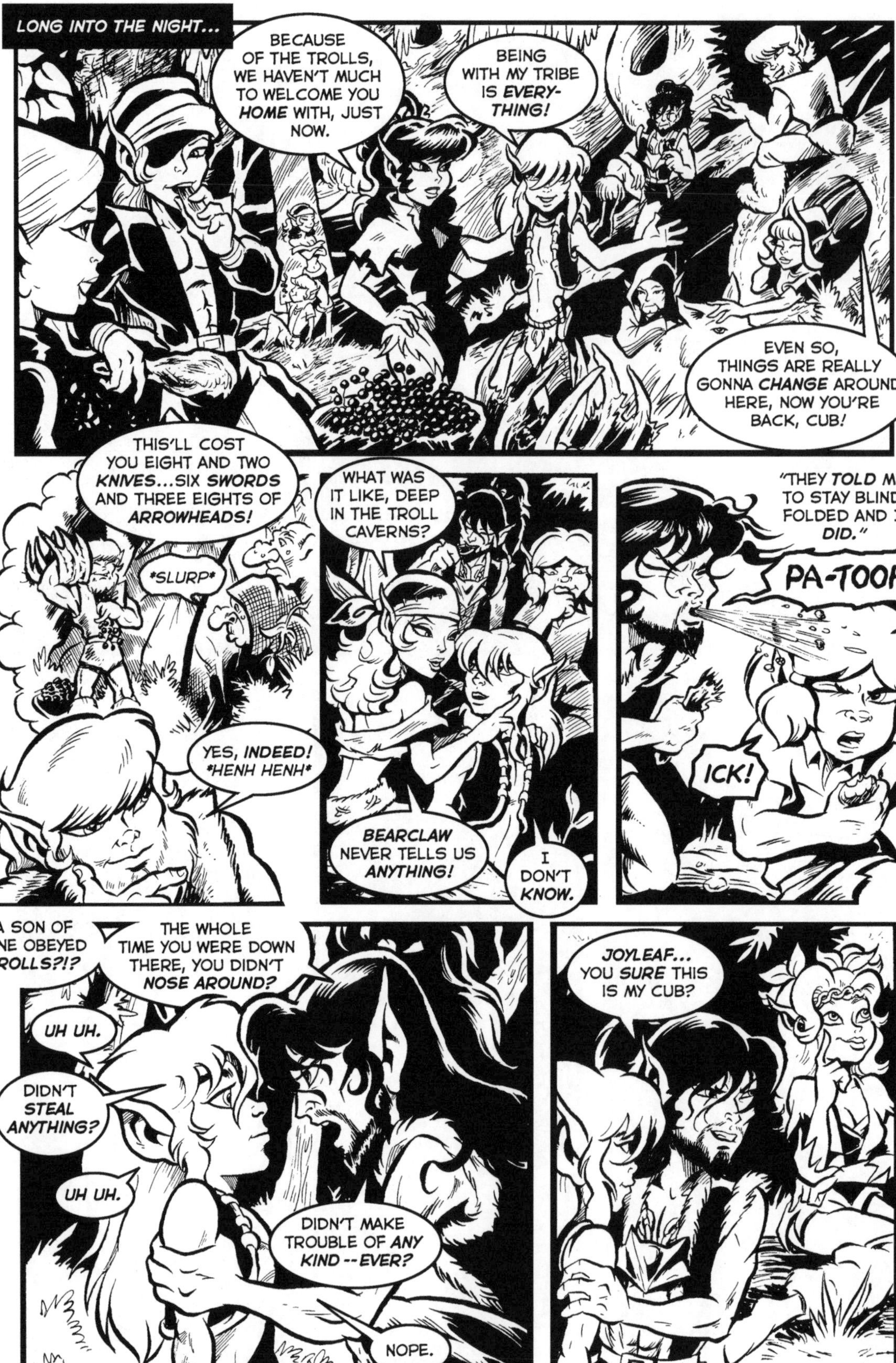
LONG INTO THE NIGHT...
BECAUSE OF THE TROLLS, WE HAVEN'T MUCH TO WELCOME YOU HOME WITH, JUST NOW.
BEING WITH MY TRIBE IS EVERY-THING!
EVEN SO, THINGS ARE REALLY GONNA CHANGE AROUND HERE, NOW YOU'RE BACK, CUB!
THIS'LL COST YOU EIGHT AND TWO KNIVES...SIX SWORDS AND THREE EIGHTS OF ARROWHEADS!
SLURP
YES, INDEED! *HENH HENH*
WHAT WAS IT LIKE, DEEP IN THE TROLL CAVERNS?
BEARCLAW NEVER TELLS US ANYTHING!
I DON'T KNOW.
"THEY TOLD ME TO STAY BLIND-FOLDED AND I DID."
PA-TOOF!
ICK!
A SON OF MINE OBEYED TROLLS?!?
THE WHOLE TIME YOU WERE DOWN THERE, YOU DIDN'T NOSE AROUND?
UH UH.
DIDN'T STEAL ANYTHING?
UH UH.
DIDN'T MAKE TROUBLE OF ANY KIND -- EVER?
NOPE.
JOYLEAF... YOU SURE THIS IS MY CUB?

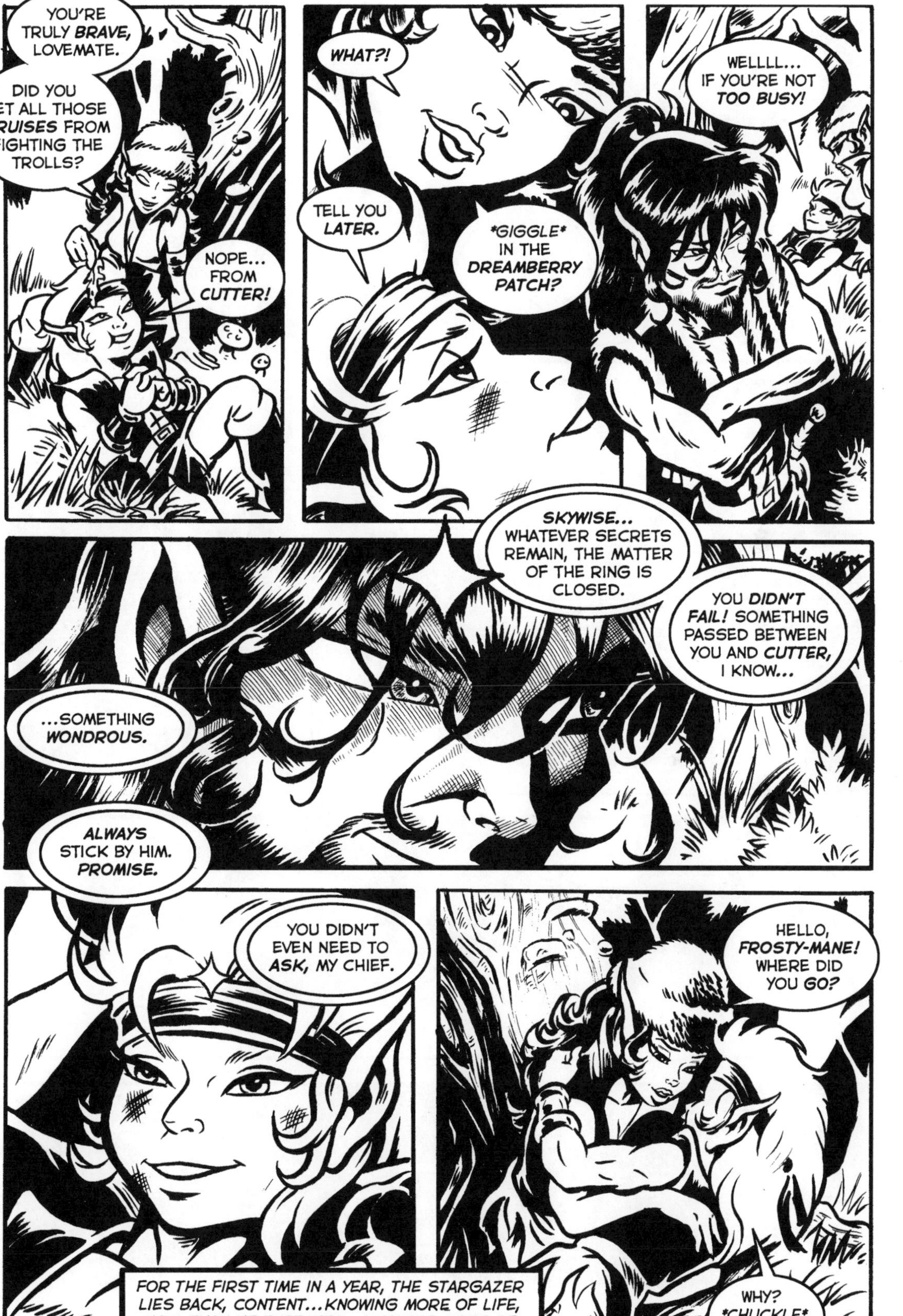
YOU'RE TRULY BRAVE, LOVEMATE.
DID YOU GET ALL THOSE BRUISES FROM FIGHTING THE TROLLS?
NOPE... FROM CUTTER!
WHAT?!
TELL YOU LATER.
GIGGLE IN THE DREAMBERRY PATCH?
WELLLL... IF YOU'RE NOT TOO BUSY!
SKYWISE... WHATEVER SECRETS REMAIN, THE MATTER OF THE RING IS CLOSED.
YOU DIDN'T FAIL! SOMETHING PASSED BETWEEN YOU AND CUTTER, I KNOW...
...SOMETHING WONDROUS.
ALWAYS STICK BY HIM. PROMISE.
YOU DIDN'T EVEN NEED TO ASK, MY CHIEF.
FOR THE FIRST TIME IN A YEAR, THE STARGAZER LIES BACK, CONTENT...KNOWING MORE OF LIFE, NOW, THAN HE EXPECTED...KNOWING MORE OF SHARING IN IT THAN HE EVER HOPED.
HELLO, FROSTY-MANE! WHERE DID YOU GO?
WHY? *CHUCKLE* MISS ME?

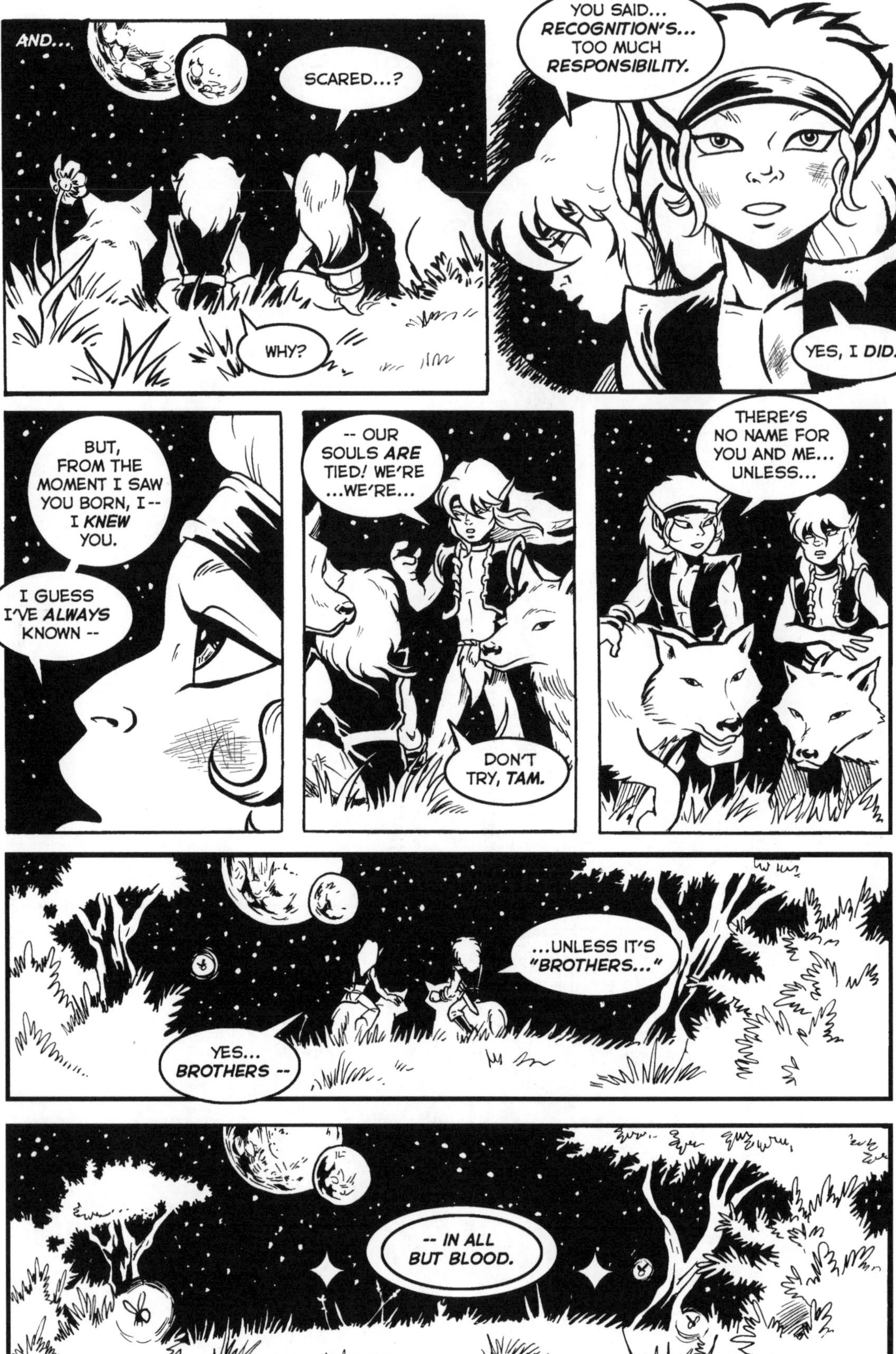
AND...
SCARED...?
WHY?
YOU SAID... RECOGNITION'S... TOO MUCH RESPONSIBILITY.
YES, I DID.
BUT, FROM THE MOMENT I SAW YOU BORN, I-- I KNEW YOU.
I GUESS I'VE ALWAYS KNOWN --
-- OUR SOULS ARE TIED! WE'RE ...WE'RE...
DON'T TRY, TAM.
THERE'S NO NAME FOR YOU AND ME... UNLESS...
...UNLESS IT'S "BROTHERS..."
YES... BROTHERS --
-- IN ALL BUT BLOOD.
THE END

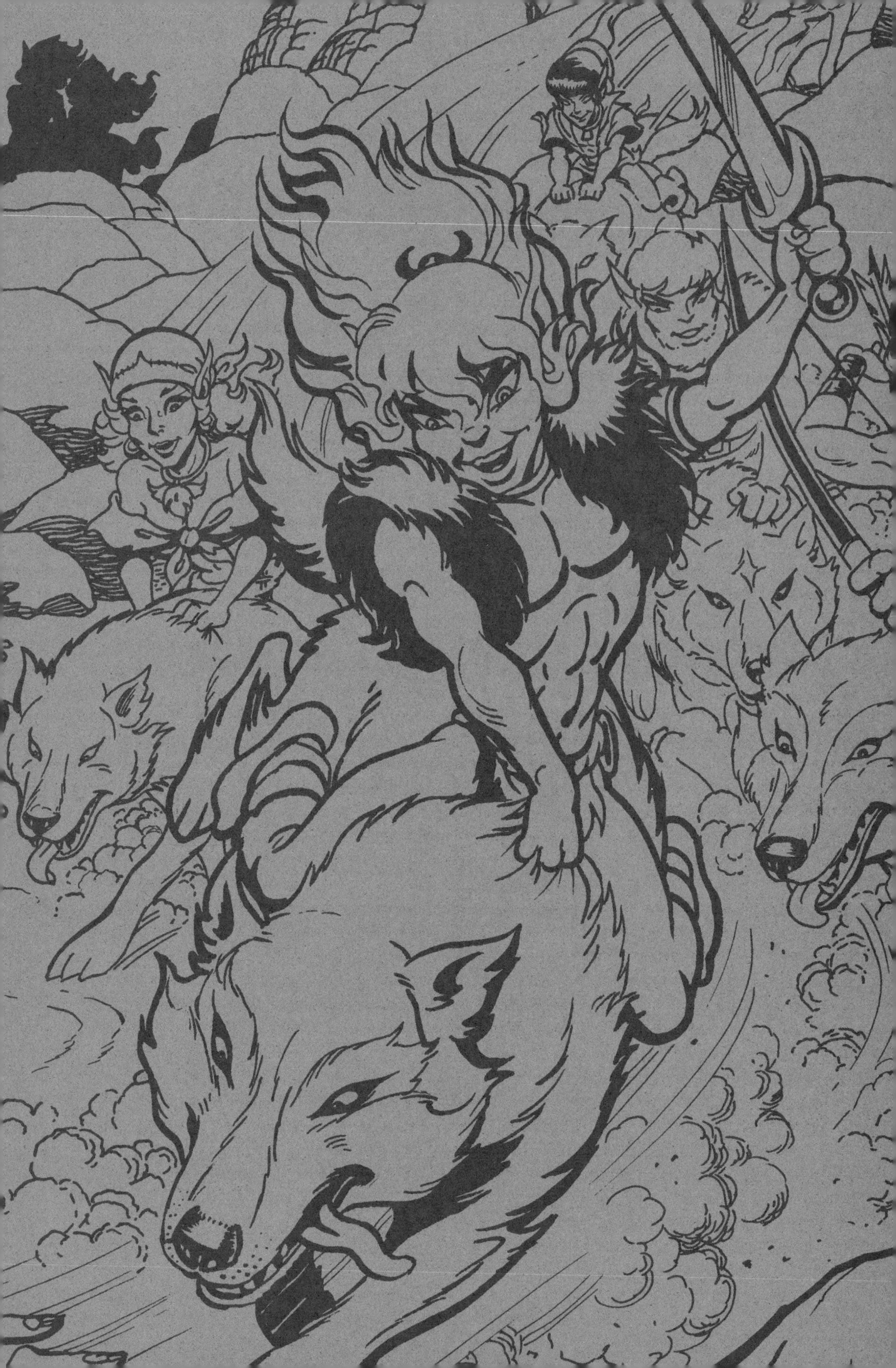

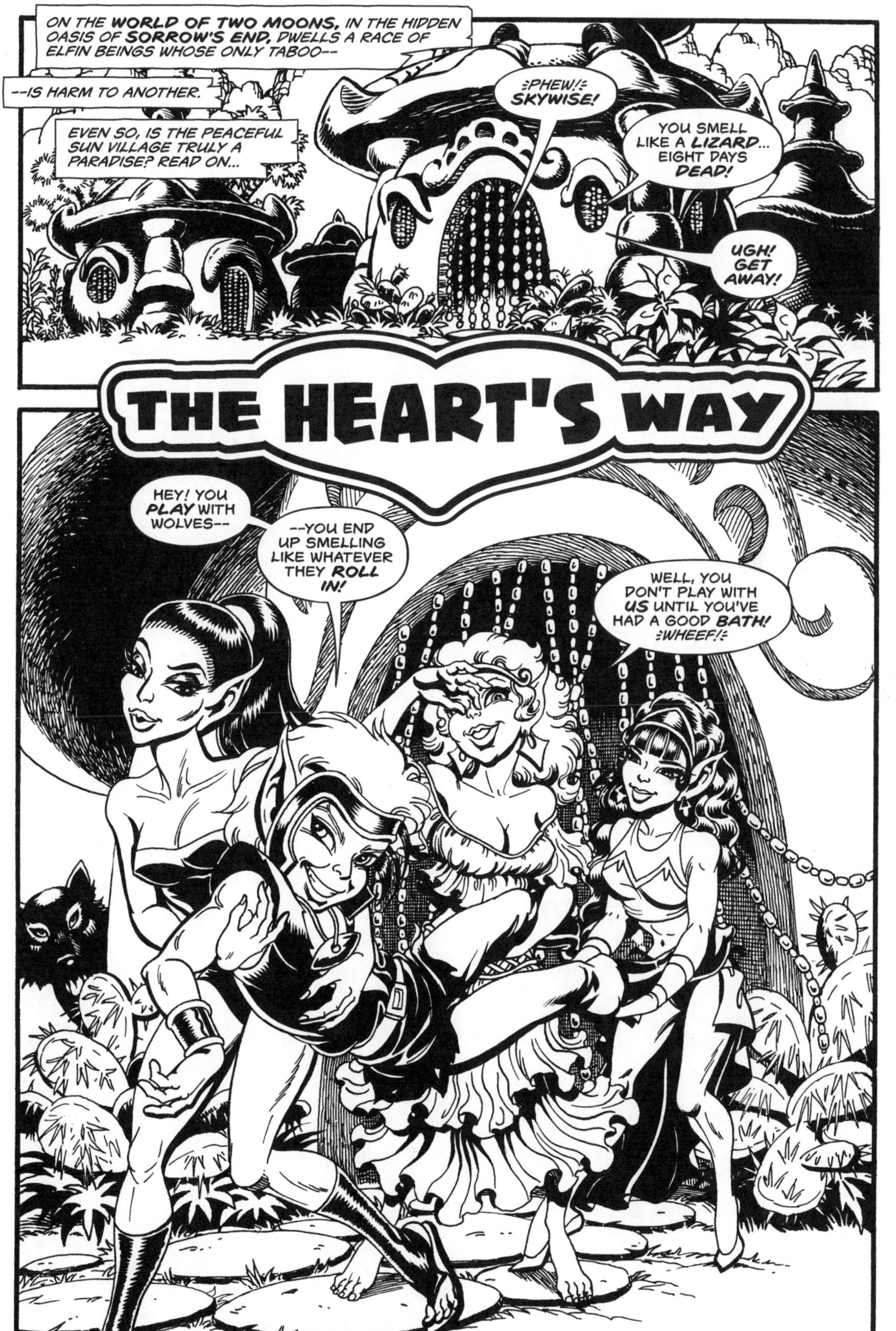
ON THE WORLD OF TWO MOONS, IN THE HIDDEN OASIS OF SORROW'S END, DWELLS A RACE OF ELFIN BEINGS WHOSE ONLY TABOO--
--IS HARM TO ANOTHER.
EVEN SO, IS THE PEACEFUL SUN VILLAGE TRULY A PARADISE? READ ON...
:PHEW!: SKYWISE!
YOU SMELL LIKE A LIZARD... EIGHT DAYS DEAD!
UGH! GET AWAY!
THE HEART'S WAY
HEY! YOU PLAY WITH WOLVES--
--YOU END UP SMELLING LIKE WHATEVER THEY ROLL IN!
WELL, YOU DON'T PLAY WITH US UNTIL YOU'VE HAD A GOOD BATH! :WHEEF!:

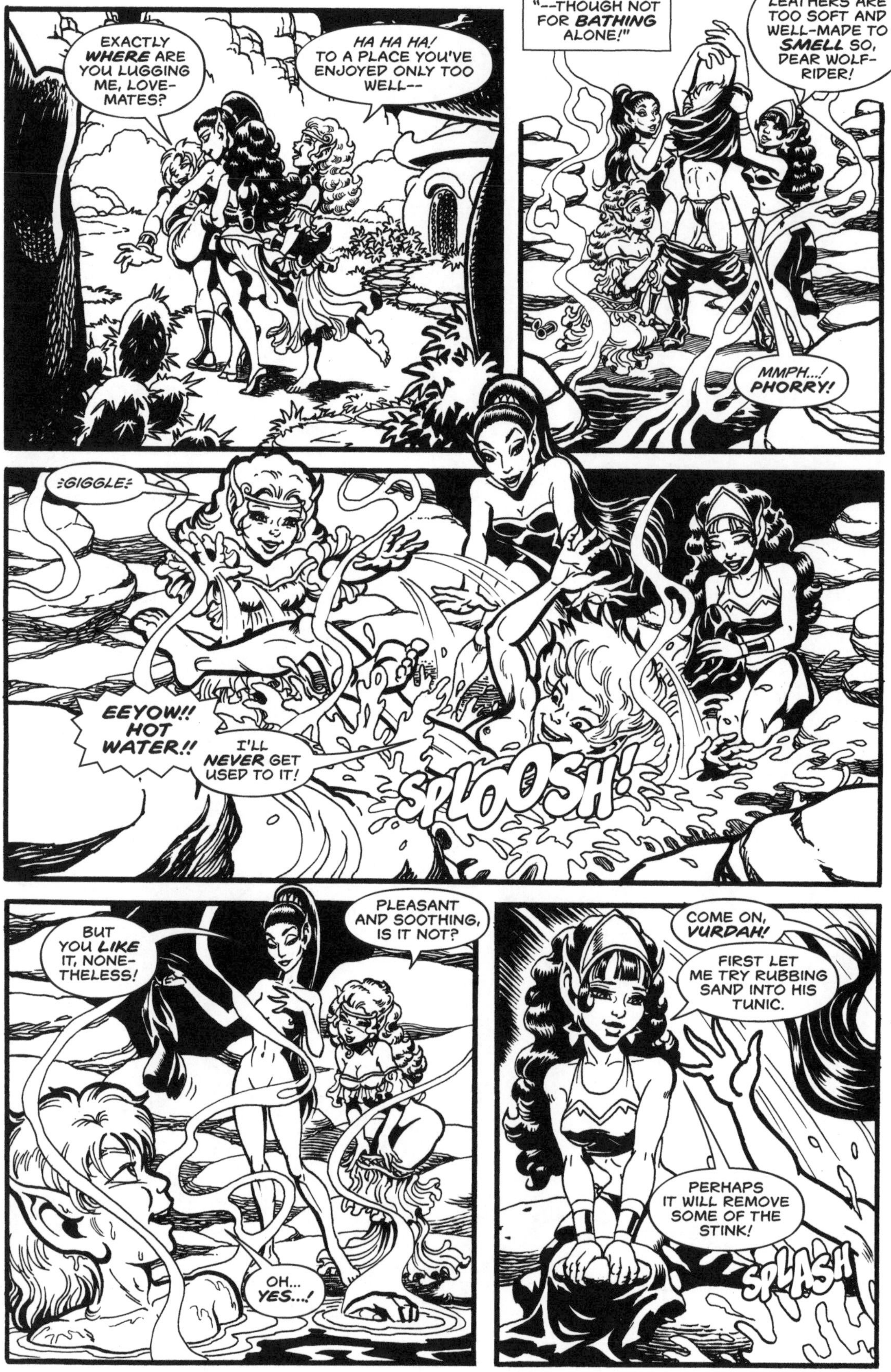
EXACTLY WHERE ARE YOU LUGGING ME, LOVE-MATES?
HA HA HA! TO A PLACE YOU'VE ENJOYED ONLY TOO WELL--
"--THOUGH NOT FOR BATHING ALONE!"
YOUR LEATHERS ARE TOO SOFT AND WELL-MADE TO SMELL SO, DEAR WOLF-RIDER!
MMPH...! PHORRY!
GIGGLE
EEYOW!! HOT WATER!!
I'LL NEVER GET USED TO IT!
SPLOOSH!
BUT YOU LIKE IT, NONE-THELESS!
PLEASANT AND SOOTHING, IS IT NOT?
OH... YES...!
COME ON, VURDAH!
FIRST LET ME TRY RUBBING SAND INTO HIS TUNIC.
PERHAPS IT WILL REMOVE SOME OF THE STINK!
SPLASH

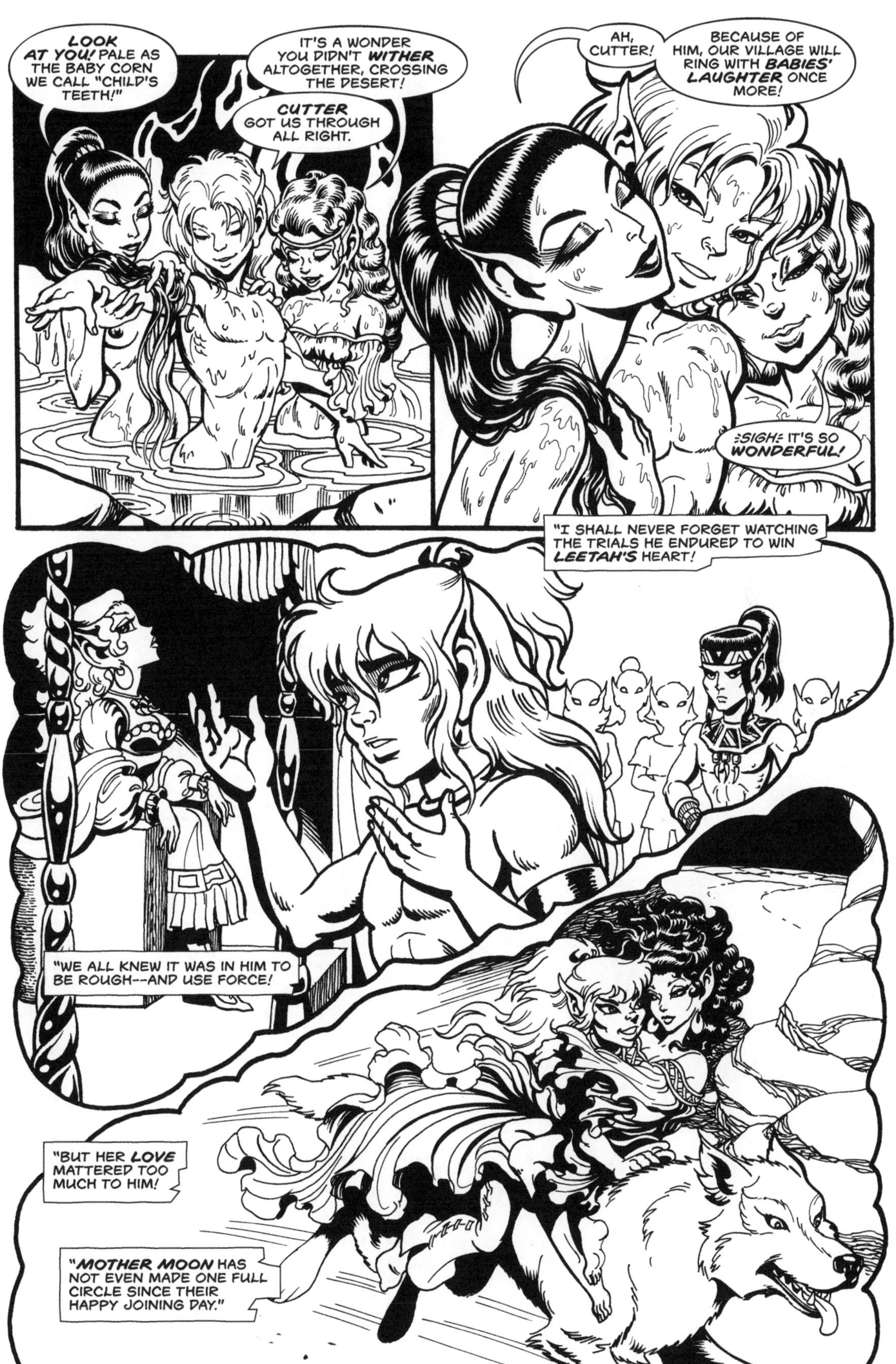
LOOK AT YOU! PALE AS THE BABY CORN WE CALL "CHILD'S TEETH!"
IT'S A WONDER YOU DIDN'T WITHER ALTOGETHER, CROSSING THE DESERT!
CUTTER GOT US THROUGH ALL RIGHT.
AH, CUTTER!
BECAUSE OF HIM, OUR VILLAGE WILL RING WITH BABIES' LAUGHTER ONCE MORE!
SIGH IT'S SO WONDERFUL!
"I SHALL NEVER FORGET WATCHING THE TRIALS HE ENDURED TO WIN LEETAH'S HEART!
"WE ALL KNEW IT WAS IN HIM TO BE ROUGH--AND USE FORCE!
"BUT HER LOVE MATTERED TOO MUCH TO HIM!
"MOTHER MOON HAS NOT EVEN MADE ONE FULL CIRCLE SINCE THEIR HAPPY JOINING DAY."

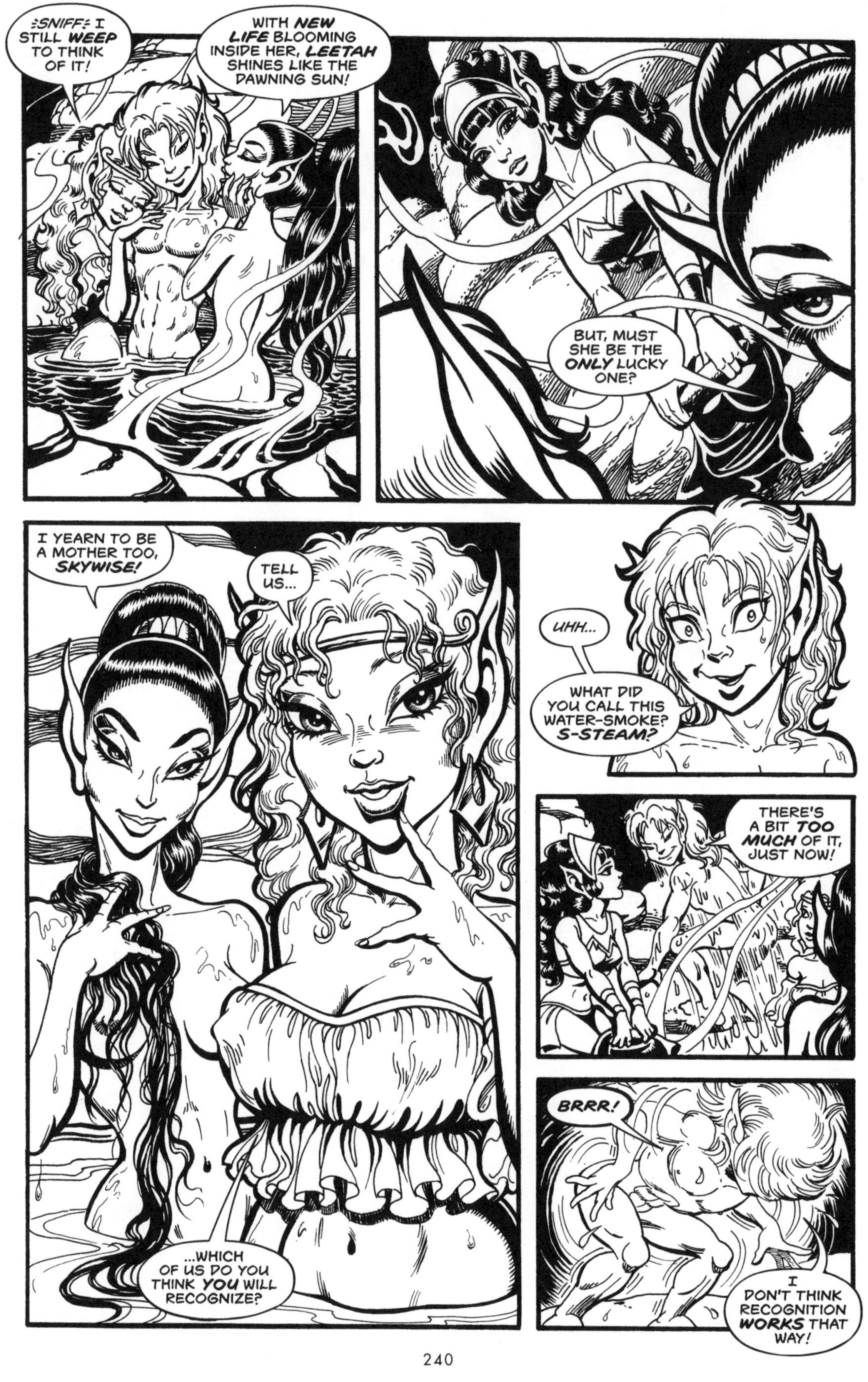
:SNIFF: I STILL WEEP TO THINK OF IT!
WITH NEW LIFE BLOOMING INSIDE HER, LEETAH SHINES LIKE THE DAWNING SUN!
BUT, MUST SHE BE THE ONLY LUCKY ONE?
I YEARN TO BE A MOTHER TOO, SKYWISE!
TELL US...
...WHICH OF US DO YOU THINK YOU WILL RECOGNIZE?
UHH...
WHAT DID YOU CALL THIS WATER-SMOKE? S-STEAM?
THERE'S A BIT TOO MUCH OF IT, JUST NOW!
BRRR!
I DON'T THINK RECOGNITION WORKS THAT WAY!

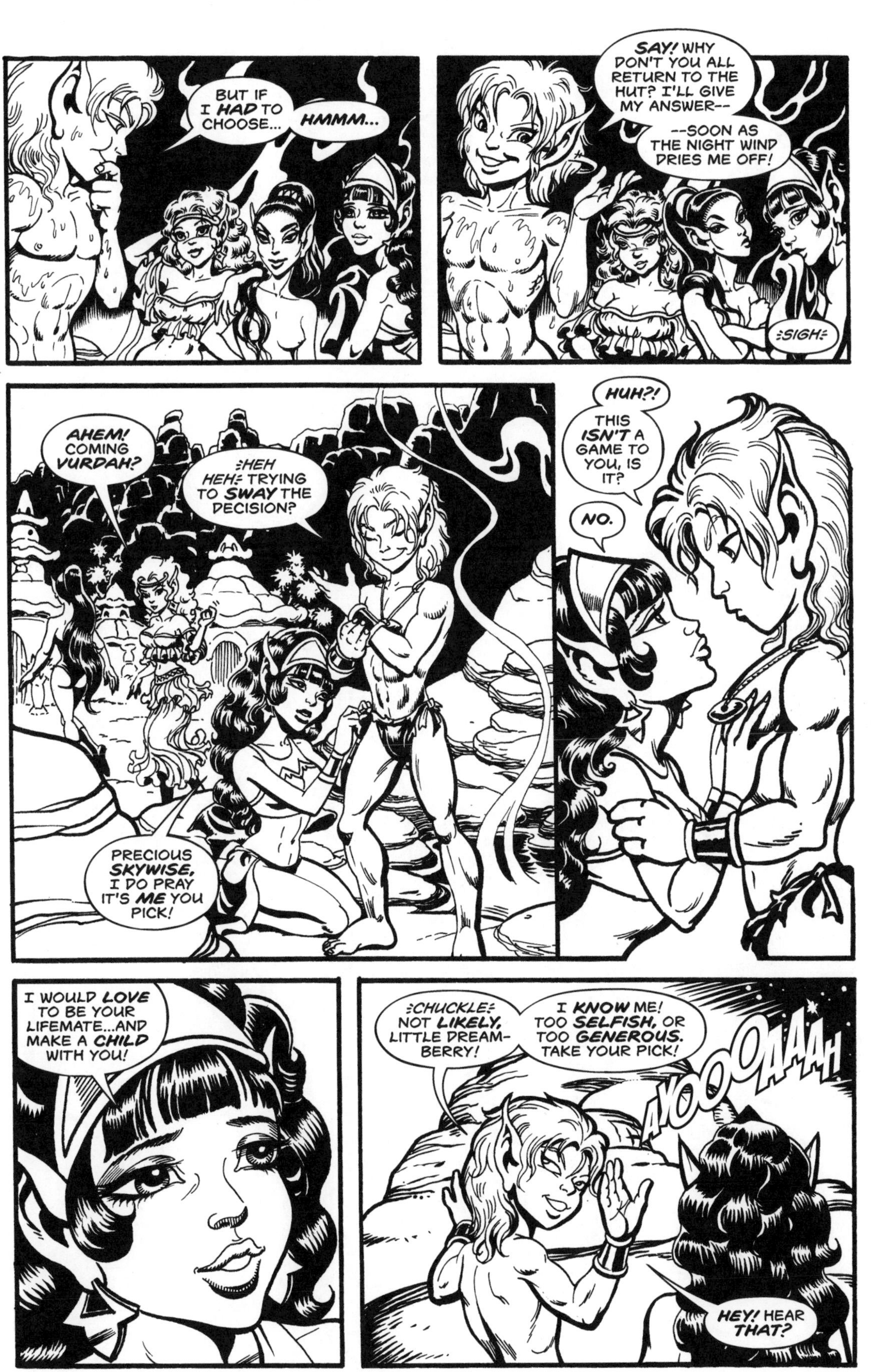

BUT IF I **HAD** TO CHOOSE...
HMMM...
SAY! WHY DON'T YOU ALL RETURN TO THE HUT? I'LL GIVE MY ANSWER--
--SOON AS THE NIGHT WIND DRIES ME OFF!
SIGH
AHEM! COMING **VURDAH?**
HEH HEH TRYING TO **SWAY** THE DECISION?
PRECIOUS **SKYWISE,** I DO PRAY IT'S **ME** YOU PICK!
HUH?!
THIS **ISN'T** A GAME TO YOU, IS IT?
NO.
I WOULD **LOVE** TO BE YOUR LIFEMATE...AND MAKE A **CHILD** WITH YOU!
CHUCKLE NOT **LIKELY,** LITTLE DREAMBERRY!
I **KNOW** ME! TOO **SELFISH,** OR TOO **GENEROUS.** TAKE YOUR PICK!
AYOOOAAAH
HEY! HEAR **THAT?**

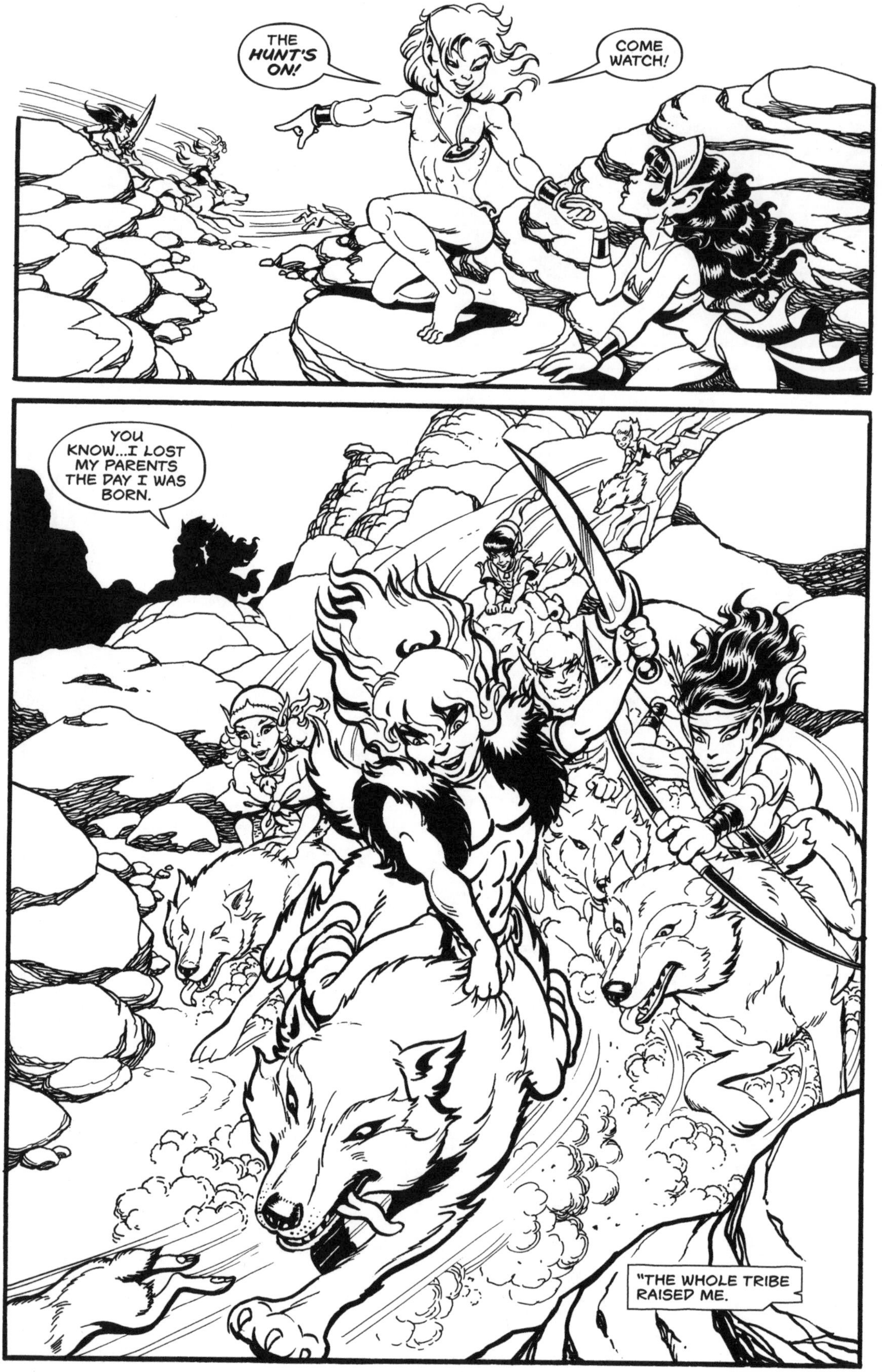
THE *HUNT'S* ON!
COME WATCH!
YOU KNOW...I LOST MY PARENTS THE DAY I WAS BORN.
"THE WHOLE TRIBE RAISED ME.

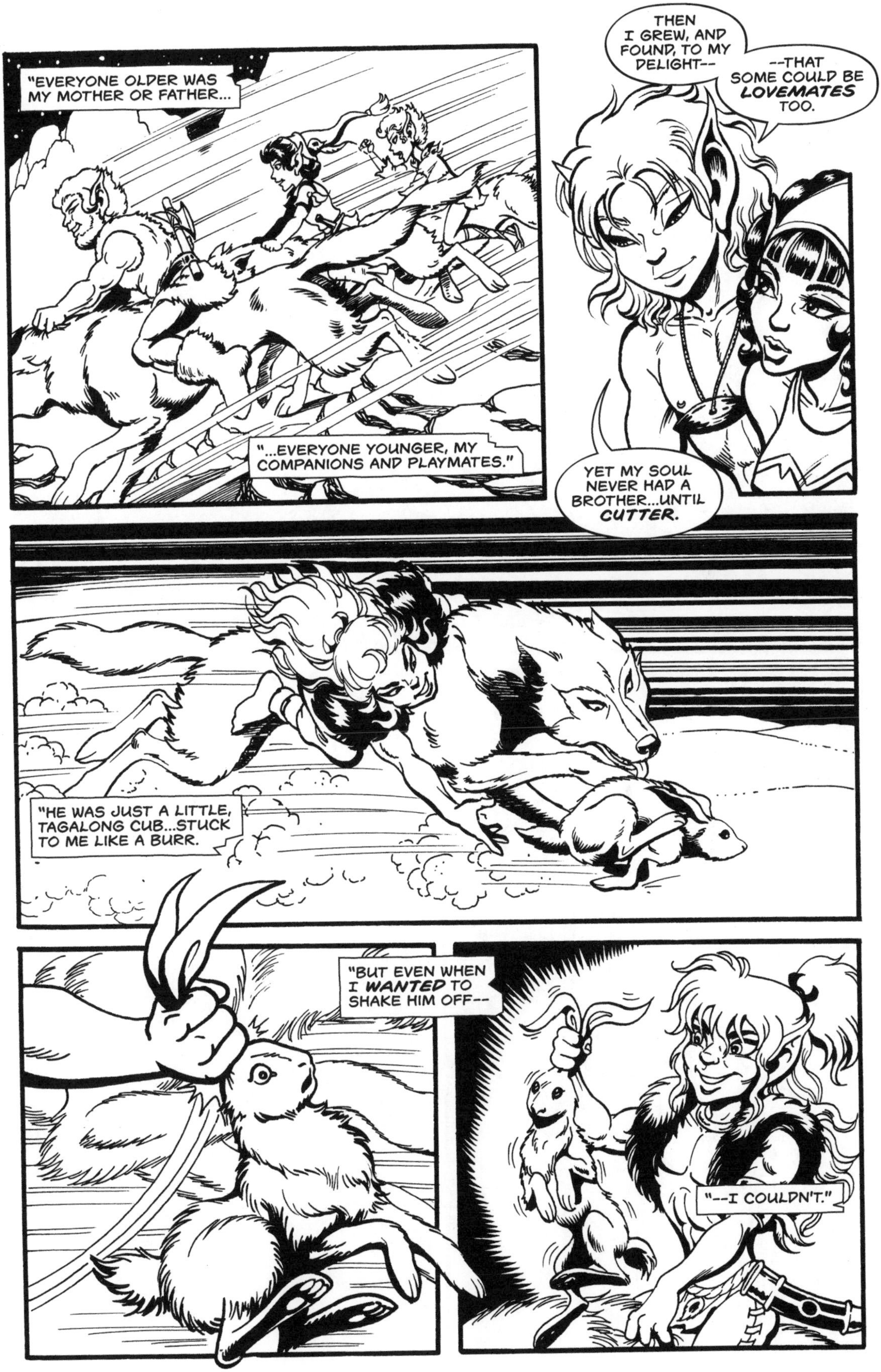
"EVERYONE OLDER WAS MY MOTHER OR FATHER...
"...EVERYONE YOUNGER, MY COMPANIONS AND PLAYMATES."
THEN I GREW, AND FOUND, TO MY DELIGHT--
--THAT SOME COULD BE LOVEMATES TOO.
YET MY SOUL NEVER HAD A BROTHER...UNTIL CUTTER.
"HE WAS JUST A LITTLE, TAGALONG CUB...STUCK TO ME LIKE A BURR.
"BUT EVEN WHEN I WANTED TO SHAKE HIM OFF--
"--I COULDN'T."

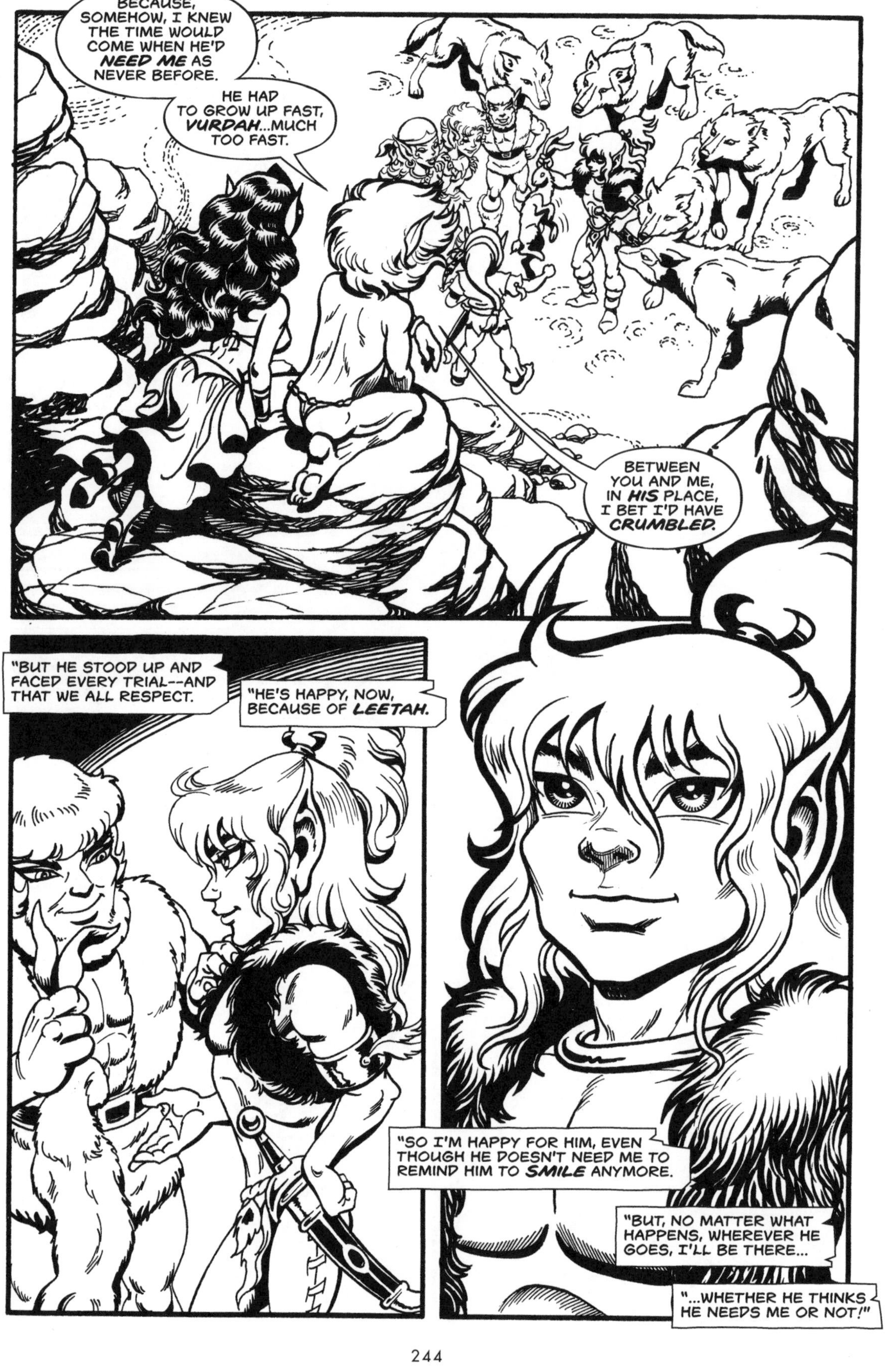
BECAUSE, SOMEHOW, I KNEW THE TIME WOULD COME WHEN HE'D NEED ME AS NEVER BEFORE.
HE HAD TO GROW UP FAST, VURDAH...MUCH TOO FAST.
BETWEEN YOU AND ME, IN HIS PLACE, I BET I'D HAVE CRUMBLED.
"BUT HE STOOD UP AND FACED EVERY TRIAL--AND THAT WE ALL RESPECT.
"HE'S HAPPY, NOW, BECAUSE OF LEETAH.
"SO I'M HAPPY FOR HIM, EVEN THOUGH HE DOESN'T NEED ME TO REMIND HIM TO SMILE ANYMORE.
"BUT, NO MATTER WHAT HAPPENS, WHEREVER HE GOES, I'LL BE THERE...
"...WHETHER HE THINKS HE NEEDS ME OR NOT!"

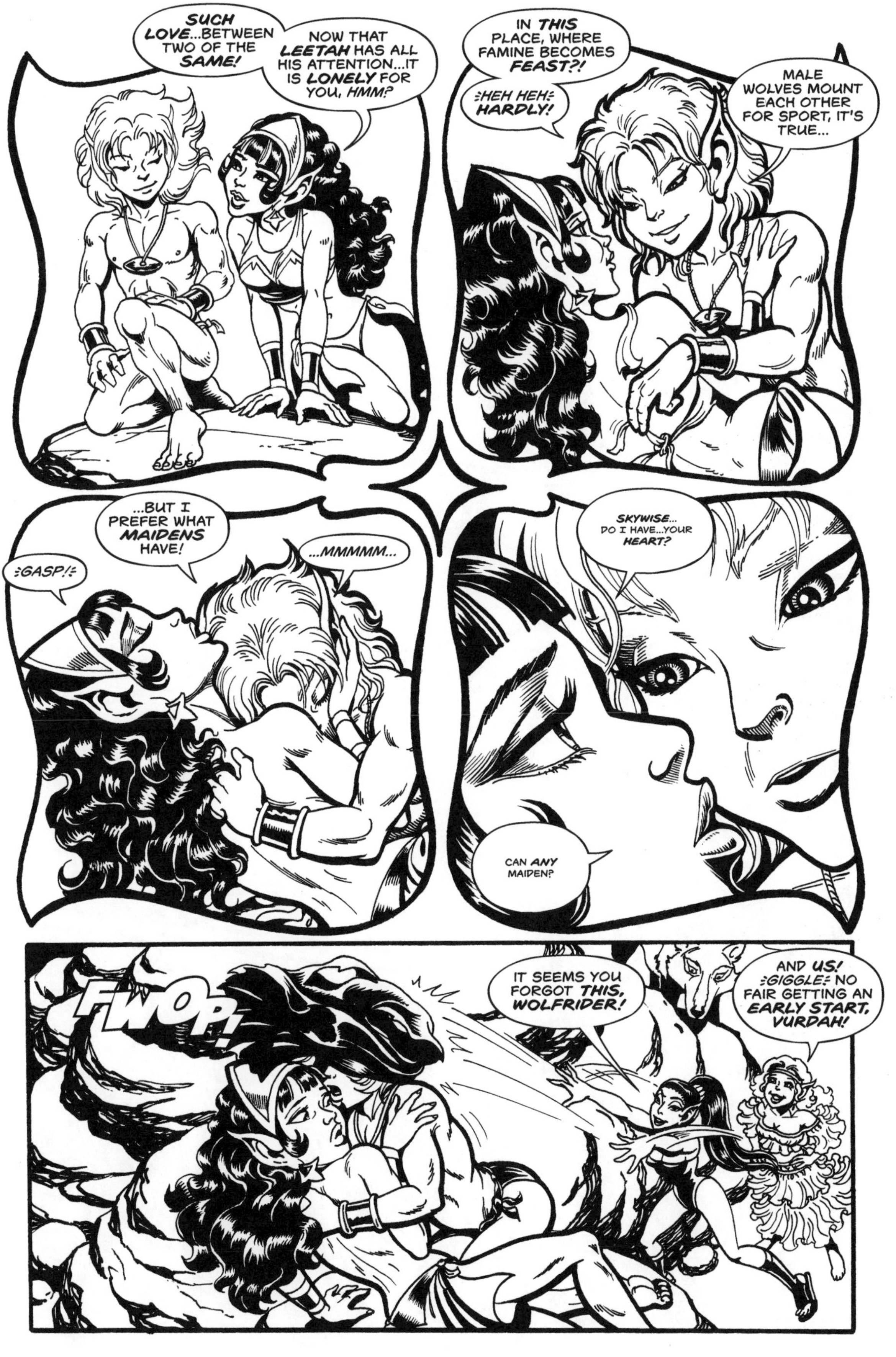
SUCH LOVE...BETWEEN TWO OF THE SAME!
NOW THAT LEETAH HAS ALL HIS ATTENTION...IT IS LONELY FOR YOU, HMM?
IN THIS PLACE, WHERE FAMINE BECOMES FEAST?!
HEH HEH HARDLY!
MALE WOLVES MOUNT EACH OTHER FOR SPORT, IT'S TRUE...
...BUT I PREFER WHAT MAIDENS HAVE!
GASP!
...MMMMM...
SKYWISE... DO I HAVE...YOUR HEART?
CAN ANY MAIDEN?
FWOP!
IT SEEMS YOU FORGOT THIS, WOLFRIDER!
AND US! GIGGLE NO FAIR GETTING AN EARLY START, VURDAH!

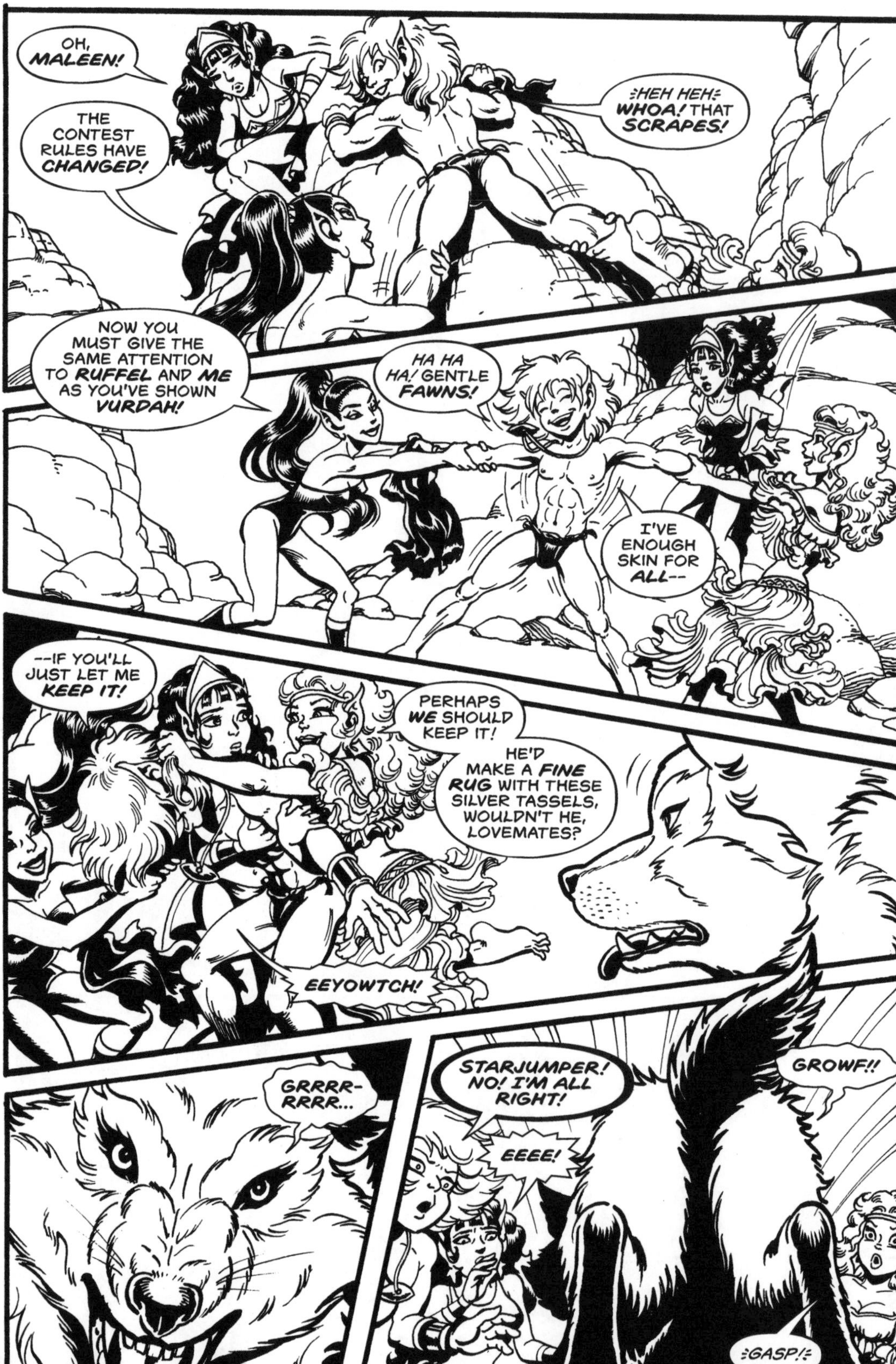
OH, MALEEN!
THE CONTEST RULES HAVE CHANGED!
HEH HEH! WHOA! THAT SCRAPES!
NOW YOU MUST GIVE THE SAME ATTENTION TO RUFFEL AND ME AS YOU'VE SHOWN VURDAH!
HA HA HA! GENTLE FAWNS!
I'VE ENOUGH SKIN FOR ALL--
--IF YOU'LL JUST LET ME KEEP IT!
PERHAPS WE SHOULD KEEP IT!
HE'D MAKE A FINE RUG WITH THESE SILVER TASSELS, WOULDN'T HE, LOVEMATES?
EEYOWTCH!
GRRRR-RRRR...
STARJUMPER! NO! I'M ALL RIGHT!
GROWF!!
EEEE!
GASP!

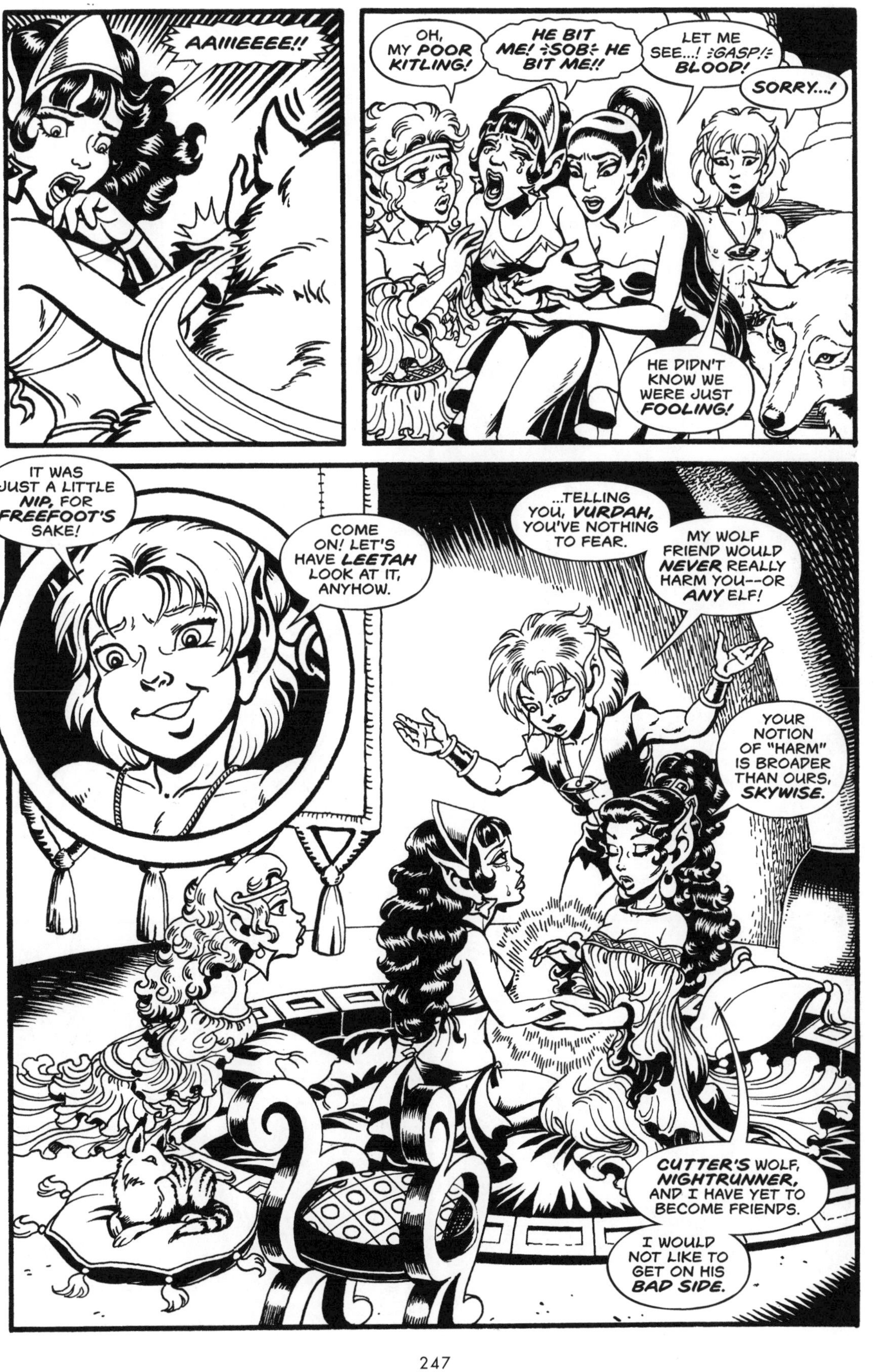
AAIIEEEE!!
OH, MY POOR KITLING!
HE BIT ME! ⁐SOB⁐ HE BIT ME!!
LET ME SEE...! ⁐GASP!⁐ BLOOD!
SORRY...!
HE DIDN'T KNOW WE WERE JUST FOOLING!
IT WAS JUST A LITTLE NIP, FOR FREEFOOT'S SAKE!
COME ON! LET'S HAVE LEETAH LOOK AT IT, ANYHOW.
...TELLING YOU, VURDAH, YOU'VE NOTHING TO FEAR.
MY WOLF FRIEND WOULD NEVER REALLY HARM YOU--OR ANY ELF!
YOUR NOTION OF "HARM" IS BROADER THAN OURS, SKYWISE.
CUTTER'S WOLF, NIGHTRUNNER, AND I HAVE YET TO BECOME FRIENDS.
I WOULD NOT LIKE TO GET ON HIS BAD SIDE.

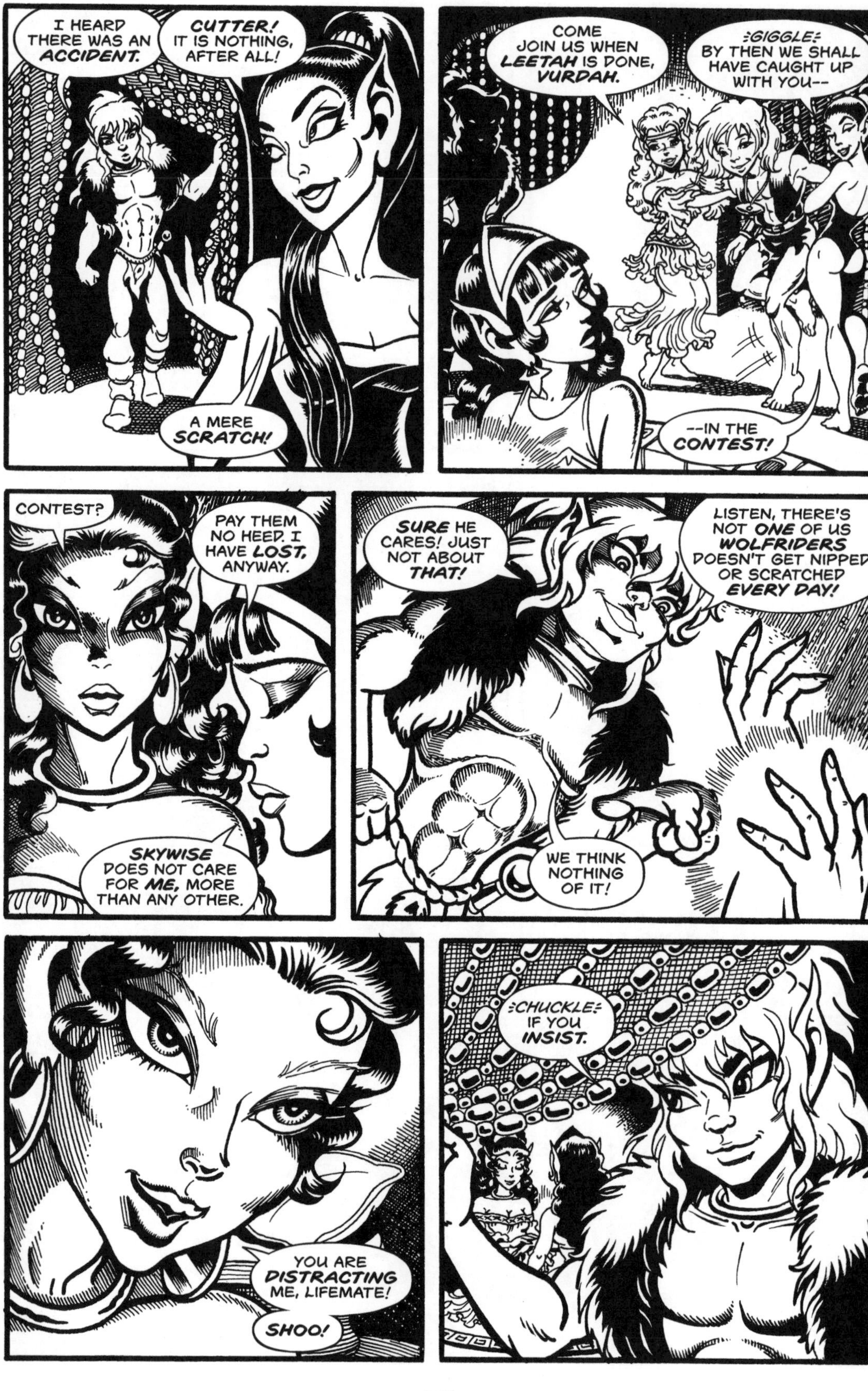

I HEARD THERE WAS AN ACCIDENT.
CUTTER! IT IS NOTHING, AFTER ALL!
A MERE SCRATCH!
COME JOIN US WHEN LEETAH IS DONE, VURDAH.
GIGGLE BY THEN WE SHALL HAVE CAUGHT UP WITH YOU--
--IN THE CONTEST!
CONTEST?
PAY THEM NO HEED. I HAVE LOST, ANYWAY.
SKYWISE DOES NOT CARE FOR ME, MORE THAN ANY OTHER.
SURE HE CARES! JUST NOT ABOUT THAT!
LISTEN, THERE'S NOT ONE OF US WOLFRIDERS DOESN'T GET NIPPED OR SCRATCHED EVERY DAY!
WE THINK NOTHING OF IT!
YOU ARE DISTRACTING ME, LIFEMATE!
SHOO!
CHUCKLE IF YOU INSIST.

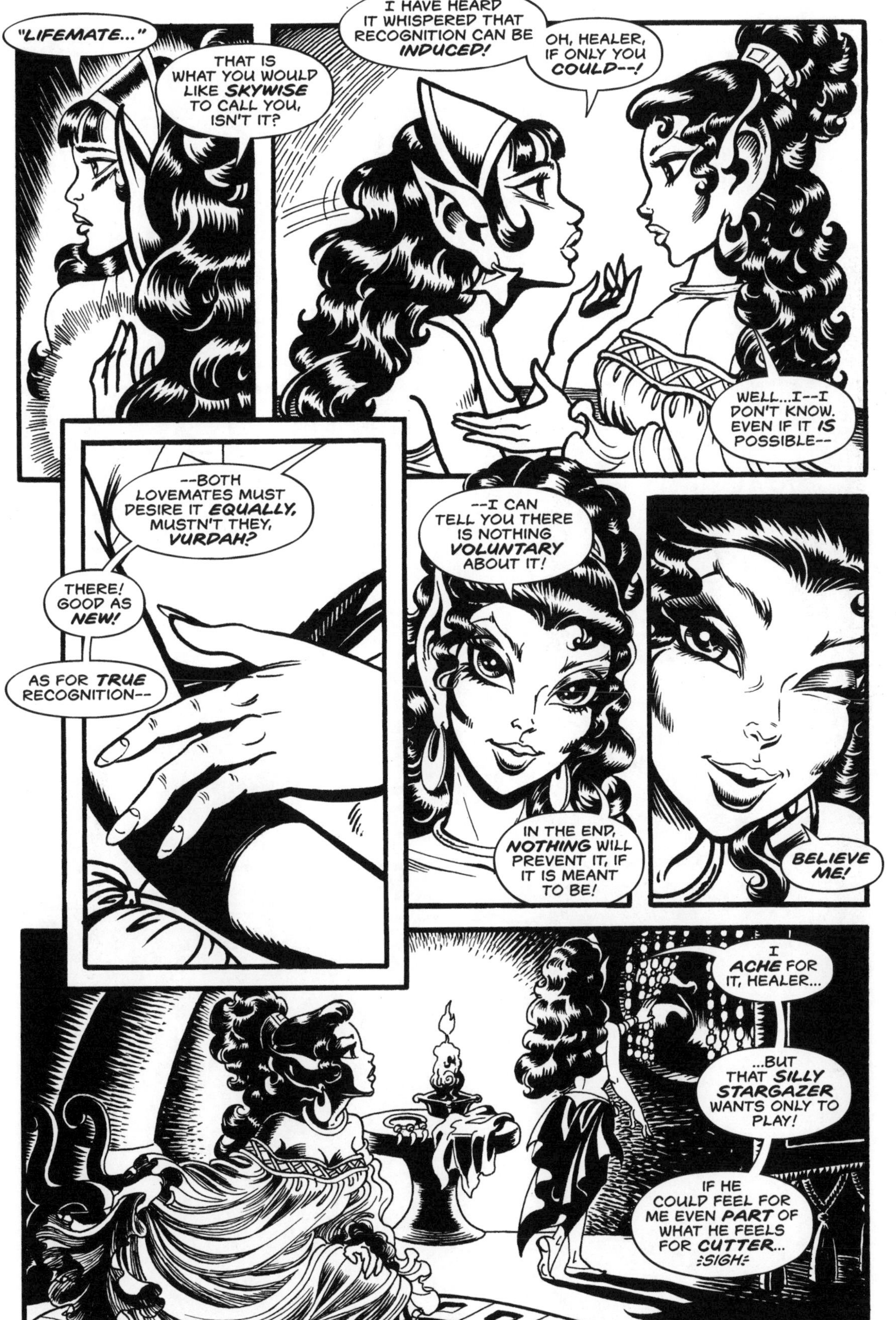
"LIFEMATE..."
THAT IS WHAT YOU WOULD LIKE SKYWISE TO CALL YOU, ISN'T IT?
I HAVE HEARD IT WHISPERED THAT RECOGNITION CAN BE INDUCED!
OH, HEALER, IF ONLY YOU COULD--!
WELL...I--I DON'T KNOW. EVEN IF IT IS POSSIBLE--
--BOTH LOVEMATES MUST DESIRE IT EQUALLY, MUSTN'T THEY, VURDAH?
THERE! GOOD AS NEW!
AS FOR TRUE RECOGNITION--
--I CAN TELL YOU THERE IS NOTHING VOLUNTARY ABOUT IT!
IN THE END, NOTHING WILL PREVENT IT, IF IT IS MEANT TO BE!
BELIEVE ME!
I ACHE FOR IT, HEALER...
...BUT THAT SILLY STARGAZER WANTS ONLY TO PLAY!
IF HE COULD FEEL FOR ME EVEN PART OF WHAT HE FEELS FOR CUTTER... :SIGH:

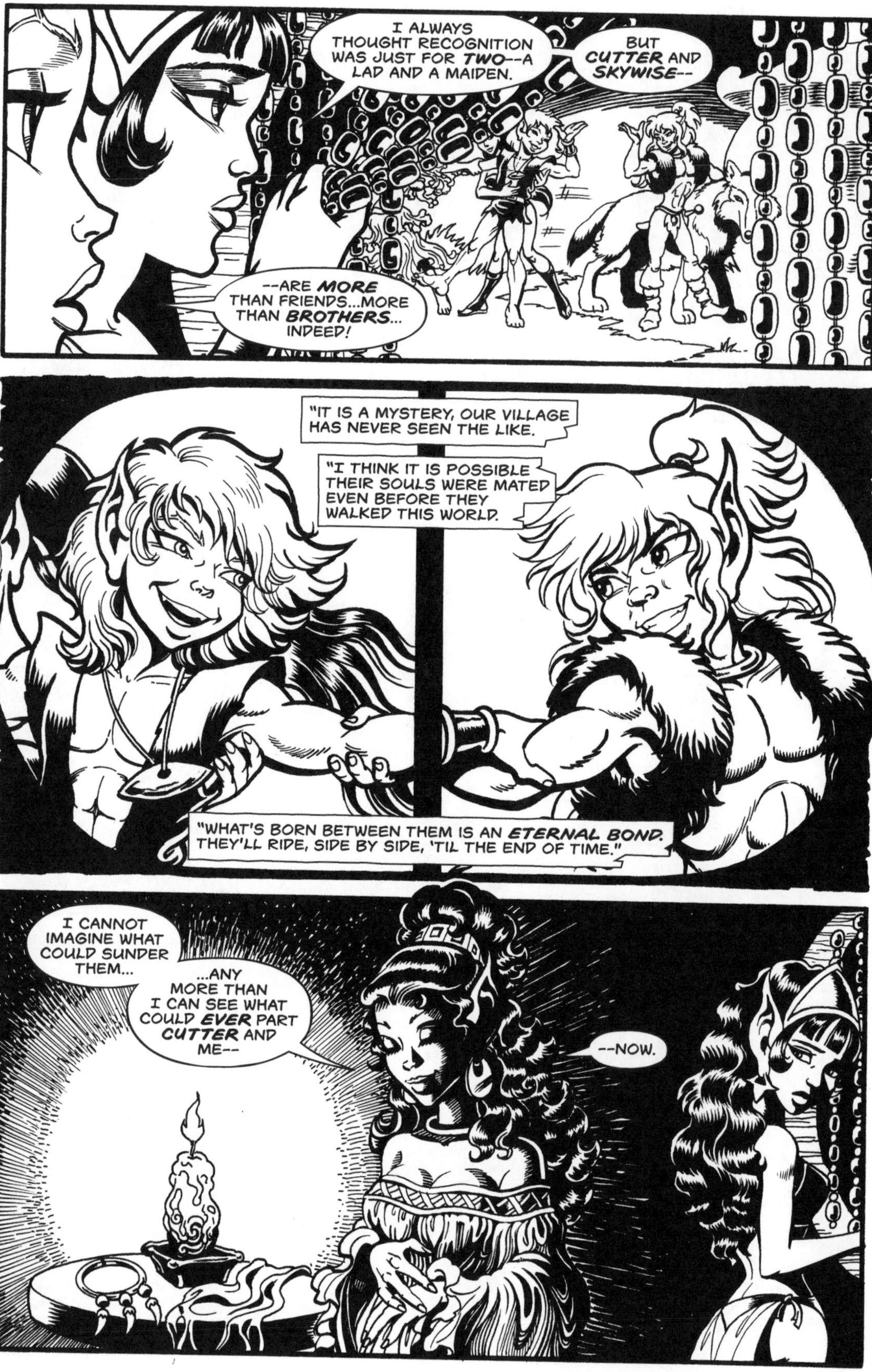
I ALWAYS THOUGHT RECOGNITION WAS JUST FOR TWO--A LAD AND A MAIDEN.
BUT CUTTER AND SKYWISE--
--ARE MORE THAN FRIENDS...MORE THAN BROTHERS... INDEED!
"IT IS A MYSTERY, OUR VILLAGE HAS NEVER SEEN THE LIKE.
"I THINK IT IS POSSIBLE THEIR SOULS WERE MATED EVEN BEFORE THEY WALKED THIS WORLD.
"WHAT'S BORN BETWEEN THEM IS AN ETERNAL BOND. THEY'LL RIDE, SIDE BY SIDE, 'TIL THE END OF TIME."
I CANNOT IMAGINE WHAT COULD SUNDER THEM...
...ANY MORE THAN I CAN SEE WHAT COULD EVER PART CUTTER AND ME--
--NOW.

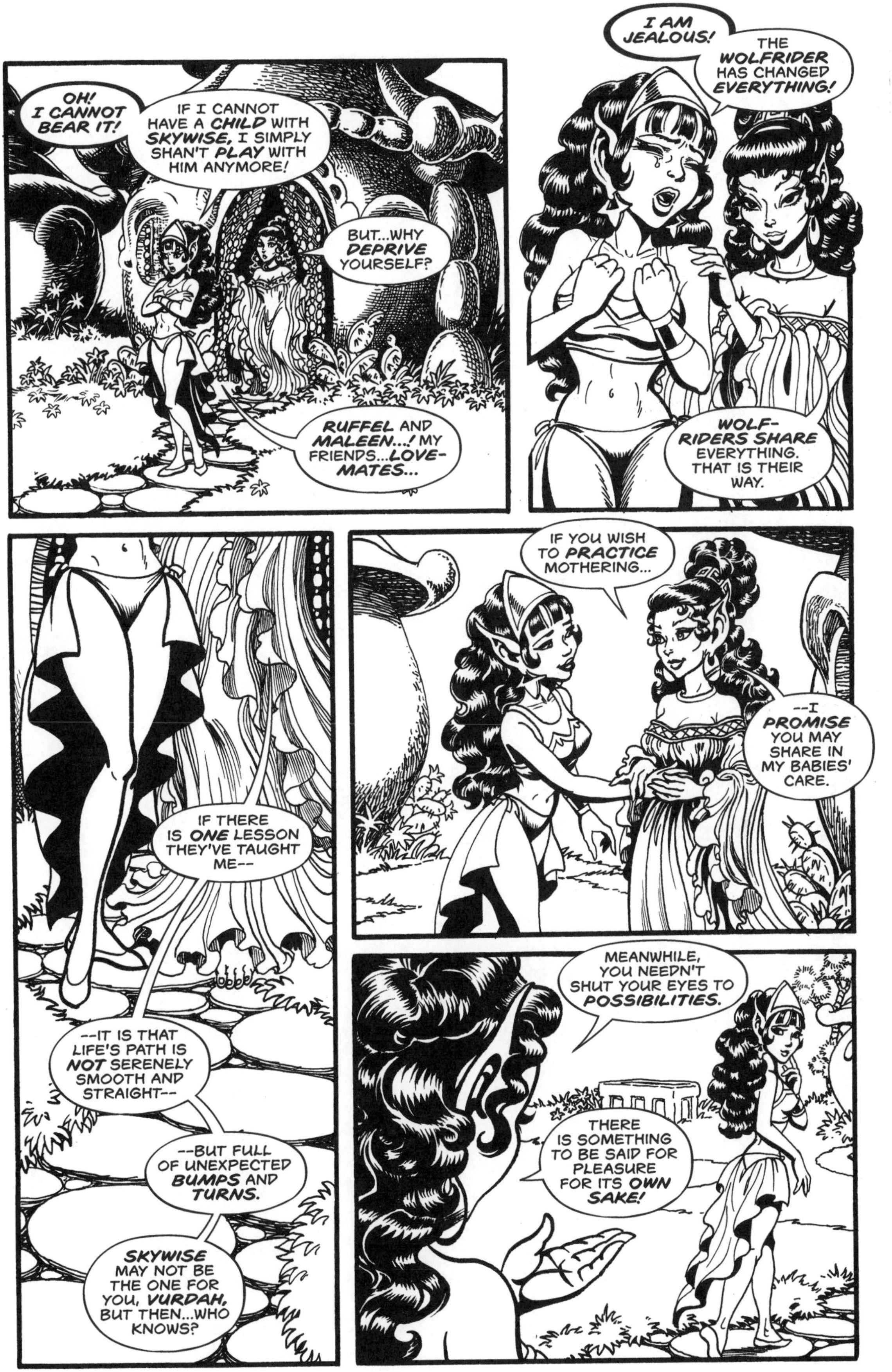
OH! I CANNOT BEAR IT!
IF I CANNOT HAVE A CHILD WITH SKYWISE, I SIMPLY SHAN'T PLAY WITH HIM ANYMORE!
BUT...WHY DEPRIVE YOURSELF?
RUFFEL AND MALEEN...! MY FRIENDS...LOVE-MATES...
I AM JEALOUS!
THE WOLFRIDER HAS CHANGED EVERYTHING!
WOLF-RIDERS SHARE EVERYTHING. THAT IS THEIR WAY.
IF THERE IS ONE LESSON THEY'VE TAUGHT ME--
--IT IS THAT LIFE'S PATH IS NOT SERENELY SMOOTH AND STRAIGHT--
--BUT FULL OF UNEXPECTED BUMPS AND TURNS.
SKYWISE MAY NOT BE THE ONE FOR YOU, VURDAH, BUT THEN...WHO KNOWS?
IF YOU WISH TO PRACTICE MOTHERING...
--I PROMISE YOU MAY SHARE IN MY BABIES' CARE.
MEANWHILE, YOU NEEDN'T SHUT YOUR EYES TO POSSIBILITIES.
THERE IS SOMETHING TO BE SAID FOR PLEASURE FOR ITS OWN SAKE!

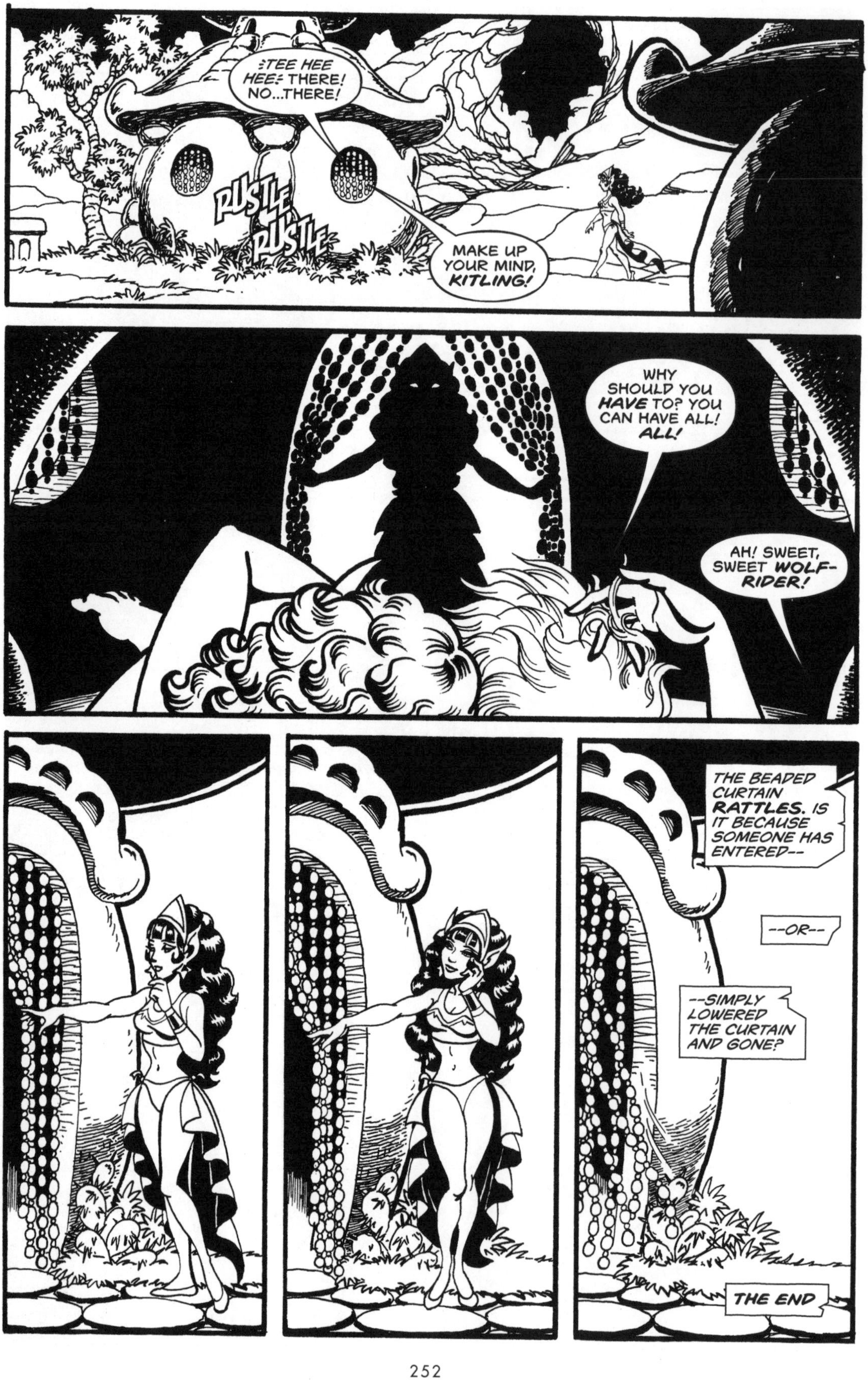

TEE HEE HEE THERE! NO...THERE!
RUSTLE RUSTLE
MAKE UP YOUR MIND, KITLING!
WHY SHOULD YOU HAVE TO? YOU CAN HAVE ALL! ALL!
AH! SWEET, SWEET WOLF-RIDER!
THE BEADED CURTAIN RATTLES. IS IT BECAUSE SOMEONE HAS ENTERED--
--OR--
--SIMPLY LOWERED THE CURTAIN AND GONE?
THE END

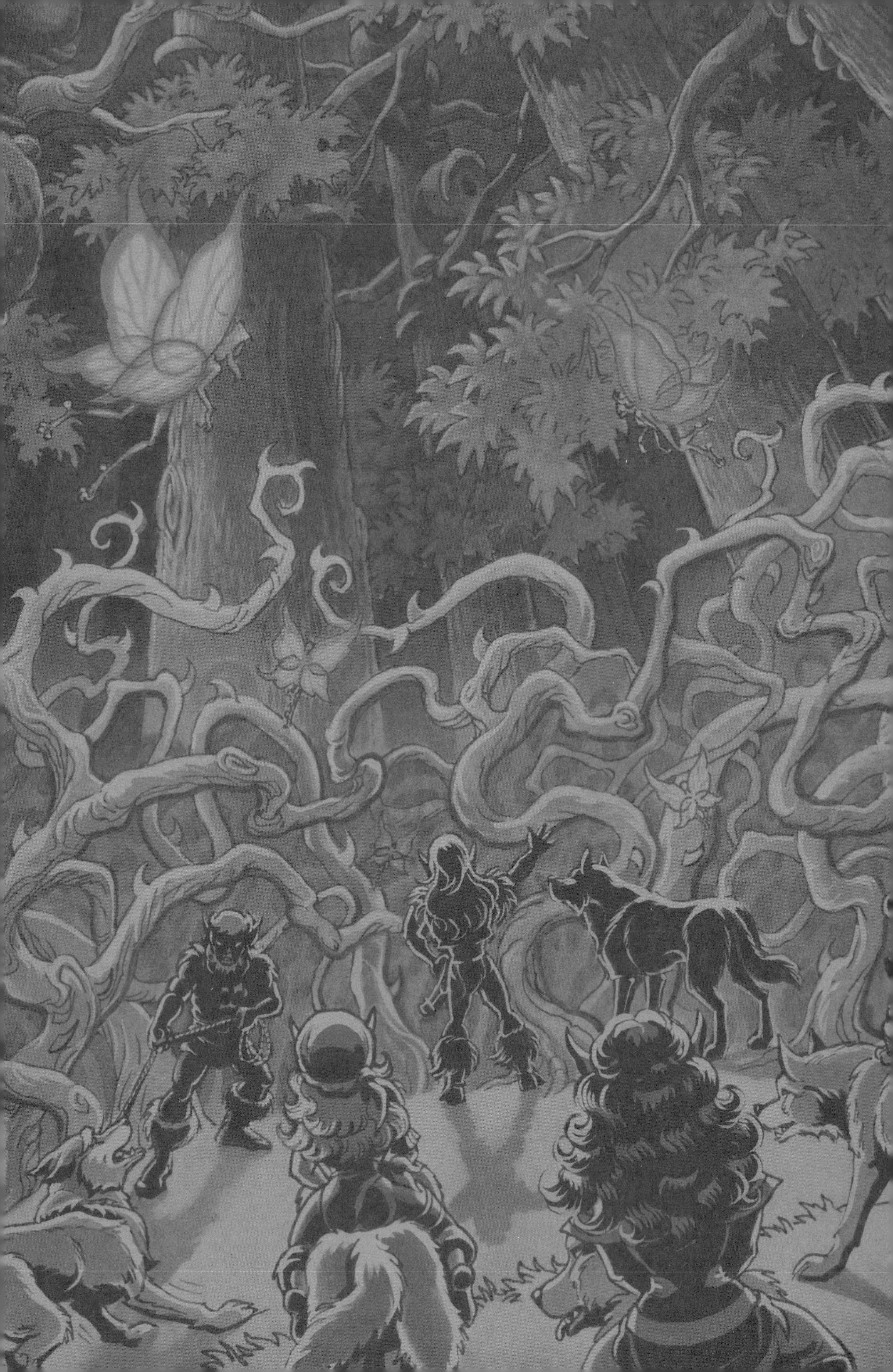

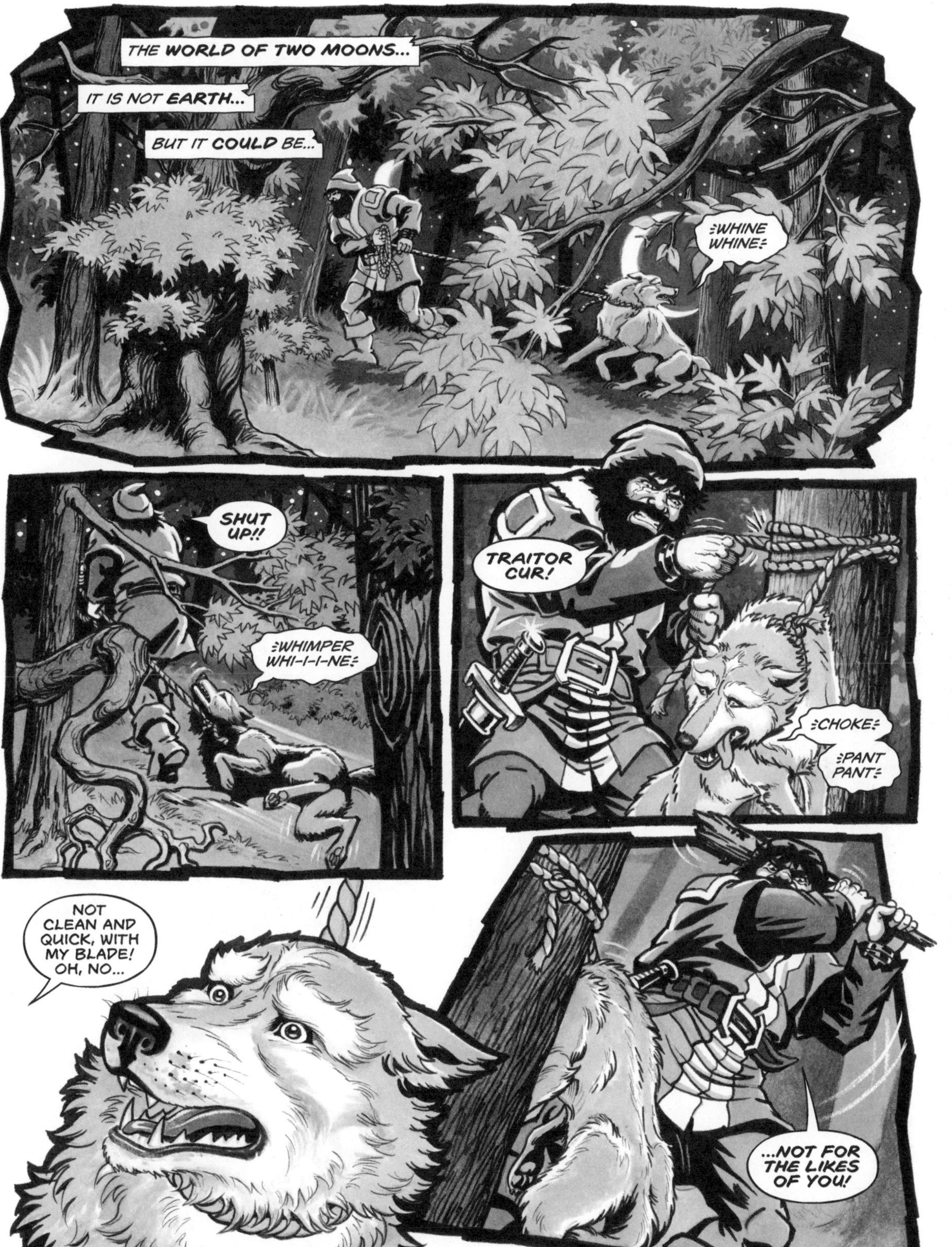
THE WORLD OF TWO MOONS...
IT IS NOT EARTH...
BUT IT COULD BE...
WHINE WHINE
SHUT UP!!
WHIMPER WHI-I-I-NE
TRAITOR CUR!
CHOKE
PANT PANT
NOT CLEAN AND QUICK, WITH MY BLADE! OH, NO...
...NOT FOR THE LIKES OF YOU!

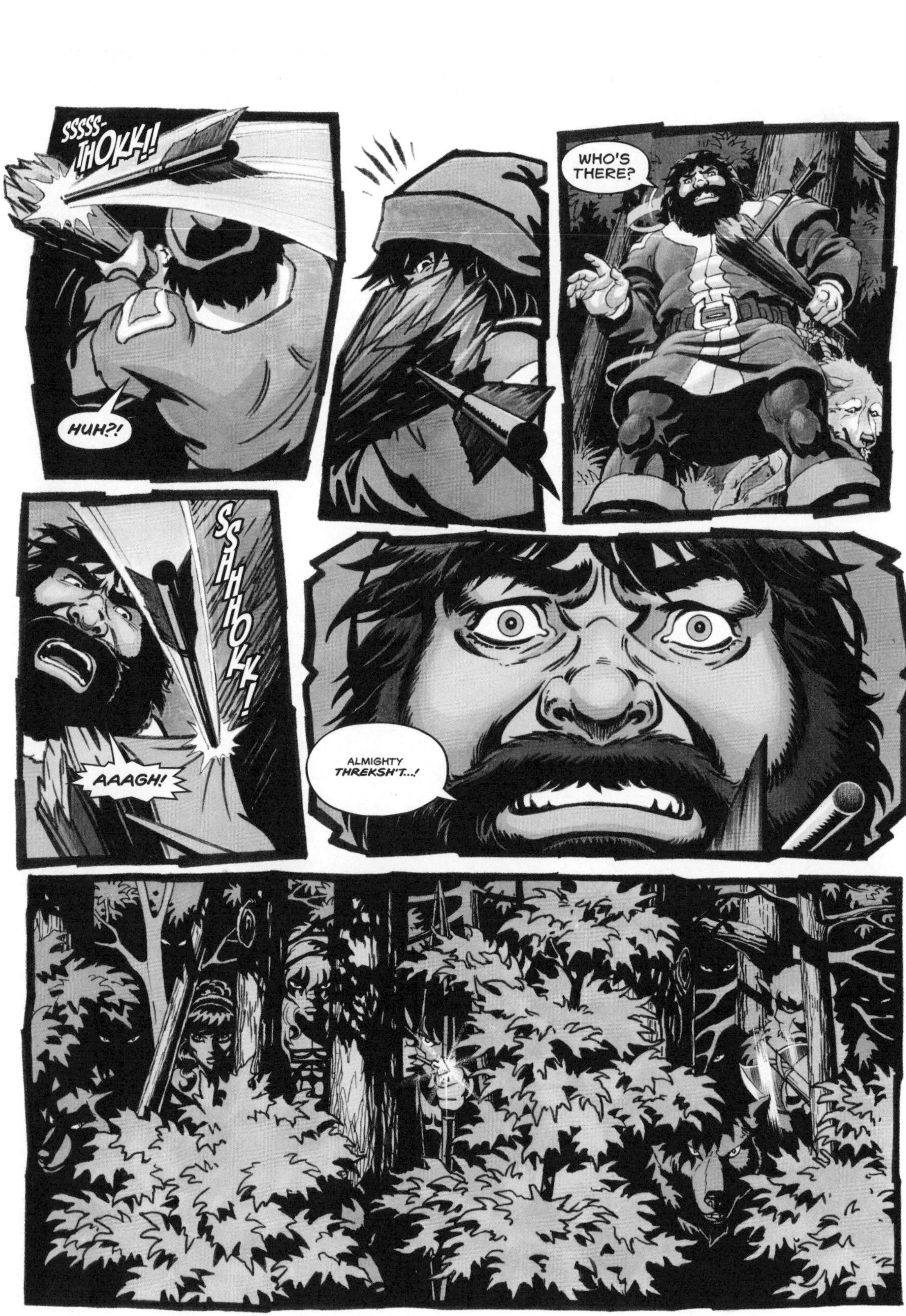
SSSSS-THOKK!!
HUH?!
WHO'S THERE?
SSHHOKK!
AAAGH!
ALMIGHTY THREKSH'T...!

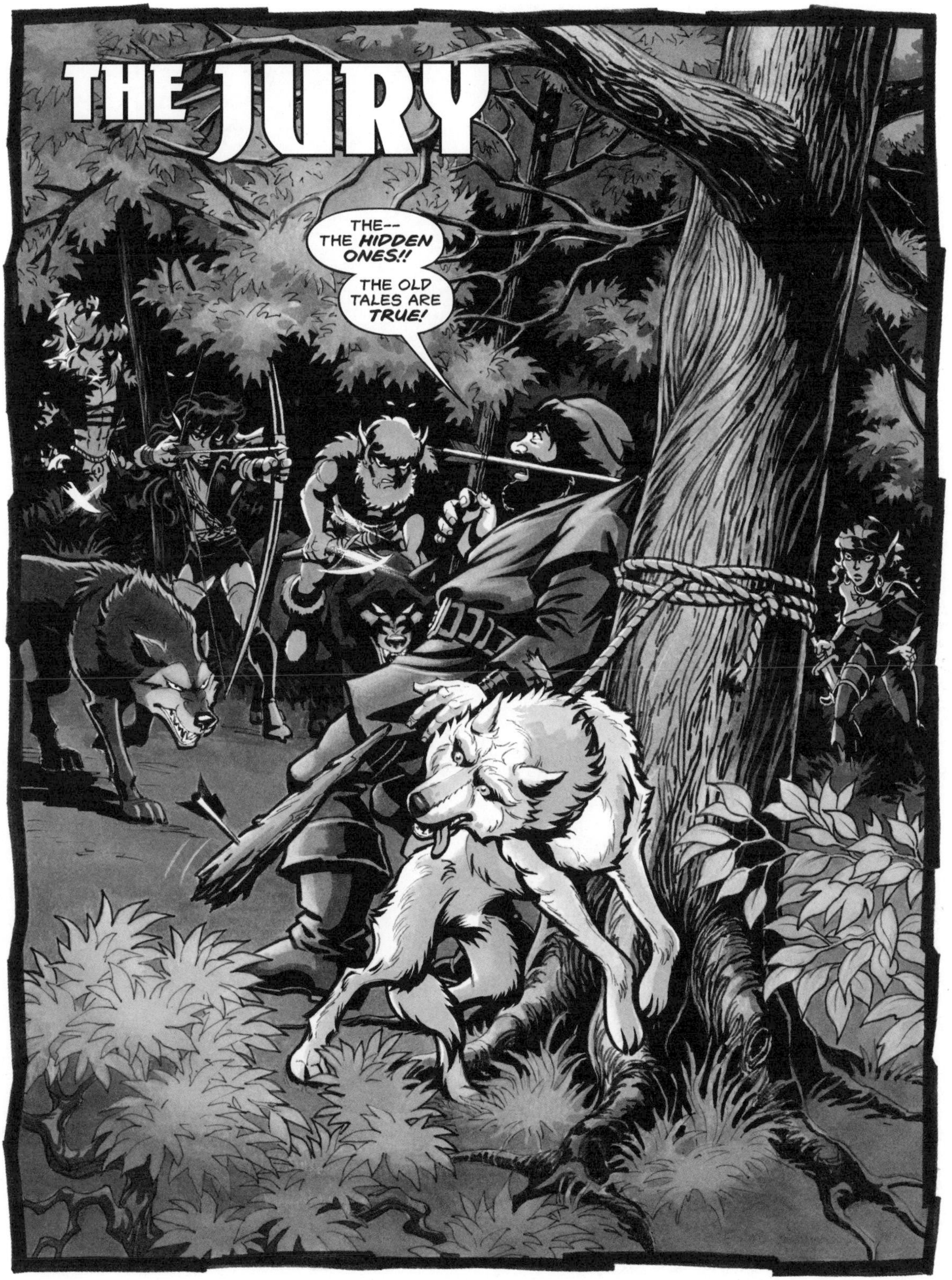
THE JURY
THE-- THE HIDDEN ONES!!
THE OLD TALES ARE TRUE!

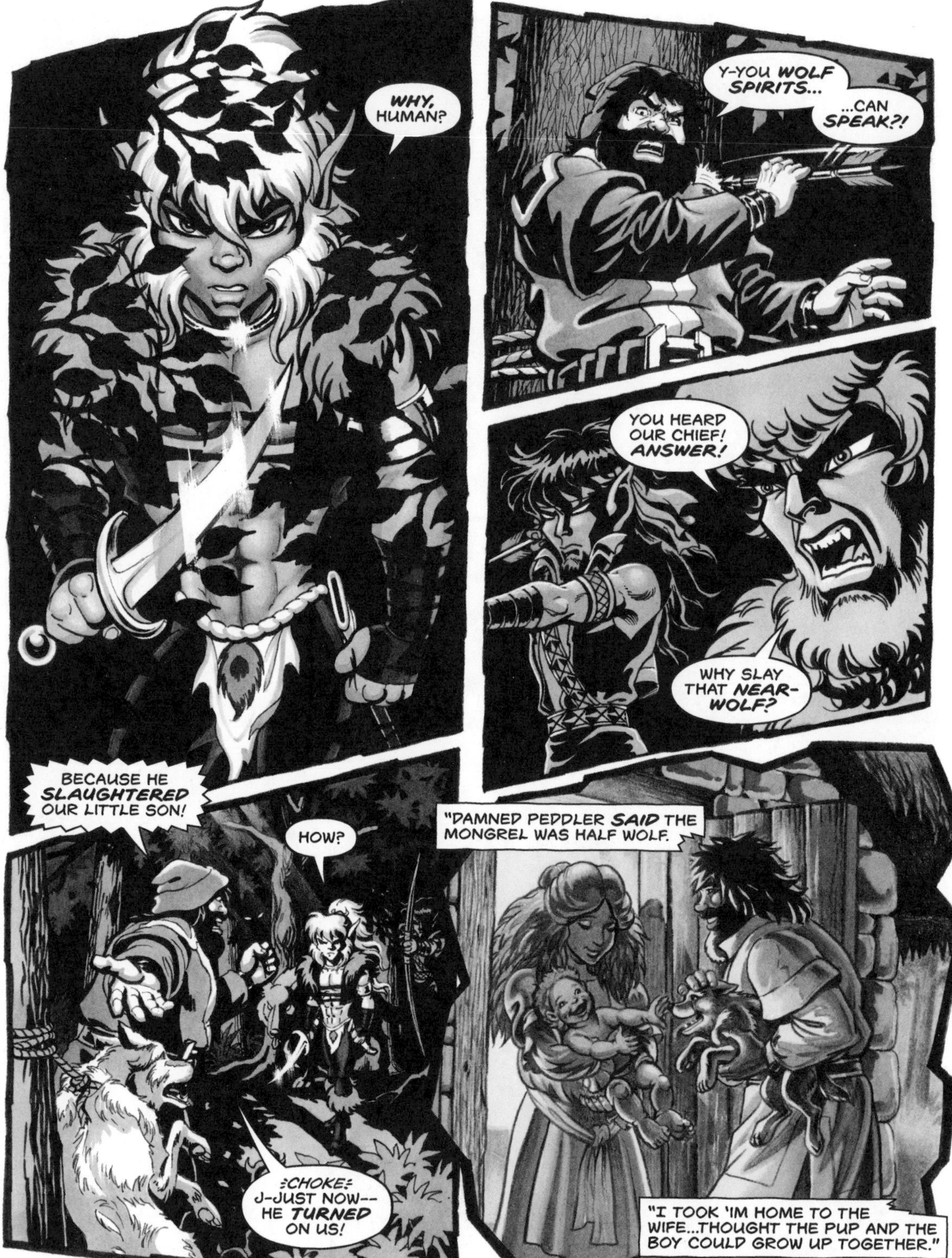

WHY, HUMAN?
Y-YOU WOLF SPIRITS...
...CAN SPEAK?!
YOU HEARD OUR CHIEF! ANSWER!
WHY SLAY THAT NEAR-WOLF?
BECAUSE HE SLAUGHTERED OUR LITTLE SON!
HOW?
:CHOKE: J-JUST NOW-- HE TURNED ON US!
"DAMNED PEDDLER SAID THE MONGREL WAS HALF WOLF.
"I TOOK 'IM HOME TO THE WIFE...THOUGHT THE PUP AND THE BOY COULD GROW UP TOGETHER."

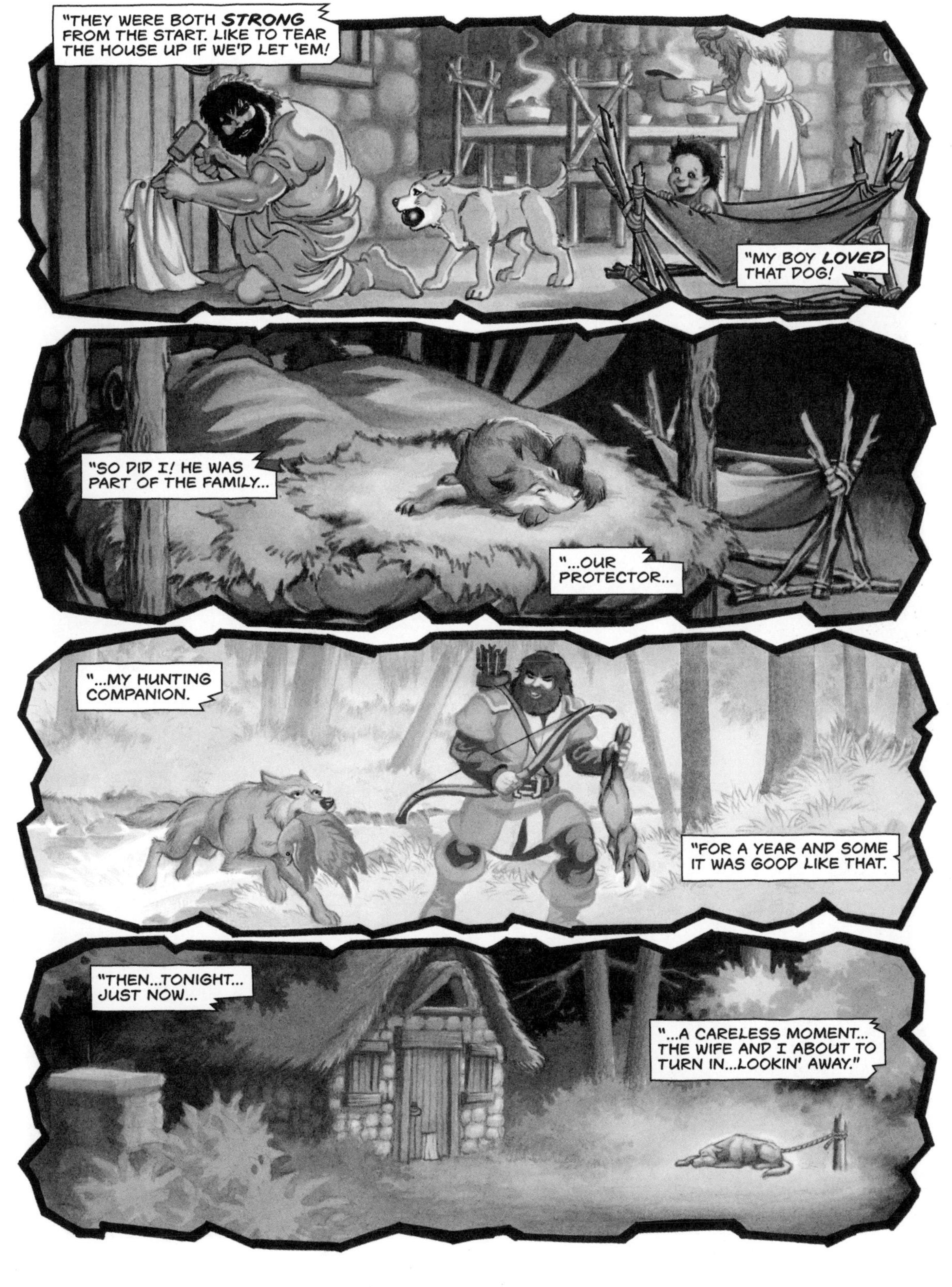
"THEY WERE BOTH STRONG FROM THE START. LIKE TO TEAR THE HOUSE UP IF WE'D LET 'EM!
"MY BOY LOVED THAT DOG!
"SO DID I! HE WAS PART OF THE FAMILY...
"...OUR PROTECTOR...
"...MY HUNTING COMPANION.
"FOR A YEAR AND SOME IT WAS GOOD LIKE THAT.
"THEN...TONIGHT... JUST NOW...
"...A CARELESS MOMENT... THE WIFE AND I ABOUT TO TURN IN...LOOKIN' AWAY."

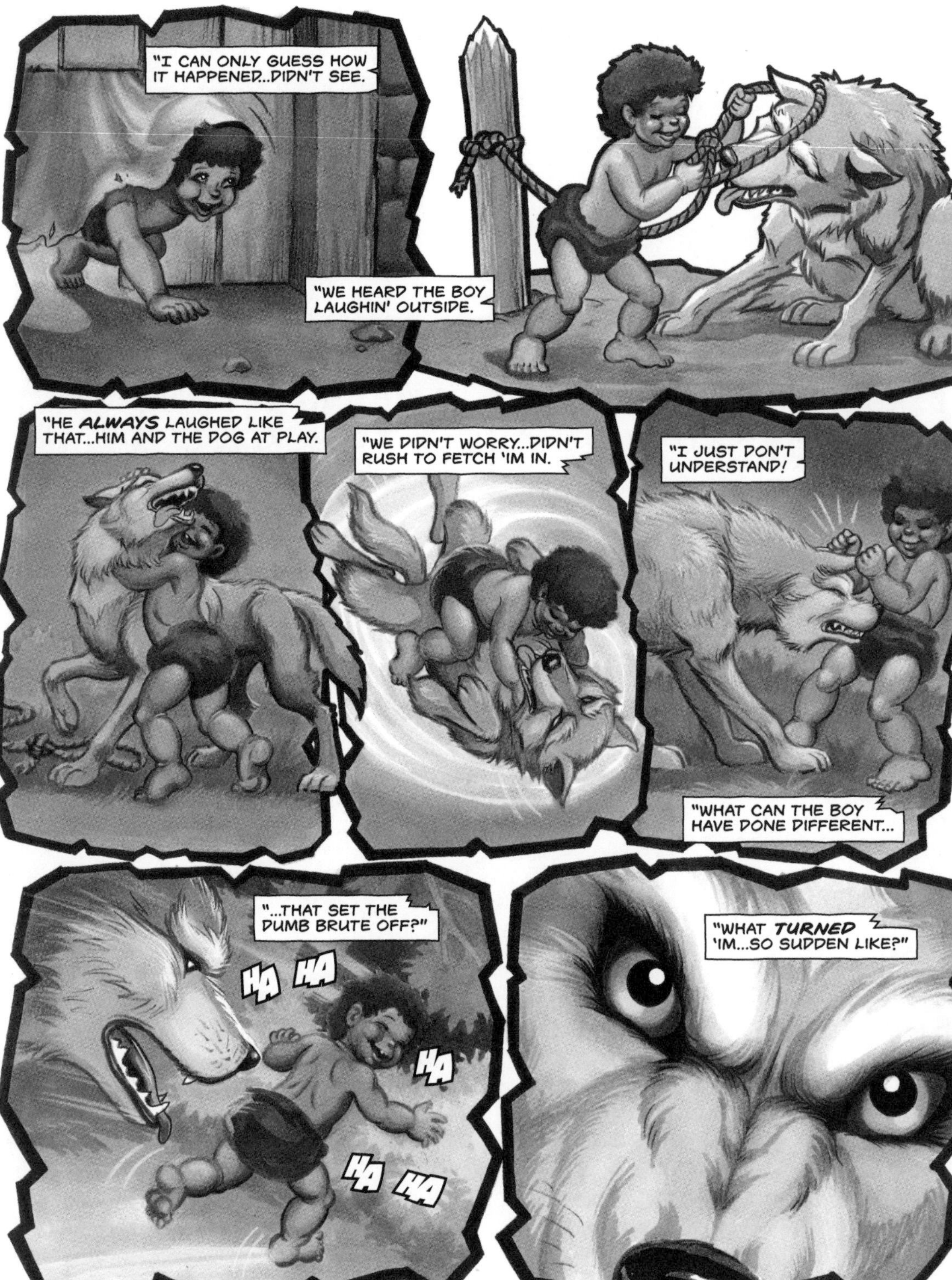
"I CAN ONLY GUESS HOW IT HAPPENED...DIDN'T SEE.
"WE HEARD THE BOY LAUGHIN' OUTSIDE.
"HE ALWAYS LAUGHED LIKE THAT...HIM AND THE DOG AT PLAY.
"WE DIDN'T WORRY...DIDN'T RUSH TO FETCH 'IM IN.
"I JUST DON'T UNDERSTAND!
"WHAT CAN THE BOY HAVE DONE DIFFERENT...
"...THAT SET THE DUMB BRUTE OFF?"
HA HA
HA
HA HA
"WHAT TURNED 'IM...SO SUDDEN LIKE?"

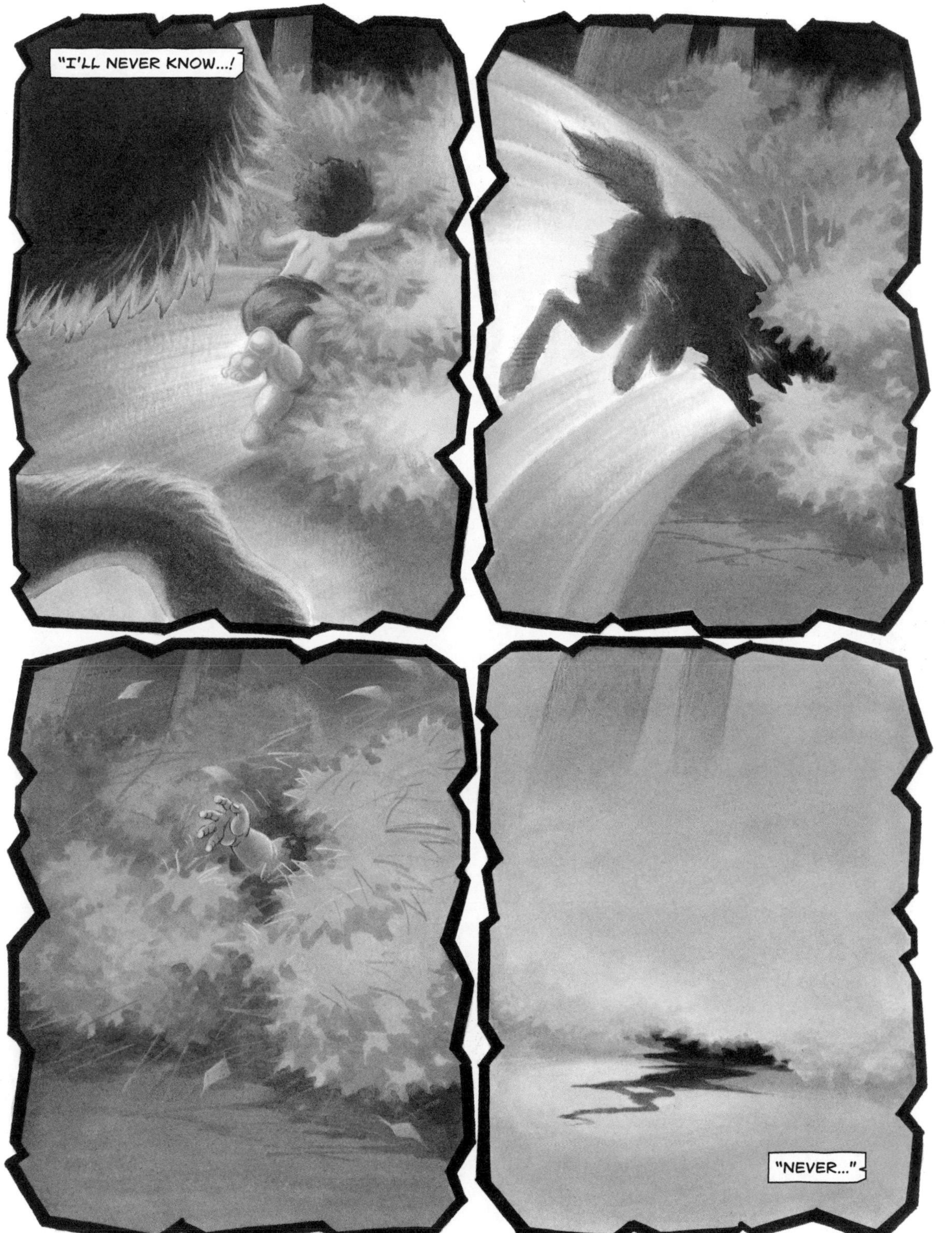
"I'LL NEVER KNOW...!
"NEVER..."

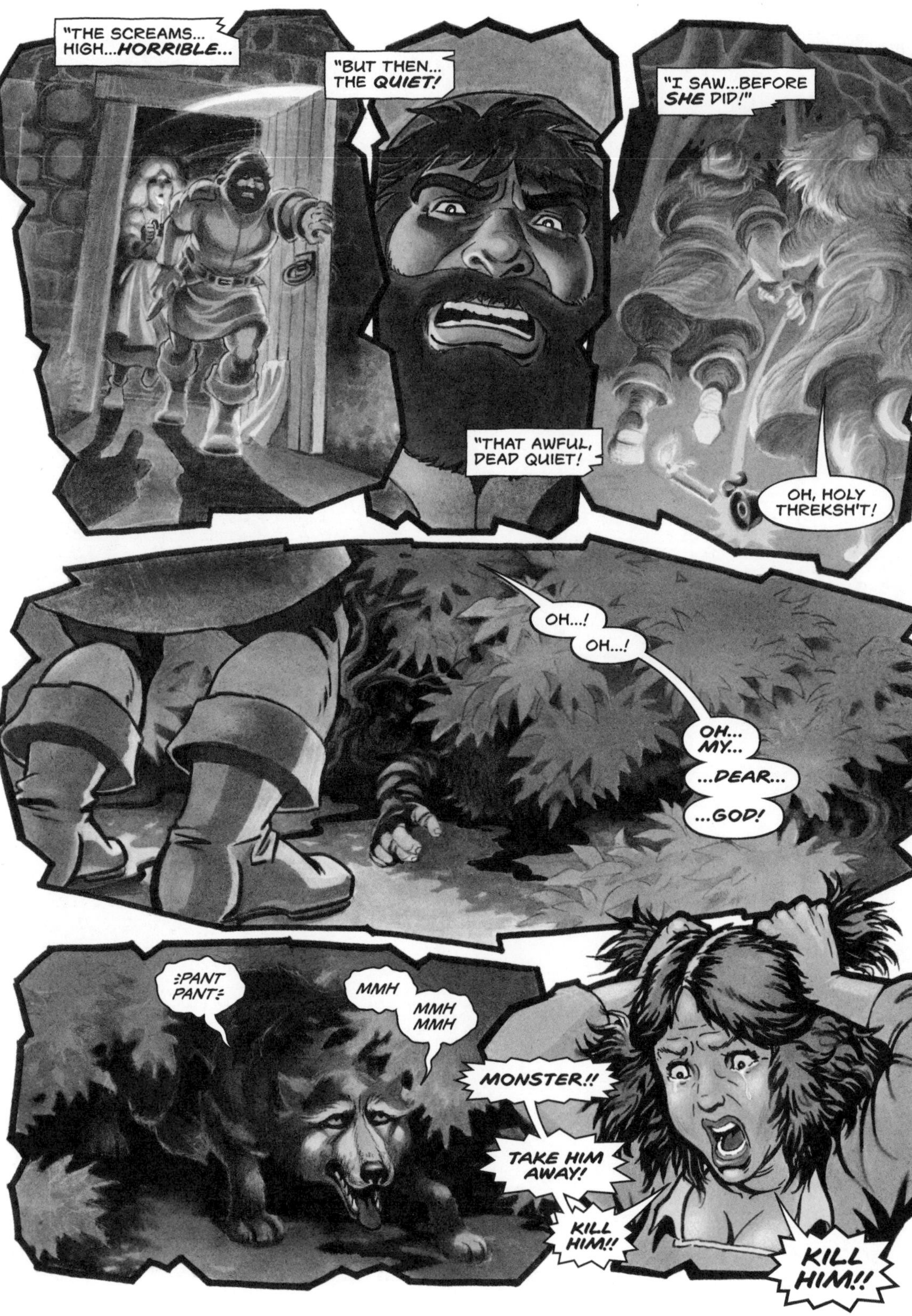

"THE SCREAMS... HIGH...HORRIBLE...
"BUT THEN... THE QUIET!
"THAT AWFUL, DEAD QUIET!
"I SAW...BEFORE SHE DID!"
OH, HOLY THREKSH'T!
OH...!
OH...!
OH... MY...
...DEAR...
...GOD!
PANT PANT
MMH
MMH MMH
MONSTER!!
TAKE HIM AWAY!
KILL HIM!!
KILL HIM!!

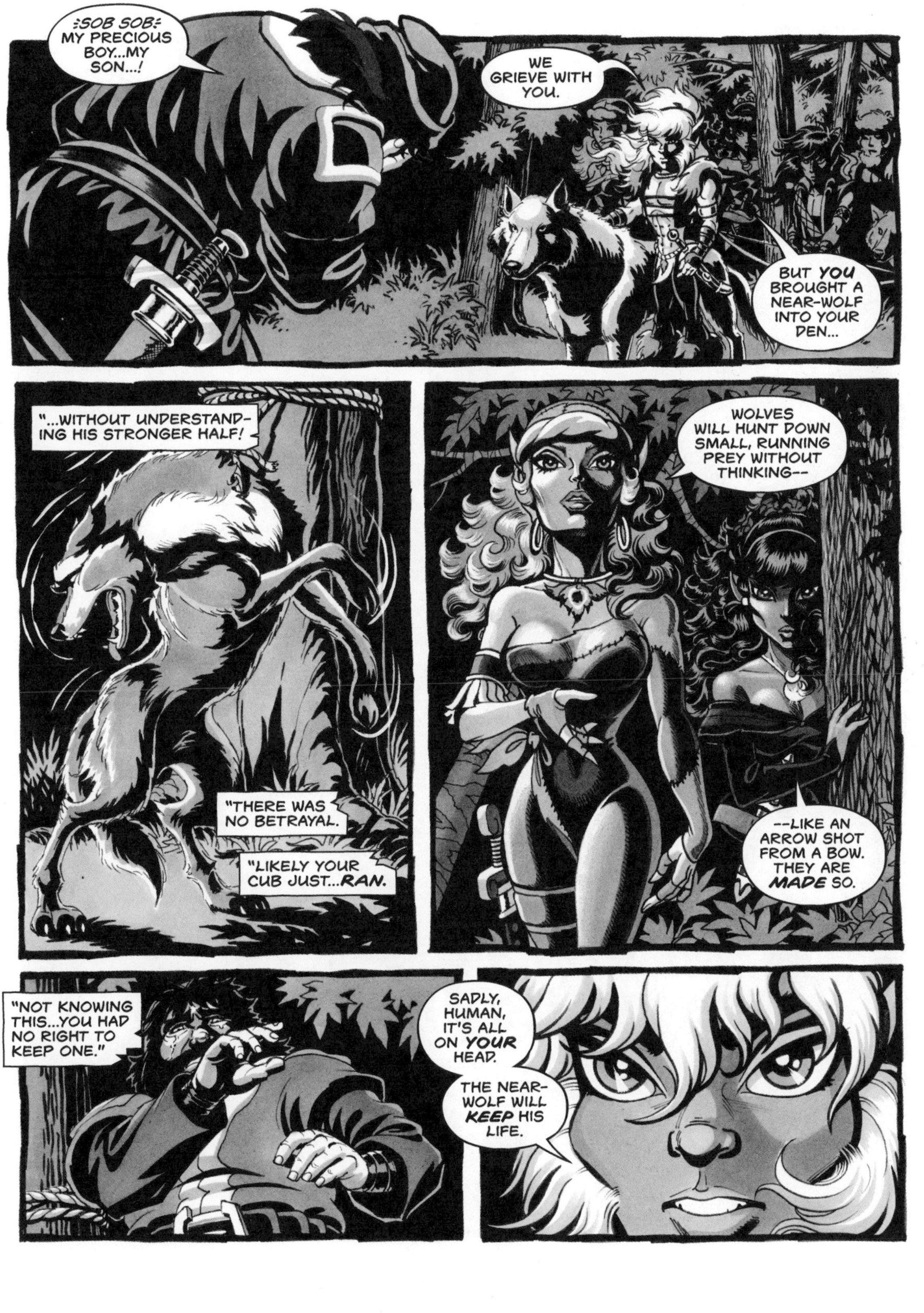
:SOB SOB: MY PRECIOUS BOY...MY SON...!
WE GRIEVE WITH YOU.
BUT *YOU* BROUGHT A NEAR-WOLF INTO YOUR DEN...
"...WITHOUT UNDERSTANDING HIS STRONGER HALF!
"THERE WAS NO BETRAYAL.
"LIKELY YOUR CUB JUST...*RAN.*
WOLVES WILL HUNT DOWN SMALL, RUNNING PREY WITHOUT THINKING--
--LIKE AN ARROW SHOT FROM A BOW. THEY ARE *MADE* SO.
"NOT KNOWING THIS...YOU HAD NO RIGHT TO KEEP ONE."
SADLY, HUMAN, IT'S ALL ON *YOUR* HEAD.
THE NEAR-WOLF WILL *KEEP* HIS LIFE.

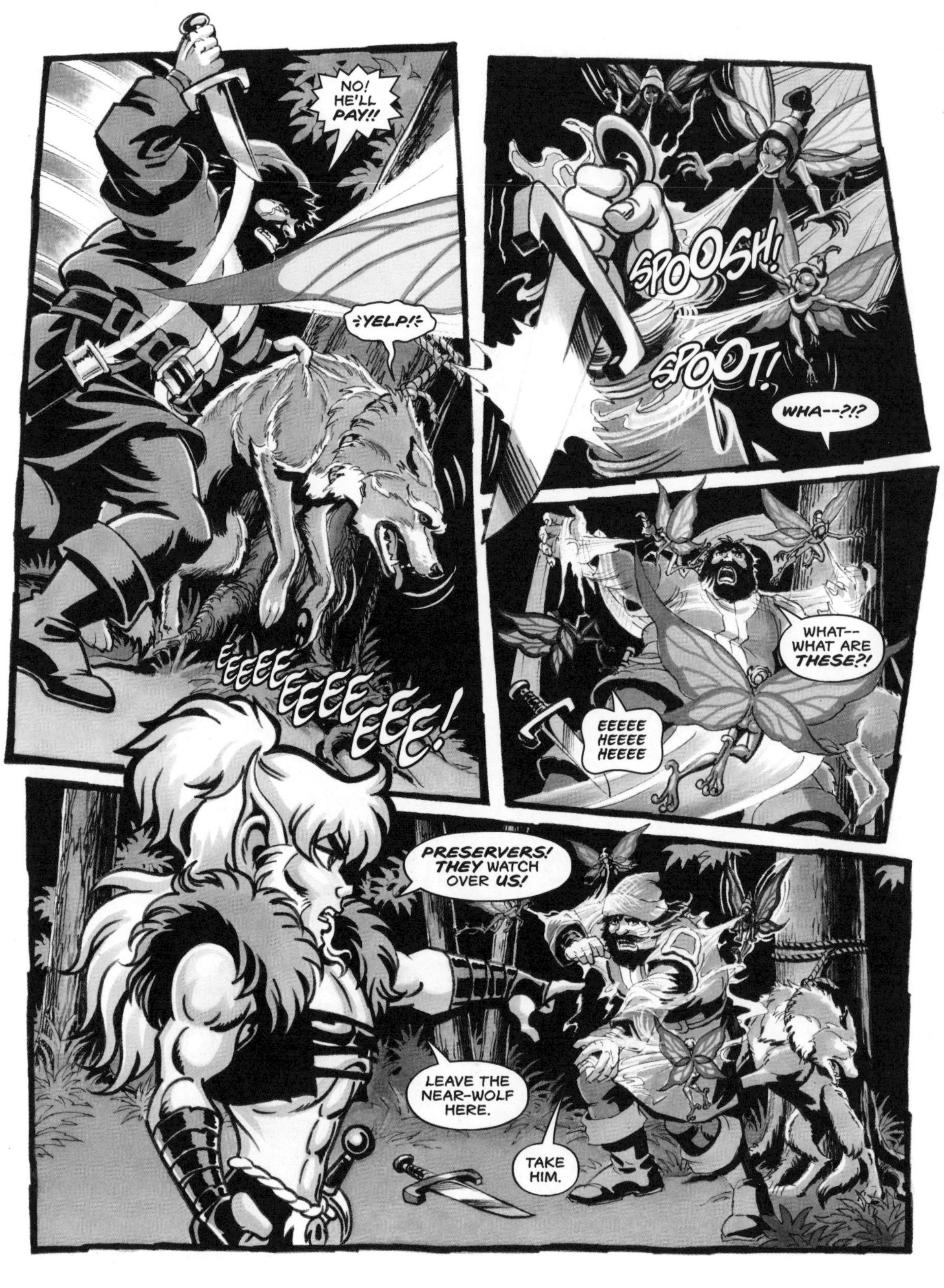
NO! HE'LL PAY!!
YELP!
EEEEEEEEEEEEE!
SPOOSH!
SPOOT!
WHA--?!?
WHAT-- WHAT ARE THESE?!
EEEEE HEEEE HEEEE
PRESERVERS! THEY WATCH OVER US!
LEAVE THE NEAR-WOLF HERE.
TAKE HIM.

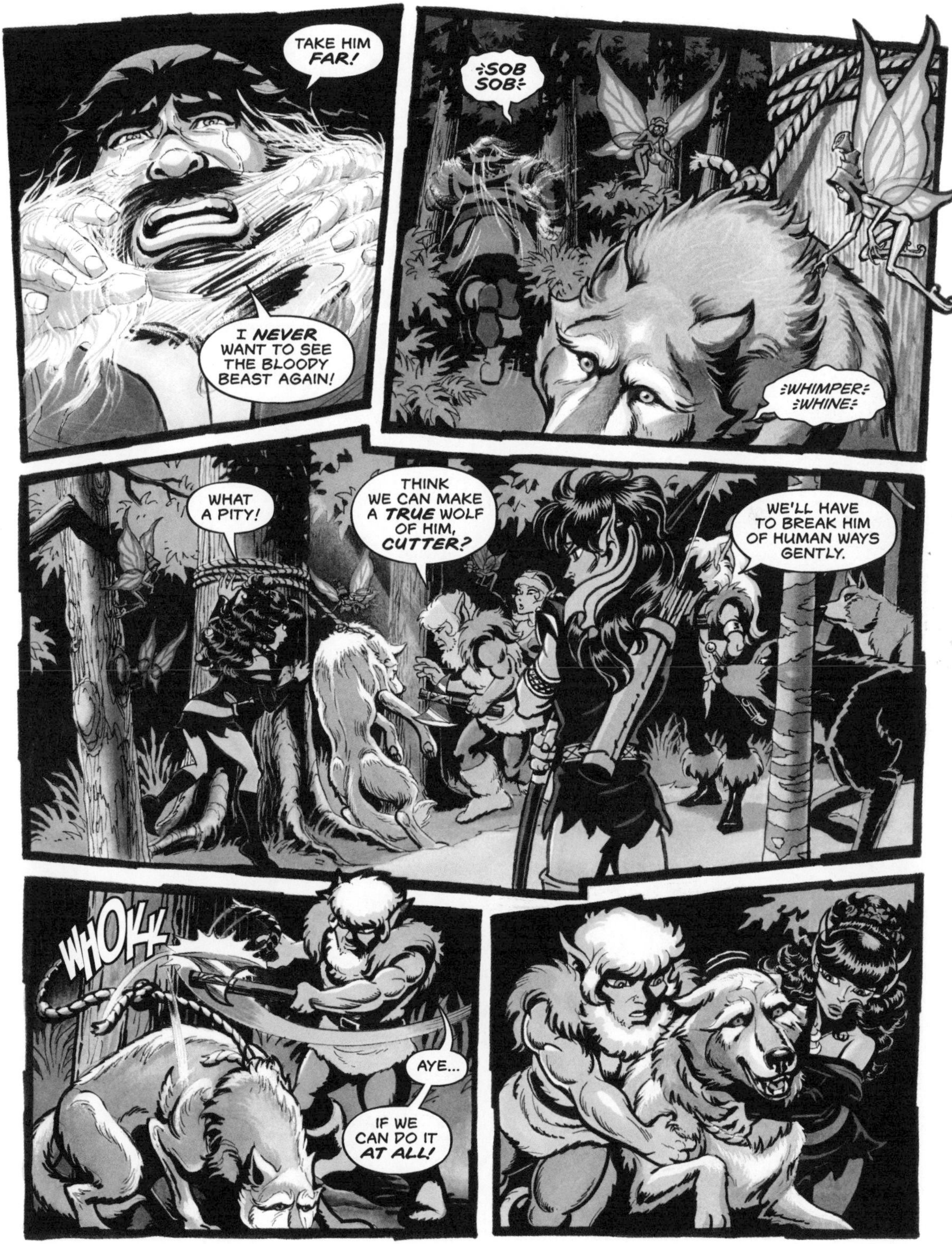
TAKE HIM FAR!
I NEVER WANT TO SEE THE BLOODY BEAST AGAIN!
SOB SOB
WHIMPER WHINE
WHAT A PITY!
THINK WE CAN MAKE A TRUE WOLF OF HIM, CUTTER?
WE'LL HAVE TO BREAK HIM OF HUMAN WAYS GENTLY.
WHOKK
AYE...
IF WE CAN DO IT AT ALL!

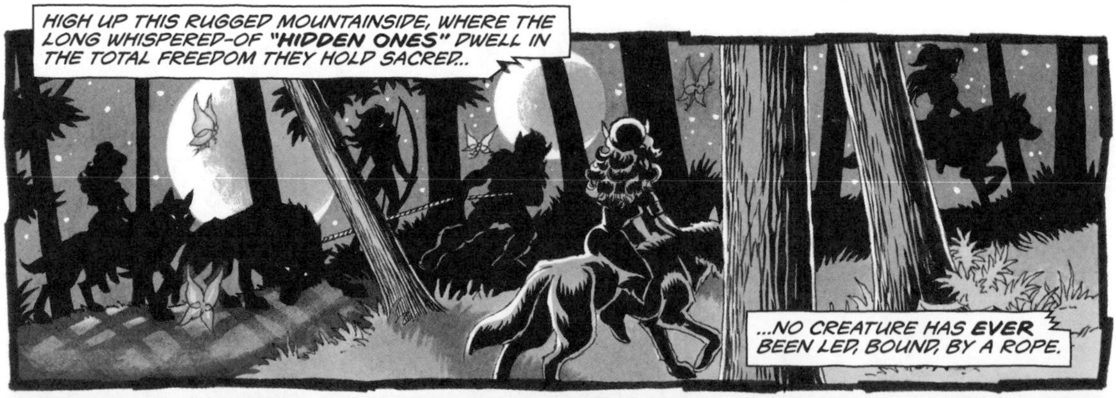

HIGH UP THIS RUGGED MOUNTAINSIDE, WHERE THE LONG WHISPERED-OF "HIDDEN ONES" DWELL IN THE TOTAL FREEDOM THEY HOLD SACRED...
...NO CREATURE HAS EVER BEEN LED, BOUND, BY A ROPE.

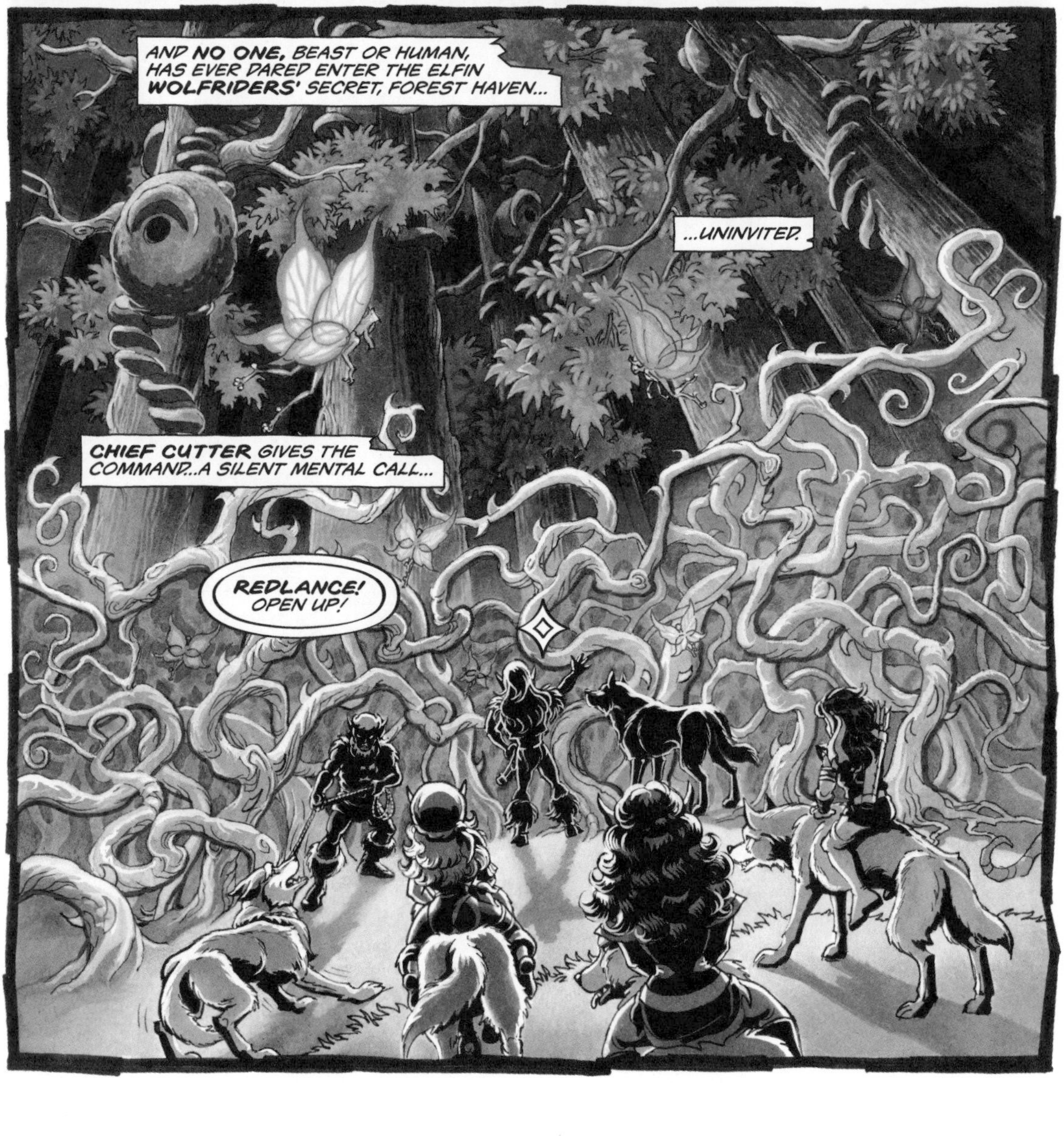

AND NO ONE, BEAST OR HUMAN, HAS EVER DARED ENTER THE ELFIN WOLFRIDERS' SECRET, FOREST HAVEN...
...UNINVITED.
CHIEF CUTTER GIVES THE COMMAND...A SILENT MENTAL CALL...
REDLANCE! OPEN UP!

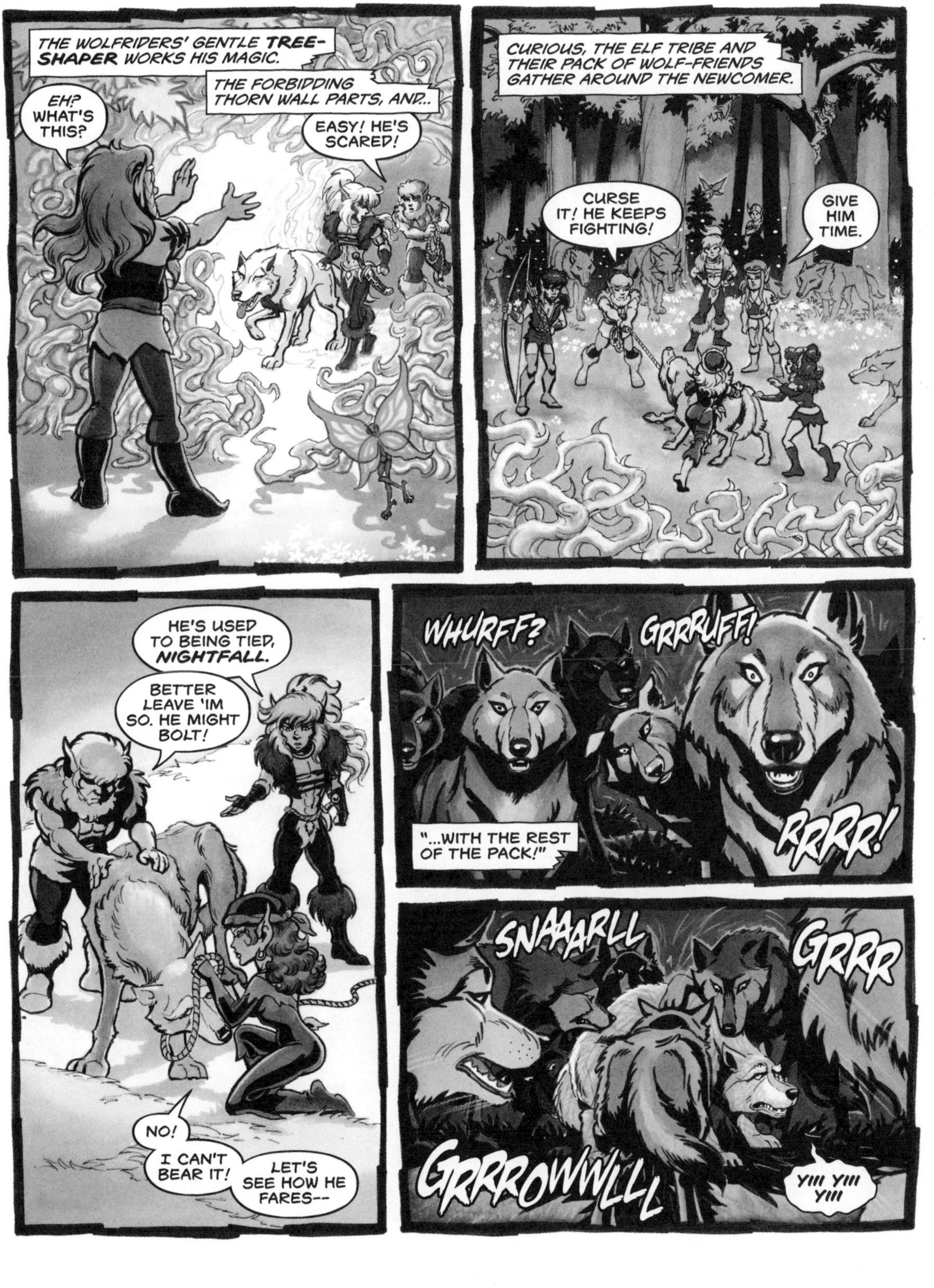
THE WOLFRIDERS' GENTLE TREE-SHAPER WORKS HIS MAGIC.
THE FORBIDDING THORN WALL PARTS, AND...
EH? WHAT'S THIS?
EASY! HE'S SCARED!
CURIOUS, THE ELF TRIBE AND THEIR PACK OF WOLF-FRIENDS GATHER AROUND THE NEWCOMER.
CURSE IT! HE KEEPS FIGHTING!
GIVE HIM TIME.
HE'S USED TO BEING TIED, NIGHTFALL.
BETTER LEAVE 'IM SO. HE MIGHT BOLT!
NO! I CAN'T BEAR IT!
LET'S SEE HOW HE FARES--
WHURFF?
GRRRUFF!
"...WITH THE REST OF THE PACK!"
RRRR!
SNAAARLL
GRRR
GRRROWWLLL
YIII YIII YIII

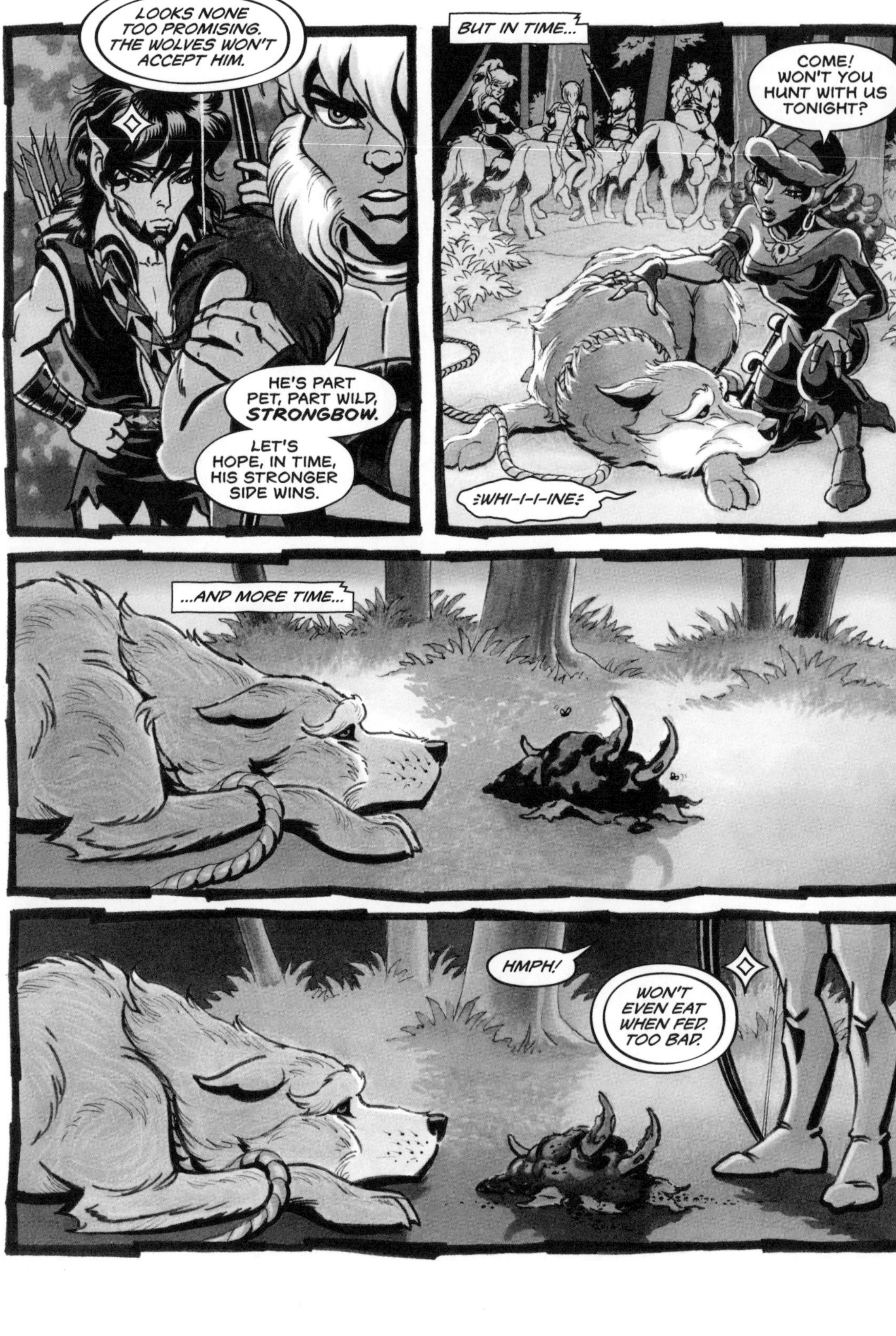
LOOKS NONE TOO PROMISING. THE WOLVES WON'T ACCEPT HIM.
HE'S PART PET, PART WILD, STRONGBOW.
LET'S HOPE, IN TIME, HIS STRONGER SIDE WINS.
BUT IN TIME...
COME! WON'T YOU HUNT WITH US TONIGHT?
WHI-I-I-INE
...AND MORE TIME...
HMPH!
WON'T EVEN EAT WHEN FED. TOO BAD.

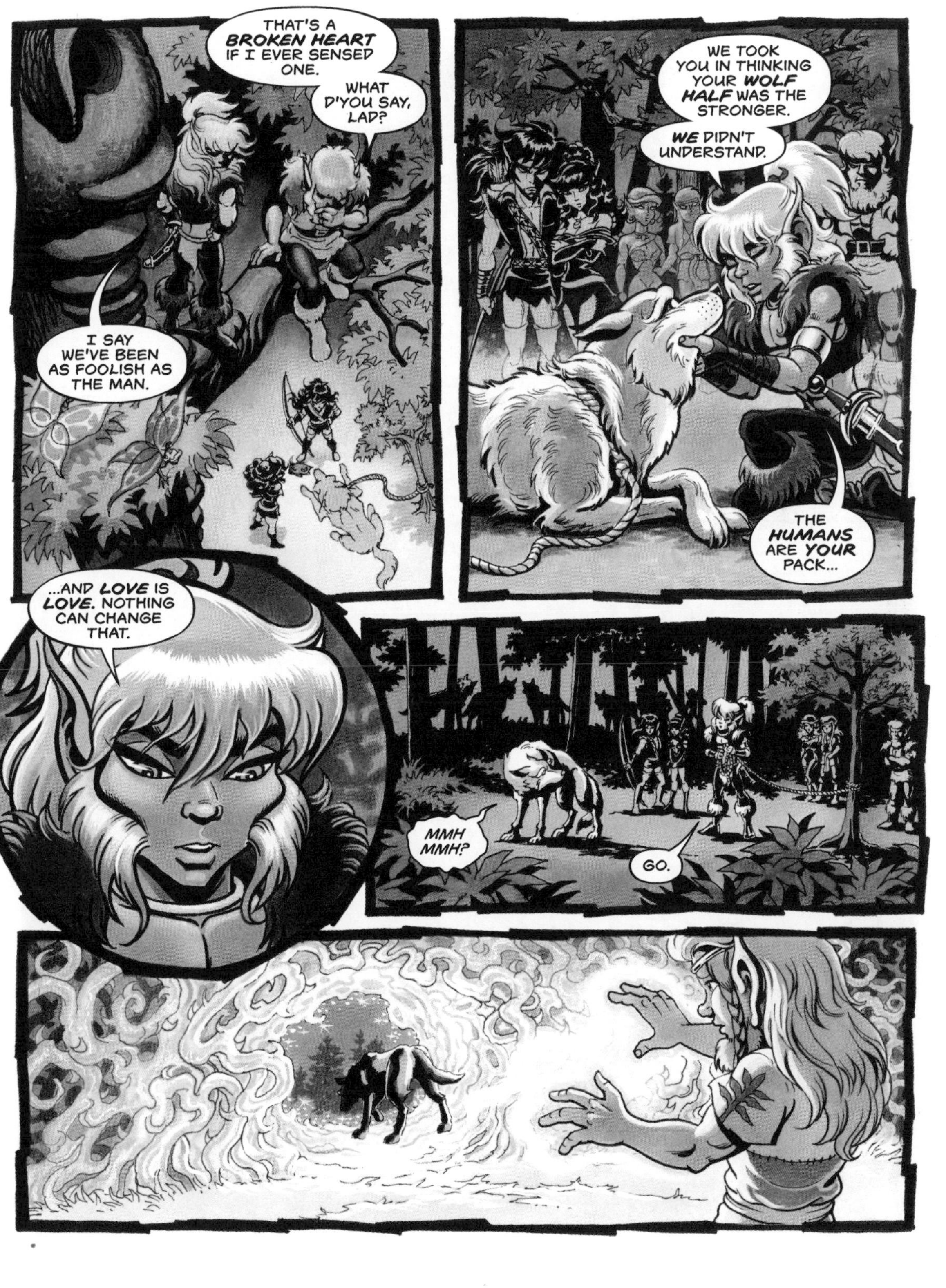

THAT'S A BROKEN HEART IF I EVER SENSED ONE.
WHAT D'YOU SAY, LAD?
I SAY WE'VE BEEN AS FOOLISH AS THE MAN.
WE TOOK YOU IN THINKING YOUR WOLF HALF WAS THE STRONGER.
WE DIDN'T UNDERSTAND.
THE HUMANS ARE YOUR PACK...
...AND LOVE IS LOVE. NOTHING CAN CHANGE THAT.
MMH MMH?
GO.

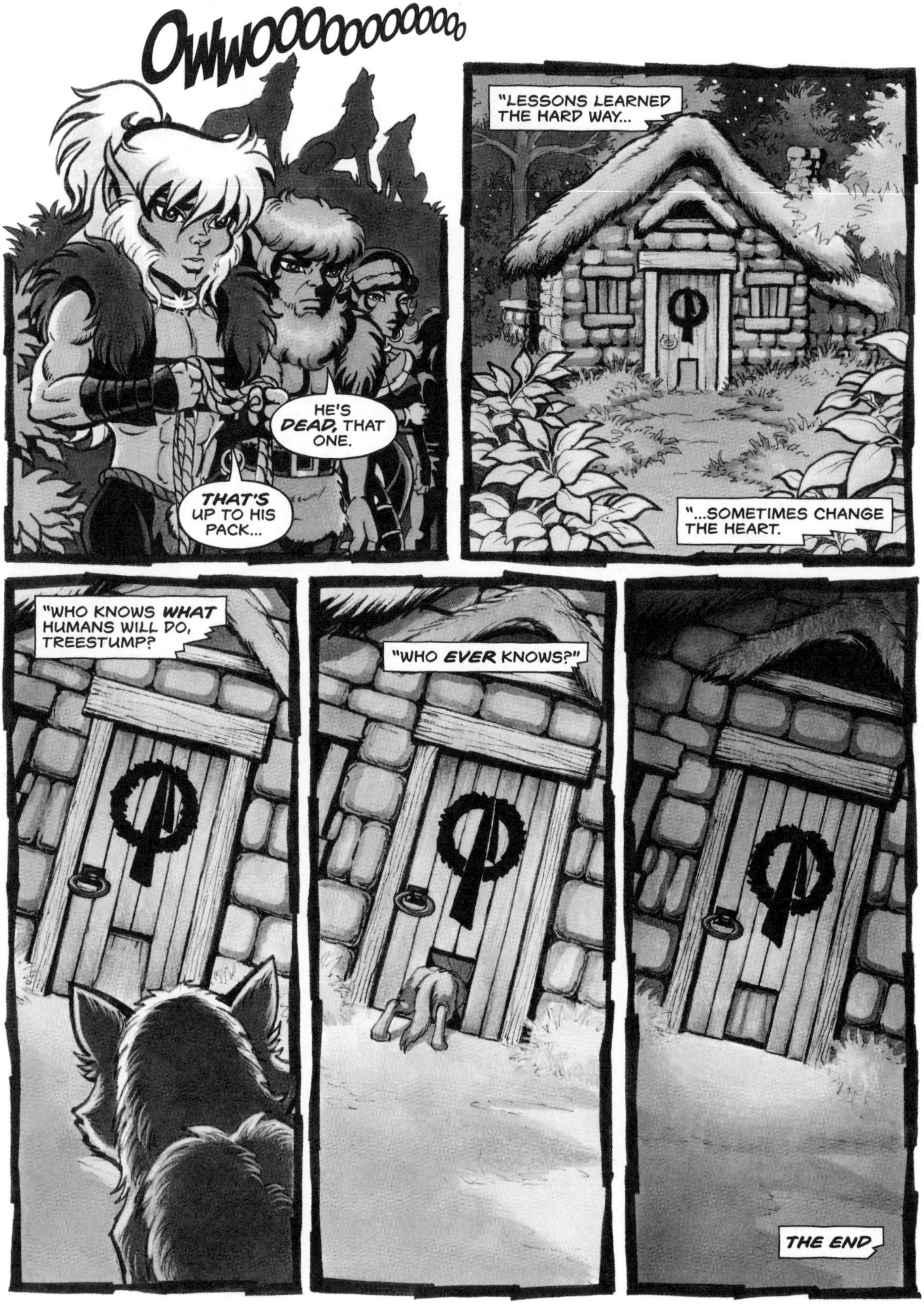

OWWOOOOOOOOOOOOO
HE'S *DEAD,* THAT ONE.
THAT'S UP TO HIS PACK...
"LESSONS LEARNED THE HARD WAY...
"...SOMETIMES CHANGE THE HEART.
"WHO KNOWS *WHAT* HUMANS WILL DO, TREESTUMP?
"WHO *EVER* KNOWS?"
THE END

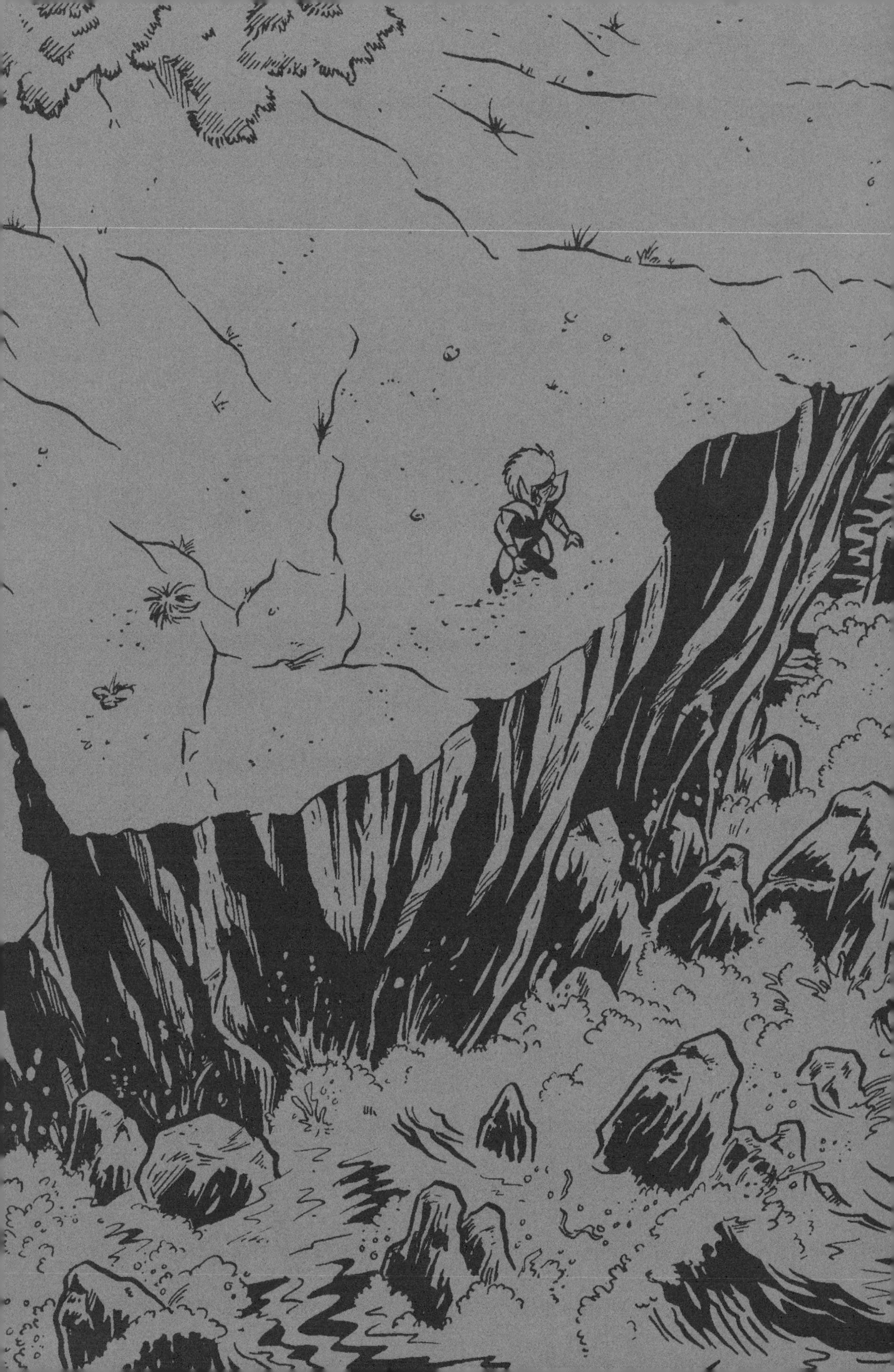

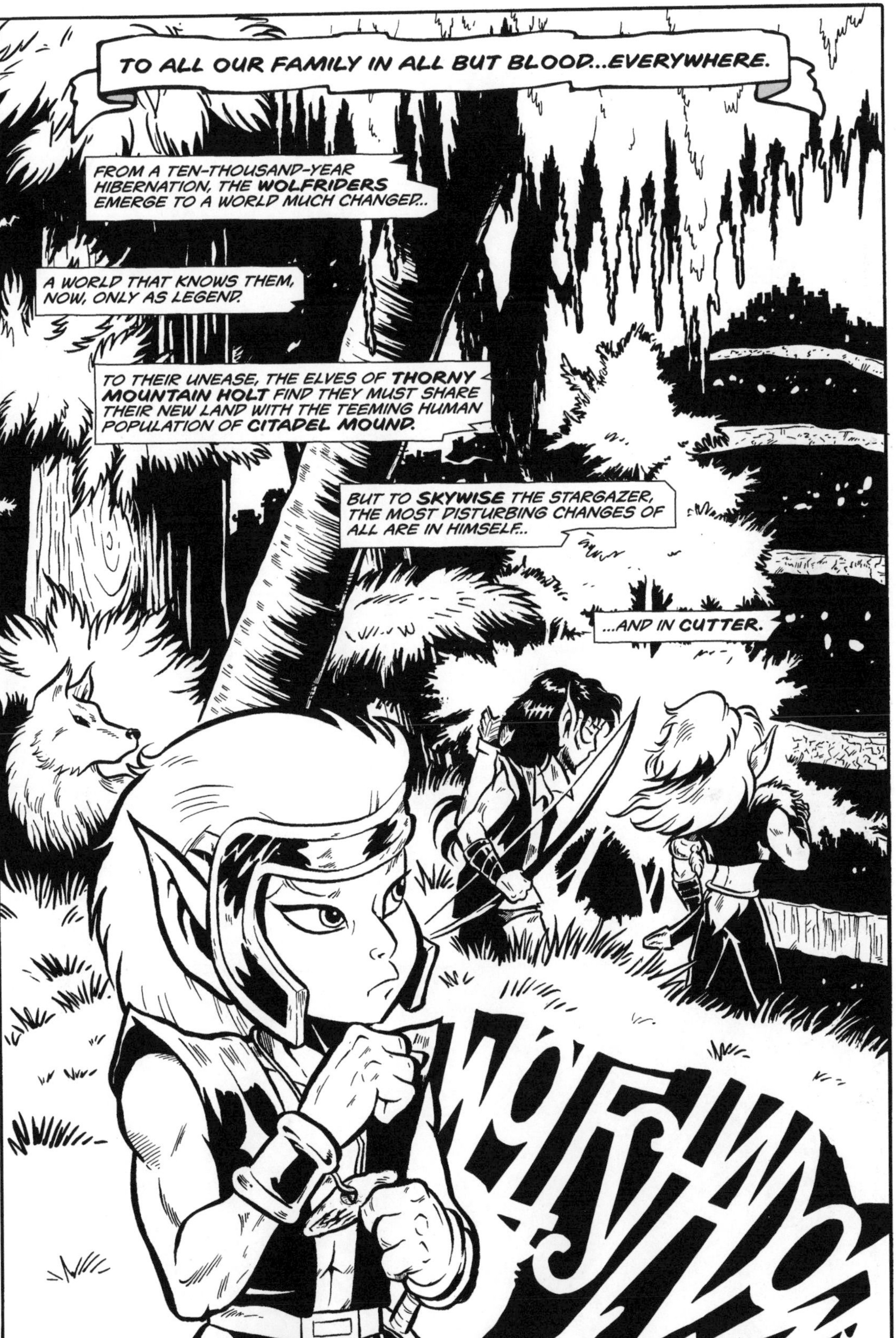
TO ALL OUR FAMILY IN ALL BUT BLOOD...EVERYWHERE.
FROM A TEN-THOUSAND-YEAR HIBERNATION, THE WOLFRIDERS EMERGE TO A WORLD MUCH CHANGED..
A WORLD THAT KNOWS THEM, NOW, ONLY AS LEGEND.
TO THEIR UNEASE, THE ELVES OF THORNY MOUNTAIN HOLT FIND THEY MUST SHARE THEIR NEW LAND WITH THE TEEMING HUMAN POPULATION OF CITADEL MOUND.
BUT TO SKYWISE THE STARGAZER, THE MOST DISTURBING CHANGES OF ALL ARE IN HIMSELF..
...AND IN CUTTER.

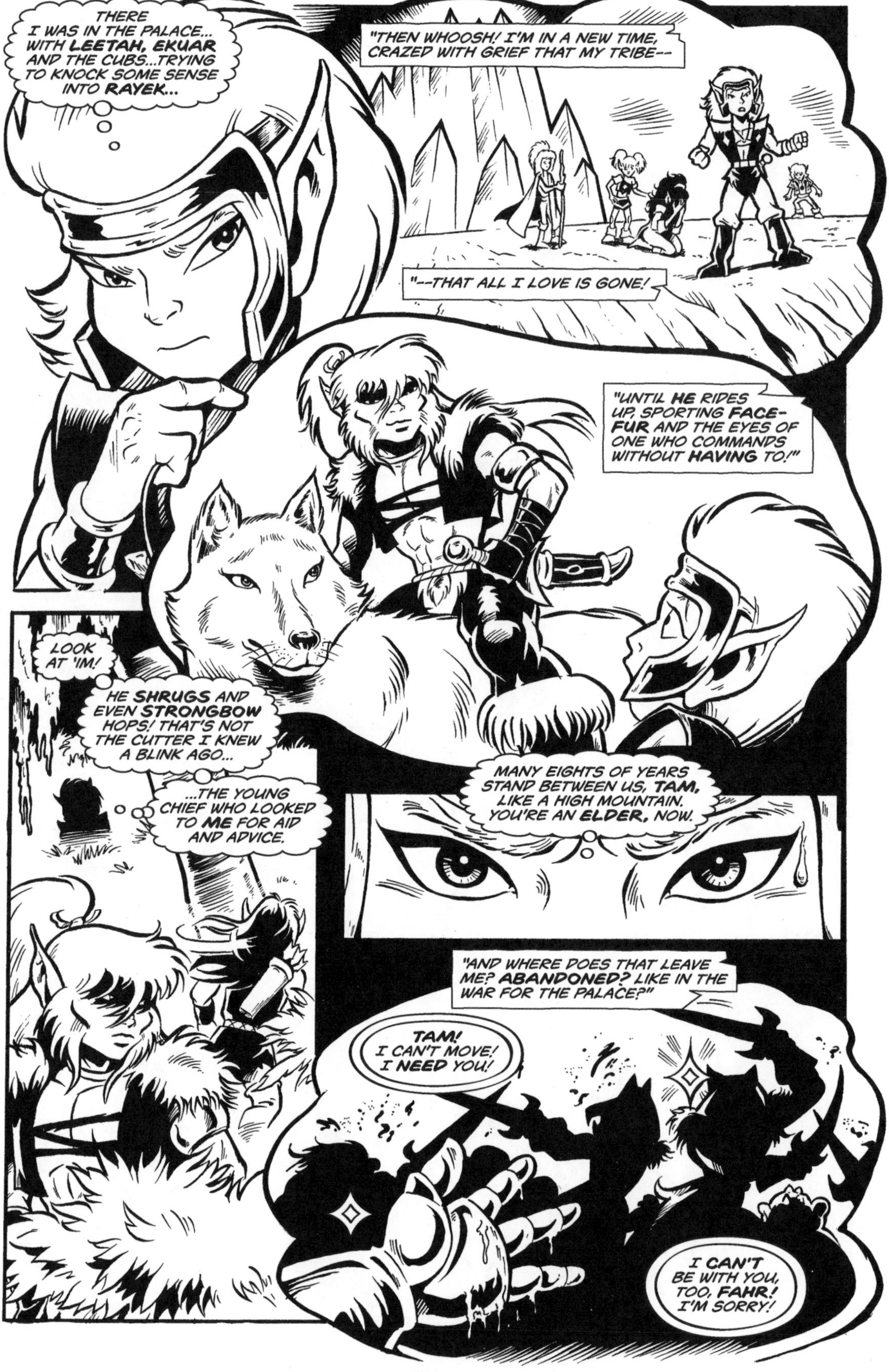
THERE I WAS IN THE PALACE... WITH LEETAH, EKUAR AND THE CUBS...TRYING TO KNOCK SOME SENSE INTO RAYEK...
"THEN WHOOSH! I'M IN A NEW TIME, CRAZED WITH GRIEF THAT MY TRIBE--
"--THAT ALL I LOVE IS GONE!
"UNTIL HE RIDES UP, SPORTING FACE-FUR AND THE EYES OF ONE WHO COMMANDS WITHOUT HAVING TO!"
LOOK AT 'IM!
HE SHRUGS AND EVEN STRONGBOW HOPS! THAT'S NOT THE CUTTER I KNEW A BLINK AGO...
...THE YOUNG CHIEF WHO LOOKED TO ME FOR AID AND ADVICE.
MANY EIGHTS OF YEARS STAND BETWEEN US, TAM, LIKE A HIGH MOUNTAIN. YOU'RE AN ELDER, NOW.
"AND WHERE DOES THAT LEAVE ME? ABANDONED? LIKE IN THE WAR FOR THE PALACE?"
TAM! I CAN'T MOVE! I NEED YOU!
I CAN'T BE WITH YOU, TOO, FAHR! I'M SORRY!

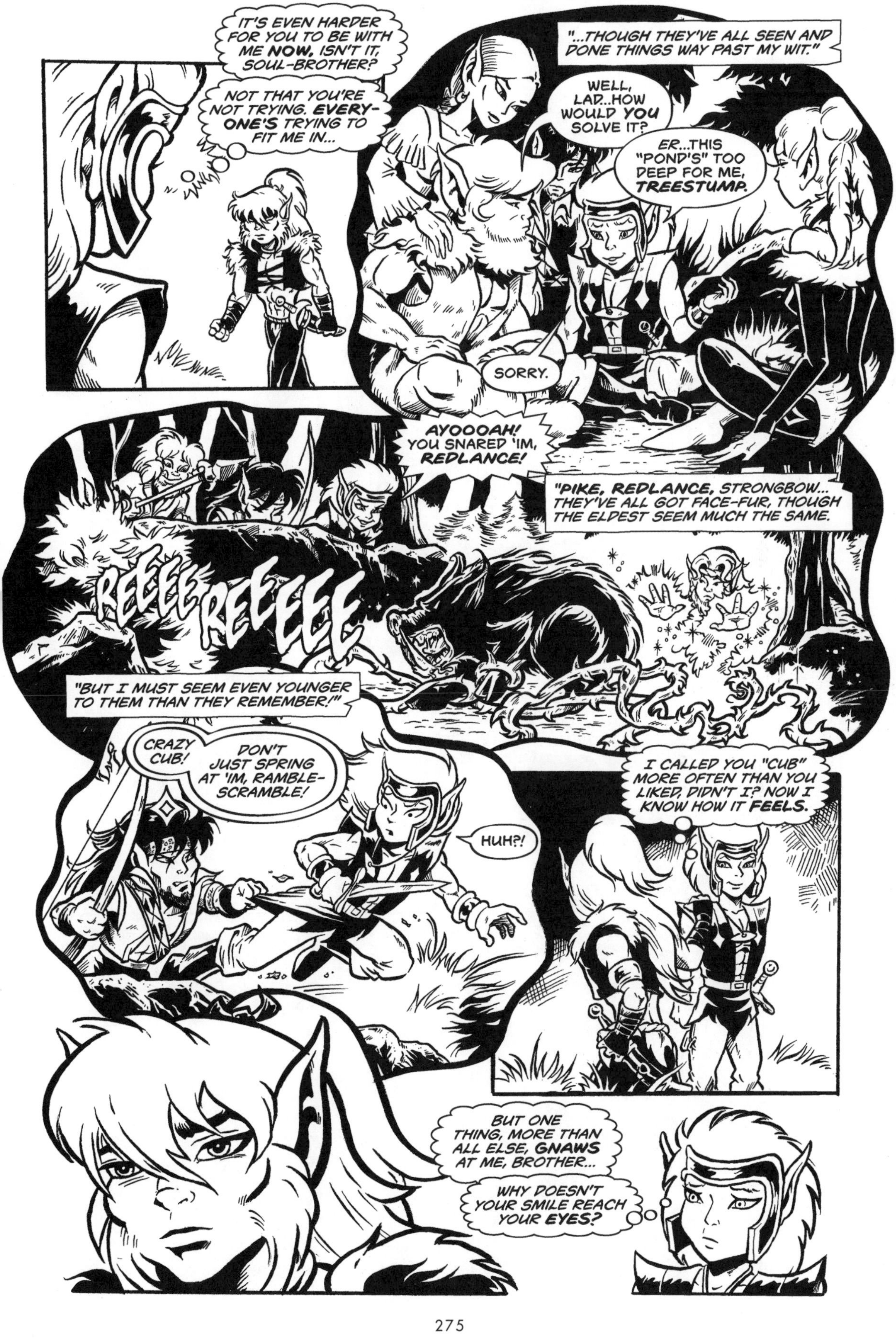
IT'S EVEN HARDER FOR YOU TO BE WITH ME NOW, ISN'T IT, SOUL-BROTHER?
NOT THAT YOU'RE NOT TRYING. EVERY-ONE'S TRYING TO FIT ME IN...
"...THOUGH THEY'VE ALL SEEN AND DONE THINGS WAY PAST MY WIT."
WELL, LAD...HOW WOULD YOU SOLVE IT?
ER...THIS "POND'S" TOO DEEP FOR ME, TREESTUMP.
SORRY.
AYOOOAH! YOU SNARED 'IM, REDLANCE!
"PIKE, REDLANCE, STRONGBOW... THEY'VE ALL GOT FACE-FUR, THOUGH THE ELDEST SEEM MUCH THE SAME.
REEEE REEEEEE
"BUT I MUST SEEM EVEN YOUNGER TO THEM THAN THEY REMEMBER!"
CRAZY CUB!
DON'T JUST SPRING AT 'IM, RAMBLE-SCRAMBLE!
HUH?!
I CALLED YOU "CUB" MORE OFTEN THAN YOU LIKED, DIDN'T I? NOW I KNOW HOW IT FEELS.
BUT ONE THING, MORE THAN ALL ELSE, GNAWS AT ME, BROTHER...
WHY DOESN'T YOUR SMILE REACH YOUR EYES?

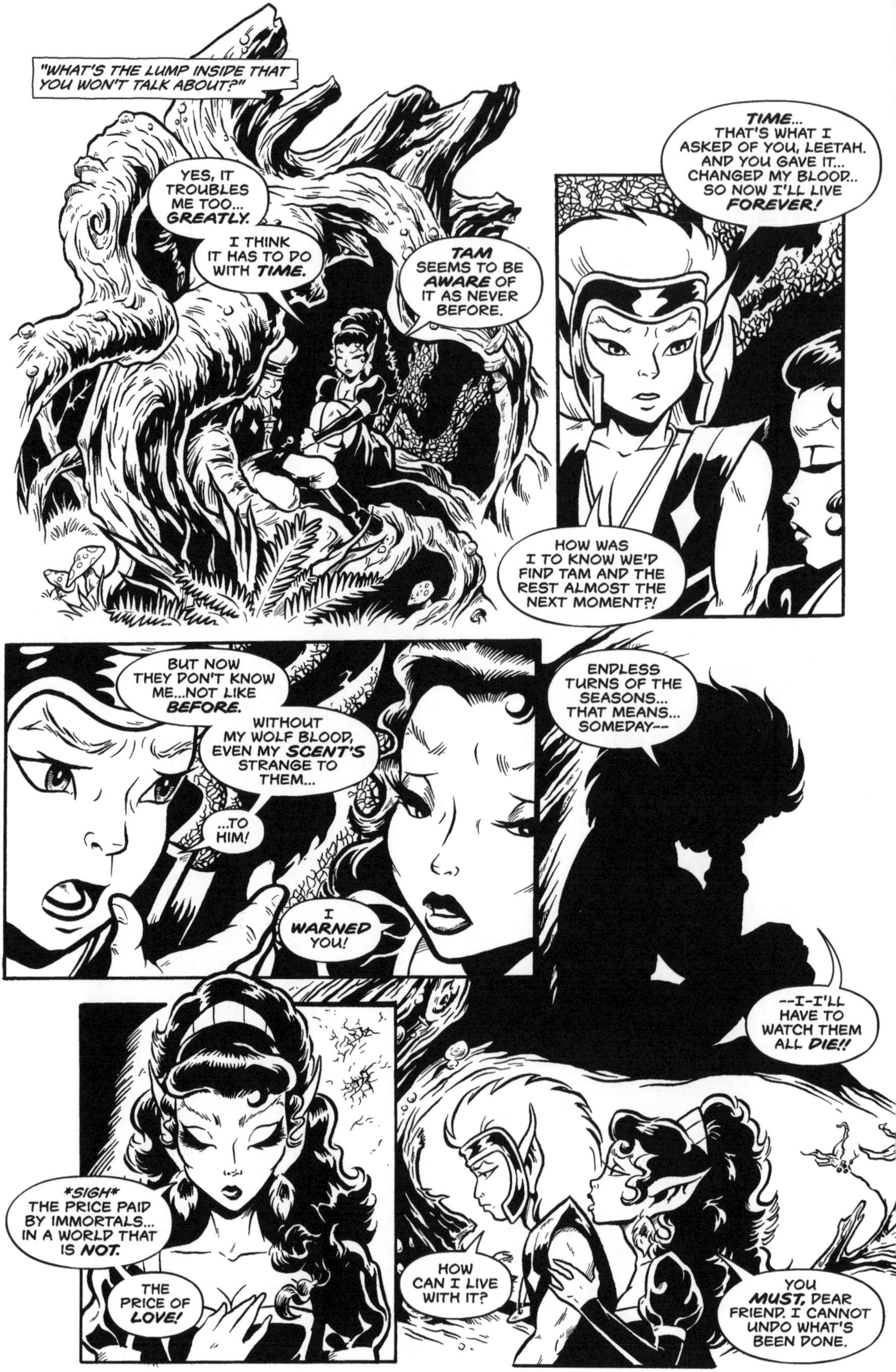
"WHAT'S THE LUMP INSIDE THAT YOU WON'T TALK ABOUT?"
YES, IT TROUBLES ME TOO... GREATLY.
I THINK IT HAS TO DO WITH TIME.
TAM SEEMS TO BE AWARE OF IT AS NEVER BEFORE.
TIME... THAT'S WHAT I ASKED OF YOU, LEETAH. AND YOU GAVE IT... CHANGED MY BLOOD.. SO NOW I'LL LIVE FOREVER!
HOW WAS I TO KNOW WE'D FIND TAM AND THE REST ALMOST THE NEXT MOMENT?!
BUT NOW THEY DON'T KNOW ME...NOT LIKE BEFORE.
WITHOUT MY WOLF BLOOD, EVEN MY SCENT'S STRANGE TO THEM...
...TO HIM!
I WARNED YOU!
ENDLESS TURNS OF THE SEASONS... THAT MEANS... SOMEDAY--
--I-I'LL HAVE TO WATCH THEM ALL DIE!!
SIGH THE PRICE PAID BY IMMORTALS... IN A WORLD THAT IS NOT.
THE PRICE OF LOVE!
HOW CAN I LIVE WITH IT?
YOU MUST, DEAR FRIEND. I CANNOT UNDO WHAT'S BEEN DONE.

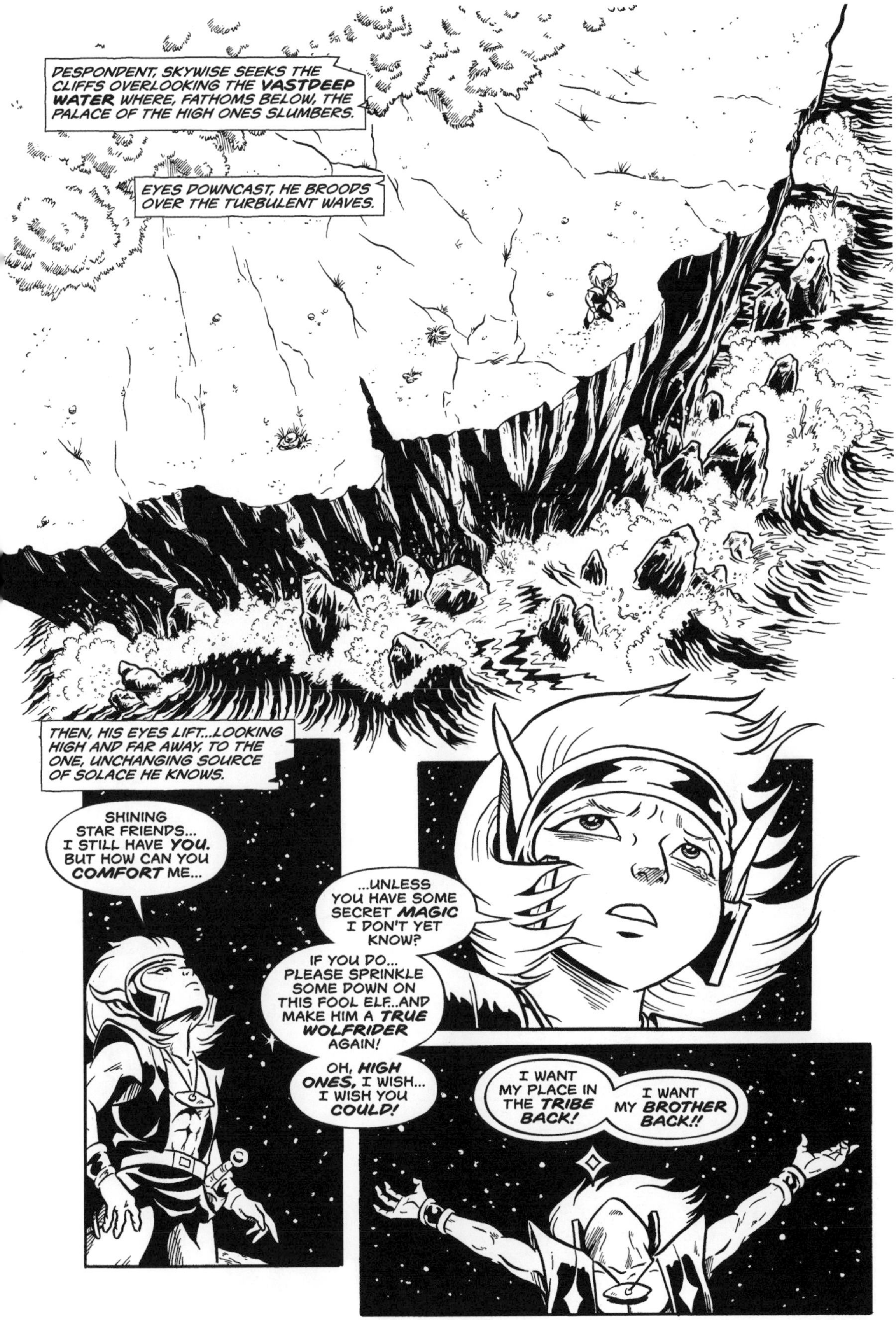
DESPONDENT, SKYWISE SEEKS THE CLIFFS OVERLOOKING THE VASTDEEP WATER WHERE, FATHOMS BELOW, THE PALACE OF THE HIGH ONES SLUMBERS.
EYES DOWNCAST, HE BROODS OVER THE TURBULENT WAVES.
THEN, HIS EYES LIFT...LOOKING HIGH AND FAR AWAY, TO THE ONE, UNCHANGING SOURCE OF SOLACE HE KNOWS.
SHINING STAR FRIENDS... I STILL HAVE YOU. BUT HOW CAN YOU COMFORT ME...
...UNLESS YOU HAVE SOME SECRET MAGIC I DON'T YET KNOW?
IF YOU DO... PLEASE SPRINKLE SOME DOWN ON THIS FOOL ELF...AND MAKE HIM A TRUE WOLFRIDER AGAIN!
OH, HIGH ONES, I WISH... I WISH YOU COULD!
I WANT MY PLACE IN THE TRIBE BACK!
I WANT MY BROTHER BACK!!

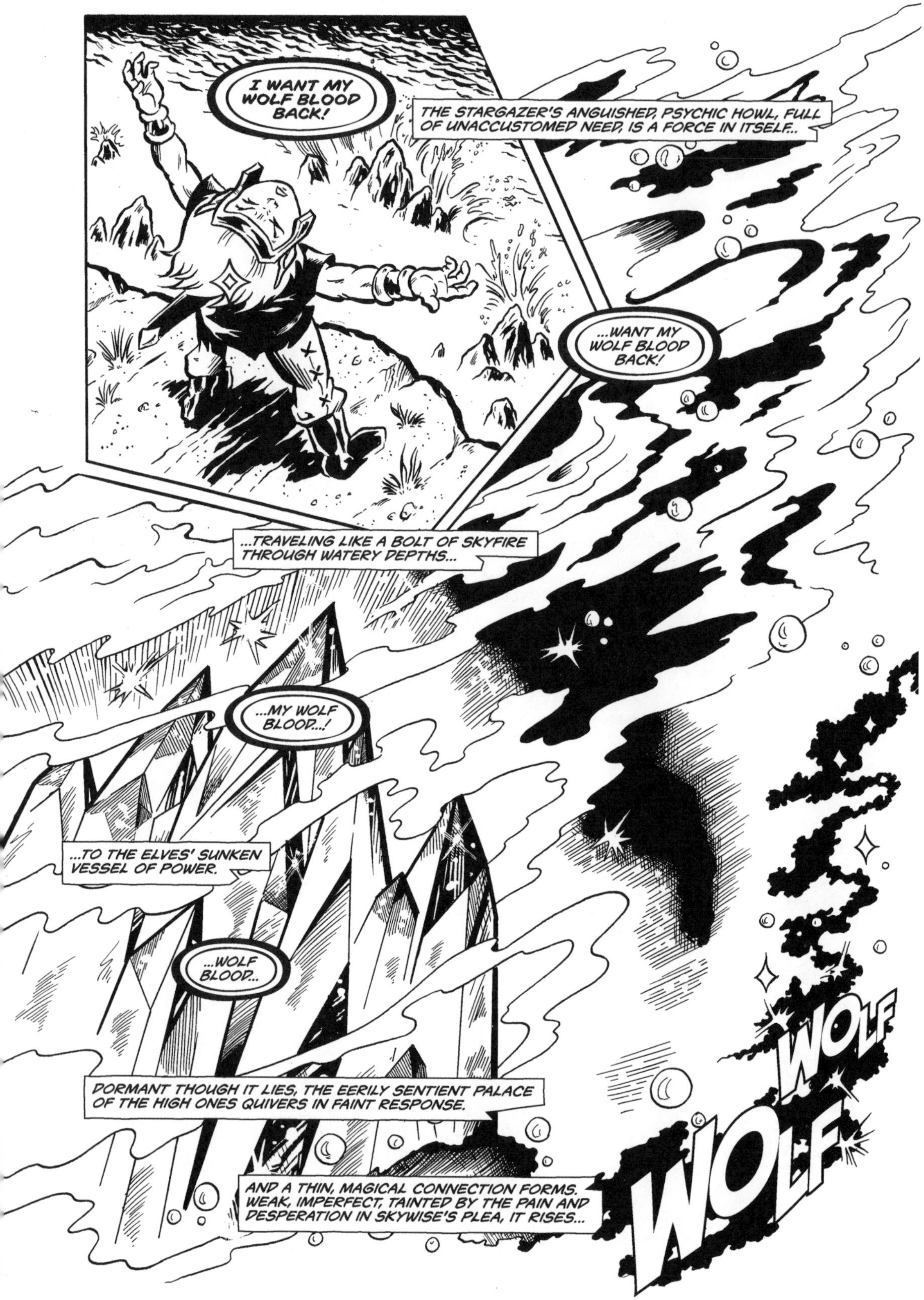
I WANT MY WOLF BLOOD BACK!
THE STARGAZER'S ANGUISHED, PSYCHIC HOWL, FULL OF UNACCUSTOMED NEED, IS A FORCE IN ITSELF...
...WANT MY WOLF BLOOD BACK!
...TRAVELING LIKE A BOLT OF SKYFIRE THROUGH WATERY DEPTHS...
...MY WOLF BLOOD...!
...TO THE ELVES' SUNKEN VESSEL OF POWER.
...WOLF BLOOD...
DORMANT THOUGH IT LIES, THE EERILY SENTIENT PALACE OF THE HIGH ONES QUIVERS IN FAINT RESPONSE.
AND A THIN, MAGICAL CONNECTION FORMS. WEAK, IMPERFECT, TAINTED BY THE PAIN AND DESPERATION IN SKYWISE'S PLEA, IT RISES...
WOLF
WOLF

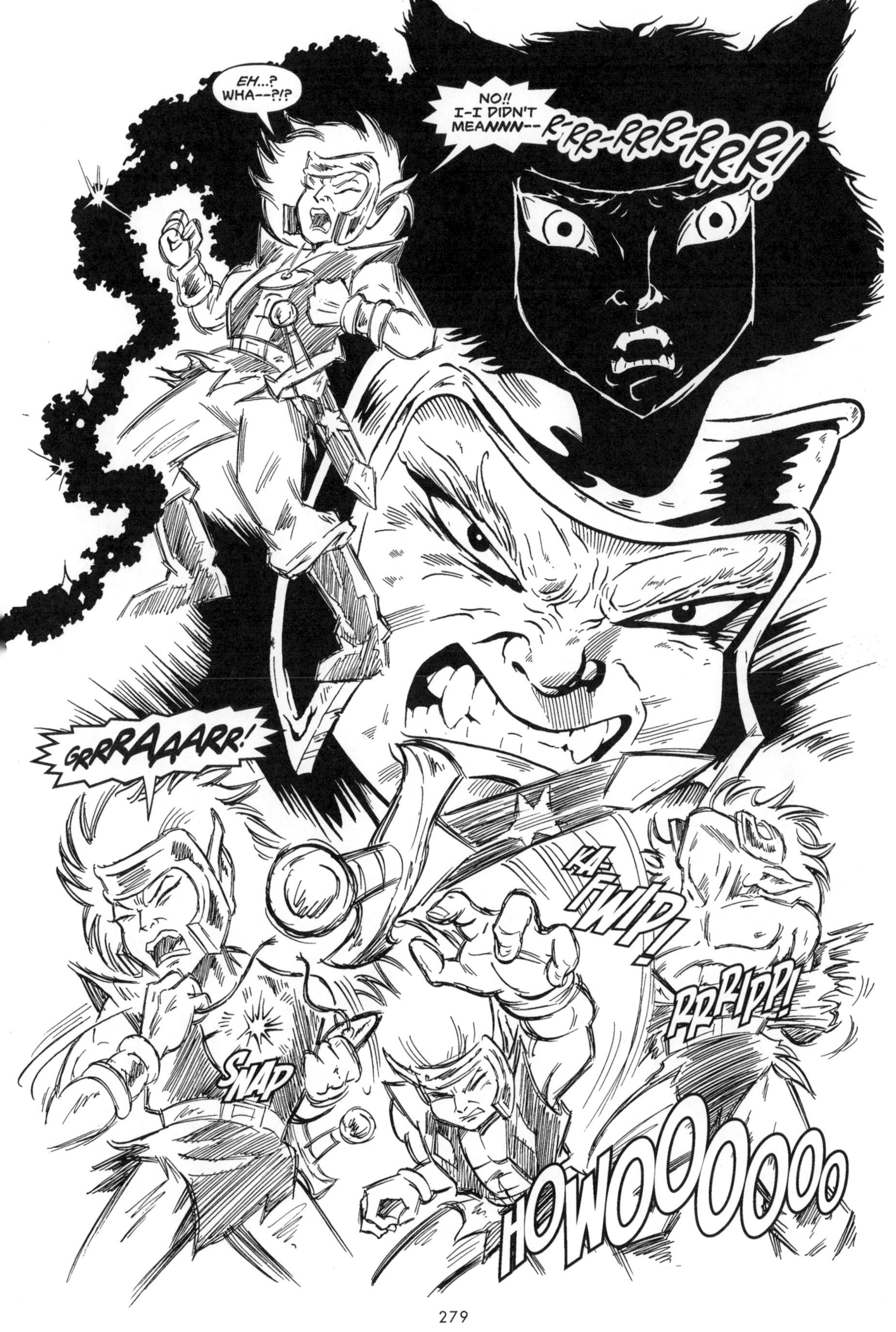
EH...? WHA--?!?
NO!! I-I DIDN'T MEANNN--R-RR-RRR-RRR!
GRRRAAARR!
KA-TWIP!
RRRIPP!
SNAP
HOWOOOOOo

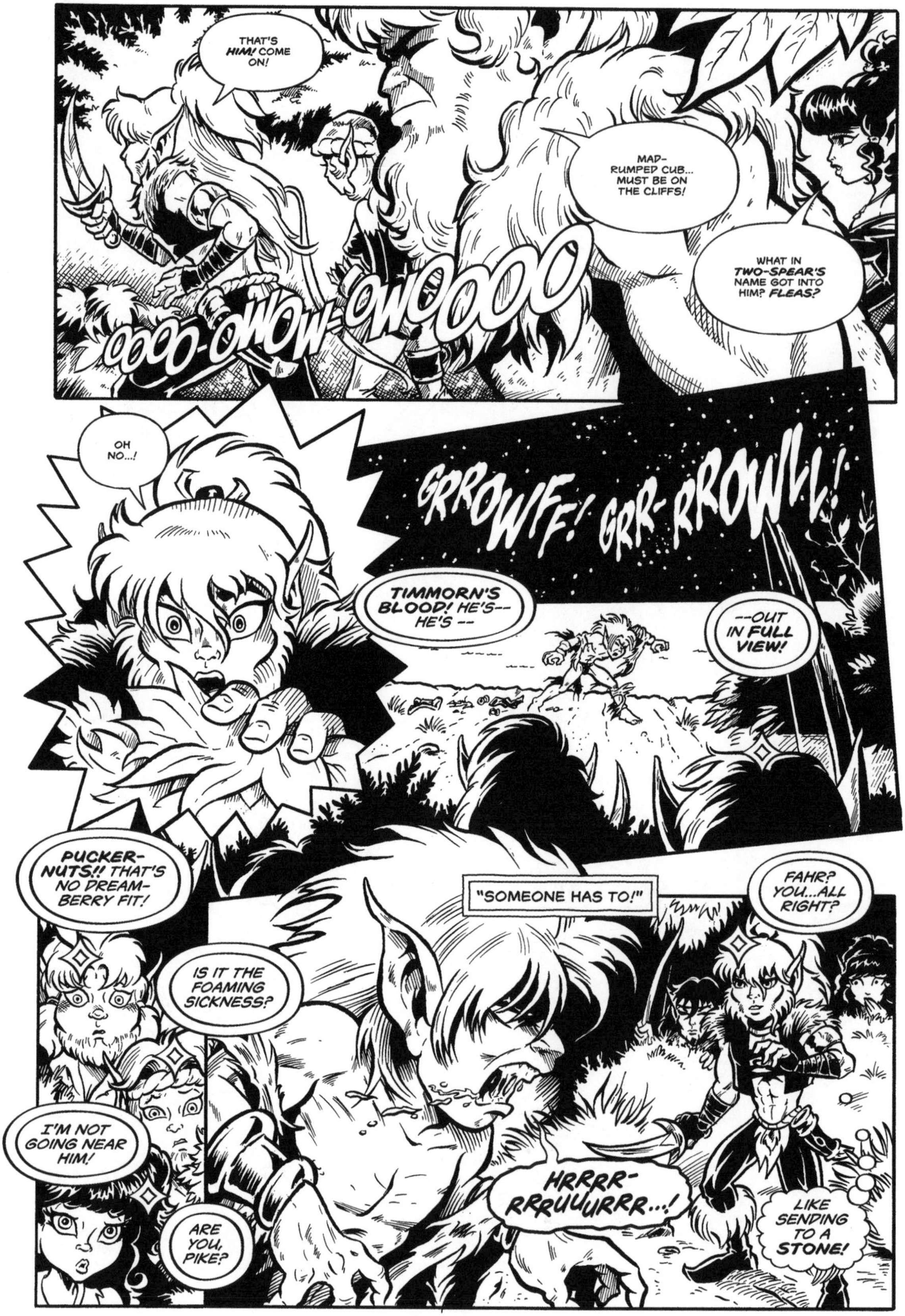

THAT'S HIM! COME ON!
MAD-RUMPED CUB... MUST BE ON THE CLIFFS!
WHAT IN TWO-SPEAR'S NAME GOT INTO HIM? FLEAS?
OOOO-OWOW-OWOOOO
OH NO...!
GRROWIFF! GRR-RROWLLL!
TIMMORN'S BLOOD! HE'S-- HE'S --
--OUT IN FULL VIEW!
PUCKER-NUTS!! THAT'S NO DREAM-BERRY FIT!
IS IT THE FOAMING SICKNESS?
I'M NOT GOING NEAR HIM!
ARE YOU, PIKE?
"SOMEONE HAS TO!"
HRRRR-RRRUUURRR...!
FAHR? YOU...ALL RIGHT?
LIKE SENDING TO A STONE!

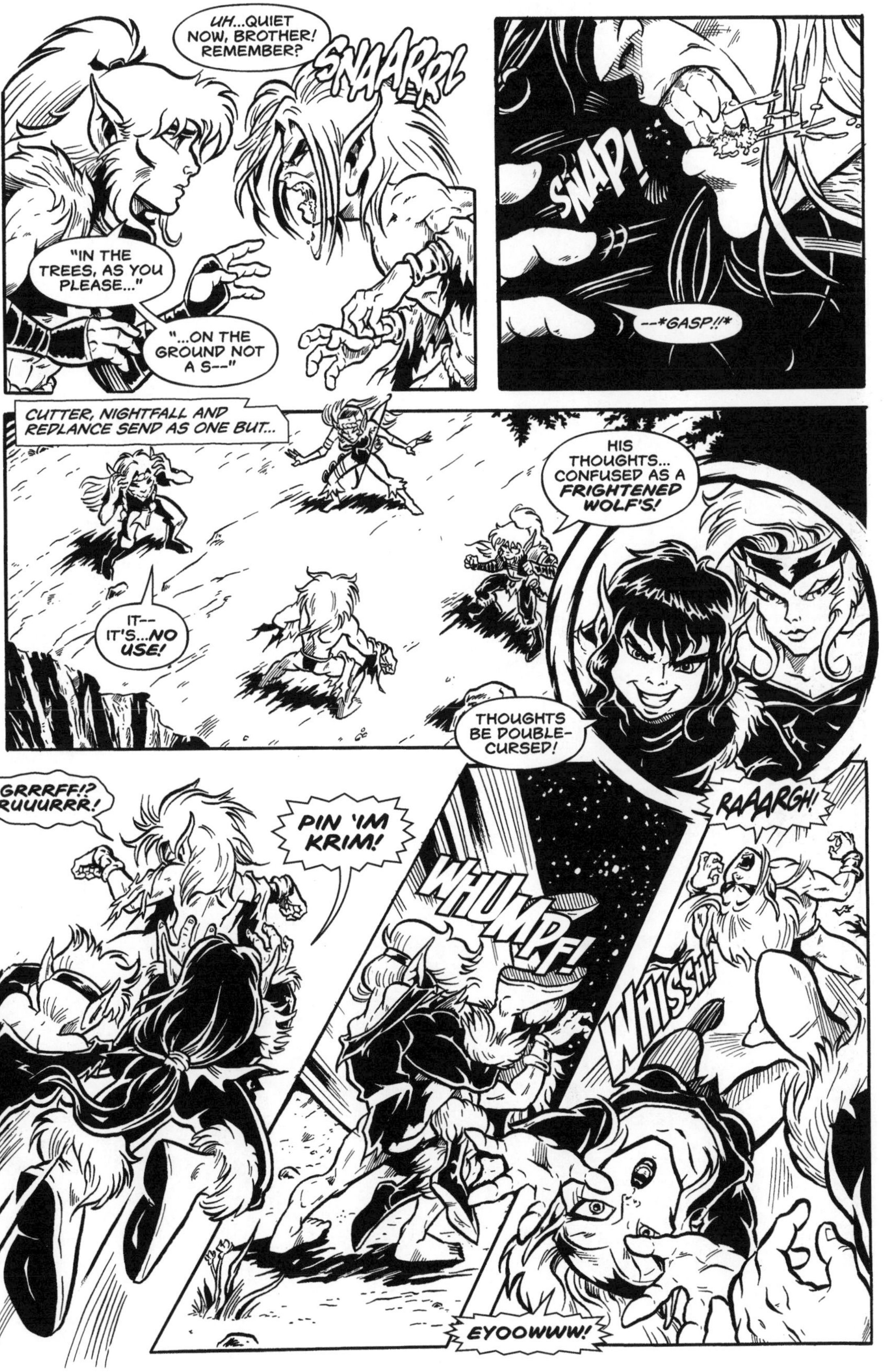
UH...QUIET NOW, BROTHER! REMEMBER?
SNAARRL
"IN THE TREES, AS YOU PLEASE..."
"...ON THE GROUND NOT A S--"
SNAP!
--*GASP!!*
CUTTER, NIGHTFALL AND REDLANCE SEND AS ONE BUT...
HIS THOUGHTS... CONFUSED AS A FRIGHTENED WOLF'S!
IT-- IT'S...NO USE!
THOUGHTS BE DOUBLE-CURSED!
GRRRFF!? RUUURRR!
PIN 'IM KRIM!
WHUMPF!
RAAARGH!
WHISSH!
EYOOWWW!

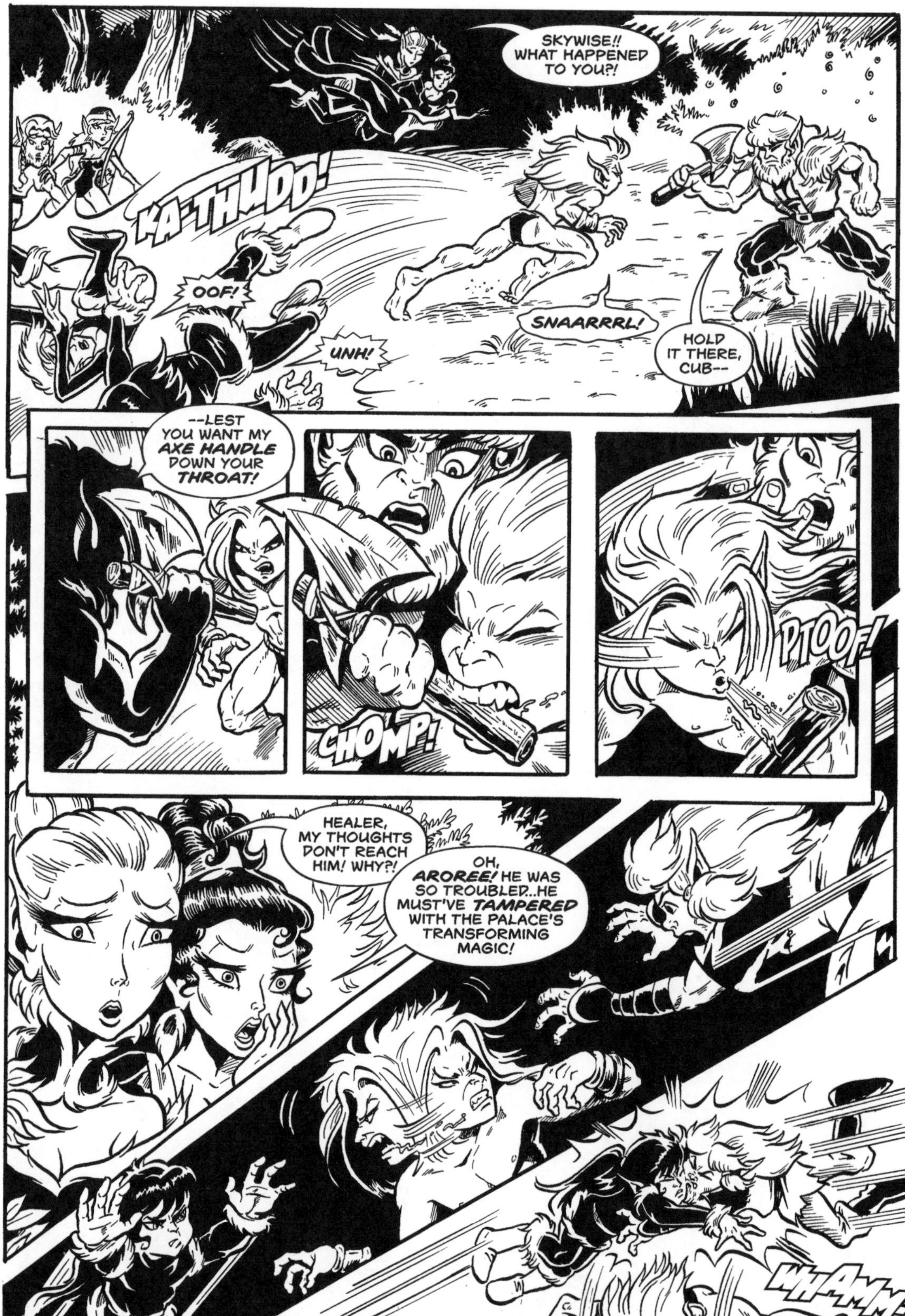
SKYWISE!! WHAT HAPPENED TO YOU?!
KA-THUDD!
OOF!
UNH!
SNAARRRL!
HOLD IT THERE, CUB--
--LEST YOU WANT MY AXE HANDLE DOWN YOUR THROAT!
CHOMP!
PTOOF!
HEALER, MY THOUGHTS DON'T REACH HIM! WHY?!
OH, AROREE! HE WAS SO TROUBLED...HE MUST'VE TAMPERED WITH THE PALACE'S TRANSFORMING MAGIC!
AND SOMEHOW...IT WENT VERY WRONG!
WHAMM!

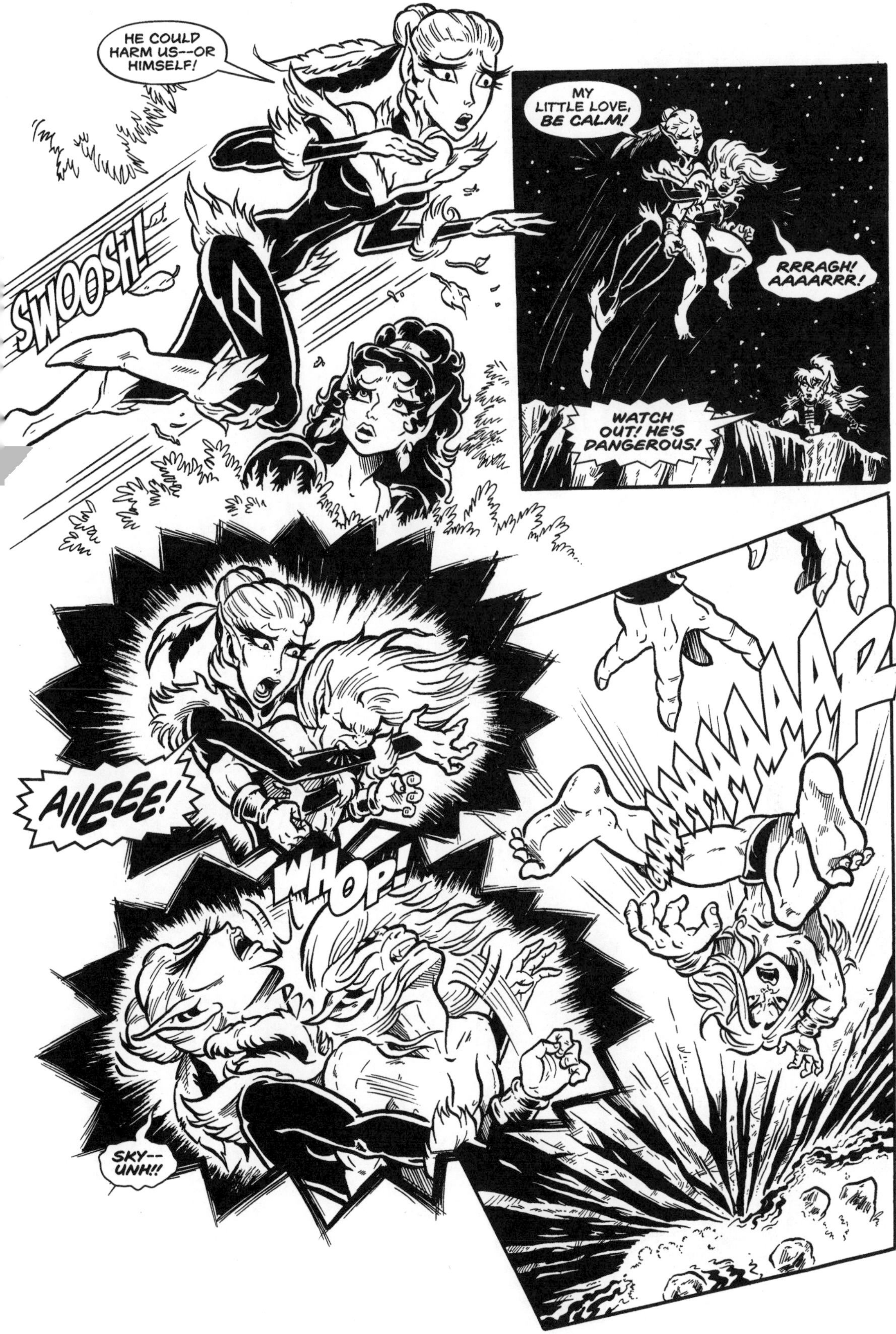
HE COULD HARM US--OR HIMSELF!
SWOOSH!
MY LITTLE LOVE, BE CALM!
RRRAGH! AAAARRR!
WATCH OUT! HE'S DANGEROUS!
AIIEEE!
WHOP!
AAAAAAAAAAR
SKY-- UNH!!

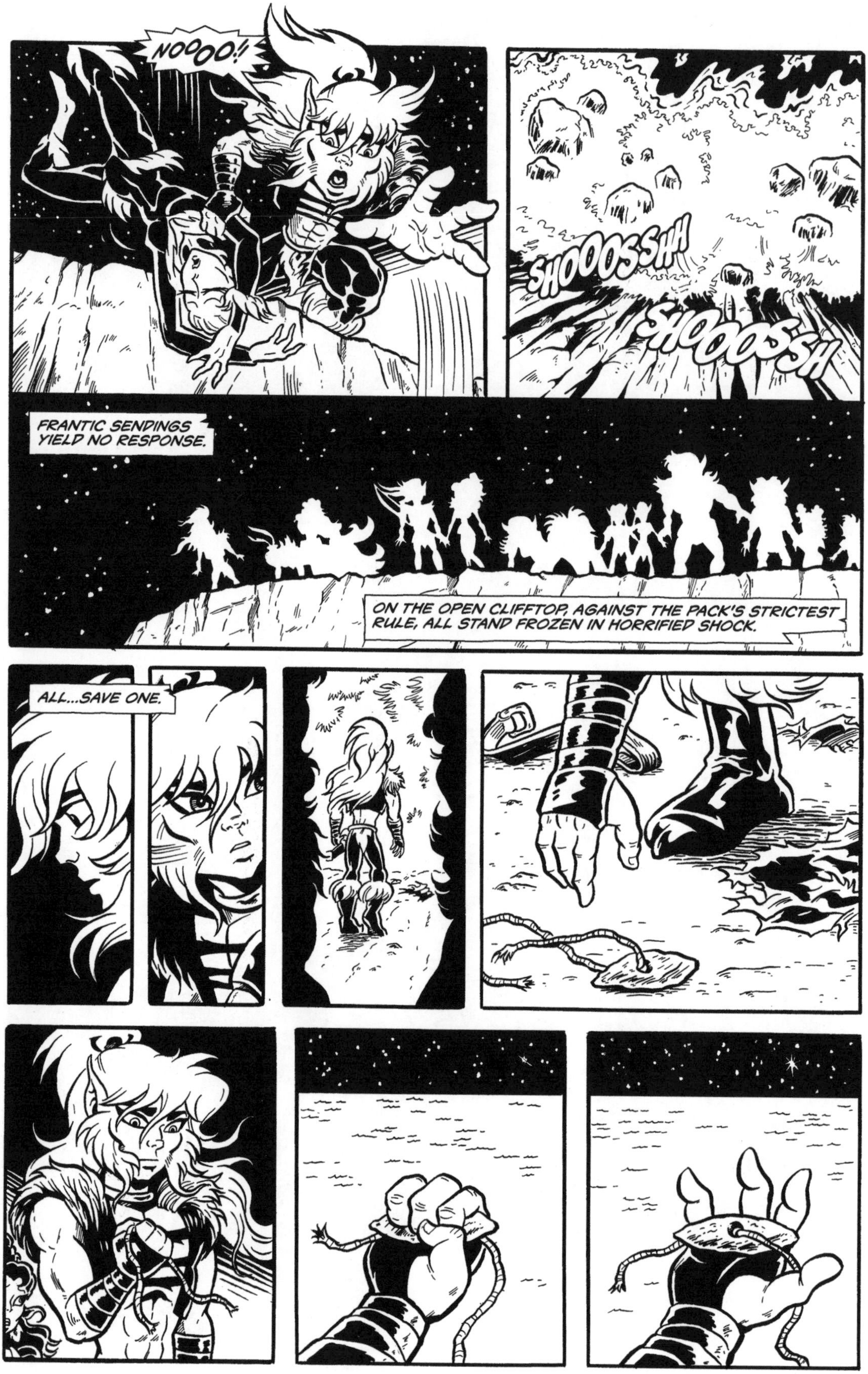
NOOOO!!
SHOOOSSHH
SHOOOSSH
FRANTIC SENDINGS YIELD NO RESPONSE.
ON THE OPEN CLIFFTOP, AGAINST THE PACK'S STRICTEST RULE, ALL STAND FROZEN IN HORRIFIED SHOCK.
ALL...SAVE ONE.

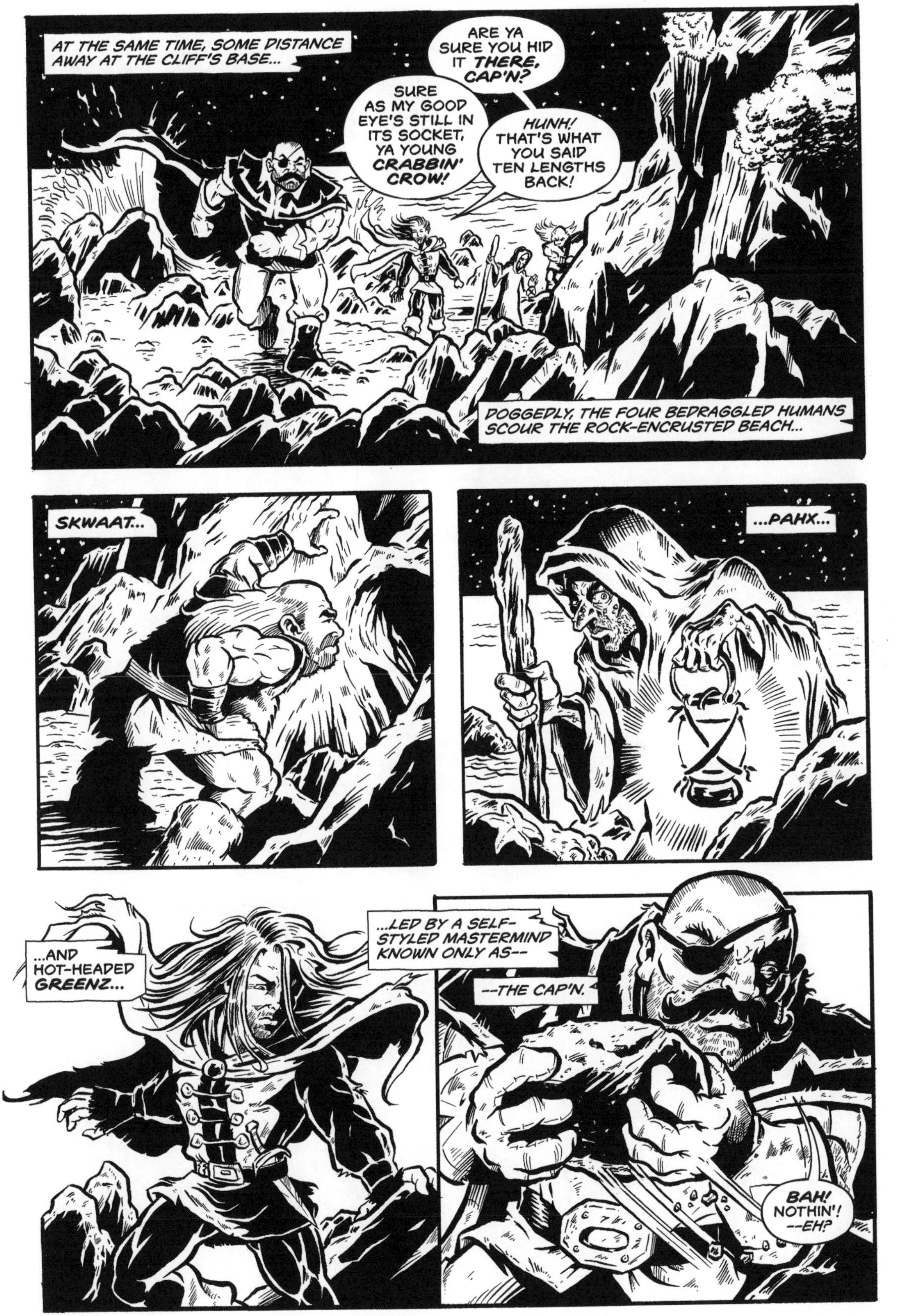
AT THE SAME TIME, SOME DISTANCE AWAY AT THE CLIFF'S BASE...
ARE YA SURE YOU HID IT THERE, CAP'N?
SURE AS MY GOOD EYE'S STILL IN ITS SOCKET, YA YOUNG CRABBIN' CROW!
HUNH! THAT'S WHAT YOU SAID TEN LENGTHS BACK!
DOGGEDLY, THE FOUR BEDRAGGLED HUMANS SCOUR THE ROCK-ENCRUSTED BEACH...
SKWAAT...
...PAHX...
...AND HOT-HEADED GREENZ...
...LED BY A SELF-STYLED MASTERMIND KNOWN ONLY AS--
--THE CAP'N.
BAH! NOTHIN'! --EH?

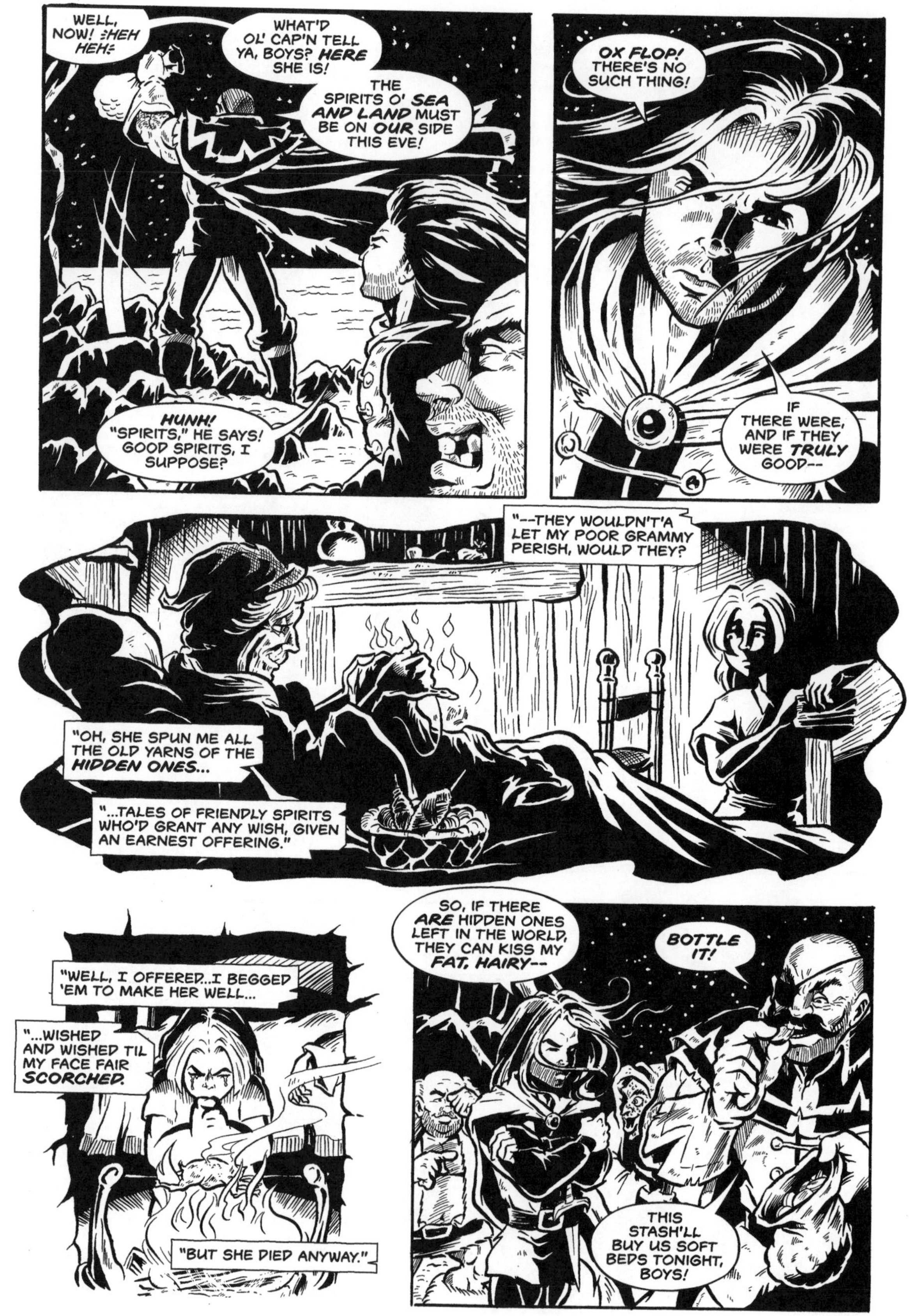
WELL, NOW! :HEH HEH:
WHAT'D OL' CAP'N TELL YA, BOYS? HERE SHE IS!
THE SPIRITS O' SEA AND LAND MUST BE ON OUR SIDE THIS EVE!
HUNH! "SPIRITS," HE SAYS! GOOD SPIRITS, I SUPPOSE?
OX FLOP! THERE'S NO SUCH THING!
IF THERE WERE, AND IF THEY WERE TRULY GOOD--
"--THEY WOULDN'T'A LET MY POOR GRAMMY PERISH, WOULD THEY?
"OH, SHE SPUN ME ALL THE OLD YARNS OF THE HIDDEN ONES...
"...TALES OF FRIENDLY SPIRITS WHO'D GRANT ANY WISH, GIVEN AN EARNEST OFFERING."
"WELL, I OFFERED...I BEGGED 'EM TO MAKE HER WELL...
"...WISHED AND WISHED TIL MY FACE FAIR SCORCHED.
"BUT SHE DIED ANYWAY."
SO, IF THERE ARE HIDDEN ONES LEFT IN THE WORLD, THEY CAN KISS MY FAT, HAIRY--
BOTTLE IT!
THIS STASH'LL BUY US SOFT BEDS TONIGHT, BOYS!

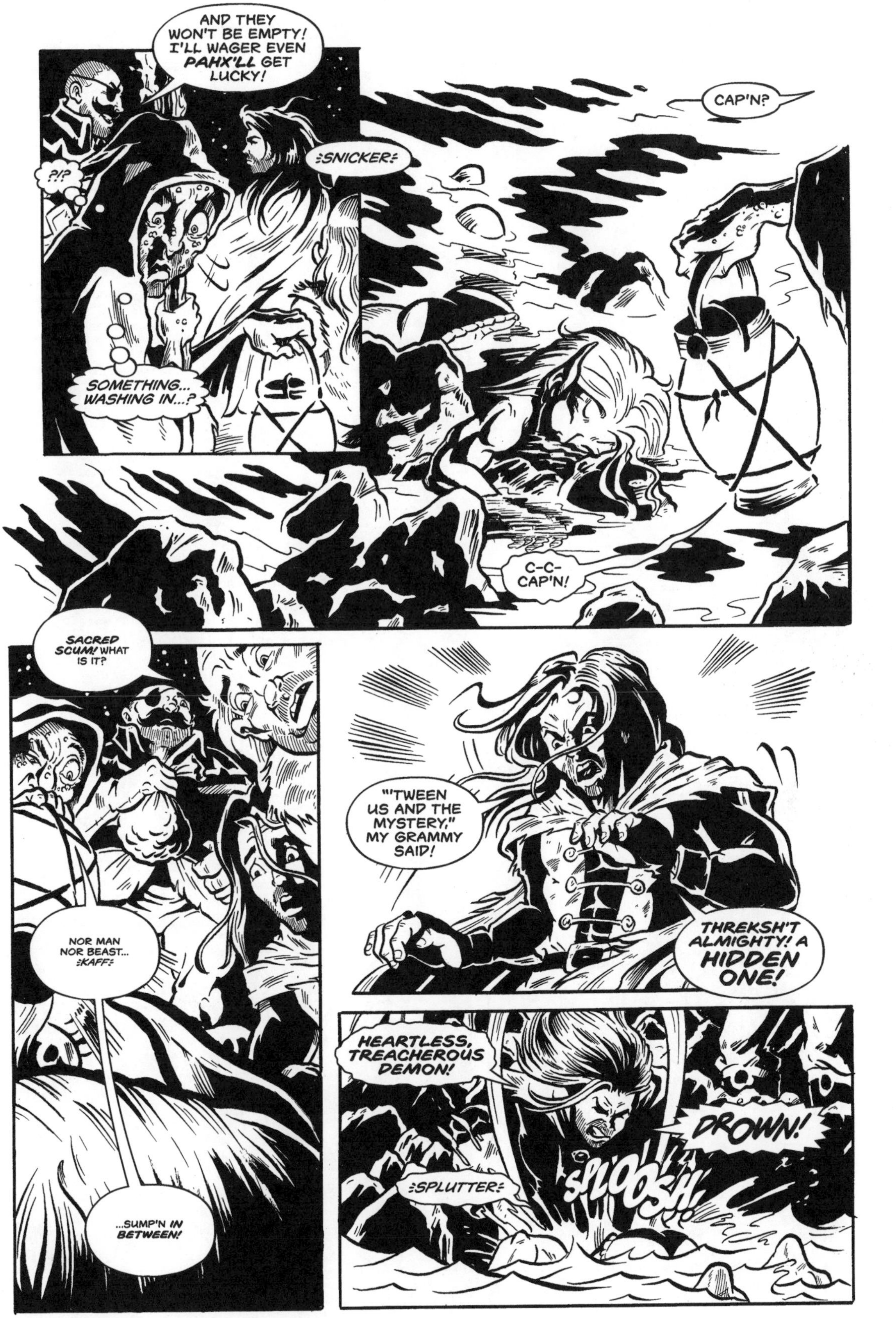
AND THEY WON'T BE EMPTY! I'LL WAGER EVEN PAHX'LL GET LUCKY!
?!?
:SNICKER:
SOMETHING... WASHING IN...?
CAP'N?
C-C-CAP'N!
SACRED SCUM! WHAT IS IT?
NOR MAN NOR BEAST... :KAFF:
...SUMP'N IN BETWEEN!
"'TWEEN US AND THE MYSTERY," MY GRAMMY SAID!
THREKSH'T ALMIGHTY! A HIDDEN ONE!
HEARTLESS, TREACHEROUS DEMON!
DROWN!
:SPLUTTER:
SPLOOSH!

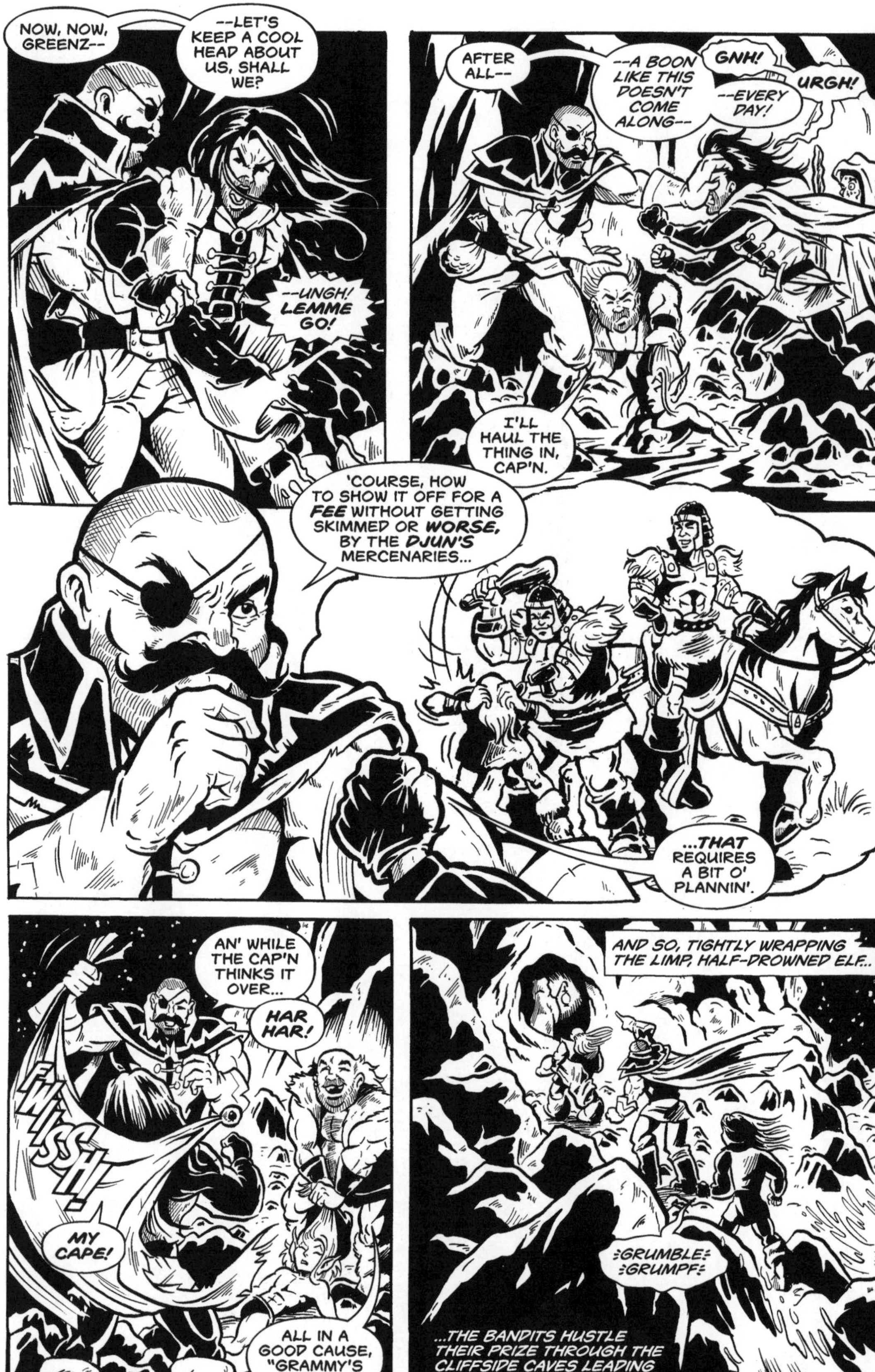
NOW, NOW, GREENZ--
--LET'S KEEP A COOL HEAD ABOUT US, SHALL WE?
--UNGH! LEMME GO!
AFTER ALL--
--A BOON LIKE THIS DOESN'T COME ALONG--
GNH!
--EVERY DAY!
URGH!
I'LL HAUL THE THING IN, CAP'N.
'COURSE, HOW TO SHOW IT OFF FOR A FEE WITHOUT GETTING SKIMMED OR WORSE, BY THE DJUN'S MERCENARIES...
...THAT REQUIRES A BIT O' PLANNIN'.
AN' WHILE THE CAP'N THINKS IT OVER...
HAR HAR!
FWISH!
MY CAPE!
ALL IN A GOOD CAUSE, "GRAMMY'S BOY!"
AND SO, TIGHTLY WRAPPING THE LIMP, HALF-DROWNED ELF...
GRUMBLE GRUMPF
...THE BANDITS HUSTLE THEIR PRIZE THROUGH THE CLIFFSIDE CAVES LEADING TO THE LOW TOWNS OF CITADEL MOUND.

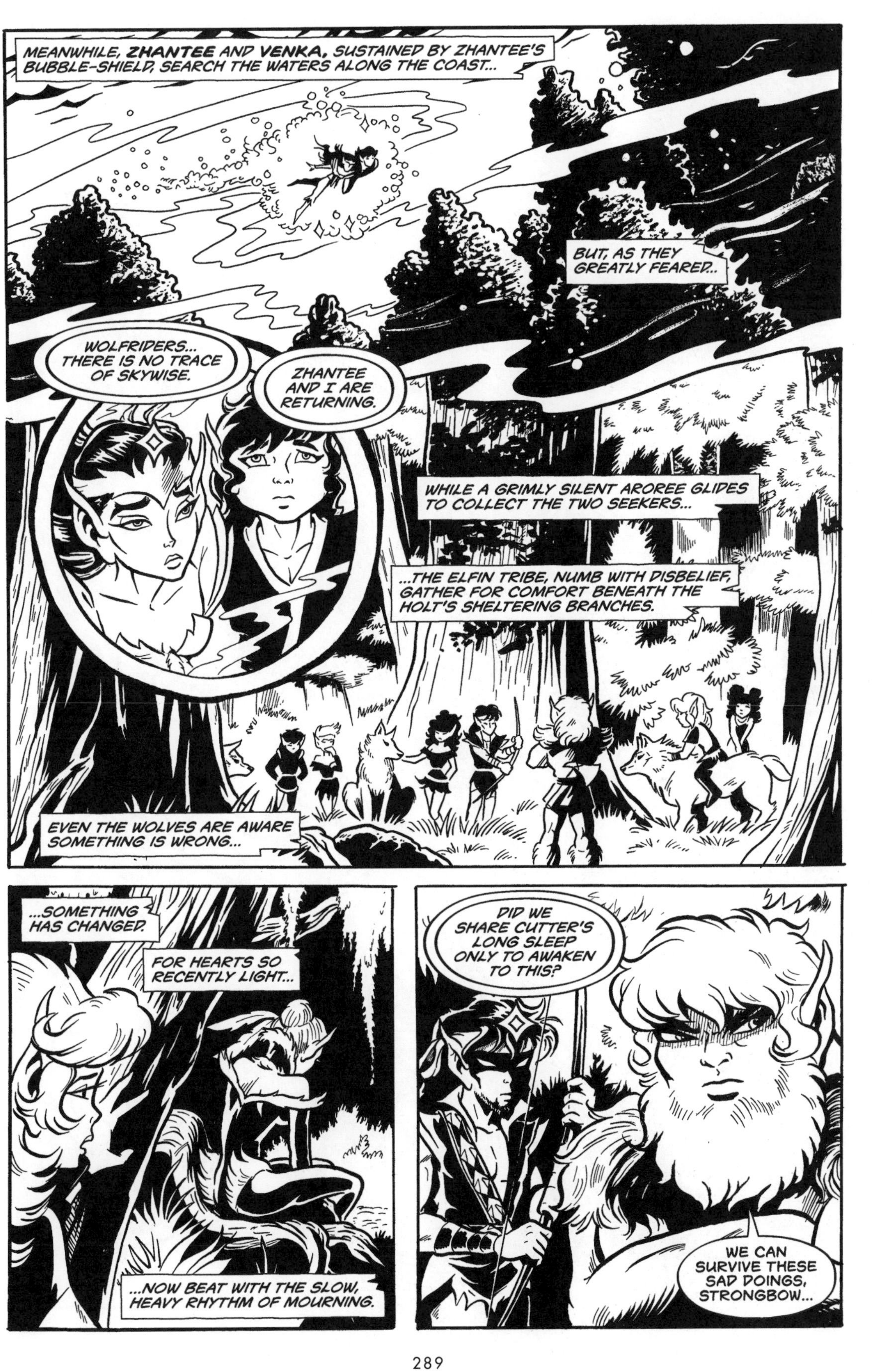
MEANWHILE, ZHANTEE AND VENKA, SUSTAINED BY ZHANTEE'S BUBBLE-SHIELD, SEARCH THE WATERS ALONG THE COAST...
BUT, AS THEY GREATLY FEARED...
WOLFRIDERS... THERE IS NO TRACE OF SKYWISE.
ZHANTEE AND I ARE RETURNING.
WHILE A GRIMLY SILENT AROREE GLIDES TO COLLECT THE TWO SEEKERS...
...THE ELFIN TRIBE, NUMB WITH DISBELIEF, GATHER FOR COMFORT BENEATH THE HOLT'S SHELTERING BRANCHES.
EVEN THE WOLVES ARE AWARE SOMETHING IS WRONG...
...SOMETHING HAS CHANGED.
FOR HEARTS SO RECENTLY LIGHT...
...NOW BEAT WITH THE SLOW, HEAVY RHYTHM OF MOURNING.
DID WE SHARE CUTTER'S LONG SLEEP ONLY TO AWAKEN TO THIS?
WE CAN SURVIVE THESE SAD DOINGS, STRONGBOW...

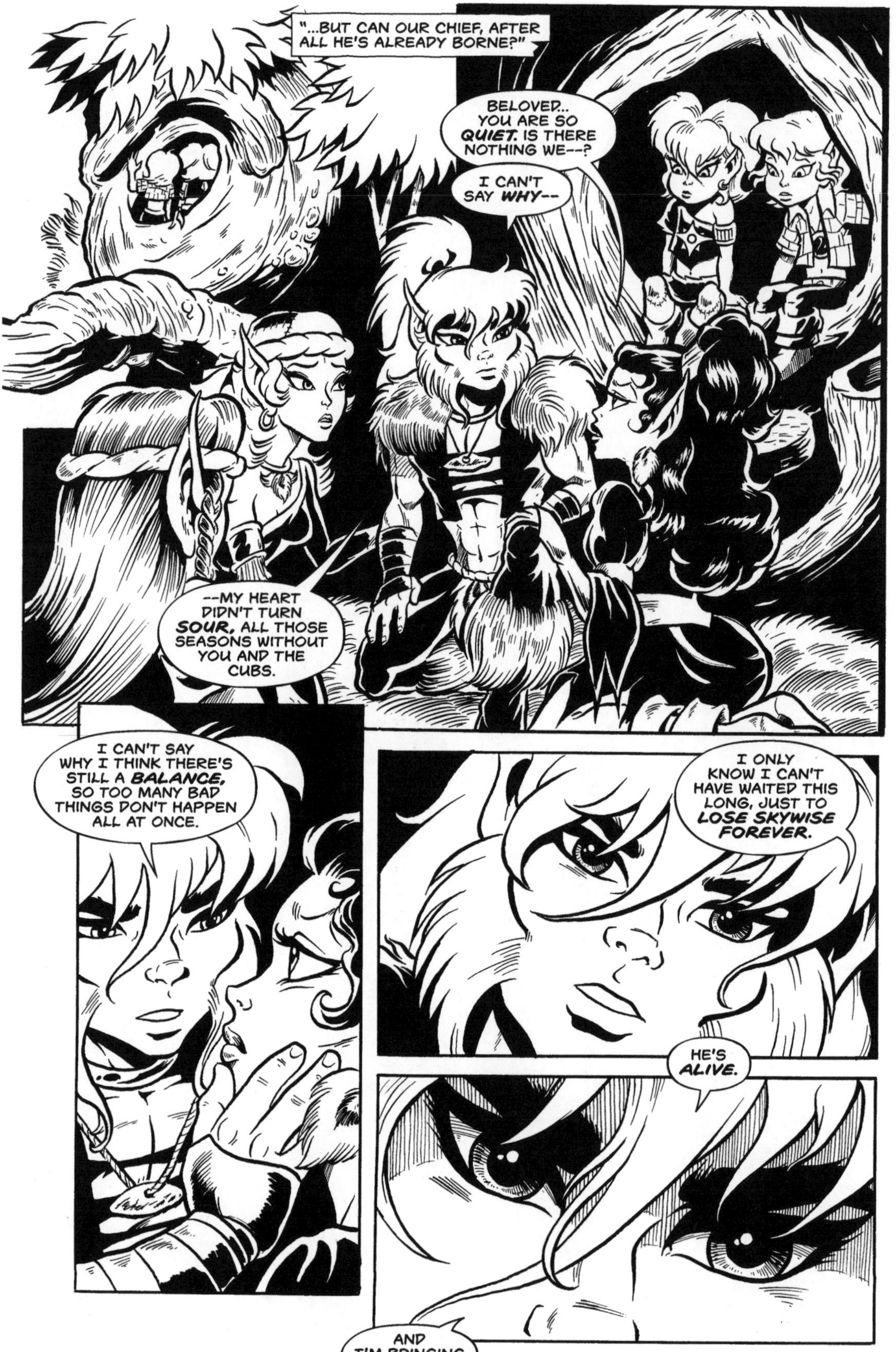
"...BUT CAN OUR CHIEF, AFTER ALL HE'S ALREADY BORNE?"
BELOVED... YOU ARE SO QUIET. IS THERE NOTHING WE--?
I CAN'T SAY WHY--
--MY HEART DIDN'T TURN SOUR, ALL THOSE SEASONS WITHOUT YOU AND THE CUBS.
I CAN'T SAY WHY I THINK THERE'S STILL A BALANCE, SO TOO MANY BAD THINGS DON'T HAPPEN ALL AT ONCE.
I ONLY KNOW I CAN'T HAVE WAITED THIS LONG, JUST TO LOSE SKYWISE FOREVER.
HE'S ALIVE.
AND I'M BRINGING HIM HOME!

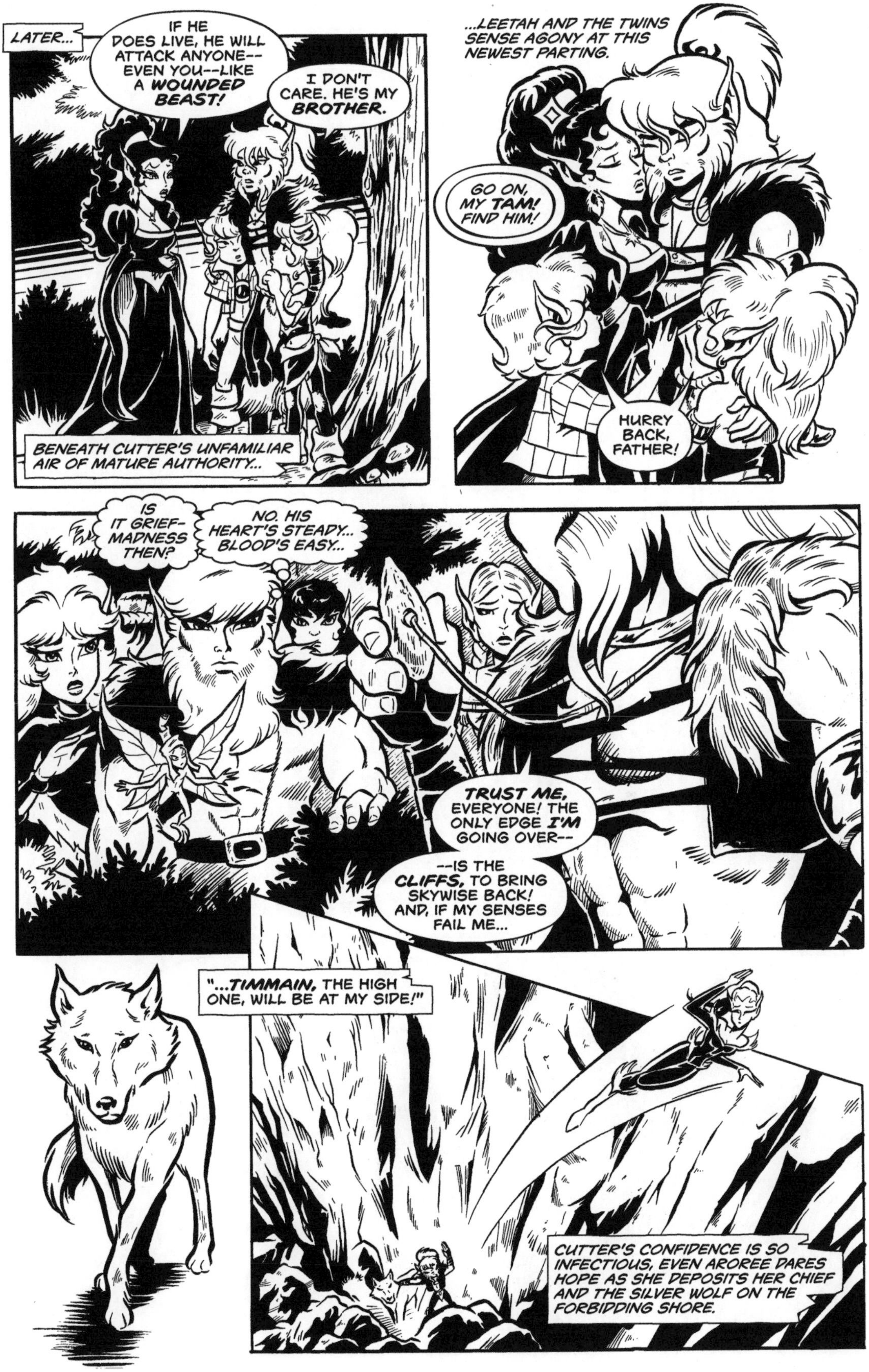
LATER...
IF HE DOES LIVE, HE WILL ATTACK ANYONE--EVEN YOU--LIKE A WOUNDED BEAST!
I DON'T CARE. HE'S MY BROTHER.
BENEATH CUTTER'S UNFAMILIAR AIR OF MATURE AUTHORITY...
...LEETAH AND THE TWINS SENSE AGONY AT THIS NEWEST PARTING.
GO ON, MY TAM! FIND HIM!
HURRY BACK, FATHER!
IS IT GRIEF-MADNESS THEN?
NO. HIS HEART'S STEADY... BLOOD'S EASY...
TRUST ME, EVERYONE! THE ONLY EDGE I'M GOING OVER--
--IS THE CLIFFS, TO BRING SKYWISE BACK! AND, IF MY SENSES FAIL ME...
"...TIMMAIN, THE HIGH ONE, WILL BE AT MY SIDE!"
CUTTER'S CONFIDENCE IS SO INFECTIOUS, EVEN AROREE DARES HOPE AS SHE DEPOSITS HER CHIEF AND THE SILVER WOLF ON THE FORBIDDING SHORE.

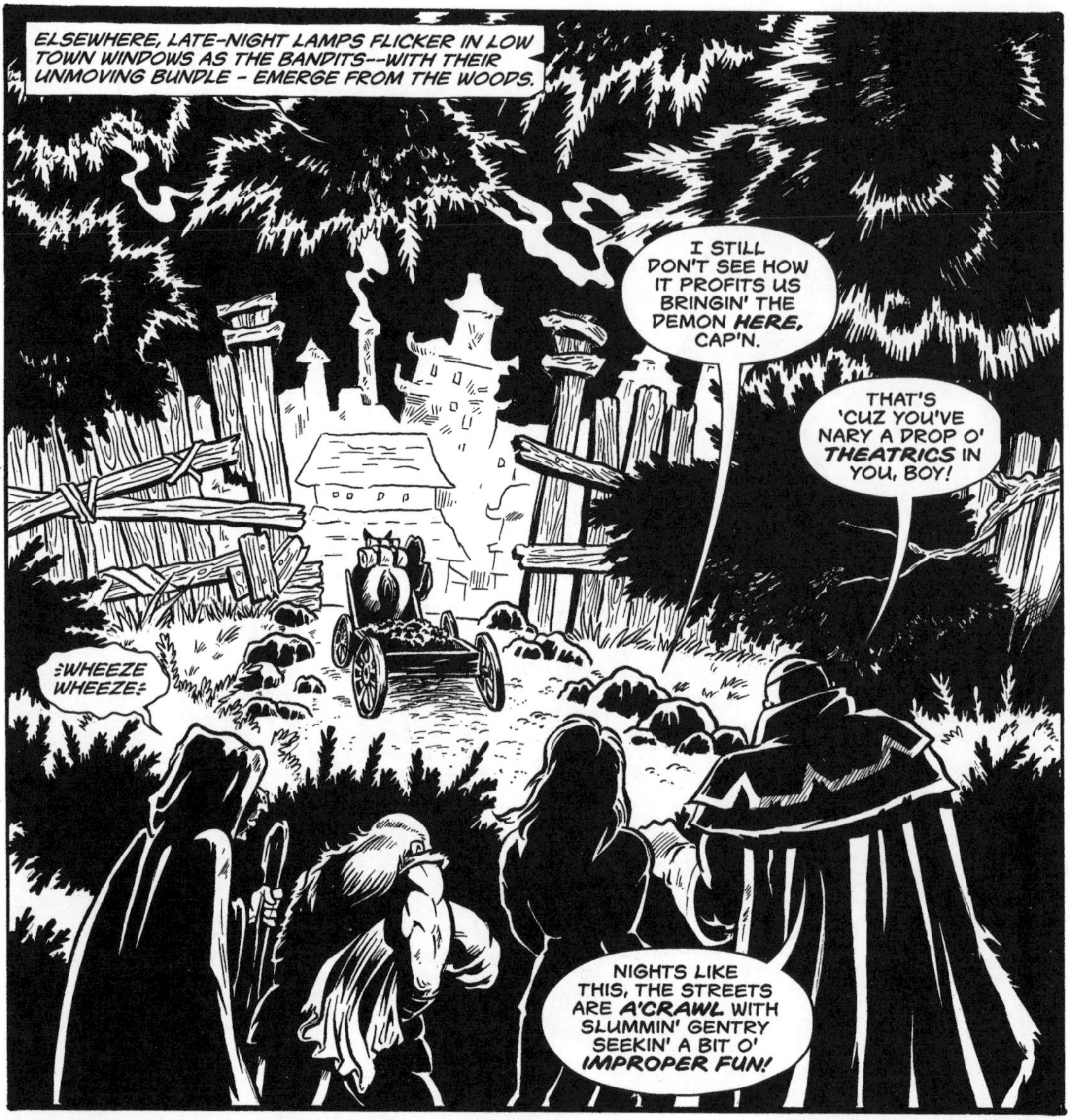
ELSEWHERE, LATE-NIGHT LAMPS FLICKER IN LOW TOWN WINDOWS AS THE BANDITS--WITH THEIR UNMOVING BUNDLE - EMERGE FROM THE WOODS.
I STILL DON'T SEE HOW IT PROFITS US BRINGIN' THE DEMON HERE, CAP'N.
THAT'S 'CUZ YOU'VE NARY A DROP O' THEATRICS IN YOU, BOY!
WHEEZE WHEEZE
NIGHTS LIKE THIS, THE STREETS ARE A'CRAWL WITH SLUMMIN' GENTRY SEEKIN' A BIT O' IMPROPER FUN!

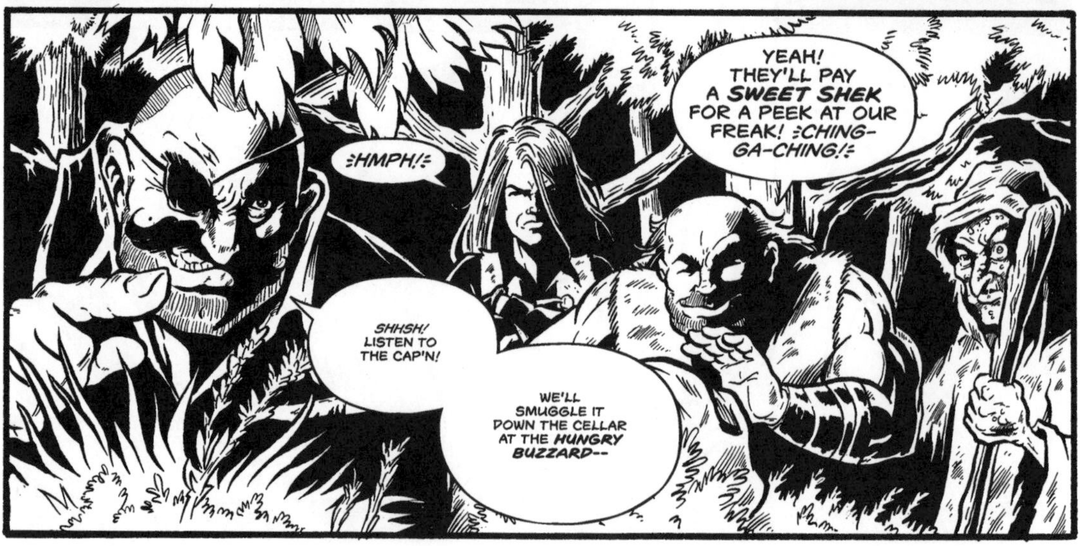
HMPH!
YEAH! THEY'LL PAY A SWEET SHEK FOR A PEEK AT OUR FREAK! CHING-GA-CHING!
SHHSH! LISTEN TO THE CAP'N!
WE'LL SMUGGLE IT DOWN THE CELLAR AT THE HUNGRY BUZZARD--

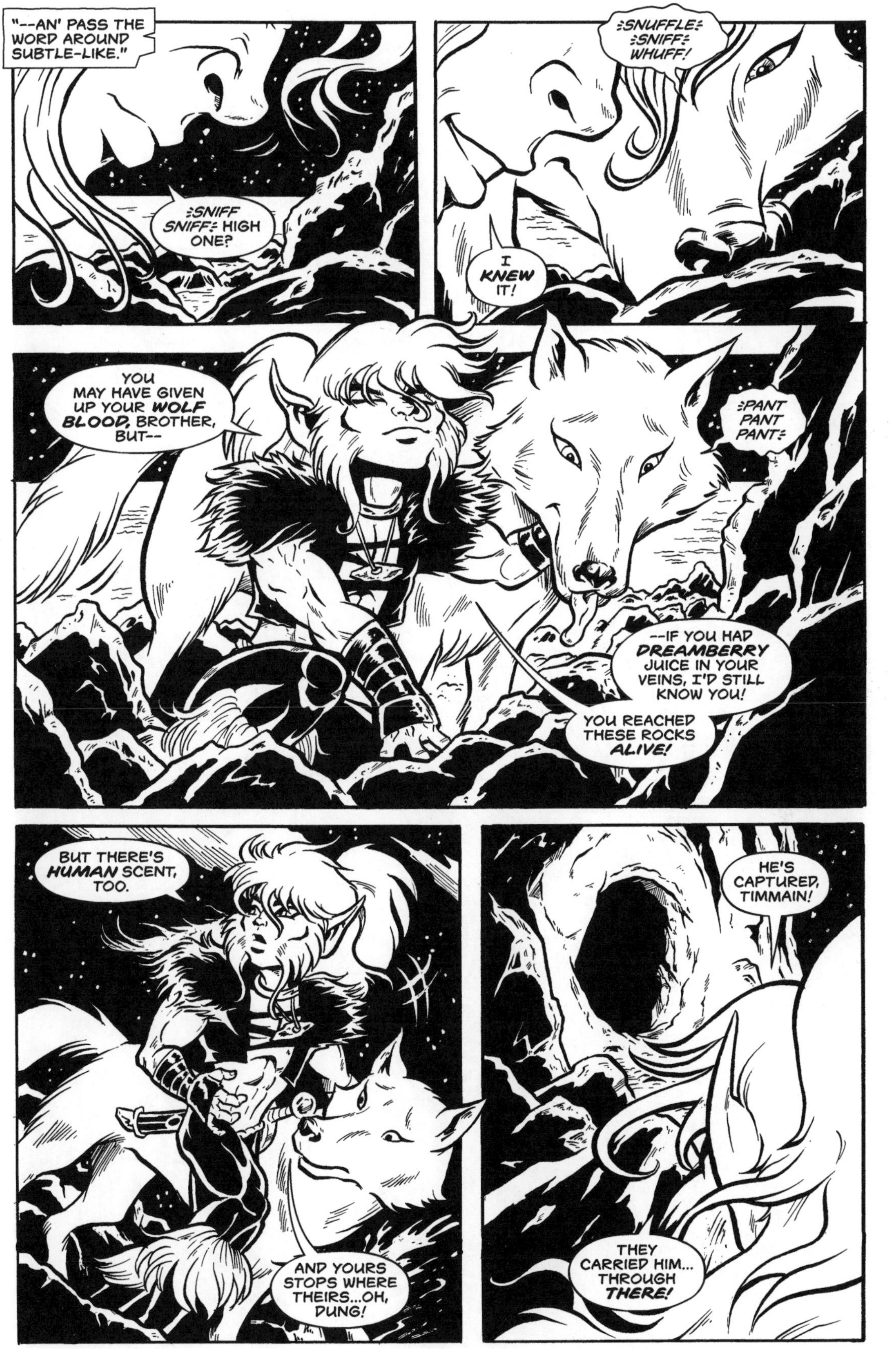
"--AN' PASS THE WORD AROUND SUBTLE-LIKE."
:SNIFF SNIFF: HIGH ONE?
:SNUFFLE: :SNIFF: WHUFF!
I KNEW IT!
YOU MAY HAVE GIVEN UP YOUR WOLF BLOOD, BROTHER, BUT--
:PANT PANT PANT:
--IF YOU HAD DREAMBERRY JUICE IN YOUR VEINS, I'D STILL KNOW YOU!
YOU REACHED THESE ROCKS ALIVE!
BUT THERE'S HUMAN SCENT, TOO.
AND YOURS STOPS WHERE THEIRS...OH, DUNG!
HE'S CAPTURED, TIMMAIN!
THEY CARRIED HIM... THROUGH THERE!

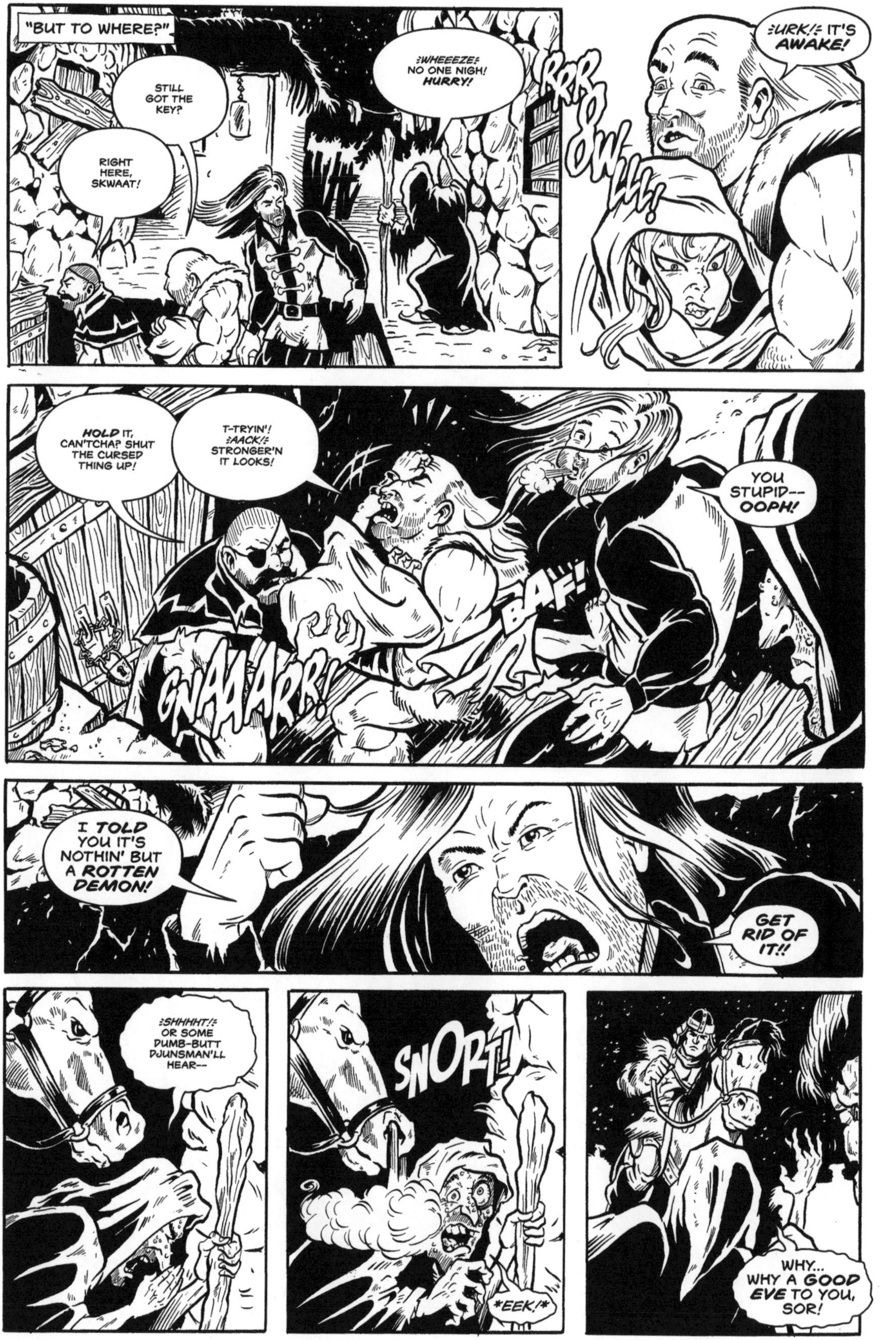
"BUT TO WHERE?"
STILL GOT THE KEY?
RIGHT HERE, SKWAAT!
:WHEEEZE: NO ONE NIGH! HURRY!
RRROWLLL!
:URK!: IT'S AWAKE!
HOLD IT, CAN'TCHA? SHUT THE CURSED THING UP!
T-TRYIN'! :AACK!: STRONGER'N IT LOOKS!
YOU STUPID-- OOPH!
BAF!
GNAAARR!
I TOLD YOU IT'S NOTHIN' BUT A ROTTEN DEMON!
GET RID OF IT!!
:SHHHHT!: OR SOME DUMB-BUTT DJUNSMAN'LL HEAR--
SNORT!
EEK!
WHY... WHY A GOOD EVE TO YOU, SOR!

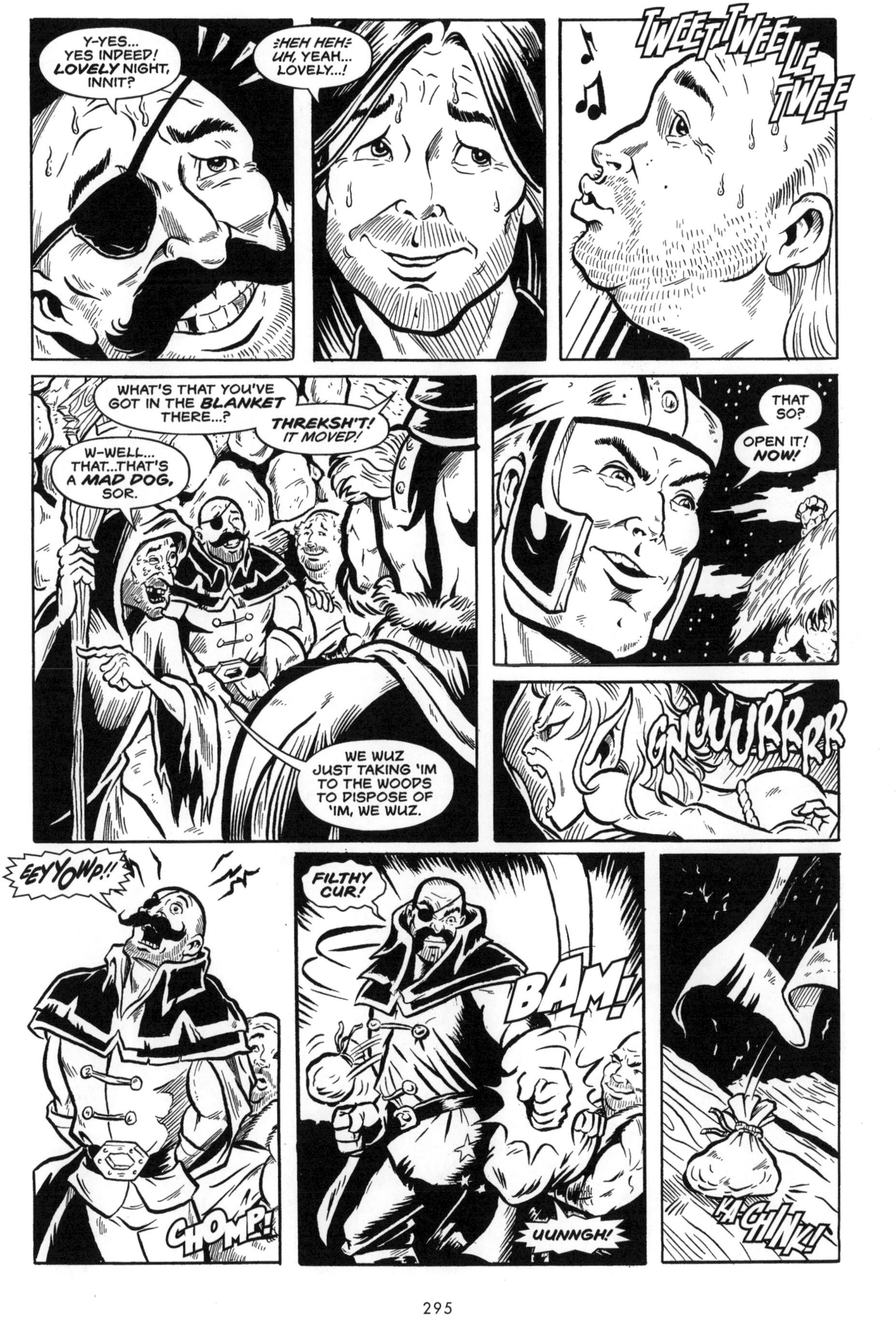

Y-YES... YES INDEED! LOVELY NIGHT, INNIT?
:HEH HEH: UH, YEAH... LOVELY...!
TWEET TWEET LE TWEE
WHAT'S THAT YOU'VE GOT IN THE BLANKET THERE...?
THREKSH'T! IT MOVED!
W-WELL... THAT...THAT'S A MAD DOG, SOR.
WE WUZ JUST TAKING 'IM TO THE WOODS TO DISPOSE OF 'IM, WE WUZ.
THAT SO?
OPEN IT! NOW!
GNUUURRRR
EEYYOWP!!
CHOMP!
FILTHY CUR!
BAM!
UUNNGH!
KA-CHINK!

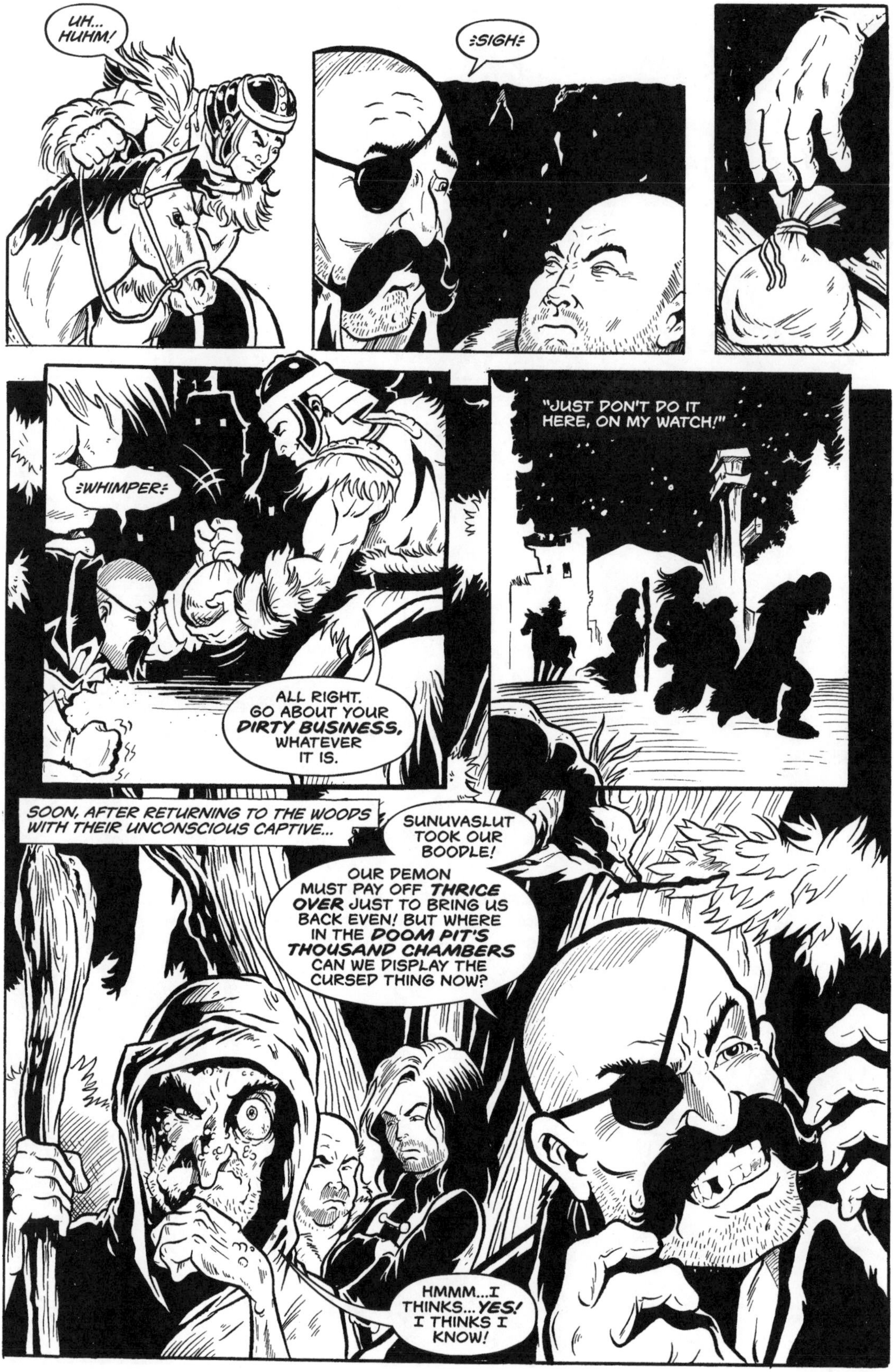
UH... HUHM!
:SIGH:
:WHIMPER:
ALL RIGHT. GO ABOUT YOUR DIRTY BUSINESS, WHATEVER IT IS.
"JUST DON'T DO IT HERE, ON MY WATCH!"
SOON, AFTER RETURNING TO THE WOODS WITH THEIR UNCONSCIOUS CAPTIVE...
SUNUVASLUT TOOK OUR BOODLE!
OUR DEMON MUST PAY OFF THRICE OVER JUST TO BRING US BACK EVEN! BUT WHERE IN THE DOOM PIT'S THOUSAND CHAMBERS CAN WE DISPLAY THE CURSED THING NOW?
HMMM...I THINKS... YES! I THINKS I KNOW!

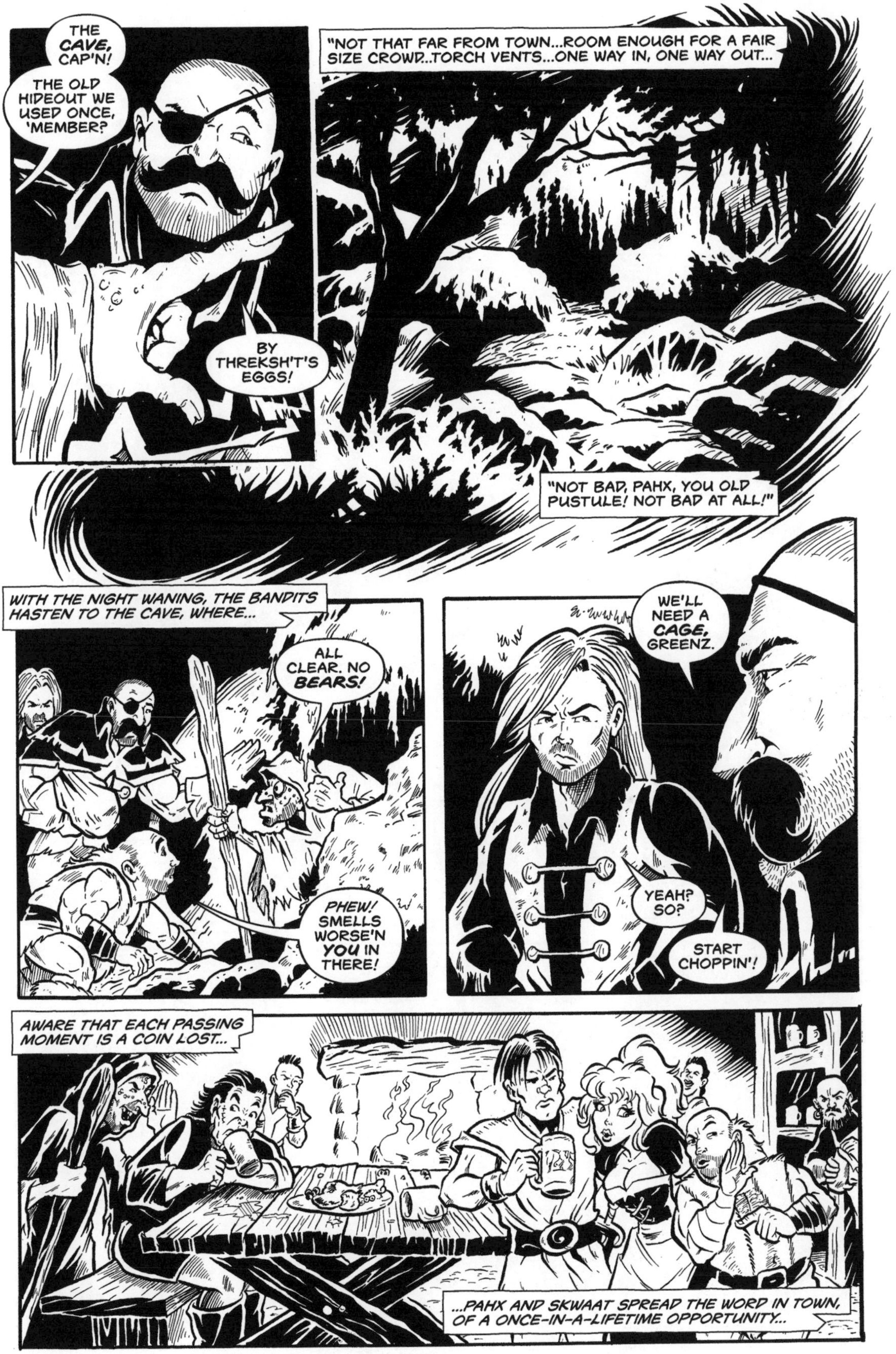
THE CAVE, CAP'N!
THE OLD HIDEOUT WE USED ONCE, 'MEMBER?
BY THREKSH'T'S EGGS!
"NOT THAT FAR FROM TOWN...ROOM ENOUGH FOR A FAIR SIZE CROWD...TORCH VENTS...ONE WAY IN, ONE WAY OUT...
"NOT BAD, PAHX, YOU OLD PUSTULE! NOT BAD AT ALL!"
WITH THE NIGHT WANING, THE BANDITS HASTEN TO THE CAVE, WHERE...
ALL CLEAR. NO BEARS!
PHEW! SMELLS WORSE'N YOU IN THERE!
WE'LL NEED A CAGE, GREENZ.
YEAH? SO?
START CHOPPIN'!
AWARE THAT EACH PASSING MOMENT IS A COIN LOST...
...PAHX AND SKWAAT SPREAD THE WORD IN TOWN, OF A ONCE-IN-A-LIFETIME OPPORTUNITY...

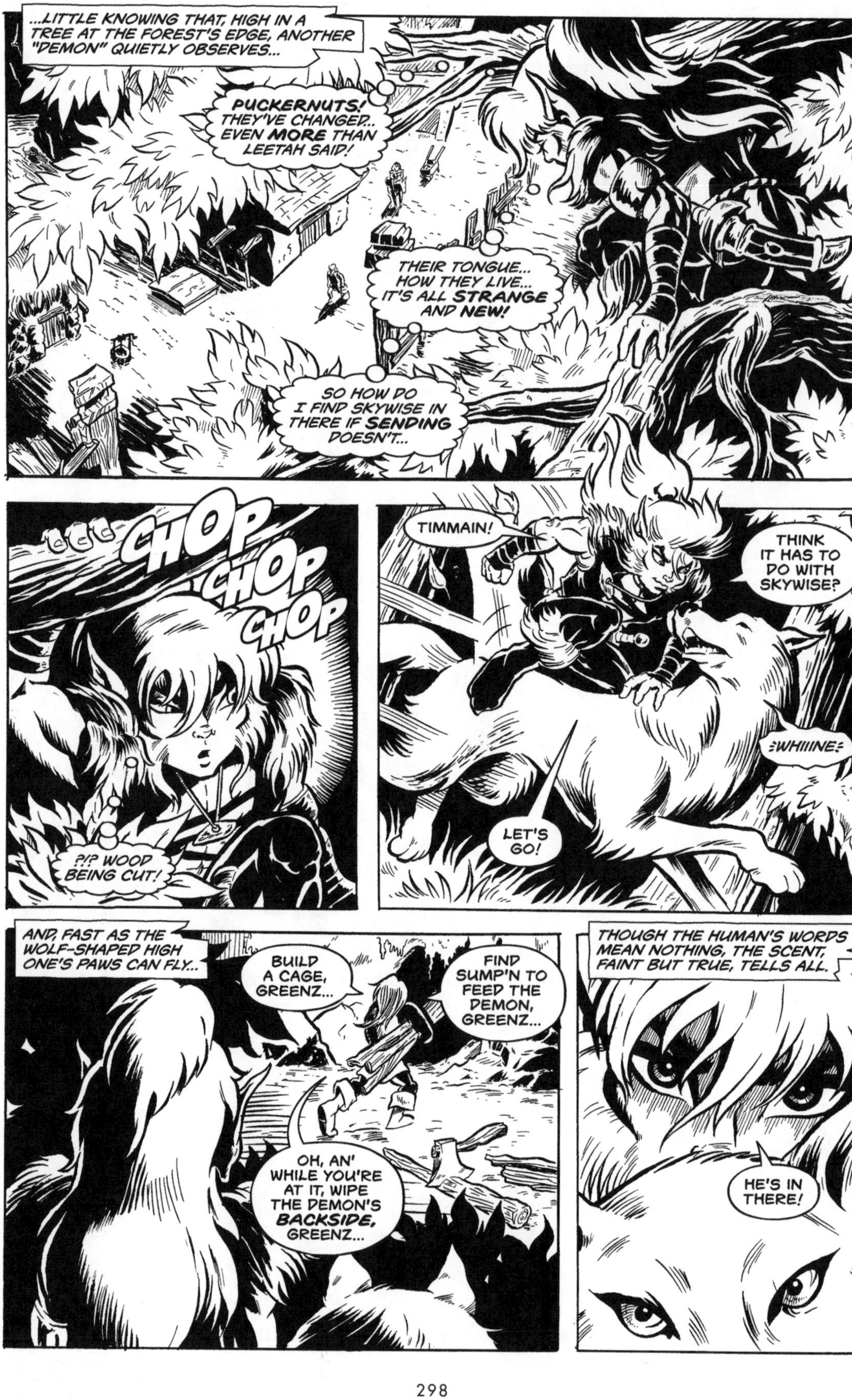
...LITTLE KNOWING THAT, HIGH IN A TREE AT THE FOREST'S EDGE, ANOTHER "DEMON" QUIETLY OBSERVES...
PUCKERNUTS! THEY'VE CHANGED... EVEN MORE THAN LEETAH SAID!
THEIR TONGUE... HOW THEY LIVE... IT'S ALL STRANGE AND NEW!
SO HOW DO I FIND SKYWISE IN THERE IF SENDING DOESN'T...
CHOP CHOP CHOP
?!? WOOD BEING CUT!
TIMMAIN!
THINK IT HAS TO DO WITH SKYWISE?
:WHIIINE:
LET'S GO!
AND, FAST AS THE WOLF-SHAPED HIGH ONE'S PAWS CAN FLY...
BUILD A CAGE, GREENZ...
FIND SUMP'N TO FEED THE DEMON, GREENZ...
OH, AN' WHILE YOU'RE AT IT, WIPE THE DEMON'S BACKSIDE, GREENZ...
THOUGH THE HUMAN'S WORDS MEAN NOTHING, THE SCENT, FAINT BUT TRUE, TELLS ALL.
HE'S IN THERE!

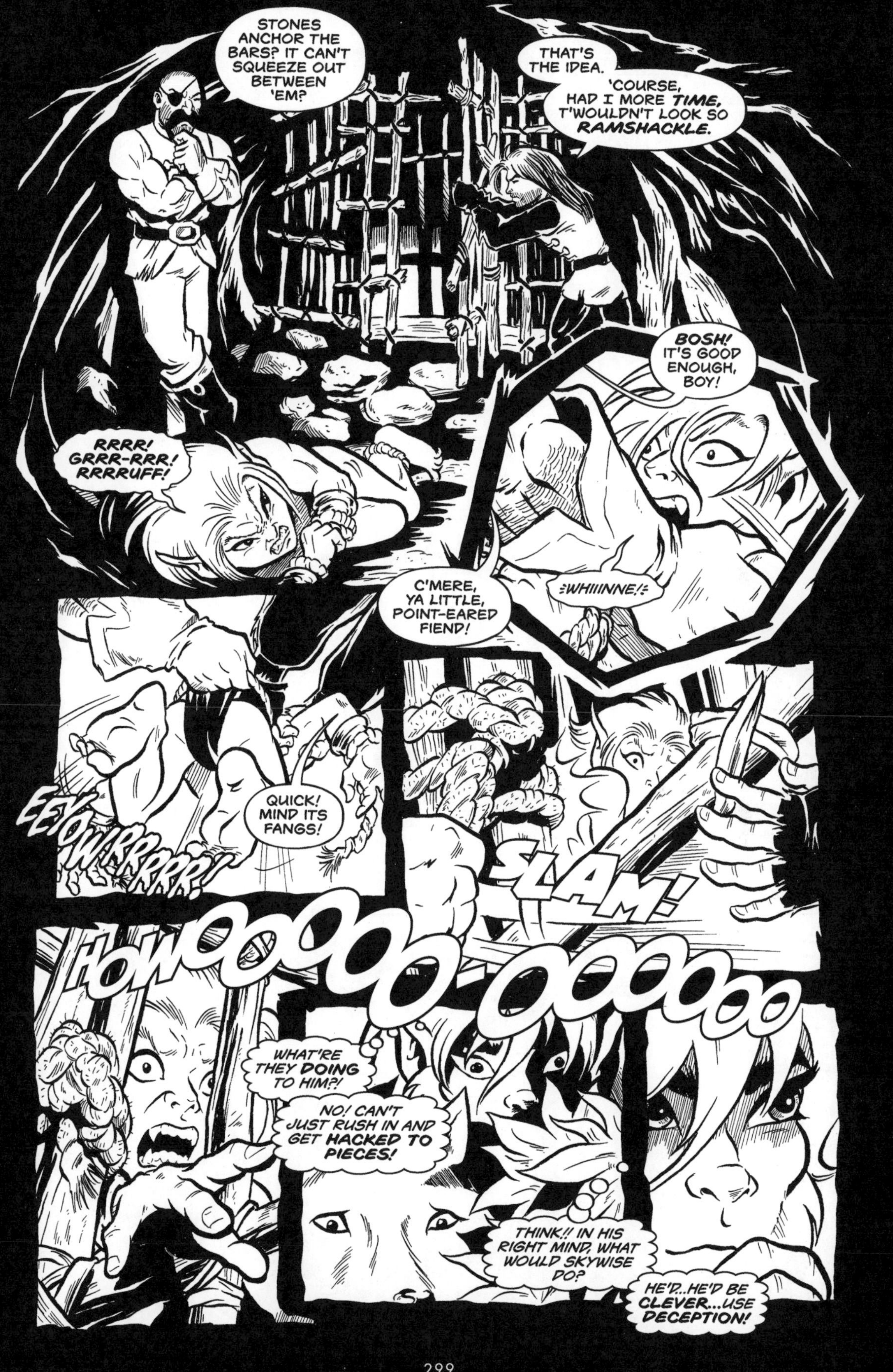
STONES ANCHOR THE BARS? IT CAN'T SQUEEZE OUT BETWEEN 'EM?
THAT'S THE IDEA.
'COURSE, HAD I MORE TIME, T'WOULDN'T LOOK SO RAMSHACKLE.
BOSH! IT'S GOOD ENOUGH, BOY!
RRRR! GRRR-RRR! RRRRUFF!
C'MERE, YA LITTLE, POINT-EARED FIEND!
WHIIINNE!
QUICK! MIND ITS FANGS!
EEYOWRRRRR!
SLAM!
HOWOOOOO-OOOOOO
WHAT'RE THEY DOING TO HIM?!
NO! CAN'T JUST RUSH IN AND GET HACKED TO PIECES!
THINK!! IN HIS RIGHT MIND, WHAT WOULD SKYWISE DO?
HE'D...HE'D BE CLEVER...USE DECEPTION!

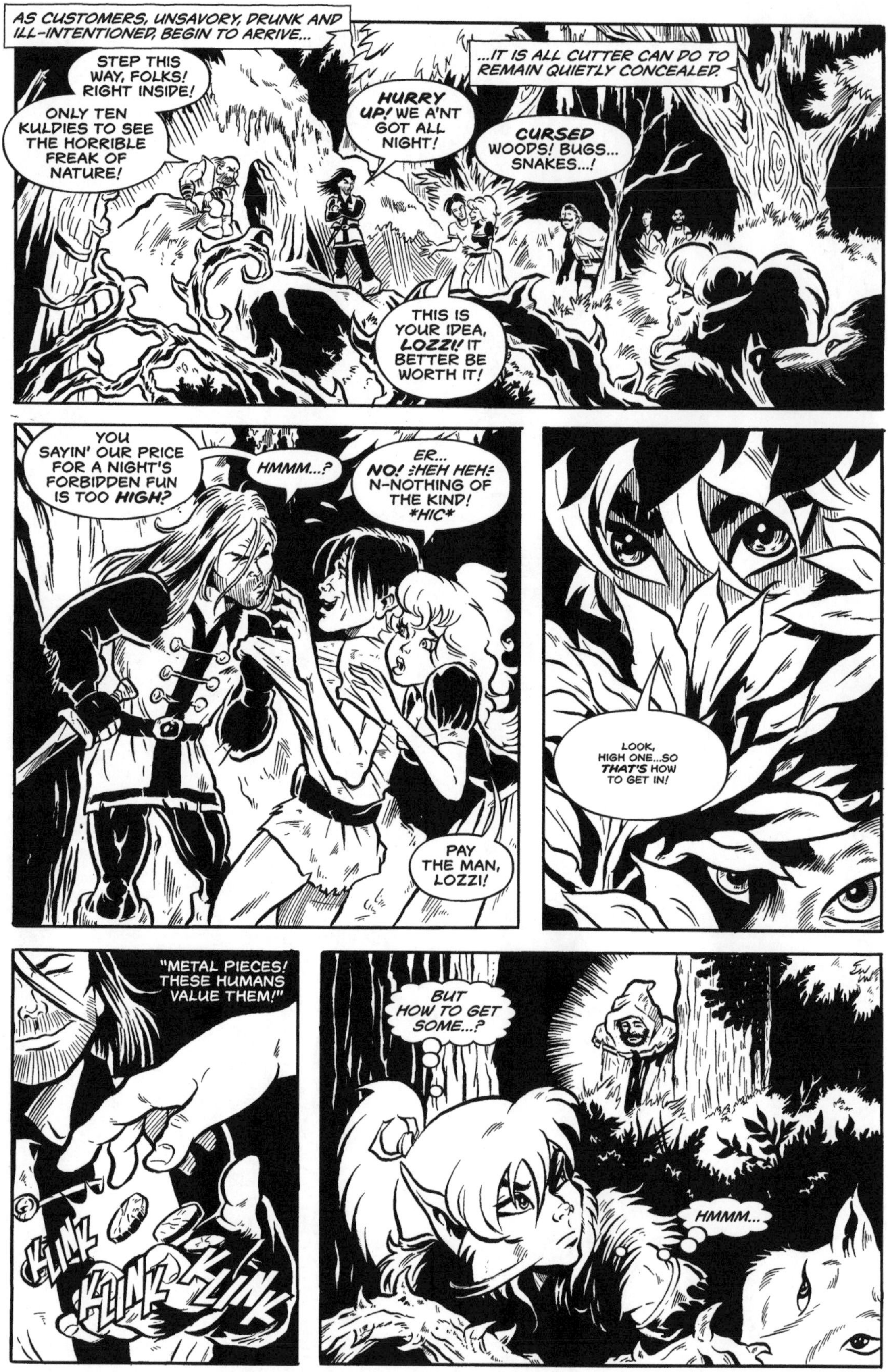
AS CUSTOMERS, UNSAVORY, DRUNK AND ILL-INTENTIONED, BEGIN TO ARRIVE...
STEP THIS WAY, FOLKS! RIGHT INSIDE!
ONLY TEN KULDIES TO SEE THE HORRIBLE FREAK OF NATURE!
HURRY UP! WE A'NT GOT ALL NIGHT!
...IT IS ALL CUTTER CAN DO TO REMAIN QUIETLY CONCEALED.
CURSED WOODS! BUGS... SNAKES...!
THIS IS YOUR IDEA, LOZZI! IT BETTER BE WORTH IT!
YOU SAYIN' OUR PRICE FOR A NIGHT'S FORBIDDEN FUN IS TOO HIGH?
HMMM...?
ER... NO! HEH HEH N-NOTHING OF THE KIND! *HIC*
PAY THE MAN, LOZZI!
LOOK, HIGH ONE...SO THAT'S HOW TO GET IN!
"METAL PIECES! THESE HUMANS VALUE THEM!"
KLINK KLINK KLINK
BUT HOW TO GET SOME...?
HMMM...

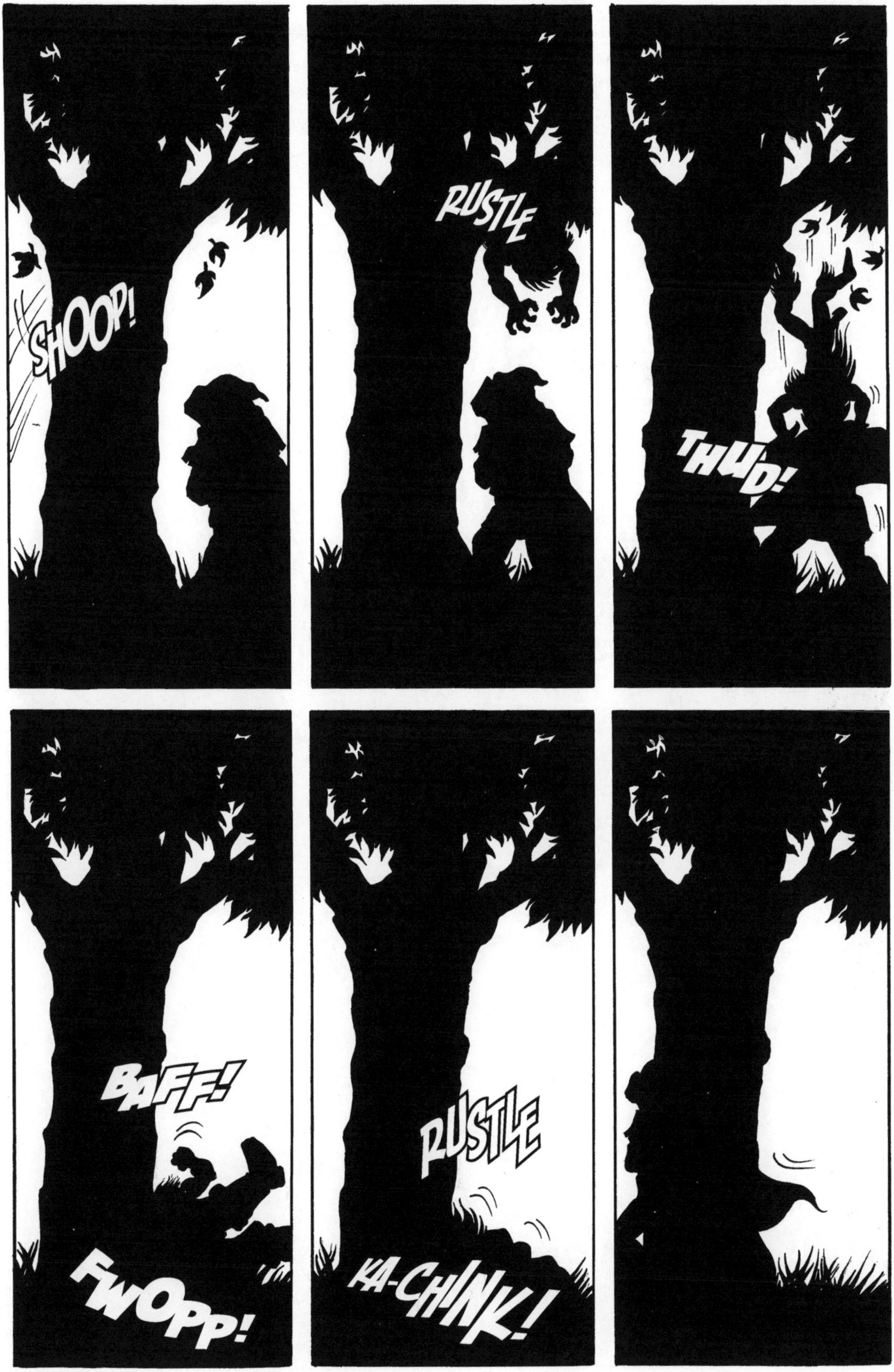
SHOOP!
RUSTLE
THUD!
BAFF!
FWOPP!
RUSTLE
KA-CHINK!

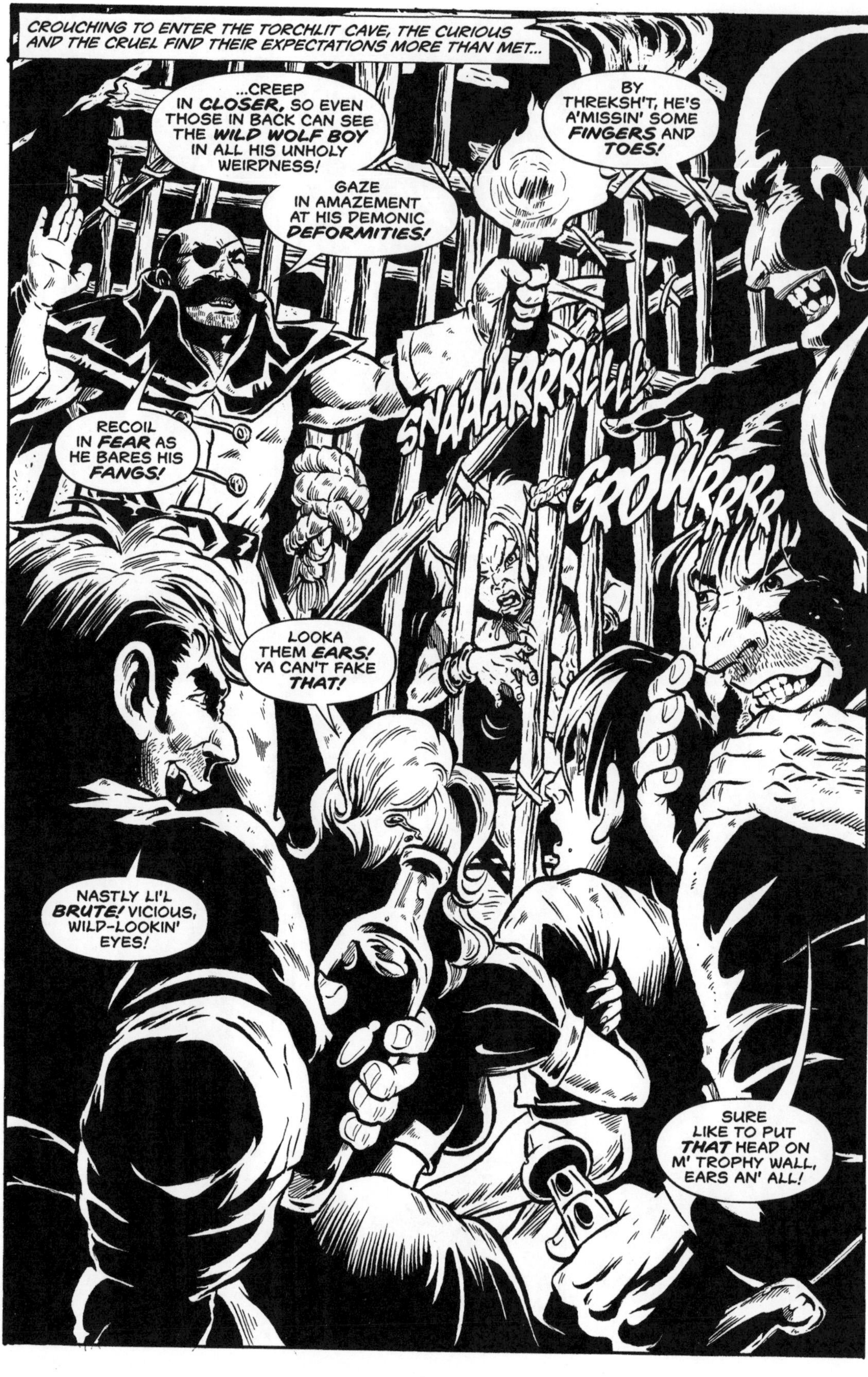
CROUCHING TO ENTER THE TORCHLIT CAVE, THE CURIOUS AND THE CRUEL FIND THEIR EXPECTATIONS MORE THAN MET...
...CREEP IN CLOSER, SO EVEN THOSE IN BACK CAN SEE THE WILD WOLF BOY IN ALL HIS UNHOLY WEIRDNESS!
BY THREKSH'T, HE'S A'MISSIN' SOME FINGERS AND TOES!
GAZE IN AMAZEMENT AT HIS DEMONIC DEFORMITIES!
RECOIL IN FEAR AS HE BARES HIS FANGS!
SNAAARRRLLLL
GROWRRRR
LOOKA THEM EARS! YA CAN'T FAKE THAT!
NASTLY LI'L BRUTE! VICIOUS, WILD-LOOKIN' EYES!
SURE LIKE TO PUT THAT HEAD ON M' TROPHY WALL, EARS AN' ALL!

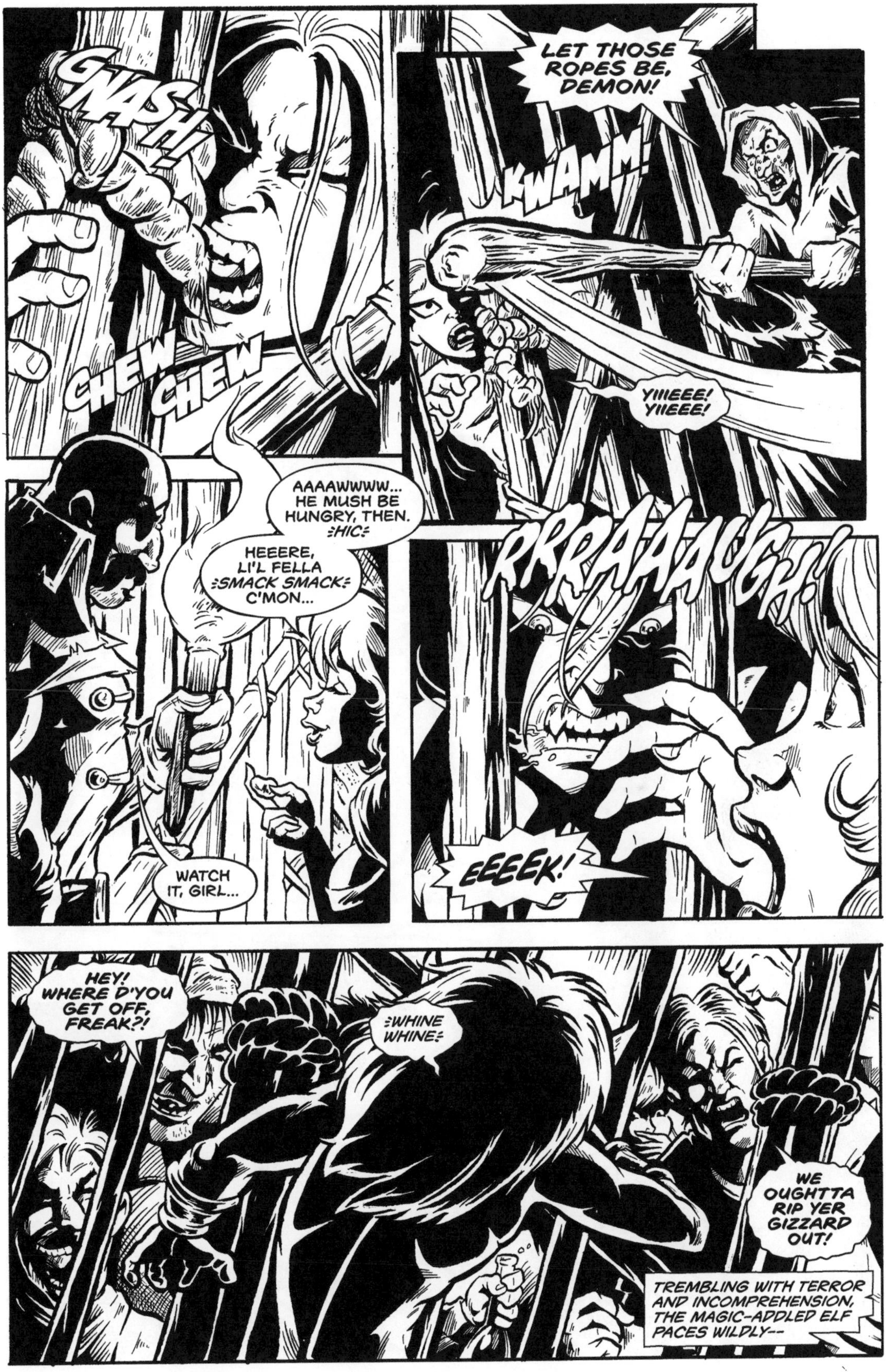
GNASH!
CHEW CHEW
LET THOSE ROPES BE, DEMON!
KWAMM!
YIIEEE! YIIEEE!
AAAAWWWW... HE MUSH BE HUNGRY, THEN. HIC
HEEERE, LI'L FELLA SMACK SMACK C'MON...
WATCH IT, GIRL...
RRRAAAAUGH!
EEEEK!
HEY! WHERE D'YOU GET OFF, FREAK?!
WHINE WHINE
WE OUGHTTA RIP YER GIZZARD OUT!
TREMBLING WITH TERROR AND INCOMPREHENSION, THE MAGIC-ADDLED ELF PACES WILDLY--

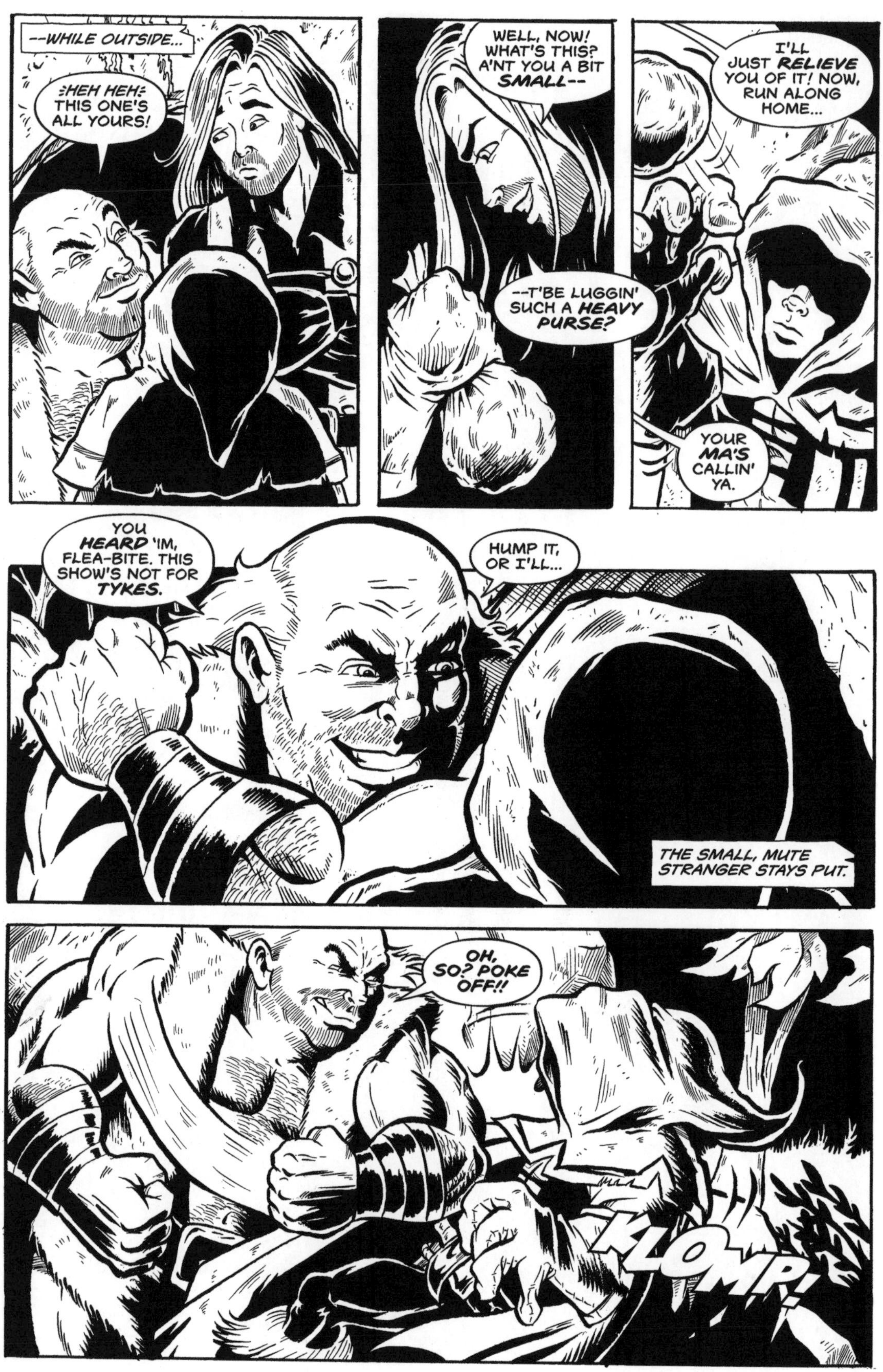
--WHILE OUTSIDE...
HEH HEH
THIS ONE'S ALL YOURS!
WELL, NOW! WHAT'S THIS? A'NT YOU A BIT SMALL--
--T'BE LUGGIN' SUCH A HEAVY PURSE?
I'LL JUST RELIEVE YOU OF IT! NOW, RUN ALONG HOME...
YOUR MA'S CALLIN' YA.
YOU HEARD 'IM, FLEA-BITE. THIS SHOW'S NOT FOR TYKES.
HUMP IT, OR I'LL...
THE SMALL, MUTE STRANGER STAYS PUT.
OH, SO? POKE OFF!!
KLOMP!

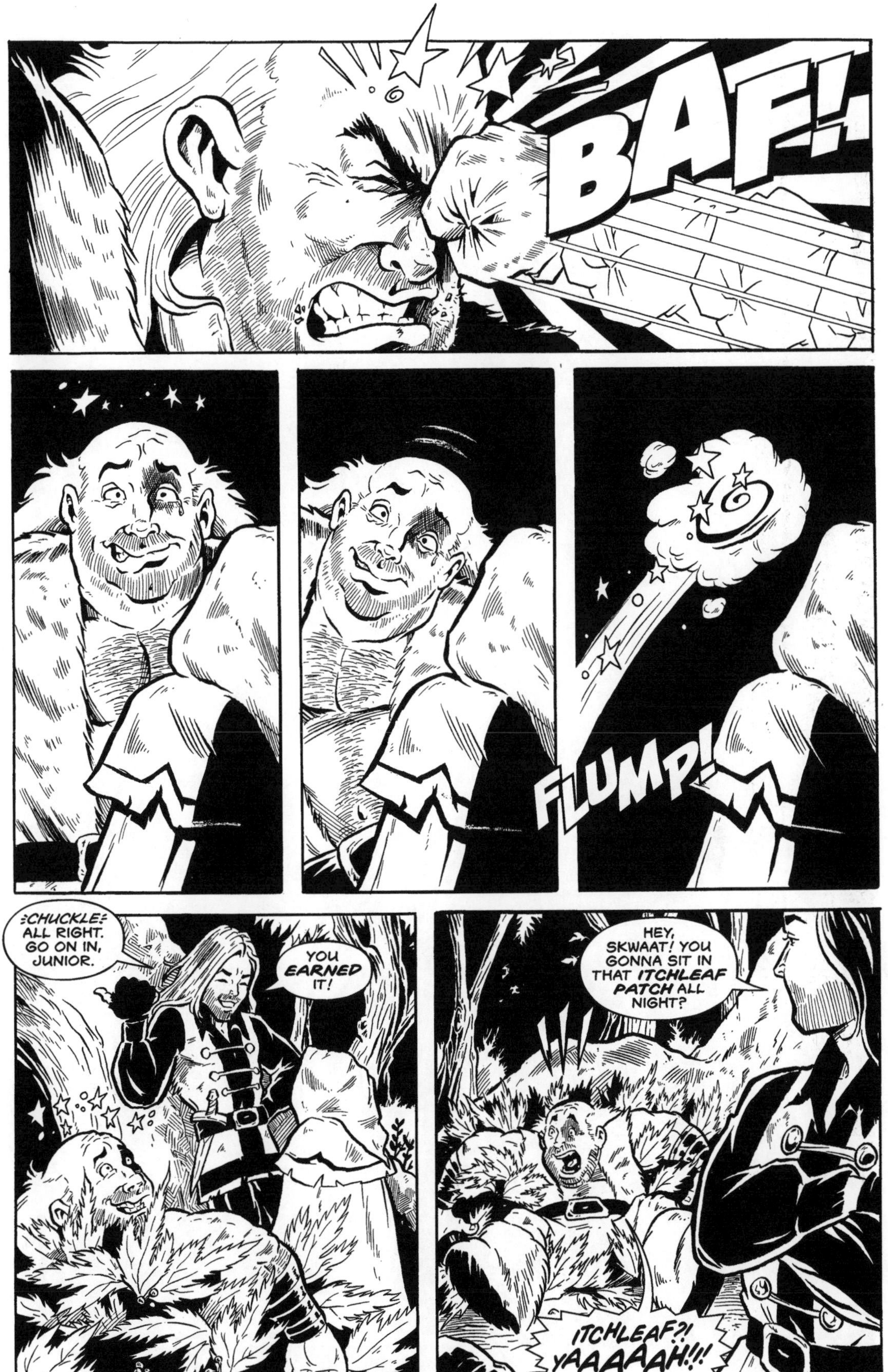
BAF!
FLUMP!
CHUCKLE ALL RIGHT. GO ON IN, JUNIOR.
YOU EARNED IT!
HEY, SKWAAT! YOU GONNA SIT IN THAT ITCHLEAF PATCH ALL NIGHT?
ITCHLEAF?! YAAAAAH!!!

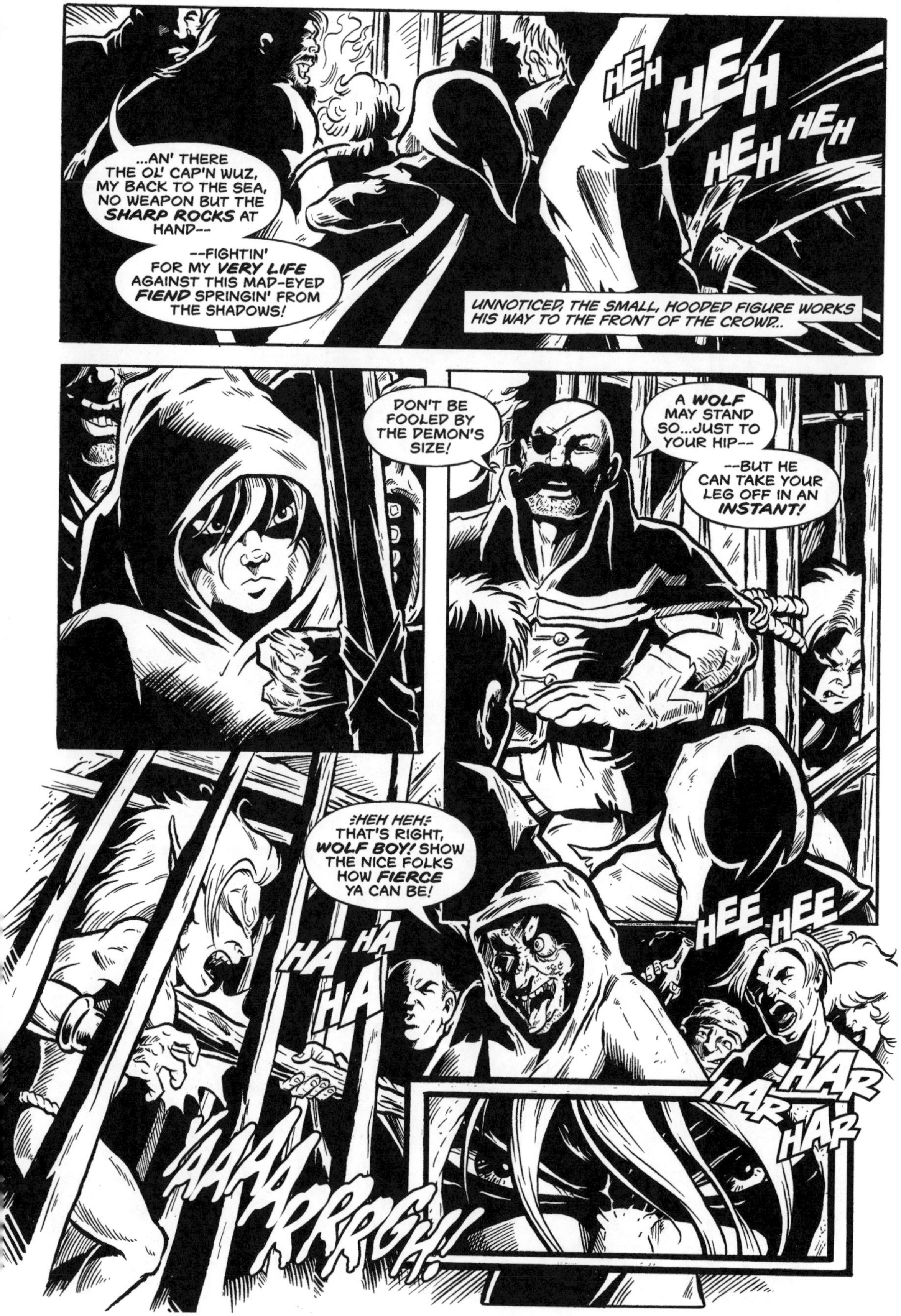
...AN' THERE THE OL' CAP'N WUZ, MY BACK TO THE SEA, NO WEAPON BUT THE SHARP ROCKS AT HAND--
--FIGHTIN' FOR MY VERY LIFE AGAINST THIS MAD-EYED FIEND SPRINGIN' FROM THE SHADOWS!
HEH HEH HEH HEH
UNNOTICED, THE SMALL, HOODED FIGURE WORKS HIS WAY TO THE FRONT OF THE CROWD...
DON'T BE FOOLED BY THE DEMON'S SIZE!
A WOLF MAY STAND SO...JUST TO YOUR HIP--
--BUT HE CAN TAKE YOUR LEG OFF IN AN INSTANT!
HEH HEH THAT'S RIGHT, WOLF BOY! SHOW THE NICE FOLKS HOW FIERCE YA CAN BE!
HA HA HA
HEE HEE
HAR HAR HAR HAR
YAAAARRRGH!

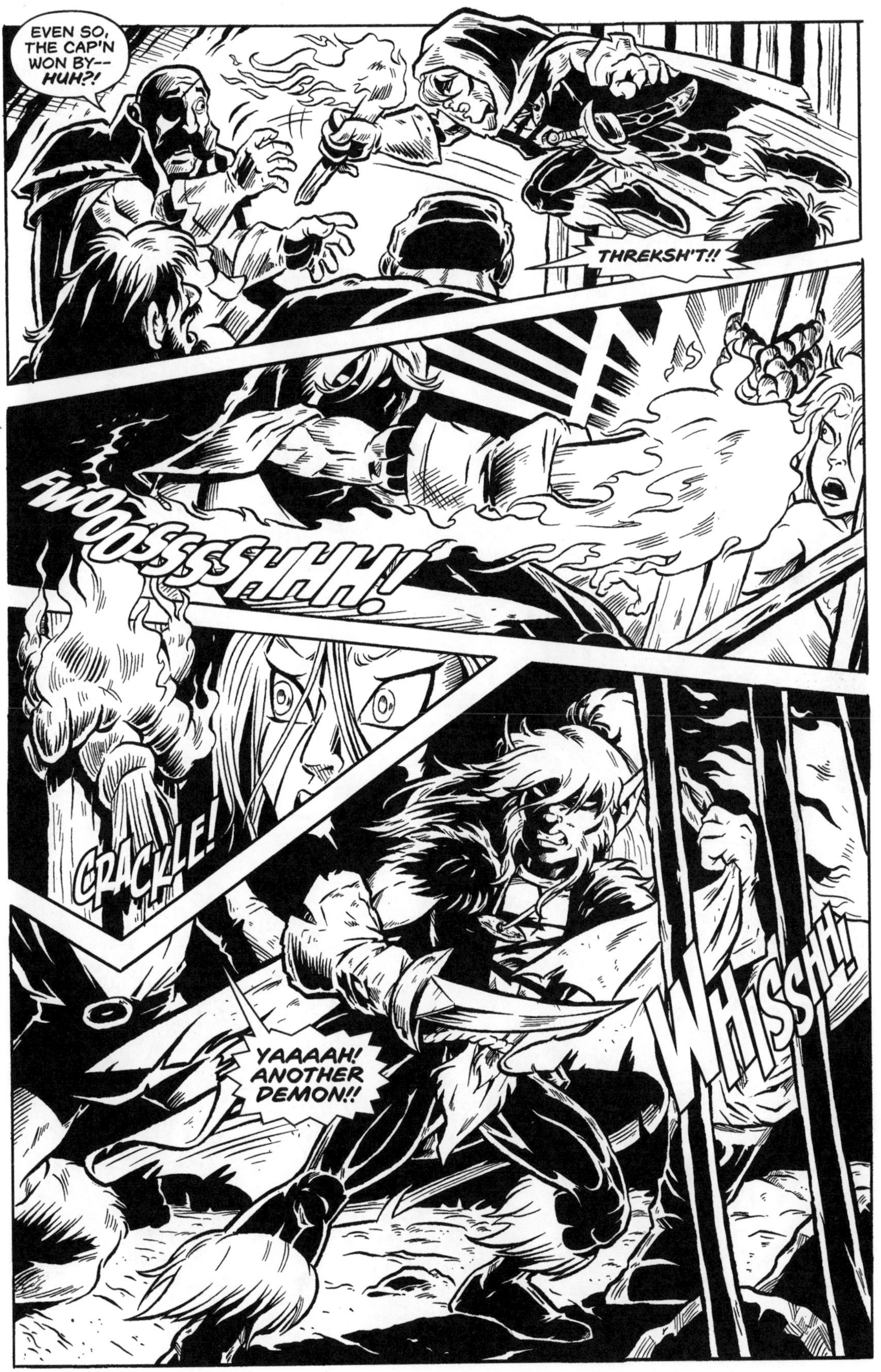
EVEN SO, THE CAP'N WON BY-- HUH?!
THREKSH'T!!
FWOOOSSSSHHHH!
CRACKLE!
WHISSH!
YAAAAH! ANOTHER DEMON!!

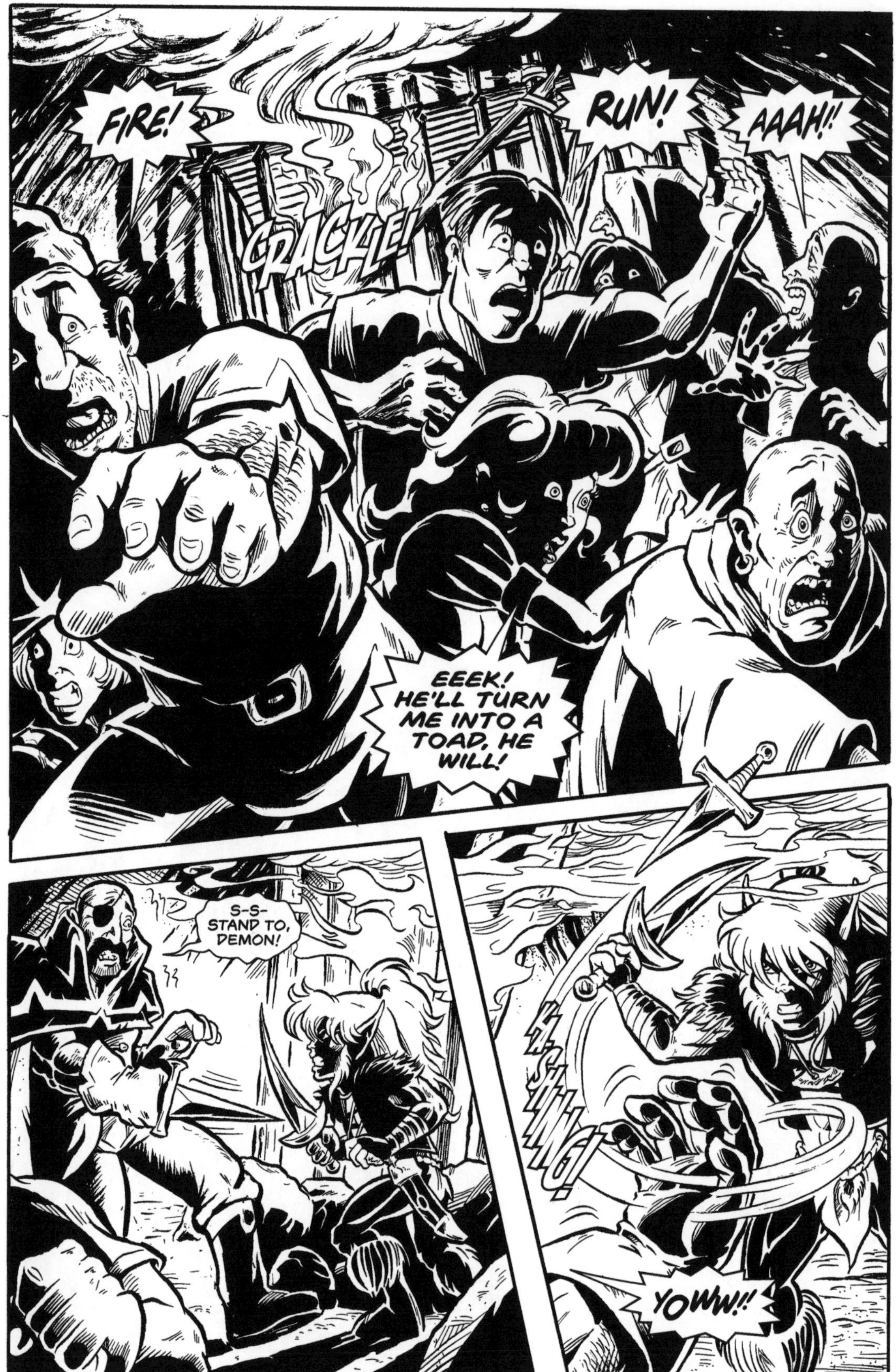
FIRE!
RUN!
AAAH!!
CRACKLE!
EEEK! HE'LL TURN ME INTO A TOAD, HE WILL!
S-S-STAND TO, DEMON!
SHING!
YOWW!!

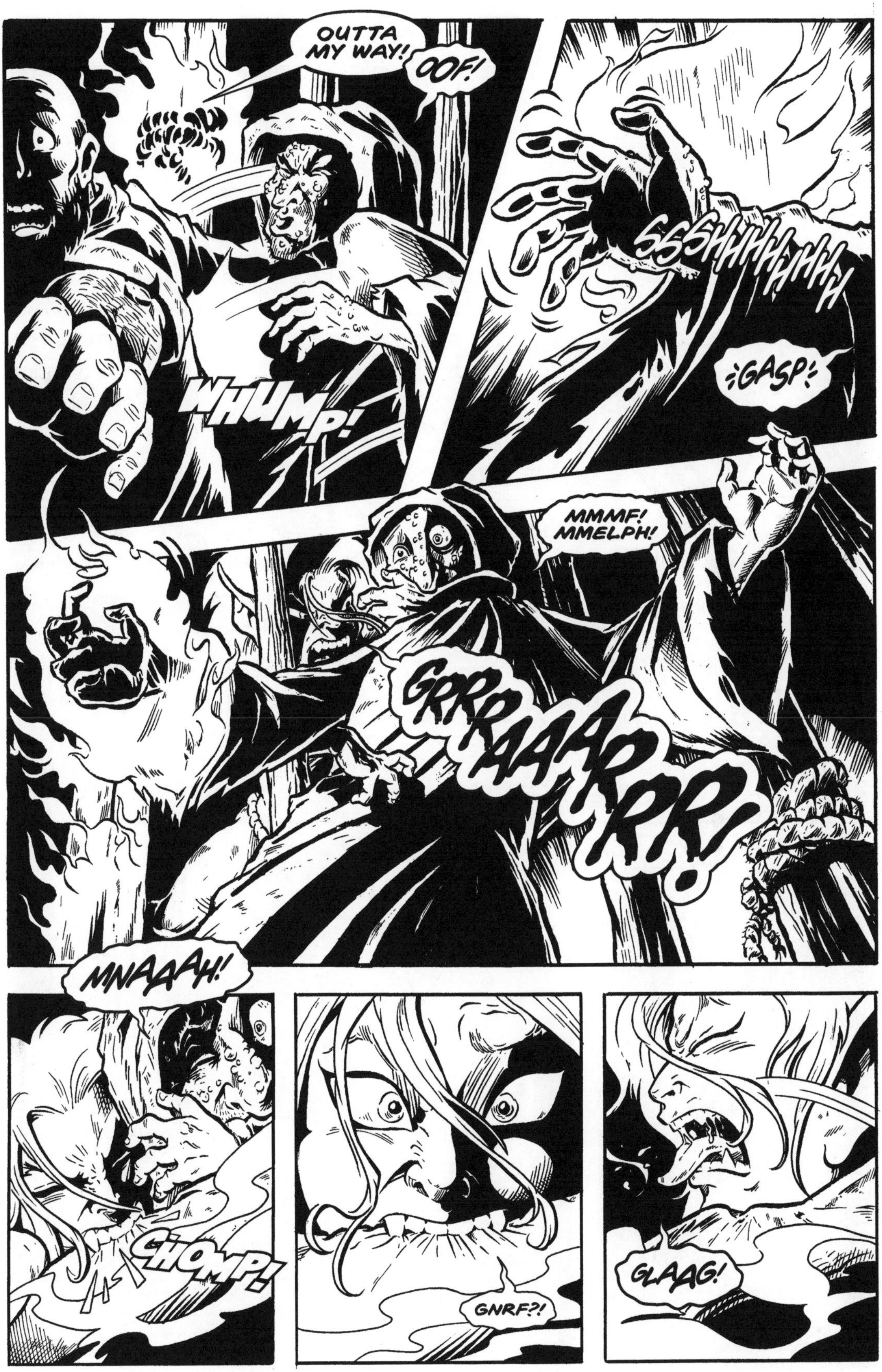
OUTTA MY WAY!
OOF!
WHUMP!
SSSHHHHHHHH
¡GASP!
MMMF! MMELPH!
GRRRAAAARRR!
MNAAAH!
CHOMP!
GNRF?!
GLAAG!

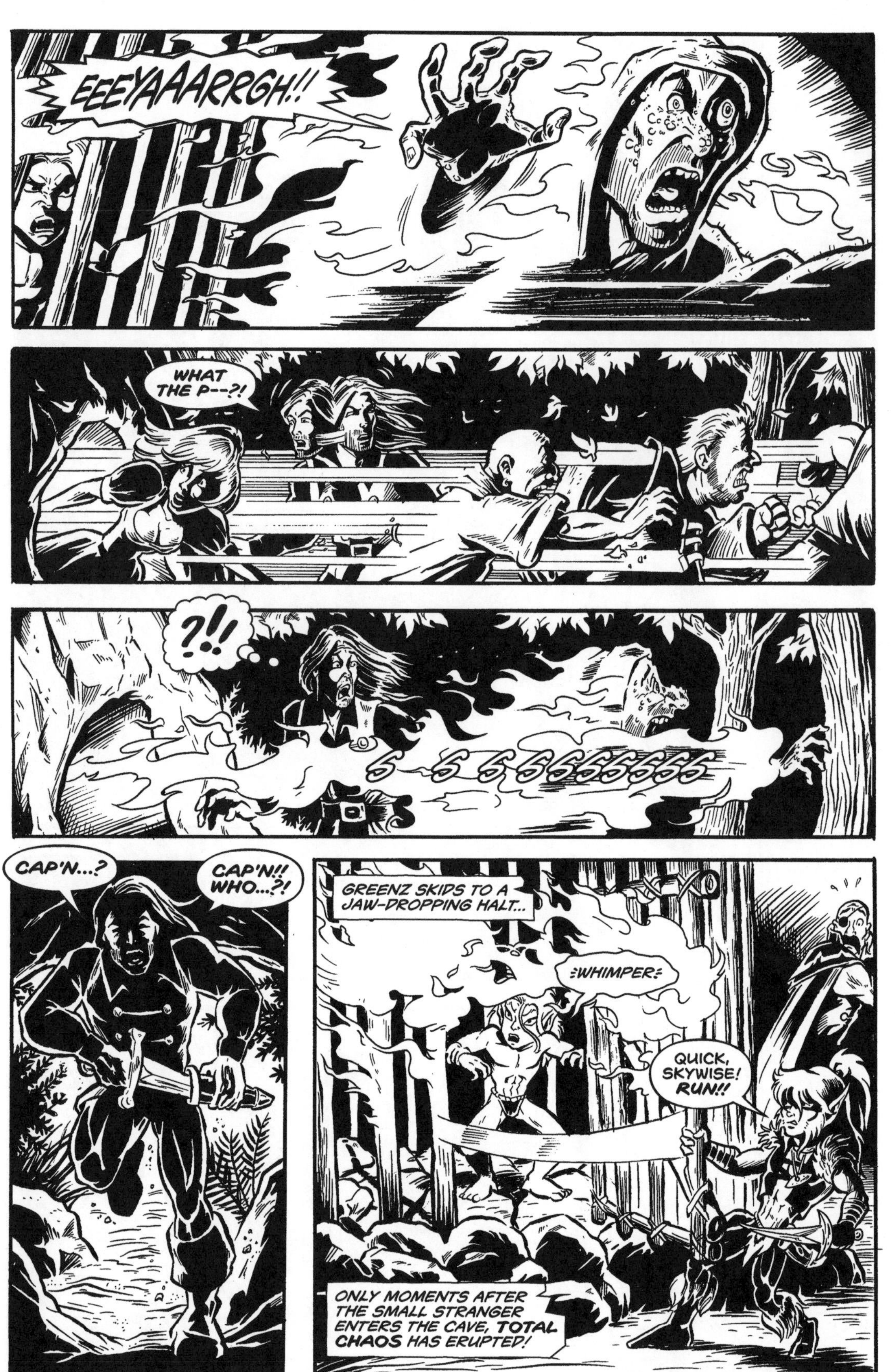
EEEYAAARRGH!!
WHAT THE P--?!
?!!
6 6 6 6666666
CAP'N...?
CAP'N!! WHO...?!
GREENZ SKIDS TO A JAW-DROPPING HALT...
WHIMPER
QUICK, SKYWISE! RUN!!
ONLY MOMENTS AFTER THE SMALL STRANGER ENTERS THE CAVE, TOTAL CHAOS HAS ERUPTED!

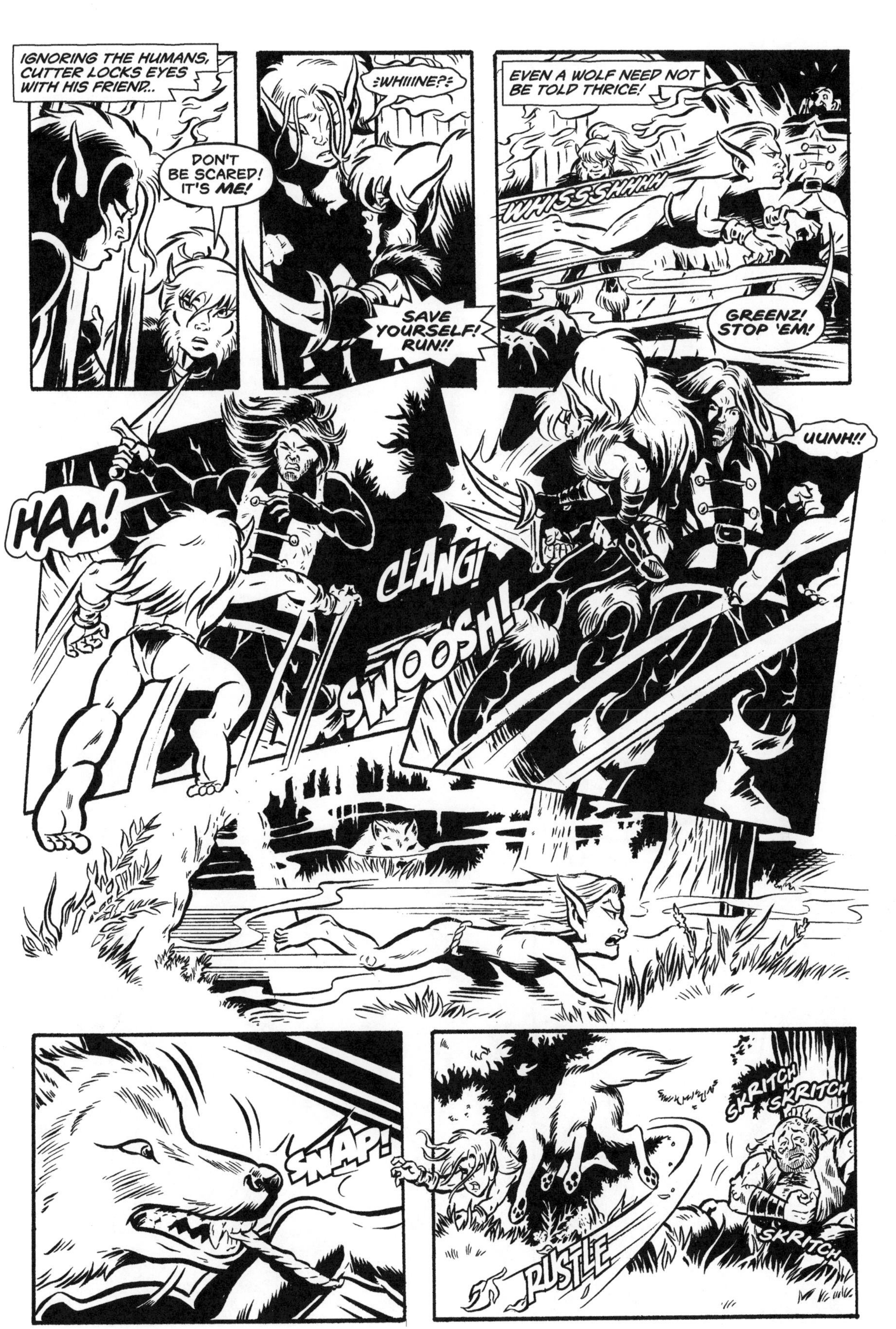
IGNORING THE HUMANS, CUTTER LOCKS EYES WITH HIS FRIEND...
DON'T BE SCARED! IT'S ME!
WHIIINE?
SAVE YOURSELF! RUN!!
EVEN A WOLF NEED NOT BE TOLD THRICE!
WHISSSHHHH
GREENZ! STOP 'EM!
HAA!
CLANG!
SWOOSH!
UUNH!!
SNAP!
SKRITCH
SKRITCH
SKRITCH
RUSTLE

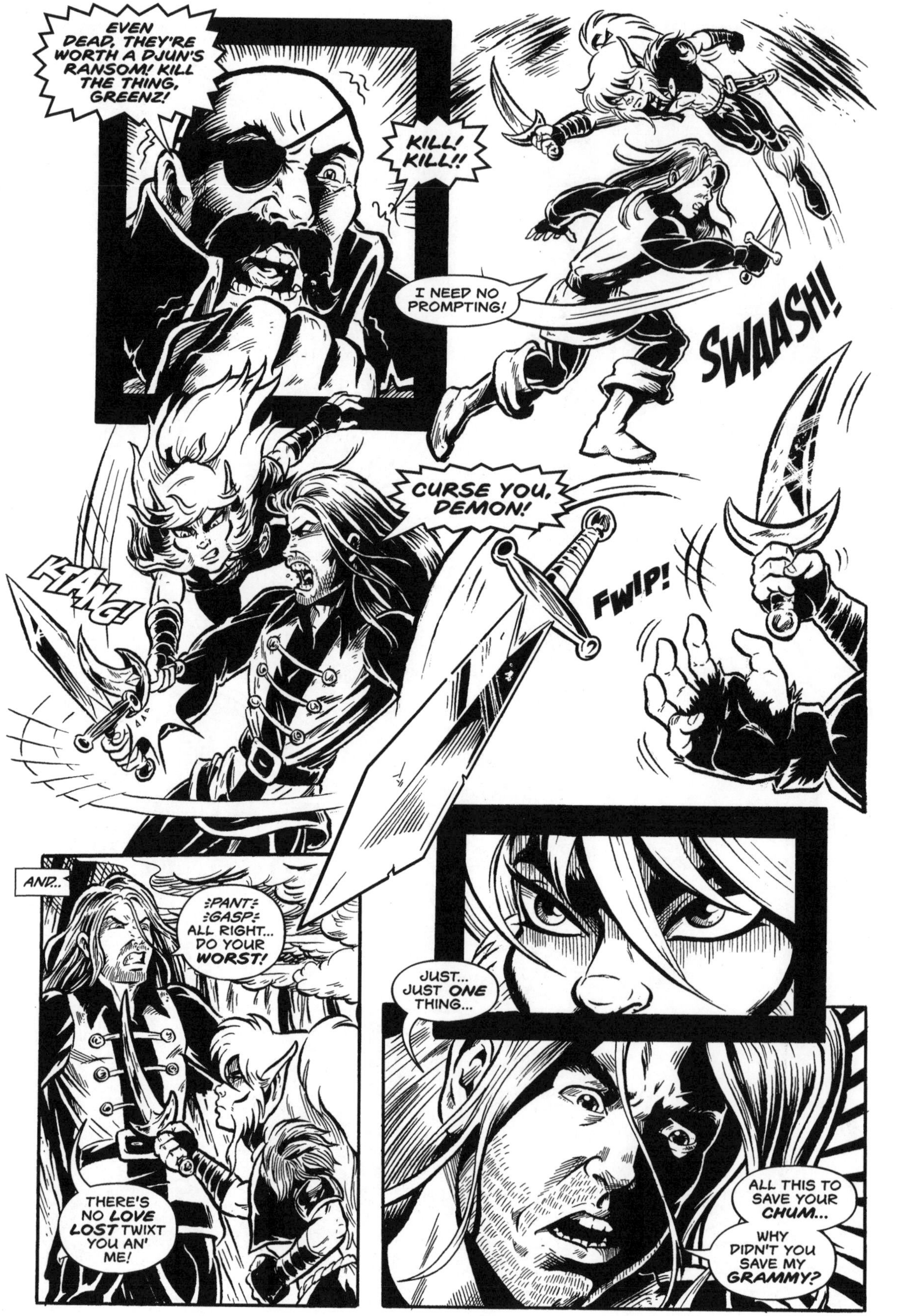

EVEN DEAD, THEY'RE WORTH A DJUN'S RANSOM! KILL THE THING, GREENZ!
KILL! KILL!!
I NEED NO PROMPTING!
SWAASH!
CURSE YOU, DEMON!
K-TANG!
FWIP!
AND...
PANT GASP ALL RIGHT... DO YOUR WORST!
THERE'S NO LOVE LOST TWIXT YOU AN' ME!
JUST... JUST ONE THING...
ALL THIS TO SAVE YOUR CHUM...
WHY DIDN'T YOU SAVE MY GRAMMY?

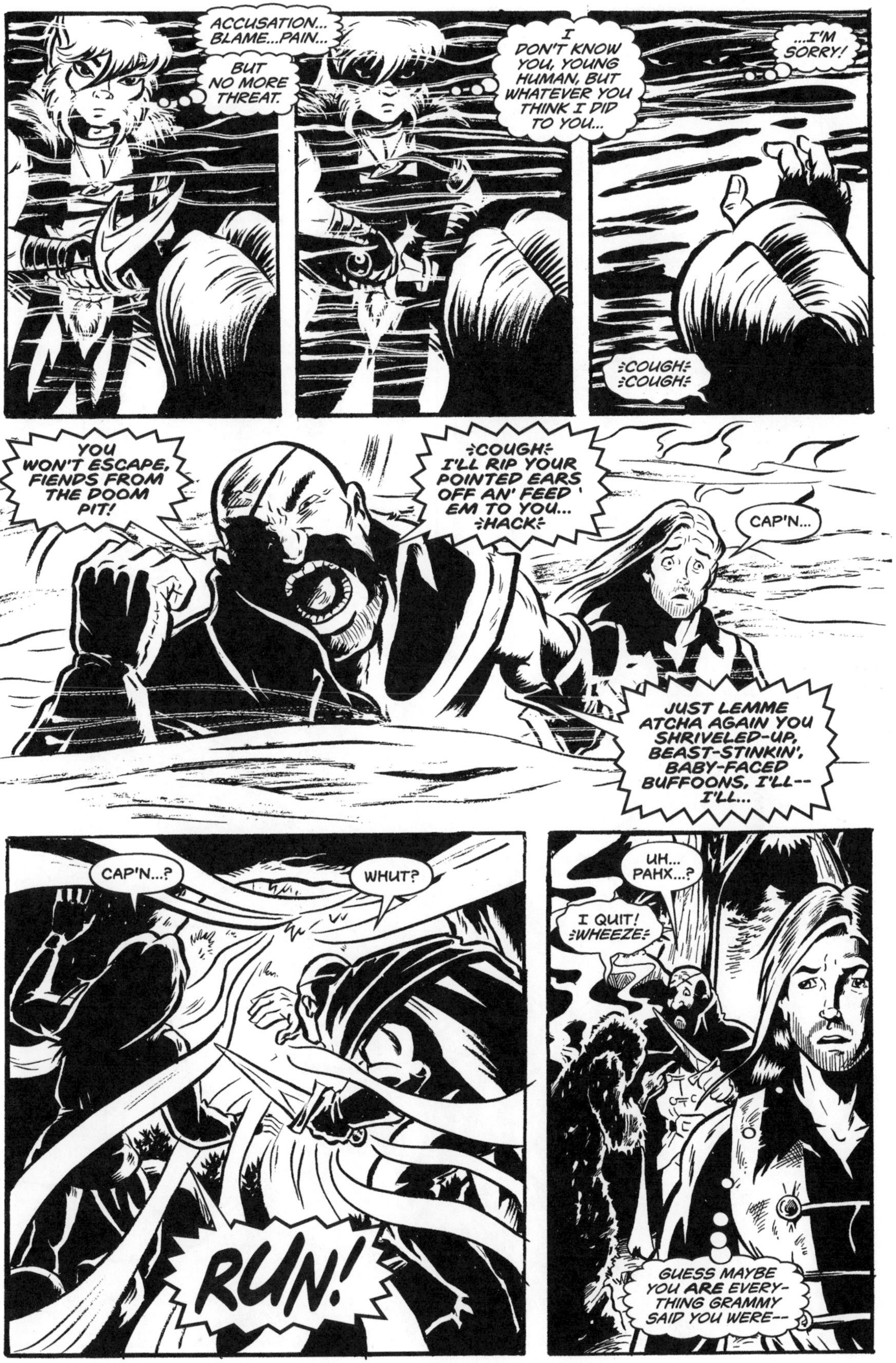

ACCUSATION... BLAME...PAIN...
BUT NO MORE THREAT.
I DON'T KNOW YOU, YOUNG HUMAN, BUT WHATEVER YOU THINK I DID TO YOU...
...I'M SORRY!
COUGH COUGH
YOU WON'T ESCAPE, FIENDS FROM THE DOOM PIT!
COUGH I'LL RIP YOUR POINTED EARS OFF AN' FEED EM TO YOU... HACK
CAP'N...
JUST LEMME ATCHA AGAIN YOU SHRIVELED-UP, BEAST-STINKIN', BABY-FACED BUFFOONS, I'LL-- I'LL...
CAP'N...?
WHUT?
RUN!
UH... PAHX...?
I QUIT! WHEEZE
GUESS MAYBE YOU ARE EVERY-THING GRAMMY SAID YOU WERE--

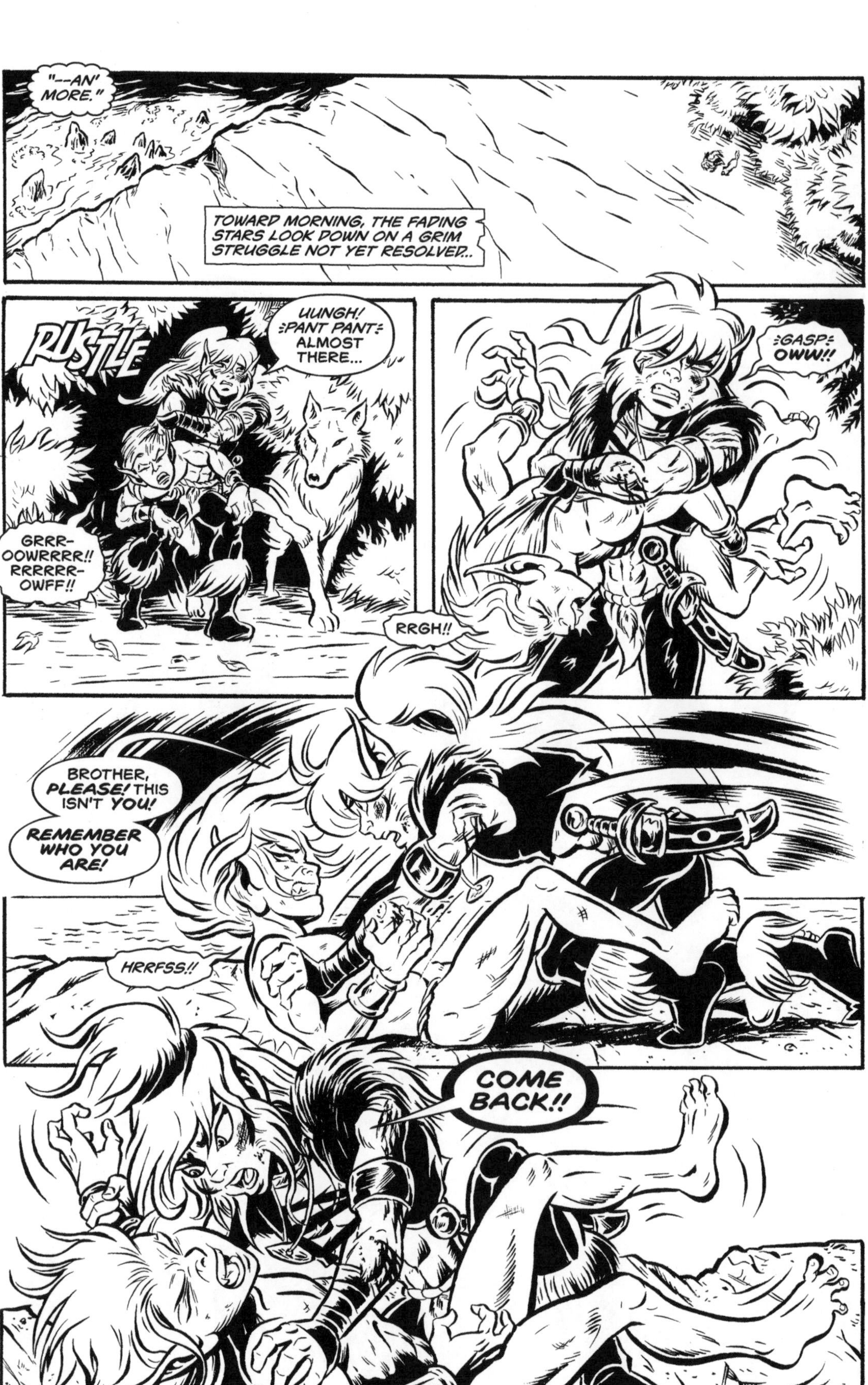
"--AN' MORE."
TOWARD MORNING, THE FADING STARS LOOK DOWN ON A GRIM STRUGGLE NOT YET RESOLVED...
RUSTLE
UUNGH! PANT PANT ALMOST THERE...
GRRR-OOWRRRR!! RRRRRR-OWFF!!
GASP OWW!!
RRGH!!
BROTHER, PLEASE! THIS ISN'T YOU!
REMEMBER WHO YOU ARE!
HRRFSS!!
COME BACK!!

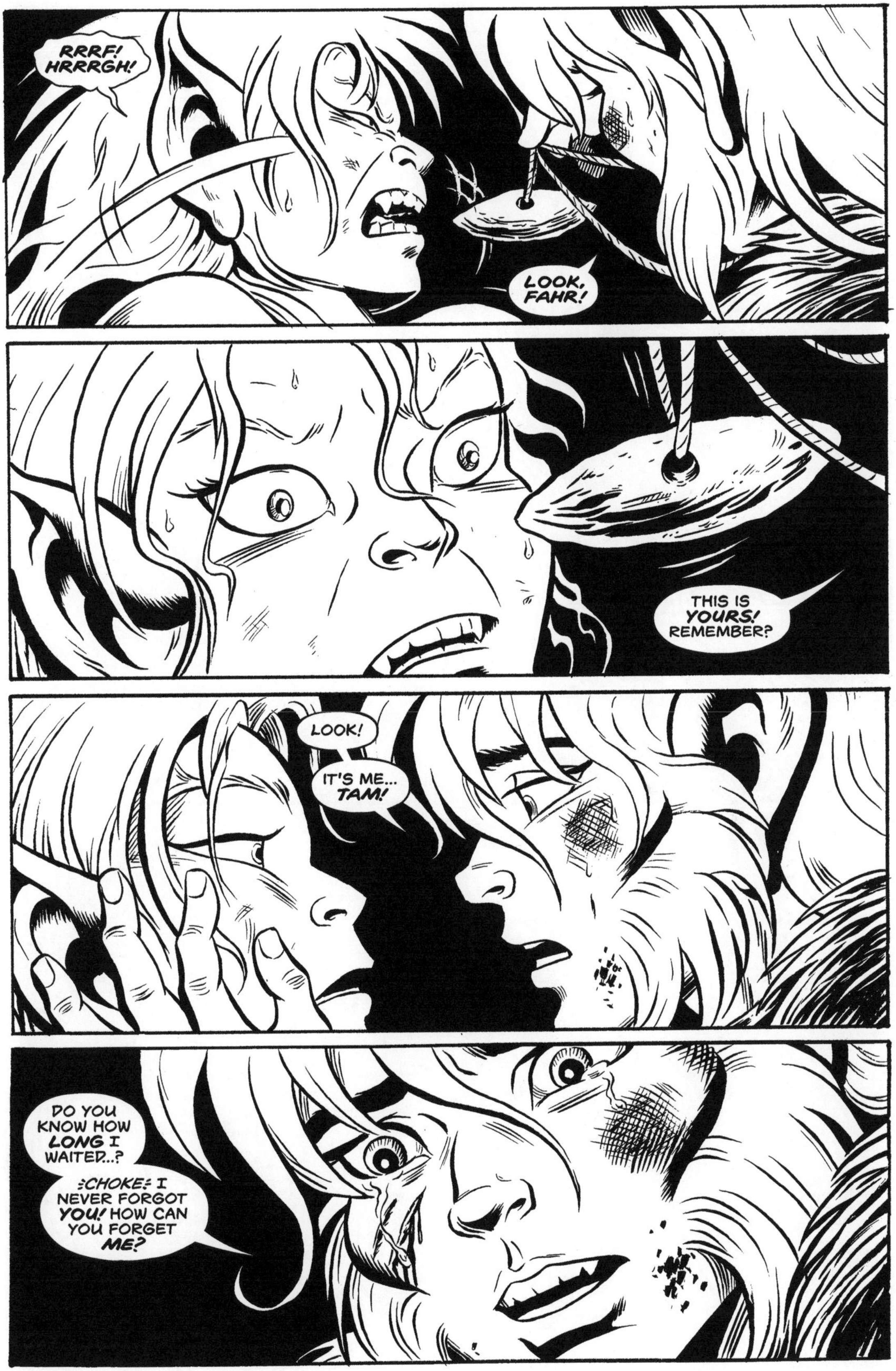
RRRF! HRRRGH!
LOOK, FAHR!
THIS IS YOURS! REMEMBER?
LOOK!
IT'S ME... TAM!
DO YOU KNOW HOW LONG I WAITED...?
:CHOKE: I NEVER FORGOT YOU! HOW CAN YOU FORGET ME?

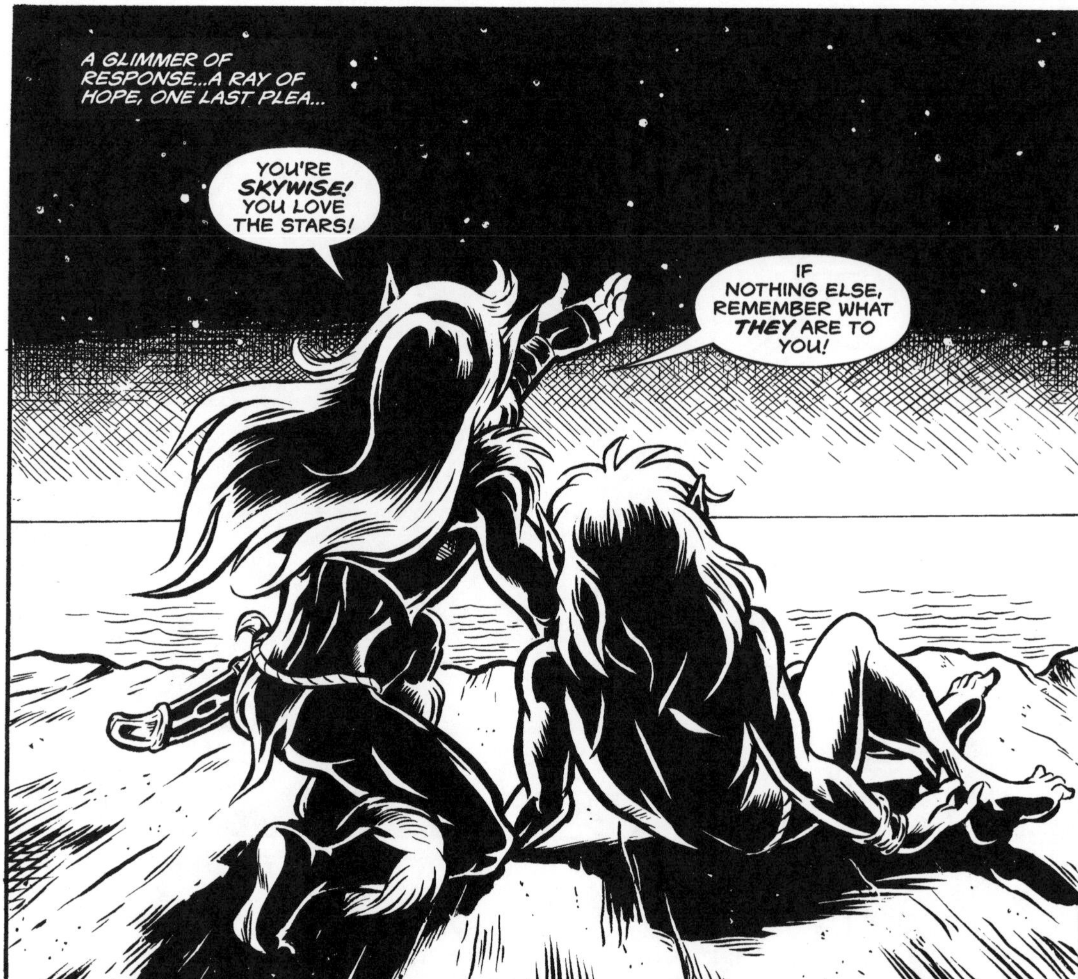
A GLIMMER OF RESPONSE...A RAY OF HOPE, ONE LAST PLEA...
YOU'RE SKYWISE! YOU LOVE THE STARS!
IF NOTHING ELSE, REMEMBER WHAT THEY ARE TO YOU!

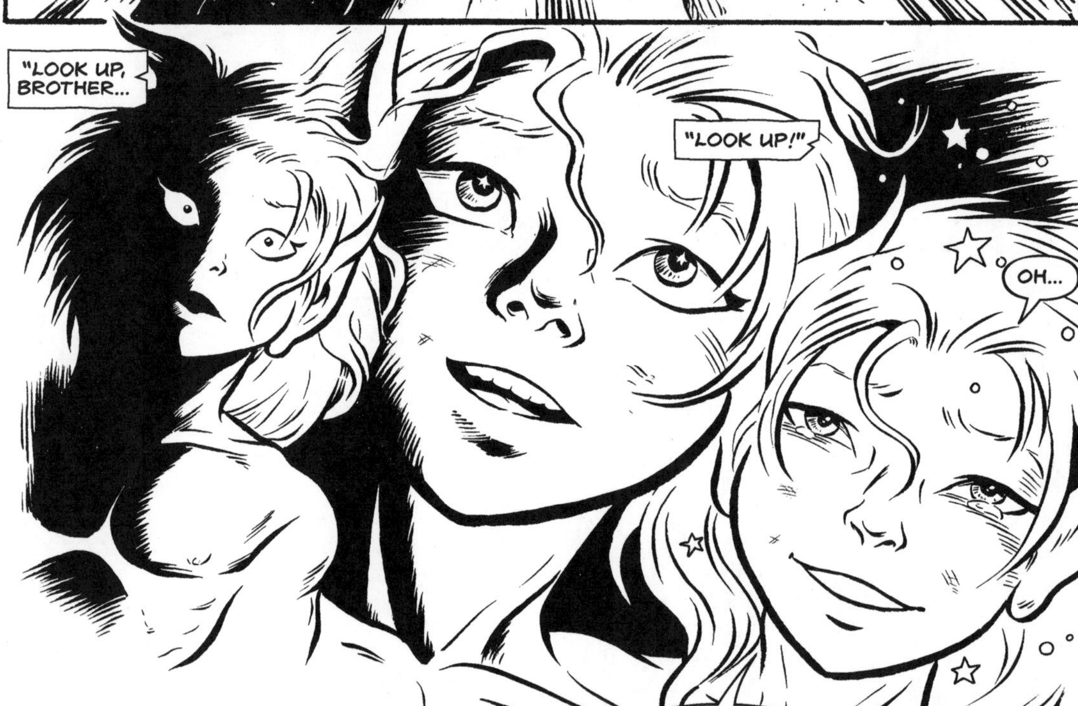
"LOOK UP, BROTHER...
"LOOK UP!"
OH...
BEAUTIFUL!

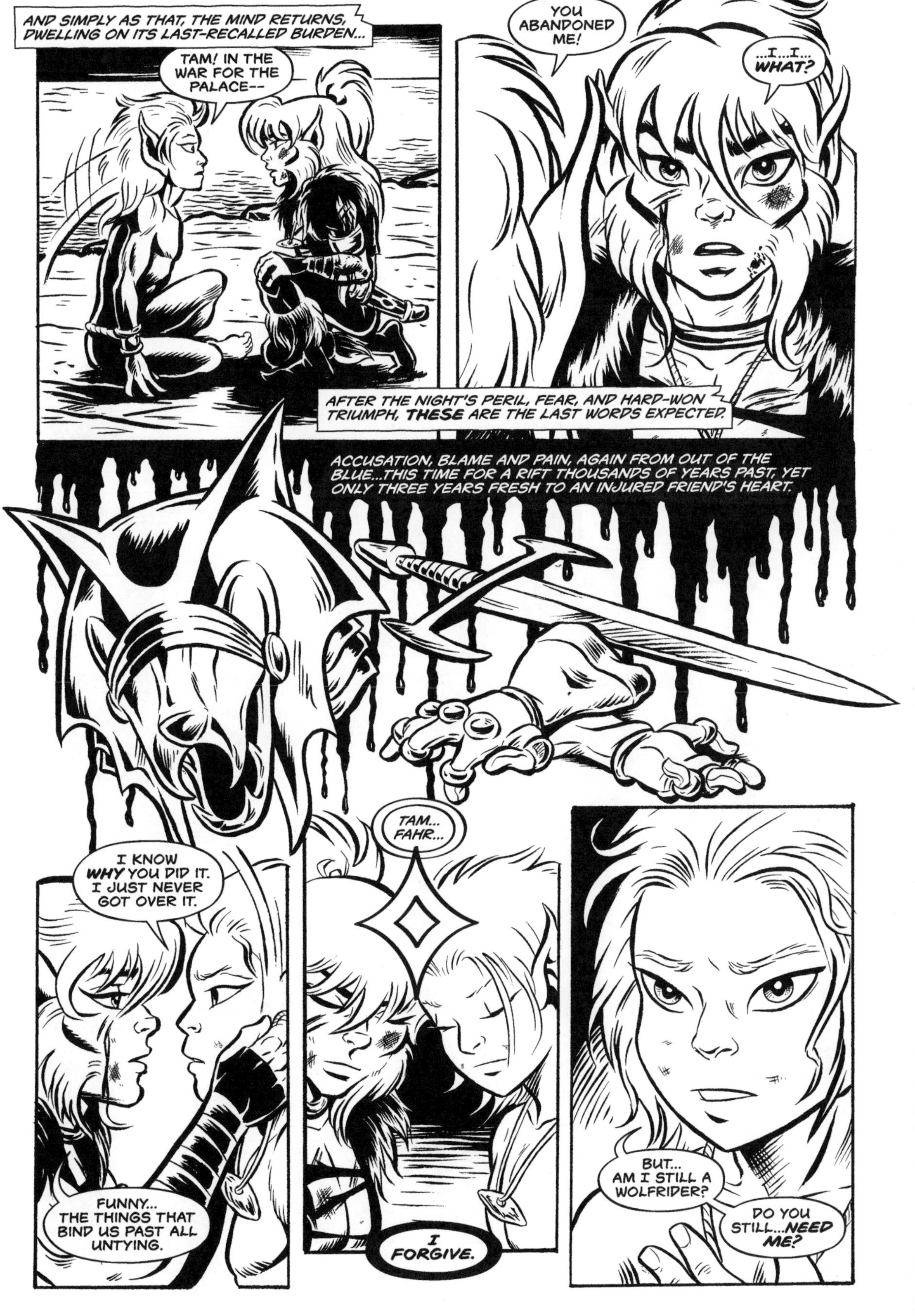
AND SIMPLY AS THAT, THE MIND RETURNS, DWELLING ON ITS LAST-RECALLED BURDEN...
TAM! IN THE WAR FOR THE PALACE--
YOU ABANDONED ME!
...I...I... WHAT?
AFTER THE NIGHT'S PERIL, FEAR, AND HARD-WON TRIUMPH, THESE ARE THE LAST WORDS EXPECTED.
ACCUSATION, BLAME AND PAIN, AGAIN FROM OUT OF THE BLUE...THIS TIME FOR A RIFT THOUSANDS OF YEARS PAST, YET ONLY THREE YEARS FRESH TO AN INJURED FRIEND'S HEART.
I KNOW WHY YOU DID IT. I JUST NEVER GOT OVER IT.
FUNNY... THE THINGS THAT BIND US PAST ALL UNTYING.
TAM... FAHR...
I FORGIVE.
BUT... AM I STILL A WOLFRIDER?
DO YOU STILL...NEED ME?

HA HA! NEED YOU?

--HA-- UUNGH!

I EVEN NEEDED TO *THINK* LIKE YOU TO SAVE YOU TONIGHT! HA HA--

TAM?! HIGH ONES! LOOK WHAT I--!

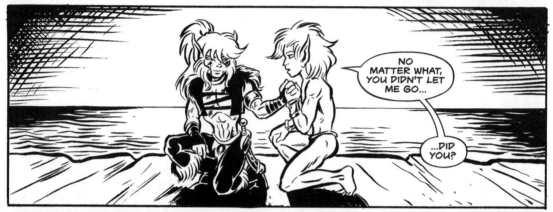

NO MATTER WHAT, YOU DIDN'T LET ME GO...

...DID YOU?

NEVER.

"NO MATTER WHAT."

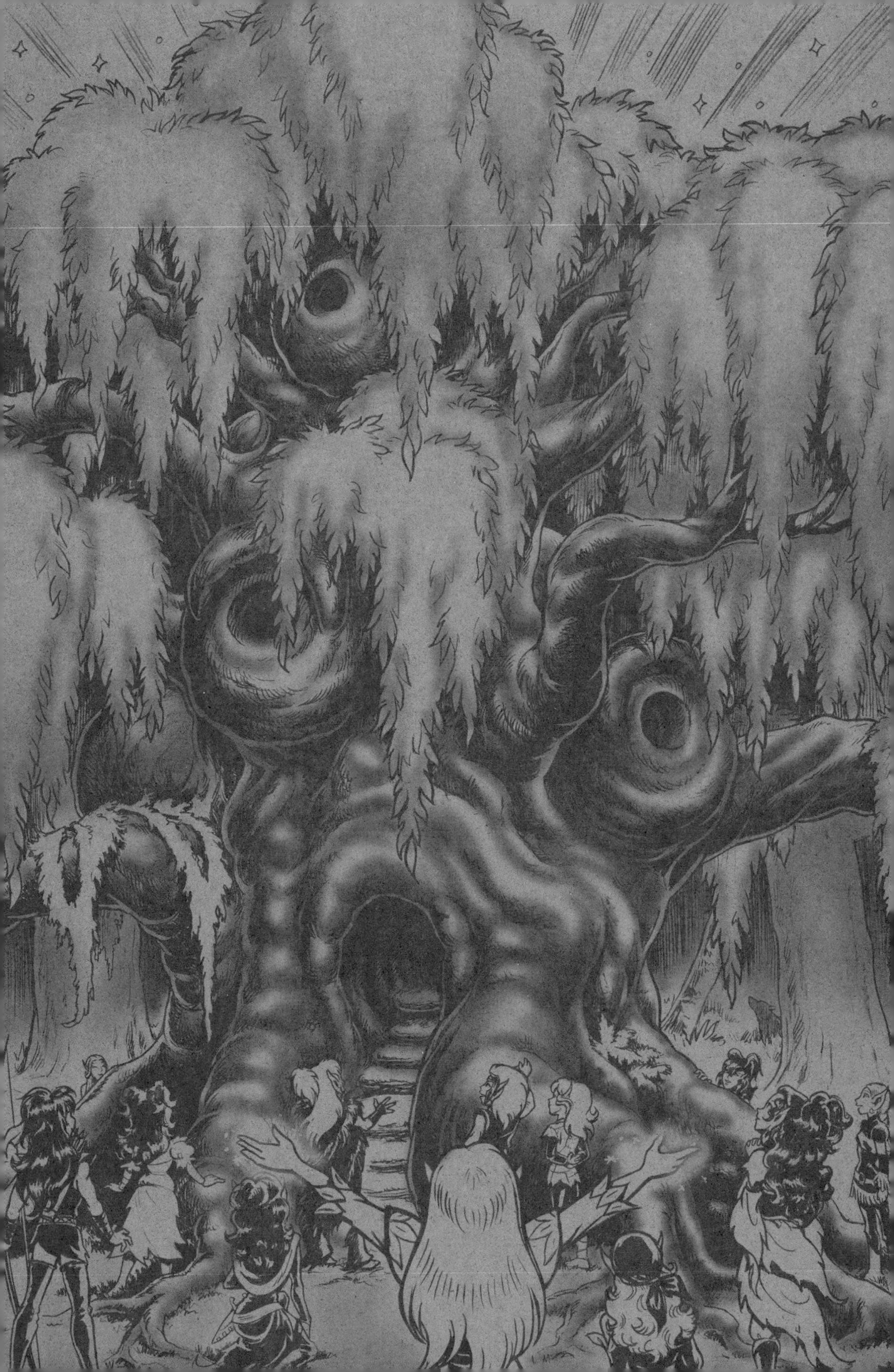

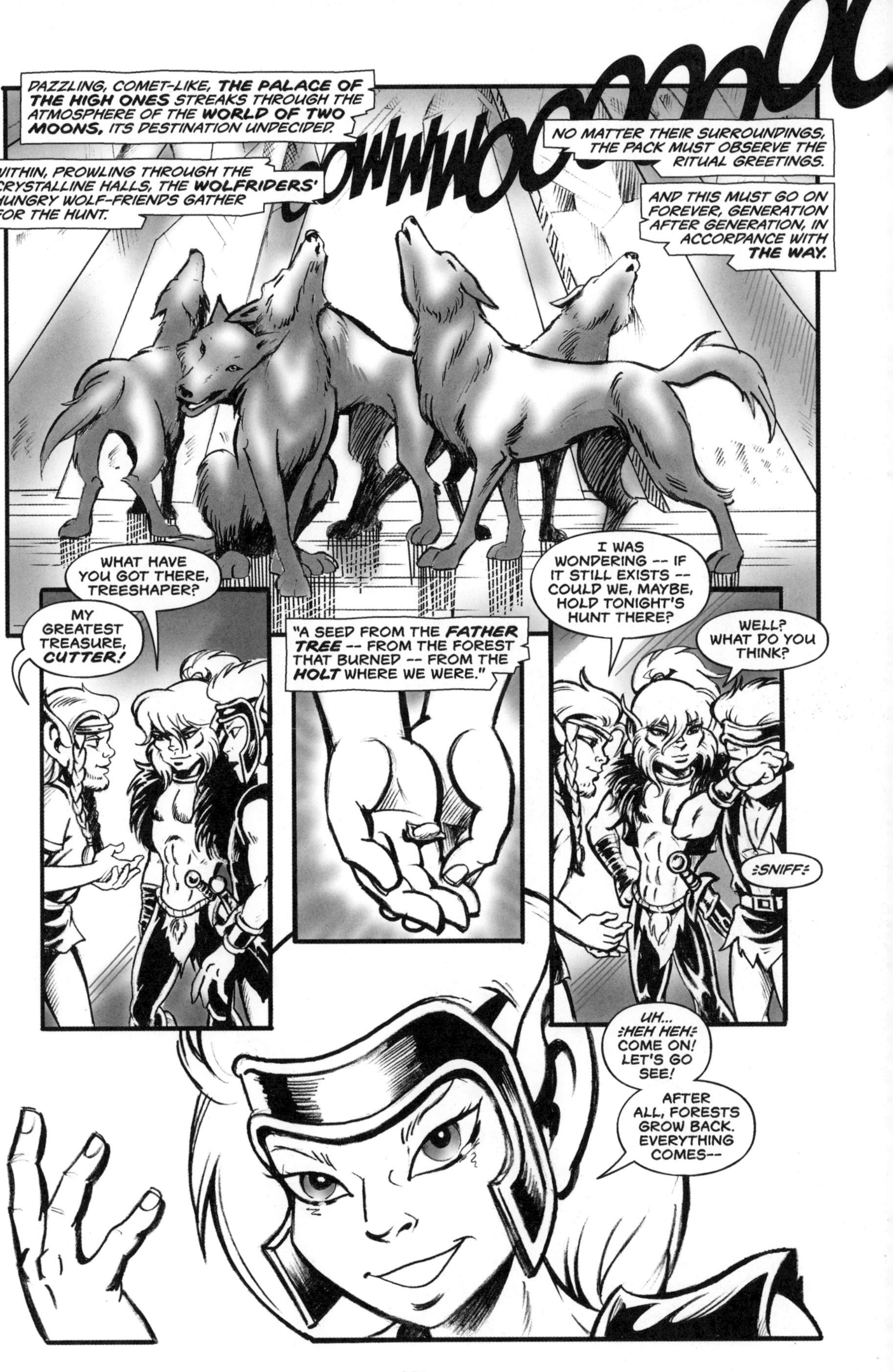

DAZZLING, COMET-LIKE, THE PALACE OF THE HIGH ONES STREAKS THROUGH THE ATMOSPHERE OF THE WORLD OF TWO MOONS, ITS DESTINATION UNDECIDED.
AOOWWWOOOOOOA
WITHIN, PROWLING THROUGH THE CRYSTALLINE HALLS, THE WOLFRIDERS' HUNGRY WOLF-FRIENDS GATHER FOR THE HUNT.
NO MATTER THEIR SURROUNDINGS, THE PACK MUST OBSERVE THE RITUAL GREETINGS.
AND THIS MUST GO ON FOREVER, GENERATION AFTER GENERATION, IN ACCORDANCE WITH THE WAY.
WHAT HAVE YOU GOT THERE, TREESHAPER?
MY GREATEST TREASURE, CUTTER!
"A SEED FROM THE FATHER TREE -- FROM THE FOREST THAT BURNED -- FROM THE HOLT WHERE WE WERE."
I WAS WONDERING -- IF IT STILL EXISTS -- COULD WE, MAYBE, HOLD TONIGHT'S HUNT THERE?
WELL? WHAT DO YOU THINK?
SNIFF
UH... HEH HEH! COME ON! LET'S GO SEE!
AFTER ALL, FORESTS GROW BACK. EVERYTHING COMES--

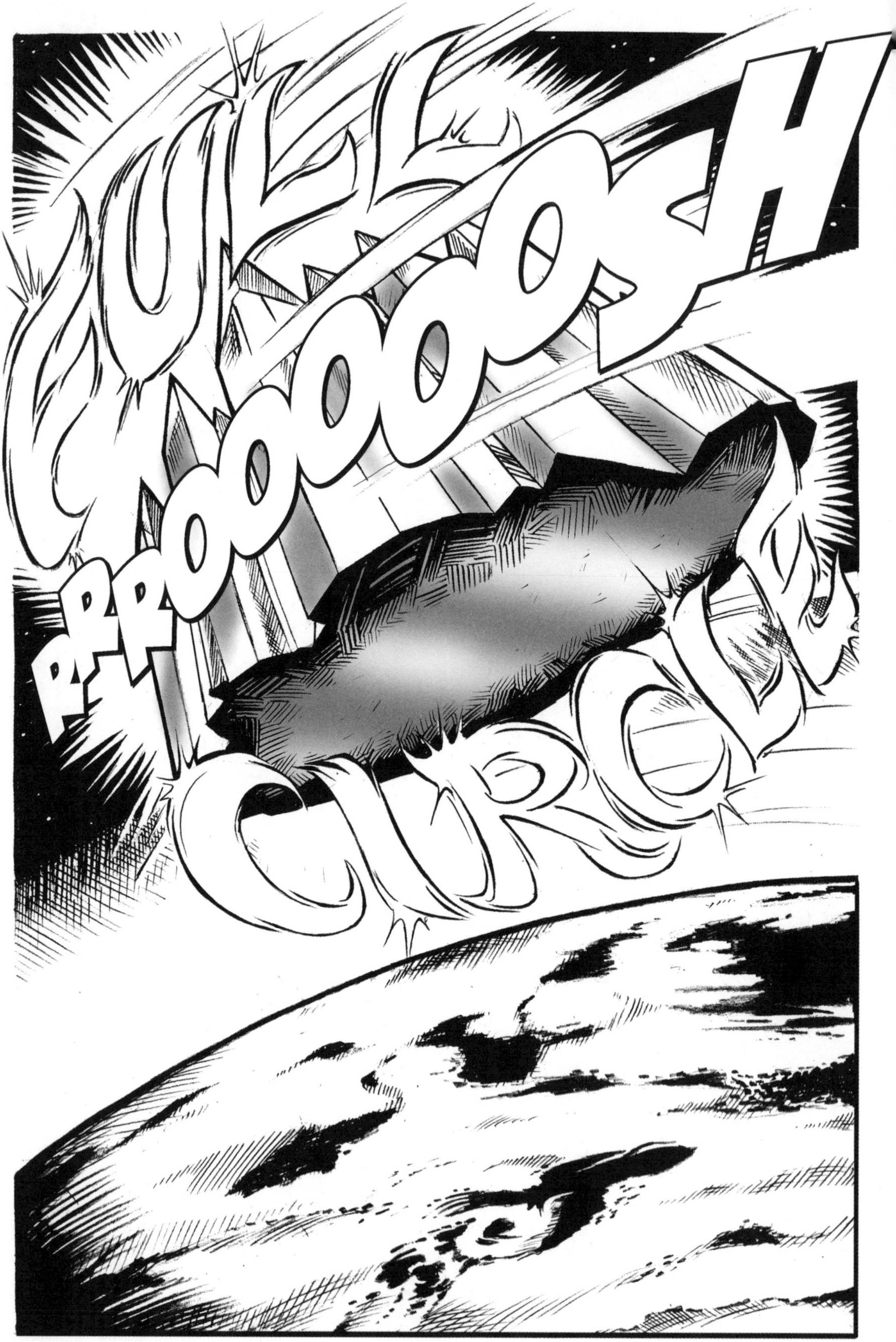

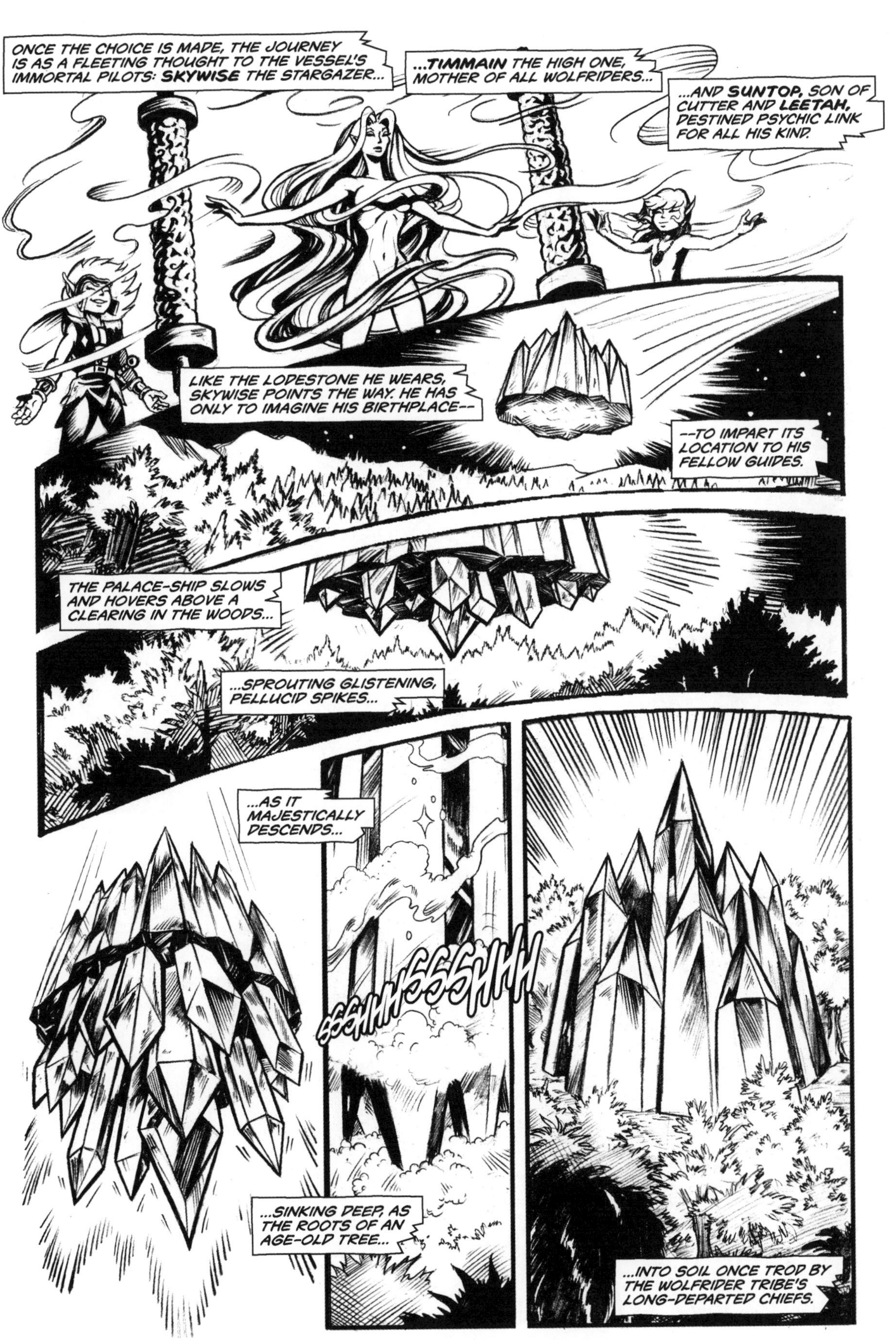
ONCE THE CHOICE IS MADE, THE JOURNEY IS AS A FLEETING THOUGHT TO THE VESSEL'S IMMORTAL PILOTS: SKYWISE THE STARGAZER...
...TIMMAIN THE HIGH ONE, MOTHER OF ALL WOLFRIDERS...
...AND SUNTOP, SON OF CUTTER AND LEETAH, DESTINED PSYCHIC LINK FOR ALL HIS KIND.
LIKE THE LODESTONE HE WEARS, SKYWISE POINTS THE WAY. HE HAS ONLY TO IMAGINE HIS BIRTHPLACE--
--TO IMPART ITS LOCATION TO HIS FELLOW GUIDES.
THE PALACE-SHIP SLOWS AND HOVERS ABOVE A CLEARING IN THE WOODS...
...SPROUTING GLISTENING, PELLUCID SPIKES...
...AS IT MAJESTICALLY DESCENDS...
...SINKING DEEP, AS THE ROOTS OF AN AGE-OLD TREE...
...INTO SOIL ONCE TROD BY THE WOLFRIDER TRIBE'S LONG-DEPARTED CHIEFS.

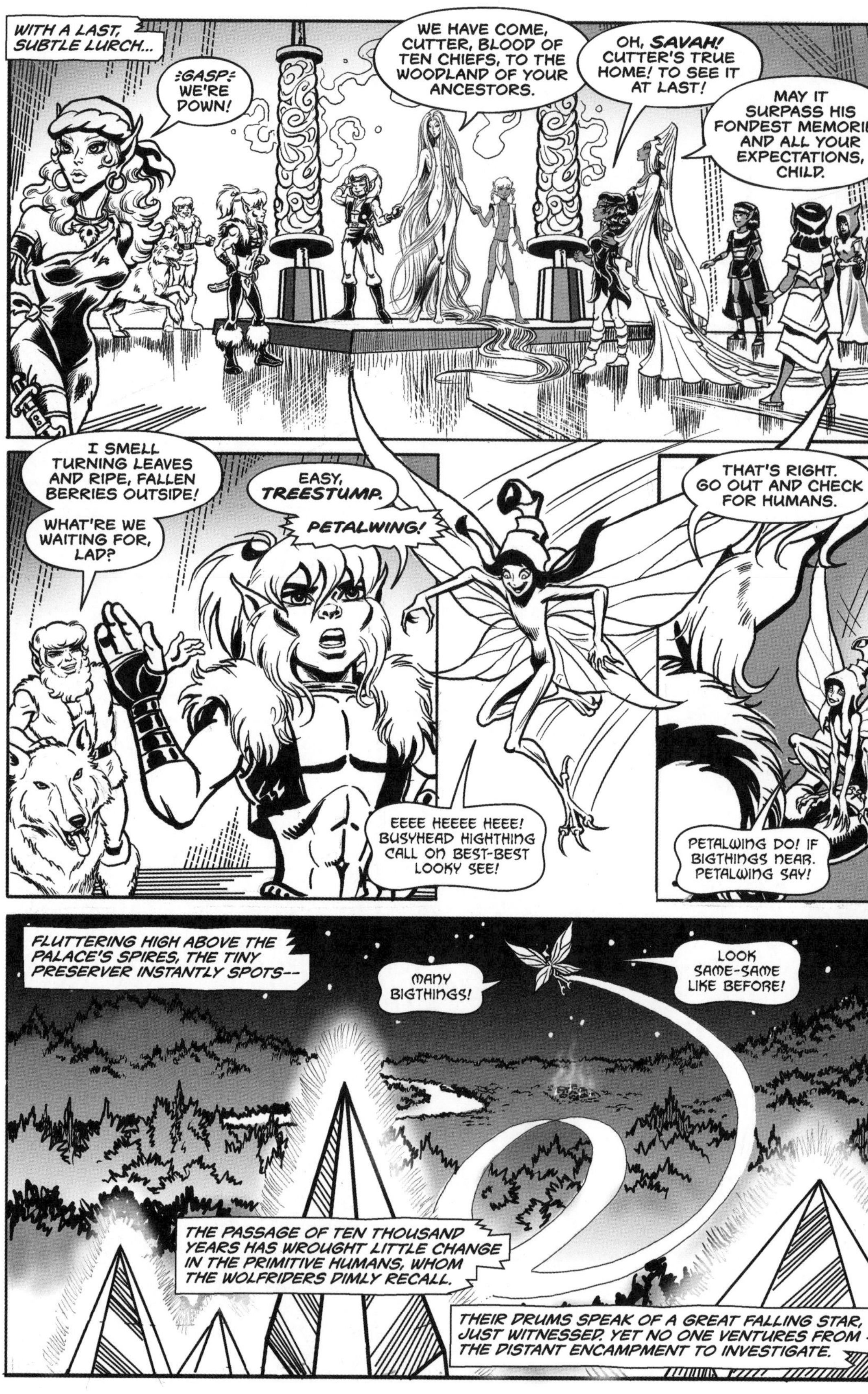
WITH A LAST, SUBTLE LURCH...
:GASP: WE'RE DOWN!
WE HAVE COME, CUTTER, BLOOD OF TEN CHIEFS, TO THE WOODLAND OF YOUR ANCESTORS.
OH, SAVAH! CUTTER'S TRUE HOME! TO SEE IT AT LAST!
MAY IT SURPASS HIS FONDEST MEMORIES AND ALL YOUR EXPECTATIONS, CHILD.
I SMELL TURNING LEAVES AND RIPE, FALLEN BERRIES OUTSIDE!
WHAT'RE WE WAITING FOR, LAD?
EASY, TREESTUMP.
PETALWING!
EEEE HEEEE HEEE! BUSYHEAD HIGHTHING CALL ON BEST-BEST LOOKY SEE!
THAT'S RIGHT. GO OUT AND CHECK FOR HUMANS.
PETALWING DO! IF BIGTHINGS NEAR. PETALWING SAY!
FLUTTERING HIGH ABOVE THE PALACE'S SPIRES, THE TINY PRESERVER INSTANTLY SPOTS--
MANY BIGTHINGS!
LOOK SAME-SAME LIKE BEFORE!
THE PASSAGE OF TEN THOUSAND YEARS HAS WROUGHT LITTLE CHANGE IN THE PRIMITIVE HUMANS, WHOM THE WOLFRIDERS DIMLY RECALL.
THEIR DRUMS SPEAK OF A GREAT FALLING STAR, JUST WITNESSED. YET NO ONE VENTURES FROM THE DISTANT ENCAMPMENT TO INVESTIGATE.

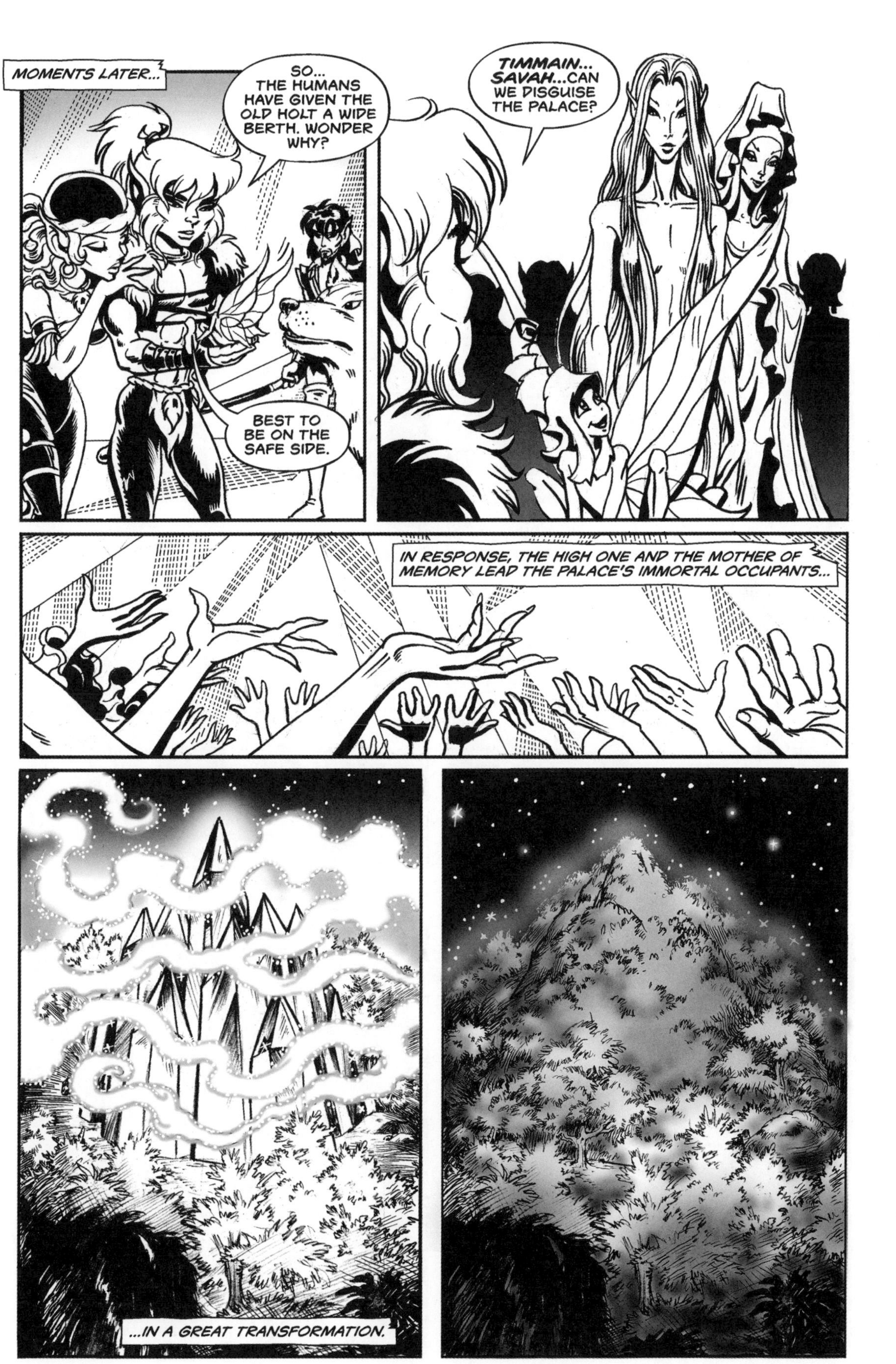
MOMENTS LATER...
SO... THE HUMANS HAVE GIVEN THE OLD HOLT A WIDE BERTH. WONDER WHY?
BEST TO BE ON THE SAFE SIDE.
TIMMAIN... SAVAH...CAN WE DISGUISE THE PALACE?
IN RESPONSE, THE HIGH ONE AND THE MOTHER OF MEMORY LEAD THE PALACE'S IMMORTAL OCCUPANTS...
...IN A GREAT TRANSFORMATION.

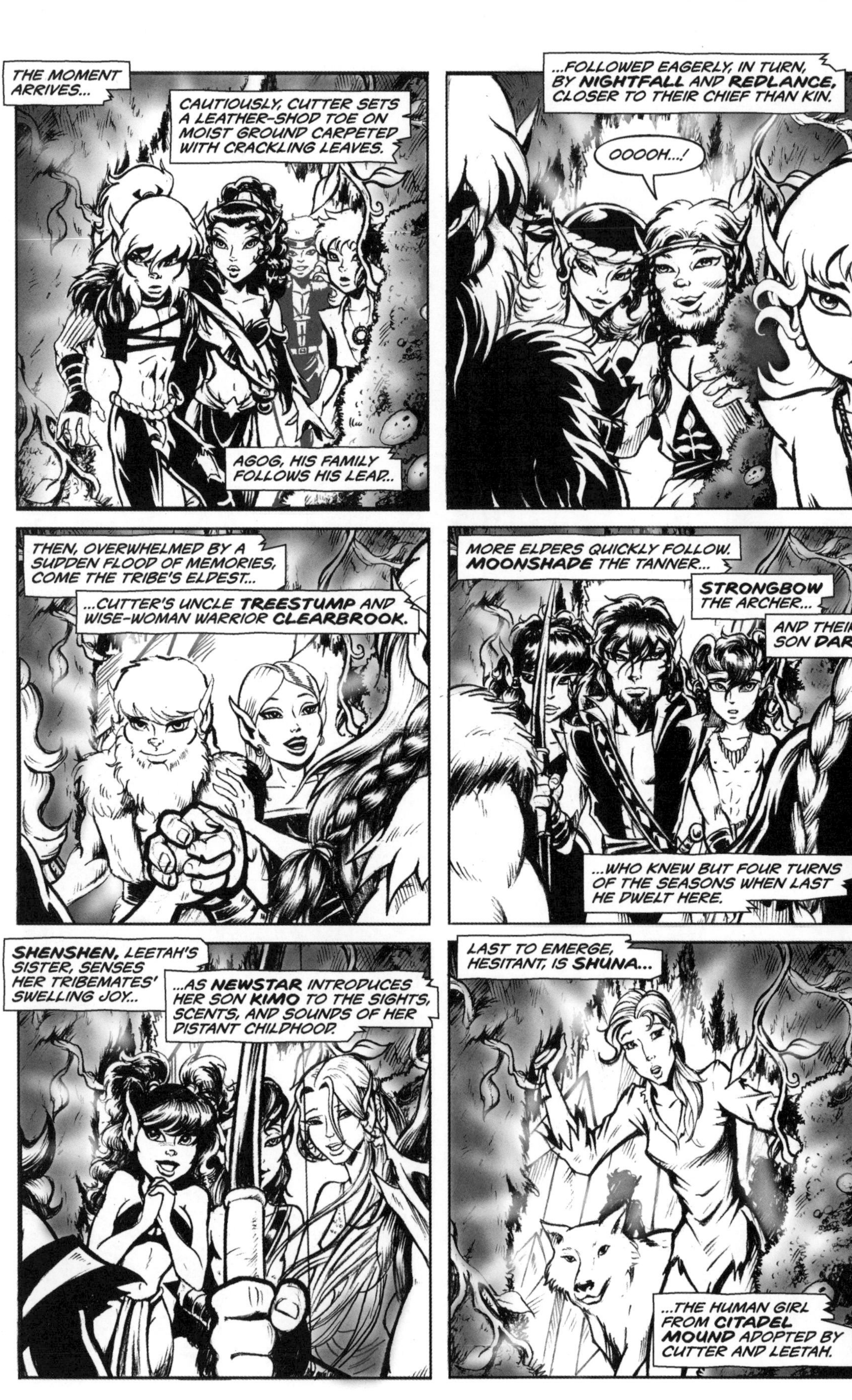
THE MOMENT ARRIVES...
CAUTIOUSLY, CUTTER SETS A LEATHER-SHOD TOE ON MOIST GROUND CARPETED WITH CRACKLING LEAVES.
AGOG, HIS FAMILY FOLLOWS HIS LEAD...
...FOLLOWED EAGERLY, IN TURN, BY NIGHTFALL AND REDLANCE, CLOSER TO THEIR CHIEF THAN KIN.
OOOOH...!
THEN, OVERWHELMED BY A SUDDEN FLOOD OF MEMORIES, COME THE TRIBE'S ELDEST...
...CUTTER'S UNCLE TREESTUMP AND WISE-WOMAN WARRIOR CLEARBROOK.
MORE ELDERS QUICKLY FOLLOW. MOONSHADE THE TANNER...
STRONGBOW THE ARCHER...
AND THEIR SON DART...
...WHO KNEW BUT FOUR TURNS OF THE SEASONS WHEN LAST HE DWELT HERE.
SHENSHEN, LEETAH'S SISTER, SENSES HER TRIBEMATES' SWELLING JOY...
...AS NEWSTAR INTRODUCES HER SON KIMO TO THE SIGHTS, SCENTS, AND SOUNDS OF HER DISTANT CHILDHOOD.
LAST TO EMERGE, HESITANT, IS SHUNA...
...THE HUMAN GIRL FROM CITADEL MOUND ADOPTED BY CUTTER AND LEETAH.

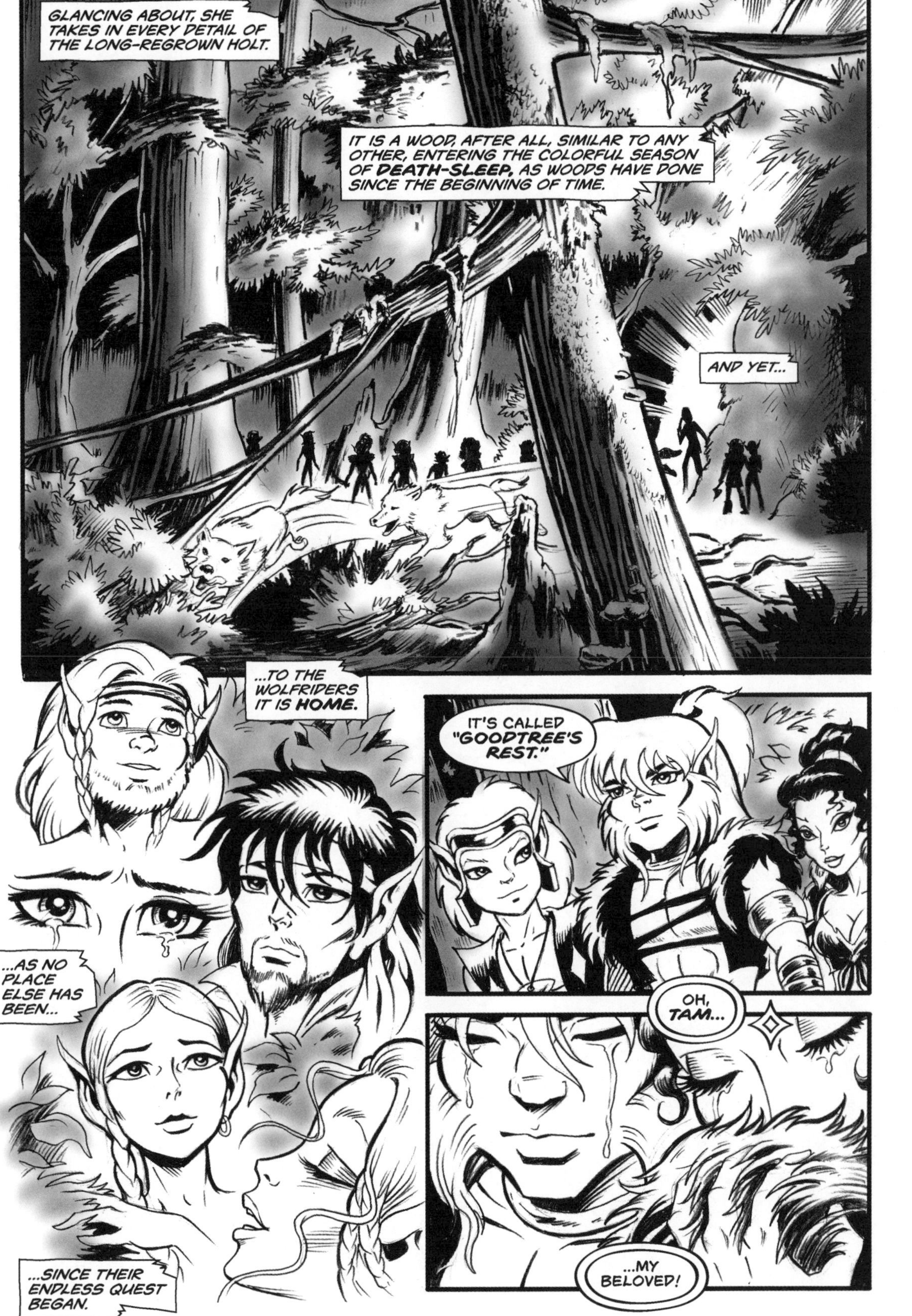
GLANCING ABOUT, SHE TAKES IN EVERY DETAIL OF THE LONG-REGROWN HOLT.
IT IS A WOOD, AFTER ALL, SIMILAR TO ANY OTHER, ENTERING THE COLORFUL SEASON OF DEATH-SLEEP, AS WOODS HAVE DONE SINCE THE BEGINNING OF TIME.
AND YET...
...TO THE WOLFRIDERS IT IS HOME.
...AS NO PLACE ELSE HAS BEEN...
...SINCE THEIR ENDLESS QUEST BEGAN.
IT'S CALLED "GOODTREE'S REST."
OH, TAM...
...MY BELOVED!

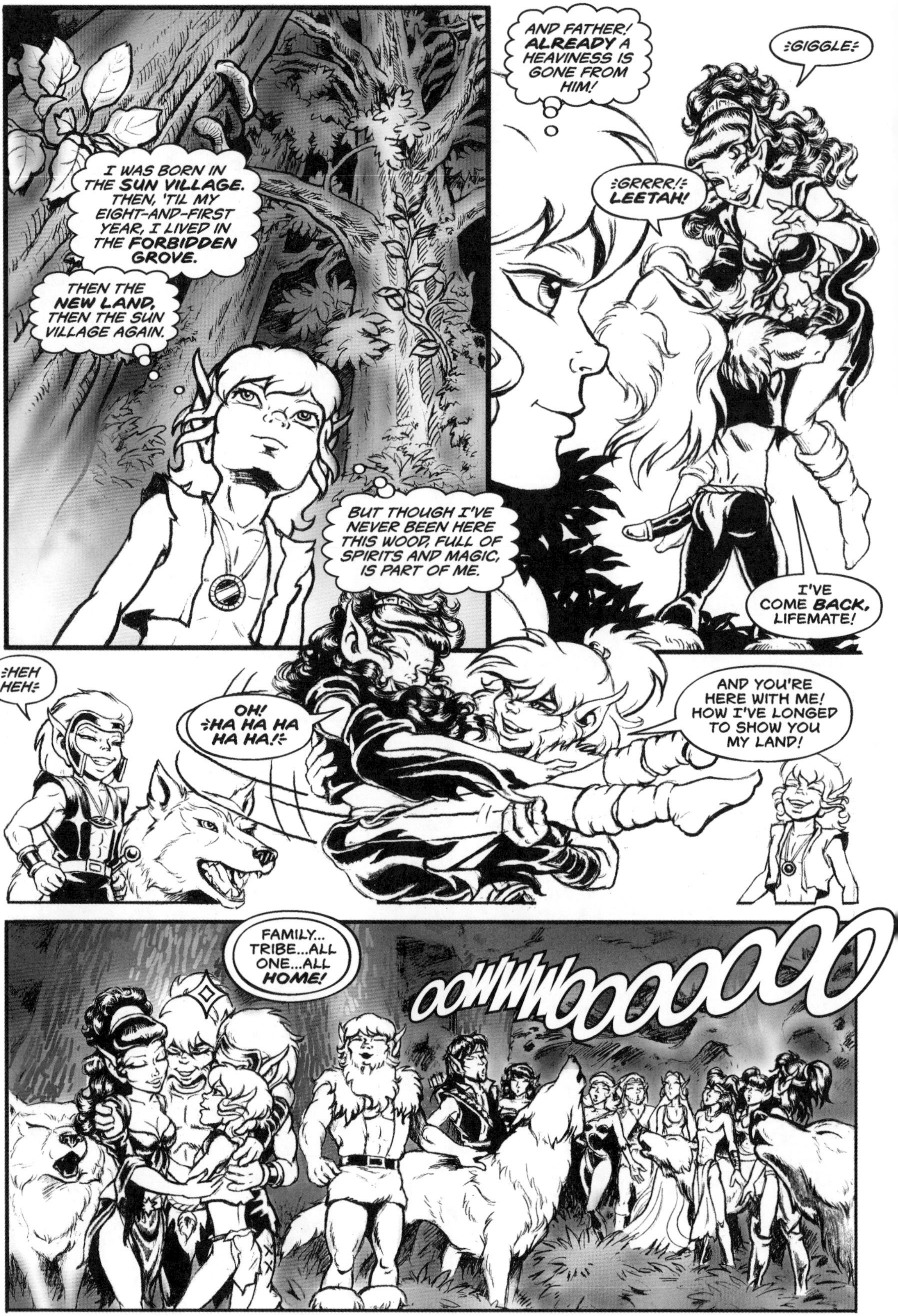
I WAS BORN IN THE SUN VILLAGE. THEN, 'TIL MY EIGHT-AND-FIRST YEAR, I LIVED IN THE FORBIDDEN GROVE.
THEN THE NEW LAND, THEN THE SUN VILLAGE AGAIN.
BUT THOUGH I'VE NEVER BEEN HERE THIS WOOD, FULL OF SPIRITS AND MAGIC, IS PART OF ME.
AND FATHER! ALREADY A HEAVINESS IS GONE FROM HIM!
:GIGGLE:
:GRRRR!: LEETAH!
I'VE COME BACK, LIFEMATE!
:HEH HEH:
OH! :HA HA HA HA HA!:
AND YOU'RE HERE WITH ME! HOW I'VE LONGED TO SHOW YOU MY LAND!
FAMILY... TRIBE...ALL ONE...ALL HOME!
OOWWWOOOOOOO

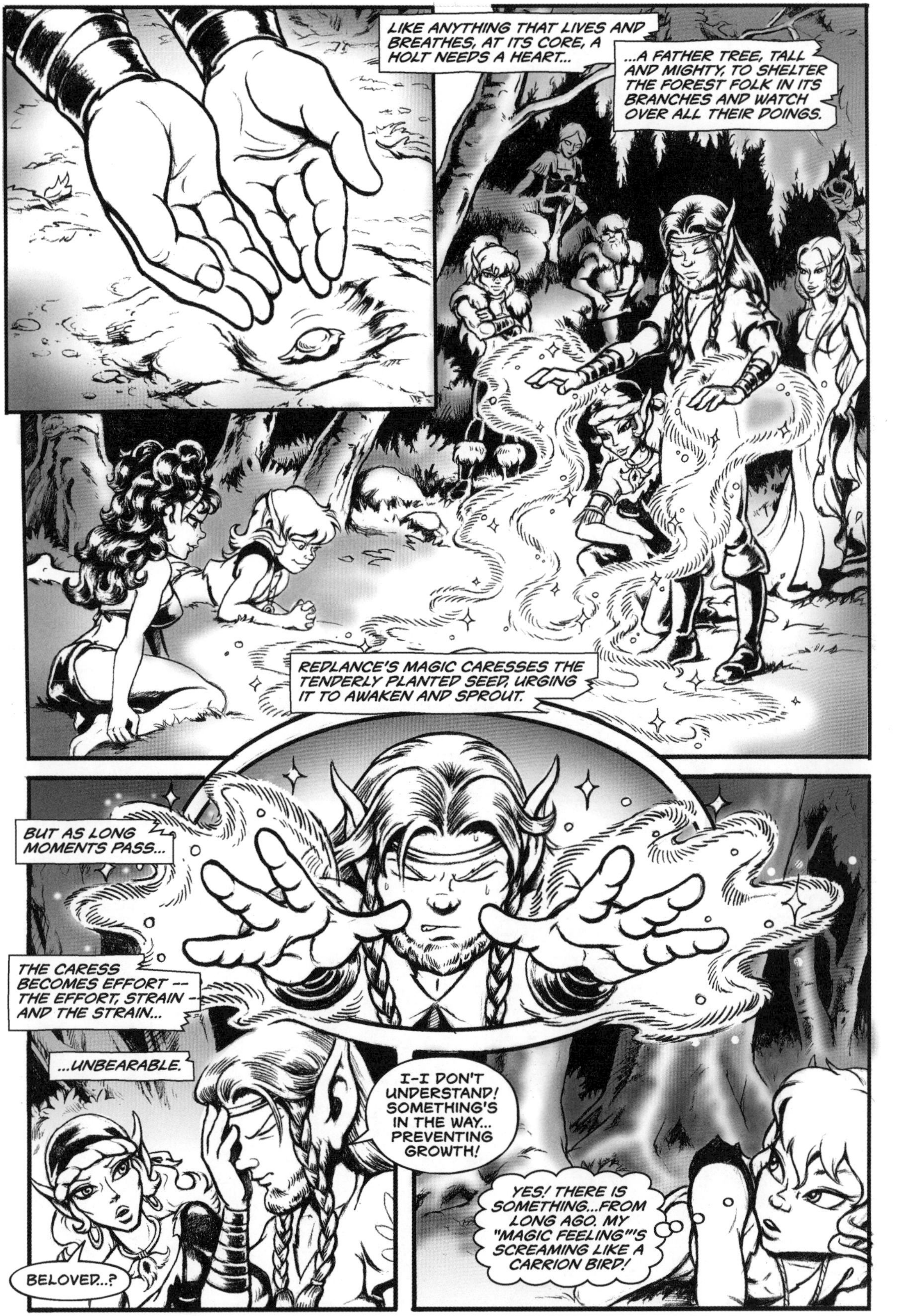
LIKE ANYTHING THAT LIVES AND BREATHES, AT ITS CORE, A HOLT NEEDS A HEART...
...A FATHER TREE, TALL AND MIGHTY, TO SHELTER THE FOREST FOLK IN ITS BRANCHES AND WATCH OVER ALL THEIR DOINGS.
REDLANCE'S MAGIC CARESSES THE TENDERLY PLANTED SEED, URGING IT TO AWAKEN AND SPROUT.
BUT AS LONG MOMENTS PASS...
THE CARESS BECOMES EFFORT -- THE EFFORT, STRAIN -- AND THE STRAIN...
...UNBEARABLE.
I-I DON'T UNDERSTAND! SOMETHING'S IN THE WAY... PREVENTING GROWTH!
BELOVED...?
YES! THERE IS SOMETHING...FROM LONG AGO. MY "MAGIC FEELING"'S SCREAMING LIKE A CARRION BIRD!

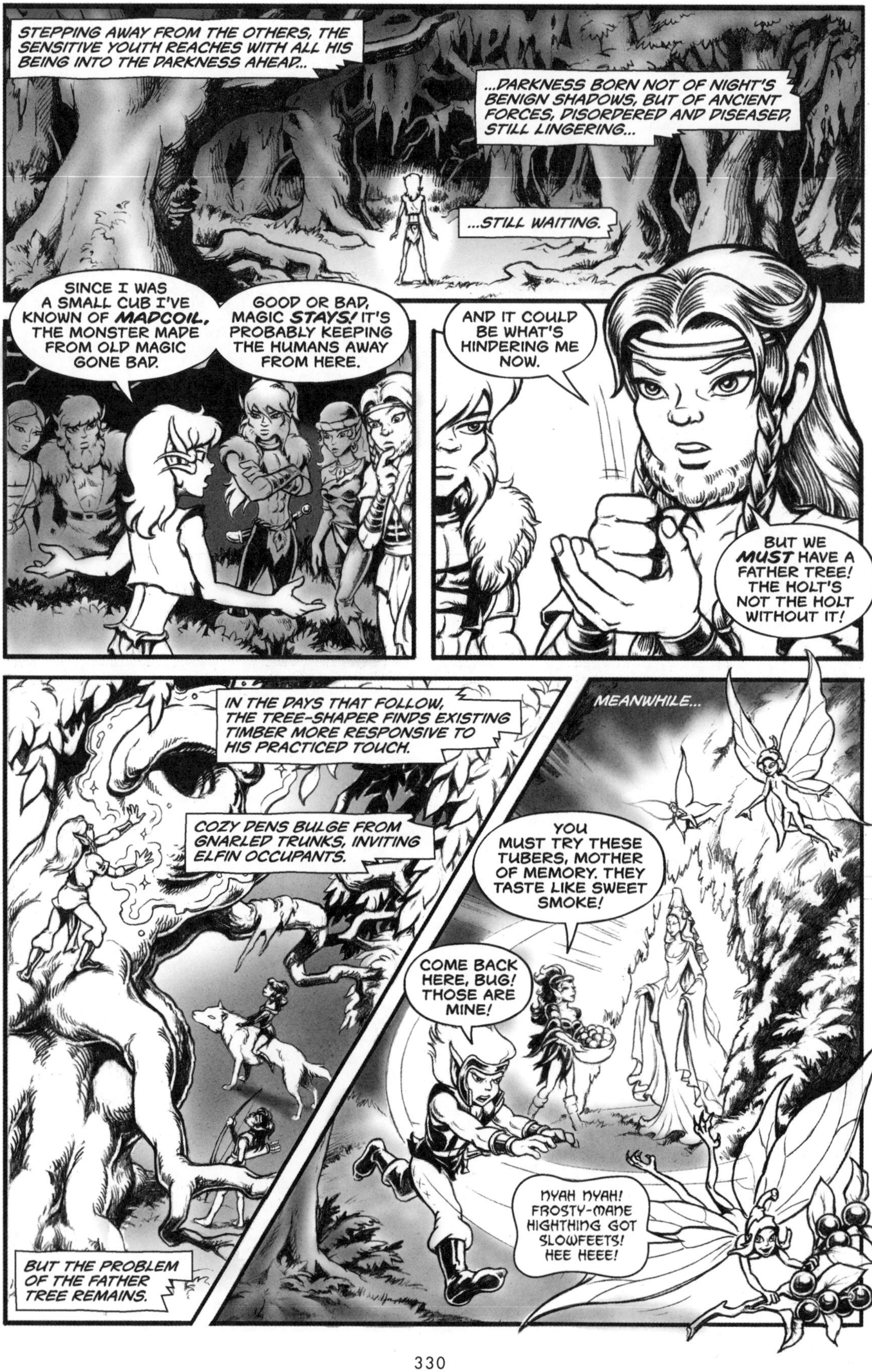
STEPPING AWAY FROM THE OTHERS, THE SENSITIVE YOUTH REACHES WITH ALL HIS BEING INTO THE DARKNESS AHEAD...
...DARKNESS BORN NOT OF NIGHT'S BENIGN SHADOWS, BUT OF ANCIENT FORCES, DISORDERED AND DISEASED, STILL LINGERING...
...STILL WAITING.
SINCE I WAS A SMALL CUB I'VE KNOWN OF MADCOIL, THE MONSTER MADE FROM OLD MAGIC GONE BAD.
GOOD OR BAD, MAGIC STAYS! IT'S PROBABLY KEEPING THE HUMANS AWAY FROM HERE.
AND IT COULD BE WHAT'S HINDERING ME NOW.
BUT WE MUST HAVE A FATHER TREE! THE HOLT'S NOT THE HOLT WITHOUT IT!
IN THE DAYS THAT FOLLOW, THE TREE-SHAPER FINDS EXISTING TIMBER MORE RESPONSIVE TO HIS PRACTICED TOUCH.
COZY DENS BULGE FROM GNARLED TRUNKS, INVITING ELFIN OCCUPANTS.
BUT THE PROBLEM OF THE FATHER TREE REMAINS.
MEANWHILE...
YOU MUST TRY THESE TUBERS, MOTHER OF MEMORY. THEY TASTE LIKE SWEET SMOKE!
COME BACK HERE, BUG! THOSE ARE MINE!
NYAH NYAH! FROSTY-MANE HIGHTHING GOT SLOWFEETS! HEE HEEE!

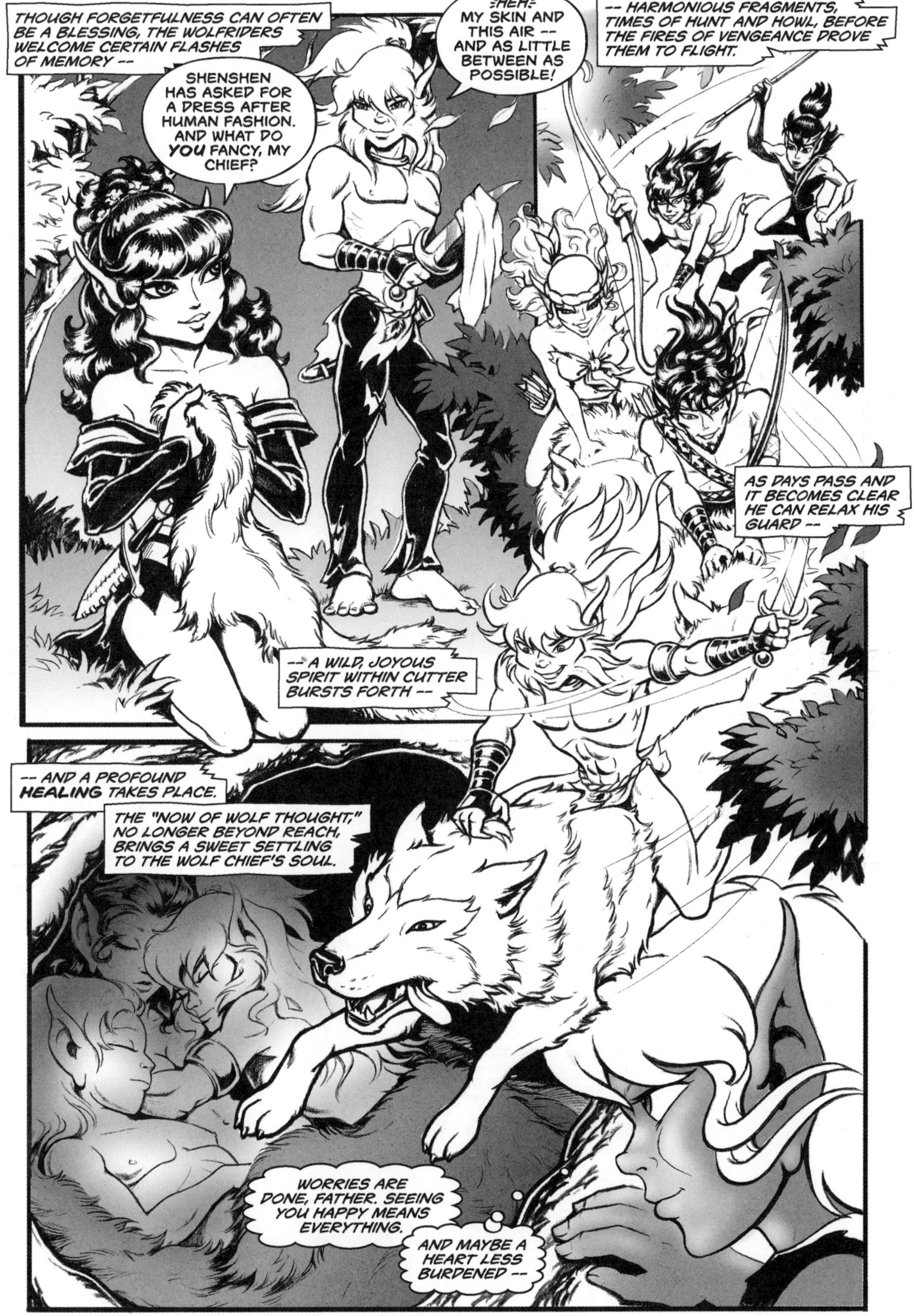

THOUGH FORGETFULNESS CAN OFTEN BE A BLESSING, THE WOLFRIDERS WELCOME CERTAIN FLASHES OF MEMORY --
SHENSHEN HAS ASKED FOR A DRESS AFTER HUMAN FASHION. AND WHAT DO YOU FANCY, MY CHIEF?
HEH MY SKIN AND THIS AIR -- AND AS LITTLE BETWEEN AS POSSIBLE!
-- HARMONIOUS FRAGMENTS, TIMES OF HUNT AND HOWL, BEFORE THE FIRES OF VENGEANCE DROVE THEM TO FLIGHT.
AS DAYS PASS AND IT BECOMES CLEAR HE CAN RELAX HIS GUARD --
-- A WILD, JOYOUS SPIRIT WITHIN CUTTER BURSTS FORTH --
-- AND A PROFOUND HEALING TAKES PLACE.
THE "NOW OF WOLF THOUGHT," NO LONGER BEYOND REACH, BRINGS A SWEET SETTLING TO THE WOLF CHIEF'S SOUL.
WORRIES ARE DONE, FATHER. SEEING YOU HAPPY MEANS EVERYTHING.
AND MAYBE A HEART LESS BURDENED --

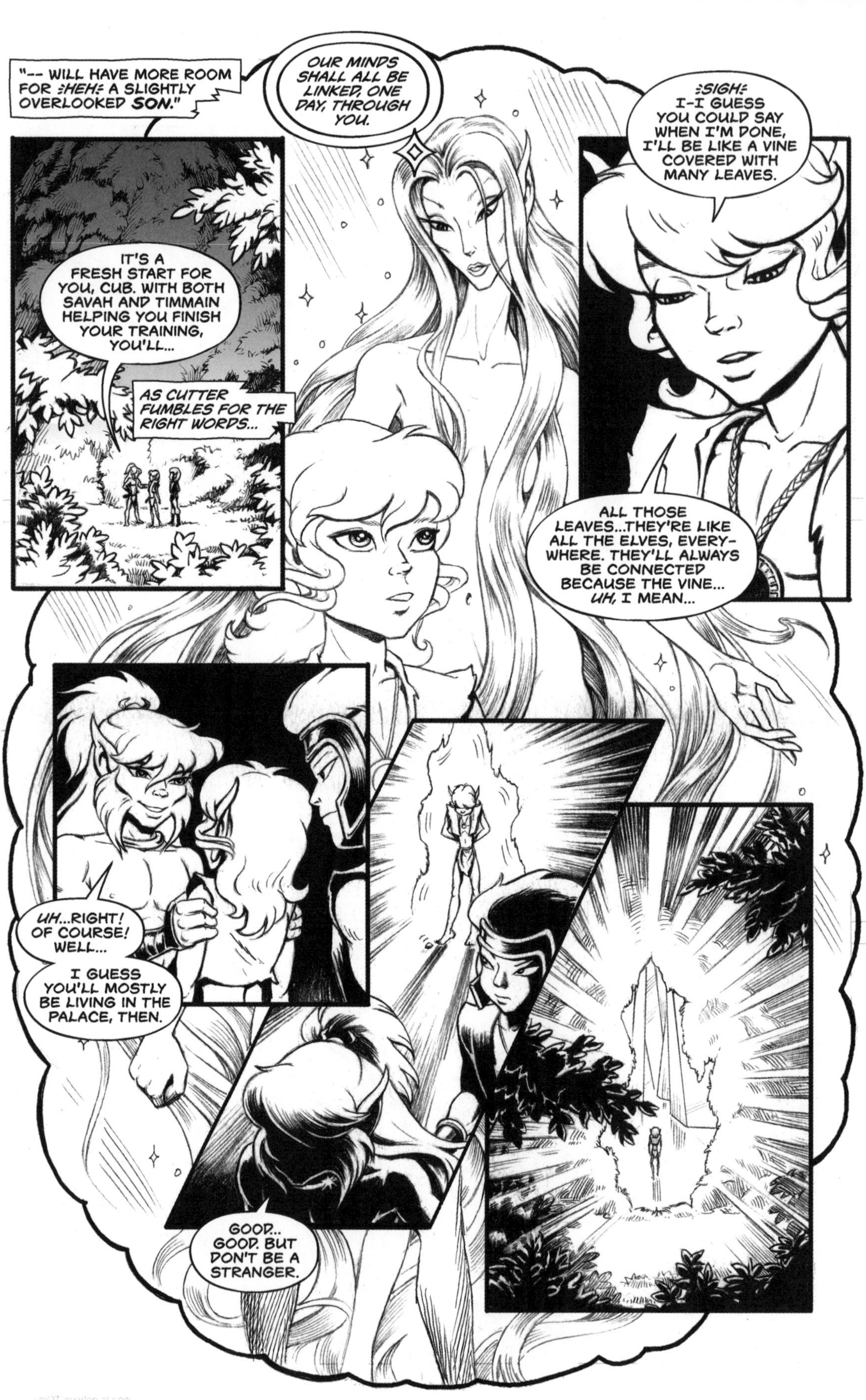
"-- WILL HAVE MORE ROOM FOR :HEH: A SLIGHTLY OVERLOOKED SON."
OUR MINDS SHALL ALL BE LINKED, ONE DAY, THROUGH YOU.
:SIGH: I-I GUESS YOU COULD SAY WHEN I'M DONE, I'LL BE LIKE A VINE COVERED WITH MANY LEAVES.
IT'S A FRESH START FOR YOU, CUB. WITH BOTH SAVAH AND TIMMAIN HELPING YOU FINISH YOUR TRAINING, YOU'LL...
AS CUTTER FUMBLES FOR THE RIGHT WORDS...
ALL THOSE LEAVES...THEY'RE LIKE ALL THE ELVES, EVERY-WHERE. THEY'LL ALWAYS BE CONNECTED BECAUSE THE VINE... UH, I MEAN...
UH...RIGHT! OF COURSE! WELL...
I GUESS YOU'LL MOSTLY BE LIVING IN THE PALACE, THEN.
GOOD... GOOD. BUT DON'T BE A STRANGER.

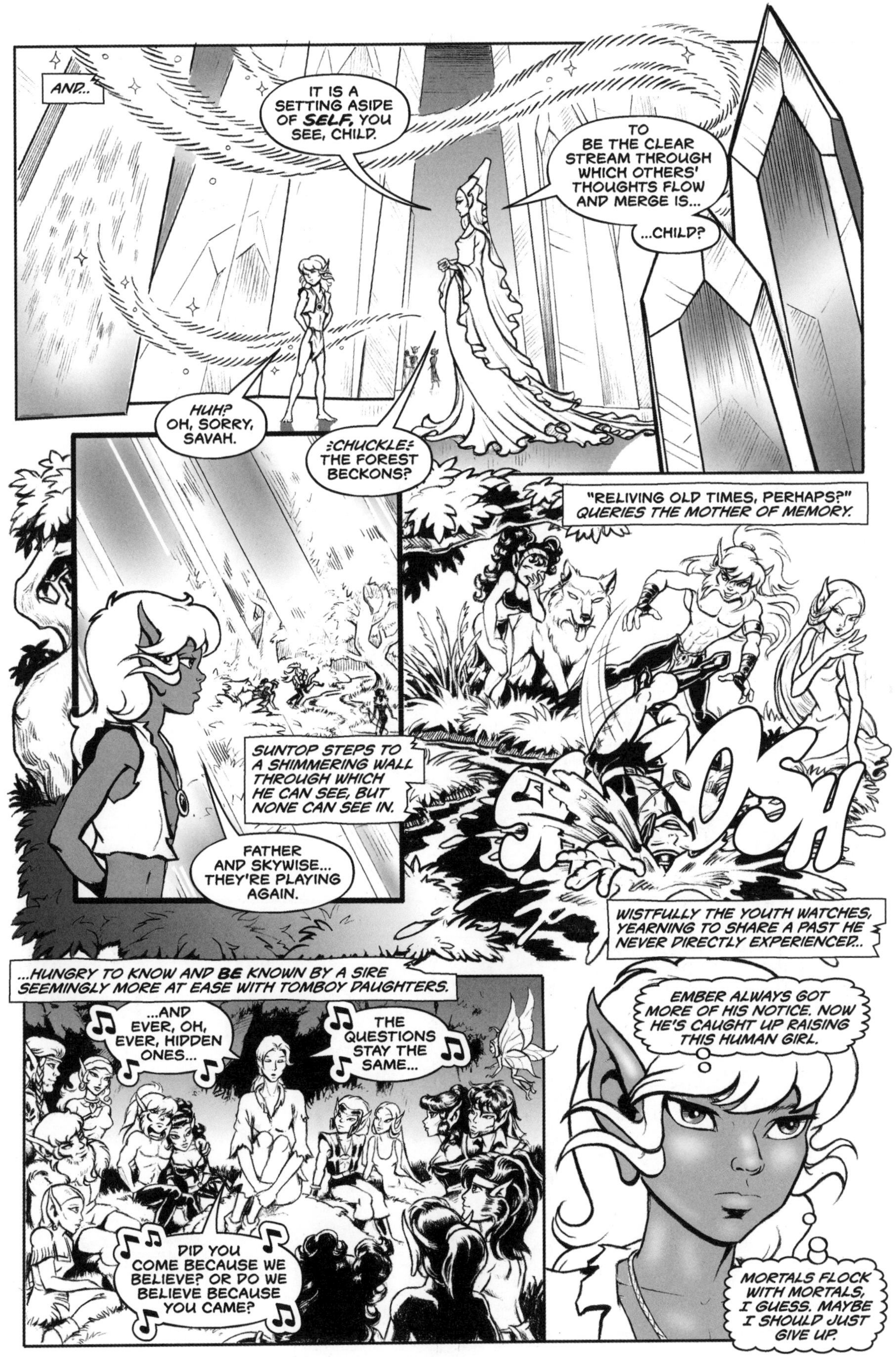
AND...
IT IS A SETTING ASIDE OF SELF, YOU SEE, CHILD.
TO BE THE CLEAR STREAM THROUGH WHICH OTHERS' THOUGHTS FLOW AND MERGE IS...
...CHILD?
HUH? OH, SORRY, SAVAH.
CHUCKLE THE FOREST BECKONS?
"RELIVING OLD TIMES, PERHAPS?" QUERIES THE MOTHER OF MEMORY.
SUNTOP STEPS TO A SHIMMERING WALL THROUGH WHICH HE CAN SEE, BUT NONE CAN SEE IN.
FATHER AND SKYWISE... THEY'RE PLAYING AGAIN.
SPLOOSH
WISTFULLY THE YOUTH WATCHES, YEARNING TO SHARE A PAST HE NEVER DIRECTLY EXPERIENCED...
...HUNGRY TO KNOW AND BE KNOWN BY A SIRE SEEMINGLY MORE AT EASE WITH TOMBOY DAUGHTERS.
...AND EVER, OH, EVER, HIDDEN ONES...
THE QUESTIONS STAY THE SAME...
DID YOU COME BECAUSE WE BELIEVE? OR DO WE BELIEVE BECAUSE YOU CAME?
EMBER ALWAYS GOT MORE OF HIS NOTICE. NOW HE'S CAUGHT UP RAISING THIS HUMAN GIRL.
MORTALS FLOCK WITH MORTALS, I GUESS. MAYBE I SHOULD JUST GIVE UP.

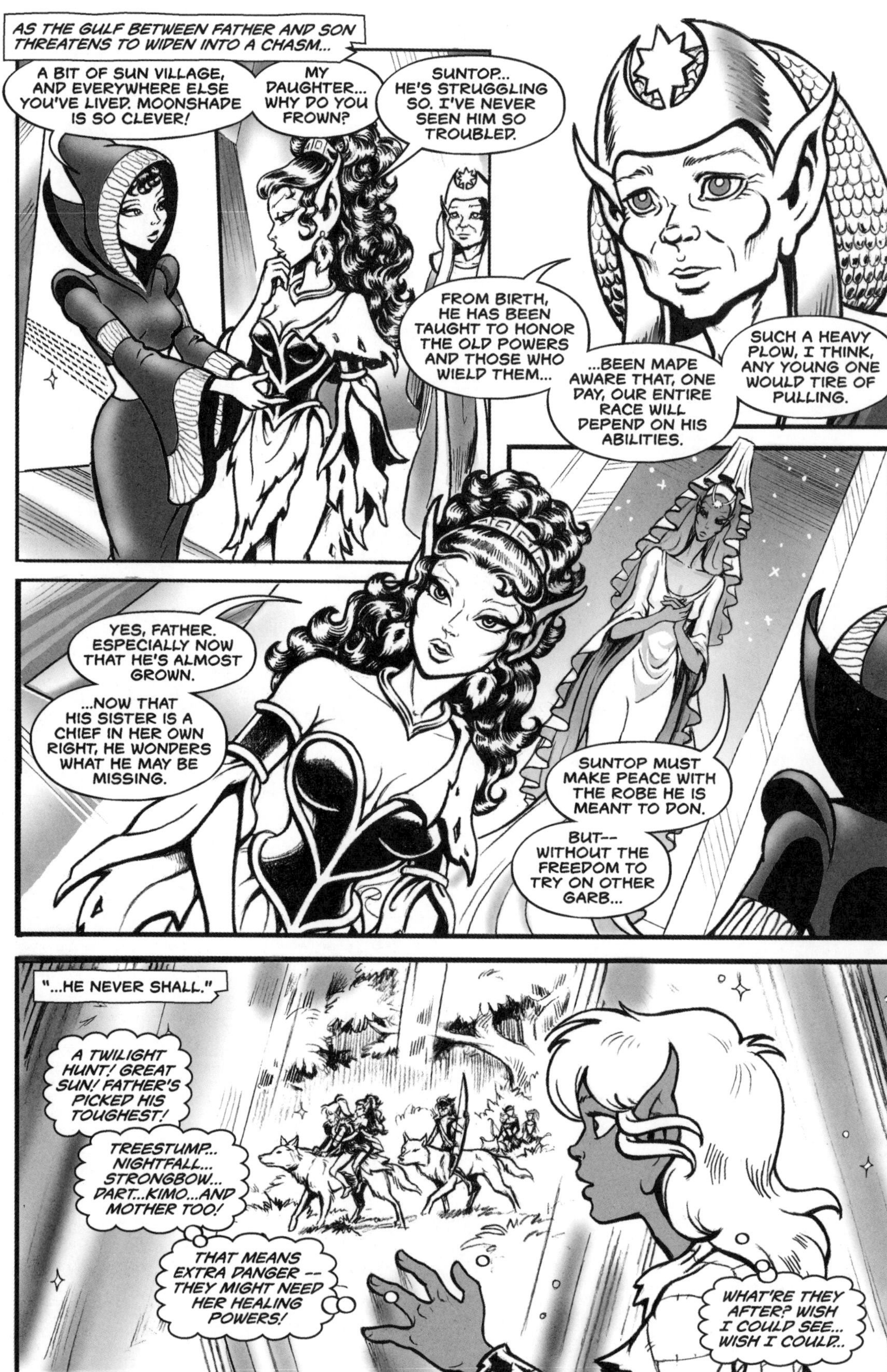
AS THE GULF BETWEEN FATHER AND SON THREATENS TO WIDEN INTO A CHASM...
A BIT OF SUN VILLAGE, AND EVERYWHERE ELSE YOU'VE LIVED. MOONSHADE IS SO CLEVER!
MY DAUGHTER... WHY DO YOU FROWN?
SUNTOP... HE'S STRUGGLING SO. I'VE NEVER SEEN HIM SO TROUBLED.
FROM BIRTH, HE HAS BEEN TAUGHT TO HONOR THE OLD POWERS AND THOSE WHO WIELD THEM...
...BEEN MADE AWARE THAT, ONE DAY, OUR ENTIRE RACE WILL DEPEND ON HIS ABILITIES.
SUCH A HEAVY PLOW, I THINK, ANY YOUNG ONE WOULD TIRE OF PULLING.
YES, FATHER. ESPECIALLY NOW THAT HE'S ALMOST GROWN.
...NOW THAT HIS SISTER IS A CHIEF IN HER OWN RIGHT, HE WONDERS WHAT HE MAY BE MISSING.
SUNTOP MUST MAKE PEACE WITH THE ROBE HE IS MEANT TO DON.
BUT-- WITHOUT THE FREEDOM TO TRY ON OTHER GARB...
"...HE NEVER SHALL."
A TWILIGHT HUNT! GREAT SUN! FATHER'S PICKED HIS TOUGHEST!
TREESTUMP... NIGHTFALL... STRONGBOW... DART...KIMO...AND MOTHER TOO!
THAT MEANS EXTRA DANGER -- THEY MIGHT NEED HER HEALING POWERS!
WHAT'RE THEY AFTER? WISH I COULD SEE... WISH I COULD..

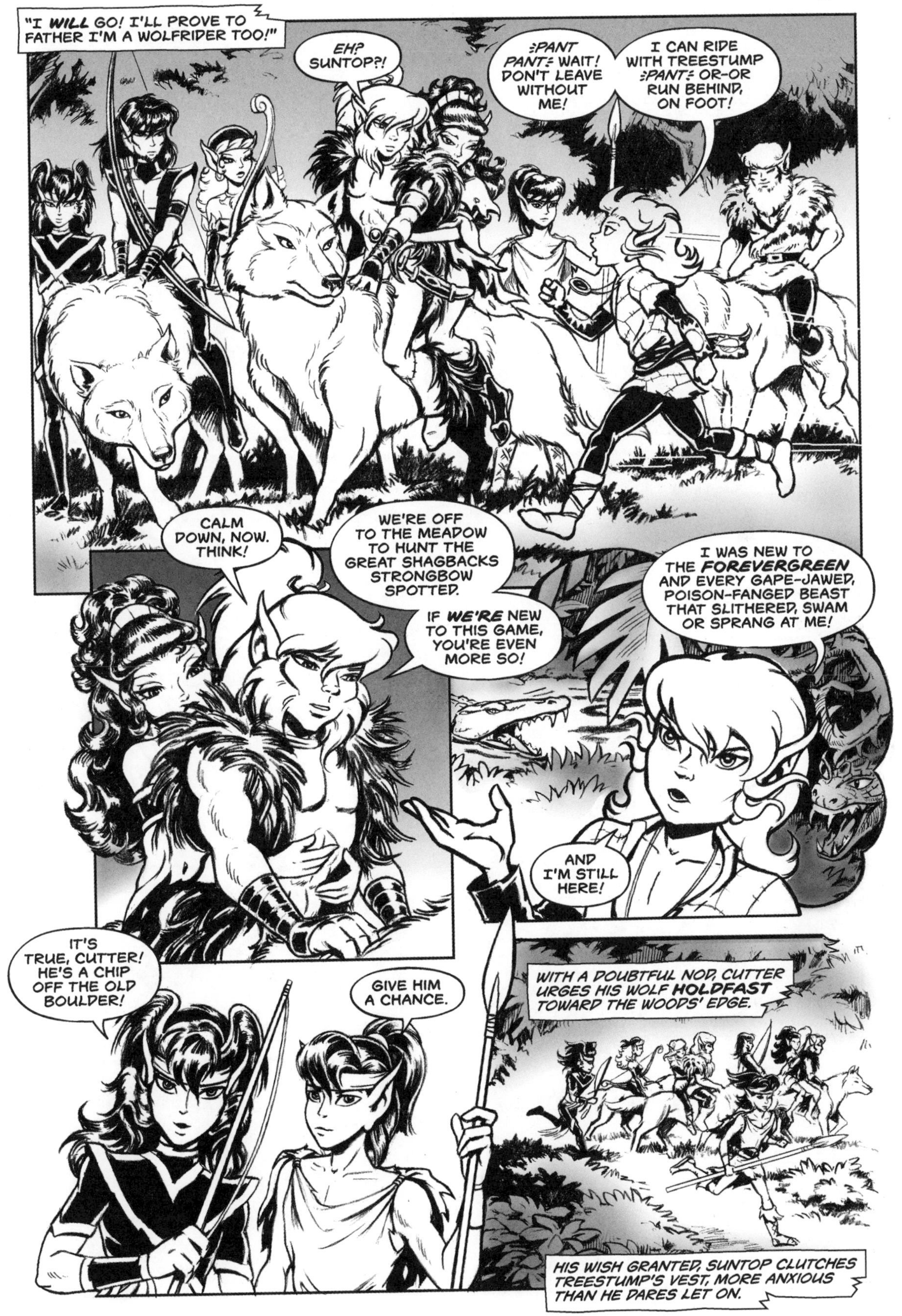

"I WILL GO! I'LL PROVE TO FATHER I'M A WOLFRIDER TOO!"
EH? SUNTOP?!
:PANT PANT: WAIT! DON'T LEAVE WITHOUT ME!
I CAN RIDE WITH TREESTUMP :PANT: OR-OR RUN BEHIND, ON FOOT!
CALM DOWN, NOW. THINK!
WE'RE OFF TO THE MEADOW TO HUNT THE GREAT SHAGBACKS STRONGBOW SPOTTED.
IF WE'RE NEW TO THIS GAME, YOU'RE EVEN MORE SO!
I WAS NEW TO THE FOREVERGREEN AND EVERY GAPE-JAWED, POISON-FANGED BEAST THAT SLITHERED, SWAM OR SPRANG AT ME!
AND I'M STILL HERE!
IT'S TRUE, CUTTER! HE'S A CHIP OFF THE OLD BOULDER!
GIVE HIM A CHANCE.
WITH A DOUBTFUL NOD, CUTTER URGES HIS WOLF HOLDFAST TOWARD THE WOODS' EDGE.
HIS WISH GRANTED, SUNTOP CLUTCHES TREESTUMP'S VEST, MORE ANXIOUS THAN HE DARES LET ON.

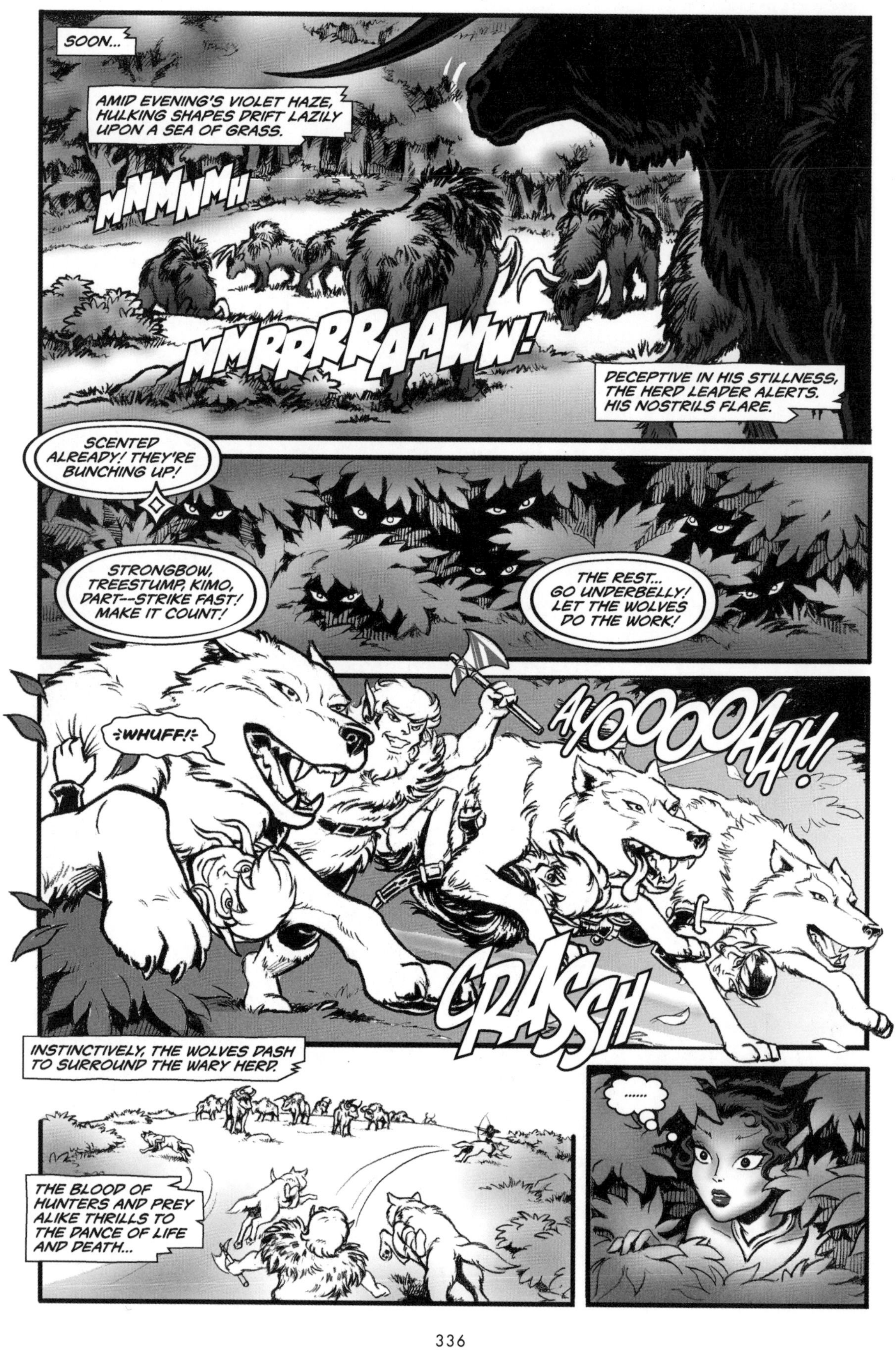
SOON...
AMID EVENING'S VIOLET HAZE, HULKING SHAPES DRIFT LAZILY UPON A SEA OF GRASS.
MNMNMH
MMRRRRAAWW!
DECEPTIVE IN HIS STILLNESS, THE HERD LEADER ALERTS. HIS NOSTRILS FLARE.
SCENTED ALREADY! THEY'RE BUNCHING UP!
STRONGBOW, TREESTUMP, KIMO, DART--STRIKE FAST! MAKE IT COUNT!
THE REST... GO UNDERBELLY! LET THE WOLVES DO THE WORK!
WHUFF!
AYOOOOAAH!
CRASSH
INSTINCTIVELY, THE WOLVES DASH TO SURROUND THE WARY HERD.
THE BLOOD OF HUNTERS AND PREY ALIKE THRILLS TO THE DANCE OF LIFE AND DEATH...
......

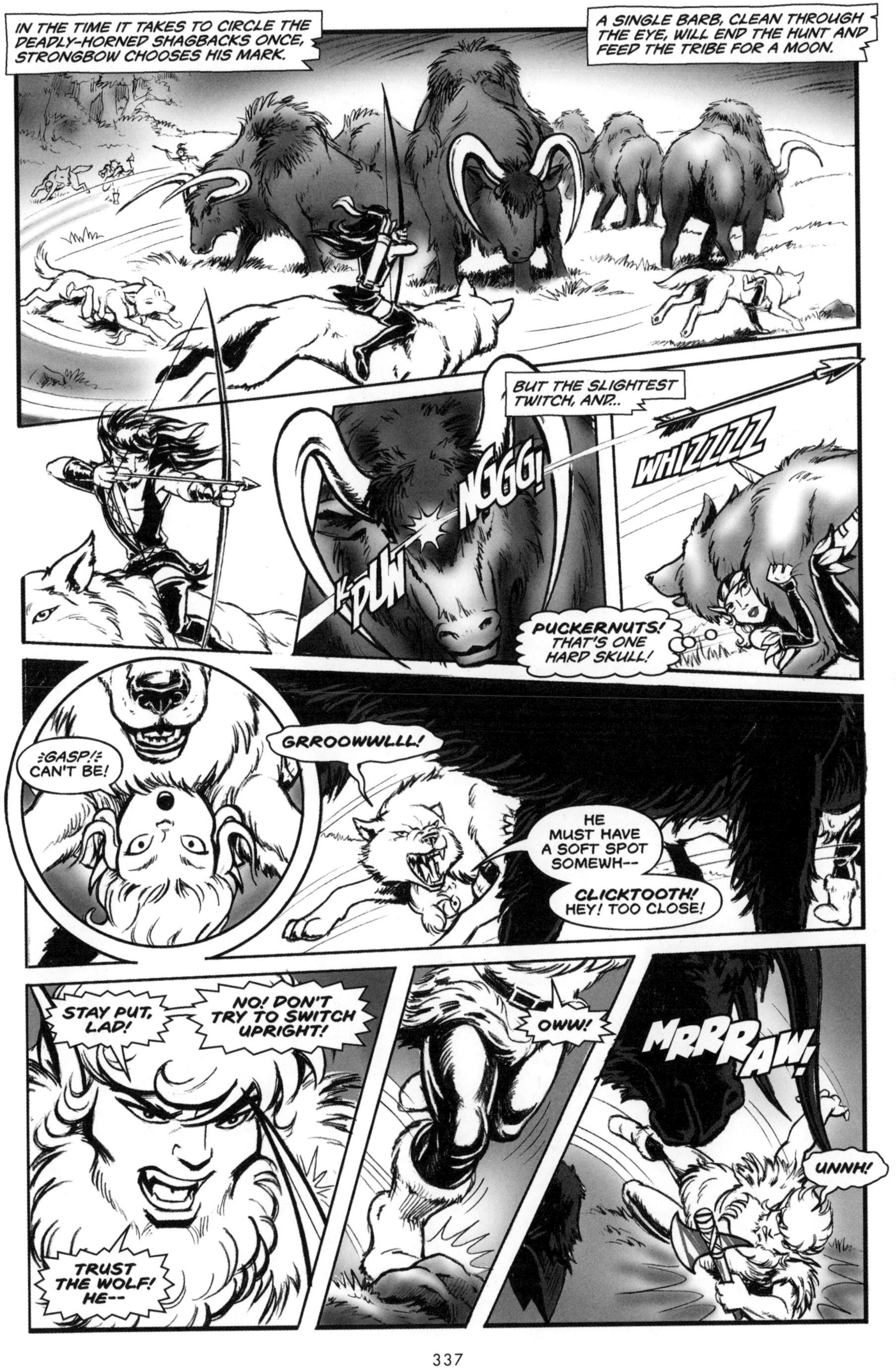
IN THE TIME IT TAKES TO CIRCLE THE DEADLY-HORNED SHAGBACKS ONCE, STRONGBOW CHOOSES HIS MARK.
A SINGLE BARB, CLEAN THROUGH THE EYE, WILL END THE HUNT AND FEED THE TRIBE FOR A MOON.
BUT THE SLIGHTEST TWITCH, AND...
K-PUW
NGGG!
WHIZZZZ
PUCKERNUTS! THAT'S ONE HARD SKULL!
:GASP!: CAN'T BE!
GRROOWWLLL!
HE MUST HAVE A SOFT SPOT SOMEWH--
CLICKTOOTH! HEY! TOO CLOSE!
STAY PUT, LAD!
NO! DON'T TRY TO SWITCH UPRIGHT!
TRUST THE WOLF! HE--
OWW!
MRRRAW!
UNNH!

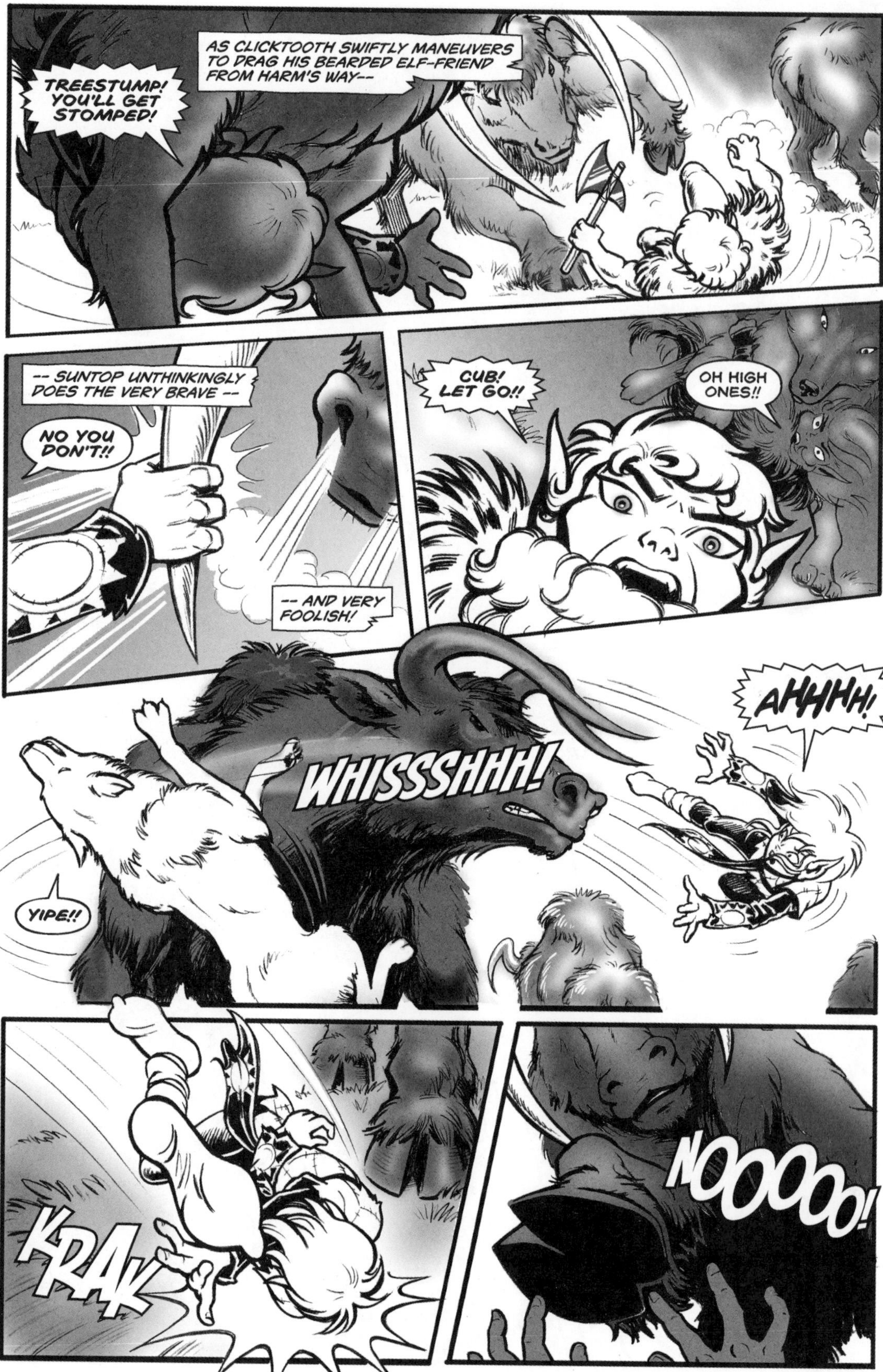

AS CLICKTOOTH SWIFTLY MANEUVERS TO DRAG HIS BEARDED ELF-FRIEND FROM HARM'S WAY--
TREESTUMP! YOU'LL GET STOMPED!
-- SUNTOP UNTHINKINGLY DOES THE VERY BRAVE --
NO YOU DON'T!!
-- AND VERY FOOLISH!
CUB! LET GO!!
OH HIGH ONES!!
WHISSSHHH!
AHHHH!
YIPE!!
KRAK
NOOOOO!

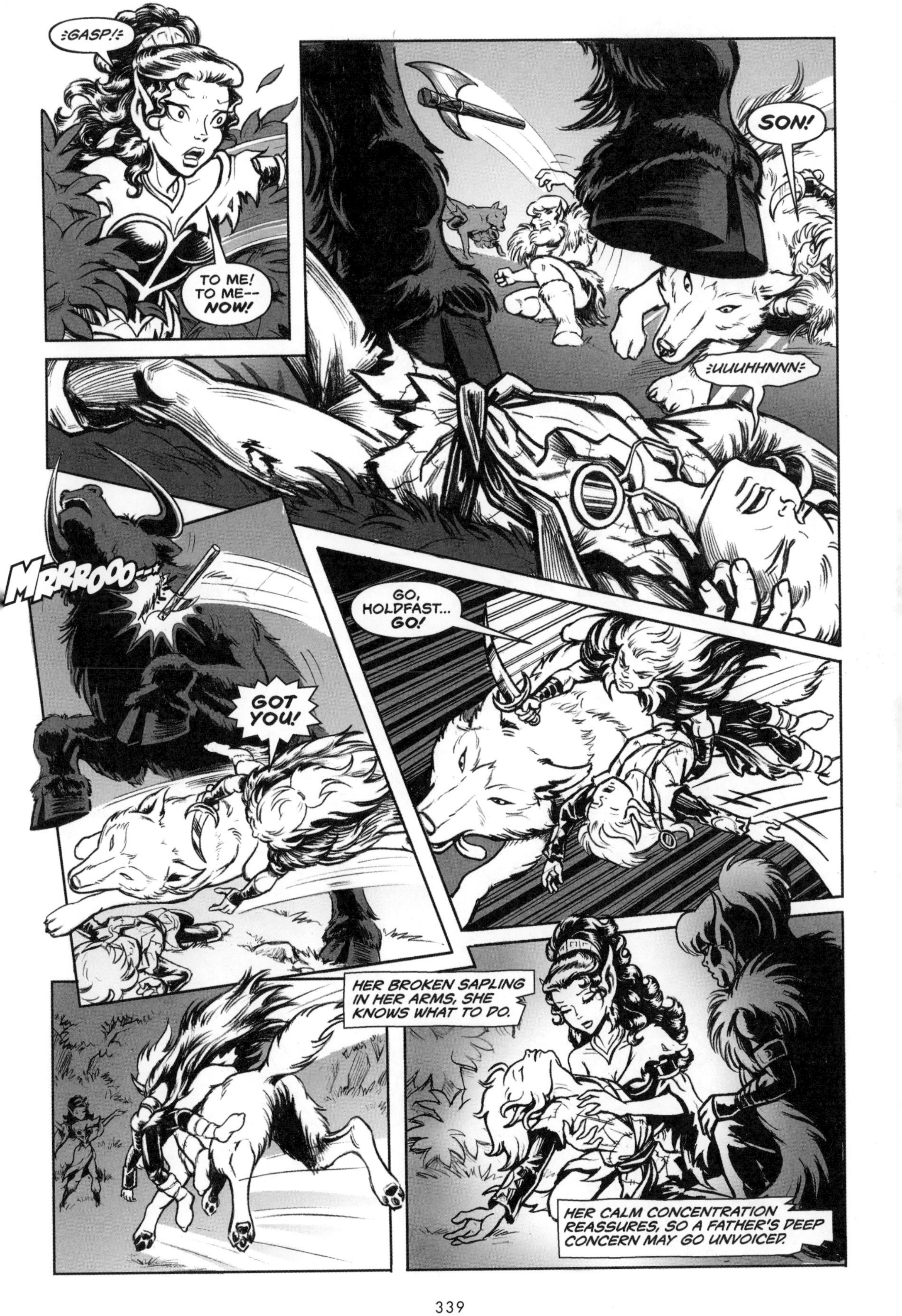
GASP!
TO ME! TO ME-- NOW!
SON!
UUUHHNNN
MRRROOO--
GO, HOLDFAST... GO!
GOT YOU!
HER BROKEN SAPLING IN HER ARMS, SHE KNOWS WHAT TO DO.
HER CALM CONCENTRATION REASSURES, SO A FATHER'S DEEP CONCERN MAY GO UNVOICED.

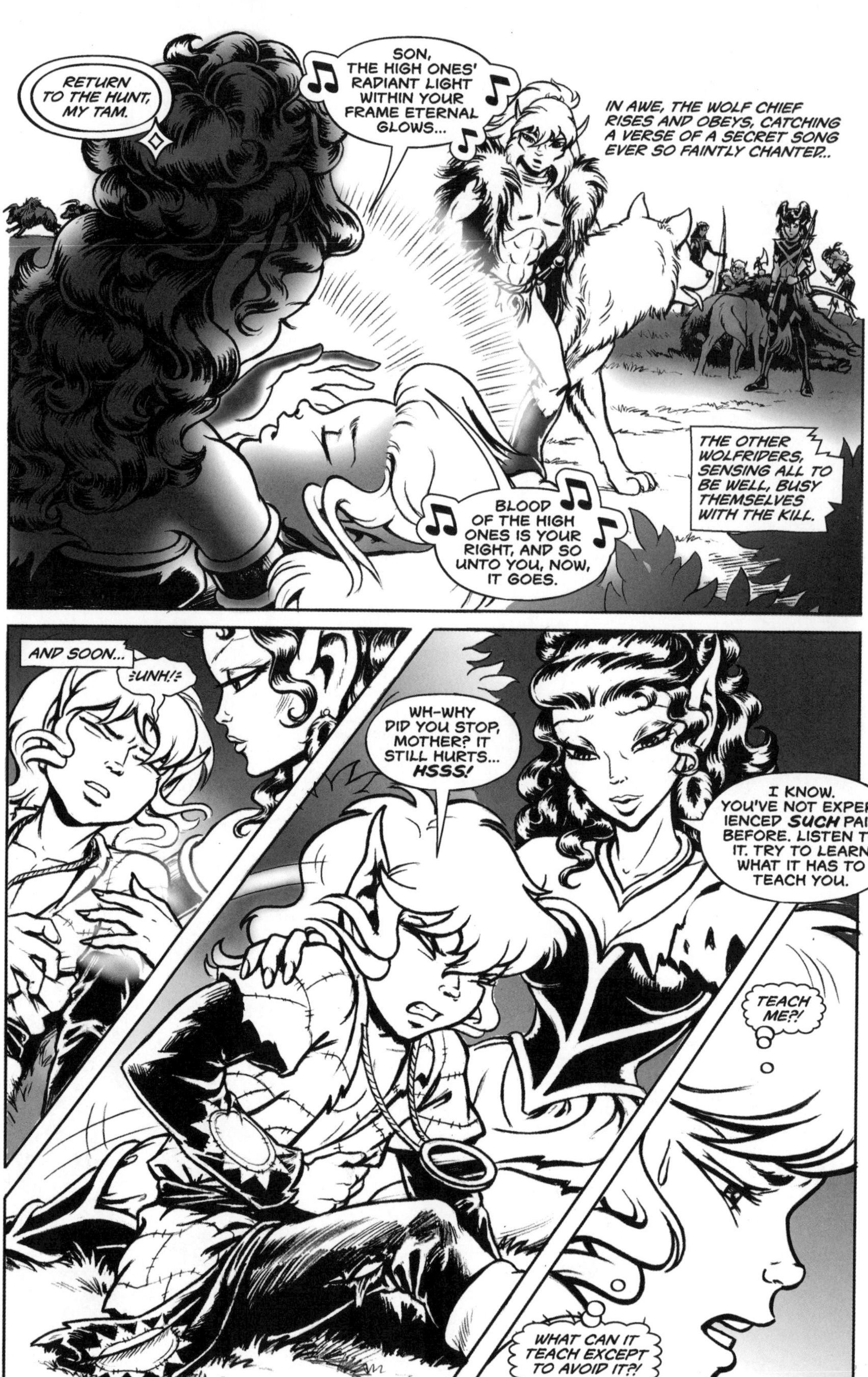
RETURN TO THE HUNT, MY TAM.
SON, THE HIGH ONES' RADIANT LIGHT WITHIN YOUR FRAME ETERNAL GLOWS...
IN AWE, THE WOLF CHIEF RISES AND OBEYS, CATCHING A VERSE OF A SECRET SONG EVER SO FAINTLY CHANTED...
THE OTHER WOLFRIDERS, SENSING ALL TO BE WELL, BUSY THEMSELVES WITH THE KILL.
BLOOD OF THE HIGH ONES IS YOUR RIGHT, AND SO UNTO YOU, NOW, IT GOES.
AND SOON...
UNH!
WH-WHY DID YOU STOP, MOTHER? IT STILL HURTS... HSSS!
I KNOW. YOU'VE NOT EXPERIENCED SUCH PAIN BEFORE. LISTEN TO IT. TRY TO LEARN WHAT IT HAS TO TEACH YOU.
TEACH ME?!
WHAT CAN IT TEACH EXCEPT TO AVOID IT?!

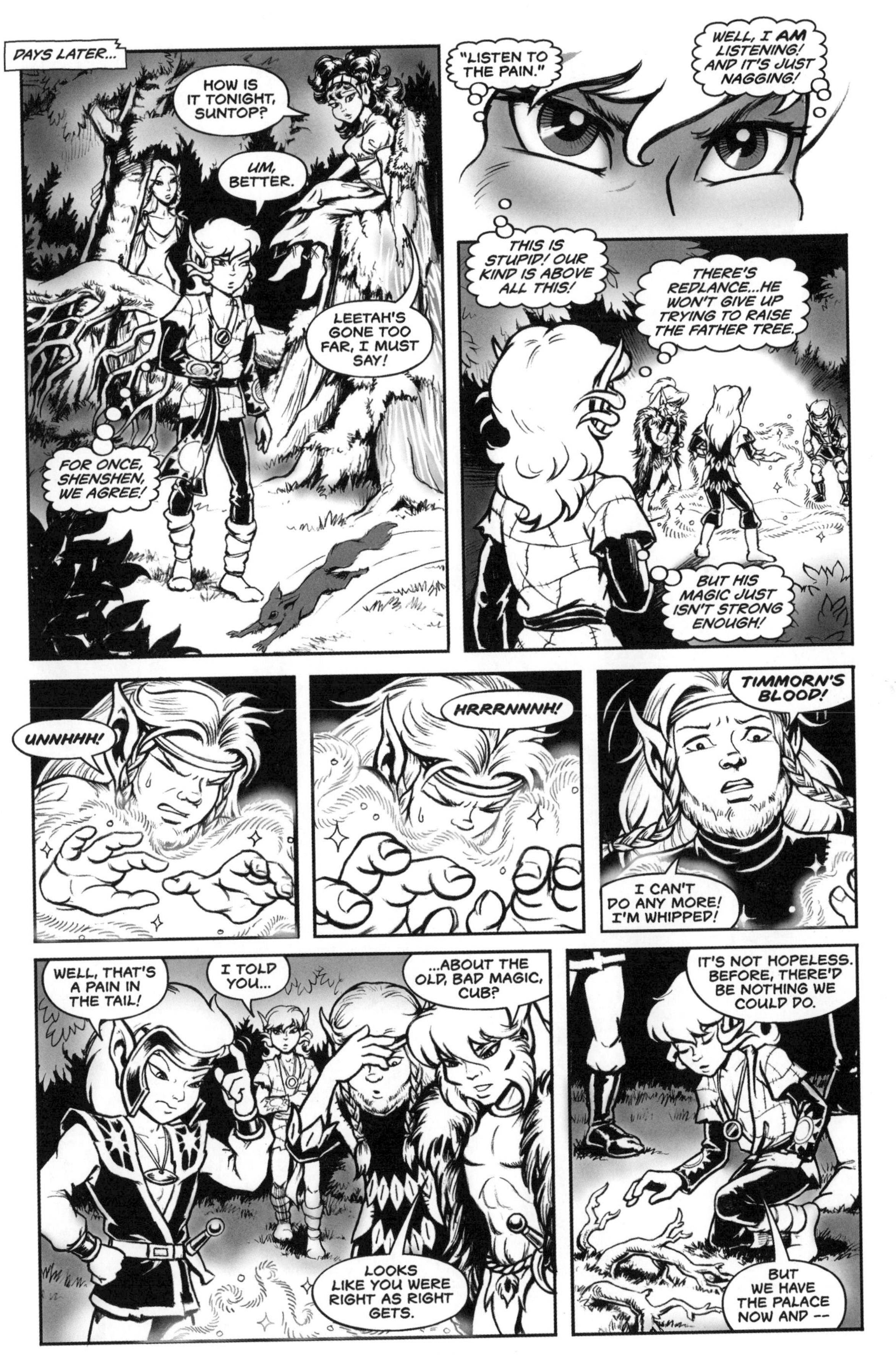
DAYS LATER...
HOW IS IT TONIGHT, SUNTOP?
UM, BETTER.
LEETAH'S GONE TOO FAR, I MUST SAY!
FOR ONCE, SHENSHEN, WE AGREE!
"LISTEN TO THE PAIN."
WELL, I AM LISTENING! AND IT'S JUST NAGGING!
THIS IS STUPID! OUR KIND IS ABOVE ALL THIS!
THERE'S REDLANCE...HE WON'T GIVE UP TRYING TO RAISE THE FATHER TREE.
BUT HIS MAGIC JUST ISN'T STRONG ENOUGH!
UNNHHH!
HRRRNNNH!
TIMMORN'S BLOOD!
I CAN'T DO ANY MORE! I'M WHIPPED!
WELL, THAT'S A PAIN IN THE TAIL!
I TOLD YOU...
...ABOUT THE OLD, BAD MAGIC, CUB?
LOOKS LIKE YOU WERE RIGHT AS RIGHT GETS.
IT'S NOT HOPELESS. BEFORE, THERE'D BE NOTHING WE COULD DO.
BUT WE HAVE THE PALACE NOW AND --

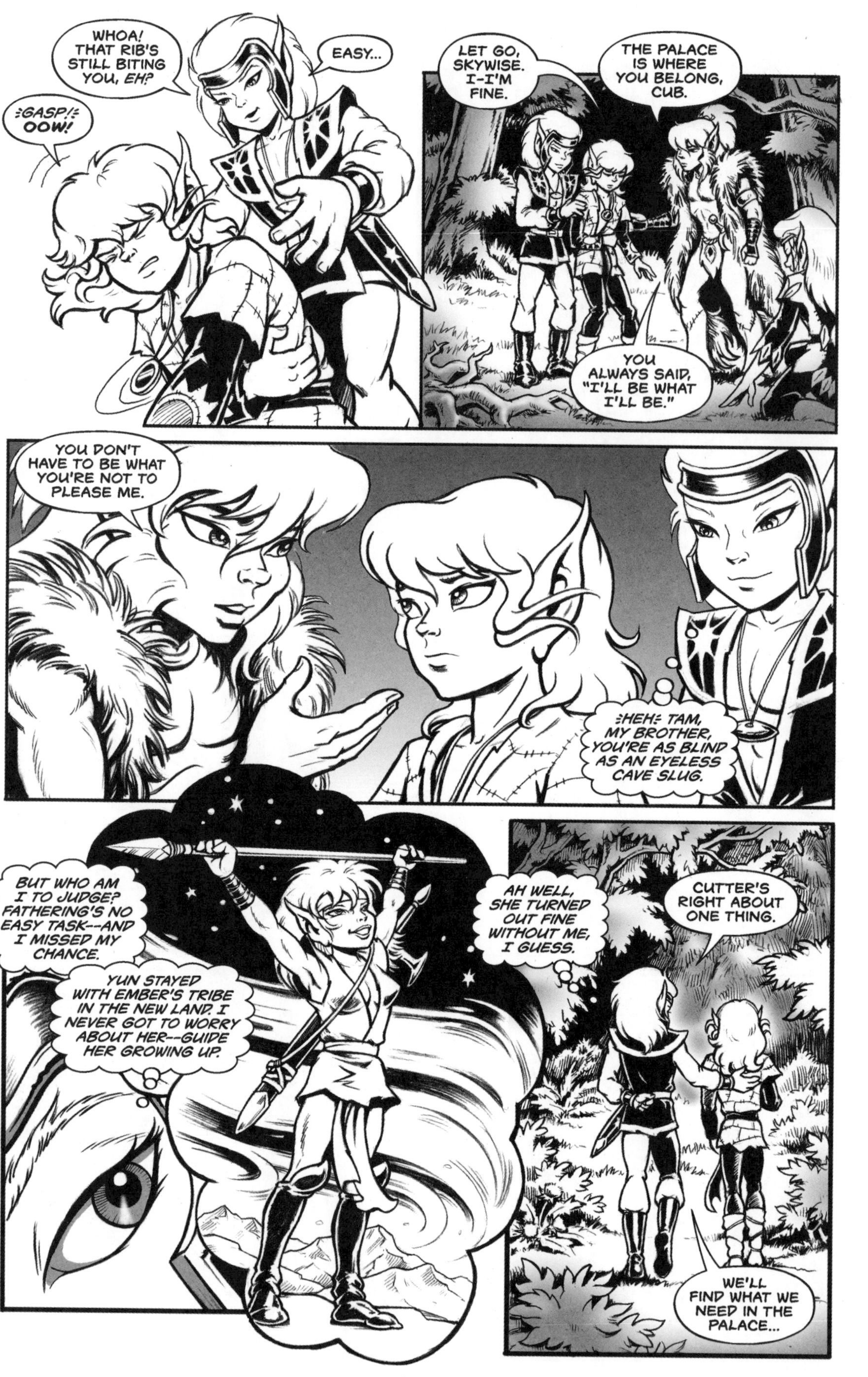
WHOA! THAT RIB'S STILL BITING YOU, EH?
EASY...
:GASP!: OOW!
LET GO, SKYWISE. I-I'M FINE.
THE PALACE IS WHERE YOU BELONG, CUB.
YOU ALWAYS SAID, "I'LL BE WHAT I'LL BE."
YOU DON'T HAVE TO BE WHAT YOU'RE NOT TO PLEASE ME.
:HEH: TAM, MY BROTHER, YOU'RE AS BLIND AS AN EYELESS CAVE SLUG.
BUT WHO AM I TO JUDGE? FATHERING'S NO EASY TASK--AND I MISSED MY CHANCE.
YUN STAYED WITH EMBER'S TRIBE IN THE NEW LAND. I NEVER GOT TO WORRY ABOUT HER--GUIDE HER GROWING UP.
AH WELL, SHE TURNED OUT FINE WITHOUT ME, I GUESS.
CUTTER'S RIGHT ABOUT ONE THING.
WE'LL FIND WHAT WE NEED IN THE PALACE...

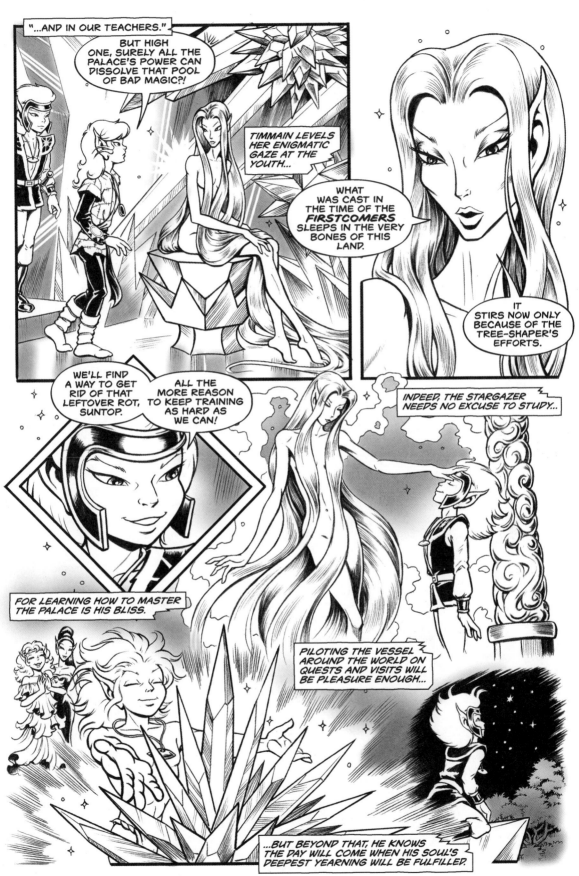

"...AND IN OUR TEACHERS."

BUT HIGH ONE, SURELY ALL THE PALACE'S POWER CAN DISSOLVE THAT POOL OF BAD MAGIC?!

TIMMAIN LEVELS HER ENIGMATIC GAZE AT THE YOUTH...

WHAT WAS CAST IN THE TIME OF THE *FIRSTCOMERS* SLEEPS IN THE VERY BONES OF THIS LAND.

IT STIRS NOW ONLY BECAUSE OF THE TREE-SHAPER'S EFFORTS.

WE'LL FIND A WAY TO GET RID OF THAT LEFTOVER ROT, SUNTOP.

ALL THE MORE REASON TO KEEP TRAINING AS HARD AS WE CAN!

INDEED, THE STARGAZER NEEDS NO EXCUSE TO STUDY...

FOR LEARNING HOW TO MASTER THE PALACE IS HIS BLISS.

PILOTING THE VESSEL AROUND THE WORLD ON QUESTS AND VISITS WILL BE PLEASURE ENOUGH...

...BUT BEYOND THAT, HE KNOWS THE DAY WILL COME WHEN HIS SOUL'S DEEPEST YEARNING WILL BE FULFILLED.

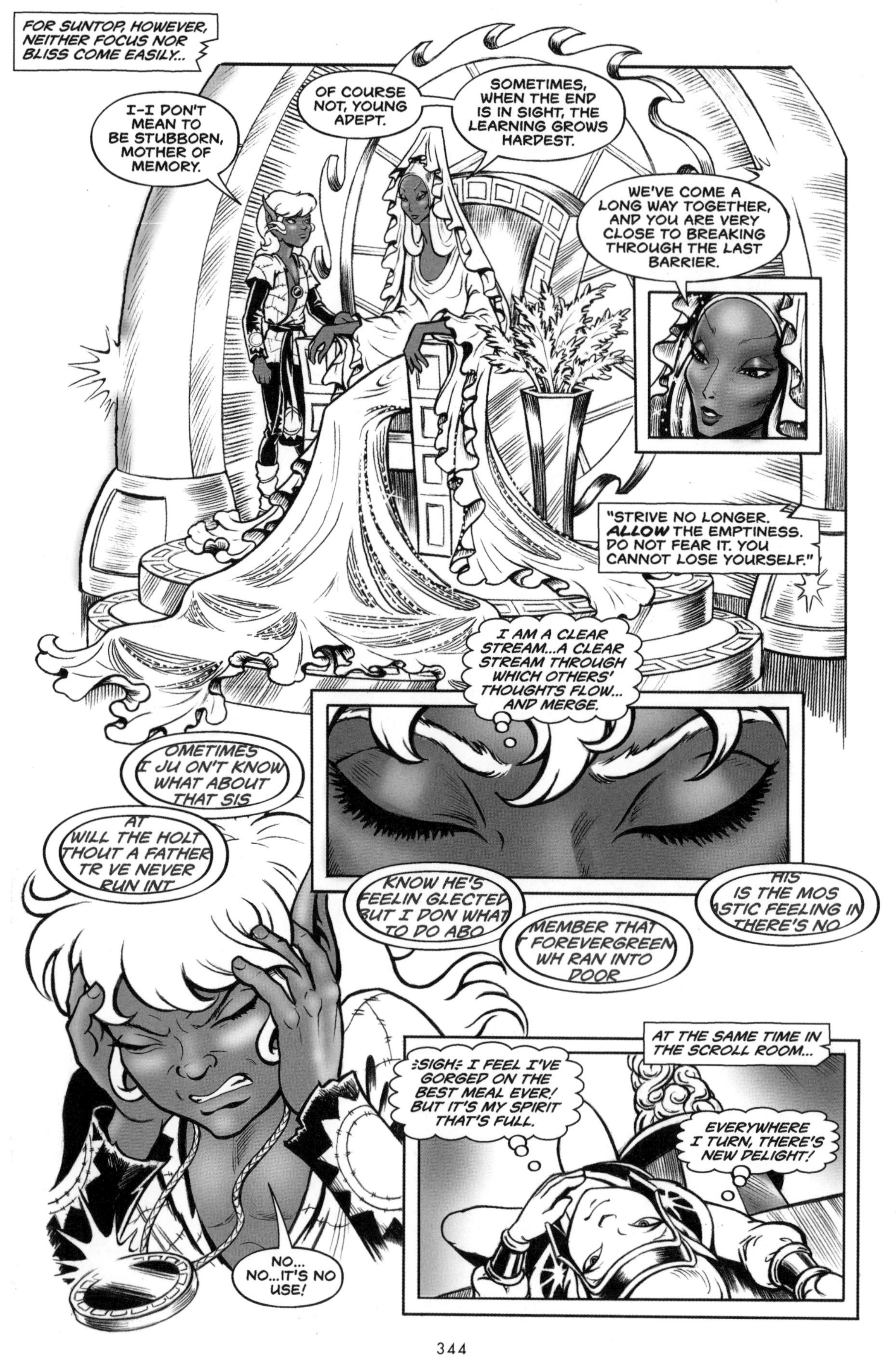

FOR SUNTOP, HOWEVER, NEITHER FOCUS NOR BLISS COME EASILY...
I-I DON'T MEAN TO BE STUBBORN, MOTHER OF MEMORY.
OF COURSE NOT, YOUNG ADEPT.
SOMETIMES, WHEN THE END IS IN SIGHT, THE LEARNING GROWS HARDEST.
WE'VE COME A LONG WAY TOGETHER, AND YOU ARE VERY CLOSE TO BREAKING THROUGH THE LAST BARRIER.
"STRIVE NO LONGER. ALLOW THE EMPTINESS. DO NOT FEAR IT. YOU CANNOT LOSE YOURSELF."
I AM A CLEAR STREAM...A CLEAR STREAM THROUGH WHICH OTHERS' THOUGHTS FLOW... AND MERGE.
OMETIMES I JU ON'T KNOW WHAT ABOUT THAT SIS
AT WILL THE HOLT THOUT A FATHER TR VE NEVER RUN INT
KNOW HE'S FEELIN GLECTED BUT I DON WHAT TO DO ABO
MEMBER THAT FOREVERGREEN WH RAN INTO DOOR
HIS IS THE MOS ASTIC FEELING IN THERE'S NO
NO... NO...IT'S NO USE!
AT THE SAME TIME IN THE SCROLL ROOM...
:SIGH: I FEEL I'VE GORGED ON THE BEST MEAL EVER! BUT IT'S MY SPIRIT THAT'S FULL.
EVERYWHERE I TURN, THERE'S NEW DELIGHT!

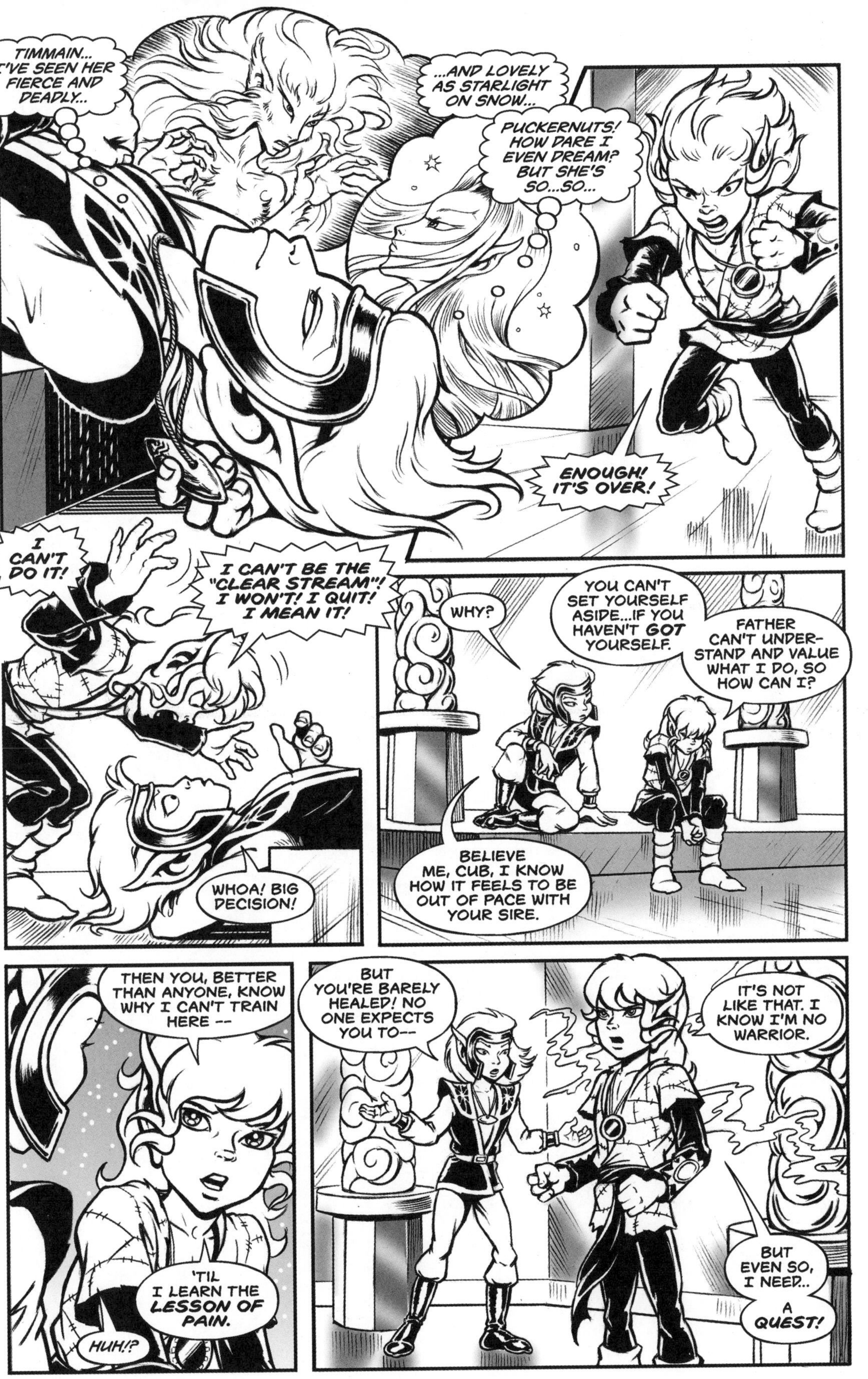
TIMMAIN... I'VE SEEN HER FIERCE AND DEADLY...
...AND LOVELY AS STARLIGHT ON SNOW...
PUCKERNUTS! HOW DARE I EVEN DREAM? BUT SHE'S SO...SO...
ENOUGH! IT'S OVER!
I CAN'T DO IT!
I CAN'T BE THE "CLEAR STREAM"! I WON'T! I QUIT! I MEAN IT!
WHOA! BIG DECISION!
WHY?
YOU CAN'T SET YOURSELF ASIDE...IF YOU HAVEN'T GOT YOURSELF.
FATHER CAN'T UNDERSTAND AND VALUE WHAT I DO, SO HOW CAN I?
BELIEVE ME, CUB, I KNOW HOW IT FEELS TO BE OUT OF PACE WITH YOUR SIRE.
THEN YOU, BETTER THAN ANYONE, KNOW WHY I CAN'T TRAIN HERE --
'TIL I LEARN THE LESSON OF PAIN.
HUH!?
BUT YOU'RE BARELY HEALED! NO ONE EXPECTS YOU TO--
IT'S NOT LIKE THAT. I KNOW I'M NO WARRIOR.
BUT EVEN SO, I NEED... A QUEST!

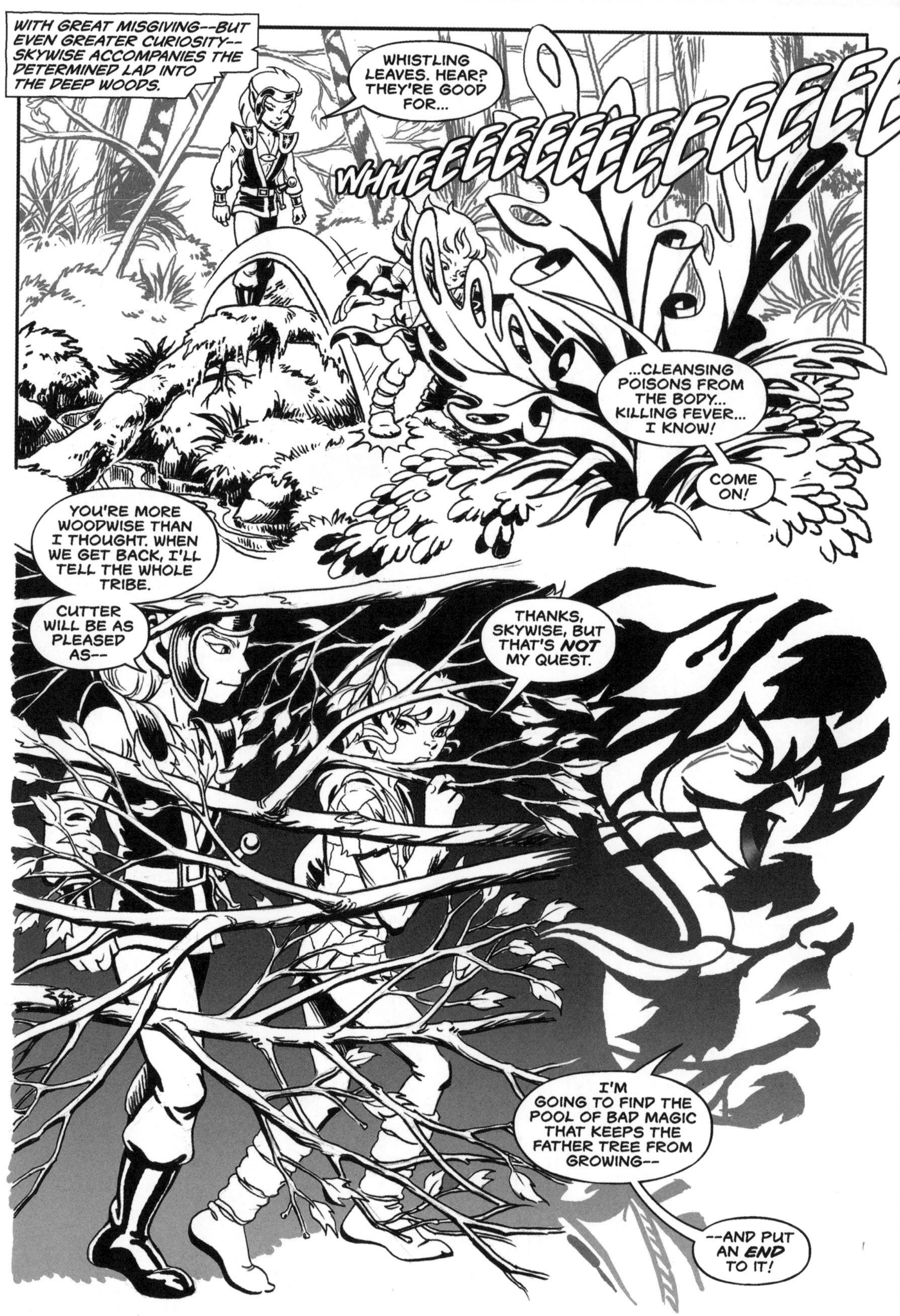
WITH GREAT MISGIVING--BUT EVEN GREATER CURIOSITY--SKYWISE ACCOMPANIES THE DETERMINED LAD INTO THE DEEP WOODS.
WHISTLING LEAVES. HEAR? THEY'RE GOOD FOR...
WHHEEEEEEEEEEEEEEEE
...CLEANSING POISONS FROM THE BODY... KILLING FEVER... I KNOW!
COME ON!
YOU'RE MORE WOODWISE THAN I THOUGHT. WHEN WE GET BACK, I'LL TELL THE WHOLE TRIBE.
CUTTER WILL BE AS PLEASED AS--
THANKS, SKYWISE, BUT THAT'S NOT MY QUEST.
I'M GOING TO FIND THE POOL OF BAD MAGIC THAT KEEPS THE FATHER TREE FROM GROWING--
--AND PUT AN END TO IT!

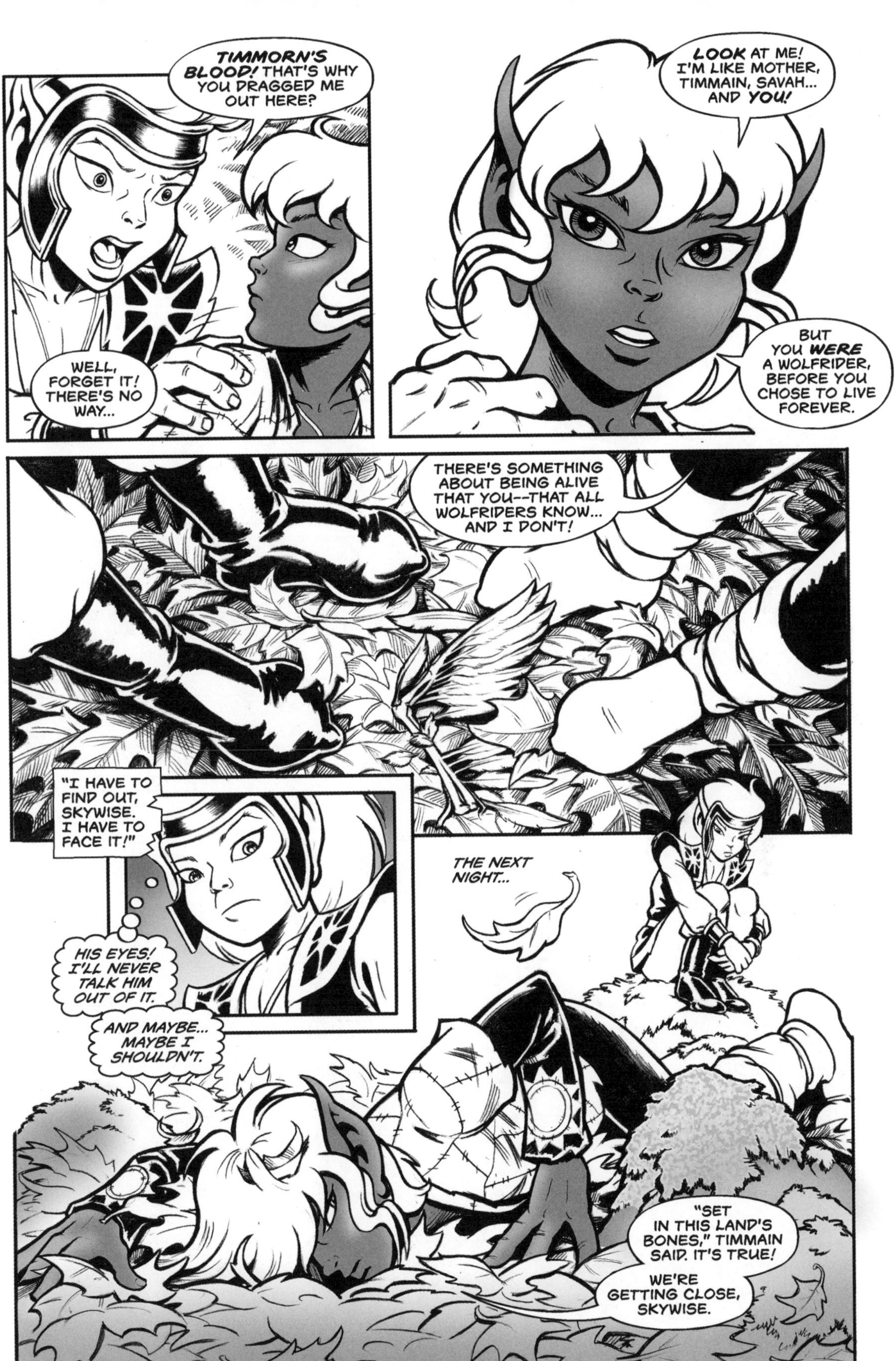
TIMMORN'S BLOOD! THAT'S WHY YOU DRAGGED ME OUT HERE?
WELL, FORGET IT! THERE'S NO WAY...
LOOK AT ME! I'M LIKE MOTHER, TIMMAIN, SAVAH... AND YOU!
BUT YOU WERE A WOLFRIDER, BEFORE YOU CHOSE TO LIVE FOREVER.
THERE'S SOMETHING ABOUT BEING ALIVE THAT YOU--THAT ALL WOLFRIDERS KNOW... AND I DON'T!
"I HAVE TO FIND OUT, SKYWISE. I HAVE TO FACE IT!"
HIS EYES! I'LL NEVER TALK HIM OUT OF IT.
AND MAYBE... MAYBE I SHOULDN'T.
THE NEXT NIGHT...
"SET IN THIS LAND'S BONES," TIMMAIN SAID. IT'S TRUE!
WE'RE GETTING CLOSE, SKYWISE.

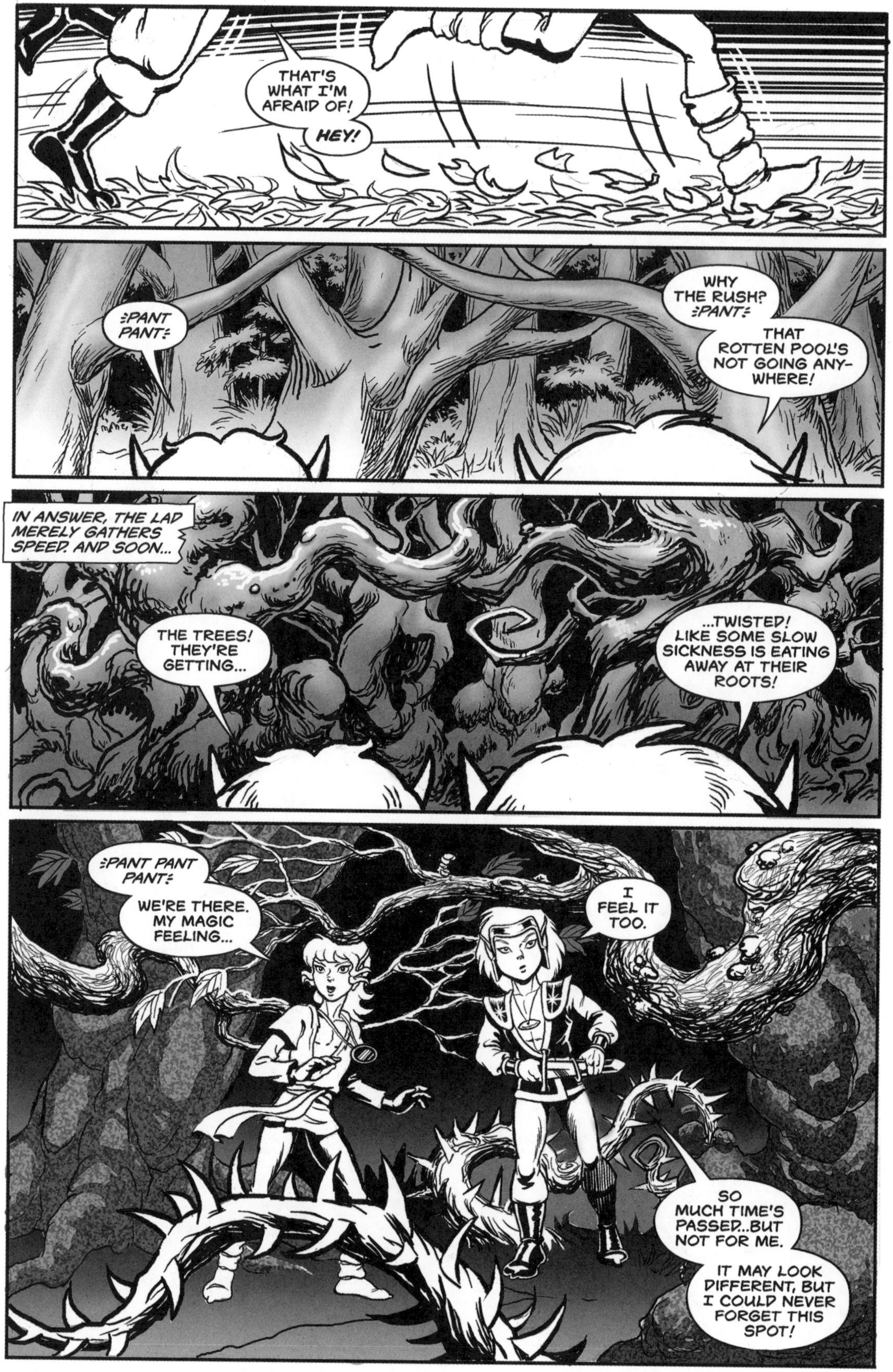
THAT'S WHAT I'M AFRAID OF!
HEY!
:PANT PANT:
WHY THE RUSH? :PANT:
THAT ROTTEN POOL'S NOT GOING ANY-WHERE!
IN ANSWER, THE LAD MERELY GATHERS SPEED. AND SOON...
THE TREES! THEY'RE GETTING...
...TWISTED! LIKE SOME SLOW SICKNESS IS EATING AWAY AT THEIR ROOTS!
:PANT PANT PANT:
WE'RE THERE. MY MAGIC FEELING...
I FEEL IT TOO.
SO MUCH TIME'S PASSED...BUT NOT FOR ME.
IT MAY LOOK DIFFERENT, BUT I COULD NEVER FORGET THIS SPOT!

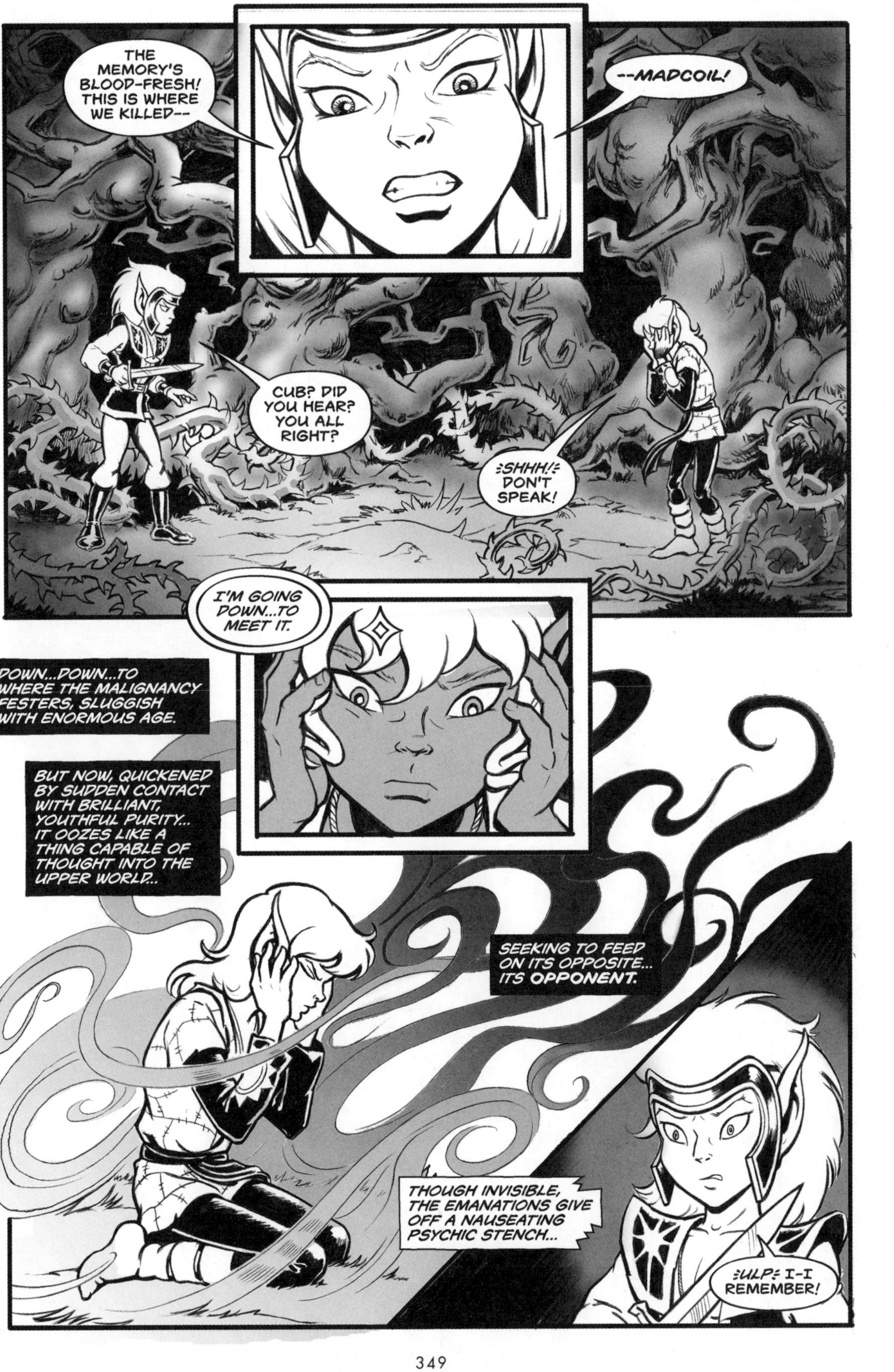
THE MEMORY'S BLOOD-FRESH! THIS IS WHERE WE KILLED--
--MADCOIL!
CUB? DID YOU HEAR? YOU ALL RIGHT?
SHHH! DON'T SPEAK!
I'M GOING DOWN...TO MEET IT.
DOWN...DOWN...TO WHERE THE MALIGNANCY FESTERS, SLUGGISH WITH ENORMOUS AGE.
BUT NOW, QUICKENED BY SUDDEN CONTACT WITH BRILLIANT, YOUTHFUL PURITY... IT OOZES LIKE A THING CAPABLE OF THOUGHT INTO THE UPPER WORLD..
SEEKING TO FEED ON ITS OPPOSITE... ITS OPPONENT.
THOUGH INVISIBLE, THE EMANATIONS GIVE OFF A NAUSEATING PSYCHIC STENCH...
ULP I-I REMEMBER!

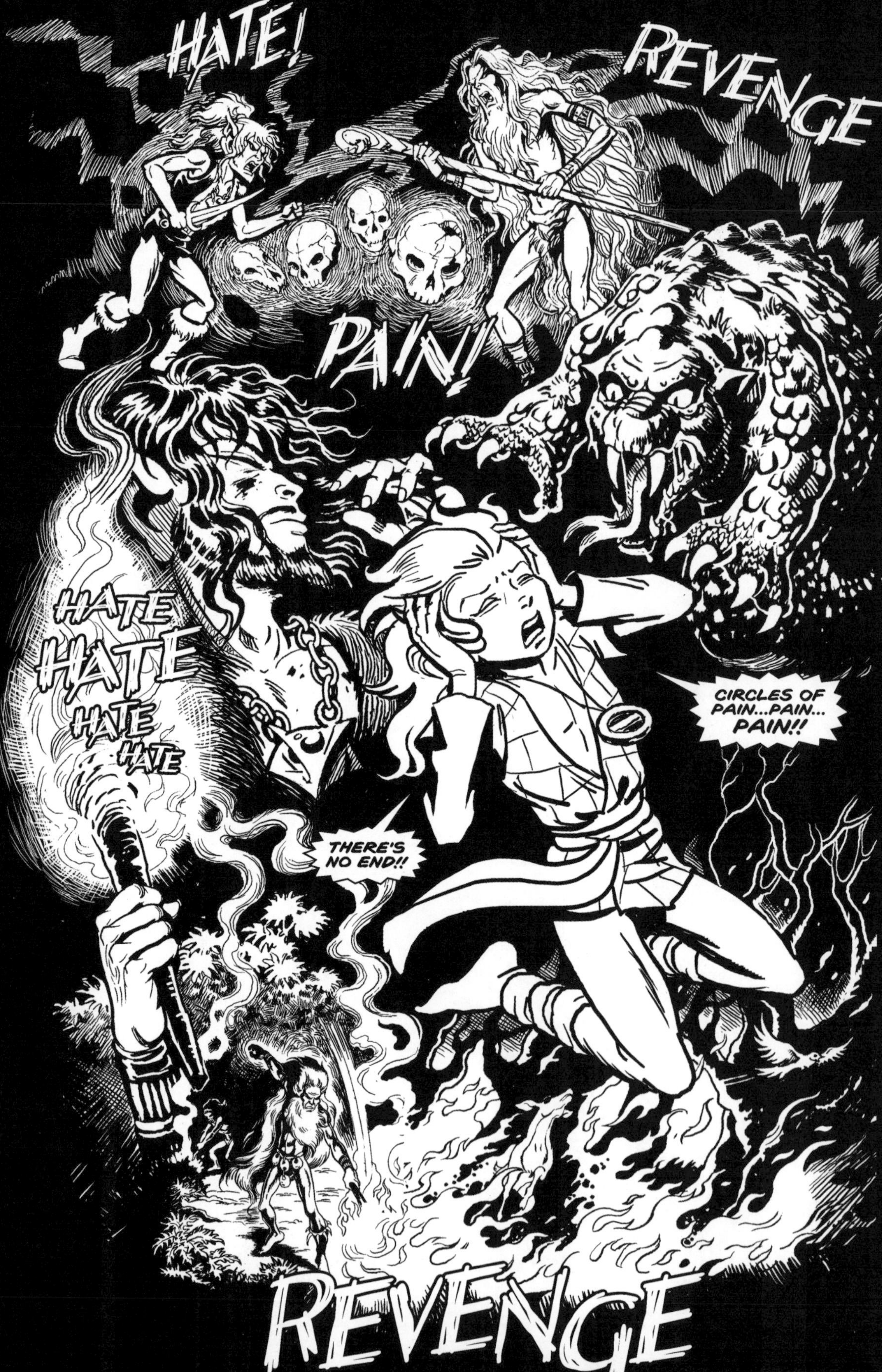
HATE!
REVENGE
PAIN!
HATE
HATE
HATE
HATE
CIRCLES OF PAIN...PAIN... PAIN!!
THERE'S NO END!!
REVENGE

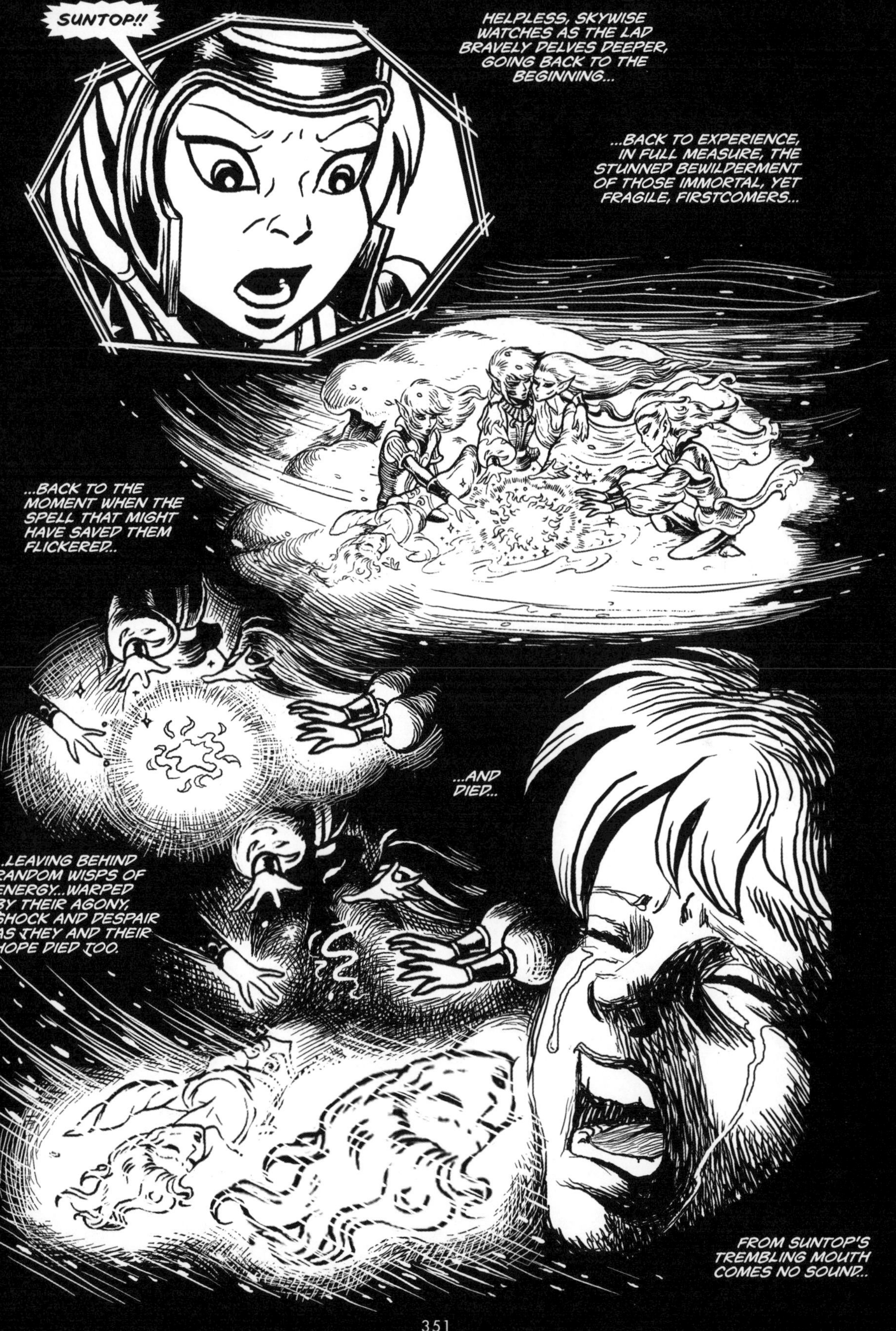
SUNTOP!!
HELPLESS, SKYWISE WATCHES AS THE LAD BRAVELY DELVES DEEPER, GOING BACK TO THE BEGINNING...
...BACK TO EXPERIENCE, IN FULL MEASURE, THE STUNNED BEWILDERMENT OF THOSE IMMORTAL, YET FRAGILE, FIRSTCOMERS...
...BACK TO THE MOMENT WHEN THE SPELL THAT MIGHT HAVE SAVED THEM FLICKERED...
...AND DIED...
...LEAVING BEHIND RANDOM WISPS OF ENERGY...WARPED BY THEIR AGONY, SHOCK AND DESPAIR AS THEY AND THEIR HOPE DIED TOO.
FROM SUNTOP'S TREMBLING MOUTH COMES NO SOUND...

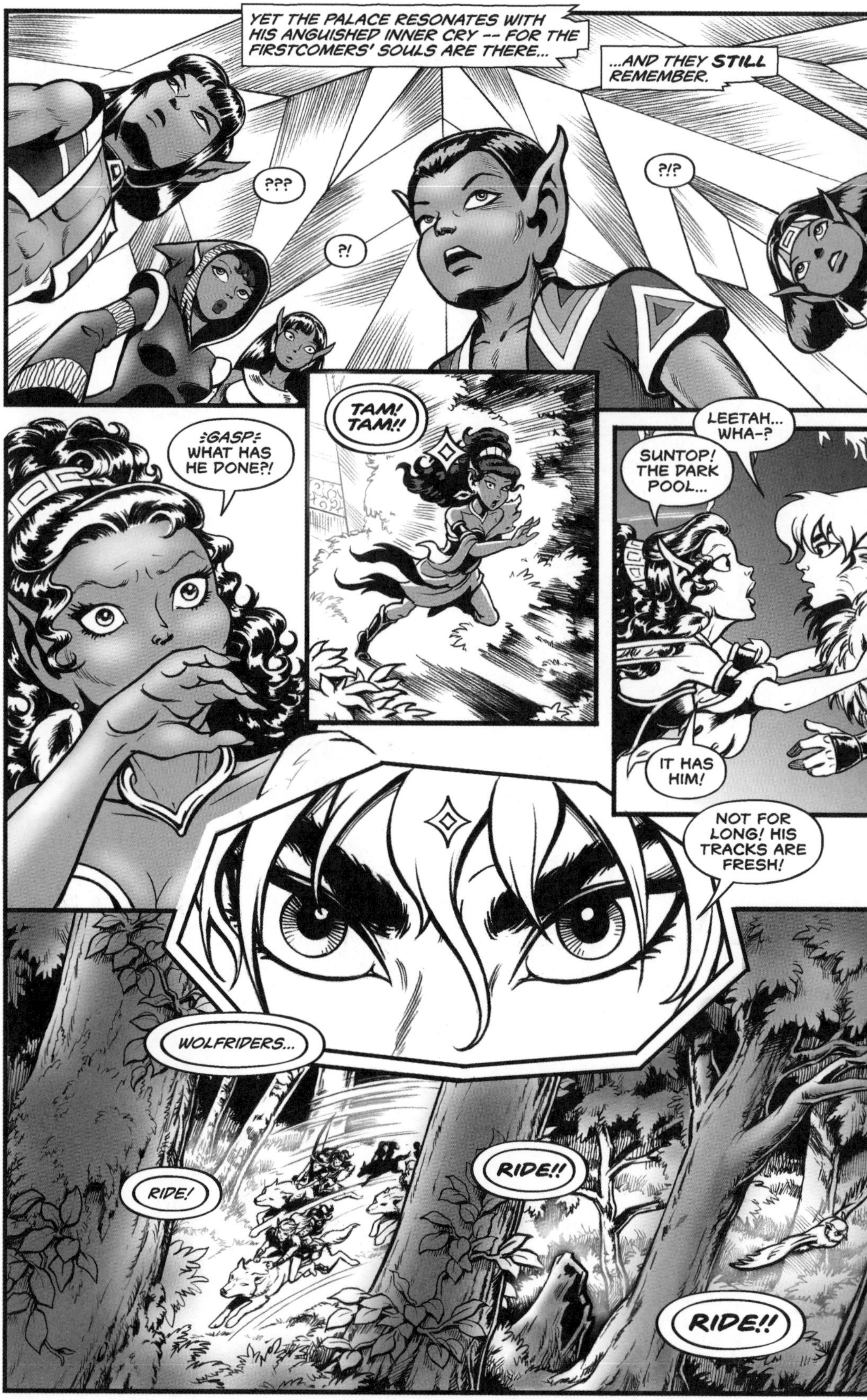

YET THE PALACE RESONATES WITH HIS ANGUISHED INNER CRY -- FOR THE FIRSTCOMERS' SOULS ARE THERE...
...AND THEY STILL REMEMBER.
???
?!
?!?
GASP WHAT HAS HE DONE?!
TAM! TAM!!
LEETAH... WHA-?
SUNTOP! THE DARK POOL...
IT HAS HIM!
NOT FOR LONG! HIS TRACKS ARE FRESH!
WOLFRIDERS...
RIDE!
RIDE!!
RIDE!!

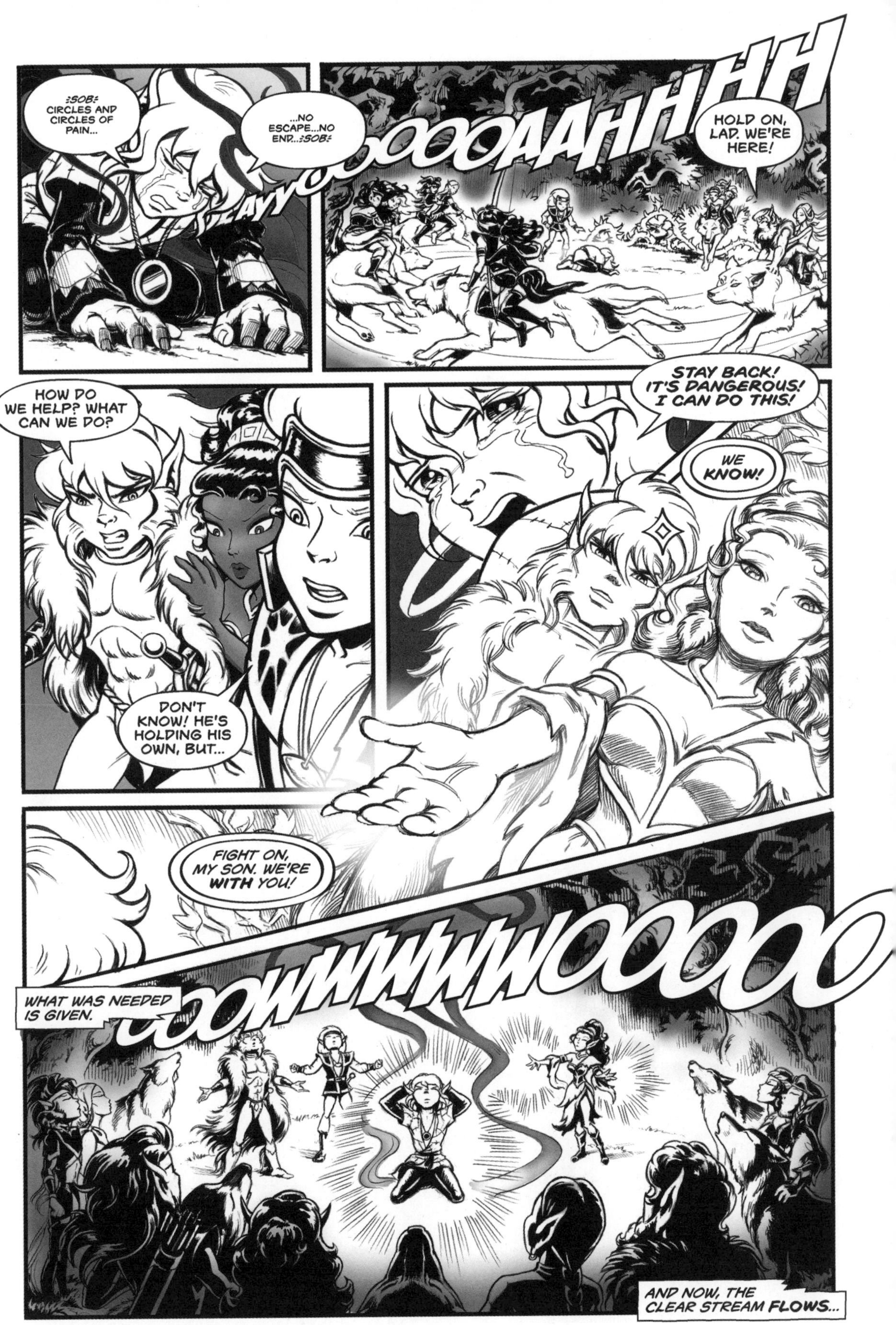

:SOB: CIRCLES AND CIRCLES OF PAIN...
...NO ESCAPE...NO END...:SOB:
AYYOOOOOOAAHHHHH
HOLD ON, LAD. WE'RE HERE!
HOW DO WE HELP? WHAT CAN WE DO?
DON'T KNOW! HE'S HOLDING HIS OWN, BUT...
STAY BACK! IT'S DANGEROUS! I CAN DO THIS!
WE KNOW!
FIGHT ON, MY SON. WE'RE **WITH** YOU!
OOOWWWWWOOOOO
WHAT WAS NEEDED IS GIVEN.
AND NOW, THE CLEAR STREAM **FLOWS**...

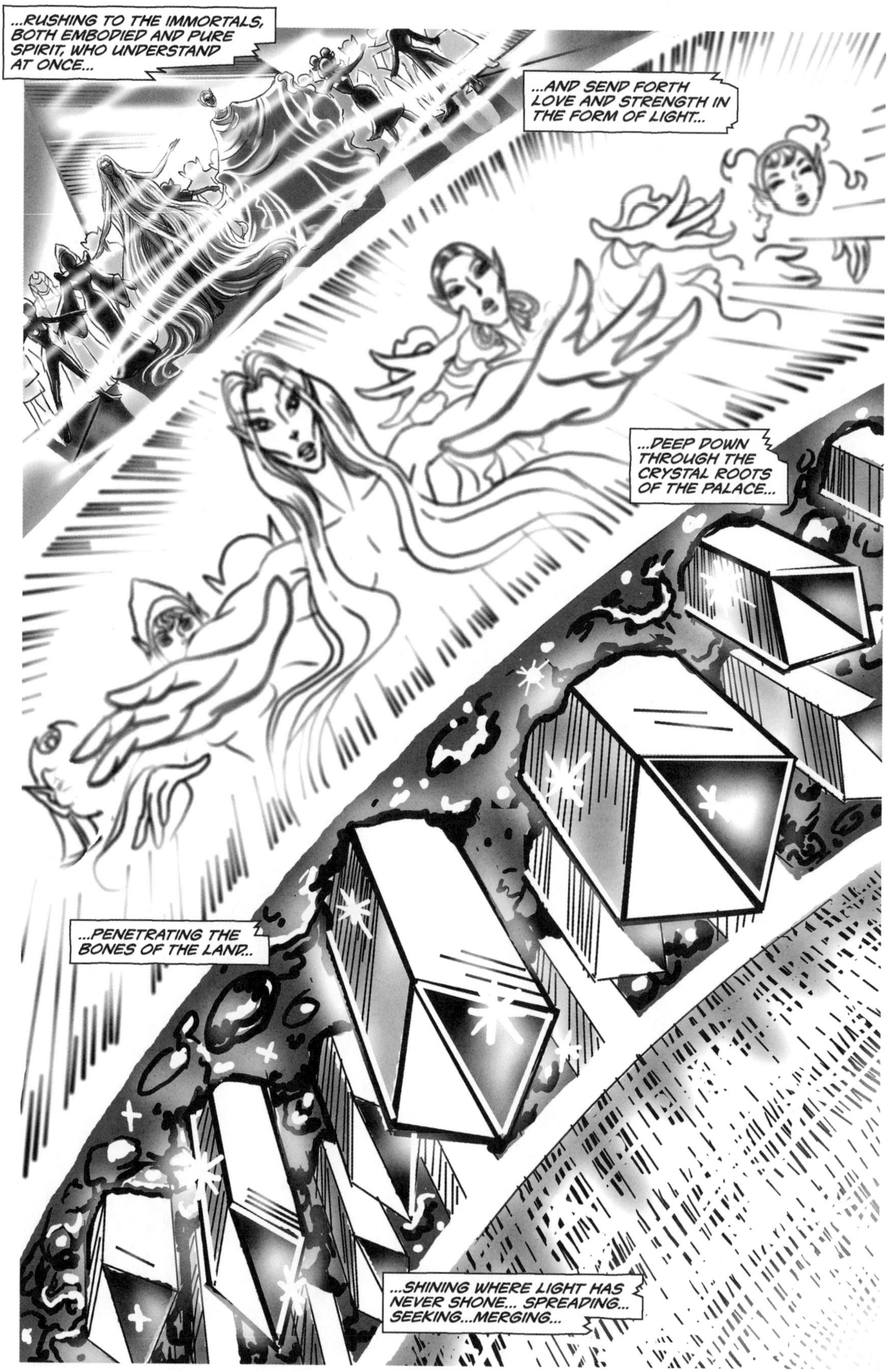
...RUSHING TO THE IMMORTALS, BOTH EMBODIED AND PURE SPIRIT, WHO UNDERSTAND AT ONCE...
...AND SEND FORTH LOVE AND STRENGTH IN THE FORM OF LIGHT...
...DEEP DOWN THROUGH THE CRYSTAL ROOTS OF THE PALACE...
...PENETRATING THE BONES OF THE LAND...
...SHINING WHERE LIGHT HAS NEVER SHONE... SPREADING... SEEKING...MERGING...

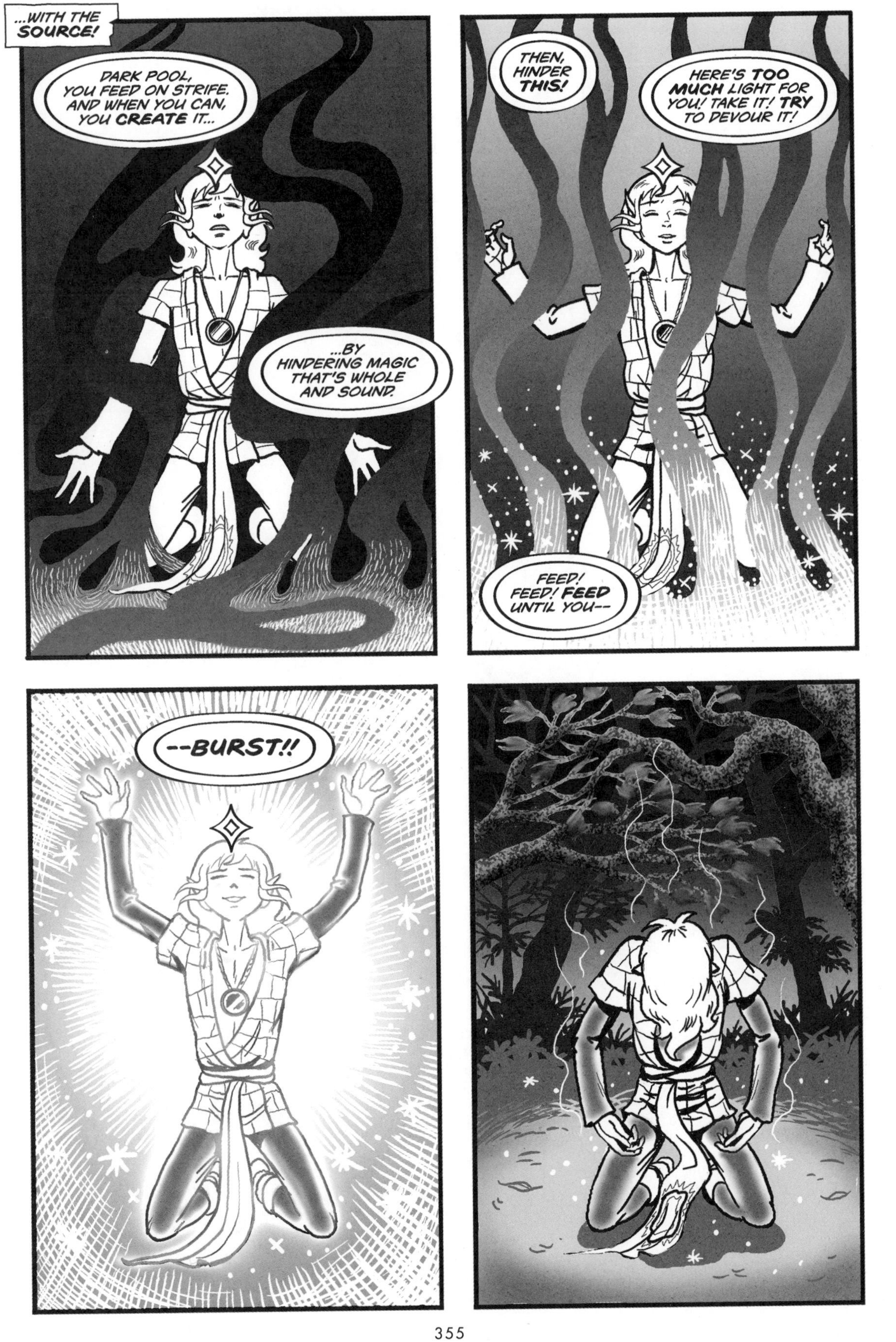
...WITH THE SOURCE!
DARK POOL, YOU FEED ON STRIFE. AND WHEN YOU CAN, YOU CREATE IT...
...BY HINDERING MAGIC THAT'S WHOLE AND SOUND.
THEN, HINDER THIS!
HERE'S TOO MUCH LIGHT FOR YOU! TAKE IT! TRY TO DEVOUR IT!
FEED! FEED! FEED UNTIL YOU--
--BURST!!

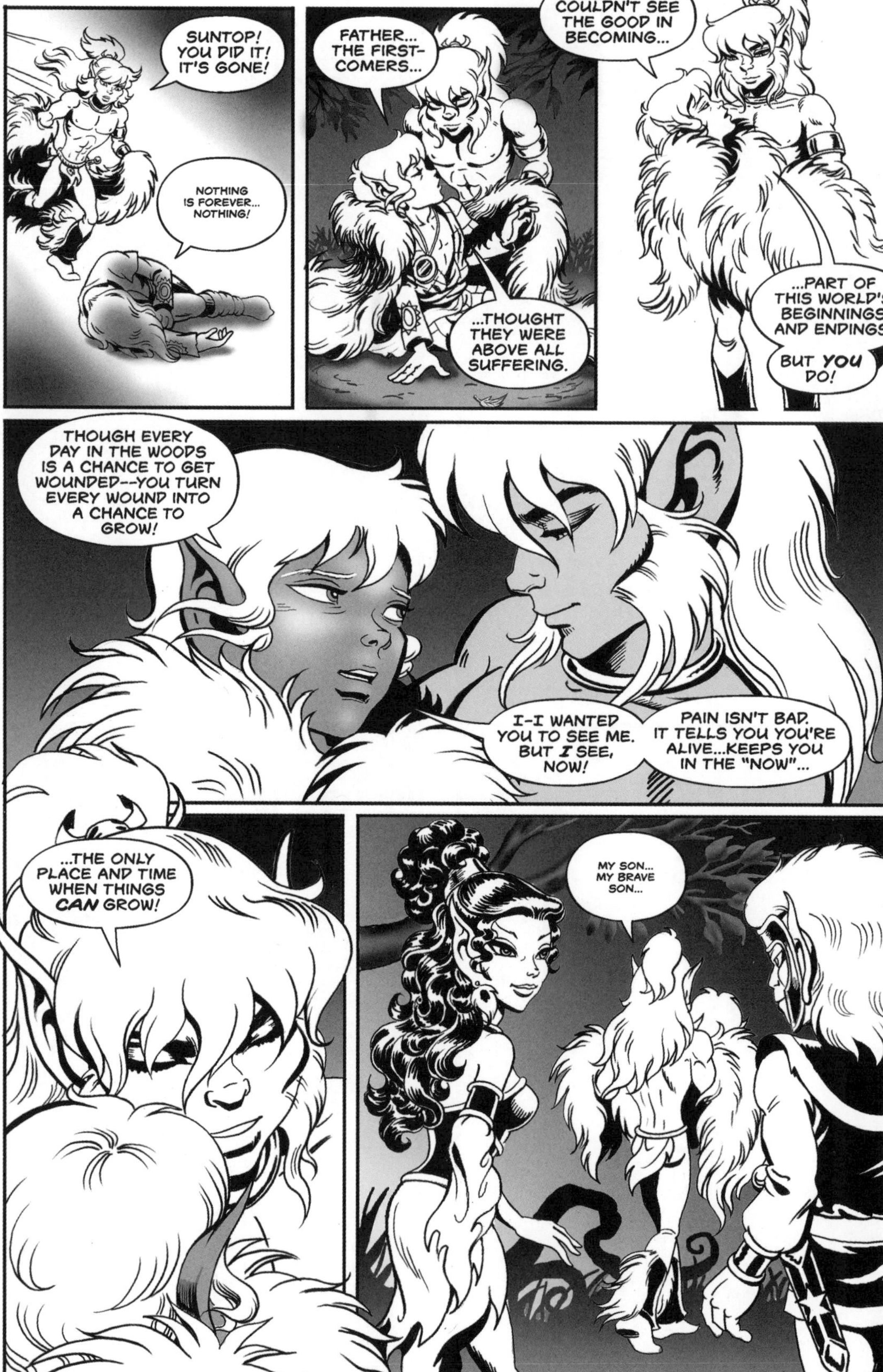
SUNTOP! YOU DID IT! IT'S GONE!
NOTHING IS FOREVER... NOTHING!
FATHER... THE FIRST-COMERS...
...THOUGHT THEY WERE ABOVE ALL SUFFERING.
THEY COULDN'T SEE THE GOOD IN BECOMING...
...PART OF THIS WORLD'S BEGINNINGS AND ENDINGS.
BUT YOU DO!
THOUGH EVERY DAY IN THE WOODS IS A CHANCE TO GET WOUNDED--YOU TURN EVERY WOUND INTO A CHANCE TO GROW!
I-I WANTED YOU TO SEE ME. BUT I SEE, NOW!
PAIN ISN'T BAD. IT TELLS YOU YOU'RE ALIVE...KEEPS YOU IN THE "NOW"...
...THE ONLY PLACE AND TIME WHEN THINGS CAN GROW!
MY SON... MY BRAVE SON...

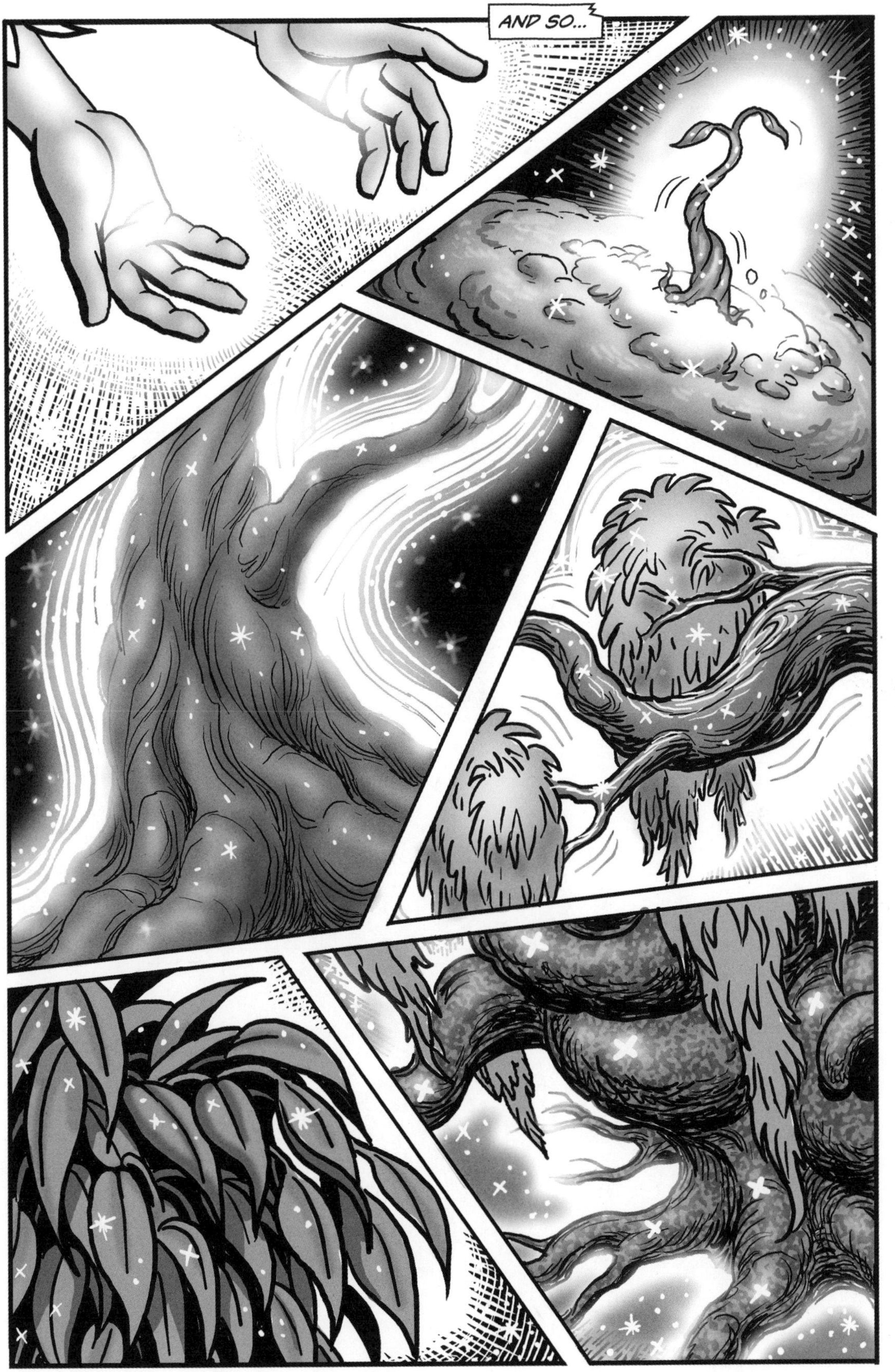
AND SO...

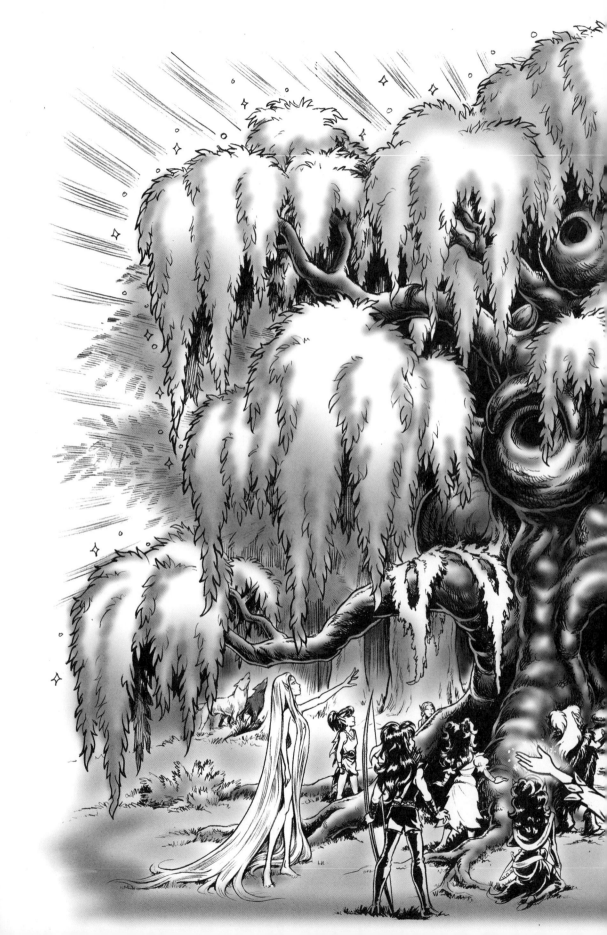

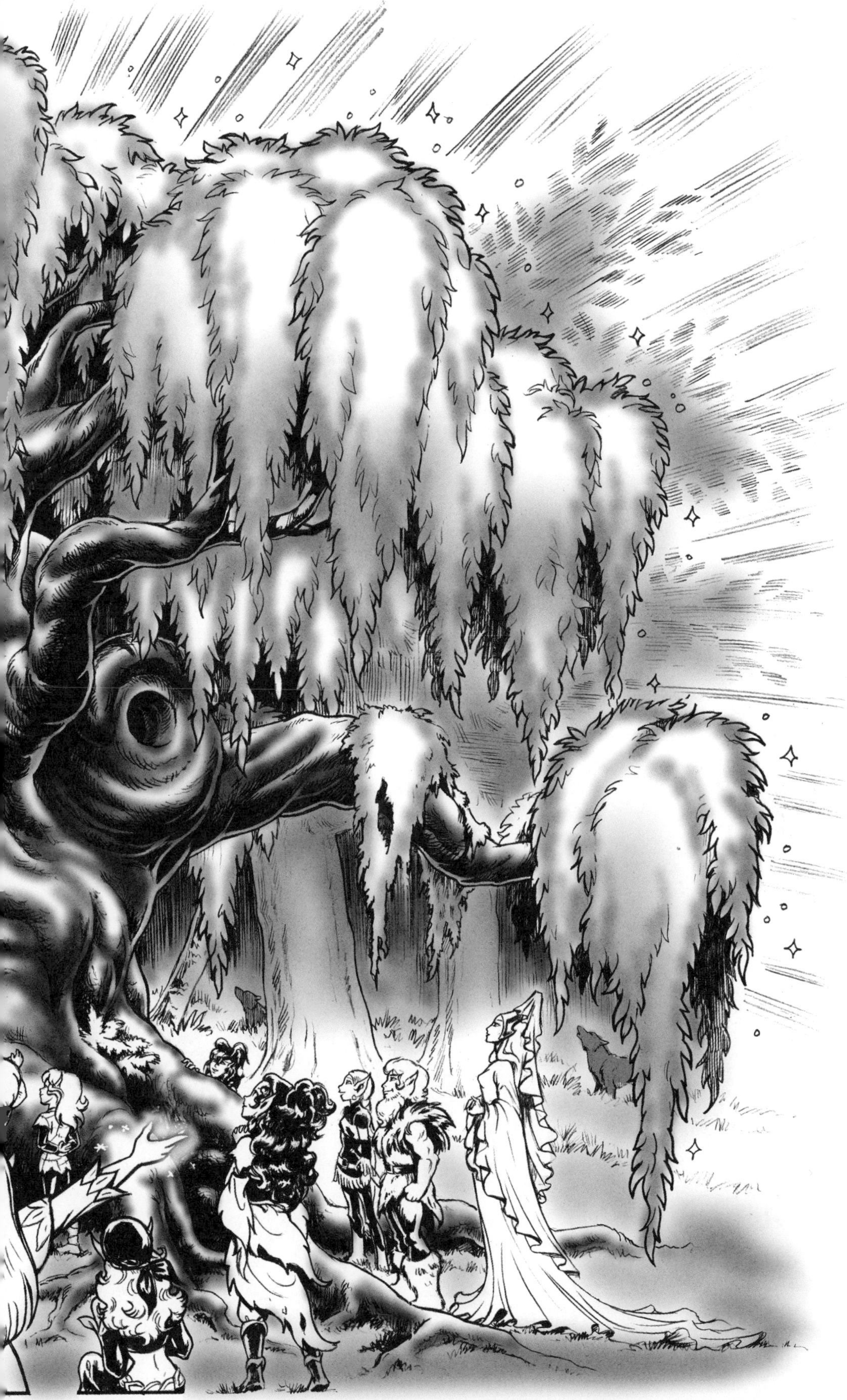

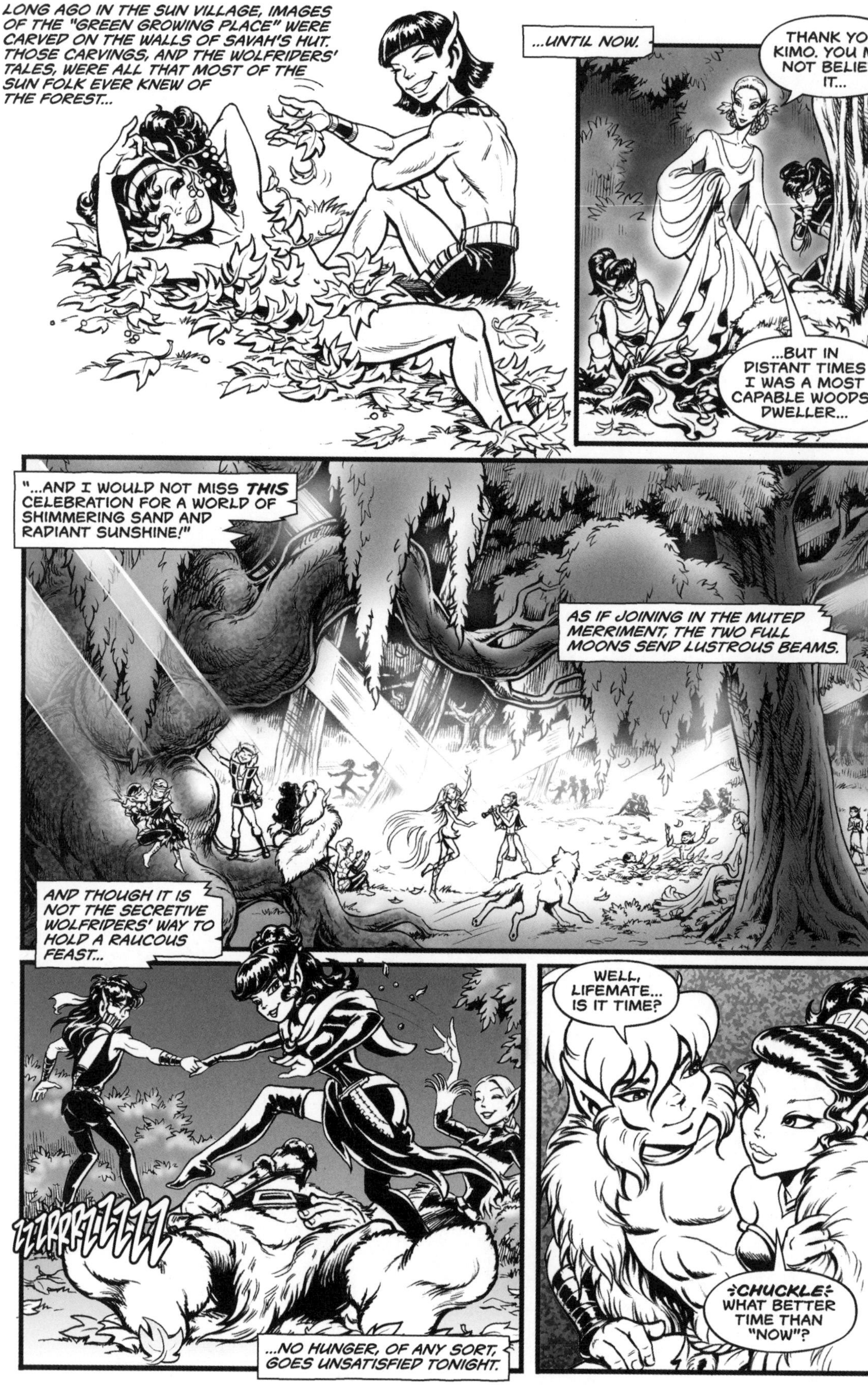

LONG AGO IN THE SUN VILLAGE, IMAGES OF THE "GREEN GROWING PLACE" WERE CARVED ON THE WALLS OF SAVAH'S HUT. THOSE CARVINGS, AND THE WOLFRIDERS' TALES, WERE ALL THAT MOST OF THE SUN FOLK EVER KNEW OF THE FOREST...
...UNTIL NOW.
THANK YOU, KIMO. YOU MAY NOT BELIEVE IT...
...BUT IN DISTANT TIMES I WAS A MOST CAPABLE WOODS-DWELLER...
"...AND I WOULD NOT MISS THIS CELEBRATION FOR A WORLD OF SHIMMERING SAND AND RADIANT SUNSHINE!"
AS IF JOINING IN THE MUTED MERRIMENT, THE TWO FULL MOONS SEND LUSTROUS BEAMS.
AND THOUGH IT IS NOT THE SECRETIVE WOLFRIDERS' WAY TO HOLD A RAUCOUS FEAST...
ZZZRRRZZZZZZ
...NO HUNGER, OF ANY SORT, GOES UNSATISFIED TONIGHT.
WELL, LIFEMATE... IS IT TIME?
CHUCKLE WHAT BETTER TIME THAN "NOW"?

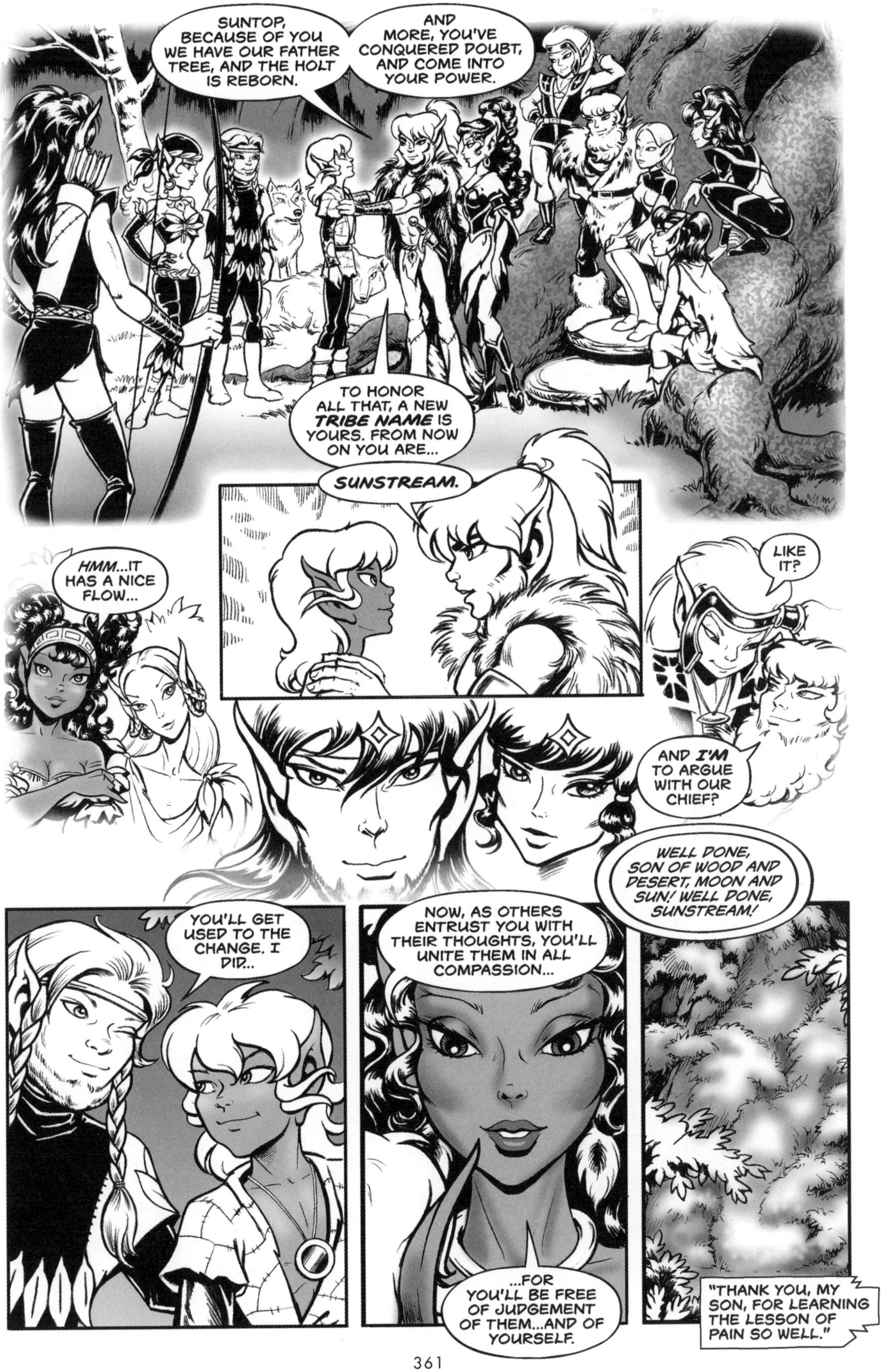
SUNTOP, BECAUSE OF YOU WE HAVE OUR FATHER TREE, AND THE HOLT IS REBORN.
AND MORE, YOU'VE CONQUERED DOUBT, AND COME INTO YOUR POWER.
TO HONOR ALL THAT, A NEW TRIBE NAME IS YOURS. FROM NOW ON YOU ARE...
SUNSTREAM.
HMM...IT HAS A NICE FLOW...
LIKE IT?
AND I'M TO ARGUE WITH OUR CHIEF?
WELL DONE, SON OF WOOD AND DESERT, MOON AND SUN! WELL DONE, SUNSTREAM!
YOU'LL GET USED TO THE CHANGE. I DID...
NOW, AS OTHERS ENTRUST YOU WITH THEIR THOUGHTS, YOU'LL UNITE THEM IN ALL COMPASSION...
...FOR YOU'LL BE FREE OF JUDGEMENT OF THEM...AND OF YOURSELF.
"THANK YOU, MY SON, FOR LEARNING THE LESSON OF PAIN SO WELL."

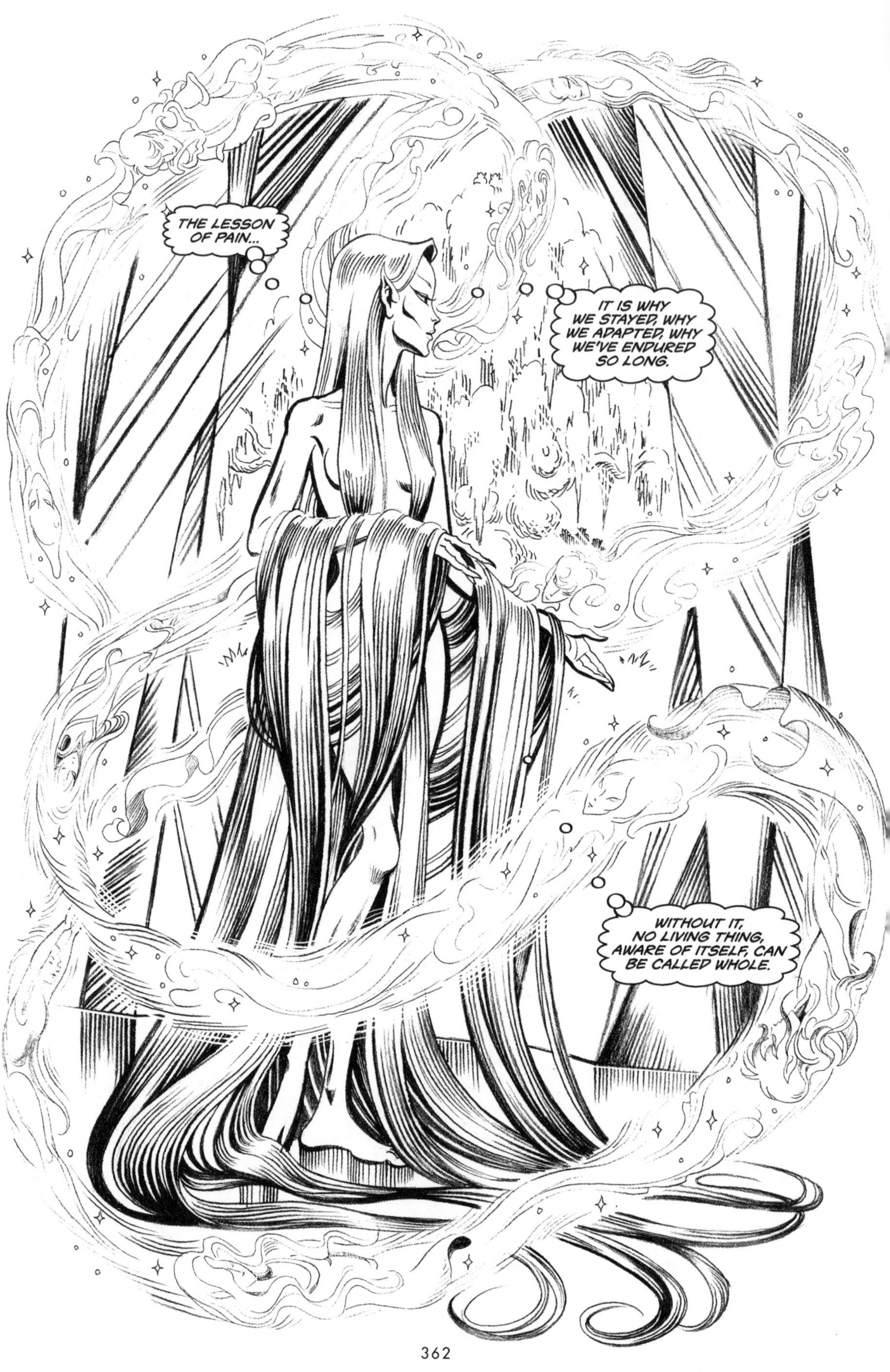
THE LESSON OF PAIN...
IT IS WHY WE STAYED, WHY WE ADAPTED, WHY WE'VE ENDURED SO LONG.
WITHOUT IT, NO LIVING THING, AWARE OF ITSELF, CAN BE CALLED WHOLE.

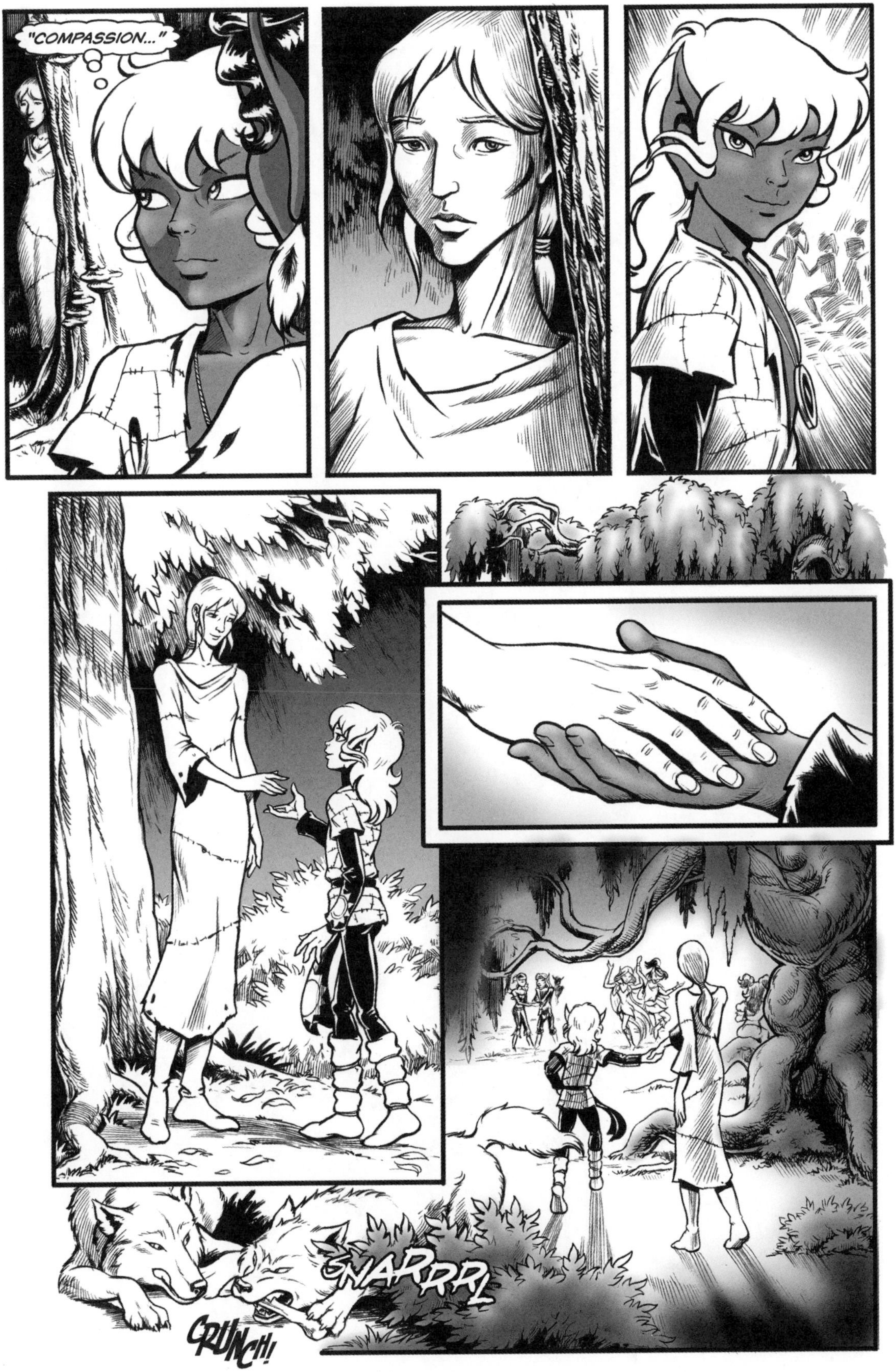
"COMPASSION..."
SNARRRL
CRUNCH!

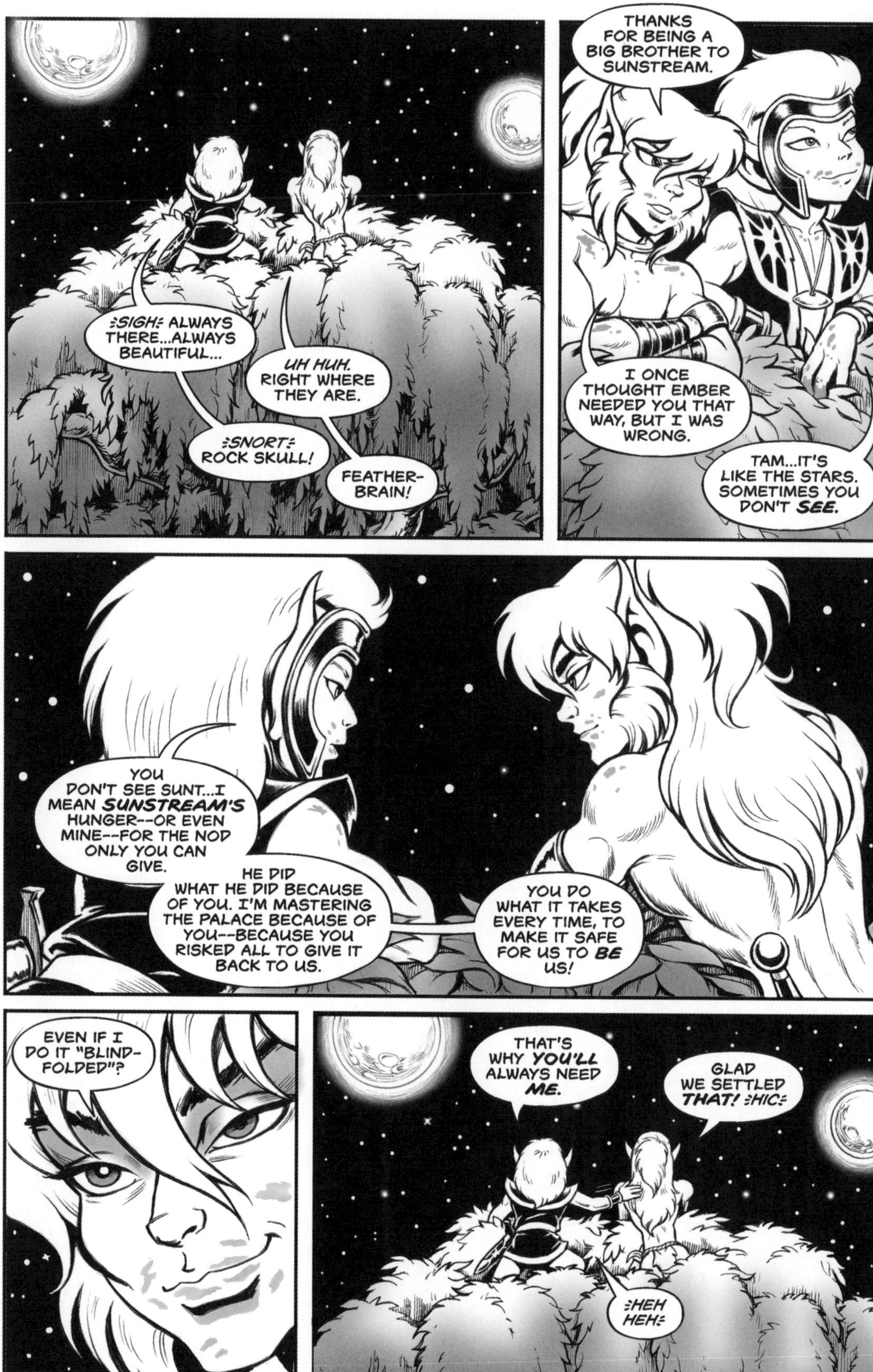

:SIGH: ALWAYS THERE...ALWAYS BEAUTIFUL...
UH HUH. RIGHT WHERE THEY ARE.
:SNORT: ROCK SKULL!
FEATHER-BRAIN!
THANKS FOR BEING A BIG BROTHER TO SUNSTREAM.
I ONCE THOUGHT EMBER NEEDED YOU THAT WAY, BUT I WAS WRONG.
TAM...IT'S LIKE THE STARS. SOMETIMES YOU DON'T SEE.
YOU DON'T SEE SUNT...I MEAN SUNSTREAM'S HUNGER--OR EVEN MINE--FOR THE NOD ONLY YOU CAN GIVE.
HE DID WHAT HE DID BECAUSE OF YOU. I'M MASTERING THE PALACE BECAUSE OF YOU--BECAUSE YOU RISKED ALL TO GIVE IT BACK TO US.
YOU DO WHAT IT TAKES EVERY TIME, TO MAKE IT SAFE FOR US TO BE US!
EVEN IF I DO IT "BLIND-FOLDED"?
THAT'S WHY YOU'LL ALWAYS NEED ME.
GLAD WE SETTLED THAT! :HIC:
:HEH HEH:
THE END

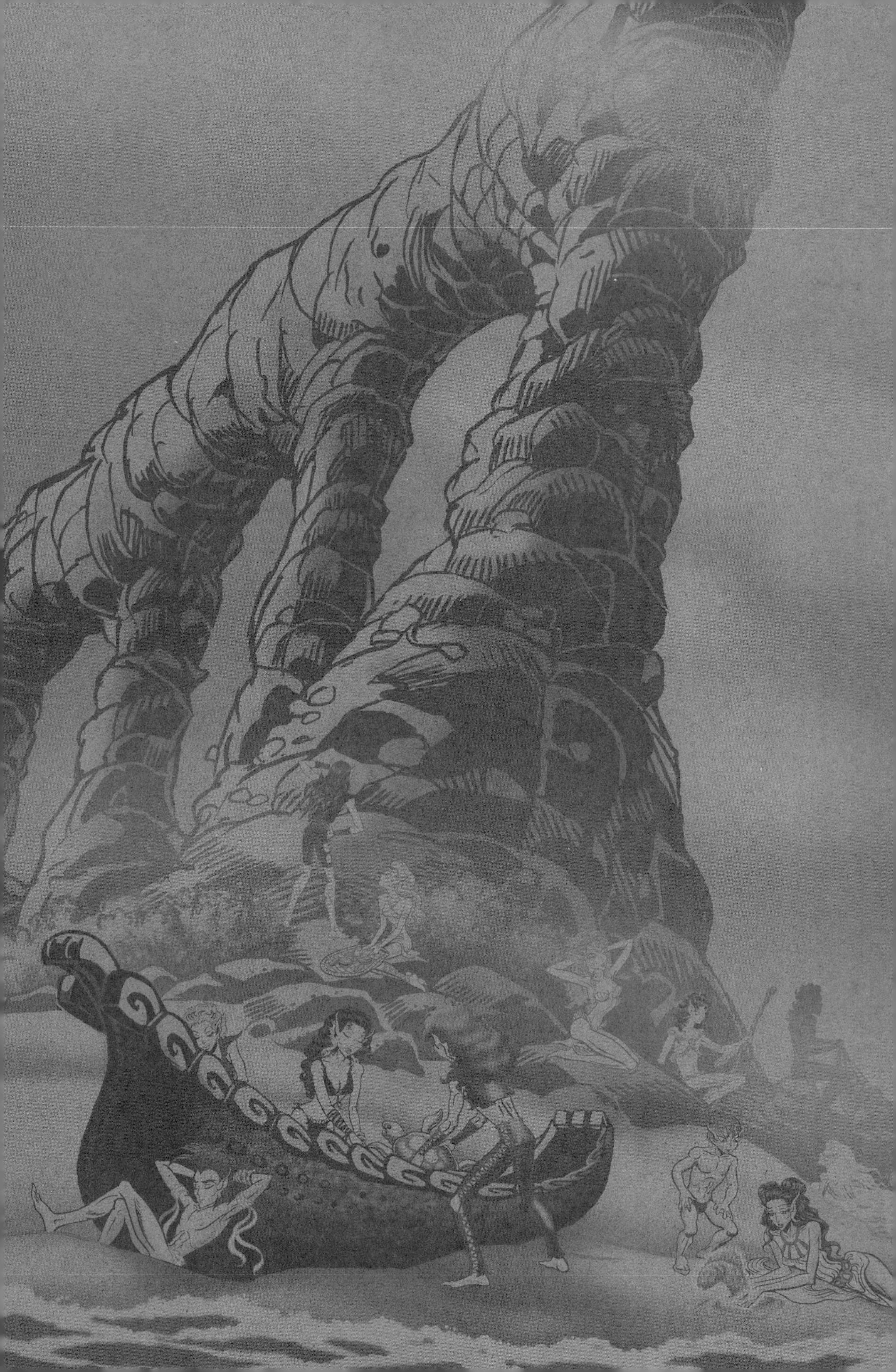

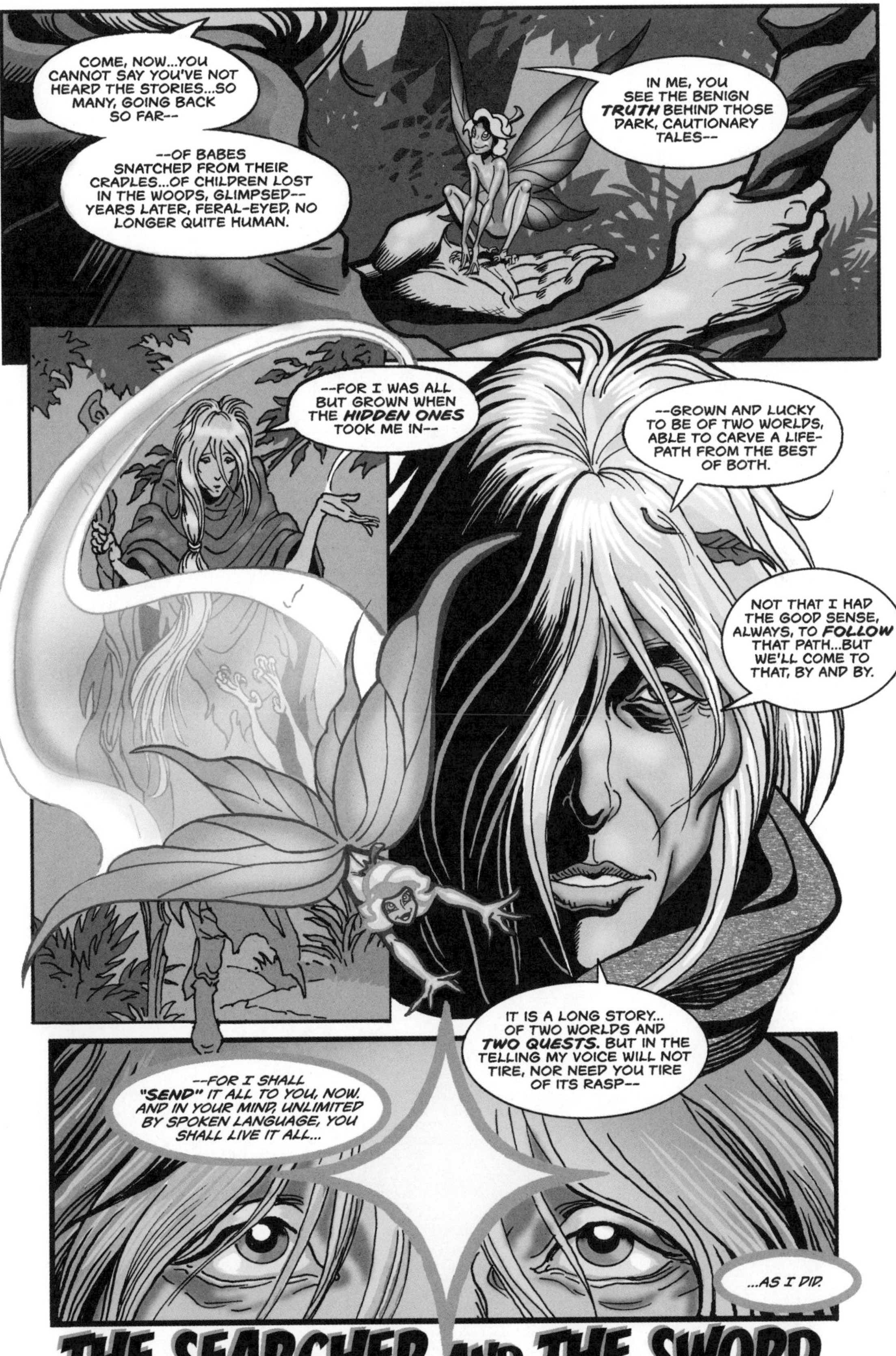

COME, NOW...YOU CANNOT SAY YOU'VE NOT HEARD THE STORIES...SO MANY, GOING BACK SO FAR--
--OF BABES SNATCHED FROM THEIR CRADLES...OF CHILDREN LOST IN THE WOODS, GLIMPSED--YEARS LATER, FERAL-EYED, NO LONGER QUITE HUMAN.
IN ME, YOU SEE THE BENIGN TRUTH BEHIND THOSE DARK, CAUTIONARY TALES--
--FOR I WAS ALL BUT GROWN WHEN THE HIDDEN ONES TOOK ME IN--
--GROWN AND LUCKY TO BE OF TWO WORLDS, ABLE TO CARVE A LIFE-PATH FROM THE BEST OF BOTH.
NOT THAT I HAD THE GOOD SENSE, ALWAYS, TO FOLLOW THAT PATH...BUT WE'LL COME TO THAT, BY AND BY.
IT IS A LONG STORY...OF TWO WORLDS AND TWO QUESTS. BUT IN THE TELLING MY VOICE WILL NOT TIRE, NOR NEED YOU TIRE OF ITS RASP--
--FOR I SHALL "SEND" IT ALL TO YOU, NOW. AND IN YOUR MIND, UNLIMITED BY SPOKEN LANGUAGE, YOU SHALL LIVE IT ALL...
...AS I DID.
THE SEARCHER AND THE SWORD

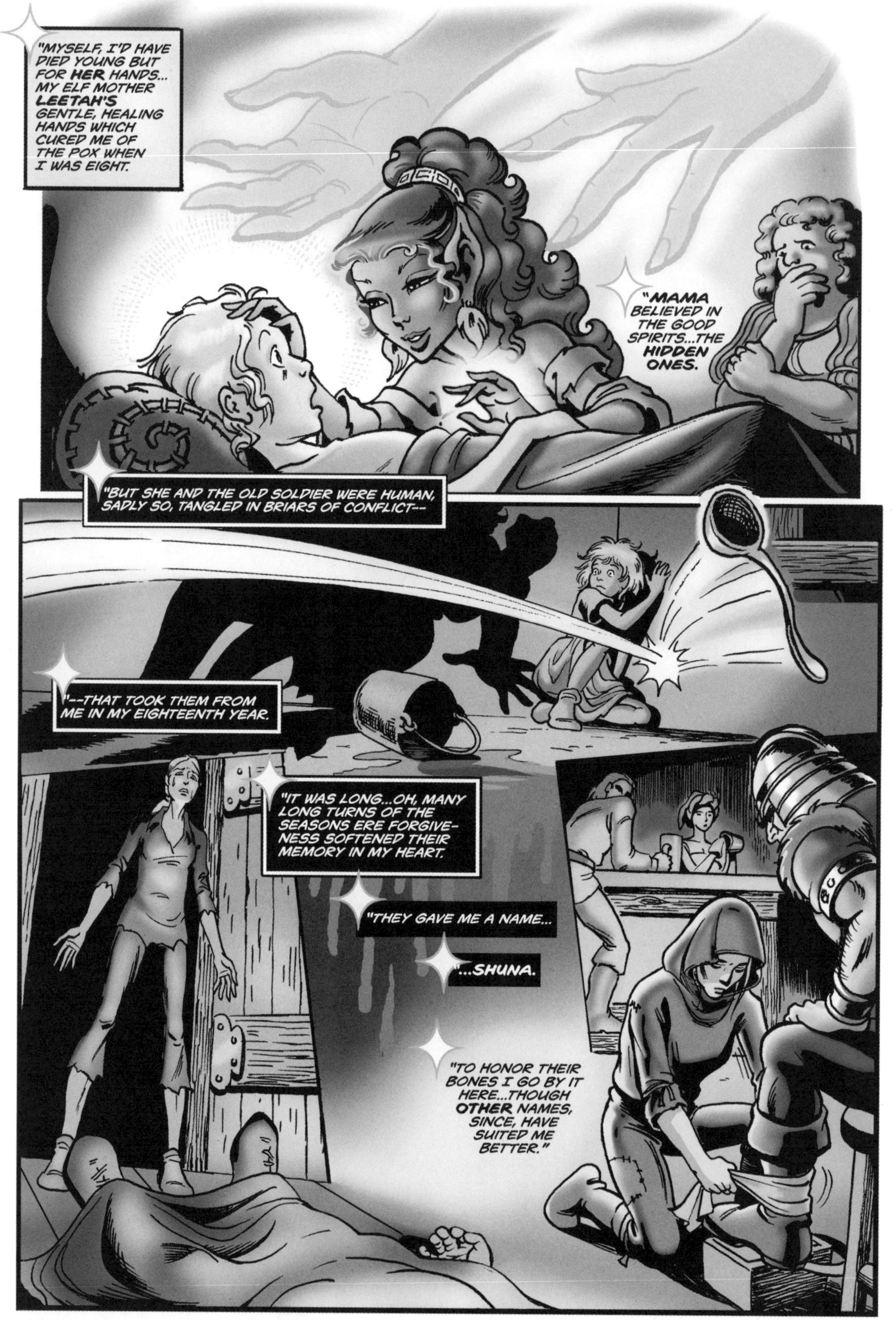
"MYSELF, I'D HAVE DIED YOUNG BUT FOR HER HANDS... MY ELF MOTHER LEETAH'S GENTLE, HEALING HANDS WHICH CURED ME OF THE POX WHEN I WAS EIGHT.
"MAMA BELIEVED IN THE GOOD SPIRITS...THE HIDDEN ONES.
"BUT SHE AND THE OLD SOLDIER WERE HUMAN, SADLY SO, TANGLED IN BRIARS OF CONFLICT--
"--THAT TOOK THEM FROM ME IN MY EIGHTEENTH YEAR.
"IT WAS LONG...OH, MANY LONG TURNS OF THE SEASONS ERE FORGIVENESS SOFTENED THEIR MEMORY IN MY HEART.
"THEY GAVE ME A NAME...
"...SHUNA.
"TO HONOR THEIR BONES I GO BY IT HERE...THOUGH OTHER NAMES, SINCE, HAVE SUITED ME BETTER."

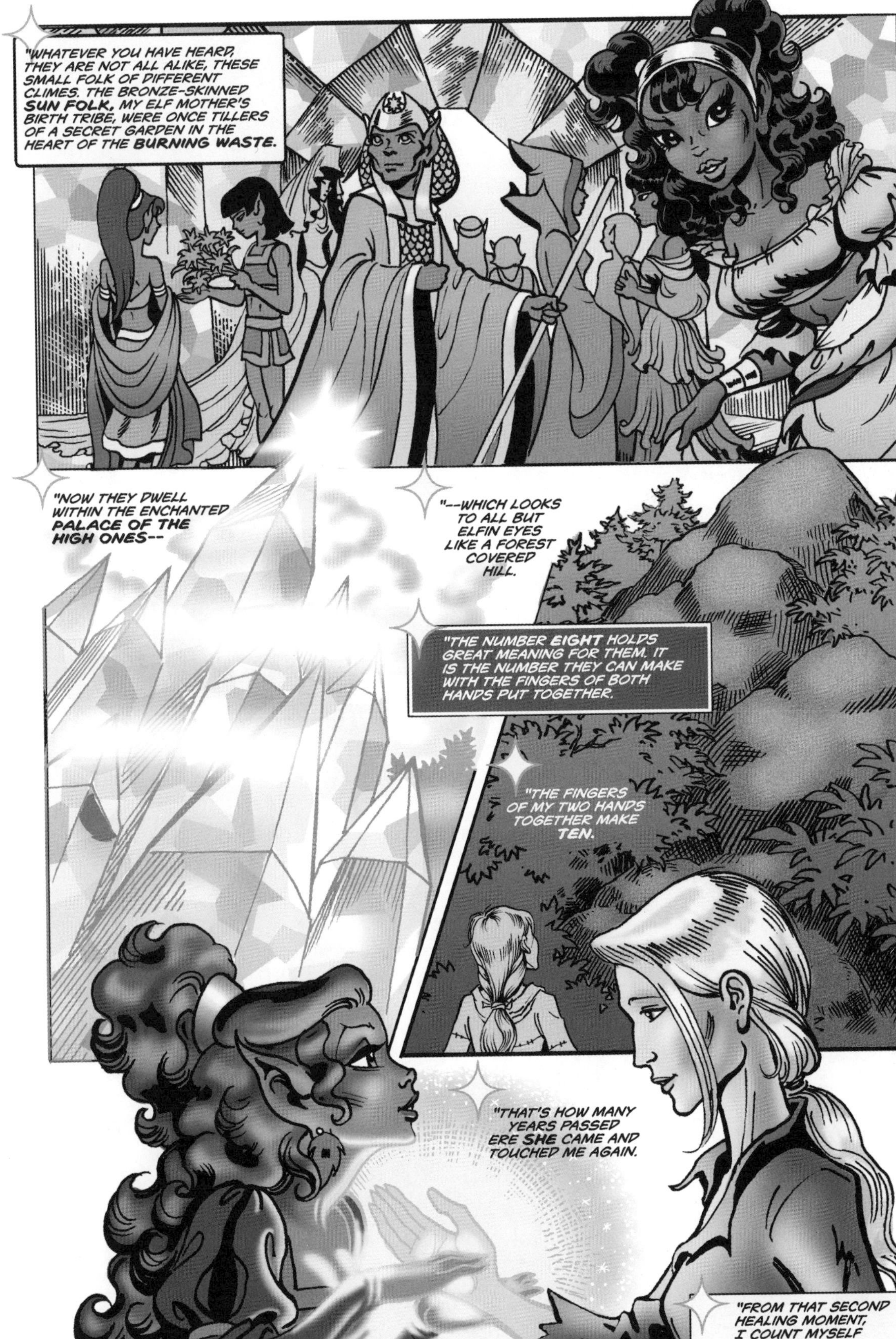
"WHATEVER YOU HAVE HEARD, THEY ARE NOT ALL ALIKE, THESE SMALL FOLK OF DIFFERENT CLIMES. THE BRONZE-SKINNED SUN FOLK, MY ELF MOTHER'S BIRTH TRIBE, WERE ONCE TILLERS OF A SECRET GARDEN IN THE HEART OF THE BURNING WASTE.
"NOW THEY DWELL WITHIN THE ENCHANTED PALACE OF THE HIGH ONES--
"--WHICH LOOKS TO ALL BUT ELFIN EYES LIKE A FOREST COVERED HILL.
"THE NUMBER EIGHT HOLDS GREAT MEANING FOR THEM. IT IS THE NUMBER THEY CAN MAKE WITH THE FINGERS OF BOTH HANDS PUT TOGETHER.
"THE FINGERS OF MY TWO HANDS TOGETHER MAKE TEN.
"THAT'S HOW MANY YEARS PASSED ERE SHE CAME AND TOUCHED ME AGAIN.
"FROM THAT SECOND HEALING MOMENT, I COUNT MYSELF TRULY BORN."

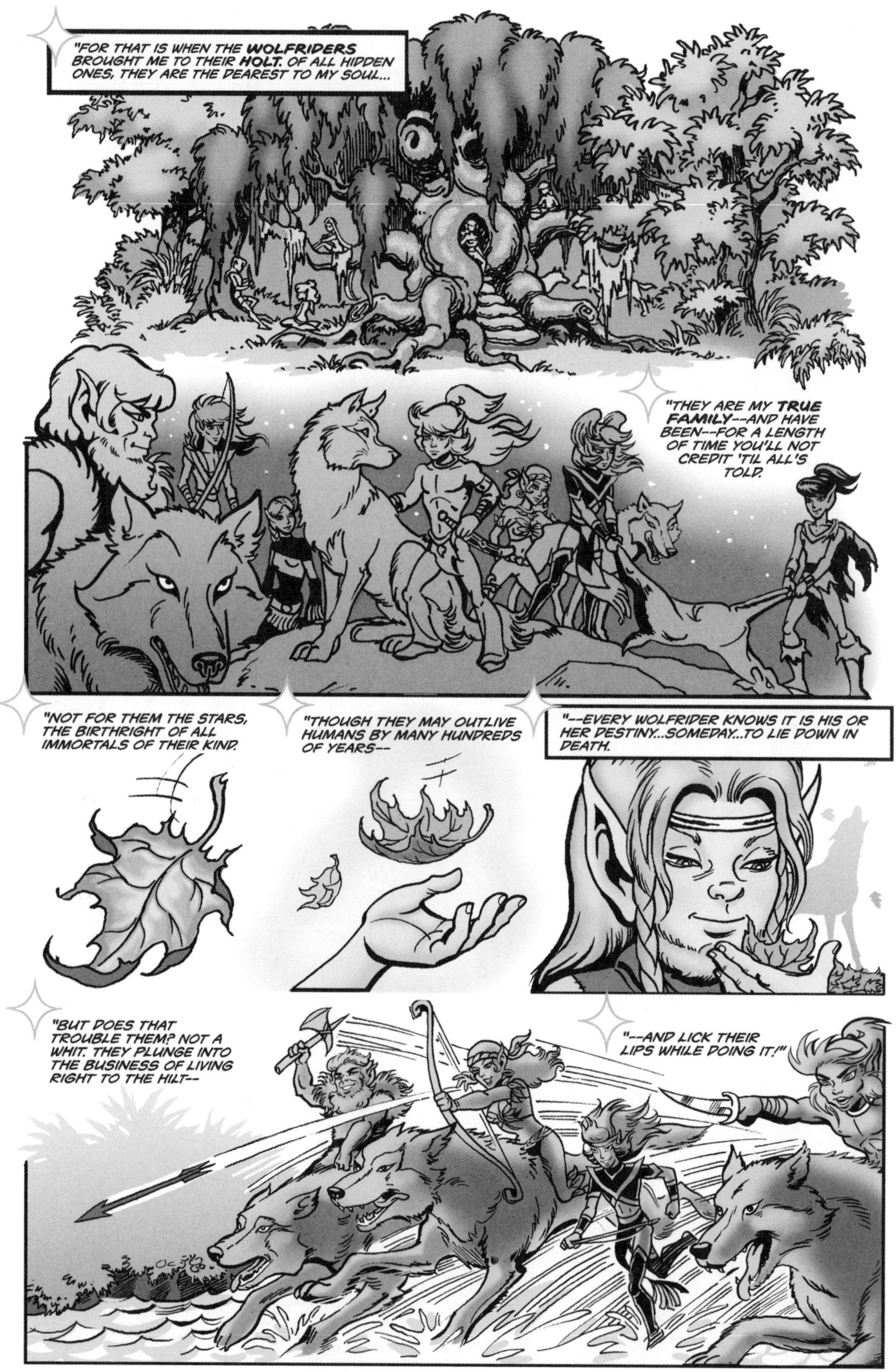
"FOR THAT IS WHEN THE **WOLFRIDERS** BROUGHT ME TO THEIR **HOLT**. OF ALL HIDDEN ONES, THEY ARE THE DEAREST TO MY SOUL...
"THEY ARE MY **TRUE FAMILY**--AND HAVE BEEN--FOR A LENGTH OF TIME YOU'LL NOT CREDIT 'TIL ALL'S TOLD.
"NOT FOR THEM THE STARS, THE BIRTHRIGHT OF ALL IMMORTALS OF THEIR KIND.
"THOUGH THEY MAY OUTLIVE HUMANS BY MANY HUNDREDS OF YEARS--
"--EVERY WOLFRIDER KNOWS IT IS HIS OR HER DESTINY...SOMEDAY...TO LIE DOWN IN DEATH.
"BUT DOES THAT TROUBLE THEM? NOT A WHIT. THEY PLUNGE INTO THE BUSINESS OF LIVING RIGHT TO THE HILT--
"--AND LICK THEIR LIPS WHILE DOING IT!"

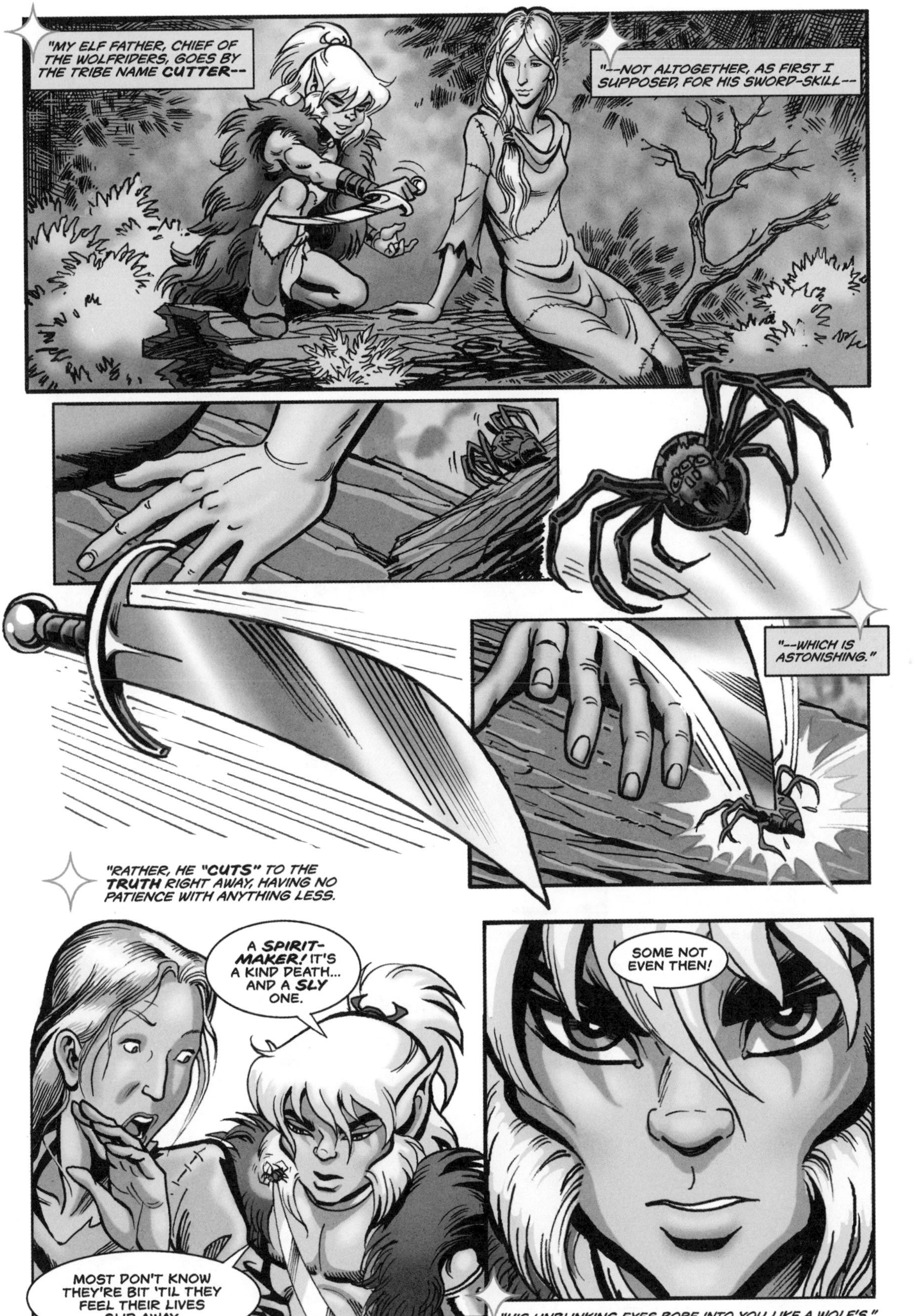
"MY ELF FATHER, CHIEF OF THE WOLFRIDERS, GOES BY THE TRIBE NAME CUTTER--
"--NOT ALTOGETHER, AS FIRST I SUPPOSED, FOR HIS SWORD-SKILL--
"--WHICH IS ASTONISHING."
"RATHER, HE "CUTS" TO THE TRUTH RIGHT AWAY, HAVING NO PATIENCE WITH ANYTHING LESS.
A SPIRIT-MAKER! IT'S A KIND DEATH... AND A SLY ONE.
MOST DON'T KNOW THEY'RE BIT 'TIL THEY FEEL THEIR LIVES SLIP AWAY.
SOME NOT EVEN THEN!
"HIS UNBLINKING EYES BORE INTO YOU LIKE A WOLF'S."

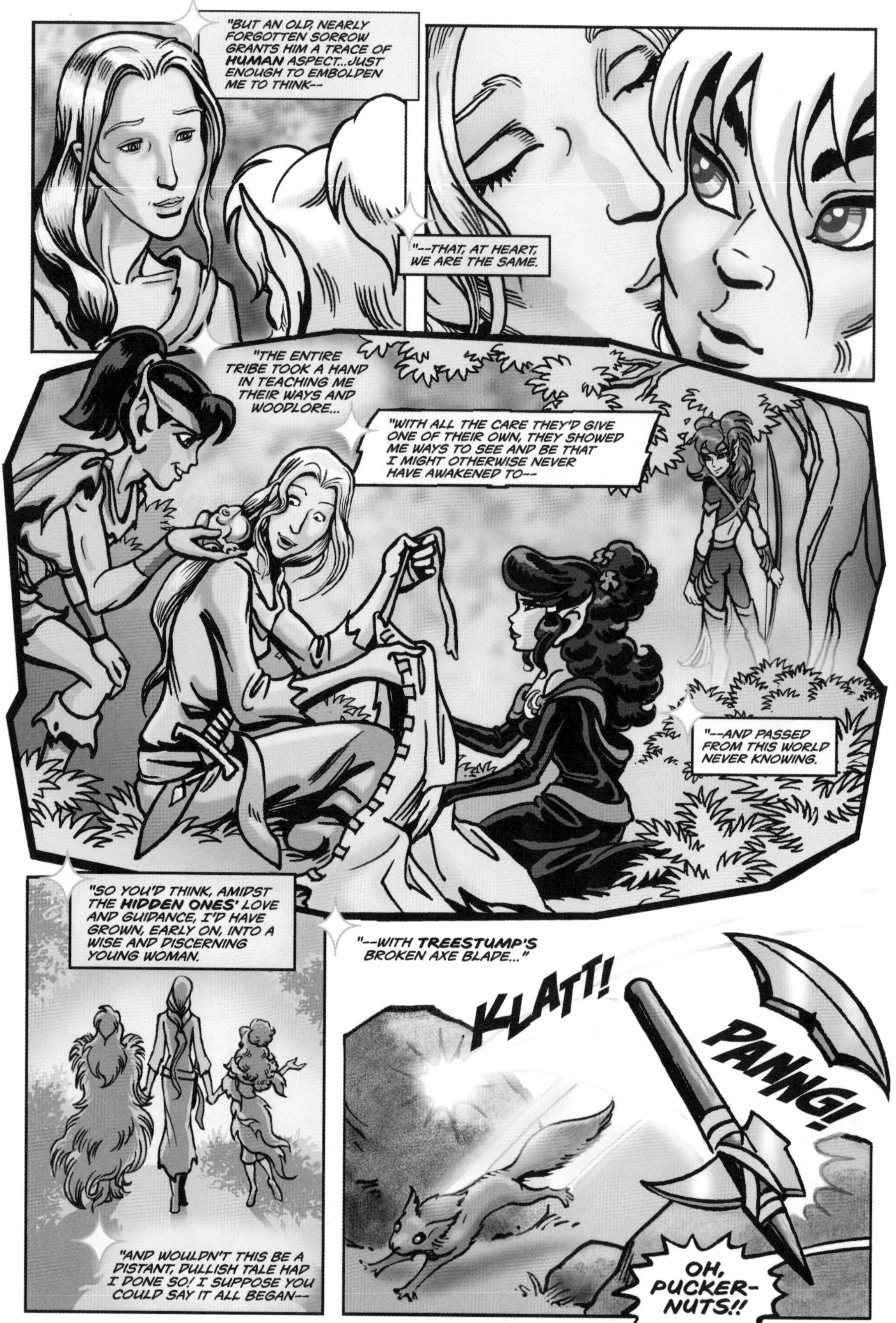
"BUT AN OLD, NEARLY FORGOTTEN SORROW GRANTS HIM A TRACE OF HUMAN ASPECT...JUST ENOUGH TO EMBOLDEN ME TO THINK--
"--THAT, AT HEART, WE ARE THE SAME.
"THE ENTIRE TRIBE TOOK A HAND IN TEACHING ME THEIR WAYS AND WOODLORE...
"WITH ALL THE CARE THEY'D GIVE ONE OF THEIR OWN, THEY SHOWED ME WAYS TO SEE AND BE THAT I MIGHT OTHERWISE NEVER HAVE AWAKENED TO--
"--AND PASSED FROM THIS WORLD NEVER KNOWING.
"SO YOU'D THINK, AMIDST THE HIDDEN ONES' LOVE AND GUIDANCE, I'D HAVE GROWN, EARLY ON, INTO A WISE AND DISCERNING YOUNG WOMAN.
"AND WOULDN'T THIS BE A DISTANT, DULLISH TALE HAD I DONE SO! I SUPPOSE YOU COULD SAY IT ALL BEGAN--
"--WITH TREESTUMP'S BROKEN AXE BLADE..."
KLATT!
PANNG!
OH, PUCKER-NUTS!!

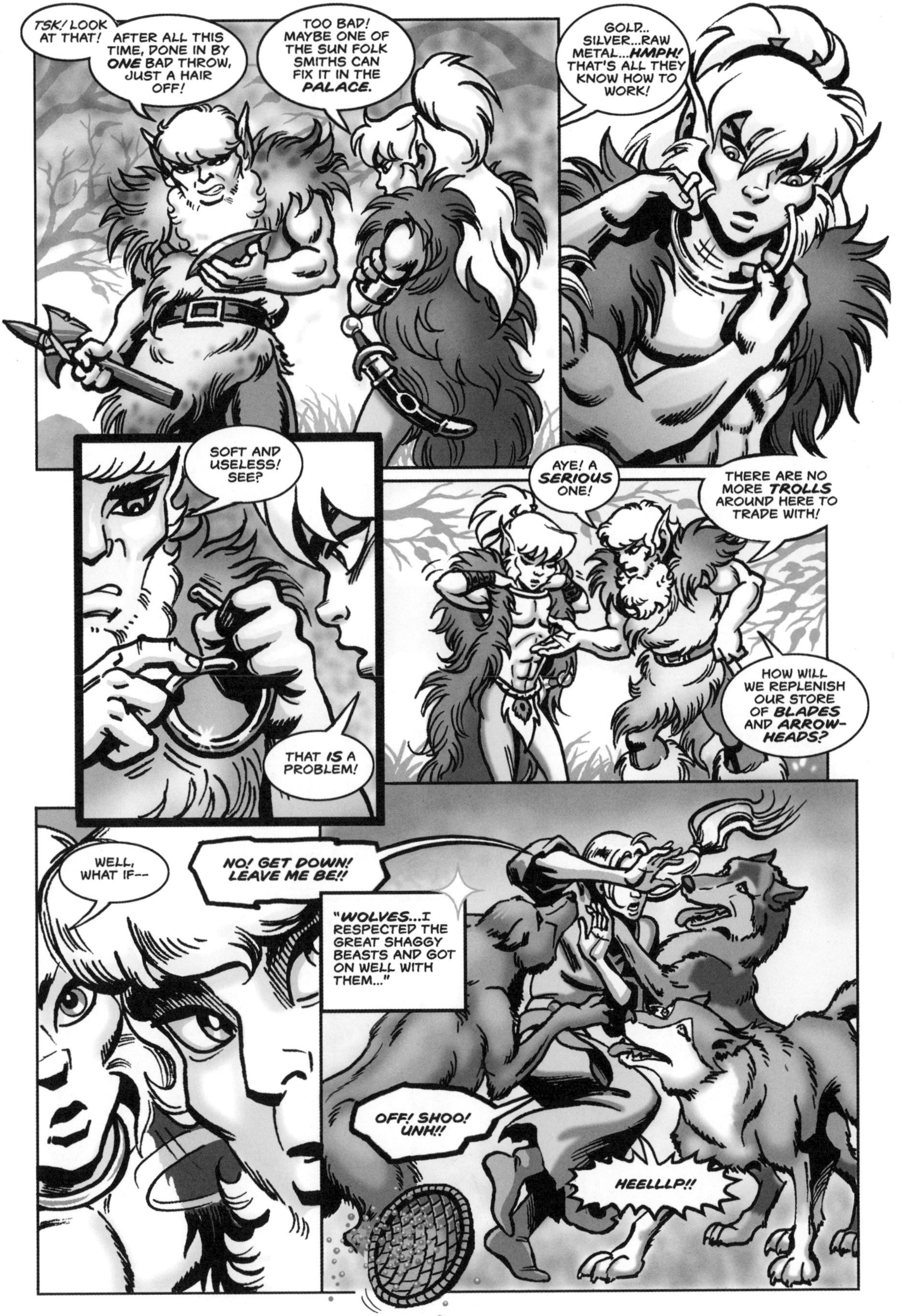
TSK! LOOK AT THAT!
AFTER ALL THIS TIME, DONE IN BY ONE BAD THROW, JUST A HAIR OFF!
TOO BAD! MAYBE ONE OF THE SUN FOLK SMITHS CAN FIX IT IN THE PALACE.
GOLD... SILVER...RAW METAL...HMPH! THAT'S ALL THEY KNOW HOW TO WORK!
SOFT AND USELESS! SEE?
THAT IS A PROBLEM!
AYE! A SERIOUS ONE!
THERE ARE NO MORE TROLLS AROUND HERE TO TRADE WITH!
HOW WILL WE REPLENISH OUR STORE OF BLADES AND ARROW-HEADS?
WELL, WHAT IF--
NO! GET DOWN! LEAVE ME BE!!
"WOLVES...I RESPECTED THE GREAT SHAGGY BEASTS AND GOT ON WELL WITH THEM..."
OFF! SHOO! UNH!!
HEELLLP!!

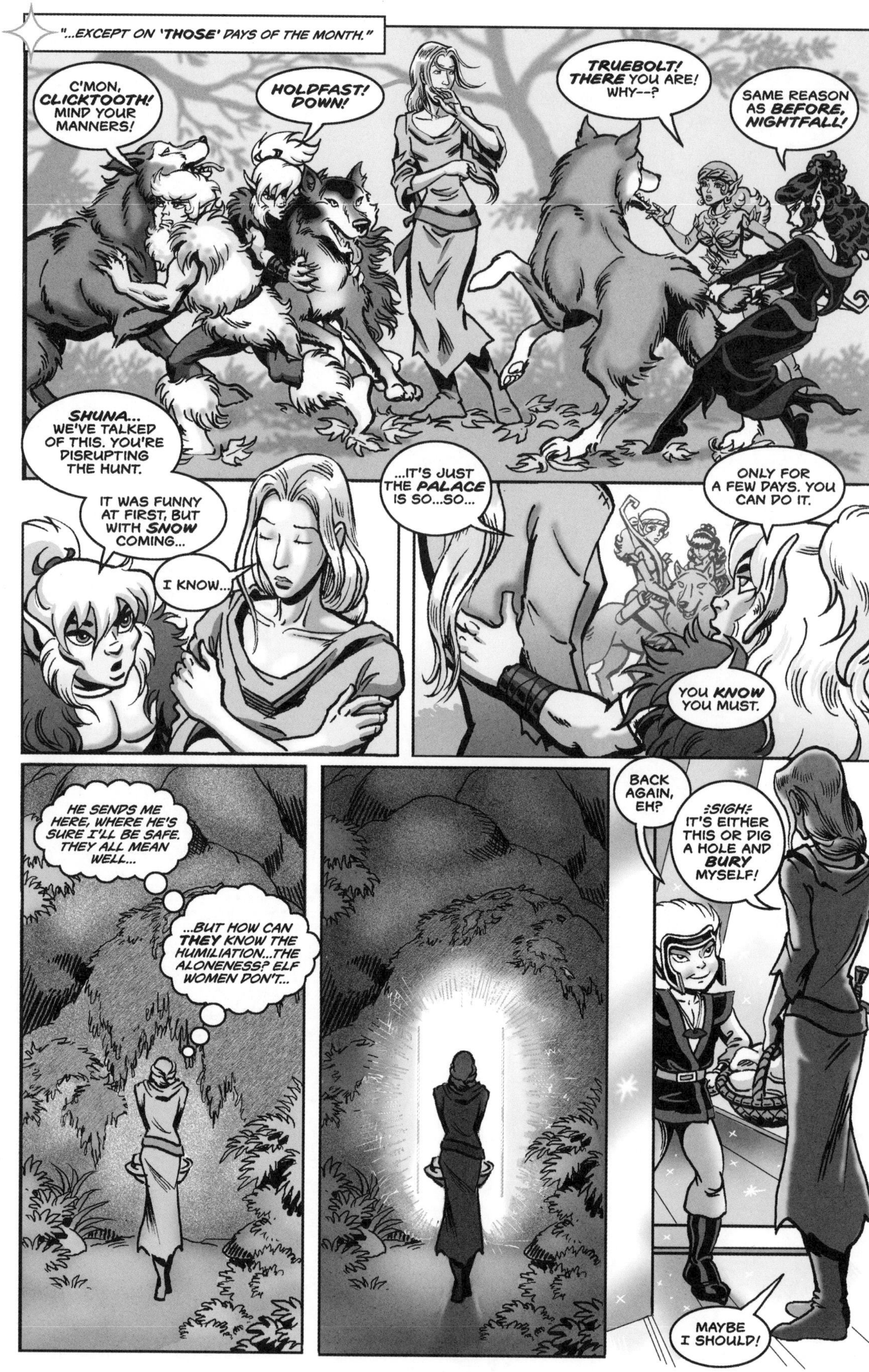
"...EXCEPT ON 'THOSE' DAYS OF THE MONTH."
C'MON, CLICKTOOTH! MIND YOUR MANNERS!
HOLDFAST! DOWN!
TRUEBOLT! THERE YOU ARE! WHY--?
SAME REASON AS BEFORE, NIGHTFALL!
SHUNA... WE'VE TALKED OF THIS. YOU'RE DISRUPTING THE HUNT.
IT WAS FUNNY AT FIRST, BUT WITH SNOW COMING...
I KNOW...
...IT'S JUST THE PALACE IS SO...SO...
ONLY FOR A FEW DAYS. YOU CAN DO IT.
YOU KNOW YOU MUST.
HE SENDS ME HERE, WHERE HE'S SURE I'LL BE SAFE. THEY ALL MEAN WELL...
...BUT HOW CAN THEY KNOW THE HUMILIATION...THE ALONENESS? ELF WOMEN DON'T...
BACK AGAIN, EH?
:SIGH: IT'S EITHER THIS OR DIG A HOLE AND BURY MYSELF!
MAYBE I SHOULD!

UH OH...IN ONE OF OUR *MOODS*, ARE WE? C'MON.

TO THE TOP TURRET? WHY--SO I CAN THROW MYSELF OFF?

‹HEH HEH HEH...›

"*SKYWISE* FOUND EVERYTHING I SAID FUNNY. STILL DOES."

"THAT AND HIS HABITUAL LOW OPINION OF HUMANS DID NOT EXACTLY ENDEAR HIM TO ME THAT EVE..."

YES, *SUN-TOUCHER*. I THOUGHT THE STARS MIGHT CHEER HER UP.

SKYWISE...? AND THE YOUNG WOMAN?

I'M AFRAID YOU'LL SEE VERY FEW TONIGHT. THE SEASON OF THE *WHITE COLD* COMES UPON US EARLY.

IS *SHUNA* PREPARED?

"SUN-TOUCHER...CUTTER...UNTIL I KNEW THEM, I KNEW NOTHING OF WISE AND CARING FATHERS."

"FOR ONE WHO COULD NOT SEE, LEETAH'S GENTLE SIRE WAS FAR FROM BLIND."

"HE SENSED MY SECRET DREAD."

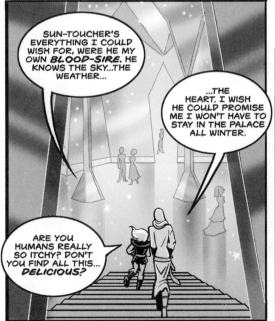

SUN-TOUCHER'S EVERYTHING I COULD WISH FOR, WERE HE MY OWN *BLOOD-SIRE*. HE KNOWS THE SKY...THE WEATHER...

...THE HEART. I WISH HE COULD PROMISE ME I WON'T HAVE TO STAY IN THE PALACE ALL WINTER.

ARE YOU HUMANS REALLY SO ITCHY? DON'T YOU FIND ALL THIS... *DELICIOUS?*

YOU DON'T UNDER--*WAIT!* NOT THIS WAY...NOT THE *SCROLL ROOM!*

DON'T BE SILLY! SHE DOESN'T *BITE!*

IN *WOLF FORM* SHE DOES!

WELL... THAT'S TRUE.

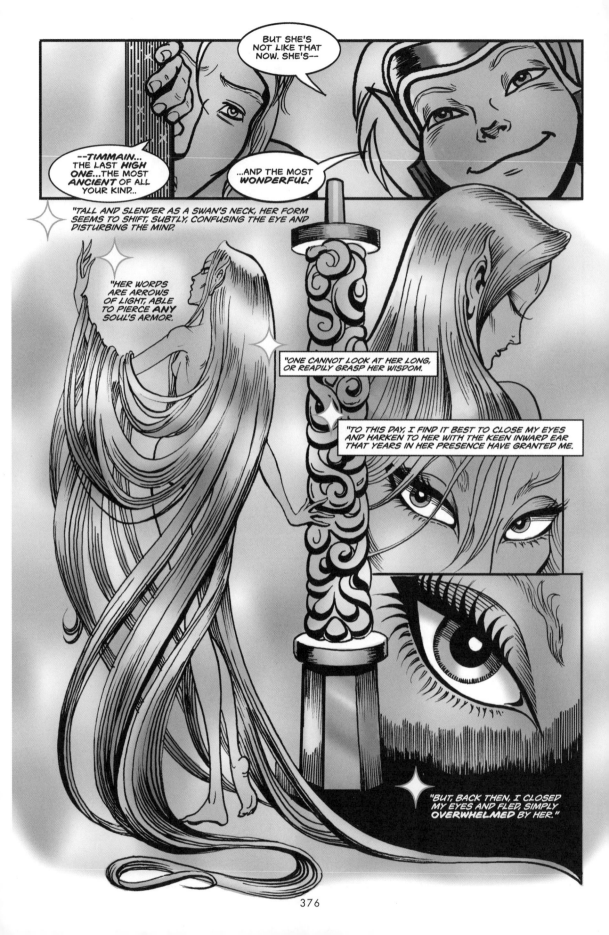

BUT SHE'S NOT LIKE THAT NOW. SHE'S--

--TIMMAIN... THE LAST *HIGH ONE*...THE MOST *ANCIENT* OF ALL YOUR KIND...

...AND THE MOST *WONDERFUL!*

"TALL AND SLENDER AS A SWAN'S NECK, HER FORM SEEMS TO SHIFT, SUBTLY, CONFUSING THE EYE AND DISTURBING THE MIND."

"HER WORDS ARE ARROWS OF LIGHT, ABLE TO PIERCE *ANY* SOUL'S ARMOR."

"ONE CANNOT LOOK AT HER LONG, OR READILY GRASP HER WISDOM."

"TO THIS DAY, I FIND IT BEST TO CLOSE MY EYES AND HARKEN TO HER WITH THE KEEN INWARD EAR THAT YEARS IN HER PRESENCE HAVE GRANTED ME."

"BUT, BACK THEN, I CLOSED MY EYES AND FLED, SIMPLY *OVERWHELMED* BY HER."

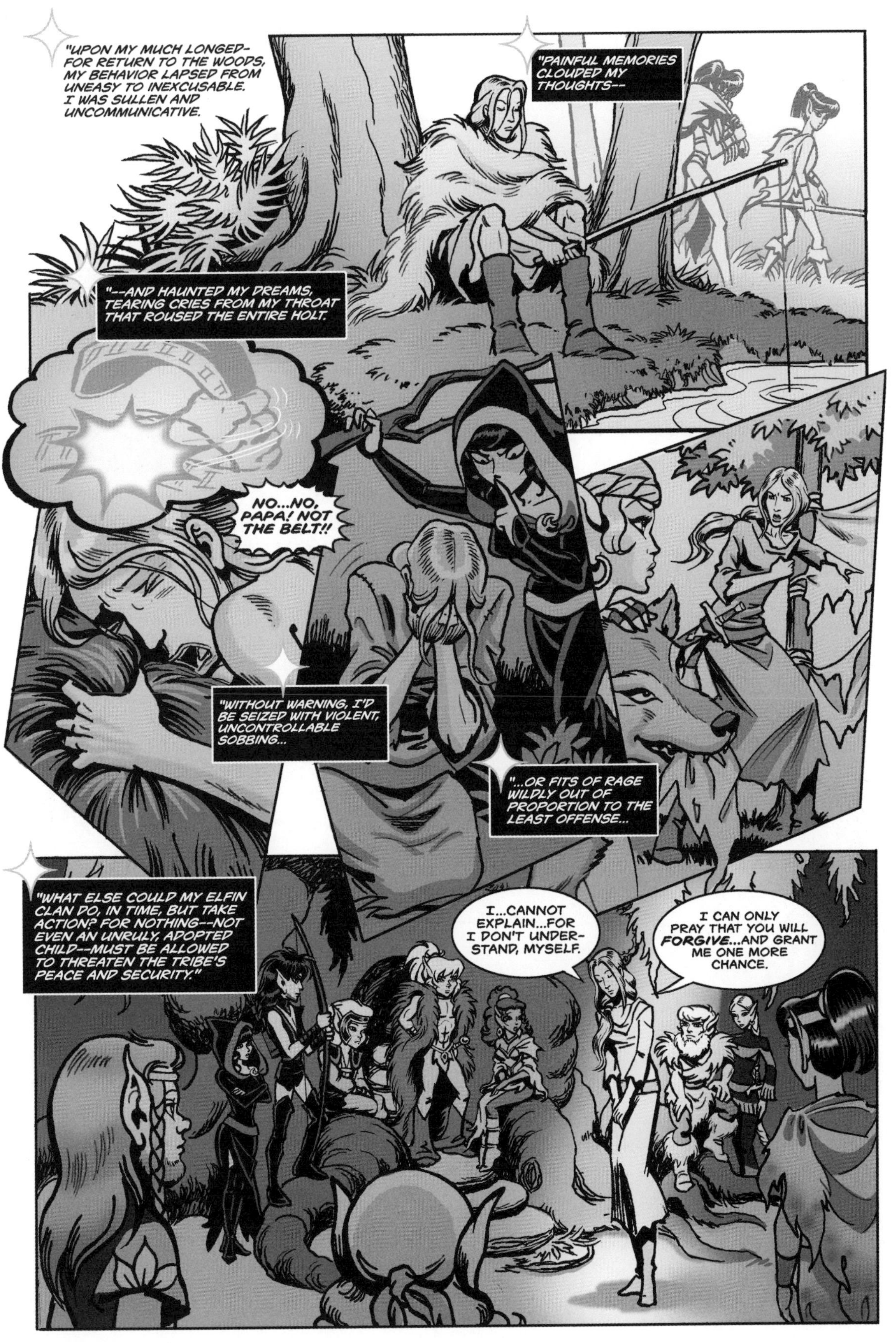
"UPON MY MUCH LONGED-FOR RETURN TO THE WOODS, MY BEHAVIOR LAPSED FROM UNEASY TO INEXCUSABLE. I WAS SULLEN AND UNCOMMUNICATIVE.
"PAINFUL MEMORIES CLOUDED MY THOUGHTS--
"--AND HAUNTED MY DREAMS, TEARING CRIES FROM MY THROAT THAT ROUSED THE ENTIRE HOLT.
NO...NO, PAPA! NOT THE BELT!!
"WITHOUT WARNING, I'D BE SEIZED WITH VIOLENT, UNCONTROLLABLE SOBBING...
"...OR FITS OF RAGE WILDLY OUT OF PROPORTION TO THE LEAST OFFENSE...
"WHAT ELSE COULD MY ELFIN CLAN DO, IN TIME, BUT TAKE ACTION? FOR NOTHING--NOT EVEN AN UNRULY, ADOPTED CHILD--MUST BE ALLOWED TO THREATEN THE TRIBE'S PEACE AND SECURITY."
I...CANNOT EXPLAIN...FOR I DON'T UNDERSTAND, MYSELF.
I CAN ONLY PRAY THAT YOU WILL FORGIVE...AND GRANT ME ONE MORE CHANCE.

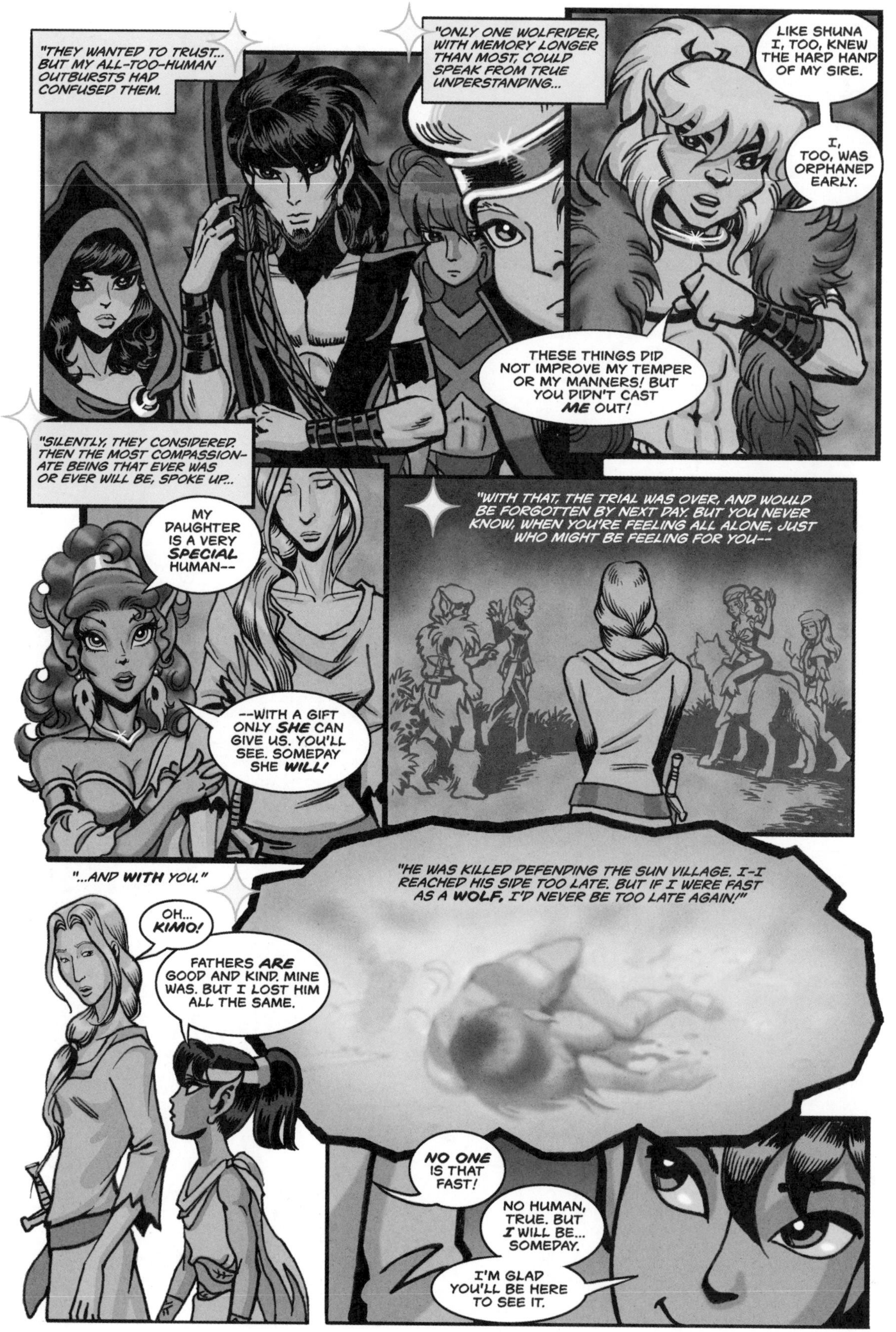
"THEY WANTED TO TRUST... BUT MY ALL-TOO-HUMAN OUTBURSTS HAD CONFUSED THEM.
"ONLY ONE WOLFRIDER, WITH MEMORY LONGER THAN MOST, COULD SPEAK FROM TRUE UNDERSTANDING...
LIKE SHUNA I, TOO, KNEW THE HARD HAND OF MY SIRE.
I, TOO, WAS ORPHANED EARLY.
THESE THINGS DID NOT IMPROVE MY TEMPER OR MY MANNERS! BUT YOU DIDN'T CAST ME OUT!
"SILENTLY, THEY CONSIDERED. THEN THE MOST COMPASSIONATE BEING THAT EVER WAS OR EVER WILL BE, SPOKE UP...
MY DAUGHTER IS A VERY SPECIAL HUMAN--
--WITH A GIFT ONLY SHE CAN GIVE US. YOU'LL SEE. SOMEDAY SHE WILL!
"WITH THAT, THE TRIAL WAS OVER, AND WOULD BE FORGOTTEN BY NEXT DAY. BUT YOU NEVER KNOW, WHEN YOU'RE FEELING ALL ALONE, JUST WHO MIGHT BE FEELING FOR YOU--
"...AND WITH YOU."
OH... KIMO!
FATHERS ARE GOOD AND KIND. MINE WAS. BUT I LOST HIM ALL THE SAME.
"HE WAS KILLED DEFENDING THE SUN VILLAGE. I-I REACHED HIS SIDE TOO LATE. BUT IF I WERE FAST AS A WOLF, I'D NEVER BE TOO LATE AGAIN!"
NO ONE IS THAT FAST!
NO HUMAN, TRUE. BUT I WILL BE... SOMEDAY.
I'M GLAD YOU'LL BE HERE TO SEE IT.

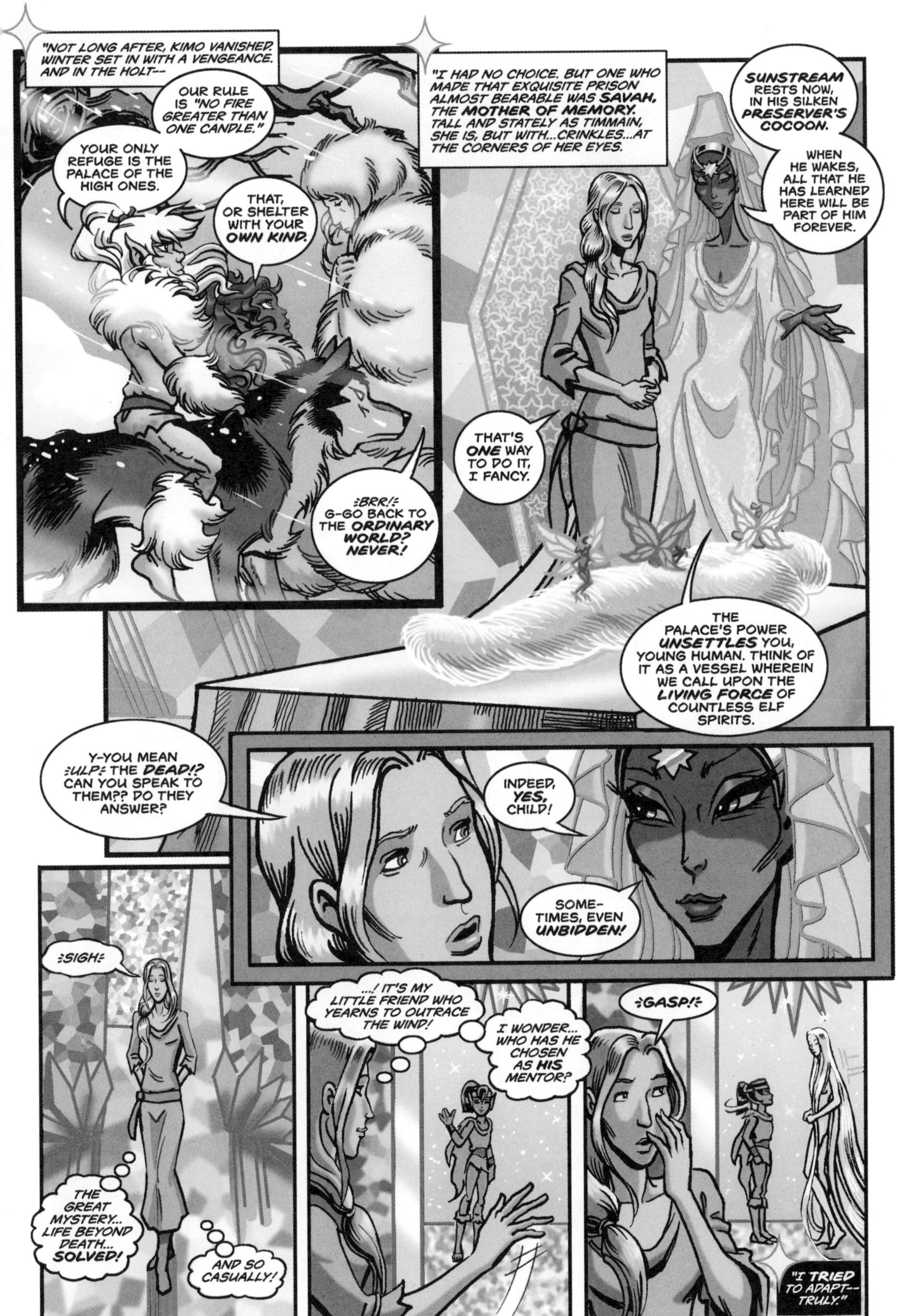
"NOT LONG AFTER, KIMO VANISHED. WINTER SET IN WITH A VENGEANCE. AND IN THE HOLT--
OUR RULE IS "NO FIRE GREATER THAN ONE CANDLE."
YOUR ONLY REFUGE IS THE PALACE OF THE HIGH ONES.
THAT, OR SHELTER WITH YOUR OWN KIND.
=BRR!= G-GO BACK TO THE ORDINARY WORLD? NEVER!
"I HAD NO CHOICE. BUT ONE WHO MADE THAT EXQUISITE PRISON ALMOST BEARABLE WAS SAVAH, THE MOTHER OF MEMORY. TALL AND STATELY AS TIMMAIN, SHE IS, BUT WITH...CRINKLES...AT THE CORNERS OF HER EYES.
SUNSTREAM RESTS NOW, IN HIS SILKEN PRESERVER'S COCOON.
WHEN HE WAKES, ALL THAT HE HAS LEARNED HERE WILL BE PART OF HIM FOREVER.
THAT'S ONE WAY TO DO IT, I FANCY.
THE PALACE'S POWER UNSETTLES YOU, YOUNG HUMAN. THINK OF IT AS A VESSEL WHEREIN WE CALL UPON THE LIVING FORCE OF COUNTLESS ELF SPIRITS.
Y-YOU MEAN =ULP= THE DEAD!? CAN YOU SPEAK TO THEM?? DO THEY ANSWER?
INDEED, YES, CHILD!
SOME-TIMES, EVEN UNBIDDEN!
=SIGH=
THE GREAT MYSTERY... LIFE BEYOND DEATH... SOLVED!
AND SO CASUALLY!
...! IT'S MY LITTLE FRIEND WHO YEARNS TO OUTRACE THE WIND!
I WONDER... WHO HAS HE CHOSEN AS HIS MENTOR?
=GASP!=
"I TRIED TO ADAPT--TRULY."

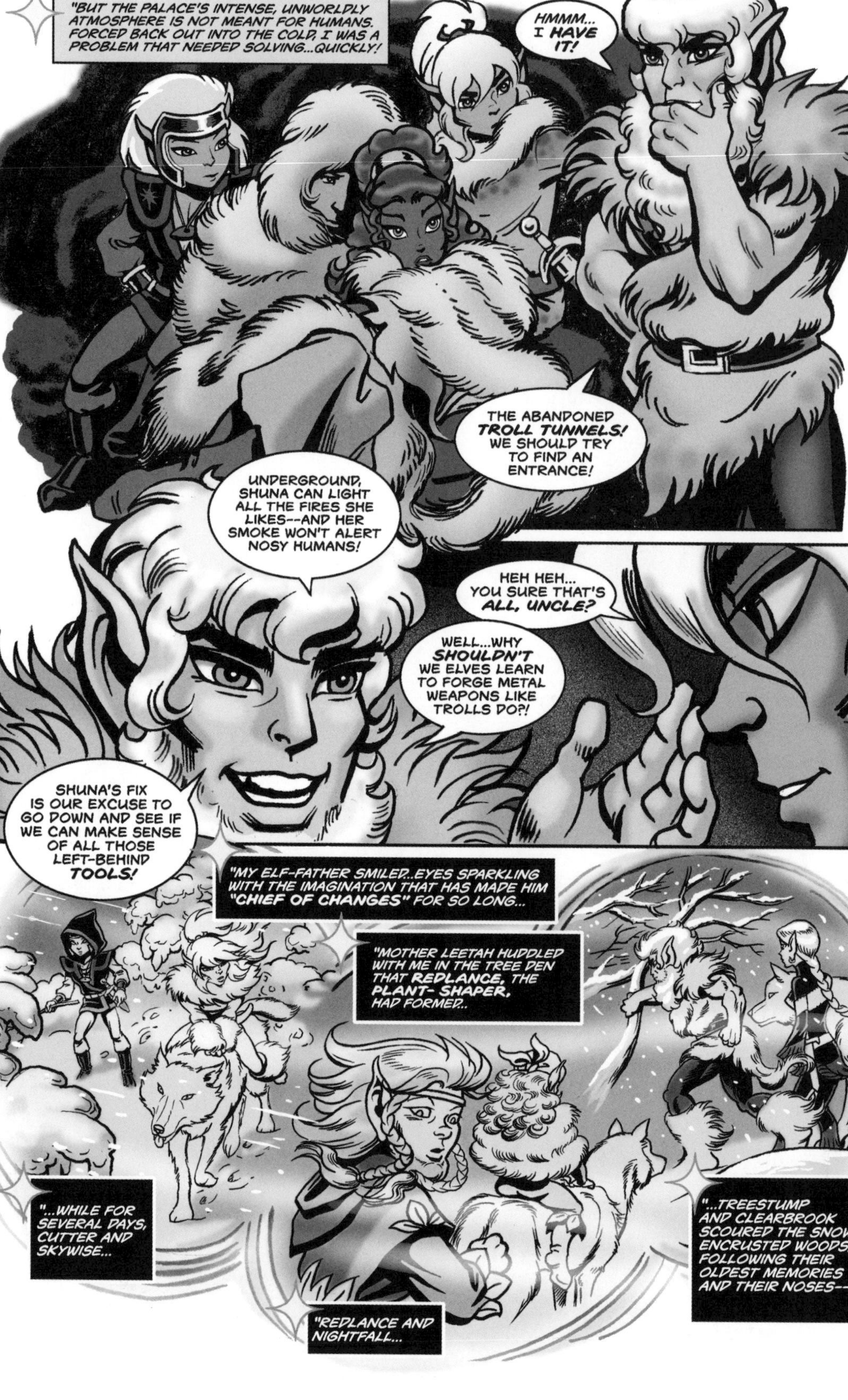
"BUT THE PALACE'S INTENSE, UNWORLDLY ATMOSPHERE IS NOT MEANT FOR HUMANS. FORCED BACK OUT INTO THE COLD, I WAS A PROBLEM THAT NEEDED SOLVING...QUICKLY!
HMMM... I HAVE IT!
THE ABANDONED TROLL TUNNELS! WE SHOULD TRY TO FIND AN ENTRANCE!
UNDERGROUND, SHUNA CAN LIGHT ALL THE FIRES SHE LIKES--AND HER SMOKE WON'T ALERT NOSY HUMANS!
HEH HEH... YOU SURE THAT'S ALL, UNCLE?
WELL...WHY SHOULDN'T WE ELVES LEARN TO FORGE METAL WEAPONS LIKE TROLLS DO?!
SHUNA'S FIX IS OUR EXCUSE TO GO DOWN AND SEE IF WE CAN MAKE SENSE OF ALL THOSE LEFT-BEHIND TOOLS!
"MY ELF-FATHER SMILED...EYES SPARKLING WITH THE IMAGINATION THAT HAS MADE HIM "CHIEF OF CHANGES" FOR SO LONG...
"MOTHER LEETAH HUDDLED WITH ME IN THE TREE DEN THAT REDLANCE, THE PLANT- SHAPER, HAD FORMED..
"...WHILE FOR SEVERAL DAYS, CUTTER AND SKYWISE...
"REDLANCE AND NIGHTFALL...
"...TREESTUMP AND CLEARBROOK SCOURED THE SNOW ENCRUSTED WOODS, FOLLOWING THEIR OLDEST MEMORIES AND THEIR NOSES--"

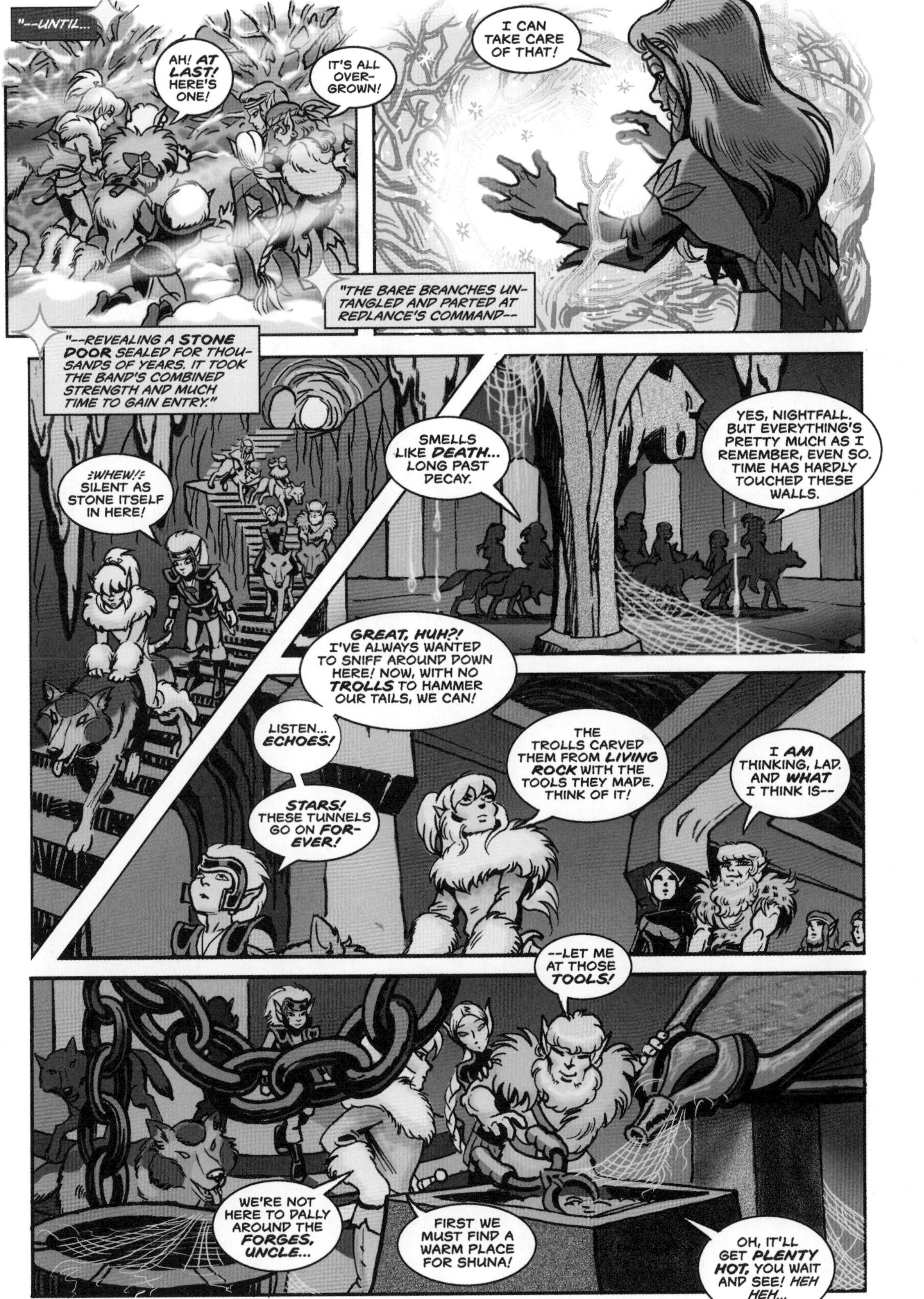
"--UNTIL...
AH! AT LAST! HERE'S ONE!
IT'S ALL OVER-GROWN!
I CAN TAKE CARE OF THAT!
"THE BARE BRANCHES UNTANGLED AND PARTED AT REDLANCE'S COMMAND--
"--REVEALING A STONE DOOR SEALED FOR THOUSANDS OF YEARS. IT TOOK THE BAND'S COMBINED STRENGTH AND MUCH TIME TO GAIN ENTRY."
WHEW! SILENT AS STONE ITSELF IN HERE!
SMELLS LIKE DEATH... LONG PAST DECAY.
YES, NIGHTFALL. BUT EVERYTHING'S PRETTY MUCH AS I REMEMBER, EVEN SO. TIME HAS HARDLY TOUCHED THESE WALLS.
GREAT, HUH?! I'VE ALWAYS WANTED TO SNIFF AROUND DOWN HERE! NOW, WITH NO TROLLS TO HAMMER OUR TAILS, WE CAN!
LISTEN... ECHOES!
STARS! THESE TUNNELS GO ON FOR-EVER!
THE TROLLS CARVED THEM FROM LIVING ROCK WITH THE TOOLS THEY MADE. THINK OF IT!
I AM THINKING, LAD. AND WHAT I THINK IS--
--LET ME AT THOSE TOOLS!
WE'RE NOT HERE TO DALLY AROUND THE FORGES, UNCLE...
FIRST WE MUST FIND A WARM PLACE FOR SHUNA!
OH, IT'LL GET PLENTY HOT, YOU WAIT AND SEE! HEH HEH...

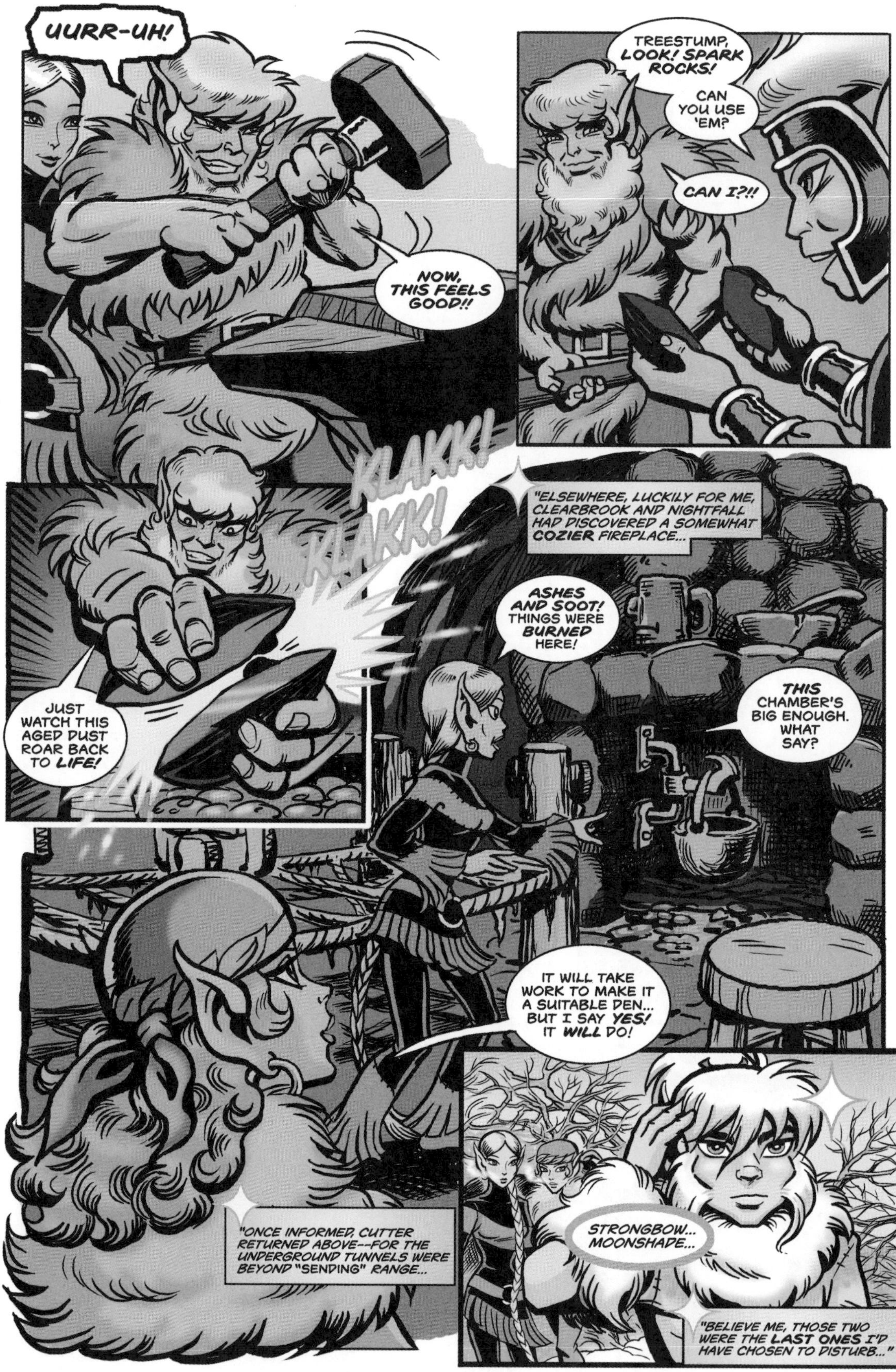
UURR-UH!
NOW, THIS FEELS GOOD!!
TREESTUMP, LOOK! SPARK ROCKS!
CAN YOU USE 'EM?
CAN I?!!
KLAKK! KLAKK!
JUST WATCH THIS AGED DUST ROAR BACK TO LIFE!
"ELSEWHERE, LUCKILY FOR ME, CLEARBROOK AND NIGHTFALL HAD DISCOVERED A SOMEWHAT COZIER FIREPLACE...
ASHES AND SOOT! THINGS WERE BURNED HERE!
THIS CHAMBER'S BIG ENOUGH. WHAT SAY?
IT WILL TAKE WORK TO MAKE IT A SUITABLE DEN... BUT I SAY YES! IT WILL DO!
"ONCE INFORMED, CUTTER RETURNED ABOVE--FOR THE UNDERGROUND TUNNELS WERE BEYOND "SENDING" RANGE...
STRONGBOW... MOONSHADE...
"BELIEVE ME, THOSE TWO WERE THE LAST ONES I'D HAVE CHOSEN TO DISTURB..."

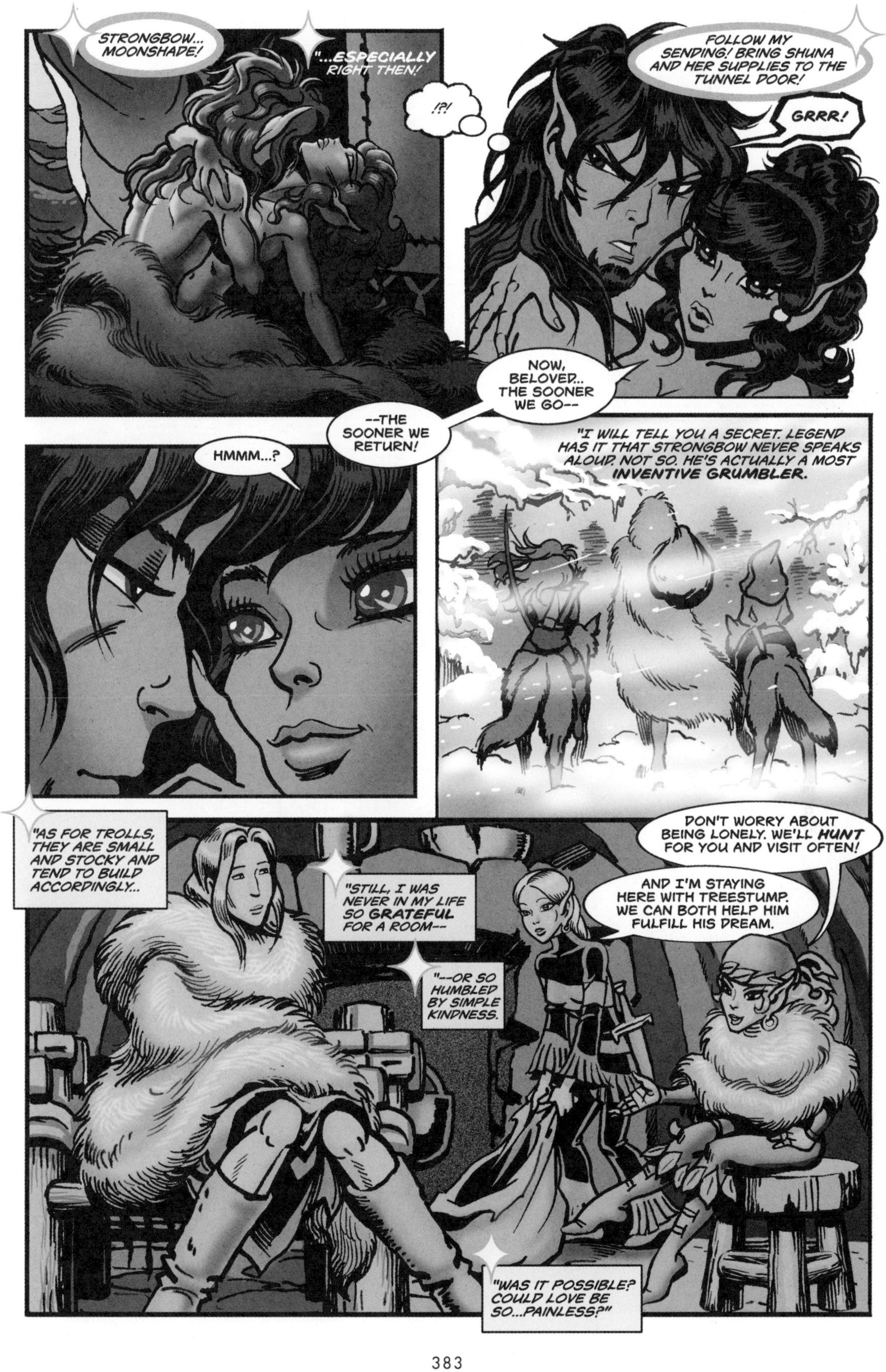

STRONGBOW... MOONSHADE!
"...ESPECIALLY RIGHT THEN!
!?!
FOLLOW MY SENDING! BRING SHUNA AND HER SUPPLIES TO THE TUNNEL DOOR!
GRRR!
NOW, BELOVED... THE SOONER WE GO--
--THE SOONER WE RETURN!
HMMM...?
"I WILL TELL YOU A SECRET. LEGEND HAS IT THAT STRONGBOW NEVER SPEAKS ALOUD. NOT SO. HE'S ACTUALLY A MOST INVENTIVE GRUMBLER.
"AS FOR TROLLS, THEY ARE SMALL AND STOCKY AND TEND TO BUILD ACCORDINGLY...
"STILL, I WAS NEVER IN MY LIFE SO GRATEFUL FOR A ROOM--
"--OR SO HUMBLED BY SIMPLE KINDNESS.
DON'T WORRY ABOUT BEING LONELY. WE'LL HUNT FOR YOU AND VISIT OFTEN!
AND I'M STAYING HERE WITH TREESTUMP. WE CAN BOTH HELP HIM FULFILL HIS DREAM.
"WAS IT POSSIBLE? COULD LOVE BE SO...PAINLESS?"

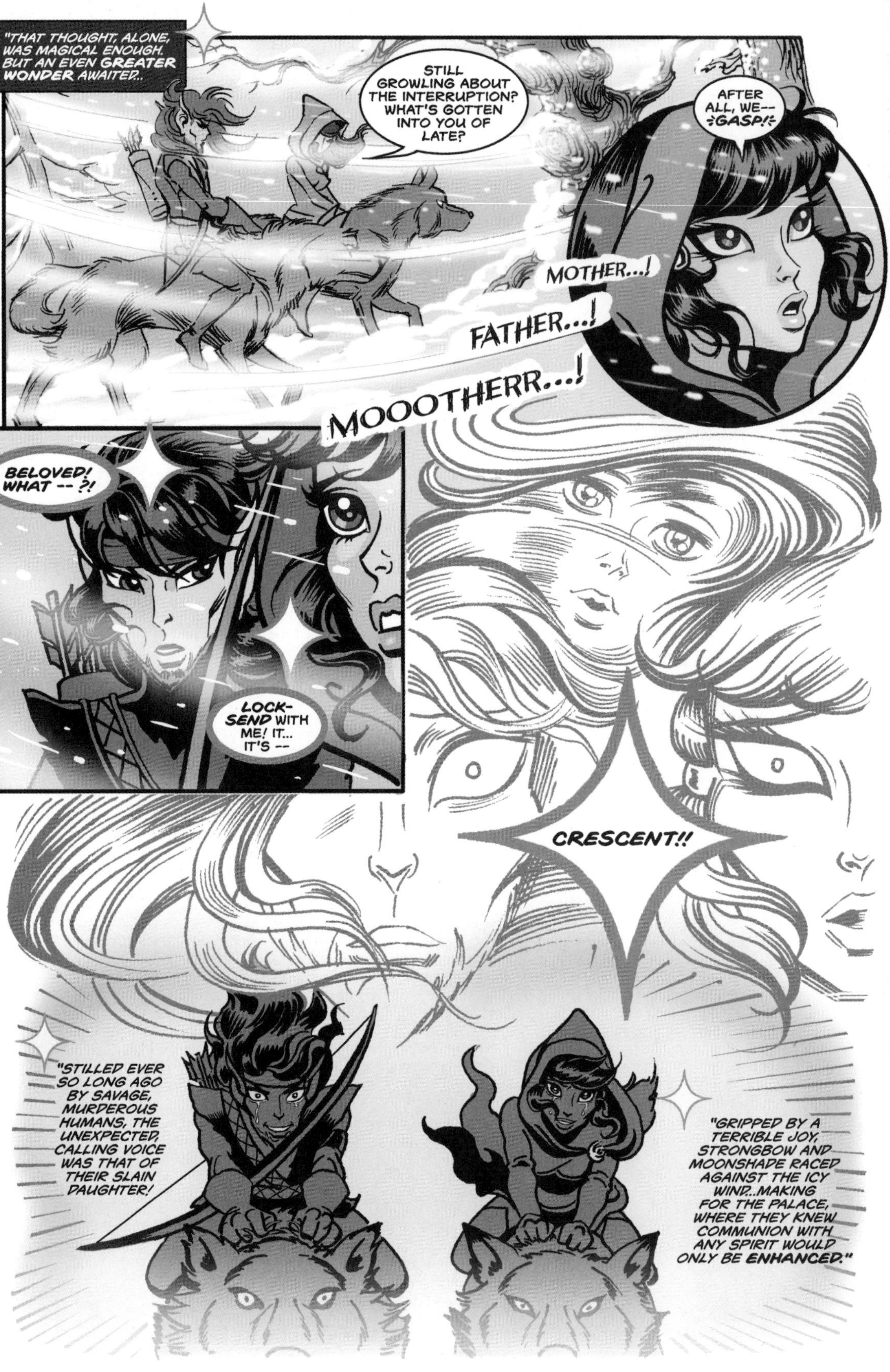
"THAT THOUGHT, ALONE, WAS MAGICAL ENOUGH. BUT AN EVEN GREATER WONDER AWAITED..
STILL GROWLING ABOUT THE INTERRUPTION? WHAT'S GOTTEN INTO YOU OF LATE?
AFTER ALL, WE-- GASP!
MOTHER...!
FATHER...!
MOOOTHERR...!
BELOVED! WHAT -- ?!
LOCK-SEND WITH ME! IT... IT'S --
CRESCENT!!
"STILLED EVER SO LONG AGO BY SAVAGE, MURDEROUS HUMANS, THE UNEXPECTED, CALLING VOICE WAS THAT OF THEIR SLAIN DAUGHTER!
"GRIPPED BY A TERRIBLE JOY, STRONGBOW AND MOONSHADE RACED AGAINST THE ICY WIND...MAKING FOR THE PALACE, WHERE THEY KNEW COMMUNION WITH ANY SPIRIT WOULD ONLY BE ENHANCED."

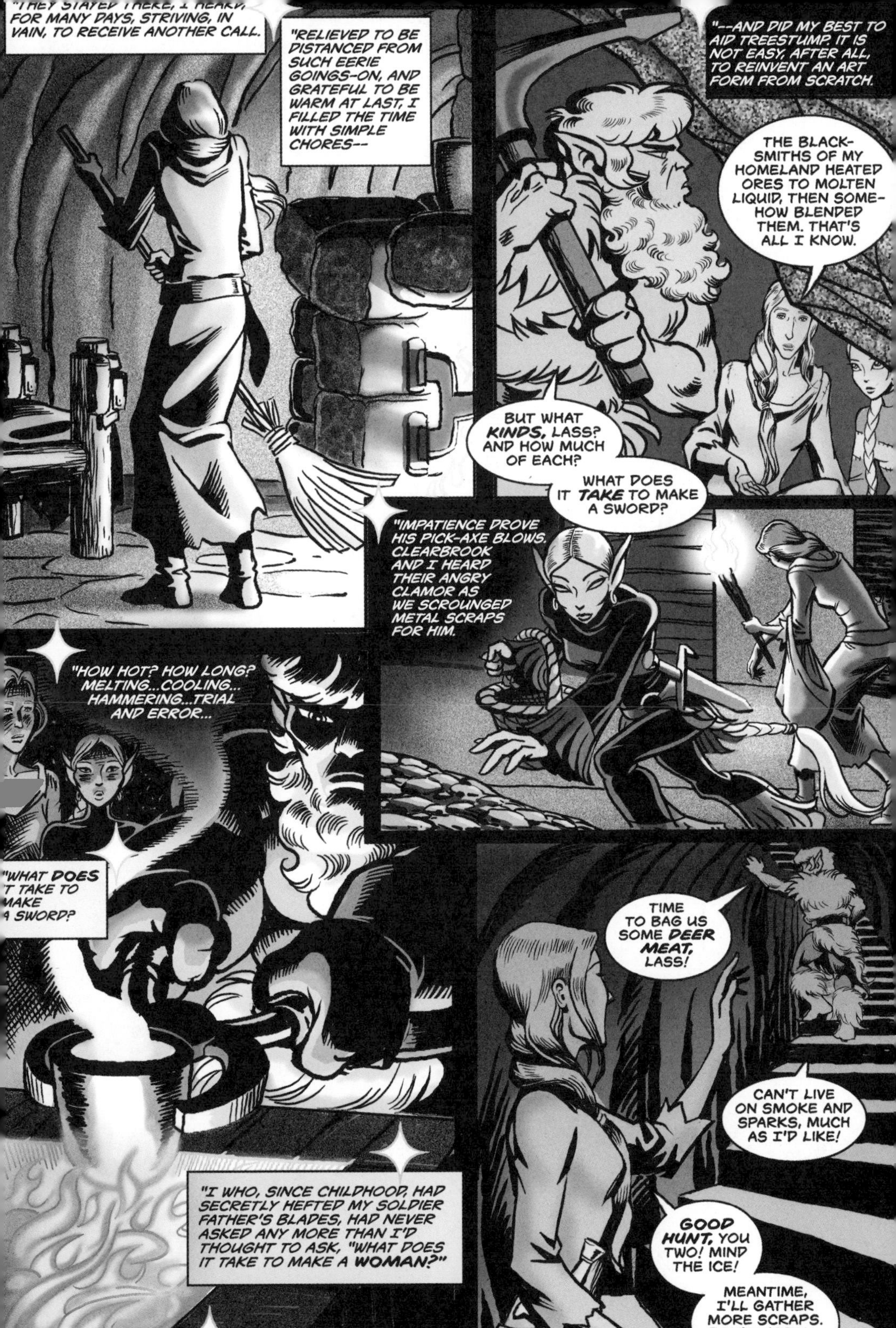
"THEY STAYED THERE, I HEARD, FOR MANY DAYS, STRIVING, IN VAIN, TO RECEIVE ANOTHER CALL.
"RELIEVED TO BE DISTANCED FROM SUCH EERIE GOINGS-ON, AND GRATEFUL TO BE WARM AT LAST, I FILLED THE TIME WITH SIMPLE CHORES--
"--AND DID MY BEST TO AID TREESTUMP. IT IS NOT EASY, AFTER ALL, TO REINVENT AN ART FORM FROM SCRATCH.
THE BLACK-SMITHS OF MY HOMELAND HEATED ORES TO MOLTEN LIQUID, THEN SOME-HOW BLENDED THEM. THAT'S ALL I KNOW.
BUT WHAT KINDS, LASS? AND HOW MUCH OF EACH?
WHAT DOES IT TAKE TO MAKE A SWORD?
"IMPATIENCE DROVE HIS PICK-AXE BLOWS. CLEARBROOK AND I HEARD THEIR ANGRY CLAMOR AS WE SCROUNGED METAL SCRAPS FOR HIM.
"HOW HOT? HOW LONG? MELTING...COOLING... HAMMERING...TRIAL AND ERROR...
"WHAT DOES IT TAKE TO MAKE A SWORD?
TIME TO BAG US SOME DEER MEAT, LASS!
CAN'T LIVE ON SMOKE AND SPARKS, MUCH AS I'D LIKE!
"I WHO, SINCE CHILDHOOD, HAD SECRETLY HEFTED MY SOLDIER FATHER'S BLADES, HAD NEVER ASKED ANY MORE THAN I'D THOUGHT TO ASK, "WHAT DOES IT TAKE TO MAKE A WOMAN?"
GOOD HUNT, YOU TWO! MIND THE ICE!
MEANTIME, I'LL GATHER MORE SCRAPS. DON'T WORRY... I'LL BE FINE!
"NOW I COULD NOT WAIT TO LEARN THE ANSWERS TO BOTH QUESTIONS!"

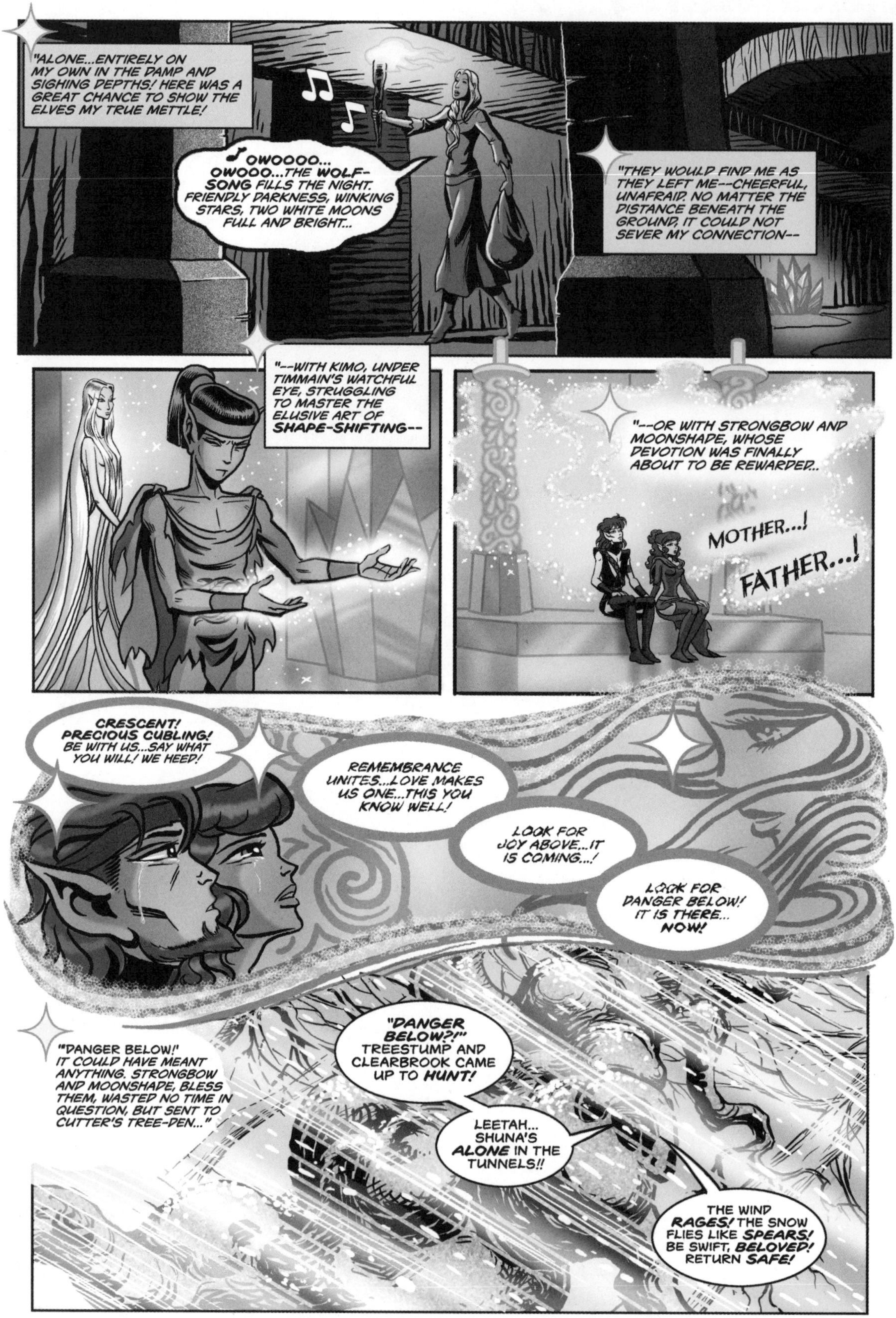
"ALONE...ENTIRELY ON MY OWN IN THE DAMP AND SIGHING DEPTHS! HERE WAS A GREAT CHANCE TO SHOW THE ELVES MY TRUE METTLE!
OWOOOO... OWOOO...THE WOLF-SONG FILLS THE NIGHT. FRIENDLY DARKNESS, WINKING STARS, TWO WHITE MOONS FULL AND BRIGHT...
"THEY WOULD FIND ME AS THEY LEFT ME--CHEERFUL, UNAFRAID. NO MATTER THE DISTANCE BENEATH THE GROUND, IT COULD NOT SEVER MY CONNECTION--
"--WITH KIMO, UNDER TIMMAIN'S WATCHFUL EYE, STRUGGLING TO MASTER THE ELUSIVE ART OF SHAPE-SHIFTING--
"--OR WITH STRONGBOW AND MOONSHADE, WHOSE DEVOTION WAS FINALLY ABOUT TO BE REWARDED...
MOTHER...!
FATHER...!
CRESCENT! PRECIOUS CUBLING! BE WITH US...SAY WHAT YOU WILL! WE HEED!
REMEMBRANCE UNITES...LOVE MAKES US ONE...THIS YOU KNOW WELL!
LOOK FOR JOY ABOVE...IT IS COMING...!
LOOK FOR DANGER BELOW! IT IS THERE... NOW!
"DANGER BELOW!" IT COULD HAVE MEANT ANYTHING. STRONGBOW AND MOONSHADE, BLESS THEM, WASTED NO TIME IN QUESTION, BUT SENT TO CUTTER'S TREE-DEN..."
"DANGER BELOW?!" TREESTUMP AND CLEARBROOK CAME UP TO HUNT!
LEETAH... SHUNA'S ALONE IN THE TUNNELS!!
THE WIND RAGES! THE SNOW FLIES LIKE SPEARS! BE SWIFT, BELOVED! RETURN SAFE!

"ALL UNAWARES, I BOLDLY ENTERED AN UNFAMILIAR CHAMBER...
"WHEN SUDDENLY..."
MMRRMMRRMMMMRR...
:GASP!: WH-WHO'S THERE...?!
MMRRMMRRMMMMRR
SOMETHING'S IN HERE...WITH ME! TROLLS? NO... TROLLS DON'T SOUND LIKE --
MMMRRRMMMM
OH, THREKSH'T! WHAT IS IT?!!
WHAT IS IT?!!
AAIIEEEEE!!!
EEEE... EEEE...
GOT TO GET OUT!!
GET OUT...
...OUT... OUT... OUT....

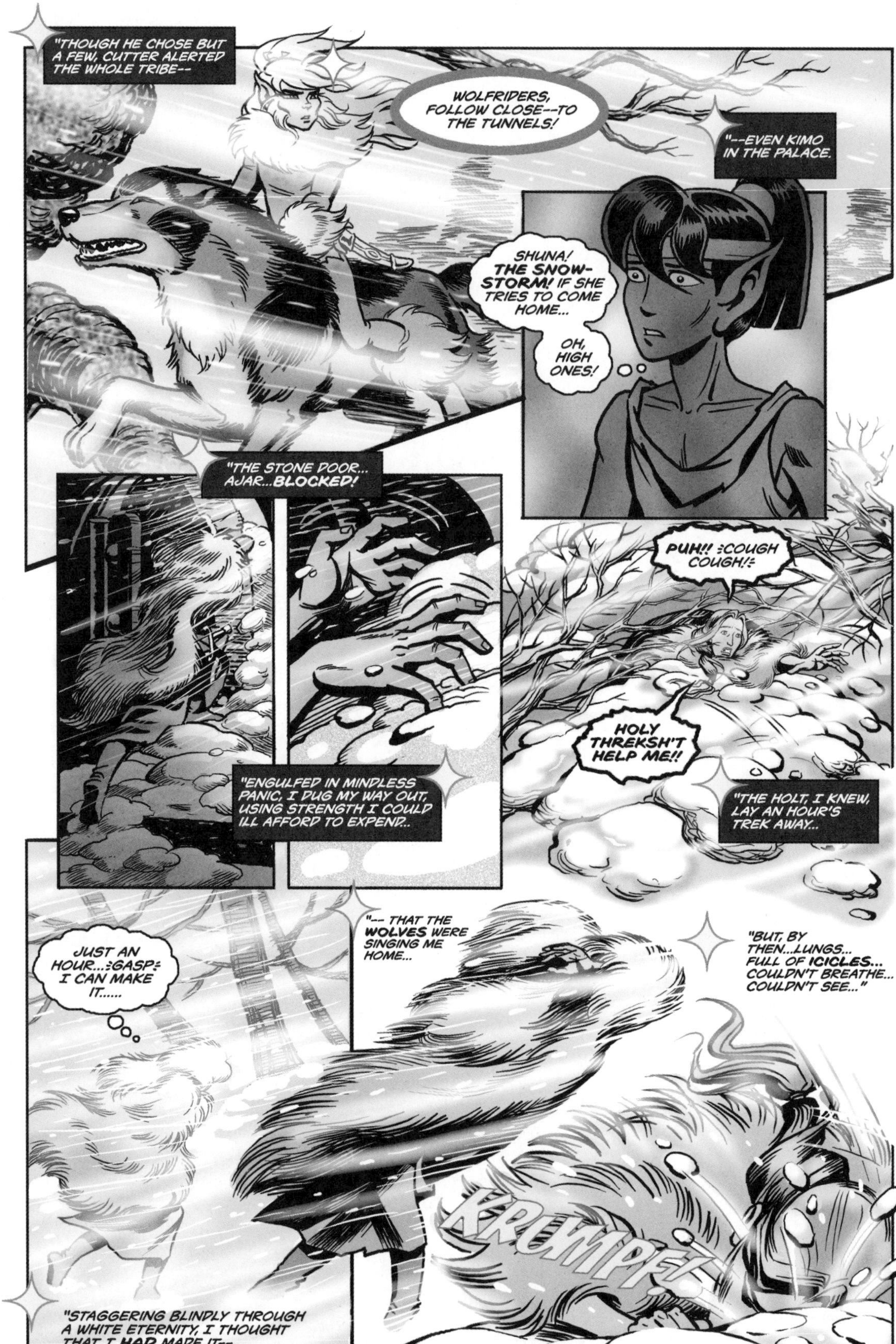
"THOUGH HE CHOSE BUT A FEW, CUTTER ALERTED THE WHOLE TRIBE--
WOLFRIDERS, FOLLOW CLOSE--TO THE TUNNELS!
"--EVEN KIMO IN THE PALACE.
SHUNA! THE SNOW-STORM! IF SHE TRIES TO COME HOME...
OH, HIGH ONES!
"THE STONE DOOR... AJAR...BLOCKED!
"ENGULFED IN MINDLESS PANIC, I DUG MY WAY OUT, USING STRENGTH I COULD ILL AFFORD TO EXPEND...
PUH!! :COUGH COUGH!:
HOLY THREKSH'T HELP ME!!
"THE HOLT, I KNEW, LAY AN HOUR'S TREK AWAY...
JUST AN HOUR... :GASP: I CAN MAKE IT......
"STAGGERING BLINDLY THROUGH A WHITE ETERNITY, I THOUGHT THAT I HAD MADE IT--
"-- THAT THE WOLVES WERE SINGING ME HOME...
"BUT, BY THEN...LUNGS... FULL OF ICICLES... COULDN'T BREATHE... COULDN'T SEE..."
KRUMPF!

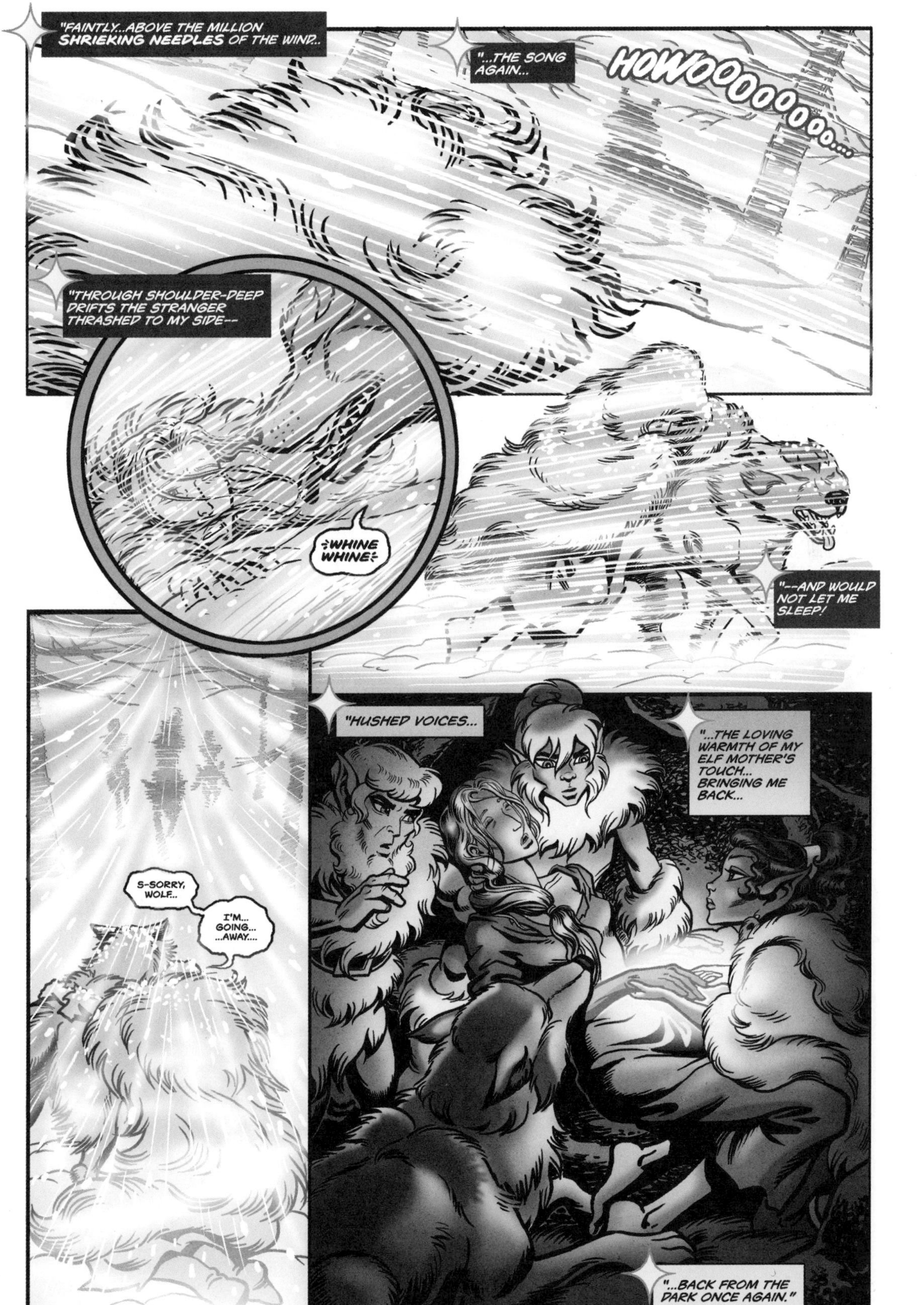
"FAINTLY...ABOVE THE MILLION SHRIEKING NEEDLES OF THE WIND...
"...THE SONG AGAIN...
HOWOOOOOOOOo...
"THROUGH SHOULDER-DEEP DRIFTS THE STRANGER THRASHED TO MY SIDE--
WHINE WHINE
"--AND WOULD NOT LET ME SLEEP!
S-SORRY, WOLF...
I'M... GOING... ...AWAY....
"HUSHED VOICES...
"...THE LOVING WARMTH OF MY ELF MOTHER'S TOUCH... BRINGING ME BACK...
"...BACK FROM THE DARK ONCE AGAIN."

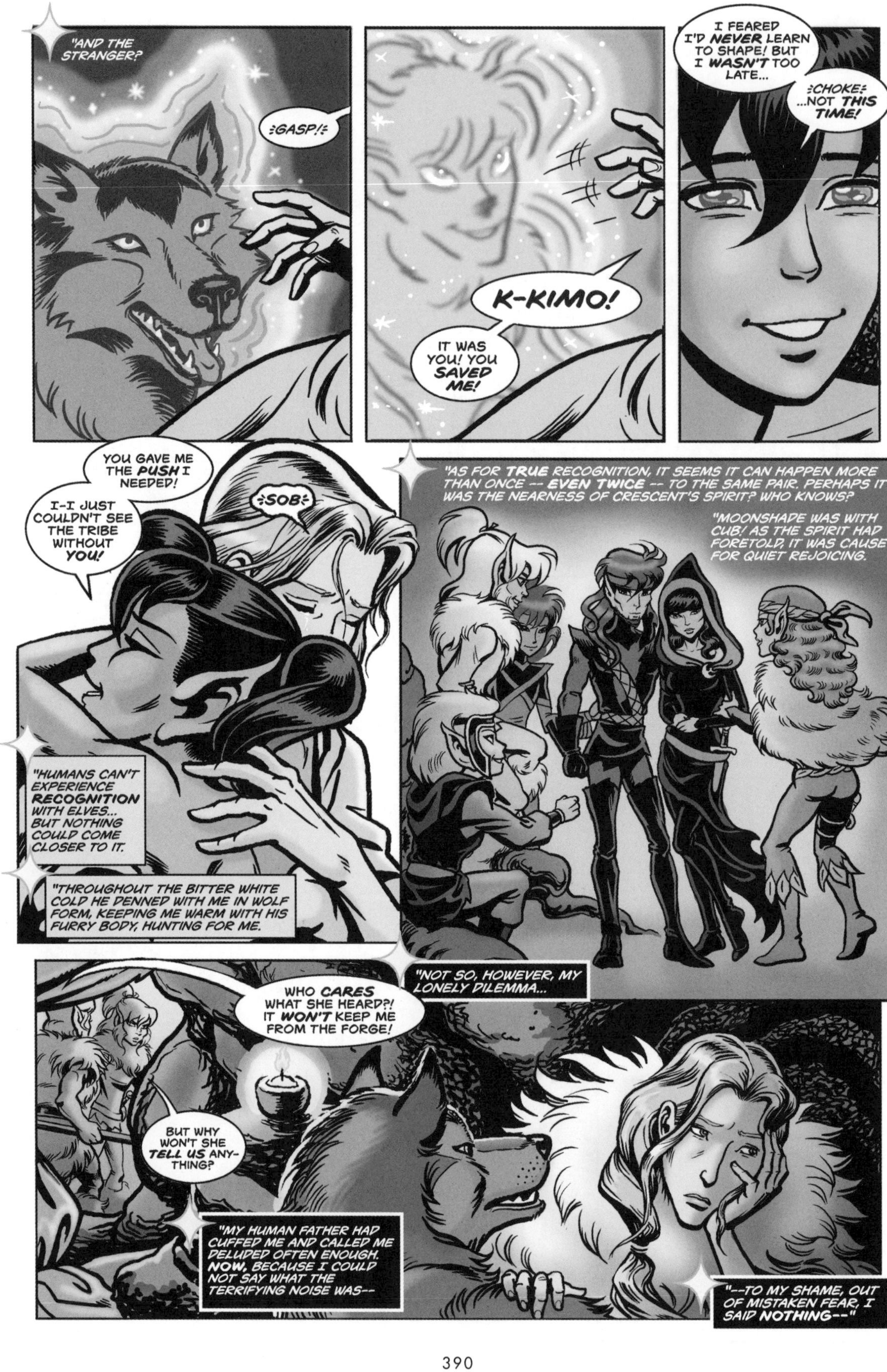
"AND THE STRANGER?
:GASP!:
K-KIMO!
IT WAS YOU! YOU SAVED ME!
I FEARED I'D NEVER LEARN TO SHAPE! BUT I WASN'T TOO LATE...
:CHOKE: ...NOT THIS TIME!
YOU GAVE ME THE PUSH I NEEDED!
:SOB:
I-I JUST COULDN'T SEE THE TRIBE WITHOUT YOU!
"HUMANS CAN'T EXPERIENCE RECOGNITION WITH ELVES... BUT NOTHING COULD COME CLOSER TO IT.
"THROUGHOUT THE BITTER WHITE COLD HE DENNED WITH ME IN WOLF FORM, KEEPING ME WARM WITH HIS FURRY BODY, HUNTING FOR ME.
"AS FOR TRUE RECOGNITION, IT SEEMS IT CAN HAPPEN MORE THAN ONCE -- EVEN TWICE -- TO THE SAME PAIR. PERHAPS IT WAS THE NEARNESS OF CRESCENT'S SPIRIT? WHO KNOWS?
"MOONSHADE WAS WITH CUB! AS THE SPIRIT HAD FORETOLD, IT WAS CAUSE FOR QUIET REJOICING.
"NOT SO, HOWEVER, MY LONELY DILEMMA...
WHO CARES WHAT SHE HEARD?! IT WON'T KEEP ME FROM THE FORGE!
BUT WHY WON'T SHE TELL US ANY-THING?
"MY HUMAN FATHER HAD CUFFED ME AND CALLED ME DELUDED OFTEN ENOUGH. NOW, BECAUSE I COULD NOT SAY WHAT THE TERRIFYING NOISE WAS--
"--TO MY SHAME, OUT OF MISTAKEN FEAR, I SAID NOTHING--"

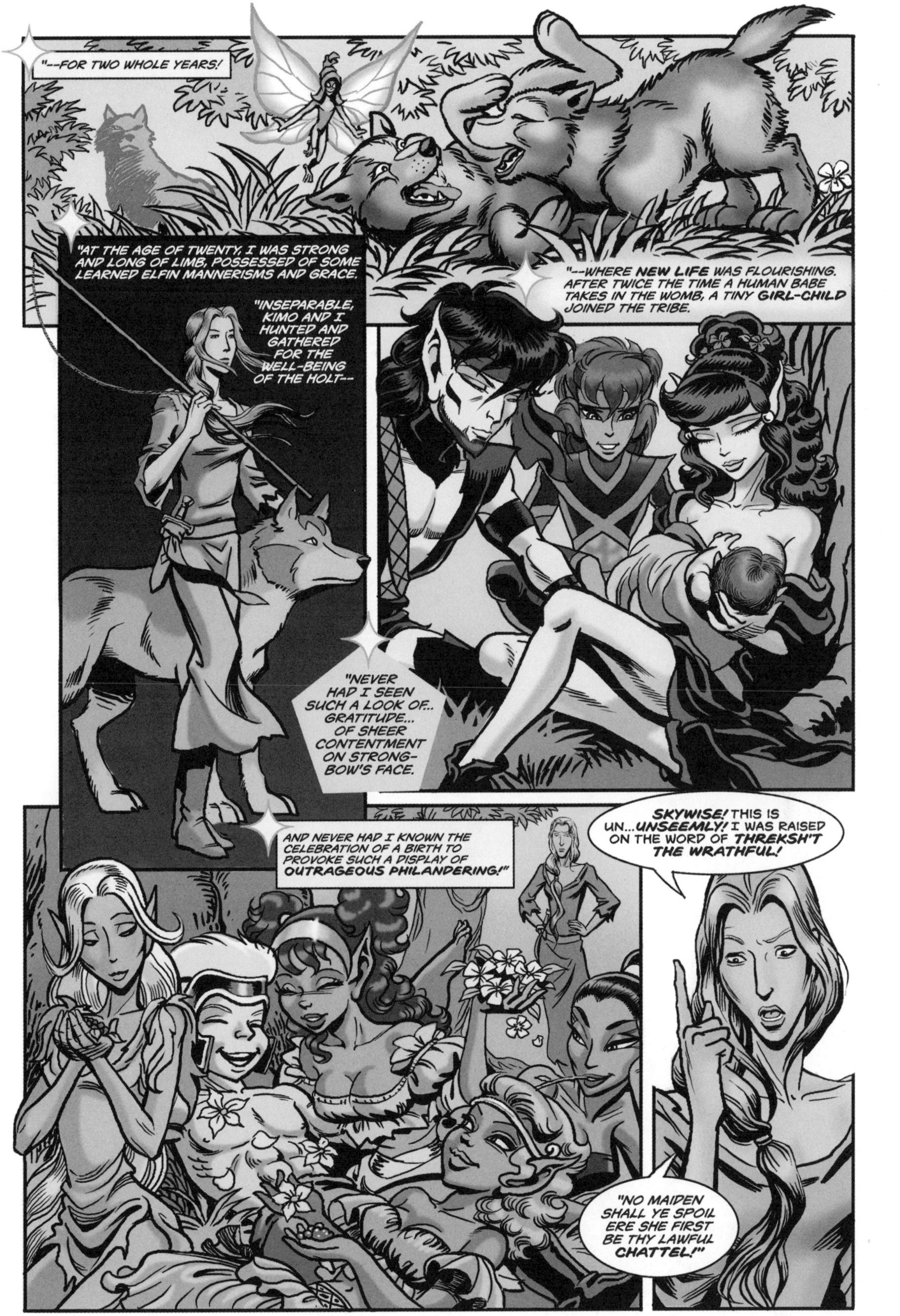
"--FOR TWO WHOLE YEARS!
"AT THE AGE OF TWENTY, I WAS STRONG AND LONG OF LIMB, POSSESSED OF SOME LEARNED ELFIN MANNERISMS AND GRACE.
"INSEPARABLE, KIMO AND I HUNTED AND GATHERED FOR THE WELL-BEING OF THE HOLT--
"--WHERE NEW LIFE WAS FLOURISHING. AFTER TWICE THE TIME A HUMAN BABE TAKES IN THE WOMB, A TINY GIRL-CHILD JOINED THE TRIBE.
"NEVER HAD I SEEN SUCH A LOOK OF... GRATITUDE... OF SHEER CONTENTMENT ON STRONG-BOW'S FACE.
AND NEVER HAD I KNOWN THE CELEBRATION OF A BIRTH TO PROVOKE SUCH A DISPLAY OF OUTRAGEOUS PHILANDERING!"
SKYWISE! THIS IS UN...UNSEEMLY! I WAS RAISED ON THE WORD OF THREKSH'T THE WRATHFUL!
"NO MAIDEN SHALL YE SPOIL ERE SHE FIRST BE THY LAWFUL CHATTEL!"

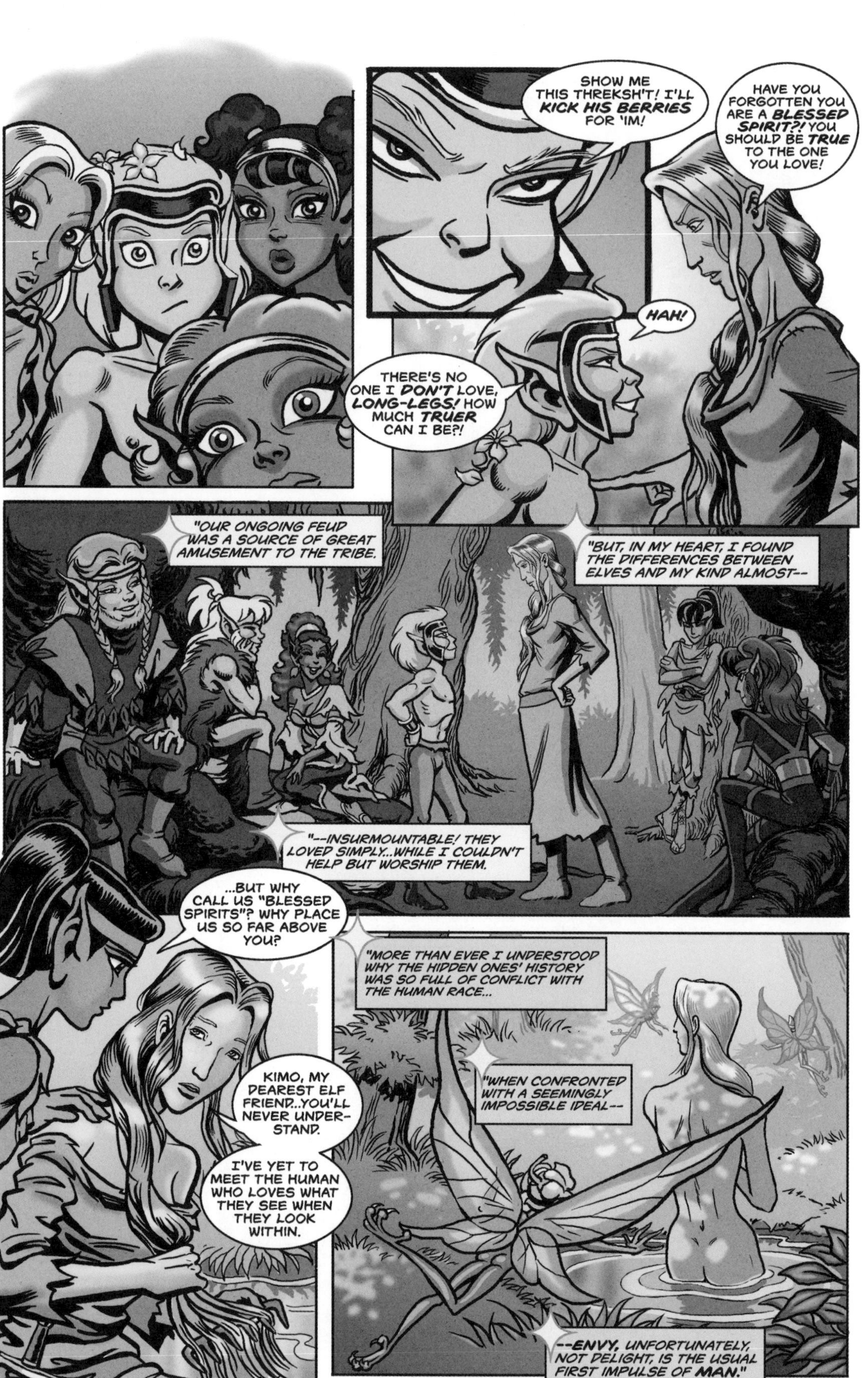
SHOW ME THIS THREKSH'T! I'LL KICK HIS BERRIES FOR 'IM!
HAVE YOU FORGOTTEN YOU ARE A BLESSED SPIRIT?! YOU SHOULD BE TRUE TO THE ONE YOU LOVE!
HAH!
THERE'S NO ONE I DON'T LOVE, LONG-LEGS! HOW MUCH TRUER CAN I BE?!
"OUR ONGOING FEUD WAS A SOURCE OF GREAT AMUSEMENT TO THE TRIBE.
"BUT, IN MY HEART, I FOUND THE DIFFERENCES BETWEEN ELVES AND MY KIND ALMOST--
"--INSURMOUNTABLE! THEY LOVED SIMPLY...WHILE I COULDN'T HELP BUT WORSHIP THEM.
...BUT WHY CALL US "BLESSED SPIRITS"? WHY PLACE US SO FAR ABOVE YOU?
KIMO, MY DEAREST ELF FRIEND...YOU'LL NEVER UNDERSTAND.
I'VE YET TO MEET THE HUMAN WHO LOVES WHAT THEY SEE WHEN THEY LOOK WITHIN.
"MORE THAN EVER I UNDERSTOOD WHY THE HIDDEN ONES' HISTORY WAS SO FULL OF CONFLICT WITH THE HUMAN RACE...
"WHEN CONFRONTED WITH A SEEMINGLY IMPOSSIBLE IDEAL--
--ENVY, UNFORTUNATELY, NOT DELIGHT, IS THE USUAL FIRST IMPULSE OF MAN."

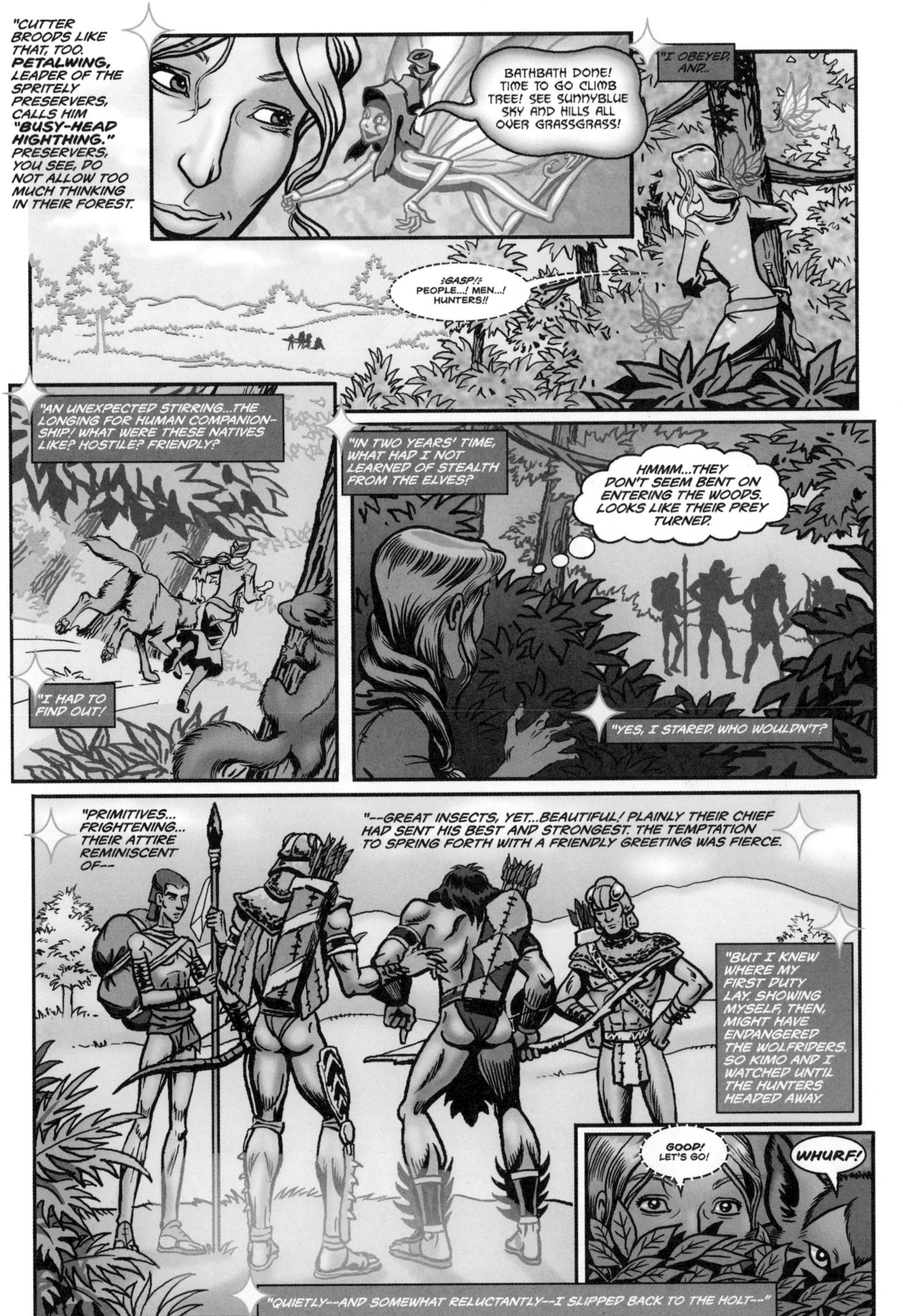
"CUTTER BROODS LIKE THAT, TOO. PETALWING, LEADER OF THE SPRITELY PRESERVERS, CALLS HIM "BUSY-HEAD HIGHTHING." PRESERVERS, YOU SEE, DO NOT ALLOW TOO MUCH THINKING IN THEIR FOREST.
BATHBATH DONE! TIME TO GO CLIMB TREE! SEE SUNNYBLUE SKY AND HILLS ALL OVER GRASSGRASS!
"I OBEYED, AND...
:GASP!: PEOPLE...! MEN...! HUNTERS!!
"AN UNEXPECTED STIRRING...THE LONGING FOR HUMAN COMPANIONSHIP! WHAT WERE THESE NATIVES LIKE? HOSTILE? FRIENDLY?
"I HAD TO FIND OUT!
"IN TWO YEARS' TIME, WHAT HAD I NOT LEARNED OF STEALTH FROM THE ELVES?
HMMM...THEY DON'T SEEM BENT ON ENTERING THE WOODS. LOOKS LIKE THEIR PREY TURNED.
"YES, I STARED. WHO WOULDN'T?
"PRIMITIVES... FRIGHTENING... THEIR ATTIRE REMINISCENT OF--
"--GREAT INSECTS, YET...BEAUTIFUL! PLAINLY THEIR CHIEF HAD SENT HIS BEST AND STRONGEST. THE TEMPTATION TO SPRING FORTH WITH A FRIENDLY GREETING WAS FIERCE.
"BUT I KNEW WHERE MY FIRST DUTY LAY. SHOWING MYSELF, THEN, MIGHT HAVE ENDANGERED THE WOLFRIDERS. SO KIMO AND I WATCHED UNTIL THE HUNTERS HEADED AWAY.
GOOD! LET'S GO!
WHURF!
"QUIETLY--AND SOMEWHAT RELUCTANTLY--I SLIPPED BACK TO THE HOLT--"

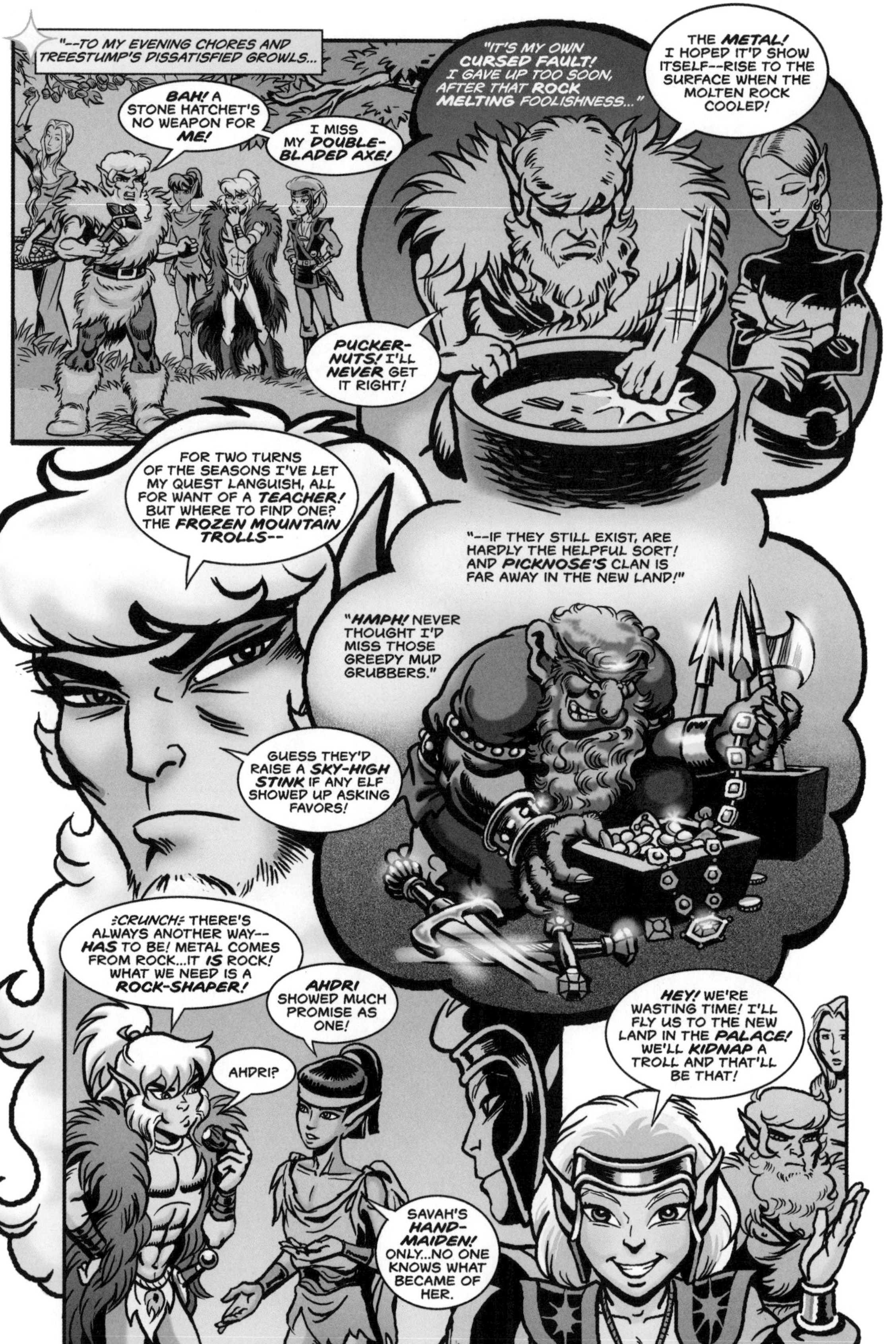
"--TO MY EVENING CHORES AND TREESTUMP'S DISSATISFIED GROWLS...
BAH! A STONE HATCHET'S NO WEAPON FOR ME!
I MISS MY DOUBLE-BLADED AXE!
"IT'S MY OWN CURSED FAULT! I GAVE UP TOO SOON, AFTER THAT ROCK MELTING FOOLISHNESS..."
THE METAL! I HOPED IT'D SHOW ITSELF--RISE TO THE SURFACE WHEN THE MOLTEN ROCK COOLED!
PUCKER-NUTS! I'LL NEVER GET IT RIGHT!
FOR TWO TURNS OF THE SEASONS I'VE LET MY QUEST LANGUISH, ALL FOR WANT OF A TEACHER! BUT WHERE TO FIND ONE? THE FROZEN MOUNTAIN TROLLS--
"--IF THEY STILL EXIST, ARE HARDLY THE HELPFUL SORT! AND PICKNOSE'S CLAN IS FAR AWAY IN THE NEW LAND!"
"HMPH! NEVER THOUGHT I'D MISS THOSE GREEDY MUD GRUBBERS."
GUESS THEY'D RAISE A SKY-HIGH STINK IF ANY ELF SHOWED UP ASKING FAVORS!
≡CRUNCH≡ THERE'S ALWAYS ANOTHER WAY--HAS TO BE! METAL COMES FROM ROCK...IT IS ROCK! WHAT WE NEED IS A ROCK-SHAPER!
AHDRI SHOWED MUCH PROMISE AS ONE!
AHDRI?
SAVAH'S HAND-MAIDEN! ONLY...NO ONE KNOWS WHAT BECAME OF HER.
HEY! WE'RE WASTING TIME! I'LL FLY US TO THE NEW LAND IN THE PALACE! WE'LL KIDNAP A TROLL AND THAT'LL BE THAT!

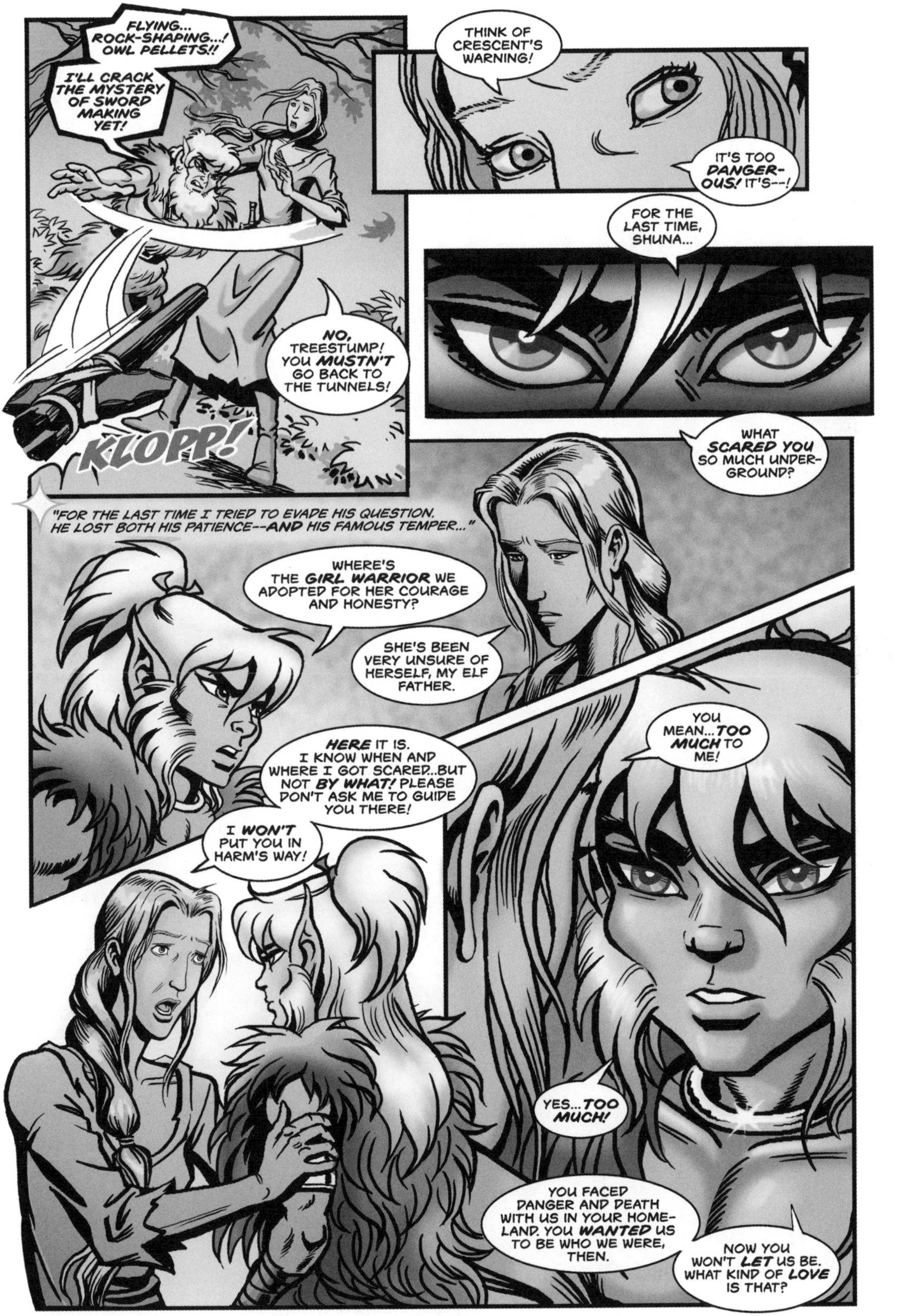
FLYING... ROCK-SHAPING...! OWL PELLETS!!
I'LL CRACK THE MYSTERY OF SWORD MAKING YET!
THINK OF CRESCENT'S WARNING!
IT'S TOO DANGER-OUS! IT'S--!
NO, TREESTUMP! YOU MUSTN'T GO BACK TO THE TUNNELS!
KLOPP!
FOR THE LAST TIME, SHUNA...
WHAT SCARED YOU SO MUCH UNDER-GROUND?
"FOR THE LAST TIME I TRIED TO EVADE HIS QUESTION. HE LOST BOTH HIS PATIENCE--AND HIS FAMOUS TEMPER..."
WHERE'S THE GIRL WARRIOR WE ADOPTED FOR HER COURAGE AND HONESTY?
SHE'S BEEN VERY UNSURE OF HERSELF, MY ELF FATHER.
HERE IT IS. I KNOW WHEN AND WHERE I GOT SCARED...BUT NOT BY WHAT! PLEASE DON'T ASK ME TO GUIDE YOU THERE!
I WON'T PUT YOU IN HARM'S WAY!
YOU MEAN...TOO MUCH TO ME!
YES...TOO MUCH!
YOU FACED DANGER AND DEATH WITH US IN YOUR HOME-LAND. YOU WANTED US TO BE WHO WE WERE, THEN.
NOW YOU WON'T LET US BE. WHAT KIND OF LOVE IS THAT?

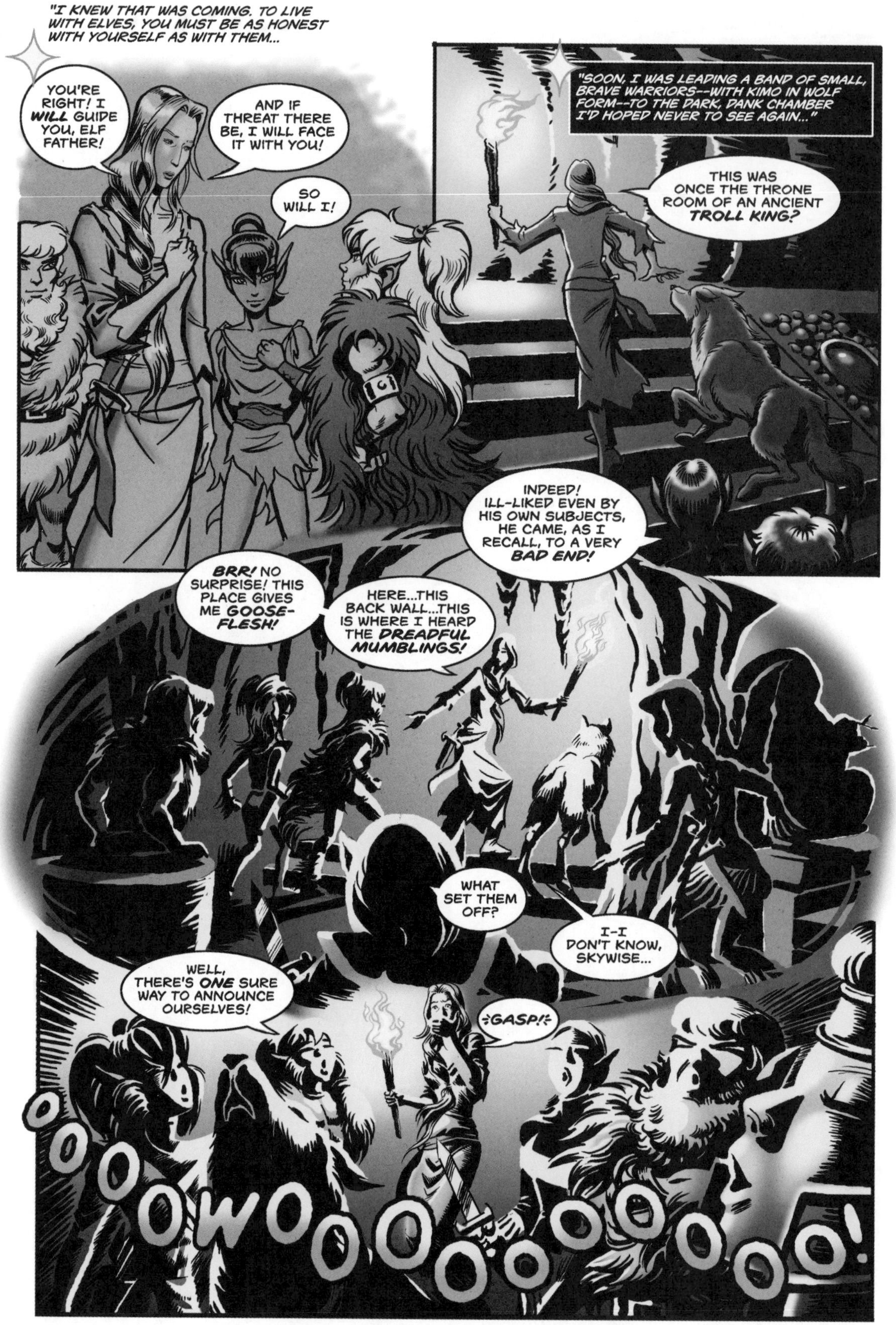

"I KNEW THAT WAS COMING. TO LIVE WITH ELVES, YOU MUST BE AS HONEST WITH YOURSELF AS WITH THEM...
YOU'RE RIGHT! I WILL GUIDE YOU, ELF FATHER!
AND IF THREAT THERE BE, I WILL FACE IT WITH YOU!
SO WILL I!
"SOON, I WAS LEADING A BAND OF SMALL, BRAVE WARRIORS--WITH KIMO IN WOLF FORM--TO THE DARK, DANK CHAMBER I'D HOPED NEVER TO SEE AGAIN..."
THIS WAS ONCE THE THRONE ROOM OF AN ANCIENT TROLL KING?
INDEED! ILL-LIKED EVEN BY HIS OWN SUBJECTS, HE CAME, AS I RECALL, TO A VERY BAD END!
BRR! NO SURPRISE! THIS PLACE GIVES ME GOOSE-FLESH!
HERE...THIS BACK WALL...THIS IS WHERE I HEARD THE DREADFUL MUMBLINGS!
WHAT SET THEM OFF?
I-I DON'T KNOW, SKYWISE...
WELL, THERE'S ONE SURE WAY TO ANNOUNCE OURSELVES!
GASP!
OOOOWOOOOOOOOOOOOOOOO!

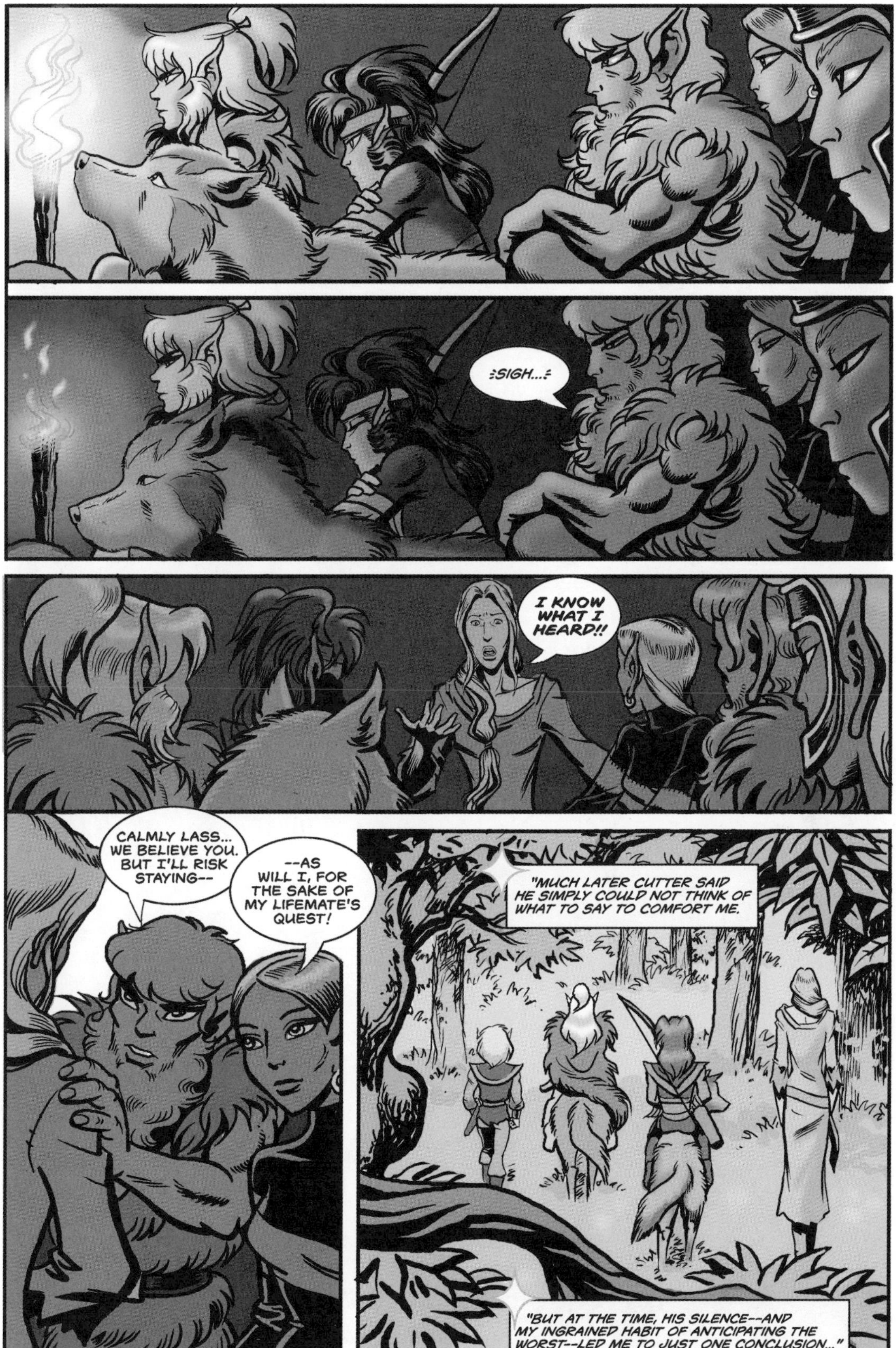

:SIGH...:
I KNOW WHAT I HEARD!!
CALMLY LASS... WE BELIEVE YOU. BUT I'LL RISK STAYING--
--AS WILL I, FOR THE SAKE OF MY LIFEMATE'S QUEST!
"MUCH LATER CUTTER SAID HE SIMPLY COULD NOT THINK OF WHAT TO SAY TO COMFORT ME.
"BUT AT THE TIME, HIS SILENCE--AND MY INGRAINED HABIT OF ANTICIPATING THE WORST--LED ME TO JUST ONE CONCLUSION..."

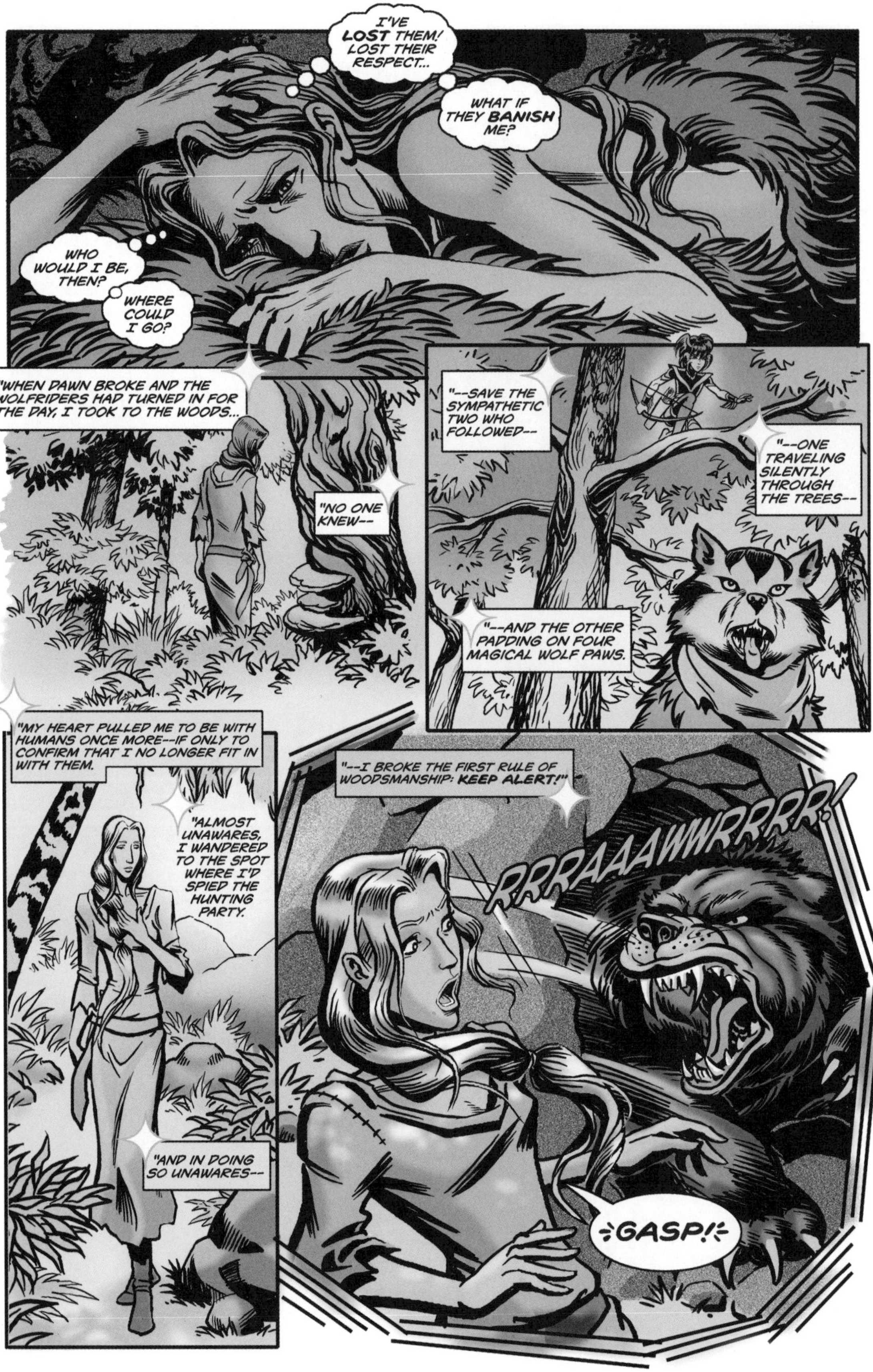
I'VE LOST THEM! LOST THEIR RESPECT...
WHAT IF THEY BANISH ME?
WHO WOULD I BE, THEN?
WHERE COULD I GO?
"WHEN DAWN BROKE AND THE WOLFRIDERS HAD TURNED IN FOR THE DAY, I TOOK TO THE WOODS...
"NO ONE KNEW--
"--SAVE THE SYMPATHETIC TWO WHO FOLLOWED--
"--ONE TRAVELING SILENTLY THROUGH THE TREES--
"--AND THE OTHER PADDING ON FOUR MAGICAL WOLF PAWS.
"MY HEART PULLED ME TO BE WITH HUMANS ONCE MORE--IF ONLY TO CONFIRM THAT I NO LONGER FIT IN WITH THEM.
"ALMOST UNAWARES, I WANDERED TO THE SPOT WHERE I'D SPIED THE HUNTING PARTY.
"AND IN DOING SO UNAWARES--
"--I BROKE THE FIRST RULE OF WOODSMANSHIP: KEEP ALERT!"
RRRAAAAWWRRRR!
GASP!

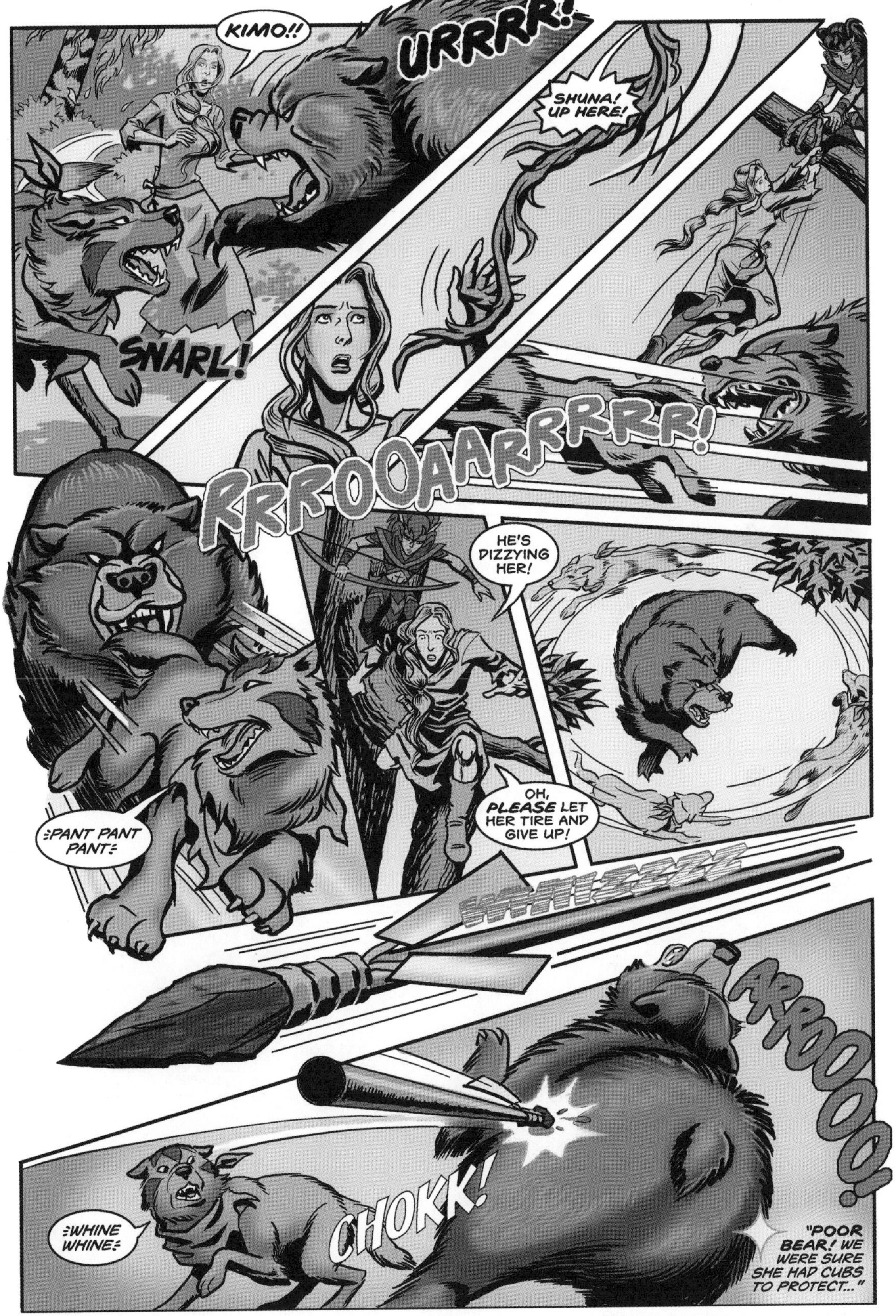
KIMO!!
URRRR!
SNARL!
SHUNA! UP HERE!
RRROOAARRRRR!
HE'S DIZZYING HER!
PANT PANT PANT
OH, PLEASE LET HER TIRE AND GIVE UP!
WHIZZZZ
AROOOOO!
CHOKK!
WHINE WHINE
"POOR BEAR! WE WERE SURE SHE HAD CUBS TO PROTECT..."

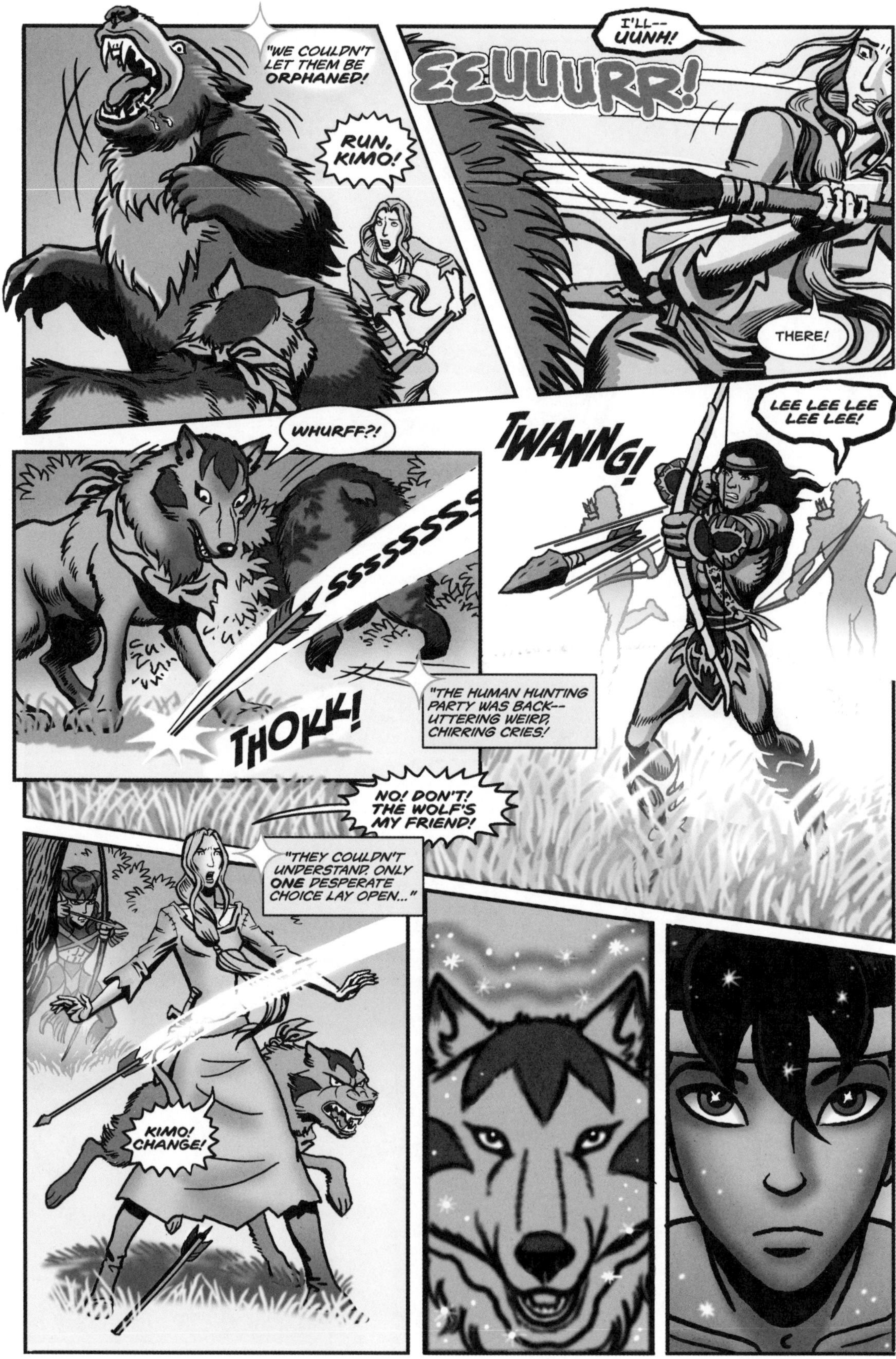
"WE COULDN'T LET THEM BE ORPHANED!
RUN, KIMO!
I'LL-- UUNH!
EEUUUURR!
THERE!
WHURFF?!
SSSSSSSSS
THOKK!
"THE HUMAN HUNTING PARTY WAS BACK-- UTTERING WEIRD, CHIRRING CRIES!
TWANNG!
LEE LEE LEE LEE LEE!
NO! DON'T! THE WOLF'S MY FRIEND!
"THEY COULDN'T UNDERSTAND. ONLY ONE DESPERATE CHOICE LAY OPEN..."
KIMO! CHANGE!

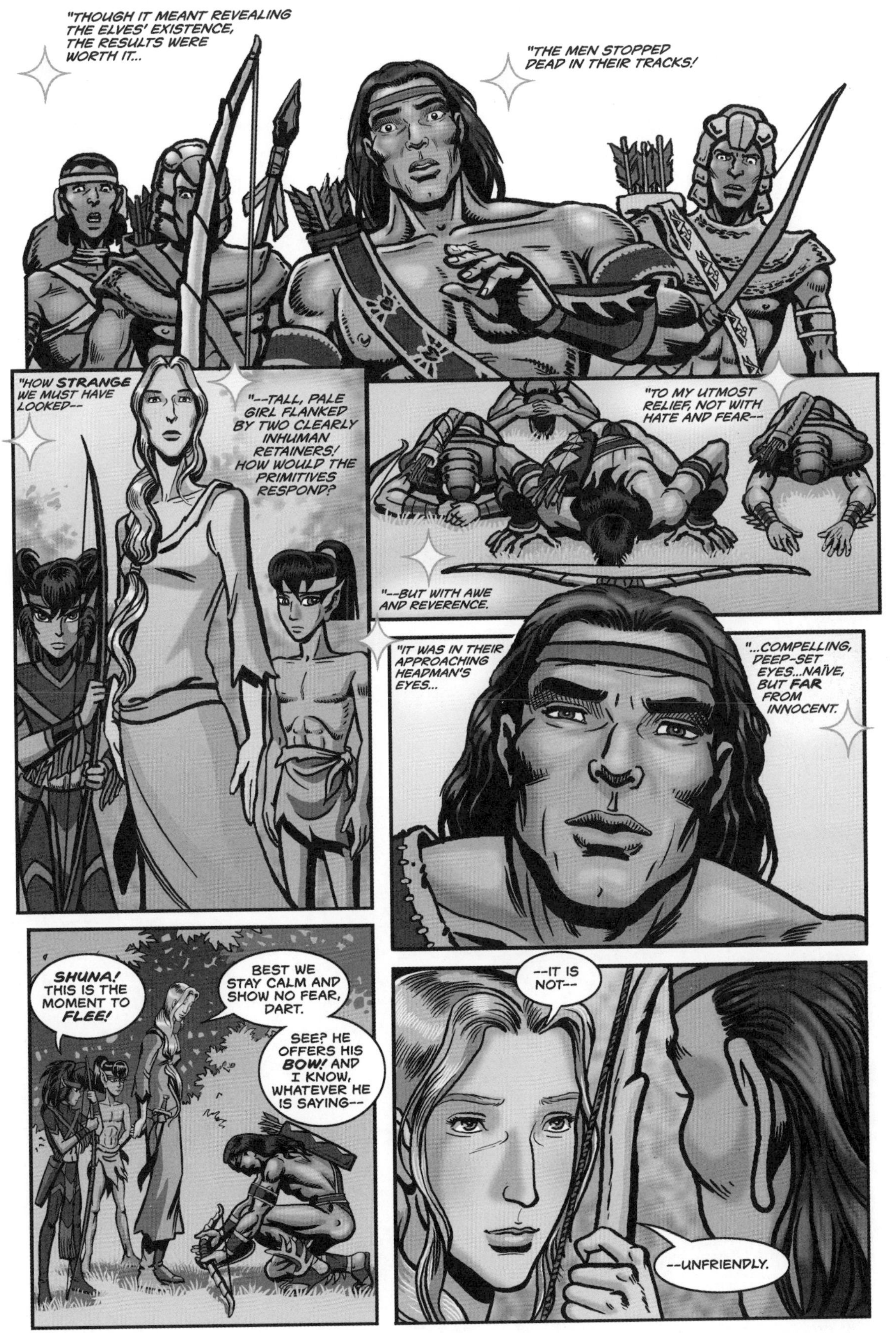
"THOUGH IT MEANT REVEALING THE ELVES' EXISTENCE, THE RESULTS WERE WORTH IT...
"THE MEN STOPPED DEAD IN THEIR TRACKS!
"HOW STRANGE WE MUST HAVE LOOKED--
"--TALL, PALE GIRL FLANKED BY TWO CLEARLY INHUMAN RETAINERS! HOW WOULD THE PRIMITIVES RESPOND?
"TO MY UTMOST RELIEF, NOT WITH HATE AND FEAR--
"--BUT WITH AWE AND REVERENCE.
"IT WAS IN THEIR APPROACHING HEADMAN'S EYES...
"...COMPELLING, DEEP-SET EYES...NAÏVE, BUT FAR FROM INNOCENT.
SHUNA! THIS IS THE MOMENT TO FLEE!
BEST WE STAY CALM AND SHOW NO FEAR, DART.
SEE? HE OFFERS HIS BOW! AND I KNOW, WHATEVER HE IS SAYING--
--IT IS NOT--
--UNFRIENDLY.

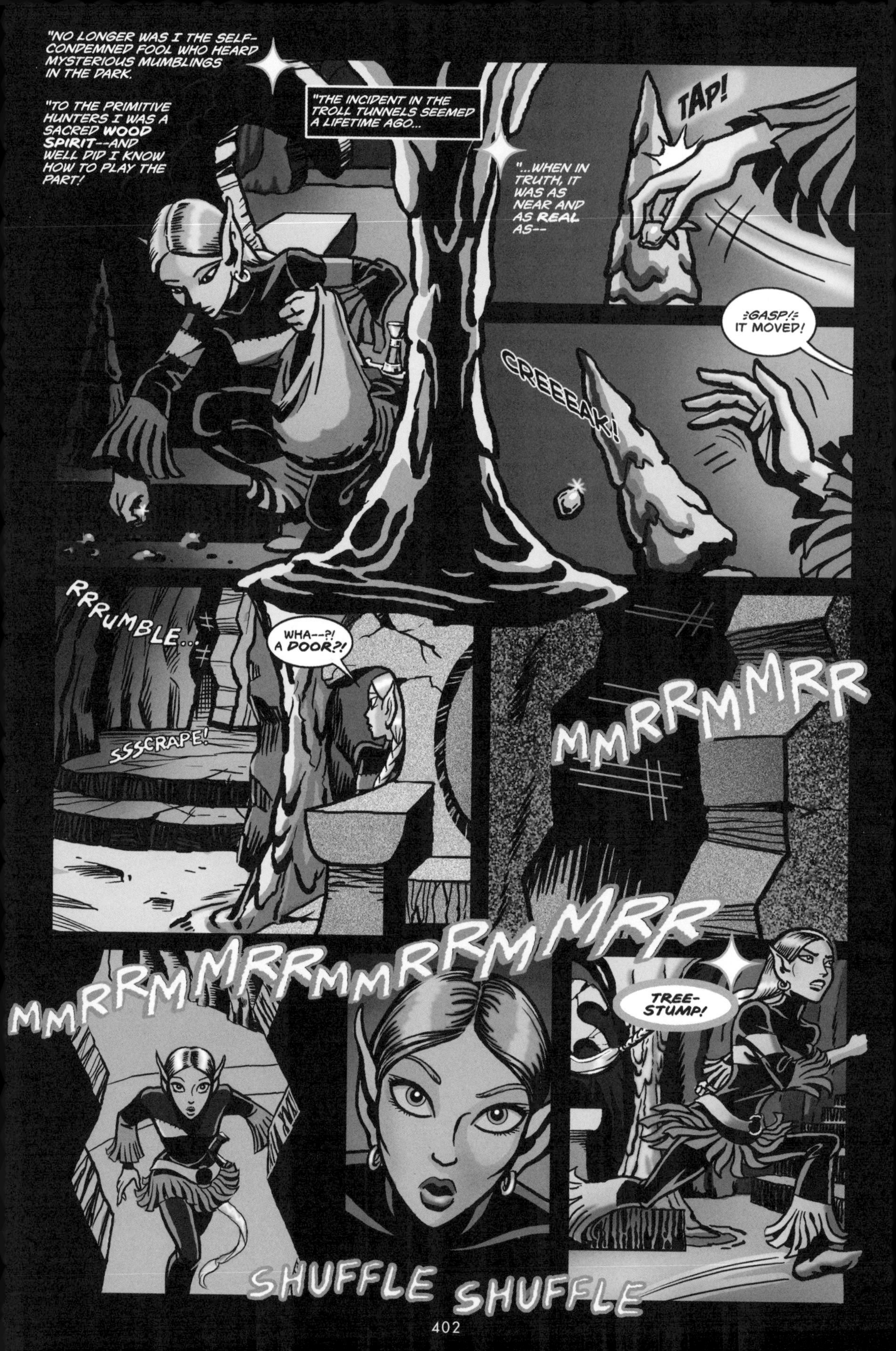
"NO LONGER WAS I THE SELF-CONDEMNED FOOL WHO HEARD MYSTERIOUS MUMBLINGS IN THE DARK.
"TO THE PRIMITIVE HUNTERS I WAS A SACRED WOOD SPIRIT--AND WELL DID I KNOW HOW TO PLAY THE PART!
"THE INCIDENT IN THE TROLL TUNNELS SEEMED A LIFETIME AGO...
"...WHEN IN TRUTH, IT WAS AS NEAR AND AS REAL AS--
TAP!
:GASP!: IT MOVED!
CREEEAK!
RRRUMBLE...
SSSCRAPE!
WHA--?! A DOOR?!
MMRRMMRR
MMRRMMRRMMRRMMRR
TREE-STUMP!
SHUFFLE SHUFFLE

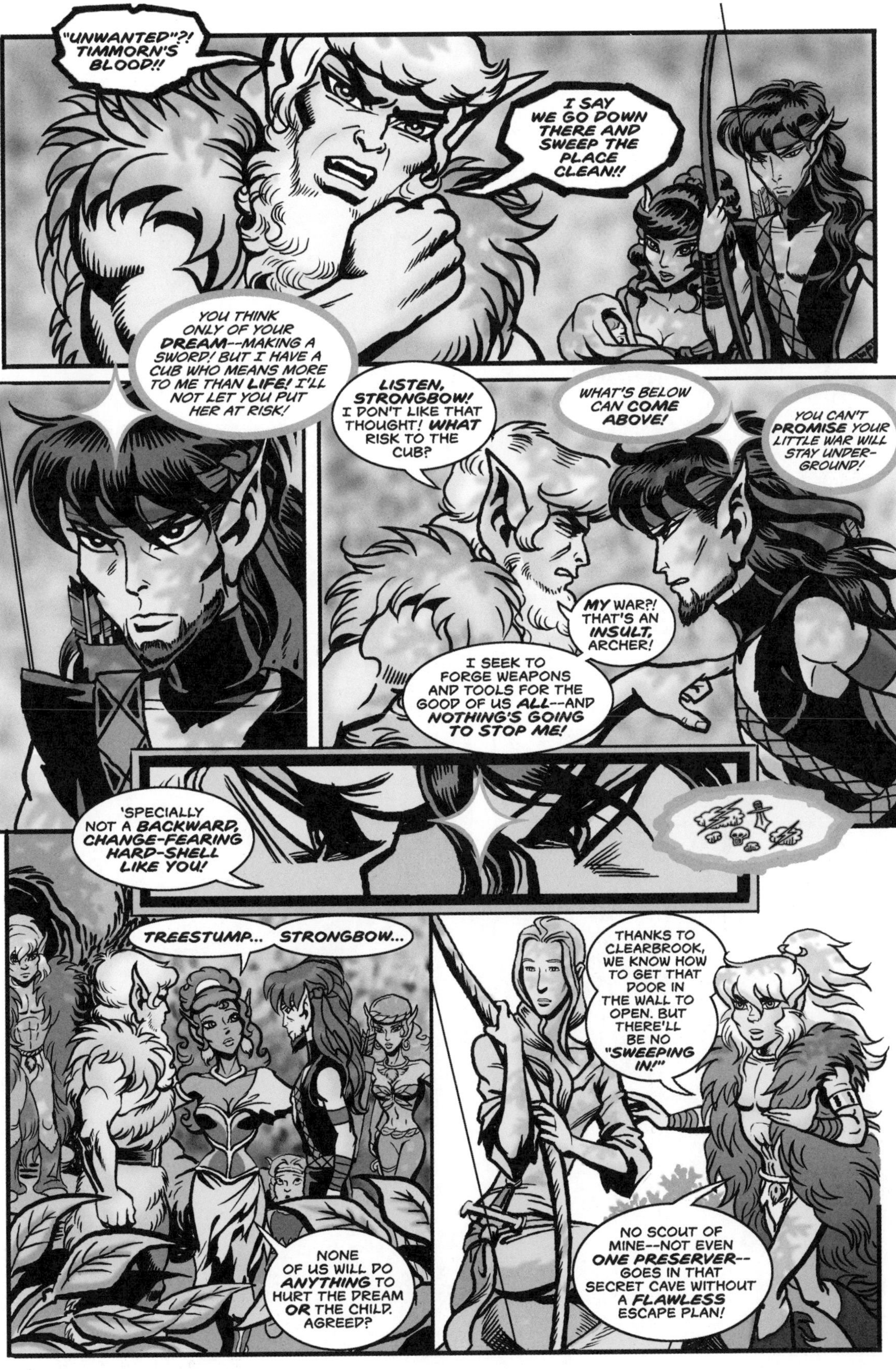
"UNWANTED"?! TIMMORN'S BLOOD!!
I SAY WE GO DOWN THERE AND SWEEP THE PLACE CLEAN!!
YOU THINK ONLY OF YOUR DREAM--MAKING A SWORD! BUT I HAVE A CUB WHO MEANS MORE TO ME THAN LIFE! I'LL NOT LET YOU PUT HER AT RISK!
LISTEN, STRONGBOW! I DON'T LIKE THAT THOUGHT! WHAT RISK TO THE CUB?
WHAT'S BELOW CAN COME ABOVE!
YOU CAN'T PROMISE YOUR LITTLE WAR WILL STAY UNDER-GROUND!
MY WAR?! THAT'S AN INSULT, ARCHER!
I SEEK TO FORGE WEAPONS AND TOOLS FOR THE GOOD OF US ALL--AND NOTHING'S GOING TO STOP ME!
'SPECIALLY NOT A BACKWARD, CHANGE-FEARING HARD-SHELL LIKE YOU!
TREESTUMP... STRONGBOW...
NONE OF US WILL DO ANYTHING TO HURT THE DREAM OR THE CHILD. AGREED?
THANKS TO CLEARBROOK, WE KNOW HOW TO GET THAT DOOR IN THE WALL TO OPEN. BUT THERE'LL BE NO "SWEEPING IN!"
NO SCOUT OF MINE--NOT EVEN ONE PRESERVER--GOES IN THAT SECRET CAVE WITHOUT A FLAWLESS ESCAPE PLAN!

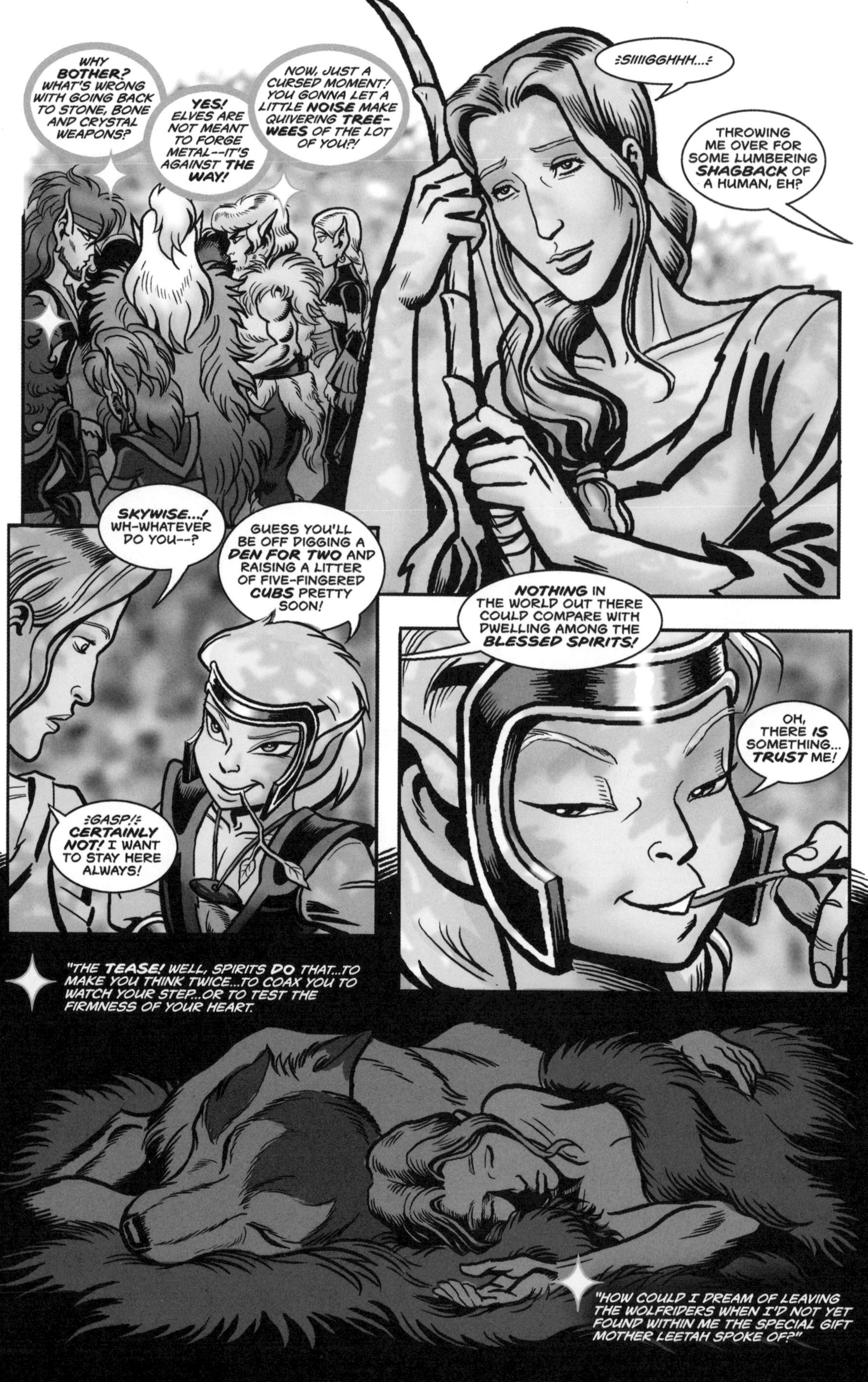
WHY BOTHER? WHAT'S WRONG WITH GOING BACK TO STONE, BONE AND CRYSTAL WEAPONS?
YES! ELVES ARE NOT MEANT TO FORGE METAL--IT'S AGAINST THE WAY!
NOW, JUST A CURSED MOMENT! YOU GONNA LET A LITTLE NOISE MAKE QUIVERING TREE-WEES OF THE LOT OF YOU?!
:SIIIIGGHHH...:
THROWING ME OVER FOR SOME LUMBERING SHAGBACK OF A HUMAN, EH?
SKYWISE...! WH-WHATEVER DO YOU--?
GUESS YOU'LL BE OFF DIGGING A DEN FOR TWO AND RAISING A LITTER OF FIVE-FINGERED CUBS PRETTY SOON!
:GASP!: CERTAINLY NOT! I WANT TO STAY HERE ALWAYS!
NOTHING IN THE WORLD OUT THERE COULD COMPARE WITH DWELLING AMONG THE BLESSED SPIRITS!
OH, THERE IS SOMETHING... TRUST ME!
"THE TEASE! WELL, SPIRITS DO THAT...TO MAKE YOU THINK TWICE...TO COAX YOU TO WATCH YOUR STEP...OR TO TEST THE FIRMNESS OF YOUR HEART.
"HOW COULD I DREAM OF LEAVING THE WOLFRIDERS WHEN I'D NOT YET FOUND WITHIN ME THE SPECIAL GIFT MOTHER LEETAH SPOKE OF?"

"A GIFT...MADE OF WHAT?
"THE ABILITY TO TAKE MY DRUNKARD SIRE'S BLOWS WITH-OUT A WHIMPER?
"PERHAPS COURAGE THAT CAME, FROM I KNOW NOT WHERE, TO DON HARNESS--
"--AND RAISE SWORD AGAINST A VICIOUS TYRANT FOR THE RIGHT OF ALL PEOPLE TO THINK AND BELIEVE AS THEY CHOOSE...
"...COURAGE THAT MADE THE ELVES NOT JUST ALLIES, BUT FAMILY?
"GOOD QUALITIES, ALL. BUT, TO THE WOLFRIDERS, NOT SPECIAL--NO MORE HEROIC THAN THEIR RUGGED WAYS DEMAND.
"MY GIFT, MOTHER LEETAH... WHAT IS IT?
"CAN THE HANDSOME HUNTER SHOW ME?
"YES... YES! I SEE HIM DANCING IN CELEBRATION-- AS BEAUTIFUL, IN HIS WAY, AS ANY ELF...
"AND WATCHING HIM, SIDE BY SIDE, WOLFRIDERS AND HUMANS IN A CIRCLE OF FRIENDSHIP AND TRUST!"

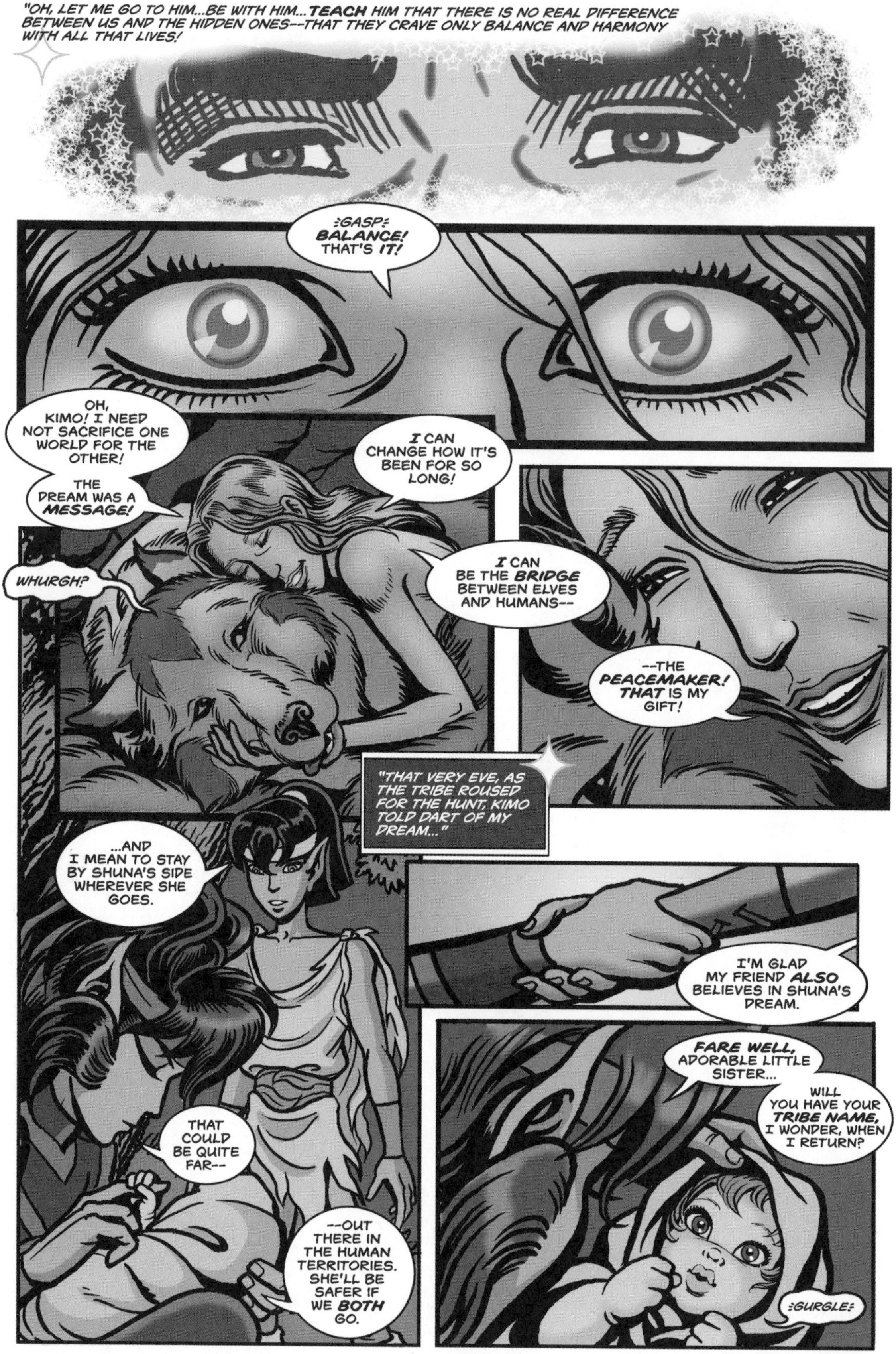
"OH, LET ME GO TO HIM...BE WITH HIM...TEACH HIM THAT THERE IS NO REAL DIFFERENCE BETWEEN US AND THE HIDDEN ONES--THAT THEY CRAVE ONLY BALANCE AND HARMONY WITH ALL THAT LIVES!
:GASP: BALANCE! THAT'S IT!
OH, KIMO! I NEED NOT SACRIFICE ONE WORLD FOR THE OTHER!
THE DREAM WAS A MESSAGE!
I CAN CHANGE HOW IT'S BEEN FOR SO LONG!
WHURGH?
I CAN BE THE BRIDGE BETWEEN ELVES AND HUMANS--
--THE PEACEMAKER! THAT IS MY GIFT!
"THAT VERY EVE, AS THE TRIBE ROUSED FOR THE HUNT, KIMO TOLD DART OF MY DREAM..."
...AND I MEAN TO STAY BY SHUNA'S SIDE WHEREVER SHE GOES.
THAT COULD BE QUITE FAR--
--OUT THERE IN THE HUMAN TERRITORIES. SHE'LL BE SAFER IF WE BOTH GO.
I'M GLAD MY FRIEND ALSO BELIEVES IN SHUNA'S DREAM.
FARE WELL, ADORABLE LITTLE SISTER...
WILL YOU HAVE YOUR TRIBE NAME, I WONDER, WHEN I RETURN?
:GURGLE:

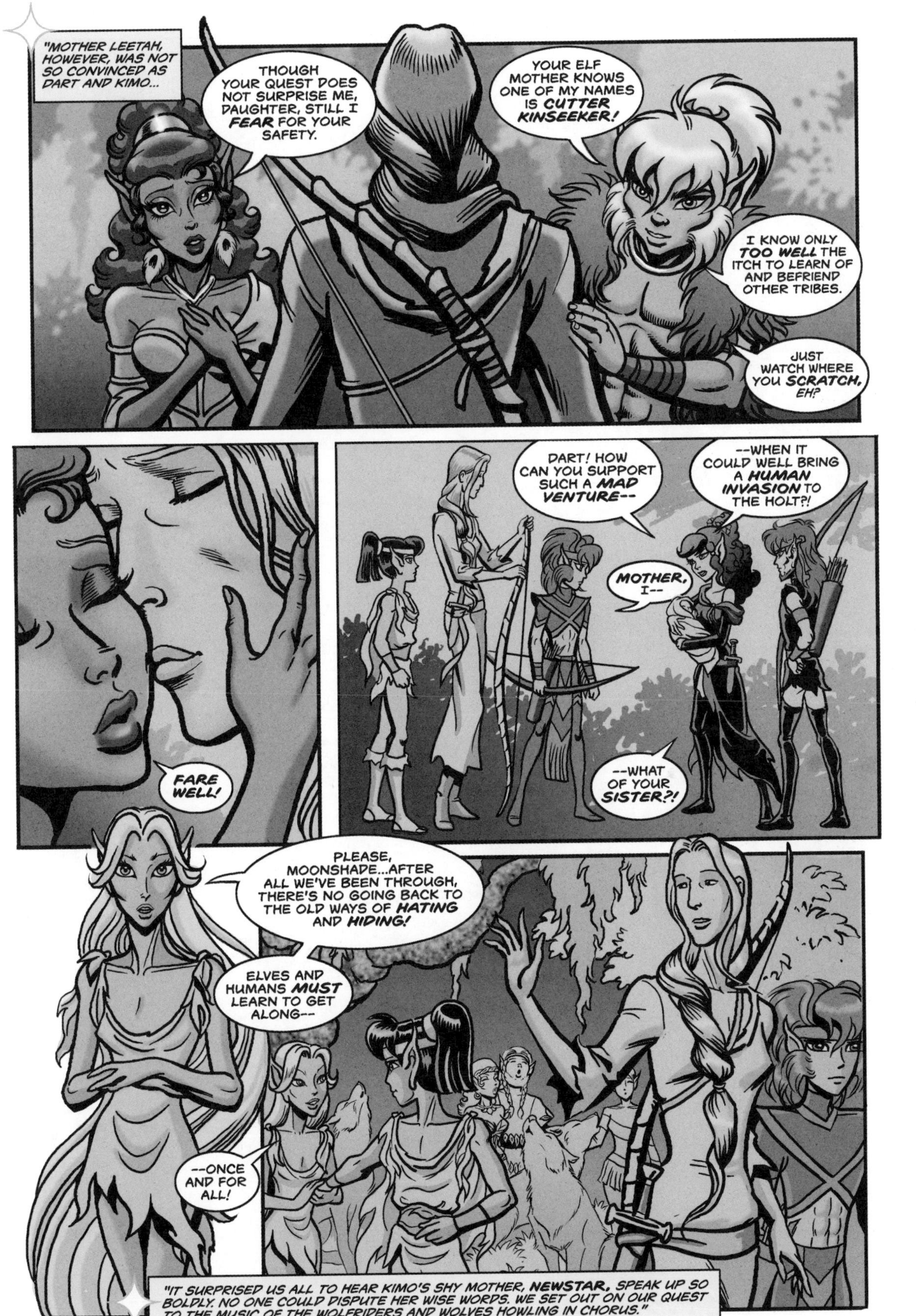
"MOTHER LEETAH, HOWEVER, WAS NOT SO CONVINCED AS DART AND KIMO...
THOUGH YOUR QUEST DOES NOT SURPRISE ME, DAUGHTER, STILL I FEAR FOR YOUR SAFETY.
YOUR ELF MOTHER KNOWS ONE OF MY NAMES IS CUTTER KINSEEKER!
I KNOW ONLY TOO WELL THE ITCH TO LEARN OF AND BEFRIEND OTHER TRIBES.
JUST WATCH WHERE YOU SCRATCH, EH?
FARE WELL!
DART! HOW CAN YOU SUPPORT SUCH A MAD VENTURE--
--WHEN IT COULD WELL BRING A HUMAN INVASION TO THE HOLT?!
MOTHER, I--
--WHAT OF YOUR SISTER?!
PLEASE, MOONSHADE...AFTER ALL WE'VE BEEN THROUGH, THERE'S NO GOING BACK TO THE OLD WAYS OF HATING AND HIDING!
ELVES AND HUMANS MUST LEARN TO GET ALONG--
--ONCE AND FOR ALL!
"IT SURPRISED US ALL TO HEAR KIMO'S SHY MOTHER, NEWSTAR, SPEAK UP SO BOLDLY. NO ONE COULD DISPUTE HER WISE WORDS. WE SET OUT ON OUR QUEST TO THE MUSIC OF THE WOLFRIDERS AND WOLVES HOWLING IN CHORUS."

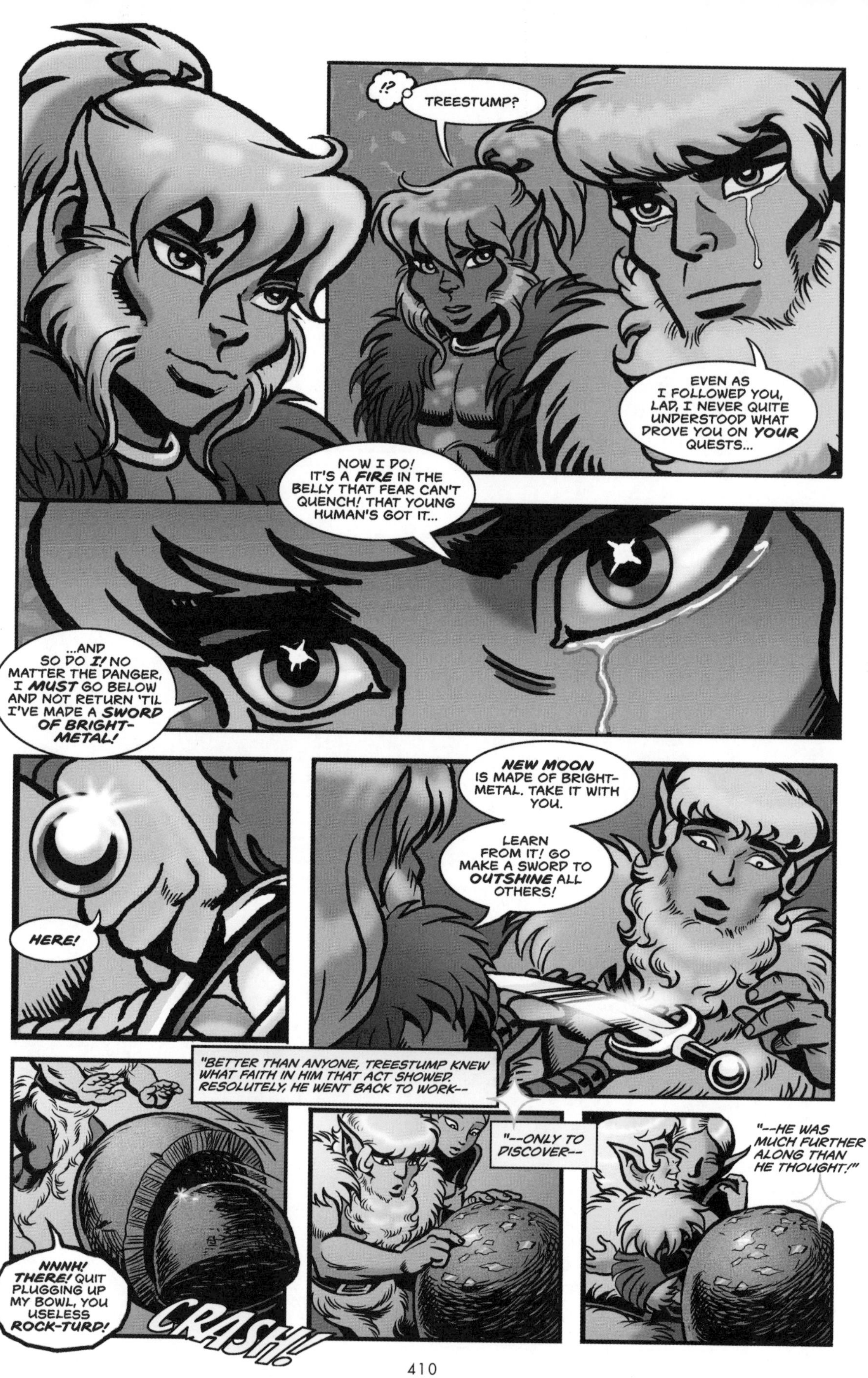
!?
TREESTUMP?
EVEN AS I FOLLOWED YOU, LAD, I NEVER QUITE UNDERSTOOD WHAT DROVE YOU ON YOUR QUESTS...
NOW I DO! IT'S A FIRE IN THE BELLY THAT FEAR CAN'T QUENCH! THAT YOUNG HUMAN'S GOT IT...
...AND SO DO I! NO MATTER THE DANGER, I MUST GO BELOW AND NOT RETURN 'TIL I'VE MADE A SWORD OF BRIGHT-METAL!
HERE!
NEW MOON IS MADE OF BRIGHT-METAL. TAKE IT WITH YOU.
LEARN FROM IT! GO MAKE A SWORD TO OUTSHINE ALL OTHERS!
"BETTER THAN ANYONE, TREESTUMP KNEW WHAT FAITH IN HIM THAT ACT SHOWED. RESOLUTELY, HE WENT BACK TO WORK--
NNNH! THERE! QUIT PLUGGING UP MY BOWL, YOU USELESS ROCK-TURD!
CRASH!
"--ONLY TO DISCOVER--
"--HE WAS MUCH FURTHER ALONG THAN HE THOUGHT!"

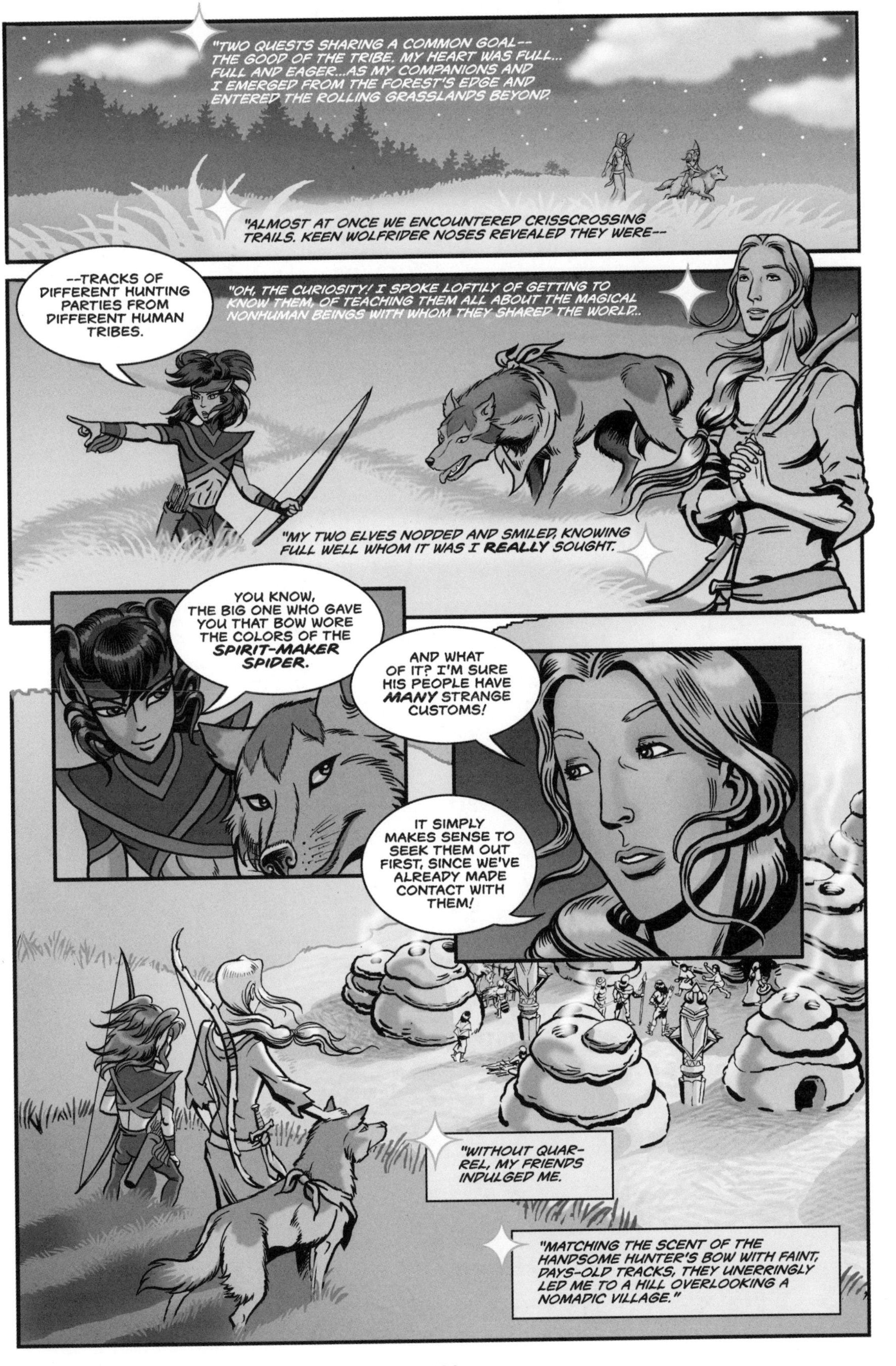
"TWO QUESTS SHARING A COMMON GOAL-- THE GOOD OF THE TRIBE. MY HEART WAS FULL... FULL AND EAGER...AS MY COMPANIONS AND I EMERGED FROM THE FOREST'S EDGE AND ENTERED THE ROLLING GRASSLANDS BEYOND.
"ALMOST AT ONCE WE ENCOUNTERED CRISSCROSSING TRAILS. KEEN WOLFRIDER NOSES REVEALED THEY WERE--
--TRACKS OF DIFFERENT HUNTING PARTIES FROM DIFFERENT HUMAN TRIBES.
"OH, THE CURIOSITY! I SPOKE LOFTILY OF GETTING TO KNOW THEM, OF TEACHING THEM ALL ABOUT THE MAGICAL NONHUMAN BEINGS WITH WHOM THEY SHARED THE WORLD...
"MY TWO ELVES NODDED AND SMILED, KNOWING FULL WELL WHOM IT WAS I REALLY SOUGHT.
YOU KNOW, THE BIG ONE WHO GAVE YOU THAT BOW WORE THE COLORS OF THE SPIRIT-MAKER SPIDER.
AND WHAT OF IT? I'M SURE HIS PEOPLE HAVE MANY STRANGE CUSTOMS!
IT SIMPLY MAKES SENSE TO SEEK THEM OUT FIRST, SINCE WE'VE ALREADY MADE CONTACT WITH THEM!
"WITHOUT QUARREL, MY FRIENDS INDULGED ME.
"MATCHING THE SCENT OF THE HANDSOME HUNTER'S BOW WITH FAINT, DAYS-OLD TRACKS, THEY UNERRINGLY LED ME TO A HILL OVERLOOKING A NOMADIC VILLAGE."

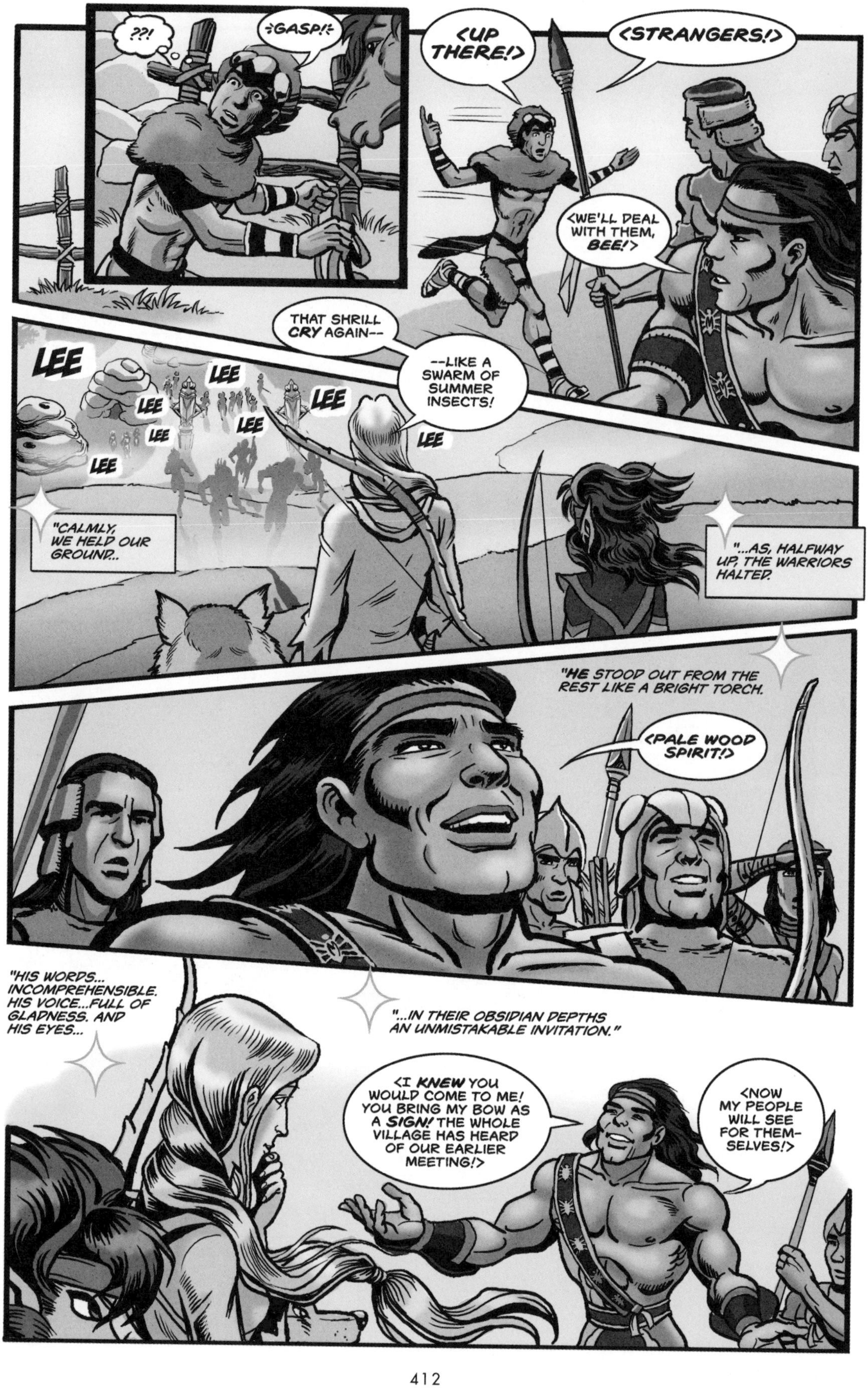
??!
-GASP!-
<UP THERE!>
<STRANGERS!>
<WE'LL DEAL WITH THEM, BEE!>
THAT SHRILL CRY AGAIN--
--LIKE A SWARM OF SUMMER INSECTS!
LEE
LEE
LEE
LEE
LEE
LEE
LEE
LEE
"CALMLY, WE HELD OUR GROUND...
"...AS, HALFWAY UP, THE WARRIORS HALTED.
"HE STOOD OUT FROM THE REST LIKE A BRIGHT TORCH.
<PALE WOOD SPIRIT!>
"HIS WORDS... INCOMPREHENSIBLE. HIS VOICE...FULL OF GLADNESS. AND HIS EYES...
"...IN THEIR OBSIDIAN DEPTHS AN UNMISTAKABLE INVITATION."
<I KNEW YOU WOULD COME TO ME! YOU BRING MY BOW AS A SIGN! THE WHOLE VILLAGE HAS HEARD OF OUR EARLIER MEETING!>
<NOW MY PEOPLE WILL SEE FOR THEMSELVES!>

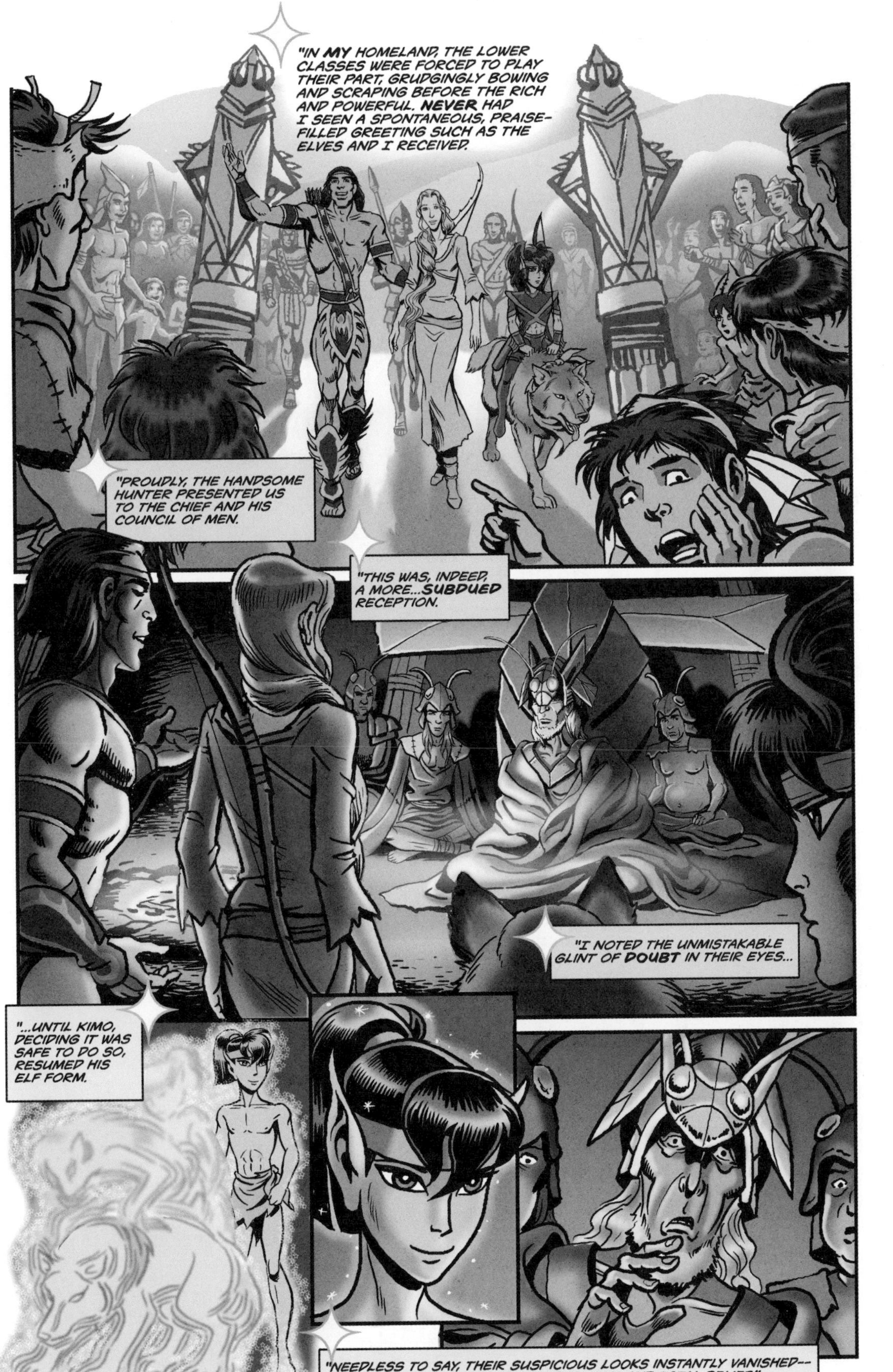
"IN MY HOMELAND, THE LOWER CLASSES WERE FORCED TO PLAY THEIR PART, GRUDGINGLY BOWING AND SCRAPING BEFORE THE RICH AND POWERFUL. NEVER HAD I SEEN A SPONTANEOUS, PRAISE-FILLED GREETING SUCH AS THE ELVES AND I RECEIVED.
"PROUDLY, THE HANDSOME HUNTER PRESENTED US TO THE CHIEF AND HIS COUNCIL OF MEN.
"THIS WAS, INDEED, A MORE... SUBDUED RECEPTION.
"I NOTED THE UNMISTAKABLE GLINT OF DOUBT IN THEIR EYES...
"...UNTIL KIMO, DECIDING IT WAS SAFE TO DO SO, RESUMED HIS ELF FORM.
"NEEDLESS TO SAY, THEIR SUSPICIOUS LOOKS INSTANTLY VANISHED-- REPLACED, THANKFULLY, BY WONDERMENT AND TOTAL BELIEF."

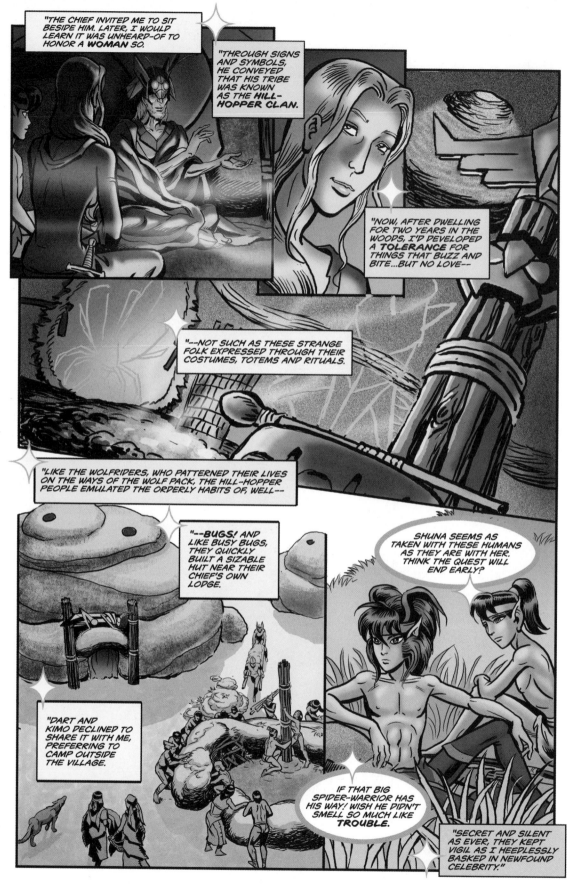

"THE CHIEF INVITED ME TO SIT BESIDE HIM. LATER, I WOULD LEARN IT WAS UNHEARD-OF TO HONOR A **WOMAN** SO.

"THROUGH SIGNS AND SYMBOLS, HE CONVEYED THAT HIS TRIBE WAS KNOWN AS THE HILL-HOPPER CLAN.

"NOW, AFTER DWELLING FOR TWO YEARS IN THE WOODS, I'D DEVELOPED A **TOLERANCE** FOR THINGS THAT BUZZ AND BITE...BUT NO LOVE--

"--NOT SUCH AS THESE STRANGE FOLK EXPRESSED THROUGH THEIR COSTUMES, TOTEMS AND RITUALS.

"LIKE THE WOLFRIDERS, WHO PATTERNED THEIR LIVES ON THE WAYS OF THE WOLF PACK, THE HILL-HOPPER PEOPLE EMULATED THE ORDERLY HABITS OF, WELL--

"--**BUGS!** AND LIKE BUSY BUGS, THEY QUICKLY BUILT A SIZABLE HUT NEAR THEIR CHIEF'S OWN LODGE.

"DART AND KIMO DECLINED TO SHARE IT WITH ME, PREFERRING TO CAMP OUTSIDE THE VILLAGE.

SHUNA SEEMS AS TAKEN WITH THESE HUMANS AS THEY ARE WITH HER. THINK THE QUEST WILL END EARLY?

IF THAT BIG SPIDER-WARRIOR HAS HIS WAY! WISH HE DIDN'T SMELL SO MUCH LIKE **TROUBLE.**

"SECRET AND SILENT AS EVER, THEY KEPT VIGIL AS I HEEDLESSLY BASKED IN NEWFOUND CELEBRITY."

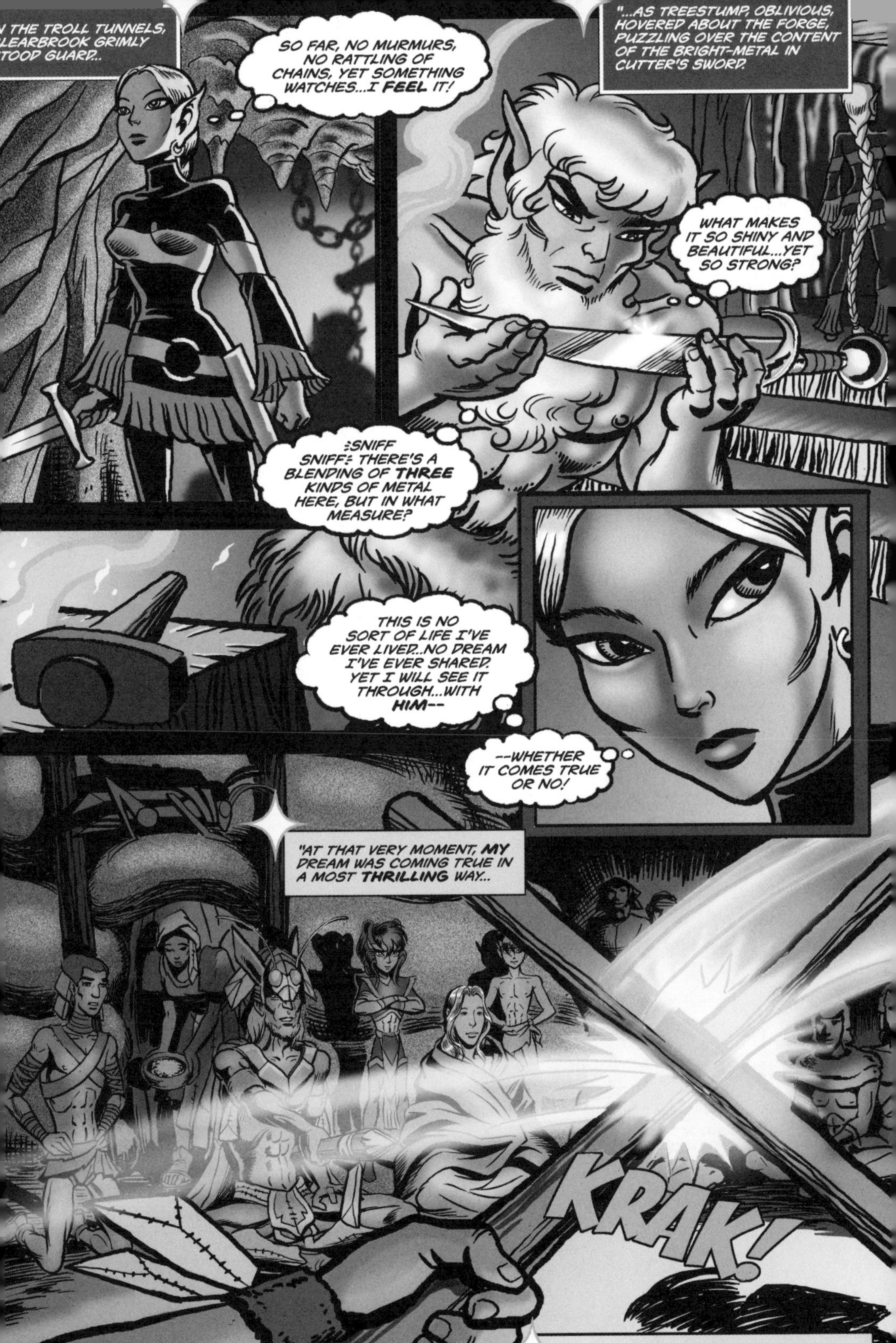

N THE TROLL TUNNELS, LEARBROOK GRIMLY STOOD GUARD..
SO FAR, NO MURMURS, NO RATTLING OF CHAINS, YET SOMETHING WATCHES...I FEEL IT!
"...AS TREESTUMP, OBLIVIOUS, HOVERED ABOUT THE FORGE, PUZZLING OVER THE CONTENT OF THE BRIGHT-METAL IN CUTTER'S SWORD.
WHAT MAKES IT SO SHINY AND BEAUTIFUL...YET SO STRONG?
:SNIFF SNIFF: THERE'S A BLENDING OF THREE KINDS OF METAL HERE, BUT IN WHAT MEASURE?
THIS IS NO SORT OF LIFE I'VE EVER LIVED...NO DREAM I'VE EVER SHARED. YET I WILL SEE IT THROUGH...WITH HIM--
--WHETHER IT COMES TRUE OR NO!
"AT THAT VERY MOMENT, MY DREAM WAS COMING TRUE IN A MOST THRILLING WAY...
KRAK!
"...A SPECTACLE OF COMBAT SKILLS AND DANCE TO HONOR THE "WOOD SPIRITS." A FEAST FOR THE SENSES...AND AN EDUCATION FOR THE MIND AND HEART."

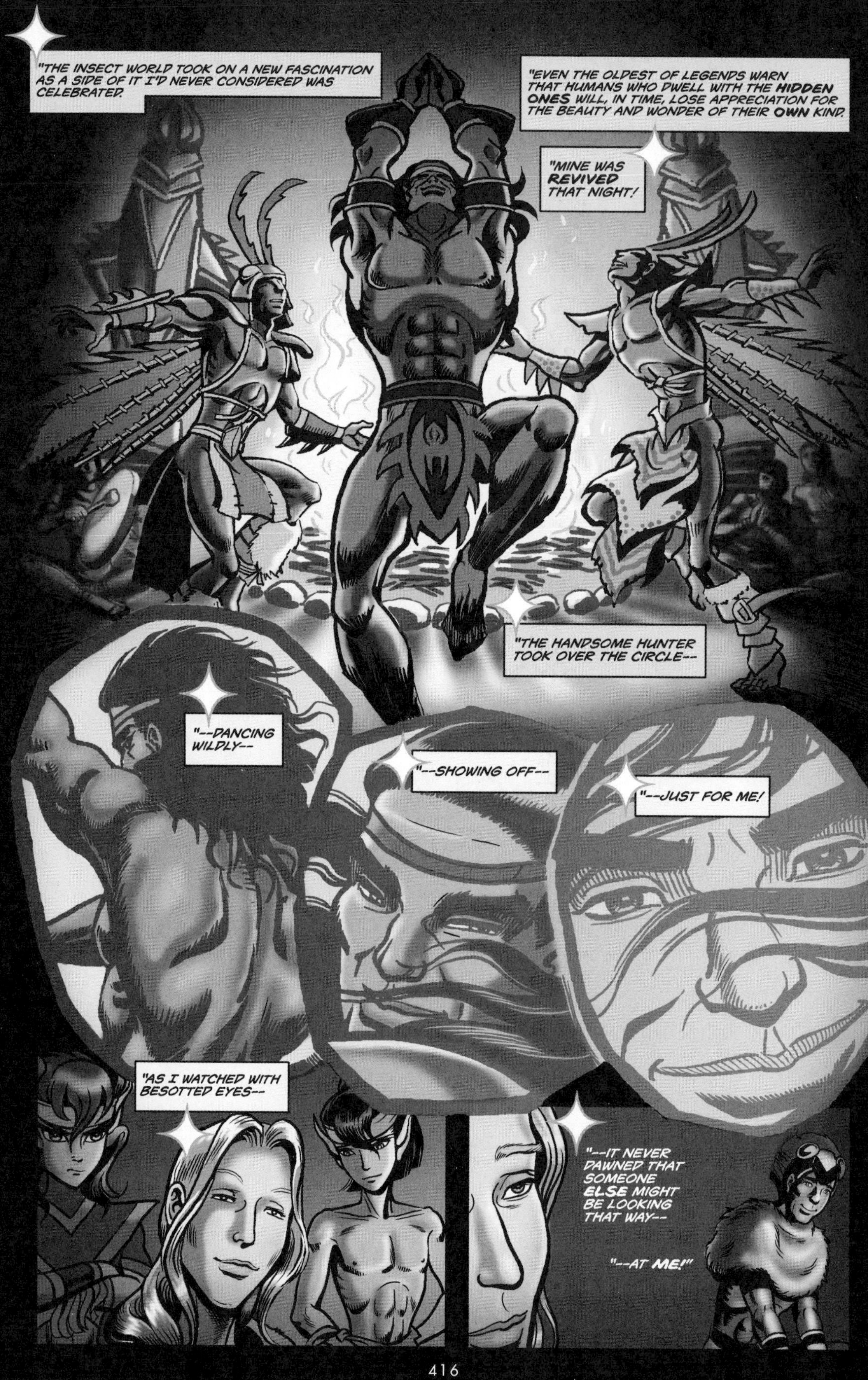
"THE INSECT WORLD TOOK ON A NEW FASCINATION AS A SIDE OF IT I'D NEVER CONSIDERED WAS CELEBRATED.
"EVEN THE OLDEST OF LEGENDS WARN THAT HUMANS WHO DWELL WITH THE HIDDEN ONES WILL, IN TIME, LOSE APPRECIATION FOR THE BEAUTY AND WONDER OF THEIR OWN KIND.
"MINE WAS REVIVED THAT NIGHT!
"THE HANDSOME HUNTER TOOK OVER THE CIRCLE--
"--DANCING WILDLY--
"--SHOWING OFF--
"--JUST FOR ME!
"AS I WATCHED WITH BESOTTED EYES--
"--IT NEVER DAWNED THAT SOMEONE ELSE MIGHT BE LOOKING THAT WAY--
"--AT ME!"

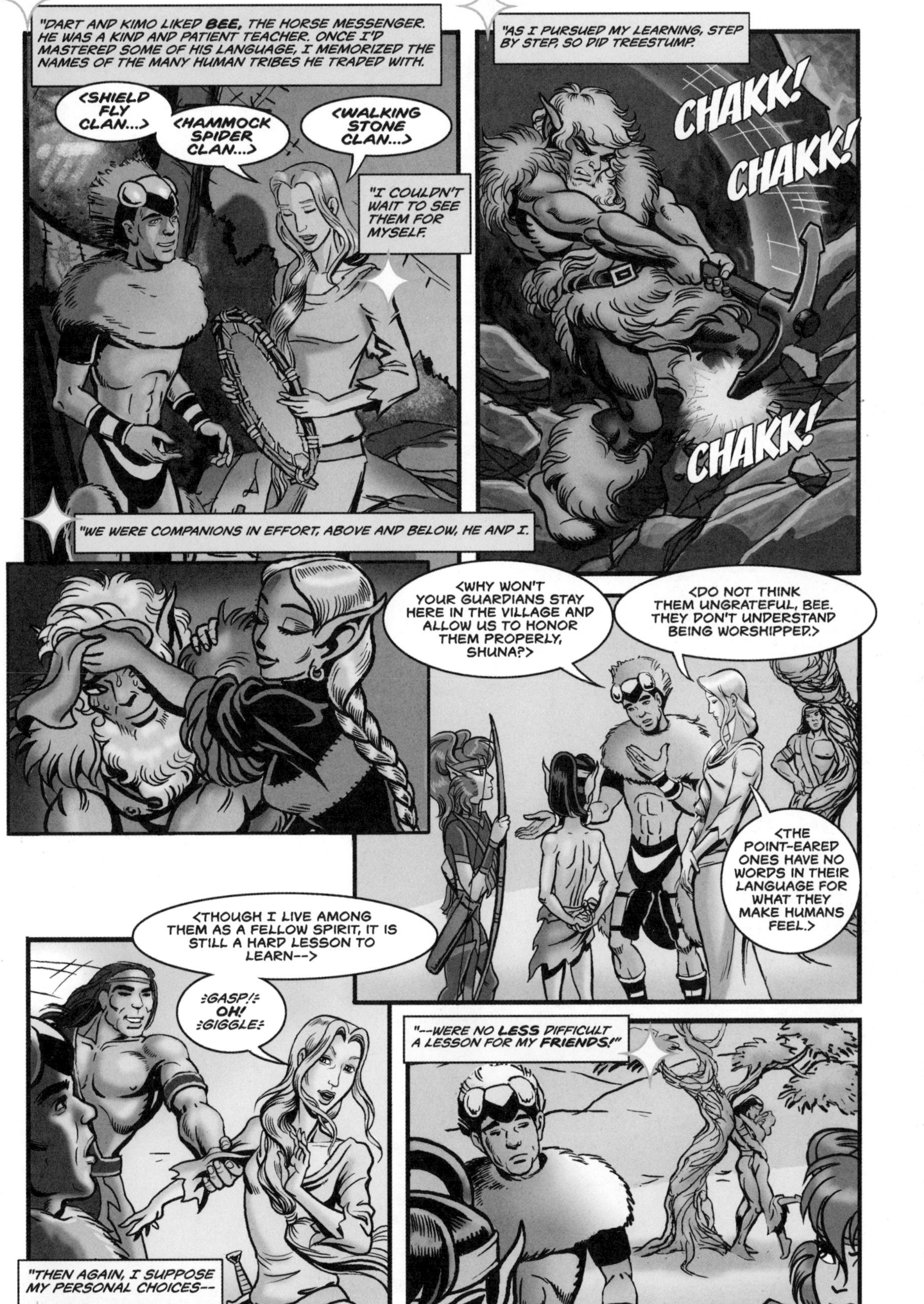
"DART AND KIMO LIKED BEE, THE HORSE MESSENGER. HE WAS A KIND AND PATIENT TEACHER. ONCE I'D MASTERED SOME OF HIS LANGUAGE, I MEMORIZED THE NAMES OF THE MANY HUMAN TRIBES HE TRADED WITH.
<SHIELD FLY CLAN...>
<HAMMOCK SPIDER CLAN...>
<WALKING STONE CLAN...>
"I COULDN'T WAIT TO SEE THEM FOR MYSELF.
"WE WERE COMPANIONS IN EFFORT, ABOVE AND BELOW, HE AND I.
"AS I PURSUED MY LEARNING, STEP BY STEP, SO DID TREESTUMP.
CHAKK!
CHAKK!
CHAKK!
<WHY WON'T YOUR GUARDIANS STAY HERE IN THE VILLAGE AND ALLOW US TO HONOR THEM PROPERLY, SHUNA?>
<DO NOT THINK THEM UNGRATEFUL, BEE. THEY DON'T UNDERSTAND BEING WORSHIPPED.>
<THE POINT-EARED ONES HAVE NO WORDS IN THEIR LANGUAGE FOR WHAT THEY MAKE HUMANS FEEL.>
<THOUGH I LIVE AMONG THEM AS A FELLOW SPIRIT, IT IS STILL A HARD LESSON TO LEARN-->
:GASP!: OH! :GIGGLE:
"THEN AGAIN, I SUPPOSE MY PERSONAL CHOICES--
"--WERE NO LESS DIFFICULT A LESSON FOR MY FRIENDS!"

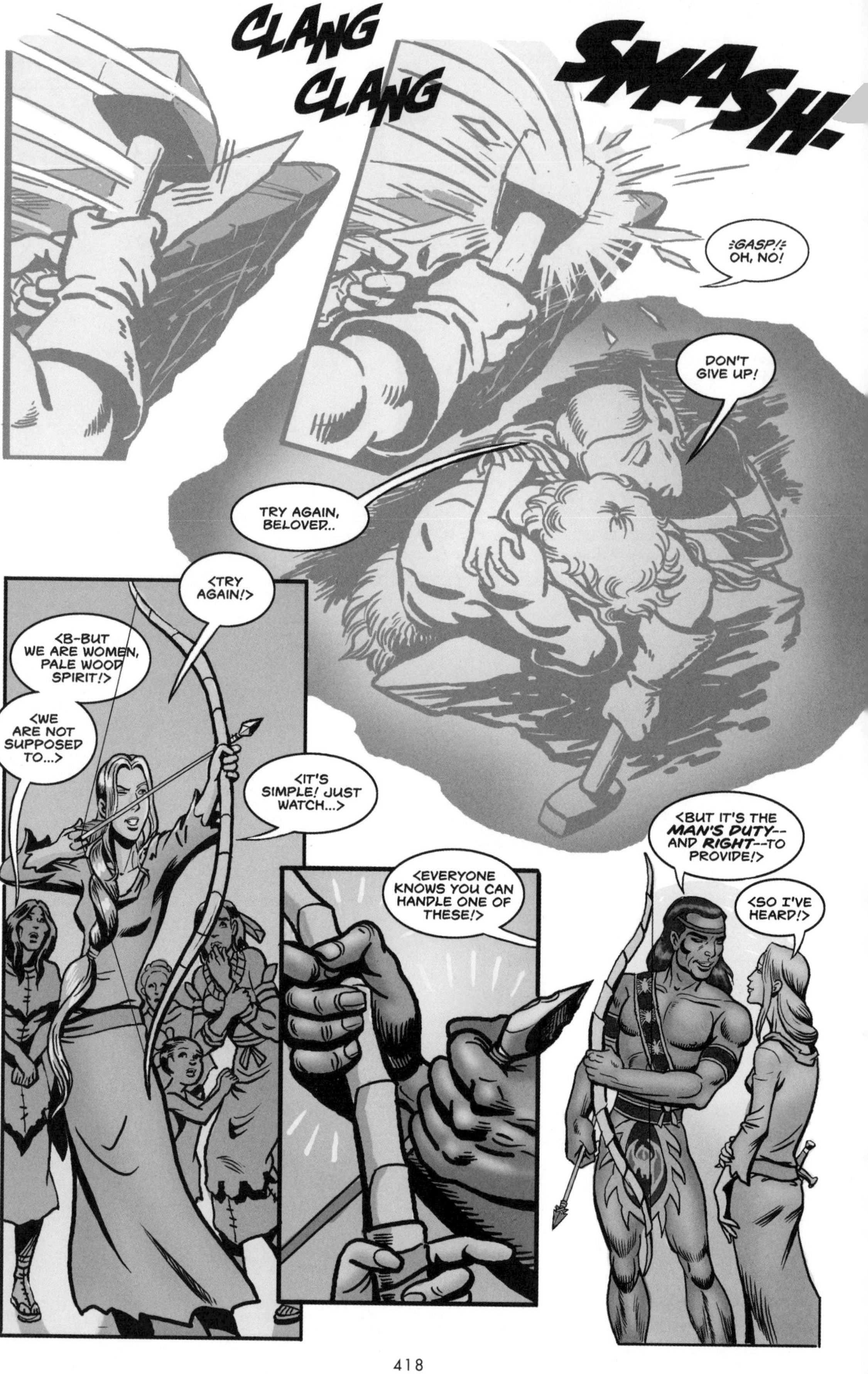
CLANG
CLANG
SMASH!
:GASP!: OH, NO!
DON'T GIVE UP!
TRY AGAIN, BELOVED...
<TRY AGAIN!>
<B-BUT WE ARE WOMEN, PALE WOOD SPIRIT!>
<WE ARE NOT SUPPOSED TO...>
<IT'S SIMPLE! JUST WATCH...>
<EVERYONE KNOWS YOU CAN HANDLE ONE OF THESE!>
<BUT IT'S THE MAN'S DUTY-- AND RIGHT--TO PROVIDE!>
<SO I'VE HEARD!>

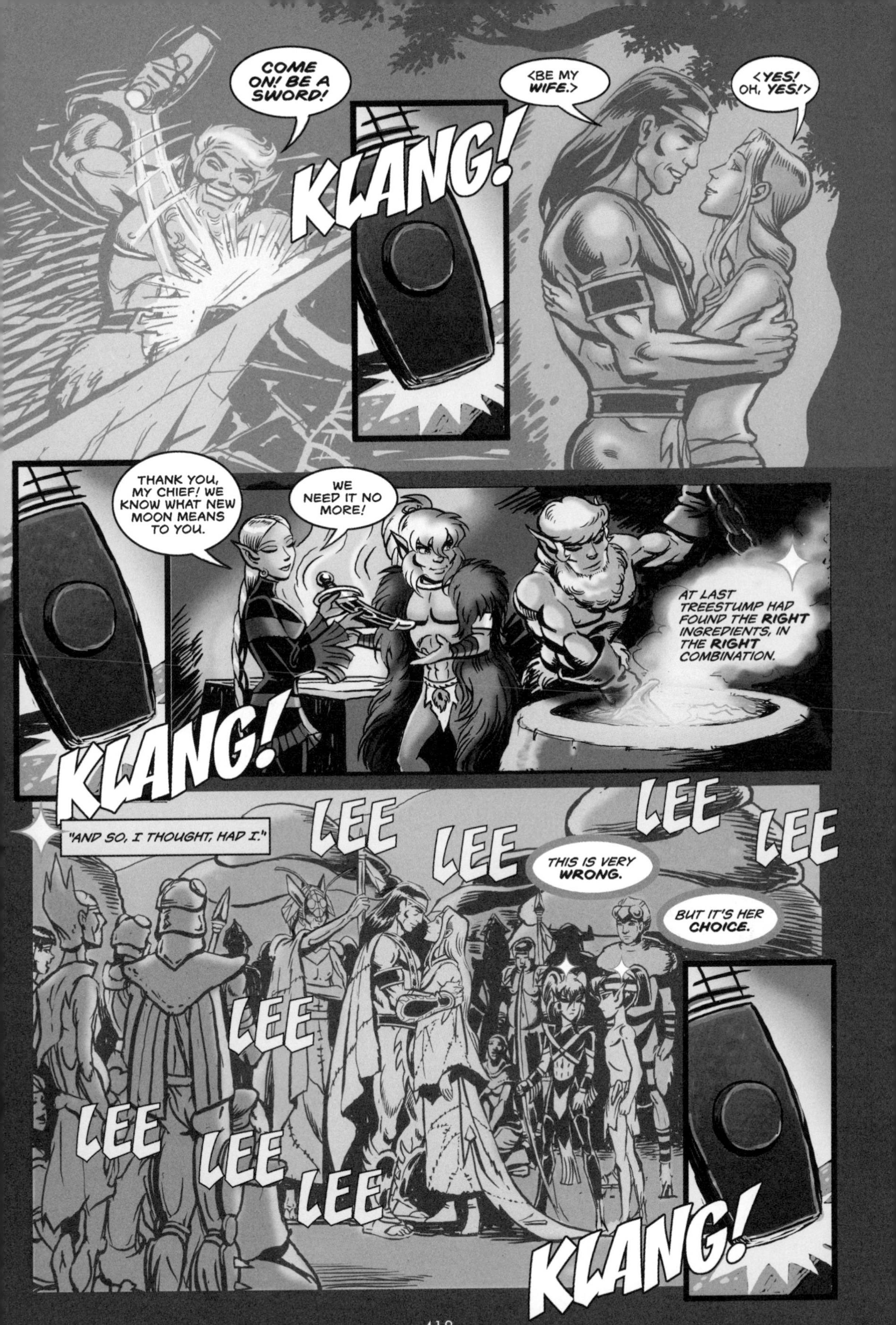
COME ON! BE A SWORD!
KLANG!
<BE MY WIFE.>
<YES! OH, YES!>
THANK YOU, MY CHIEF! WE KNOW WHAT NEW MOON MEANS TO YOU.
WE NEED IT NO MORE!
AT LAST TREESTUMP HAD FOUND THE RIGHT INGREDIENTS, IN THE RIGHT COMBINATION.
KLANG!
"AND SO, I THOUGHT, HAD I."
LEE LEE LEE LEE
THIS IS VERY WRONG.
BUT IT'S HER CHOICE.
LEE LEE LEE LEE
KLANG!

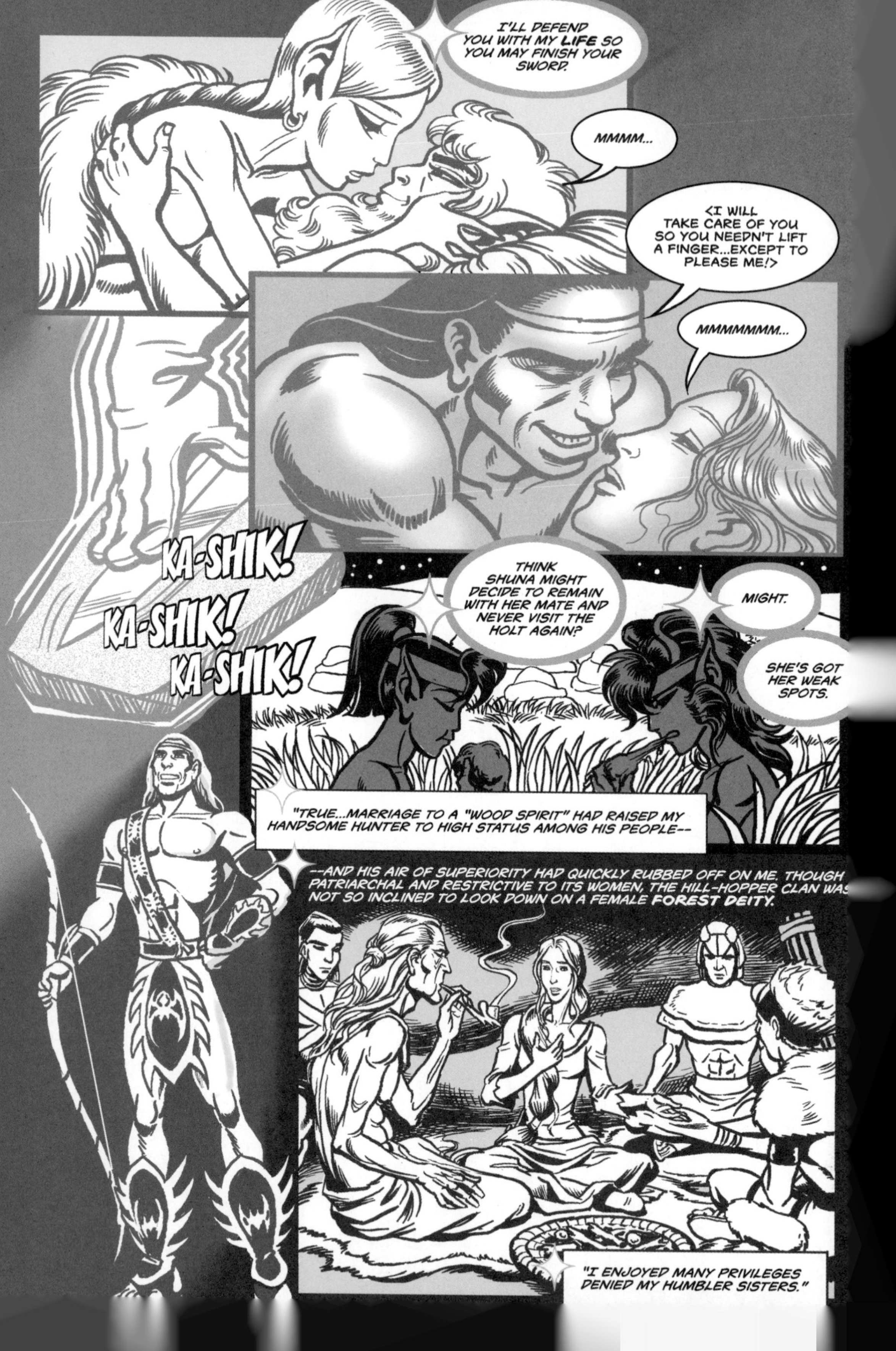
I'LL DEFEND YOU WITH MY LIFE SO YOU MAY FINISH YOUR SWORD.
MMMM...
<I WILL TAKE CARE OF YOU SO YOU NEEDN'T LIFT A FINGER...EXCEPT TO PLEASE ME!>
MMMMMMM...
KA-SHIK!
KA-SHIK!
KA-SHIK!
THINK SHUNA MIGHT DECIDE TO REMAIN WITH HER MATE AND NEVER VISIT THE HOLT AGAIN?
MIGHT.
SHE'S GOT HER WEAK SPOTS.
"TRUE...MARRIAGE TO A "WOOD SPIRIT" HAD RAISED MY HANDSOME HUNTER TO HIGH STATUS AMONG HIS PEOPLE--
--AND HIS AIR OF SUPERIORITY HAD QUICKLY RUBBED OFF ON ME. THOUGH PATRIARCHAL AND RESTRICTIVE TO ITS WOMEN, THE HILL-HOPPER CLAN WAS NOT SO INCLINED TO LOOK DOWN ON A FEMALE FOREST DEITY.
"I ENJOYED MANY PRIVILEGES DENIED MY HUMBLER SISTERS."

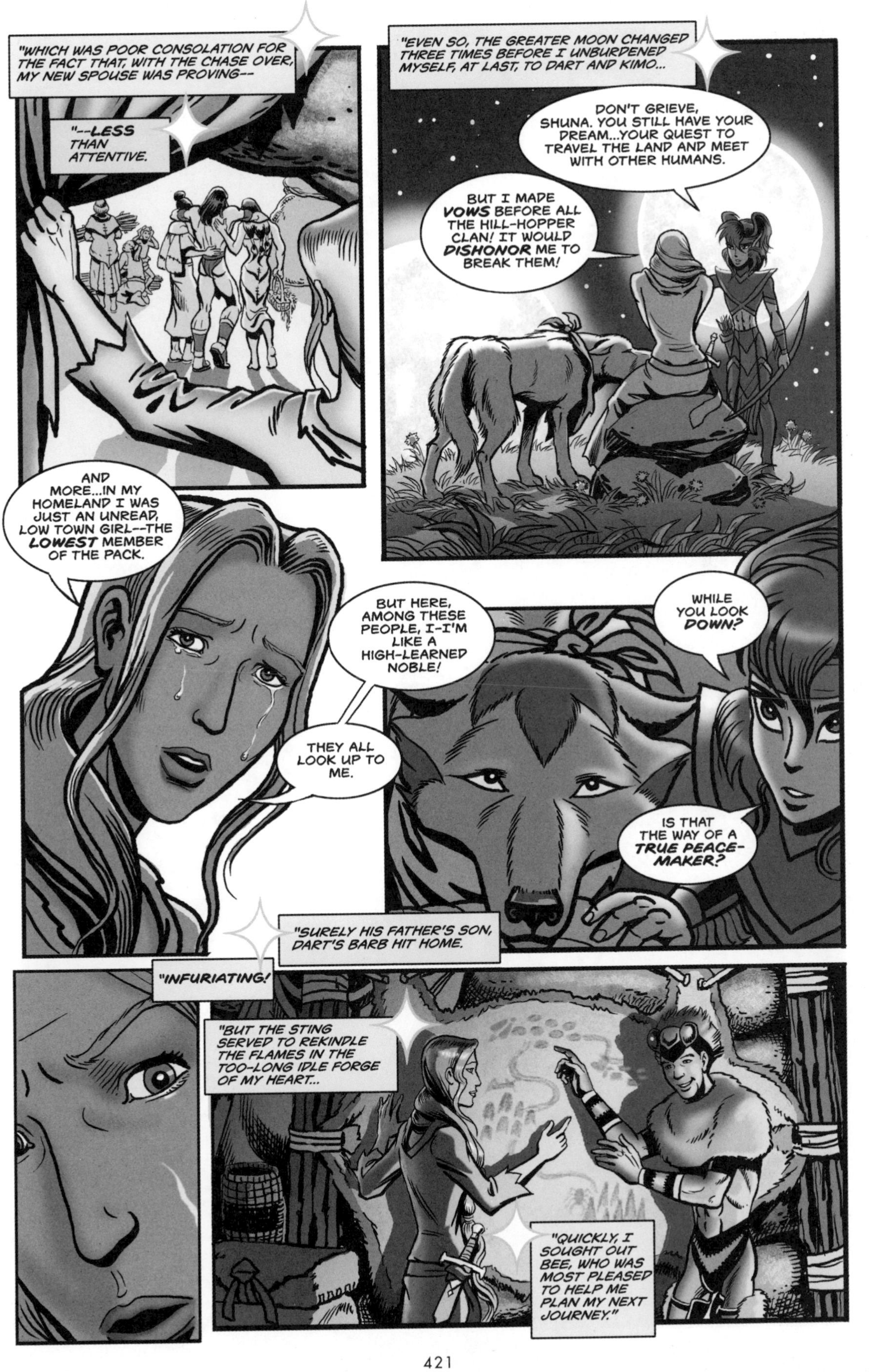
"WHICH WAS POOR CONSOLATION FOR THE FACT THAT, WITH THE CHASE OVER, MY NEW SPOUSE WAS PROVING--
"--LESS THAN ATTENTIVE.
"EVEN SO, THE GREATER MOON CHANGED THREE TIMES BEFORE I UNBURDENED MYSELF, AT LAST, TO DART AND KIMO...
DON'T GRIEVE, SHUNA. YOU STILL HAVE YOUR DREAM...YOUR QUEST TO TRAVEL THE LAND AND MEET WITH OTHER HUMANS.
BUT I MADE VOWS BEFORE ALL THE HILL-HOPPER CLAN! IT WOULD DISHONOR ME TO BREAK THEM!
AND MORE...IN MY HOMELAND I WAS JUST AN UNREAD, LOW TOWN GIRL--THE LOWEST MEMBER OF THE PACK.
BUT HERE, AMONG THESE PEOPLE, I-I'M LIKE A HIGH-LEARNED NOBLE!
THEY ALL LOOK UP TO ME.
WHILE YOU LOOK DOWN?
IS THAT THE WAY OF A TRUE PEACE-MAKER?
"SURELY HIS FATHER'S SON, DART'S BARB HIT HOME.
"INFURIATING!
"BUT THE STING SERVED TO REKINDLE THE FLAMES IN THE TOO-LONG IDLE FORGE OF MY HEART...
"QUICKLY, I SOUGHT OUT BEE, WHO WAS MOST PLEASED TO HELP ME PLAN MY NEXT JOURNEY."

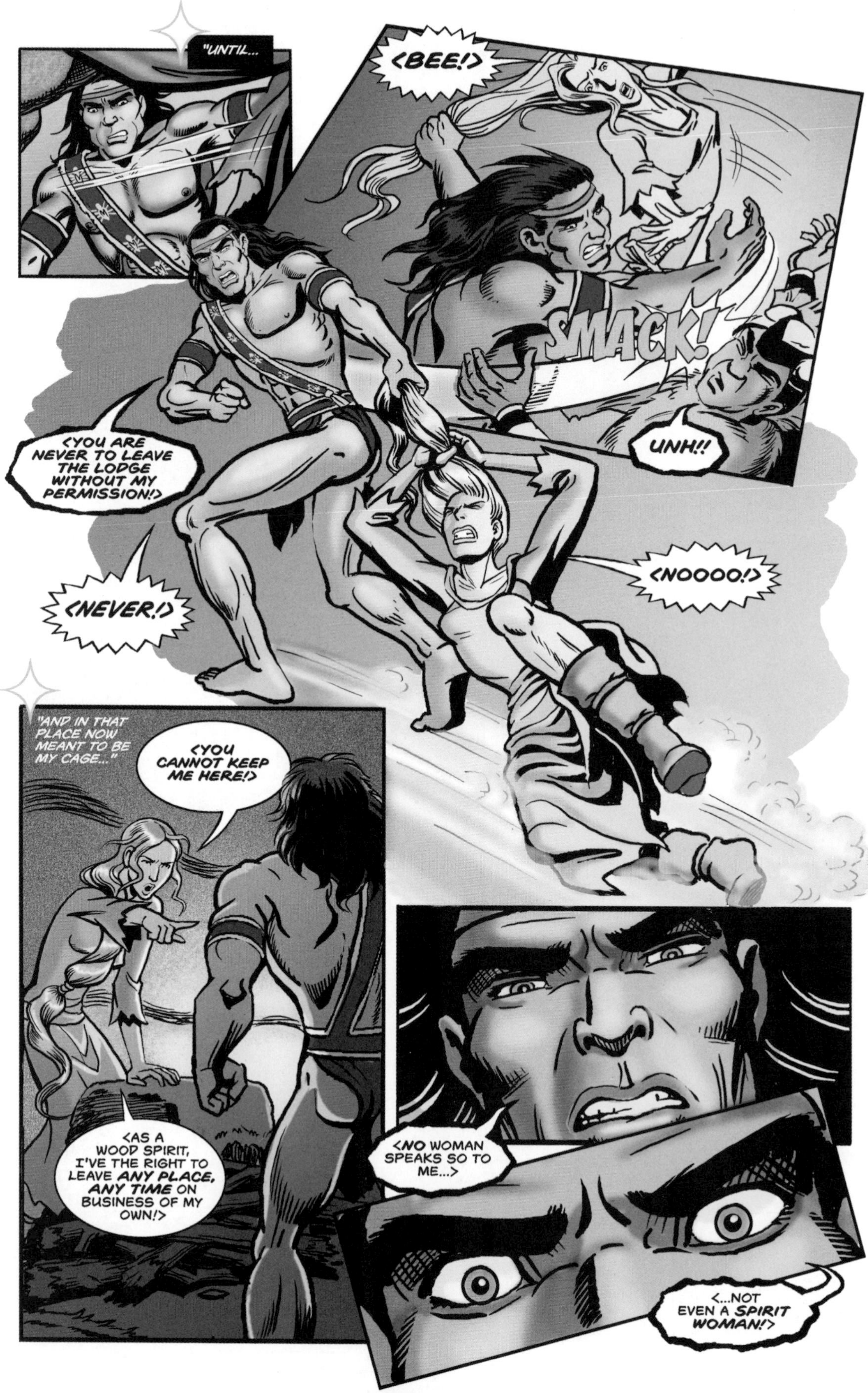
"UNTIL...
<BEE!>
SMACK!
UNH!!
<YOU ARE NEVER TO LEAVE THE LODGE WITHOUT MY PERMISSION!>
<NEVER!>
<NOOOO!>
"AND IN THAT PLACE NOW MEANT TO BE MY CAGE..."
<YOU CANNOT KEEP ME HERE!>
<AS A WOOD SPIRIT, I'VE THE RIGHT TO LEAVE ANY PLACE, ANY TIME ON BUSINESS OF MY OWN!>
<NO WOMAN SPEAKS SO TO ME...>
<...NOT EVEN A SPIRIT WOMAN!>

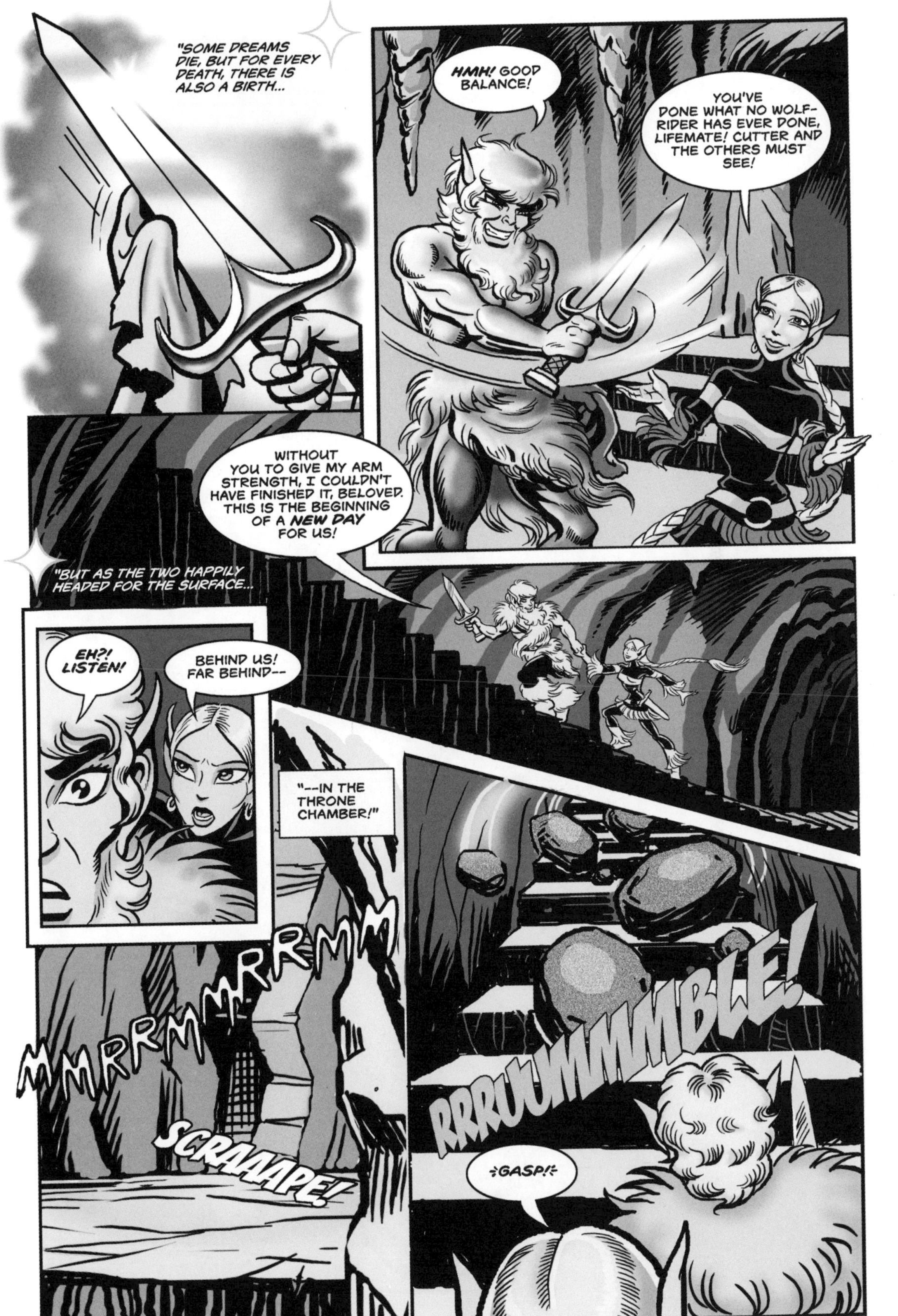
"SOME DREAMS DIE, BUT FOR EVERY DEATH, THERE IS ALSO A BIRTH...
HMH! GOOD BALANCE!
YOU'VE DONE WHAT NO WOLF-RIDER HAS EVER DONE, LIFEMATE! CUTTER AND THE OTHERS MUST SEE!
WITHOUT YOU TO GIVE MY ARM STRENGTH, I COULDN'T HAVE FINISHED IT, BELOVED. THIS IS THE BEGINNING OF A NEW DAY FOR US!
"BUT AS THE TWO HAPPILY HEADED FOR THE SURFACE...
EH?! LISTEN!
BEHIND US! FAR BEHIND--
"--IN THE THRONE CHAMBER!"
MMRRMMRRMM
SCRAAAPE!
RRRUMMMMBLE!
GASP!

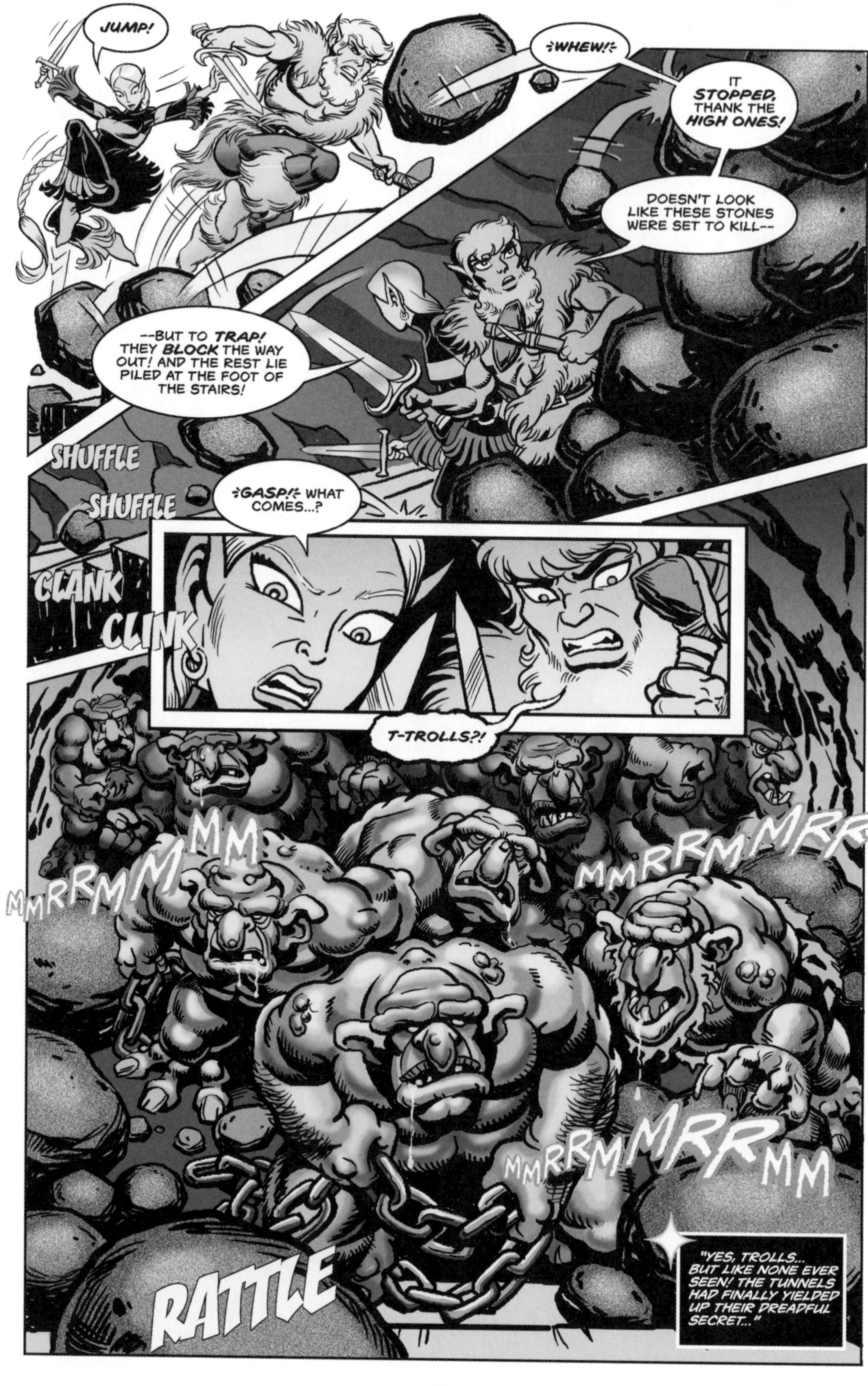

JUMP!
WHEW!
IT STOPPED, THANK THE HIGH ONES!
DOESN'T LOOK LIKE THESE STONES WERE SET TO KILL--
--BUT TO TRAP! THEY BLOCK THE WAY OUT! AND THE REST LIE PILED AT THE FOOT OF THE STAIRS!
SHUFFLE
SHUFFLE
GASP! WHAT COMES...?
CLANK
CLINK
T-TROLLS?!
MMRRMMMM
MMRRMMMRR
MMRRMMRRMM
RATTLE
"YES, TROLLS... BUT LIKE NONE EVER SEEN! THE TUNNELS HAD FINALLY YIELDED UP THEIR DREADFUL SECRET..."

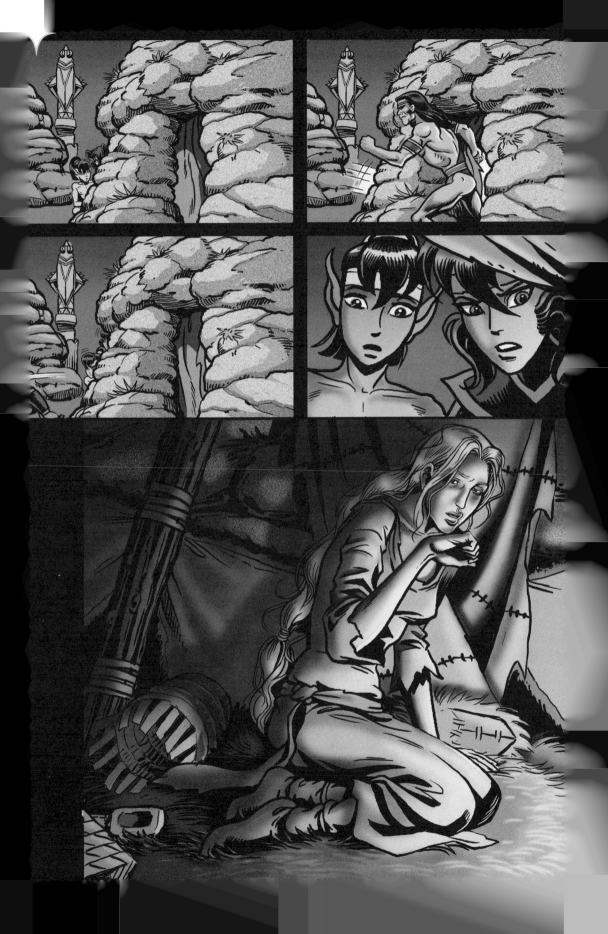

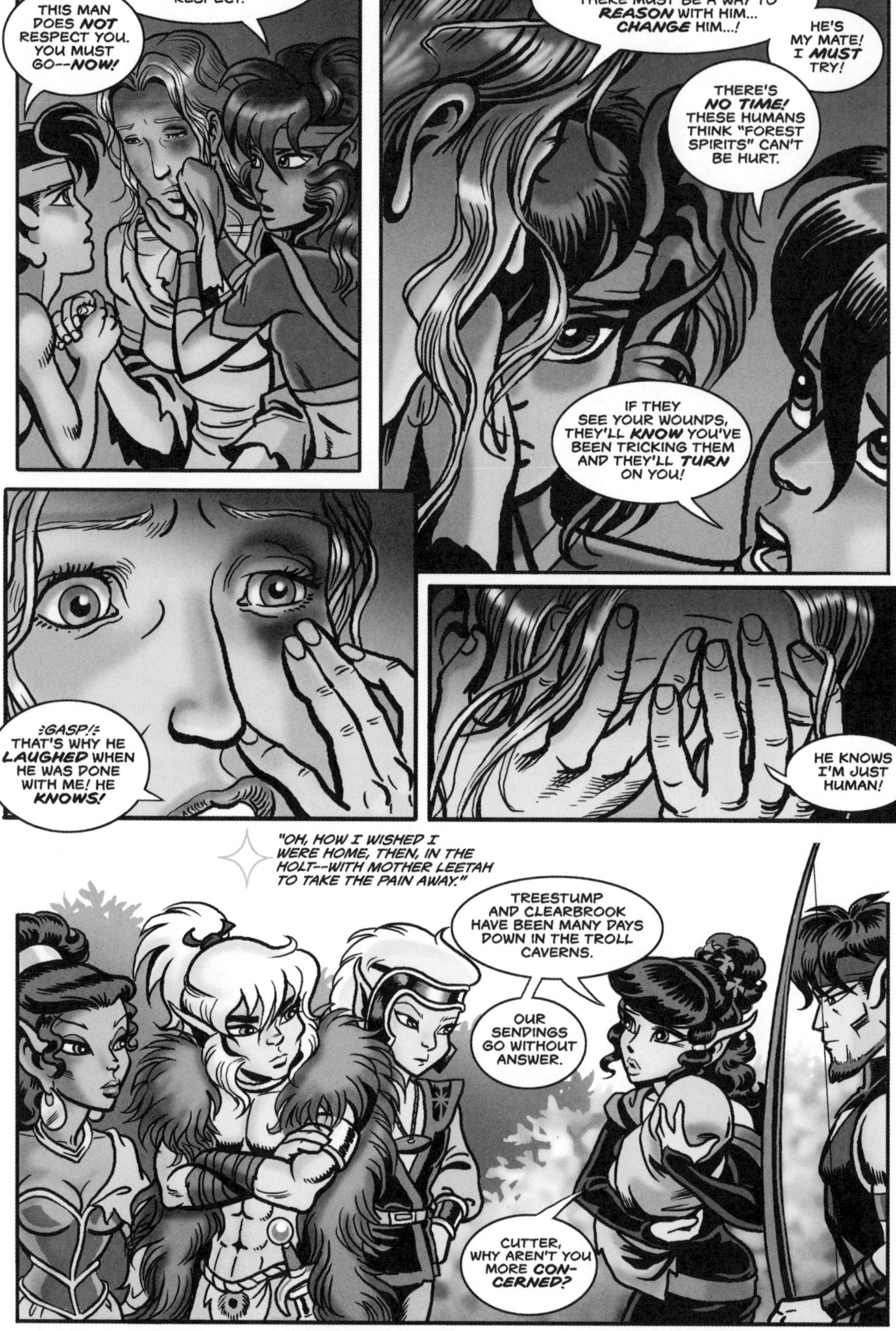
LIFEMATES QUARREL...EVEN FIGHT... BUT NEVER WITHOUT RESPECT.
THIS MAN DOES NOT RESPECT YOU. YOU MUST GO--NOW!
BUT...I CAN'T RUN AWAY, A FAILURE, NOW THAT THIS HAS HAPPENED! THERE MUST BE A WAY TO REASON WITH HIM... CHANGE HIM...!
HE'S MY MATE! I MUST TRY!
THERE'S NO TIME! THESE HUMANS THINK "FOREST SPIRITS" CAN'T BE HURT.
IF THEY SEE YOUR WOUNDS, THEY'LL KNOW YOU'VE BEEN TRICKING THEM AND THEY'LL TURN ON YOU!
GASP! THAT'S WHY HE LAUGHED WHEN HE WAS DONE WITH ME! HE KNOWS!
HE KNOWS I'M JUST HUMAN!
"OH, HOW I WISHED I WERE HOME, THEN, IN THE HOLT--WITH MOTHER LEETAH TO TAKE THE PAIN AWAY."
TREESTUMP AND CLEARBROOK HAVE BEEN MANY DAYS DOWN IN THE TROLL CAVERNS.
OUR SENDINGS GO WITHOUT ANSWER.
CUTTER, WHY AREN'T YOU MORE CON-CERNED?

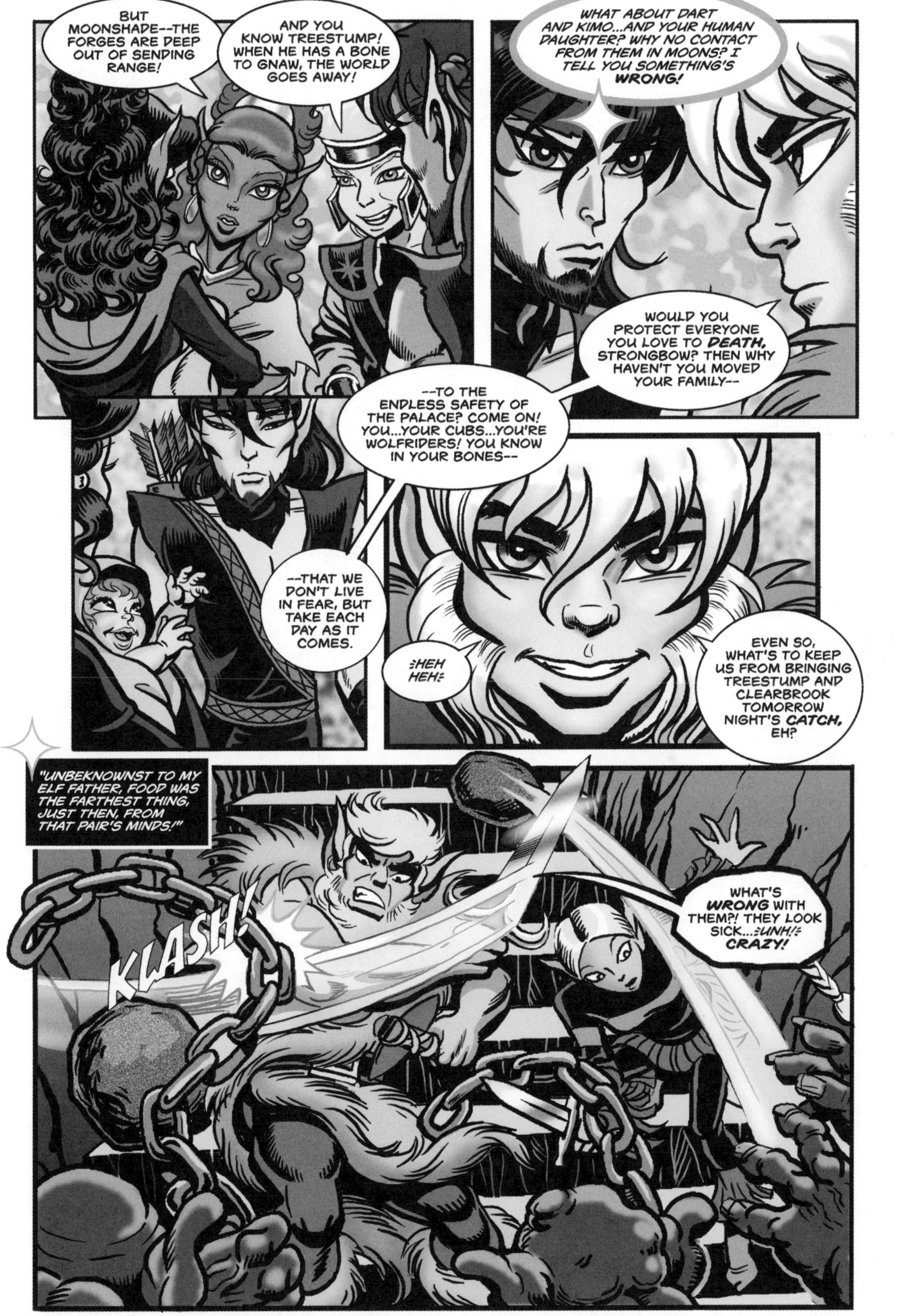

BUT MOONSHADE--THE FORGES ARE DEEP OUT OF SENDING RANGE!
AND YOU KNOW TREESTUMP! WHEN HE HAS A BONE TO GNAW, THE WORLD GOES AWAY!
WHAT ABOUT DART AND KIMO...AND YOUR HUMAN DAUGHTER? WHY NO CONTACT FROM THEM IN MOONS? I TELL YOU SOMETHING'S WRONG!
WOULD YOU PROTECT EVERYONE YOU LOVE TO DEATH, STRONGBOW? THEN WHY HAVEN'T YOU MOVED YOUR FAMILY--
--TO THE ENDLESS SAFETY OF THE PALACE? COME ON! YOU...YOUR CUBS...YOU'RE WOLFRIDERS! YOU KNOW IN YOUR BONES--
--THAT WE DON'T LIVE IN FEAR, BUT TAKE EACH DAY AS IT COMES.
HEH HEH
EVEN SO, WHAT'S TO KEEP US FROM BRINGING TREESTUMP AND CLEARBROOK TOMORROW NIGHT'S CATCH, EH?
"UNBEKNOWNST TO MY ELF FATHER, FOOD WAS THE FARTHEST THING, JUST THEN, FROM THAT PAIR'S MINDS!"
KLASH!
WHAT'S WRONG WITH THEM?! THEY LOOK SICK...UNH! CRAZY!

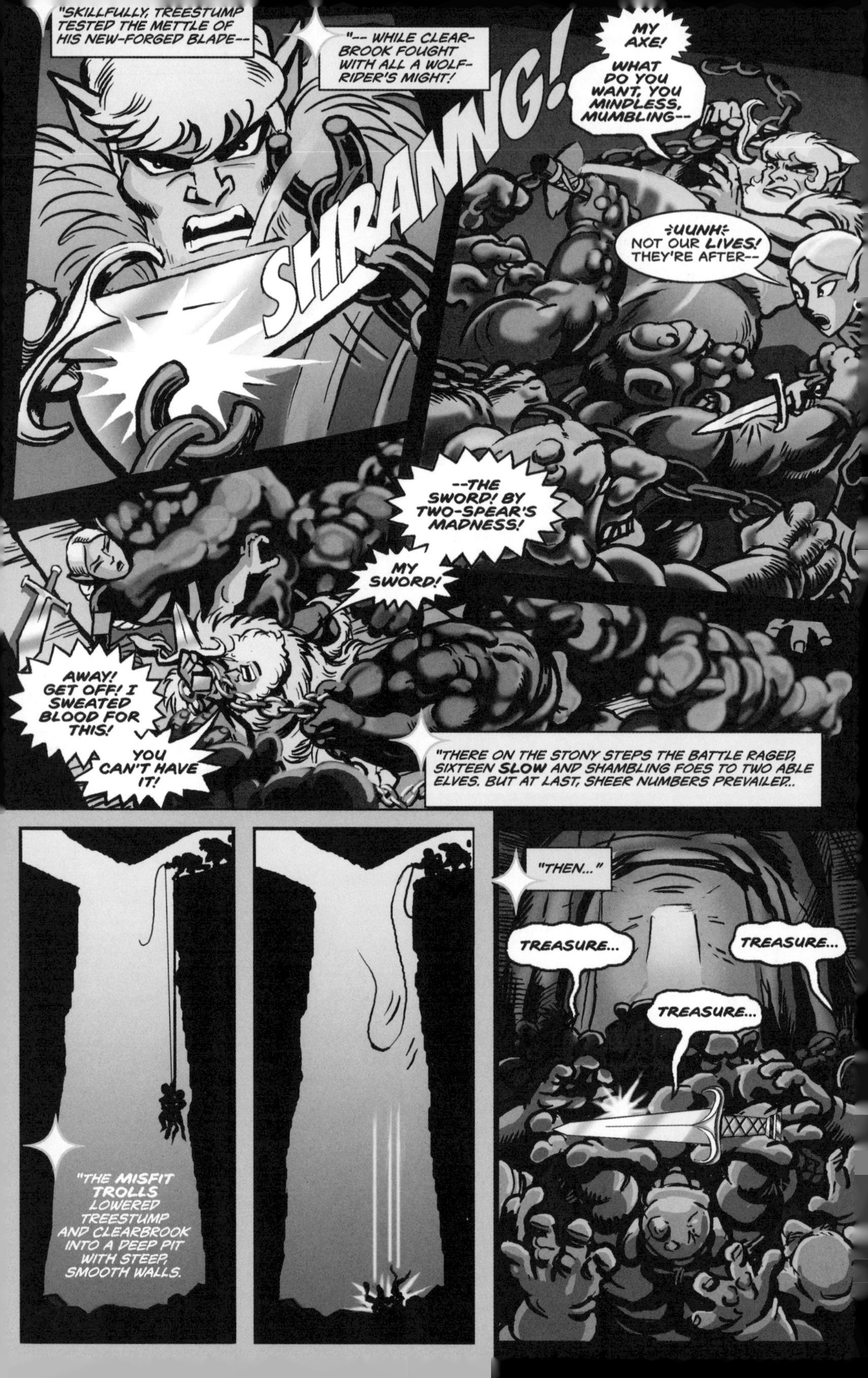
"SKILLFULLY, TREESTUMP TESTED THE METTLE OF HIS NEW-FORGED BLADE--
"-- WHILE CLEARBROOK FOUGHT WITH ALL A WOLF-RIDER'S MIGHT!
SHRANNG!
MY AXE! WHAT DO YOU WANT, YOU MINDLESS, MUMBLING--
UUNH! NOT OUR LIVES! THEY'RE AFTER--
--THE SWORD! BY TWO-SPEAR'S MADNESS!
MY SWORD!
AWAY! GET OFF! I SWEATED BLOOD FOR THIS!
YOU CAN'T HAVE IT!
"THERE ON THE STONY STEPS THE BATTLE RAGED, SIXTEEN SLOW AND SHAMBLING FOES TO TWO ABLE ELVES. BUT AT LAST, SHEER NUMBERS PREVAILED..
"THE MISFIT TROLLS LOWERED TREESTUMP AND CLEARBROOK INTO A DEEP PIT WITH STEEP, SMOOTH WALLS.
"THEN..."
TREASURE...
TREASURE...
TREASURE...

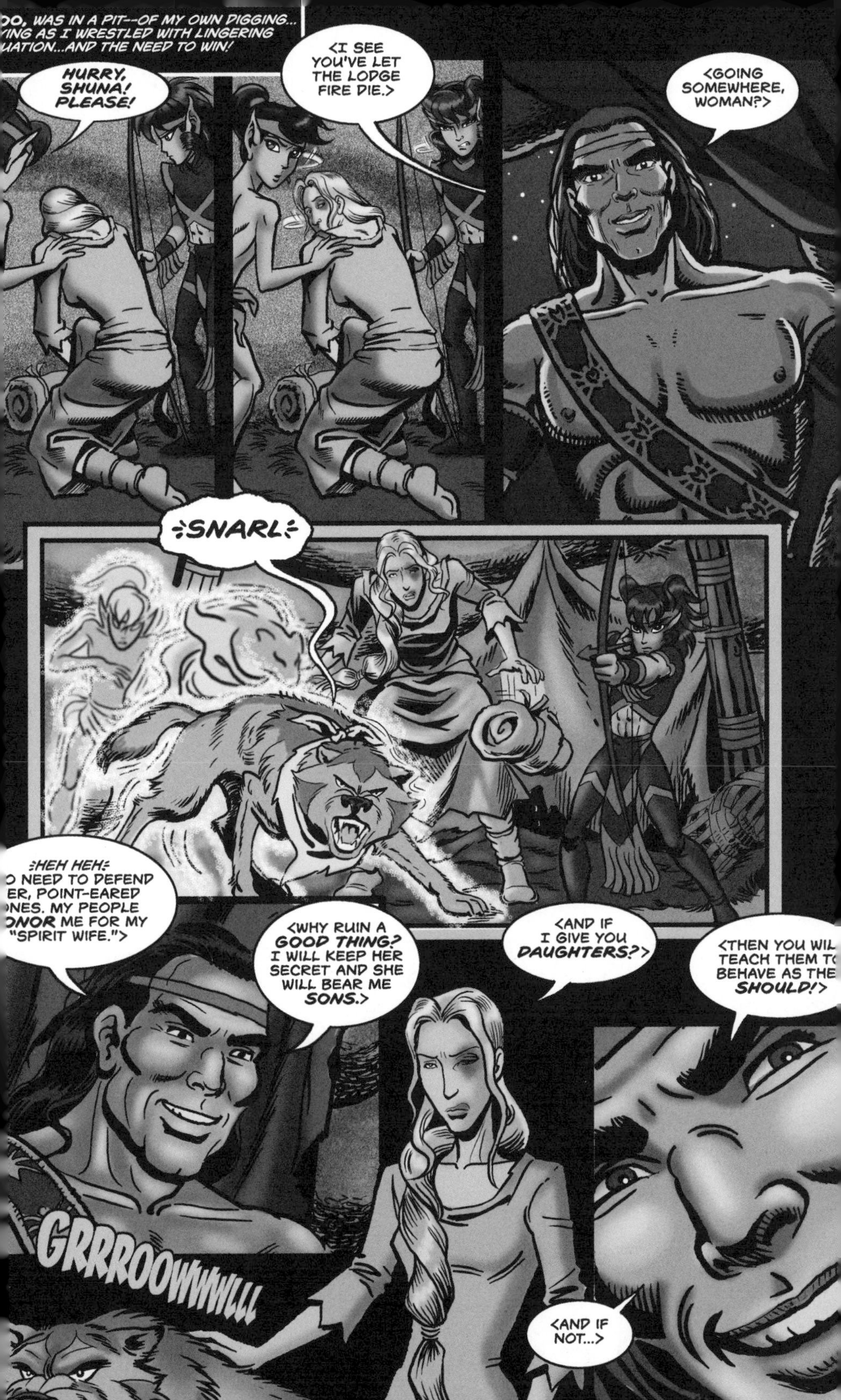
OO, WAS IN A PIT--OF MY OWN DIGGING... YING AS I WRESTLED WITH LINGERING UATION...AND THE NEED TO WIN!
HURRY, SHUNA! PLEASE!
<I SEE YOU'VE LET THE LODGE FIRE DIE.>
<GOING SOMEWHERE, WOMAN?>
SNARL
HEH HEH
O NEED TO DEFEND ER, POINT-EARED ONES. MY PEOPLE ONOR ME FOR MY "SPIRIT WIFE.">
<WHY RUIN A GOOD THING? I WILL KEEP HER SECRET AND SHE WILL BEAR ME SONS.>
<AND IF I GIVE YOU DAUGHTERS?>
<THEN YOU WIL TEACH THEM T BEHAVE AS THE SHOULD!>
GRRROOWWWLLL
<AND IF NOT...>
<I WILL!>

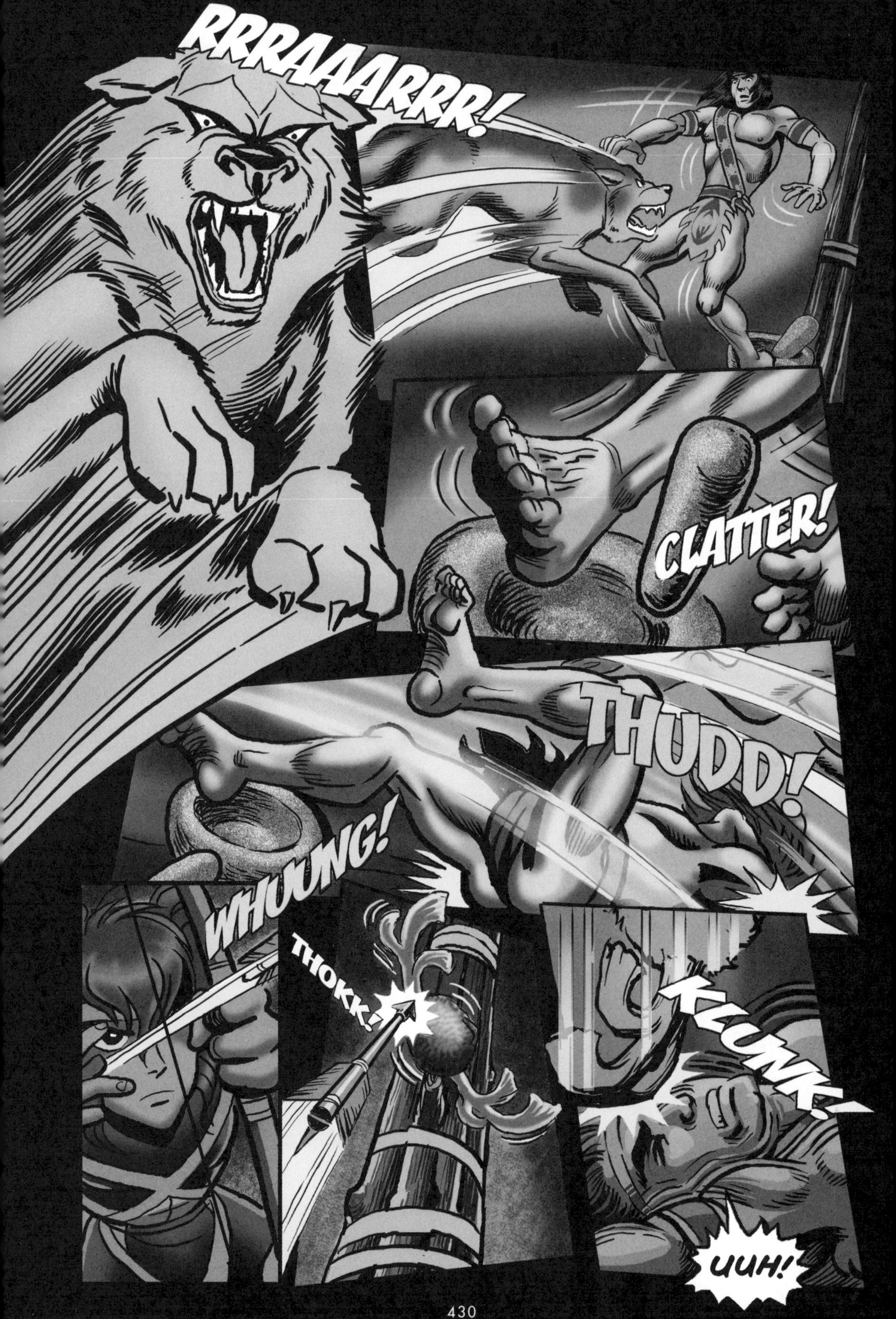
RRRAAAARRRR!
CLATTER!
THUDD!
WHUUNG!
THOKK!
KLUNK!
UUH!

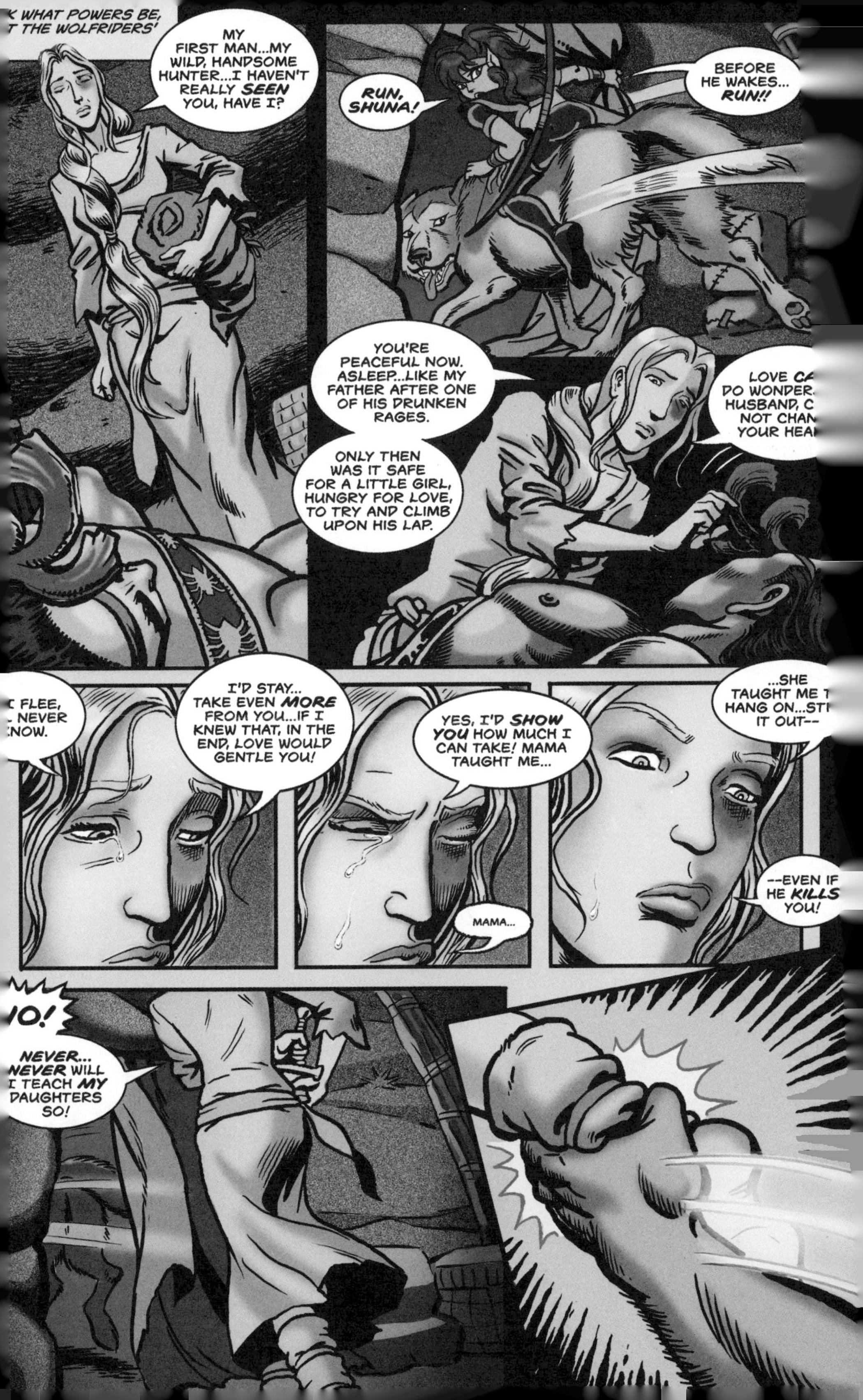
K WHAT POWERS BE,
T THE WOLFRIDERS'
MY FIRST MAN...MY WILD, HANDSOME HUNTER...I HAVEN'T REALLY SEEN YOU, HAVE I?
RUN, SHUNA!
BEFORE HE WAKES... RUN!!
YOU'RE PEACEFUL NOW. ASLEEP...LIKE MY FATHER AFTER ONE OF HIS DRUNKEN RAGES.
ONLY THEN WAS IT SAFE FOR A LITTLE GIRL, HUNGRY FOR LOVE, TO TRY AND CLIMB UPON HIS LAP.
LOVE CA DO WONDER HUSBAND, C NOT CHAN YOUR HEA
FLEE, NEVER NOW.
I'D STAY... TAKE EVEN MORE FROM YOU...IF I KNEW THAT, IN THE END, LOVE WOULD GENTLE YOU!
YES, I'D SHOW YOU HOW MUCH I CAN TAKE! MAMA TAUGHT ME...
MAMA...
...SHE TAUGHT ME T HANG ON...ST IT OUT--
--EVEN IF HE KILLS YOU!
IO!
NEVER... NEVER WILL I TEACH MY DAUGHTERS SO!

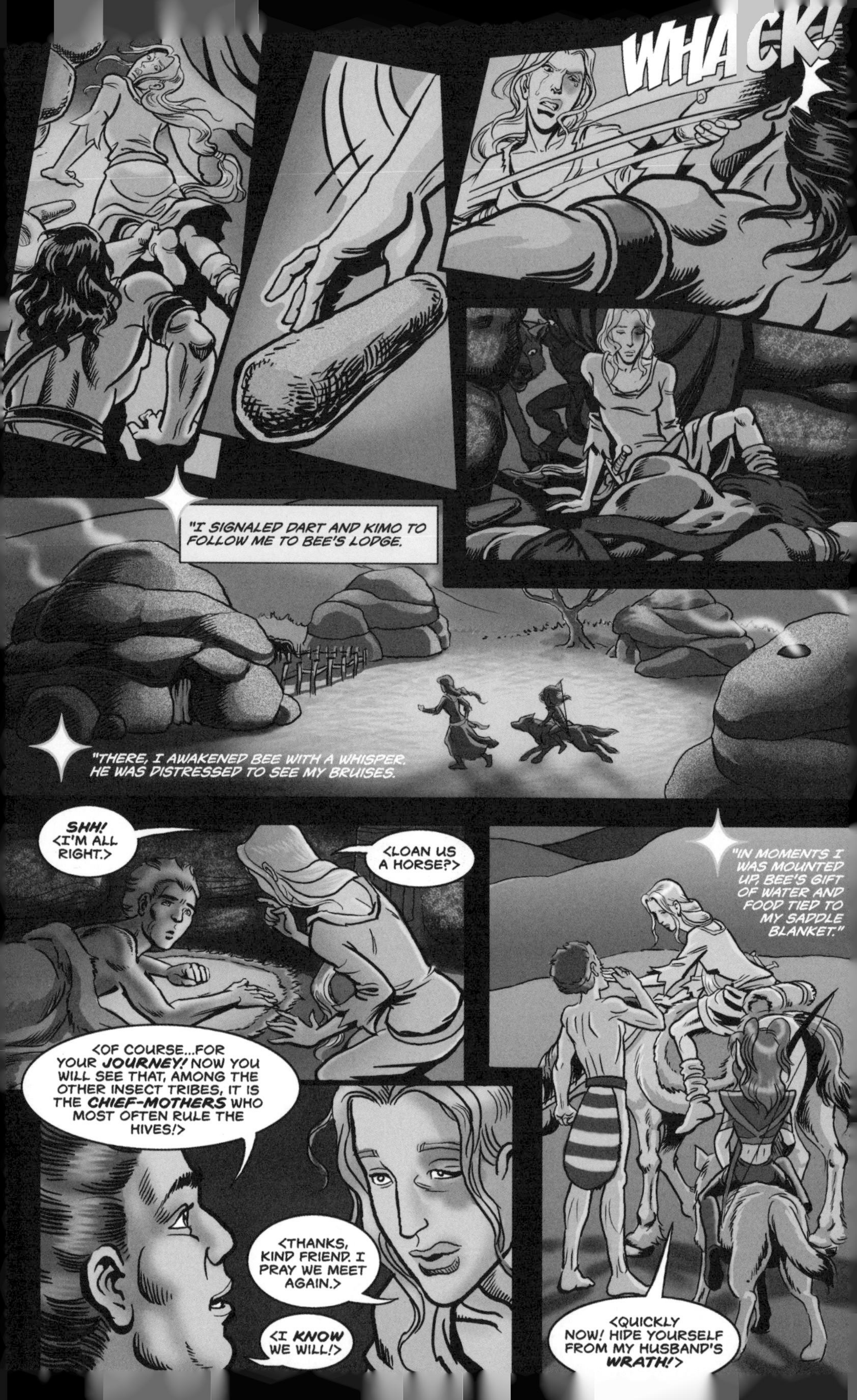
WHACK!
"I SIGNALED DART AND KIMO TO FOLLOW ME TO BEE'S LODGE.
"THERE, I AWAKENED BEE WITH A WHISPER. HE WAS DISTRESSED TO SEE MY BRUISES.
SHH! <I'M ALL RIGHT.>
<LOAN US A HORSE?>
<OF COURSE...FOR YOUR JOURNEY! NOW YOU WILL SEE THAT, AMONG THE OTHER INSECT TRIBES, IT IS THE CHIEF-MOTHERS WHO MOST OFTEN RULE THE HIVES!>
<THANKS, KIND FRIEND. I PRAY WE MEET AGAIN.>
<I KNOW WE WILL!>
"IN MOMENTS I WAS MOUNTED UP, BEE'S GIFT OF WATER AND FOOD TIED TO MY SADDLE BLANKET."
<QUICKLY NOW! HIDE YOURSELF FROM MY HUSBAND'S WRATH!>

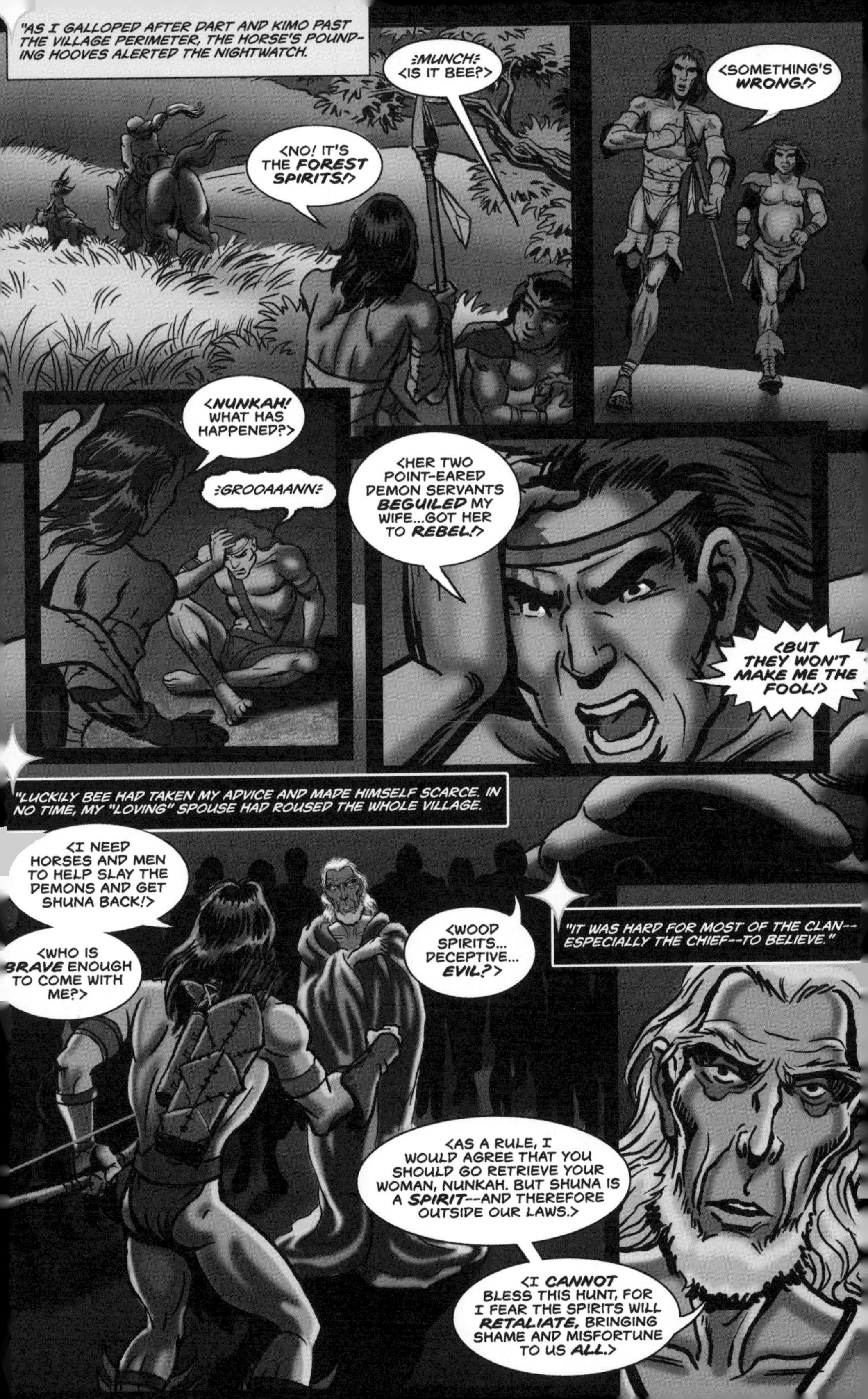
"AS I GALLOPED AFTER DART AND KIMO PAST THE VILLAGE PERIMETER, THE HORSE'S POUNDING HOOVES ALERTED THE NIGHTWATCH.
:MUNCH: <IS IT BEE?>
<NO! IT'S THE FOREST SPIRITS!>
<SOMETHING'S WRONG!>
<NUNKAH! WHAT HAS HAPPENED?>
:GROOAAANN:
<HER TWO POINT-EARED DEMON SERVANTS BEGUILED MY WIFE...GOT HER TO REBEL!>
<BUT THEY WON'T MAKE ME THE FOOL!>
"LUCKILY BEE HAD TAKEN MY ADVICE AND MADE HIMSELF SCARCE. IN NO TIME, MY "LOVING" SPOUSE HAD ROUSED THE WHOLE VILLAGE.
<I NEED HORSES AND MEN TO HELP SLAY THE DEMONS AND GET SHUNA BACK!>
<WHO IS BRAVE ENOUGH TO COME WITH ME?>
<WOOD SPIRITS... DECEPTIVE... EVIL?>
"IT WAS HARD FOR MOST OF THE CLAN--ESPECIALLY THE CHIEF--TO BELIEVE."
<AS A RULE, I WOULD AGREE THAT YOU SHOULD GO RETRIEVE YOUR WOMAN, NUNKAH. BUT SHUNA IS A SPIRIT--AND THEREFORE OUTSIDE OUR LAWS.>
<I CANNOT BLESS THIS HUNT, FOR I FEAR THE SPIRITS WILL RETALIATE, BRINGING SHAME AND MISFORTUNE TO US ALL.>

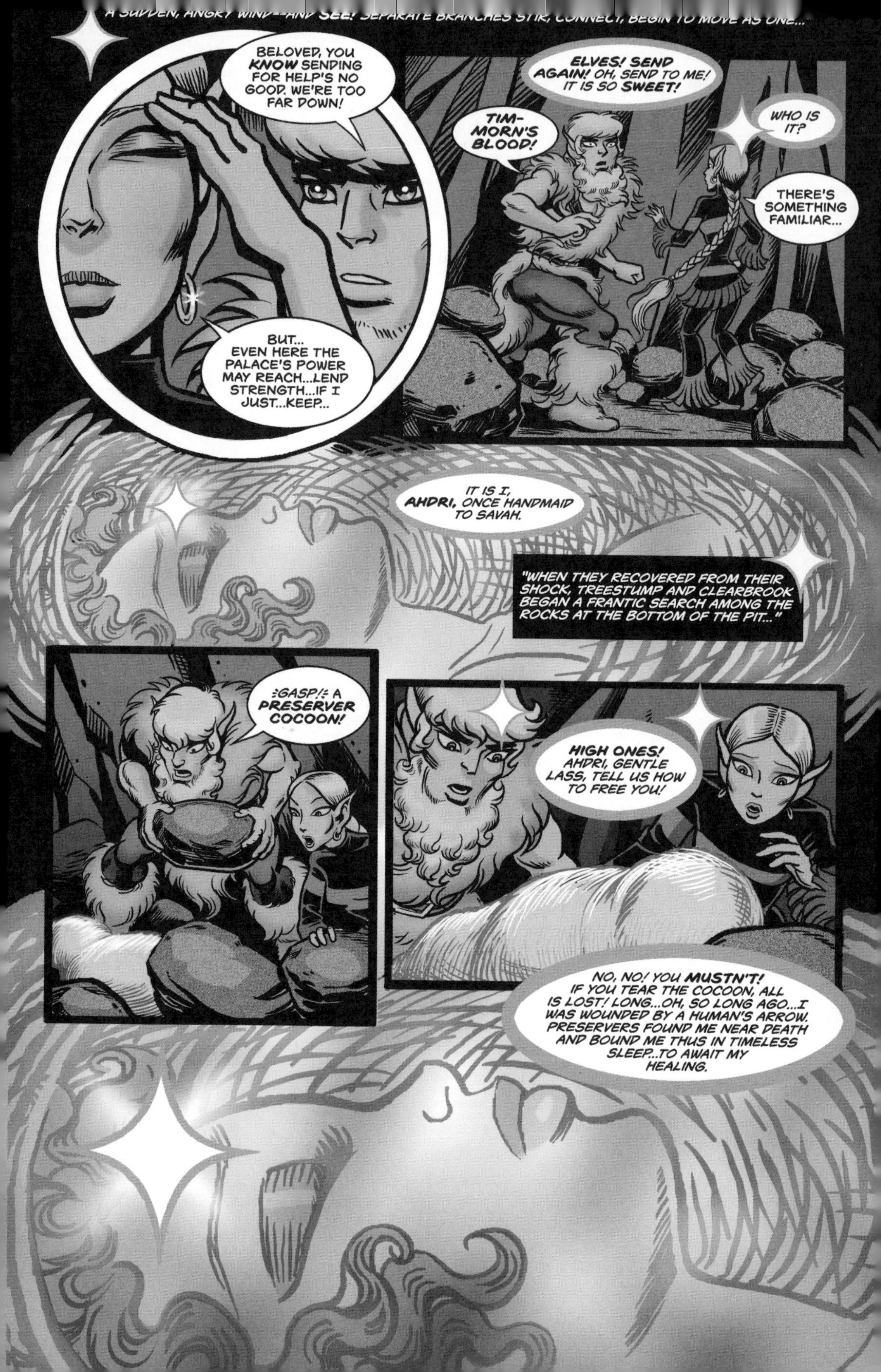

A SUDDEN, ANGRY WIND--AND SEE! SEPARATE BRANCHES STIR, CONNECT, BEGIN TO MOVE AS ONE...
BELOVED, YOU KNOW SENDING FOR HELP'S NO GOOD. WE'RE TOO FAR DOWN!
BUT... EVEN HERE THE PALACE'S POWER MAY REACH...LEND STRENGTH...IF I JUST...KEEP...
ELVES! SEND AGAIN! OH, SEND TO ME! IT IS SO SWEET!
TIM-MORN'S BLOOD!
WHO IS IT?
THERE'S SOMETHING FAMILIAR...
IT IS I, AHDRI, ONCE HANDMAID TO SAVAH.
"WHEN THEY RECOVERED FROM THEIR SHOCK, TREESTUMP AND CLEARBROOK BEGAN A FRANTIC SEARCH AMONG THE ROCKS AT THE BOTTOM OF THE PIT..."
:GASP!: A PRESERVER COCOON!
HIGH ONES! AHDRI, GENTLE LASS, TELL US HOW TO FREE YOU!
NO, NO! YOU MUSTN'T! IF YOU TEAR THE COCOON, ALL IS LOST! LONG...OH, SO LONG AGO...I WAS WOUNDED BY A HUMAN'S ARROW. PRESERVERS FOUND ME NEAR DEATH AND BOUND ME THUS IN TIMELESS SLEEP...TO AWAIT MY HEALING.

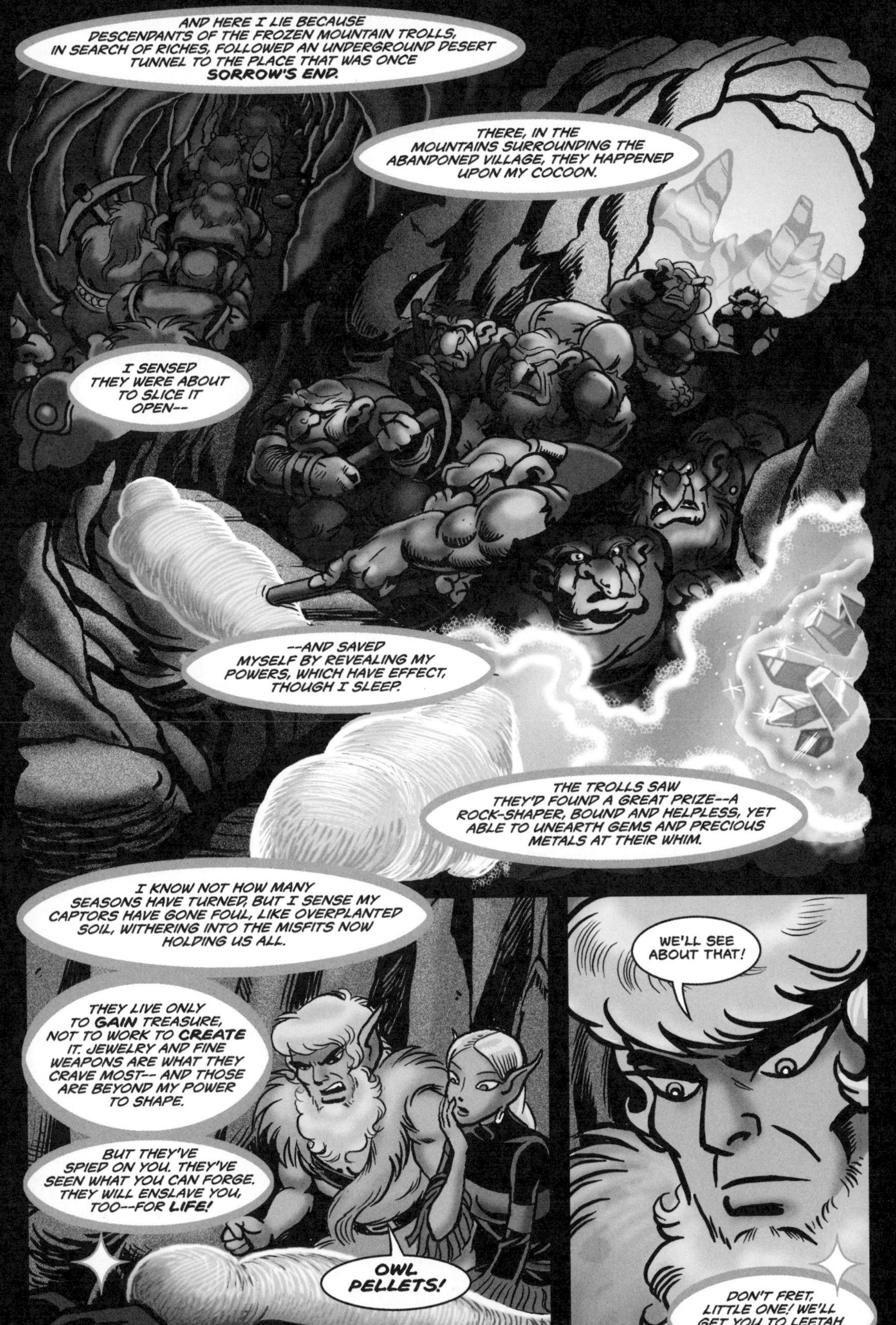
AND HERE I LIE BECAUSE DESCENDANTS OF THE FROZEN MOUNTAIN TROLLS, IN SEARCH OF RICHES, FOLLOWED AN UNDERGROUND DESERT TUNNEL TO THE PLACE THAT WAS ONCE SORROW'S END.
THERE, IN THE MOUNTAINS SURROUNDING THE ABANDONED VILLAGE, THEY HAPPENED UPON MY COCOON.
I SENSED THEY WERE ABOUT TO SLICE IT OPEN--
--AND SAVED MYSELF BY REVEALING MY POWERS, WHICH HAVE EFFECT, THOUGH I SLEEP.
THE TROLLS SAW THEY'D FOUND A GREAT PRIZE--A ROCK-SHAPER, BOUND AND HELPLESS, YET ABLE TO UNEARTH GEMS AND PRECIOUS METALS AT THEIR WHIM.
I KNOW NOT HOW MANY SEASONS HAVE TURNED, BUT I SENSE MY CAPTORS HAVE GONE FOUL, LIKE OVERPLANTED SOIL, WITHERING INTO THE MISFITS NOW HOLDING US ALL.
THEY LIVE ONLY TO GAIN TREASURE, NOT TO WORK TO CREATE IT. JEWELRY AND FINE WEAPONS ARE WHAT THEY CRAVE MOST-- AND THOSE ARE BEYOND MY POWER TO SHAPE.
BUT THEY'VE SPIED ON YOU. THEY'VE SEEN WHAT YOU CAN FORGE. THEY WILL ENSLAVE YOU, TOO--FOR LIFE!
OWL PELLETS!
WE'LL SEE ABOUT THAT!
DON'T FRET, LITTLE ONE! WE'LL GET YOU TO LEETAH FOR HEALING.

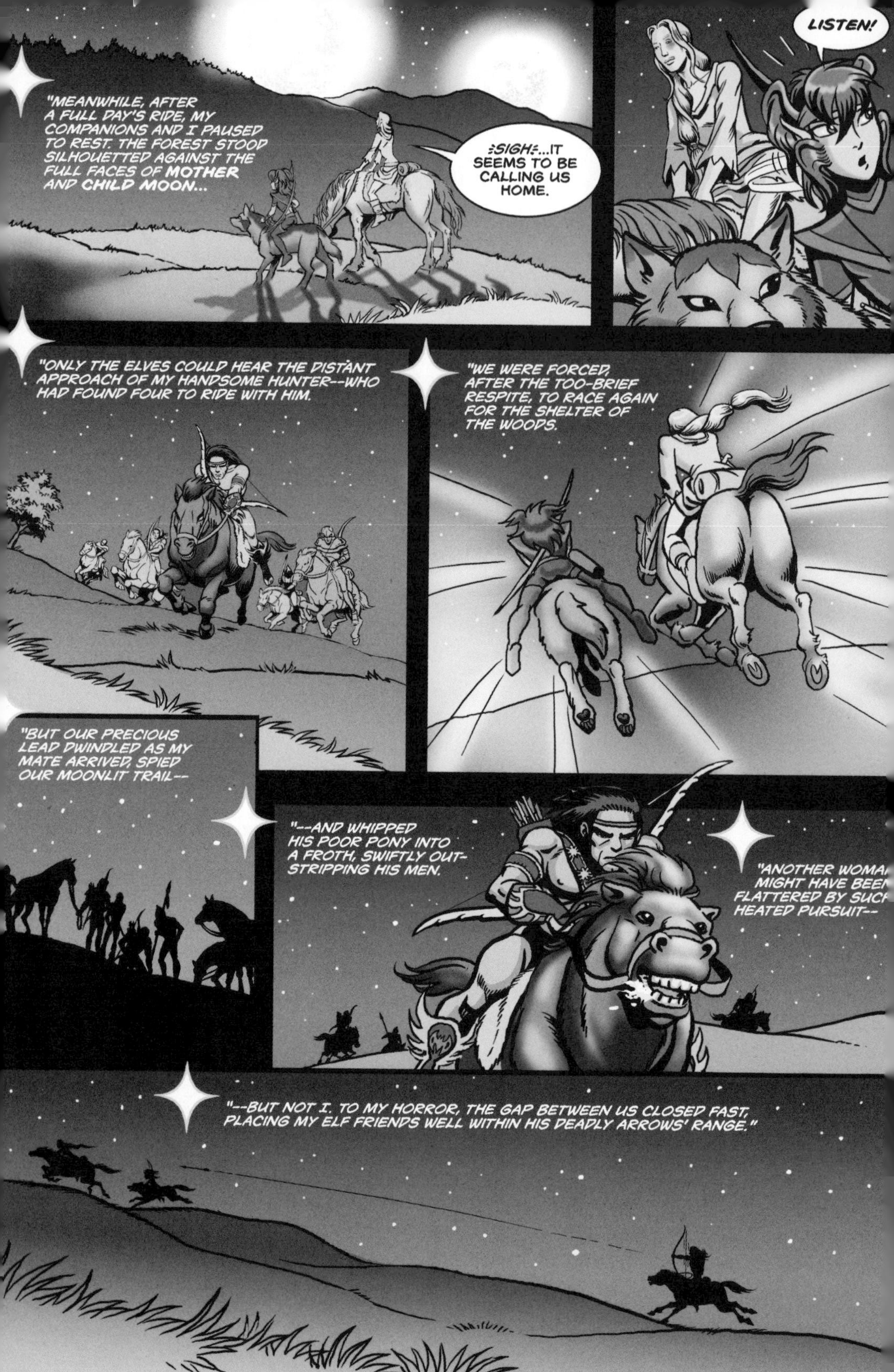
"MEANWHILE, AFTER A FULL DAY'S RIDE, MY COMPANIONS AND I PAUSED TO REST. THE FOREST STOOD SILHOUETTED AGAINST THE FULL FACES OF MOTHER AND CHILD MOON...
:SIGH:...IT SEEMS TO BE CALLING US HOME.
LISTEN!
"ONLY THE ELVES COULD HEAR THE DISTANT APPROACH OF MY HANDSOME HUNTER--WHO HAD FOUND FOUR TO RIDE WITH HIM.
"WE WERE FORCED, AFTER THE TOO-BRIEF RESPITE, TO RACE AGAIN FOR THE SHELTER OF THE WOODS.
"BUT OUR PRECIOUS LEAD DWINDLED AS MY MATE ARRIVED, SPIED OUR MOONLIT TRAIL--
"--AND WHIPPED HIS POOR PONY INTO A FROTH, SWIFTLY OUT-STRIPPING HIS MEN.
"ANOTHER WOMA MIGHT HAVE BEEN FLATTERED BY SUC HEATED PURSUIT--
"--BUT NOT I. TO MY HORROR, THE GAP BETWEEN US CLOSED FAST, PLACING MY ELF FRIENDS WELL WITHIN HIS DEADLY ARROWS' RANGE."

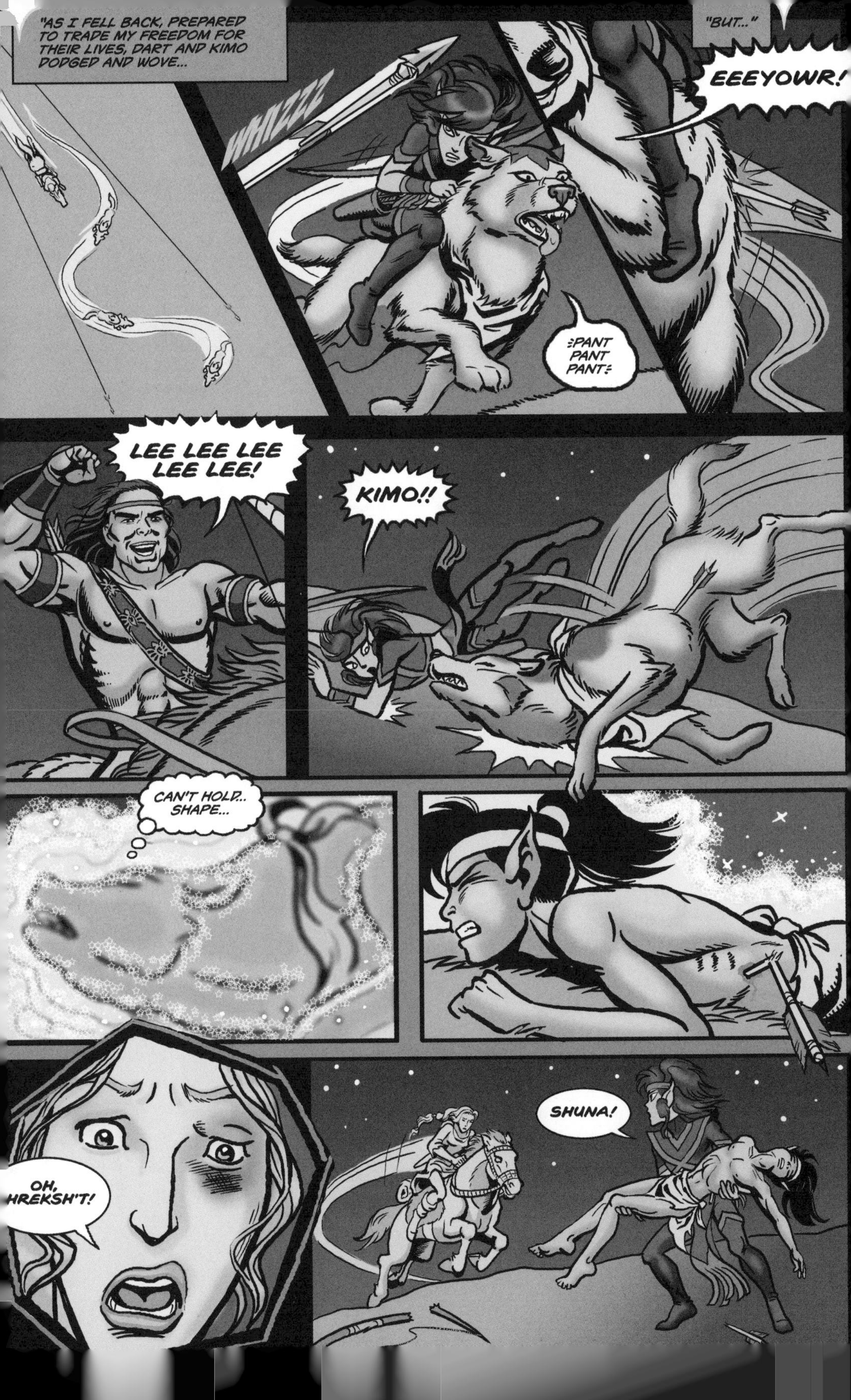
"AS I FELL BACK, PREPARED TO TRADE MY FREEDOM FOR THEIR LIVES, DART AND KIMO DODGED AND WOVE...
WHIZZZ
"BUT..."
EEEYOWR!
PANT PANT PANT
LEE LEE LEE LEE LEE!
KIMO!!
CAN'T HOLD... SHAPE...
OH, HREKSH'T!
SHUNA!

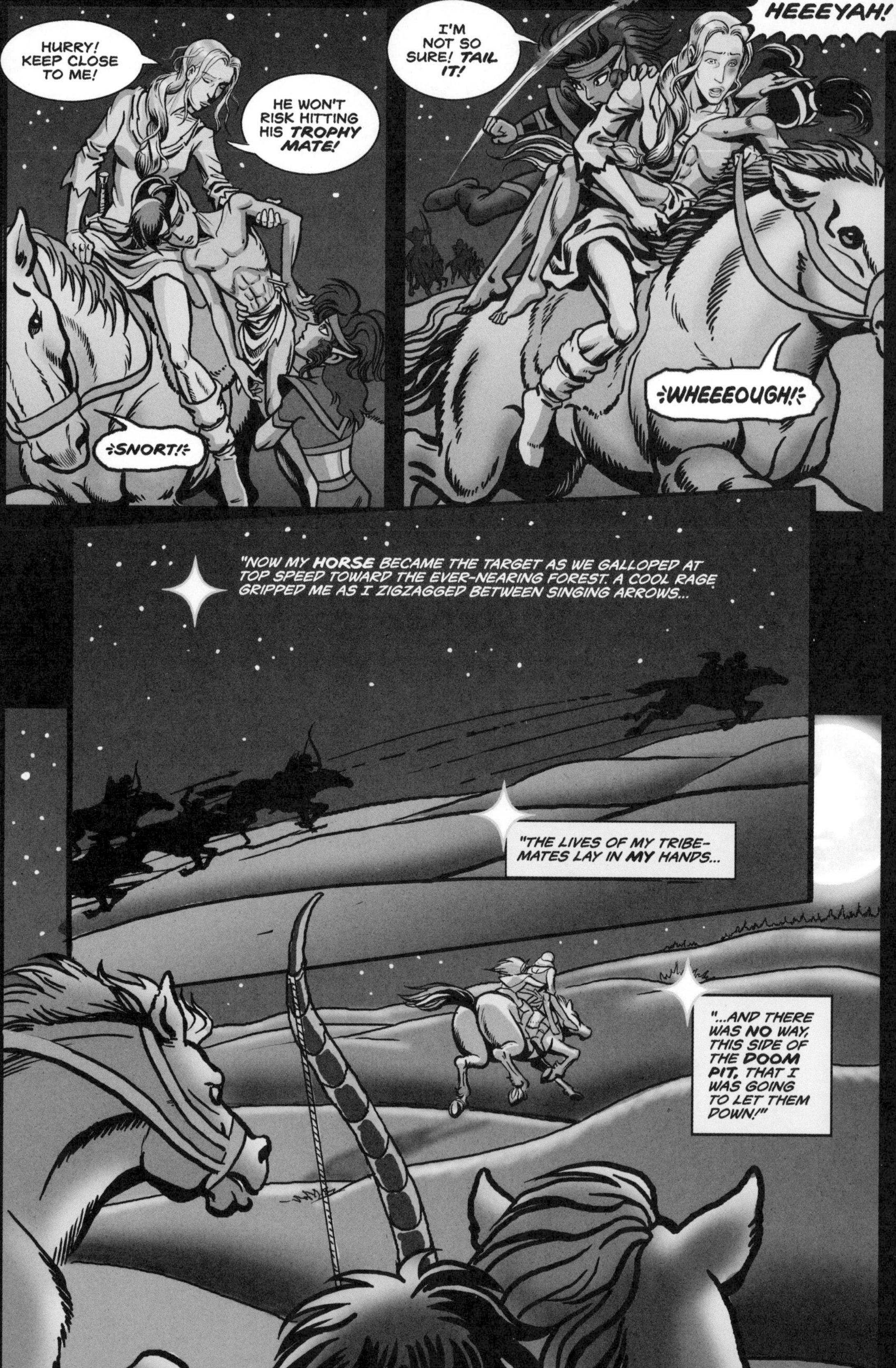
HURRY! KEEP CLOSE TO ME!
HE WON'T RISK HITTING HIS TROPHY MATE!
SNORT!
I'M NOT SO SURE! TAIL IT!
HEEEYAH!
WHEEEOUGH!
"NOW MY HORSE BECAME THE TARGET AS WE GALLOPED AT TOP SPEED TOWARD THE EVER-NEARING FOREST. A COOL RAGE GRIPPED ME AS I ZIGZAGGED BETWEEN SINGING ARROWS...
"THE LIVES OF MY TRIBE-MATES LAY IN MY HANDS...
"...AND THERE WAS NO WAY, THIS SIDE OF THE DOOM PIT, THAT I WAS GOING TO LET THEM DOWN!"

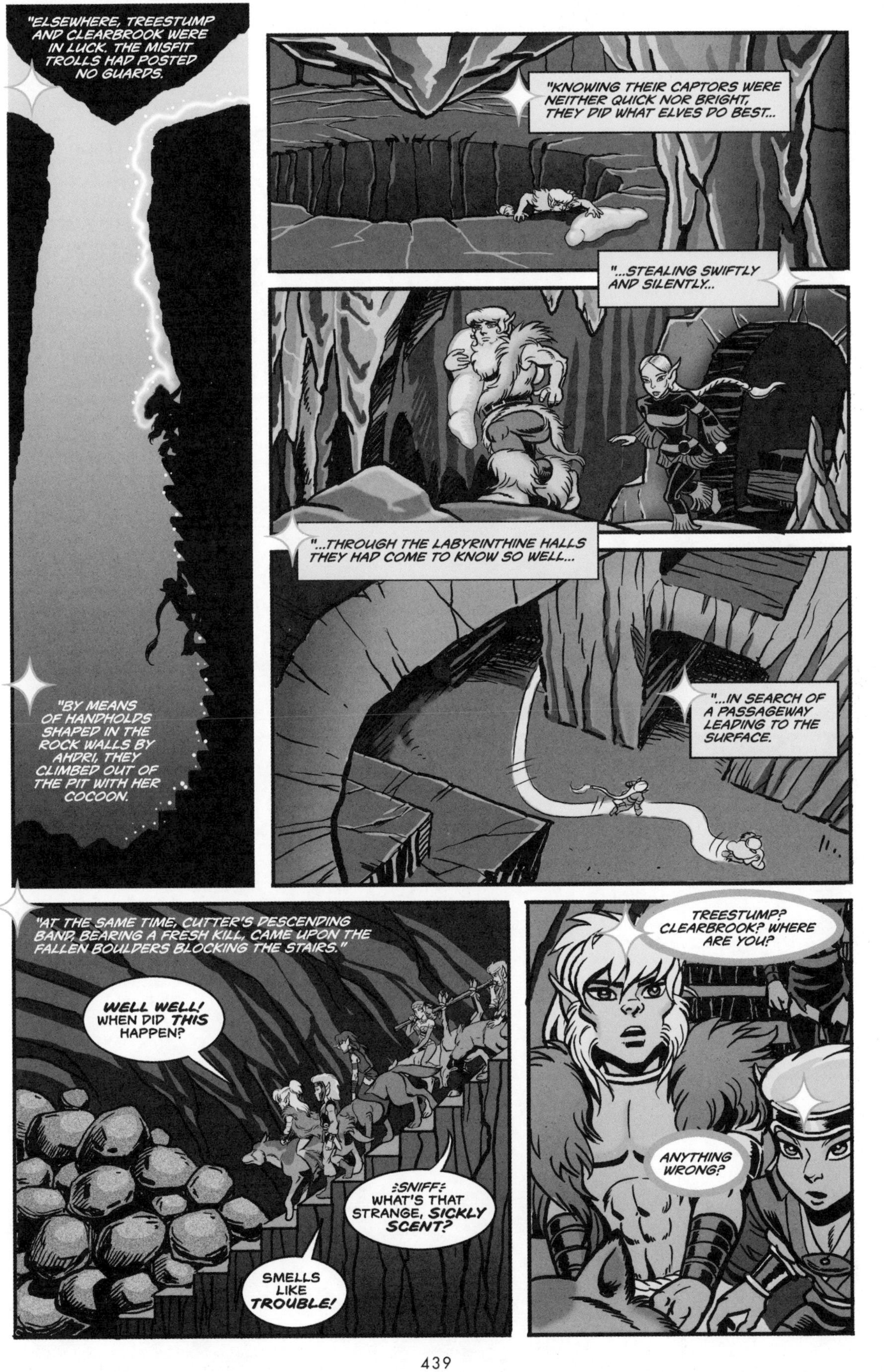
"ELSEWHERE, TREESTUMP AND CLEARBROOK WERE IN LUCK. THE MISFIT TROLLS HAD POSTED NO GUARDS.
"BY MEANS OF HANDHOLDS SHAPED IN THE ROCK WALLS BY AHDRI, THEY CLIMBED OUT OF THE PIT WITH HER COCOON.
"KNOWING THEIR CAPTORS WERE NEITHER QUICK NOR BRIGHT, THEY DID WHAT ELVES DO BEST...
"...STEALING SWIFTLY AND SILENTLY...
"...THROUGH THE LABYRINTHINE HALLS THEY HAD COME TO KNOW SO WELL...
"...IN SEARCH OF A PASSAGEWAY LEADING TO THE SURFACE.
"AT THE SAME TIME, CUTTER'S DESCENDING BAND, BEARING A FRESH KILL, CAME UPON THE FALLEN BOULDERS BLOCKING THE STAIRS."
WELL WELL! WHEN DID THIS HAPPEN?
SNIFF WHAT'S THAT STRANGE, SICKLY SCENT?
SMELLS LIKE TROUBLE!
TREESTUMP? CLEARBROOK? WHERE ARE YOU?
ANYTHING WRONG?

"OVERJOYED TO LEARN THAT THEIR TRIBEMATES WERE NEAR, THE ESCAPED PAIR SENT BACK THE FULL TALE OF THEIR IMPRISONMENT, PLUS A WARNING!"

MISFIT TROLLS! ABOUT TWO EIGHTS OF 'EM, YOU SAY?

DON'T FOOL WITH THEM! BRING AHDRI! AND COME TO US--FAST AS YOU CAN!

BUT HOW CAN THEY? THE STAIRS ARE BLOCKED!

THERE'S A WAY TO FIX THAT, NIGHTFALL--

--IF WE USE OUR HEADS!

HMMM...LOOKS LIKE THE PULL OF THE WORLD'S IN OUR FAVOR.

THIS STONE'S THE KEY TO DISLODGING THE WHOLE THING.

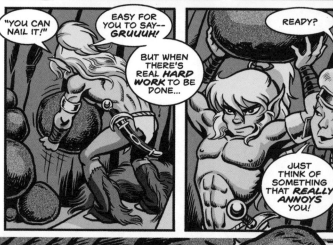

KNOCK THIS ONE LOOSE AND THEY'LL ALL TUMBLE AWAY.

DO TELL!

AND I SUPPOSE IT'D BETTER BE A CURSED CAREFUL TAP!

AW C'MON! YOU CAN NAIL IT!

"YOU CAN NAIL IT!"

EASY FOR YOU TO SAY-- GRUUUH!

BUT WHEN THERE'S REAL HARD WORK TO BE DONE...

READY?

JUST THINK OF SOMETHING THAT REALLY ANNOYS YOU!

OR... SOME... ONE...!

WHAM!

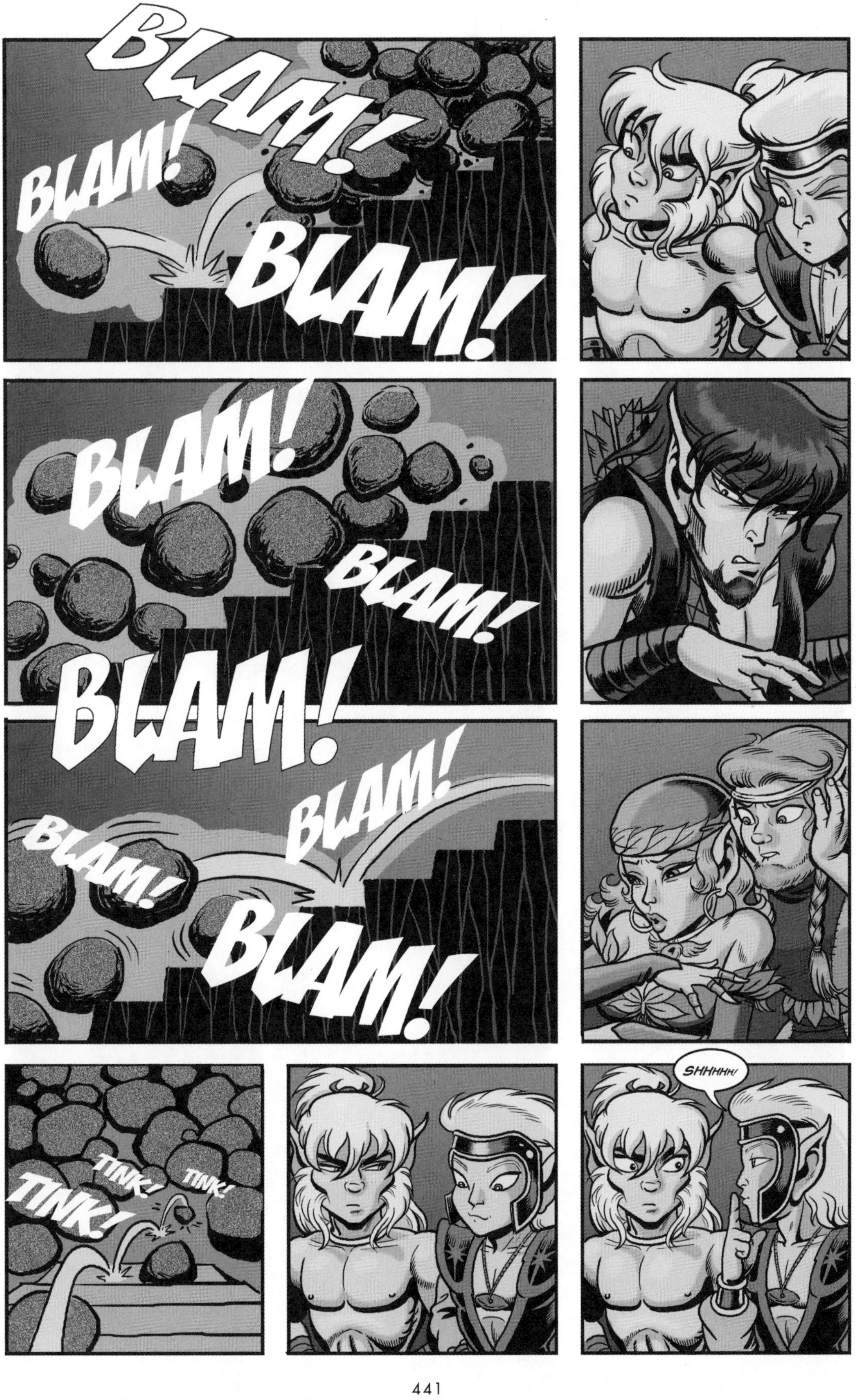
BLAM!
BLAM!
BLAM!
BLAM!
BLAM!
BLAM!
BLAM!
BLAM!
BLAM!
TINK!
TINK!
TINK!
SHHHHH!

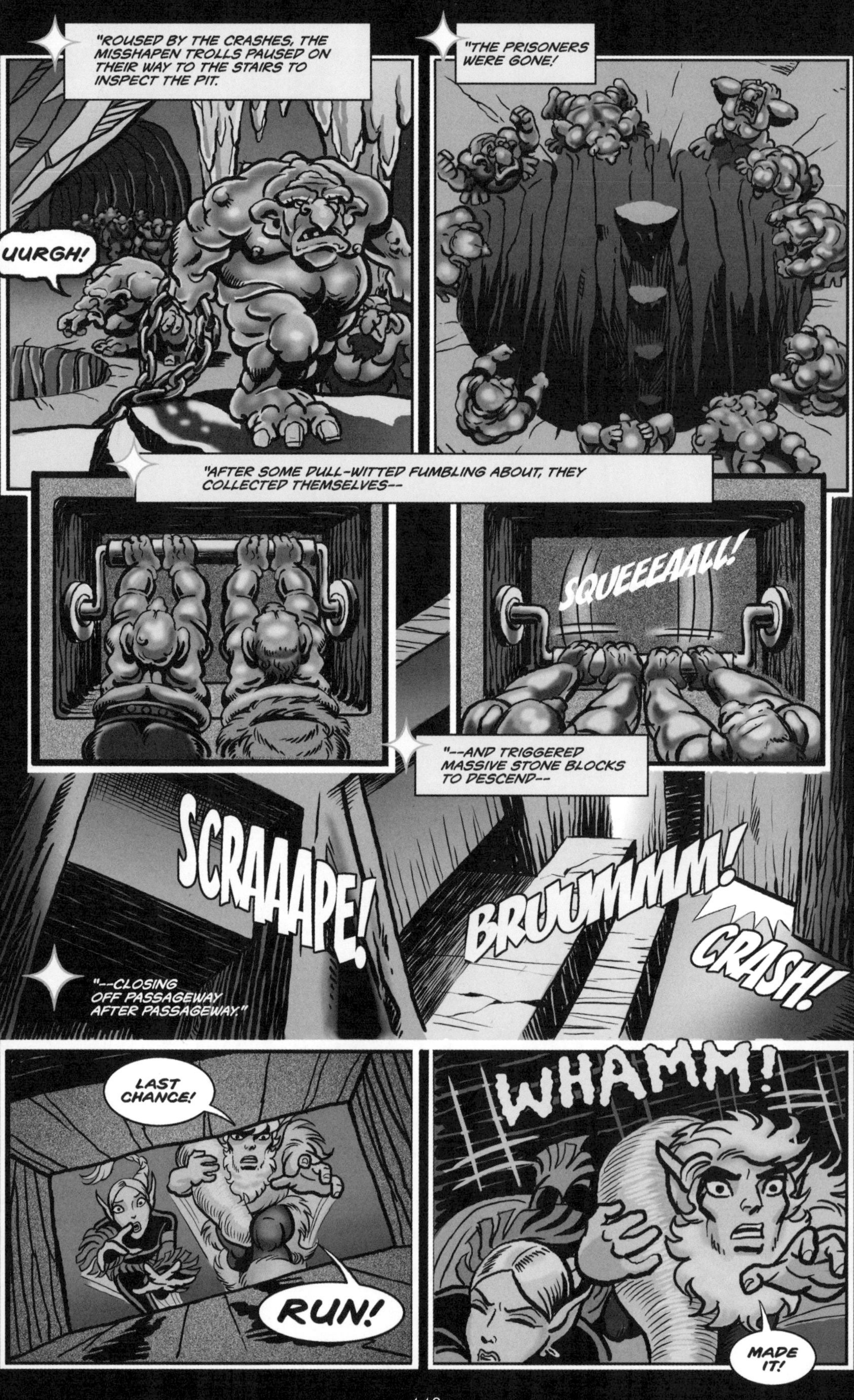

"ROUSED BY THE CRASHES, THE MISSHAPEN TROLLS PAUSED ON THEIR WAY TO THE STAIRS TO INSPECT THE PIT.
UURGH!
"THE PRISONERS WERE GONE!
"AFTER SOME DULL-WITTED FUMBLING ABOUT, THEY COLLECTED THEMSELVES--
SQUEEEAALL!
"--AND TRIGGERED MASSIVE STONE BLOCKS TO DESCEND--
SCRAAAPE!
BRUUMMM!
CRASH!
"--CLOSING OFF PASSAGEWAY AFTER PASSAGEWAY."
LAST CHANCE!
RUN!
WHAMM!
MADE IT!

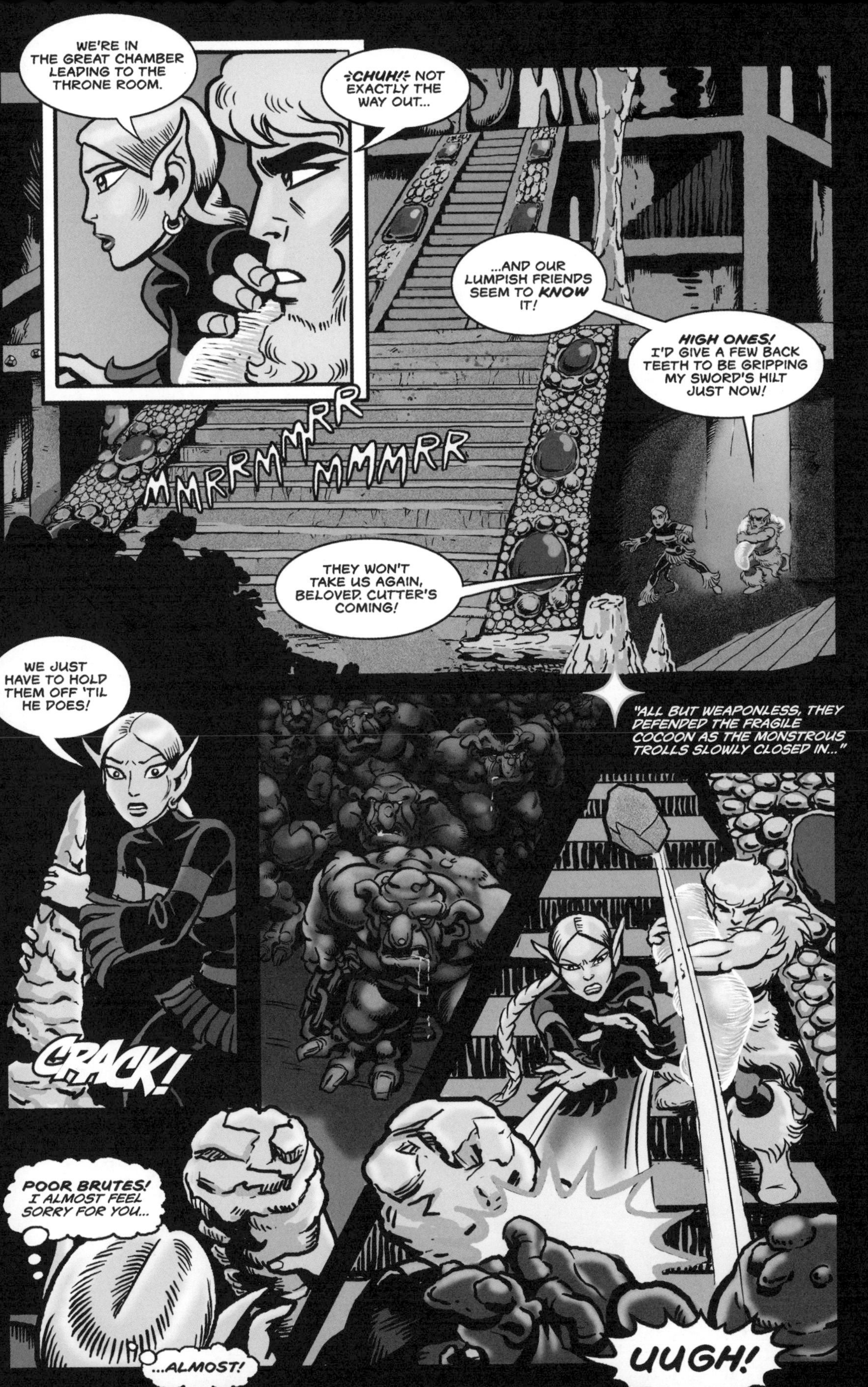

WE'RE IN THE GREAT CHAMBER LEADING TO THE THRONE ROOM.
CHUH! NOT EXACTLY THE WAY OUT...
...AND OUR LUMPISH FRIENDS SEEM TO KNOW IT!
HIGH ONES! I'D GIVE A FEW BACK TEETH TO BE GRIPPING MY SWORD'S HILT JUST NOW!
MMRRMMRR MMMRR
THEY WON'T TAKE US AGAIN, BELOVED. CUTTER'S COMING!
WE JUST HAVE TO HOLD THEM OFF 'TIL HE DOES!
"ALL BUT WEAPONLESS, THEY DEFENDED THE FRAGILE COCOON AS THE MONSTROUS TROLLS SLOWLY CLOSED IN..."
CRACK!
POOR BRUTES! I ALMOST FEEL SORRY FOR YOU...
...ALMOST!
UUGH!

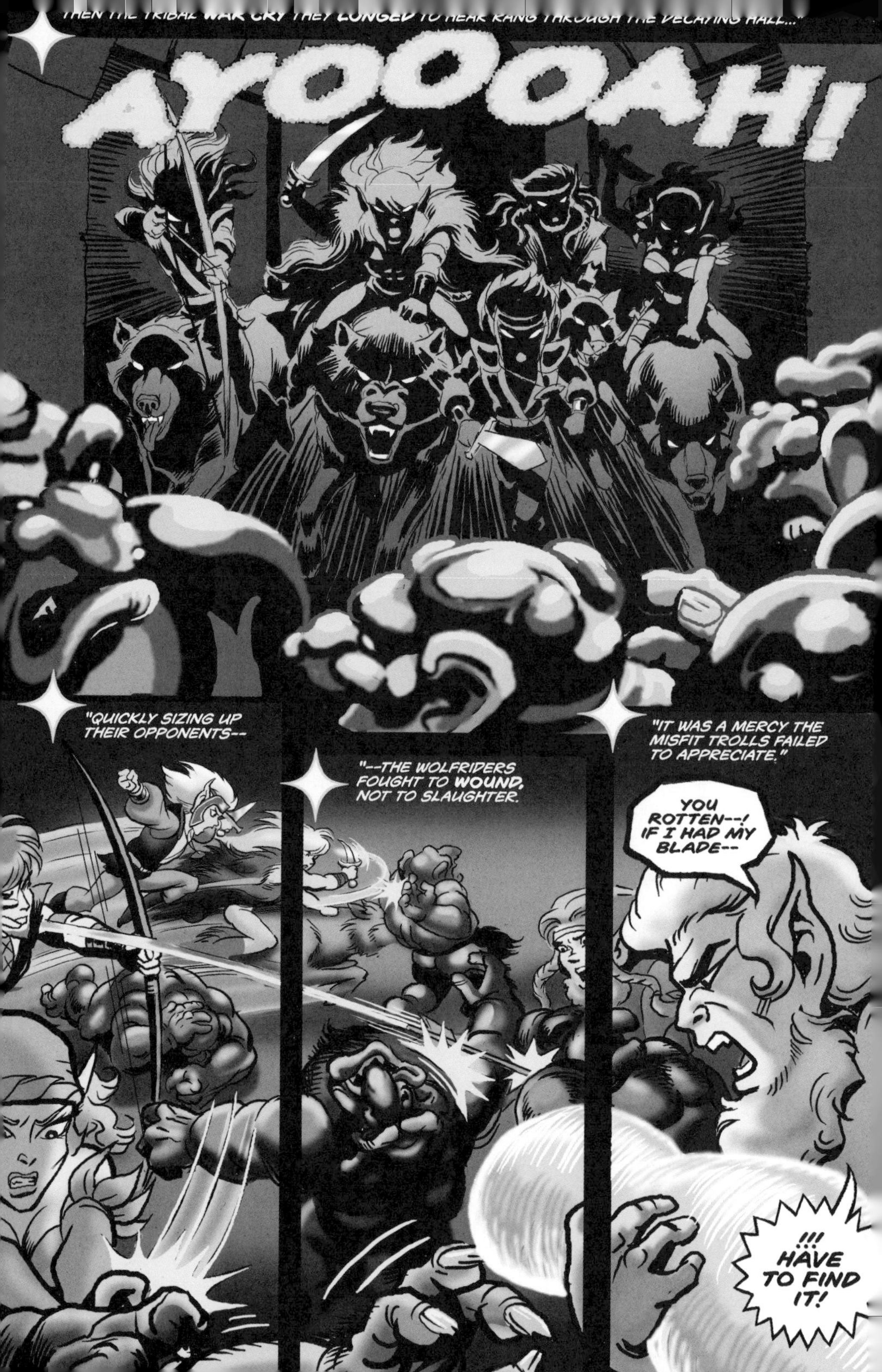
THEN THE TRIBAL WAR CRY THEY LONGED TO HEAR RANG THROUGH THE DECAYING HALL..."
AYOOOAH!
"QUICKLY SIZING UP THEIR OPPONENTS--
"--THE WOLFRIDERS FOUGHT TO WOUND, NOT TO SLAUGHTER.
"IT WAS A MERCY THE MISFIT TROLLS FAILED TO APPRECIATE."
YOU ROTTEN--! IF I HAD MY BLADE--
!!! HAVE TO FIND IT!

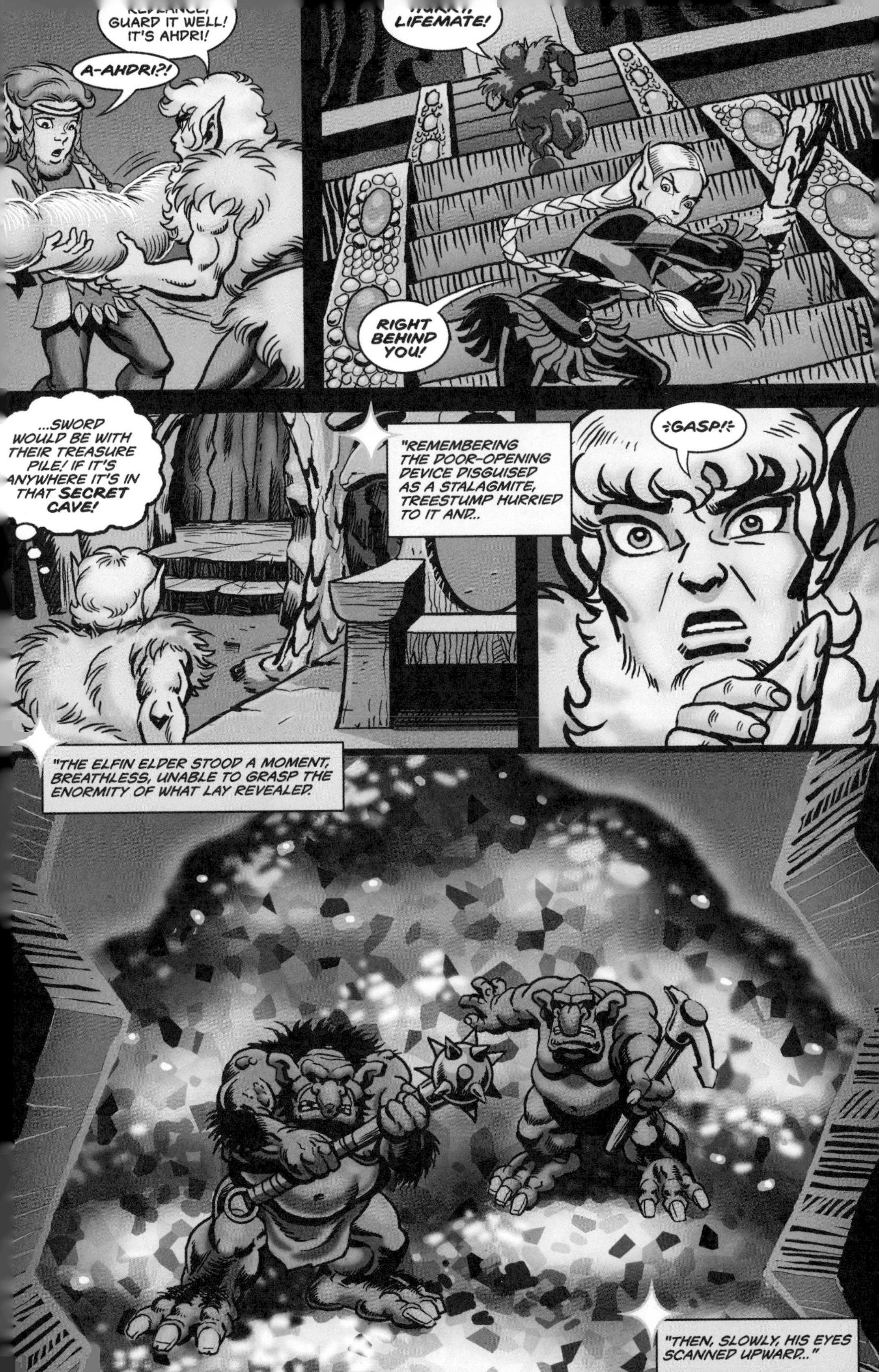
GUARD IT WELL! IT'S AHDRI!
A-AHDRI?!
LIFEMATE!
RIGHT BEHIND YOU!
...SWORD WOULD BE WITH THEIR TREASURE PILE! IF IT'S ANYWHERE IT'S IN THAT SECRET CAVE!
"REMEMBERING THE DOOR-OPENING DEVICE DISGUISED AS A STALAGMITE, TREESTUMP HURRIED TO IT AND...
GASP!
"THE ELFIN ELDER STOOD A MOMENT, BREATHLESS, UNABLE TO GRASP THE ENORMITY OF WHAT LAY REVEALED.
"THEN, SLOWLY, HIS EYES SCANNED UPWARD..."

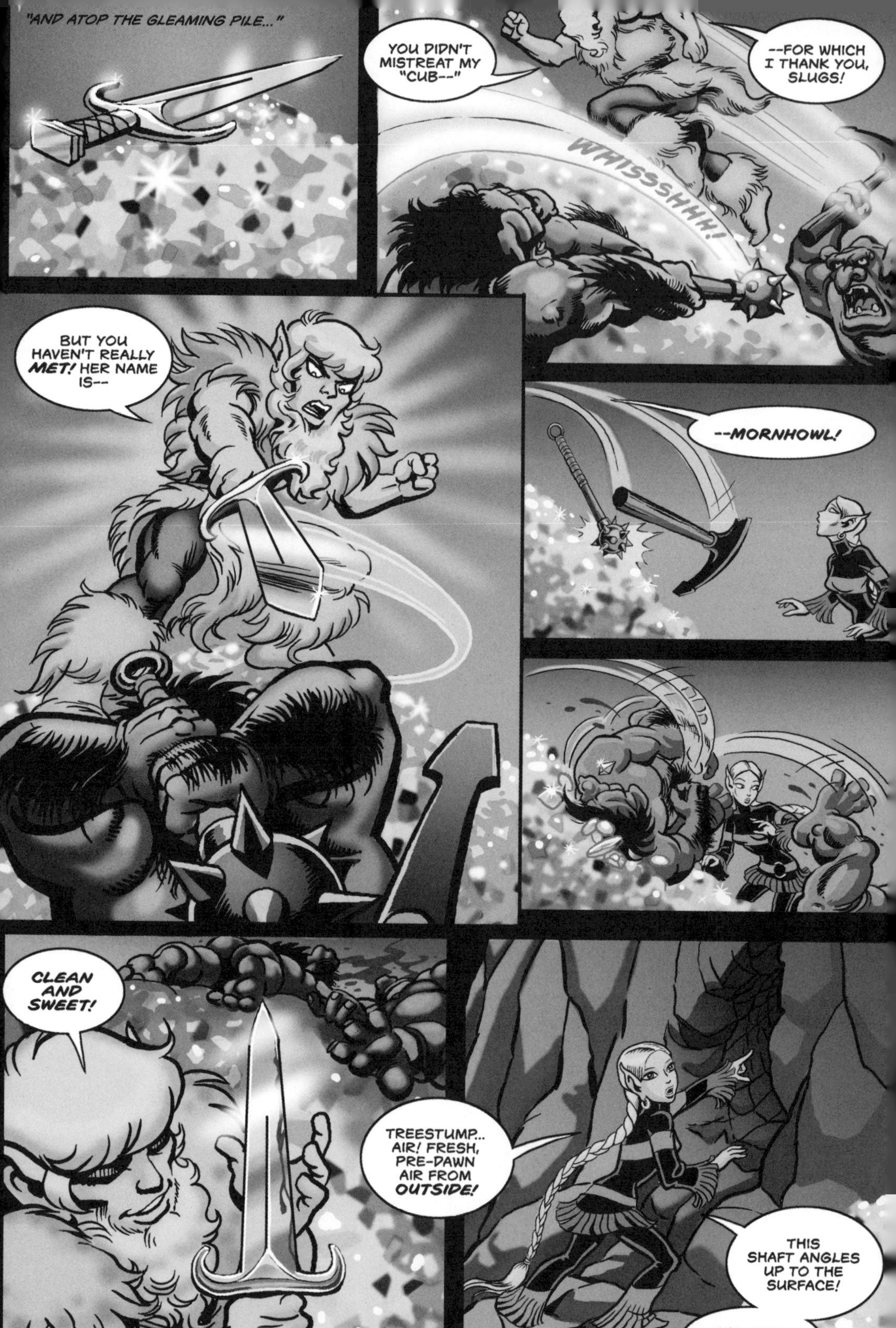
"AND ATOP THE GLEAMING PILE..."
YOU DIDN'T MISTREAT MY "CUB--"
--FOR WHICH I THANK YOU, SLUGS!
WHISSSHHH!
BUT YOU HAVEN'T REALLY MET! HER NAME IS--
--MORNHOWL!
CLEAN AND SWEET!
TREESTUMP... AIR! FRESH, PRE-DAWN AIR FROM OUTSIDE!
THIS SHAFT ANGLES UP TO THE SURFACE!
IT'S JUST BIG ENOUGH!

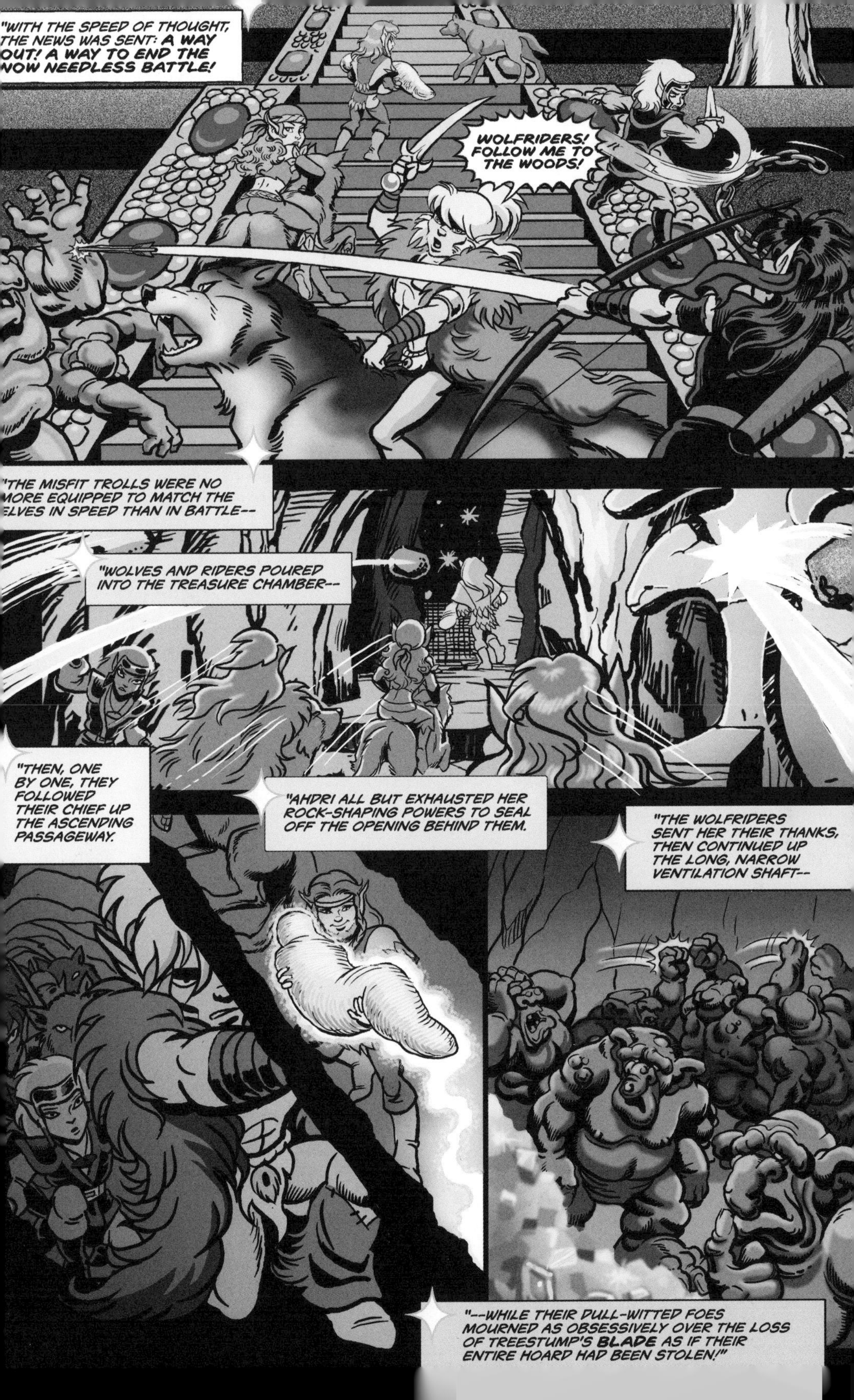
"WITH THE SPEED OF THOUGHT, THE NEWS WAS SENT: A WAY OUT! A WAY TO END THE NOW NEEDLESS BATTLE!
WOLFRIDERS! FOLLOW ME TO THE WOODS!
"THE MISFIT TROLLS WERE NO MORE EQUIPPED TO MATCH THE ELVES IN SPEED THAN IN BATTLE--
"WOLVES AND RIDERS POURED INTO THE TREASURE CHAMBER--
"THEN, ONE BY ONE, THEY FOLLOWED THEIR CHIEF UP THE ASCENDING PASSAGEWAY.
"AHDRI ALL BUT EXHAUSTED HER ROCK-SHAPING POWERS TO SEAL OFF THE OPENING BEHIND THEM.
"THE WOLFRIDERS SENT HER THEIR THANKS, THEN CONTINUED UP THE LONG, NARROW VENTILATION SHAFT--
"--WHILE THEIR DULL-WITTED FOES MOURNED AS OBSESSIVELY OVER THE LOSS OF TREESTUMP'S BLADE AS IF THEIR ENTIRE HOARD HAD BEEN STOLEN!"

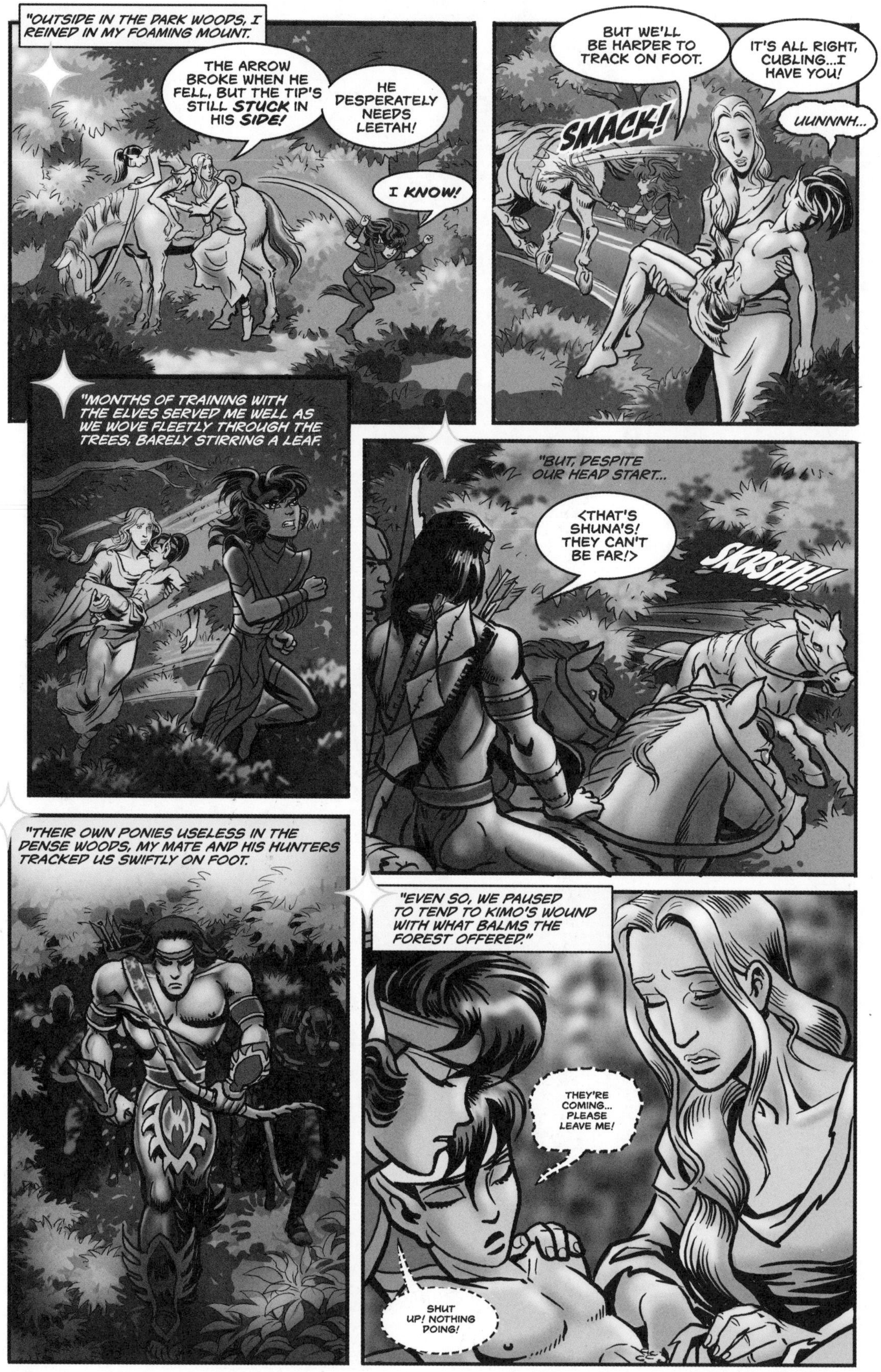
"OUTSIDE IN THE DARK WOODS, I REINED IN MY FOAMING MOUNT.
THE ARROW BROKE WHEN HE FELL, BUT THE TIP'S STILL STUCK IN HIS SIDE!
HE DESPERATELY NEEDS LEETAH!
I KNOW!
BUT WE'LL BE HARDER TO TRACK ON FOOT.
IT'S ALL RIGHT, CUBLING...I HAVE YOU!
SMACK!
UUNNNH...
"MONTHS OF TRAINING WITH THE ELVES SERVED ME WELL AS WE WOVE FLEETLY THROUGH THE TREES, BARELY STIRRING A LEAF.
"BUT, DESPITE OUR HEAD START...
<THAT'S SHUNA'S! THEY CAN'T BE FAR!>
SKRSHH!
"THEIR OWN PONIES USELESS IN THE DENSE WOODS, MY MATE AND HIS HUNTERS TRACKED US SWIFTLY ON FOOT.
"EVEN SO, WE PAUSED TO TEND TO KIMO'S WOUND WITH WHAT BALMS THE FOREST OFFERED."
THEY'RE COMING... PLEASE LEAVE ME!
SHUT UP! NOTHING DOING!

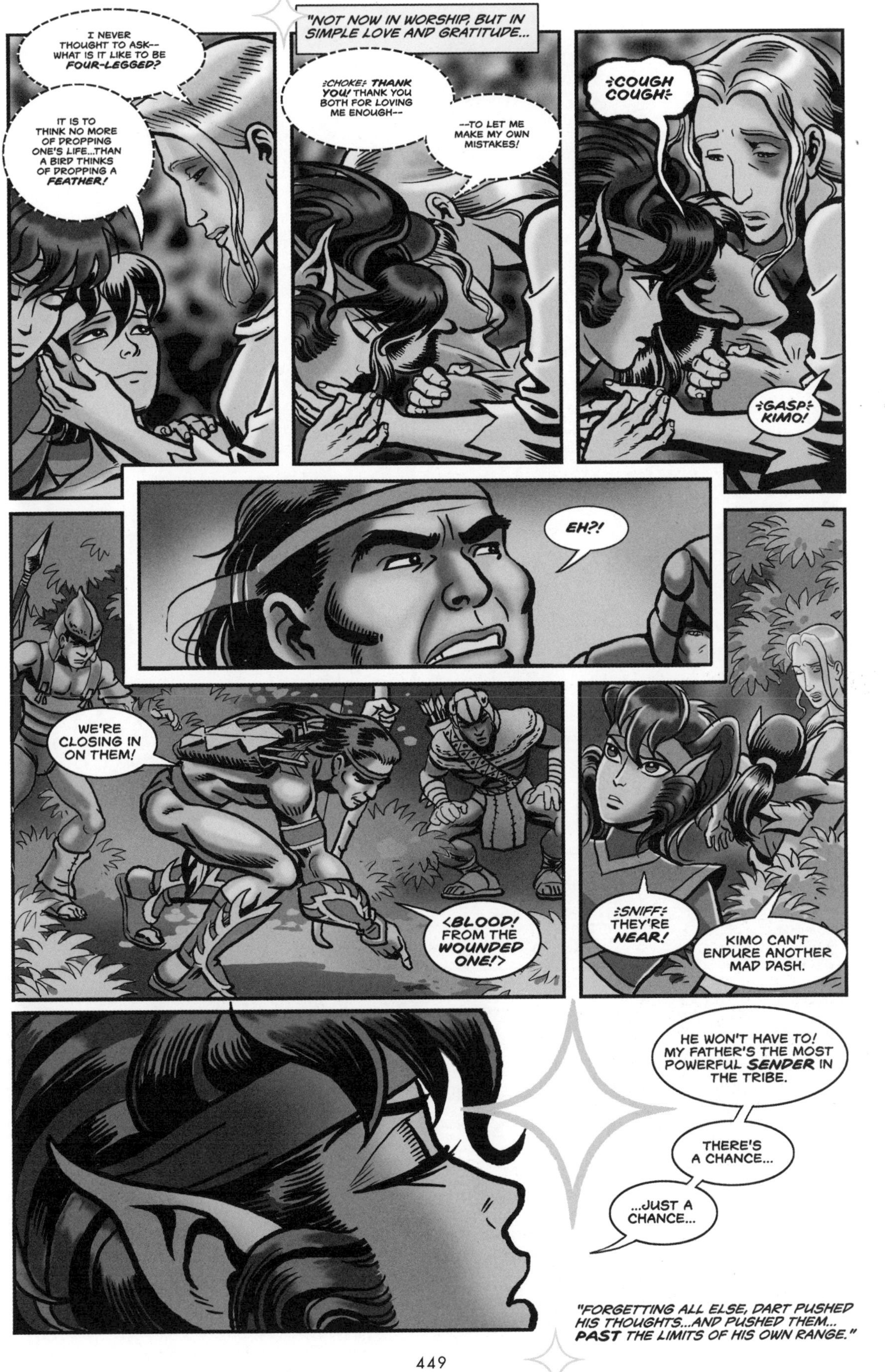

"NOT NOW IN WORSHIP, BUT IN SIMPLE LOVE AND GRATITUDE...
I NEVER THOUGHT TO ASK--WHAT IS IT LIKE TO BE FOUR-LEGGED?
IT IS TO THINK NO MORE OF DROPPING ONE'S LIFE...THAN A BIRD THINKS OF DROPPING A FEATHER!
CHOKE THANK YOU! THANK YOU BOTH FOR LOVING ME ENOUGH--
--TO LET ME MAKE MY OWN MISTAKES!
COUGH COUGH
GASP KIMO!
EH?!
WE'RE CLOSING IN ON THEM!
<BLOOD! FROM THE WOUNDED ONE!>
SNIFF THEY'RE NEAR!
KIMO CAN'T ENDURE ANOTHER MAD DASH.
HE WON'T HAVE TO! MY FATHER'S THE MOST POWERFUL SENDER IN THE TRIBE.
THERE'S A CHANCE...
...JUST A CHANCE...
"FORGETTING ALL ELSE, DART PUSHED HIS THOUGHTS...AND PUSHED THEM... PAST THE LIMITS OF HIS OWN RANGE."

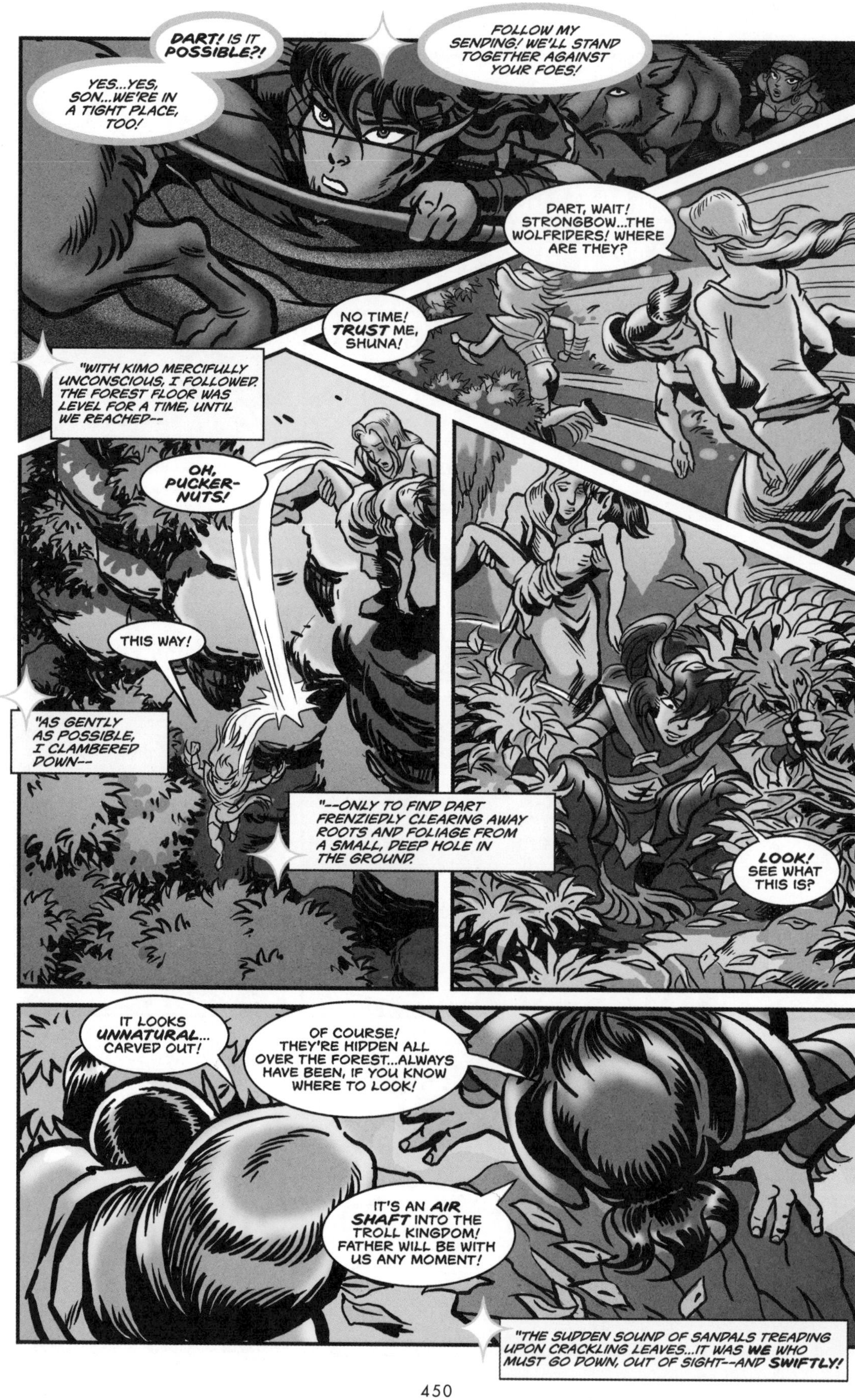
DART! IS IT POSSIBLE?!
YES...YES, SON...WE'RE IN A TIGHT PLACE, TOO!
FOLLOW MY SENDING! WE'LL STAND TOGETHER AGAINST YOUR FOES!
DART, WAIT! STRONGBOW...THE WOLFRIDERS! WHERE ARE THEY?
NO TIME! TRUST ME, SHUNA!
"WITH KIMO MERCIFULLY UNCONSCIOUS, I FOLLOWED. THE FOREST FLOOR WAS LEVEL FOR A TIME, UNTIL WE REACHED--
OH, PUCKER-NUTS!
THIS WAY!
"AS GENTLY AS POSSIBLE, I CLAMBERED DOWN--
"--ONLY TO FIND DART FRENZIEDLY CLEARING AWAY ROOTS AND FOLIAGE FROM A SMALL, DEEP HOLE IN THE GROUND.
LOOK! SEE WHAT THIS IS?
IT LOOKS UNNATURAL... CARVED OUT!
OF COURSE! THEY'RE HIDDEN ALL OVER THE FOREST...ALWAYS HAVE BEEN, IF YOU KNOW WHERE TO LOOK!
IT'S AN AIR SHAFT INTO THE TROLL KINGDOM! FATHER WILL BE WITH US ANY MOMENT!
"THE SUDDEN SOUND OF SANDALS TREADING UPON CRACKLING LEAVES...IT WAS WE WHO MUST GO DOWN, OUT OF SIGHT--AND SWIFTLY!

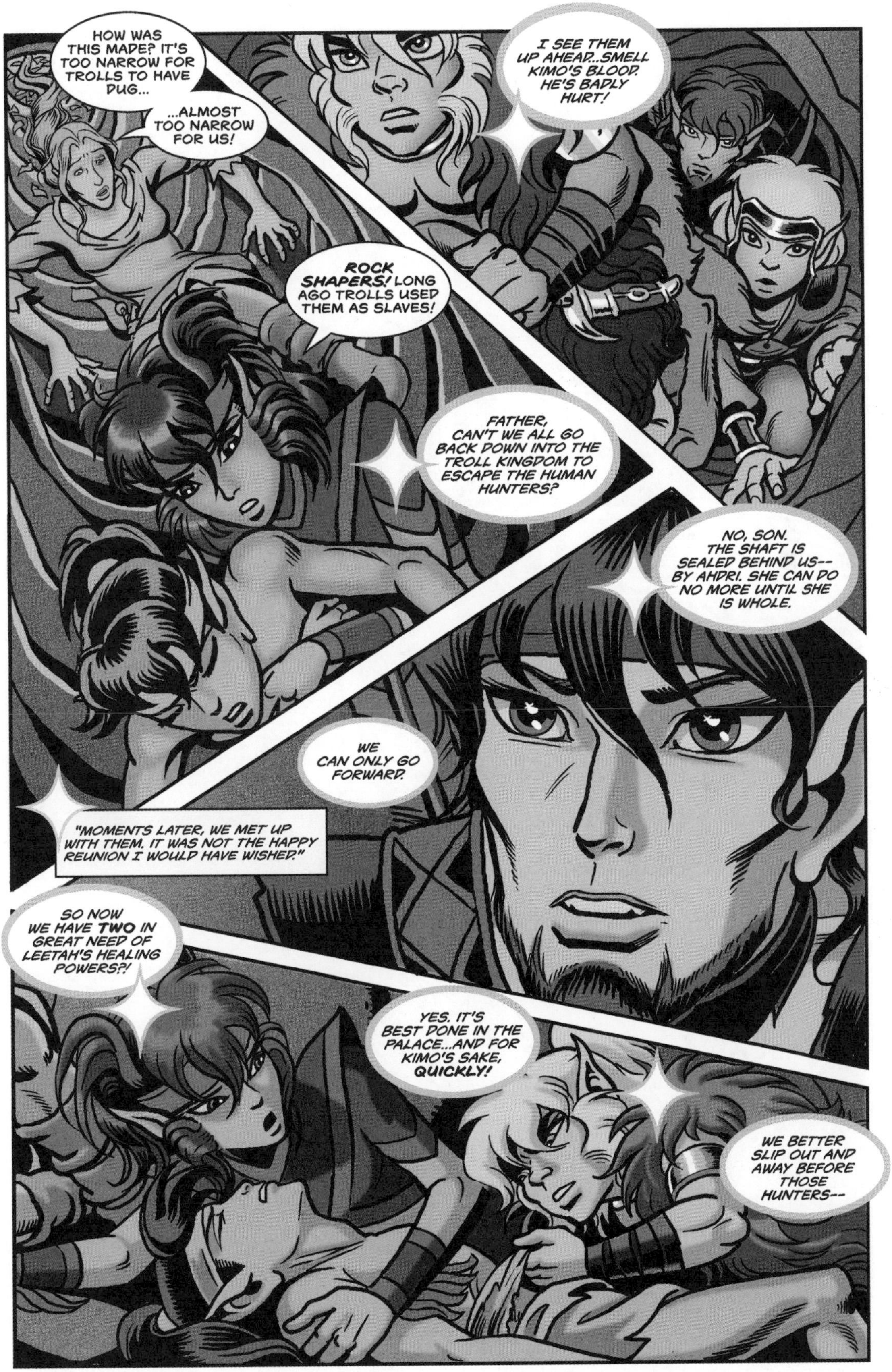
HOW WAS THIS MADE? IT'S TOO NARROW FOR TROLLS TO HAVE DUG...
...ALMOST TOO NARROW FOR US!
I SEE THEM UP AHEAD...SMELL KIMO'S BLOOD. HE'S BADLY HURT!
ROCK SHAPERS! LONG AGO TROLLS USED THEM AS SLAVES!
FATHER, CAN'T WE ALL GO BACK DOWN INTO THE TROLL KINGDOM TO ESCAPE THE HUMAN HUNTERS?
NO, SON. THE SHAFT IS SEALED BEHIND US--BY AHDRI. SHE CAN DO NO MORE UNTIL SHE IS WHOLE.
WE CAN ONLY GO FORWARD.
"MOMENTS LATER, WE MET UP WITH THEM. IT WAS NOT THE HAPPY REUNION I WOULD HAVE WISHED."
SO NOW WE HAVE TWO IN GREAT NEED OF LEETAH'S HEALING POWERS?!
YES. IT'S BEST DONE IN THE PALACE...AND FOR KIMO'S SAKE, QUICKLY!
WE BETTER SLIP OUT AND AWAY BEFORE THOSE HUNTERS--

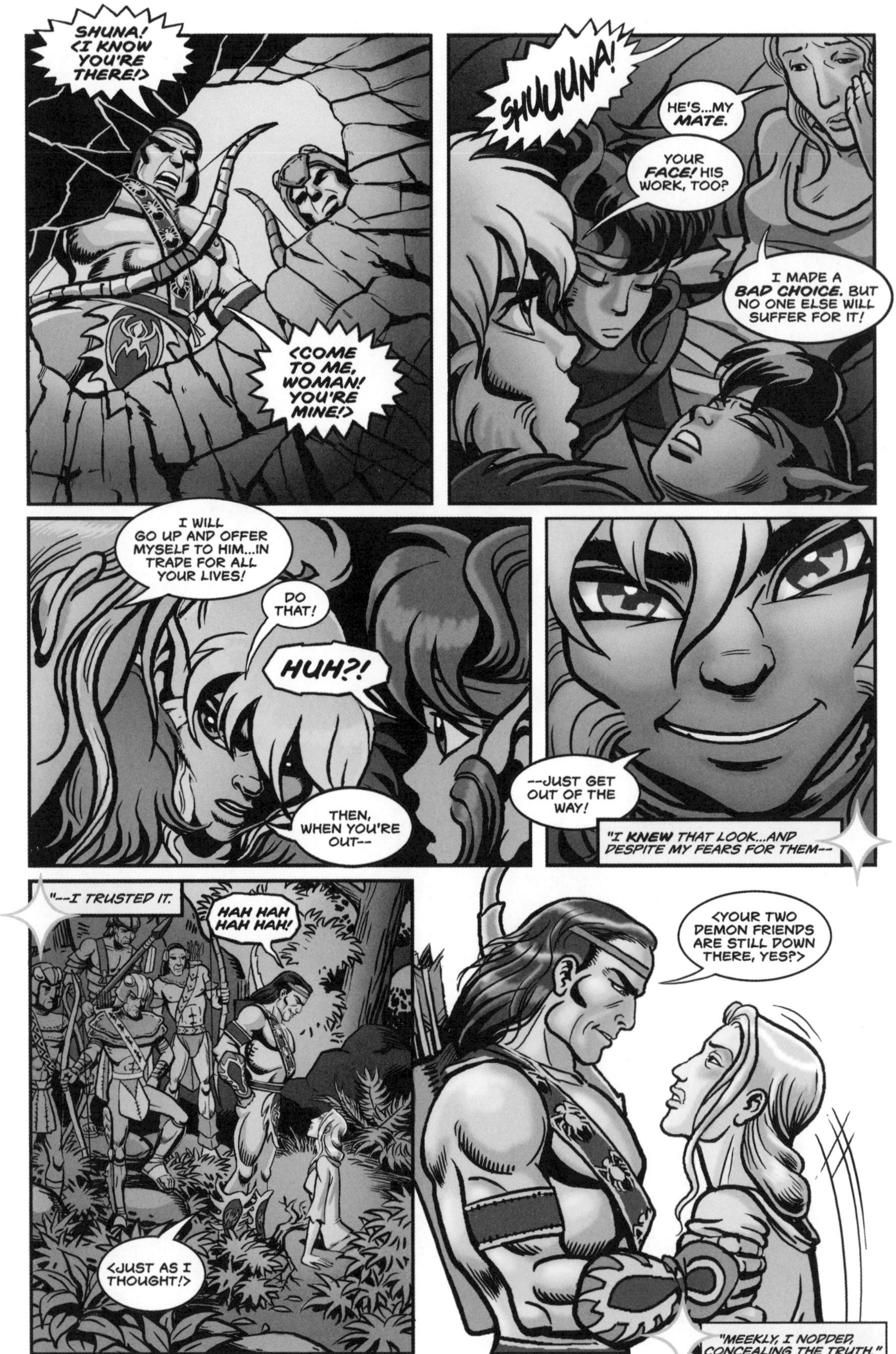
SHUNA! <I KNOW YOU'RE THERE!>
<COME TO ME, WOMAN! YOU'RE MINE!>--
SHUUUNA!
HE'S...MY MATE.
YOUR FACE! HIS WORK, TOO?
I MADE A BAD CHOICE. BUT NO ONE ELSE WILL SUFFER FOR IT!
I WILL GO UP AND OFFER MYSELF TO HIM...IN TRADE FOR ALL YOUR LIVES!
DO THAT!
HUH?!
THEN, WHEN YOU'RE OUT--
--JUST GET OUT OF THE WAY!
"I KNEW THAT LOOK...AND DESPITE MY FEARS FOR THEM--
"--I TRUSTED IT.
HAH HAH HAH HAH!
<JUST AS I THOUGHT!>
<YOUR TWO DEMON FRIENDS ARE STILL DOWN THERE, YES?>
"MEEKLY, I NODDED, CONCEALING THE TRUTH."

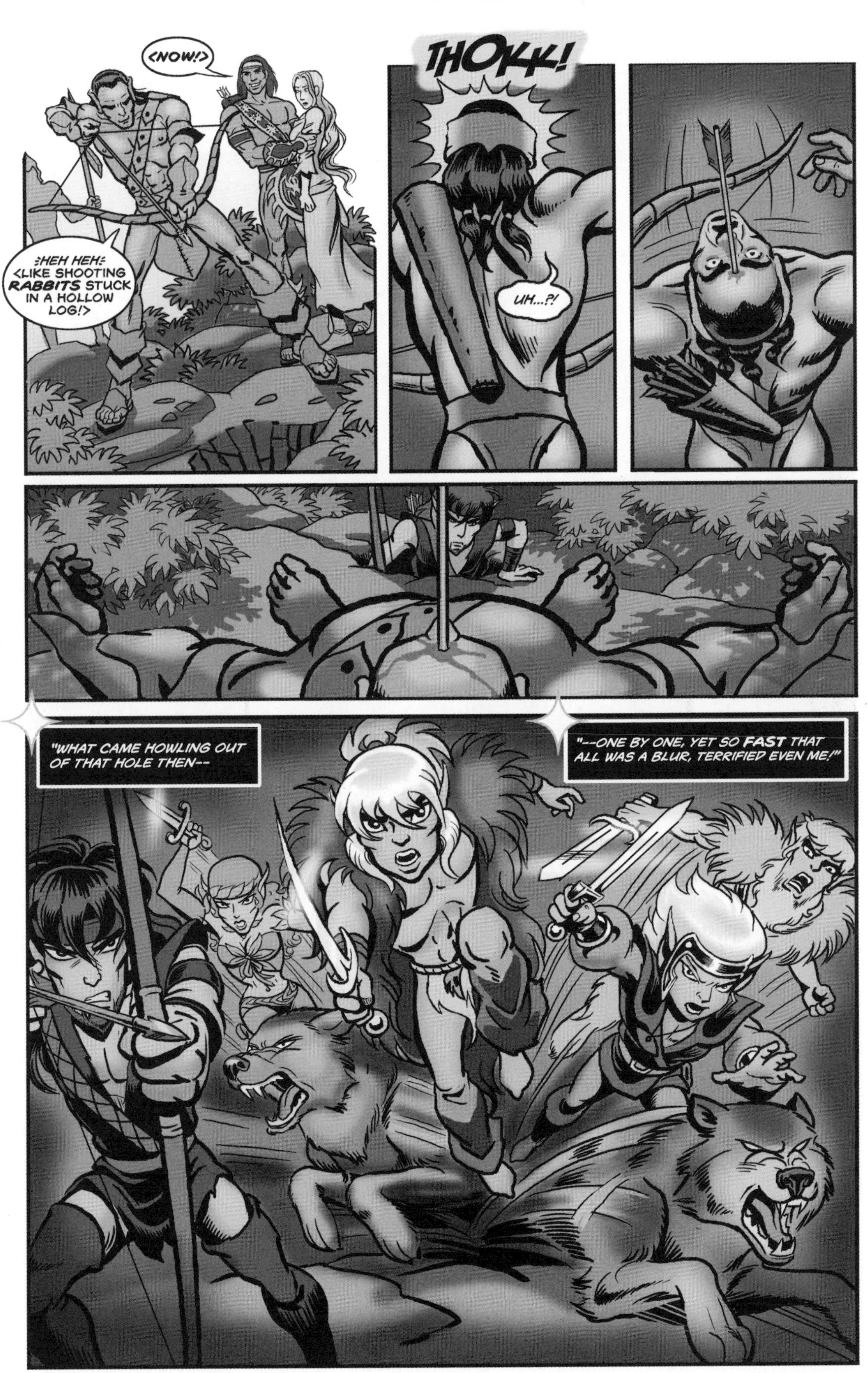
<NOW!>
:HEH HEH: <LIKE SHOOTING RABBITS STUCK IN A HOLLOW LOG!>
THOKK!
UH...?!
"WHAT CAME HOWLING OUT OF THAT HOLE THEN--
"--ONE BY ONE, YET SO FAST THAT ALL WAS A BLUR, TERRIFIED EVEN ME!"

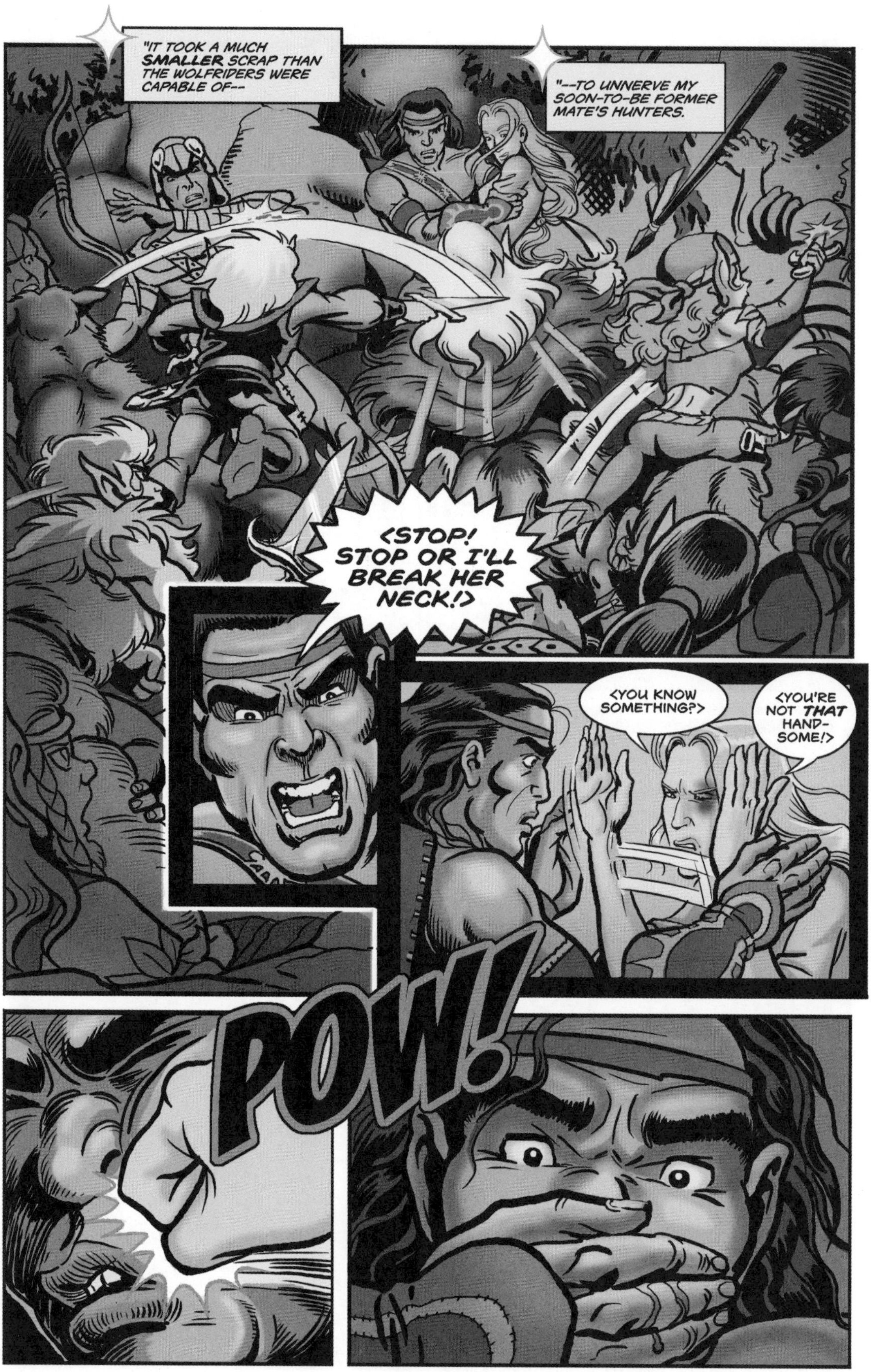
"IT TOOK A MUCH SMALLER SCRAP THAN THE WOLFRIDERS WERE CAPABLE OF--
"--TO UNNERVE MY SOON-TO-BE FORMER MATE'S HUNTERS.
<STOP! STOP OR I'LL BREAK HER NECK!>
<YOU KNOW SOMETHING?>
<YOU'RE NOT THAT HAND-SOME!>
POW!

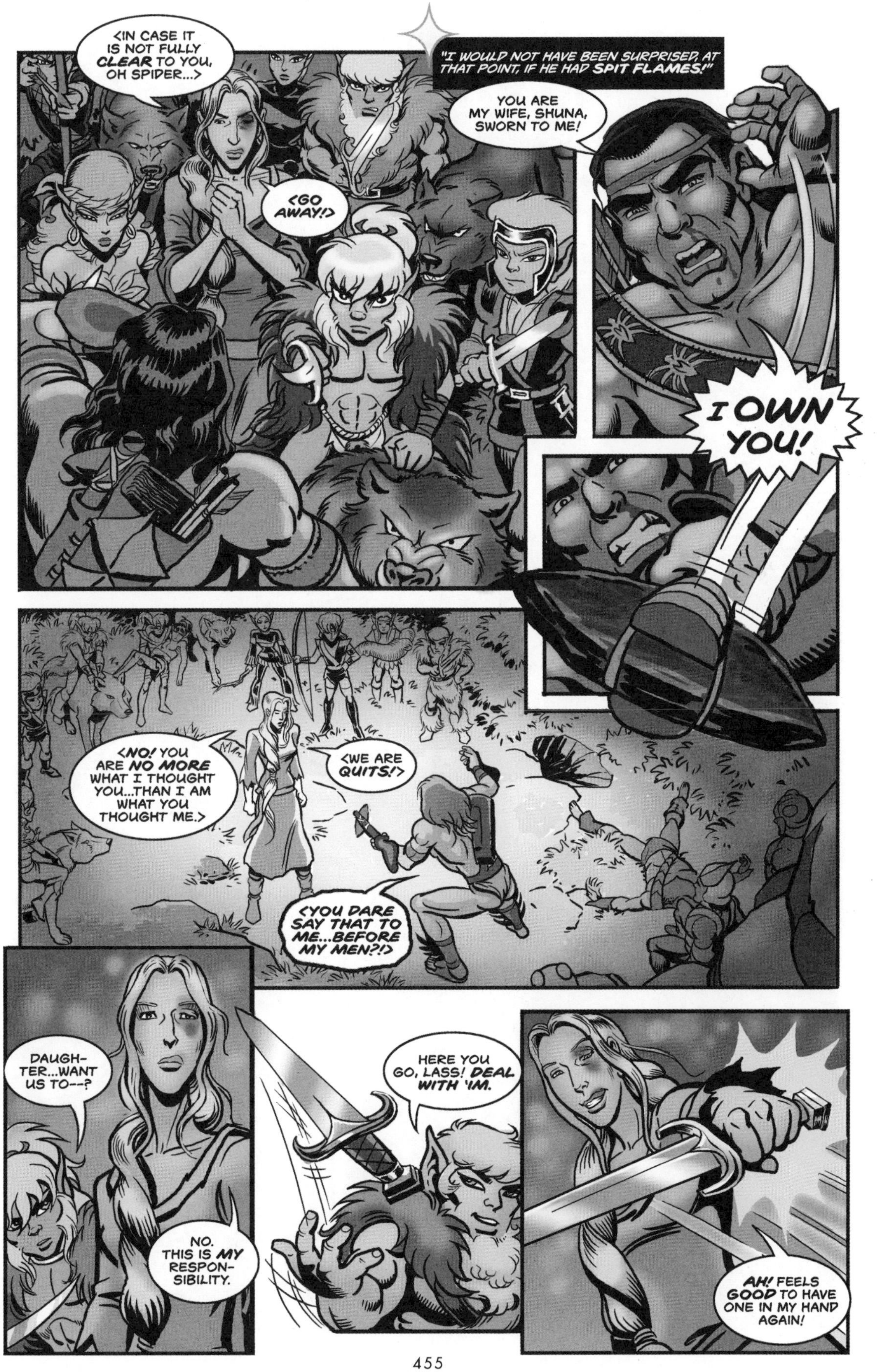
<IN CASE IT IS NOT FULLY CLEAR TO YOU, OH SPIDER...>
<GO AWAY!>
"I WOULD NOT HAVE BEEN SURPRISED, AT THAT POINT, IF HE HAD SPIT FLAMES!"
YOU ARE MY WIFE, SHUNA, SWORN TO ME!
I OWN YOU!
<NO! YOU ARE NO MORE WHAT I THOUGHT YOU...THAN I AM WHAT YOU THOUGHT ME.>
<WE ARE QUITS!>
<YOU DARE SAY THAT TO ME...BEFORE MY MEN?!>
DAUGHTER...WANT US TO--?
NO. THIS IS MY RESPONSIBILITY.
HERE YOU GO, LASS! DEAL WITH 'IM.
AH! FEELS GOOD TO HAVE ONE IN MY HAND AGAIN!

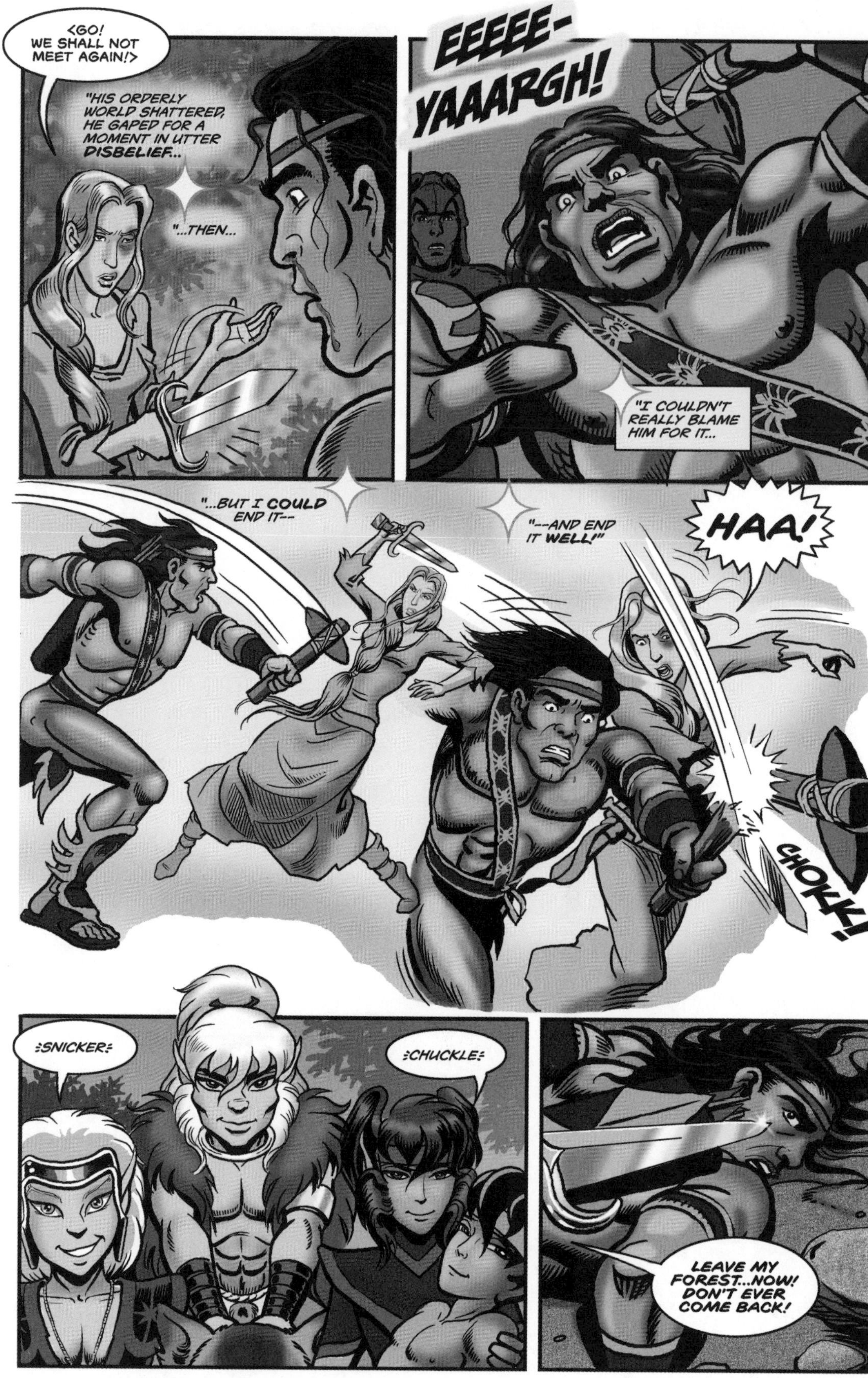

<GO! WE SHALL NOT MEET AGAIN!>
"HIS ORDERLY WORLD SHATTERED, HE GAPED FOR A MOMENT IN UTTER DISBELIEF...
"...THEN...
EEEEE-YAAARGH!
"I COULDN'T REALLY BLAME HIM FOR IT...
"...BUT I COULD END IT--
"--AND END IT WELL!"
HAA!
CHOKK!
:SNICKER:
:CHUCKLE:
LEAVE MY FOREST...NOW! DON'T EVER COME BACK!

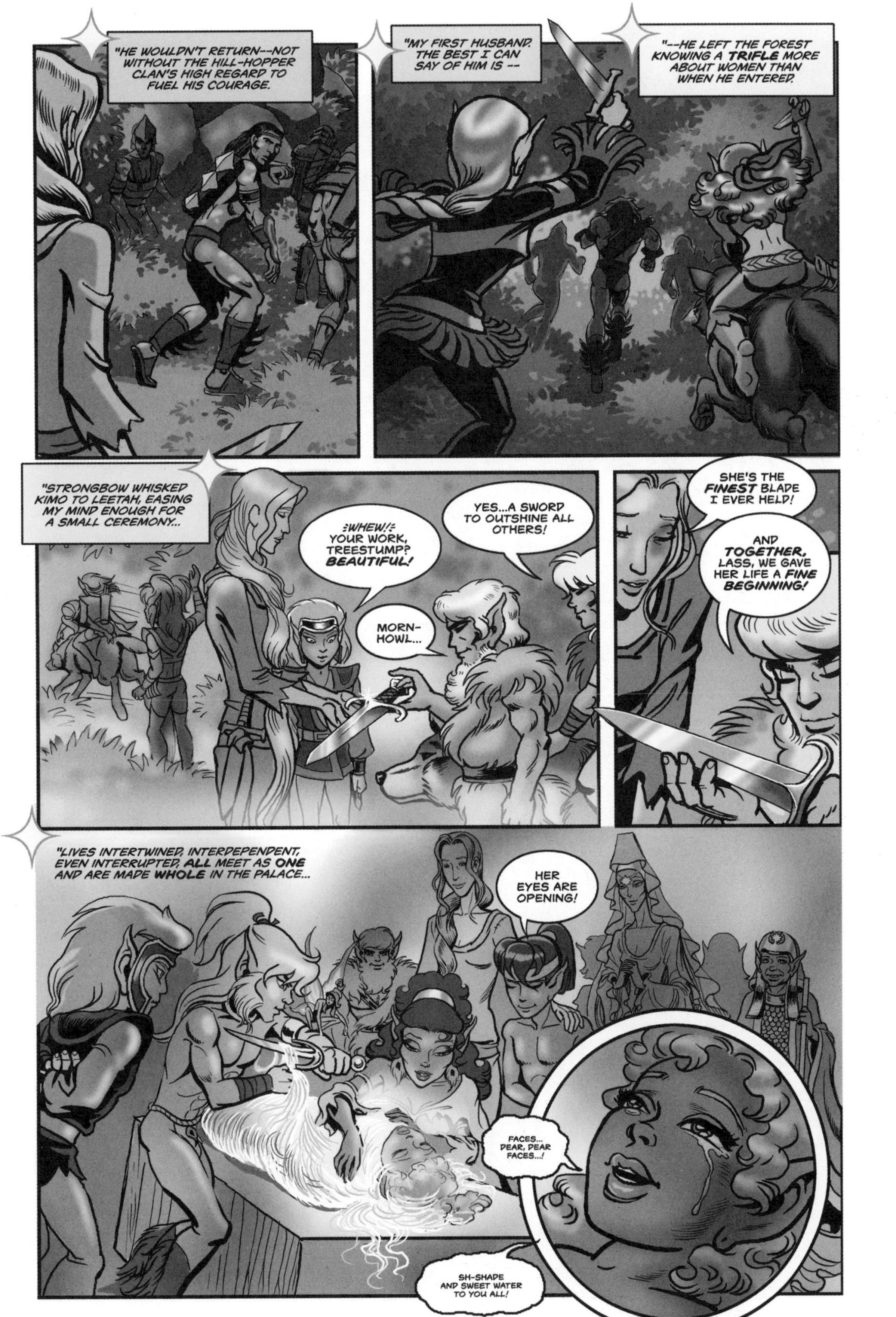
"HE WOULDN'T RETURN--NOT WITHOUT THE HILL-HOPPER CLAN'S HIGH REGARD TO FUEL HIS COURAGE.
"MY FIRST HUSBAND. THE BEST I CAN SAY OF HIM IS --
"--HE LEFT THE FOREST KNOWING A TRIFLE MORE ABOUT WOMEN THAN WHEN HE ENTERED.
"STRONGBOW WHISKED KIMO TO LEETAH, EASING MY MIND ENOUGH FOR A SMALL CEREMONY...
WHEW! YOUR WORK, TREESTUMP? BEAUTIFUL!
YES...A SWORD TO OUTSHINE ALL OTHERS!
MORN-HOWL...
SHE'S THE FINEST BLADE I EVER HELD!
AND TOGETHER, LASS, WE GAVE HER LIFE A FINE BEGINNING!
"LIVES INTERTWINED, INTERDEPENDENT, EVEN INTERRUPTED, ALL MEET AS ONE AND ARE MADE WHOLE IN THE PALACE...
HER EYES ARE OPENING!
FACES... DEAR, DEAR FACES...!
SH-SHADE AND SWEET WATER TO YOU ALL!

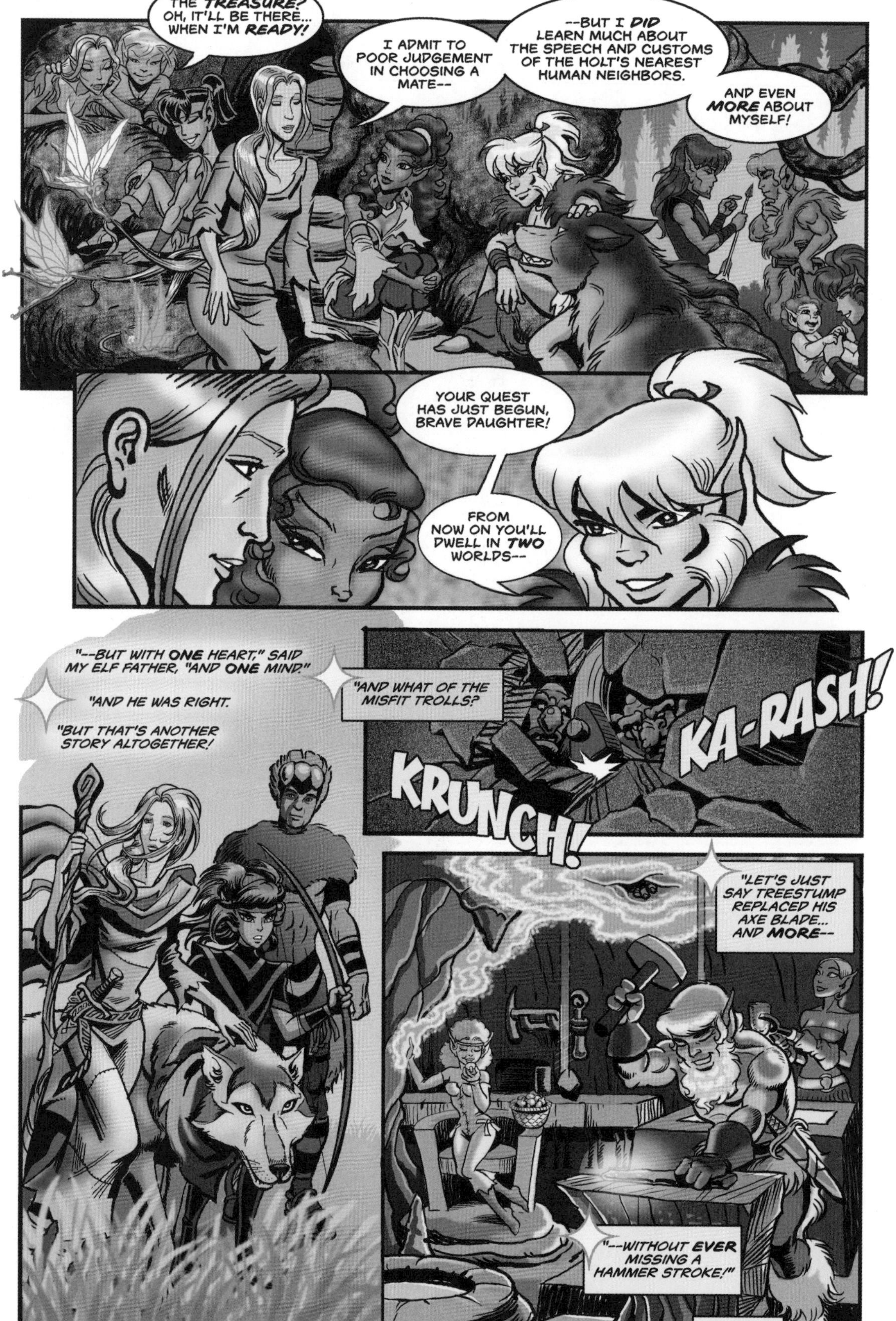
THE TREASURE? OH, IT'LL BE THERE... WHEN I'M READY!
I ADMIT TO POOR JUDGEMENT IN CHOOSING A MATE--
--BUT I DID LEARN MUCH ABOUT THE SPEECH AND CUSTOMS OF THE HOLT'S NEAREST HUMAN NEIGHBORS.
AND EVEN MORE ABOUT MYSELF!
YOUR QUEST HAS JUST BEGUN, BRAVE DAUGHTER!
FROM NOW ON YOU'LL DWELL IN TWO WORLDS--
"--BUT WITH ONE HEART," SAID MY ELF FATHER, "AND ONE MIND."
"AND HE WAS RIGHT.
"BUT THAT'S ANOTHER STORY ALTOGETHER!
"AND WHAT OF THE MISFIT TROLLS?
KA-RASH!
KRUNCH!
"LET'S JUST SAY TREESTUMP REPLACED HIS AXE BLADE... AND MORE--
"--WITHOUT EVER MISSING A HAMMER STROKE!"
THE END

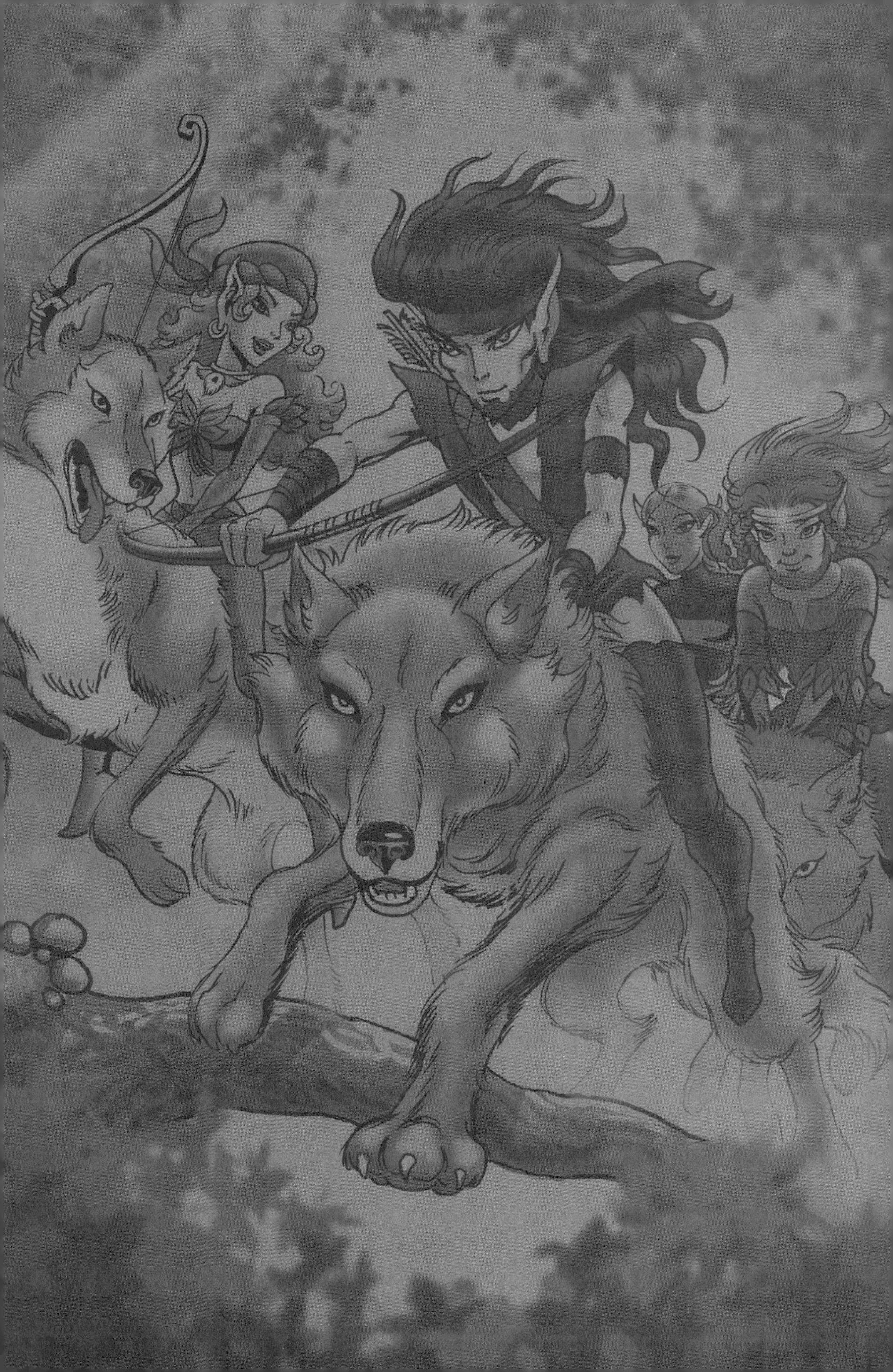

Once upon a time...

The forest-born elves called Wolfriders fought a brutal human
warlord to regain their most precious possession: the crystal
Palace of the High Ones, the star-faring vessel that had brought the
elves' ancestors to the World of Two Moons.

The battle was a bloody one, and the Wolfriders' chief Cutter
suffered wrenching losses -- of more than one kind.
But new alliances were made as well. The sweetest of these saw
Cutter and his lifemate Leetah adopt the human girl Shuna (who had
fought alongside the elves) into their tribe. Strange and wonderful
were the new ways she learned under their guidance.

The Palace once again theirs, the Wolfriders turned to recreating
a home in the forest of their birth -- a new Holt, a place of
safety and peace. But even as they went about their nightly hunts
and howls, the elves could sense that something was amiss.

Unsettling tendrils of ancient magical energy gone bad slithered
from the deep woods. Cutter's son Suntop, a young mystic,
took it upon himself to battle the stagnant pool of foul magic alone.
Calling upon all the elfin spirits dwelling in the
crystal Palace, Suntop used his own body as a conduit
to hurl their Living Light against the festering darkness.

Exhausted but triumphant, Suntop was given the new tribe-name
of Sunstream. The last living High One, Timmain, took Cutter's son
into the Palace as her student, shrouding him in magical Preserver
"wrapstuff" so that his body might sleep and heal even as
his mind absorbed wisdom.

Since then, the Wolfriders have gone about their lives, following
the seasons. Shuna and Treestump embarked on quests of their own,
and came out much the wiser for their experiences.

Cutter still keeps alive his dream of reuniting
the scattered children of the High Ones.

And Sunstream, his body yet slumbering but his powerful
spirit active, is almost ready to emerge and fulfill that dream --
in a way that no one on the World of Two Moons
could begin to imagine!

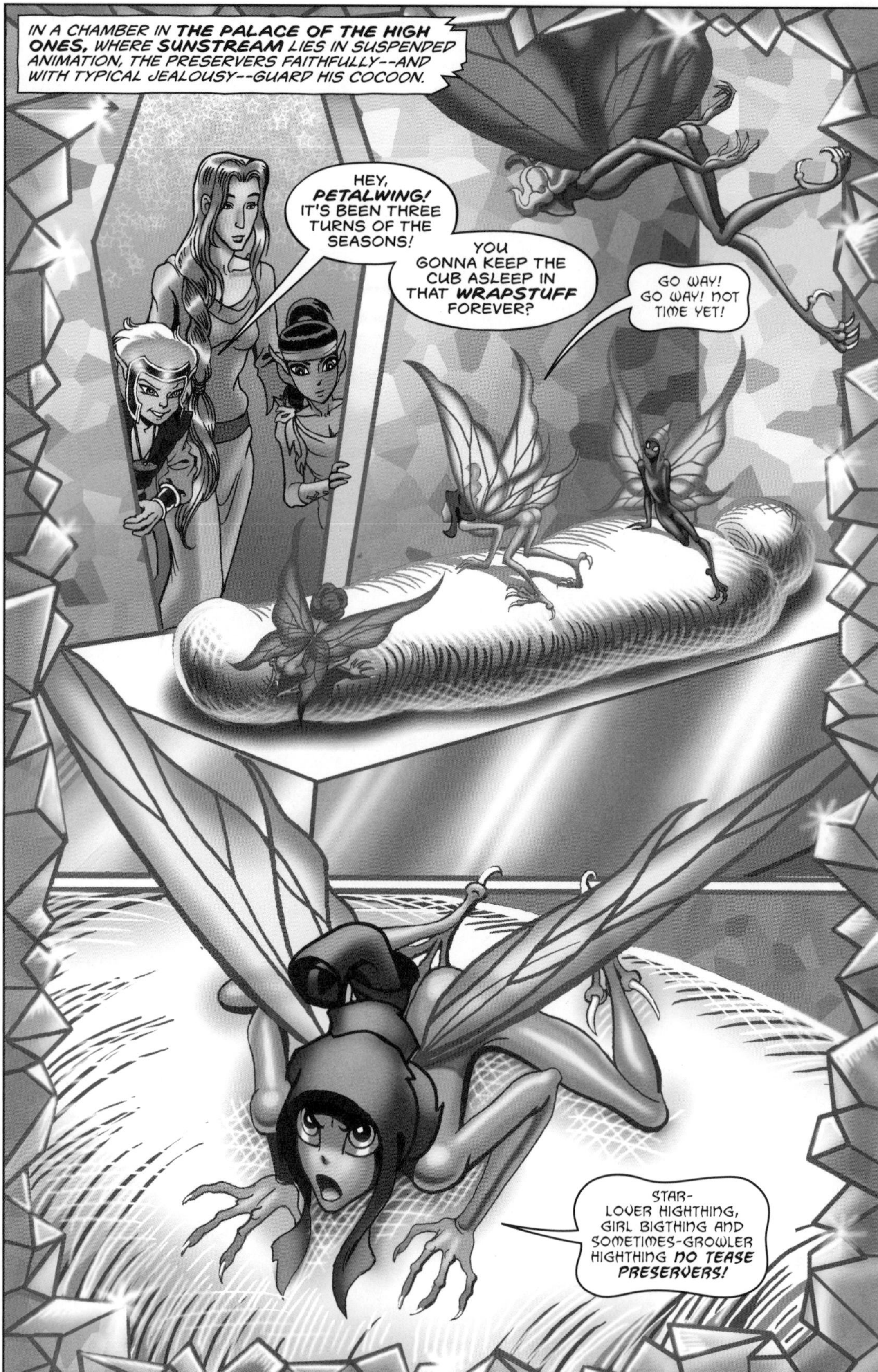
IN A CHAMBER IN THE PALACE OF THE HIGH ONES, WHERE SUNSTREAM LIES IN SUSPENDED ANIMATION, THE PRESERVERS FAITHFULLY--AND WITH TYPICAL JEALOUSY--GUARD HIS COCOON.
HEY, PETALWING! IT'S BEEN THREE TURNS OF THE SEASONS!
YOU GONNA KEEP THE CUB ASLEEP IN THAT WRAPSTUFF FOREVER?
GO WAY! GO WAY! NOT TIME YET!
STAR-LOVER HIGHTHING, GIRL BIGTHING AND SOMETIMES-GROWLER HIGHTHING NO TEASE PRESERVERS!

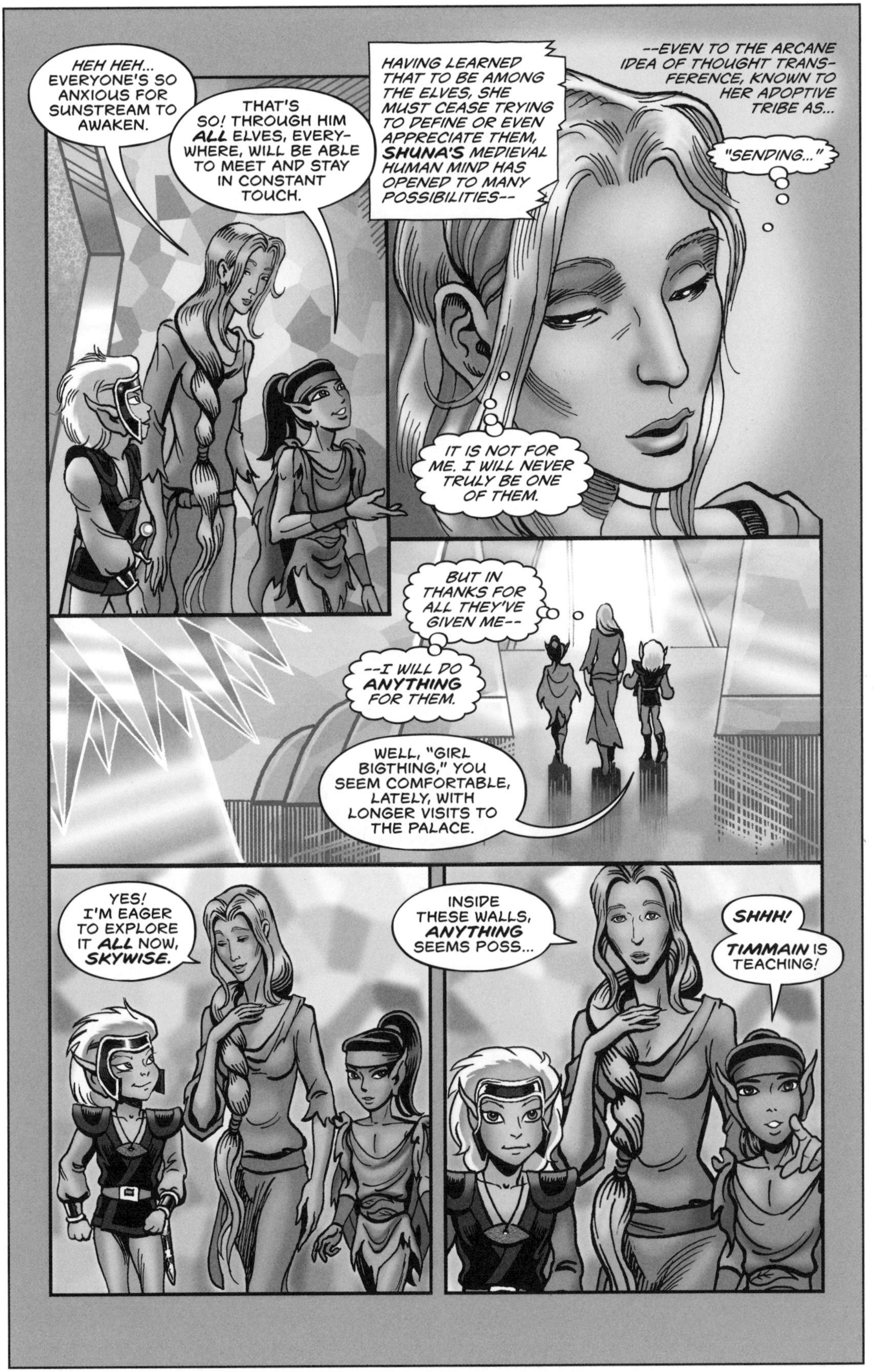
HEH HEH... EVERYONE'S SO ANXIOUS FOR SUNSTREAM TO AWAKEN.
THAT'S SO! THROUGH HIM ALL ELVES, EVERYWHERE, WILL BE ABLE TO MEET AND STAY IN CONSTANT TOUCH.
HAVING LEARNED THAT TO BE AMONG THE ELVES, SHE MUST CEASE TRYING TO DEFINE OR EVEN APPRECIATE THEM, SHUNA'S MEDIEVAL HUMAN MIND HAS OPENED TO MANY POSSIBILITIES--
--EVEN TO THE ARCANE IDEA OF THOUGHT TRANSFERENCE, KNOWN TO HER ADOPTIVE TRIBE AS...
"SENDING..."
IT IS NOT FOR ME. I WILL NEVER TRULY BE ONE OF THEM.
BUT IN THANKS FOR ALL THEY'VE GIVEN ME--
--I WILL DO ANYTHING FOR THEM.
WELL, "GIRL BIGTHING," YOU SEEM COMFORTABLE, LATELY, WITH LONGER VISITS TO THE PALACE.
YES! I'M EAGER TO EXPLORE IT ALL NOW, SKYWISE.
INSIDE THESE WALLS, ANYTHING SEEMS POSS...
SHHH!
TIMMAIN IS TEACHING!

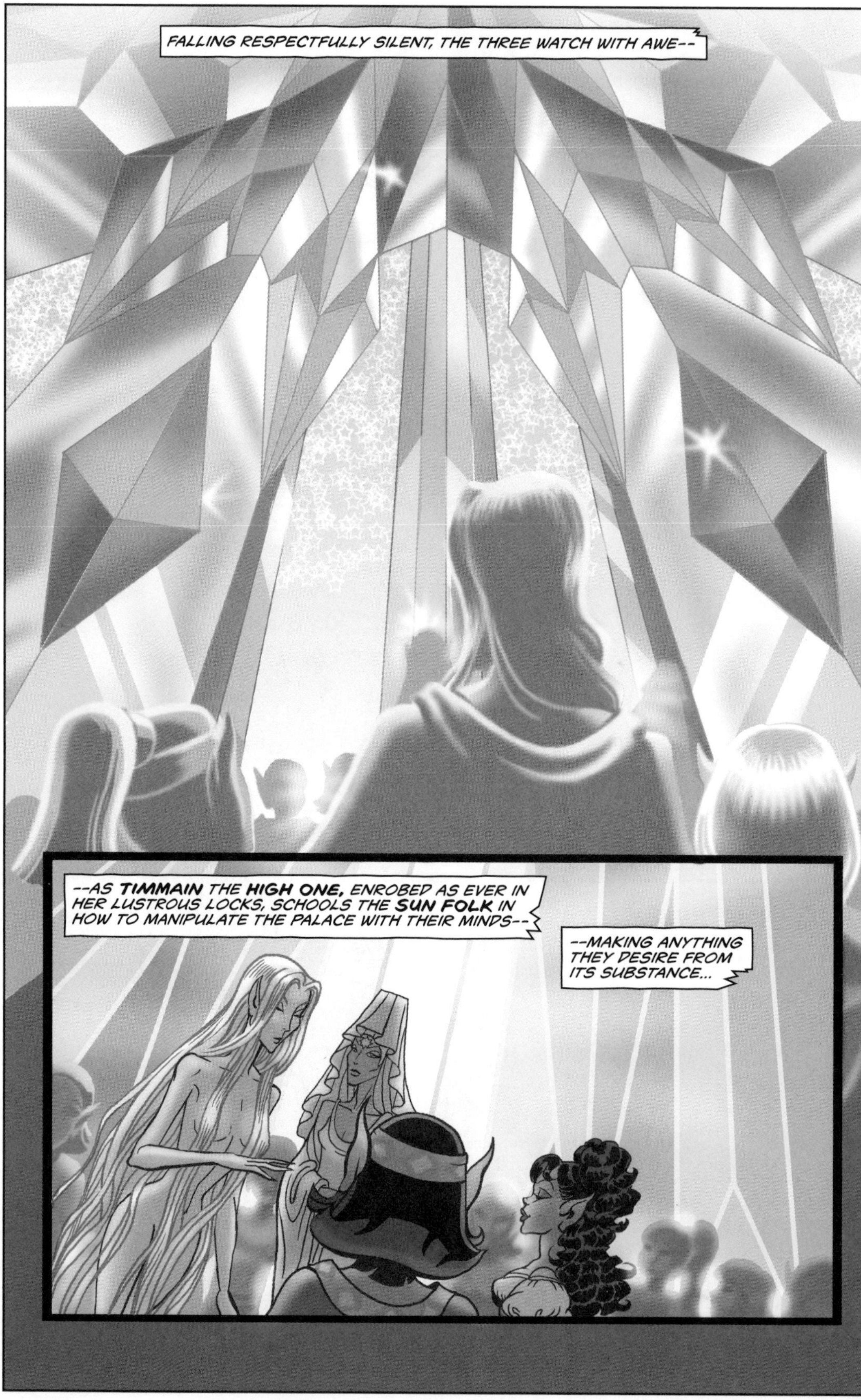
FALLING RESPECTFULLY SILENT, THE THREE WATCH WITH AWE--
--AS **TIMMAIN** THE **HIGH ONE,** ENROBED AS EVER IN HER LUSTROUS LOCKS, SCHOOLS THE **SUN FOLK** IN HOW TO MANIPULATE THE PALACE WITH THEIR MINDS--
--MAKING ANYTHING THEY DESIRE FROM ITS SUBSTANCE...

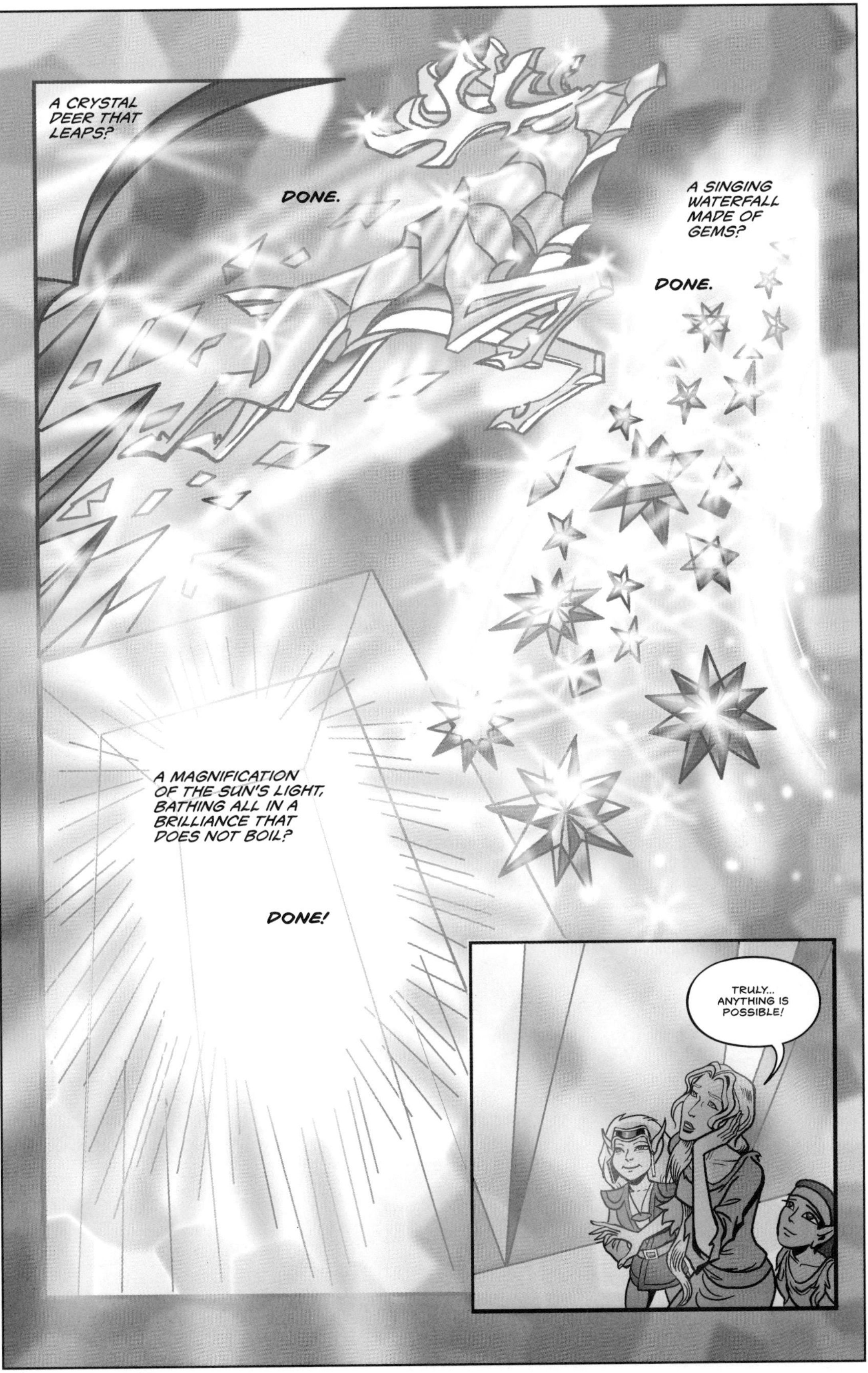
A CRYSTAL DEER THAT LEAPS?
DONE.
A SINGING WATERFALL MADE OF GEMS?
DONE.
A MAGNIFICATION OF THE SUN'S LIGHT, BATHING ALL IN A BRILLIANCE THAT DOES NOT BOIL?
DONE!
TRULY... ANYTHING IS POSSIBLE!

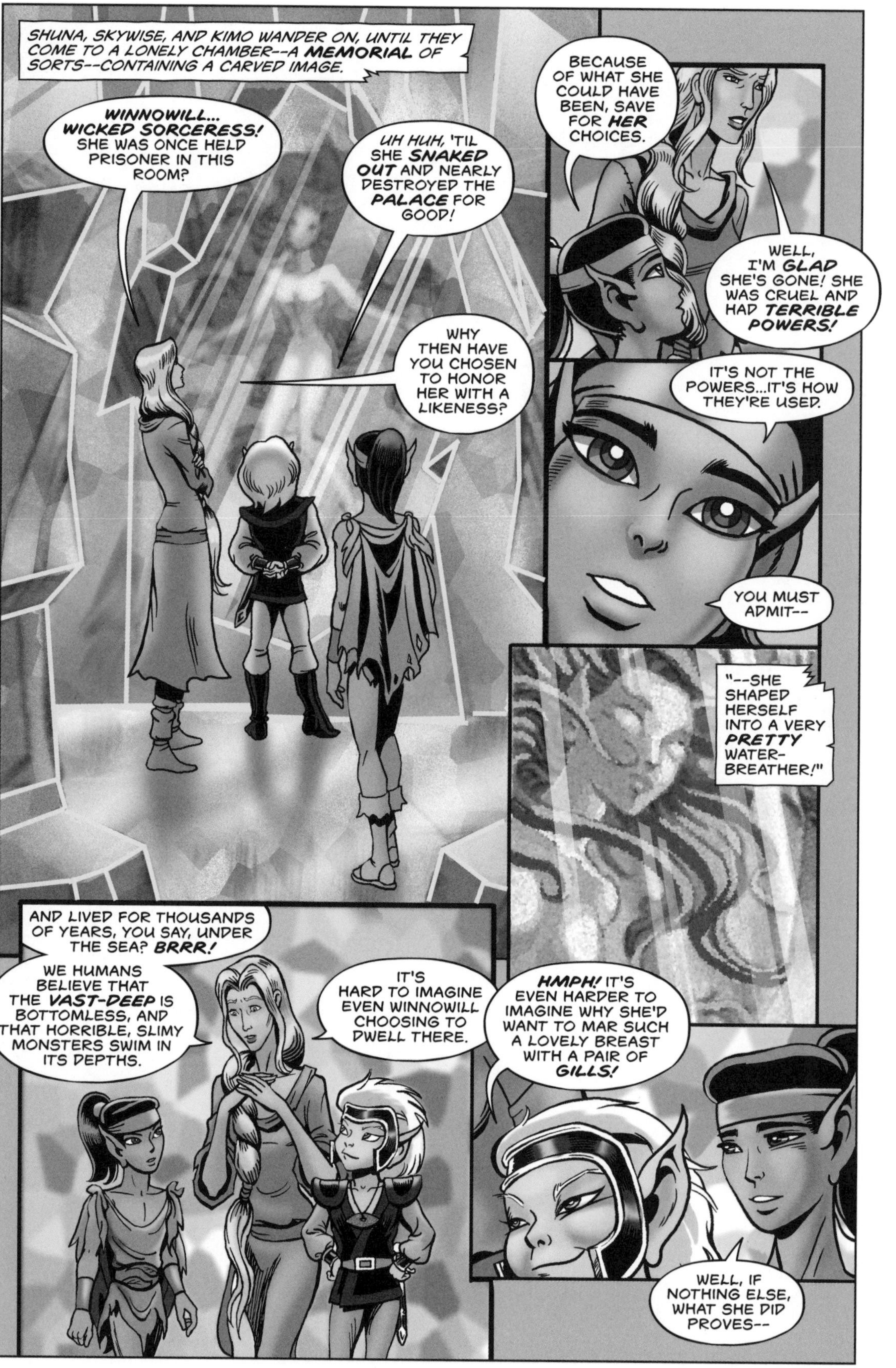

SHUNA, SKYWISE, AND KIMO WANDER ON, UNTIL THEY COME TO A LONELY CHAMBER--A MEMORIAL OF SORTS--CONTAINING A CARVED IMAGE.
WINNOWILL... WICKED SORCERESS! SHE WAS ONCE HELD PRISONER IN THIS ROOM?
UH HUH, 'TIL SHE SNAKED OUT AND NEARLY DESTROYED THE PALACE FOR GOOD!
WHY THEN HAVE YOU CHOSEN TO HONOR HER WITH A LIKENESS?
BECAUSE OF WHAT SHE COULD HAVE BEEN, SAVE FOR HER CHOICES.
WELL, I'M GLAD SHE'S GONE! SHE WAS CRUEL AND HAD TERRIBLE POWERS!
IT'S NOT THE POWERS...IT'S HOW THEY'RE USED.
YOU MUST ADMIT--
"--SHE SHAPED HERSELF INTO A VERY PRETTY WATER-BREATHER!"
AND LIVED FOR THOUSANDS OF YEARS, YOU SAY, UNDER THE SEA? BRRR!
WE HUMANS BELIEVE THAT THE VAST-DEEP IS BOTTOMLESS, AND THAT HORRIBLE, SLIMY MONSTERS SWIM IN ITS DEPTHS.
IT'S HARD TO IMAGINE EVEN WINNOWILL CHOOSING TO DWELL THERE.
HMPH! IT'S EVEN HARDER TO IMAGINE WHY SHE'D WANT TO MAR SUCH A LOVELY BREAST WITH A PAIR OF GILLS!
WELL, IF NOTHING ELSE, WHAT SHE DID PROVES--

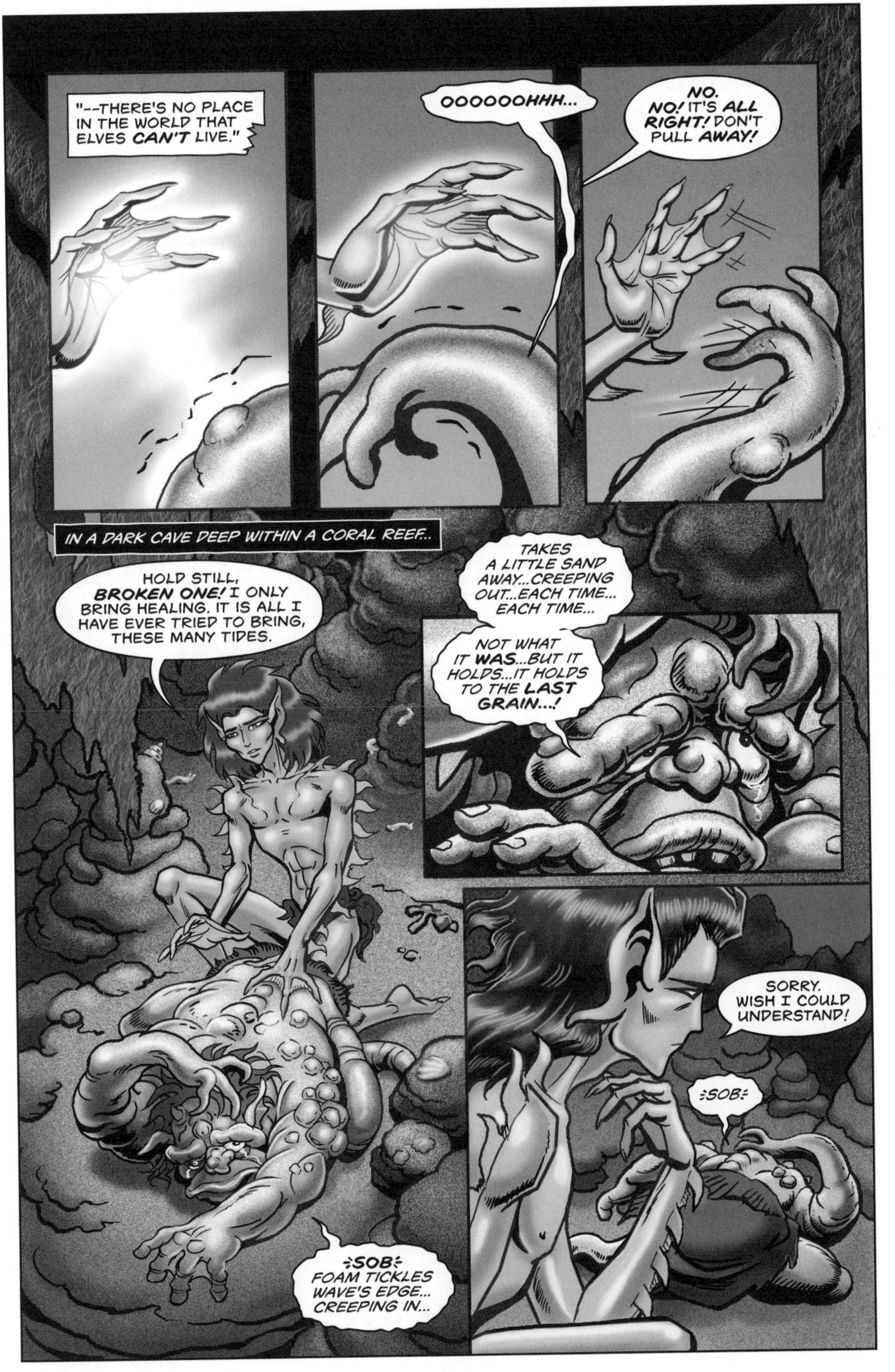
"--THERE'S NO PLACE IN THE WORLD THAT ELVES CAN'T LIVE."
OOOOOOHHH...
NO. NO! IT'S ALL RIGHT! DON'T PULL AWAY!
IN A DARK CAVE DEEP WITHIN A CORAL REEF...
HOLD STILL, BROKEN ONE! I ONLY BRING HEALING. IT IS ALL I HAVE EVER TRIED TO BRING, THESE MANY TIDES.
TAKES A LITTLE SAND AWAY...CREEPING OUT...EACH TIME... EACH TIME...
NOT WHAT IT WAS...BUT IT HOLDS...IT HOLDS TO THE LAST GRAIN...!
SOB FOAM TICKLES WAVE'S EDGE... CREEPING IN...
SORRY. WISH I COULD UNDERSTAND!
SOB

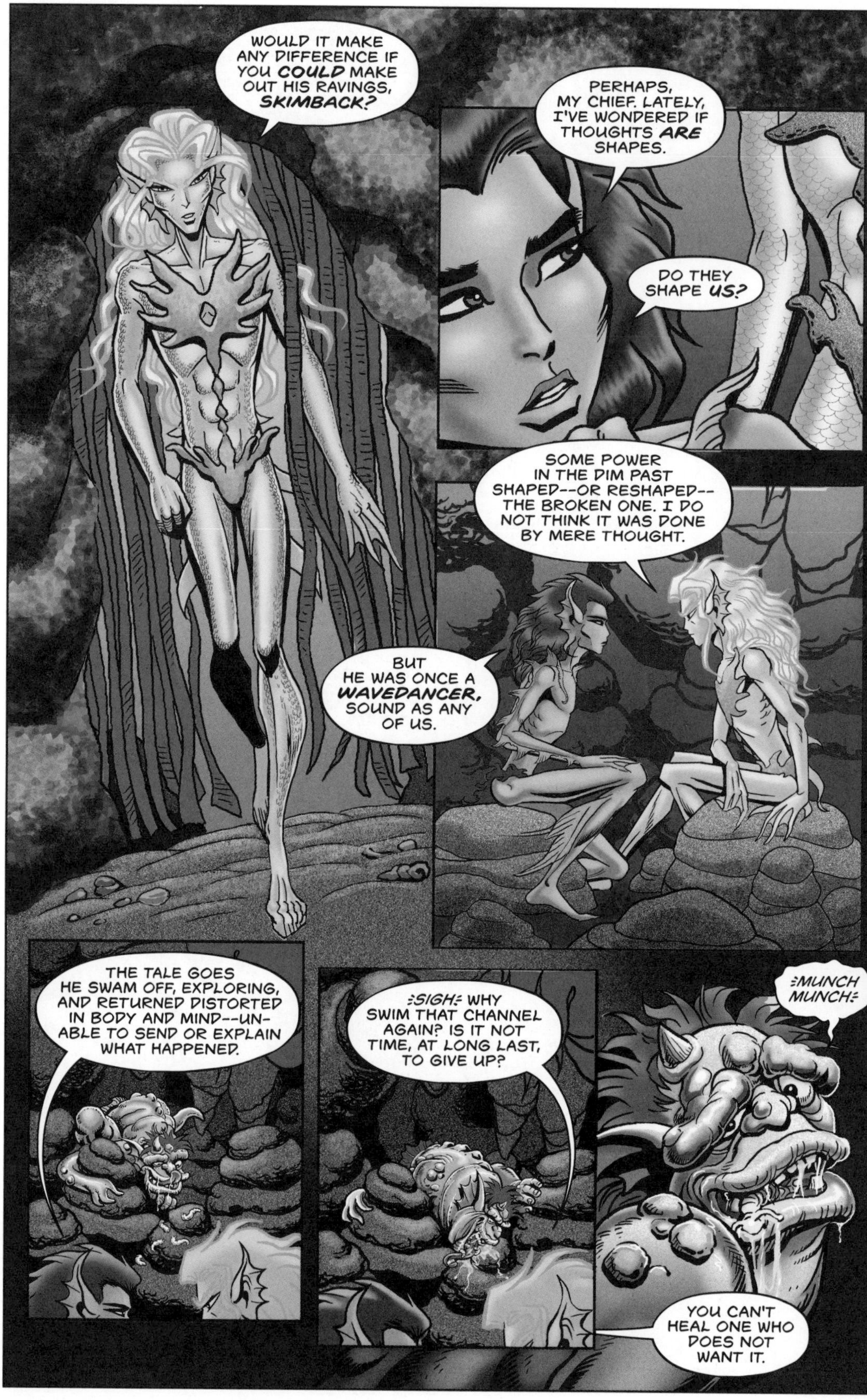
WOULD IT MAKE ANY DIFFERENCE IF YOU COULD MAKE OUT HIS RAVINGS, SKIMBACK?
PERHAPS, MY CHIEF. LATELY, I'VE WONDERED IF THOUGHTS ARE SHAPES.
DO THEY SHAPE US?
SOME POWER IN THE DIM PAST SHAPED--OR RESHAPED--THE BROKEN ONE. I DO NOT THINK IT WAS DONE BY MERE THOUGHT.
BUT HE WAS ONCE A WAVEDANCER, SOUND AS ANY OF US.
THE TALE GOES HE SWAM OFF, EXPLORING, AND RETURNED DISTORTED IN BODY AND MIND--UNABLE TO SEND OR EXPLAIN WHAT HAPPENED.
:SIGH: WHY SWIM THAT CHANNEL AGAIN? IS IT NOT TIME, AT LONG LAST, TO GIVE UP?
:MUNCH MUNCH:
YOU CAN'T HEAL ONE WHO DOES NOT WANT IT.

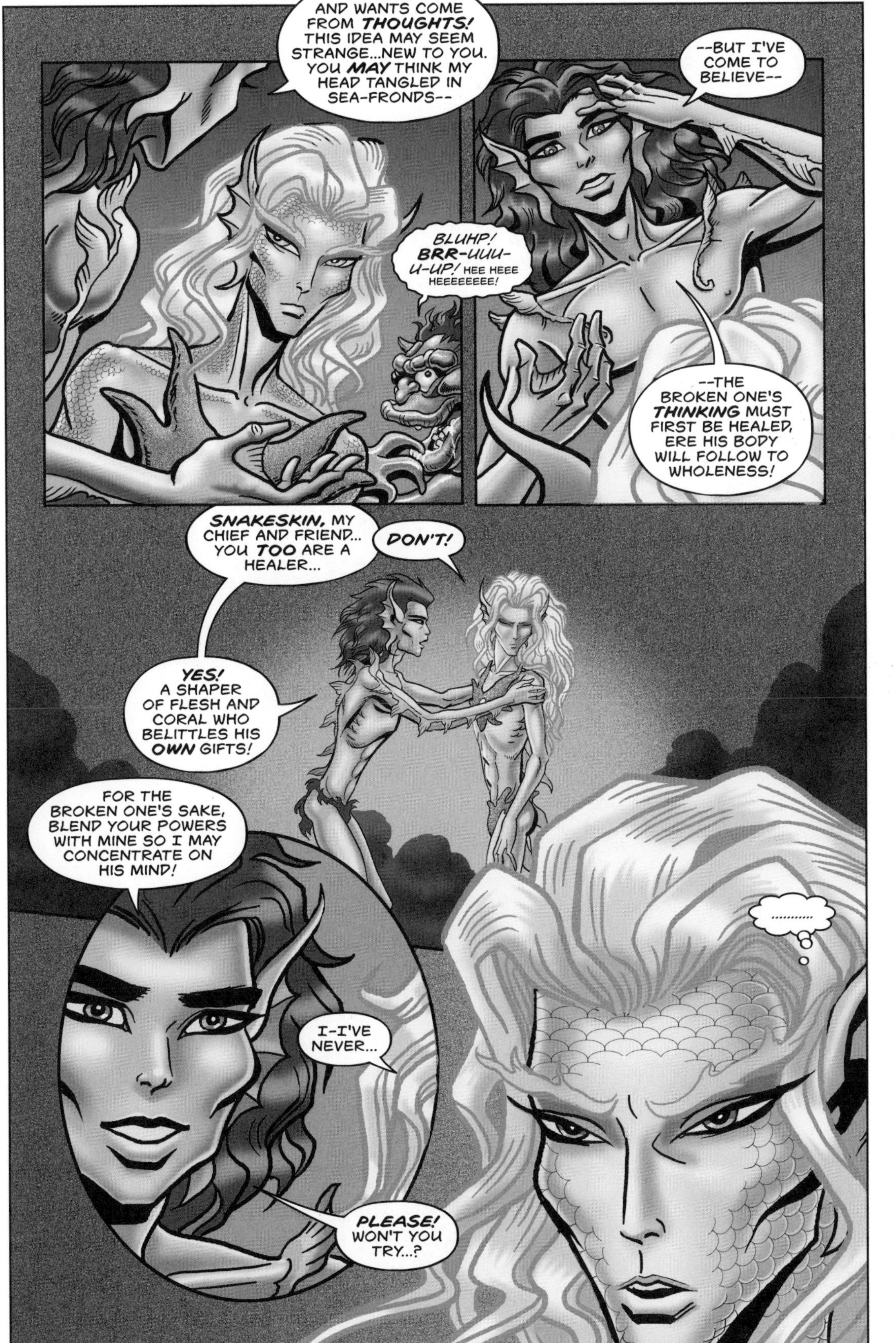
TRUE! AND WANTS COME FROM THOUGHTS! THIS IDEA MAY SEEM STRANGE...NEW TO YOU. YOU MAY THINK MY HEAD TANGLED IN SEA-FRONDS--
BLUHP! BRR-UUU-U-UP! HEE HEEE HEEEEEEEE!
--BUT I'VE COME TO BELIEVE--
--THE BROKEN ONE'S THINKING MUST FIRST BE HEALED, ERE HIS BODY WILL FOLLOW TO WHOLENESS!
SNAKESKIN, MY CHIEF AND FRIEND... YOU TOO ARE A HEALER...
DON'T!
YES! A SHAPER OF FLESH AND CORAL WHO BELITTLES HIS OWN GIFTS!
FOR THE BROKEN ONE'S SAKE, BLEND YOUR POWERS WITH MINE SO I MAY CONCENTRATE ON HIS MIND!
....
I-I'VE NEVER...
PLEASE! WON'T YOU TRY...?

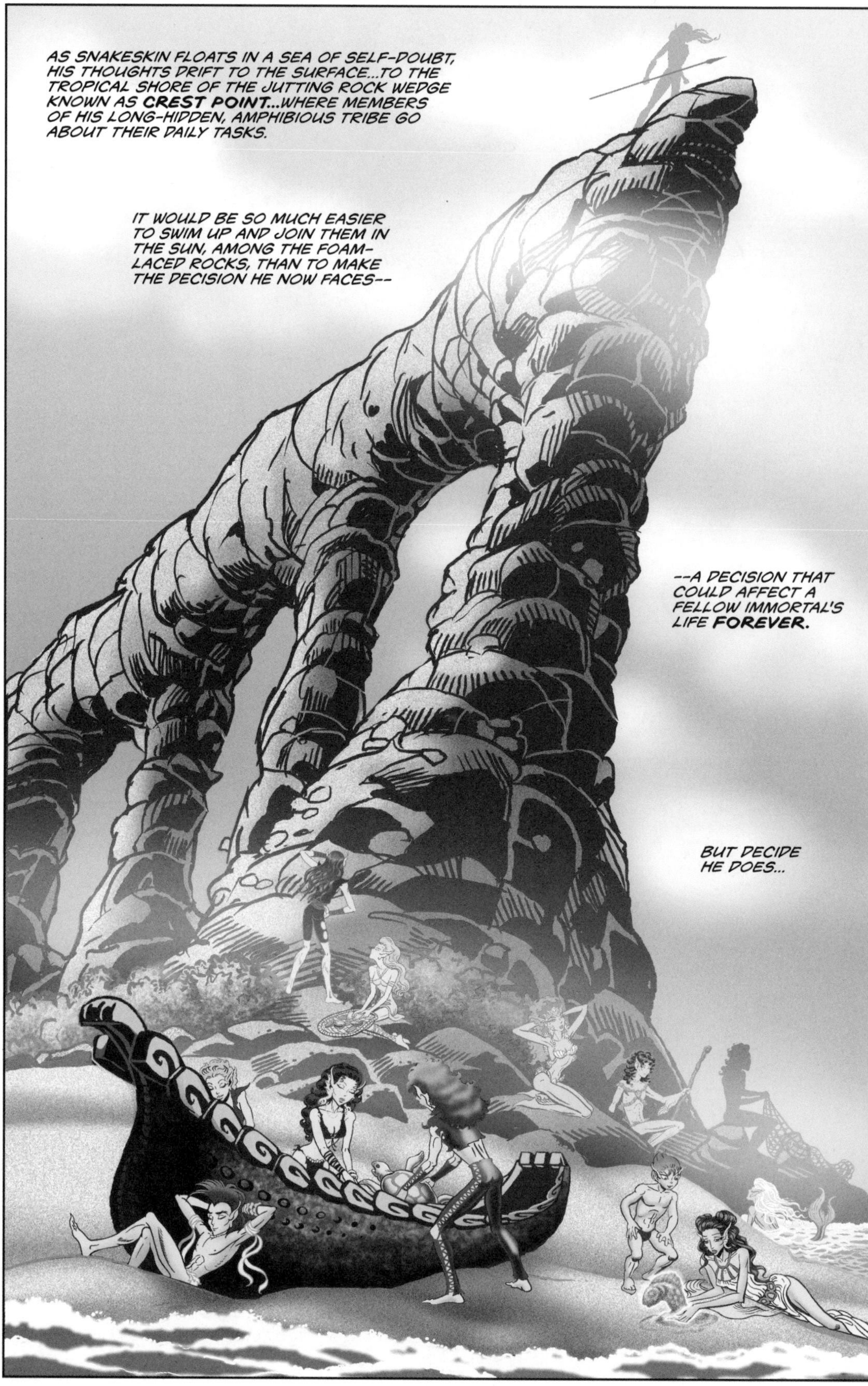
AS SNAKESKIN FLOATS IN A SEA OF SELF-DOUBT, HIS THOUGHTS DRIFT TO THE SURFACE...TO THE TROPICAL SHORE OF THE JUTTING ROCK WEDGE KNOWN AS **CREST POINT**...WHERE MEMBERS OF HIS LONG-HIDDEN, AMPHIBIOUS TRIBE GO ABOUT THEIR DAILY TASKS.
IT WOULD BE SO MUCH EASIER TO SWIM UP AND JOIN THEM IN THE SUN, AMONG THE FOAM-LACED ROCKS, THAN TO MAKE THE DECISION HE NOW FACES--
--A DECISION THAT COULD AFFECT A FELLOW IMMORTAL'S LIFE **FOREVER.**
BUT DECIDE HE DOES...

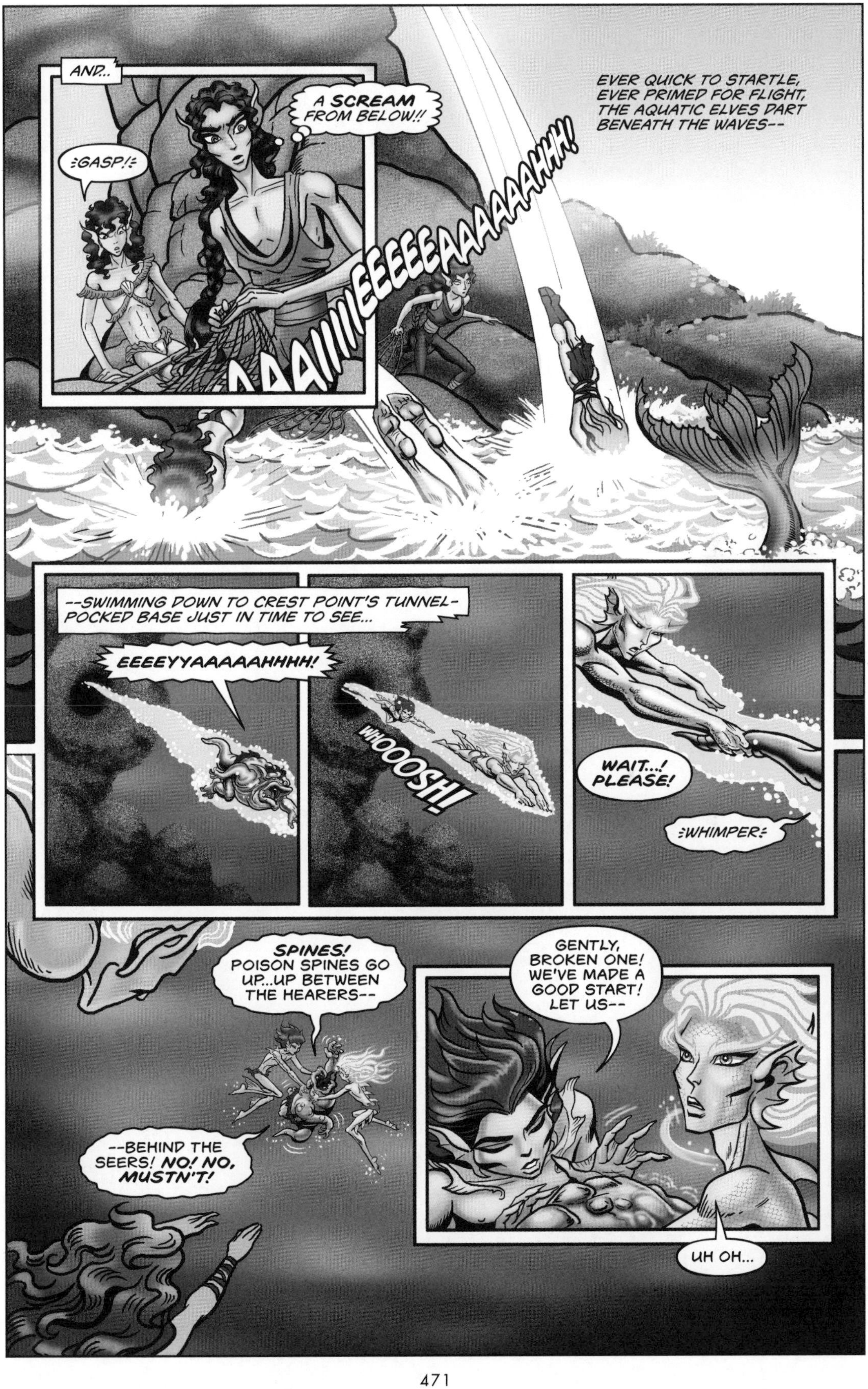
AND...
A SCREAM FROM BELOW!!
:GASP!:
EVER QUICK TO STARTLE, EVER PRIMED FOR FLIGHT, THE AQUATIC ELVES DART BENEATH THE WAVES--
AAAIIIIEEEEEAAAAAAAHHH!
--SWIMMING DOWN TO CREST POINT'S TUNNEL-POCKED BASE JUST IN TIME TO SEE...
EEEEYYAAAAAAHHHH!
WHOOOSH!
WAIT...! PLEASE!
:WHIMPER:
SPINES! POISON SPINES GO UP...UP BETWEEN THE HEARERS--
--BEHIND THE SEERS! NO! NO, MUSTN'T!
GENTLY, BROKEN ONE! WE'VE MADE A GOOD START! LET US--
UH OH...

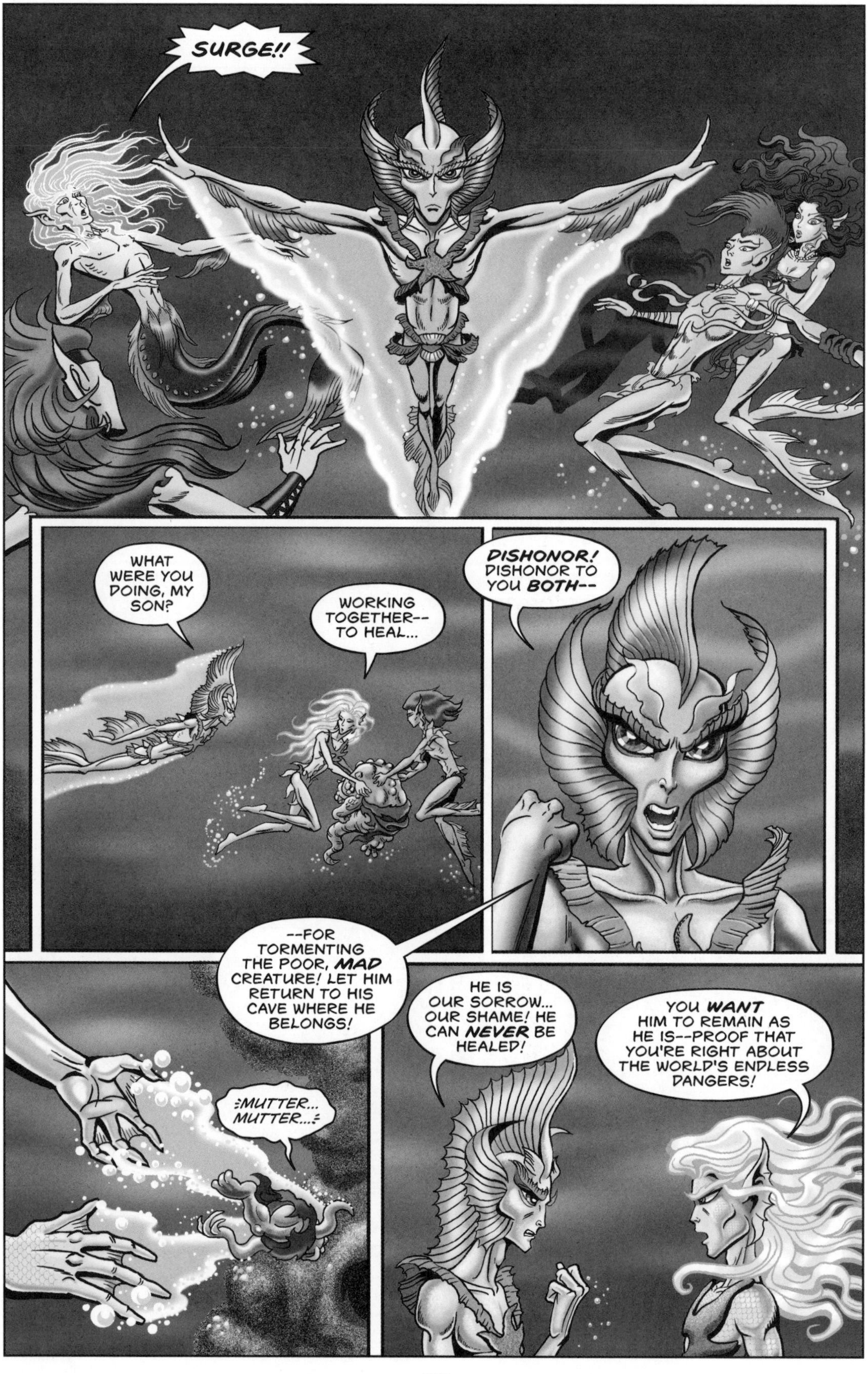
SURGE!!
WHAT WERE YOU DOING, MY SON?
WORKING TOGETHER-- TO HEAL...
DISHONOR! DISHONOR TO YOU BOTH--
--FOR TORMENTING THE POOR, MAD CREATURE! LET HIM RETURN TO HIS CAVE WHERE HE BELONGS!
:MUTTER... MUTTER...:
HE IS OUR SORROW... OUR SHAME! HE CAN NEVER BE HEALED!
YOU WANT HIM TO REMAIN AS HE IS--PROOF THAT YOU'RE RIGHT ABOUT THE WORLD'S ENDLESS DANGERS!

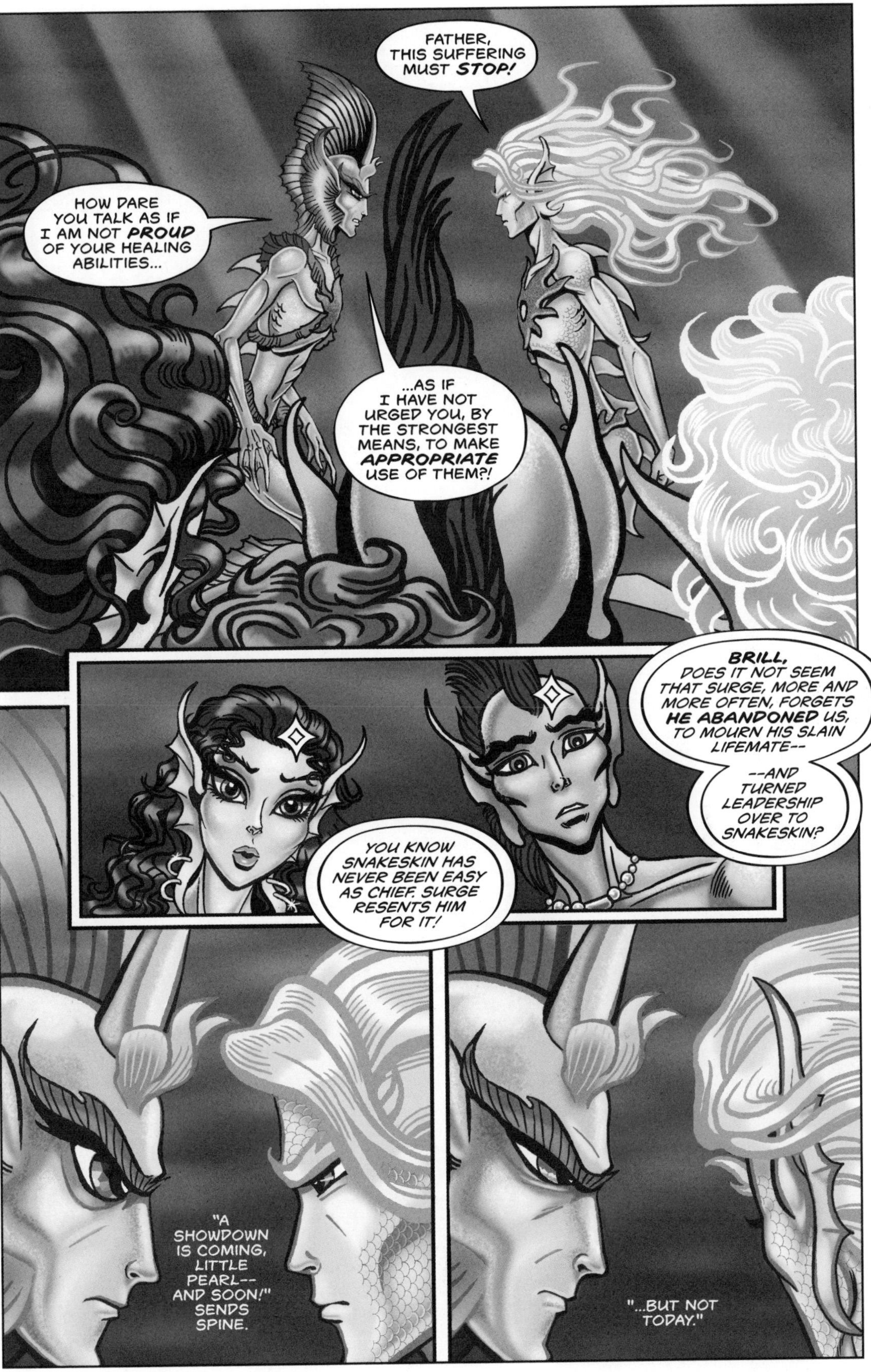
FATHER, THIS SUFFERING MUST **STOP!**
HOW DARE YOU TALK AS IF I AM NOT **PROUD** OF YOUR HEALING ABILITIES...
...AS IF I HAVE NOT URGED YOU, BY THE STRONGEST MEANS, TO MAKE **APPROPRIATE** USE OF THEM?!
BRILL, DOES IT NOT SEEM THAT SURGE, MORE AND MORE OFTEN, FORGETS HE ABANDONED US, TO MOURN HIS SLAIN LIFEMATE--
--AND TURNED LEADERSHIP OVER TO SNAKESKIN?
YOU KNOW SNAKESKIN HAS NEVER BEEN EASY AS CHIEF. SURGE RESENTS HIM FOR IT!
"A SHOWDOWN IS COMING, LITTLE PEARL--AND SOON!" SENDS SPINE.
"...BUT NOT TODAY."

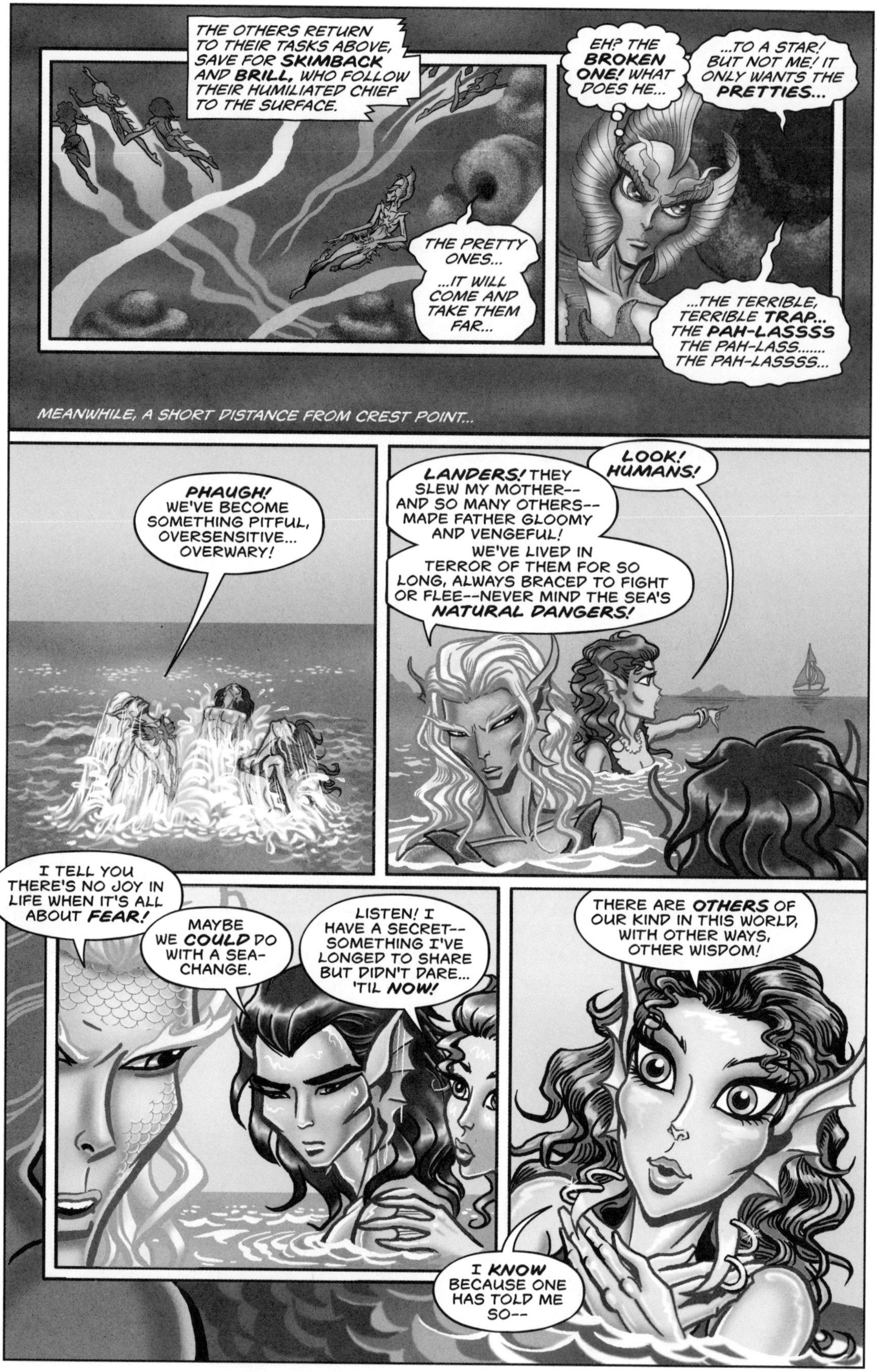
THE OTHERS RETURN TO THEIR TASKS ABOVE, SAVE FOR SKIMBACK AND BRILL, WHO FOLLOW THEIR HUMILIATED CHIEF TO THE SURFACE.
THE PRETTY ONES... ...IT WILL COME AND TAKE THEM FAR...
EH? THE BROKEN ONE! WHAT DOES HE...
...TO A STAR! BUT NOT ME! IT ONLY WANTS THE PRETTIES...
...THE TERRIBLE, TERRIBLE TRAP... THE PAH-LASSSS THE PAH-LASS....... THE PAH-LASSSS...
MEANWHILE, A SHORT DISTANCE FROM CREST POINT...
PHAUGH! WE'VE BECOME SOMETHING PITFUL, OVERSENSITIVE... OVERWARY!
LANDERS! THEY SLEW MY MOTHER-- AND SO MANY OTHERS-- MADE FATHER GLOOMY AND VENGEFUL!
WE'VE LIVED IN TERROR OF THEM FOR SO LONG, ALWAYS BRACED TO FIGHT OR FLEE--NEVER MIND THE SEA'S NATURAL DANGERS!
LOOK! HUMANS!
I TELL YOU THERE'S NO JOY IN LIFE WHEN IT'S ALL ABOUT FEAR!
MAYBE WE COULD DO WITH A SEA-CHANGE.
LISTEN! I HAVE A SECRET-- SOMETHING I'VE LONGED TO SHARE BUT DIDN'T DARE... 'TIL NOW!
THERE ARE OTHERS OF OUR KIND IN THIS WORLD, WITH OTHER WAYS, OTHER WISDOM!
I KNOW BECAUSE ONE HAS TOLD ME SO--

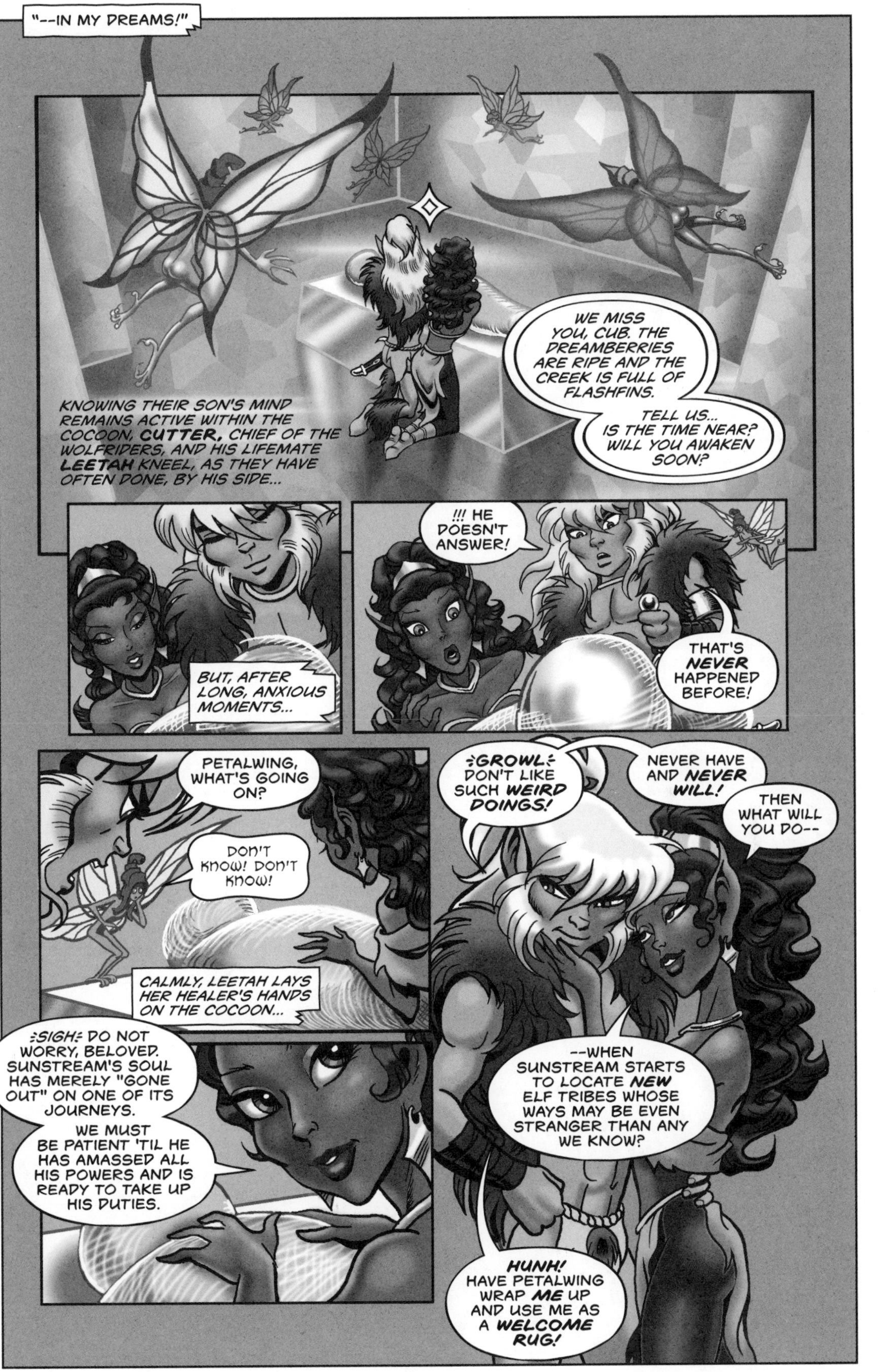
"--IN MY DREAMS!"
WE MISS YOU, CUB. THE DREAMBERRIES ARE RIPE AND THE CREEK IS FULL OF FLASHFINS.
TELL US... IS THE TIME NEAR? WILL YOU AWAKEN SOON?
KNOWING THEIR SON'S MIND REMAINS ACTIVE WITHIN THE COCOON, CUTTER, CHIEF OF THE WOLFRIDERS, AND HIS LIFEMATE LEETAH KNEEL, AS THEY HAVE OFTEN DONE, BY HIS SIDE...
BUT, AFTER LONG, ANXIOUS MOMENTS...
!!! HE DOESN'T ANSWER!
THAT'S NEVER HAPPENED BEFORE!
PETALWING, WHAT'S GOING ON?
DON'T KNOW! DON'T KNOW!
CALMLY, LEETAH LAYS HER HEALER'S HANDS ON THE COCOON...
:SIGH: DO NOT WORRY, BELOVED. SUNSTREAM'S SOUL HAS MERELY "GONE OUT" ON ONE OF ITS JOURNEYS.
WE MUST BE PATIENT 'TIL HE HAS AMASSED ALL HIS POWERS AND IS READY TO TAKE UP HIS DUTIES.
:GROWL: DON'T LIKE SUCH WEIRD DOINGS!
NEVER HAVE AND NEVER WILL!
THEN WHAT WILL YOU DO--
--WHEN SUNSTREAM STARTS TO LOCATE NEW ELF TRIBES WHOSE WAYS MAY BE EVEN STRANGER THAN ANY WE KNOW?
HUNH! HAVE PETALWING WRAP ME UP AND USE ME AS A WELCOME RUG!

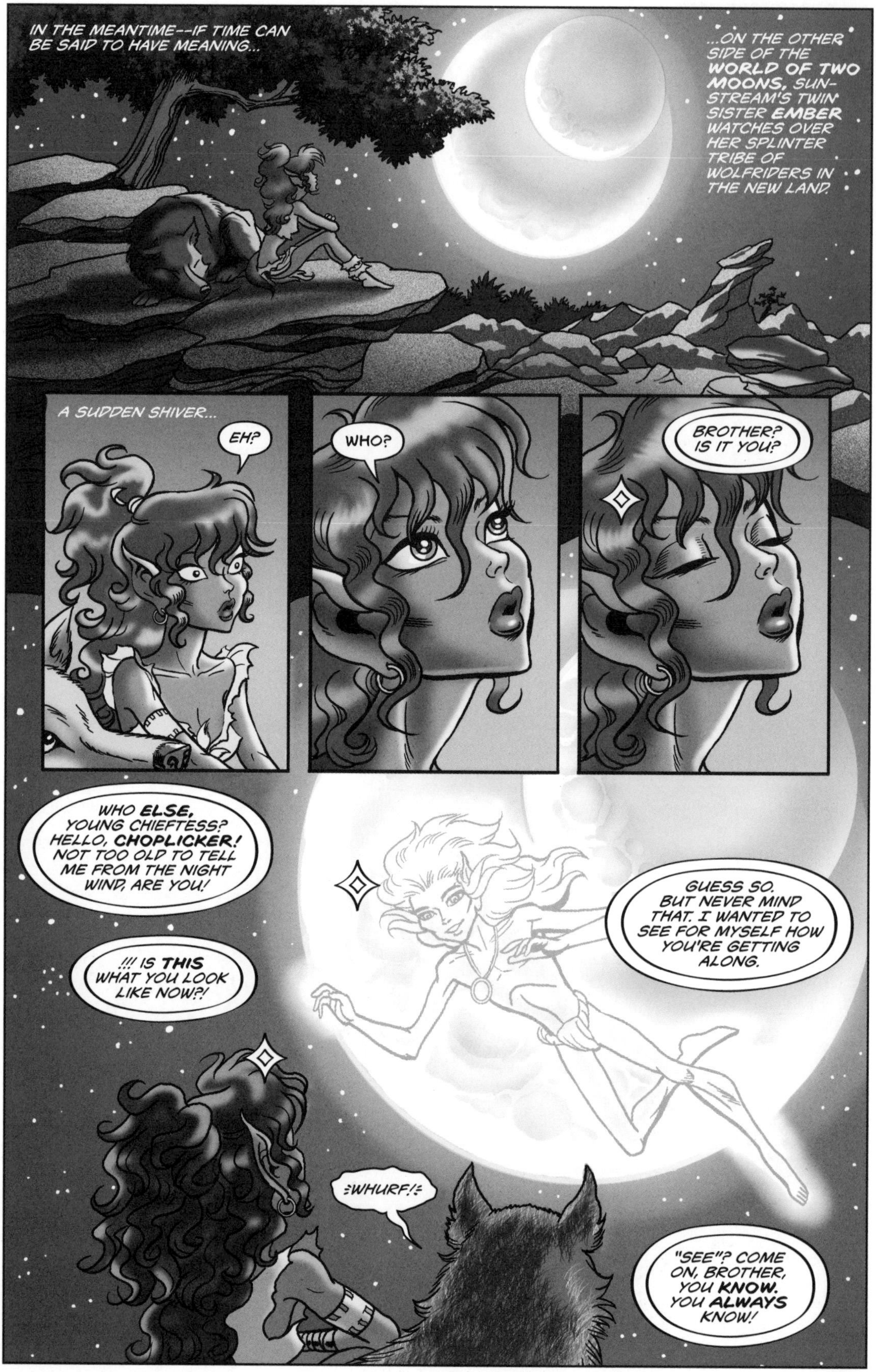
IN THE MEANTIME--IF TIME CAN BE SAID TO HAVE MEANING...
...ON THE OTHER SIDE OF THE WORLD OF TWO MOONS, SUNSTREAM'S TWIN SISTER EMBER WATCHES OVER HER SPLINTER TRIBE OF WOLFRIDERS IN THE NEW LAND.
A SUDDEN SHIVER...
EH?
WHO?
BROTHER? IS IT YOU?
WHO ELSE, YOUNG CHIEFTESS? HELLO, CHOPLICKER! NOT TOO OLD TO TELL ME FROM THE NIGHT WIND, ARE YOU!
!!! IS THIS WHAT YOU LOOK LIKE NOW?!
GUESS SO. BUT NEVER MIND THAT. I WANTED TO SEE FOR MYSELF HOW YOU'RE GETTING ALONG.
:WHURF!:
"SEE"? COME ON, BROTHER, YOU KNOW. YOU ALWAYS KNOW!

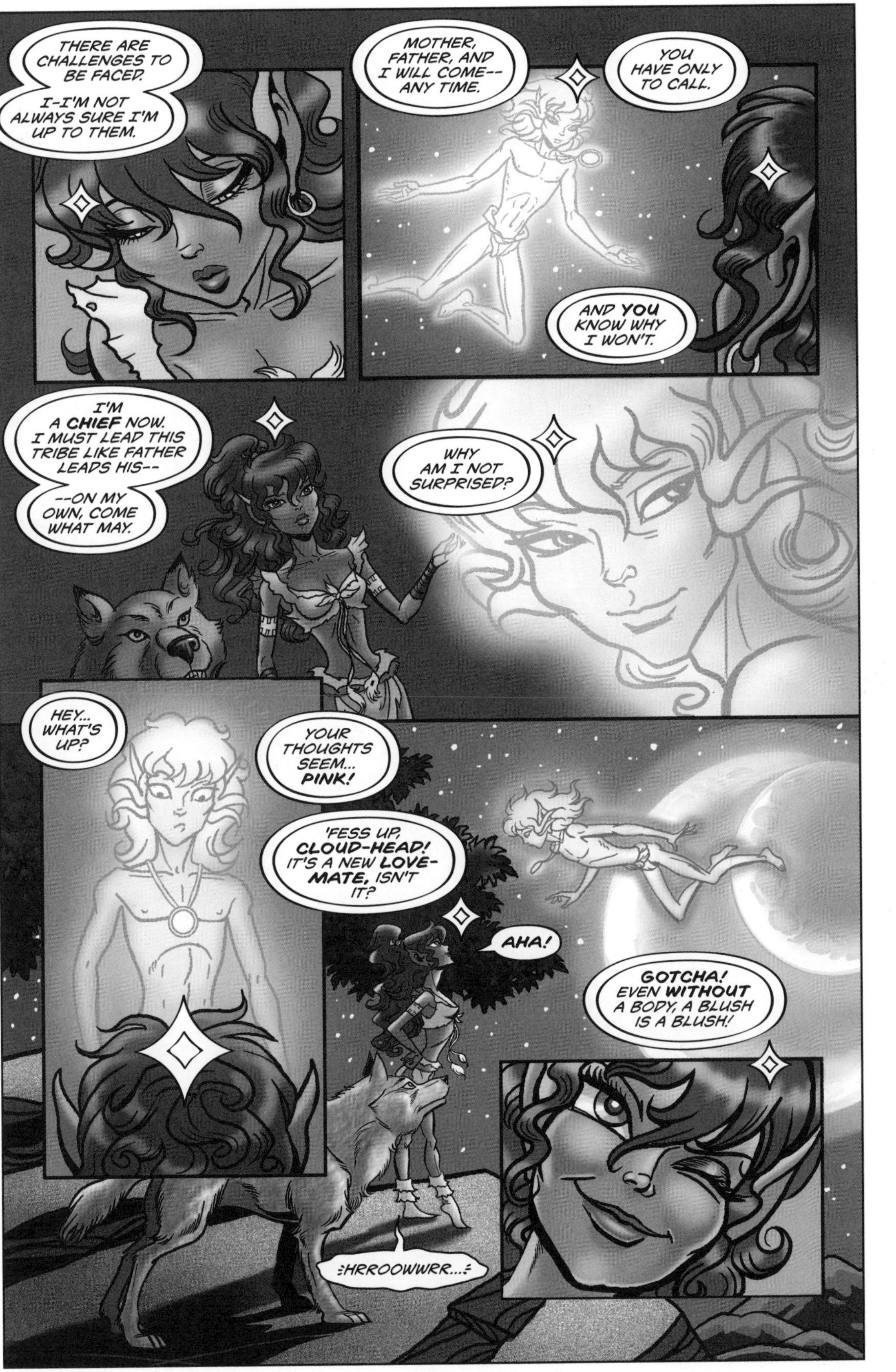
THERE ARE CHALLENGES TO BE FACED.
I-I'M NOT ALWAYS SURE I'M UP TO THEM.
MOTHER, FATHER, AND I WILL COME-- ANY TIME.
YOU HAVE ONLY TO CALL.
AND YOU KNOW WHY I WON'T.
I'M A CHIEF NOW. I MUST LEAD THIS TRIBE LIKE FATHER LEADS HIS--
--ON MY OWN, COME WHAT MAY.
WHY AM I NOT SURPRISED?
HEY... WHAT'S UP?
YOUR THOUGHTS SEEM... PINK!
'FESS UP, CLOUD-HEAD! IT'S A NEW LOVE-MATE, ISN'T IT?
AHA!
GOTCHA! EVEN WITHOUT A BODY, A BLUSH IS A BLUSH!
HRROOWWRR...

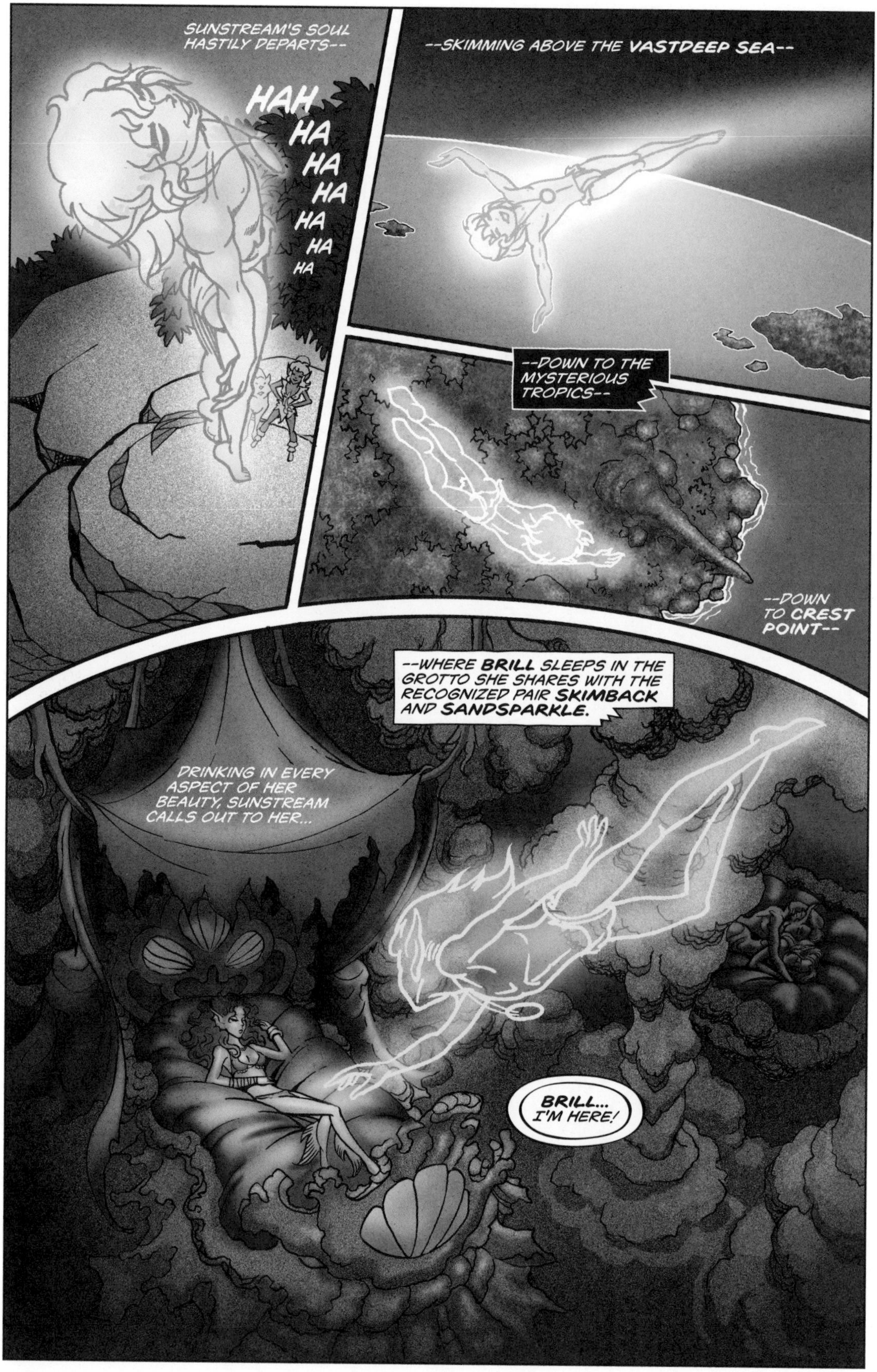
SUNSTREAM'S SOUL HASTILY DEPARTS--
HAH HA HA HA HA HA HA
--SKIMMING ABOVE THE VASTDEEP SEA--
--DOWN TO THE MYSTERIOUS TROPICS--
--DOWN TO CREST POINT--
--WHERE BRILL SLEEPS IN THE GROTTO SHE SHARES WITH THE RECOGNIZED PAIR SKIMBACK AND SANDSPARKLE.
DRINKING IN EVERY ASPECT OF HER BEAUTY, SUNSTREAM CALLS OUT TO HER...
BRILL... I'M HERE!

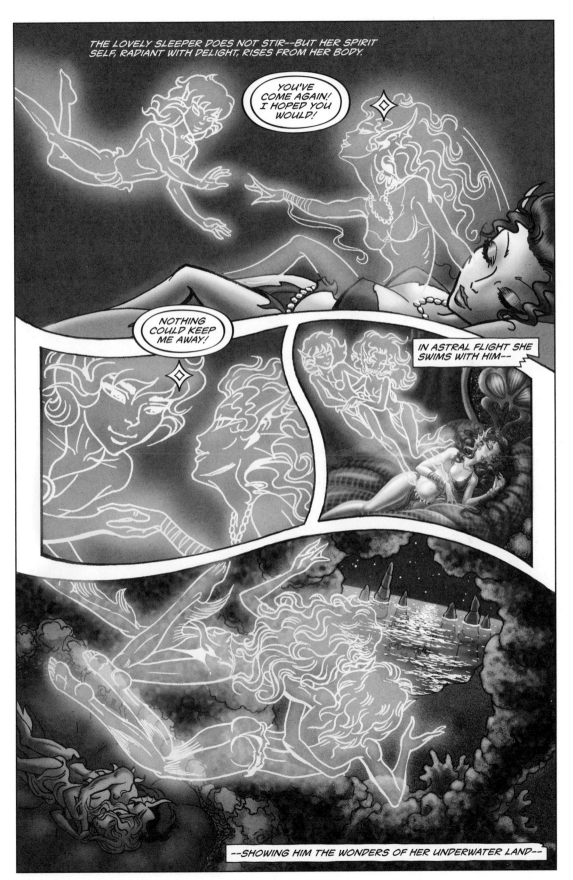

THE LOVELY SLEEPER DOES NOT STIR--BUT HER SPIRIT SELF, RADIANT WITH DELIGHT, RISES FROM HER BODY.

YOU'VE COME AGAIN! I HOPED YOU WOULD!

NOTHING COULD KEEP ME AWAY!

IN ASTRAL FLIGHT SHE SWIMS WITH HIM--

--SHOWING HIM THE WONDERS OF HER UNDERWATER LAND--

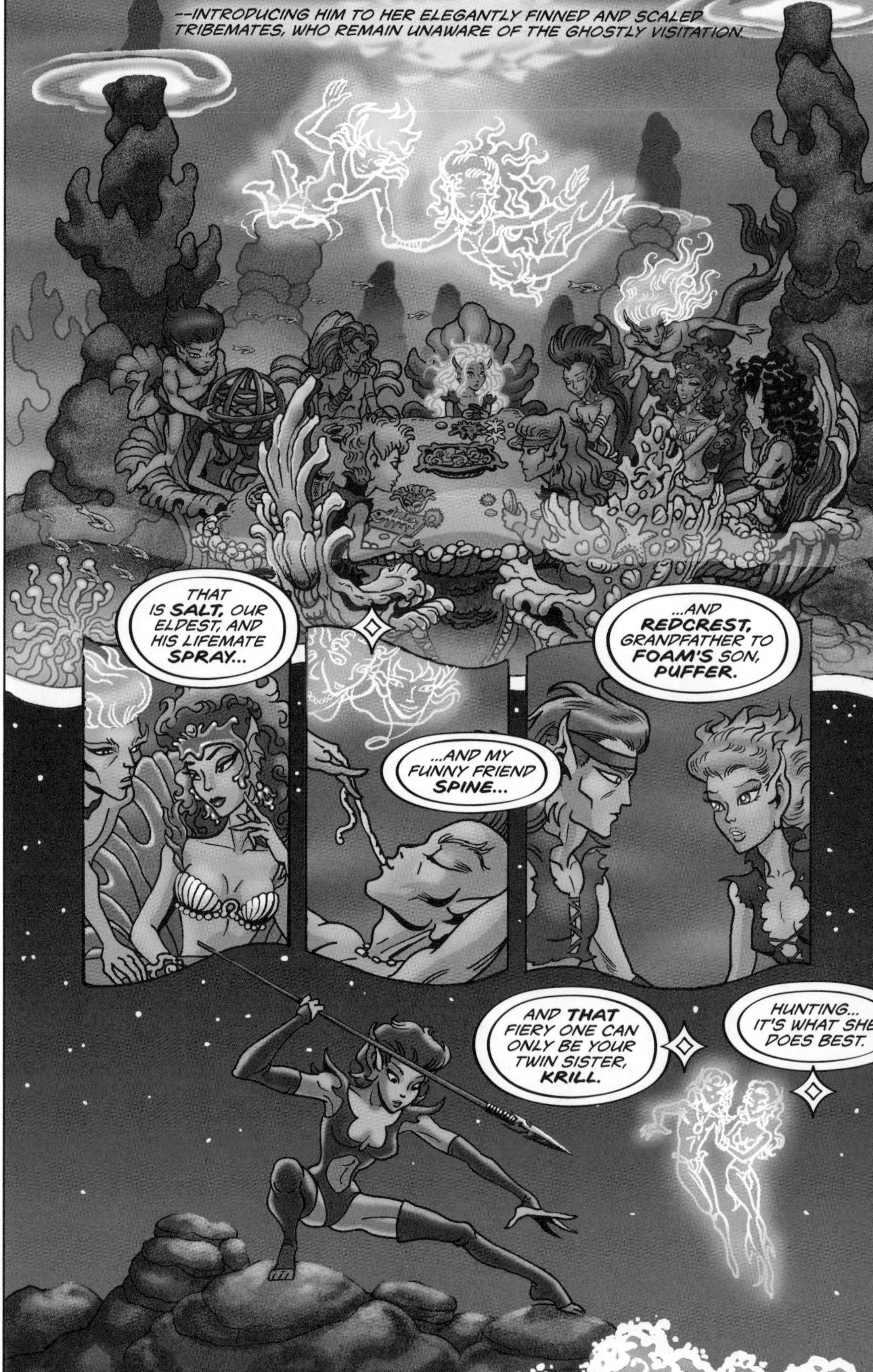
--INTRODUCING HIM TO HER ELEGANTLY FINNED AND SCALED TRIBEMATES, WHO REMAIN UNAWARE OF THE GHOSTLY VISITATION.
THAT IS SALT, OUR ELDEST, AND HIS LIFEMATE SPRAY...
...AND MY FUNNY FRIEND SPINE...
...AND REDCREST, GRANDFATHER TO FOAM'S SON, PUFFER.
AND THAT FIERY ONE CAN ONLY BE YOUR TWIN SISTER, KRILL.
HUNTING... IT'S WHAT SHE DOES BEST.

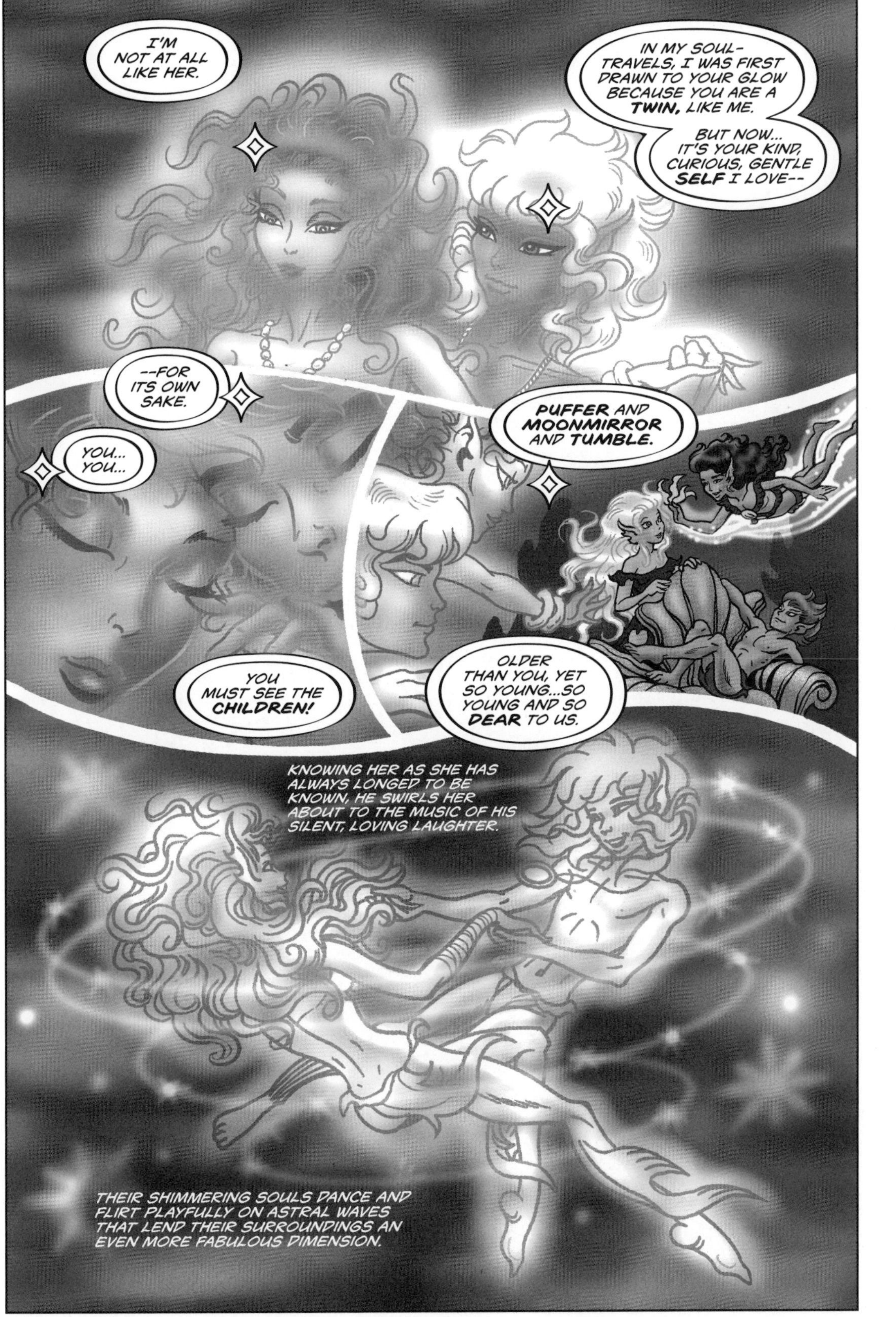
I'M NOT AT ALL LIKE HER.
IN MY SOUL-TRAVELS, I WAS FIRST DRAWN TO YOUR GLOW BECAUSE YOU ARE A TWIN, LIKE ME.
BUT NOW... IT'S YOUR KIND, CURIOUS, GENTLE SELF I LOVE--
--FOR ITS OWN SAKE.
YOU... YOU...
YOU MUST SEE THE CHILDREN!
PUFFER AND MOONMIRROR AND TUMBLE.
OLDER THAN YOU, YET SO YOUNG...SO YOUNG AND SO DEAR TO US.
KNOWING HER AS SHE HAS ALWAYS LONGED TO BE KNOWN, HE SWIRLS HER ABOUT TO THE MUSIC OF HIS SILENT, LOVING LAUGHTER.
THEIR SHIMMERING SOULS DANCE AND FLIRT PLAYFULLY ON ASTRAL WAVES THAT LEND THEIR SURROUNDINGS AN EVEN MORE FABULOUS DIMENSION.

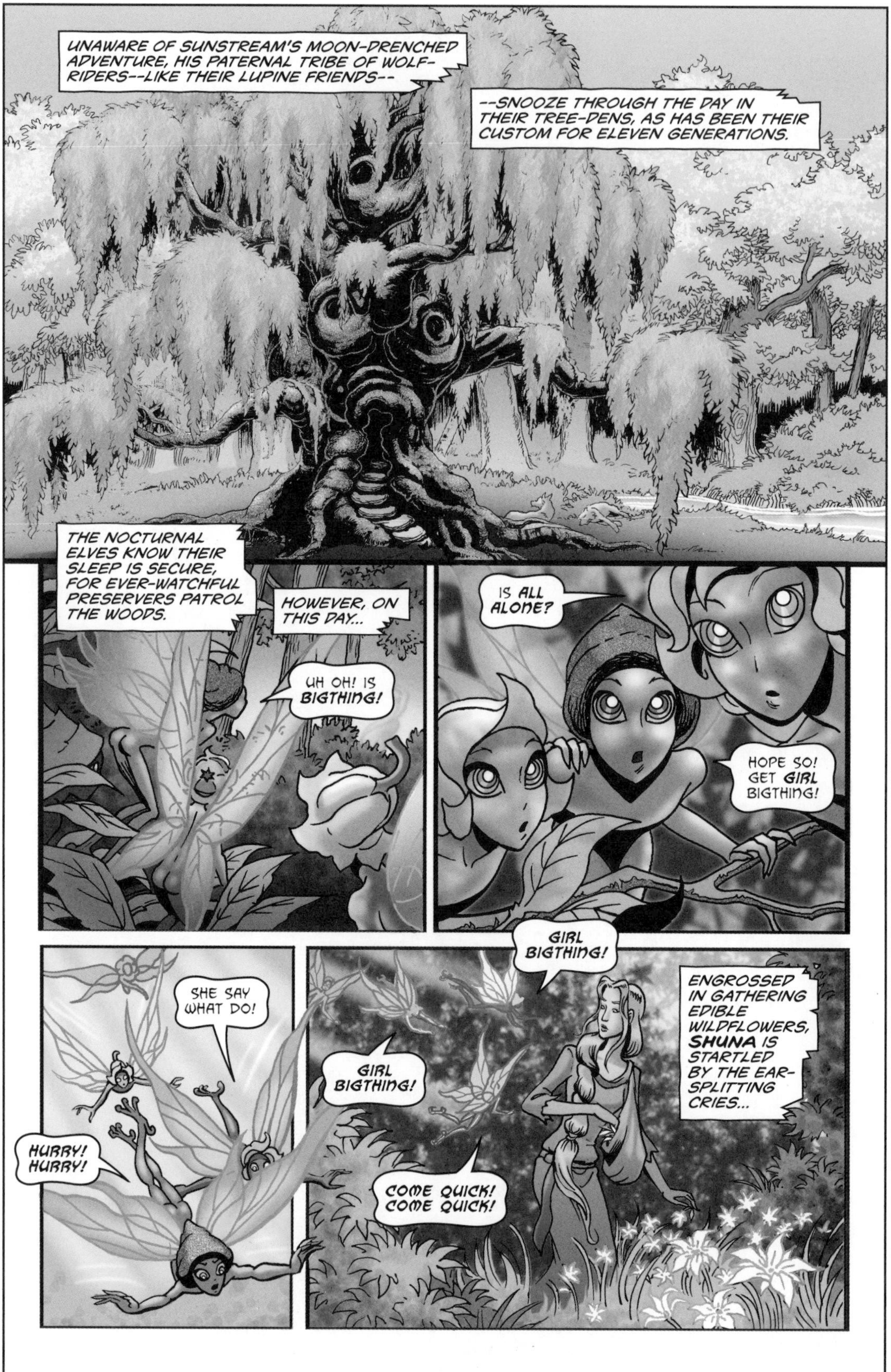
UNAWARE OF SUNSTREAM'S MOON-DRENCHED ADVENTURE, HIS PATERNAL TRIBE OF WOLF-RIDERS--LIKE THEIR LUPINE FRIENDS--
--SNOOZE THROUGH THE DAY IN THEIR TREE-DENS, AS HAS BEEN THEIR CUSTOM FOR ELEVEN GENERATIONS.
THE NOCTURNAL ELVES KNOW THEIR SLEEP IS SECURE, FOR EVER-WATCHFUL PRESERVERS PATROL THE WOODS.
HOWEVER, ON THIS DAY...
UH OH! IS BIGTHING!
IS ALL ALONE?
HOPE SO! GET GIRL BIGTHING!
SHE SAY WHAT DO!
HURRY! HURRY!
GIRL BIGTHING!
GIRL BIGTHING!
COME QUICK! COME QUICK!
ENGROSSED IN GATHERING EDIBLE WILDFLOWERS, SHUNA IS STARTLED BY THE EAR-SPLITTING CRIES...

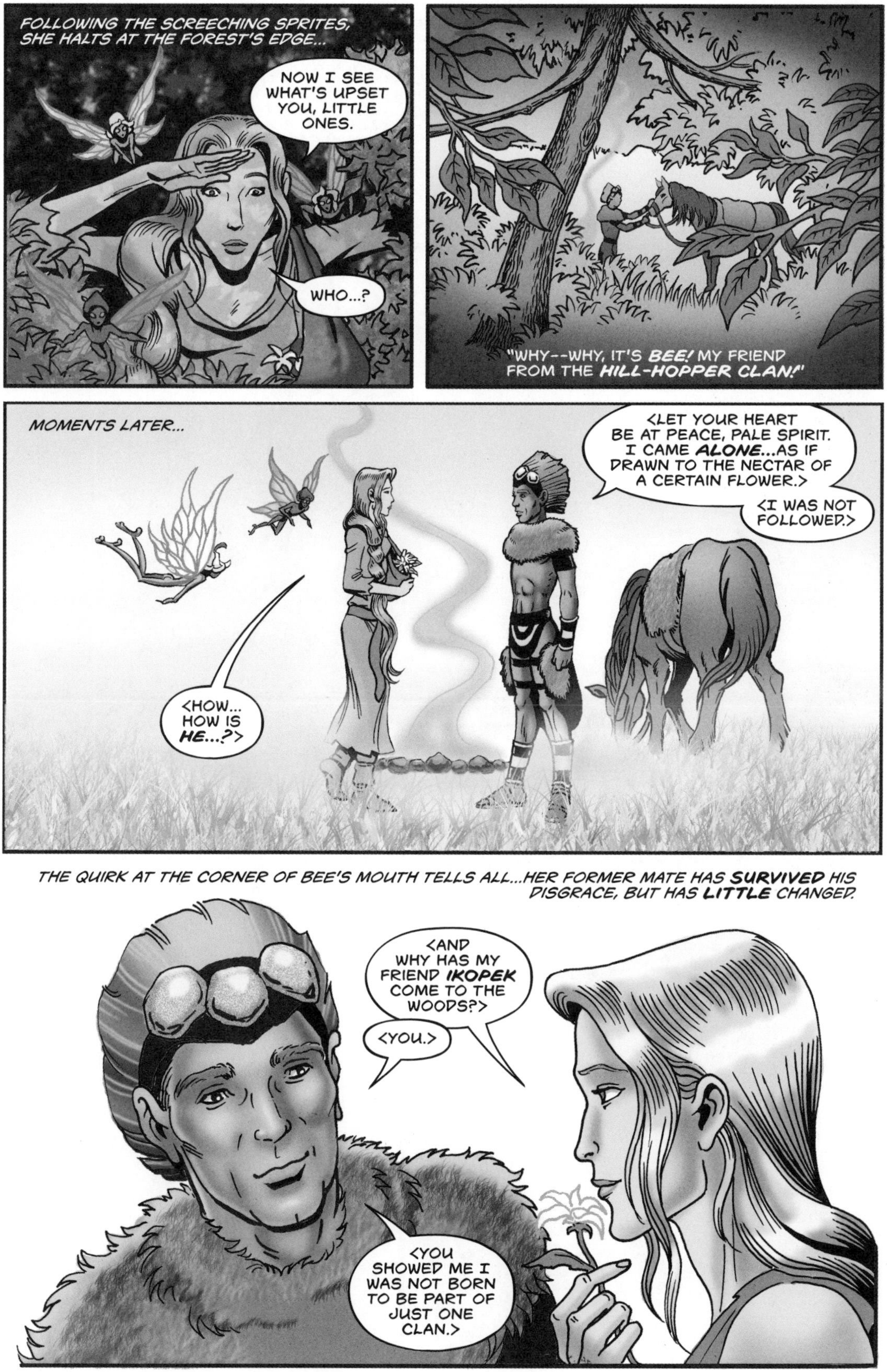
FOLLOWING THE SCREECHING SPRITES, SHE HALTS AT THE FOREST'S EDGE...
NOW I SEE WHAT'S UPSET YOU, LITTLE ONES.
WHO...?
"WHY--WHY, IT'S BEE! MY FRIEND FROM THE HILL-HOPPER CLAN!"
MOMENTS LATER...
<LET YOUR HEART BE AT PEACE, PALE SPIRIT. I CAME ALONE...AS IF DRAWN TO THE NECTAR OF A CERTAIN FLOWER.>
<I WAS NOT FOLLOWED.>
<HOW... HOW IS HE...?>
THE QUIRK AT THE CORNER OF BEE'S MOUTH TELLS ALL...HER FORMER MATE HAS SURVIVED HIS DISGRACE, BUT HAS LITTLE CHANGED.
<AND WHY HAS MY FRIEND IKOPEK COME TO THE WOODS?>
<YOU.>
<YOU SHOWED ME I WAS NOT BORN TO BE PART OF JUST ONE CLAN.>

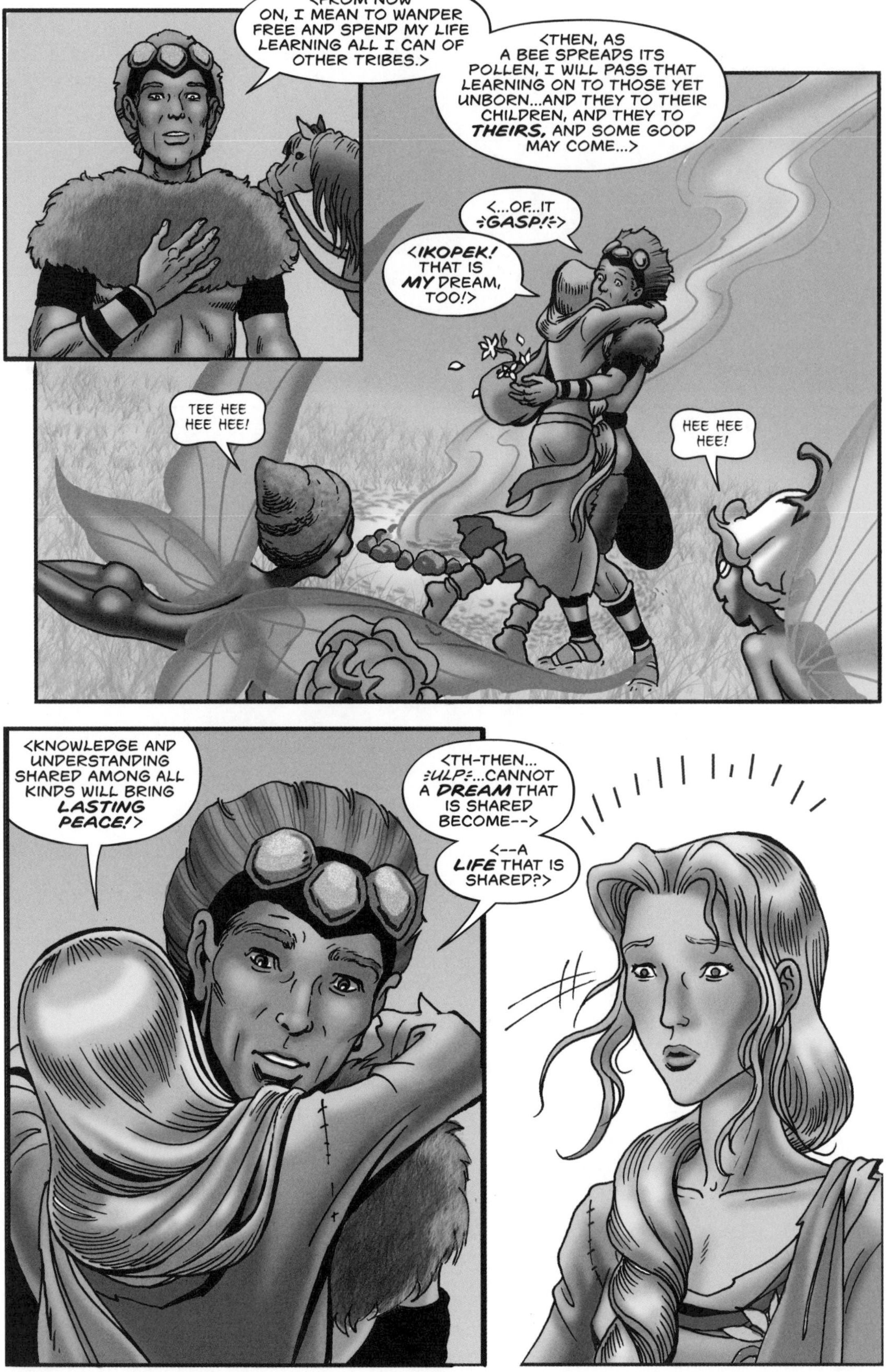
<FROM NOW ON, I MEAN TO WANDER FREE AND SPEND MY LIFE LEARNING ALL I CAN OF OTHER TRIBES.>
<THEN, AS A BEE SPREADS ITS POLLEN, I WILL PASS THAT LEARNING ON TO THOSE YET UNBORN...AND THEY TO THEIR CHILDREN, AND THEY TO THEIRS, AND SOME GOOD MAY COME...>
<...OF...IT GASP!>
<IKOPEK! THAT IS MY DREAM, TOO!>
TEE HEE HEE HEE!
HEE HEE HEE!
<KNOWLEDGE AND UNDERSTANDING SHARED AMONG ALL KINDS WILL BRING LASTING PEACE!>
<TH-THEN... ULP...CANNOT A DREAM THAT IS SHARED BECOME-->
<--A LIFE THAT IS SHARED?>

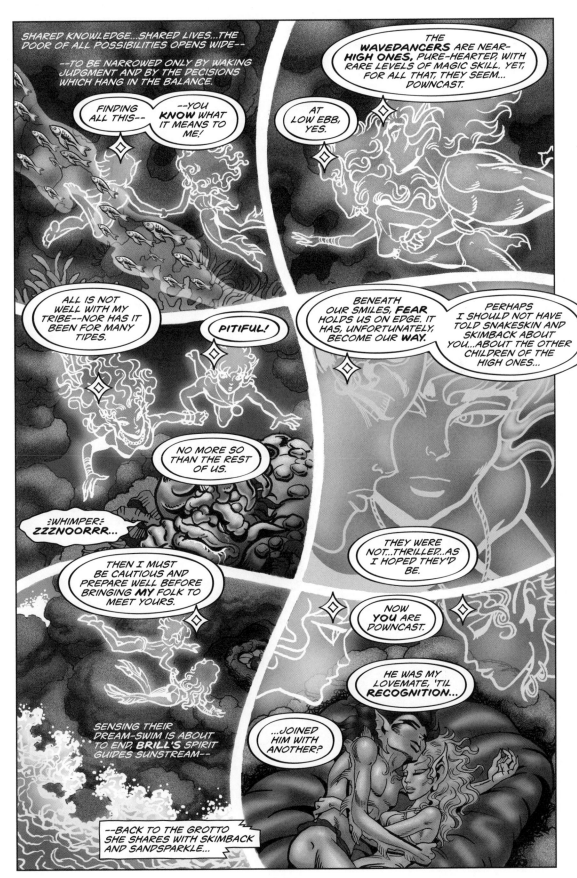

SHARED KNOWLEDGE...SHARED LIVES...THE DOOR OF ALL POSSIBILITIES OPENS WIDE--

--TO BE NARROWED ONLY BY WAKING JUDGMENT AND BY THE DECISIONS WHICH HANG IN THE BALANCE.

FINDING ALL THIS--

--YOU **KNOW** WHAT IT MEANS TO ME!

THE **WAVEDANCERS** ARE NEAR-**HIGH ONES,** PURE-HEARTED, WITH RARE LEVELS OF MAGIC SKILL. YET, FOR ALL THAT, THEY SEEM... DOWNCAST.

AT LOW EBB, YES.

ALL IS NOT WELL WITH MY TRIBE--NOR HAS IT BEEN FOR MANY TIDES.

PITIFUL!

BENEATH OUR SMILES, **FEAR** HOLDS US ON EDGE. IT HAS, UNFORTUNATELY, BECOME OUR **WAY.**

PERHAPS I SHOULD NOT HAVE TOLD SNAKESKIN AND SKIMBACK ABOUT YOU...ABOUT THE OTHER CHILDREN OF THE HIGH ONES...

NO MORE SO THAN THE REST OF US.

:WHIMPER: **ZZZNOORRR...**

THEN I MUST BE CAUTIOUS AND PREPARE WELL BEFORE BRINGING **MY** FOLK TO MEET YOURS.

THEY WERE NOT...THRILLED...AS I HOPED THEY'D BE.

NOW **YOU** ARE DOWNCAST.

HE WAS MY LOVEMATE, 'TIL **RECOGNITION...**

SENSING THEIR DREAM-SWIM IS ABOUT TO END, **BRILL'S** SPIRIT GUIDES SUNSTREAM--

...JOINED HIM WITH ANOTHER?

--BACK TO THE GROTTO SHE SHARES WITH SKIMBACK AND SANDSPARKLE...

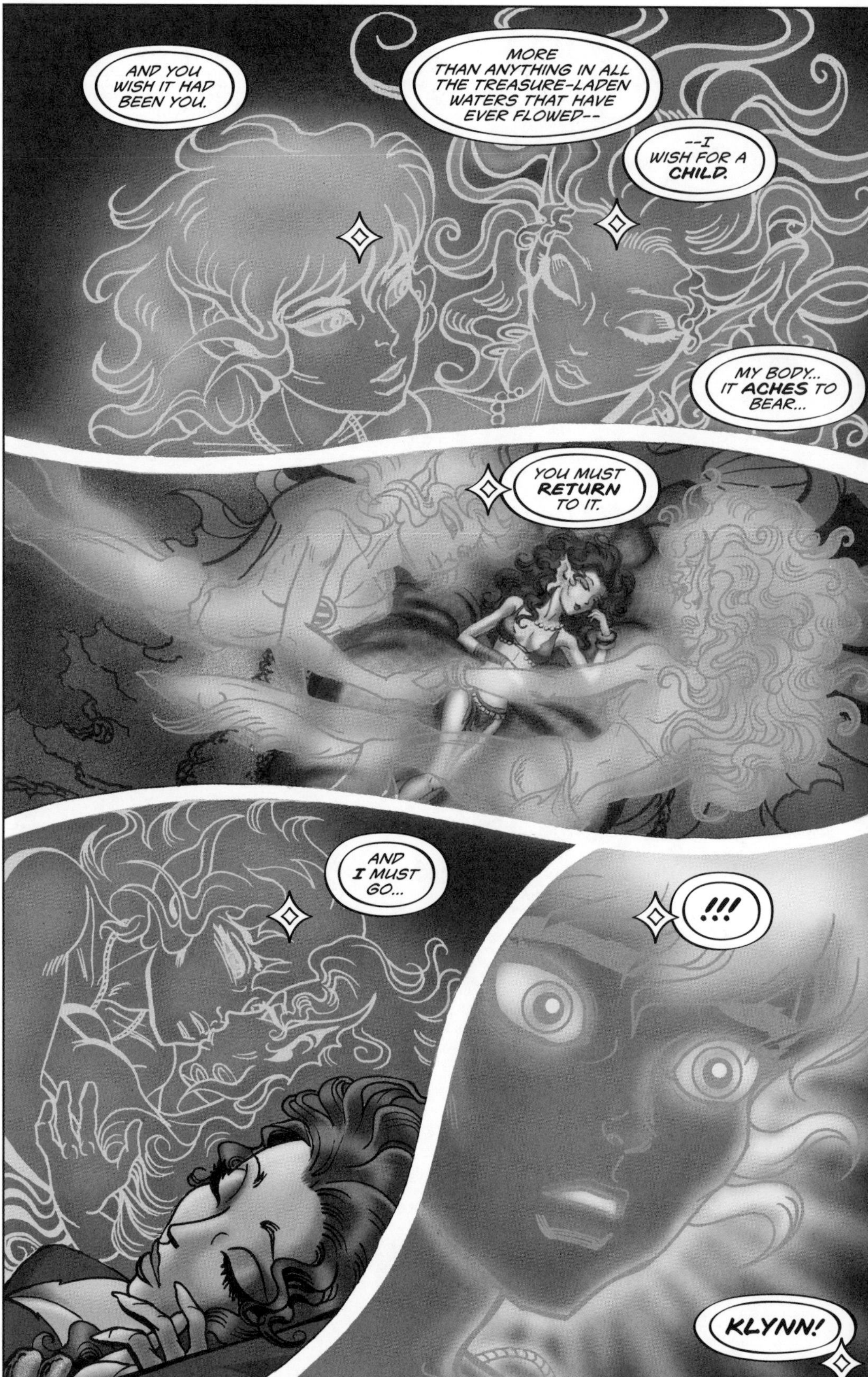
AND YOU WISH IT HAD BEEN YOU.
MORE THAN ANYTHING IN ALL THE TREASURE-LADEN WATERS THAT HAVE EVER FLOWED--
--I WISH FOR A CHILD.
MY BODY... IT ACHES TO BEAR...
YOU MUST RETURN TO IT.
AND I MUST GO...
!!!
KLYNN!

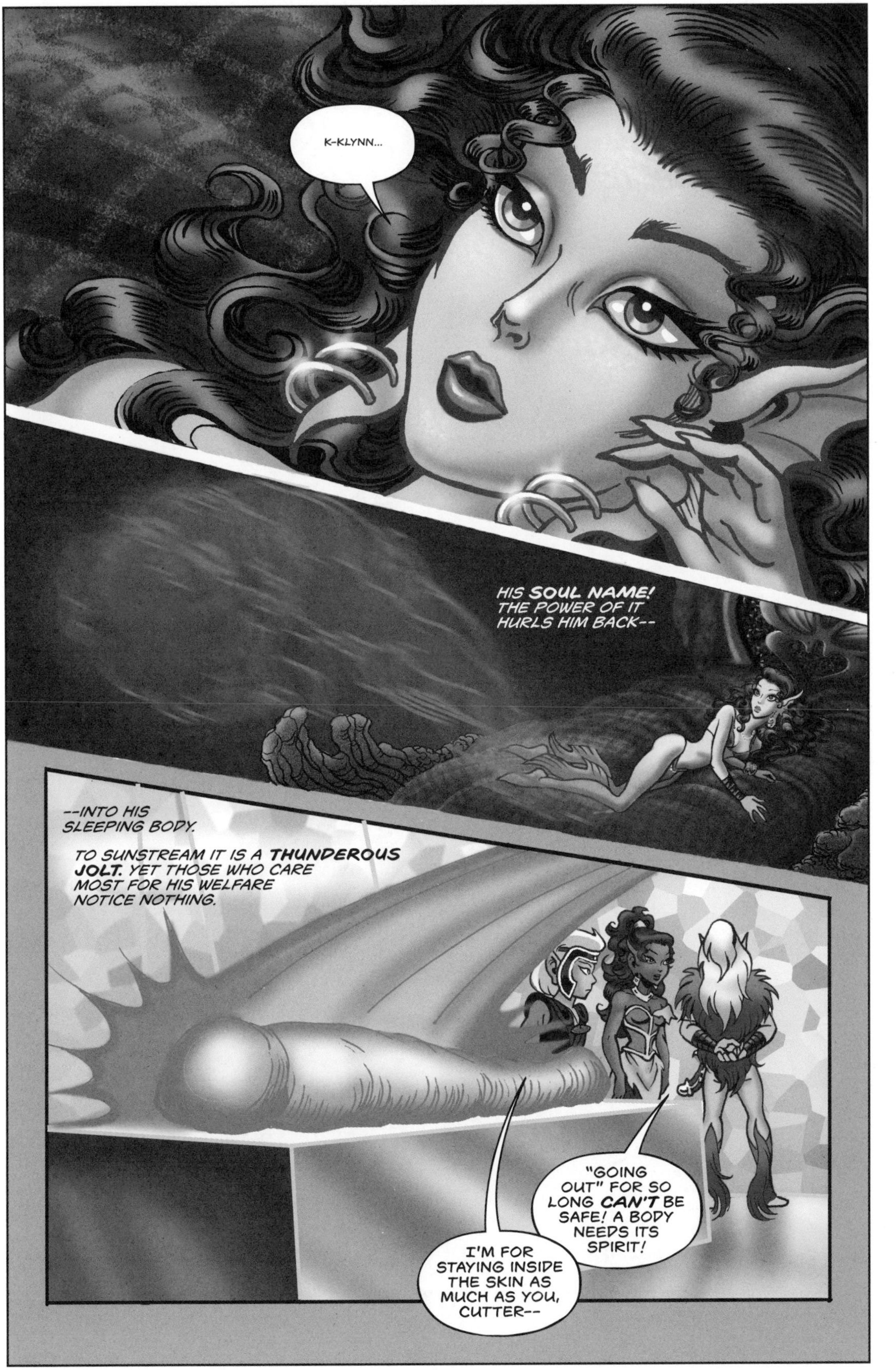
K-KLYNN...
HIS **SOUL NAME!** THE POWER OF IT HURLS HIM BACK--
--INTO HIS SLEEPING BODY.
TO SUNSTREAM IT IS A **THUNDEROUS JOLT.** YET THOSE WHO CARE MOST FOR HIS WELFARE NOTICE NOTHING.
"GOING OUT" FOR SO LONG ***CAN'T*** BE SAFE! A BODY NEEDS ITS SPIRIT!
I'M FOR STAYING INSIDE THE SKIN AS MUCH AS YOU, CUTTER--

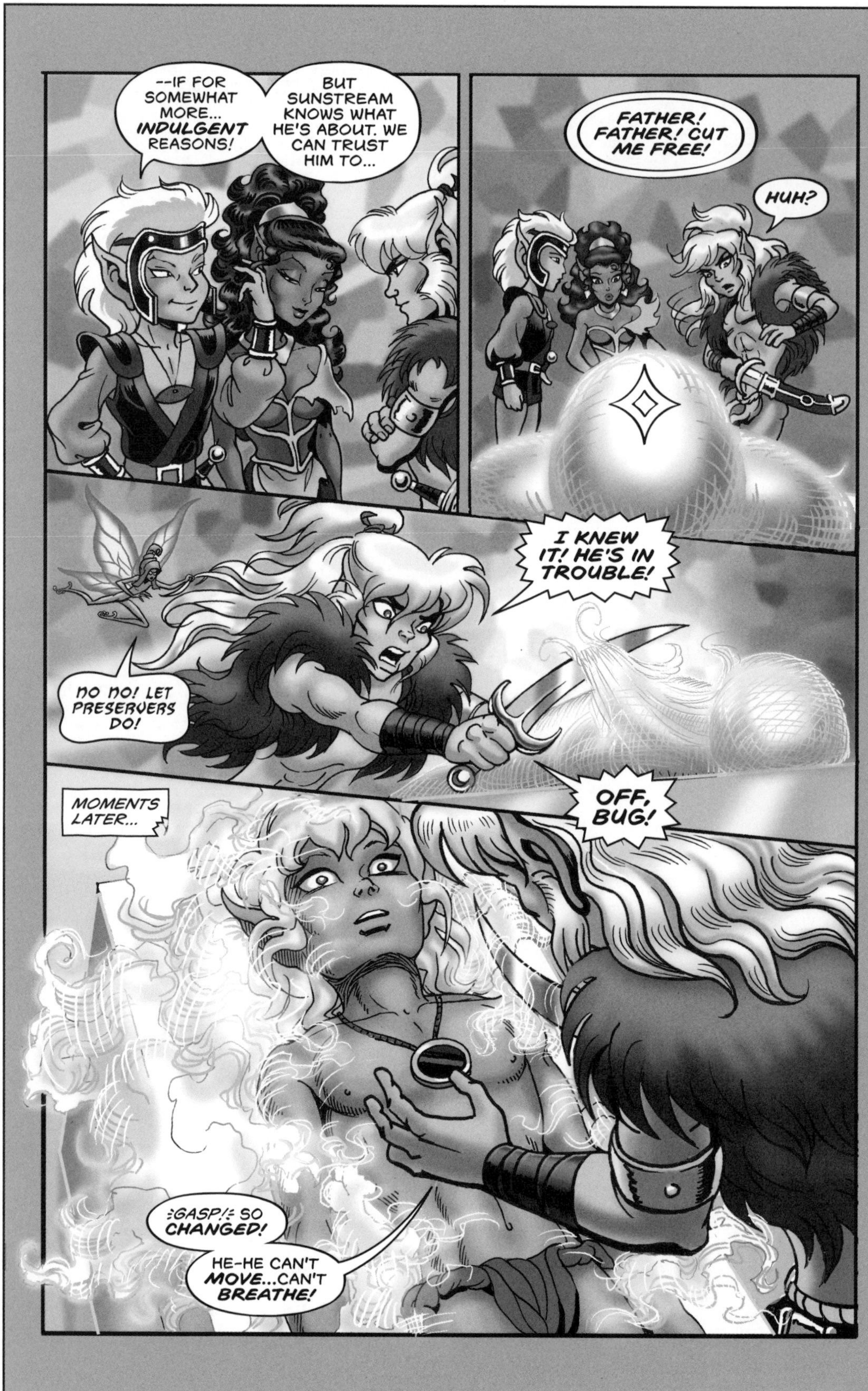
--IF FOR SOMEWHAT MORE... INDULGENT REASONS!
BUT SUNSTREAM KNOWS WHAT HE'S ABOUT. WE CAN TRUST HIM TO...
FATHER! FATHER! CUT ME FREE!
HUH?
I KNEW IT! HE'S IN TROUBLE!
NO NO! LET PRESERVERS DO!
OFF, BUG!
MOMENTS LATER...
:GASP!: SO CHANGED!
HE-HE CAN'T MOVE...CAN'T BREATHE!

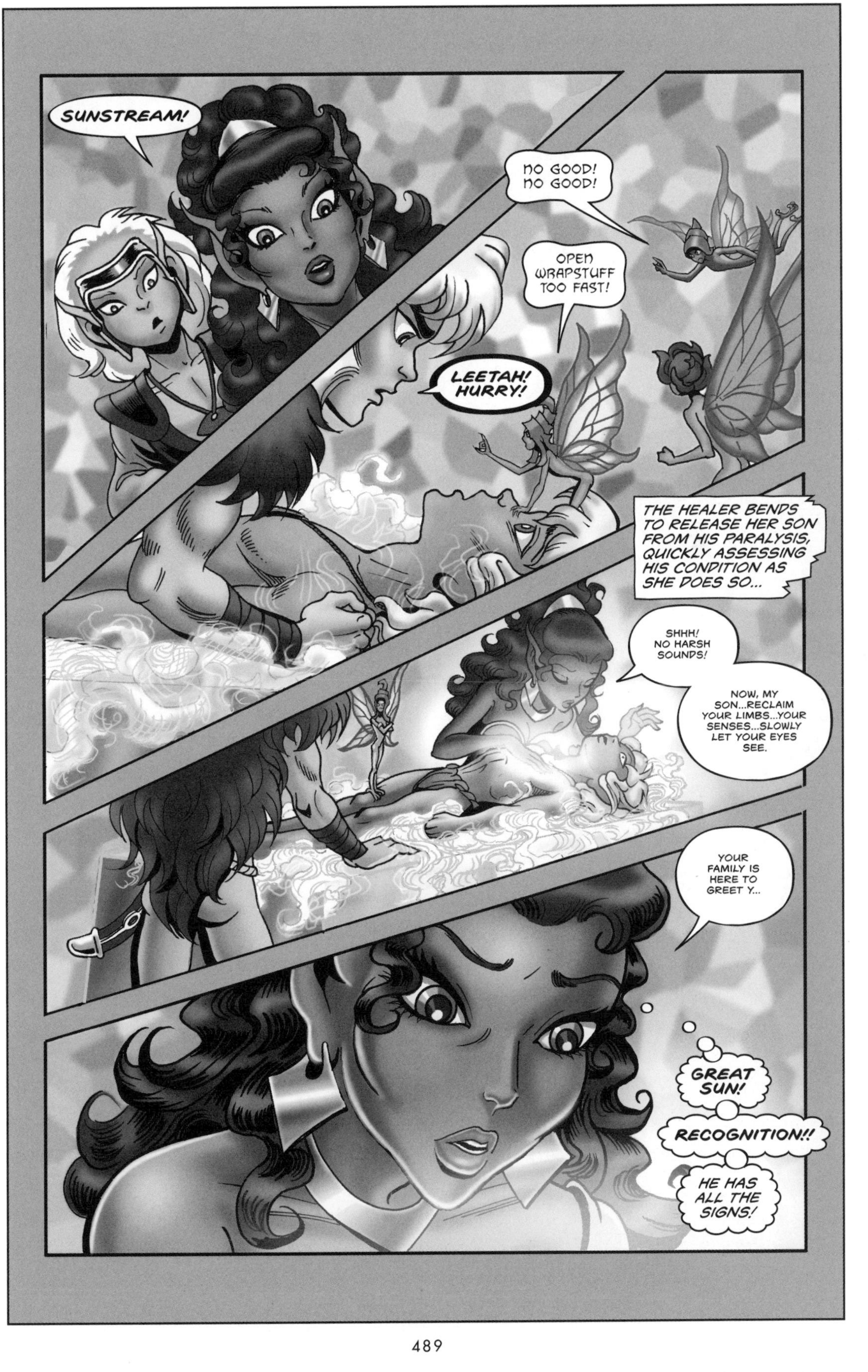
SUNSTREAM!
NO GOOD! NO GOOD!
OPEN WRAPSTUFF TOO FAST!
LEETAH! HURRY!
THE HEALER BENDS TO RELEASE HER SON FROM HIS PARALYSIS, QUICKLY ASSESSING HIS CONDITION AS SHE DOES SO...
SHHH! NO HARSH SOUNDS!
NOW, MY SON...RECLAIM YOUR LIMBS...YOUR SENSES...SLOWLY LET YOUR EYES SEE.
YOUR FAMILY IS HERE TO GREET Y...
GREAT SUN!
RECOGNITION!!
HE HAS ALL THE SIGNS!

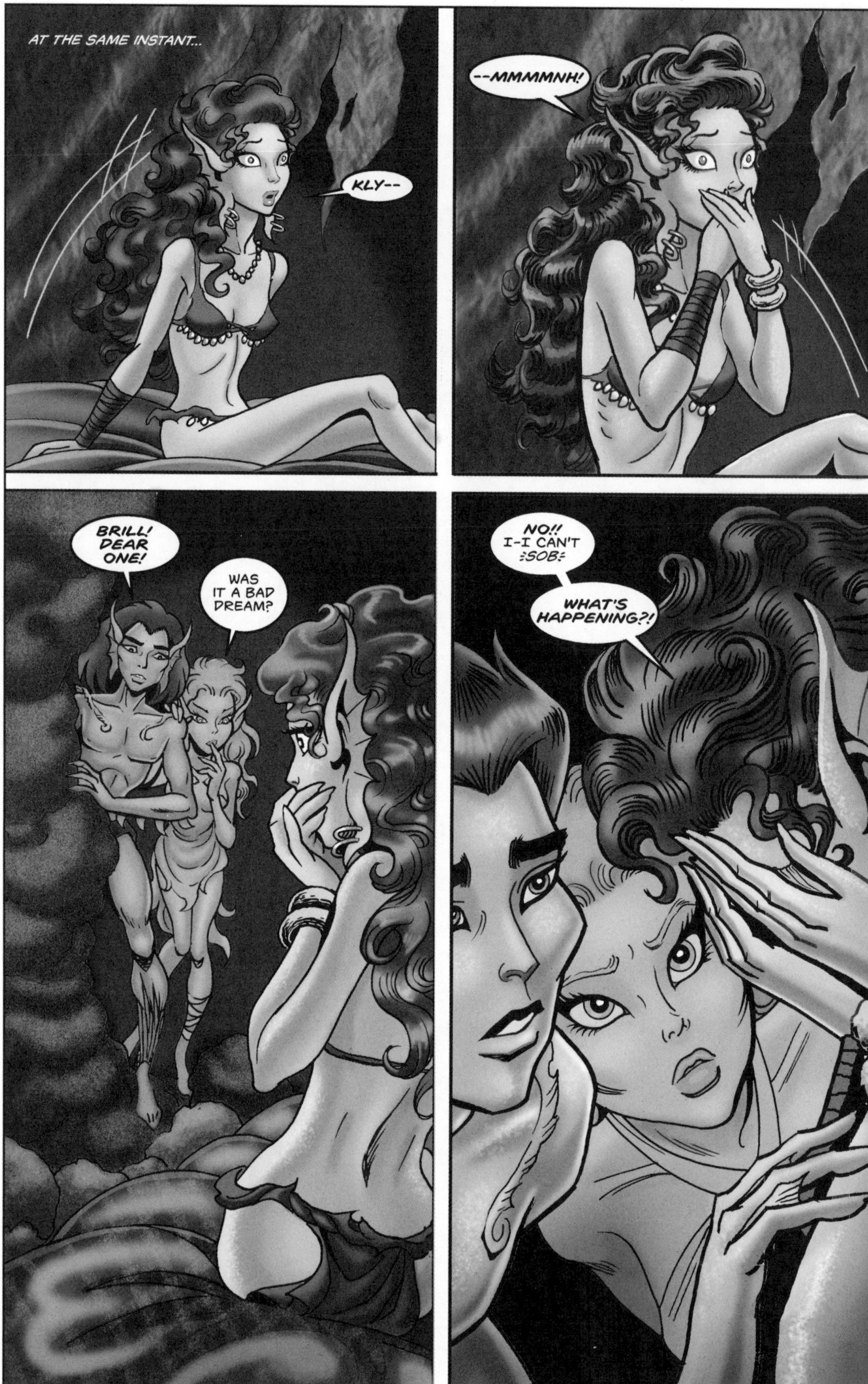
AT THE SAME INSTANT...
KLY--
--MMMMNH!
BRILL! DEAR ONE!
WAS IT A BAD DREAM?
NO!! I-I CAN'T -SOB-
WHAT'S HAPPENING?!

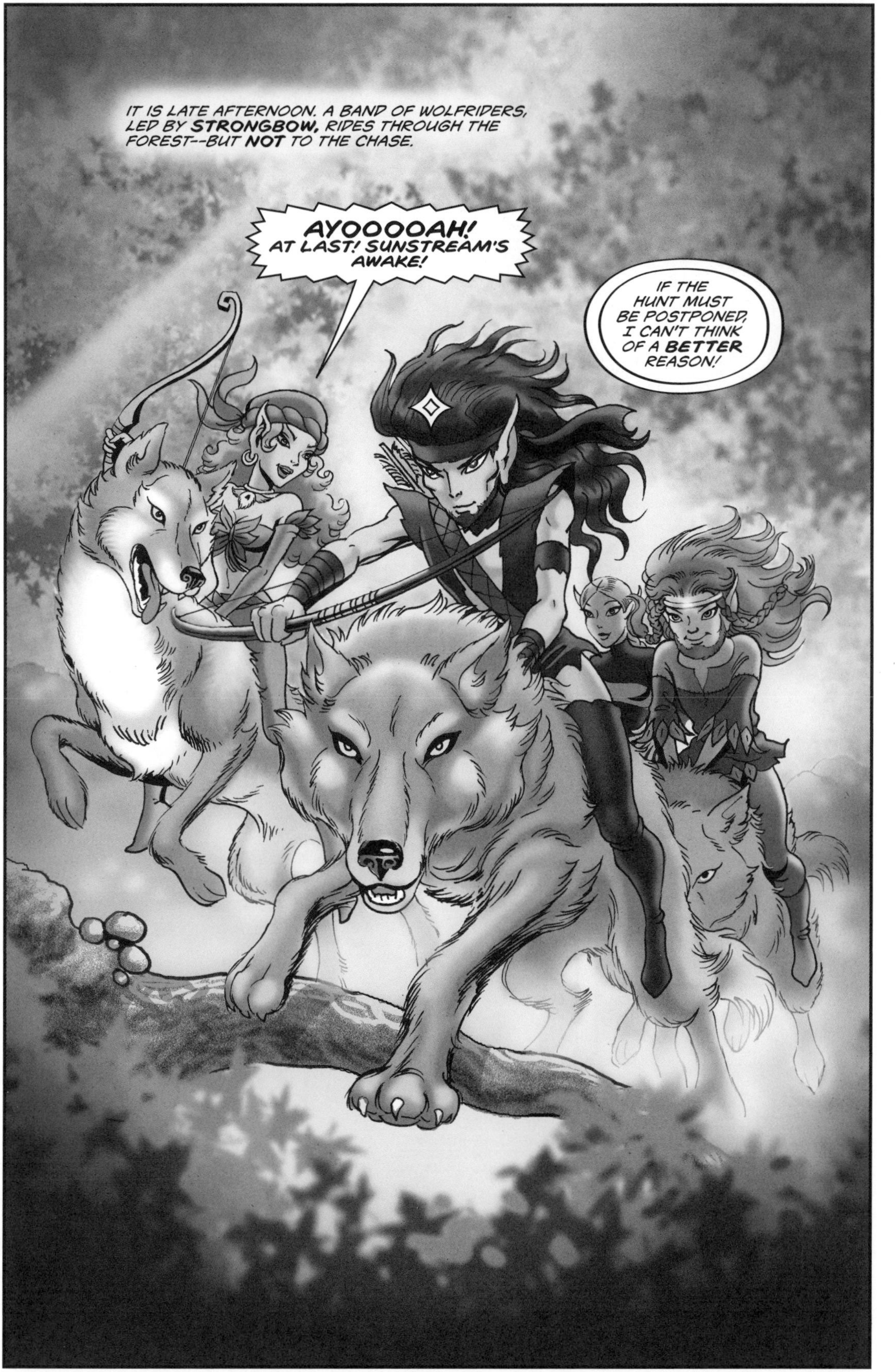
IT IS LATE AFTERNOON. A BAND OF WOLFRIDERS, LED BY **STRONGBOW**, RIDES THROUGH THE FOREST--BUT **NOT** TO THE CHASE.
AYOOOOAH! AT LAST! SUNSTREAM'S AWAKE!
IF THE HUNT MUST BE POSTPONED, I CAN'T THINK OF A **BETTER** REASON!

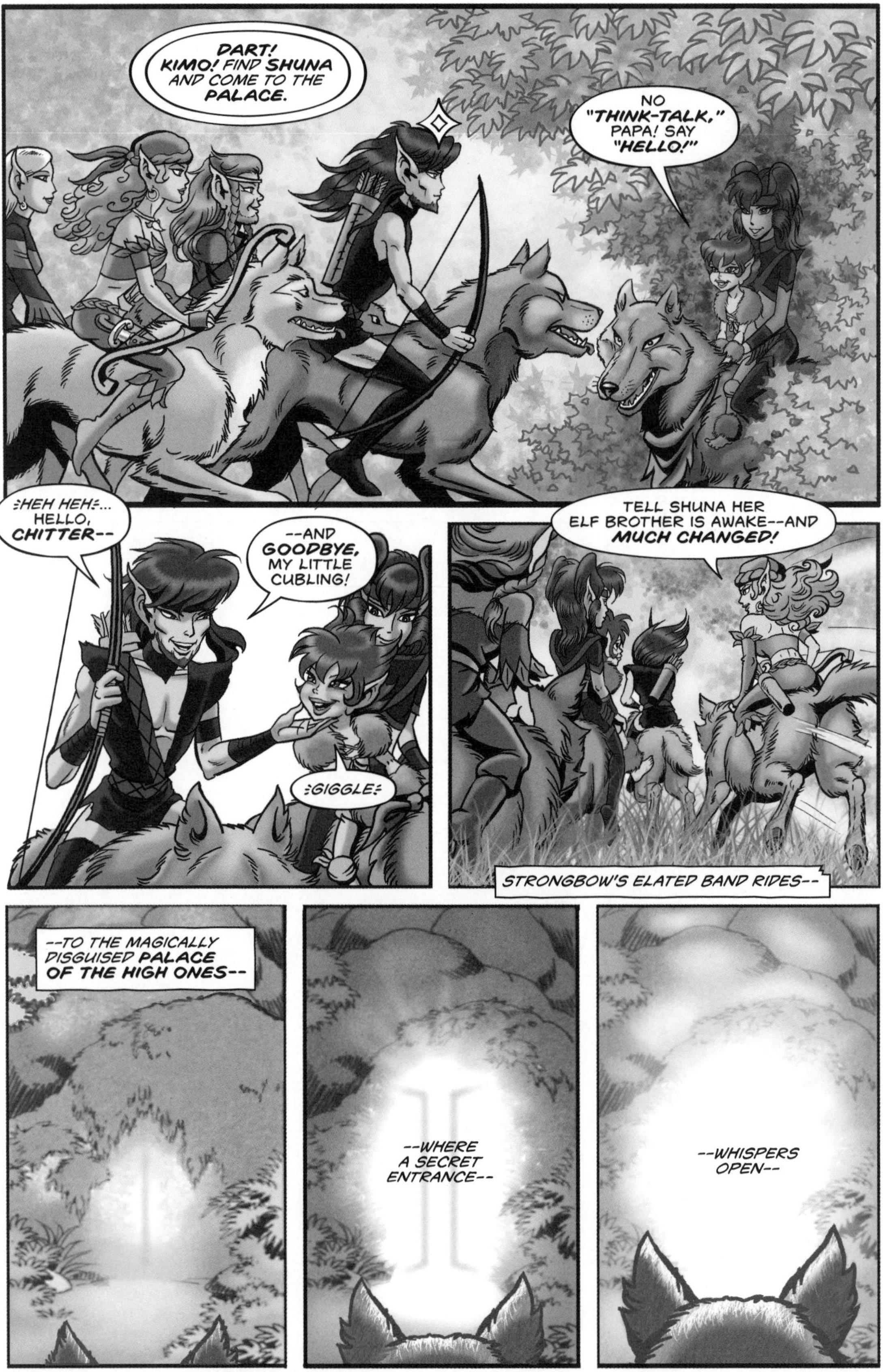
DART! KIMO! FIND SHUNA AND COME TO THE PALACE.
NO "THINK-TALK," PAPA! SAY "HELLO!"
HEH HEH... HELLO, CHITTER--
--AND GOODBYE, MY LITTLE CUBLING!
GIGGLE
TELL SHUNA HER ELF BROTHER IS AWAKE--AND MUCH CHANGED!
STRONGBOW'S ELATED BAND RIDES--
--TO THE MAGICALLY DISGUISED PALACE OF THE HIGH ONES--
--WHERE A SECRET ENTRANCE--
--WHISPERS OPEN--

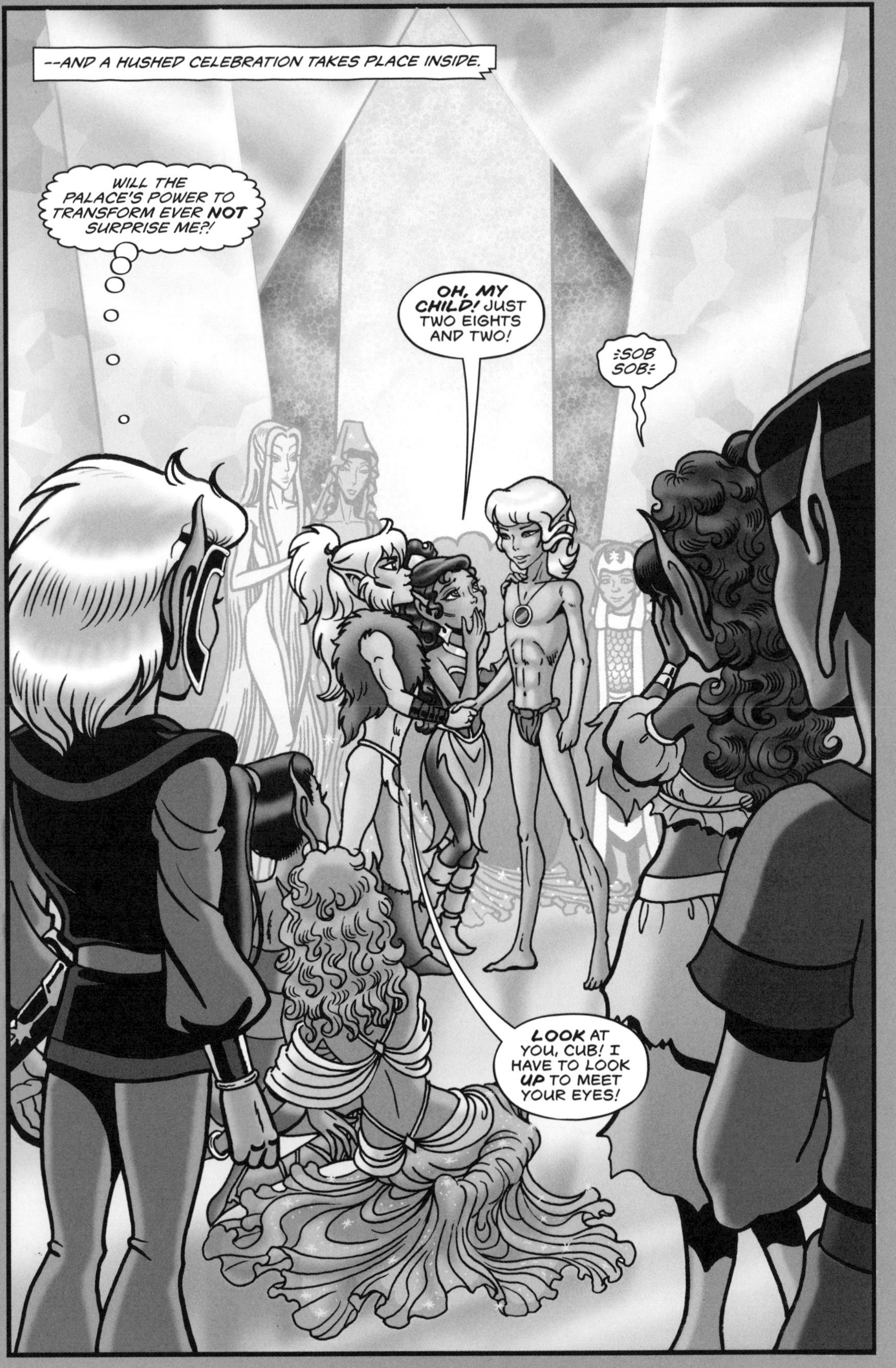
--AND A HUSHED CELEBRATION TAKES PLACE INSIDE.
WILL THE PALACE'S POWER TO TRANSFORM EVER NOT SURPRISE ME?!
OH, MY CHILD! JUST TWO EIGHTS AND TWO!
SOB SOB
LOOK AT YOU, CUB! I HAVE TO LOOK UP TO MEET YOUR EYES!

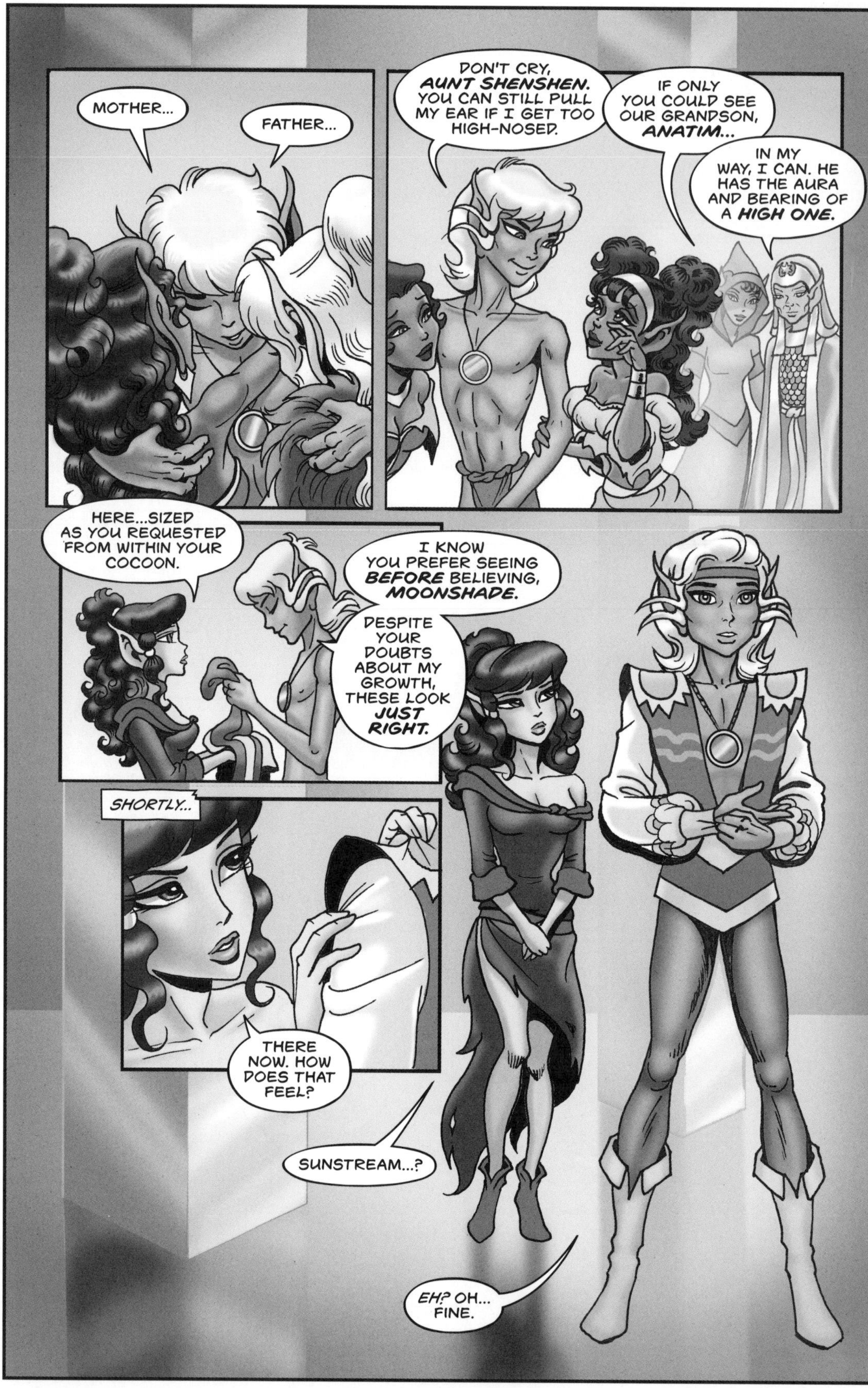
MOTHER...
FATHER...
DON'T CRY, AUNT SHENSHEN. YOU CAN STILL PULL MY EAR IF I GET TOO HIGH-NOSED.
IF ONLY YOU COULD SEE OUR GRANDSON, ANATIM...
IN MY WAY, I CAN. HE HAS THE AURA AND BEARING OF A HIGH ONE.
HERE...SIZED AS YOU REQUESTED FROM WITHIN YOUR COCOON.
I KNOW YOU PREFER SEEING BEFORE BELIEVING, MOONSHADE.
DESPITE YOUR DOUBTS ABOUT MY GROWTH, THESE LOOK JUST RIGHT.
SHORTLY...
THERE NOW. HOW DOES THAT FEEL?
SUNSTREAM...?
EH? OH... FINE.

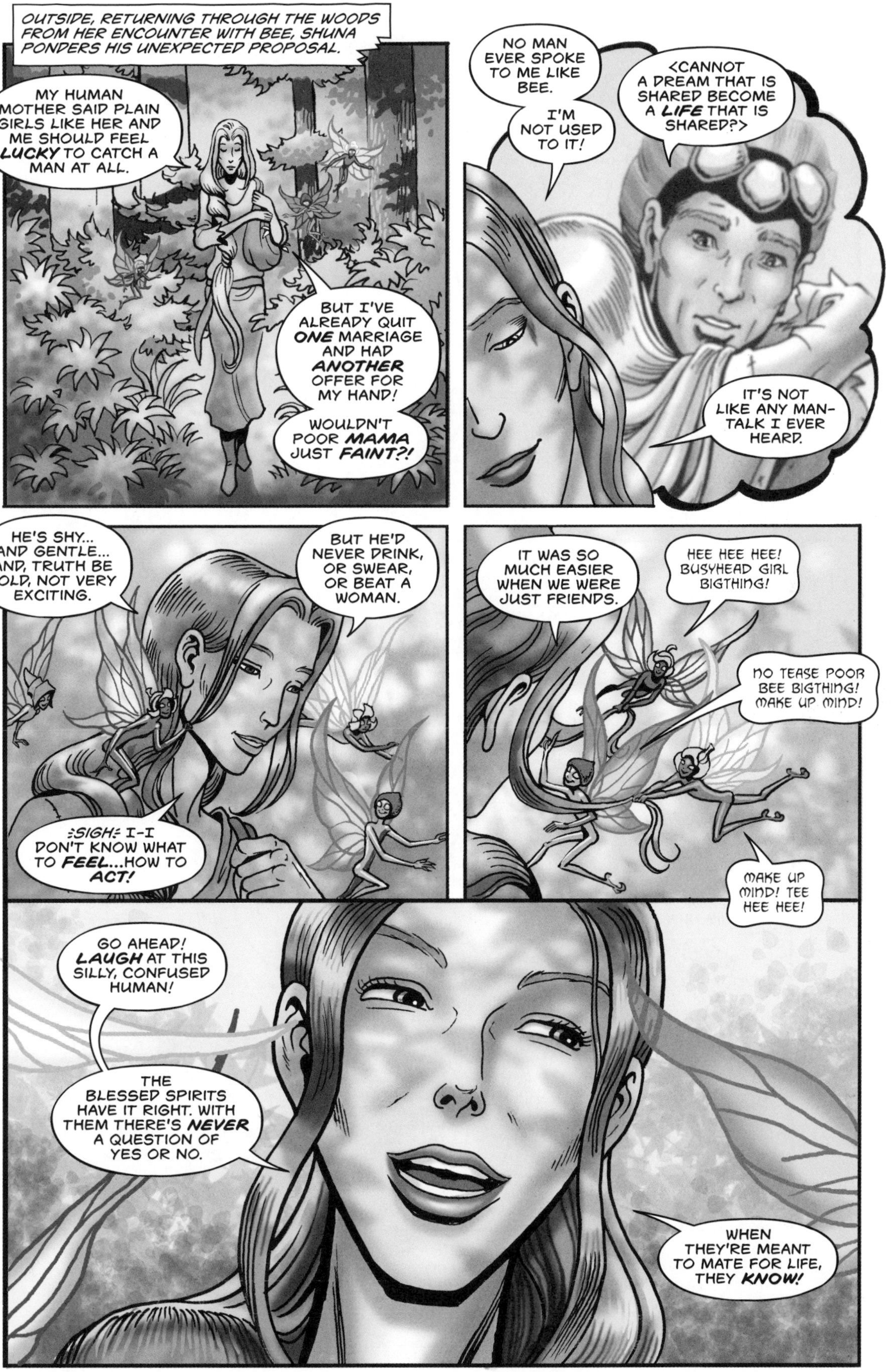
OUTSIDE, RETURNING THROUGH THE WOODS FROM HER ENCOUNTER WITH BEE, SHUNA PONDERS HIS UNEXPECTED PROPOSAL.
MY HUMAN MOTHER SAID PLAIN GIRLS LIKE HER AND ME SHOULD FEEL LUCKY TO CATCH A MAN AT ALL.
BUT I'VE ALREADY QUIT ONE MARRIAGE AND HAD ANOTHER OFFER FOR MY HAND!
WOULDN'T POOR MAMA JUST FAINT?!
NO MAN EVER SPOKE TO ME LIKE BEE.
I'M NOT USED TO IT!
<CANNOT A DREAM THAT IS SHARED BECOME A LIFE THAT IS SHARED?>
IT'S NOT LIKE ANY MAN-TALK I EVER HEARD.
HE'S SHY... AND GENTLE... AND, TRUTH BE TOLD, NOT VERY EXCITING.
BUT HE'D NEVER DRINK, OR SWEAR, OR BEAT A WOMAN.
SIGH I-I DON'T KNOW WHAT TO FEEL...HOW TO ACT!
IT WAS SO MUCH EASIER WHEN WE WERE JUST FRIENDS.
HEE HEE HEE! BUSYHEAD GIRL BIGTHING!
NO TEASE POOR BEE BIGTHING! MAKE UP MIND!
MAKE UP MIND! TEE HEE HEE!
GO AHEAD! LAUGH AT THIS SILLY, CONFUSED HUMAN!
THE BLESSED SPIRITS HAVE IT RIGHT. WITH THEM THERE'S NEVER A QUESTION OF YES OR NO.
WHEN THEY'RE MEANT TO MATE FOR LIFE, THEY KNOW!

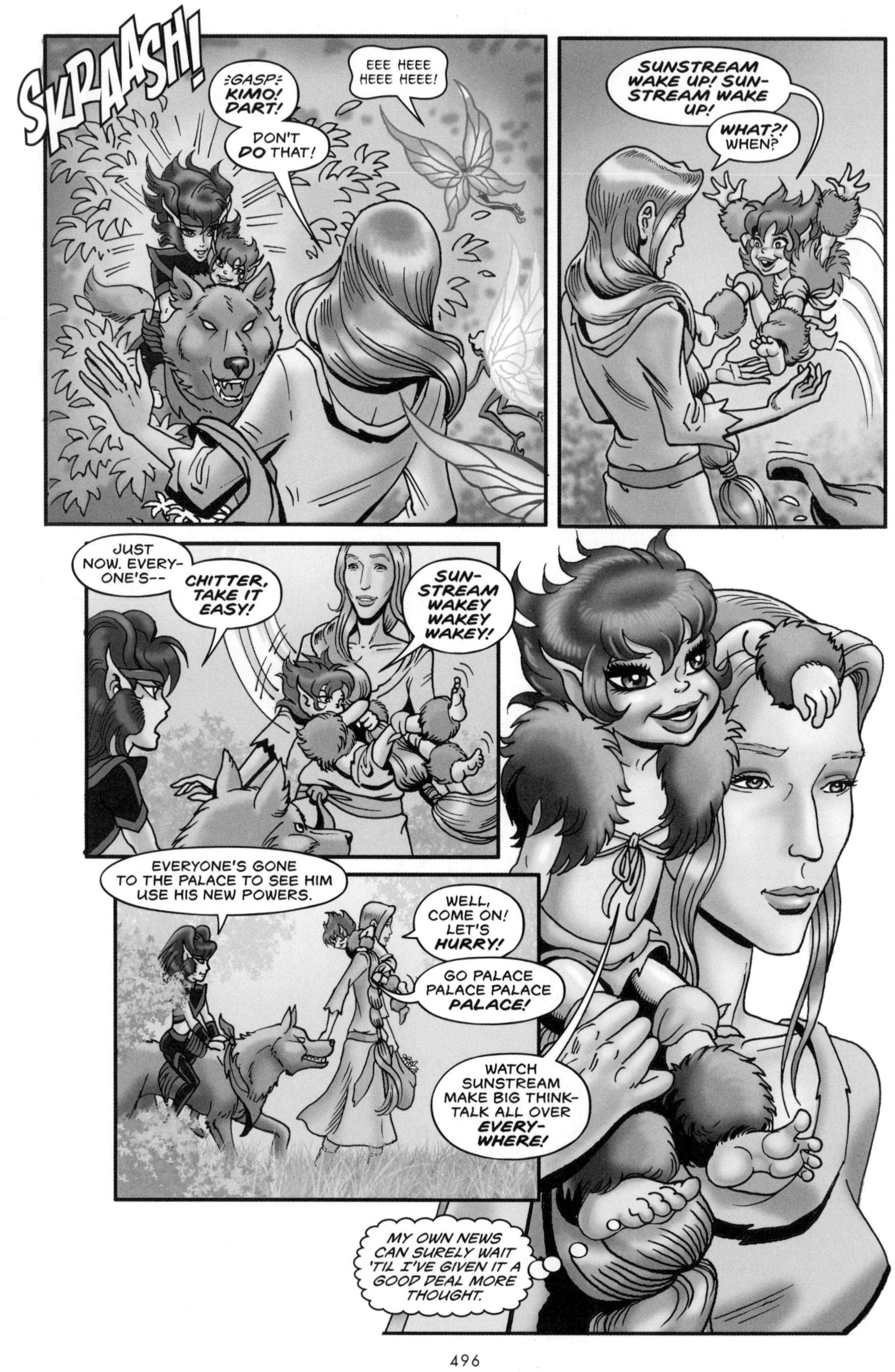
SKRAASH!
GASP KIMO! DART!
DON'T DO THAT!
EEE HEEE HEEE HEEE!
SUNSTREAM WAKE UP! SUN-STREAM WAKE UP!
WHAT?! WHEN?
JUST NOW. EVERY-ONE'S--
CHITTER, TAKE IT EASY!
SUN-STREAM WAKEY WAKEY WAKEY!
EVERYONE'S GONE TO THE PALACE TO SEE HIM USE HIS NEW POWERS.
WELL, COME ON! LET'S HURRY!
GO PALACE PALACE PALACE PALACE!
WATCH SUNSTREAM MAKE BIG THINK-TALK ALL OVER EVERY-WHERE!
MY OWN NEWS CAN SURELY WAIT 'TIL I'VE GIVEN IT A GOOD DEAL MORE THOUGHT.

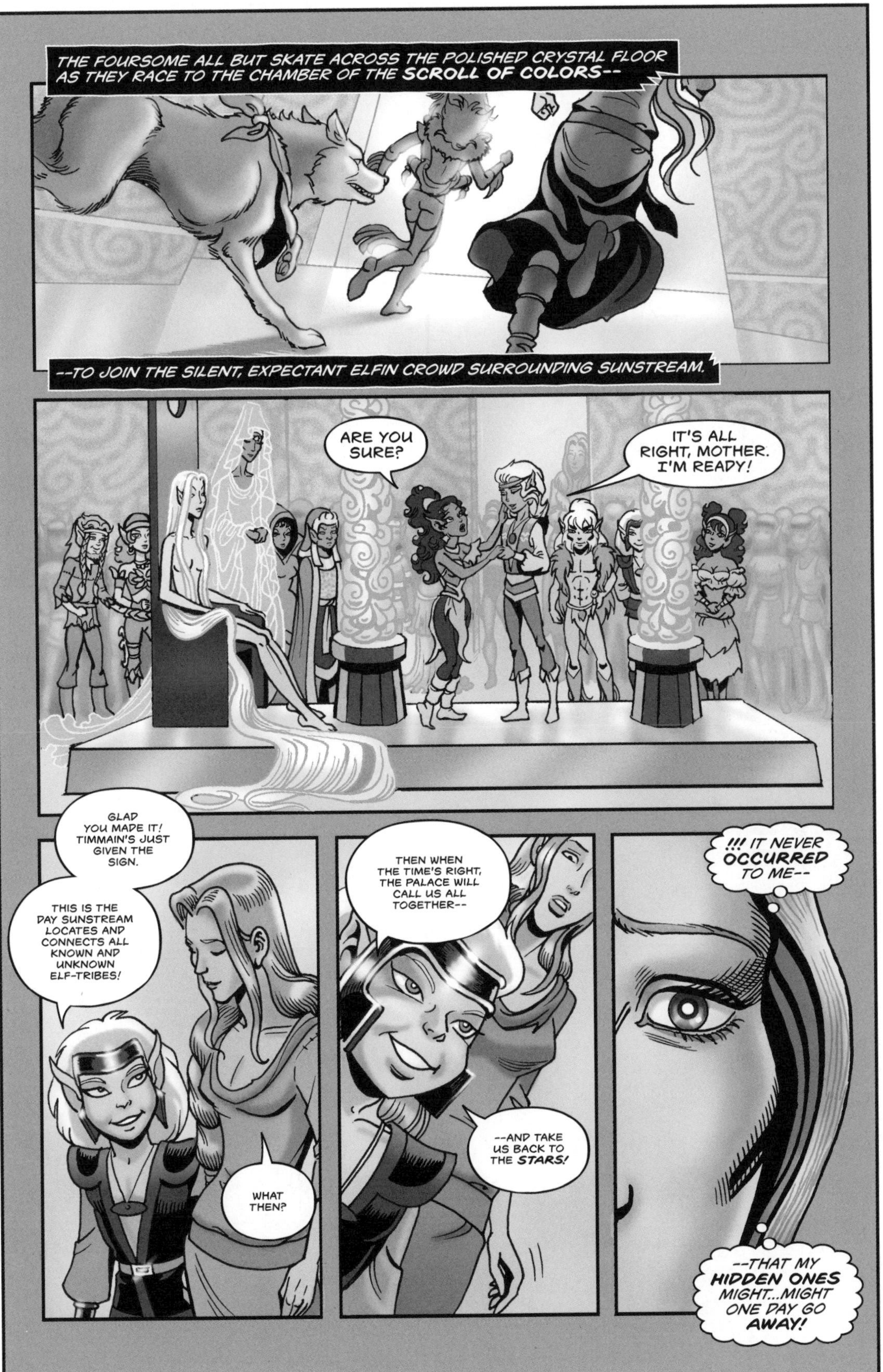
THE FOURSOME ALL BUT SKATE ACROSS THE POLISHED CRYSTAL FLOOR AS THEY RACE TO THE CHAMBER OF THE SCROLL OF COLORS--
--TO JOIN THE SILENT, EXPECTANT ELFIN CROWD SURROUNDING SUNSTREAM.
ARE YOU SURE?
IT'S ALL RIGHT, MOTHER. I'M READY!
GLAD YOU MADE IT! TIMMAIN'S JUST GIVEN THE SIGN.
THIS IS THE DAY SUNSTREAM LOCATES AND CONNECTS ALL KNOWN AND UNKNOWN ELF-TRIBES!
WHAT THEN?
THEN WHEN THE TIME'S RIGHT, THE PALACE WILL CALL US ALL TOGETHER--
--AND TAKE US BACK TO THE STARS!
!!! IT NEVER OCCURRED TO ME--
--THAT MY HIDDEN ONES MIGHT...MIGHT ONE DAY GO AWAY!

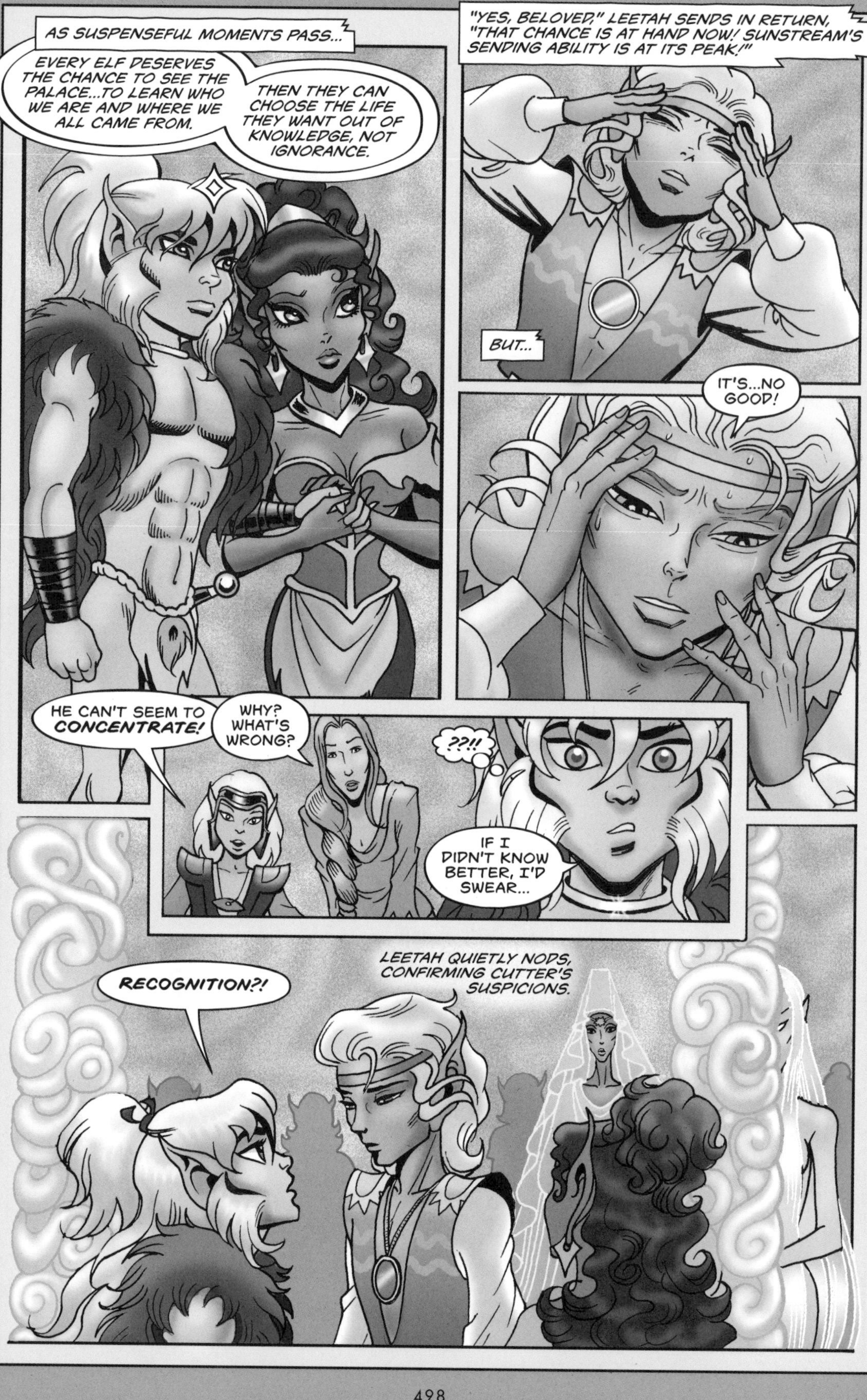
AS SUSPENSEFUL MOMENTS PASS...
EVERY ELF DESERVES THE CHANCE TO SEE THE PALACE...TO LEARN WHO WE ARE AND WHERE WE ALL CAME FROM.
THEN THEY CAN CHOOSE THE LIFE THEY WANT OUT OF KNOWLEDGE, NOT IGNORANCE.
"YES, BELOVED," LEETAH SENDS IN RETURN, "THAT CHANCE IS AT HAND NOW! SUNSTREAM'S SENDING ABILITY IS AT ITS PEAK!"
BUT...
IT'S...NO GOOD!
HE CAN'T SEEM TO CONCENTRATE!
WHY? WHAT'S WRONG?
??!!
IF I DIDN'T KNOW BETTER, I'D SWEAR...
RECOGNITION?!
LEETAH QUIETLY NODS, CONFIRMING CUTTER'S SUSPICIONS.

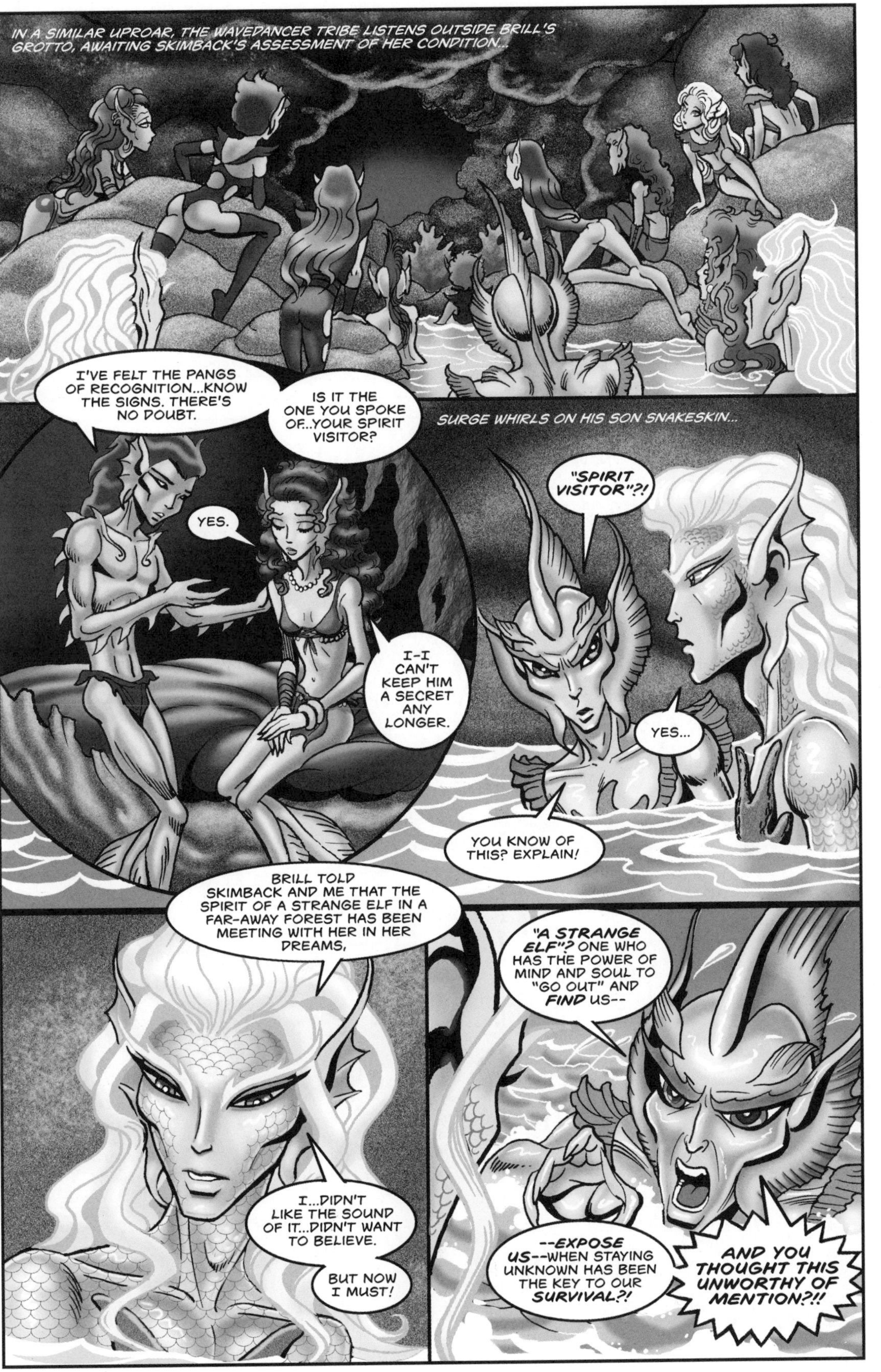
IN A SIMILAR UPROAR, THE WAVEDANCER TRIBE LISTENS OUTSIDE BRILL'S GROTTO, AWAITING SKIMBACK'S ASSESSMENT OF HER CONDITION...
I'VE FELT THE PANGS OF RECOGNITION...KNOW THE SIGNS. THERE'S NO DOUBT.
IS IT THE ONE YOU SPOKE OF...YOUR SPIRIT VISITOR?
YES.
I-I CAN'T KEEP HIM A SECRET ANY LONGER.
SURGE WHIRLS ON HIS SON SNAKESKIN...
"SPIRIT VISITOR"?!
YES...
YOU KNOW OF THIS? EXPLAIN!
BRILL TOLD SKIMBACK AND ME THAT THE SPIRIT OF A STRANGE ELF IN A FAR-AWAY FOREST HAS BEEN MEETING WITH HER IN HER DREAMS,
I...DIDN'T LIKE THE SOUND OF IT...DIDN'T WANT TO BELIEVE.
BUT NOW I MUST!
"A STRANGE ELF"? ONE WHO HAS THE POWER OF MIND AND SOUL TO "GO OUT" AND FIND US--
--EXPOSE US--WHEN STAYING UNKNOWN HAS BEEN THE KEY TO OUR SURVIVAL?!
AND YOU THOUGHT THIS UNWORTHY OF MENTION?!!

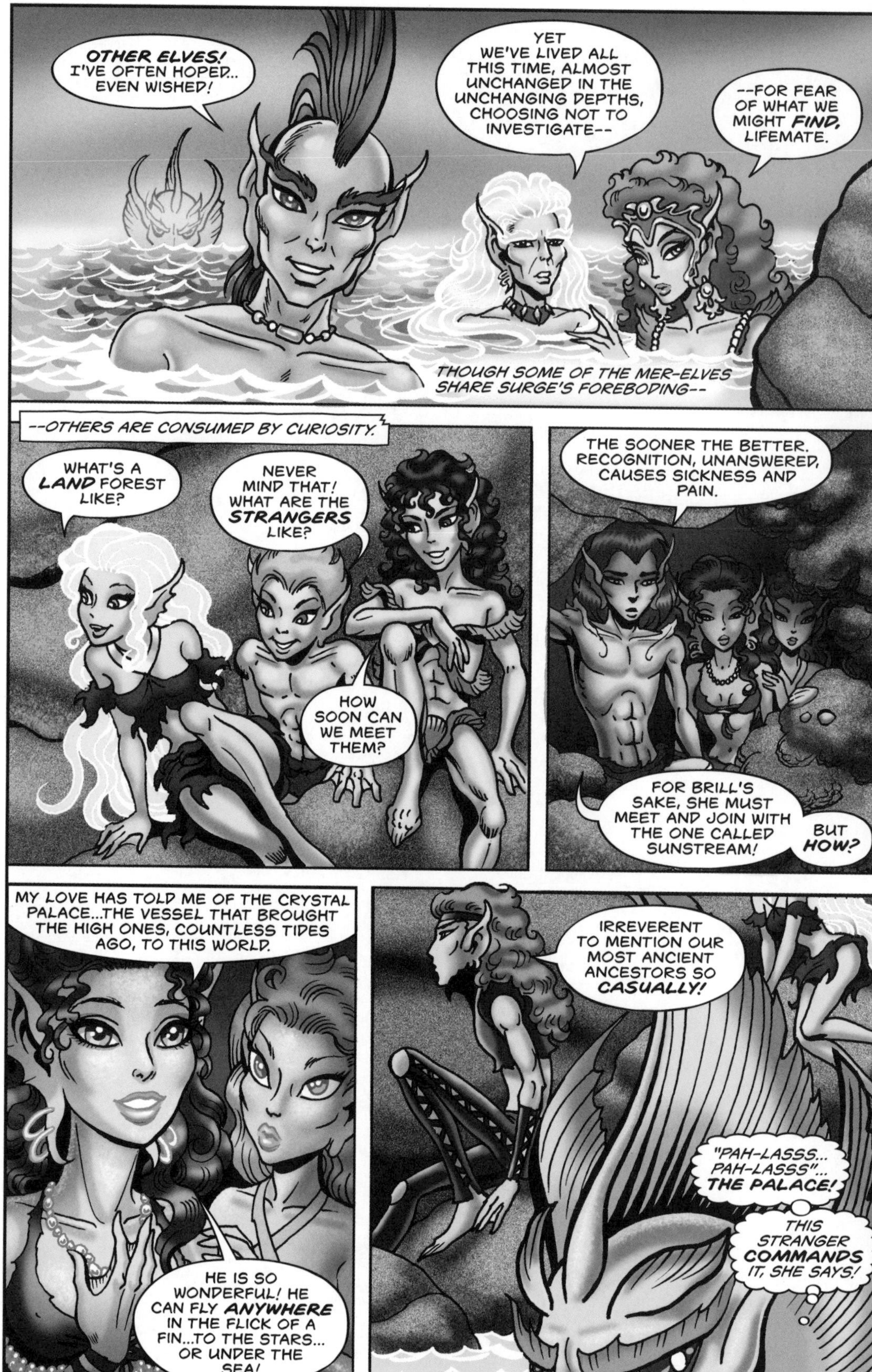
OTHER ELVES! I'VE OFTEN HOPED... EVEN WISHED!
YET WE'VE LIVED ALL THIS TIME, ALMOST UNCHANGED IN THE UNCHANGING DEPTHS, CHOOSING NOT TO INVESTIGATE--
--FOR FEAR OF WHAT WE MIGHT FIND, LIFEMATE.
THOUGH SOME OF THE MER-ELVES SHARE SURGE'S FOREBODING--
--OTHERS ARE CONSUMED BY CURIOSITY.
WHAT'S A LAND FOREST LIKE?
NEVER MIND THAT! WHAT ARE THE STRANGERS LIKE?
HOW SOON CAN WE MEET THEM?
THE SOONER THE BETTER. RECOGNITION, UNANSWERED, CAUSES SICKNESS AND PAIN.
FOR BRILL'S SAKE, SHE MUST MEET AND JOIN WITH THE ONE CALLED SUNSTREAM!
BUT HOW?
MY LOVE HAS TOLD ME OF THE CRYSTAL PALACE...THE VESSEL THAT BROUGHT THE HIGH ONES, COUNTLESS TIDES AGO, TO THIS WORLD.
HE IS SO WONDERFUL! HE CAN FLY ANYWHERE IN THE FLICK OF A FIN...TO THE STARS... OR UNDER THE SEA!
IRREVERENT TO MENTION OUR MOST ANCIENT ANCESTORS SO CASUALLY!
"PAH-LASSS... PAH-LASSS"... THE PALACE!
THIS STRANGER COMMANDS IT, SHE SAYS!

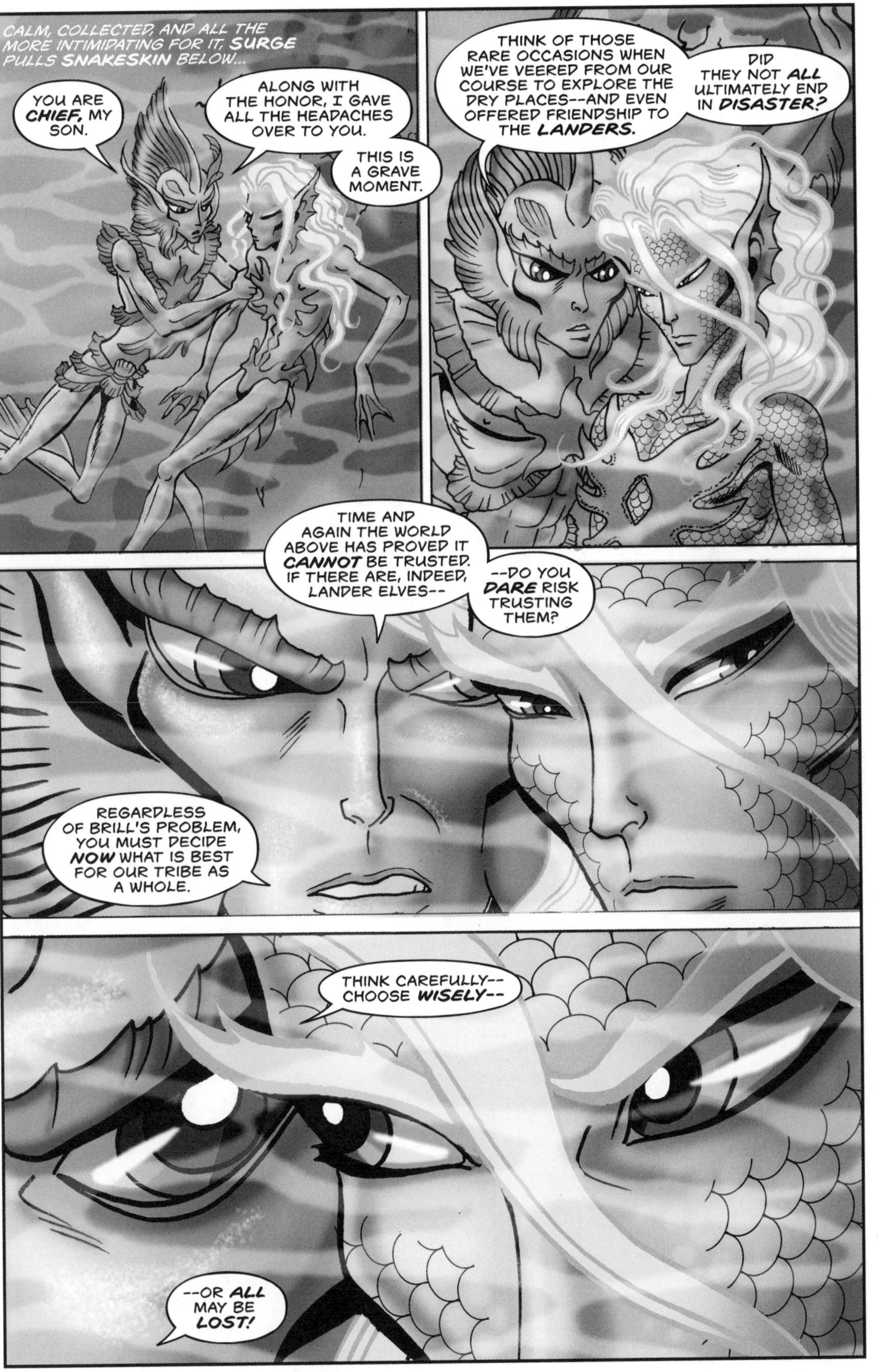
CALM, COLLECTED, AND ALL THE MORE INTIMIDATING FOR IT, SURGE PULLS SNAKESKIN BELOW...
YOU ARE CHIEF, MY SON.
ALONG WITH THE HONOR, I GAVE ALL THE HEADACHES OVER TO YOU.
THIS IS A GRAVE MOMENT.
THINK OF THOSE RARE OCCASIONS WHEN WE'VE VEERED FROM OUR COURSE TO EXPLORE THE DRY PLACES--AND EVEN OFFERED FRIENDSHIP TO THE LANDERS.
DID THEY NOT ALL ULTIMATELY END IN DISASTER?
TIME AND AGAIN THE WORLD ABOVE HAS PROVED IT CANNOT BE TRUSTED. IF THERE ARE, INDEED, LANDER ELVES--
--DO YOU DARE RISK TRUSTING THEM?
REGARDLESS OF BRILL'S PROBLEM, YOU MUST DECIDE NOW WHAT IS BEST FOR OUR TRIBE AS A WHOLE.
THINK CAREFULLY--CHOOSE WISELY--
--OR ALL MAY BE LOST!

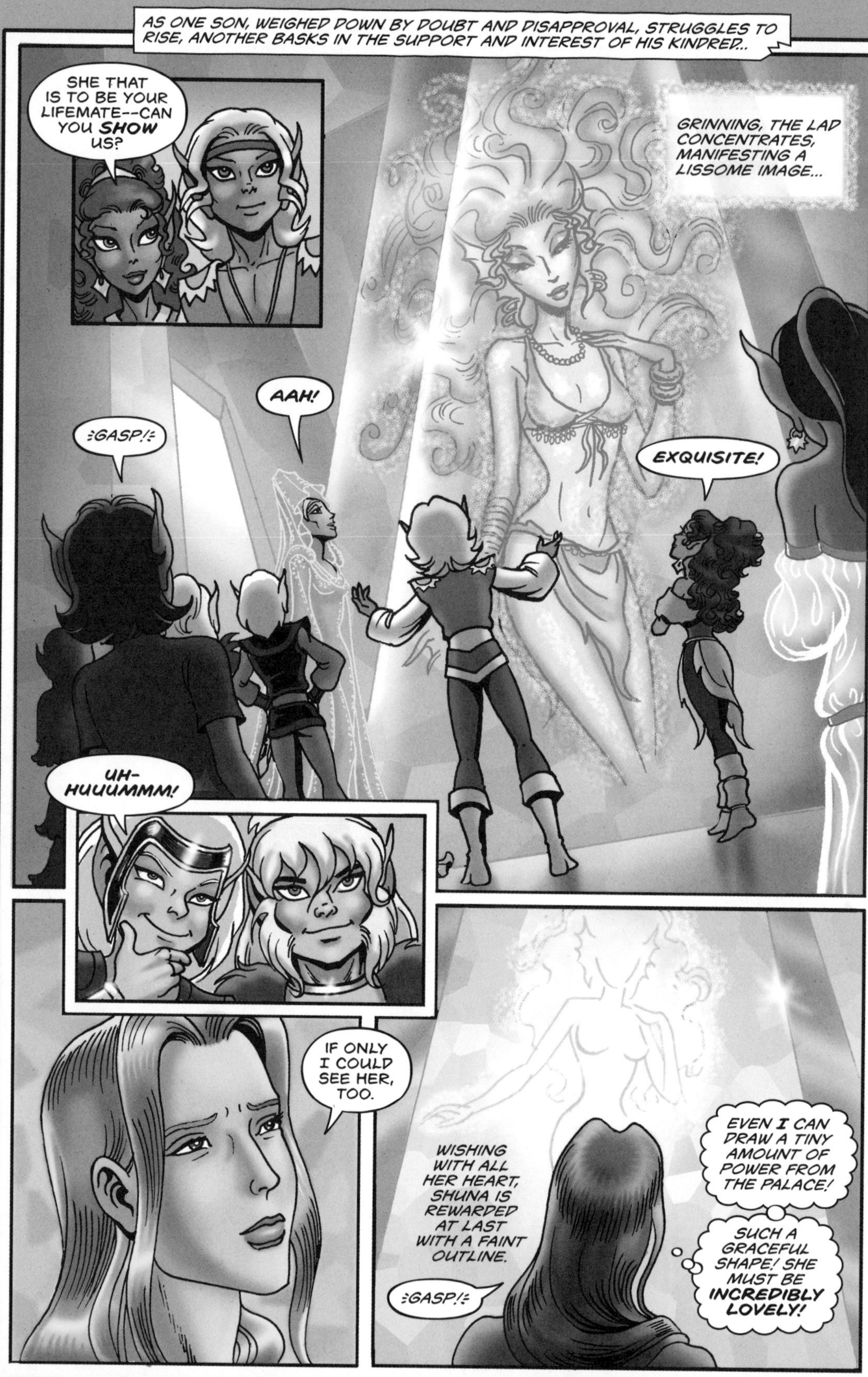
AS ONE SON, WEIGHED DOWN BY DOUBT AND DISAPPROVAL, STRUGGLES TO RISE, ANOTHER BASKS IN THE SUPPORT AND INTEREST OF HIS KINDRED...
SHE THAT IS TO BE YOUR LIFEMATE--CAN YOU **SHOW** US?
GRINNING, THE LAD CONCENTRATES, MANIFESTING A LISSOME IMAGE...
AAH!
:GASP!:
EXQUISITE!
UH-HUUUMMM!
IF ONLY I COULD SEE HER, TOO.
WISHING WITH ALL HER HEART, SHUNA IS REWARDED AT LAST WITH A FAINT OUTLINE.
EVEN **I** CAN DRAW A TINY AMOUNT OF POWER FROM THE PALACE!
SUCH A GRACEFUL SHAPE! SHE MUST BE **INCREDIBLY LOVELY!**
:GASP!:

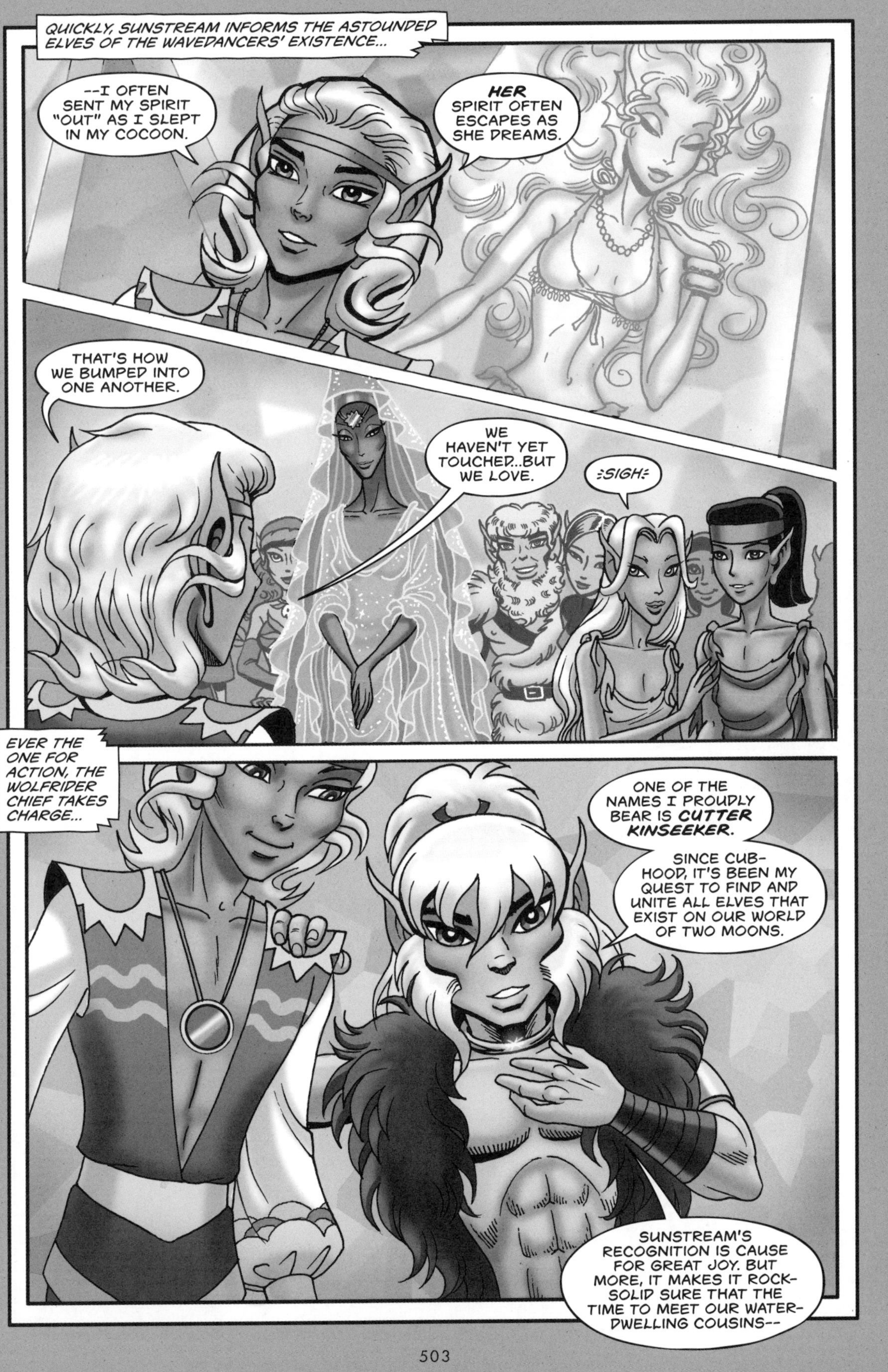
QUICKLY, SUNSTREAM INFORMS THE ASTOUNDED ELVES OF THE WAVEDANCERS' EXISTENCE...
--I OFTEN SENT MY SPIRIT "OUT" AS I SLEPT IN MY COCOON.
HER SPIRIT OFTEN ESCAPES AS SHE DREAMS.
THAT'S HOW WE BUMPED INTO ONE ANOTHER.
WE HAVEN'T YET TOUCHED...BUT WE LOVE.
SIGH
EVER THE ONE FOR ACTION, THE WOLFRIDER CHIEF TAKES CHARGE...
ONE OF THE NAMES I PROUDLY BEAR IS CUTTER KINSEEKER.
SINCE CUBHOOD, IT'S BEEN MY QUEST TO FIND AND UNITE ALL ELVES THAT EXIST ON OUR WORLD OF TWO MOONS.
SUNSTREAM'S RECOGNITION IS CAUSE FOR GREAT JOY. BUT MORE, IT MAKES IT ROCK-SOLID SURE THAT THE TIME TO MEET OUR WATER-DWELLING COUSINS--

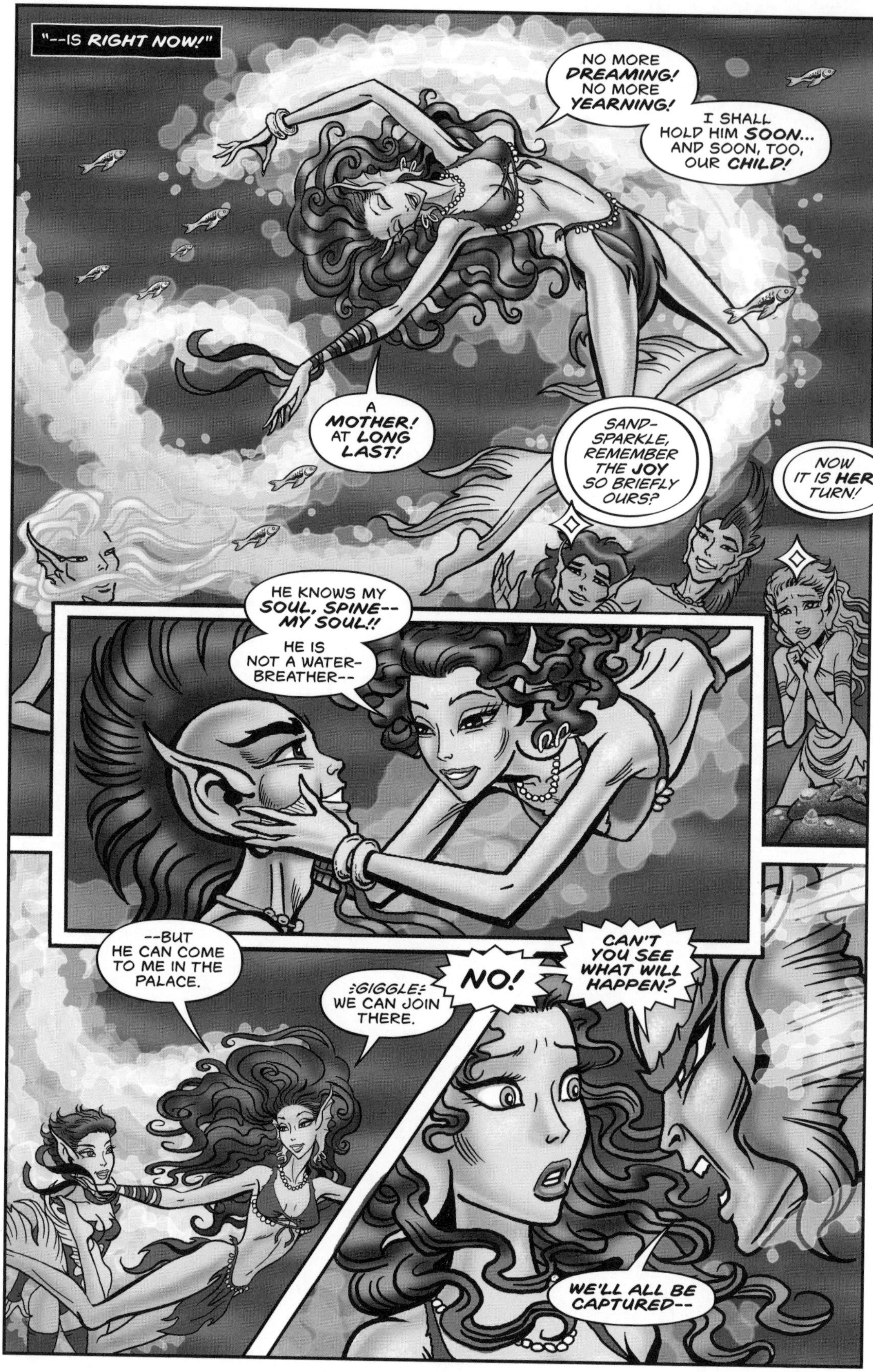
"--IS RIGHT NOW!"
NO MORE DREAMING! NO MORE YEARNING!
I SHALL HOLD HIM SOON... AND SOON, TOO, OUR CHILD!
A MOTHER! AT LONG LAST!
SAND-SPARKLE, REMEMBER THE JOY SO BRIEFLY OURS?
NOW IT IS HER TURN!
HE KNOWS MY SOUL, SPINE-- MY SOUL!!
HE IS NOT A WATER-BREATHER--
--BUT HE CAN COME TO ME IN THE PALACE.
:GIGGLE: WE CAN JOIN THERE.
NO!
CAN'T YOU SEE WHAT WILL HAPPEN?
WE'LL ALL BE CAPTURED--

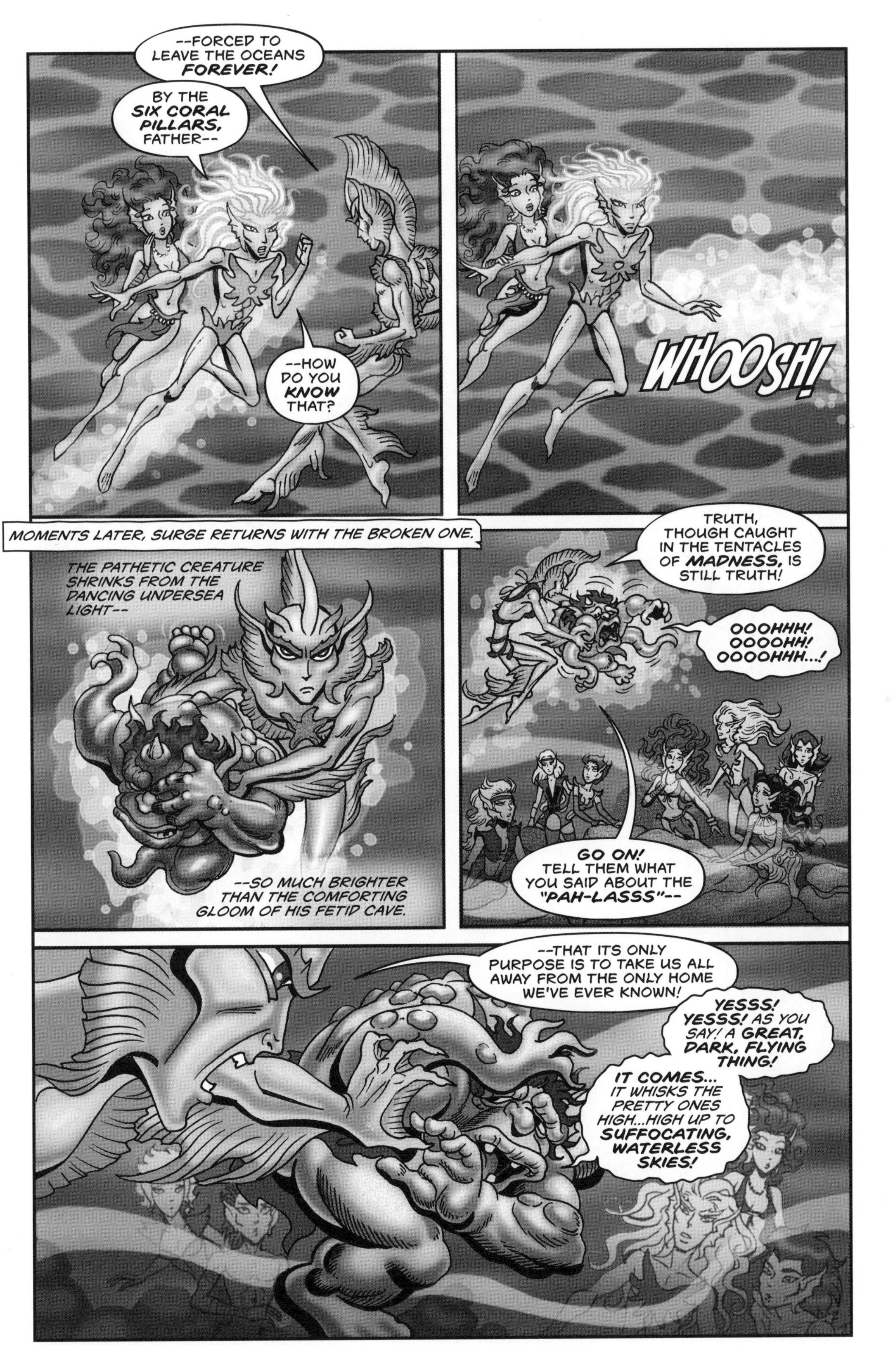
--FORCED TO LEAVE THE OCEANS FOREVER!
BY THE SIX CORAL PILLARS, FATHER--
--HOW DO YOU KNOW THAT?
WHOOSH!
MOMENTS LATER, SURGE RETURNS WITH THE BROKEN ONE.
THE PATHETIC CREATURE SHRINKS FROM THE DANCING UNDERSEA LIGHT--
--SO MUCH BRIGHTER THAN THE COMFORTING GLOOM OF HIS FETID CAVE.
TRUTH, THOUGH CAUGHT IN THE TENTACLES OF MADNESS, IS STILL TRUTH!
OOOHHH! OOOOHH! OOOOHHH...!
GO ON! TELL THEM WHAT YOU SAID ABOUT THE "PAH-LASSS"--
--THAT ITS ONLY PURPOSE IS TO TAKE US ALL AWAY FROM THE ONLY HOME WE'VE EVER KNOWN!
YESSS! YESSS! AS YOU SAY! A GREAT, DARK, FLYING THING!
IT COMES... IT WHISKS THE PRETTY ONES HIGH...HIGH UP TO SUFFOCATING, WATERLESS SKIES!

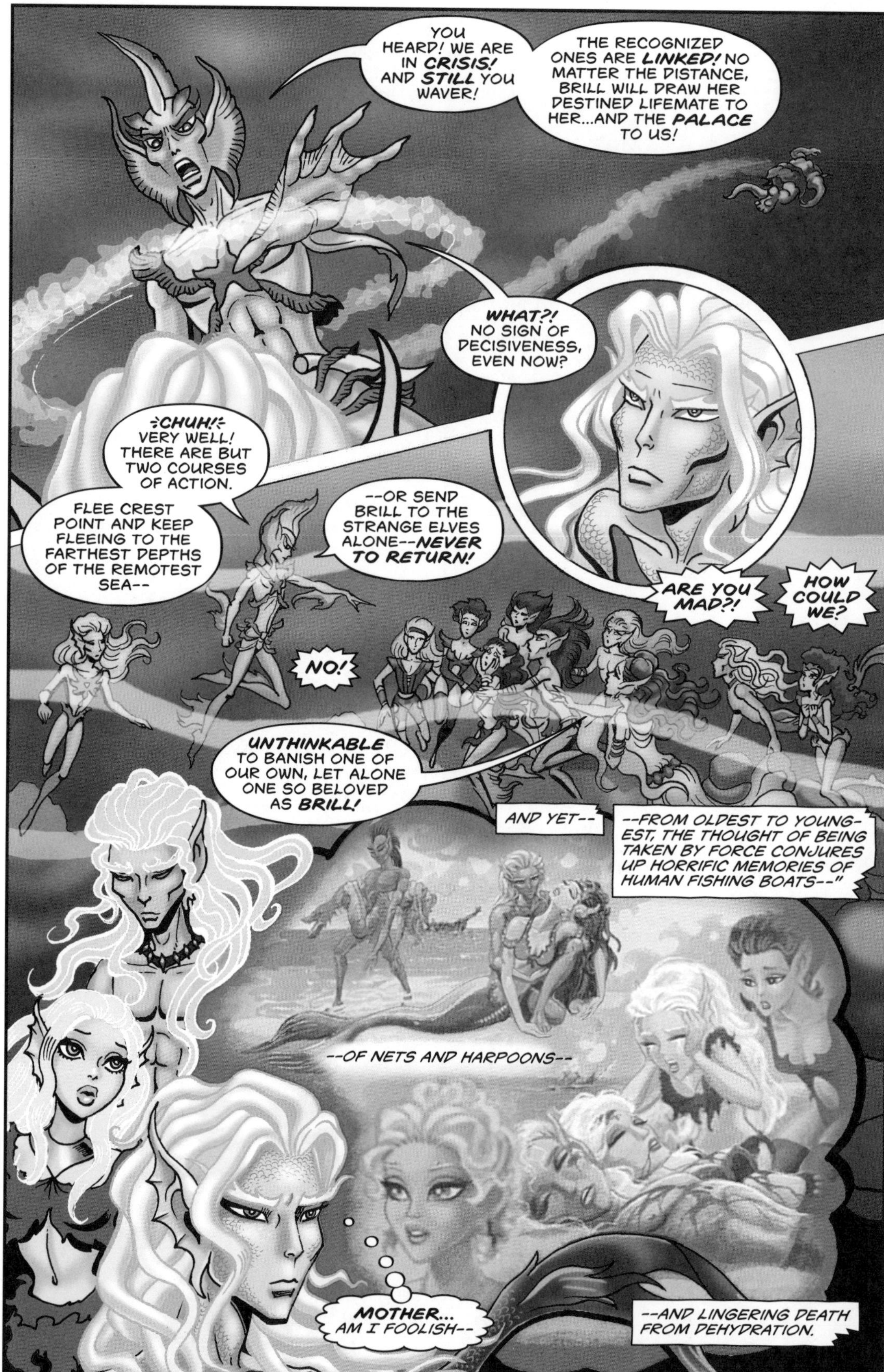
YOU HEARD! WE ARE IN CRISIS! AND STILL YOU WAVER!
THE RECOGNIZED ONES ARE LINKED! NO MATTER THE DISTANCE, BRILL WILL DRAW HER DESTINED LIFEMATE TO HER...AND THE PALACE TO US!
WHAT?! NO SIGN OF DECISIVENESS, EVEN NOW?
CHUH! VERY WELL! THERE ARE BUT TWO COURSES OF ACTION.
FLEE CREST POINT AND KEEP FLEEING TO THE FARTHEST DEPTHS OF THE REMOTEST SEA--
--OR SEND BRILL TO THE STRANGE ELVES ALONE--NEVER TO RETURN!
ARE YOU MAD?!
HOW COULD WE?
NO!
UNTHINKABLE TO BANISH ONE OF OUR OWN, LET ALONE ONE SO BELOVED AS BRILL!
AND YET--
--FROM OLDEST TO YOUNGEST, THE THOUGHT OF BEING TAKEN BY FORCE CONJURES UP HORRIFIC MEMORIES OF HUMAN FISHING BOATS--"
--OF NETS AND HARPOONS--
MOTHER... AM I FOOLISH--
--AND LINGERING DEATH FROM DEHYDRATION.

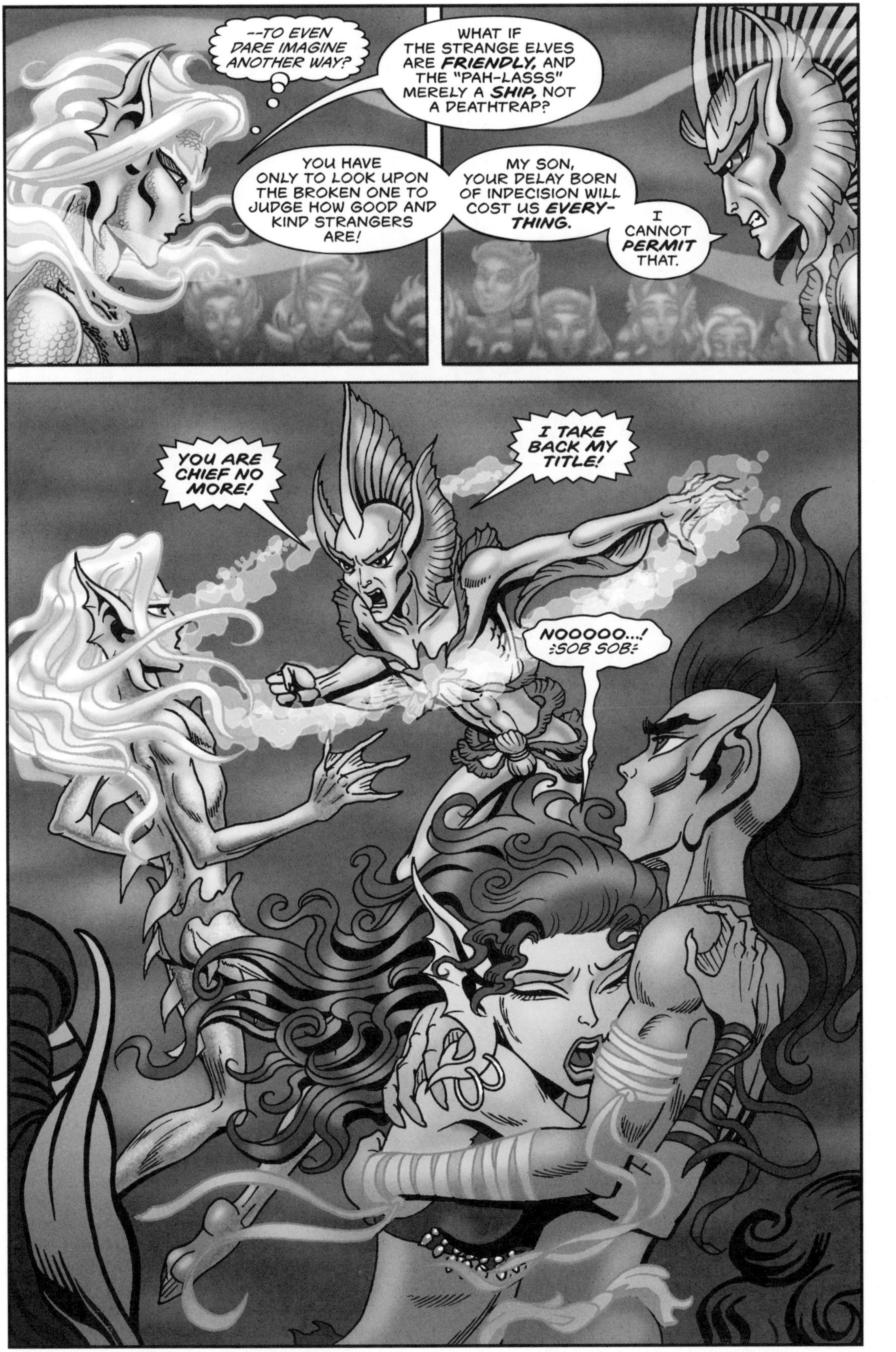
--TO EVEN DARE IMAGINE ANOTHER WAY?
WHAT IF THE STRANGE ELVES ARE FRIENDLY, AND THE "PAH-LASSS" MERELY A SHIP, NOT A DEATHTRAP?
YOU HAVE ONLY TO LOOK UPON THE BROKEN ONE TO JUDGE HOW GOOD AND KIND STRANGERS ARE!
MY SON, YOUR DELAY BORN OF INDECISION WILL COST US EVERYTHING.
I CANNOT PERMIT THAT.
YOU ARE CHIEF NO MORE!
I TAKE BACK MY TITLE!
NOOOOO...! SOB SOB

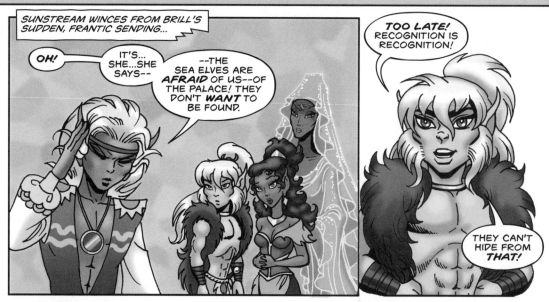

SUNSTREAM WINCES FROM BRILL'S SUDDEN, FRANTIC SENDING...

OH!

IT'S... SHE...SHE SAYS--

--THE SEA ELVES ARE *AFRAID* OF US--OF THE PALACE! THEY DON'T *WANT* TO BE FOUND.

TOO LATE! RECOGNITION IS RECOGNITION!

THEY CAN'T HIDE FROM *THAT!*

TO HER LIFE-MATE'S LESS THAN SENSITIVE BARK, LEETAH ADDS HER OWN GENTLE HUMOR...

YOU AND BRILL HAVE UNITED OUR TRIBES ALREADY, MY SON--

--AND WITHOUT THE LITTLE...DIFFERENCES OF *OPINION* YOUR FATHER AND I FACED.

I AM SURE, ONCE THEY'RE EMBRACED BY THE PALACE'S AURA, THE WAVEDANCERS WILL FEEL SAFE AND WELCOME--

--AND ONLY TOO *GLAD* TO CELEBRATE YOUR JOINING DAY.

RIGHT! FEAR IS JUST THE NOT KNOWING OF THINGS, CUB!

WE'LL SHOW 'EM THEY'VE AS MUCH RIGHT TO THE PALACE AS *ANY* ELVES!

OOF!

WHAP!

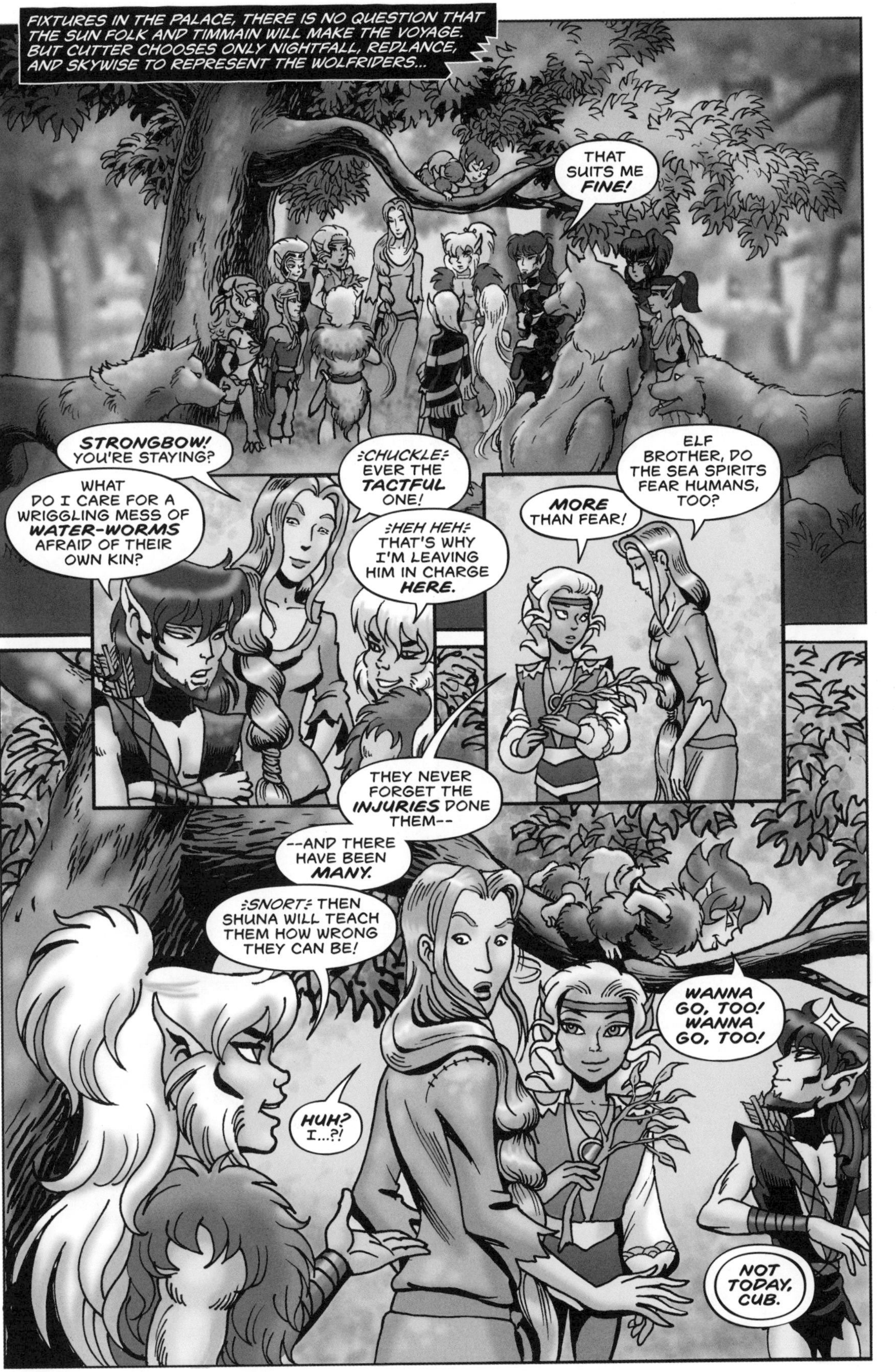
FIXTURES IN THE PALACE, THERE IS NO QUESTION THAT THE SUN FOLK AND TIMMAIN WILL MAKE THE VOYAGE. BUT CUTTER CHOOSES ONLY NIGHTFALL, REDLANCE, AND SKYWISE TO REPRESENT THE WOLFRIDERS...
THAT SUITS ME FINE!
STRONGBOW! YOU'RE STAYING?
WHAT DO I CARE FOR A WRIGGLING MESS OF WATER-WORMS AFRAID OF THEIR OWN KIN?
CHUCKLE EVER THE TACTFUL ONE!
HEH HEH THAT'S WHY I'M LEAVING HIM IN CHARGE HERE.
ELF BROTHER, DO THE SEA SPIRITS FEAR HUMANS, TOO?
MORE THAN FEAR!
THEY NEVER FORGET THE INJURIES DONE THEM--
--AND THERE HAVE BEEN MANY.
SNORT THEN SHUNA WILL TEACH THEM HOW WRONG THEY CAN BE!
HUH? I...?!
WANNA GO, TOO! WANNA GO, TOO!
NOT TODAY, CUB.

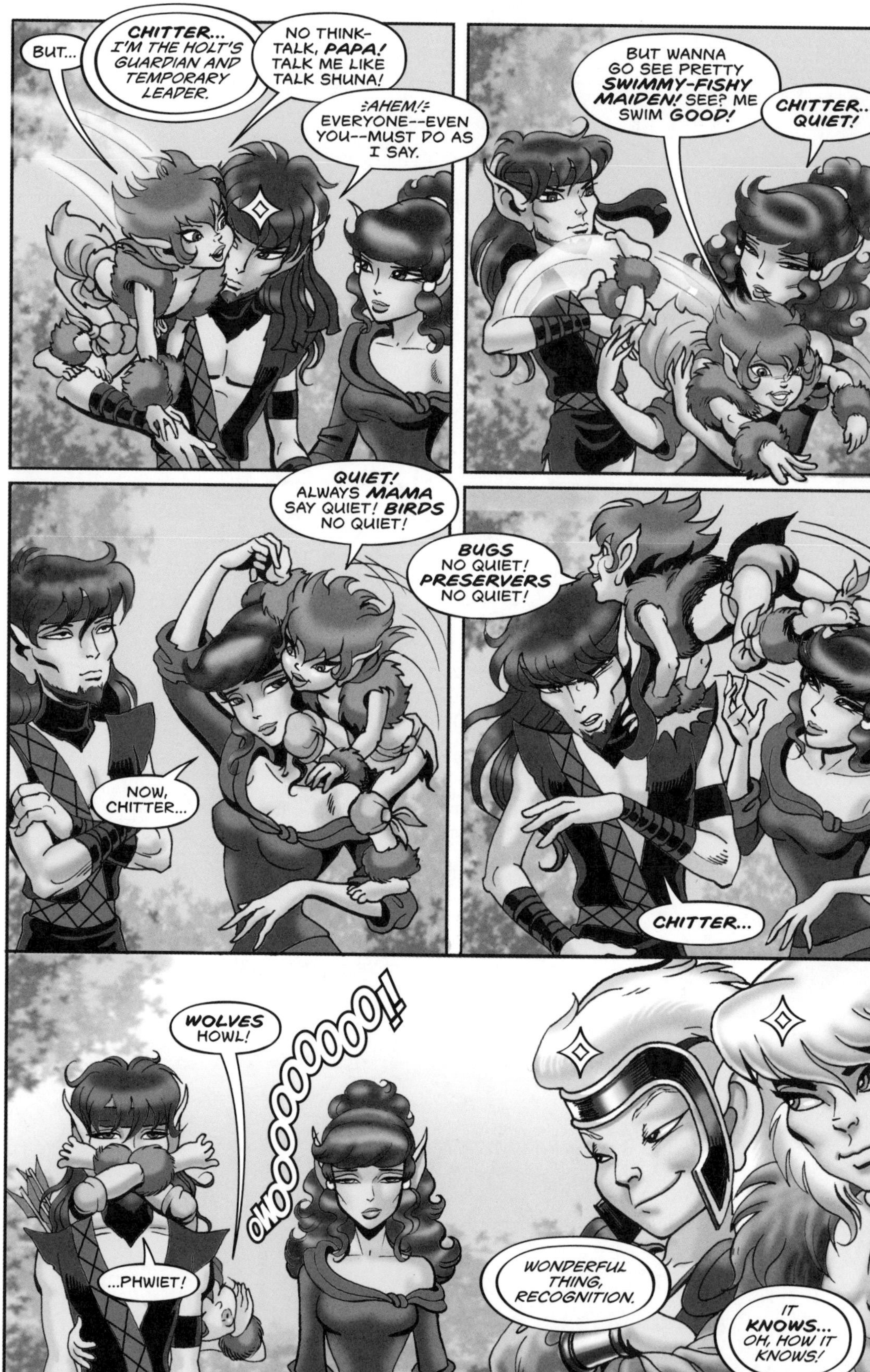
BUT...
CHITTER... I'M THE HOLT'S GUARDIAN AND TEMPORARY LEADER.
NO THINK-TALK, PAPA! TALK ME LIKE TALK SHUNA!
:AHEM!: EVERYONE--EVEN YOU--MUST DO AS I SAY.
BUT WANNA GO SEE PRETTY SWIMMY-FISHY MAIDEN! SEE? ME SWIM GOOD!
CHITTER... QUIET!
QUIET! ALWAYS MAMA SAY QUIET! BIRDS NO QUIET!
NOW, CHITTER...
BUGS NO QUIET! PRESERVERS NO QUIET!
CHITTER...
WOLVES HOWL!
OWOOOOOOOOO!!
...PHWIET!
WONDERFUL THING, RECOGNITION.
IT KNOWS... OH, HOW IT KNOWS!

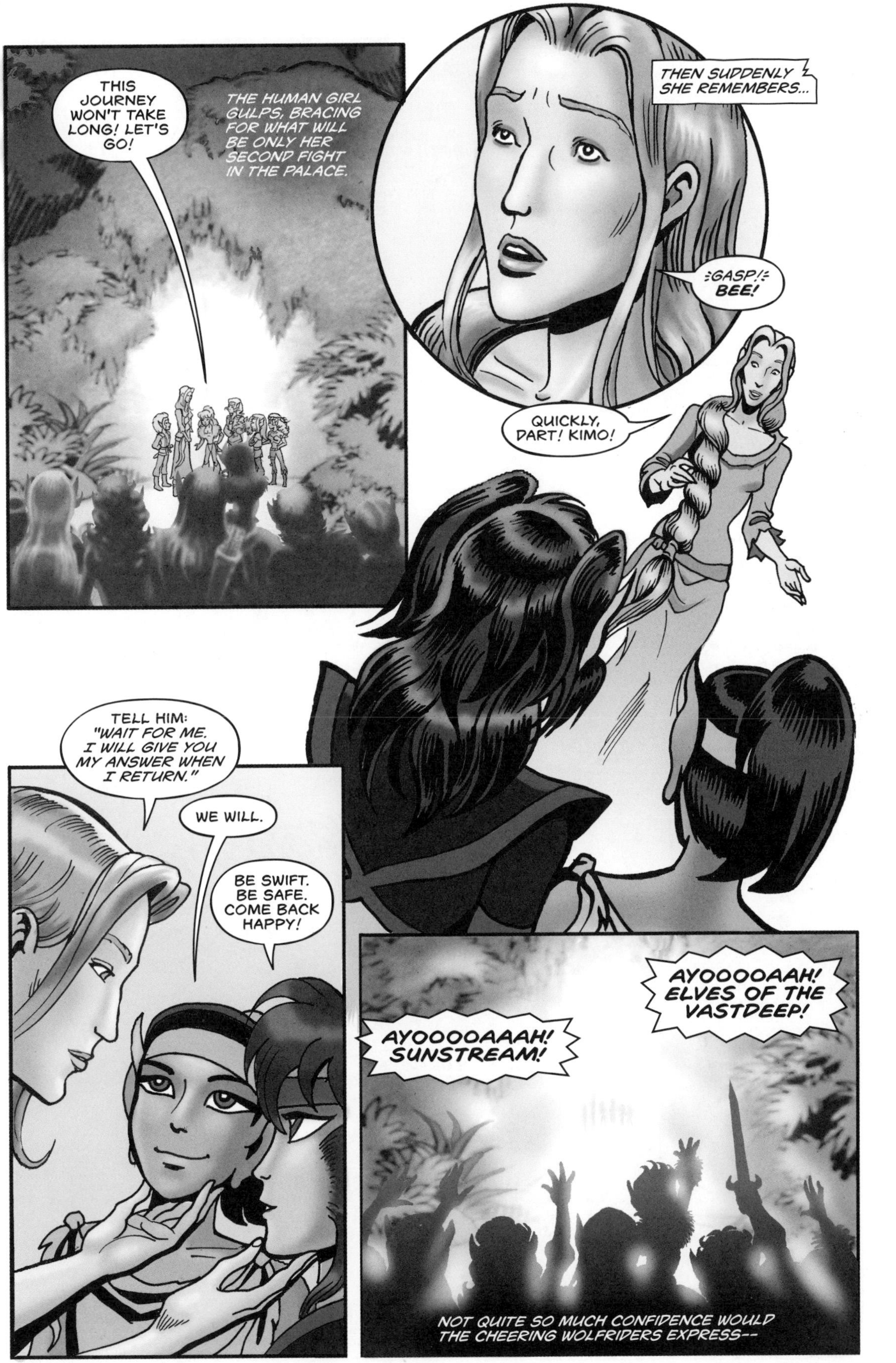
THIS JOURNEY WON'T TAKE LONG! LET'S GO!
THE HUMAN GIRL GULPS, BRACING FOR WHAT WILL BE ONLY HER SECOND FIGHT IN THE PALACE.
THEN SUDDENLY SHE REMEMBERS...
GASP! BEE!
QUICKLY, DART! KIMO!
TELL HIM: "WAIT FOR ME. I WILL GIVE YOU MY ANSWER WHEN I RETURN."
WE WILL.
BE SWIFT. BE SAFE. COME BACK HAPPY!
AYOOOOAAAH! SUNSTREAM!
AYOOOOAAH! ELVES OF THE VASTDEEP!
NOT QUITE SO MUCH CONFIDENCE WOULD THE CHEERING WOLFRIDERS EXPRESS--

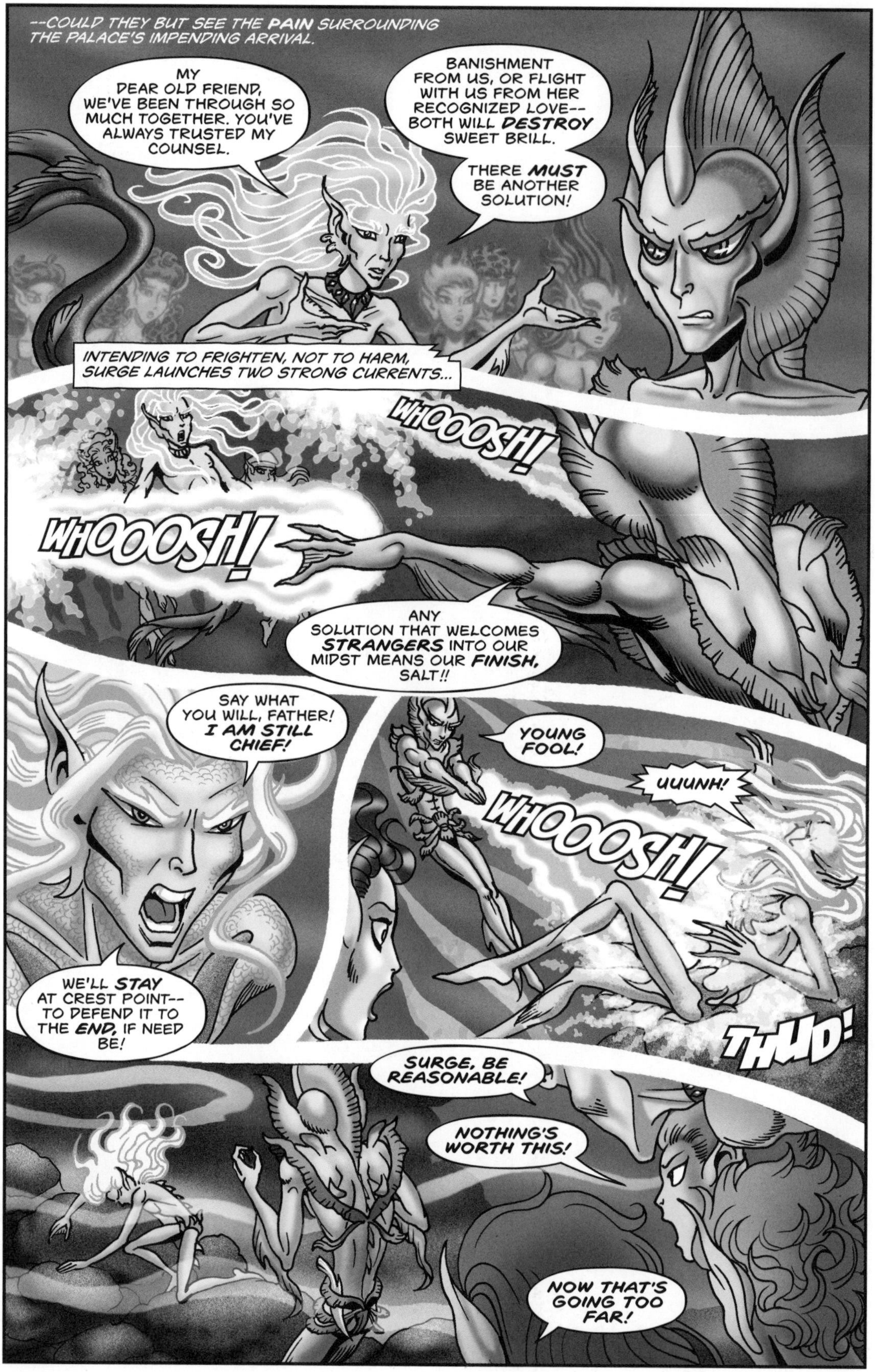
--COULD THEY BUT SEE THE PAIN SURROUNDING THE PALACE'S IMPENDING ARRIVAL.
MY DEAR OLD FRIEND, WE'VE BEEN THROUGH SO MUCH TOGETHER. YOU'VE ALWAYS TRUSTED MY COUNSEL.
BANISHMENT FROM US, OR FLIGHT WITH US FROM HER RECOGNIZED LOVE-- BOTH WILL DESTROY SWEET BRILL.
THERE MUST BE ANOTHER SOLUTION!
INTENDING TO FRIGHTEN, NOT TO HARM, SURGE LAUNCHES TWO STRONG CURRENTS...
WHOOOSH!
WHOOOSH!
ANY SOLUTION THAT WELCOMES STRANGERS INTO OUR MIDST MEANS OUR FINISH, SALT!!
SAY WHAT YOU WILL, FATHER! I AM STILL CHIEF!
WE'LL STAY AT CREST POINT-- TO DEFEND IT TO THE END, IF NEED BE!
YOUNG FOOL!
UUUNH!
WHOOOSH!
THUD!
SURGE, BE REASONABLE!
NOTHING'S WORTH THIS!
NOW THAT'S GOING TOO FAR!

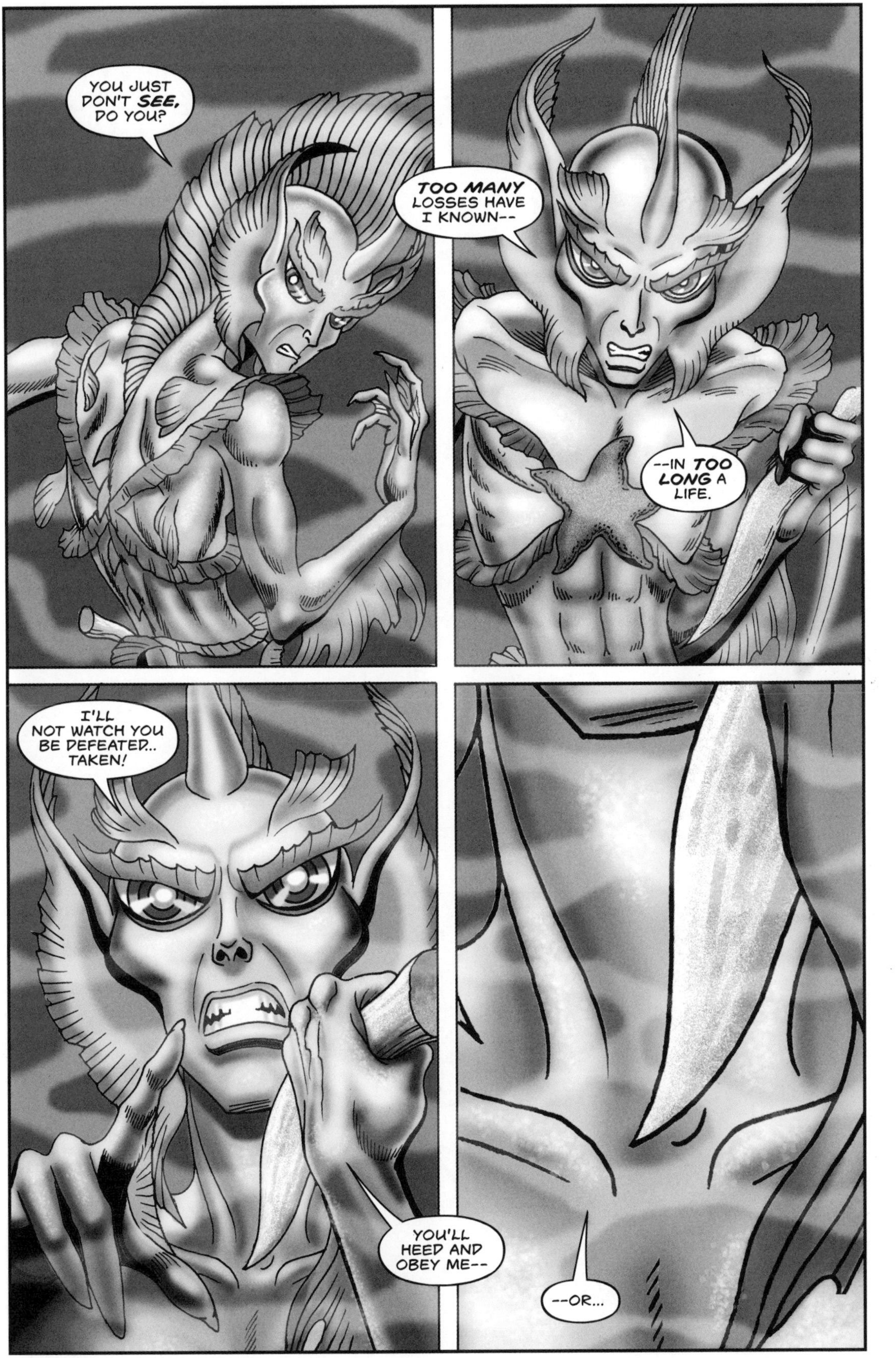
YOU JUST DON'T **SEE,** DO YOU?
TOO MANY LOSSES HAVE I KNOWN--
--IN **TOO LONG** A LIFE.
I'LL NOT WATCH YOU BE DEFEATED... TAKEN!
YOU'LL HEED AND OBEY ME--
--OR...

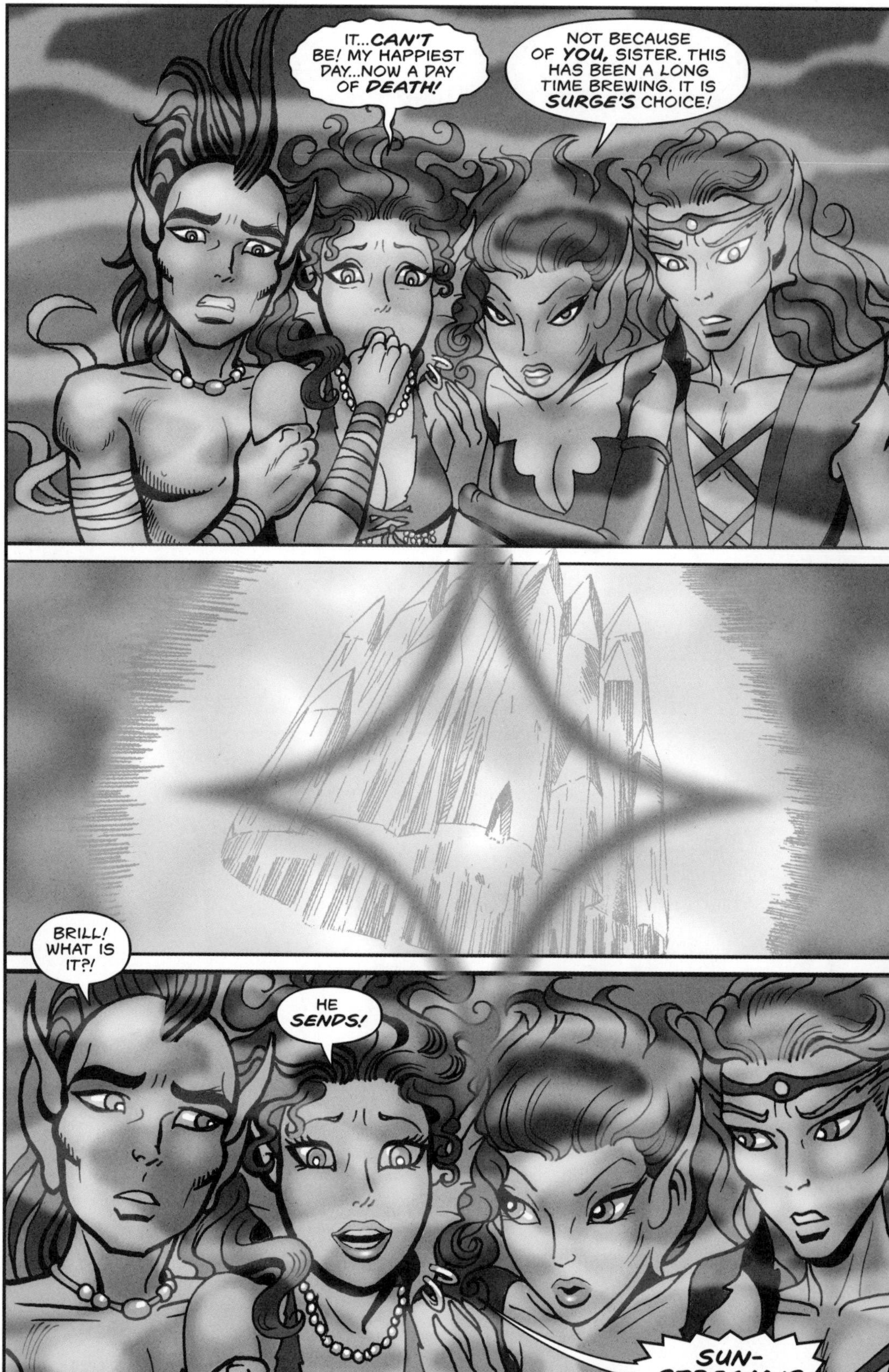
IT...CAN'T BE! MY HAPPIEST DAY...NOW A DAY OF DEATH!
NOT BECAUSE OF YOU, SISTER. THIS HAS BEEN A LONG TIME BREWING. IT IS SURGE'S CHOICE!
BRILL! WHAT IS IT?!
HE SENDS!
SUN-STREAM IS COMING!

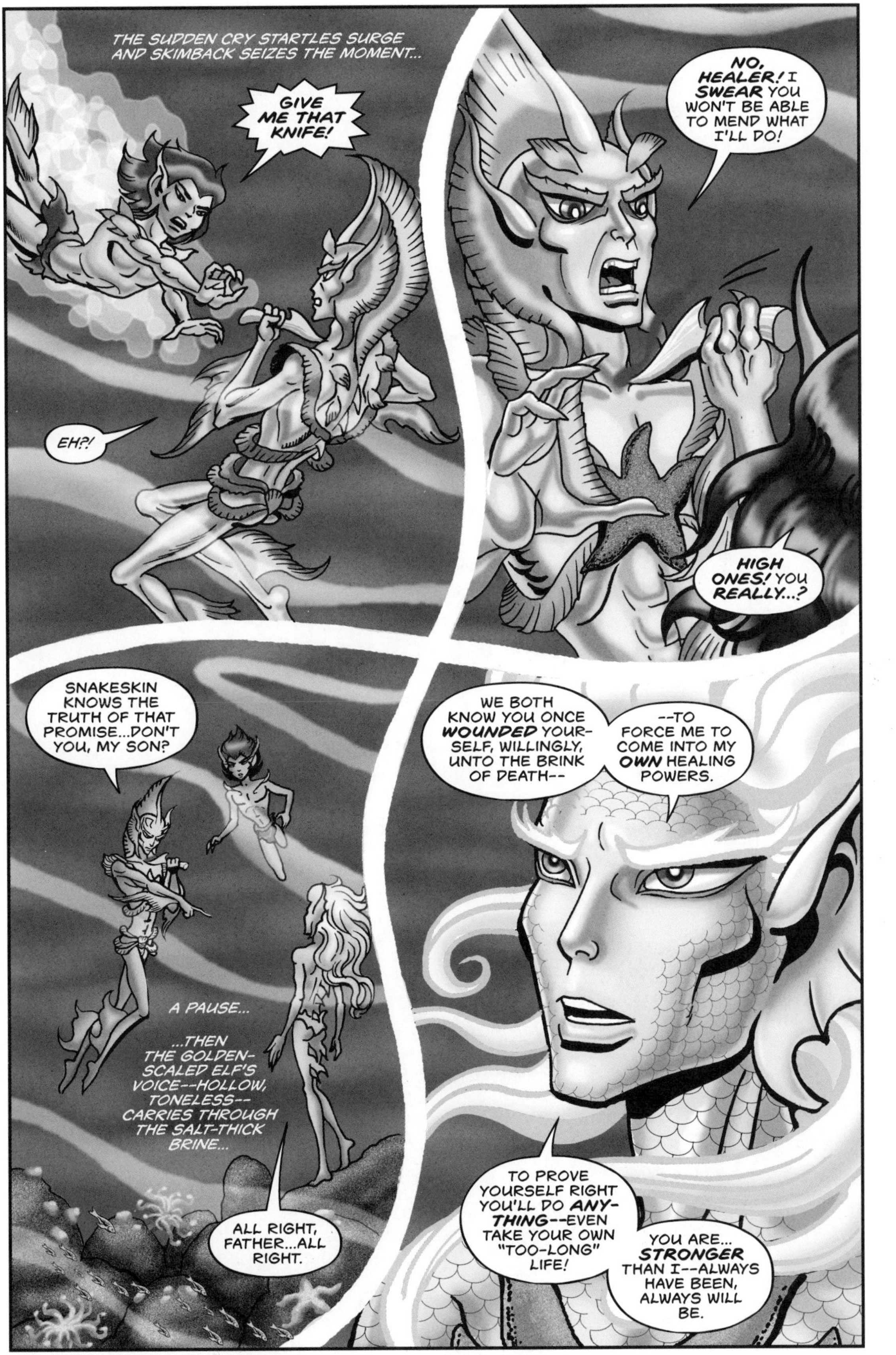

THE SUDDEN CRY STARTLES SURGE AND SKIMBACK SEIZES THE MOMENT...
GIVE ME THAT KNIFE!
EH?!
NO, HEALER! I SWEAR YOU WON'T BE ABLE TO MEND WHAT I'LL DO!
HIGH ONES! YOU REALLY...?
SNAKESKIN KNOWS THE TRUTH OF THAT PROMISE...DON'T YOU, MY SON?
A PAUSE...
...THEN THE GOLDEN-SCALED ELF'S VOICE--HOLLOW, TONELESS--CARRIES THROUGH THE SALT-THICK BRINE...
ALL RIGHT, FATHER...ALL RIGHT.
WE BOTH KNOW YOU ONCE WOUNDED YOURSELF, WILLINGLY, UNTO THE BRINK OF DEATH--
--TO FORCE ME TO COME INTO MY OWN HEALING POWERS.
TO PROVE YOURSELF RIGHT YOU'LL DO ANYTHING--EVEN TAKE YOUR OWN "TOO-LONG" LIFE!
YOU ARE... STRONGER THAN I--ALWAYS HAVE BEEN, ALWAYS WILL BE.

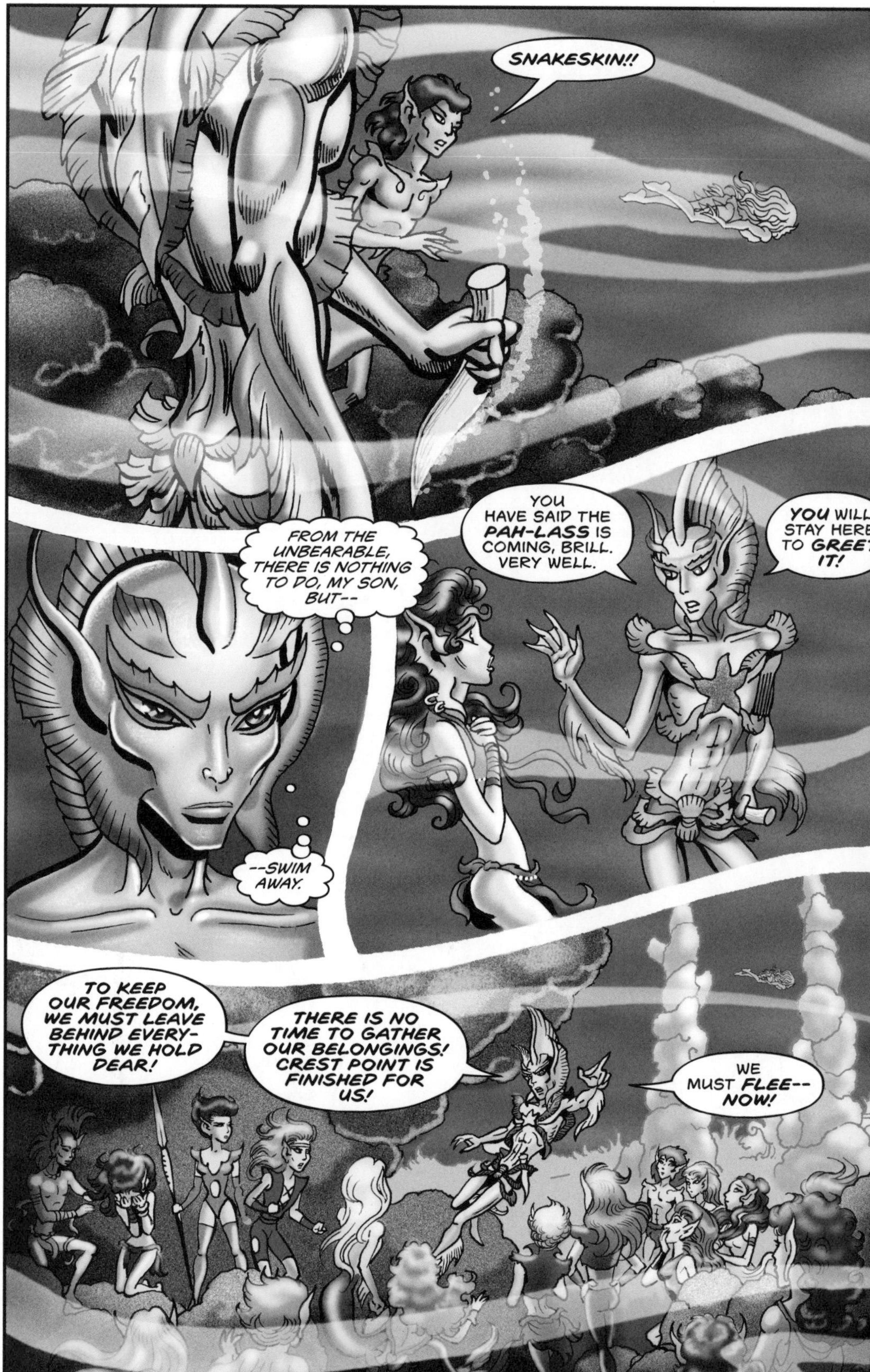
SNAKESKIN!!
FROM THE UNBEARABLE, THERE IS NOTHING TO DO, MY SON, BUT--
YOU HAVE SAID THE PAH-LASS IS COMING, BRILL. VERY WELL.
YOU WILL STAY HERE TO GREET IT!
--SWIM AWAY.
TO KEEP OUR FREEDOM, WE MUST LEAVE BEHIND EVERY-THING WE HOLD DEAR!
THERE IS NO TIME TO GATHER OUR BELONGINGS! CREST POINT IS FINISHED FOR US!
WE MUST FLEE-- NOW!

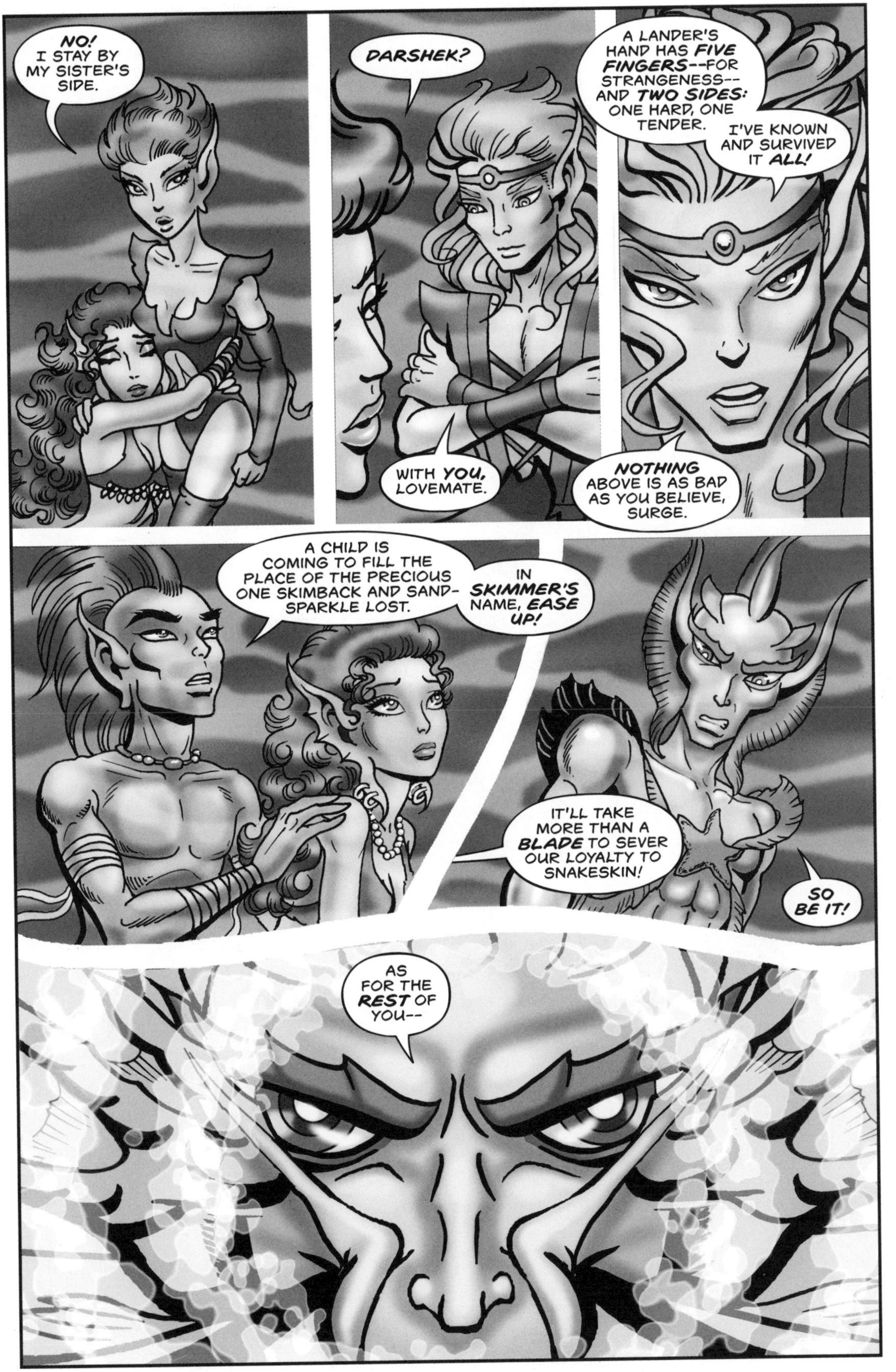
NO! I STAY BY MY SISTER'S SIDE.
DARSHEK?
WITH YOU, LOVEMATE.
A LANDER'S HAND HAS FIVE FINGERS--FOR STRANGENESS-- AND TWO SIDES: ONE HARD, ONE TENDER.
I'VE KNOWN AND SURVIVED IT ALL!
NOTHING ABOVE IS AS BAD AS YOU BELIEVE, SURGE.
A CHILD IS COMING TO FILL THE PLACE OF THE PRECIOUS ONE SKIMBACK AND SAND-SPARKLE LOST.
IN SKIMMER'S NAME, EASE UP!
IT'LL TAKE MORE THAN A BLADE TO SEVER OUR LOYALTY TO SNAKESKIN!
SO BE IT!
AS FOR THE REST OF YOU--

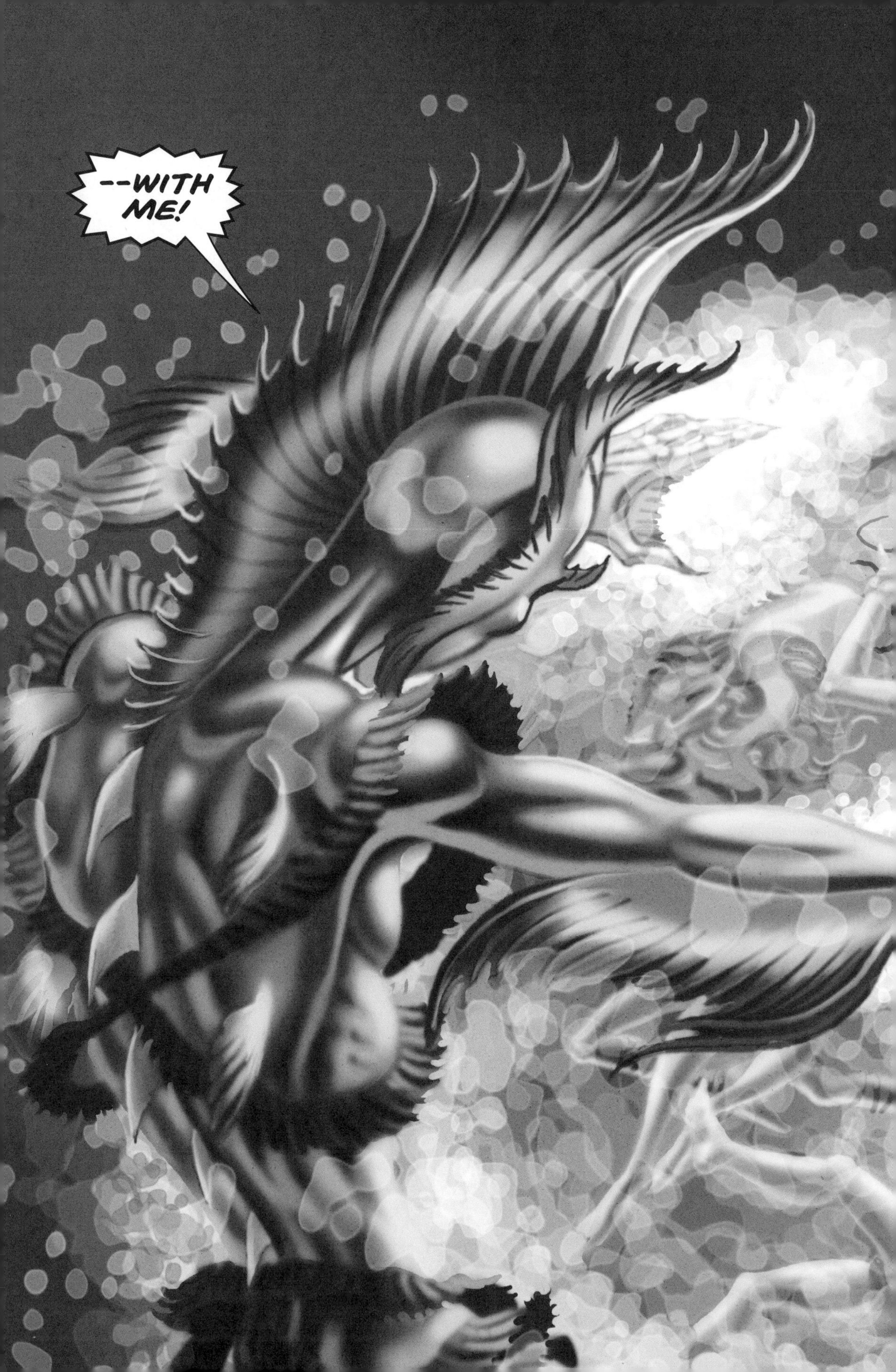
--WITH ME!

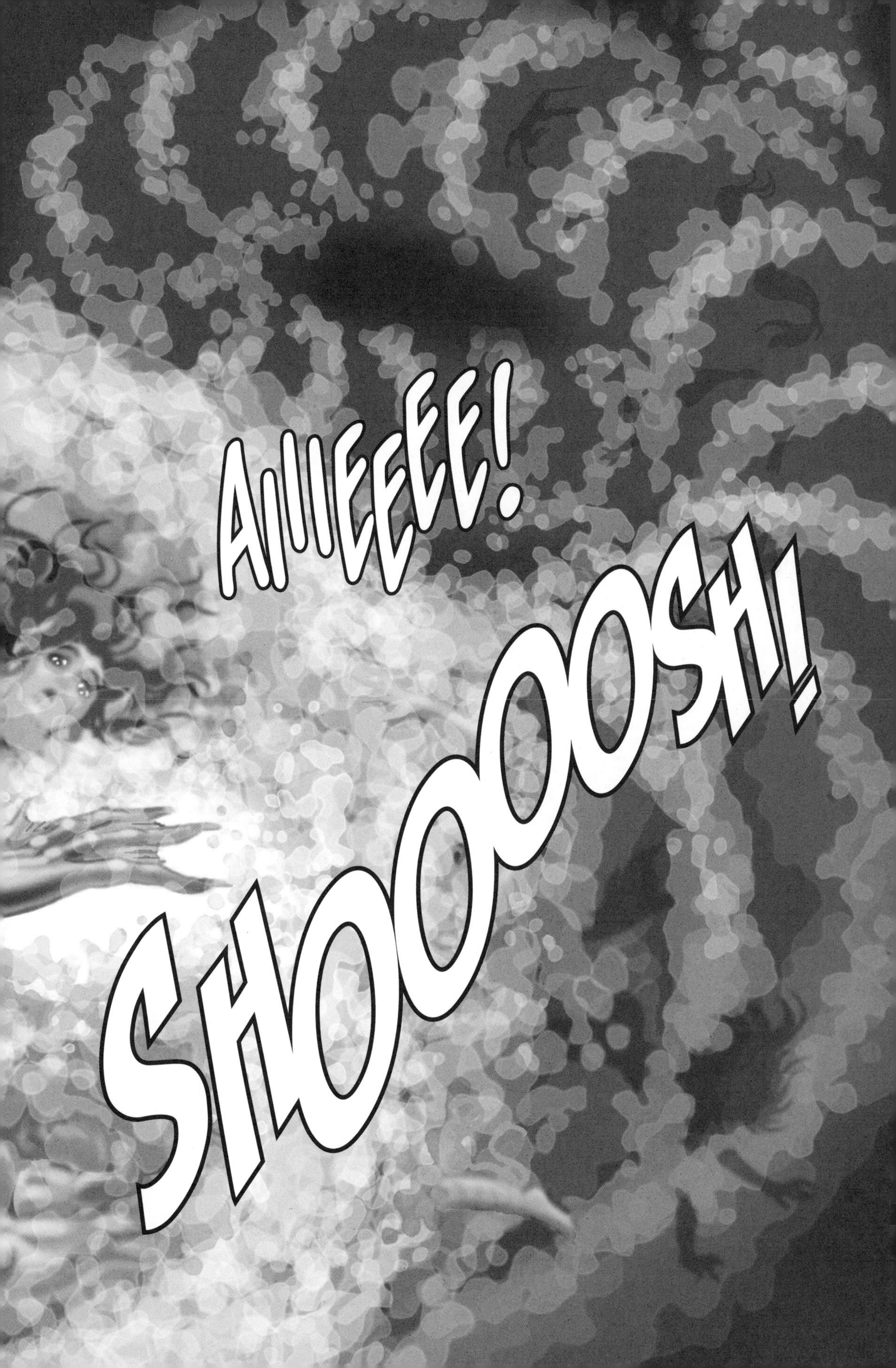
AIIIEEEE!
SHOOOOOSH!

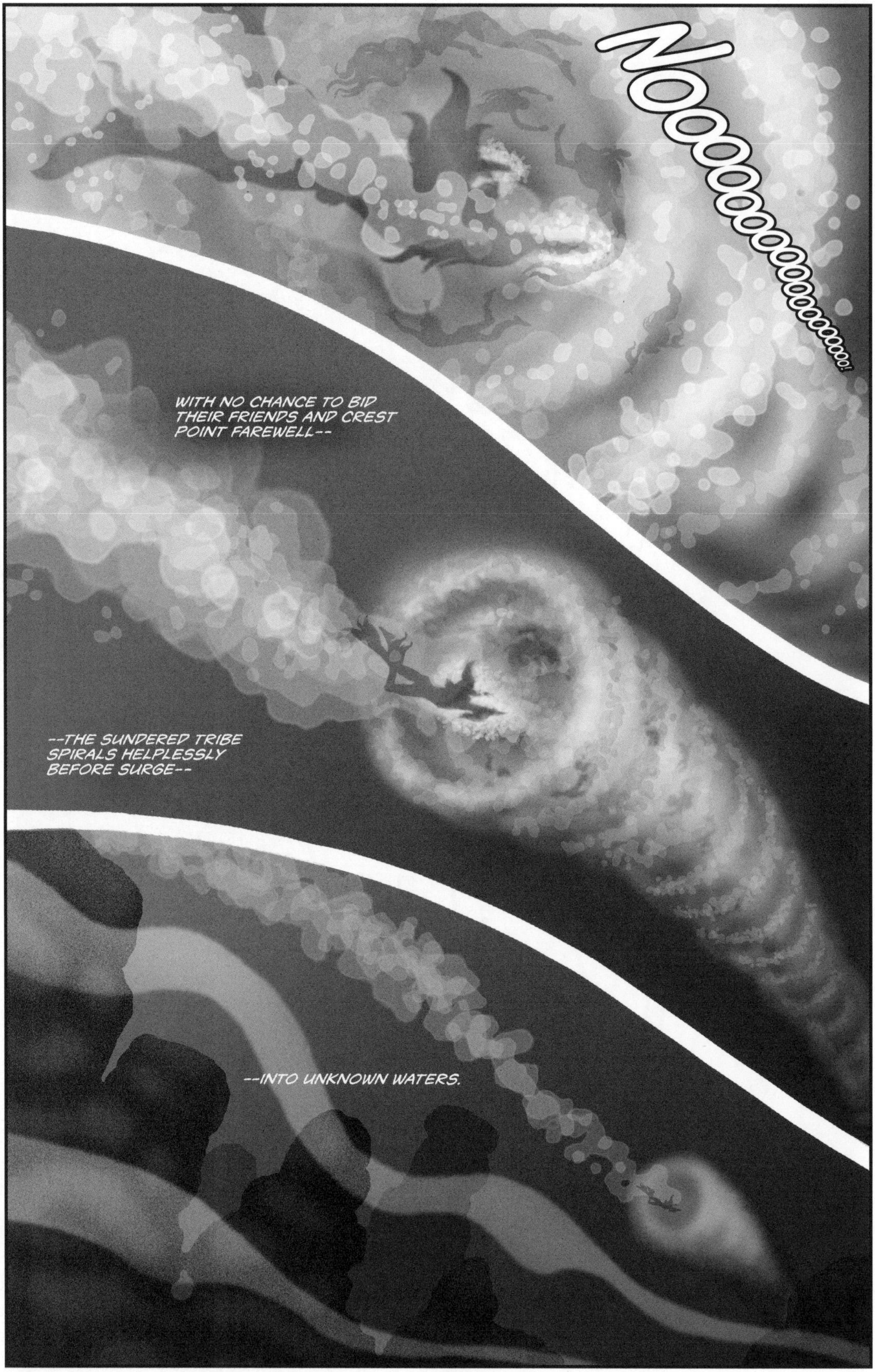
NOOOOOOOOOOOOOOOOO!
WITH NO CHANCE TO BID THEIR FRIENDS AND CREST POINT FAREWELL--
--THE SUNDERED TRIBE SPIRALS HELPLESSLY BEFORE SURGE--
--INTO UNKNOWN WATERS.

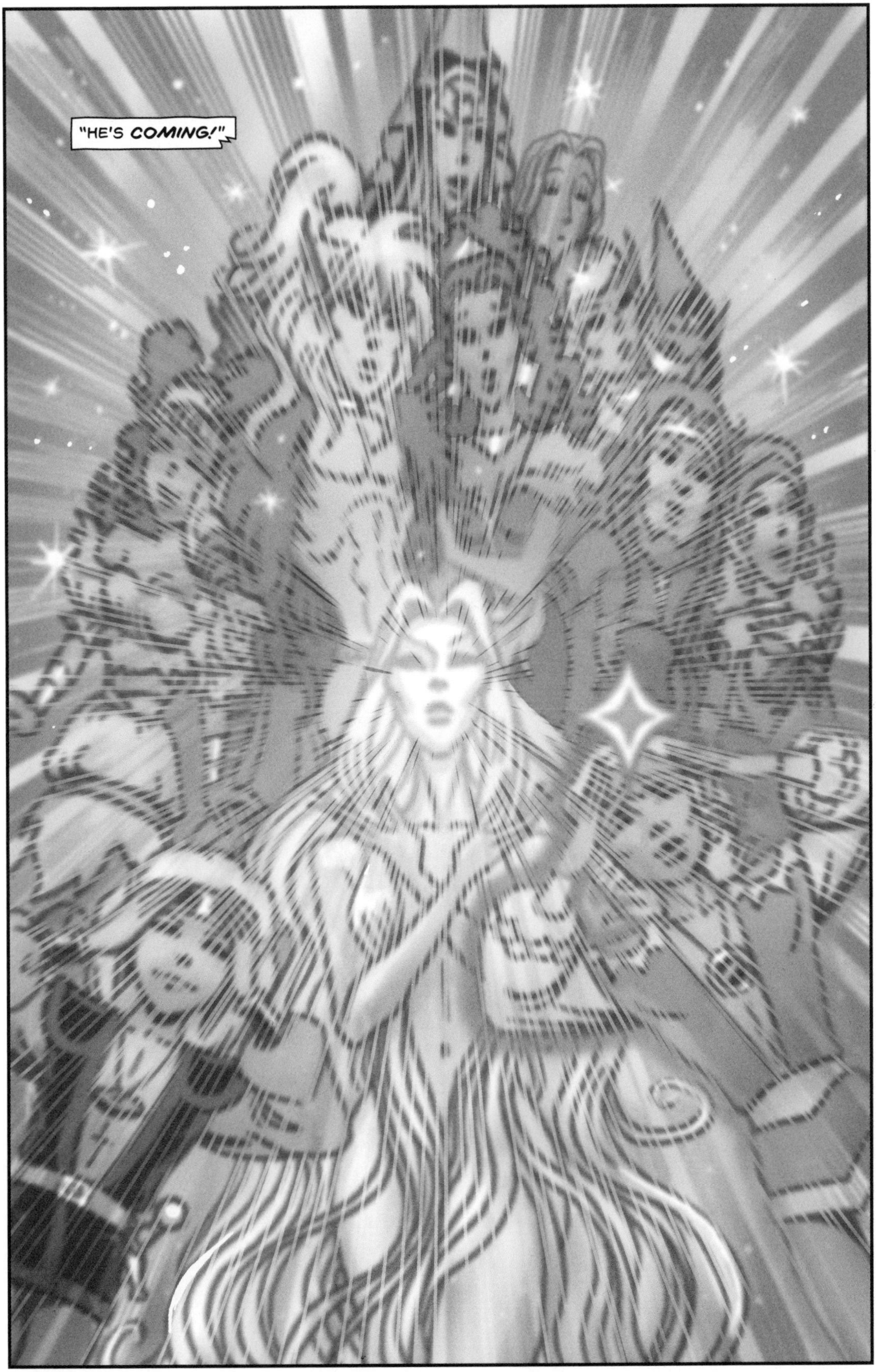
"HE'S COMING!"

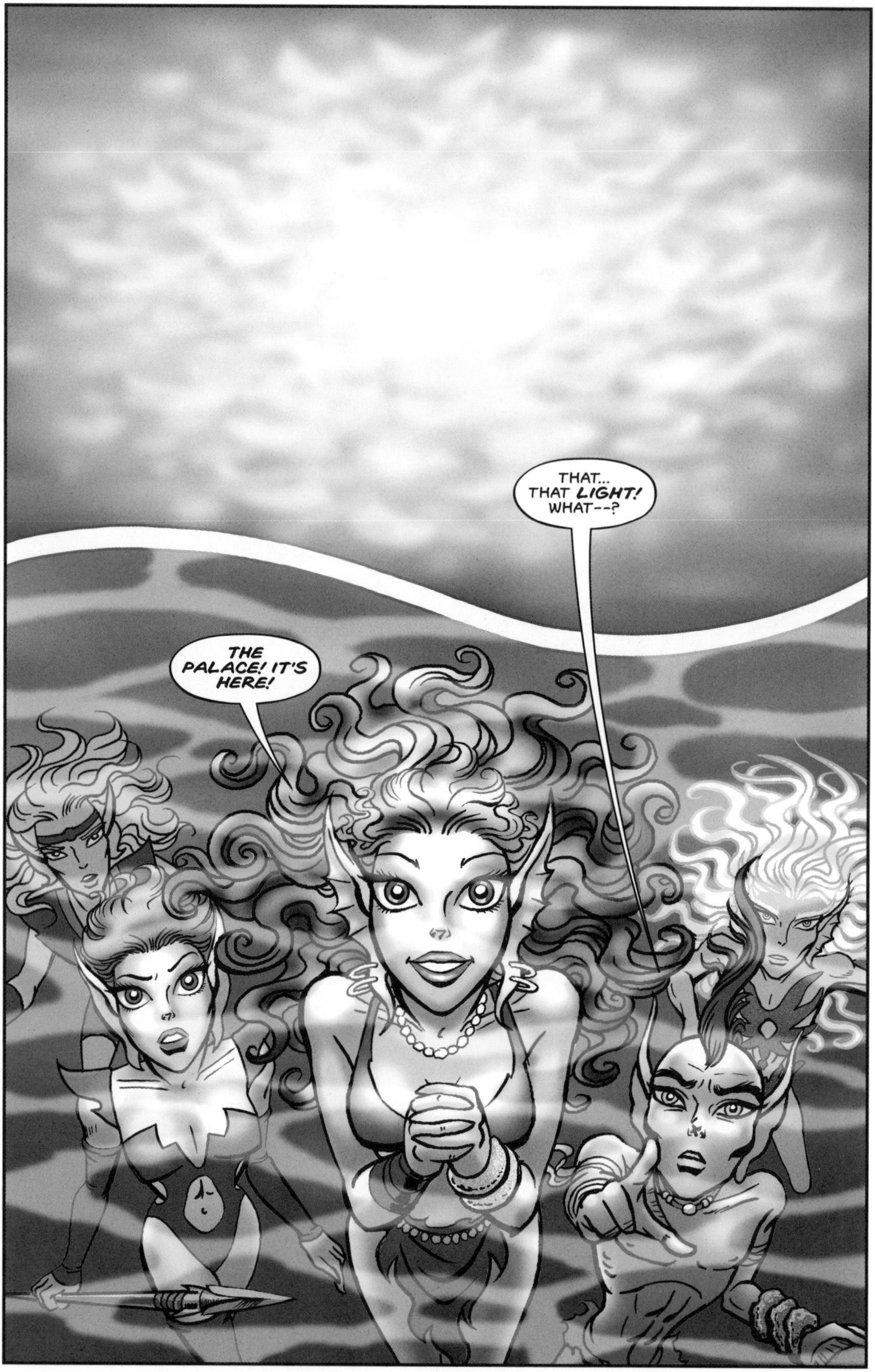
THE PALACE! IT'S HERE!
THAT... THAT LIGHT! WHAT--?

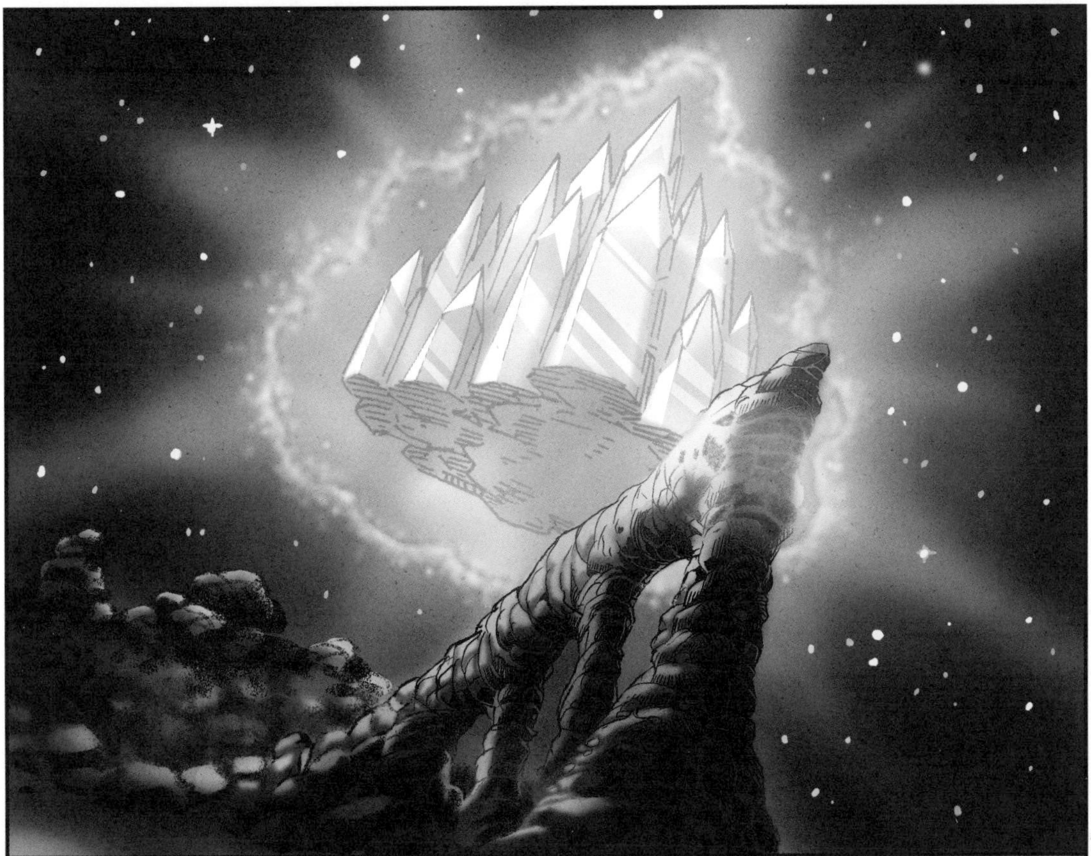

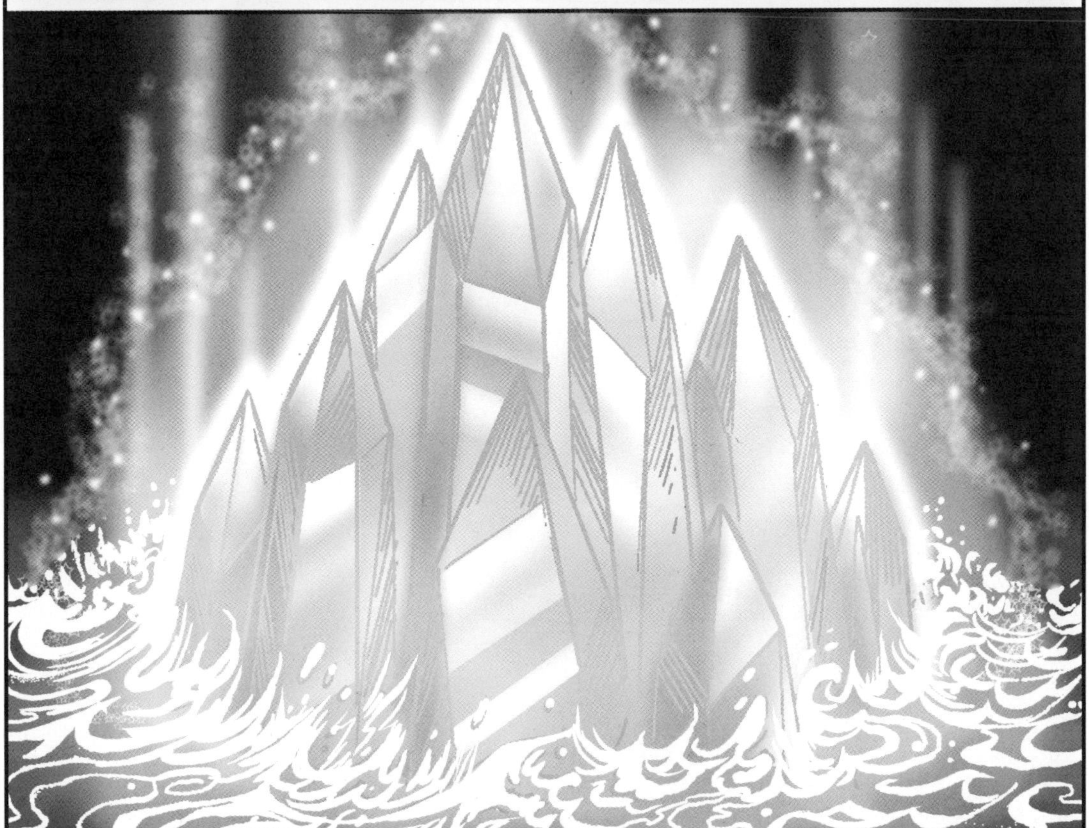

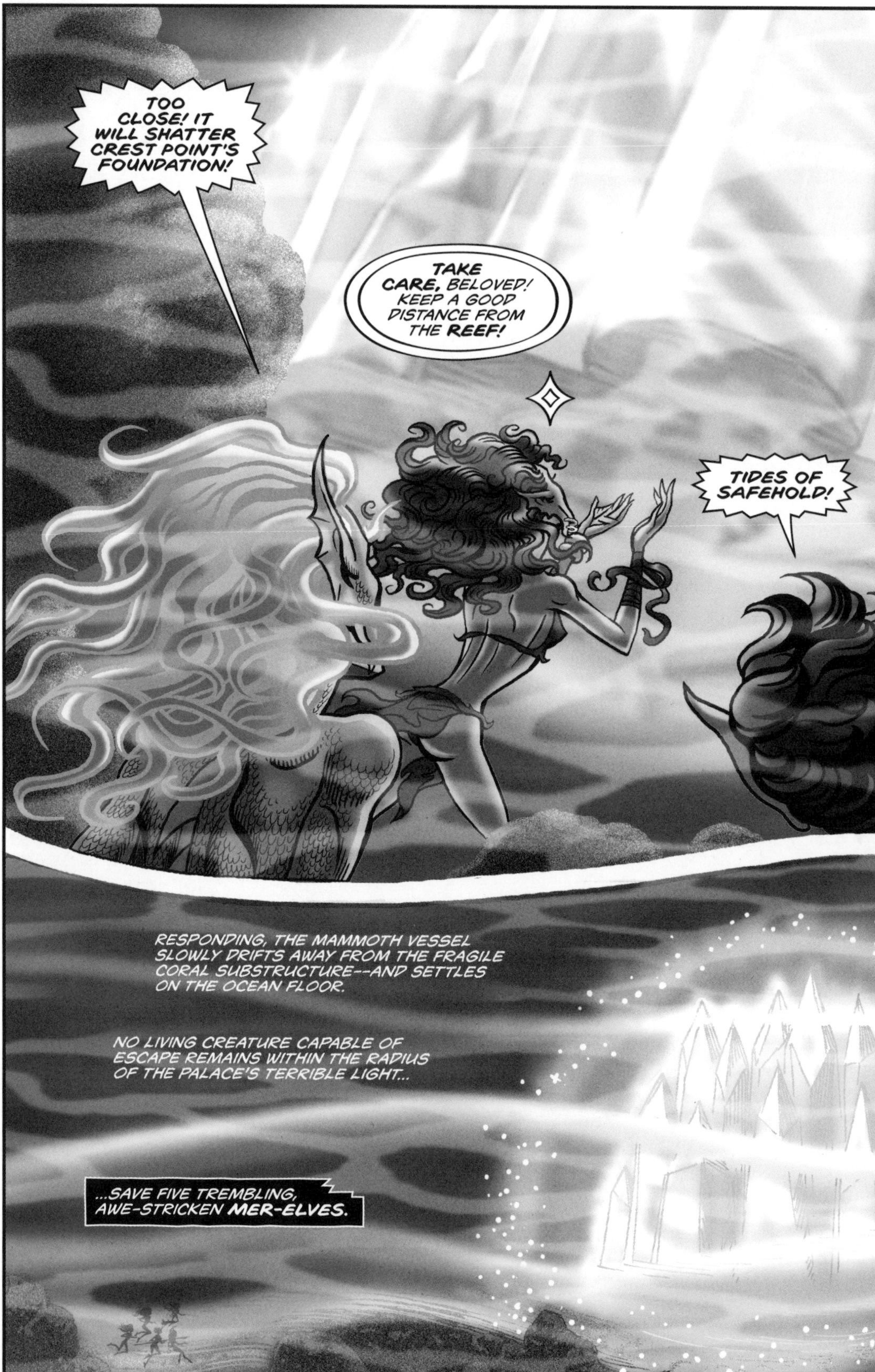
TOO CLOSE! IT WILL SHATTER CREST POINT'S FOUNDATION!
TAKE CARE, BELOVED! KEEP A GOOD DISTANCE FROM THE REEF!
TIDES OF SAFEHOLD!
RESPONDING, THE MAMMOTH VESSEL SLOWLY DRIFTS AWAY FROM THE FRAGILE CORAL SUBSTRUCTURE--AND SETTLES ON THE OCEAN FLOOR.
NO LIVING CREATURE CAPABLE OF ESCAPE REMAINS WITHIN THE RADIUS OF THE PALACE'S TERRIBLE LIGHT...
...SAVE FIVE TREMBLING, AWE-STRICKEN MER-ELVES.

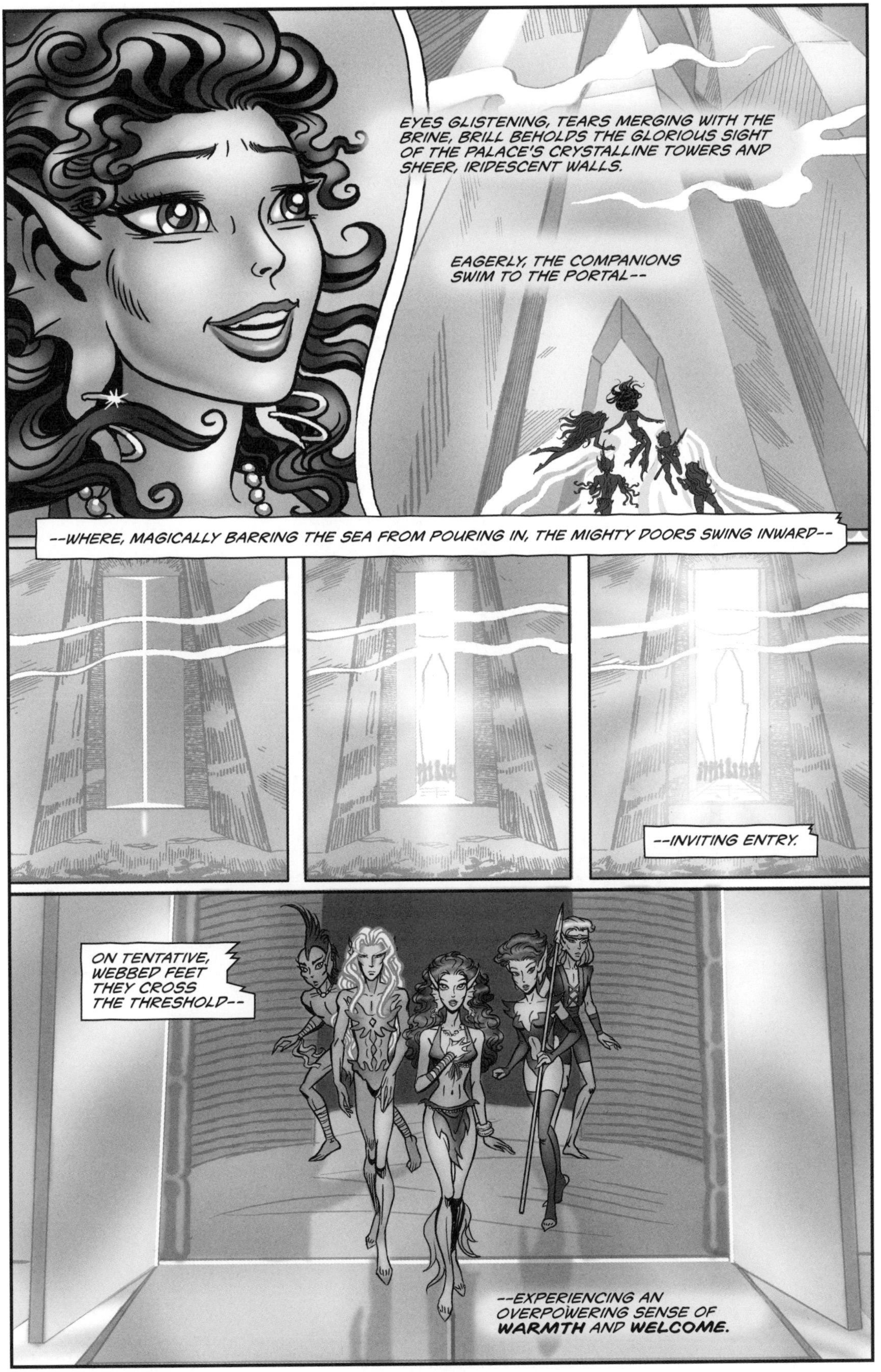
EYES GLISTENING, TEARS MERGING WITH THE BRINE, BRILL BEHOLDS THE GLORIOUS SIGHT OF THE PALACE'S CRYSTALLINE TOWERS AND SHEER, IRIDESCENT WALLS.
EAGERLY, THE COMPANIONS SWIM TO THE PORTAL--
--WHERE, MAGICALLY BARRING THE SEA FROM POURING IN, THE MIGHTY DOORS SWING INWARD--
--INVITING ENTRY.
ON TENTATIVE, WEBBED FEET THEY CROSS THE THRESHOLD--
--EXPERIENCING AN OVERPOWERING SENSE OF **WARMTH** AND **WELCOME.**

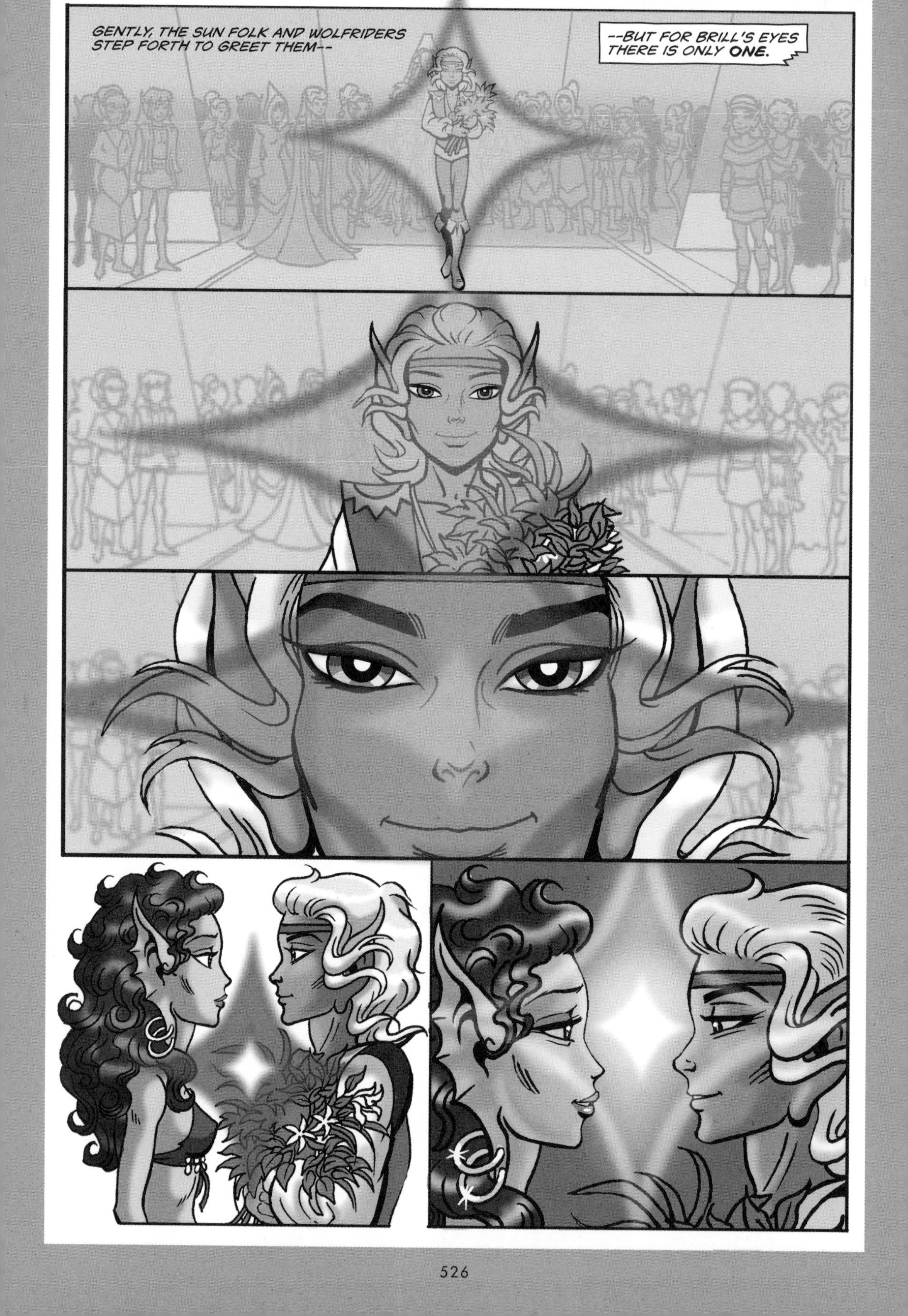
GENTLY, THE SUN FOLK AND WOLFRIDERS STEP FORTH TO GREET THEM--
--BUT FOR BRILL'S EYES THERE IS ONLY **ONE.**

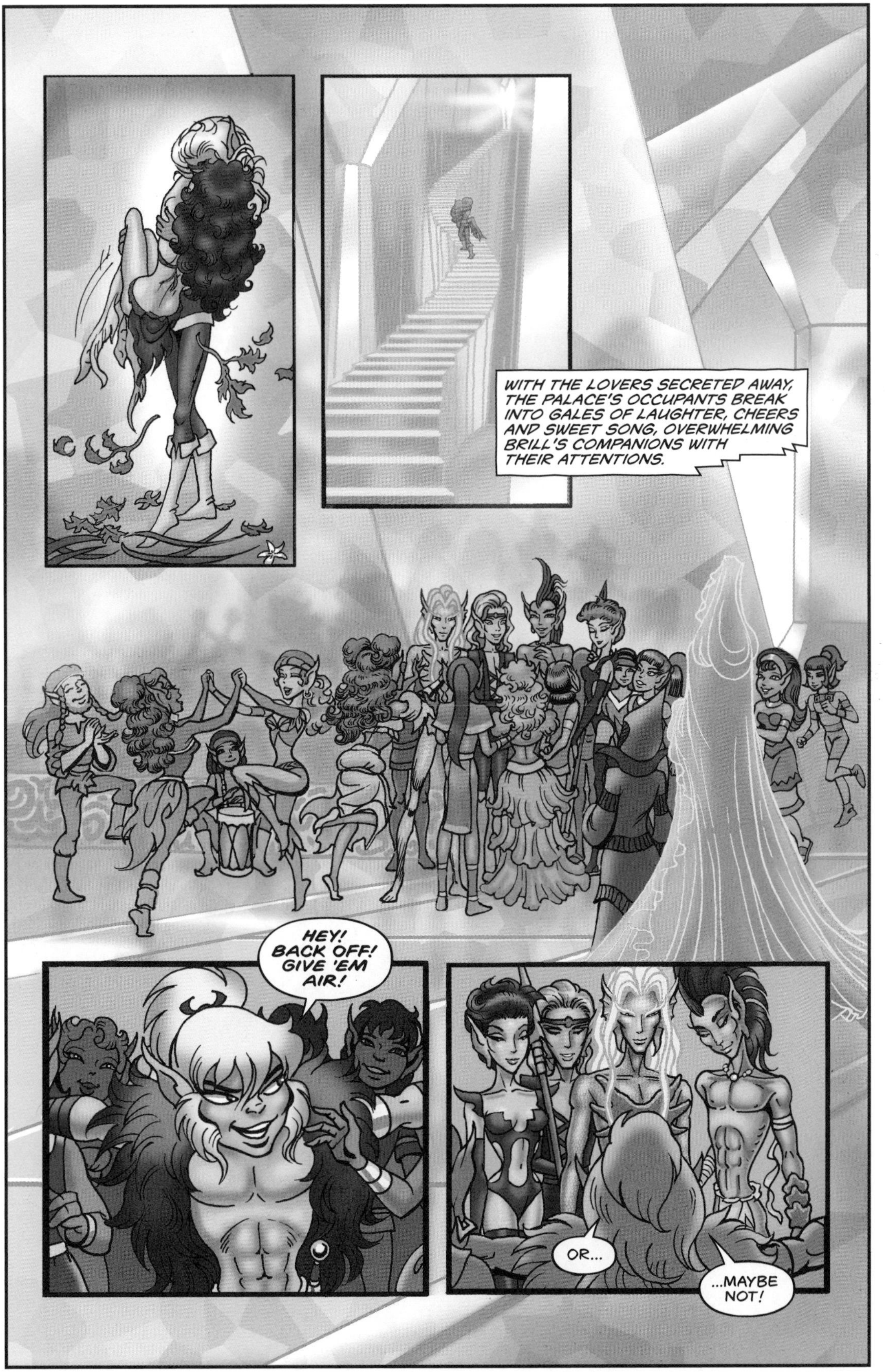
WITH THE LOVERS SECRETED AWAY, THE PALACE'S OCCUPANTS BREAK INTO GALES OF LAUGHTER, CHEERS AND SWEET SONG, OVERWHELMING BRILL'S COMPANIONS WITH THEIR ATTENTIONS.
HEY! BACK OFF! GIVE 'EM AIR!
OR...
...MAYBE NOT!

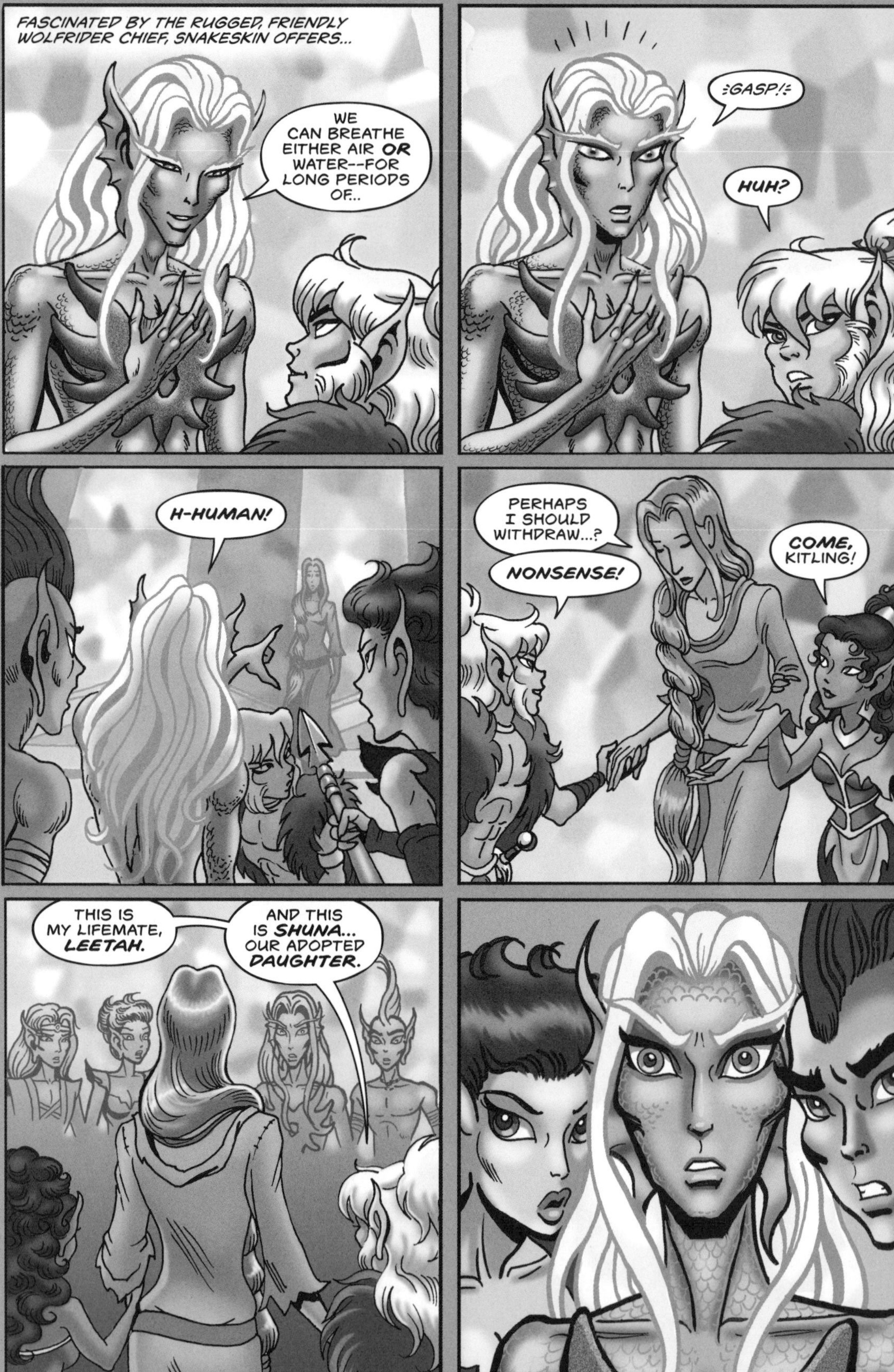
FASCINATED BY THE RUGGED, FRIENDLY WOLFRIDER CHIEF, SNAKESKIN OFFERS...
WE CAN BREATHE EITHER AIR OR WATER--FOR LONG PERIODS OF...
GASP!
HUH?
H-HUMAN!
PERHAPS I SHOULD WITHDRAW...?
NONSENSE!
COME, KITLING!
THIS IS MY LIFEMATE, LEETAH.
AND THIS IS SHUNA... OUR ADOPTED DAUGHTER.

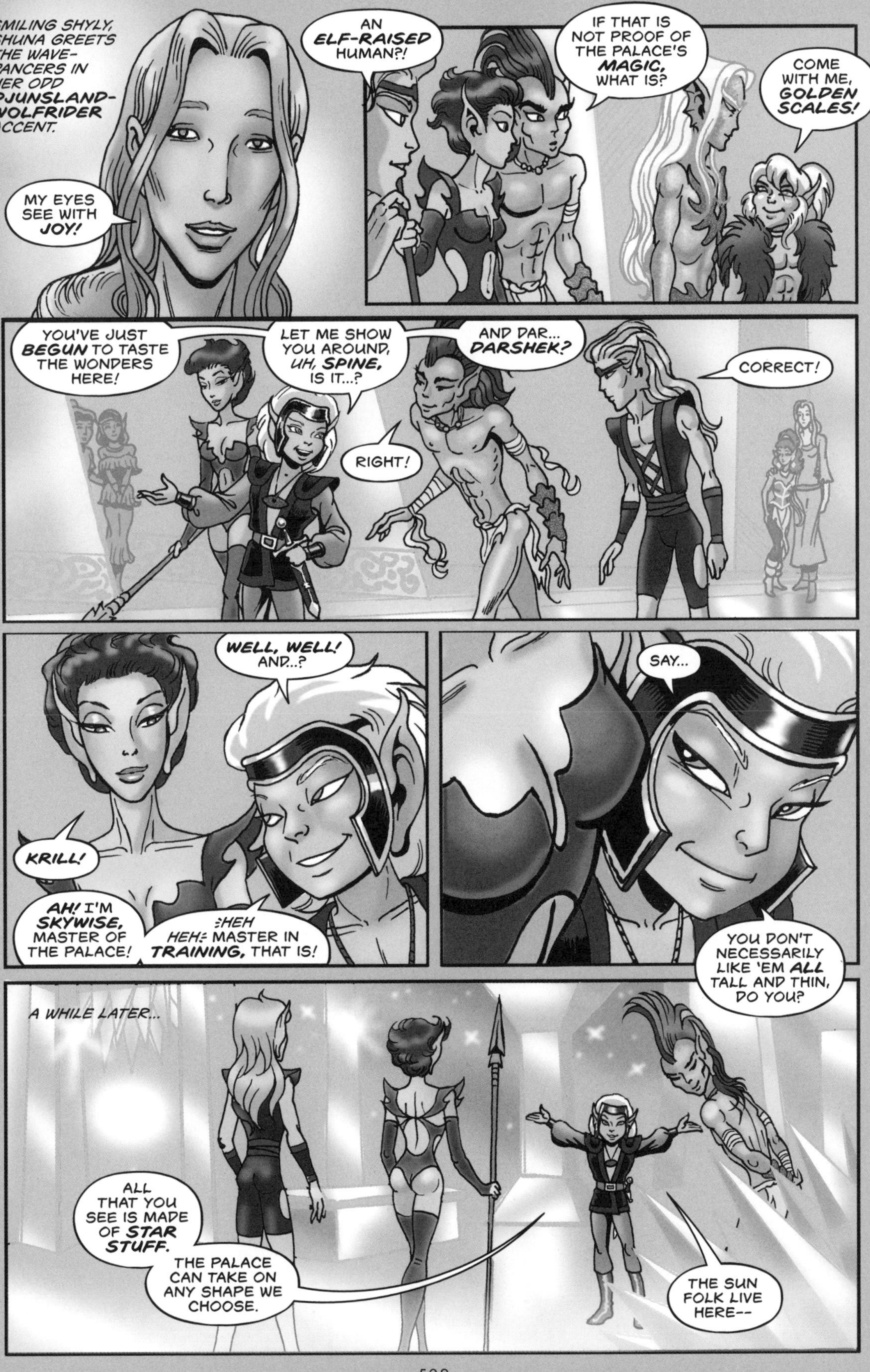

SMILING SHYLY, SHUNA GREETS THE WAVE-DANCERS IN HER ODD DJUNSLAND-WOLFRIDER ACCENT.
MY EYES SEE WITH JOY!
AN ELF-RAISED HUMAN?!
IF THAT IS NOT PROOF OF THE PALACE'S MAGIC, WHAT IS?
COME WITH ME, GOLDEN SCALES!
YOU'VE JUST BEGUN TO TASTE THE WONDERS HERE!
LET ME SHOW YOU AROUND, UH, SPINE, IS IT...?
RIGHT!
AND DAR... DARSHEK?
CORRECT!
WELL, WELL! AND...?
KRILL!
AH! I'M SKYWISE, MASTER OF THE PALACE!
HEH HEH MASTER IN TRAINING, THAT IS!
SAY...
YOU DON'T NECESSARILY LIKE 'EM ALL TALL AND THIN, DO YOU?
A WHILE LATER...
ALL THAT YOU SEE IS MADE OF STAR STUFF.
THE PALACE CAN TAKE ON ANY SHAPE WE CHOOSE.
THE SUN FOLK LIVE HERE--

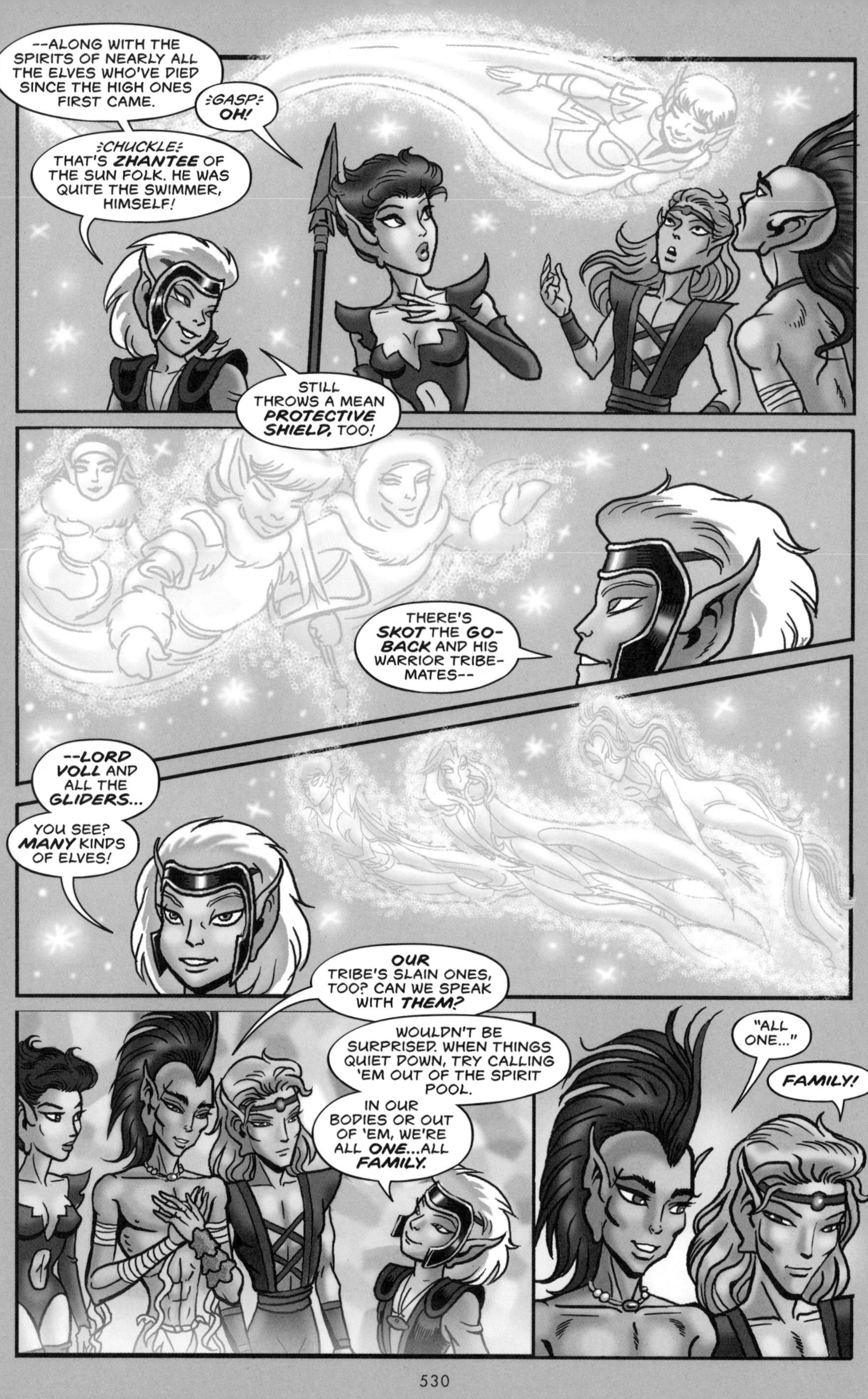
--ALONG WITH THE SPIRITS OF NEARLY ALL THE ELVES WHO'VE DIED SINCE THE HIGH ONES FIRST CAME.
:GASP: OH!
:CHUCKLE: THAT'S ZHANTEE OF THE SUN FOLK. HE WAS QUITE THE SWIMMER, HIMSELF!
STILL THROWS A MEAN PROTECTIVE SHIELD, TOO!
THERE'S SKOT THE GO-BACK AND HIS WARRIOR TRIBE-MATES--
--LORD VOLL AND ALL THE GLIDERS...
YOU SEE? MANY KINDS OF ELVES!
OUR TRIBE'S SLAIN ONES, TOO? CAN WE SPEAK WITH THEM?
WOULDN'T BE SURPRISED. WHEN THINGS QUIET DOWN, TRY CALLING 'EM OUT OF THE SPIRIT POOL.
IN OUR BODIES OR OUT OF 'EM, WE'RE ALL ONE...ALL FAMILY.
"ALL ONE..."
FAMILY!

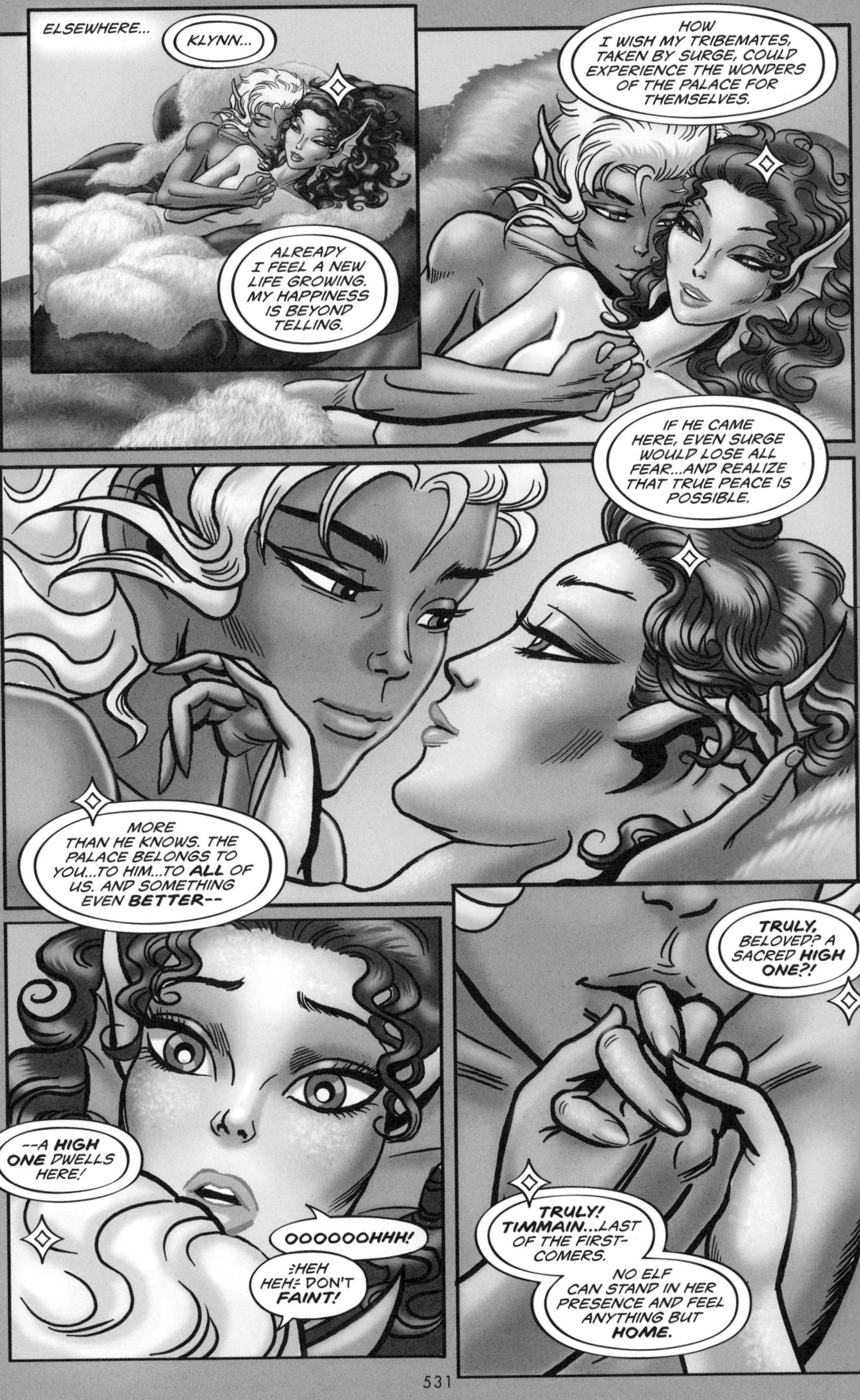
ELSEWHERE...
KLYNN...
HOW I WISH MY TRIBEMATES, TAKEN BY SURGE, COULD EXPERIENCE THE WONDERS OF THE PALACE FOR THEMSELVES.
ALREADY I FEEL A NEW LIFE GROWING. MY HAPPINESS IS BEYOND TELLING.
IF HE CAME HERE, EVEN SURGE WOULD LOSE ALL FEAR...AND REALIZE THAT TRUE PEACE IS POSSIBLE.
MORE THAN HE KNOWS. THE PALACE BELONGS TO YOU...TO HIM...TO ALL OF US. AND SOMETHING EVEN BETTER--
--A HIGH ONE DWELLS HERE!
OOOOOOHHH!
HEH HEH DON'T FAINT!
TRULY, BELOVED? A SACRED HIGH ONE?!
TRULY! TIMMAIN...LAST OF THE FIRST-COMERS.
NO ELF CAN STAND IN HER PRESENCE AND FEEL ANYTHING BUT HOME.

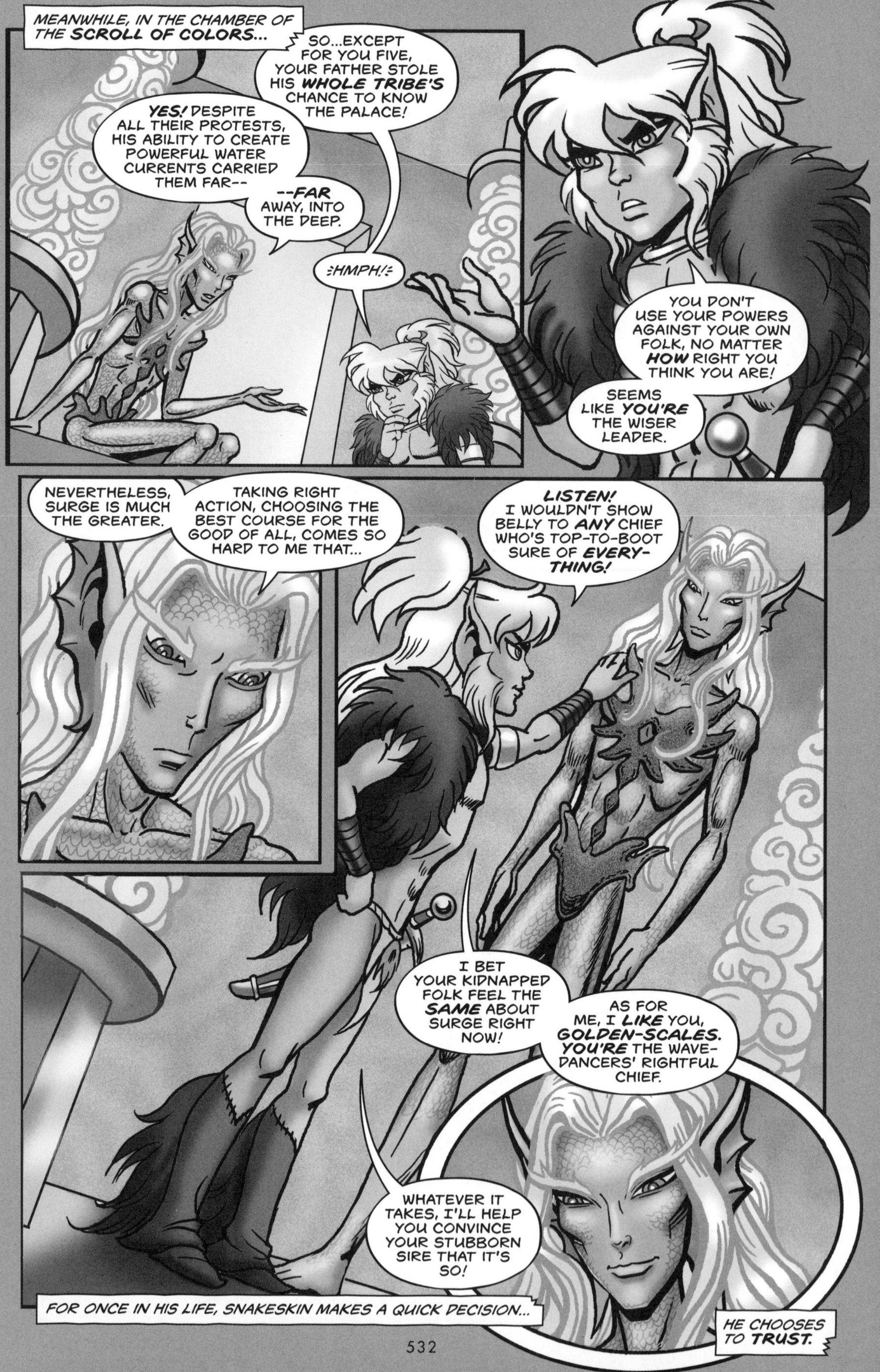

MEANWHILE, IN THE CHAMBER OF THE SCROLL OF COLORS...
SO...EXCEPT FOR YOU FIVE, YOUR FATHER STOLE HIS WHOLE TRIBE'S CHANCE TO KNOW THE PALACE!
YES! DESPITE ALL THEIR PROTESTS, HIS ABILITY TO CREATE POWERFUL WATER CURRENTS CARRIED THEM FAR--
--FAR AWAY, INTO THE DEEP.
HMPH!
YOU DON'T USE YOUR POWERS AGAINST YOUR OWN FOLK, NO MATTER HOW RIGHT YOU THINK YOU ARE!
SEEMS LIKE YOU'RE THE WISER LEADER.
NEVERTHELESS, SURGE IS MUCH THE GREATER.
TAKING RIGHT ACTION, CHOOSING THE BEST COURSE FOR THE GOOD OF ALL, COMES SO HARD TO ME THAT...
LISTEN! I WOULDN'T SHOW BELLY TO ANY CHIEF WHO'S TOP-TO-BOOT SURE OF EVERY-THING!
I BET YOUR KIDNAPPED FOLK FEEL THE SAME ABOUT SURGE RIGHT NOW!
AS FOR ME, I LIKE YOU, GOLDEN-SCALES. YOU'RE THE WAVE-DANCERS' RIGHTFUL CHIEF.
WHATEVER IT TAKES, I'LL HELP YOU CONVINCE YOUR STUBBORN SIRE THAT IT'S SO!
FOR ONCE IN HIS LIFE, SNAKESKIN MAKES A QUICK DECISION...
HE CHOOSES TO TRUST.

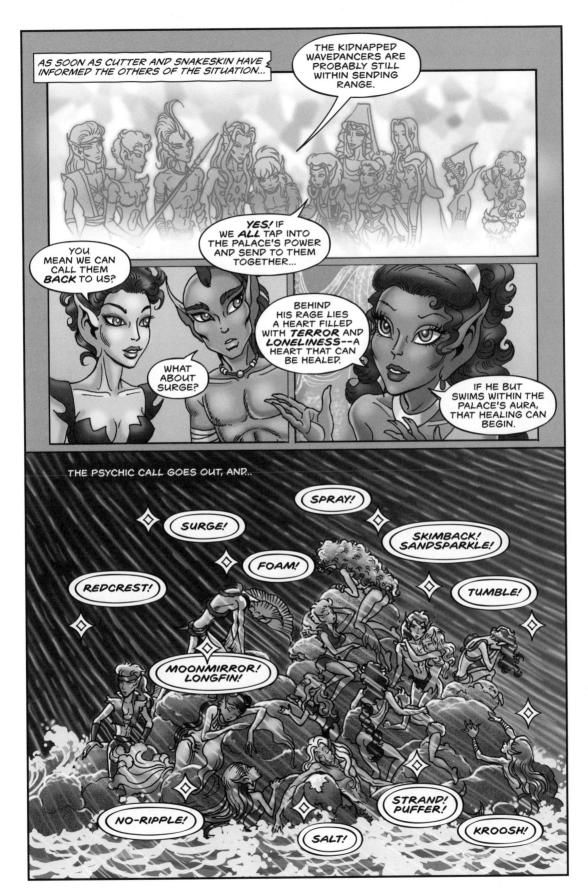

AS SOON AS CUTTER AND SNAKESKIN HAVE INFORMED THE OTHERS OF THE SITUATION...

THE KIDNAPPED WAVEDANCERS ARE PROBABLY STILL WITHIN SENDING RANGE.

YOU MEAN WE CAN CALL THEM *BACK* TO US?

YES! IF WE *ALL* TAP INTO THE PALACE'S POWER AND SEND TO THEM TOGETHER...

WHAT ABOUT SURGE?

BEHIND HIS RAGE LIES A HEART FILLED WITH *TERROR* AND *LONELINESS*--A HEART THAT CAN BE HEALED.

IF HE BUT SWIMS WITHIN THE PALACE'S AURA, THAT HEALING CAN BEGIN.

THE PSYCHIC CALL GOES OUT, AND...

SPRAY!

SURGE!

SKIMBACK! SANDSPARKLE!

FOAM!

REDCREST!

TUMBLE!

MOONMIRROR! LONGFIN!

NO-RIPPLE!

STRAND! PUFFER!

SALT!

KROOSH!

533

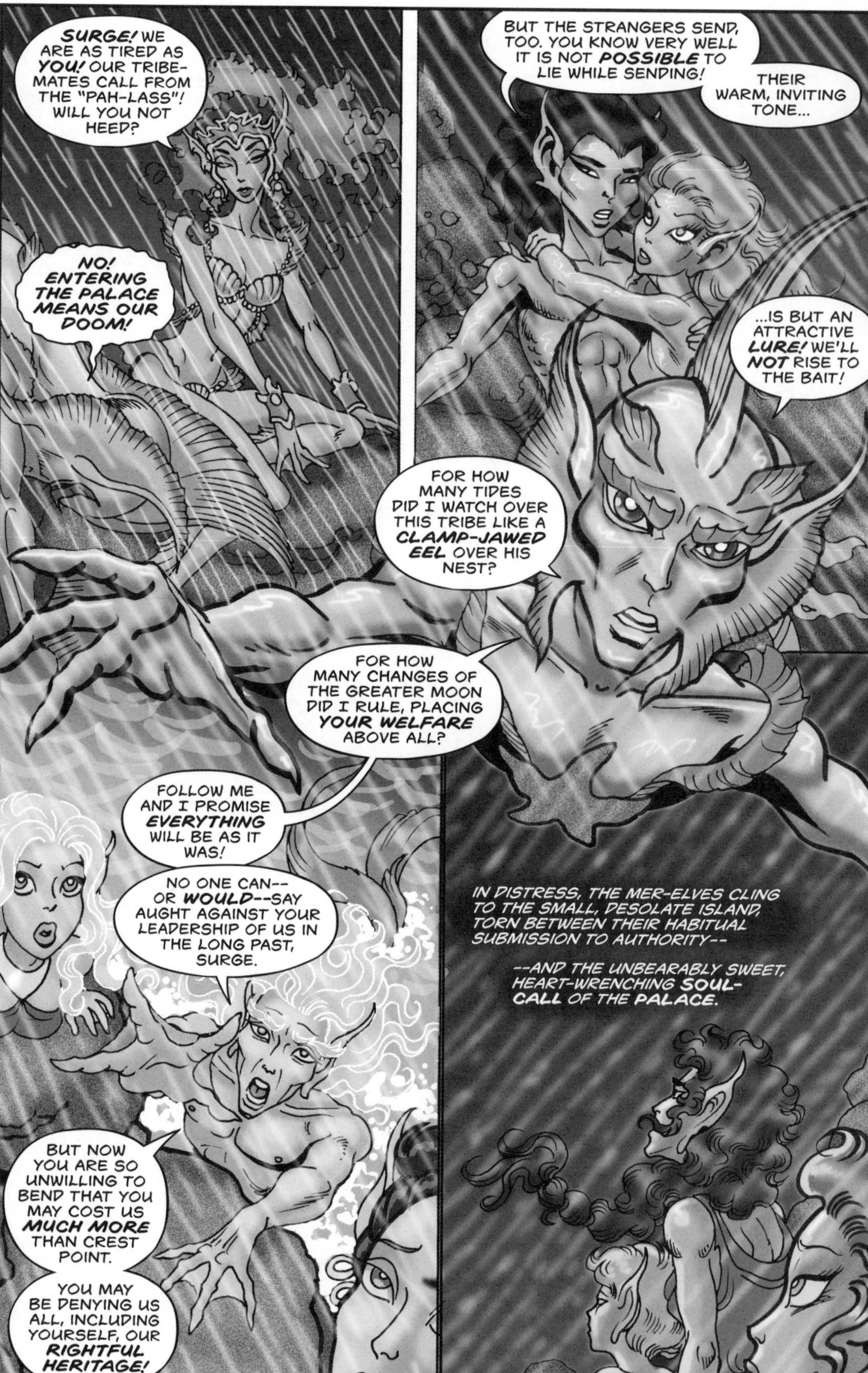

SURGE! WE ARE AS TIRED AS YOU! OUR TRIBE-MATES CALL FROM THE "PAH-LASS"! WILL YOU NOT HEED?
NO! ENTERING THE PALACE MEANS OUR DOOM!
BUT THE STRANGERS SEND, TOO. YOU KNOW VERY WELL IT IS NOT POSSIBLE TO LIE WHILE SENDING!
THEIR WARM, INVITING TONE...
...IS BUT AN ATTRACTIVE LURE! WE'LL NOT RISE TO THE BAIT!
FOR HOW MANY TIDES DID I WATCH OVER THIS TRIBE LIKE A CLAMP-JAWED EEL OVER HIS NEST?
FOR HOW MANY CHANGES OF THE GREATER MOON DID I RULE, PLACING YOUR WELFARE ABOVE ALL?
FOLLOW ME AND I PROMISE EVERYTHING WILL BE AS IT WAS!
NO ONE CAN-- OR WOULD--SAY AUGHT AGAINST YOUR LEADERSHIP OF US IN THE LONG PAST, SURGE.
BUT NOW YOU ARE SO UNWILLING TO BEND THAT YOU MAY COST US MUCH MORE THAN CREST POINT.
YOU MAY BE DENYING US ALL, INCLUDING YOURSELF, OUR RIGHTFUL HERITAGE!
IN DISTRESS, THE MER-ELVES CLING TO THE SMALL, DESOLATE ISLAND, TORN BETWEEN THEIR HABITUAL SUBMISSION TO AUTHORITY--
--AND THE UNBEARABLY SWEET, HEART-WRENCHING SOUL-CALL OF THE PALACE.

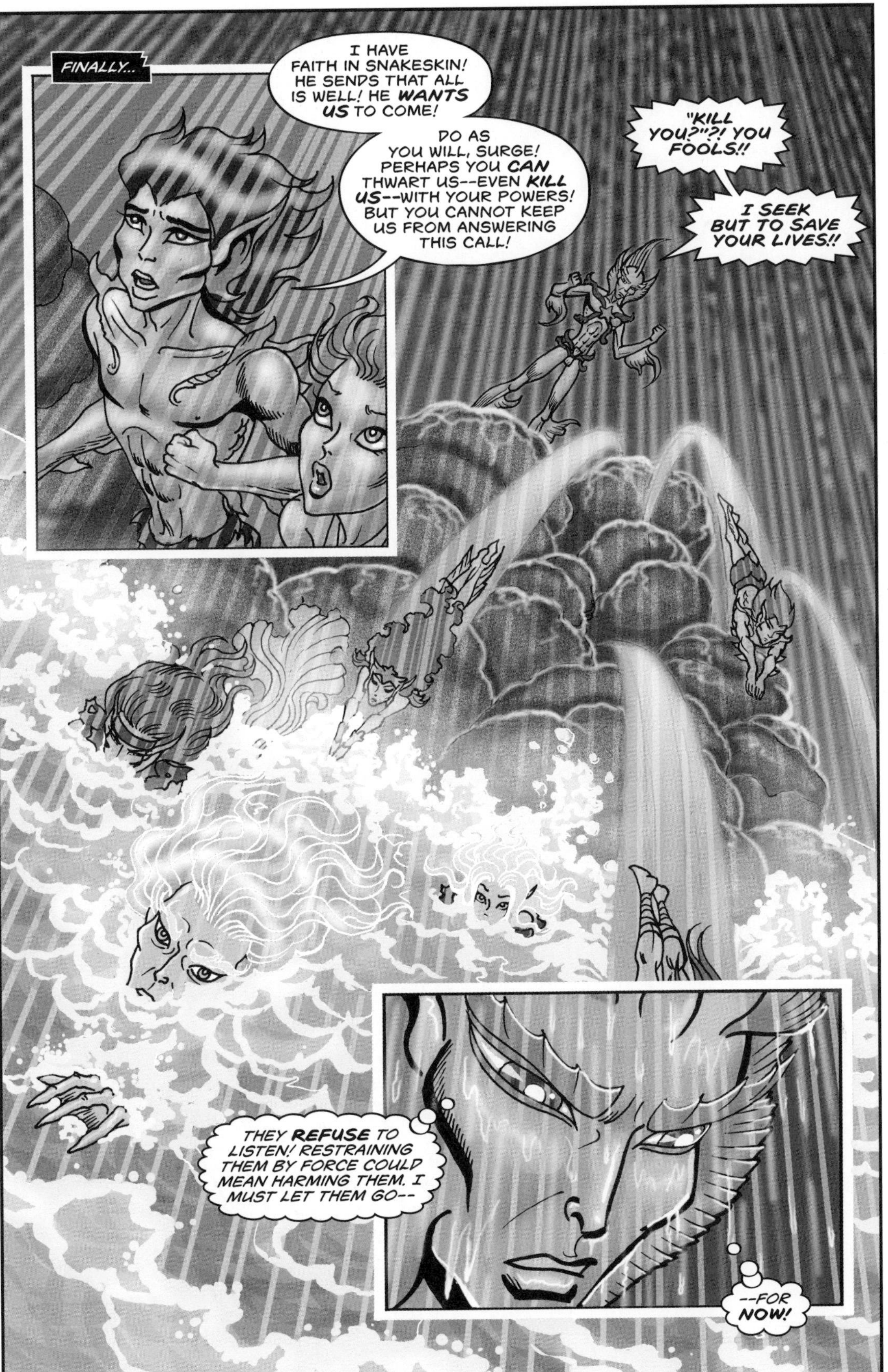
FINALLY...
I HAVE FAITH IN SNAKESKIN! HE SENDS THAT ALL IS WELL! HE WANTS US TO COME!
DO AS YOU WILL, SURGE! PERHAPS YOU CAN THWART US--EVEN KILL US--WITH YOUR POWERS! BUT YOU CANNOT KEEP US FROM ANSWERING THIS CALL!
"KILL YOU?"?! YOU FOOLS!!
I SEEK BUT TO SAVE YOUR LIVES!!
THEY REFUSE TO LISTEN! RESTRAINING THEM BY FORCE COULD MEAN HARMING THEM. I MUST LET THEM GO--
--FOR NOW!

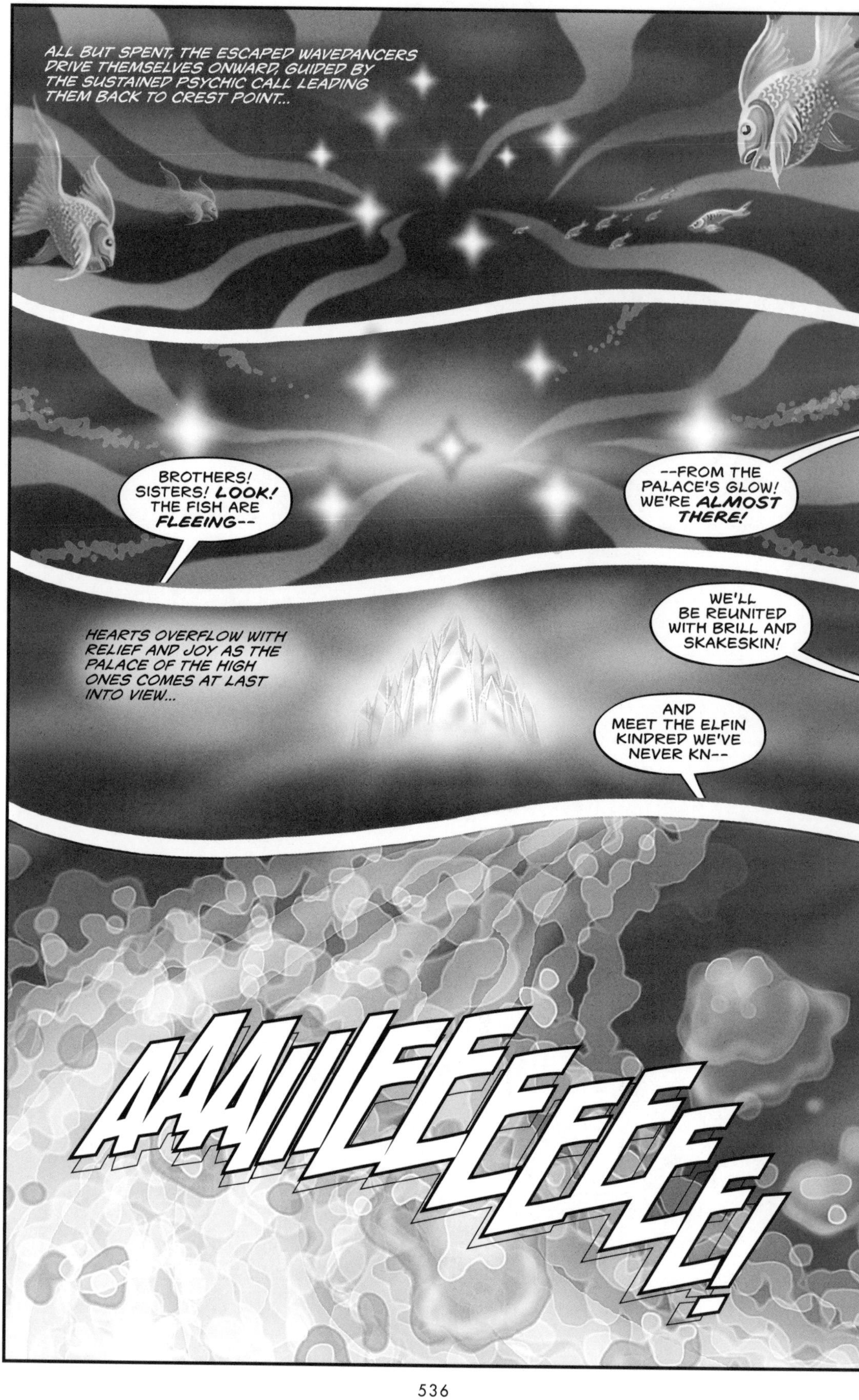
ALL BUT SPENT, THE ESCAPED WAVEDANCERS DRIVE THEMSELVES ONWARD, GUIDED BY THE SUSTAINED PSYCHIC CALL LEADING THEM BACK TO CREST POINT...
BROTHERS! SISTERS! LOOK! THE FISH ARE FLEEING--
--FROM THE PALACE'S GLOW! WE'RE ALMOST THERE!
HEARTS OVERFLOW WITH RELIEF AND JOY AS THE PALACE OF THE HIGH ONES COMES AT LAST INTO VIEW...
WE'LL BE REUNITED WITH BRILL AND SKAKESKIN!
AND MEET THE ELFIN KINDRED WE'VE NEVER KN--
AAAIIEEEEEEEE!

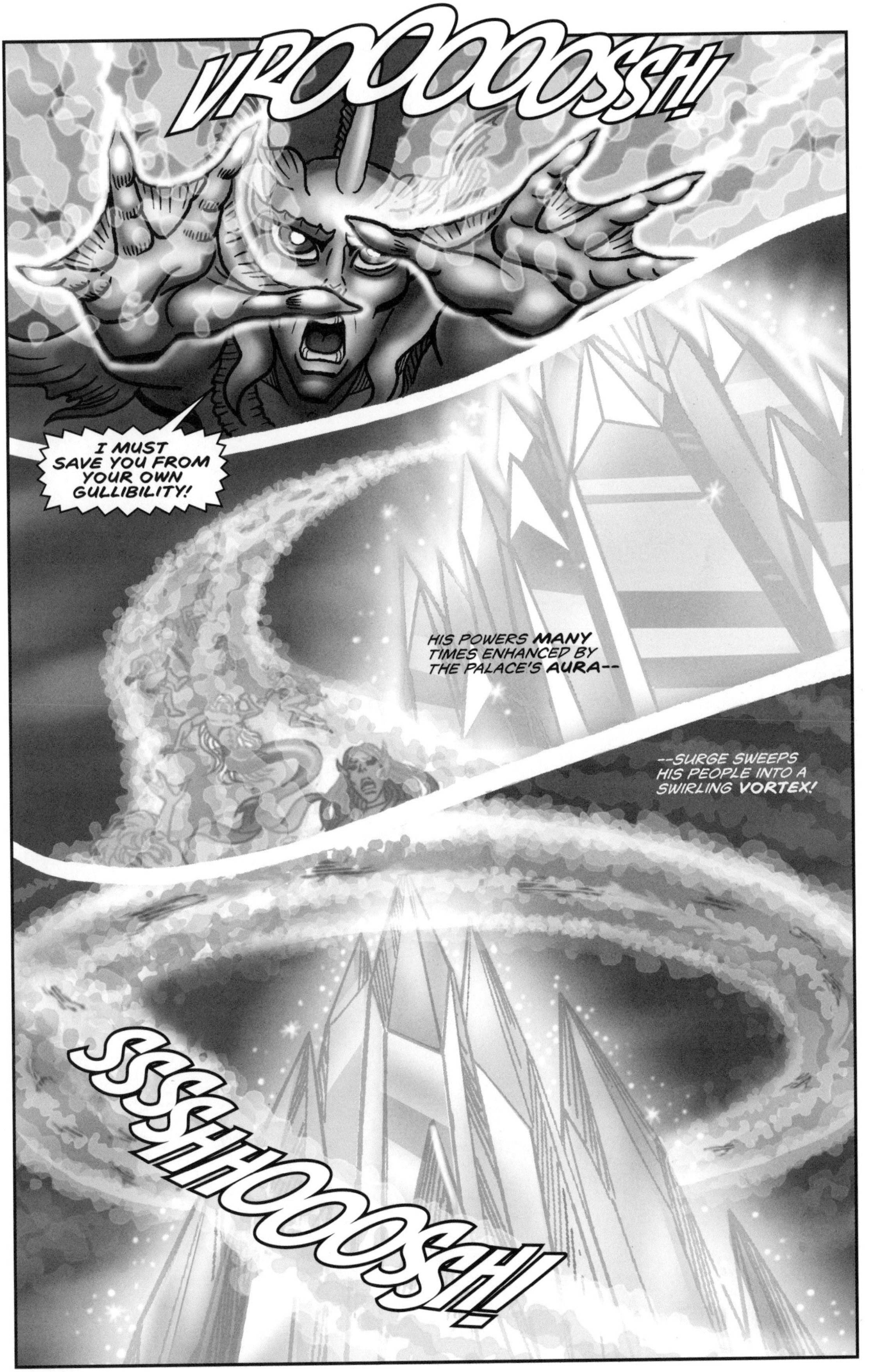
VROOOOOOSSH!
I MUST SAVE YOU FROM YOUR OWN GULLIBILITY!
HIS POWERS MANY TIMES ENHANCED BY THE PALACE'S AURA--
--SURGE SWEEPS HIS PEOPLE INTO A SWIRLING VORTEX!
SSSHHOOOSSH!

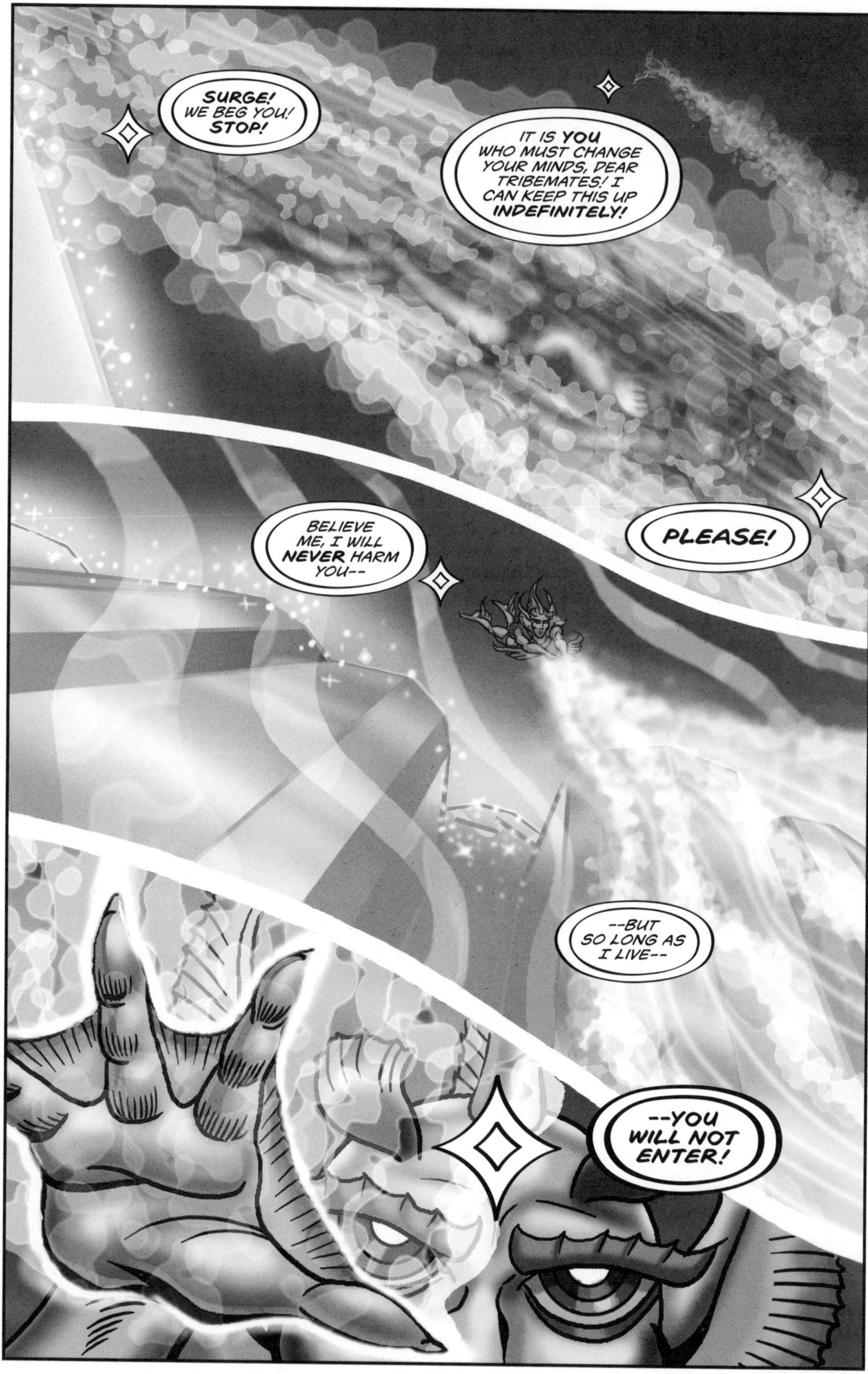
SURGE! WE BEG YOU! STOP!
IT IS YOU WHO MUST CHANGE YOUR MINDS, DEAR TRIBEMATES! I CAN KEEP THIS UP INDEFINITELY!
BELIEVE ME, I WILL NEVER HARM YOU--
PLEASE!
--BUT SO LONG AS I LIVE--
--YOU WILL NOT ENTER!

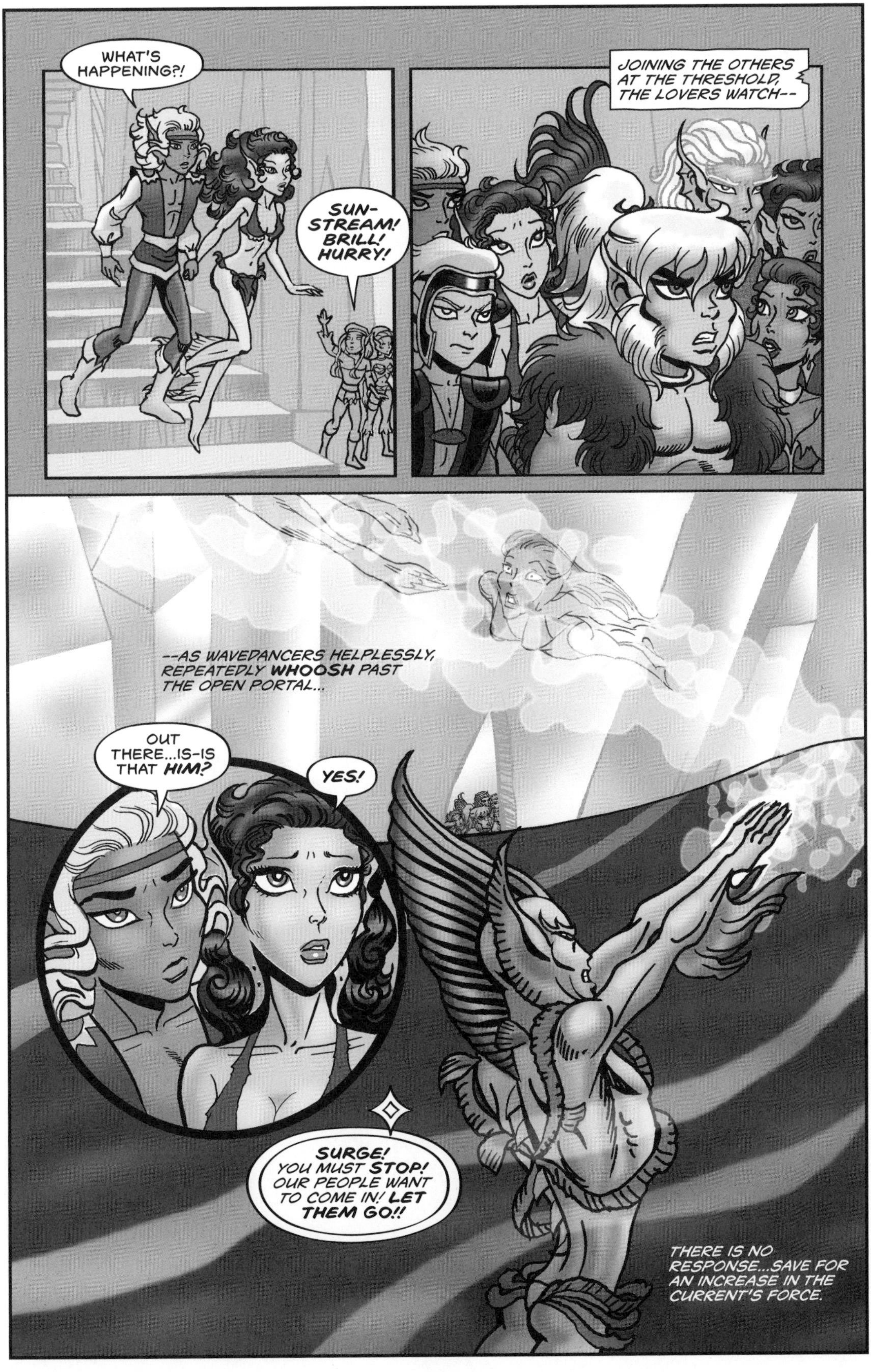
WHAT'S HAPPENING?!
SUN-STREAM! BRILL! HURRY!
JOINING THE OTHERS AT THE THRESHOLD, THE LOVERS WATCH--
--AS WAVEDANCERS HELPLESSLY, REPEATEDLY WHOOSH PAST THE OPEN PORTAL...
OUT THERE...IS-IS THAT HIM?
YES!
SURGE! YOU MUST STOP! OUR PEOPLE WANT TO COME IN! LET THEM GO!!
THERE IS NO RESPONSE...SAVE FOR AN INCREASE IN THE CURRENT'S FORCE.

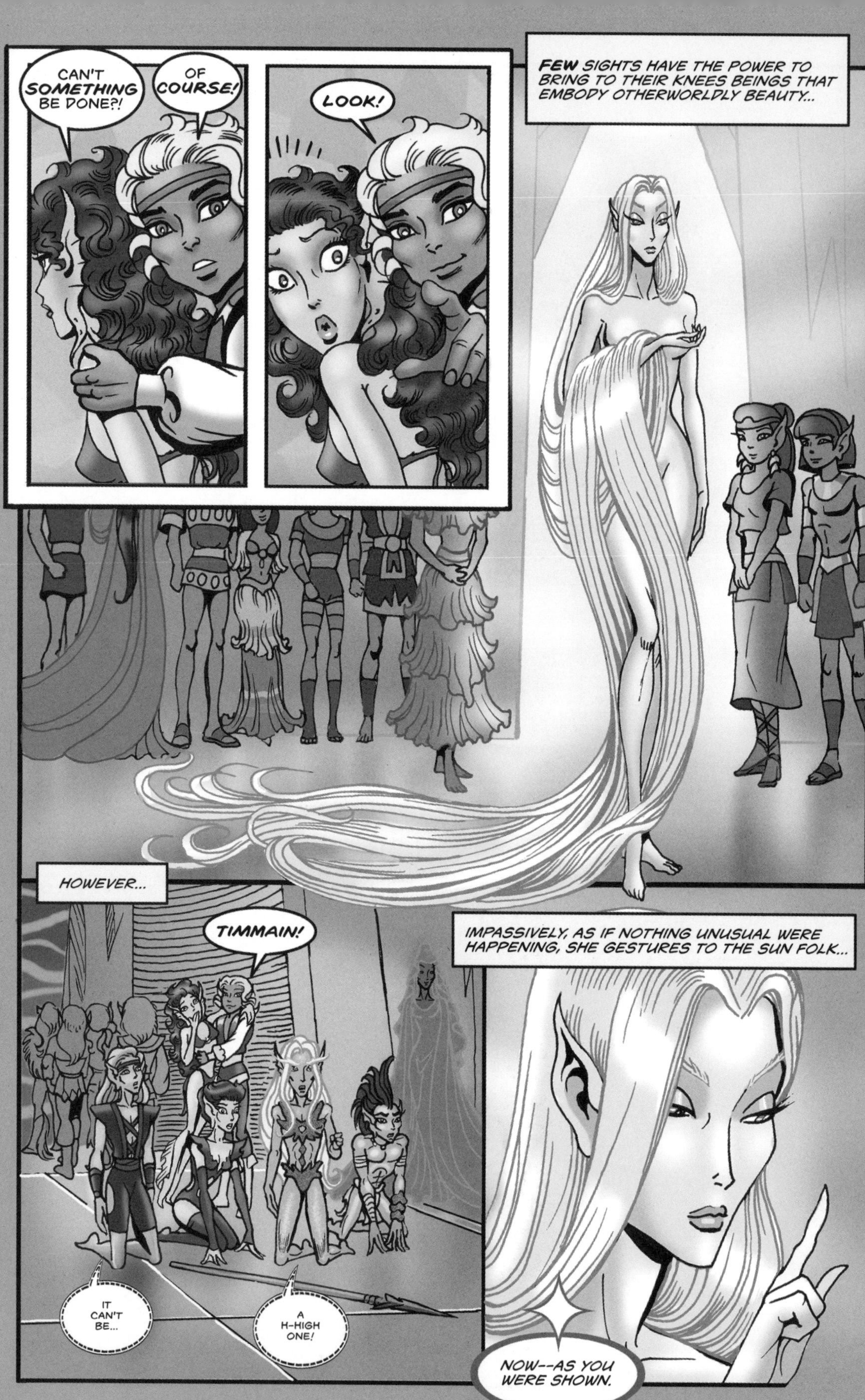
CAN'T SOMETHING BE DONE?!
OF COURSE!
LOOK!
FEW SIGHTS HAVE THE POWER TO BRING TO THEIR KNEES BEINGS THAT EMBODY OTHERWORLDLY BEAUTY...
HOWEVER...
TIMMAIN!
IT CAN'T BE...
A H-HIGH ONE!
IMPASSIVELY, AS IF NOTHING UNUSUAL WERE HAPPENING, SHE GESTURES TO THE SUN FOLK...
NOW--AS YOU WERE SHOWN.

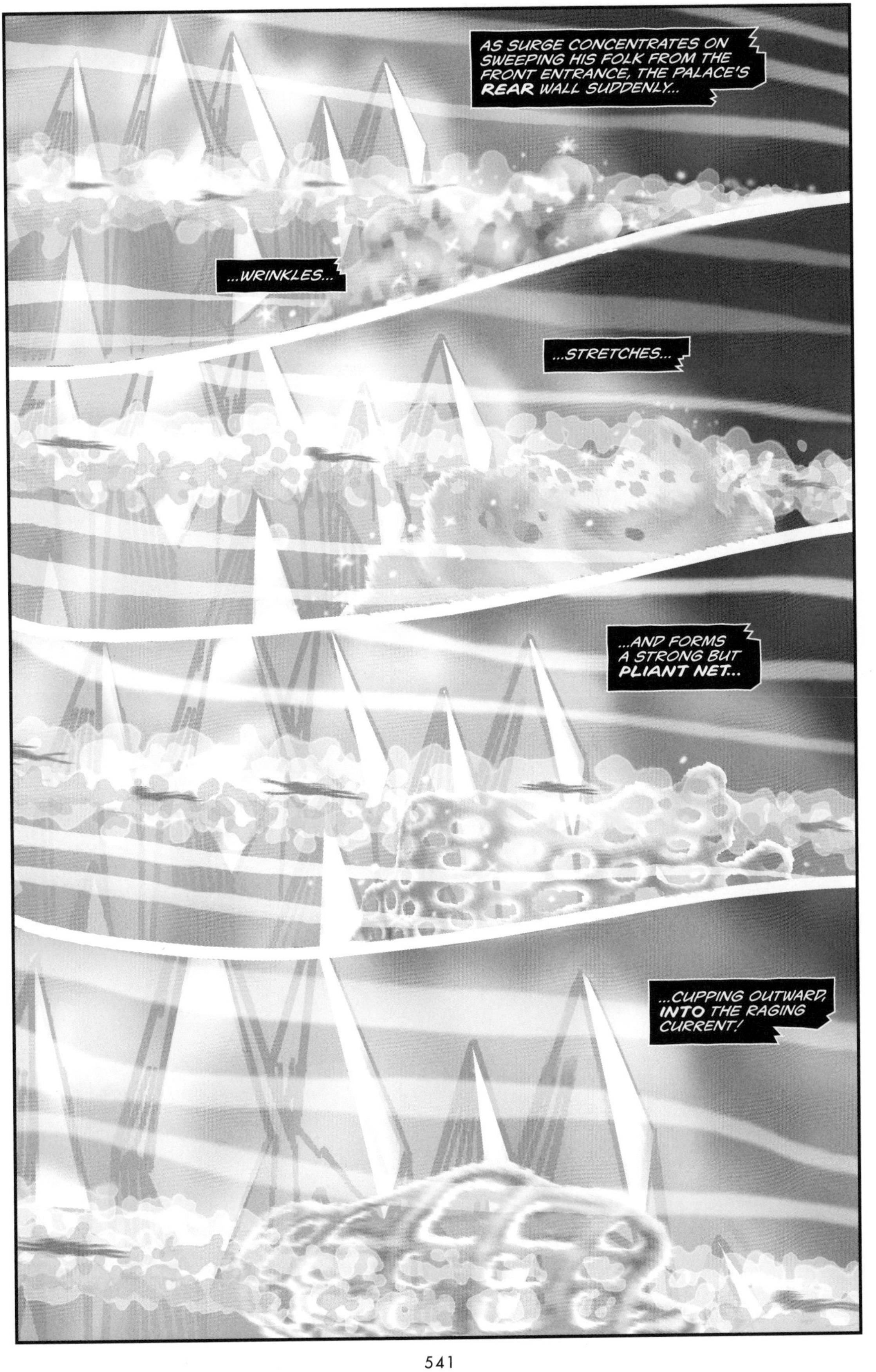
AS SURGE CONCENTRATES ON SWEEPING HIS FOLK FROM THE FRONT ENTRANCE, THE PALACE'S **REAR** WALL SUDDENLY...
...WRINKLES...
...STRETCHES...
...AND FORMS A STRONG BUT **PLIANT NET**...
...CUPPING OUTWARD, **INTO** THE RAGING CURRENT!

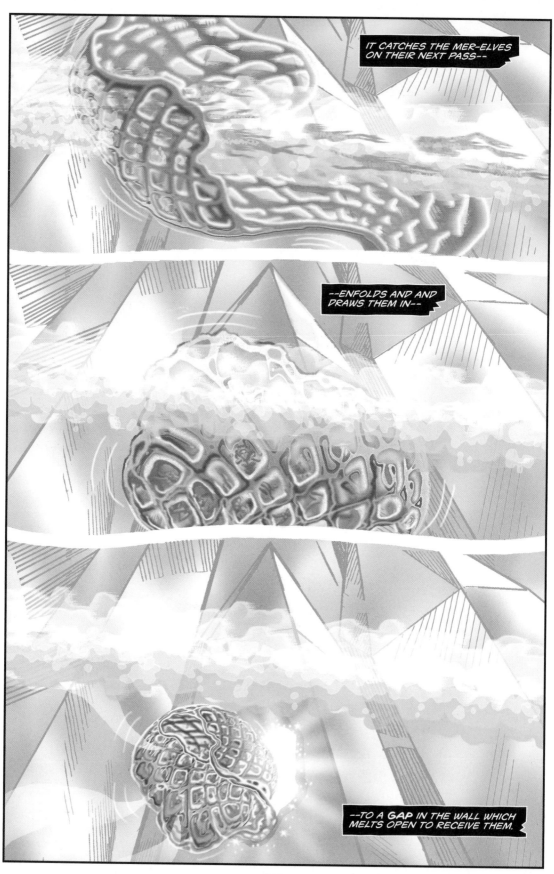

IT CATCHES THE MER-ELVES ON THEIR NEXT PASS--

--ENFOLDS AND AND DRAWS THEM IN--

--TO A **GAP** IN THE WALL WHICH MELTS OPEN TO RECEIVE THEM.

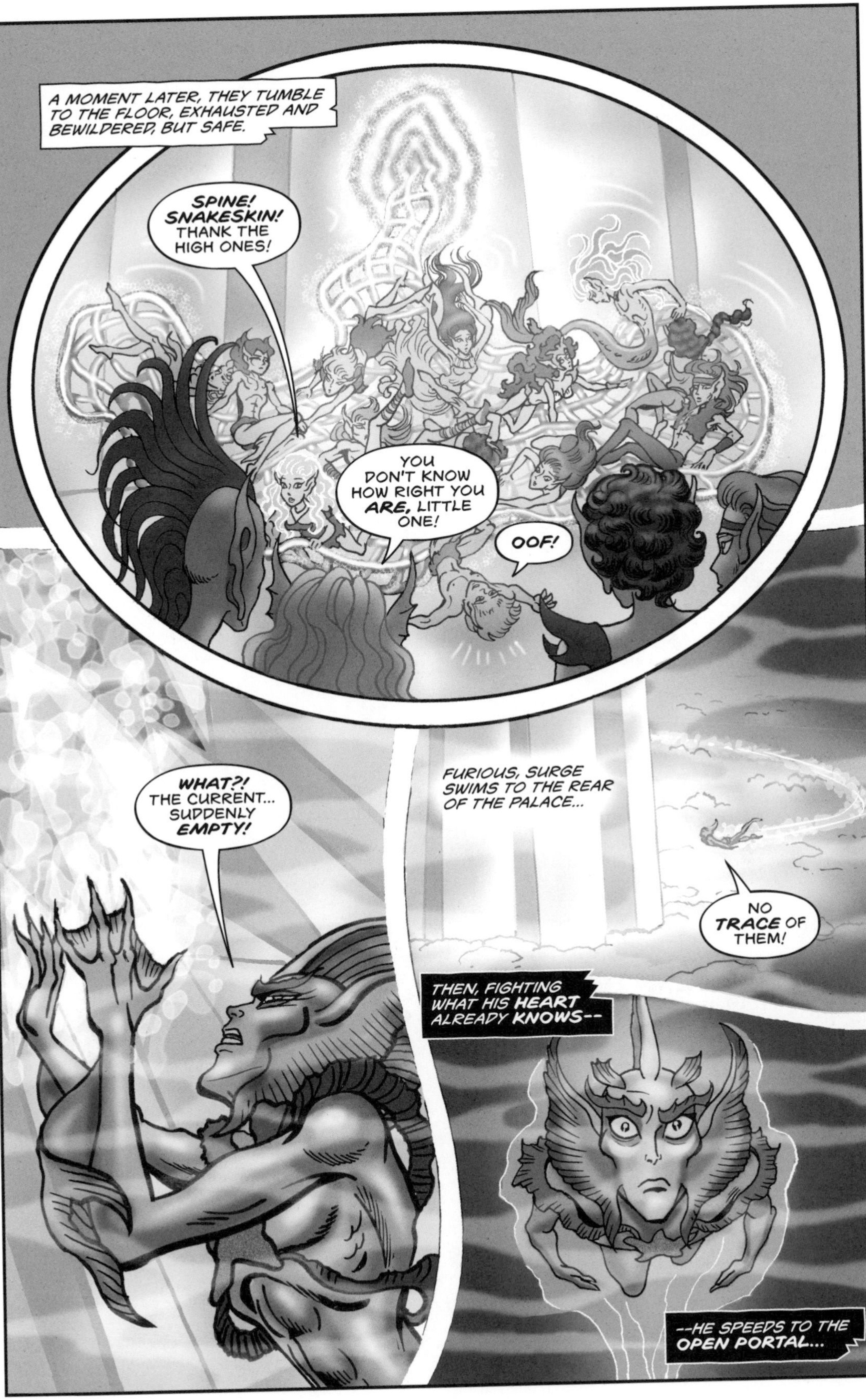

A MOMENT LATER, THEY TUMBLE TO THE FLOOR, EXHAUSTED AND BEWILDERED, BUT SAFE.
SPINE! SNAKESKIN! THANK THE HIGH ONES!
YOU DON'T KNOW HOW RIGHT YOU ARE, LITTLE ONE!
OOF!
WHAT?! THE CURRENT... SUDDENLY EMPTY!
FURIOUS, SURGE SWIMS TO THE REAR OF THE PALACE...
NO TRACE OF THEM!
THEN, FIGHTING WHAT HIS HEART ALREADY KNOWS--
--HE SPEEDS TO THE OPEN PORTAL...

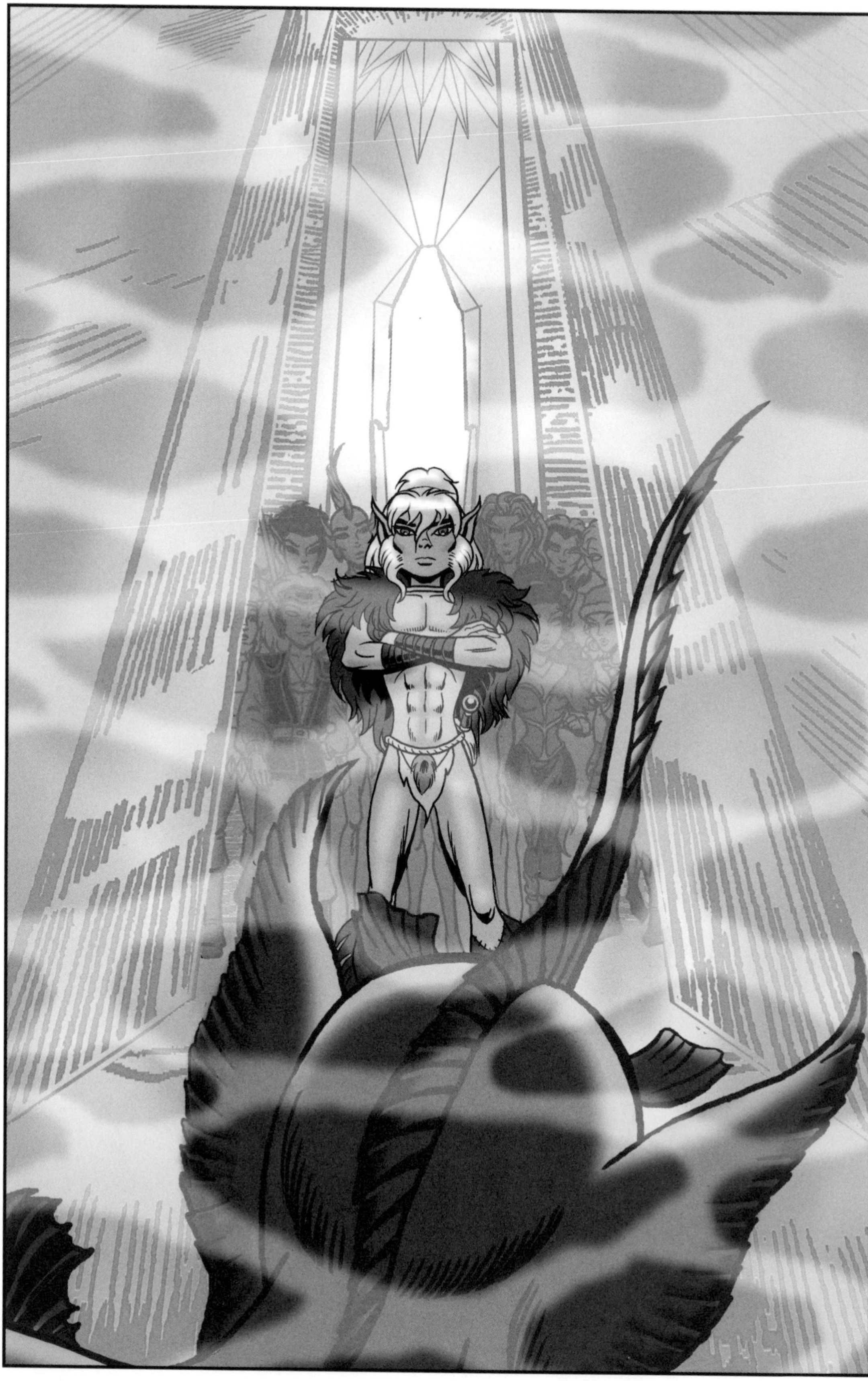

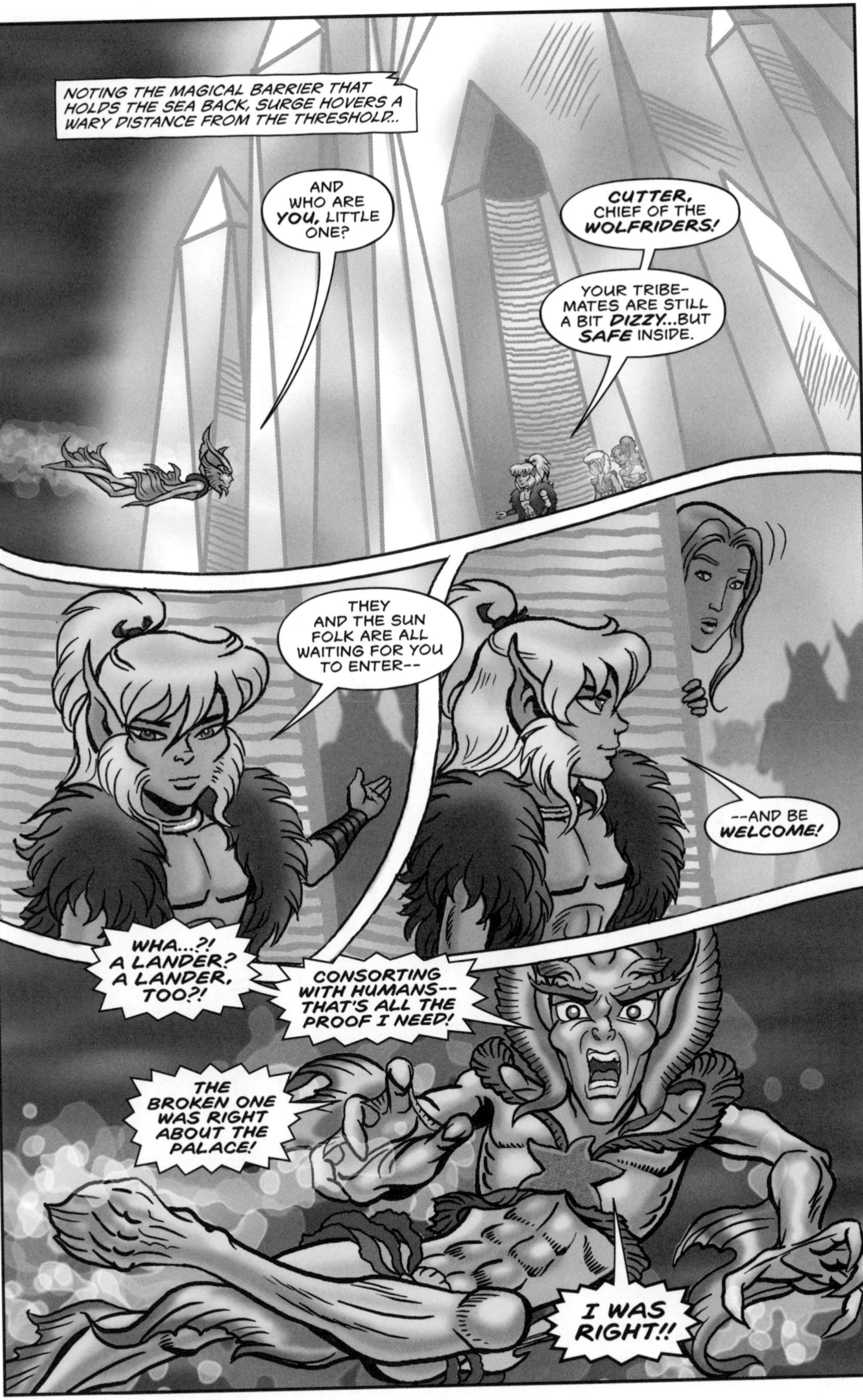
NOTING THE MAGICAL BARRIER THAT HOLDS THE SEA BACK, SURGE HOVERS A WARY DISTANCE FROM THE THRESHOLD...
AND WHO ARE YOU, LITTLE ONE?
CUTTER, CHIEF OF THE WOLFRIDERS!
YOUR TRIBE-MATES ARE STILL A BIT DIZZY...BUT SAFE INSIDE.
THEY AND THE SUN FOLK ARE ALL WAITING FOR YOU TO ENTER--
--AND BE WELCOME!
WHA...?! A LANDER? A LANDER, TOO?!
CONSORTING WITH HUMANS-- THAT'S ALL THE PROOF I NEED!
THE BROKEN ONE WAS RIGHT ABOUT THE PALACE!
I WAS RIGHT!!

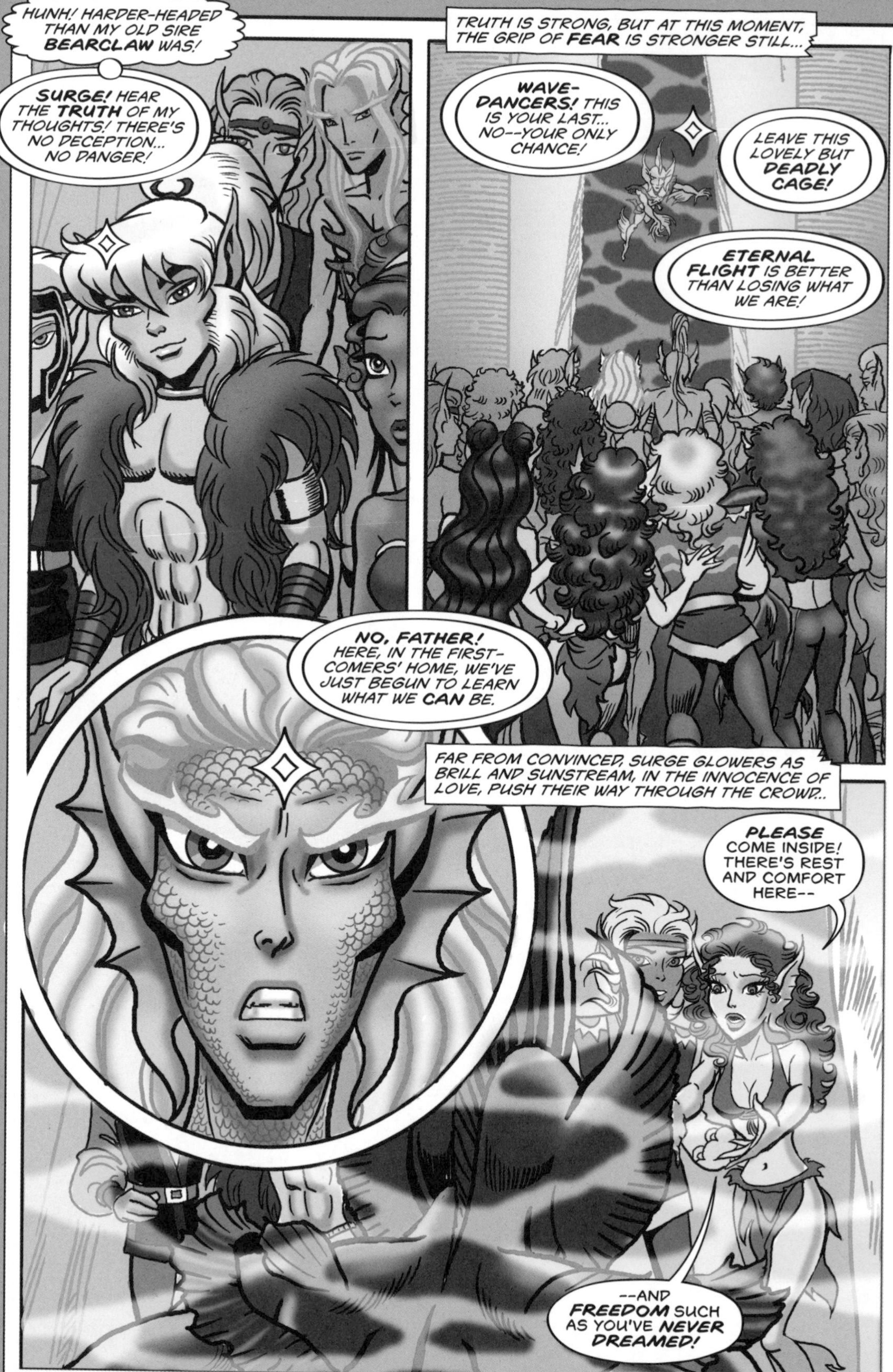
HUNH! HARDER-HEADED THAN MY OLD SIRE BEARCLAW WAS!
SURGE! HEAR THE TRUTH OF MY THOUGHTS! THERE'S NO DECEPTION... NO DANGER!
TRUTH IS STRONG, BUT AT THIS MOMENT, THE GRIP OF FEAR IS STRONGER STILL...
WAVE-DANCERS! THIS IS YOUR LAST... NO--YOUR ONLY CHANCE!
LEAVE THIS LOVELY BUT DEADLY CAGE!
ETERNAL FLIGHT IS BETTER THAN LOSING WHAT WE ARE!
NO, FATHER! HERE, IN THE FIRST-COMERS' HOME, WE'VE JUST BEGUN TO LEARN WHAT WE CAN BE.
FAR FROM CONVINCED, SURGE GLOWERS AS BRILL AND SUNSTREAM, IN THE INNOCENCE OF LOVE, PUSH THEIR WAY THROUGH THE CROWD...
PLEASE COME INSIDE! THERE'S REST AND COMFORT HERE--
--AND FREEDOM SUCH AS YOU'VE NEVER DREAMED!

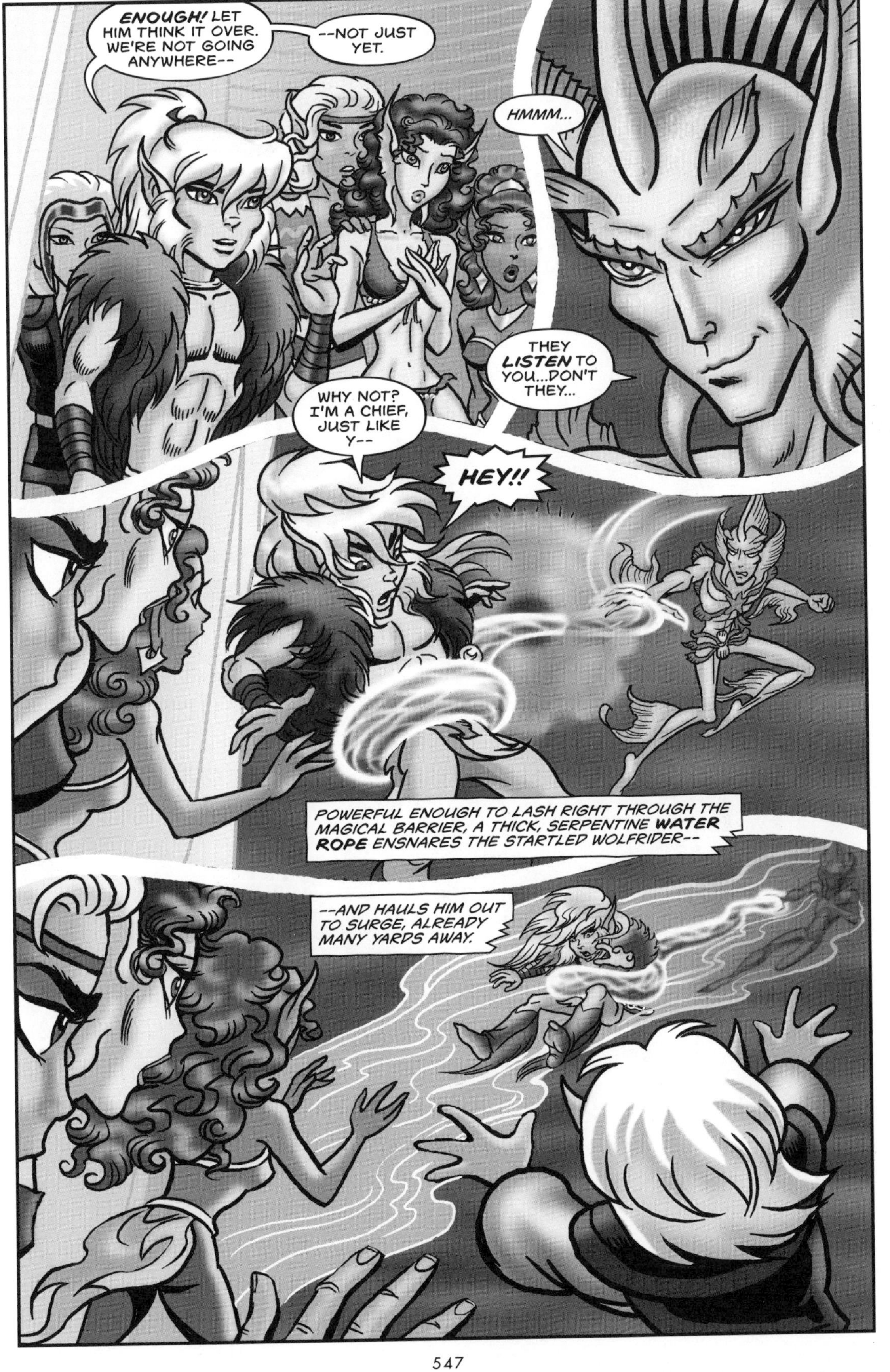
ENOUGH! LET HIM THINK IT OVER. WE'RE NOT GOING ANYWHERE--
--NOT JUST YET.
HMMM...
THEY LISTEN TO YOU...DON'T THEY...
WHY NOT? I'M A CHIEF, JUST LIKE Y--
HEY!!
POWERFUL ENOUGH TO LASH RIGHT THROUGH THE MAGICAL BARRIER, A THICK, SERPENTINE WATER ROPE ENSNARES THE STARTLED WOLFRIDER--
--AND HAULS HIM OUT TO SURGE, ALREADY MANY YARDS AWAY.

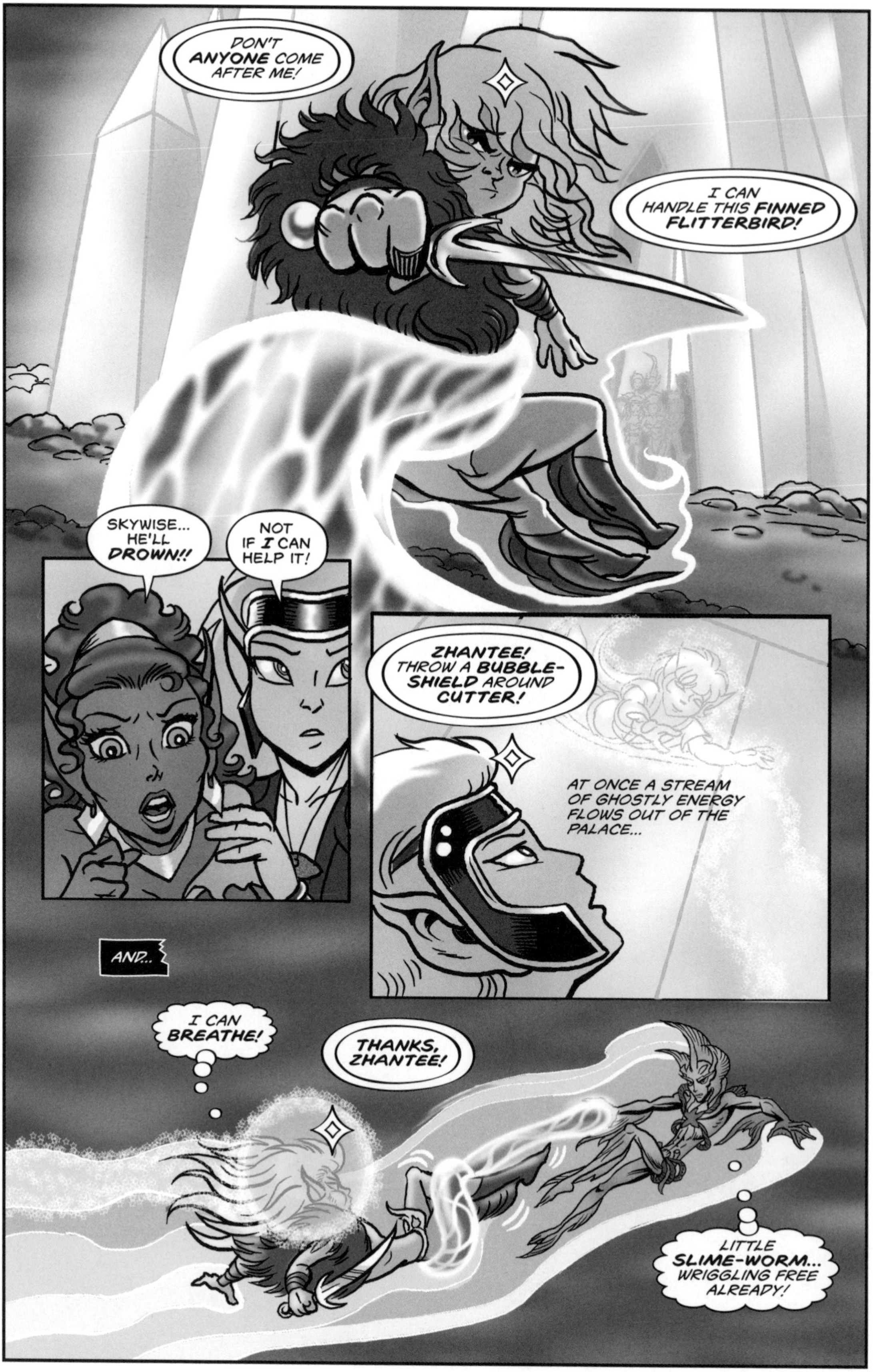
DON'T ANYONE COME AFTER ME!
I CAN HANDLE THIS FINNED FLITTERBIRD!
SKYWISE... HE'LL DROWN!!
NOT IF I CAN HELP IT!
ZHANTEE! THROW A BUBBLE-SHIELD AROUND CUTTER!
AT ONCE A STREAM OF GHOSTLY ENERGY FLOWS OUT OF THE PALACE...
AND...
I CAN BREATHE!
THANKS, ZHANTEE!
LITTLE SLIME-WORM... WRIGGLING FREE ALREADY!

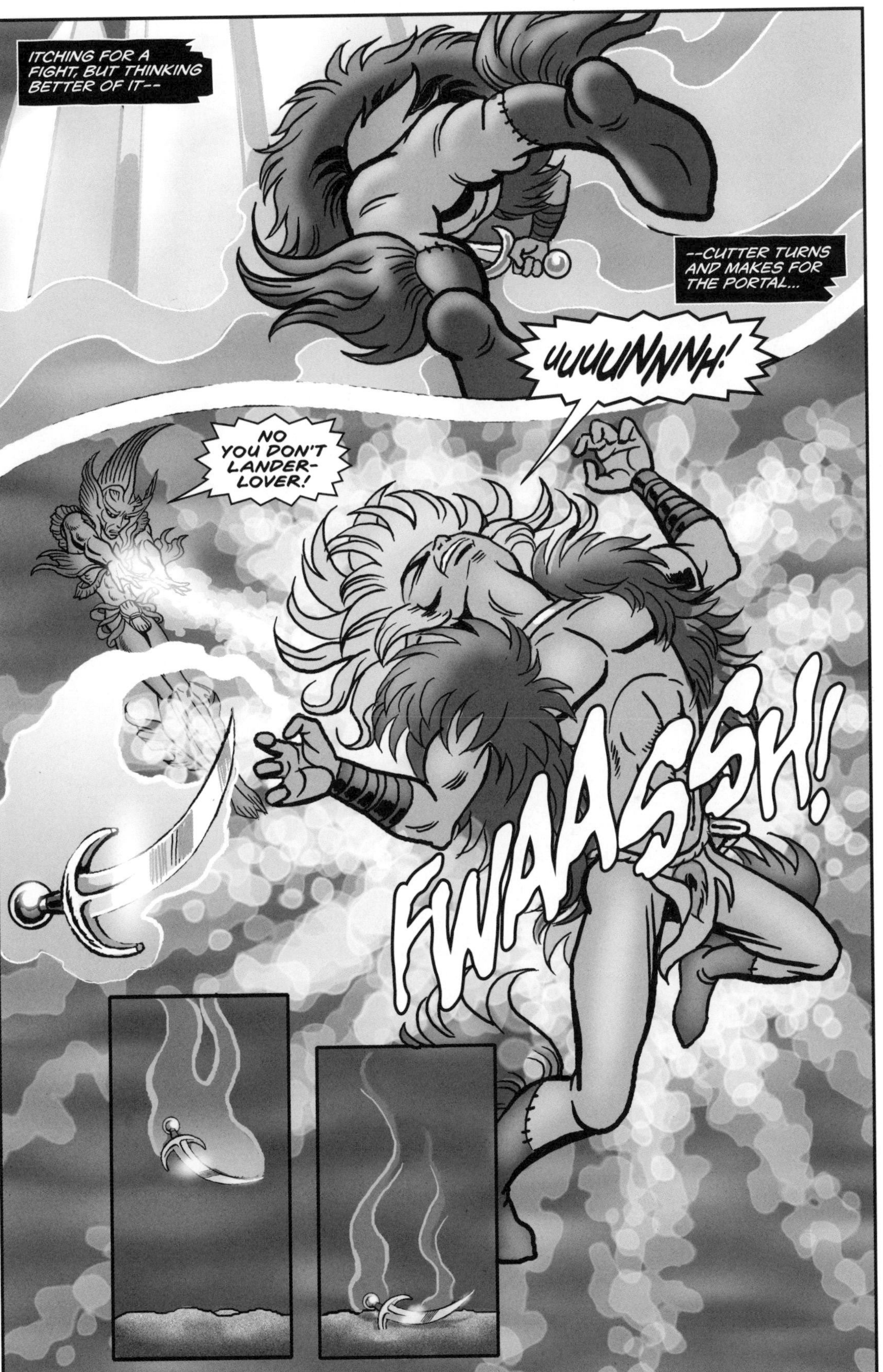
ITCHING FOR A FIGHT, BUT THINKING BETTER OF IT--
--CUTTER TURNS AND MAKES FOR THE PORTAL...
UUUUNNNH!
NO YOU DON'T LANDER-LOVER!
FWAASSH!!

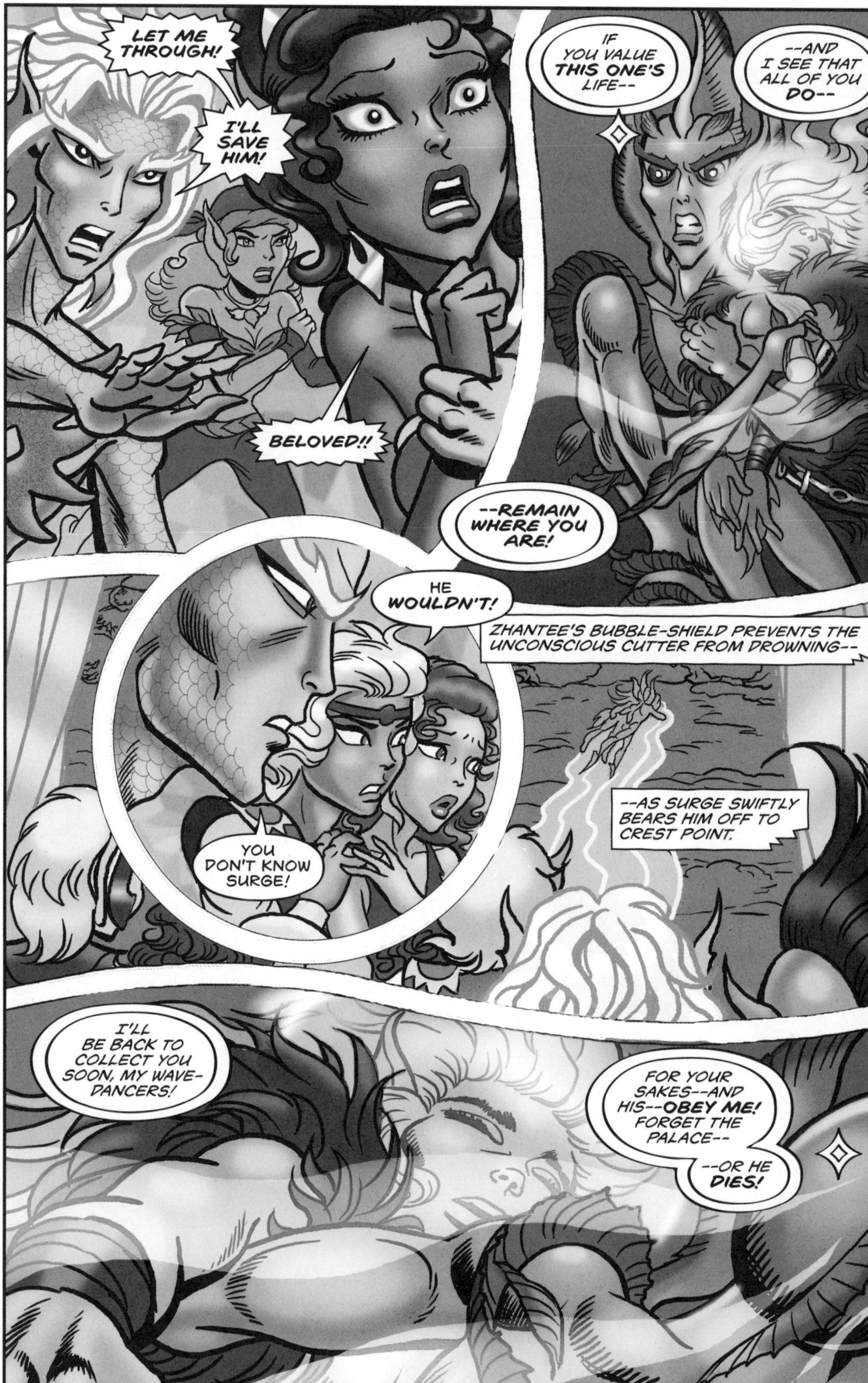
LET ME THROUGH!
I'LL SAVE HIM!
BELOVED!!
IF YOU VALUE THIS ONE'S LIFE--
--AND I SEE THAT ALL OF YOU DO--
--REMAIN WHERE YOU ARE!
HE WOULDN'T!
ZHANTEE'S BUBBLE-SHIELD PREVENTS THE UNCONSCIOUS CUTTER FROM DROWNING--
YOU DON'T KNOW SURGE!
--AS SURGE SWIFTLY BEARS HIM OFF TO CREST POINT.
I'LL BE BACK TO COLLECT YOU SOON, MY WAVE-DANCERS!
FOR YOUR SAKES--AND HIS--OBEY ME! FORGET THE PALACE--
--OR HE DIES!

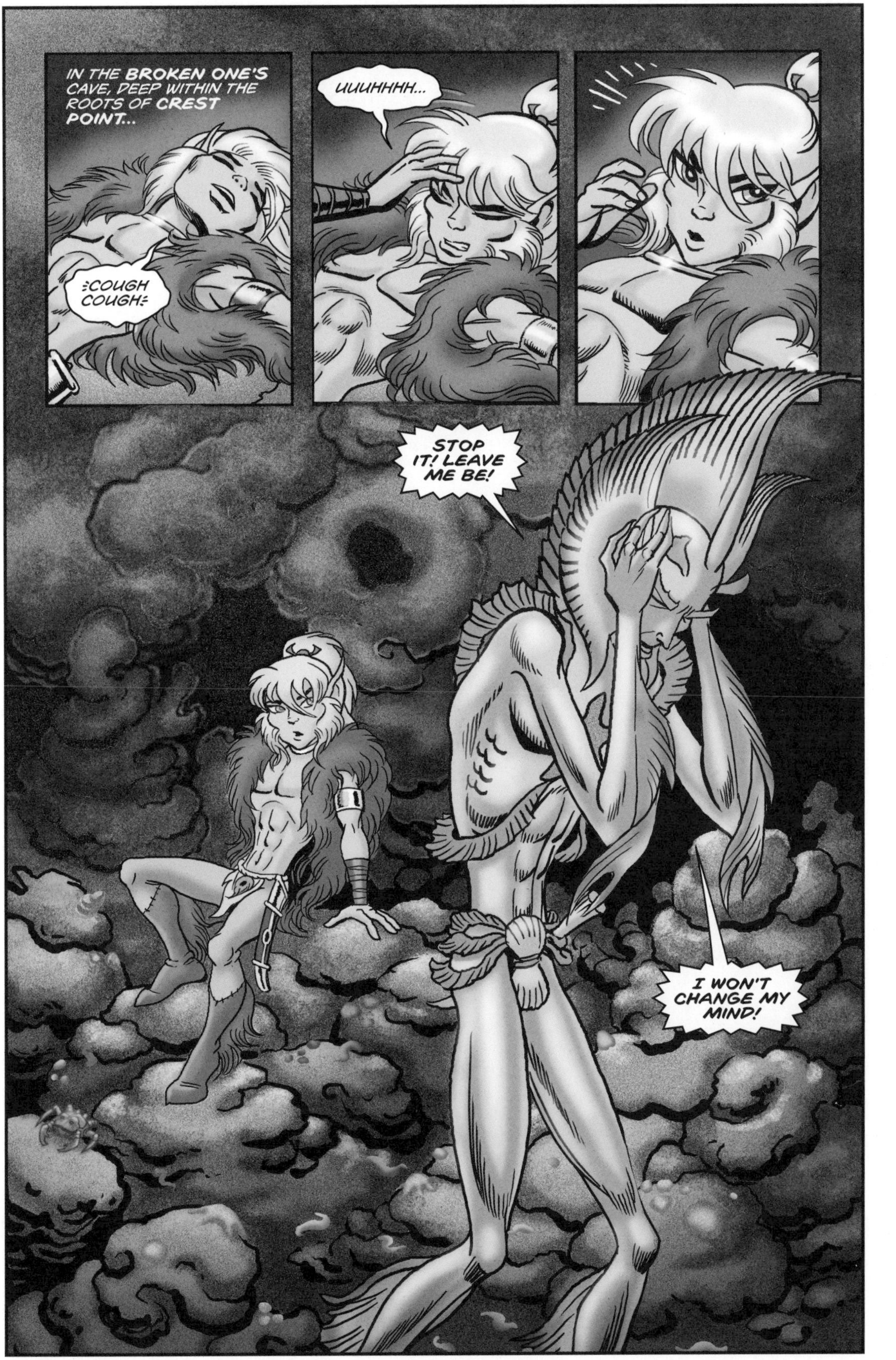
IN THE BROKEN ONE'S CAVE, DEEP WITHIN THE ROOTS OF CREST POINT...
COUGH COUGH
UUUHHHH...
STOP IT! LEAVE ME BE!
I WON'T CHANGE MY MIND!

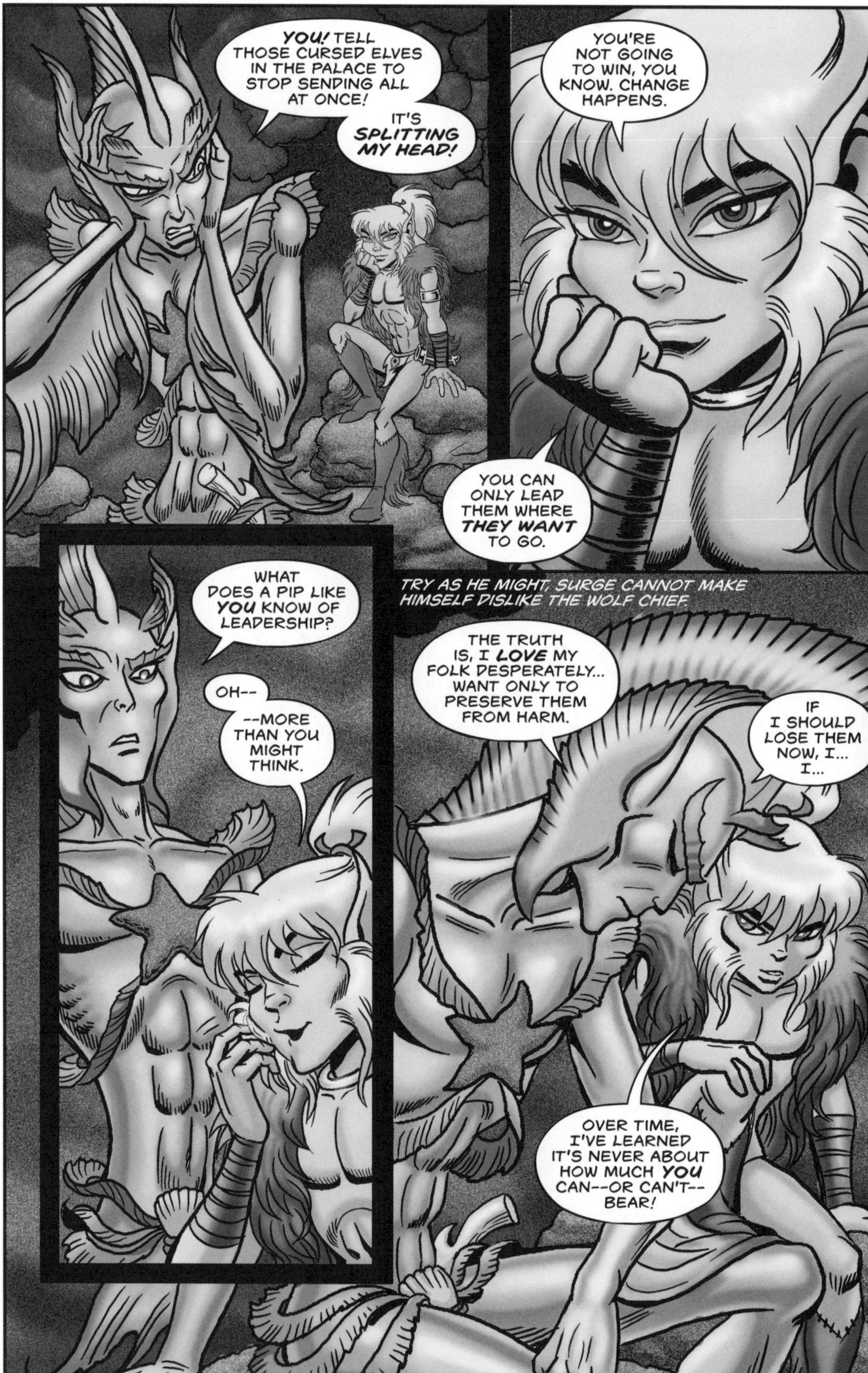
YOU! TELL THOSE CURSED ELVES IN THE PALACE TO STOP SENDING ALL AT ONCE!
IT'S SPLITTING MY HEAD!
YOU'RE NOT GOING TO WIN, YOU KNOW. CHANGE HAPPENS.
YOU CAN ONLY LEAD THEM WHERE THEY WANT TO GO.
WHAT DOES A PIP LIKE YOU KNOW OF LEADERSHIP?
OH--
--MORE THAN YOU MIGHT THINK.
TRY AS HE MIGHT, SURGE CANNOT MAKE HIMSELF DISLIKE THE WOLF CHIEF.
THE TRUTH IS, I LOVE MY FOLK DESPERATELY... WANT ONLY TO PRESERVE THEM FROM HARM.
IF I SHOULD LOSE THEM NOW, I... I...
OVER TIME, I'VE LEARNED IT'S NEVER ABOUT HOW MUCH YOU CAN--OR CAN'T--BEAR!

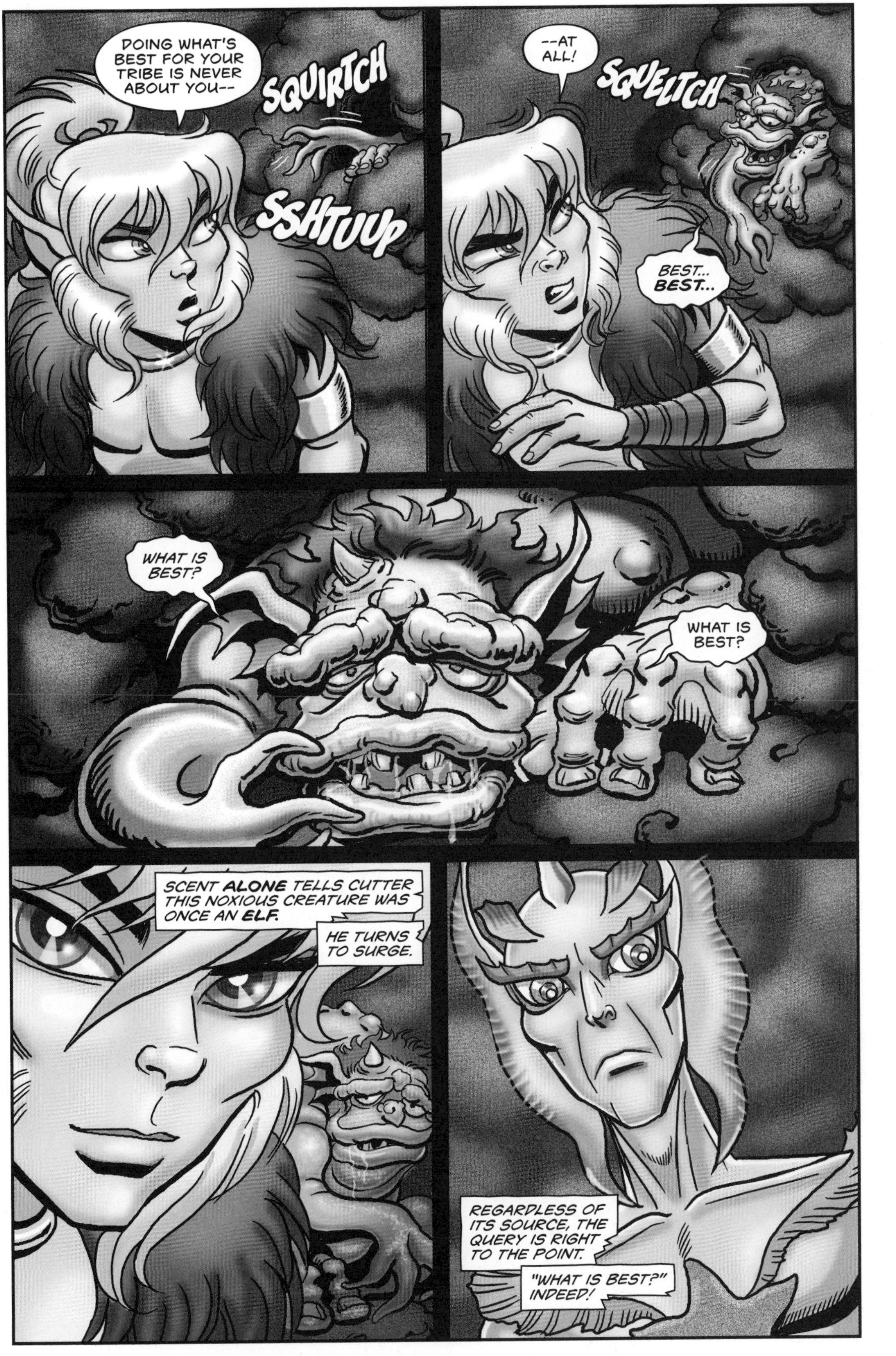
DOING WHAT'S BEST FOR YOUR TRIBE IS NEVER ABOUT YOU--
SQUIRTCH
SSHTUUP
--AT ALL!
SQUELTCH
BEST... BEST...
WHAT IS BEST?
WHAT IS BEST?
SCENT ALONE TELLS CUTTER THIS NOXIOUS CREATURE WAS ONCE AN ELF.
HE TURNS TO SURGE.
REGARDLESS OF ITS SOURCE, THE QUERY IS RIGHT TO THE POINT.
"WHAT IS BEST?" INDEED!

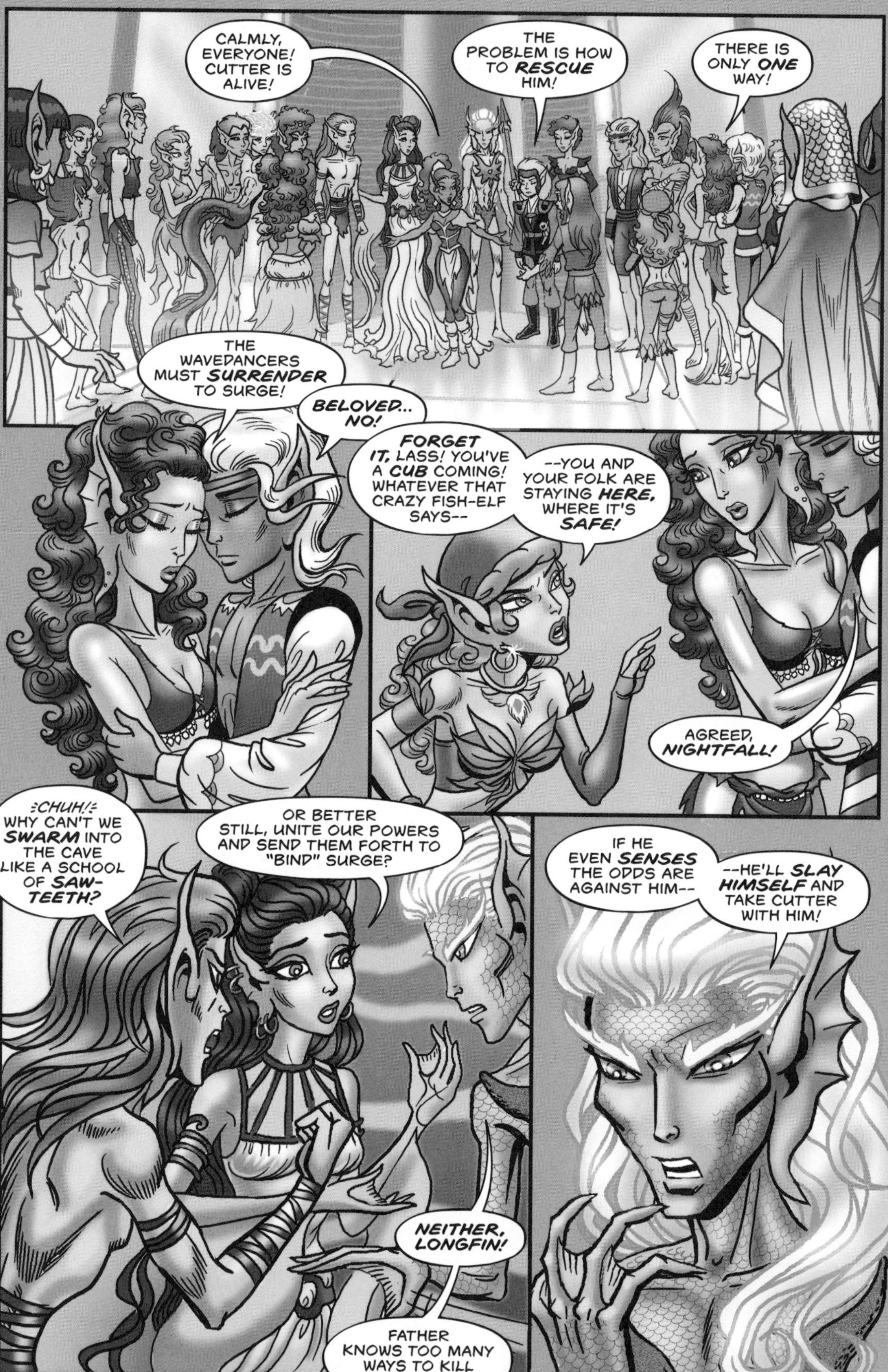
AT THE SAME TIME, IN THE PALACE...
CALMLY, EVERYONE! CUTTER IS ALIVE!
THE PROBLEM IS HOW TO RESCUE HIM!
THERE IS ONLY ONE WAY!
THE WAVEDANCERS MUST SURRENDER TO SURGE!
BELOVED... NO!
FORGET IT, LASS! YOU'VE A CUB COMING! WHATEVER THAT CRAZY FISH-ELF SAYS--
--YOU AND YOUR FOLK ARE STAYING HERE, WHERE IT'S SAFE!
AGREED, NIGHTFALL!
CHUH! WHY CAN'T WE SWARM INTO THE CAVE LIKE A SCHOOL OF SAW-TEETH?
OR BETTER STILL, UNITE OUR POWERS AND SEND THEM FORTH TO "BIND" SURGE?
NEITHER, LONGFIN!
FATHER KNOWS TOO MANY WAYS TO KILL QUICKLY!
IF HE EVEN SENSES THE ODDS ARE AGAINST HIM--
--HE'LL SLAY HIMSELF AND TAKE CUTTER WITH HIM!

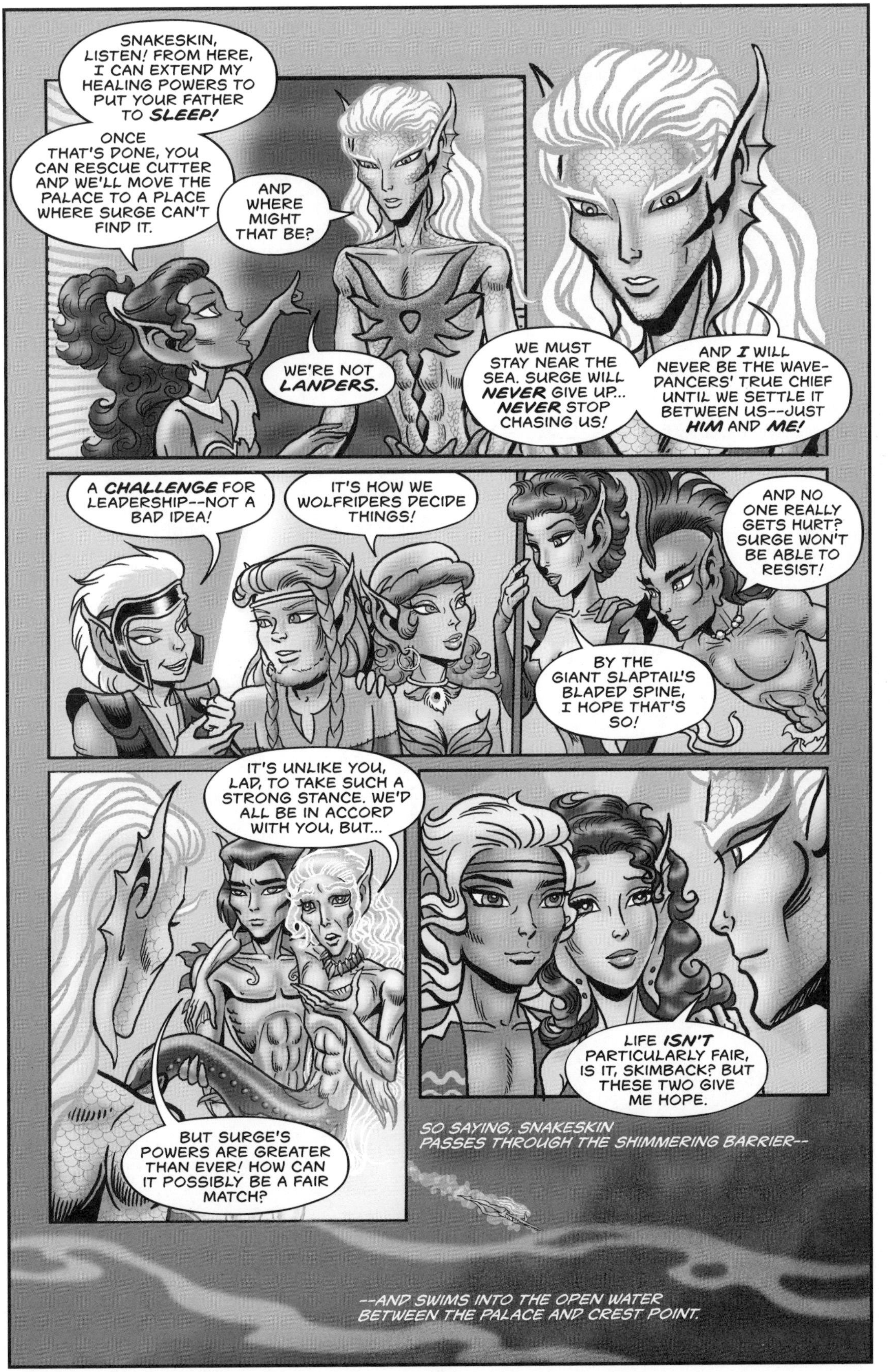
SNAKESKIN, LISTEN! FROM HERE, I CAN EXTEND MY HEALING POWERS TO PUT YOUR FATHER TO SLEEP!
ONCE THAT'S DONE, YOU CAN RESCUE CUTTER AND WE'LL MOVE THE PALACE TO A PLACE WHERE SURGE CAN'T FIND IT.
AND WHERE MIGHT THAT BE?
WE'RE NOT LANDERS.
WE MUST STAY NEAR THE SEA. SURGE WILL NEVER GIVE UP... NEVER STOP CHASING US!
AND I WILL NEVER BE THE WAVE-DANCERS' TRUE CHIEF UNTIL WE SETTLE IT BETWEEN US--JUST HIM AND ME!
A CHALLENGE FOR LEADERSHIP--NOT A BAD IDEA!
IT'S HOW WE WOLFRIDERS DECIDE THINGS!
AND NO ONE REALLY GETS HURT? SURGE WON'T BE ABLE TO RESIST!
BY THE GIANT SLAPTAIL'S BLADED SPINE, I HOPE THAT'S SO!
IT'S UNLIKE YOU, LAD, TO TAKE SUCH A STRONG STANCE. WE'D ALL BE IN ACCORD WITH YOU, BUT...
BUT SURGE'S POWERS ARE GREATER THAN EVER! HOW CAN IT POSSIBLY BE A FAIR MATCH?
LIFE ISN'T PARTICULARLY FAIR, IS IT, SKIMBACK? BUT THESE TWO GIVE ME HOPE.
SO SAYING, SNAKESKIN PASSES THROUGH THE SHIMMERING BARRIER--
--AND SWIMS INTO THE OPEN WATER BETWEEN THE PALACE AND CREST POINT.

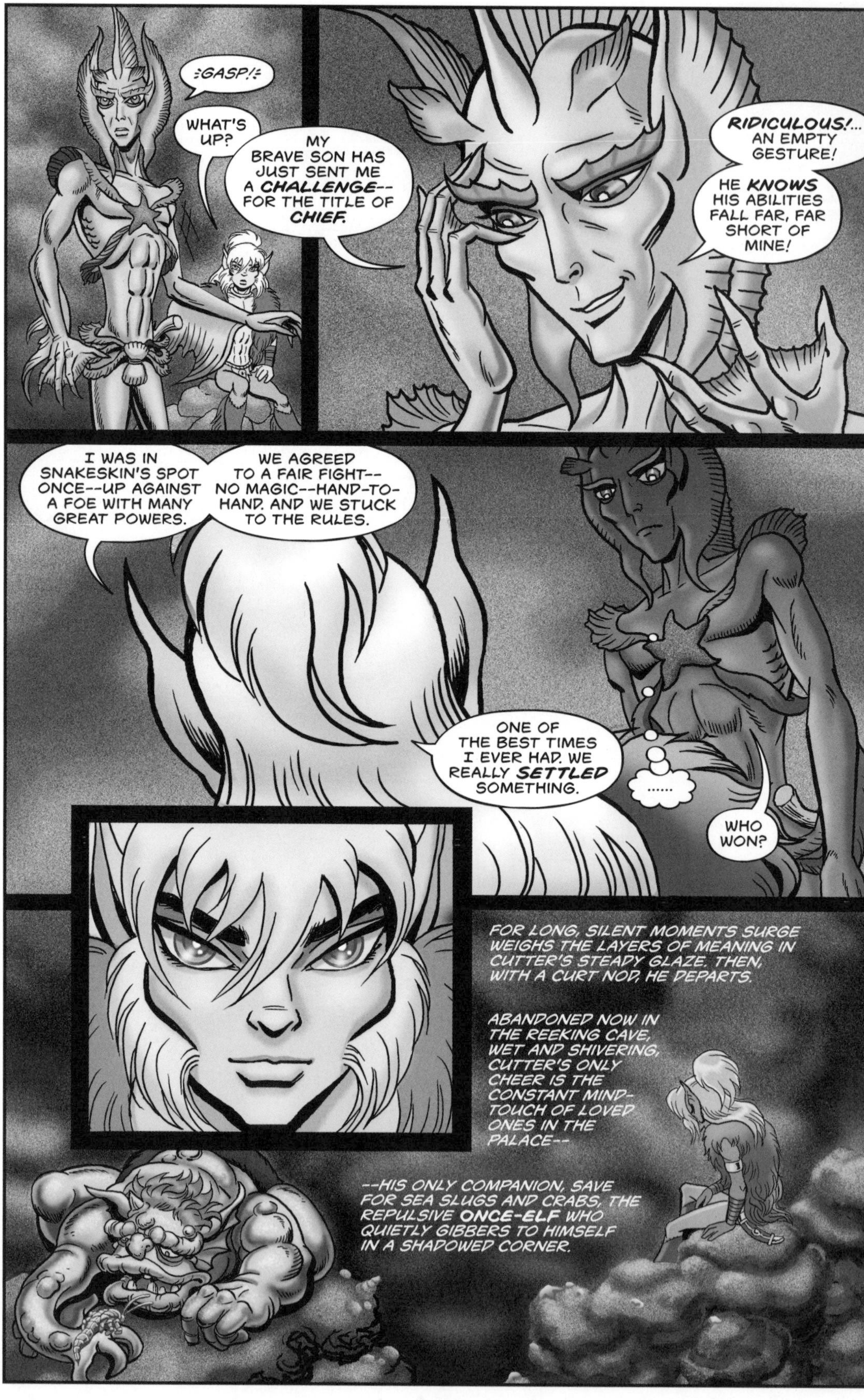

:GASP!:
WHAT'S UP?
MY BRAVE SON HAS JUST SENT ME A CHALLENGE-- FOR THE TITLE OF CHIEF.
RIDICULOUS!... AN EMPTY GESTURE!
HE KNOWS HIS ABILITIES FALL FAR, FAR SHORT OF MINE!
I WAS IN SNAKESKIN'S SPOT ONCE--UP AGAINST A FOE WITH MANY GREAT POWERS.
WE AGREED TO A FAIR FIGHT-- NO MAGIC--HAND-TO-HAND. AND WE STUCK TO THE RULES.
ONE OF THE BEST TIMES I EVER HAD. WE REALLY SETTLED SOMETHING.
......
WHO WON?
FOR LONG, SILENT MOMENTS SURGE WEIGHS THE LAYERS OF MEANING IN CUTTER'S STEADY GLAZE. THEN, WITH A CURT NOD, HE DEPARTS.
ABANDONED NOW IN THE REEKING CAVE, WET AND SHIVERING, CUTTER'S ONLY CHEER IS THE CONSTANT MIND-TOUCH OF LOVED ONES IN THE PALACE--
--HIS ONLY COMPANION, SAVE FOR SEA SLUGS AND CRABS, THE REPULSIVE ONCE-ELF WHO QUIETLY GIBBERS TO HIMSELF IN A SHADOWED CORNER.

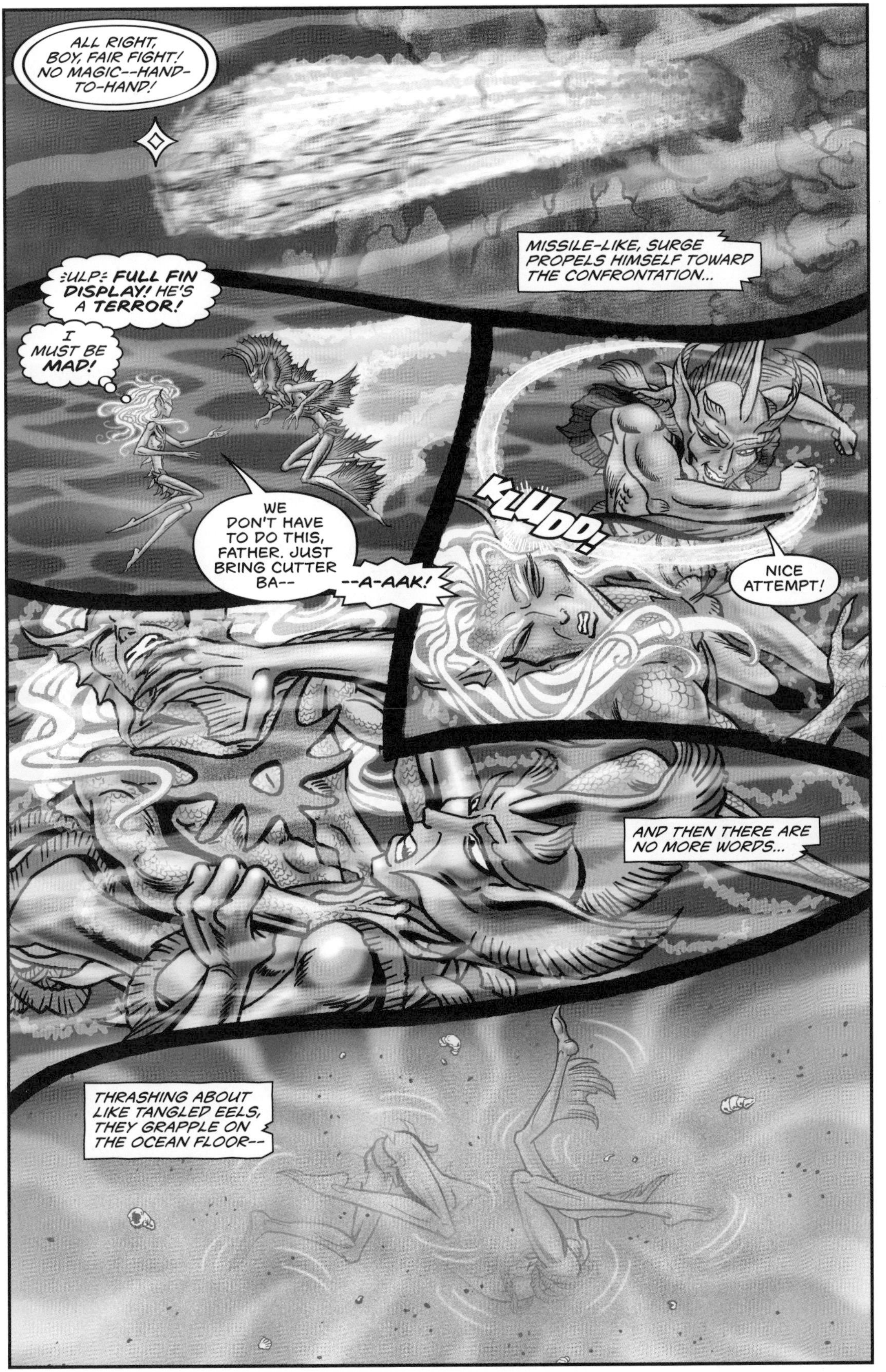
ALL RIGHT, BOY, FAIR FIGHT! NO MAGIC--HAND-TO-HAND!
MISSILE-LIKE, SURGE PROPELS HIMSELF TOWARD THE CONFRONTATION...
ULP FULL FIN DISPLAY! HE'S A TERROR!
I MUST BE MAD!
WE DON'T HAVE TO DO THIS, FATHER. JUST BRING CUTTER BA--
KLUDD!
--A-AAK!
NICE ATTEMPT!
AND THEN THERE ARE NO MORE WORDS...
THRASHING ABOUT LIKE TANGLED EELS, THEY GRAPPLE ON THE OCEAN FLOOR--

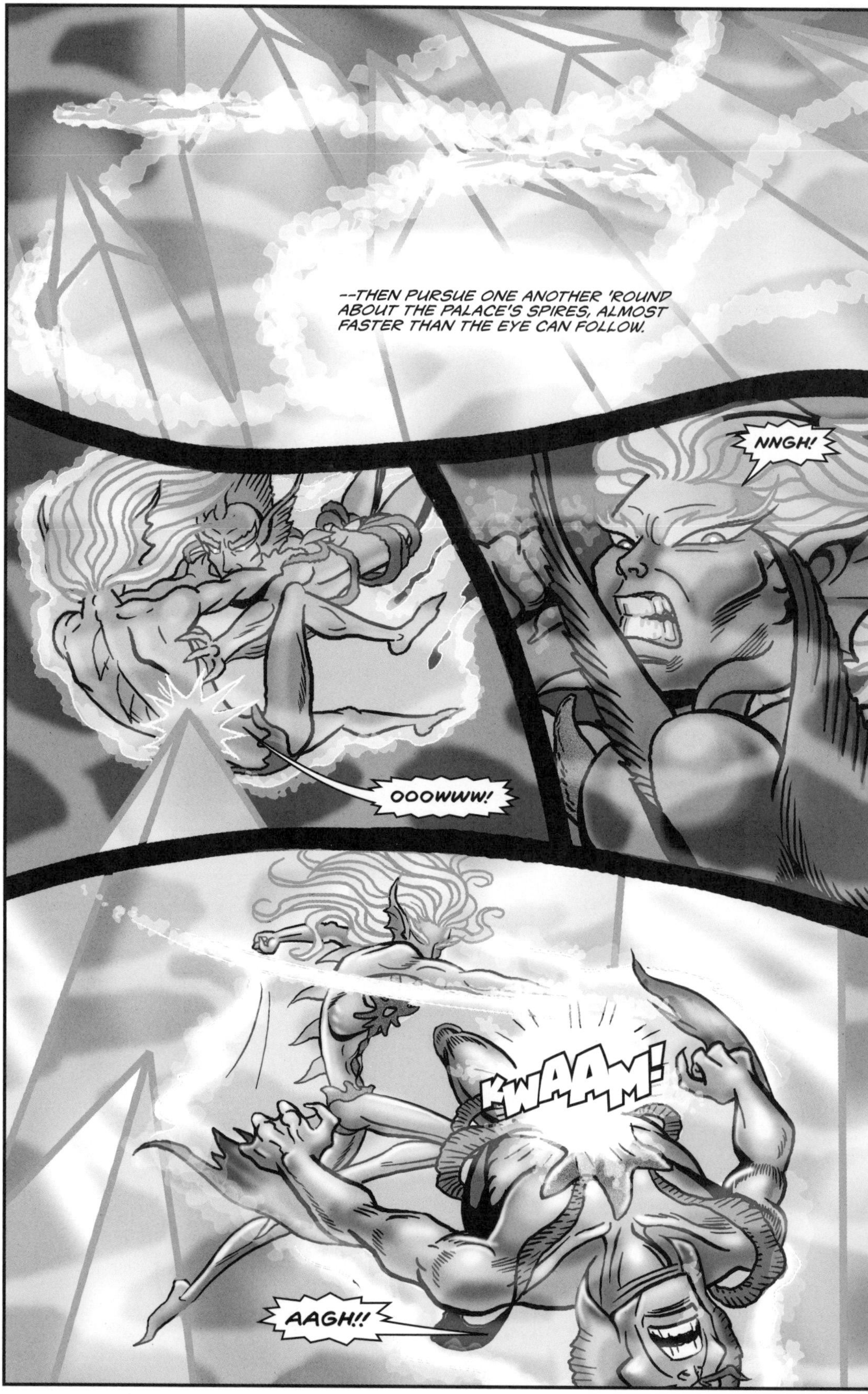
--THEN PURSUE ONE ANOTHER 'ROUND ABOUT THE PALACE'S SPIRES, ALMOST FASTER THAN THE EYE CAN FOLLOW.
NNGH!
OOOWWW!
KWAAM!
AAGH!!

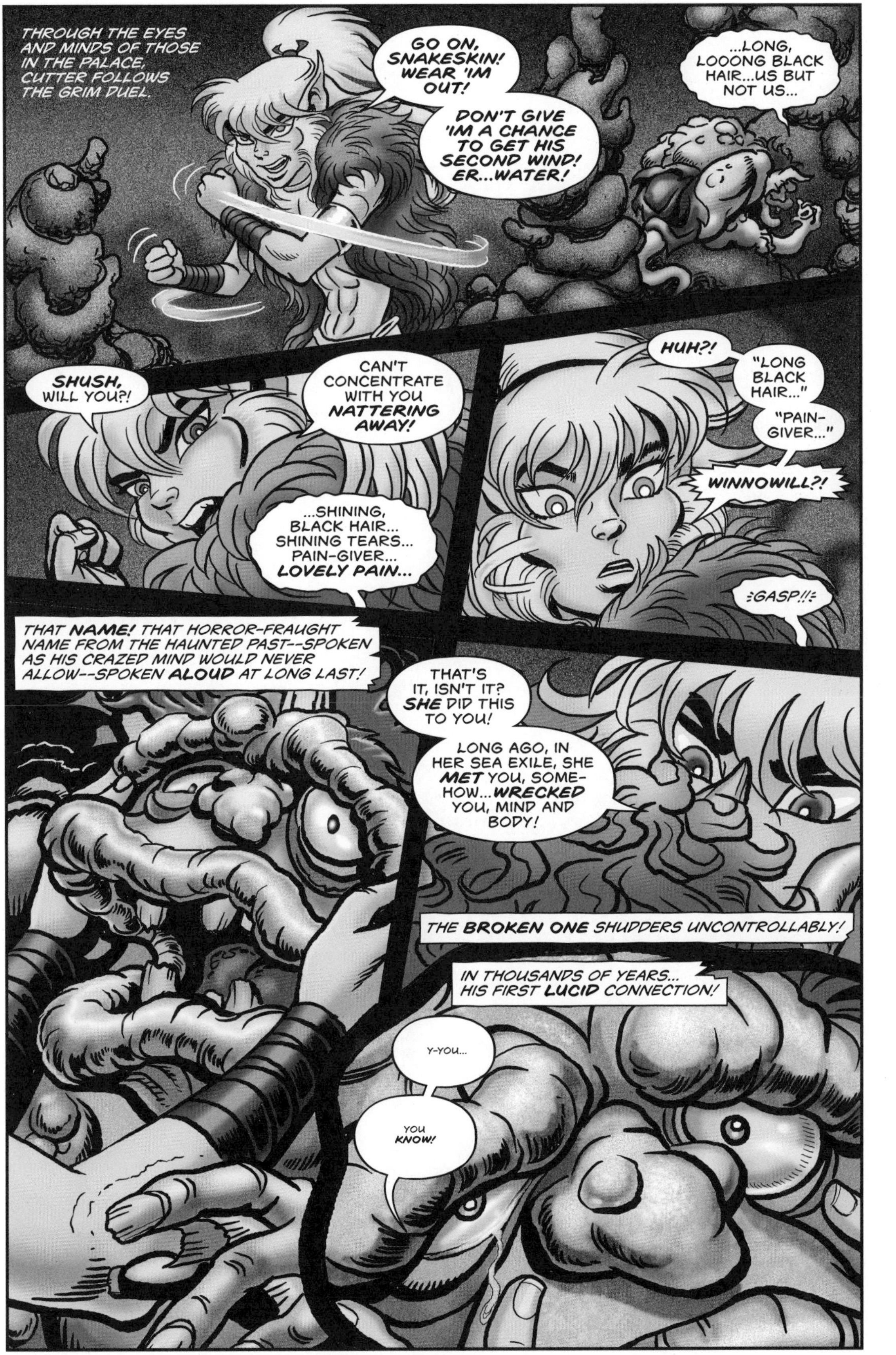
THROUGH THE EYES AND MINDS OF THOSE IN THE PALACE, CUTTER FOLLOWS THE GRIM DUEL.
GO ON, SNAKESKIN! WEAR 'IM OUT!
DON'T GIVE 'IM A CHANCE TO GET HIS SECOND WIND! ER...WATER!
...LONG, LOOONG BLACK HAIR...US BUT NOT US...
SHUSH, WILL YOU?!
CAN'T CONCENTRATE WITH YOU NATTERING AWAY!
...SHINING, BLACK HAIR... SHINING TEARS... PAIN-GIVER... LOVELY PAIN...
HUH?!
"LONG BLACK HAIR..."
"PAIN-GIVER..."
WINNOWILL?!
GASP!!
THAT NAME! THAT HORROR-FRAUGHT NAME FROM THE HAUNTED PAST--SPOKEN AS HIS CRAZED MIND WOULD NEVER ALLOW--SPOKEN ALOUD AT LONG LAST!
THAT'S IT, ISN'T IT? SHE DID THIS TO YOU!
LONG AGO, IN HER SEA EXILE, SHE MET YOU, SOME-HOW...WRECKED YOU, MIND AND BODY!
THE BROKEN ONE SHUDDERS UNCONTROLLABLY!
IN THOUSANDS OF YEARS... HIS FIRST LUCID CONNECTION!
Y-YOU...
YOU KNOW!

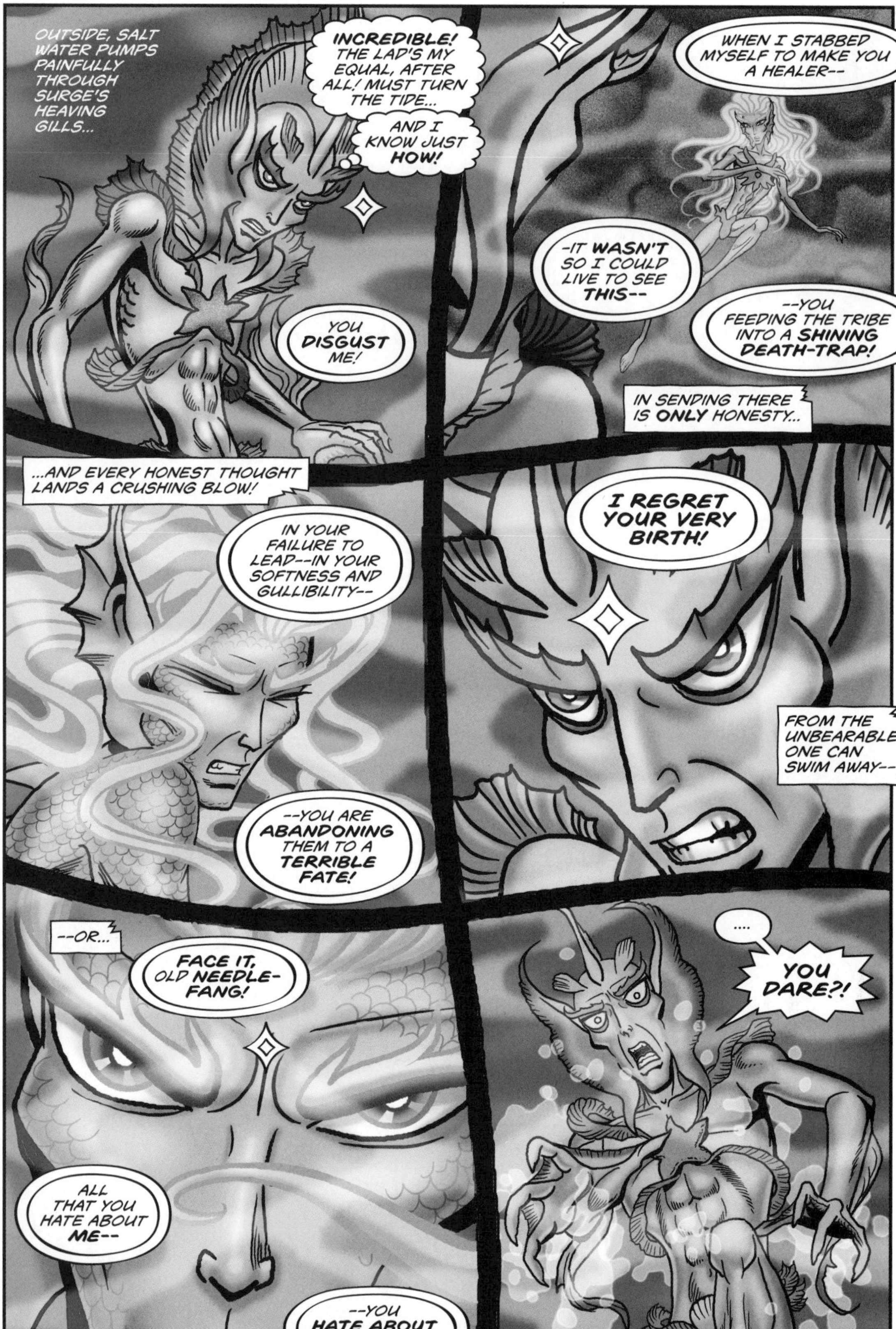
OUTSIDE, SALT WATER PUMPS PAINFULLY THROUGH SURGE'S HEAVING GILLS...
INCREDIBLE! THE LAD'S MY EQUAL, AFTER ALL! MUST TURN THE TIDE...
AND I KNOW JUST HOW!
YOU DISGUST ME!
WHEN I STABBED MYSELF TO MAKE YOU A HEALER--
-IT WASN'T SO I COULD LIVE TO SEE THIS--
--YOU FEEDING THE TRIBE INTO A SHINING DEATH-TRAP!
IN SENDING THERE IS ONLY HONESTY...
...AND EVERY HONEST THOUGHT LANDS A CRUSHING BLOW!
IN YOUR FAILURE TO LEAD--IN YOUR SOFTNESS AND GULLIBILITY--
--YOU ARE ABANDONING THEM TO A TERRIBLE FATE!
I REGRET YOUR VERY BIRTH!
FROM THE UNBEARABLE, ONE CAN SWIM AWAY--
--OR...
FACE IT, OLD NEEDLE-FANG!
ALL THAT YOU HATE ABOUT ME--
--YOU HATE ABOUT YOURSELF!
....
YOU DARE?!

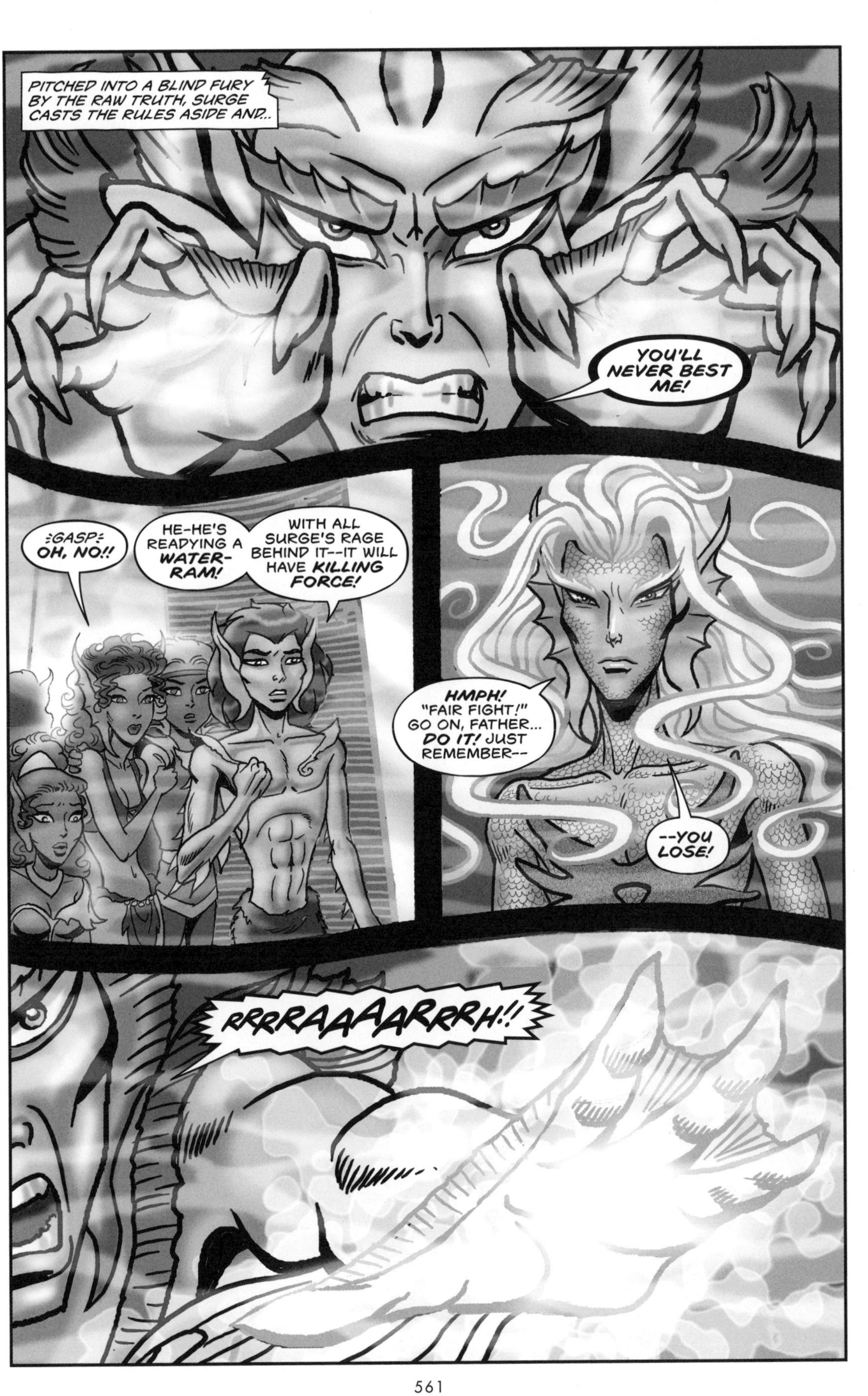
PITCHED INTO A BLIND FURY BY THE RAW TRUTH, SURGE CASTS THE RULES ASIDE AND..
YOU'LL NEVER BEST ME!
≑GASP≑ OH, NO!!
HE-HE'S READYING A WATER-RAM!
WITH ALL SURGE'S RAGE BEHIND IT--IT WILL HAVE KILLING FORCE!
HMPH! "FAIR FIGHT!" GO ON, FATHER... DO IT! JUST REMEMBER--
--YOU LOSE!
RRRRAAAAARRRRH!!

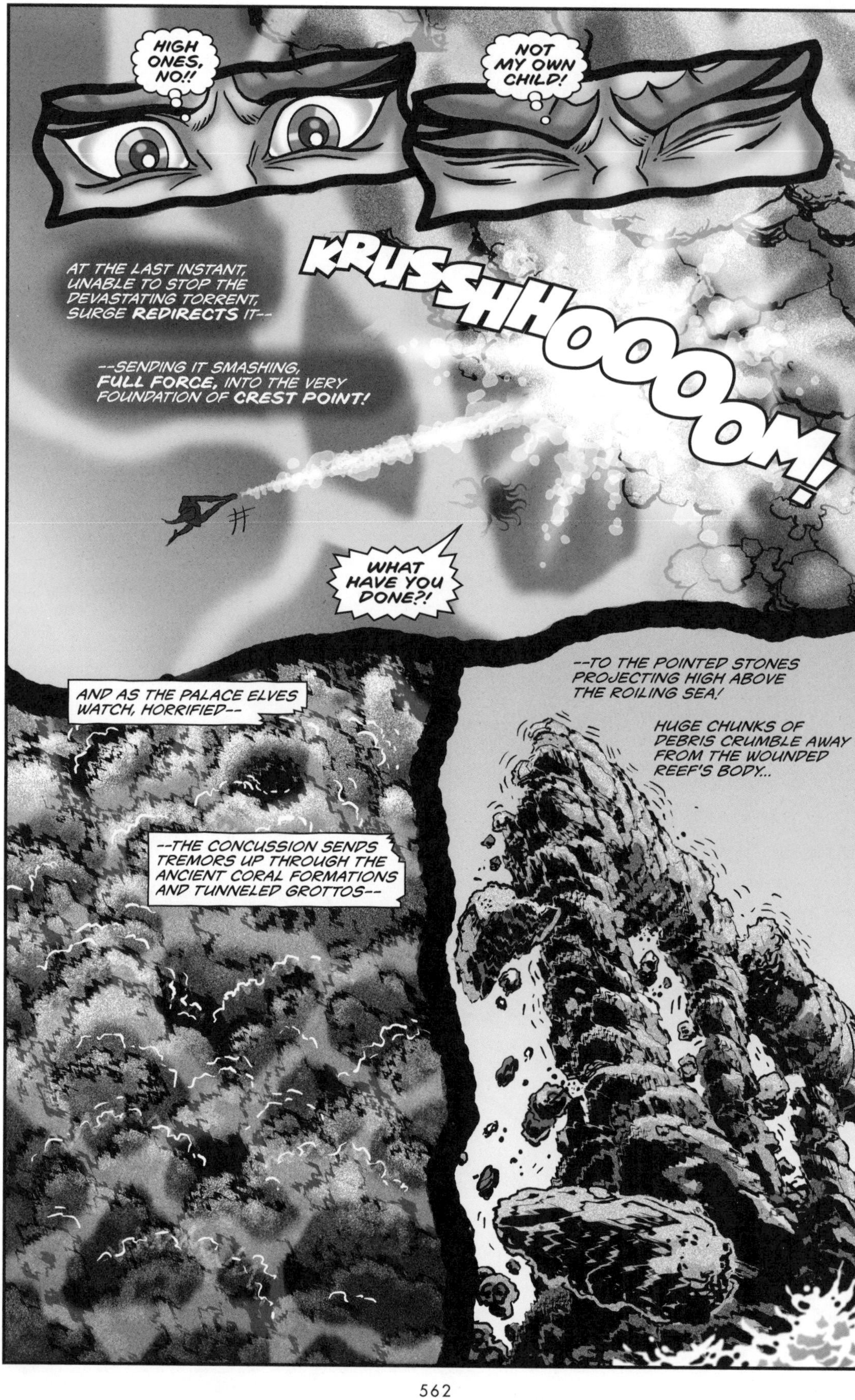
HIGH ONES, NO!!
NOT MY OWN CHILD!
AT THE LAST INSTANT, UNABLE TO STOP THE DEVASTATING TORRENT, SURGE REDIRECTS IT--
KRUSSHHOOOOOM!
--SENDING IT SMASHING, FULL FORCE, INTO THE VERY FOUNDATION OF CREST POINT!
WHAT HAVE YOU DONE?!
AND AS THE PALACE ELVES WATCH, HORRIFIED--
--THE CONCUSSION SENDS TREMORS UP THROUGH THE ANCIENT CORAL FORMATIONS AND TUNNELED GROTTOS--
--TO THE POINTED STONES PROJECTING HIGH ABOVE THE ROILING SEA!
HUGE CHUNKS OF DEBRIS CRUMBLE AWAY FROM THE WOUNDED REEF'S BODY...

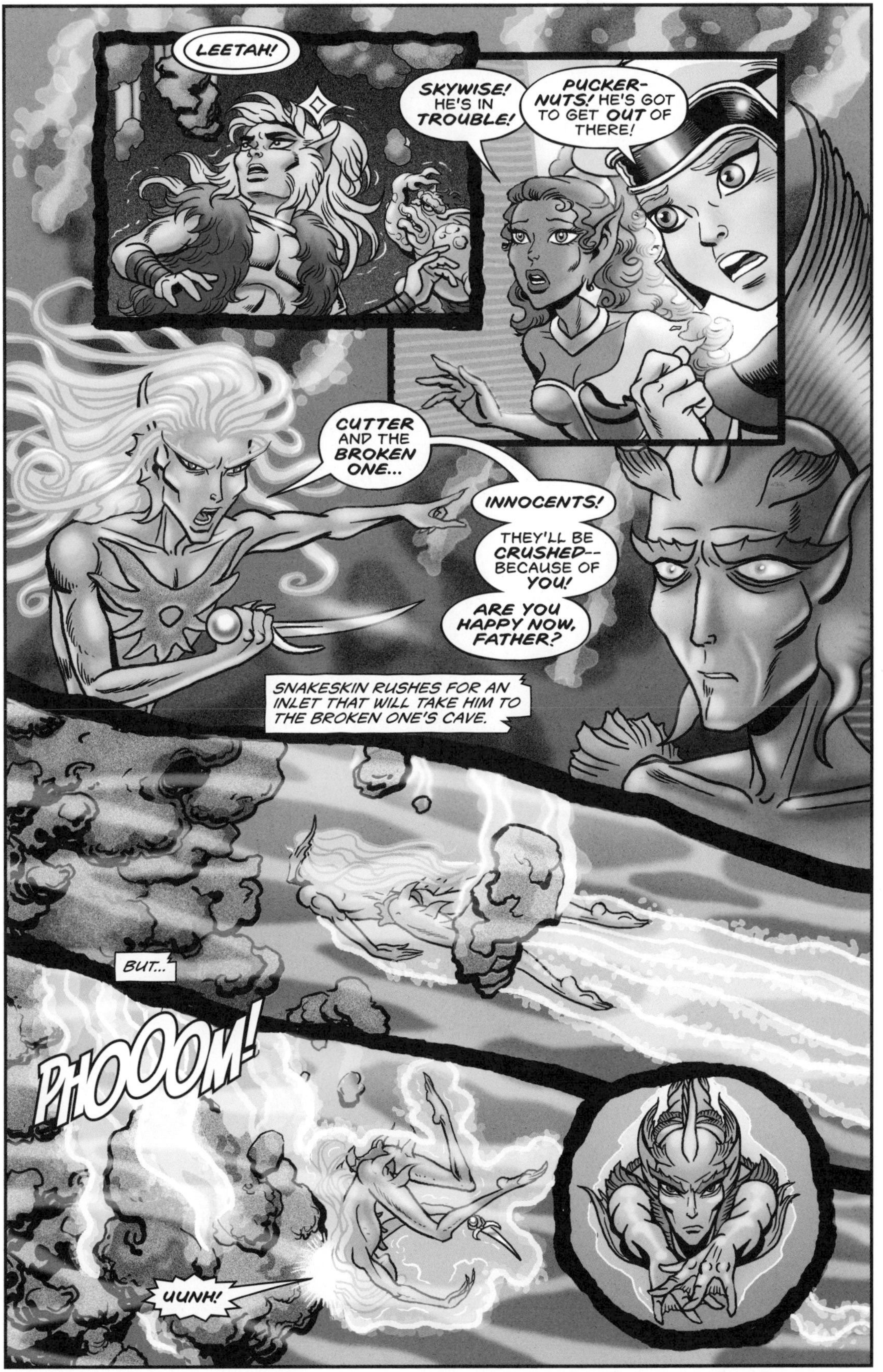
LEETAH!
SKYWISE! HE'S IN TROUBLE!
PUCKER-NUTS! HE'S GOT TO GET OUT OF THERE!
CUTTER AND THE BROKEN ONE...
INNOCENTS!
THEY'LL BE CRUSHED-- BECAUSE OF YOU!
ARE YOU HAPPY NOW, FATHER?
SNAKESKIN RUSHES FOR AN INLET THAT WILL TAKE HIM TO THE BROKEN ONE'S CAVE.
BUT...
PHOOOM!
UUNH!

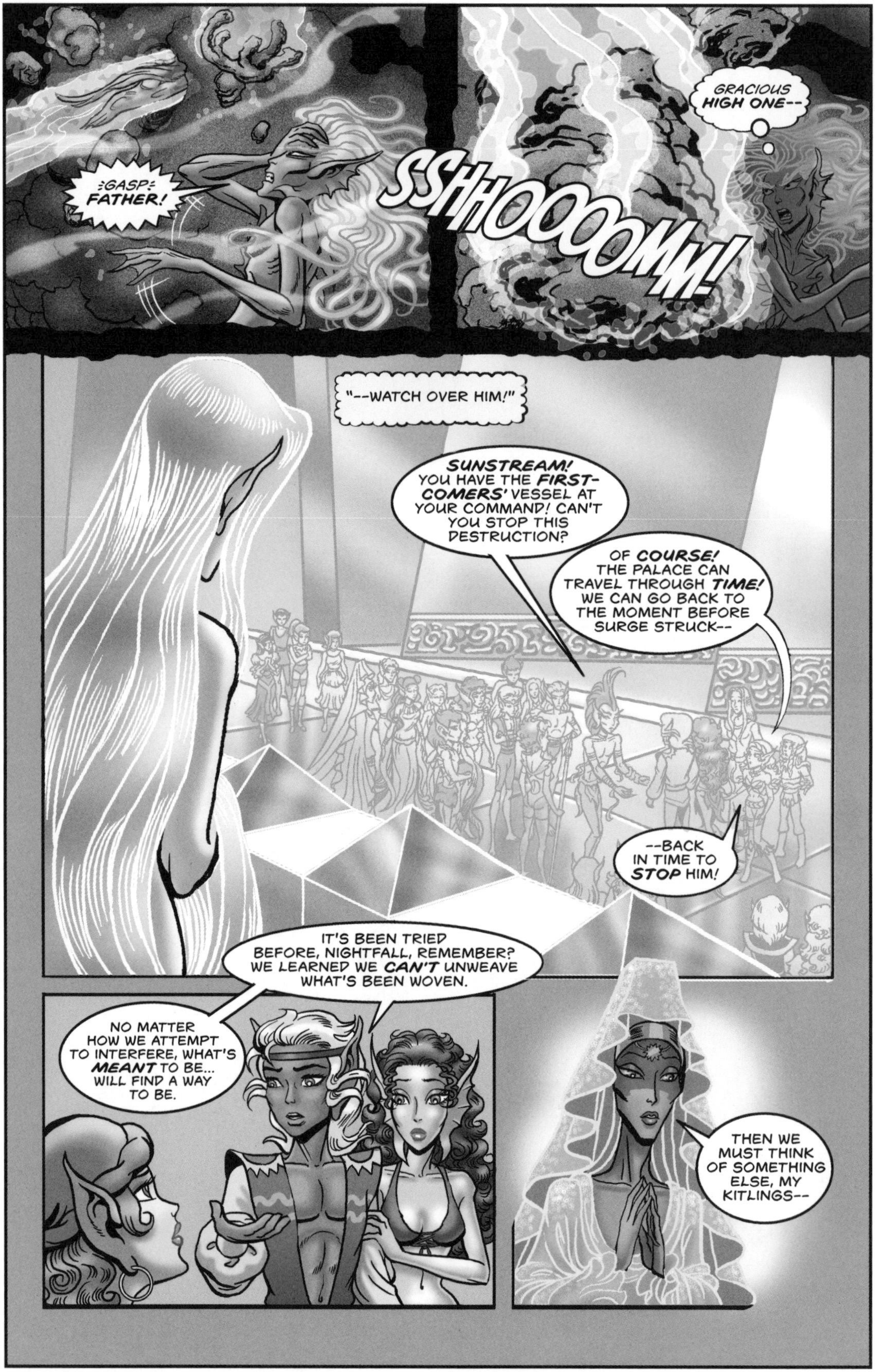

:GASP: FATHER!
SSHHOOOOOMMM!
GRACIOUS HIGH ONE--
"--WATCH OVER HIM!"
SUNSTREAM! YOU HAVE THE FIRST-COMERS' VESSEL AT YOUR COMMAND! CAN'T YOU STOP THIS DESTRUCTION?
OF COURSE! THE PALACE CAN TRAVEL THROUGH TIME! WE CAN GO BACK TO THE MOMENT BEFORE SURGE STRUCK--
--BACK IN TIME TO STOP HIM!
IT'S BEEN TRIED BEFORE, NIGHTFALL, REMEMBER? WE LEARNED WE CAN'T UNWEAVE WHAT'S BEEN WOVEN.
NO MATTER HOW WE ATTEMPT TO INTERFERE, WHAT'S MEANT TO BE... WILL FIND A WAY TO BE.
THEN WE MUST THINK OF SOMETHING ELSE, MY KITLINGS--

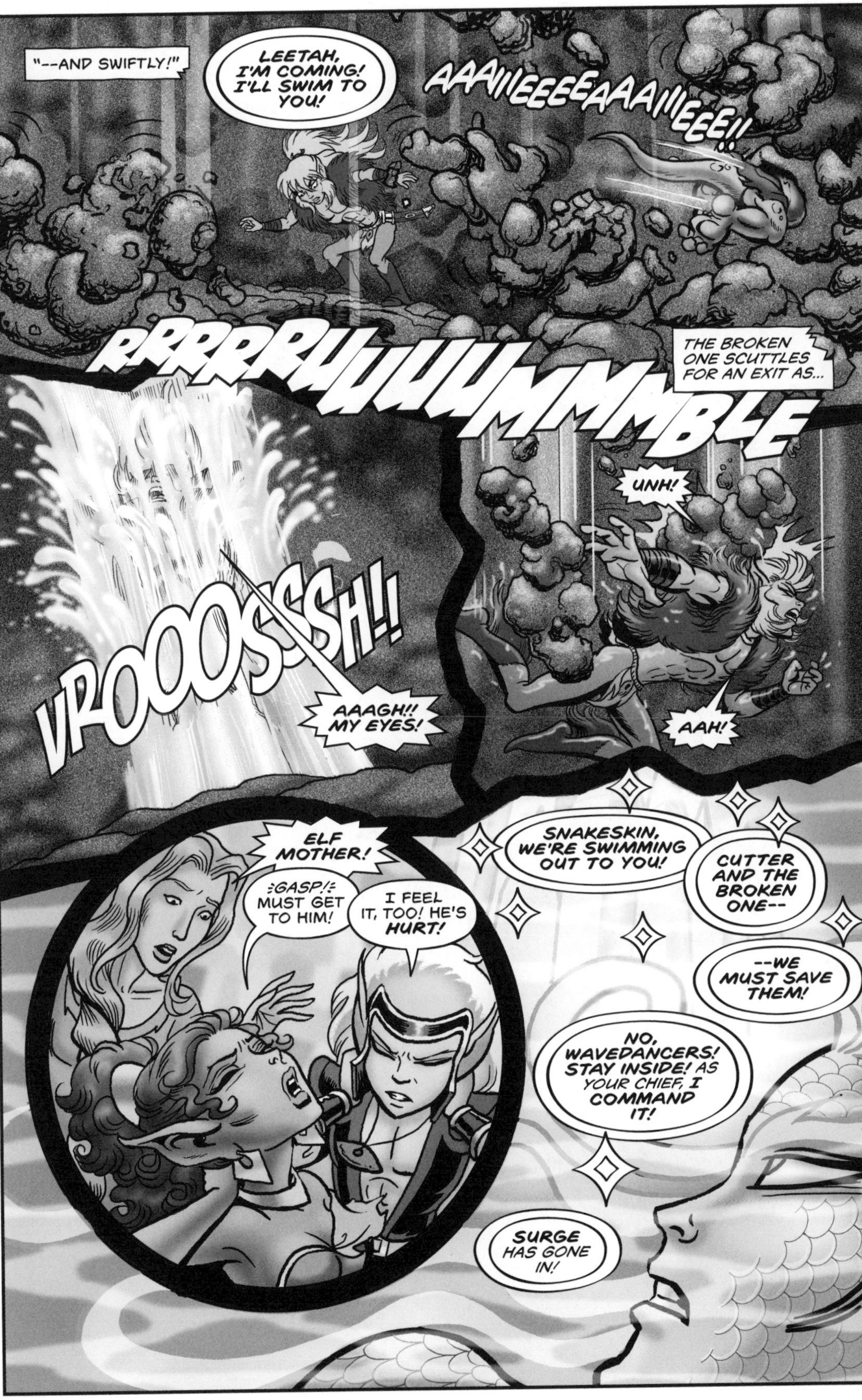

"--AND SWIFTLY!"
LEETAH, I'M COMING! I'LL SWIM TO YOU!
AAAIIIEEEEAAAIIIEEE!!
THE BROKEN ONE SCUTTLES FOR AN EXIT AS...
RRRRRUUUUUMMMMBLE
UNH!
VROOOSSSH!!
AAAGH!! MY EYES!
AAH!
ELF MOTHER!
:GASP!: MUST GET TO HIM!
I FEEL IT, TOO! HE'S HURT!
SNAKESKIN, WE'RE SWIMMING OUT TO YOU!
CUTTER AND THE BROKEN ONE--
--WE MUST SAVE THEM!
NO, WAVEDANCERS! STAY INSIDE! AS YOUR CHIEF, I COMMAND IT!
SURGE HAS GONE IN!

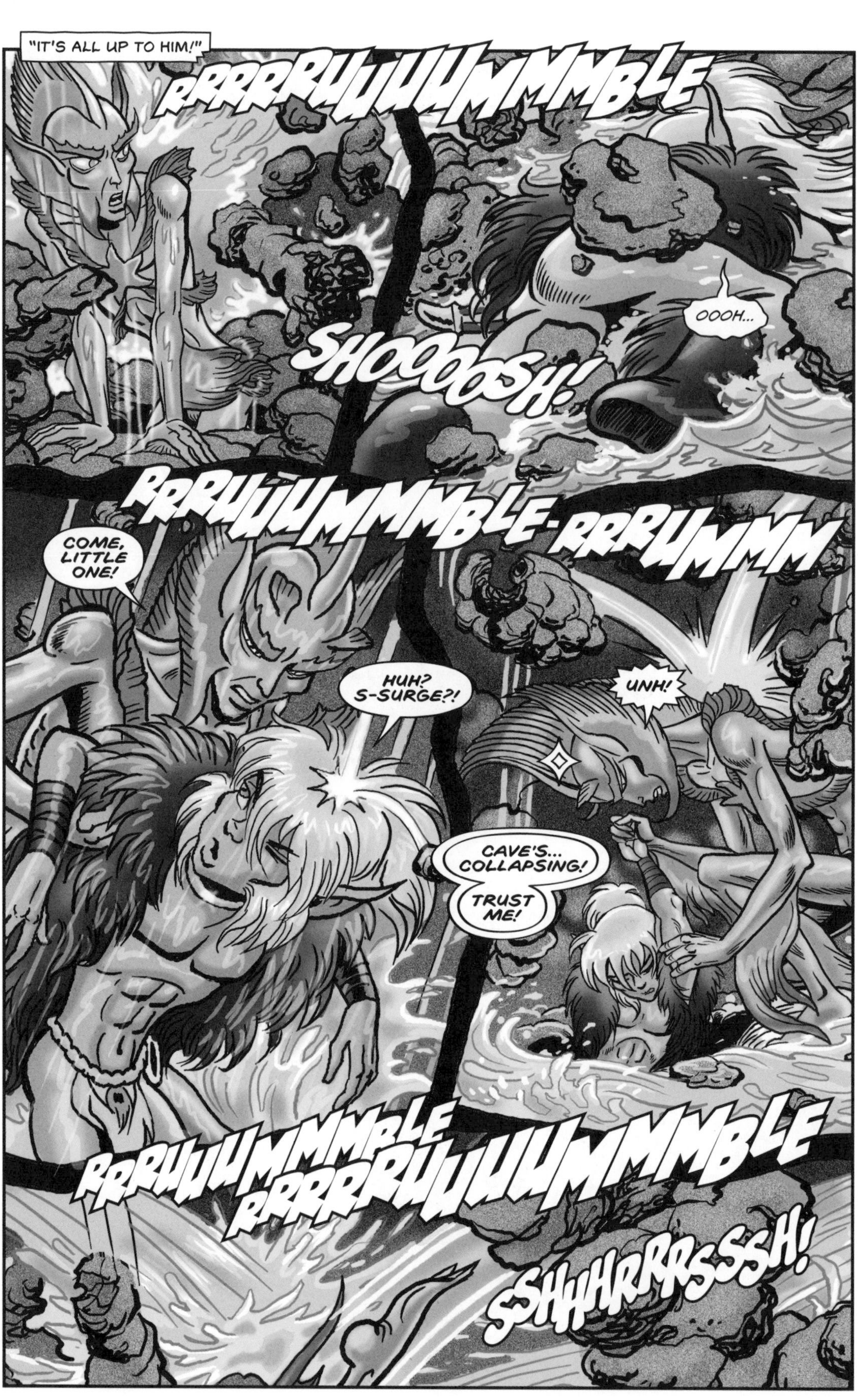
"IT'S ALL UP TO HIM!"
RRRRRUUUUMMMMBLE
SHOOOOOSH!
OOOH...
RRRUUUUMMMMBLE-RRRUMMMM
COME, LITTLE ONE!
HUH? S-SURGE?!
UNH!
CAVE'S... COLLAPSING!
TRUST ME!
RRRUUUMMMMBLE
RRRRRUUUUMMMMBLE
SSHHHRRRRSSSSH!

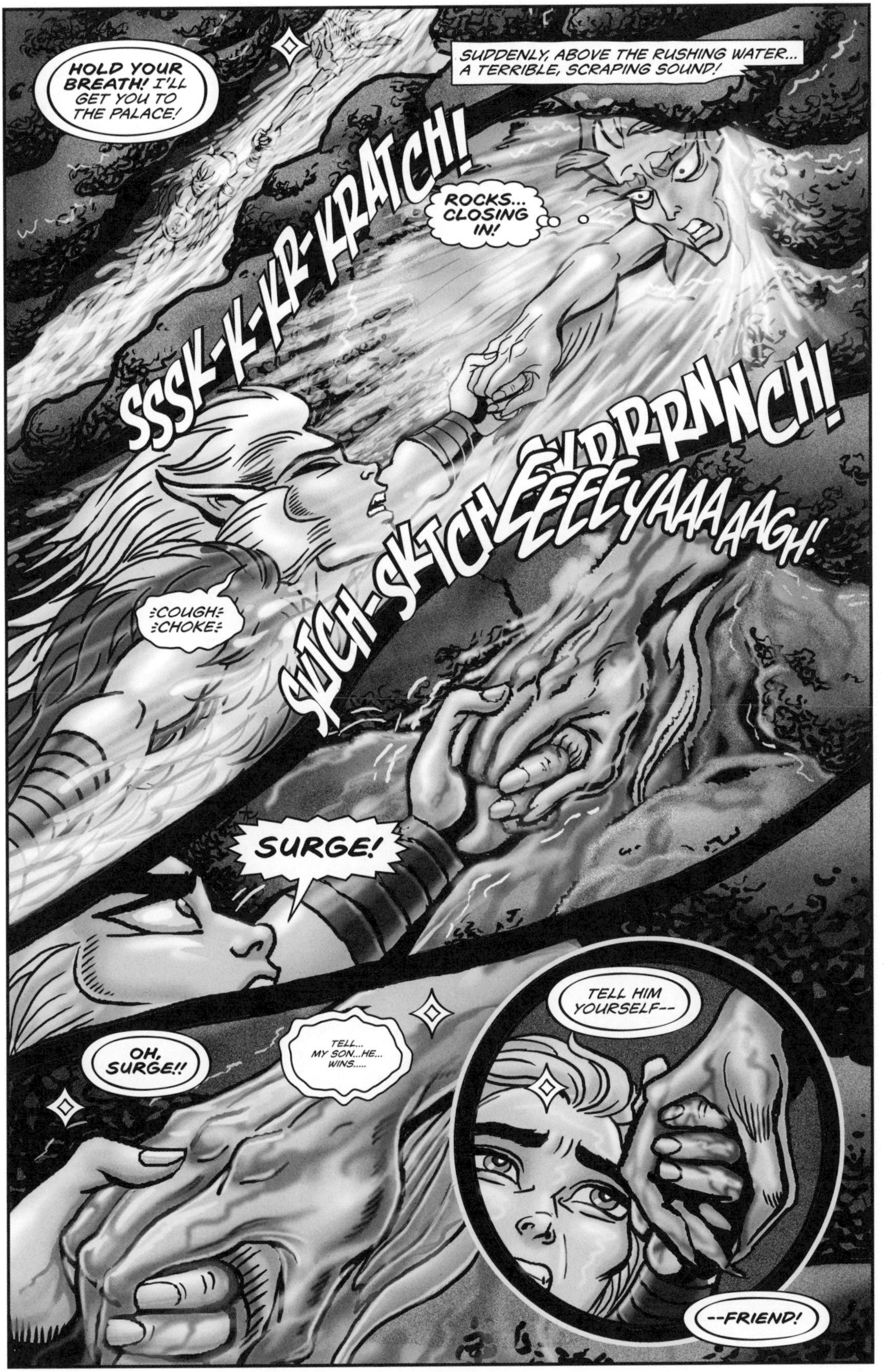
HOLD YOUR BREATH! I'LL GET YOU TO THE PALACE!
SUDDENLY, ABOVE THE RUSHING WATER... A TERRIBLE, SCRAPING SOUND!
SSSK-K-KR-KRATCH!
ROCKS... CLOSING IN!
SPTCH-SKTCH SKRRRNNCH!
EEEEYAAAAAGH!
COUGH CHOKE
SURGE!
OH, SURGE!!
TELL... MY SON...HE... WINS.....
TELL HIM YOURSELF--
--FRIEND!

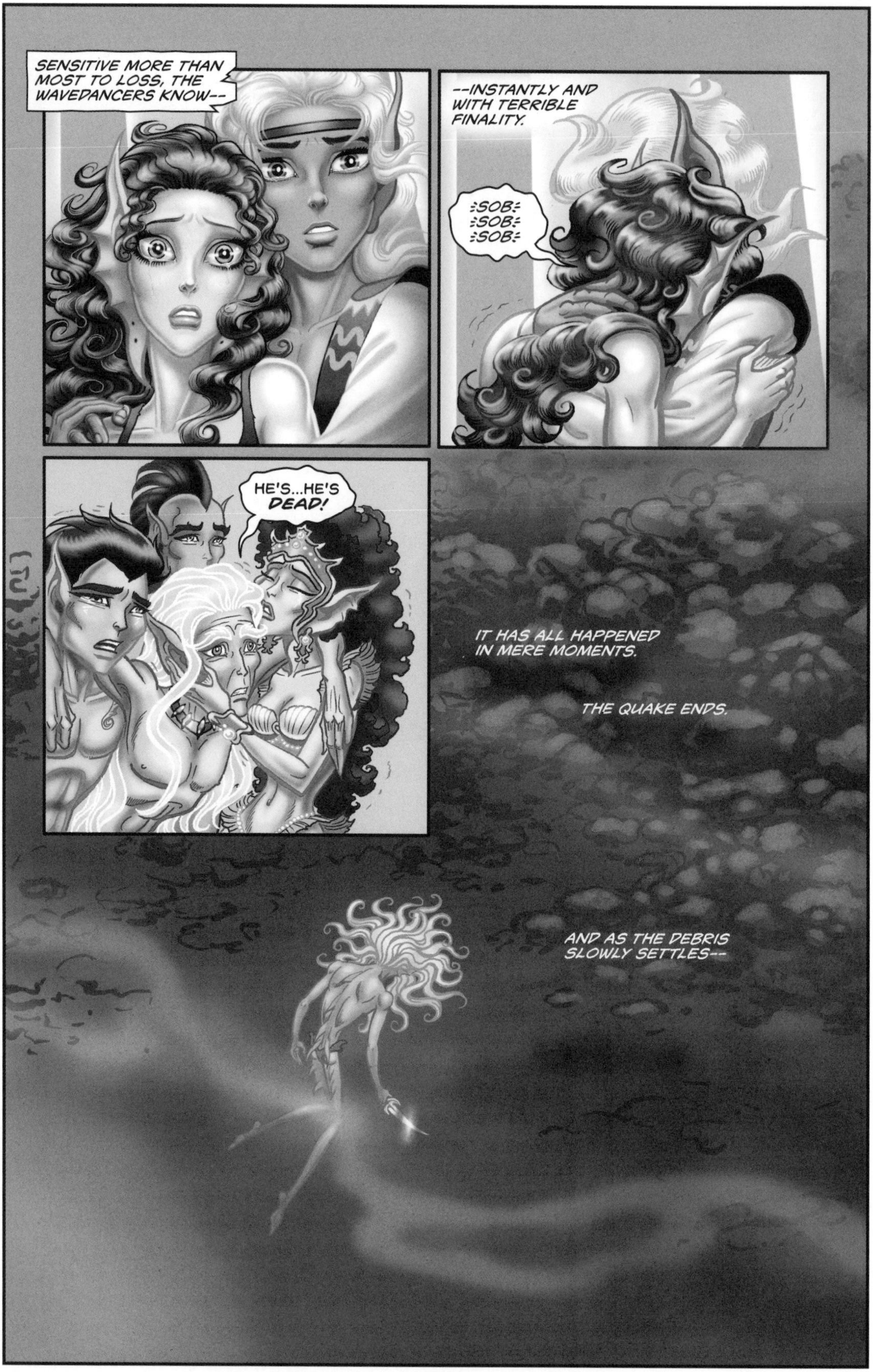
SENSITIVE MORE THAN MOST TO LOSS, THE WAVEDANCERS KNOW--
--INSTANTLY AND WITH TERRIBLE FINALITY.
:SOB: :SOB: :SOB:
HE'S...HE'S DEAD!
IT HAS ALL HAPPENED IN MERE MOMENTS.
THE QUAKE ENDS.
AND AS THE DEBRIS SLOWLY SETTLES--

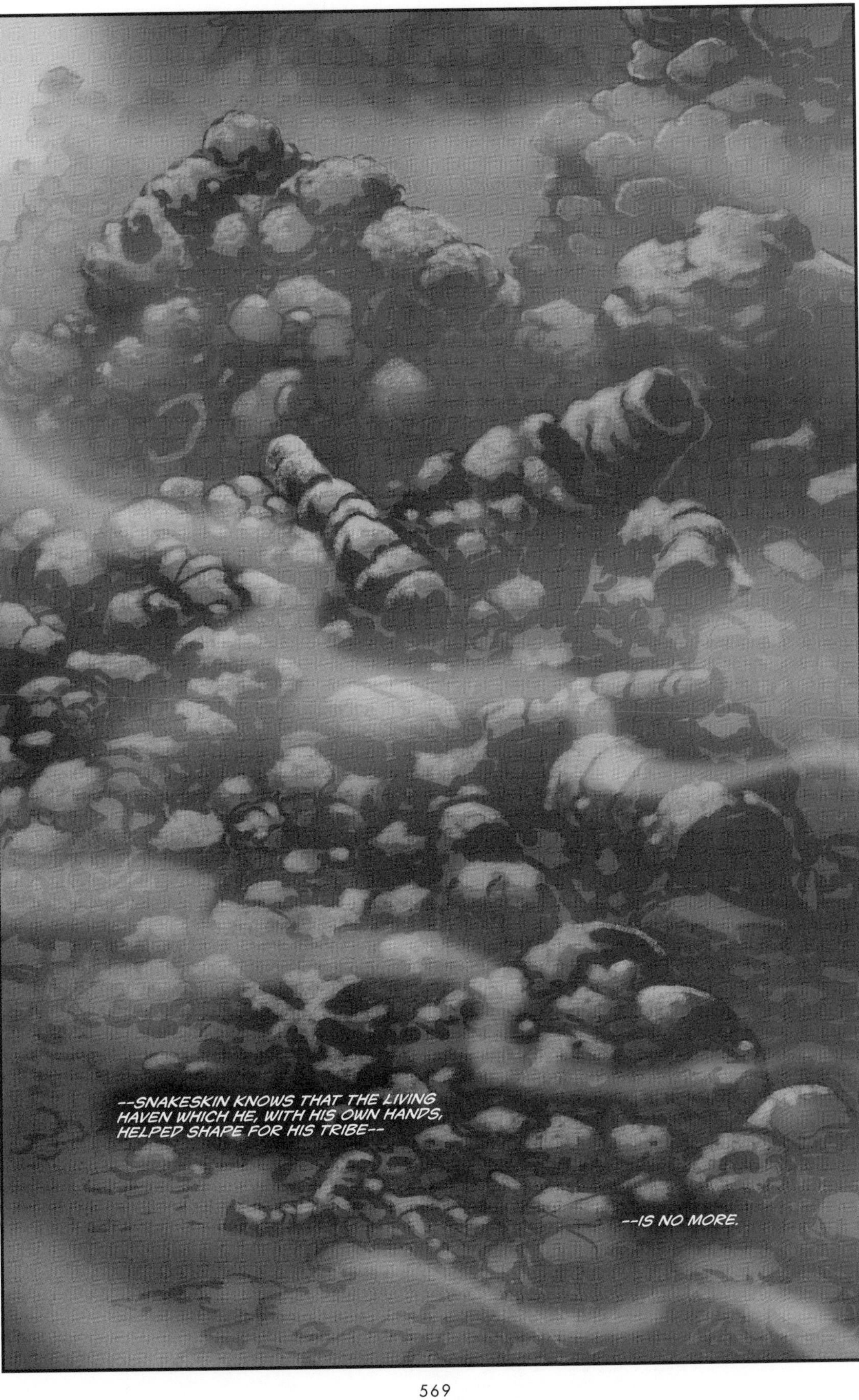
--SNAKESKIN KNOWS THAT THE LIVING HAVEN WHICH HE, WITH HIS OWN HANDS, HELPED SHAPE FOR HIS TRIBE--
--IS NO MORE.

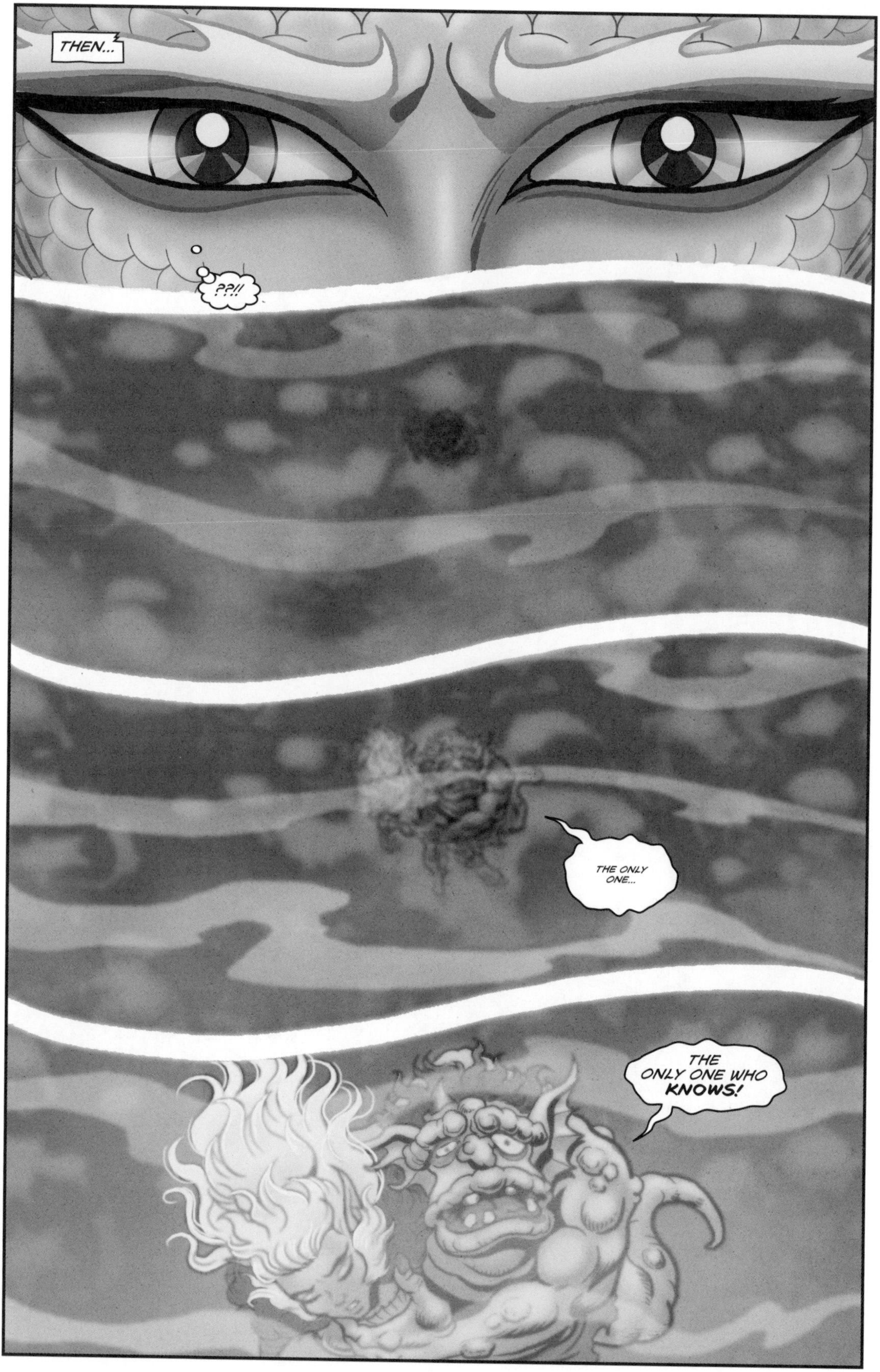
THEN...
??!!
THE ONLY ONE...
THE ONLY ONE WHO KNOWS!

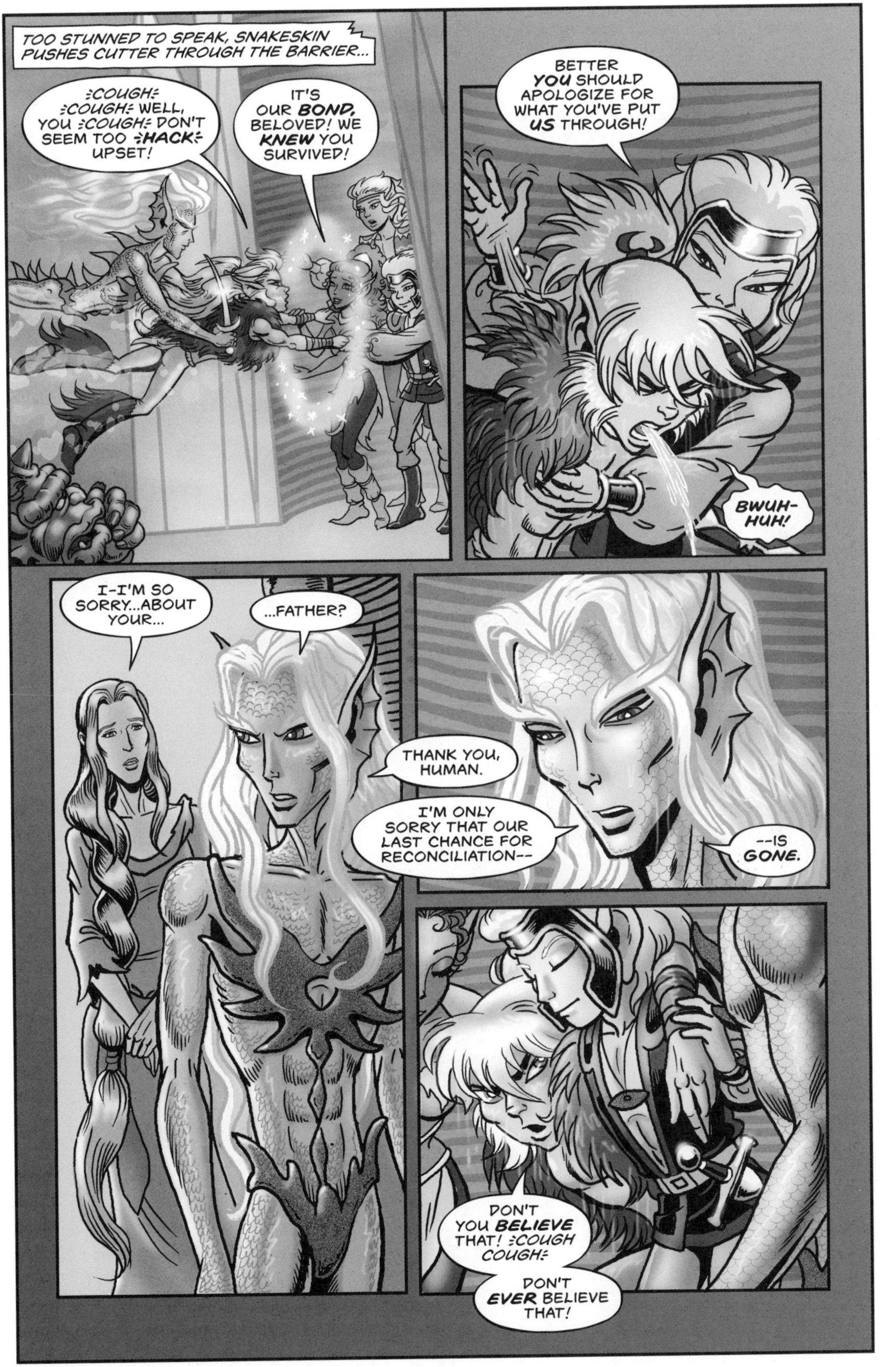
TOO STUNNED TO SPEAK, SNAKESKIN PUSHES CUTTER THROUGH THE BARRIER...
:COUGH: :COUGH: WELL, YOU :COUGH: DON'T SEEM TOO :HACK: UPSET!
IT'S OUR BOND, BELOVED! WE KNEW YOU SURVIVED!
BETTER YOU SHOULD APOLOGIZE FOR WHAT YOU'VE PUT US THROUGH!
BWUH-HUH!
I-I'M SO SORRY...ABOUT YOUR...
...FATHER?
THANK YOU, HUMAN.
I'M ONLY SORRY THAT OUR LAST CHANCE FOR RECONCILIATION--
--IS GONE.
DON'T YOU BELIEVE THAT! :COUGH COUGH:
DON'T EVER BELIEVE THAT!

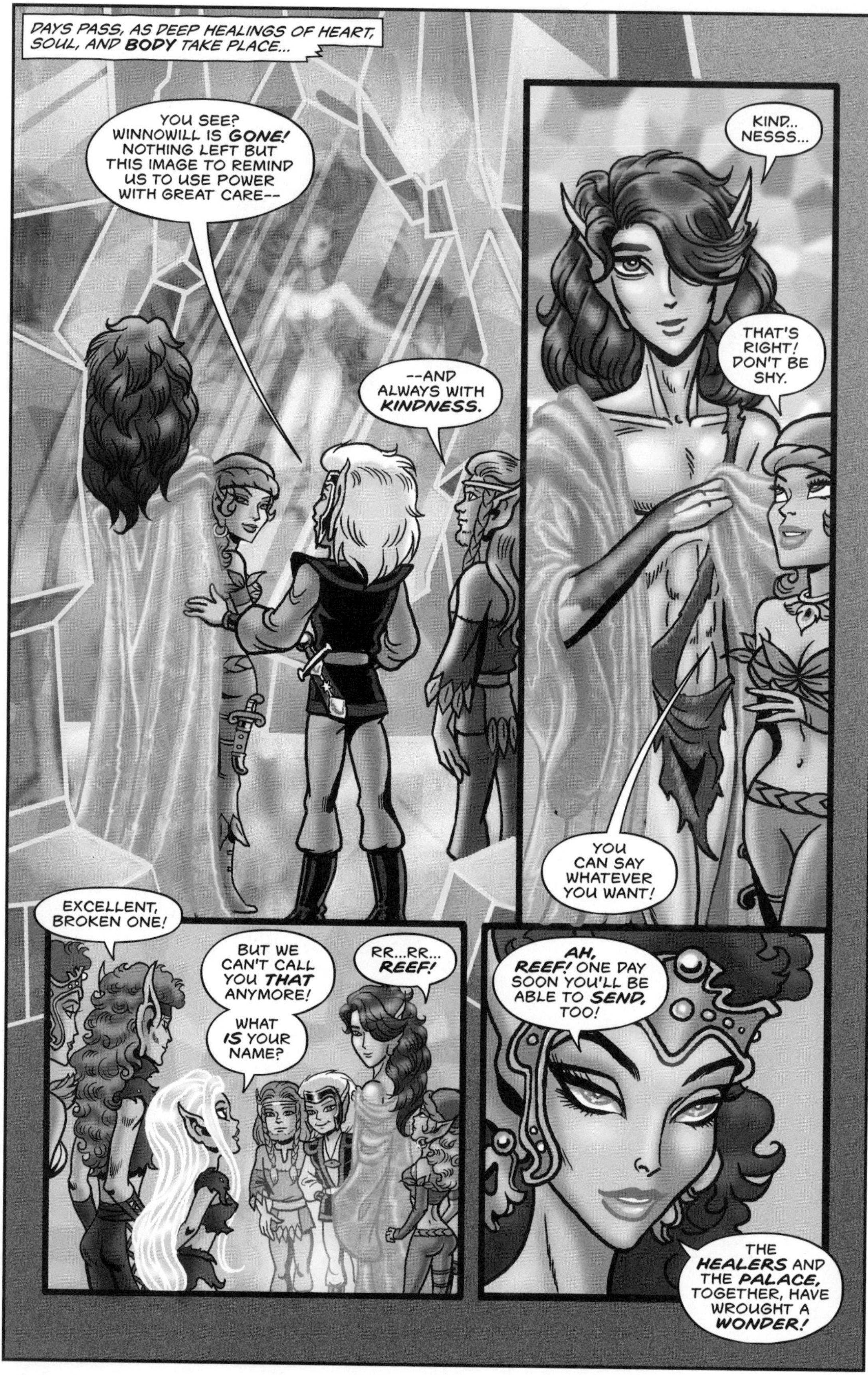
DAYS PASS, AS DEEP HEALINGS OF HEART, SOUL, AND BODY TAKE PLACE...
YOU SEE? WINNOWILL IS GONE! NOTHING LEFT BUT THIS IMAGE TO REMIND US TO USE POWER WITH GREAT CARE--
--AND ALWAYS WITH KINDNESS.
KIND... NESSS...
THAT'S RIGHT! DON'T BE SHY.
YOU CAN SAY WHATEVER YOU WANT!
EXCELLENT, BROKEN ONE!
BUT WE CAN'T CALL YOU THAT ANYMORE!
WHAT IS YOUR NAME?
RR...RR... REEF!
AH, REEF! ONE DAY SOON YOU'LL BE ABLE TO SEND, TOO!
THE HEALERS AND THE PALACE, TOGETHER, HAVE WROUGHT A WONDER!

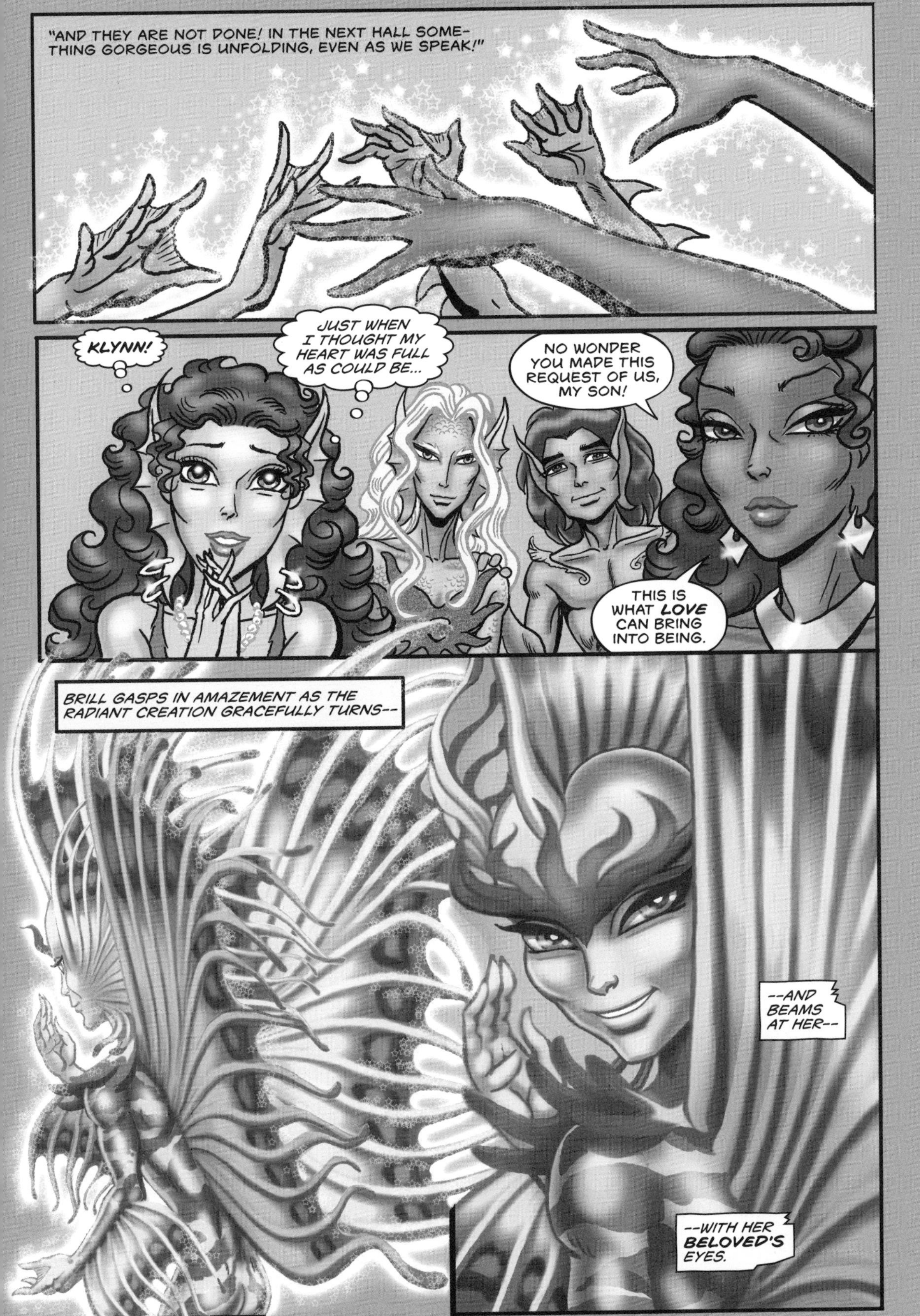
"AND THEY ARE NOT DONE! IN THE NEXT HALL SOMETHING GORGEOUS IS UNFOLDING, EVEN AS WE SPEAK!"
KLYNN!
JUST WHEN I THOUGHT MY HEART WAS FULL AS COULD BE...
NO WONDER YOU MADE THIS REQUEST OF US, MY SON!
THIS IS WHAT LOVE CAN BRING INTO BEING.
BRILL GASPS IN AMAZEMENT AS THE RADIANT CREATION GRACEFULLY TURNS--
--AND BEAMS AT HER--
--WITH HER BELOVED'S EYES.

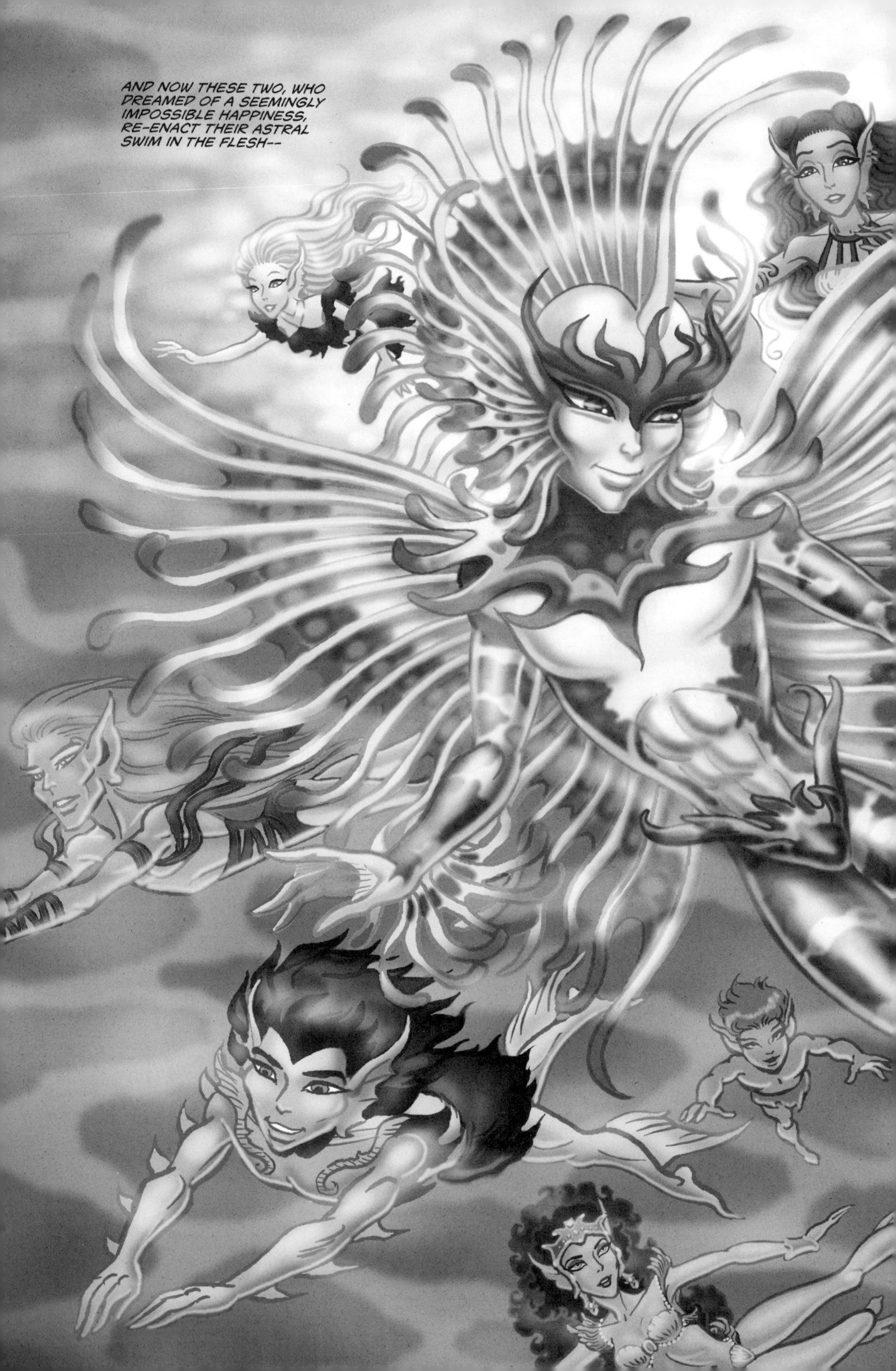
AND NOW THESE TWO, WHO DREAMED OF A SEEMINGLY IMPOSSIBLE HAPPINESS, RE-ENACT THEIR ASTRAL SWIM IN THE FLESH--

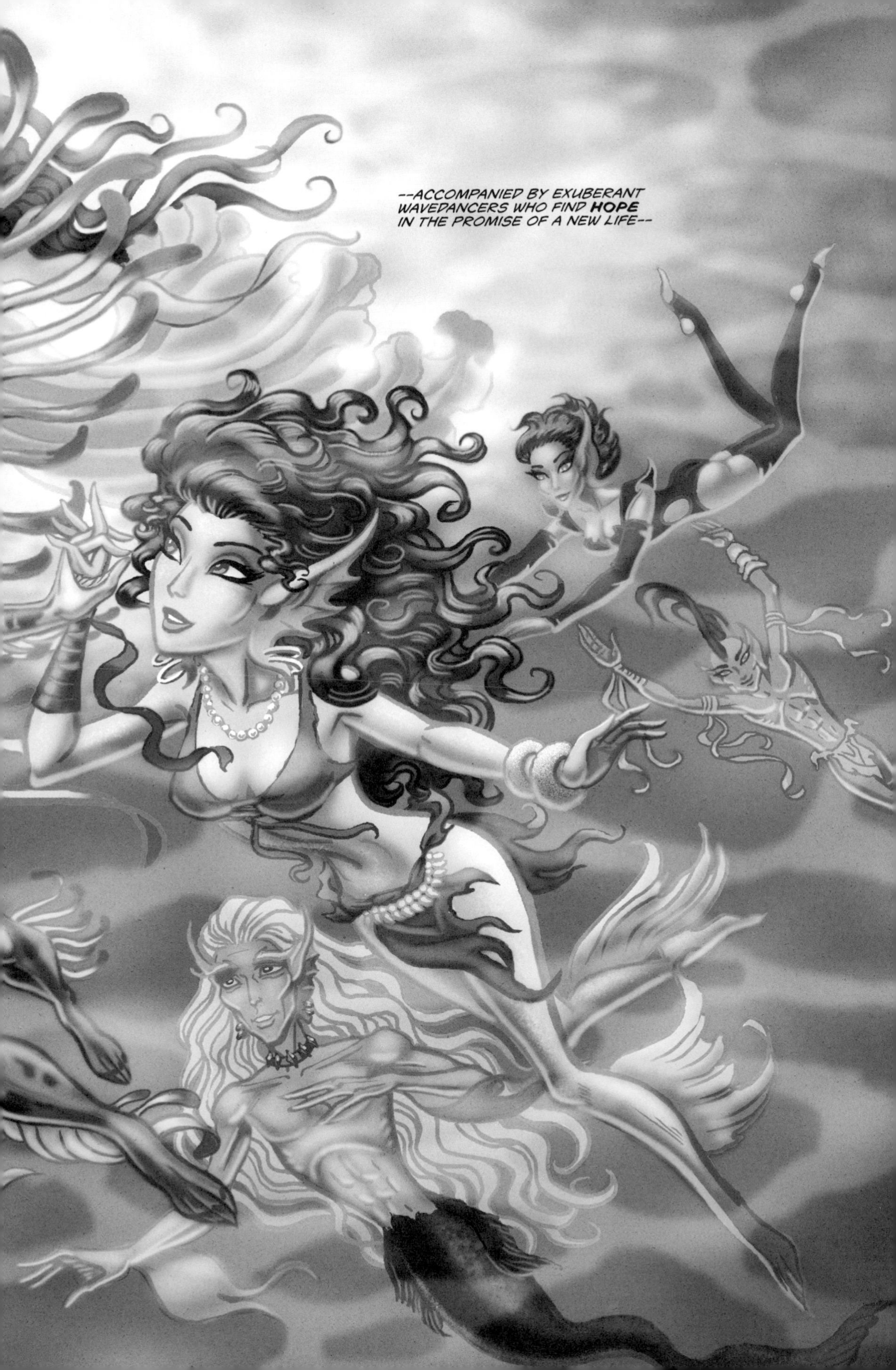
--ACCOMPANIED BY EXUBERANT WAVEDANCERS WHO FIND HOPE IN THE PROMISE OF A NEW LIFE--

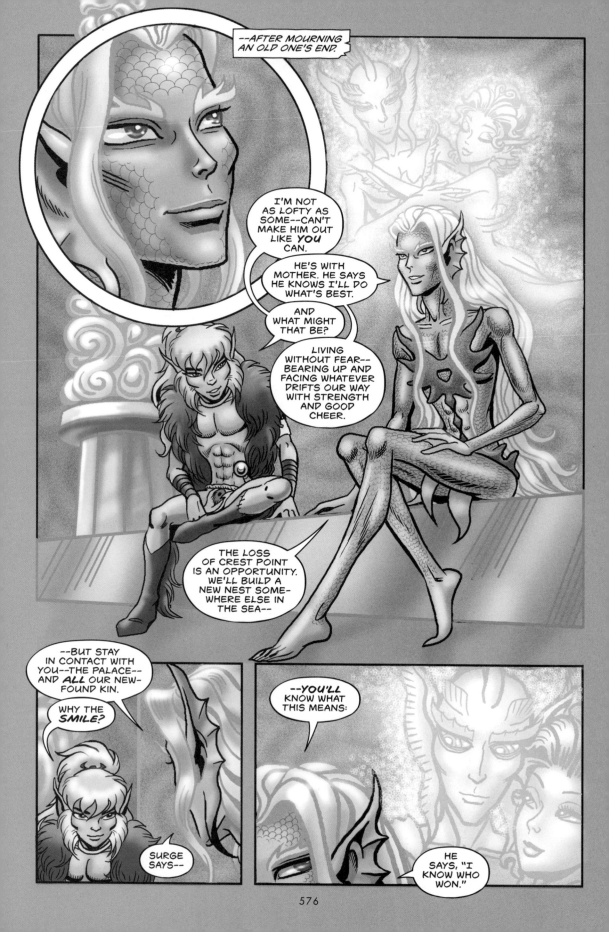

--AFTER MOURNING AN OLD ONE'S END.

I'M NOT AS LOFTY AS SOME--CAN'T MAKE HIM OUT LIKE *YOU* CAN.

HE'S WITH MOTHER. HE SAYS HE KNOWS I'LL DO WHAT'S BEST.

AND WHAT MIGHT THAT BE?

LIVING WITHOUT FEAR-- BEARING UP AND FACING WHATEVER DRIFTS OUR WAY WITH STRENGTH AND GOOD CHEER.

THE LOSS OF CREST POINT IS AN OPPORTUNITY. WE'LL BUILD A NEW NEST SOME- WHERE ELSE IN THE SEA--

--BUT STAY IN CONTACT WITH YOU--THE PALACE-- AND *ALL* OUR NEW- FOUND KIN.

WHY THE *SMILE?*

SURGE SAYS--

--YOU'LL KNOW WHAT THIS MEANS:

HE SAYS, "I KNOW WHO WON."

576

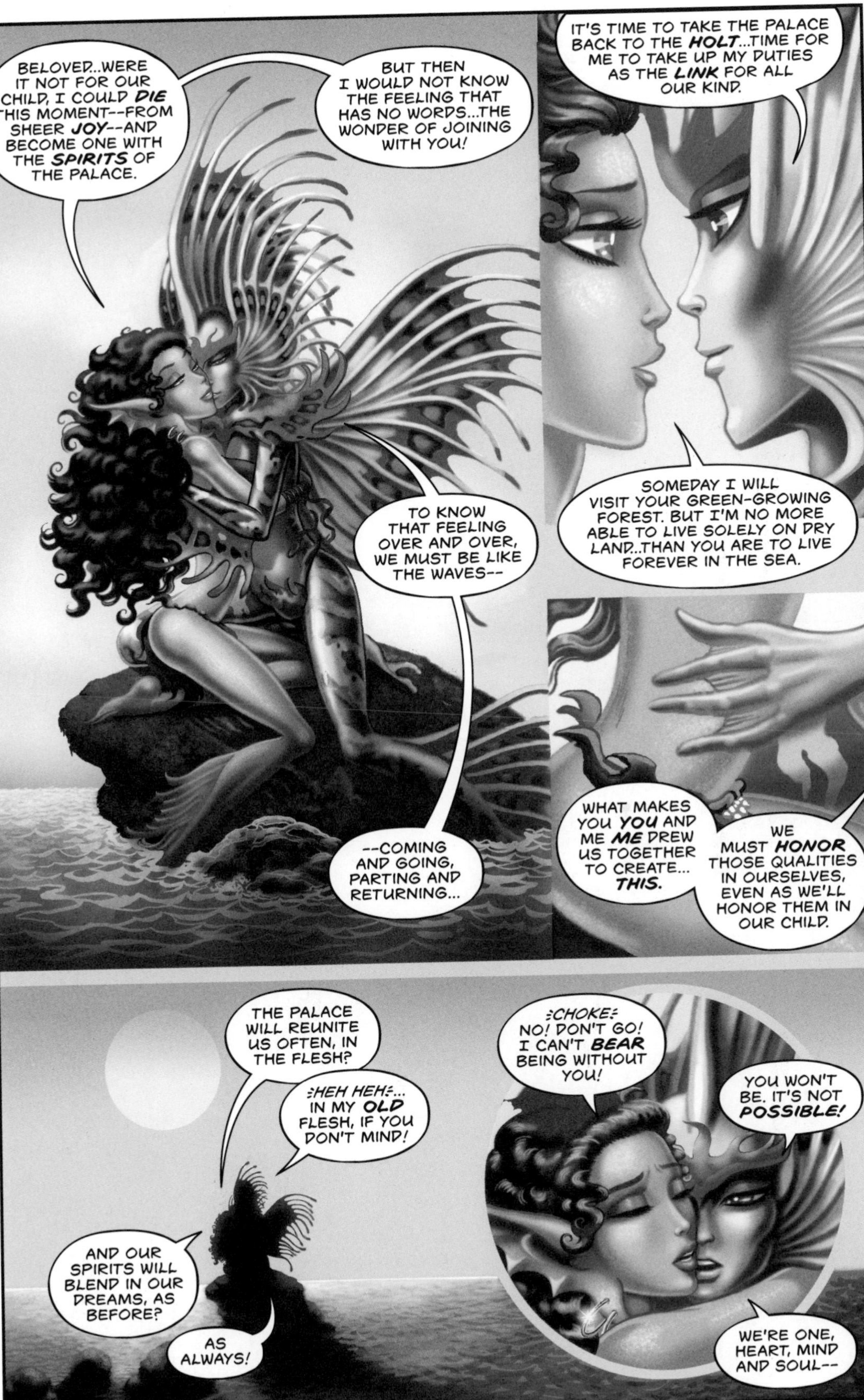
BELOVED...WERE IT NOT FOR OUR CHILD, I COULD DIE THIS MOMENT--FROM SHEER JOY--AND BECOME ONE WITH THE SPIRITS OF THE PALACE.
BUT THEN I WOULD NOT KNOW THE FEELING THAT HAS NO WORDS...THE WONDER OF JOINING WITH YOU!
TO KNOW THAT FEELING OVER AND OVER, WE MUST BE LIKE THE WAVES--
--COMING AND GOING, PARTING AND RETURNING...
IT'S TIME TO TAKE THE PALACE BACK TO THE HOLT...TIME FOR ME TO TAKE UP MY DUTIES AS THE LINK FOR ALL OUR KIND.
SOMEDAY I WILL VISIT YOUR GREEN-GROWING FOREST. BUT I'M NO MORE ABLE TO LIVE SOLELY ON DRY LAND...THAN YOU ARE TO LIVE FOREVER IN THE SEA.
WHAT MAKES YOU YOU AND ME ME DREW US TOGETHER TO CREATE... THIS.
WE MUST HONOR THOSE QUALITIES IN OURSELVES, EVEN AS WE'LL HONOR THEM IN OUR CHILD.
THE PALACE WILL REUNITE US OFTEN, IN THE FLESH?
HEH HEH... IN MY OLD FLESH, IF YOU DON'T MIND!
AND OUR SPIRITS WILL BLEND IN OUR DREAMS, AS BEFORE?
AS ALWAYS!
CHOKE NO! DON'T GO! I CAN'T BEAR BEING WITHOUT YOU!
YOU WON'T BE. IT'S NOT POSSIBLE!
WE'RE ONE, HEART, MIND AND SOUL--

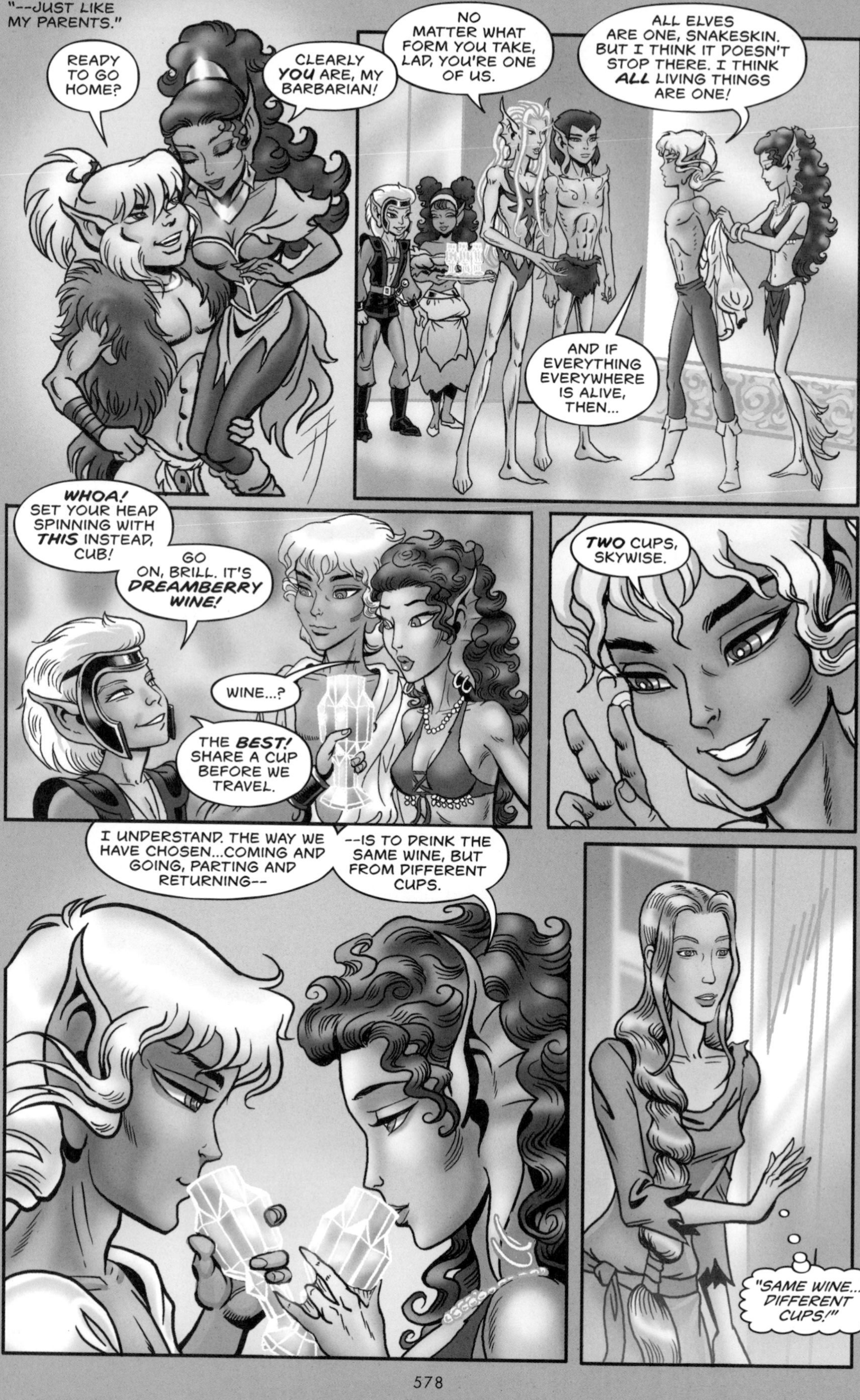
"--JUST LIKE MY PARENTS."
READY TO GO HOME?
CLEARLY YOU ARE, MY BARBARIAN!
NO MATTER WHAT FORM YOU TAKE, LAD, YOU'RE ONE OF US.
ALL ELVES ARE ONE, SNAKESKIN. BUT I THINK IT DOESN'T STOP THERE. I THINK ALL LIVING THINGS ARE ONE!
AND IF EVERYTHING EVERYWHERE IS ALIVE, THEN...
WHOA! SET YOUR HEAD SPINNING WITH THIS INSTEAD, CUB!
GO ON, BRILL. IT'S DREAMBERRY WINE!
WINE...?
THE BEST! SHARE A CUP BEFORE WE TRAVEL.
TWO CUPS, SKYWISE.
I UNDERSTAND. THE WAY WE HAVE CHOSEN...COMING AND GOING, PARTING AND RETURNING--
--IS TO DRINK THE SAME WINE, BUT FROM DIFFERENT CUPS.
"SAME WINE... DIFFERENT CUPS!"

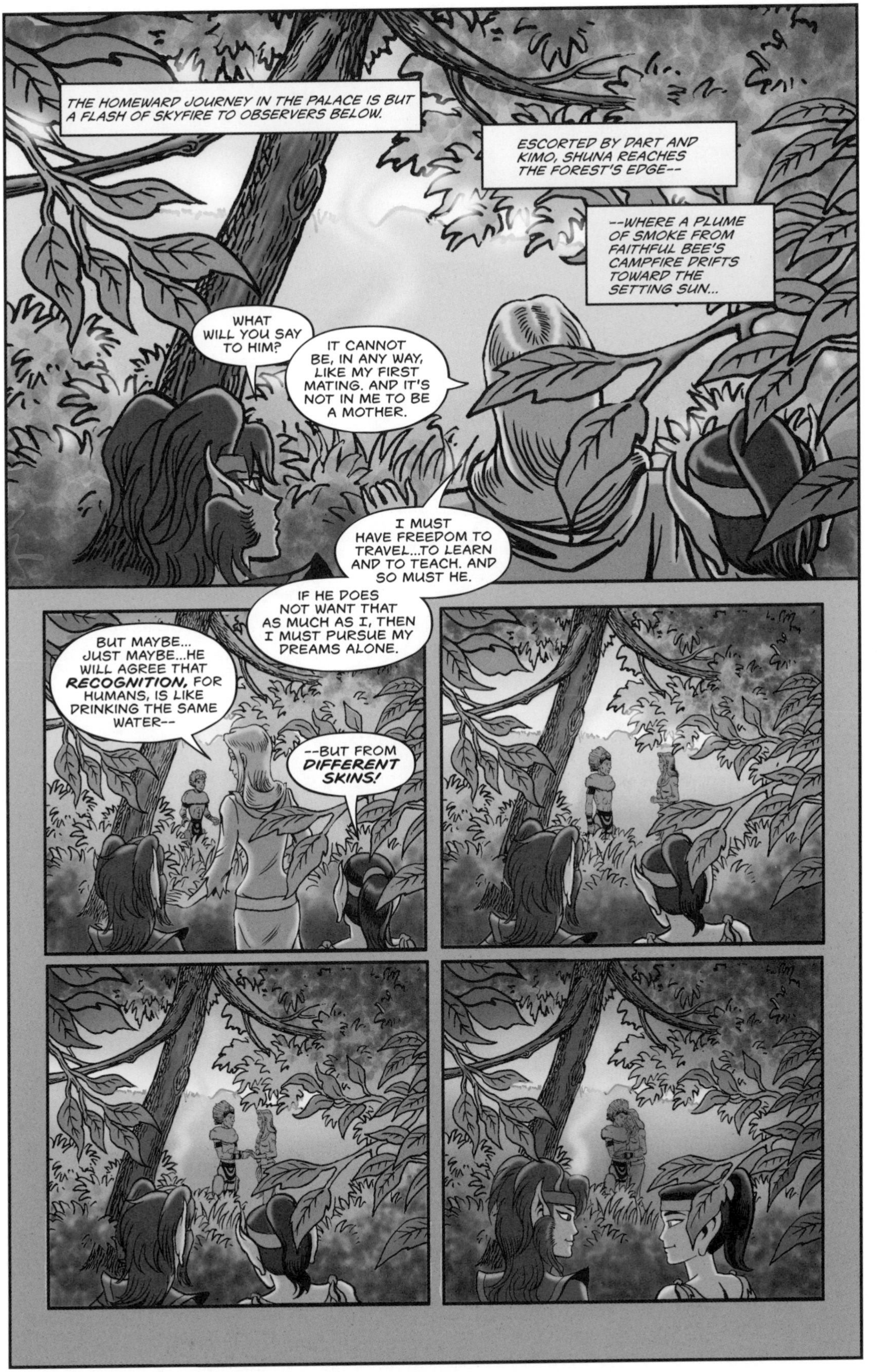

THE HOMEWARD JOURNEY IN THE PALACE IS BUT A FLASH OF SKYFIRE TO OBSERVERS BELOW.
ESCORTED BY DART AND KIMO, SHUNA REACHES THE FOREST'S EDGE--
--WHERE A PLUME OF SMOKE FROM FAITHFUL BEE'S CAMPFIRE DRIFTS TOWARD THE SETTING SUN...
WHAT WILL YOU SAY TO HIM?
IT CANNOT BE, IN ANY WAY, LIKE MY FIRST MATING. AND IT'S NOT IN ME TO BE A MOTHER.
I MUST HAVE FREEDOM TO TRAVEL...TO LEARN AND TO TEACH. AND SO MUST HE.
IF HE DOES NOT WANT THAT AS MUCH AS I, THEN I MUST PURSUE MY DREAMS ALONE.
BUT MAYBE... JUST MAYBE...HE WILL AGREE THAT **RECOGNITION,** FOR HUMANS, IS LIKE DRINKING THE SAME WATER--
--BUT FROM **DIFFERENT SKINS!**

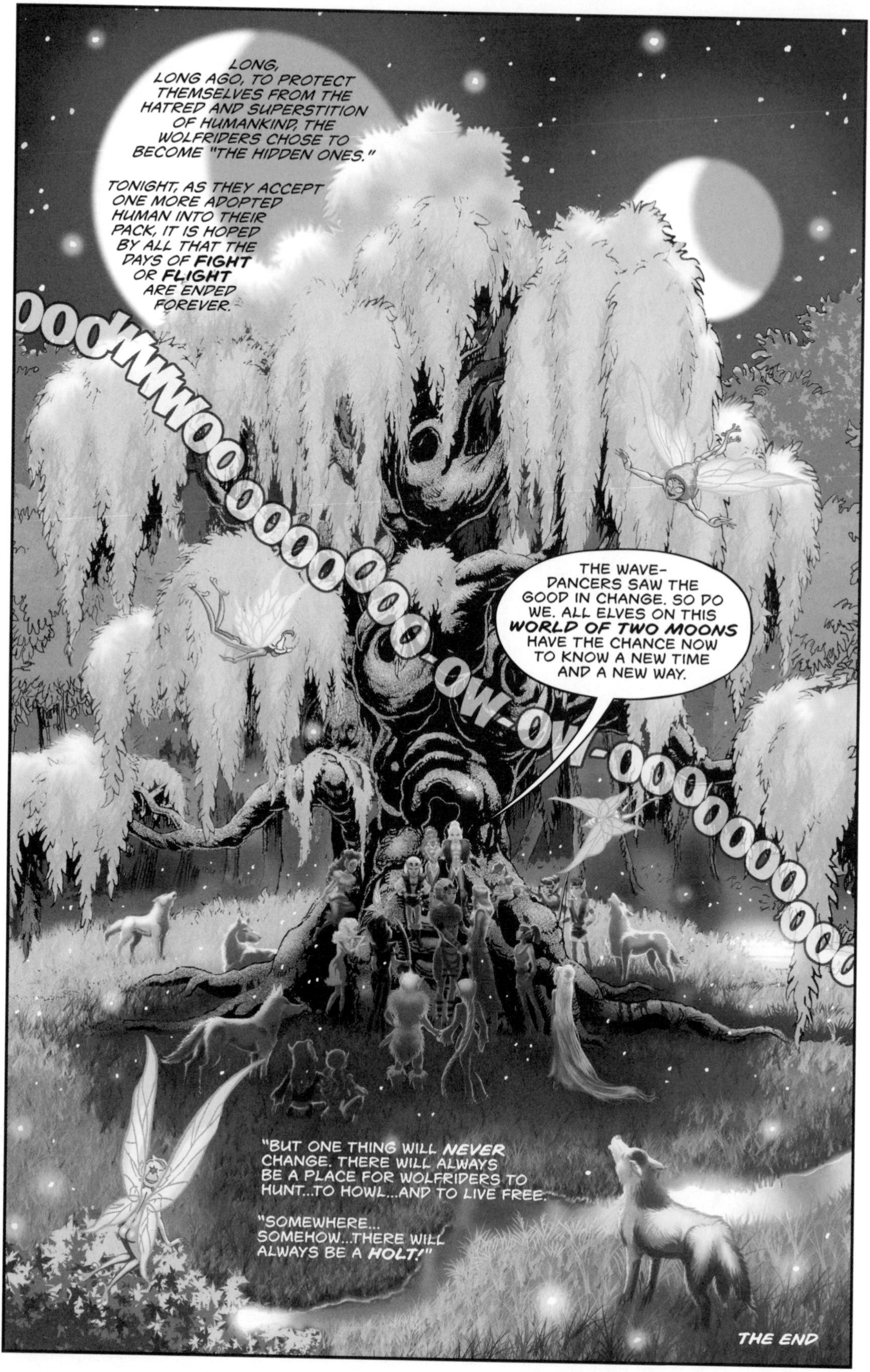
LONG, LONG AGO, TO PROTECT THEMSELVES FROM THE HATRED AND SUPERSTITION OF HUMANKIND, THE WOLFRIDERS CHOSE TO BECOME "THE HIDDEN ONES."
TONIGHT, AS THEY ACCEPT ONE MORE ADOPTED HUMAN INTO THEIR PACK, IT IS HOPED BY ALL THAT THE DAYS OF FIGHT OR FLIGHT ARE ENDED FOREVER.
OOOHWWOOOOOOOOOOOO-OW-OW-OW-OOOOOOOOOOOOO
THE WAVE-DANCERS SAW THE GOOD IN CHANGE. SO DO WE. ALL ELVES ON THIS WORLD OF TWO MOONS HAVE THE CHANCE NOW TO KNOW A NEW TIME AND A NEW WAY.
"BUT ONE THING WILL NEVER CHANGE. THERE WILL ALWAYS BE A PLACE FOR WOLFRIDERS TO HUNT...TO HOWL...AND TO LIVE FREE.
"SOMEWHERE... SOMEHOW...THERE WILL ALWAYS BE A HOLT!"
THE END

ELFQUEST

DISCOVER THE LEGEND OF *ELFQUEST*! ALLIANCES ARE FORGED, ENEMIES DISCOVERED, AND SAVAGE BATTLES FOUGHT IN THIS EPIC FANTASY ADVENTURE, HANDSOMELY PRESENTED BY DARK HORSE BOOKS!

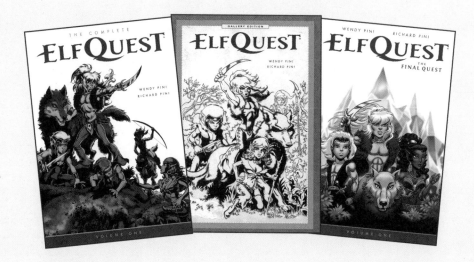

THE COMPLETE ELFQUEST
Volume 1: The Original Quest
978-1-61655-407-1 | $24.99

Volume 2
978-1-61655-408-8 | $24.99

Volume 3
978-1-50670-080-9 | $24.99

Volume 4
978-1-50670-158-5 | $24.99

Volume 5
978-1-50670-606-1 | $24.99

Volume 6
978-1-50670-607-8 | $24.99

ELFQUEST: THE ORIGINAL QUEST GALLERY EDITION
978-1-61655-411-8 | $125.00

ELFQUEST: THE FINAL QUEST
Volume 1
978-1-61655-409-5 | $17.99

Volume 2
978-1-61655-410-1 | $17.99

Volume 3
978-1-50670-138-7 | $17.99

Volume 4
978-1-50670-492-0 | $17.99

GABRIEL BÁ AND FÁBIO MOON!

"Twin Brazilian artists Fábio Moon and Gabriel Bá have made a huge mark on comics." –Publisher's Weekly